THE WORKS

OF

HUBERT HOWE BANCROFT

THE WORKS

OF

HUBERT HOWE BANCROFT

VOLUME XXIV.

HISTORY OF CALIFORNIA
VOL. VII. 1860-1890

PRINTED IN FACSIMILE FROM THE FIRST AMERICAN EDITION

PUBLISHED AT SANTA BARBARA BY WALLACE HEBBERD

To

JOE D. PAXTON

Let us all be happy and live within our means,
even if we have to borrow the money to do it with.
Artemus Ward: His Book

THE WORKS

OF

HUBERT HOWE BANCROFT

THE WORKS

OF

HUBERT HOWE BANCROFT

VOLUME XXIV

HISTORY OF CALIFORNIA
VOL. VII. 1860–1890

SAN FRANCISCO
THE HISTORY COMPANY, PUBLISHERS
1890

CONTENTS OF THIS VOLUME.

CHAPTER IV.

LIVESTOCK.

1769–1889.

CHAPTER V.

MANUFACTURES.

1848–1889.

CHAPTER VI.

FOREIGN COMMERCE.

1848–1889.

CHAPTER VII.

INLAND AND OVERLAND TRAFFIC.

1848–1888.

CHAPTER VIII.

BUSINESS METHODS AND CHARACTERISTICS.

1848–1888.

CHAPTER IX.

CRIMINAL AND JUDICIAL.

1849–1879.

CHAPTER X.

THE JUDICIARY.

1850–1872.

CHAPTER XIV.

CHINESE, THE LABOR AGITATION, AND POLITICS.

1868-1877.

CHAPTER XV.

THE NEW CONSTITUTION.

1878-1879.

CHAPTER XVI.

POLITICAL HISTORY.

1879-1889.

CHAPTER XVII.

MILITARY.

1848–1888.

CHAPTER XVIII.

EXTERMINATION OF THE INDIANS.

1849–1887.

CHAPTER XIX.

INCEPTION OF RAILWAY ROUTES.

1832–1862.

CHAPTER XX.

RAILROADS—CENTRAL PACIFIC SYSTEM.

1852–1888.

CHAPTER XXI.

CHAPTER XXII.

CHAPTER XXIII.

CHAPTER XXIV.

CONTENTS.

CHAPTER XXV.

RECENT EVENTS.

1889–1890.

HISTORY OF CALIFORNIA

CHAPTER I

THE DEVELOPMENT OF AGRICULTURE

1769–1889

THE THREE GREAT BRANCHES, GRASS, GRAIN, AND FRUIT—THE AGE OF
GRASS—PRE-AMERICAN FARMING—PROCESSES AND PRODUCTS—EXHAUS-
TION OF SOIL—FARMING MACHINERY—IRRIGATION—ARTESIAN WELLS—
RIPARIAN RIGHTS—DROUGHTS—FLOODS—PESTS—CLIMATES AND SOILS
—TEMPERATURE AND RAINFALLS—CONFIGURATIONS AS AFFECTING AGRI-
CULTURE.

AFTER the close of the pastoral period, the three
great products of California were successively gold,
grain, and fruit. Grass, gold, and grain have each
had their day, and the epoch of fruit and the vine
is upon us. These dominant devolopments had each
their collateral industries. Thus the grazing period,
which flourished during the pastoral times prior to
the gold discoveries, was attended by the hide and
tallow trade, which for three quarters of a century
constituted the basis of inland and coast commerce.
Digging for gold developed a new commerce and a
new community, while with grain-growing and fruit-
raising came social refinement and the higher culture.

The stock-raising pursuit of the Hispano-Californians was attended by a little planting, only enough
for food to sustain the inhabitants. Horses and cattle,
left to roam almost in a state of nature, must look to
nature for their sustenance. The grass, brought forward by the rains of winter, was cured by the suns of

summer; shelter for beasts was little thought of, barns almost unknown. Horses for riding were broken by quick and violent methods; few were used for draught. Little or no care was taken to improve the breed, which rather deteriorated. Ploughs were often nothing more than crooked sticks; thrashing was performed by the feet of mares; wagons consisted of rude frames upon wheels made from pieces of board.

Enterprise was mostly confined to the slowly inflowing foreign element. Sutter had in 1840 opened extensive plantations, and drilled Indians to cultivate them. Before this example Anglo-Saxon occupation spread southward, and to the north, establishing stock-farms and orchards between the Stanislaus and Russian rivers. Gold roused the country from its lethargy, and engendered new ambitions. As surface mining became less remunerative, diggers began to swell the agricultural ranks, first as raisers of potatoes and other vegetables, almost indispensable to health among miners confined to a salt-meat diet. Cereals followed, first barley as the hardier grain for the dry and sandy soil, and in demand for the large animal traffic; then others, and by 1854 the state was practically self-supporting. Then came the revelation that the large interior valleys, condemned as arid, were well adapted for wheat, and soon afterward began their cultivation, until the region took rank among the leading wheat-fields of the world. Speculation entered into the pursuit, which feature was rather stimulated than checked by the uncertain rainfall which frequently caused a failure of crops, leaving to die the herds now becoming somewhat dependent upon them in default of large portions of their otherwise occupied grazing-grounds. The drought of 1862–4 gave a fatal blow to the aspirations of cattle-men, sweeping away the pastoral importance of entire counties in the south, compelling tillage and the subdivision of ranges. Thus stock-raising was reduced to a subordinate adjunct of the farm, with greater attention given to sheep, the no-fence laws which followed almost putting an end to the business.

The possibilities of orchards and vineyards had been early understood, but the inferior quality of the mission fruit, especially the grape, offered but little employment, until in later years the gradual introduction of foreign varieties paved the way for flourishing vineyards and orange groves. The attendant formation of small holdings proved a gratifying feature, as best adapted to the general prosperity and the elevation of agricultural labor, causing a superior class to engage in such pursuits.

The high prices and the ready acquisition of wealth gave the speculative spirit a bent for operations on a grand scale on farms of vast acreage, no less than for superficial methods, with gang-ploughs for scratching rather than turning the surface, and with frequent recourse to the ready yet exhausting volunteer crop. To the predilection of Californians to experiment and change is due such results as the low pruning and other improvements in vineyards and orchards, the evolution of superior breeds in stock, the promising silk and cotton culture,[1] and the numerous labor-saving implements, as multiform gang-ploughs and combined header and thrasher, which are here more widely perfected and adopted than elsewhere. Few countries possess so varied a cultivation, or a farming community of higher general intelligence and enterprise.

This development has been wrought in the face of obstacles, notably the dryness of soil and season, with periodical droughts.[2]

[1] All countries were required to contribute their quota to the rising commonwealth. From France and Japan were obtained the silk-worm, from England and Kentucky horses and cows of superior breed, from Asia minor the Angora goat, from Mexico cotton and a host of other plants, and vines from half a dozen regions. The method of making sparkling wines and brandy were studied at Epernay and Cognac, raisin-drying at Malaga, etc. Every lesson and experiment was noted—every achievement of science.

[2] The north wind is withering, producing a suffocating, alkaline dust, which often affects the eyes and air passages. Flies and mosquitoes abound in some parts, in others ground-squirrels and rabbits; yet on the whole these

The preëminence of stock-raising in early days laid upon farmers the burden of maintaining fences; but as the cultivation of the soil increased, their interests acquired greater weight. It was shown that a free range for cattle should not be allowed in the great valleys, where timber was scarce. The discovery of the value of the San Joaquin plain for wheat-raising gave emphasis to this view. After a long delay, the legislature allowed a test to be made in a small district, and with the decline of cattle-raising subsequent to the drought of 1862–4, less difficulty was encountered in extending the area, until nearly the entire agricultural portion of the state enjoyed the benefit.[3]

afflictions are of a mild nature. Good water is not general. But while the dryness is forbidding in some respects, and at times delays ploughing, yet it also checks weeds and is a great boon in harvest-time, permitting crops to be reaped in economic and convenient security. Traffic monopoly has been inveighed against, but the evil is not worse than in many other states. More formidable is land monopoly, in taxing enterprise and retarding immigration, but the remedy lies with the people. Against these drawbacks stands an overwhelming array of advantages which inspire the most glowing pride and hope. California occupies one of the most favored zones on the globe, and compared with the sister states of the union it is a summer-land. So attests the ever-increasing influx of tourists, who seek here a period of rest and enjoyment; of invalids in quest of health and winter homes; of immigrants drawn by the expanding fame of vineyards and orange groves, by the perennial spring and balmy air of the coast region, with ever-blooming banks beneath an Italian sky. Moreover, the land lies mostly prepared for immediate tillage, with no heavy sod, or shrub, or stone to obstruct the farmer, but with light soil and clear surface which permit gang-ploughs to cover areas much larger than elsewhere, and at one third the cost. There are no cold winters to bury the ground for months; little frost, and rarely hail or levelling rain storms. Nature grants extra time for unfoldment, as shown in the perpetual green, in the faster growth of trees and of animals, both of which acquire maturity at almost half the age assigned in the eastern states, for with these the comparison is fittest. And not only can the harvesting of grain and fruit be left to the convenience of the farmer, but grain may be cut, thrashed, and sacked in one operation, ready for shipment, and many fruits may be dried in the sun for preservation. The no-fence law confers an economic boon on tillers, without real detriment to the stock-raiser, and farming has risen to supreme consideration, as the leading industry of the state, to the restriction of formerly preëminent mining rights. Thus safeguards and natural advantages lighten toil and expense, supply more wants and luxuries, and permit the formation of the nost beautiful and comfortable of homes and of prosperous fruit-growing colonies. See chapter on birth of towns, vol. vi. Colonies were formed in all parts of the state, but flourished best on the irrigated tracts of the south, where the common interests centre in a canal; which makes each small holding all-sufficient for a family, yet impels them to unite for harvesting and other operations, as wine-pressing, drying, and canning.

    [3] The *Census* of 1880 places the cost of constructing and repairing fences in 1879 at $2,120,000, the farm acreage being 16,600,000, while for the entire union it stood at $77,800,000 for an acreage of 536,000,000. Considering the

The number of farms in 1880 was placed at 36,000, a doubling within 20 years,[4] and the average size at 462 acres.[5] In 1889 the number was estimated at 55,000, with a slightly larger average. The monopolization of so much of the best land is due partially to the old land laws of Mexico, and also to the acquisition of large valley tracts by Americans before their agricultural value had become fully known.[6] The

small value of the live-stock, as compared with farms, the latter have the strength on their side. Timber fences cost as high as $600 per mile. The barbed wire fence, howsoever barbarous, has by its comparative cheapness largely supplanted the superior board structure; but in the redwood districts, the worm and post and rail fences naturally sustain themselves better. In the south the cactus was in vogue at the missions, but willow hedges were frequently grown.

[4] This gives one farm to every 24 persons, while the average for the U. S. is one for every dozen. But here must be considered the position of Cal. as a mining state, with the commercial and manufacturing industries, and the prevalence of speculative farming, as indicated by the great size of the farms and the large improved acreage in each, which require the service of a considerable proportion of the population. The increase of farms from 18,700 in 1860 to 23,700 in 1870 and over 35,900 in 1880, with an acreage of 8,700,000, 11,400,000, and 16,600,000, respectively, fully corresponds to the growth of population, from 380,000 to 560,000 and 865,000, for here must be considered the relatively greater immigration of females in late years and the expansion of families, which form neutral factors.

[5] For size of farms California exceeds every other state, and it is a peculiarity favored by her speculative spirit, which delights in operations on a large scale, by the rapid acquisition of wealth through mining and other chance efforts, and by the soil and climate, which favor vast farming enterprises. Nor is it a mere holding of farm, for the percentage of unimproved land in these tracts is only 35.7, while the average for the U. S. is 46.9.

[6] Of the Mexican ranges large lots were sold at a few dimes per acre. Under the state law of March 8, 1868, which set aside many safe restrictions, possessory rights permitted the temporary enclosure of tracts, to the prejudice of preëmptors. Under Indian and eastern agricultural college scrip large areas were bought up, one person obtaining over 300,000 acres. The railways held back large lots for higher prices. The office of U. S. sur.-gen. for Cal. was created by act of March 3, 1851, and S. D. King of the land dept at Washington became the first incumbent, arriving here on Apr. 19, 1851. He took possession of the archives then held by the military govt. J. C. Hays succeeded him in 1853, and was followed in Sept. 1857 by J. Mandeville. Meanwhile extra work had devolved upon the office at the conclusion of the labors of the land commission. E. F. Beale, later minister to Austria, held office 1861-4, L. Upston, long editor of the *Sac. Union*, 1864-8. The office is in a measure under control of the state. Mount Diablo forms the base point for surveys. Prof. Davidson criticises the system. *Californian*, i. 60-3. Reports of work done are given in *U. S. Gov. Doc.*, Cong. 32, Sess. 1, H. Ex. Doc. 2, ii. pt. ii. 8-11, 43-9, for 1851; *Id.*, Sess. 2, Doc. 14, iii. 1-11, for 1852; *Land Off. Repts*, passim; in the preceding act and in separate form, with references in *Cal. Jour. Sen.*, 1852 et seq.; and *Id., Ass.*, ap. annually; *U. S. Coast Survey*. Of the 101,000,000 of land in 157,800 sq. miles in Cal., over 52,000,000 had been surveyed by the beginning of this decade. By March 1857 over 77,000 miles of survey lands had been measured. Land-offices were recommended by the executive in 1851-2. *U. S. Gov. Doc.*, Cong. 32, Sess. 1, H.

evil is becoming more noticeable of late years, as the
increased demand for small settlements reveals that
little land of value is left in government hands, and as
the riparian question points out that numerous holders
of both small and large sections have so selected their
ground as to control still larger areas.[7]   But the abuse
is gradually lessening, under the new horticultural era
which demands for its best development the tenure of
small sections.[8]

The comparatively high value of farms here is sustained by the favorable climate and conditions, the
usually unobstructed ground, ready for immediate
cultivation, and the immense possibilities of the soil.[9]

Ex. Doc. 2, p. 15; *Id.*, Sess. 2, Doc. 1, i. pt. i. 76; and by act of March 3, 1853,
three were established at Benicia, Marysville, and Los Angeles; in 1858 three
more were added, at Humboldt, Stockton, and Visalia; and subsequently half
a dozen more, three of them east of the Sierra Nevada.   Some were consolidated. *Id.*, Cong. 33, Sess. 1, Doc. 1, i. pt. i. 78–9, etc.; *Dunlop's Laws*,
1788–91; *Van Buren's Remarks*, 1852, 1–8; *Douglas' Speech*, June 26–8, 1850;
Cal. Polit. Code, 486; *U. S. Gov. Doc.*, Cong. 47, Sess. 2, H. Ex. Doc. 45, pp.
1019 et seq.; *Cal. Jour. Ass.*, passim.
    [7] To the virtual exclusion of settlers.   The possessor of a small spring
may command sections of land dependent upon this source.
    [8] The consequent rise of land values also promotes subdivision, by tempt-
ing the large holders to sell, by pressing them with heavier taxes, and by
reducing their percentage of gain, particularly when compared with the more
thorough methods of the small cultivator, sustained by the reserve force of
the family.   So far nearly two thirds of the farms range between 100 and
500 acres, with over 2,500 exceeding 1,000 acres; but during the last few years
the sale of 20-acre lots for viniculture has become a marked feature among
land-holders in the southern counties.   Only one fifth of the total number of
farms are leased to tenants.
    [9] Of a total acreage in farms of 16,600,000, there was unimproved about one
third, or 5,920,000 acres, of which only 1,670,000 was in woodland.   Of the
improved, 6,600,000 were tilled, including fallow and grass in rotation, and
4,060,000 in permanent pastures, orchards, and vineyards.   Of the U. S. farm
acreage, 536,000,000, over 251,000,000 acres were unimproved, mostly in
timber, and 223,000,000 tilled.   Their value was placed at $10,200,000,000,
including buildings, equivalent to about $20 per acre.   In Cal. the value was
$262,000,000, equivalent to $16, which must be considered high for so new a
country.   In Arkansas the valuation is only $6, and in old settled Alabama,
little over $4.   The cost of constructing and repairing fences was placed for
1879 at $2,100,000.   Arkansas, with nearly the same acreage and population,
spent only $1,580,000.   From the other two thirds were obtained products
valued at $59,700,000, or $69 for every inhabitant, or about $750 for every
one of 79,000 persons engaged in agriculture, although the improved acre
yielded little more than $5.50, while the average acre in the union brought
nearly $8, yielding, however, only $44 to the inhabitant, or about $300 to
each farm worker.   In 1870 the census returned for California $49,900,000
from 6,200,000 acres, and the average for the U. S. was also relatively higher.
The value of the 11,400,000 farm acres was then $141,000,000 in Cal.; for
1860, 8,700,000 acres stood at only $48,700,000; and for 1850, 3,900,000,
nearly all unimproved, at $3,870,000.   The value of live-stock figured for

Great extravagance has been displayed in by raisers of grain in exhausting the soil without due attention to rest, rotation, and fertilization.[10] As a rule, the rains of November soften the summer-baked earth sufficiently for ploughing. Favored by the lightness of the soil and the absence of sod, stones, and bushes, the operation is mostly performed by gang-ploughs, cutting from four to eight inches deep,[11] and ploughing from four to eight or even more acres daily, so that the cost is reduced sometimes as low as forty cents per acre.[12]

1850, 1860, 1870, and 1880 at $3,350,000, $35,600,000, $38,000,000, and $35,500,000, respectively; and farming implements at $103,000, $2,560,000, $5,300,000, and $8,450,000, or about 80 cents per improved acre, while the average for the U. S. was nearly twice as much; but then Cal. is a new country, with ingenious ideas of economy.

[10] There are, however, numerous instances of land being cultivated year after year, especially for the less exhausting barley, with only a little falling off from the original productiveness. The only manure applied in these cases was from the burning of stubble or what was dropped by stock. Some divided their land into three parcels; one being ploughed to lie fallow; another, the last fallow, being simply sown and harrowed; the third was ploughed and sown. Some permitted volunteer crops every other year.

[11] In the San Joaquin Valley from two to five or even ten ploughs were used in a gang, each making a furrow 8 or 10 inches wide and 4 or 5 deep. A gang of 5 ploughs will turn up 6 acres in a day.

[12] While on small farms with heavy soil, the acre may cost $2 or $3. In the prevailing haste deep ploughing has been widely neglected. Farmers also overlook the capillary power induced by ploughing, for drawing moisture to the plant and attracting solar heat. Some attach a sower and harrow to the plough and complete the entire work at once; otherwise broadcast sowing is preferred as the cheapest and speediest, and the task may be delayed for weeks after ploughing. A broadcast sower with 2 men covers 100 acres a day, giving work for 7 harrows of 100 teeth each. Steam ploughs have been commended as well adapted to level fields, with stationary or locomotive engines, but experience does not favor them. Hewlett gives an account of the demand for them in his *Stat.*, MS., as do Nash & Co. in their *Rept*, MS.; *Cal. Farmer*, March 11, 1869, describes the trial of steam ploughs; *S. F. Bulletin*, March 13, 1869; Feb. 8, 1859; Nov. 22, 1866; *Sac. Union*, Nov. 12, 1873; *S. Joaq. Co. Hist.*, 71–2, on implement manuf. and inventions at Stockton, and in *Yolo Co. Hist.*, 44; *Alta Cal.*, Oct. 8, 1857, Aug. 13, 1858. The rarity of rains during the summer and autumn leave harvesters undisturbed. Grain and many root and fruit crops may be left untouched for weeks after maturity, for the latter continue to thrive, and grain capsules retain tenaciously the kernel until moistened by rain or opened by the thrasher. This gives the farmer ample time for reaping, and he may safely leave the grain loose or in sheaves, without stacking, till prepared to thrash it. Usually it is collected in piles, from which the thrasher is fed unless the cutting is performed by the favorite header, which, sweeping over from 20 to 60 acres a day, delivers the grain to the wagon attending, whence it is drawn up and pitched into the thrasher. Latterly a combined header and thrasher has been introduced, which delivers the grain in sacks along its path ready to be hauled to the granary. Thus can be saved the expense of binding, stacking, and storing, together with much other costly labor required elsewhere. The

The peculiar and scanty distribution of rain in California renders irrigation desirable for a large portion
of the soil, and indispensable for some sections.[13]
Besides assured and augmented.crops, with irrigation
is combined several additional benefits: in fertilizing
and renovating the soil;[14] in destroying, by flooding,
numerous pests, such as squirrels, gophers, and
phylloxera; in enabling the farmer to select his own
time for planting, thus economizing time and opportunity, and assisting him to obtain several crops in
one season.[15] Several advantages combine to raise the
value of irrigated lands many fold; the chief objection
lies in the sanitary aspect, but this is slight, and so
far applies only to certain conditions.[16]

Nowhere, perhaps, are the benefits of irrigation
more appreciated than in southern California, where
many tracts, before considered almost worthless, have
been transformed into the most productive lands in the
state.   On some of them towns have been built, as in
the case of Pomona, a portion of whose site was purchased in 1882 by Moses L. Wicks,[17] one of the most

machinery in use here is on a larger scale than in the east, and several Cal.
inventions have helped reduce the cost of harvesting some 50 per cent.
Descriptions under manufactures, vol. vi., and in *Mount. Dem.*, June 1, 1878;
Modesto News, June 29, July 6, 1877, etc.

[13] The rainfall, excessive in the north, decreases going southward, rendering cultivation more and more insecure.   The foothills bordering the valleys
are favored with the condensation of moisture by the ranges, and the coast
feels the vapors from the ocean.   The melting snows in March and April
form the reserve supply of water on which irrigation mainly depends.   Irrigation is becoming more important as population increases, and with it the
desire to obtain the greatest returns from the soil.   Hence, also, the growing
necessity for occupying the plains of the south, whose arid aspect possesses
the compensating advantages of a soil and climate unsurpassed, under irrigation, for productiveness and for choice and varied culture.   Their treeless
expanse, devoid of sod, lies ready, moreover, for immediate cultivation.

[14] Dissolving, as it does, the elements required for organic life.   Numerous
instances can be given of fields yielding well for decades without other manure.   The value of the Nile overflows is generally understood.   The saving
in manure is an offset to the cost of irrigation.

[15] In the southern part of San Joaquin valley 5 cuts of alfalfa are not
uncommon.   Egyptian corn and millet have yielded three crops.

[16] Partly because the cultures in vogue require only moderate irrigation,
and because the climate has features modifying the influence of malaria.   It
is supposed that rice-fields would be less healthy.

[17] Mr Wicks was born at Aberdeen, Monroe county, Mississippi, on the
22d of April 1852.   His father, Moses J. Wicks, a native of Savanna, was
a prominent banker and railroad man of Memphis, Tennessee.   The elder

enterprising and public-spirited citizens of Los Angeles county. On this property water was obtained by sinking more than a score of artesian wells and by conveying to it in pipes the waters of San Antonio cañon, whereby an almost desert region has been converted into a thriving settlement.

Irrigation was introduced during the first decade of Spanish occupation,[18] but progressed in a slow, desultory manner, at least north of Los Angeles, although aided in the gold region by mining ditches. In the seventies, however, with the extension of settlements in San Joaquin valley, capitalists turned their attention to it; and in 1871 was begun the largest canal in the state, the San Joaquin and King river,[19] carried

Wicks was the first one who contributed to the support of the confederate provisional government at Montgomery, and by him was taken its first issue of bonds. Entering the confederate service, he raised a regiment of cavalry, furnishing more than a hundred horses at his own expense, and purchasing a supply of arms in the northern states. His son completed his education at the University of Virginia, where he condensed into a single year the studies of the two years' law course. In 1875 he married Miss Elizabeth Littlejohn of Memphis and set forth for his bridal trip to Los Angeles, Cal., soon afterward opening a law office at Anaheim. Here he had the misfortune to lose his wife, a most amiable and accomplished lady, her death occurring four months after the birth of her only son. After some two years of successful practice at Anaheim and later at Los Angele he found that his real estate transactions and his various enterprises demanded all his attention. No man has done more toward developing the resources of this portion of the state. In addition to the investment above related he purchased the Dryfus tract, forming a portion of the San Rafael rancho, together with a large tract in San Bernardino county, and the Dalton portion of the San José ranch, improving and subdividing them so that many of the purchasers made from 200 to 300 per cent on their outlay. Under his management the property of the Temecula Land and Water company was developed and increased largely in value. He was one of those who organized the Savings Fund and Building association, the Los Angeles and Santa Monica railroad, the Abstract and Title Insurance company, the California bank and others of the leading corporations in southern California. On improving the harbor at Ballona he expended large amounts, though the work belonged of right to the government. He furnished the hill portion of Los Angeles with a plentiful supply of water. In a word there are few prominent enterprises in this portion of the state in which he has not been one of the leading promoters. In 1881 he was married to his second wife, Mrs Jennie L. Butler, a lady who has been to him in the truest sense of the word a consort. A man of excellent judgment, of rare business ability, and of the strictest integrity, there is no one to whom southern California is more indebted for her present era of prosperity.

[18] See preceding volumes. The southern coast counties had a number of ditches, small, and not well planned. San Joaquin county applied them early, and likewise Yolo, which by 1879 had 13,000 acres covered.

[19] Extended by 1878 from S. Joaquin river, at Fresno slough, northwestward, about 10 miles from the main river, for nearly 70 miles with subse-

by 1878 nearly 70 miles, of which the first 40 were
built by John Bensley,[20] by whom was incorporated
the San Joaquin and Kings river canal and irrigation
company. This he accomplished at his own expense,
and under the most adverse conditions, materials, implements, and supplies being conveyed at enormous
cost over a mountainous and difficult country. Several similar enterprises were undertaken from Kern
northward; so that in the begnning of the eighties
190,000 acres were irrigated[21] in the San Joaquin
valley, the price usually charged being $1.50 per
acre. At first the dry soil and the undeveloped
plant require more water than subsequently. Although flooding by means of ditches is the most
prevalent method, lateral seeping from them is partly
relied upon in sandy soil, and in some places where
water is scarce choice cultivation is supplied through

quent slight extension, including over 120 miles of branch ditches 12 ft wide.
The total cost was $1,300,000, and the receipts in 1880, $50,000, half of it
net, from 29,000 acres, while 120,000 acres could be irrigated. Chapman,
Miller, and Lux tapped the San Joaquin 12 miles above its bend, and ran a
channel northward for 30 miles, to irrigate 50,000 acres of their own land.
Friedlander and others opened a canal from Fresno river southward for 10
miles to cover 40,000 acres. The Kern river delta, a triangle of 25 miles by
about 16 and 16, containing nearly 100,000 acres, was supplied by 7 ditches
of 66 miles, costing $4,000 a mile.

[20] One of our pioneers, a native of Mass., and a graduate of Columbia college. He was among the earliest merchants of Sacramento, but after the first
of 1852 removed to San Francisco, where he was one of the first to introduce a
regular supply of water. He was on the first board of trustees of the Citizens' Gas company, the projector of the Pacific Rolling mills and the Pacific
Oil and Lead works, was one of those who organized the Electric Light company, and is or has been connected with other leading enterprises. He died
in June 1889.

Moses J. Church, who was also one of the first to develop our irrigation system, was born in Chatauqua co., N. Y., in 1818. Coming to Cal. in 1852,
after engaging in various occupations, he took up land on Kings river, near
Centerville, and in 1869, having secured a franchise to divert the waters of
that stream, surveyed and laid out a canal to Francha creek. In the face of
strong opposition from cattle-kings and riparian claimants, he pushed forward
the work, until in 1876 he had completed nearly 1,000 miles of main and lateral canals, with their ditches and feeders, thereby materially advancing the
industrial, commercial, and financial developments of the state a thousand-
fold.

[21] Or 5 per cent of the total irrigable amount. A larger proportion lay
ready for irrigation. Several other projects were vainly waiting for aid from
the government. Petitions in U. S. Gov. Doc., Cong. 41, Sess. 1, Sen. Misc.
Doc. 31; Cal. Jour. Sen., 1865-6, ap. 42, 46, 61; 1871-2, ap. 35.

perforated cement pipes.[22] Reservoirs in the mountains are less exposed to evaporation. Artesian wells supply considerable tracts of field and settlement through most of the San Joaquin counties,[23] and in the adjoining western valleys. Altogether there is sufficient water to irrigate most of the valuable soil,[24] say 70 per cent of the eastern valley side of the San Joaquin. The western side is not so well provided, yet with winter storage the limited sources here and southward may be greatly extended.

In 1854 the legislature issued an act for the appointment of water commissioners in several counties, and under acts of May 14, 1862, and April 2, 1870, most of the water appropriated for irrigation was controlled;[25] but no proper measures were taken by the state to investigate and promote this important inter-

[22] To obviate the great evaporation. To lay such pipes costs from $30 to $50 per acre.

[23] In the Sacramento Valley the geologic conditions for such wells are rare. Round Stockton in 1887 were half a score about 1,000 feet in depth, yielding on an average 150,000 gallons per minute. In Merced they were feebler, aggregating in 1884 a flow of 8.35 cubic feet per second, many giving also gas for illumination. In Tulare their number increased from twoscore in 1882 to over 100 in 1884, aggregating 30 c. ft per second, and supplying 6,000 acres. Of the score in Kern, one yielded a million gallons a day of water fairly free from the alkali which renders Tulare Lake objectionable. In some parts, as S. Joaquin and Yolo counties, water was pumped from wells wrongly called artesian. A gardener reported that such pumping, by steam instead of windmills, cost $90 a month for 15 acres. *Hittell's Com.*, 408. Pumping from streams is occasionally done. *Sac. Union*, March 18, 1864, estimates costs. New methods, in *S. F. Bulletin*, Oct. 21, Dec. 30, 1881. The number of artesian wells in 1887 was over 2,000, chiefly west of the Coast Range, and their usual depth was not over 250 feet, though the range was from 100 to over 1,000 feet. The 7-inch bore cost about $275 for 200 feet, $450 for 300 ft. The first flowing well in Los Angeles was bored near Wilmington, in 1868. *L. Ang. Exp.*, Sept. 7, 1872. For early wells and projects, see *Sac. Union*, Aug. 1, 1855; Dec. 23, 1857; Jan. 1, 12, 24, 1884; *Cal. Jour. Ass.*, 1855, ap. 14; 1856, Apr. 19.

[24] Notwithstanding the incorrect ideas of Gov. Riley and other early observers to the contrary. *U. S. Gov. Doc.*, Cong. 31, Sess. 1, H. Ex. Doc. 17, 785–6. The Sac. drains 26,600 sq. miles, of which 4,000 embrace the valley bed, from the Cosumnes to Iron Cañon. The S. Joaquin drains 31,700 sq. miles, 11,400 of which forming the valley bed, 7,700 on the east side. Of the latter nearly 70 per cent may be irrigated from current water supply. On the west side of the S. Joaquin, with its scanty drainage, only one fifth is irrigable. This leaves about 6,000 sq. miles, or 3,800,000 acres of irrigable land in the S. Joaquin, of which up to 1887 only 5 per cent was watered.

[25] The civil code adopted in 1872 provided for the acquisition of rights to use water. Yet the special spasmodic efforts of the state to promote irrigation brought no fruit.

est prior to 1878, when, under the incentive of a prior superficial examination by a federal commission, an engineer was appointed to ascertain the resources and wants of the country in this regard.[26]   The completion of his task requires time.   Meanwhile the absence of definite laws on the subject has thrown matters into confusion, with the prospect of endless litigation.

Under the laws established by custom in the early mining days, priority of occupation and appropriation gave title to claims, as well as to the water indispensable for working them, and this right was repeatedly affirmed by the courts and by act of congress.[27]   But when the appropriation was extended from the unnavigable head-waters of mining fields to agricultural districts, under the direction of companies which prepared almost to drain several tributaries, then rose in opposition the large riparian land-owners, many of whom had acquired tracts by the score containing hundreds of square miles, with a view to control the water.[28] They quoted the act of April 1850, adopting the common law of England as a rule under which riparian land-holders were entitled to an undiminished flow of the stream past their land,[29] and this claim was sustained by the supreme tribunal of the state.[30]   There are manifest equities which demand that a common

26 Wm Ham. Hall was appointed, and preliminary reports of value appeared, on which part of the preceding matter is based, but he has outlined a very exhaustive treatise on the subject in several volumes, the first of which, issued in 1886, covers the history of irrigation in Europe.   Under act of congress of March 3, 1873, *Cong. Globe*, 1872-3, iii. ap. 305, a commission was appointed to report a system of irrigation for the Sacramento and S. Joaq. valleys, with a paltry appropriation of $5,000.   Its report, with plan, 91 pp., points out both the need and value of irrigation. *U. S. Gov. Doc.*, Cong. 43, Sess. 1, H. Ex. Doc. 290; *Mendell's Report.*

27 Of July 26, 1866, confirming also right of way for ditches.

28 Thus in Kern one person bought up 200,000 acres, which controlled all the available water on 500,000 acres.   Small preëmptors of 160 acres, homestead or timber privileges, gained control over large adjoining regions dependent on the springs secured by them.

29 For water-power, navigation, and fishing.   Although they acquire no ownership in the river, no deviation of water is permitted without their consent under Cal. laws, save where such deviation has been made for five years unmolested.

30 As late as May 1886. *S. F. Chron.*, May 17-18, 1886.   It was argued in opposition that the common law being adopted before Cal. became a state, it should not operate on titles not then vested in her.

law, hastily adopted from a country so dissimilar in climate and condition to California, should not be made applicable when it imperils the vital interests of some of the richest districts of the country. The setting aside of this law under the general mining custom, which concedes right of way for ditches as well as prior appropriation, has given a precedent for another ruling, or for ready legislative amendment.[31] The interests of a few land monopolists should not be allowed to outweigh those which affect the prosperity of large communities. The rain falls alike over all the earth, on hills as well as in vales, and when gathered in channels on the way to the ocean, the property of the nations, it should still be permitted to shed its blessings on all.

A guiding rule for riparian decisions lies evidently in the universal law which reserves navigable rivers as public property. Some nations see the necessity also to retain for public use all constantly running streams, thus extending the law to meet their special wants. Now, California is an exceptional country climatically, and not being subject to the common meteorologic laws, she must perforce be governed by distinct rules and methods, applicable to this peculiarity. Nature clearly designs the rain for the land where it falls, but owing to topographic features beyond the remedy of the land-owner, the water granted to him drains, under direction of the same all-controlling power, into springs, pools, and streams upon adjoining property, there to be stored. Now such storage, in the case of navigable and running streams, pertains to the public, wherever it is of value to a district for carriage, waterpower, fishing, and so forth. Minor storages are abandoned to the land enclosing them, simply because frequent rains provide a sufficient supply for adjoining tracts, for agriculture and domestic use.

---

[31] And so has the rejection of eastern fence laws, under different conditions ruling in Cal. Even England has recognized appropriation rights in many instances.

The feeling against monopoly has been vigorously
expressed by meetings and conventions.[32]   Aware of
the danger, on the other side, of surrendering the
water to speculative canal companies, many wish the
state to assume control;[33] but this might lead to corrupt rings for the manipulation of bonds and local interests, and the work, vast and ill understood, concerns
only certain districts.   The state certainly should
assert its right of eminent domain, and condemn to
public use all necessary water; and in view of the
breadth and intricacy of the distribution system, the
common good demands that the government should
plan it, leaving the execution of the work to the districts interested, yet retaining the supervision of it.[34]
If properly distributed during a California season,

[32] Instance that at Los Angeles in 1873, *Sac. Union*, Oct. 27, 1873; that at
S. F. in 1886, *S. F. Chron.*, May 21, 1886.

[33] The question of sole right to springs on private land might be raised
where public benefit is affected.   A precedent for such encroachment lies in
rules which do not yield the ownership of minerals to the holder of the soil.
See mines, vol. vi.   The convention of 1873 urged that the state create a department for irrigation, with superintendents for each county.

[34] This idea is favored by the U. S. com. referred to above.   Farmers are
not expected to readily form proper associations for such vast enterprise, and
one district if engaged in it might not plan well and economically enough for
those adjoining.   One impartial power could alone give the system intelligent
and comprehensive scope.   This being outlined, with estimates for cost and
extent in each section, farmers might individually or jointly undertake local
construction.   The mere announcement of such a project would raise values
and permit the sale of enough land to pay the assessment.   The state and
counties would benefit by increased revenue, and could afford to aid.   Mr
Ryer advocates that farmers form districts and take possession of all available water, as condemned by the state, leaving owners to sue for damages,
and then employ engineers to plan the local ditches.   Each acre should be
assessed for the cost according to the benefit derived, and the funds deposited
in the county treasury, subject to orders from the supervisors for actual
work.   Contracts should be let to the lowest bidders, and in small sections,
so as to enable poor men to pay the assessment in labor.   The U. S. com.
favored the sale of such water-rights with the land, but this has been tried in
Lombardy and found to be fraught with selfish exactions.   Associations
might be controlled by agreement under conditions governing highways.
France assumed control of her water after a long struggle.   Chili and Italy
control theirs, the latter adding tax exemptions to the prizes issued for encouraging irrigation works.   Under Rome constantly running streams were
public property, not others.   Concerning the claim on streams for navigation
and water-power, it must be remembered that the canals do not always need
water, and least at the time when navigation most demands a filled bed, so
that navigation would suffer very little in behalf of the other greater good.
Riparian owners should be left a sufficient quantity for use.   Specimen cries
against water monopoly are given in *Sac. Union*, July 19, 1873; also in *Lowe,
the Laborer*, 1–58.

a rainfall of a dozen inches is ample for the wheat crops; but coming too much together, a fall of less than sixteen inches is sure to result in some failures. Of such the state has had fully half a dozen since the gold discovery, the driest seasons being 1850–1, 1863–4, 1876–7, indicating intervals of thirteen years, a peculiarity also noticed in colonial days.[35] The limited extent of agriculture in 1851, save in gardening, gave little scope for damage, and the lighter drought of 1855–7 proved more severe in its effect. The most disastrous drought took place in 1862–4, when crops failed over vast areas, and cattle died of starvation and were slaughtered by the hundred thousand, completely revolutionizing agricultural industries. More than one southern county changed from a pastoral to a farming district, and stock-raising received a startling curtailment throughout.[36] The season 1870–1 was a disastrous one, and that of 1876–7 more so, approaching that of 1862–4, with losses on crops and cattle of some twenty million dollars.[37] If future observations should confirm our past experience as to the rainfall and the periodicity of droughts, the forecast will be of no little benefit to the agricultural interests of California, for the nature and treatment of crops could then be adapted to foreseen conditions. As matters are at present, in the greater portion of the San Joaquin valley one good crop out of three or five is all that can be expected

[35] As shown in my preceding vols. i.–iv. The rainfall of 1850–1 was only 7 inches at S. F. and 4.7 at Sac. In 1855–6 only 8 inches fell at Stockton and 13 at Sac., followed by still less in 1856–7, and attendant suffering and loss of stock, especially in the south.

[36] With the compulsory subdivision of many Mexican grants.

[37] The average rainfall for 1862–4 at S. F. was little over 11 inches, at Los Angeles 4, and at Sac. 9. In 1870–1 S. F. had 13 inches, Stockton 6, Sac. 8, Los Angeles 7, Napa 10. Details of these droughts and their effect in *S. F. Bulletin*, May 1, Nov. 13, 1856; May 6, 1857; Apr. 16, July 2, Nov. 1863; March–Apr., June 22, Oct.–Nov. 1864; Feb. 7, March 24, 1865; Oct. 19, 1871; Apr. 13, 1873; May–Oct. 1877, etc.; *Los Angeles Herald*, June 16, Nov. 10, 1877; *L. A. Exp.*, Jan. 13, March 10, Apr. 14, Nov. 10, 1877; *Antioch Ledger*, July 22, 1877; *Alta Cal.*, Apr. 29, May 9, 1857; Nov. 7, 1859; Apr. 2, 1863; May 15, 1871; *Sac. Union; S. F. Call; Hayes' Angeles*, v. 40, etc.

without the aid of irrigation, the harvest frequently depending on a few light showers, or even on the direction of the wind at the critical moment.

There are times, however, when there is no scarcity of water, when floods sweep over the land, competing with droughts for the vexation of man. Every spring the snows of the Sierra, melted by warm and heavy rains, swell the streams, which sometimes overflow their banks and cover broad low-lying tracts, to the great damage of the inhabitants. And with the progress of time overflows are becoming more frequent, owing to the filling of the river-beds with mining débris. The first great flood since the gold discovery in 1849–50 did little harm, because the settlements in the interior valleys were few and not highly improved; but in 1852–3 the injury was greater, and in 1861–2 its course was marked, especially in the northern half, by disasters never before equalled. In Yolo Indian mounds of great antiquity were swept away. The Stanislaus washed down banks formed centuries ago. On Russian River an adobe building several decades old disappeared, and everywhere the rivers presented scenes of desolation, bearing along trees and buildings, broken fences and household commodities, and dead sheep and cattle, with now and then a human victim.[38]

[38] The official report of the flood, in *Cal. Jour. Sen.*, 1863, ap. 3, p. 42–50, 89–102, points to the cause in the excessive snowfall in the mountains during Nov. and Dec., followed by unusually heavy and warm rains in Dec. and Jan. Over 25 inches fell at Red Dog in 19 days, of which 11.32 inches were in 48 hours, on Jan. 10–11th. At Sac. over 14 inches fell between Jan. 5th and 22d. It was shown that the straits of Carquinez had little to do with detaining the flow from the two great tributaries, for the highest water at Benicia was caused by an unusual tide, several days before the highest flood. For details of damage, see *S. F. Bulletin, Sac. Union,* and *Alta,* for Dec. 1861–Feb. 1862, extending from Klamath southward, the hills of San Mateo not escaping. The legislature proposed measures for relief. Plans for improved drainage in *Cal. Jour. Sen.,* 1863, ap. iii. 25–31, 97–100; *Morse's W. Per.,* MS., 80; *Burnett's Recol.,* MS., ii. 285; *Hayes' Misc.,* 127; reports on damage in the south, *Winans' Stat.,* MS., 12; *Siskiyou Co. Aff.,* MS., 27. The fullest accounts are collected in *Cal. Floods, Scraps,* passim; including information on previous and subsequent floods, to be found also in *Alta Cal.,* March 9, 30, Dec. 20, 1852, etc.; Nov. 15, 1855; March 2, Nov. 14, 1857; March 6, 1858; March 28, July 15, Nov. 9, 1859; *Placer Times and Transcript,* March 21, 1852, etc.; *S. F. Herald,* June 6, 1852; Jan 3, 1853; Dec. 1861; *Marysville Appeal,* id.; county histories; *Grass Val. Directory.* The damage at Sacramento, Stockton, and Marysville is related in my historic sketches of those towns, in my *Hist. Cal.,* vol. vi. The legislature was driven from the capital to S. F.

Warned by the calamity, Sacramento, Stockton, and other important towns took the precaution to improve still further the levees raised after previous inundations, and so place themselves beyond all risk. Farmers generally heeded the lesson, and subsequent slighter overflows of 1867–8, 1871–2, 1877–8, 1880, and 1881 were thus lessened in their damaging effects. In the south the denuded banks offer so little check to the accumulating waters that in some places the dry bed may be converted into a raging current within a few hours.[39]

If the farmers here have some ills, others they have not. There are fewer than elsewhere of the evils arising from storms, hail, frost, excess of moisture; and we suffer, perhaps, in less degree than people to the eastward from wheat rust, potato blight, apple worm, orange scale, and cattle diseases. Yet there are pests in plenty. The spermophile, or California ground-squirrel, is exceedingly destructive to grain crops, vegetables, fruit-trees, and vines,[40] especially south of the Carquinez line, where they materially

[39] Details of these and other later and partial overflows, in *S. F. Bulletin*, Dec. 2, 7–8, 1864; Feb. 10, 1869; Nov. 25, Dec. 26–7, 1871; Jan. 15, Apr. 4, 1872; Feb. 5, 1874; March 1, 9, 1878; Feb. 3, 1880; Jan.–Feb. 1881; with account of broken levees. *Sac. Union, Alta Cal., S. F. Call, Chronicle,* for about the same dates; *Mt. Messenger*, March 16, 1878; Feb. 12, 1881; *Los Ang. News*, March 12, 1867; Jan. 3, 1868; *Monterey Dem.*, Jan. 23, 1875; *Sonoma Dem.*, March 15, 1878; *Amador Ledger*, March 2, 1878; *Ferndale Enterprise*, March 14, 1879; *San José Mercury*, Apr. 22, 1880; *Los Ang. Herald*, Jan. 3, 1880; *Oroville Merc.*, Feb. 4, 1881. Among severe avalanches which have taken place in the Sierra Nevada, *S. F. Bulletin*, Jan. 16, 1857, and Feb. 9, 1859, refers to two in Plumas and Shasta which killed 4 men each; *S. F. Post*, Jan. 21, 1875, to one which involved the loss of 28 Chinese; *S. F. (W.) Call*, March 27, 1882; *Id. (D.)*, March 12, 1884, overwhelming Woodstock. In 1878 the gov. refused assent to a bill for relieving sufferers by the flood. *Cal. Jour. Sen.*, 1877–8, 342.

[40] They are especially abundant along the central zone running from Pájaro to Amador. The most effective remedies against them are strychnine and phosphorus poison scattered in saturated wheat, and sulphur smoke blown into their burrows. Gophers are treated in the same way. The pouched cheek is the chief point of difference between the spermophiles and the regular squirrel. There are two species, distinguished by the color of a stripe along the spine. That with the yellowish hoary stripe abounds south of S. F. Bay; the other, with dark brown stripe, is found north of it and in less numbers. Concerning remedies and enactments for enforcing, see *Cal. Squirrel Law; Burnett's Recol.*, MS., ii. 217–21.

affect the value of farms in many districts. The
gopher ranks next as the destroyer of roots of fruit-
trees, vegetables, newly planted seed, and sweet buds
in the coast valleys. Along the eastern slopes of the
Sierra grasshoppers have occasionally denuded large
districts, leaving not a leaf or blade of grass. The first
notable ravage occurred in 1855 and the last in 1885.[41]

The great length of California, subdivided into narrow strips by several ranges, with cross-ridges and
lateral openings, gives rise to a variety of climates
and soils. The coast has a very equable temperature, bathed as it is by warm ocean currents, tempered
by almost daily breezes. These also modify to a great
extent the heat concentrated within the interior by
the enclosing mountain walls, and it is only in the
desert region of the south-east that the heat becomes
extreme.

In the northern part, where no heated interior
basins exist to draw the cooling currents, the prevailing wind is north-westerly, laden with summer showers.
Below Cape Mendocino this changes, and rains depend
on south-westerly currents, which are very rare between May and October, but rule through the winter
months. Their opposite exists in the dreaded Boreas,
moisture consuming and shrivelling, whether hot or
cold.[42] During the six months beginning with No-

[41] Trenches and smoke are the only partial safeguards against them. Placer
lost a large portion of its crops in 1855 by their raid, and Shasta, Yolo, Suisun,
and the S. Joaquin east counties shared more or less in the disaster. They
have penetrated to the coast counties. Other visitations are mentioned in
Id., May 8, June 27, 1856; June 21-2, 1859; June 13, 1861; *S. F. Times*,
Apr. 1, June 11, 1869, in Lassen; *S. F. Call*, June 27, 1871; *Folsom Teleg.*,
June 8, 1872; *S. F. Bulletin*, June 14, 1858; July 2, 1884; June 8, 1885. In
U. S. Gov. Doc., Cong. 45, Sess. 2, Entomolog. Rept for 1878-9, p. xviii.
322, 80, are considerations of remedies. In some parts wild geese have been
so destructive that bands of hunters were kept to exterminate them. *S. F.
Call*, May 7, 1882. *Prov. Rec.*, iii. 131, alludes to the chahuistle wheat ravage
in 1783, and to dread of locusts. Concerning worms injurious to fruit, see
Treatise on Fruit Trees; L. Lake Bull., June 19, 1880; *S. F. Times*, June 6,
1867; *Oakl. Transcr.*, Sept. 1, 1877; *Castrov. Argus*, Sept. 4, 1869; *S. José
Merc.*, Nov. 23, 1883; *Alta Cal.*, March 9, Apr. 13, July 22, 1859; *S. F. Call*,
July 18, 1871; *S. F. Bulletin*, Feb. 25, Aug. 9, 1859; *Cal. Agric. Soc., Trans.;
Rural Press*, passim.

[42] Occasionally, it has become a veritable siroces, as at Santa Bárbara in
June 1859, when trees were blasted, fruit literally roasted on the trees, and
birds and calves suffocated. *Sta B. Gazette*, June 23, 1859, etc.; *Stockton Argus*,
id.; *S. F. Bulletin*, June 14, 1864.

vember, the dried-up or shrunken streams are replenished, at first from the rains, and subsequently, in March and April, from the melting of the Sierra snow. The rainfall varies from an annual mean of 70 inches in the extreme north-west to 40 inches above Cape Mendocino, about 22 near San Francisco, 16 below Monterey, and 10 inches at San Diego. A corresponding decrease takes place along the interior valley strip, with a relatively lighter fall than that on the more humid coast, in similar latitudes. Thus the average fall at Redding is 42 inches, at Red Bluff 24, at Sacramento 18, at Modesto 9, Tulare 6, Sumner 4 inches. As the moisture-condensing Sierra is ascended, the fall increases to 34 inches at Auburn,[43] and 60 at Cisco.[44] The general average for the greater part of

[43] Or about 1 inch for every 100 or 150 feet, while the corresponding latitude in the bottom of the valley is 18 inches. The lava beds in the northeast corner are exceptionally drier. Yet the temperature up the Sierra slopes remains as warm as the valley for the first 2,000 or 2,500 feet during summer. The winter is colder.

[44] The appended tables of temperature and humidity in connection with the preceding observations, and those given in the opening chapter, will suffice for a better understanding of the present topic. The peculiarity mentioned calls for a statement of rainfall by the season.

	Temperature.			Rainfall.	Elev.
	Summer.	Winter.	Av.	Av.	
Coast Region.	Deg.	Deg.	Deg.	Inches.	Feet.
Camp Lincoln, Del Norte co........	59.5	47.2	53.9	73.4	
Fort Humboldt, Humboldt co	58.2	47.0	52.9	35.9	50
Camp Wright, Mendocino co.......	74.7	58.8	57.8	43.9	
Napa, Napa co....................	70.3	49.3	59.9	26.6	95
San Francisco..................	58.0	50.1	55.2	20.7	130
Martinez, Contra Costa co.....	70.1	48.9	60.3	16.1	
San José, Santa Clara co...........	66.7	49.5	56.8	11.4	91
Monterey, Monterey co............	59.7	50.2	55.5	15.7	140
Soledad, Monterey co....	66.9	48.8	57.8	7.9	
Santa Bárbara, Santa Bárbara co... .	67.9	54.1	61.4	16.2	20
Los Angeles, Los Angeles co....... .	73.2	55.6	64.9	12.0	265
San Diego, San Diego co...........	66.7	56.8	62.0	9.3	64
Interior Section.					
Fort Jones, Siskiyou co.............	71.1	34.1	52.3	21.7	2,570
Redding, Shasta co.................	81.6	47.3	63.4	42.1	556
Red Bluff, Tehama co......	80.8	47.5	63.7	24.0	308
Marysville, Yuba co...............	78.7	49.5	64.4	17.8	67
Sacramento, Sacramento co....	71.8	48.2	60.8	18.7	30
Stockton, San Joaquin co..........	72.5	48.2	60.8	15.8	23
Merced, Merced co.................	79.1	49.0	63.4	9.7	171
Fresno, Fresno co.................	84.1	51.3	67.6	7.0	292
Tulare, Tulare co......	83.8	45.9	64.4	6.2	282
Sumner, Kern co..................	86.2	48.7	67.3	4.2	415
Foothills.					
Auburn, Placer co....	74.1	45.4	58.6	34.0	1,360
Cisco, Placer co........	60.9	32.8	45.2	60.3	5,934

the state would be utterly inadequate for this zone,
but for its distribution during the half-year when
most needed, leaving the summer and autumn dry.
This peculiarity regulates the agricultural system,
making the winter season so busy, and the harvest-
time so early and convenient.

The agricultural value of districts depends in California less on the underlying geologic formation, which
forms the base in most countries, than on climatic conditions, the south being especially dependent on the
topography and hydrography. Yet the Sierra Nevada has left its impress, as shown by the sandy surface deposits in San Joaquin valley, and the more
clayey soil in Sacramento. Owing to the elevated
slope and vast drainage area, its foothills extend in a

The information is based in part on *U. S. Gov. Doc.*, Cong. 47, Sess. 1, H. Ex.
Doc., vii. 335–6, 385, 565–84, 626; *Cal. Climate Scraps*, 4 et seq.; *Hayes' Nat.
Phenom.*, i.–ii.; the *Smithsonian Reports*, by the railway companies and by private individuals; *Schott's Tables; Turrill's Notes*, 18–21; *Cal. Agric. Soc., Trans.*,
1868 et seq.; *Hittell's Res.*, 94, etc. The following is a fair average at various
points in the Pacific and eastern states and in Europe:

	Temperature. Degrees.			Rainfall. Inches.				
	Jan.	July.	Diff.	Spring.	Sum.	Aut.	Wint.	Year.
Fort Humboldt	40	58	18	13.5	1.2	4.9	15.	34.6
Sacramento........	45	73	'8	7.0	0.	2.6	12.1	21.7
San Francisco......	49	57	8	6.6	0.1	3.3	13.3	23.4
San Diego.........	51	72	21	2.7	0.5	1.2	5.9	10.4
Fort Yuma........	56	92	36	0.3	1.3	0.9	0.7	3.2
Astoria, Oregon....	..	..	..	16.4	4.0	21.8	44.2	86.0
New York.........	31	77	46	11.7	11.6	9.9	10.4	43.7
New Orleans.......	55	82	27	11.3	17.3	9.6	12.7	50.1
St. Louis..........	..	..	..	12.9	14.1	8.7	6.3	42.
Liverpool..........	..	..	..	6.2	9.8	10.8	7.3	34.1
Paris..............	..	..	..	5.5	5.9	6.5	4.7	22.6
Rome.............	..	..	..	7.3	3.4	10.9	9.3	30.9
Naples....	46	76	30	....	....	....	....	....
London............	37	62	25	....	....	....	....	....

Storms are rare, and the occasional severe ones have not inflicted much damage. Instances in *Alta Cal.*, Dec. 15, 1849; Jan. 3, 1855; March 2, 1861; *S. F.
Bulletin*, March 4, 1857; June 14, Aug. 6, Sept. 10, Dec. 2, 1864; Jan. 2–9,
1872; May 30, 1878; *S. F. Call*, Apr. 11, 1884. A small district in Shasta
was on May 10, 1856, damaged by a hail-storm. Cloud-bursts have, on rare
occasions, done some harm in the south and in the Sierra. *L. Ang. Exp.*,
Jan. 3, 1880; *Inyo Indep.*, Aug. 1, 1874; *Vallejo Recorder*, Nov. 18, 1870; *Red
Bluff Sentinel*, March 22, 1873; *Quincy Union*, July 16, 1864. Meteoric showers,
with meteor falls. *S. F. Times*, Feb. 23–5, Aug. 7–10, 1869; *S. F. Call*, Nov.
16, 1867; Nov. 15, 1868; Aug. 12, 1869; Apr. 21, 1871; *Sac. Union*, May 7,
1859; *Nev. Gaz.*, Dec. 29–31, 1866.

long, gentle, talus-like slope, which forms a kind of
upland plain, with a breadth in the north and centre
of 50 to 70 miles, between the elevations of 500 and
4,000 feet, but narrowing in the south, where the
transverse incisions or lateral valleys are widely bor-
dered with bare, abrupt bluffs, while in the Sacramento section they are rounded and tree-lined. On
the west side the slope from the Coast range is from
10 to 40 miles wide in Shasta and Tehama counties,
after which it lessens to a narrow strip. The lower
foothills below the altitude of 2,000 or 2,500 feet enjoy
the same temperature with greater moisture, and yield
the same products as the valley land, including semi-
tropic plants, fruit thriving relatively better.[45]

The Sacramento valley land proper is gently undu-
lating, dotted with hillocks known as hog-wallows, and
lined by strips and blocks of adobe soil. In the lower
half the river bottoms on the east side are widely covered with mining débris, termed slickens, which have
converted once fertile tracts into sterile wastes, and so
filled up the river-beds as to increase the frequency
and extent of floods, and to cause the wider spread of
this destructive deposit.[46] All this expanse of allu-
vial land is very productive, with little need for irrigation;[47] but in the San Joaquin drainage region the
lighter soil and scantier rain increase the need for
artificial watering, while in the south it becomes
absolutely necessary. The sandy and less compact
soil does not retain the moisture so well, and the
number of intermittent streams increase, especially on
the west side, with its bare and abrupt Coast range.

[45] Their soil has a general similarity in its orange-red tint, due to an iron
oxide admixture of 4 to 12 or even more per cent, with a texture varying from
moderately heavy loam to stiff clay, with rolled gravel often in excess. The
percentage of lime increases toward the central counties, and diminishes beyond the Tuolumne. The proportion of phosphates is low. Deep ploughing
is advisable.

[46] True, a small admixture of such sandy ingredients is beneficial to certain
heavy soil; but when a succession of layers is made, the benefit becomes an
evil which can be remedied only by years of costly effort, with special planting, ploughing, and counter-manuring.

[47] The rainfall ranging from 40 to 20 inches, with usually slight snow in
the winter and frost temperature at night for several months.

The Tulare section contains much delta land easily irrigated.[48]

A large portion of the valley trough, especially toward the mouths of the two converging main rivers, and round the lakes, is marshy, and known as tule land from the rush growing upon it.[49] Another large area of such lands, subject to overflow from salt water, lies along the coast, but chiefly within the bays, forming in all some 3,000,000 acres, much of it exceedingly productive. A portion has been reclaimed by levees, but these are in many places insecure, owing to the porous and buoyant nature of the foundation, which in other parts have so far baffled all efforts of engineers. In the San Joaquin delta the matted tule forms large floating islands.[50]

[48] Round Visalia is the one heavily wooded oak region of the S. Joaquin valley. From Merced to San Joaquin county stretches an irregular belt of black adobe. Round it the soil is calcareous, the lime admixture ranging from half to three per cent, and it is consequently very productive under irrigation, yet with little phosphoric acid. It has the advantage of being deep, so as to permit roots to seek compensation for dryness by wider sinking. In the uplands the phosphates will soon be exhausted. In the lake districts the prevalent alkali, which dissolves the humus, needs only the corrective of gypsum, for the soil composition is otherwise good. Between Calaveras and the American extends a great plain of rich dun-colored loam, broken only by timber belts of rivers and easily tilled. In the Sac. valley the lime admixture is generous, and by retaining the humus tends to counteract dryness; potash abounds, but phosphates are rare.

[49] Known as cat-tail, or *typha*. The round rush proper on salt marshes is the *scripus locustris*.

[50] So that the famous floating gardens of the Aztecs here find their counterpart. The lake region is so strongly impregnated with alkali as to render reclamation unpromising. Most of the reclaimed land lies within the delta region of the confluent Sac. and San Joaquin, protected by dikes of 5 to 10 feet in height, with a base of 20 to 30 feet and a summit 5 feet broad. The cost has been about 11 cents per cubic yard. The legislature of 1872 authorized the sale of bonds, in mortgage on reclaimed districts, to promote such work, but the scheme did not succeed; in time better plans may be adopted. For suggestions, reports, and state measures, see every *Cal. Jour. Sen.* and *Ass.*, including governor's message and surveyor-general's report. *Cal. Agric. Soc., Trans.*, 1860, 285-9, etc.; *Hayes' Agric.*, 233-41; *Rural Press*, etc. The first reclamation act. *Cal. Statutes*, 1851, 409. County histories of *S. Joaq., Sac., Sutter, Contra Costa*, and *Yolo*, give accounts of plans and work done. *U. S. Agric. Rept*, 1872, 179-87. Concerning special drainage canals, from Fresno slough, *Report on Canal from Fresno Slough to Antioch; Sac. Union*, Nov. 11, 1880; Jan. 17, 1881. The reclamation of Colorado desert, by turning in the waters of Colorado River, has been widely discussed. Meanwhile several oases have been formed in this quarter with the aid of wells. *U. S. Gov. Doc.*, Cong. 36, Sess. 1, Sen. Com. Rept 276, ii.; Cong. 43, Sess. 1, Sen. Misc. Doc. 84, i.; Cong. 44, Sess. 2, U. S. Statutes 377; *Wheeler's Surveys*, 1876, 70-2, 109-25; *Cal. Statutes*, 1859, 238, 392; *Cal. Agric. Soc., Trans.*, 1874, 363-6; *Hayes' S. Diego*, i. 127-34, 216-21; *Overland*, xv. 17-53.

The terrace formation noted in the great valley ranges from the low, rich bottom-land to a second poorer bench, and to a third less regular surface with comparatively little valuable land. The coast region enjoys the advantage of ocean moisture, combined with a soil which increases in heaviness and timber wealth northward. Thermal belts occur in several parts, chiefly near the bay, which are exempt from frosts.

Within recent years portions of southern California before considered almost worthless have been turned to good account as agricultural areas, their virgin soil producing abundant crops of fruit and cereals, under the improved methods which have superseded primitive systems of farming. Many of them are now occupied by thriving colonies, as in the case of the Chino ranch in San Bernardino county, which, in 1881, passed into the hands of Richard Gird,[52] a wealthy and enterprising citizen of southern California. Here families have been introduced and settlements founded on a tract of more than 20,000 acres, set apart for the purpose, every ten acres of which, it is estimated, is capable of supporting a family.

[52] Richard Gird, a native of Litchfield, N. Y., came to California in 1852, and first tried his fortune at the placer mines of El Dorado co. Here he was prostrated by Panamá fever, contracted during the voyage, and after his recovery, engaged in farming in Sonoma co., which occupation he followed till 1858, when he embarked for Chili, and was there appointed a surveyor on the first railroad built by Henry Meiggs. Returning to this coast in 1860, after a brief visit to his home, he took part in several expeditions against the Apaches in Arizona, of which territory, by order of the legislature, he made a topographical survey, and published what is to-day the only official map. In 1872, after suffering business reverses in San Francisco, we again find him in Arizona, where he arrived with a capital of $16. A few years later he became a millionaire, being one of the discoverers of the Tombstone mine, and disposing of his interest for $1,000,000. A portion of this money he invested in the Chino ranch of 36,000 acres, to which he has since added 14,000 acres, making in all 50,000 acres of the choicest land, all in one body, and under one fence. He also owns a half interest in 500,000 acres in Sonora, Mex., together with valuable oil lands and brown-stone quarries, is one of the largest share-holders in the Elsinor and Pomona railroad, and has a controlling interest in the Farmers' Exchange and Second National banks in San Bernardino. He purposes to use the bulk of his fortune in founding the largest industrial school in the world, where orphan children will receive free of charge a practical education. As a self-made man, a self-denying man, a philanthropist, and a benefactor to the community, this gentleman has no superior in the city and state of his adoption.

CHAPTER II.

CEREALS AND OTHER PRODUCTS.

1848-1889.

Leading Staples—Wheat and Barley—Oats and Corn—Yield—Effect of Irrigation—Rice—Conditions of Culture—Quality—Vegetables — Cotton — Flax — The Silk-worm Excitement — Effect of Legislation on Sericulture—Fiasco in Tobacco—Mustard—Sugar.

Notwithstanding the many other growing industries of California, cereals must always hold a conspicuous place as a staple product, favored by easy tillage and the many advantages of climate. Though not always the case, grain-growing under favorable conditions is still profitable, even if the yield does not reach the former figures of 70 bushels of wheat and 100 of barley to the acre. The latter grain was the favorite during the fifties, owing to the demand for animal feed under the increasing traffic, and to its special adaptability to the sandy soil and dry climate. In 1852 more than 2,000,000 bushels were harvested; and this quantity was nearly doubled during every succeeding decade, till it was estimated at 20,000,000 bushels by 1888, used largely for malting.[1]

[1] The crop of 9,700 bushels reported for 1850 rose to over 2,000,000 in 1852; and although soon yielding to wheat, the increase continued, under the growing demand for horse-feed and brewing, the yield for 1860, 1870, and 1880 standing at 4,400,000, 8,780,000, and 12,460,000 bushels respectively, the last from 586,000 acres, Alameda county leading with 1,200,000 bushels. The home consumption is estimated at 210,000 tons, of which 32,000 were for brewing. *Commerce and Ind.*, 282. The lower price received for barley was offset by a larger and surer yield. The assessor of Monterey county reported for 1853 a crop of 9,000 bushels from a field of 100 acres in Pájaro Valley, one acre yielding 149 bushels; Burrell of Sta Cruz was credited in 1859 with a small field of 90 bushels to the acre. See also *Alta Cal.*, Sept. 15, 1851; Apr. 19, 1859; *S. F. Bulletin*, June 18, 1856; in Yuba 100 acres averaged 69 bushels, *Sac. Union*, Jan. 27, 1858; crop in January. In volunteer

Oats suffer under the conditions favorable to barley, thriving well only in the northern and central coast counties, with an average yield surpassing that of any other cereal, yet with little prospect for increased production beyond the present million and a half bushels.[2] Rye and buckwheat are only slightly cultivated.

Maize, or Indian corn, is likewise limited by the dryness of the soil and coolness of the nights It thrives best in the sheltered valleys of the northern coast, but owing to the inherent predilection of the Spanish race, it is raised chiefly in the south, and with the aid of irrigation can be made to yield two crops. The average yield within recent years may be stated at 4,000,000 to 5,000,000 bushels.[3] The attempts to cultivate rice have so far been unpromising experiments.[4]

crops, barley excels; and in Yolo a field was said to have yielded five in succession, the last of 30 bushels to the acre. *Hittell's Res. Cal.*, 231. This was of the nepaul kind, which shares with the Chevalier in a limited cultivation, the latter being used chiefly for pearl barley, yielding about 15 per cent less than the common barley.

[2] The production for 1860, 1870, and 1880 stands at 1,043,000, 1,757,000, and 1,341,000 bushels respectively, Humboldt yielding over one fourth, and San Mateo one tenth. In 1852 it was 94,000. Heavy crops are frequently reported, especially from Del Norte, as high as 125 and even 157 bushels to the acre. *Crescent C. Herald*, Oct. 1857; in Sta Bárbara 4 acres gave 15 tons. *Sac. Union*, July 6, 1855. Of the several kinds grown, the Feather flourishes best in sandy loam, and Bare and Tucker in heavy soil. The other leading varieties are Australian, English, and Norway. Of rye and buckwheat, the former yielded for 1860, 1870, and 1880 about 52,000, 26,000, and 181,000 bushels, chiefly from San Joaquin county; the latter 76,800, 22,000, and 22,300, one third from Sac. county.

[3] Irrigation is as a rule esteemed too costly for the grain. Besides the north coast valleys, some of the moist bottom-lands of the lower Sac., and on the San Gabriel are favorable. Russian River is a favorite haunt, says *Sac. Union*, Aug. 2, 1859; see also county histories of *Mendocino, Yuba*, and *Los Angeles;* but Los Angeles county in 1879 yielded 752,000 bushels, from 22,700 acres, out of the total 1,993,000 bushels. Egyptian corn, though as yet little known or in demand, recommends itself as requiring less moisture even than barley, producing one fourth more weight of grain to the acre than other cereals, and yielding good forage. *Napa Register*, Dec. 27, 1878; *S. Diego News*, Feb. 20, 1878.

[4] The planting of rice was early suggested by the influx of Chinese and the extent of swamp-land, and under the spell of experiments so prevalent in the fifties, a feeble attempt was made therein. The state offered a premium to encourage it, but in vain. The inducements were not sufficient to overcome the many obstacles in the way. The *U. S. Census* for 1860 reports a crop of 2,140 lbs.; *Hayes' Agric.*, 242-4; *Cal. Farmer*, Sept. 1862; Jan. 26, 1871; *S. F. Bulletin*, Aug. 2, Sept. 3, 1856; Jan. 29, 1857; March 3, July 30, 1862; *Salinas Democ.*, May 16, 1874.

For none of these cereals is there any promising opening beyond the local requirement, save for wheat, whose valuable glutinous quality has made it highly esteemed, and whose flinty dryness permits it to endure, without special preparation or care, the long sea voyage to Europe. The difficulties in the way of corn obliged the Spanish-Californians to give it greater prominence, and before the gold discovery it was raised to some extent even east of the Coast Range. Toward the close of the fifties its production began to surpass that of barley; but it was not till the value of the plains of the great valley, especially the San Joaquin, burst like a revelation upon its decriers that wheatlands began to be fully appreciated. Under the facilities for shipment presented by a large fleet, whose predecessors had to depart in ballast, the yield increased rapidly from less than 6,000,000 bushels in 1860 to over 30,000,000 in the early eighties, with Stanislaus county in the front rank, followed by Colusa and San Joaquin. The crop for 1889, one of the largest in the history of the state, was estimated at nearly 50,000,000 bushels, the product of about 3,250,000 acres, and realizing at tide-water $35,000,-000. The export rose from nearly three quarters of a million bushels in 1867 to more than treble that amount by 1888. Under hasty methods of farming, the average crop has fallen to about 16 bushels to the acre, or about one fourth more than the average for the union, and even less with diminished rains and withering north winds. Nevertheless, when conducted on a large scale, it is still a fairly profitable industry, even at the low prices prevailing within recent years. With steam machinery, now largely used, as a motive power, it is estimated that, where cheap communication exists, wheat can be sown, reaped, and forwarded to market from interior valleys at a cost of from thirty to forty cents per bushel.

[5] According to the census of 1850, the crop was only 17,328 bushels. By 1852 it had risen to 297,000, by 1860 to 5,900,000, by 1870 to 16,000,000, by 1880 to 29,000,000, of which Colusa county leads with over 4,500,000, Glenn

After the gold excitement had begun to subside, attention was first of all directed, as I have said, to the

being the prominent farmer, followed by San Joaquin with 3,500,000 bushels, Butte with 2,200,000, and Yolo and Solano with 2,000,000 each, several others having over 1,000,000. By 1883 Stanislaus had assumed the lead with 4,600,-000 bushels out of a total of 32,600,000. The 1880 figure represents an average yield of only 16.1 bushels to the acre.

The Hispano-Californians planted wheat from the first, and at the opening of the century it was surpassing the favorite maize for which the climate was not so well adapted. By 1784 the grain crop reached 20,000 fanegas and shipments from Mexico for the garrisons were declared needless. *Cal. Prov. Rec.*, i. 184. The dryness of some districts combined with fickleness of climate in discouraging growers, as in San Diego, where crops failed in 1776 and 1781. *S. Diego Arch.; Parr. Mont.*, 24 et seq.; *Bandini, Doc.*, 2, etc.; *Sta Bárb. Arch.*, v., ix.-x.; *S. P. Miss.*, i. 18, 68–71; *Prov. S. P.*, v., vi.; *Dept. S. P., S. José*, i. 7–10; *Vallejo, Doc.*, iii. 228–30. Mexicans carried it in 1834 to the north side of the bay, where Russians had prior to this made a beginning. Sutter introduced it with the forties into Sac. valley, and in 1845 it was cultivated in Yolo and Placer. In 1847, the *Californian* of July 10th boasts of the expanding wheat culture, which had brought flour down to $6 per 100 lbs. at S. F., which is one fourth above the average for the U. S., but far below that of several larger wheat-producing western states. Nevertheless it is widely assumed that the soil, in favorable seasons, and with the precautions prevalent elsewhere, can be made to yield more to the acre than perhaps any other country on the globe. Brewer, in *U. S. Census*, 1880, ii. 78, admits that the soil and climate are peculiarly well adapted for wheat, yielding marvellous crops. Several cases of over 70 bushels to the acre were reported to him, and he saw 'crops reputed to be heavier than that.' Bidwell responded to the premiums offered by the State Agric. Soc. by harvesting 'upward of 73 bushels per acre on 10 acres...in the presence of witnesses.' Mission records, ubi sup., refer to 30 and 33 fold yields, which Colton, *Three Years*, 442–5, speaks of over 100-fold, as does Bryant, *Cal.*, 304. At San Ramon 90 bushels to the acre, reports the *S. F. Call*, Oct. 3, 1865; near S. José, 87 bushels. *Sac. Union*, Aug. 10, 1855. See also *Hittell's Res. Cal.*, 227. The average was higher in earlier years before the non-rotation in crops tended to impoverish the soil. Other drawbacks lie in volunteer crops and hasty cultivation of the soil, especially among the speculative tillers of San Joaquin valley, and under such neglect the average has fallen, as in 1871, to 9 bushels. The lack of timely rain has been the trouble, excess of rain seldom doing harm, and the beating down of crops by storms is rare; but hot winds come at times to shrivel the grain while it is in milk. Smut does comparatively little damage. Allusions to, in *Sac. Union*, June 15, Oct. 15, Nov. 15, 1855; *Marin Tocsin*, Apr. 24, 1879. The Australian shows the greatest tendency toward this disease. As it is, the treatment with sulphate of copper is almost general among wheat-growers. Odessa, or old Californian, is the favorite variety in the southern part of the state. Elsewhere the Chile holds the sway; with a decided concession to club, red Mediterranean, and Sonora, and a proportion of Oregon white, bald, and Egyptian. The last, while yielding well, lacks gluten. The Sonora, while smaller in head, ripens early, so as to escape the shrivelling northers. The winter-wheat of the east does not thrive till the second year, when it has become acclimated and converted into spring-wheat, as all California varieties may be called. Red seeds turn white during this conversion. The great merit of California wheat lies in its gluten, of which it possesses a larger proportion than that of any other North American state. It is therefore sought as an admixture to the weaker grain of countries not favored with sunshine and the loose soil of El Dorado. The sheltered coast valleys excel in this respect the moister ocean slopes and the over-heated San Joaquin and Sacramento. Another advantage is its extreme dryness, which permits it to be shipped through the tropics without danger of sweating, although taken di-

raising of various kinds of vegetables, immigrants and miners, who had hitherto lived mainly on a diet of salt meat, having a more decided taste for these esculents than the shiftless Mexicans, who cared for little in this respect save beans. The first who engaged in gardening were rewarded by high prices, which enabled them to make money. The consequent rush of competitors, especially foreigners of the Latin race who had been

rect from the field. Even the kiln-dried and pressed flour of the Altantic does not keep so well. The hot winds of the great valley often injure the plumpness and size of the grain, which nevertheless compares well with the eastern; in weight it exceeds eastern, the bushel being over 60 lbs., seldom less, sometimes 65 lbs. Whiteness and thin skin appear coördinate, for where the coast fogs impart an exceptional darkness of color, there the skin increases in thickness and bran. Objections have been raised to the lack of sifting, and more attention is now given to grain cleaners and separators, as instanced in *Sac. Union*, Aug. 14, 1865; Jan. 1, 1881; *Napa Reg.*, March 4, 1879; *Petal. Courier*, Aug. 14, 1878; and to improving the grade of the flour. *S. F. Chron.*, Apr. 6, 1881.

Wheat-sowing extends during the last two and the first three months of the year, preferably during Jan. and Feb., the latter succeeding best with heavy spring rains, while earlier fields gain their strength from moderate moisture. Glenn used 90 lbs. of seed on early fields, and 100 lbs. for late sowing. In Los Angeles 45 lbs. was deemed sufficient. *U. S. Census*, 1880, iii. 76-7. The immunity from rain during the summer and early autumn allows the grain to be left standing for weeks after maturity, while awaiting its turn in the harvest. Little is lost by shaking from wind or machinery, the club grain especially holding itself remarkably well till the first rains relax the capsules. The average cost of production ranges between $6 and $9 per acre; ploughing $1 to $1.50; seed 80 cents to $1.50; sowing and harrowing 50 to 75 cents; heading $1.20 to $1.50; thrashing $1.25; sacks $1; hauling 50 cents to $1; add rent and taxes. In the great valley a saving is widely effected by combining the sowing and harrowing operation with the ploughing, at a total cost of $1 per acre, and ploughing has been done as low as 50 cents. With an average yield of 16 bushels there is a fair return, even with wheat at $1.25 per bushel. The lightness of the soil, with freedom from sod, stones, and shrubs, permits ready cultivation; combination machinery, so widely adopted, whether rented or owned, reduces the cost, especially of man power; the dry climate gives time for harvesting and obviates the need for barns and attendant handling; add to this volunteer crops, and Cal. presents numerous advantages over other wheat countries. Standing crops are widely insured against fire. By burning the high stubble left by headers, the injury to the soil by deficient rotation or fallowing is greatly counteracted. England offers the best market for Cal. wheat, which there commands an extra price for its glutinous properties. Frisbie, *Remin.*, MS., 37, speaks of the first regular cargo in 1860. In 1867 nearly a quarter of a million tons were exported, and in 1881 more than three times this quantity, leaving nearly as much behind for lack of tonnage. High freights and competition from Russia and the eastern states in the limited markets tend to reduce profits, so that the average net return has fallen to 4 per cent. During the preceding decade prices for wheat ranged from a minimum of $1.05 during the winter 1869-70, and an average of $1.55 in 1872, 1874-5, 1876, to a maximum of $3.20 in 1877, and an average of $3.10 in May 1871. Hence with rent and heavy hauling and handling even fair crops failed at times to remunerate. Cal. obtained a gold medal for cereals at the Paris exhibition. *S. F. Times*, Aug. 27, 1868.

driven from the mines, rapidly reduced values, but an encouraging compensation was found in the susprisingly large yield, the uninterrupted growth of most vegetables throughout the year, and their generally thriving condition, marked by size and weight greatly in excess of products in the eastern states, potatoes sometimes weighing several pounds, cabbages 50 pounds, and squashes over 300 pounds. There was one drawback in the comparatively inferior flavor, owing partly to the rapidity of growth; and choice potatoes were imported. Within recent years, however, this has been remedied, and in 1889 some 250 carloads of vegetables were sent to the eastern states.[6]

[6] Comments on early neglect of vegetables, in *Cal. Star.*, March 11, 1848. Miners planted patches round their cabins, after the lessons taught by scurvy and hunger, and gardeners followed the advancing prospectors to reap a rich harvest. Gardens sprang up in 1849 round Coloma. *El Dor. Co. Hist.*, 110–11. Lassen raised vegetables on the Feather in 1851, *Plumas, Id.*, 295, and Siskiyou boasted of her potatoes in 1852. Established farmers around the bay and near Sac. applied themselves with especial zeal, and the earliest in the field made much money. Four men near Sac. received $40,000 from 16 acres. A tomato crop of 1½ acres was valued at $18,000. *S. F. Herald*, Aug. 1, 1850. Homer, near San José, cultivated 150 acres, raising potatoes, onions, and tomatoes, and realizing over $200,000 net, for 1850. Several gardens yielded over $3,000 per acre in 1849. *Sac. Transcript*, Oct. 14, Nov. 29, 1850; Feb. 28, March 14, May 15, 1851; *Farnham's Cal.*, 142–3; *Lambertie, Voy.*, 208–9; *Matthewson's Stat.*, MS., 4–7. Many Frenchmen and Italians abandoned the gold-fields before Anglo-Saxon persecution and sought the safer occupation of gardening. *Willey's Mem.*, 100–2; *Hayes' Agric.*, 191–2, 216; *Sac. Directory*, 1871, 76; *Pac. News*, Apr. 26, May 3, 1850; Jan. 25, Feb. 15, 1851; *Cal. Courier*, Aug. 9, Sept. 2, Nov. 13, Dec. 27, 1850; Feb. 18, Apr. 10, 1851; *S. F. Herald*, Jan 6, 1851; *Alta Cal.*, Oct. 4, Nov. 14, 1851; *Taylor's El Dorado*, i. 122–4. The high prices brought shipments from Oregon to compete with the growing production, and carry disappointment and loss to many. On the other hand came large crops, and general surprise was created by the size and beauty of the fruit. Potatoes were, as a rule, much larger than those of New England, with numerous specimens weighing 1 lb., and some of 4 and even 7 lbs. Pájaro Valley sent a sack of tubers, none of which weighed less than 3 lbs. A Santa Cruz farmer raised 2,500 bushels from 25. *S. F. Picayune*, Oct. 28, 1850. Onions have been displayed measuring 22 inches in circumference and weighing 47 oz. *Burnett's Rec.*, MS., ii. 233–6. Carrots 15½ lbs. *Golden Era*, Dec. 26, 1868. Turnips of 26 lbs., it is said; tomatoes 26 inches in circumference; one vine bore 608 lbs. *Id.*, Dec. 30, 1855; *S. F. Times*, Oct. 19, 1869. Squashes or pumpkins, 265, 279, and 340 lbs., with several fellows on the same vine of over 100 lbs. each. *Alta Cal.*, Oct. 5, 26, 1856; Oct. 1, 1857. Melons 64½ lbs., 3 weighed 178½ lbs. *Id.*, Sept. 20, 1856; Oct. 9, 1858. *Pac. News*, Aug. 1, 1850; Apr. 11, 1851. 1,331 full pods grown from 2 beans. *S. F. Bulletin*, March 29, 1856; *Sac. Union*, Dec. 1, 1858. Cabbages of over 50 lbs., with solid heads, are recorded, and others converted into evergreen tree-like plants, with stalks several feet high. *Alta Cal.*, Aug. 25, 1853; Oct. 26, 1859; *Sac. Union*, May 3, 1860; Sept. 15, 1862. Most of the vegetables can be found in the

The Spaniards brought with them from Mexico the indigenous cotton-plant, and one mission father cultivated it to some extent at Pala, for a time. Subsequently planters from the southern states brought their knowledge to bear, but only in experimental form, and no real effort was made until the offer of premiums by the state. In 1865 several fields of a hundred acres each were exhibited in Los Angeles and the valley of the San Joaquin; but the cultivation was finally reduced to a limited section in Merced and Kern, where a yield of one ton to eight acres brought an estimated profit of ten dollars per acre. With improving methods and quality of fibre there are prospects for a revival in cultivation.[7]

market throughout the year; others, as pease, melons, tomatoes, asparagus, enjoy here an extra long season. Potatoes were found to thrive best in the light sandy loam and misty atmosphere of the coast region, notably from Tomales to Pájaro, and along the warm Sac. sloughs, where the sweet potato flourishes. At Suisun 15-lb. specimens have been grown. *Id.*, Sept. 29, 1857; Oct. 26, 1858. Both potatoes are inferior in flavor to the eastern, and the Irish is subject to blights. These as well as many other roots may be left in the ground all winter. In 1852 the state raised 1,350,000 bushels Irish potatoes, of which 277,000 were in Sonoma, which also had a large proportion of the 10,000,000 lbs. of onions for that season. In 1860, 1870, and 1880 the potato crop stood at 1,789,000, 2,049,000, and 4,550,000 bushels, increasing to 5,000,000 bushels before 1890, while the crop of sweet potatoes diminished during the same years. *Pac. Rural Press*, Jan. 13, March 3, 1877, etc.; *Hittell's Res. Cal.*, 232–8. In 1889 over 10,000 tons of beans were forwarded to the eastern states. Lima beans are a specialty at Carpenteria, Santa Bárbara. At present vegetables are mainly cultivated for the market by Italians, Portuguese, and Chinese, whose windmills for irrigation form a striking feature in the outskirts of towns.

[7] For early efforts, see *Hist. Cal.*, ii.–iii., this series; *S. Diego Co. Hist.*, 189; *Cal. Courier*, Sept. 19, 1850, commended; and *S. F. Herald*, Oct. 21, 1852, referred to experiments; and *Sac. Union* of Dec. 5, 1854, spoke of a small fourth crop. In 1856 the state agricultural society began to offer premiums, and reported upon a patch in Los Angeles, where several subsequent efforts were made, although not so sustained as indicated in *Los Angeles Co. Hist.*, 85. *Alta Cal.*, Oct. 9, Nov. 8, Dec. 9, 1856, alludes to plants raised in Shasta, and in San Joaquin by Holden. There is good cotton land in San Diego county. In 1865 Calaveras had a 12-acre crop. *S. F. Bulletin*, May 8, 1865. In 1863 the state itself offered several prizes of from $1,000 to $3,000 for plantations of not less than 10 acres and for the first 100 bales of cotton, and Los Angeles in 1865 obtained $3,000 for 100 acres, the yield being one third of a bale per acre. Several other plantations existed here and in Fresno and Tulare, here one of 130 acres. *Cal. St. Agric. Soc., Transac.*, 1856, et seq., with résumé in 1872; *U. S. Agric. Rept.*, 1864 et seq.; *Hilgard's Report*, 72–5; *Nordhoff's Cal.*, 225; *Hayes' Ang.*, vii. 261; *Overland*, vi. 326–35; xiii. 18–25; *McPherson's Angeles*, 55–8; *Lake Co. Hist.*, 85, refers to experiments in the Lake valley. Early in the seventies wider efforts were made, and San Diego, San Bernardino, Yolo, and Sac. counties entered the field, which soon, however, was yielded to Merced and Kern, the former varying

Flax was also commended to the early colonists by the authorities, but no one has so far seen any profit in it. Nevertheless a considerable area has been planted in common with castor-beans, to raise seed for oil-mills. As regards fibre, attention is turning rather to the somi-tropic ramie and jute, the latter largely imported for the manufacture of bags.[8]

A singular episode in the history of California agriculture is the silk-worm excitement, which had

during 1879–81 from 240, 695, and 550 acres, the yield being about one ton to 8 acres, bringing 12 cents a pound. The expenses for 60 acres in Kern were: ploughing $104.50, irrigating $120.50, hoeing $295.50, picking $578, ginning and baling $99.61, rope, burlap, and seed $89.31, total $1,287.42, leaving a net profit of $9.24 per acre. Other calculations lower the cost and raise the prospective price, so that the outlook is by no means discouraging. Further details in *Alta Cal.*, Aug. 16, 1861; Sept. 27, Oct. 13, 1862; Apr.–July, 1863, etc. On Jan. 11, 1864, it speaks of the first cotton-press; *S. F. Bulletin*, Oct. 26, 1861; Dec. 6, 1862; Feb. 11, March 27, 1863; Apr. 13, 1864; Nov. 29, 1871; Nov. 25, 1881; Jan. 3, 1882; *Sac. Union*, Jan. 11, 1855; Oct. 12, 1858, concerning El Dorado; Oct. 24, Nov. 11, 1861; March 31, 1864; Nov. 17, 1868; *Com. Herald*, Nov.–Dec. 1870; *Stockton Rep.*, Nov. 30, 1872; *Fresno Expos.*, Nov. 20, 1872; *Kern Courier*, Nov. 30, Dec. 7, 1872; *S. Diego Union*, Nov. 15, 1872; *Snelling Argus*, Dec. 7, 1872; *Bakersfield Cal.*, July 8, 1880; *Sta Rosa Dem.*, Jan. 8, 1881; *S. F. Call*, Aug. 16, 1874; Jan. 31, 1882.

[8] Flax grows wild in California and has led many to advocate its cultivation. Even the colonial authorities of the preceding century sought to foster it. *Azanza, Instruct.*, 89; *Cal. St. Pap.*, Sac., iv. 6–7. But farmers failed to become interested until the establishment in the sixties of oil-mills encouraged them to plant it for seed. The stalk proved vigorous and yielded 1,500 lbs. of seed to the acre. In 1867 they produced 150 tons, partly from Sta Cruz. *S. F. Bulletin*, May 30, 1867. In 1879 Los Angeles had 400 acres, with prospects that encouraged others. *Los Ang. Co. Hist.*, 62. San Mateo held the lead in production, however, with 28,300 bushels out of a total 45,700 for that year, Ventura following with 13,000, Sta Bárbara, Solano, and S. Joaquin having each 1,000 to 1,300. *U. S. Census*, 1880, 215, reports no fibre, only 823 tons flax straw. *Ventura Co. Pict.*, 24; *Anaheim Gaz.*, Apr. 28, 1877; *Castrov. Argus*, Dec. 18, 1869; Nov. 29, 1879; *Petal. Argus*, March 29, 1878; *San Benito Advance*, Oct. 2, 1879; *Lake Democ.*, May 24, 1879; *S. L. Ob. Tribune*, Oct. 27, 1877; *Stockton Herald*, March 11, 1878; *Sac. Union*, July 14, 1855, reports a crop; *S. F. Times*, March 22, 1867; June 23, 1869; *Cal. Farmer*, Aug. 29, 1867, etc.; *Scientific Press*, July 16, 1875, et seq. Hemp has been still more neglected. *Alta Cal.*, Nov. 4, 1862. *Napa Reg.*, March 20, 27, 1880, points to the soil as favorable to jute. Arguments for ramie culture in *S. F. Call*, Oct. 9, 1870; June 6, 1871; May 31, 1872; Feb. 3, 1873; *Salinas Dem.*, Feb. 7, 1874; *Antioch Ledger*, March 28, 1874. *S. José Mercury*, Sept. 22, 1883, describes the pampas plume industry at Sta Bárbara; *Alta Cal.*, May 11, 1863, comments on teasel; *S. F. Bulletin*, Oct. 31, 1865, *S. F. Times*, March 9, 1869, give accounts of broom-corn fields, which in 1874 yielded 191,600 lbs., chiefly in Sutter county. Besides flaxseed the castor-bean is cultivated for oil. Los Angeles having in 1879 fully 350 acres, yielding 525,000 lbs. *Los Ang. Hist.*, 62; *Sutter Co. Hist.*, 84; *S. F. Times*, March 23, 1867; *Cal. Farmer*, Oct. 27, 1870; *S. J. Mercury*, Dec. 25, 1879. The sunflower is grown to a limited extent. *S. F. Alta*, Oct. 20, 1858, illustrates its flourishing condition. Los Angeles grows canary-seed, and the soap-plant or amole, *chlorogalum pomeridianum*, is gathered for its fibre.

its beginning in the experiments of L. Prevost at San
José, in 1853. The favorable reports from France
upon his products lent confirmation to the claim that
the state was well adapted for sericulture. The equable climate was free from the storms and cold which interfered with the growth and quality of the mulberry-
tree and silk in Europe, and gave rise to destructive
diseases among the worms. Trees here acquired in
three years a growth equivalent to that of five years
in Europe, produced more and superior leaves, and
showed such power of recuperation as to permit the
pruning of entire branches for feeding, keeping the
leaves fresher and cleaner, and affording the worm a
more spacious field, while preventing the waste of
leaves, and enabling one person to do the work of six.
Two crops could be raised if required, with an average
yield for each cocoon of 400 yards of silk, more than
one eighth above the yield in Europe. Impressed by
these advantages, the state was rashly induced in 1866
to offer heavy premiums without due restrictions;
whereupon a host of speculators entered the field,
intent only upon planting by any makeshift process
a sufficient number of trees, and raising inferior Japanese bivoltines and trivoltines, till immature trees and
diseased cocoons multiplied into the millions, with a
prospect of swamping the state treasury. The alarmed
legislature hastened to reform the premium act, and
the governor very properly refused to pay claims for
worthless productions. The bubble burst with a
heavy loss to those concerned. No market having as
yet been opened for the proportion of good ware, the
enterprise received a further check. In 1880 it was
revived by some philanthropic women to build up a
congenial occupation for their sex, for the prospects
had again brightened under the efforts of a few stanch
sericulturists, who, by selecting superior trees and
annual cocoons, were gradually finding a market for
their silk. The culture by 1888 was developing on a
sound basis, stimulated by the wide margin for profit

held out by the import duty on silk fabrics, and by
the undeniable advantages of the climate as an offset
to higher wages and other obstacles.[9]

[9] In addition to the advantages already mentioned, the comparative cheapness of land must be considered, which permits trees to be more readily given
their due space, two-year-old shoots thriving best when standing from 1 to 2 feet
apart in rows 3 to 4 feet apart. Two crops of cocoons can be raised in May
and July without need for kilns to kill the insect, although the annual is
preferable, and even those yield an average of 400 yards of silk each, or $\frac{1}{8}$ to
$\frac{1}{4}$ more than in Europe. Details in *Prevost, Mem. Silk Culture*, 1868; *Silk-
growers' Manual of 1882: Pioneer Silk-growers' Rept; Neumann's Mem.*, in *Cal.
Jour. Sen.*, 1867–8, ap. 24, 76, 84, ii.–iii.; 1869–70, ap. 105, iii.; *Cal. St. Agric.
Soc., Trans.*, 1864, pp. 256, 289; 1866, pp. 469–81. Assisted by the Swiss
banker, H. Hentsch, of S. F., Prevost, a French nurseryman of San José had
in 1853–4 planted mulberry seed and sent twice to China for eggs. Both consignments were spoiled or sent in unfertilized condition by the suspicious
Orientals, and Prevost in his disappointment destroyed a part of his 25,000
trees. Hentsch, in 1859, obtained eggs from France which produced the
most encouraging results, notwithstanding the drawbacks attending a first
experiment. The cocoons were in France declared to be of superior quality,
and several orders came for eggs, also from Italy and Mexico. Prevost continued his efforts, and pointed out zealously the advantages for silk culture.
He obtained several small premiums at the fairs, and in 1862 the state offered
a bounty of $2,000 for the first ten bales of raw silk, 100 lbs. each. *Cal. Stat.*,
1862, p. 416. Herein could lie no inducement for beginners, and so in 1866
the legislature rushed to the extreme of offering for 4 years a premium of $250
for each plantation of 5,000 trees two years old, and $300 for each 1,000 cocoons.
Id., 1865–6, p. 660. Such liberality, without restrictions as to method, quality of tree or silk, when cocoons brought only some $2 per 1,000 in the mar-
ket, brought into the field a number of speculators, who, regardless of the
future or for the requirements of real plantations, sought to win the bounty
by the readiest and cheapest means. The *morus multicaulis* were planted in
nursery rows by the thousands, on a space suitable only for a hundred, and
the best annual worms were discarded for the inferior Japanese bivoltines and
trivoltines, which produced several times more cocoons. Trees rose by the
hundred thousand, and in 1868 over 1,000,000 cocoons appeared, with the sure
prospect of treble the quantity in 1869, and quadruple this number for 1870.
Legislators then demanded the repeal of the act to save the state from bankruptcy, but were induced in 1868 by the Pioneer Silk Growers' and Manuf.
Assoc., then formed, to issue a modified offer, whereby the prize of $250 was
limited, once to each person, for properly laid out plantations, and $300 prize
for 100,000 cocoons. *Cal. Stat.*, 1867–8, p. 699. Concerning the spread of the
culture, see *Cal. St. Agric. Soc., Trans.*, and county histories for Los Angeles,
Contra Costa, Sta Clara, Yolo, Nevada. *West Shore Gaz.*, 1867, p. 106–9, and
notices on state and county fairs in 1867–71 in the journals. With unmethodic
culture, cocooneries in unwholesome situations, and worms mismanaged, disease broke out, worms died in large numbers, eggs became infected and cocoons
worthless. In addition, the governor, sustained by the courts, refused to pay
bounties under either act for the unmerchantable ware, and the disappointed
speculators retired with losses entering into the hundred thousand. *Governor's
Message*, 1869–70, p. 53. Sup. court opinion in 38 *Cal.* 291. The legislature
was sufficiently startled by the stormy claimants to repeal the act. *Cal. Stat.*,
1869–70, p. 79; *Id., Jour. Sen.*, 55–6, ap. 6, p. 6. In addition to this, the
Franco-German war intervened to cut off the only market, leaving a large
supply of cocoons and eggs upon the hands of producers. This caused the
abandonment of many excellent plantations, so that only a limited number
were left. Even the pioneer association lost interest, of which I. N. Hoag of
Sac. had been the sustaining pillar. The depressed condition of labor in the

The sericultural bubble was followed by an equally costly, though less wide-spread fiasco in tobacco. Its cultivation had early commended itself to inwandering southerners, but the dry climate was found to be detrimental to the quality. J. D. Culp sought a remedy for the defect in a patent process for curing the leaf which was claimed by the inventor to be economic as well as improving to the flavor. A company undertook in 1872 to carry out the idea on a large scale without due preliminary experiments. The process proved less satisfactory than expected, and reckless management assisted to bring about failure and discouragement, so that production fell from 1,240,000 pounds in 1874 to 73,000 in 1879, yet not without the prospect of a gradual revival under growing experience.[10]

latter part of the seventies led Mrs T. Hittell in 1880 to organize the Silk Culture Association, and to give fresh impulse to the industry, especially among women. Within a brief period more than half of the counties in the state gave evidence of participation on a small scale, the state created a board of silk culture, with an appropriation of $5,000 toward establishing a filature. A school was established, in which young women were taught reeling and other arts, and two factories arranged to offer them employment. Greater attention is given to cultivating the superior morus alba tree for annual cocoons, so that the Cal. silk by 1888 was rising in favor, and the prospects for an expansion of the industry was promising. Hoag states that in 1868 he cleared $3,920 from 3½ acres, while the expense amounted to only $472. The receipts came mainly from eggs sold at $4 per ounce. He calculated that even the low Japanese silk would at $7 per lb. yield $4,480 per acre, less an expense of $2,140, of which $800 was for cultivating land and feeding, $50 for rent of land and cocoonery, and $1,280 for reeling 640 lbs. of silk by girls or Chinamen at $1 a day. A yard of silk dress goods weighing 3 ounces costs the European manufacturer $2.15; import duty and freight brings the price in S. F. to over $4, leaving a wide margin for higher wages. Cal. St. Agric. Soc., Trans., 1866, p. 452; 1868-9, p. 251-6. The California Silk-growers' Manual, 14 et seq., states that 5 acres may be safely calculated to yield 4,000 lbs. of cocoons, worth $1,400, and that the profit cannot fall below $425. For extent of culture and methods, see, further, Sac. Union, Jan. 1, 1884; S. F. Call, Apr. 21, 1883; Nov. 9, Dec. 9, 1884; S. F. Bulletin, Jan. 20, 1882; S. F. Chron., Feb. 8, June 4, 1881; Cal. Res., March 1881; Cronise Cal., 393-5; Cal. Farmer, Dec. 9, 1868; Sept. 16, 1869; May 19, 1870, etc. See also under manufactures, this history.

[10] As early as 1854 a number of planters were raising the leaf. The rise in prices with the outbreak of the union war in 1861 gave a stimulus which blinded farmers to the mediocrity of results so far, and opened a large area to the plant, notably in the Napa and Russian River regions. See county histories for Mendocino, Butte, Sta Bárbara, Los Angeles; Alta Cal., June 3, 1854; Oct. 28, 1857; Feb. 7, 1859; March 11, July 17, Sept. 22, 1861; Aug. 2, 20, 1862; Feb. 14-15, May, 3, June 22, 1863; Jan. 2, March 13, 1872; Sept. 7, 1873, etc.; Sac. Union, Feb. 22, Apr. 3, May 18, June 6, Sept. 13, Oct. 31, 1855; Feb. 13, 1856; Apr. 22, 1858; Nov. 12, 1861; Sept. 17, 1863, etc. Unfortunately the dryness of the climate proved detrimental to the

Experiments have been and continue to be made with different plants, chiefly by model farmers, and in course of time additional sources of profit will no doubt be revealed, although there is so far a sufficient number of incipient productions to tempt a wide expansion. The mustard-plant, which is a veritable pest to wheat-fields in many directions, has become valued for its spice as well as oil;[11] and for hops the climate has been found exceptionably favorable in its

quality, and the decline in prices added to the discouragement. A decade later J. D. Culp obtained patents for his improved curing process, consisting of alternately piling the plant for fermentation and drying it in horizontal position in close, heated buildings, an operation of 3 to 6 weeks, followed by a six months' stacking in bulk. He claimed that this method not only overcame the climatic difficulties, but obviated the damage inflicted by the variable eastern weather, and imparted a superior and uniform quality to the leaf, diminishing the expense of curing it and saving more tobacco. So promising was the showing that the American Tobacco Co., incorporated in 1872 to wield the patents, planted in the following year some 400 acres, and prepared to extend the plantation to 1,000 acres, besides stimulating a large cultivation in other counties. The production for 1874 was reported at 800,000 lbs. in Sta Clara and San Benito, in addition to more than 100,000 lbs. each in Los Angeles and Alameda, 70,000 lbs. each in Sta Cruz and Sta Bárbara, 60,000 in Lake, and 40,000 in S. Mateo, total 1,240,000 lbs. *Cal. Agric. Soc., Trans.*, 1874, p. 287. But the management was bad, the process failed to work so well as expected, and the company proved a disastrous failure. The experience served, however, to guide the prudent survivors of the tobacco excitement. The acreage for 1879 had fallen to 84 with a yield of 73,300 lbs., of 64 acres with 59,000 being in S. Benito, 10 acres with 8,200 lbs. in Los Angeles, and 1 or 2 acres in several other counties, chiefly on the northern coast, yet the prospects in 1888 were deemed good for a steady growth of the industry, as shown also by the increasing production, from 1,000 lbs. in 1850, and 3,150 lbs. in 1860, to 63,800 lbs. in 1870. Details of progress and method in *S. F. Call*, Nov. 24, Dec. 2, 1868; Apr. 21, June 29, 1871; Sept. 7, 1872; Jan. 20, July 17, Aug. 6, 23, 1873; Aug. 18, Oct. 12, 1874, etc; *Stockton Indep.*, Apr. 19, 1879; *Ukiah Dem.*, Sept. 21, 1878; *Shasta Courier*, Sept. 14, 1878; *Sta Barb. Press*, March 11, 1876; *Antioch Ledger*, Nov. 14, 1874; *S. Benito Advo.; Salinas Dem.*, June 20, 1874; *Com. Herald*, Sept. 10, 1867; Sept. 10, 1874; *Scient. Press*, Oct. 1, 1870; March 23, 1872; Dec. 11, 1875. It is pointed out that the plant grows wild in Tehama, *S. F. Bulletin*, Feb. 8, 1859, and that the long seasons permit 4 crops of cigar and 2 of chewing tobacco.

[11] *S. F. Call*, Sept. 21, 1865; Dec. 10, 1868, etc.; *S. F. Bulletin*, Nov. 24, 1865. Nutmeg-trees, *S. F. Bulletin*, Aug. 25, 1859; March 16, 1869; *Sac. Union* recommended June 18, 1869. Red pepper grows in Los Angeles. Concerning peppermint, see *S. J. Herald*, March 12, 1877. Camphor, *S. F. Alta*, Apr. 2, 1859. Sumach is found wild in S. Diego, and its cultivation has been tried in Sta Clara. *Alameda Encinal*, July 20, 1878. Chikcot, or Giant Bitter Root, is treated of in *S. F. Bulletin*, July 17, 1865. Opium culture in *Id.*, Dec. 1, 1879; *Sta Rosa Times*, Dec. 17, 1879; *Alta Cal.*, Aug. 13, 1871. Insect powder. *Pr. Dent. Zeitung*, July 13, 1878; *Jackson Ledger*, July 21, 1877. Indigo and cochineal prospects in *Alta Cal.*, May 1, 1856; Sept. 7, 1859; *S. F. Bulletin*, Oct. 27, 1859; *Scient. Press*, May 6, 1871. These and other odd cultures are considered especially in the *Rural Press; Cal. Agric. Soc., Trans.; Commerce and Industries*, and in numerous other places.

freedom from summer rains and heavy dews and fogs, which produce the destructive blights and wash away the strength of the flower. The result is surer and superior crops, as well as safer and easier means for curing them, than in the eastern states. The cultivation has developed since the fifties, yielding by 1880 a million and a half of pounds, with the prospect of a large increase.[12]

Several materials have been tested for sugar-making, among them grapes and melons, which proved as unsuccessful, from an economic point of view, as the sugar-cane, of which only a small quantity is raised in the south for chewing; sorghum is reserved for fodder. Sugar-beet has alone been found to answer, and sufficiently so to encourage a larger cultivation of it, with a marked increase in sweetness that places it far above European beets.[13]

[12] By low trailing the roots are sheltered from excessive heat, and three years suffice for attaining the maturity elsewhere requiring five or six. An extraordinary proportion of the valued lupuline is here obtained, and the fresh green color is well preserved. A St Helena crop took the premium at the Centennial Exposition in 1876. *Napa Co. Hist.*, 11. The total yield in 1879 was 1,444,000 lbs. from 1,119 acres. Sacramento leading with 684,500 lbs. from 402 acres, followed by Mendocino with 229,600 lbs. from 279 acres, and Napa, S. Joaquin, and Alameda with from 99,000 to 73,000 lbs. The census of 1870 reported 625,000 lbs., and that of 1860 only 80 lbs., showing a rapid increase. For reports on development and methods, see *Pac. Rural Press*, May 8, 1875; Jan. 6, June 2, 1877; July 6, 1878; *Napa Reg.*, July 10–13, 1878; *Anaheim Gaz.*, March 10, June 9, July 14, 1877; *Merced Argus*, Oct. 12, 1878; *Sac. Union* of Dec. 11, 1855, Jan. 1, 1884, records attempts; also July 11, Nov. 14, 1863; *S. F. Herald*, Sept. 15, 1859; *S. F. Times*, Feb. 12, June 30, 1868; Aug. 12, 1369; *S. F. Call*, June 6, Sept. 22, 1871; Aug. 17, 1874; March 15, 1882; *St Helena Star*, Sept. 29, 1876; Aug. 3, 1877; *S. F. Bulletin*, Apr. 16, 1884.

[13] Chinese sugar-cane has been cultivated in Los Angeles since 1854, and syrup made, but not successfully enough. The *U. S. Census* mentions, however, for 1879, 2,459 gallons of sorghum molasses, mostly in Kern and Tulare. *Sutter Co. Hist.*, 84—culture abandoned lately. Sugar-beet has alone answered. During the greater part of the last decade the only mill in operation for the manufacture of beet sugar was at Alvarado. Besides paying $4.50 a ton for beets, it offered premiums for beet culture. In 1887 a large refinery was built at Watsonville, and has thus far met with fair success. See, further, under manufactures; *Los Ang. Co. Hist.*, 62; *Com. and Ind.*, 540; *Cal. Agric. Soc., Trans.*, 1868–9, 272–302; 1873, 323–444; *Sac. Union*, March 25, Oct. 16. 1857; Dec. 31, 1870; *Kern Co. Cal.*, Jan. 8, 1880; *S. F. Call*, Dec. 23, 1868; Jan. 21, 1870; *S. F. Chron.*, Dec. 29, 1889.

As one who has done much to develop the agricultural and other interests of Los Angeles co. and of southern California should be mentioned James Boon

Lankershim, who came to San Francisco in 1860, and after graduating at the high school, began farming in connection with his father, first in Fresno and then in San Diego co. In 1873 he removed to Los Angeles, where he was the first one to engage extensively in wheat-raising, and to prove that such farming was profitable. He helped to build the first flouring mill in Los Angeles, and to organize the Lankershim Land and Water company, 12,000 acres of whose domain were sold in small tracts for colonization purposes. A director of the Farmers' and Merchants' bank, the Los Angeles Savings bank, and many other prominent institutions, he is known as one of the most public-spirited men in this portion of the state.

Daniel Freeman, a native of Ontario, Canada, who, after practising for some years as a barrister, came to this coast in 1873, was also among the first in Los Angeles co. who engaged largely in farming. Leasing and afterward purchasing from a Scotch baronet the Centinela ranch, containing more than 25,000 acres, he began raising cereals in 1877; in 1884 his crop was about 1,000,000 bushels. Two years later he sold one half of this estate for $25 an acre, and in 1887 most of the remainder for $125 an acre, with two fifths of the profits made by its sale and subdivision. Here the town of Inglewood has since been laid out by the purchasing company.

Probably the largest farmer and land-owner in Tehama county is Joseph S. Cone, on whose ranch of nearly 100,000 acres in the neighborhood of Red Bluff the average crop of wheat is 125,000 bushels, and of wool 275,000 pounds, in addition to a large amount of citrus and other fruits. A native of Marietta, O., and of noble lineage, Mr Cone came across the plains to California in 1850, and after engaging in various occupations, in 1860 began stock-raising on Alder creek. His present estate he purchased, as opportunity offered, for $50,000. In 1876, in conjunction with Charles Cadwallader, he established the bank of Tehama co., one of the most successful in the state, and of which he is vice-president. He is also at the head of the large mercantile firm of Cone, Kimball, & Co. As one of the railroad commissioners selected under the new constitution, he rendered most faithful and efficient service.

One of the most successful among those who adopted the coöperative system of farming was the late Wm F. Downing, who at his decease in 1887 ranked among the wealthiest men in the Santa Clara valley. From his birthplace at Newark, Mo., where he worked on his father's farm until the age of twenty-one, he started in 1859 for Pike's peak, Col., and some two years later came to Cal., where, after engaging in various occupations, he began farming and stock-raising in Santa Clara co.

Worthy of mention among the leading farmers of northern Cal. is Neuschwander D. Julien, a native of the Canton de Vaud in Switzerland, who came to this coast in 1849, and after engaging in store-keeping, hotel-keeping, and cattle-dealing, began farming and fruit-raising in Siskiyou co. He is also connected with the bank of Yreka, in which he holds a one-fifth interest.

CHAPTER III.

FRUIT-GROWING AND GRAPES.

1769-1889.

CERES AND POMONA—ITALY EXCELLED—COMPARATIVE YIELD—FRUIT SEASON
AND FLAVOR—PRODUCTS AND PESTS—DRYING AND CANNING—SHIPPING
—FARM ORCHARDS—APPLES—CITRUS FRUITS—THE ORANGE—PEARS—
COST OF CULTIVATION—SCALE INFLICTION—FIGS—ALMONDS AND OTHER
NUTS—THE OLIVE—BERRIES—THE GRAPE—WINE-MAKING—RAISINS—
FLOWERS AND FOREST TREES.

FRUIT culture and the vine are the rising industries
of California, and although Ceres may retain control
over the large areas, Pomona will count under her
sway a greater number of subjects, with votaries of
high intelligence and prosperity, who shall vest in this
Italy of America the choicest treasures of southern
Europe.

Few countries can display so great a variety of excellent fruit, some of which, like the grape and pear,
seem to have found here their best development, while
others, as the apricot, olive, and fig thrive nowhere
better throughout the United States. The loose
soil and sunny climate combine to give the trees and
shrubs a strong and rapid growth, with early bearing
and large and abundant fruit. As compared with the
eastern states, the yield is about double, and trees
begin bearing at half the age. Vines and many other
plants yield about twice the quantity of fruit obtained
in Europe, and for product as well as size our orchards excel. Cherries are in the market from May
to October; strawberries nearly all the year, in the

south. Indeed, fruit-picking never ceases, for the citrus season covers all the months when other orchards sleep. Owing to the equable temperature, failures of crops are rare, and partial at the most, and pests are comparatively few and mild in their ravages, particularly under the remedial measures favored by climate, irrigation, low training of trees and shrubs, and other methods. There is also the advantage that fruit may be left upon the trees long after maturity. The principal drawback lies in the inferior flavor of our apples, peaches, and strawberries, but other fruits compare well with foreign varieties, some, as the pear, being unsurpassed, under the improvements effected within recent years.

The state has experienced several excitements in horticulture, first in the products of colder climates, then for vines and oranges, with relapses due to rash selections of seedlings and soil, inexperience in methods, and overstocked markets; but the revivals have been strengthened by each ordeal. Of late years better facilities are offered by the railways for transporting fresh fruit eastward, and canneries assist in opening wider outlets. Their business has steadily augmented, from 4,500,000 cans in 1875 to more than 11,000,000 two-and-a-half-pound cans in 1881, including 4,700,000 cans of vegetables. The climate gives the advantage that raisins, figs, and prunes can be safely and cheaply dried in the sun, although fruit requiring slicing demands kilns and other means to protect it from dust, insect, and the like.[1]

[1] The Hispano-Californians planted numerous orchards in the south, especially with semi-tropic fruit and pears, as shown in my preceding volumes, but mostly of an inferior kind, and which deteriorated by neglect. North of the bay Russians had planted a few slips, and in the third decade the missionaries followed the example, providing also means for succeeding American settlers to do likewise. Sacramento had an irrigated orchard in 1849. Placer and counties farther north began to plant in 1846-8; Trinity had fruit-trees in 1853, and Siskiyou about the same time; Coloma became famous for certain fruits. See county histories for Sac. districts and northward. American garden seeds and apple slips were brought from Oregon in 1849. *Or. Specta-tor*, Apr. 29, 1849, *Pac. News*, May 27, 1850, and *Sac. Transc.*, i. no, 5, refer to scarcity of fruit, and urge planting. H. Lewelling of N. Carolina carried seedlings to Oregon in 1847, and his brother John took a selection from him

The predilection of Anglo-Saxons for apples is
marked by the great predominance of this fruit in the

to Cal. in 1851, establishing an orchard at S. Lorenzo, from which locality
seeds were later sent to many foreign countries. Kilburn of Napa had a peach
orchard in 1852, the trees having come by sea from the east. *Bartlett's Nar.*,
ii. 14–25. Greeley, *Journey*, 328, is enthusiastic over Cal. fruits. All during
the fifties orchard-planting kept pace with the spread of settlement, but
the cost and difficulty of obtaining good seed, and the inexperience with
regard to soil and irrigation, led to numerous failures. In the sixties came the
grape excitement; and this resulting through similar causes in more disappointment than success, orchards revived in favor, and with more discrimination,
promoted by the greater choice of cheap and good varieties, and vine-planting
shared subsequently in this improvement. L. J. Rose, W. Wolfskill of Angeles, G. G. Briggs, near the Yuba, and W. Meek, were among the leading orchardists in 1888. Lord, *B. C. Nat*, 230, says that a peach orchard of 200 acres
near Marysville yielded $80,000 for the year. *Alta Cal.*, June 21, 1858; *Hunt's
Mag.*, xxxi. 129, refer to another large orchard of early days. The rapid
recuperation in this climate encourages the replanting of inferior orchards.
For the supposed counteraction in early decay there seems to be no ground,
for the old mission orchards show themselves fully as enduring as the eastern.
As for growth, there are instances of cherry-trees attaining to a height of 14
feet in one year, and peach-tree trunks to a diameter of 2 or 3 inches. Vaca
and Pleasant valleys are noted for early spring fruit. Cherries are in the
market from the middle of May to October, yet *Alta Cal.*, Jan. 30, 1869,
alludes to ripe cherries in Jan.; *Sac. Union*, of July 14, 1855, boasts of ripe
peaches and apples early in July; strawberries grow in the open garden in
Dec., observes *S. F Call*, Dec. 18, 1868; *Id.*, Dec. 21, 1867; *Sac. Union*, Oct.
27, 1857; Nov. 19, 1859; Oct. 9, 1861; *S. F. Bulletin*, Oct. 6, 1856, refer
glowingly to second crops of pears and apples. The second crop from vines
is discouraged as injurious to the quality. The Sta Bárbara region failed to
respond to efforts for raising early fruit. *Sta Bárb. Co. Hist.*, 131, 398–9.
Instances of large fruit exist in pears of 3½ lbs., cherries 3 inches in circumference, and strawberries 1½ ounces in weight. The state in 1888 was practically free from the curculio pest; plums suffered but little from the
aphis, and apples from borers, only during the first year; yet since 1877 the
codling worm has become troublesome; in some parts bugs and bees attack
the apricot, peach is becoming more subject to the curled-leaf disease, and
the scale frightened orange growers a while; but these troubles are not extensive, and remedies have been found for checking several of them. By training trees low, with the lower limbs one or two feet from the ground, the
trunk is protected against sun-scald, and the roots are kept moist, the effect
of winds being also lessened. As a further protection against sun and wind,
trees are planted nearer together than in the east, without diminishing their
productiveness; the intervening space is seldom used for cultivation. Fruit
can be left on the trees long after maturity without risk, the citrus for over
half a year. The outlet for this growing interest lies partly through the overland railway, with its improving arrangements for special cars and speedy
transmission, favored by the early maturity of fruits here. Cal. shippers can
with proper precautions be assured of fair profits. Freight trains, occupying
18 to 21 days in the journey to N. York, charged about $2.50 per 100 lbs.
early in the eighties; passenger trains, occupying 8 days, charged double.
The shipments have largely increased during the last 15 years. The chief
outlet, however, is provided by means of drying, canning, and other preserving processes, which open wider markets and render growers less dependent
on fluctuating demands. The growing favor of such goods attest the quality
of the fruit. Raisins, figs, and prunes are cheaply and safely dried in the
sun, but for fruit that requires slicing, and would suffer from dust and insects,
kilns and other means are used. Several special fruit-drying factories have

farm orchards, exceeding that of all the other trees of temperate climes combined. The peach follows with 800,000; yet the pear, only one half as numerous, is gaining in favor as the best among this class of fruit, led by the famous Bartlett, which is finding a wide market in the east. Some old trees bear 40 bushels annually. Apricots are both prolific and delicious, and in demand eastward, and prunes are acquiring a deserving reputation, the crop for 1889 being estimated at 18,000,000 pounds.[2]

been started to this end, as described in *Napa Reg.*, July 20, 1878; *Amador Ledger*, July 12, 1877; *Hall's Cal.*, 25; *Los Ang. Hist.*, 70, 157; *Sonora Union Dem.*, Dec. 15, 1877; March 23, 1878. Different driers are described in *Castrov. Argus*, Feb. 28, 1878; *Monterey Dem.*, May 18, July 27, 1878; *Calaveras Citizen*, March 24, Apr. 14, 1877; *S. L. Ob. Tribune*, Nov. 19, 1879. Several large canneries exist, to be noticed in the chapter on manufactures. In the stress of competition, some firms have resorted to inferior fruit, glucose, poor tins, and low weight, to the injury of the state. Nevertheless their production has steadily increased from 4,500,000 cans of 2 lbs., fruit and vegetables, in 1875, to over 11,000,000 2½-lb. cans in 1881, the latter including 4,700,000 of vegetables, chiefly tomatoes, and 700,000 of jams and jellies; S. F. furnished 8,000,000, and S. José 2,000,000. The price in 1881 ranged between $1.85 and $2.50 per dozen cans of table fruit; one third less for pie-fruit. Canneries paid in 1880 $40 to $60 per ton for pears, plums, and peaches, $70 to $80 for apricots, $100 to $200 for cherries. Conventions of fruit-growers, as instanced in *S. F. Call*, Dec. 7, 1881, have taken steps to check frauds. At the close of the last decade California was estimated to possess 2,400,000 apple-trees, 800,000 peach, 350,000 pear, 260,000 plum and prune, 250,000 apricot, 130,000 cherry, 50,000 fig, 30,000 nectarine, 140,000 lemon, and 200,000 oranges in bearing, with rapid increase. The value of orchard products for 1879 is placed by the *U. S. Census* at $2,017,000, in which Sta Clara leads with $228,000, followed by Alameda with $210,000, Sac. $179,000, Sonoma $169,000, Los Angeles $123,000, then Solano, El Dorado, and Napa, with from $92,000 to $82,000, Placer 65,000, Modoc and Mono standing lowest. For detailed information on fruit culture, I refer to *U. S. Agric. Reports, Cal. Agric. Soc., Trans.; Pac. Rural Press; Cal. Horticulturist; Hayes' Agric.; S. Joaq. Agric. Soc., Trans.; Overland*, xi. 239; *Nordhoff's Cal.*, 166–73; *Cook's Treatise on Fruit*.

[2] Although the average California apple is inferior in flavor and for keeping, the different climates presented by lowland and foothill, moist and windy coast and warm valleys, permit many excellent varieties to be grown, even of the so-called winter apple. Of these, the Spitzenberg and Wine Sap flourish at 1,000 to 3,000 feet up the Sierra Nevada slope. Other kinds are named in *Hittell's Res.*, 259–60. For size and beauty they are unsurpassed anywhere in the world; the Gloria Mundi attaining to 20 ounces, or even to 2½ lbs. The best of the temperate zone fruits is the pear, for size and delicacy of flavor, and for abundant yield. It thrives everywhere, and suffers little from pests, except the codling worm. It was the favorite among the Mexicans, though inferior to the present varieties. At S. José are old trees which produce 2,500 lbs., or 40 bushels, annually. The Bartlett flourishes in the so-called Bartlett belt of the Sac. Valley foothills, also in Contra Costa county, and has netted $300 per acre. Peaches of the Sierra foothills equal the eastern, surpassing those of the coast and along the Sac. *Barnes, Or., MS.*, 15, assumes that some were planted in Butte in 1849. *Tyler's Bidwell's Bar, MS.*,

The orange is fast outnumbering the preceding fruits under periodic citrus excitements, and the improved arrangements for export. The fruit thrives throughout the Sacramento valley, and at an elevation of 1,000 feet it here ripens earlier than in Los Angeles, the centre of the orange region, which is generally assumed to be south of 35° latitude. The crop for 1889 was estimated at about 850,000 boxes, and its total value at nearly $1,500,000, or an average of $1.75 per box. The lemon and lime form a large percentage in the groves. Irrigation adds to the expenses, so that the care of an orchard for five years, or until bearing begins, may be placed at from $400 to $500 per acre.[3]

The fig is very prolific, and flourishes in the same zones, but the black Turkey, which so far forms the

6-7. *S. F. Bulletin*, Sept. 1, 1858, alludes to trees bearing nearly a ton of peaches, some 22 ounces in weight and over a foot in circumference. Apricots, almost unknown in the east, are here most prolific and delicious, especially in warm districts. Quinces are increasing. Cherries are widely grown in Alameda. Plums thrive best in Sonoma and adjoining valleys, where prunes are produced equal to all but the very choicest French. *S. José Mercury*, March 11, 1885, comments on the spread of the fruit.

[3] Of the 200,000 orange-trees in bearing early in 1880, Los Angeles contained 193,000, largely at S. Gabriel and Riverside; S. Bernardino had 9,000, S. Diego 2,500, and Sonoma, Sta Clara, and Placer somewhat over 6,000 together. Placer had several in 1860, and Solano and Butte a few. See their county histories. W. Wolfskill appears to have been the first foreigner to imitate the early missionaries in planting the citrus, and the large profits made by him attracted others, L. J. Rose being the only large grower, however. The appearance of the scale pest began to check progress as early as 1857, and the prospect of having to wait half a dozen years before the first good crop could be obtained was not encouraging. Of late, however, a decided revival has taken place in fruit culture, the number of trees by 1888 entering far into the millions. The net profits in former times reached $500 per acre. In 1882 shipments were made to the east at $300 per car-load. The disadvantages are exposure to scale bugs and gophers, and need for irrigation, with only a slight demand for preserves. But with increasing railway facilities wide markets are waiting in the east. The lemon and lime form a large percentage in the citrus groves. See county histories for *Ventura, Sta Bárbara, Butte*, and above all *Los Angeles*, for details; *Hayes' Agric.*, and other general references under fruit. A valued contribution comes from Rose, *Stat.*, MS., one of the early growers; *Gunnison's Rambles*, 159-78; *Contra C. Gaz.*, of Feb. 1863, glows over the first open-air product in its vicinity. *Napa Reg.*, Dec. 14, 1878; *Calaveras Citizen*, Apr. 20, 1877; *Id., Chron.*, Apr. 14, 1877; *S. F. Chron.*, Feb. 16, 1885, concerns Butte; *Los Ang. Exp.*, Jan. 10, 1880, on frost damage. *Id.*, March 19, 1874, alludes to the discussion concerning origin, showing that S. Gabriel can claim only the first large grove, not the first tree. See *Overland*, xii. 235, 560; and *Vallejo, Doc.*, xxxvi., no. 283.

staple, is not in favor for export, and varieties such as the Smyrna and White Adriatic are introduced to improve upon it.[4] Almonds planted in Placer county in 1846 took the premium at the first state fair, but in parts it blooms without yielding fruit. Several other varieties of nuts are grown, from walnuts to peanuts.[5] The olive is a promising product, for which the dry and otherwise comparatively worthless hill lands of the south are well suited, though the valley lands are better. The tree is exceedingly healthy and prolific, free from the pests which, along the Mediterranean, cause failures at frequent intervals, although not yielding equally large crops every year.[6] Strawberries, which are practically in bearing nearly all the year round, are cultivated for market chiefly in Santa Clara and Alameda, together with several other berries.[7]

Chief among all first products, however, is the grape, the cultivation of which has, within the past

[4] Nevada had fig-trees in 1859. *Sac. Union*, Nov. 24, 1859.

[5] Concerning early almonds, see *Placer Co. Hist.*, 239; *Sta Bárb.* and *Los Ang. Co. Hist.* Although less numerous, there are more than 100,000 English walnut trees, yielding in 1881 about 10 lbs. to the tree. Owing to slow growth, 15–20 years, and blights, they are not in favor. Madeira nuts exist. *Id.;* also *Ventura; S. José Mercury*, Dec. 8, 1880. Chestnuts and butternuts have been tried. Peanuts of a fine quality are grown in different parts, on about 500 acres, greatly by Chinese. In Los Angeles 75 acres yielded 75,000 lbs. *West S. Gaz.*, Yolo, 104–6; *S. F. Bull.*, Nov. 7, 1866; county histories of *Los Ang.* and *Butte.* Pine-nuts, etc. *Cal. Scient. Press*, May 15, 1869; *S. F. Call*, Oct. 24, 1872; *Sac. Union*, Oct. 25, 1859. There are dates and bananas in the south. *S. F. Bulletin*, Dec. 22, 1884; *Los Ang. Times*, Nov. 17, 1883; *Sta Bárb. Press*, July 28, 1877.

[6] Its slow growth has checked planting, and in the beginning of this decade there were only 13,000 trees in orchard, some of which have returned $500 to the acre. See *Cooper's Treatise Olive*, MS.; *Hayes' Ang.*, vii. 264; *Californian*, March 1881; *S. F. Chron.*, May 19, 1878; Jan. 4, 1885; *Sac. Union*, Feb. 10, 1855, refers to early bearing at S. José; also county histories for *S. Diego*, *Los Ang.*, *Sta Bárb.*

[7] At the close of the last decade there were 12,000,000 strawberry vines and 1,000,000 raspberry bushes. The Alameda raspberry production is about 1,500 lbs. to the acre; 5 tons from 4 acres, says *Alta Cal.*, Jan. 8, 1858. Strawberries for the S. F. markets are supplied chiefly from Alameda, and near S. José. Here 300 acres are under irrigation, 34 of which are said to have yielded 100 tons. They are usually cultivated by Chinese, on shares. *S. José Pioneer*, March 24, 1877, states that Shelton introduced them at Sta Clara in 1852. Gooseberries are in small demand. *S. F. Bull.*, Nov. 16, 1881. Raspberries, blackberries, and currants enjoy fair attention

decade, roused the interest of the entire community
and absorbed the chief attention among inflowing
land-tillers, who are assisting to extend our neat
and attractive vineyards over valleys and foothills
throughout the state. During the first years of
Spanish occupation were introduced from Mexico the
two leading varieties of the deteriorated yet hardy
fruit of South Spanish stock now known as the mission grape, first the reddish black grape of Los Angeles, rich in sweet juice, then the fruitier bluish
black Sonoma, which yields a lighter wine. Los
Angeles long retained the supremacy in viniculture,
producing in 1850 some 57,000 gallons of wine; but
the high prices realized led to a rapid extension even
far up the Sacramento valley, where the vine had
been planted shortly before the gold discovery.

Well-known varieties were brought from central
Europe, such as the Zinfandel, yielding the popular
red table-wine, and the Reisling, esteemed for its
light dry wine. Toward the close of the fifties it was
recognized that these foreign cuttings yielded a superior product, although the doubt as to their relative
value served to sustain the mission grape, while the inferior quality of the wine tended to restrict the culture.
The state took an interest in the matter, and A. Haraszthy, whose efforts in behalf of the industry have
procured for him the appellation of father of viniculture in California, was induced to visit Europe as commissioner to study the subject and bring back cuttings.
The experiments then introduced led in due time to
another fever, which received a check from the phylloxera, and other more threatening than actually
serious troubles. This had the effect of confining the
business more among thorough viniculturists, whose
experience and caution induced them to seek superior
and reliable varieties and improve the wine-making.
Their success gave rise toward the close of the seventies to a healthier revival, which has steadily unfolded,
stimulated to some extent by the misfortunes of France.

The south still retains the preponderance, reënforced by the southern counties of San Joaquin valley, while the essentially vinicultural regions of the north, Sonoma and Napa, are strongly supplemented by El Dorado and districts beyond it in the Sacramento valley. By 1889 about 150,000 acres were planted with some 120,000,000 vines, half of them in bearing, and fully half as yet in mission grapes; but a few years hence the area will be doubled, with a preponderance of foreign varieties. In 1888 about 800 vines were planted to the acre. An advantage here gained is the self-supporting stalk after the third year. It is pruned to a height of about 18 inches, a process which hastens maturity and reduces the danger from wind and frost. At full maturity a yield of three to four tons of grapes to the acre may be expected, although some vineyards produce double that quantity, and occasionally even 16 tons. The average from each vine may be placed at seven pounds, and from a ton of grapes may be obtained 130 gallons of wine. So far, about half the crop is pressed, two per cent exported fresh, four per cent made into raisins, the product of which increased from 1,800,000 pounds in 1881 to 28,000,000 pounds in 1889, besides a percentage equivalent to 2,000,000 gallons of wine for conversion into one fifth that amount of brandy. The total wine product for 1889 was estimated at 14,000,-000 gallons, with the promise of a rapid increase through the growing home and eastern demand.

With nearly double the amount of sugar contained in European grapes, the California wines are as a whole strong, and lacking in delicacy of flavor, the heavier southern resembling those of Spain, Hungary, and Greece, while the central and northern resemble German and French standards. The defect is greatly due to the lowland soil and irrigation, which being necessary in the dry south was long advocated elsewhere, and favored as more convenient; but Haraszthy upheld non-irrigation, and it is now becoming recognized that the poorer hill lands, though yielding less and involving more work, are the best. With the additional care bestowed by wine merchants in pressing their own grapes, the improvement, already so marked, will make steady progress, until the brands of California acquire a general recognition, based on their merits. The champagne now made is winning favor. The different advantages enumerated tend, indeed, to sustain the claim for the state of being one of the best grape regions in the world.[8]

[8] In my *Hist. Mex.*, ii.–iii., this series, reference is made to the introduction and spread of viniculture in Mexico. Lower California, as the mother province for Alta, Cal., supplied the first slips. Vina Madre, of San Gabriel, as its name implies, claims to be the mother vineyard of California, but Padre Serra and his missionaries made the first planting at San Diego, whence San Gabriel was provided. Discussion in *Hayes' Legal Hist. S. Diego*, i. 29–32. Some regard this vine as derived from a Malaga stock, much changed by transplanting in Mexico; others, like Barrows, identify it with the Alicante. *Los Ang. Co. Hist.*, 64. It is the so-called Los Angeles grape, to be found in all old vineyards, and throughout the south, a reddish black berry, rich in sweet juice. The Sonoma grape, introduced north of S. F. Bay about 1820, is smaller, of bluish black color, covered at maturity with a grayish dust, and has more meat and fruitiness of flavor, yielding a lighter wine. It is ascribed to Madeiran stock, and prevails more widely throughout the northern valleys. Both are classed under the term of Mission, native, or California grape, and recognized as hardy, productive, and of early bearing; but even in these qualities they are surpassed by several foreign varieties, which, as a rule, far excel in flavor. Los Angeles was the vine region of the flush times, and as early as 1831 its present city limits claimed numerous vineyards, covering fully 100 acres, with half of the nearly 200,000 vines of the country. Hayes, *Los Ang.*, 29, increases this estimate. *Froebel's Aus. Am.*, i. 521–2. The census of 1850 credits Los Angeles with 57,355 gallons of wine, and Sta Bárbara with 700, yet Sonoma and other sections had in all a large additional amount. Vallejo, for instance, expected to clear $25,000 from his small crop. *Sac. Transcript*, Oct. 14, 1850. In 1852, Sta Clara figured for 16,800 vines, Solano for 5,811, Sta Bárbara for 46 barrels of wine. *U. S. Census*, 1850, 985. Wilkes, *Ex. Exp.*, condemned the wine as 'miserable stuff,' but this applied rather to the light kind, for port, angelica, and other sweet varieties were by no means so bad. W. Wolfskill appears to have been the first in 1849 to ship wine to S. F. The high prices realized, especially for the luscious grapes—Sonoma bringing 3 bits a lb., *Pac. News*, Oct. 16, 1850—led quickly to increased planting, even in the mining region. A man has just set out 1,000 grape cuttings on the Calaveras—noted for its wild vines—and quite a number have done likewise in different places, observes *Sac. Transcript*, March 14, 1851; *S. Joaq. Co. Hist.*, 71–2, claims wine-making for Stockton in 1850. It is pressed in S. Diego, says *S. F. Herald*, Feb. 26, 1853. Haraszthy, who had planted a vineyard here in 1851, began in 1853 to introduce vines from the eastern states and Europe, notably the now famous Zinfandel, as before stated. Not long after he bought the Kelsey or Buena Vista vineyard of Sonoma, the largest north of the bay. Delmas, in 1854 and later, introduced other varieties, especially the black Malvoisie and Charbonneau, and other French grape-growers obtained cuttings of different varieties, but the native plant commending itself as the readiest and cheapest, the inexperienced beginners had recourse to it, so that few out of

Many of the preceding plants find places in the ornamental gardens which form so attractive a feature of

the 1,500,000 bearing vines reported for 1855 were foreign. In 1856 three vineyards of Los Angeles had 27,000, 20,000, and 18,000 vines, respectively. 'I have 16,000 vines, each promising a gallon of wine,' writes White in *Sac. Union*, Oct. 9, 1855; Sept. 25, 1854. The grape interest was carefully nursed by the press, as instanced in *Alta Cal.*, Sept. 25, Dec. 18, 1854; *S. F. Bulletin*, May 1, 1856; Oct. 11, 15, 1856; and by such publications as *Haraszthy's Treatise on Culture of Grapes*, 1858, 1-21. Los Angeles continued to lead, as shown by the census report of 1860 conceding to her 163,000 of the total 246,500 gallons of wine, and she claimed in 1858 nearly 2,000,000 vines, half of them in bearing. Sta Bárbara and Mariposa ranked next with some 10,500 each. Sonoma figures for only 2,000, for her grapes went to S. F. Before the real gold excitement began vines had been planted north of the American, on Bear River, *Placer Co. Hist.*, 239, and thence it spread 2 or 3 years later to Sutter, Yuba, and Butte, Trinity boasting of it here about 1853. *Cox's Annals*, 56, 43, 177. Merced had started the first vineyard in 1855. *Merced Co. Hist.*, 121. In Fresno, subsequently so promising, the first vine was planted only in 1873, and 200 gallons of wine were pressed out in 1875. *Fresno Co. Hist.*, 211.

Toward the close of the fifties it became recognized that the foreign grape was superior to the Mission. The state lent its aid toward raising the standard for the culture, besides exempting it from tax, *Cal. Statutes*, 1859, 260, and Haraszthy's importations reached 500 varieties. But a doubt long prevailed as to the relative value of these strange kinds, which it would take years to solve, so that although the Mission vine declined in appreciation, it was sustained to some extent by the uncertainty and by its value for certain sweet wines. The planting of both classes continued, stimulated by the record of profits for early years, and by the belief in a growing foreign demand. But the inferior quality of the wine assisted the established brands of Europe to overshadow it, and so reduce prices as to render the culture largely unprofitable. Mildew, phylloxera, and other troubles came to ruin many vineyardists. Nevertheless, the steady gains of certain prudent ones, either by improving the manufacture of sweet wine from old vines, or by gaining recognition for the value of new plants, restored confidence, and toward the close of the seventies a sounder excitement set in, fostered greatly by the misfortunes of the French viniculturists. By 1882 she had about 80,000 acres in vines, which at an average of 800 to the acre indicated 64,000,000 vines, of which half were in good bearing condition, about equally divided between European and Mission, less than 10 per cent of the total being diseased or valueless. Of the foreign varieties which are now almost exclusively planted or grafted upon old stock, the Alexandrian Muscat is most esteemed for its size and flavor, and value for raisins as well as wine, and for table. It thrives best in gravelly loam, especially in Sonoma, where in good years it yields 9,000 lbs. to the acre, and inclines to two crops a year, although this is not favored by prudent culturists. The French Muscat is esteemed for vinegar. Zinfandel yields the now most popular red table-wine. Reisling is insipid as a grape, but growing in favor with its dry white wine. Early July grapes are the White St Peter, Madeline Blanche, Black July, Sweetwater, Shasselas, and Fontainebleau. In Oct. the Alexandrian Muscat, Muscatel, White Malaga, Rose of Peru, Red Tokay, and Cornichon become abundant. Berger, Malvoisie, Charbonneau, and seedless Sultana are among the well yielding. The American Catawba, Isabella, and Concord are less valued, as inferior in yield and fine quality, and costly to train; yet the Vitis Riparia and Æstivalis are recommended for grafting stock, as exempt from phylloxera.

The long absence of rain led to the planting of vineyards in bottom-lands open to irrigation, which also proved more convenient to cultivate. Subse-

California towns   The climate admits not alone a vast
variety, but forces them rapidly to maturity, and keeps

quently Haraszthy and others began to advocate non-irrigation as conducive
to superior quality, and of late years hill lands, as significantly pointed out
in the Germantown weinberg, are gaining in favor; yet the value of flooding
in the case of certain pests has been urged with effect, and south of 35° lat.
it is considered necessary.   In planting, the flattened crowbar is preferred to
the spade.   The vines are placed from 6½ to 8 feet apart, the former distance
prevailing in Los Angeles, the latter in Sonoma; wide apart rows gaining in
favor, thus leaving plenty of room for the branches and cultivation, and with
frequent intersection in large fields for wagon roads, to save hand carriage.
In old vineyards the stalks stand 3 to 5 feet high.   Now the custom is to prune
them to 18 inches, a proximity to the ground which hastens maturity and
reduces the danger from wind and frost.   During the first year there is little
increase of wood.   In the second the rooted vines may bear a few grapes.
The third year 3 to 4 lbs. of grapes should be obtained from each vine.   After
this the stalks are self-supporting.   The increase in yield continues till full
maturity in the sixth and seventh year.   One writer refers to vines 70 years
old, fruitful as ever.   There are vines in different parts with trunks a foot in
diameter and with branches sufficient to cover an arbor fourscore feet square,
as at Coloma, San Buenaventura, Blakes in Napa, Cajon Valley.   That of
Montecito, dating since 1795, is widely celebrated. *Alta Cal.*, March 27, 1858;
S. F. Call, Sept. 12, 16, 1875; *Vischer's Miss.*, 41.   It is supported by an arbor 115 by 78 feet, and has borne 4 tons of grapes in favorable years.   The
largest vineyard in Cal. and in the world is that of Leland Stanford in Tehama
co., named the Viña.   In 1888 it included 3,575 acres, planted with 2,860,000
vines, and formed a part of the endowment of the Leland Stanford Junior university.   A list of others, below 400 acres, is given in *Com. and Ind.*, 244–5;
Hayes' Angeles, v. 46; *Hyatt's Grape Culture*, ap. 1–6, 27–9.   The average production is far above that of European vineyards, 12,000 lbs. of grapes per acre being
as common as half that quantity in France, and 20,000 lbs. not unfrequent,
while 16 tons had been gathered, or equivalent to 2,000 gallons of wine.
The average is probably 7 lbs. to the 34,000,000 well-bearing vines of 1881, or
about 120,000 tons, half of which may be set aside for wine, equivalent to
fully 8,000,000 gallons, at the rate of 130 gallons to the ton, or one gallon to
15 lbs.; about 4 per cent is made into raisins, 2 per cent are exported fresh,
leaving a very large amount, say fourscore lbs., for each inhabitant, to be consumed in the country, or wasted, and a percentage corresponding to 2,000,000
gallons to be converted into 400,000 gallons of brandy.   Sixty per cent of the
wine is supposed to be received at S. F., amounting in 1881 to 4,885,000 gallons, of which Napa and Sonoma supplied half, and southern California one
fifth.   In 1877 the S. F. receipts were 3,337,000 gallons.   The export for
1881 rose to somewhat over 3,000,000 gallons, with a slight preponderance
in favor of railway shipments, 300,000 being from Sacramento, and 40,000
from Los Angeles; of the total 98 per cent passed through S. F.   As more
vines are rapidly coming into bearing, and as each acre can be estimated to
yield 500 gallons, the calculation for 1886–7 might not unreasonably be placed
at 30,000,000, and yet this would amount to only 1½ per cent of the yield by
France before the phylloxera ravage.   In 1867 the production was hardly
2,000,000, by 1871 it had risen to 4,540,000.   Haraszthy assumes 10,000,000
gallons for 1880, less than 7 per cent of which were sweet wine, worth on an
average 60 cents per gallon, the rest dry wine, for which the producers obtained 25 cents from the wine dealer, the latter buying within 10 months
after the vintage.

Owing to the growth of small vineyards, a large portion of the grapes are
now pressed by special wine makers, or by wine dealers, who are thus
enabled to better sustain the reputation of their labels, for the advantage of
the country in general.   The first of the regular wine merchants was Charles

most of them green throughout the winter, with larger and brilliant flowers though less perfume. The rose

Kohler, a German, who arrived at S. F. in 1853, and is now deceased. In the following year he formed a partnership with J. Frohling, who bought a vineyard in Los Angeles, while Kohler opened and managed the cellar at the bay city. For a long time the business was unprofitable, but Kohler's enthusiasm and energy succeeded in building up a large trade, and to him was largely due the impulse given to viniculture. His *Wine Production*, MS., dictated for my work, has furnished many of the facts here given. Fermentation has usually been effected in 140-gallon casks, at first filled only with about 115 gallons of must. The southern wine stands preëminent for sweetness, with much spirit and little aroma; the Coast Range district, especially of Napa and Sonoma, yield more acid white and red wines; and from the foothills of the Sierra Nevada come the larger proportion of sherry, Madeira, and high aroma German wines. Of late the vinicultural development, particularly in the great valley, has been so immense and varied as to require a new classification. The grape ripens so rapidly as to produce an excess of sugar, nearly double that of the average European. Hence a haste to press in advance of full maturity. The proportion of alcohol in the lighter wine is from 10 to 14 per cent, which renders fermentation difficult and lessens the delicacy. The selection for cellars is improving, and the advisability is considered of using fire to modify the temperature. In the south more adobe houses have been used. Hill tunnels are commended. The rejection of rotten or unripe grapes is so small as to speak highly for their quality. Grapes were shipped to the Atlantic states in 1854, *Hayes' Ang.*, v. 21, and wine consignments began soon after. By 1881 the latter had risen to more than 3,000,000 gallons, of which 45 per cent consisted of light red wine, 35 per cent of light white, and the remainder of port, sherry, and angelica, the latter verging toward a cordial. This proportion answers well enough for estimates of the total. The Zinfandel now leads the dry red, and Reisling the dry white. Golden Chasselas and Berger follow the latter; Pinot, Charbonneau, and Malvoisie the former. In the latter part of the sixties the eastern demand preferred the hock, port, (whereof 150,000 gallons sold at New York in 1867), angelica, sherry, champagne, muscat, and claret in the order named. *Cronise's Cal.*, 390. California will no doubt in time assert herself for special new brands, rather than cling to imitations. Noteworthy are the efforts of Arpad Haraszthy to foster a taste for pure champagne, free even from the flavoring so widely practised in France, and at a sufficiently low price to gain advantage over the machine-aerated productions so widely circulated under forged labels. Champagne was made at S. Gabriel prior to 1856. *Sac. Union*, Oct. 9, 1855. Sansevain tried shortly after to manufacture it for the market, but failed. Haraszthy studied the process at Epernay, and after costly failures to produce the sparkling wine he attained success, as related in *Com. and Ind.*, 249–52; *Id., Agric.*, MS., 21–2. Brandy has also been improved in quality, after long contentment with crude processes and inferior grapes. Naglee of S. José made it his specialty, Baldwin and Rose of Los Angeles rank as chief producers in the south, and the Johnson and Brighton distilleries on the Sac. lead in the north. Codman, *Round Trip*, 106–8, describes Naglee's efforts. A growing proportion of culturists devote themselves to making raisins. This began as an industry at Los Angeles in 1859, says *Los Ang. Co. Hist.*, 65, but it dates commercially only since 1872, when the first good American raisins appeared. See also *S. Bern. Co. Hist.*, and *S. Diego Co. Hist.* In 1875 the crop was 18,000 boxes of 20 lbs.; in 1880 fully 160,000, with prospective large increase. The raisin region extends from S. Diego far into the Sac. Valley, and the demand in the U. S. alone is sufficient to encourage a wide cultivation. The white Muscats are preferred. They are dried in the sun on trays, and ready for the sweat-box within two weeks. In 1881 Riverside growers reported a yield of 200 boxes to the acre, worth nearly $2 a box,

and many others bloom the year round. The streets
of the interior towns are as a rule profusely adorned
with trees, which, being ever green, help to relieve
their plainness, and to provide the shade so much
needed during a rainless summer. The Australian
gum is preferred for its rapid growth and stately bearing, as well as its sanitary qualities, though sapping
the soil of its strength for some distance around. Timber cultivation has also been considered for the bare

while the cost of preparing and packing amounted to only one third, leaving a
net yield of $250 per acre. The common price of grapes for wine in that
year was $25 per ton, or nearly $100 per acre.
   The foregoing shows that California has exceptional advantages for viniculture, and may be regarded as perhaps the best grape country in the world.
The yield is double that of European vineyards, with a larger, juicier fruit and
sounder stalks, which in being self-supporting obviate much labor and risk, as
does the speedier growth. A greater variety of grapes thrive here, and fermentation is easier to effect. Failure of crops is almost unknown, owing to
the equability of the climate, devoid of the severe frosts, hails, and storms
which do so much damage in Europe. Abundant time is afforded for gathering
the grape. Its afflictions, as phylloxera, mildew, and grape-fly, promise to be
mild. The first has beset one eighth of the field in northern and central districts, but destroyed only a small proportion. The south owes its immunity
probably to irrigation. The mildew is arrested by sulphur sprinkling, and the
fly by letting sheep enter after the crop is gathered to eat the egg-speckled
leaves. Report on phylloxera treatment. *Cal. Jour. Sen.*, 1875–6, ap. 55, v.
Several of the above features offset the prevailing higher wages, while the bad
situation of so much vine-land and the inexperience concerning soil and methods
are disadvantages fast dwindling. The comparative cheapness of land has
helped to draw attention, especially after the disasters which reduced the production and quality of French vineyards. These have also tended to open a
wider market for wine from other regions, to justify the rapid expansion of
viniculture in California, so that promises to become the leading industry of
the state. Grape-growers, who had held more than one convention before
1872, then organized for the protection of Cal. wines. In 1880 the state viticultural commission organized. *Sta Rosa Dem.*, June 5, 1850; *S. F. Chron.*,
Apr. 20, 1883; *S. F. Call*, May 8, 1870; Dec. 20, 1872. In 1859 vines and
olives were exempt from taxes. *Cal. Stat.*, 1859, p. 210. Resolutions against
wine tax, etc. *U. S. Govt Doc.*, Cong. 38, Sess. 1, H. Misc. Doc. 7, i. 8, in *Id.*,
Cong. 41, Sess. 2, Sen. Misc. Doc. 103, etc. See also essays and reports in
Cal. Agric. Soc., Trans., 1858, et seq.; *Cal. Jour. Sen.*, 1861, p. 253–60, ap.
13; 1862, ap. 13, 28; 1863, ap. 27; 1865–6, ap. 44; 1867–8, ap. 72; 1869–70,
ap. 43, 54, etc.; *Viticulture, 1st An. Rept*, et seq.; *Cal. 1st Bien., Rept Labor
Stat.*, 1883–4, p. 178–80; with reference to openings for labor; *U. S. Pat. Off.
Rept*, 1858, etc.; *Overland*, Jan. 1884, 1–5, etc.; *Harper's Mag.*, xxix. 22–30;
local journals, like *Anaheim Gaz., Napa Reg.*, etc., as well as scattered articles
in S. F. and Sac. newspapers; *Cal. Sports, Scraps*, 44, etc.; county histories, passim; *Pet. Crescent*, Jan. 31, 1872, refers to a dance in the then largest
vat of 50,000 gallons; *Folsom Teleg.*, Jan. 20, 1872; *Hayes' Ang.*, iv. 63; v.
46; viii. 21; *Id., Misc.*, 64, 76; *Id., Agric.*, passim; *Id., Cal. Notes*, iii. 79;
Hunt's Mag., lviii. 387; *Mechanics' Instit., Exhib. Repts; Langley's Trade Pac.*,
i. 4–5, 15; *Powers' Afoot*, 274–6; *Player-Frowd's Cal.*, 142–6; *McPherson's
Los Ang.*, 14 et seq.; *Codman's Rd Trip*, 64–9, 100–10; *Price's Two Amer.*,
196, 234; *Nordhoff's Cal.*, 215–22.

valleys, for which, as is shown by the several groves of giant trees so much admired by tourists, they are well adapted.[9] The planting of forests would undoubtedly tend to modify the objectionable features of the interior valleys, and promote greater humidity, and besides providing material for fuel and fences, would diminish the withering effect of the northers.[10]

[9] The first grove of blue gum planted for timber was set out in 1869, in Castro Valley, being over 10 acres, with nearly 1,000 to the acre; seven years later they were thinned to 100, yielding over $900 net for fuel and telegraph poles. A rental for grain would not have produced so much. The gum-tree, however, was introduced earlier. *S. F. Call*, Dec. 8, 1868; Apr. 7, 1871; Feb. 27, 1873; Aug. 14, 1874, etc. Pertinent points for tree culture are given. *Sonora Indep.*, Jan. 6, 1877; *Marysv. Appeal*, Dec. 13, 1878; *Merced Argus*, Dec. 7, 1878; *Castroville Argus*, Sept. 4, 1869; *Salinas Dem.*, Jan. 17, 1874; *Calav. Citizen*, June 22, 1878. While the gum is valuable for fuel, drainage, and durable wood, other useful trees could be added, as the cork, growing in Sta Bárbara, *S. F. Bulletin*, March 22, 29, May 27, 1859, the bamboo, *Scient. Press*, June 19, 1869, the Peruvian bark, the Japan varnish tree, etc. The useful date-palm and banana-tree are grown. *S. F. Call*, Apr. 30, 1871; July 1, 1877. Transplanting from nursery soil requires special care, owing to the tendency of the tree in this drier atmosphere to send down deep pump roots. Despite its adaptability the country has furnished few of the garden plants; the ceonothus is the chief ornamental shrub. Yet it has some striking peculiarities, as in the mammoth *sequoia* and the Monterey cypress; and more or less broad differences stamp the vegetation, as may be expected from the isolated position of the state, bounded on one side by the ocean and on others by lofty ranges and deserts.

[10] The legislature made a wise enactment on March 30, 1868, in encouraging the planting of fruit and shade trees along the highways. *Cal. Statutes; Cal. Agric. Soc., Trans.*, 1872, p. 27.

One of the earliest fruit-growers in Cal. was O. W. Childs, who was born in Vt in 1824, and came to this coast in Aug. 1850, with but $12 in his pocket. After engaging in various occupations, he began this business at Los Angeles, clearing in a short time $100,000. In 1856 he purchased a tract of land in the suburbs of that city, planting it as a nursery and with fruit trees, whereby he realized handsome profits, though the bulk of his fortune was made by judicious investments in real estate.

CHAPTER IV.

PASTURE CULTIVATION — EASTERN GRASS AND ALFALFA — EARLY STOCK-
RAISING—CATTLE AND SHEEP—NOTABLE RANGES—MILK AND CHEESE—
HORSES—IMPROVEMENT OF BREEDS—MULES AND OXEN—WOOL-GROWING
—GOATS—SWINE—POULTRY—THE HONEY BEE—AGRICULTURAL SOCIE-
TIES—PATRONS OF HUSBANDRY—THE GRANGE SYSTEM—FARMERS' PRO-
TECTIVE UNION LEAGUE.

So far there has been little cultivation of pasture, but with the extension of farming interests and the consequent limitation of cattle ranges, and the effort to improve the breed of animals for different purposes, the industry is gaining ground. Among the reasons for the neglect is the mildness of the winter, which obviates the need for special winter fodder, and the dryness of the summer, which kills most of the favorite grasses, and obliges frequent replanting.[1]

---

[1] For this reason the alfalfa, or lucerne, is gaining favor, as it sends down deep roots, and thrives luxuriantly with irrigation. *Cal. Agric. Soc., Trans.*, 1877; 150–9; *Alta Cal.*, June 29, 1851; May 19, 1860; *Eureka Times*, Sept. 29, 1877; *S. F. Bulletin*, Oct. 27, 1858; Nov. 20, 1871; *Reno Jour.*, June 18, Sept. 27, 1873; May 23, 1874. Hay worth 12 cents per lb. in 1849. *Woodward's Stat.*, MS., 7; *Kern Co. Hist.*, 113. Ensilage system introduced by J. W. Green. *Hist. Mont. Co.*, 164. Of wild grasses, the bunch-grass in small detached tufts affords almost perpetual pasture on dry hills, in being proof against drought. The flattened tufts of the alfilleria also endures well. The lupin, which is cultivated in France, grows here wild among the sand hills. The bur clover, mostly in the south, sustains the stock during autumn with its rich oily seed, scattered almost invisibly on the ground. Among sheep it injures the wool, and at times the throat. The most striking pasture is presented by the wild oats, with small grains, and bent, bearded projections, which is frequently cut for hay, yielding on an average one ton per acre. Cultivated oats are preferred to barley, which, like green wheat, is widely harvested for hay. The rough tule-grass saved many cattle during the drought of 1864. The hay harvest occurs about May 1st. One turning and

(52)

Stock-raising was the chief occupation of colonial days, and hides were almost the only medium of exchange. The animals introduced from Mexico, of deteriorated Spanish breed, increased rapidly, until in 1834, the last year of mission prosperity, they numbered scores of thousands. They roamed in untamed freedom, and a portion overran the interior valleys in a wild state, a condition which by no means served to improve the quality, distinguished as it was by 'scrub' colors and light weight; the cattle by long, thin legs, heads high and slender, wide-spread horns; and the sheep by short, coarse wool. The incoming Americans brought at first stock valued chiefly for strength and endurance. A large special importation followed in response to the high prices of early mining days, partly for breeding, and by 1862 the number of cattle had increased to over 2,000,000, as compared with 262,000 in 1850. Then came the disastrous droughts of 1862--4, which destroyed several hundred thousand by starvation and forced slaughter, and created so wide-spread a mistrust as to greatly curtail the industry. It made a perfect revolution in the business, by giving prominence to sheep, by changing many cattle districts to farming regions, and by obliging the adoption of more careful methods, such as the better apportionment of cattle to pasture, and the wide introduction of fencing, partly under compulsory laws. But compensation was found in the improved feeding and breeding, marked also by greater and better yield of beef and milk, and by reduced loss from diseases and accidents, with diminished expenses for herding. Cows calve before they are two years old. The business is now mostly combined with farming, with a desire to still further raise the breed. Few of the Spanish stock remain, for the south had suffered most from the droughts. The census for 1870 returned

one day's curing is enough. The *Census* gives the hay harvest for 1850, 1860, 1870, and 1880 at 2,000, 305,000, 551,000, and 1,135,000 tons, the last named from 758,000 acres, Sta Clara leading with 71,000 tons.

only 631,000 cattle, and the increase since has been
slow, partly owing to the increased price of land, under the steady encroachments of agriculture.   In 1889
the number was estimated at about 725,000, worth
from $13,000,000 to $14,000,000, while the total value
of all live-stock might be placed at nearly $60,000,000.[2]

[2] The first live-stock was brought with the first exploring expedition from
L. Cal. in 1769, followed by frequent additions for private and official
account, as shown in my preceding volumes.   By 1784 there was enough to
feed the settlers regularly, and after 1800 even Indians were not stinted.
Alvavado, Hist., i. 32–3.   Horses were invoiced at $9 in 1776.   In 1781 they
rose to $10, mares $4, cows $5, mules $20. *Prov. St. Pap., Ben. Mil.*, i. 45.
Official regulations were issued for the care and utilization of the herds.
Cows were not permitted to be killed for a long period.   Slaughterings were
ordered for May and June.   Settlers were loaned stock, to be repaid in kind.
The 18 heads of cattle allowed to each mission at founding had by 1784 increased, among 9 of them, to 5,384, besides 5,629 sheep and 4,294 goats.
Palou, Vida, 172; *Prov. St. Pap.*, i. 196, 201; iii. 141–3; vi. 154–5; *Dept. St.
Pap., S. José*, i. 11.   By 1800 there were reported 74,000 cattle, 24,000
horses, and 88,000 sheep.   Of these, a large proportion belonged to the missions, but their secularization, begun at this time, led to a rapid spoliation
and scattering of the animals, some of which ran wild in the ranges and valleys to the eastward. *Pac. News*, Dec. 28, 1850; *Sac. Transcript*, Jan. 14,
1851.   The stock was light and hardy, tough of flesh, and the cows yielding
little milk.   Emigrants from the United States brought a superior breed.
Almost every early journal from Aug. to Dec. contained notices of overland
arrivals with stock.   Crow left Pike co. in May 1850, with 800 cows, and arrived with 524 in Sept., which were placed on the Stanislaus. *Sac. Transcript*,
Oct. 14, 1850; Feb. 14, 28, 1851.   Sac. became a great stock market.   The
price of cows fell from $300 and $500 at the close of 1849 to $50 and $150
early in 1851. *Hayes' Agric.*, 133–46; *Nev. Jour.*, Nov. 10, 1854, refer to
losses from poisonous grass and Indians.   Some 40,000 on the way, writes
Alta Cal., Aug. 11, 1856; Sept. 13, 1857; *Cal. Jour. Sen.*, 1855, pp. 43–4.
Oregon and New Mexico sent special droves.   Cal. subsequently repaid by
export to adjoining mining regions, etc., partly for breeding.   In 1880 she
sent 7,500 cattle, 180,000 sheep, and 6,400 swine, the cattle chiefly to Oregon
and Arizona, the sheep to Montana and Utah. *U. S. Census*, 1880, iii. 1045;
Salinas Dem., Aug. 22, 1874.   The increase was rapid under the efforts to
continue the former staple industry, and with free and vast ranges.   The
census figure of 262,000 cattle for 1850 rose by 1860 to 1,180,000, and the
generally accepted estimate for 1862 was 3,000,000, the maximum.   Then
came the several severe droughts.   Those of 1862–4 are said to have destroyed
half the stock in Los Angeles, while that of Sta Bárbara was reduced from
200,000 to a mere remnant. *Sta Bárb. Co. Hist.*, 125.   The total loss by starvation was estimated at 300,000, and by compulsory slaughter still more.
The loss of confidence in the industry led to wide curtailments, and by 1870
the census returned only 631,000 cattle, and 815,000 for 1880, the county assessors giving only 621,000.   Preference was now accorded to the hardier and
more profitable small stock, notably sheep, which increased from a little over
1,000,000 in 1860 to fully 6,000,000 within a few years.   Of the cattle on
farms, the census of 1880 enumerates only 664,000, of which 210,000 were
milch cows, and 2,200 working oxen.   Of the 815,000 total, 250,000 were
classed as American stock, assessed at $18, 425,000 as seven eighths blood
American, assessed at $10.39, 110,000 as one half to three fourths blood, as-
sessed at $9.49 29,000 California or Spanish, at $8, and 1,000 thoroughbred,
at $57.   It will be seen that only a small proportion of the Spanish stock re-

The new restrictive methods are particularly favorable to the development of dairying, which was

mains, under the constant introduction of the heavier American, which is far superior for milk and beef, though excelled for special purposes by Jerseys, Durhams, Ayrshires, and Alderneys. These growing favorites deteriorate on the wild pastures, but with the growing price of land and expansion of farming and horticulture, the ranges are being reduced, and cattle-raising is becoming more and more associated with other branches, within cultivated fields and pastures more suited for the finer breed. The greater part is confined to farms, serving to glean stubble and weed, and returning manure. Some farmers are still able to send their stock to the mountains, if numerous, and so impart to it the benefit of continued pasture, together with an invigorating climate. The plains begin to dry in July. The mountains supply the deficiency better until Oct.; then, till Jan., follows a season of scanty feed, under which the stock grows thin, a percentage dying of starvation almost every year. The available acreage under these conditions is greatly reduced in value. In the rugged northern border counties an average range of 35 acres is calculated for every head, from Shasta to 35° lat. 25 acres, although some assume 5 acres of valley land, or 20 of mountain slopes, to suffice in central California, and so in Los Angeles; others insist upon 10 acres on S. Joaquin plains. In the more humid coast counties of Humboldt and Mendocino, 7 acres are sufficient. Of sheep, 4 to 5 subsist on the acreage for 1 cow. The return per acre is not large in a stock-raising business alone. The effort of stock-raisers is to secure water, so as to control much of the adjoining government land. Thus, El Tejon rancho of 200,000 acres, which contains all the available water, controls 300,000 acres of public land. Miller & Lux own 750,000 acres, costing them on an average $6, 500,000 acres being under fence, and estimated to sustain one head on every three acres. Their success is due to an admirable business tact, associated with prudence and personal supervision, ever eliminating the wasteful and applying improved methods. William Dunphy and Gen. Beale rank among the first in importance, and J. D. Carr, P. Saxe, C. Younger, and J. Bidwell are among leading breeders of fine stock.

Mr Dunphy was a pioneer of 1849, a man of great ability and merit, who associated himself with T. Hildreth to form one of the leading cattle firms on the coast, with Nevada as chief range for his 20,000 head of cattle, and S. F. for a market. In the north-east section of the state, chiefly dedicated to stock-raising, Irvin Ayres holds a corresponding position. He was born on March 30, 1832, in Montgomery county, N. York, where his father practised as physician. Reaching California in 1853 he became agent for the Cal. Stage Co. at Tehama, and drifted, after a brief experience as livery-stable keeper, into the trading, notably at Fort Bidwell, at present as member of the firm of D. L. Beck & Sons. During the union war he drilled several companies for service, and was barely restrained by business pressure from joining the fortunes of his brother, Gen. R. B. Ayres, a graduate of West Point, stationed in Cal. in 1854 and 1859, who acheived a brilliant record as one of the five foremest artillerists during that war.

Miller & Lux are able to brand 90 per cent of calves, while on some of the open ranges of Kern only 60 per cent are branded. The increase in weight since in 1855, under improved breed, feed, and method, has been fully 200 lbs. per head, the average weight of yearlings in 1855 being 250 to 400 lbs. net, and in 1880, 400 to 450, and of beeves 450 to 500 lbs. as compared with 750 to 800 in 1880. The live weight of American three-and-a-half-year-old beeves is placed at 1,100 lbs., worth $24; graded American 1,150 lbs., worth $25; three-fourths American 950 lbs., $21; half-breed Californian 875 lbs., $21; California 800 lbs., $19. U. S. Census, 1880, iii. 1035. The average value of cows, $17; of calves, $7. Every 100 cows are estimated to drop 80 calves, 73 surviving to yearlings. The percentage of loss among cattle over

much neglected by the Spanish colonists, partly because their cows gave but little milk. The Americans
infused new life into the business, and hastened to improve their stock for dairy purposes from the best
eastern and English sources. In 1889 there were
about 260,000 milch cows, the production of butter
being then placed at 17,000,000 pounds, and cheese
at 3,000,000 pounds. The business is chiefly confined
to the moister pastures of the coast, especially north
of and near San Francisco, as the principal market.[3]

12 months old was in 1880 placed at 4.9. The ruling diseases are big head
or big jaw, bloat, black leg, abscess of liver, and Texas or splenic fever.
The latter, originating probably about Tulare Lake, killed 10,000 head for a
Kern breeder in 1879. The remedy seems to be removal from low to elevated
districts, the exercise itself being beneficial. The finer breeds suffer most.
Abscess of liver is supposed to result from excess of dry food and from alkali,
the latter reducing more speedily the breeding power. Storms and poisonous
grasses assist to bring the loss in some parts of Kern to 5 or 7 per cent. The
loco plant and its effect is considered in *U. S. Agric. Rept*, 1874, 159–60.
With increased fencing, herding expenses are greatly reduced. Miller & Lux,
with 100,000 cattle and 80,000 sheep, require 200 regular men. One man looks
after several pastures. Branding takes place about April 1st. The market
season for purely grass-fed cattle is from February to July, when the pasture
fails, although beef is turned off at all times for S. F., which in the beginning
of this decade consumed annually 96,000 beeves, 24,000 calves, 440,000 sheep,
225,000 lambs, and 150,000 hogs. *Com. and Ind.*, 268. One bull for 20 cows
is deemed best. Cows calve before they are two years old, with instances
before attaining the age of 14 or 18 months. Calves suckle from 6 to 10
months. The largest herd, probably in San Bernardino, numbered about
1,300 head.

The rodeo has lost the gay and romantic aspect imparted to it during
Hispano-Californian times, when families gathered from afar in festive assembly, the older folk to exchange business ideas and gossip, the young to court,
with serenade and dance and sports, the cavaliers striving above all to win
admiration by dashing feats of horsemanship during the rodeo, or during
games attending it. In the south a gathering of owners is still held for picking
out strayed stock, but as a rule it now implies merely a driving in of animals
for the annual branding. Several regulations appeared in colonial days concerning brands. In case of frequent sale the shoulder as well as hip become
covered with marks. *Cal. Statutes* have regulated these matters. A law of
1851 made the annual rodeo compulsory, and gave unmarked cattle to the
owner of the rancho where found when the mothers were unknown. This
gave rise to much stealing, observes Barton, *Tulare*, MS., 12. American
herders have become expert in the use of the reata or raw-hide rope for lasso-
ing. Further details on methods and development are given in *Cal. Agric.
Soc., Trans.; S. Joaq. Agric. Soc., Trans.*, 1861, etc.; *Hayes' Agric.; Pac.
Rural Press; Cal. Farmer;* surveyor reports in *Cal. Jour. Sen.; First Nat.
Convention Cattlemen, Proceedings*, 1884, 12–13; *Stebbins' Industry*, 37–68; *Barstow's Stat.*, 14; *Hollister's Stat.*, MS., 11; and *Cal. Pastoral*, this series.

[3] The Mexicans did not take kindly to milking, and little of it was done
save for the children, and for a little cheese. Americans introduced high-
bred animals, that is, eastern, crossed with British stock, together with a few
of pure blood, for producing the best quality and the largest quantity of milk.
The census of 1880 enumerates 210,000 milch cows, and 12,000,000 gallons of

The achievements lately performed on eastern courses by California race-horses have gained for the state a wide reputation as an exceptionally favorable breeding ground, both for swift and enduring animals. The Spanish horse, introduced by Cortés into Mexico and thence into California, is small and deficient in strength and beauty, and little fitted for cart or plough, yet quick and tough, and with a record since 1846 for remarkable riding feats. He is, however, of a base and blotchy color, and neither honest nor gentle. This stock by 1888 was reduced to less than a fourth

milk sold or sent to factories. Of butter, 14,000,000 lbs. were made, against 8,000,000 in 1870, 3,100,000 in 1860, and 705 in 1850; of cheese, 2,560,000 in 1880, against 3,400,000 in 1870, 1,340,000 in 1860, and 150 in 1850. S. F. is placed far above any other county as a milk producer, with over 5,400,000 gallons, perhaps without due credit for supplies from San Mateo, which is credited with only 740,000 gallons. Marin, properly the leading dairy county, is accorded 3,170,000 gallons of milk, 2,500,000 lbs. of butter, its staple article, and 65,000 lbs. of cheese. Next comes Sac., partly owing to its swamp-land, with 1,240,000 gallons of milk, 540,000 lbs. of butter, and 182,000 lbs. of cheese; then S. Mateo with 283,000 lbs. of butter, and 288,000 lbs. of cheese. Both are, however, surpassed as butter counties by Sonoma, with 1,900,000 lbs., S. L. Obispo with 1,150,000 lbs. and Humboldt with 993,000 lbs , while Santa Clara leads as a cheese producer, with 740,000 lbs., followed by S. Mateo and Sonoma. The immediate vicinity of S. F. excels in milk, and the largest milk dairy in the state is the Jersey farm, near S. Bruno, which milks 500 or 600 cows daily, yielding 400,000 gallons a year, nearly all carted into S. F. The next nearest line predominates in butter and cheese, as shown by San Mateo, Sonoma, and Sta Clara. The chief butter district is Point Reyes, in Marin, covered by 6 dairy tracts of 54,000 acres, with about 5,000 cows, upon some 30 tenant farms. The proprietors lease them at a rental of $20 or $25 for each cow and a portion of the calves. Each cow yields nearly 200 lbs. of butter, equivalent to $40. Other sources produce $10 more. The average life of a cow is 10 years. J. Russ of Humboldt sustained over 2,000 cows on 13,700 acres. Details in *Humboldt Co. Hist.*, 135 et seq., and *Marin, Id.;* also for *Sta Bárb.*, *Sta Cruz*, etc. Cheese is made as a rule from unskimmed milk and sold while new. The Limburger and Swiss varieties are well imitated. A few factories exist, yet large dairymen prefer to manufacture for themselves. The largest cheese-makers are Steel Brothers of S. L. Obispo, who keep fully 1,500 cows. *S. L. Ob. Co. Hist.*, 224–7; *Pac. News*, Apr. 30, 1850, commends the cheese made by Wilkes near San José. Reports on dairies in *U. S. Agric. Rept*, 1870, 326–9, etc.; *Cal. Agric. Soc., Trans.;* Hayes, and other general authorities already given. Premium cheeses mentioned in *Sac. Union*, Dec. 3, 1855; Sept. 24, 1859; *S. F. Bulletin*, Dec. 5, 1864; Oct. 24, 1873. Oleomargarine was rousing attention already in 1873. *S. F. Chron.*, Sept. 20–2, March 1, 8, Oct. 28, 1874; *Cronise's Cal.*, 368–70. The dependence on indigenous grasses by dairies is indicated by the great fluctuation in butter prices, from about 24 cents from April to June, to 40 cents from Oct. to Dec. Many dairymen of the great valley drive their cows to the mountains after May, returning in Oct. with their butter to seek the high market. Yet a good deal of green corn, beets, and alfalfa is cultivated for butter dairies. Round S. F. refuse malt is largely given to stimulate the yield of milk, notwithstanding the deteriorating effect.

of the total 237,700, given by the census of 1880,
under constant admixture with the larger, finer, and
stronger American breed, which is also more trac-
table, though less tough and healthy. Its further
improvement with thoroughbred blood is promoted
by the general and commendable ambition among
farmers to possess fine animals.[4]

Mules are regarded by small farmers as too dear
and unattractive, but for packing and hauling trains
they present the advantage of superior strength and
endurance, with less need for care. Working oxen
are condemned as too slow in this progressive land.[5]

[4] Leland Stanford has done much to raise the grade of Cal. horses and
achieve a record in the eastern fields. His stock farm at Palo Alto is probably the most complete horse-breeding establishment in the world, celebrated,
moreover, for new training methods. The peculiar features of Palo Alto are
the liberal scale on which the breeding and training is performed, the great
care given to the brood mares, with due use of stalls, sheds, and fields, the
feeding of colts with steamed grain, and their daily paddock practice at high
speed, though of short duration. Over 500 horses of the finest blood have
been collected here, two costing $25,000. In 1881 the best eastern record
for two-year-old trotters was here reduced to 2.21, and that of yearlings to
2.36½. Like other live-stock, the horse develops in Cal. faster in weight and
other qualities. Of Spanish horses, a large proportion is still allowed to run
semi-wild, in bands of 30 or 60, led by the garañon or stallion, which guards
the mares with jealous care, and exhibits remarkable intelligence in seeking
out good pastures, and thwarting the interference of herders. The mares foal
with great regularity before the third year. Colts are weaned at 8 or 10
months old, and broken in the third or fourth year, after which they are sent
to the broken herd. Mexicans have a prejudice against breaking mares. S.
Joaquin and Sonoma have the largest proportion of horses, 13,000 and 10,700,
respectively. The totals for 1850, 1860, and 1870 stand at 21,700, 160,000,
and 192,000, respectively. Dissensions have risen concerning the first American horse here, in Sac. Union, July 6, 1872; Yreka Union, July 10, 1869;
Marysville Appeal, Dec. 26, 1874, which refer it to 1849, but immigrants
brought the animal long before. S. F. Call, May 3, 1871; Alta Cal., Apr. 16,
1873; S. F. Bulletin, Apr. 19–26, 1873, 1875, etc. English and American
thoroughbreds are widely distributed, trotters having so far been the favorites. The Blydesdale, crossed with both American and Spanish stocks, had
supplied most of the heavy draught-horses. A half-blood of this breed, from
Spanish stock, weighs 1,300 when four years old; a three-quarter blood,
1,500 lbs. Pac. News, Jan. 10, 1850, refers to 4 stallions brought from New
South Wales for breeding. See also Alta Cal., May 31, 1857. Concerning
advantages for breeding, Rose, Stat., 15–19, has glowing opinions. See also
Hayes' Mont., 209, etc.; Berry's Up and Down, 111–14; Cal. Agric. Soc.,
Trans., etc. Although horses ran wild in S. Joaquin Valley, S. F. Herald,
Jan. 16, 1853, yet prices were high at early mining camps; $100 for broken
horses, $50 for wild. Bauer's Stat., MS., 7. Later in 1882, Vallejo sold
mares and stallion at $20. Vallejo, Doc., xxxiii. 263; Alta Cal., June 6, 1852.

[5] And have declined from 26,000 in 1860 to 2,290 in 1880. Camels have
been tried in the south, but abandoned. Vischer's Cal., 66–7. Jacks and she-
asses were early introduced, costing in 1784 $5. Prov. Rec., iii. 249–50.
Fully 100 mules came in 1776. Palou, Vida, vii. 209–11. Black were preferred,

California may not be especially adapted for large cattle, despite its early pastoral rank, yet for sheep it presents exceptional advantages. The mild climate permits an uninterrupted growth, so that at two years of age they are as well developed as those of three years in the eastern states. They give a larger increase and more wool; they require only grass for food, and little care, save shelter in some parts from wild beasts, and are remarkably free from disease. The low grade Spanish-Mexican stock, introduced also during early mining years from New Mexico, and marked by short, coarse wool, were mostly consigned to the butcher; and wool-raising began properly with the introduction of American sheep in 1853. Attention was soon given to improve the breed with Spanish merinos from Vermont, till the high-grade merinos number three fourths of the total of about 4,000,000 assigned for 1889. Although checked like cattle by droughts, their hardier nature induced stock-raisers largely to turn to them after the disaster of 1862-4; since when their predominance dates. The profit on them is increased by their adaptability to cheaper pastures, their large natural increase of fully 80 per cent, sustained by a large proportion of twins, and the heavy yield of wool, averaging in 1888 over seven pounds for ewes and wethers, from two clippings, as against four pounds for the United States. The clip for 1880 reached 23,000 tons, after which it declined. The average price for a dozen years has exceeded 19 cents per pound. It may be asserted that no branch of agriculture has paid so well throughout as sheep-raising, and with the reputation acquired by California wool factories, the prospect continues favorable.[6]

as hardier. *Alvarado, Hist.*, i. 31. If mules 20 years old are brought to Cal. from the east they take a second growth, observes McDaniel, *Early Days*, MS., 10. The *Census* of 1880 places the number of mules and asses at 28,300, 4,000 being in Colusa, and 2,000 in Stanislaus. In 1850, 1860, and 1878 there were 1,660, 3,680, and 17,500, respectively.

[6] In the early colonial period there were large flocks in the south, of a poor stock, with short, coarse wool; but they were mostly killed after the secularization, the rest falling into neglect. Similar low-grade animals were brought in large numbers from New Mexico to supply the mining markets. In 1849-51

Goats receive little attention, although a number
are always found in the outskirts of towns and vil-

large numbers came. *Cerruti's Ramblings*, MS., 39–40; 1852, 40,000, some selling for $16; in 1853, 135,000, selling for $9; and by 1858 over 376,000 more,
with prices falling to $3.37. The loss on the way from dust, thirst, Indians,
etc., tended to stop the traffic after 1860. *Hayes' Agric.*, 127–32; *Id., Ind.*, i.
211–16; *Alta Cal.*, Feb. 8, 1852, etc., for imports prior to 1853; for subsequent,
see *Hayes' Misc.*, 64; *Van Tramp's Adv.*, 306; *U. S. Census*, 1880, iii. 1035.
From Hawaii came some in 1847. *Pickett's Expos.*, 15. The first to introduce
American sheep for wool-raising was W. W. Hollister, in 1853, and he quickly
made his fortune thereby, as related in his *Stat.*, MS., 2–4. He became the
worthy magnate of S. Benito county, which has named its seat after him.
Flint, Bixby, and Cole were other prominent breeders. *Monterey Co. Hist.*,
157, etc. Attention was specially directed to improve the breed with Spanish
merinos, for which Vermont ranked as the centre in the U. S., and during
the rapid growth of the industry during 20 years 75 per cent of the sheep
have become high-grade merinos. Among the largest flocks is Strobridge's
at Haywards, which has brought an average of $30 for breeding ewes. A few
Southdowns and Cotswolds were here, and it is supposed that with the modifications of closer settlements, the English sheep will grow in favor, with its longer
fleece and savory mutton. Hoyt of Suisun is the leading breeder of Shropshires.
So far the Spanish thrives best. The *U. S. Census* of 1880, iii. 781,046, assigns
California 4,150,000 sheep, exclusive of spring lambs, and unenumerated range
flocks, which would make the total 5,700,000. Fresno and Los Angeles lead
from the first total with 383.000 and 330,000, respectively, followed by Mendocino with 296,000, Humboldt 186,000, S. Joaquin 182,000, Colusa 168,000,
Merced 167,000, Sonoma 156,000. Gordon's report in *Id.* raises the number
greatly. The total census figures for 1850, 1852, 1860, and 1870 stand at
17,500, 35,800, 1,088,000, and 2,768,000, respectively. In 1875–6 the dept of
agriculture raised the total to 6,700,000, reducing it to 3,700,000 in 1879. The
increase has been checked by severe droughts, such as in 1861–2 and 1863–4,
when several southern districts were almost stripped of sheep; in 1871 they
lost 20 per cent; in 1877 about 2,500,000, it is claimed, owing to overstocked
pastures; 1874–5 and 1879–80 were particularly severe for the north. The
growth of settlements, with increased cost of land and fence laws is now imposing restrictions. The average range required is two acres for each sheep;
in the north one acre is frequently enough. The expense is calculated at 35
to 50 cents per head, exclusive of land, which can be leased at 10 to 25 cents
per acre, or bought at $2 to $5. See *U. S. Census*, 1880, 1037–43, for estimates.
Only a proportion of the fine breed receive shelter and cultivated food. The
sheep are reckoned at $2.20 a head. The receipts may be placed at $1.50 for
wool, and the increase at fully 80 per cent, an average sustained by early
bearing, often before the sheep are a year old, and by a large proportion of
twins and triplets, the average twin-bearing being over 30 per cent between
the third and tenth year. A loss of ten per cent may be ascribed to straying
and neglect, to storms and wild beasts and dogs, poisonous weeds, and diseases. The only wide-spread malady is scab, which exists only in mild form.
Fluke, water on the brain, and foot-rot are still less prevalent. Droughts,
fluctuating prices, and bad management bring occasional heavy inflictions.
The two annual shearings, in May and September, lambs preferably in July
and August, yield 4 lbs. and 3 lbs. 'in the grease,' respectively. The average
in 1880 was 8.11 lbs. from wethers, 6.33 from ewes, and 5.40 from lambs. The
average for the U. S. is little over 4 lbs. The aim is to improve the breed to
a larger yield. Strobridge's merinos yielded an average of 20 lbs., and Griz-
zly's 14-month-old fleece weighed 42 lbs. *Hittell's Res.*, 273. Shropshires
yield 7 to 14 lbs. The loss in scouring is about 65 per cent. The Oregon
annual 6-lb. fleece loses 60 per cent. The rainier north districts have cleaner
wool, but the southern claim heavier fleeces from their more nourishing though

lages. Angoras were introduced with great flourish in the fifties, but failed to meet expectations. They and the cashmeres form the only herd animals, but with very few of high grade, and not of great value for the wool.[7]

The raising of swine is restricted by dry pastures; the warm climate interferes with pork packing, and fence laws have proved a check in some quarters; nevertheless, there are favorable localities, especially in the tule regions of San Joaquin and Sacramento, and the rapid increase, the ready markets, and the growth of irrigation are promoting the expansion of the industry.[8]

dry and bur-infested pastures; and they assume the advantage in breed. *U. S. Census*, 1880, 1043. The Cal. wool is fine, though, and the products of her factories are widely esteemed. Griser's tables place the total wool yield at 150 tons in 1855, 1,500 in 1860, 10,000 in 1870, 28,000 in 1876, 20,400 in 1878, 23,000 in 1880, and 21,500 in 1881. The census reduces the spring fleece for 1880 to 16,800,000 lbs. from 4,150,000 sheep. The price rose from 14 cents per lb. in 1870 to 29 in 1872, declined gradually to 14½ in 1876, and revived to 22 in 1880; average for 11 years 19¼ cents, equivalent to $78,000,000. Review in *Cal. Agric. Soc., Trans.*, notably 1873–7; concerning frauds, *Cal. Jour. Sen.*, 1867–8, Apr. 87. Wool-growers' conventions touching these points, etc., are noted in *Sac. Union*, Sept. 20, 1861; *S. F. Call*, Jan. 22, 1874. Of late years only occasional choice animals have been introduced, but the export has been growing, from 50,000 in 1877 to nearly 150,000 in 1880 to Idaho, Montana, Arizona, and New Mexico, which latter seeks the superior merinos. The drive across Arizona occupies fully seven months. In Cal. one ram can serve 100 ewes for three years. A few dogs are used. One shepherd is regarded as sufficient for 1,000 to 2,000 sheep. The flock is usually driven into corrals or pens during the night to escape wild animals. The change of pasture from the drying valleys to the mountains in summer is undoubtedly beneficial. With proper care during certain seasons, especially after rains, the ranges rather profit by sheep, although some claim that the quality of the grass deteriorates.

[7] Yet they are hardy, easily herded, and there is room to expand in order to meet the demand for skins, etc. The Sierra Nevada slopes present the best ground for them. *Pac. Rural Press*, May 15, 1875; May 10, June 7, 1879; *Sta Bárb. Press*, Jan. 8, March–Aug., Nov.–Dec., 1876; *S. José Times*, Aug. 26, 1879; *Colusa Sun*, May 27, 1876; *Jackson Ledger*, March 30, 1878; *Placero Repub.*, Jan. 11, 1877; March 28, 1878; *Watsonville Transcr.*, June 2, 1877; Sept. 13, 1878; *Yreka Union*, Oct. 27, 1877; Oct. 26, 1878; *Petal. Courier*, Dec. 21, 1876; *S. L. Ob. Tribune*, Feb. 23, 1878; *S. F. Call*, May 28, July 13, Dec. 29, 1871; Sept. 21, 1875; *Plumas Nat.*, June 15, 1872; *S. F. Bulletin*, Oct. 31, 1865; July 17, 1868; July 25, 1871; Jan. 28, 1880. For laws to restrain and protect sheep, see especially *Cal. Statutes*, 1857, 227; 1858, 165; 1859, 119; 1860, 332; also 1862, 1866, 1870, 1874; *Thompson's Law of Farm;* essays and reports on sheep in *Cal. Agric. Soc., Trans.*, 1863, 134–45; 1864–5, 63–5, 279–86, 406; 1874, 449–510, 563–9; *Butler's Monterey*, 14–16; *Cal. Jour. Sen.*, 1865–6; ap. 15, pp. 13–15; *Overland*, viii. 489–97; xii. 358–63; *Nordhoff's Cal.*, 234–7; *L. Ang. Exp.*, Nov. 12, 1883; *Hayes' Agric.*, 53–7, 95, et seq.; *Nidever's Life*, MS., 141. C. B. Bailey of Wadsworth, Nevada, is the leading breeder of Angoras, owning 7,000.

[8] The number of swine has increased from 2,700 in 1850 to 456,000 in

Poultry have been profitable on a small scale, but attempts to extend the business have for the most part proved failures.[9]

The honey-bee was not found in California prior to 1852, when the first hive was brought from the east. Although suffering in some districts from drought, it increased rapidly along the streams, and especially in San Diego county.[10]

1860, 444,600 in 1870, and 603,500 in 1880. Tulare, with its rich tule region, leads with 36,000, followed by Los Angeles, rich in maize-fields, with 33,600; by Colusa, Ventura, Sonoma, Yolo. For early droves, see *Los Ang. Co. Hist.*, and *Sonoma Id.*; and for first arrivals, *Prov. St. Pap., Ben. Mil.*, i. 18; *Monterey Parr.*, 22. Berkshires were introduced in 1847. *Pickett's Expos.*, 15; *Alta Cal.*, Nov. 15, 1857; *S. F. Bulletin*, July 11, 1859; Nov. 21, 1860, etc.; *Sta Bárb. Press*, March 9, 1878; May 17, 1879.

[9] The collection, exceeding say 500 hens, attracts a sweeping apoplectic epidemic. Artificial hatching establishments are increasing. The census of 1880 places the number of poultry at 1,600,000, producing 5,770,000 dozen eggs in 1879. *Alta Cal.*, Aug. 8, 1854, comments on the growth of poultry-raising. *Prov. St. Pap., Ben. Mil.*, i. 18, refers to introductions in 1772. Ostrich farming has of late years become an industry in Los Angeles. *S. F. W. Call*, Dec. 21, 1882; *S. F. Bull.*, Oct. 18, 1883; Oct. 30, 1885, refer to its introduction from South Africa and the favorable progress.

[10] W. A. Buckley brought the first hive from New York. *Alta Cal.*, July 1, 1852. T. Shelton, wrongly claimed to be the first, in *S. J. Pioneer*, Jan. 27, 1877. He obtained 12 swarms from a disgusted passenger at Aspinwall, and landed one in safety in March 1853, which threw off three swarms the first season. Two of these sold in Dec. 1853 for $105 and $110. The same year some of the small and stingless Mexican bees arrived. In 1855-6, several large importations were made, from which honey sold at $1.50 to $2 per lb. Among the importers was Harbison, subsequently the leading apiarist of the state, who published *The Bee-keeper's Directory*, S. F., 1861, 12°, 440 pp., to guide the rising industry. This in 1859-60 embraced 6,000 swarms, but soon met with reverses from diseases and inexperience, and from declining prices, 25 cents per lb. in 1867. *Cronise's Cal.*, 373. Los Angeles was then the leading producer. Harbison, so far at Sacramento, opened about this time in San Diego, which soon assumed the head, claiming 20,000 stands in 1880. It was followed by S. Bernardino, Sta Bárbara, Ventura, Los Angeles, Kern, and S. Joaquin, whose production of honey, according to the *U. S. Census* of 1880, stand respectively at 91,000, 83,600, 55,000, 48,000, 44,500, 29,700, and 25,000 lbs., the total for the state being 574,000 lbs. of honey, and 14,600 of wax. It was at first supposed that the bee could not thrive in so dry a summer region, and indeed, heavy losses have occurred through droughts as in 1877, but they do well along streams and also in mountain regions. Many a hive has made 200 lbs. in a season. Horticulturists have frequently raised an outcry against them, *Hayes' Monterey*, 90, *Taylor's Bet. Gates*, 268-9, for feeding on grapes, and especially apricots. The wild sage of the mountains yields a fine honey, and some apiarists of the great valley used to send their hives to the Sierra slopes for fresh pasture. The honey of the coast valleys, with their varied flowers, has a peculiar flavor resembling that of Mt Hymettus. That from the honey dew deposited by the aphis is coarse and unfit for market. The great enemy of the bee is the bee-moth, which enters the hives and ruins them, unless closely watched; the bee-bird and lizard confine their raids to bees on the flowers. Estimates of expenses are given in *Com. and Ind.*, 275; in *Harbison; McPherson's Los Ang.*, 32-4; *Hayes' Agric.*, 186; *Hawley's Ange-*

Agriculturists took an early opportunity to impress upon the community, by means of exhibitions, that the wealth of California was not restricted to the fields, but that her countless valleys contained the most prolific of soils and the most attractive features for building homes and yielding sure competence and even riches. Enterprises of this nature, being left to private efforts, were led by T. Shelton, who in November 1851 gave at San Francisco a display dignified by the appellation of agricultural and mineral fair, with fine specimens from farms and gardens in the bay counties, and even from Nevada and Tuolumne.[11] His success induced Warren & Son to open a more imposing exhibition at Sacramento on September 20, 1852, and another at San Francisco on October 5, 1853, with mineral collections, art treasures, lectures, and other attractions, and a number of valuable premiums.[12]

With so encouraging an example, a number of prominent agriculturists united to organize in 1854 the State Agricultural Society,[13] which henceforth

[footnotes]

les, 101–2; *Century*, July 1882; *S. F. Chron.*, Nov. 12, 1883; *Cal. Argic. Soc., Trans.*, 1859, 292–308.

[11] Yet chiefly from Sta Clara. A few prizes were distributed, notably one to a hat manufacturer. *S. F. Herald*, Nov. 14, 1851; *Alta*, etc.

[12] In cups, medals, etc. In Oct. 1853 a church congregation held a World's Miniature Fair with curious and artistic exhibits representing different countries. *Alta Cal.*, Oct. 6, 1853; *Id.*, Sept. 20 to Oct. 1852; Oct. 3, Nov. 14, 1853; *Herald*, etc.; *Cal. State Fair Scraps*, 9 et seq.

[13] Under the presidency of F. W Macondray, with six vice-pres. Incorporated May 13, 1854, with power to buy land and erect buildings for model farms and exhibitions. After shifting from place to place it was in 1860 permanently located at Sac. By act of March 20, 1858, the management was intrusted to a board, consisting of a president and nine directors, to be elected after 1862 by an annual convention of members of said society, and delegates from county and district agric. societies. An act of March 21, 1872, appropriated $5,000 for the society, $3,000 for the Bay District Agric. Soc., and $2,000 each for a number of county and district societies, solely toward premiums. Any person was admitted a member on paying $5 a year, with privilege to use the library. *Cal. Statutes*, 1854, 1858, 1872, etc.; *Cal. Agric. Soc., Trans.*, prefaces, etc. It long struggled under a debt which at one time reached $30,000, but this was cleared off by 1870. The need for new buildings, grand-stand, and improvements in the park caused an expenditure of $45,000 in 1872–5, toward which the state contributed, besides adding to premiums, leaving only $16,000 debt. Since then the society has prospered. Report in *Cal. Jour. Sen.*, 1875–6, ap. 43; *Id.*, 1862, ap. 34; 1854, 1858, etc.; *Hittell's Code*, ii. 1660. Park inauguration. *Alta Cal.*, July 24, 1870.

assumed the lead in such exhibitions, beginning with 1854, and fostering improvements in farming, horticulture, stock-breeding, and cognate industries, aided by the state with premiums and means to sustain experimental grounds. It became the head for the county and district agricultural societies, which sprang up throughout the state, with similar local aims and exhibits.[14]

These organizations lent interest to the general and special meetings, such as conventions of stock-raisers, wheat and fruit growers, gardeners,[15] and sericulturists for promoting certain objects. They did much to sustain the excitement in various industries that agitated the state at different times, and to seek protection against opposing interests. At one time apiarists and horticulturists were in array against each other. Then raisers of cereals and live-stock, during the fence-law movement of the sixties. Then again all these united together to face the merchants, freight carriers,

[14] An act of 1866, *Cal. Statutes*, sought to encourage their formation, and by act of 1872 $2,000 each were granted for premiums to those of Sta Clara, Sonoma and Marin, S. Joaquin, Northern district, Upper Sac., Siskiyou, Los Angeles, Bay District Horticultural and Cal. Vine Growers. For their development, see *S. José Pioneer*, June 8, 1878; *Bay Dist. Hortic. Soc., Trans.*, 1772, etc.; *S. Joaq. Agric. Soc., Trans.*, 1861, etc., the latter organized in 1859, when Sac. also formed a special agric. soc. The Southern Cal. Ag. Soc. had troubles in 1873. The Sonoma formed in 1855, and also the Yuba-Sutter. *Sac. Union*, May 14, July 24, Aug. 17, 1855. The state horticultural society proposed a fair in 1856. *Id.*, Dec. 19, 1856. The transactions of many of these societies are published in *Cal. Agric. Soc., Trans.* See also county histories in *Hayes' Agric.*, *Cal. Farmer*, *Rural Press*. Citrus fairs have lately become a feature in Los Angeles, Sta Bárbara, and S. Diego. *L. Ang. Herald*, March 6, 1880; March 17, 22, 1881; May 24, 1882; *S. F. Call*, March 16, 1882. S. F. and Sac. follow the example. *S. F. Chron.*, Jan. 14, 26, 1886. In early days female equestriennes formed a feature at the fairs. *Alta Cal.*, Sept. 29, 1855. Later gambling has risen into an evil. Agric. displays form a feature also in the industrial exhibitions under auspices of the Mechanics' Institute, organized in 1855, and opening its first fair at S. F. on Sept. 7, 1857, for three weeks. *Mech. Instit., Report First Indust. Exh.*, 1–157; *Williams' Stat.*, MS., 16, comment on its site, corner of Sutter and Montgomery sts, and its success. *Alta Cal., Bulletin*, Sept. 1857. The legislature created a state agric. board to foster farming. See report by it in *Cal. Jour. Sen.*, 1865-6, ap. 15. But the agric. soc. carry out its aims equally well.

[15] A general convention held at Sac. in 1855 is reported in *Hayes' Agric.*, 46–50; *Sac. Union*, Apr. 26, 1855. Wheat-growers proposed an organization in 1881. *S. F. Chron.*, Sept. 15, 1881. Fruit-growers met in enthusiastic spirit in 1859, *S. F. Bulletin*, Sept. 10, 1859, and organized in 1885. *S. F. Chron.*, Oct. 15, Nov. 12, 1885; Jan. 22, 1886. The Gardeners' Ass., dating since 1874, is composed chiefly of Italians.

and other middle-men, who, not content with growing rich at the expense of producers, combined in rings and monopolies to manipulate markets and rates for ruinous extortion. These evils had already roused the farmers of the eastern states to organize in 1867 the order of patrons of husbandry, centring in a national grange. After an attempt in 1871 to create a special union, the farmers of California in 1873 joined this successful movement and formed a state grange, which within six months counted more than 100 subordinate granges, in 24 counties. At first an established business firm was chosen to export and sell their surplus grain and produce, and fifteen cargoes were despatched in 1874; but this house failing, the grangers' business association was organized, which also undertook by direct arrangement with importers and manufacturers to procure and forward implements, groceries, and other goods at low rates. The grange and its branches further promoted the establishment of farmers' banks, warehouses, and coöperative stores in several towns, even the construction of railways; all aiming to defeat speculators and extortion, and obtain ready and direct markets, saving in commissions and profits from 5 to 50 per cent, on sales as well as purchases, and benefiting the farming community throughout by forcing competing middle-men to greater compliance.[16]

[16] This very compliance, and the growth of carrying enterprises, in which many farmers were interested, served in a measure to check the ardor which marked the first enrolment for the grange and its tributary undertakings. They prosper, nevertheless, sufficiently to continue their task so widely beneficent, direct and indirect. The success of the no-fence-law agitation had served to reveal to the farmers their growing strength, and to encourage them to band for resistance against other extortions and encroachments. They had long clamored against the merchants and middle-men, who availed themselves of the helpless condition of a large proportion among husbandmen. Transportation had fallen into the hands of monopolists, who forced the producers to pay enormous prices for moving their grain and fruit. The banks also conspired to demand a higher percentage for loans upon county property than upon city estate. For these ills lay remedy in coöperation. On Dec. 7, 1871, a farmers' club was formed at Sac., followed by similar associations in other towns, and soon after their representatives met in convention to organize the Farmers' Protective Union League, of which J. Bidwell became the first president. At the first meeting of the board, in January 1872, were discussed plans for a produce exchange, loan bank, etc., with appeals for

local clubs to form and sustain them. *Cal. Agric. Soc., Trans.*, 1872, 777-84. The S. Joaquin Farmers' Union formed at Stockton, and so forth. At the second meeting in April 1873, petitions were framed for the legislature to advocate reduction of duty on sacks, jute, etc. By this time the members had become impressed with the superior features of the grange movement in the eastern states, and this meeting with general favor, the union disbanded.

O. H. Kelley, of the bureau of agriculture at Washington, had in 1866 been struck by the helpless condition of the farming interests, and conferring with W. M. Ireland, of the post-office, and others, he compiled a plan for the Order of Patrons of Husbandry. W. Saunders, of the agricultural dept, gave it his active support, and established the National Grange on Dec. 4, 1867. *Martin's Hist. Grange Movement*, 407-9. At first the expansion was gradual, and in 1873 it embraced only 10 states, but by 1874 over 30 had joined, and in 1875 over 1,400,000 members stood enlisted, with over $18,000,000 invested in warehouses, elevators, mills, bag factories, fruit canneries, cotton gins, etc. In Iowa more than half the elevators were controlled by Patrons. The grange promoted the formation of mutual insurance companies, published information on crops and markets, fostered arbitration in lieu of costly litigation, and established agencies in all parts for exchanging produce and arranging for cheaper groceries, implements, clothing, etc. In Indiana alone the agency did a business of over $250,000, saving to Patrons on implements 35 to 50 per cent, and on groceries and clothing 5 to 20 per cent. W. H. Baxter, of Napa, had communicated with the national grange in 1871, and received a commission as deputy. He took part in the deliberations of the Farmers' Union, and prepared the way for the special deputy, N. W. Garretson, who organized the requisite number of subordinate granges toward forming, at Napa, on July 15, 1873, the Cal. State Grange of Patrons of Husbandry, with J. W. A. Wright as first master. Its members to be composed of masters of sub-granges, and their wives, as matrons; its officers to be chosen every two years, including an executive committee of six; meeting annually, on the first Tuesday in Oct. Any person interested in agricultural pursuits might be admitted as a member of sub-granges; fee $5 for males, $2 for females; minimum monthly dues 10 cents from each member, a percentage going to the state grange; officers elected annually; the sick must be visited and cared for; cruelty to animals forbidden. Further general rules and by-laws in *Carr's Husbandry*, 153-7. Special laws in *Patrons of Husbandry, Linden Grange* (no. 56), *Constit.*, 1-21. At the first annual meeting held in Oct. 1873, at S. José, 104 granges from 24 counties were represented. *Alta Cal.*, Oct. 15, 1873. It was here resolved to employ business agents at S. F., and the best proposals coming from A. F. Walcott, of the firm E. E. Morgan's Sons, of N. York and Liverpool, he received the appointment, G. P. Kellogg being the first special agent for the grange to watch the operations of this firm, and arrange with importers and dealers in implements, groceries, etc., for reduced rates to Patrons. Roused by this independence of action, the opposition bestirred themselves to inflate the market, to transfer to Walcott their chartered vessels at a heavy advance, and to excite him to make heavy advances and rash purchases. The grange of only one year's existence saw with pride the departure of 15 vessels in 1874, laden with their grain; but before they reached their transatlantic market Walcott had succumbed in bankruptcy, leaving a host of farmers to rue their confidence. The grange had nevertheless demonstrated its value by the large savings effected through its own agent on grain commissions, shipping charges, and tonnage, and on implements and groceries, by promoting dealings direct with principals. Carr, *Husbandry*, 160, estimates the saving to patrons alone at over $5,000,000 for the first year. This prospect had encouraged the grange in April 1874 to promote a system of warehouses and banks, connected with a central establishment at S. F. That year, accordingly, the Grangers' Bank of California was organized, with a capital of $5,000,000. Within a year 1,500 patrons subscribed for half the capital, and others helped to bring deposits to $2, 000,000. A Farmers' Saving and Loan society had formed in Stanislaus in 1873, and now other farmers' banks opened in Solano,

Colusa, and elsewhere. At Modesto and other places were opened grangers' warehouses and coöperative unions and stores, one at S. José proving a marked success, dealing as it did in almost everything required by the community, implements, groceries, etc., and all at greatly reduced prices. For rules governing such stores, see *Carr's Husbandry*, 167. A farmers' Mutual Insurance Company was formed, and after Walcott's failure, the grange promoted the organization, on Feb. 18, 1875, of the Grangers' Business Association of California, with a capital of $1,000,000. By-laws in *Id.*, 207-9. It proposed to deal in all kinds of produce, goods, and implements, and act as factors and brokers in shipping and selling grain. In 1882 it assumed wider powers to borrow money, acquire real estate, etc. *S. F. Call*, March 16, 1882. The prudent management of its eleven directors, annually elected, has produced most gratifying results. A further instance of the energetic efforts of the grangers exists in the narrow-gauge railway from Salinas to Monterey, affording a cheap outlet for the grain of this valley.

The largest stock-raiser in Cal., and one of the largest in the world, is Henry Miller, a native of Brackenheim, Wurtemburg, who came to San Francisco in 1850, and soon afterward became the leading wholesale butcher in the state. In 1857 he entered into a partnership with Charles Lux, which lasted until the decease of the latter, more than a quarter of a century afterward. Purchasing lands and stock as opportunity offered, they became the owners of 750,000 acres in eleven counties of Cal., besides large possessions in Or. and Nev. On them were depastured in 1888 about 100,000 cattle and 80,000 sheep, the sales of meat amounting for that year to $1,500,000. To Mr Miller is largely due the successful operation of the San Joaquin and Kings river canal company, the largest irrigation enterprise on the coast.

Among others in southern California is Jefferson G. James, a Missourian by birth, who came to this country in 1850, and after a brief mining experience engaged in cattle-farming, first in Los Angeles co., and afterward at the head of Fresno slough, where he was one of the pioneer stock-raisers, and where are still his headquarters. Here and at other points he now controls about 100,000 acres, on which are depastured some 15,000 head of cattle. In 1882 he was elected to the S. F. board of supervisors, and in 1888 to the board of education, rendering good service in both capacities.

Albert H. Denny, a native of New Jersey, and one of the oldest settlers in Siskiyou co., is also one of the most successful stock-raisers and merchants in that section. Reaching Cal. in 1852, after a somewhat harsh experience at the mines, he began dairy-farming in the Shasta valley. In 1865 he engaged in business at the town of Callahan's, where the sales of his firm up to 1890 exceeded $1,000,000.

Among other stock-raisers of Siskiyou co. may be mentioned Samuel Jackson, a prominent citizen of Yreka, and a native of Frederick co., Va. Landing in San Francisco in 1852, after a somewhat checkered experience as a miner, a farmer, and in various other occupations, he became the owner of several valuable ranches in Siskiyou co., to the management of which his attention is now devoted.

One of the leading cattle-farmers in Humboldt co. is Hy Curtner, a native of Fountain co., Ind., who came to this coast in 1852 with $20 in his pocket, and is now the owner of several large ranches in Cal. and Nev., and of several thousand head of stock. In 1857 he engaged in fruit-raising, his orchard in the thermal belt of the Alameda foothills being among the choicest in the state.

CHAPTER V.

MANUFACTURES.

1848–1889.

Mission Work—Agricultural and Mining Manufactures—High Wages —Iron and Lead Works—Lumber and Leather—Pottery and Paper —Conditions and Climate—Material—Forest Trees—Saw-mills— Charcoal—Planing-mills—Ship-building—Dry-dock—Wagons— Cooperage and Box-making—Willow-ware—Brooms—Furniture— Billiard-tables — Pianos — Fish-curing — Whaling — Oysters — Flour — Confectionery — Beer — Spirits — Fruit canning — Meat-packing—Sugar and Tobacco—Wool, Cotton, and Silk—Cloth-ing—Leather—Miscellaneous Articles—Soap—Iron—Jewelry —Glass and Clay Works—Soda—Powder.

It has long been predicted by political economists that the manufacturing interests of California will eventually surpass both mining and agriculture in volume and value of output. Although this prophecy has not as yet come to pass, its fulfilment, not-withstanding many obstacles, would appear by no means improbable, in view of the ever-increasing sup-ply of cheaper labor and capital, of superior facilities, and of the steady, if slow and in some directions still inadequate, demand for manufactured goods of home production.

The main check here interposed has been in the high cost of labor, weighing alike on the production of raw material and on refining processes, and opening wide the portals for goods from eastern and European fac-tories. Certain advantages remained with California, by reason of the long distance from these sources of supplies, brought in early days by the circuitous routes over the Isthmus or round Cape Horn, which involved loss of time—then of exceeding value—and high freights, particularly on bulky and dangerous articles, both presenting a wide margin for the application of costlier and inferior local efforts to the vast resources near at hand. An impetus was accordingly given to saw and flour mills, fisheries, and other primary branches of industry. The sudden expansion of a vast traffic gave rise to wagon-making and ship-building, the latter embracing the putting together and the repair of steamboats, which added important departments to foundries and cognate establishments for the supply of mining implements. The large amount of repairs required was sufficient to give a foothold to a number of enterprises, and so to strengthen their means, capacity, and skill as to permit the acceptance of large special orders, and in time to prepare stock for the trade.

To the obstacle of high wages came that of novel features and conditions, both of which the self-reliant American undertook to overcome with characteristic energy and originality. Thus in mining a number of methods were evolved of such importance and scope as to revolutionize the industry, and extend operations to unparalleled magnitude, notably in placers and deep mines. Instance the development of the sluice from the tom, rocker, and pan, and of the hydraulic pipe, which enabled one man to perform the labor of hundreds, and undertake tasks that once appeared impossible, thus opening to enterprise new fields and hitherto neglected regions. A demand rose in consequence for peculiar implements and machinery, suggested by obstacles and requirements as they occurred. This served to retain for California also their manufacture, and to attract foreign orders for apparatus alone invented and understood here. Thus it is that the foundry business of San Francisco acquired a vast importance, notwithstanding the high cost of labor and the necessity of importing the raw material. The dry climate and special wants called for ditches, aqueducts, and windmills, which gave wider opportunities for mills and shops, and led to such inventions as the inverted syphon and peculiar frames. Deep mines demanded novel and strong machinery for sinking, and hydraulic pumps, air compressors and hoisting gear, to overcome heat, water, and distance. Different kinds of ore, crumbling, rebellious, or mixed with tenacious substances, had to be treated on different plans, and crushers and amalgamators multiplied. New explosives were introduced for blasting, and extended here to submarine operations. A high-pressure accumulator facilitated the use of hydraulic power. Rolling-mills found their origin in the accumulation of old rails, which could not profitably be exported. The lead brought to light in the search for precious metals gave an opening for shot-towers and lead-works. The difficulty of mountain transport, and the irregular topography of San Francisco, suggested wire-rope ways and cable roads, which overcame the obstacles presented by hills and ravines.

The V-flume did a similar service for lumbering, by giving easy and cheap access to mountain timber scores of miles distant from available points, and hitherto valueless. The loading chute remedied the lack of good shipping-places; the adjustable saw-tooth proved of great importance for saw-mills; and the triple circular saw, the logging, gang-slicing machines, the guides and levers, were designed in particular for manipulating the enormous and valuable redwood and other trees of the state;—all assisting to raise the lumber industry within its different limits to an extraordinary magnitude and excellence, the fountain-head for a number of others.

In agriculture, the straw-burning machine, the combined harvester, the multiple gang-ploughs, and a number of other improvements, have tended to reduce the cost of field-work fully fifty per cent, and to make California conspicuous for vast and cheap operations. Her superior wheat encouraged the grinding of flour to the extent of more than a dozen million dollars, largely for export. The fine malt and hops, and the difficulty of introducing beer by sea in good condition, favored breweries, whose production in 1888 exceeded four million dollars. Fine and abundant fruit, vegetables, and salmon led to the establishment of numerous canneries, which sustained several vinegar factories, and consumed a large proportion of the seven million dollars' worth and more of sugar from the local refineries. Proximity to the Hawaiian Islands for raw sugar was a fostering factor. The excellence of the chestnut-oak bark raised tannery products to three and a half million dollars, and brought a foreign demand, which extended to saddlery, shoes, gloves, and belting, with a total out-turn of more than six million dollars. The abundance of tallow and other substances account for soap factories. A fine quality of wool and a substantial weft sustained the mills against many adverse influences. Simplicity of fabrication and nearness of sources for raw material built up jute and bag factories, while paper-mills found an abundance of good straw and rags. The discovery of antimony brought type foundries to the front. The risk and cost of transporting crockery and glassware gave an opening for potteries and glassworks. The possession of quartz promoted a special branch of jewelry. The lead joint for water-pipes, the pneumatic clock, and the photography of animals in motion are also among California's inventions. A number of other devices might be named which have contributed to her fame, and to the increasing development of her resources.

The general wealth has maintained large orders at high rates for domestic purposes, so as to support many otherwise impracticable industries. A number of others are due entirely to Chinese, whose cheap and in many respects undesirable labor is largely forced upon the country by white workingmen.

High wages have been sustained by a variety of

causes,[1] such as the fascinations of the gold-fields, cheap lands, and other undeveloped resources, the falling off of immigration, and the indolent and unyielding habits among a large class, fostered by interruptions from seasons and unstable conditions. These drawbacks, especially the irregularity, affected employers seriously, and compelled them to have recourse to Chinese. To a certain stage the latter have undoubtedly been a useful and even necessary element, for without their aid must have been deferred the construction of railroads to facilitate the introduction of white labor, the opening of ditches, reclamation of land, the planting of vineyards, and the establishment of many manufactures, such as woollen-mills, which all help to provide more employment for superior white men and for capital.[2] But before the Chinese came it was said that the Indians were degrading labor, when white men were too lazy to work. The gold excitement with its immense influx of people soon dissipated this idea by a healthy democratic feeling, the maintenance of which is particularly desirable in

[1] The gold-fields held out prospects of independence and fair returns for labor, gilded by occasional glittering prizes, so as to greatly lower the attractions of other pursuits. This field was ever extended by new discoveries, sufficient to greatly counteract the effects of immigration. Agriculture presented in somewhat less degree similar attractions, with the charm of home-building. The mass of undeveloped resources offered avenues to wealth and opportunity for independent enterprise. The magnetism of the first gold discoveries gone, the cost, length, and danger of the journey to the Pacific, and the attractions of nearer countries, interposed a check on the influx of workingmen, and with every slight decline in wages a number of branches appeared to compete for labor, to enlarge the field for employment, and retard the decline in earnings, so that they still rule higher than in the eastern states. For early rates, see my chapter on trade. To this must be added the periodical indulgence in idleness by a large class, fostered by the nomadic and independent mining life, with its gambling spirit, its irresponsible bachelorhood, the scanty and insecure inducements in early days for saving and investing, the liberal revenue which provided ample means for enjoyment and rest, the compulsory interruptions caused by climate and agricultural seasons, by new and irregular industries, and the stress upon employers to eliminate in the training process less valuable hands. Men preferred also to wait for the higher pay of the busy periods, and hold back at other times rather than accept reductions.

[2] Without them a number of industries, like the making of shoes, underclothing, and cigars, could not have been maintained. Yet the question arises whether it might not have been better to await the cheapening of white labor. No people can be permanently benefited by the introduction of a low foreign element, black, white, or copper colored.

a republican country. In California it would tend to redeem the youth, which, on the plea of shunning the labor-levelling Chinese,[3] is drifting into deplorable idleness, vagabondage, and lawlessness, which retard progress and desirable immigration, and deter capital from opening new avenues for employment and wealth.

Among other obstacles may be mentioned a high rate of interest,[4] the larger profits of elementary industries, the lack of water-power in eligible quarters, the cost of transportation, the high value of good sites, and doubtful land titles, scanty population, unsettled conditions, the limited quantity of iron and hard wood, and the high price of coal.

The civil war gave a decided impulse to industries, by increasing the cost and risk of transportation. But the opening of the overland railway undermined many kinds of business by bringing cheap markets so much nearer, and it disturbed many more by unsteady rates and other attendant insecurity. The speculative spirit of Californians had, moreover, tempted to many undertakings, with insufficient capital and experience, and the consequent failures spread discouragement and lowered industrial credit. Nevertheless, progress has been rapid for so young a state, dating properly from 1849, and this in face of so many obstacles and the naturally slow unfolding of manufactures. In the accompanying end note I give an outline of the leading industries, chiefly with respect to their beginning. Their development is best compared by an examination of the census reports. That of 1860 enumerates nearly 1,450 establishments, with a capital of $11,000,000, employing 6,400 hands, paying $5,500,000 in wages, using $11,000,000 worth of

[3] This undesirable competition and consequent hostility, and the irregularity of employment, hold back much desirable immigration and capital. Australia has pointed a way in not only imposing a protective tariff against cheap foreign production, but against the entry of undesirable labor in the form of an inferior and unassimilating race.

[4] Two and three per cent monthly in early years, and one per cent until lately.

raw material, and producing goods to the value of $23,500,000.[5] By 1870 the establishments numbered 3,980, with $40,000,000 capital, 25,400 hands, receiving $13,000,000 in wages, using $35,000,000 of material, and producing $66,000,000 worth of goods. In 1880 the figures had risen to 5,890 establishments, with $61,000,000 capital, 43,700 hands, $21,000,000 wages, $72,600,000 of raw material, and $116,200,000 of products,[6] increased to $160,000,000 by 1889.

San Francisco, as the chief harbor of the coast, and the main depôt for most of the raw and refined material, has naturally become the centre for manufactures; and the congregation here of Chinese for mutual protection has assisted to so maintain it for branches not requiring proximity to existing local sources.

The annual mechanics' fair, as well as the county fairs, has exerted a fostering influence in a marked degree, and gives evidence of continual advance in all branches. This, indeed, is to be expected with the possession of so many natural resources, with an ever-augmenting surplus of raw products, with the disclosure of additional coal-beds, and the rapid exploitation of iron deposits so essential to the development of other branches. The planting of the eucalyptus and other trees promises in time to remedy the sensible defect in hard and elastic woods. Along the Sierra slopes is water-power in abundance, and with spreading settlements they will become more eligible; while the increasing population will provide hands at sufficiently low rates to encourage the launch of new enterprises,

[5] Of which S. F. produced $19,600,000. Flour leads with over $4,600,000, lumber $3,900,000, sugar $1,586,000, machinery $5,575,000. The rest all fall below the million, save liquor. This order was very nearly maintained in 1870.

[6] Fisheries excluded. S. F. leads with 2,970 estab., 28,400 hands, and $77,800,000 products; Alameda following with $5,300,000 worth of products, Sac. $4,200,000, S. Joaquin $3,200,000, Sta Clara $2,890,000, Solano $2,760,-000. Seven other counties exceed $1,000,000. Flour leads with $12,700,000; next come slaughtering and meat-packing $8,000,000, leather $6,200,000, sugar $5,930,000, foundry-work $4,800,000, lumber $4,400,000, clothing $4,000,000, cigars, etc., $3,950,000, liquor, shoes, printing, exceed $3,000,000 each, bread and bags exceed $2,000,000.

and the training of workers for more refined productions. The greater part of the wool still exported can thus be retained to swell the list of woollen fabrics which enjoy so high a reputation abroad; and so with leather and several other products. With increasing railway competition, the raw material will be cheapened, and it is calculated that cotton can be brought from Texas at nearly as low a rate as to Lowell, and so open the prospect for a resumption of cotton spinning, to be sustained also by local plantations. The effort for fine productions should be especially fostered, for these form the chief drain upon remittances from California, which makes plenty of flannels and blankets, but imports fine cloth; exports sole leather, but buys uppers for shoes and fine gloves; produces common crockery and bottles, but introduces table-ware and window-glass; manufactures printing-paper, but sends for writing-paper.

In addition to the preceding prospects, the advantage remains with California of a protective tariff in the shape of freight and risk on transports from the east, most foreign goods being restricted by duty, and by the demand for special urgent work. Favorable conditions are, moreover, presented by the equable climate, which permits almost uninterrupted work throughout the year, obviates the necessity for the substantial and costly buildings required in the eastern states, to the saving also of rent and fuel. California possesses facilities for manufactures decidedly superior to those of several interior states and regions to the south, so that a vast area of the Pacific slope, already made tributary by her geographic position and trade channels, may be counted upon to sustain her industrial aspirations.[7]

[7] The area covered by forests in California is very small in proportion to its size, 478,000 acres in a total acreage of 11,400,000, according to the forestry statistics in *U. S. Agric. Rept*, 1875, pp. 245, 328–30, which place it lowest among the 36 states there listed. This gives an average of only 4.1 per cent of forest land, S. Diego and Alameda ranking lowest, with 0.1 and 0.2 per cent, and Nevada, Mariposa, and Santa Cruz highest, with 55.9, 53.2, and 52.8 per cent, respectively. The valuable timber belts are confined to the

humid coast and mountain regions in central and northern parts, from 37°
lat. to the Oregon border; and the interior valleys and the south are comparatively bare, relieved by clumps along the streams, and occasionally
by a scanty vegetation on the less arid north side of the hills. The trees
have their peculiarity, like the other flora as well as fauna, the country
being remarkable for containing the largest coniferous trees in the world,
growing to a height of 300 feet, and a thickness of 8 feet and more.
The best known are the redwood, the *sequoia sempervirens*, to which belong .
the mammoth tree; the sugar-pine, *pinus lambertiana*, the red and yellow
fir, and the arbor-vitæ. Then there are the laurel, madroño, evergreen oak,
and the nut-pine—evergreen trees. The few deciduous trees are of small industrial value. The foremost place commercially is held by the redwood,
which extends along the coast from Santa Cruz for 350 miles, with an average breadth of 10 miles, and 20,000 feet of standing lumber to the acre,
equivalent to over 40,000,000,000 feet, and sufficient for two centuries, without counting the self-renewal of cut forests. On Eel, Mud, and Little rivers
are nearly 100,000 acres, averaging from 100,000 to 250,000 feet each, and
there are acres bearing 2,000,000 feet. In the Sierra groves are clusters
of trees 20 feet in diameter, standing so close together that a wagon cannot
pass between them. A common height is 200 feet, and in Humboldt the
average saw-log is nearly 5 feet thick, with many reaching as high as 20,
and yielding 100,000 feet of lumber. It is unequalled for ready and smooth
splitting along its straight grain, remarkably free from knots for the first 100
feet, trebly superior in this respect to eastern timber, and exceedingly dura-
ble, offering the readiest and cheapest of material for railway-ties, fence-rails,
etc. Notwithstanding its softness for working, it is not brittle, coarse, flinty,
or gummy, and for size, beauty, and density, and general value, it is one of
the most precious of trees. Hardly inferior is the sugar-pine, which forms a
large proportion in the forests of the Sierra Nevada, but owing to its remoteness from markets, only certain sections, chiefly along the railway lines, have
been invaded. The red fir and yellow pine are also much sought, as well as
the cedar of the north-west; but hard, elastic wood, like the hickory and
white oak of the Atlantic slopes, is rare, and the scanty walnut, maple, wild
cherry, and ash are too small for general use.

The Spanish Californians gave little heed to the timber resources, and
even in the forest regions they preferred adobe houses. The few boards required were mostly imported before the entry of the Anglo-Saxons, who, with
their training in Canada, Maine, etc., felt a natural inclination for lumbering.
The first regular whip-saw pit for manufacturing lumber for sale is attributed
to Jas Dawson of Bodega, in 1835, according to *Son. Co. Hist.*, 203. Soon
after 1840, Read opened a mill on Corta de Madera, and Isaac Graham another near Sta Cruz. In 1843, S. Smith, who had long laid his plans, arrived
at Bodega with machinery for the first steam mill, saw and grist, an effort
which was rewarded by a large grant of land. *Cal. Dept. St. Pap.*, v. MS.,
15–17; *Alvarado, Hist.*, v. MS., 5–7. His example went for little, however,
and not until after the U. S. conquest did mills begin to rise. After opening
a pit near Amador Creek in 1846, Sutter built the water-power mill at Coloma in 1847–8, which proved instrumental in discovering gold. Napa
claimed a similar smaller mill in 1847, and San Mateo one in 1848. See my
preceding vols. In 1849 several were erected as far north as Yuba, with the
first circular saw, it is said, and Nevada, with application of steamboat and
other engines for motive power. *Placer Times*, May 19, 1849. Mills followed
close upon the heels of the advancing miners, Sierra obtaining one in 1850,
Plumas in 1851, after using whip-saws for a time; first on Mill Creek, says
Boynton, *Stat.*, MS., 3; Siskiyou in 1852, when lumbering began on a large
scale, for shipment, in Mendocino, under H. Meiggs, and in Humboldt. Even
Tulare co. was then erecting a mill. *Alta Cal.*, Dec. 11, 1852. The *Census* for
1852 credits Butte with 3 steam and 11 water-power mills; S. F. (S. Mateo)
with 5; Marin with 4 steam mills, producing 9,000,000 feet a year, capital,
$150,000; Yuba, 18 mills, producing the same quantity, capital, $81,000; Nevada had $129,000 in mills, Mendocino $66,000, of which $6,000 represented

water-power, and Calaveras $60,000. See also *Williams' Rec.*, MS., 4; *Branham's Remin.*, MS., which dates the first Sta Cruz Mt mill 1847; *Stockton Repub.*, Dec. 1852; *Sac. Union*, June 16, 1882; *Skellenger's Remin.*, MS.; *Banning's Wilmington*, MS., 5, refers to first steam mill in the south; *Polynesian*, v. 150; *S. F. Bulletin*, June 8, 1875; *Lake Co., Rept. Co. Clerk*, 71; surveyor's reports, in *Cal. Jour. Sen.*, passim; *S. F. Herald*, Sept. 22, 1852, etc.; *Cal. Register*, 1857, 240-9, etc.; *Cal. Lumber Scraps*, 20 et seq.

The lack of roads and minor harbors, the high wages and the large size of the trees, called for the application of improved methods, to which Californians contributed several valuable inventions, such as Dolbeer's steam logging machine for moving timber, the treble circular saw for cutting the extraordinarily thick logs here prevailing, and adjustable teeth for such saws, the carriage for handling long logs, and the V-shaped flumes, some over 40 miles in length, along the Sierra slope, from Madera northward, which tend not alone to cheapen lumber by means of their ready and economic transport, but to open otherwise inaccessible forest regions. Concerning the experiments of J. W. Haines of Genoa, and his claims to the invention, see *Com. and Ind.*, 420-1. The largest fluming enterprise is that of the Sierra Flume and Lumber Co. of 1875, which bought 60,000 acres of sugar and yellow pine timber land in Sierra region in and near Plumas, built 10 mills, and 150 miles of flume to carry the lumber to the valley. An investment of $2,500,000 was followed by failure, but the creditors continued the business successfully. Drives and booms are used, and the slide has been applied to novel chutes for loading vessels anchored at some distance from the harborless shore. These different methods and features, calling for large and varied machinery and vast and expeditious operations, impart to the lumber industry in the state an extraordinary magnitude and excellence. The tracts owned by many mill companies are veritable principalities, exceeding 50,000 acres, with towns, harbors, water routes, special railways, and electric lights for night labor. The *Census* of 1860 enumerated 279 saw-mills, with $1,923,000 capital, and 1,870 hands receiving $1,443,000 in wages and producing $3,944,000 worth of material. That of 1880 reduced the establishments to 251, but of increased magnitude with the aid of improved appliances and capital, the latter being placed at $6,454,000. The hands had increased to 3,430, while the wages amounted to only $1,096,000; and the vaster production, including 305,000,000 feet of lumber (board measure), was valued at only $4,430,000, half of which figured as value of material. The motive power was obtained from 211 steam-engines, of 8,760 horse-power, and 90 water-wheels of 2,230 horse-power. This production was half as much more than that of Washington territory, and double that of Oregon. For railway ties fully 24,000,000 feet were required, and for fenceposts 10,000,000. Shingle machines were offered in 1850, *Pac. News*, Jan. 15, 1850; and Shingle Springs in El D. obtained its name from one in use there in 1849, it is said. The demand upon the yellow pine of the Sierra, chiefly in Butte, for turpentine and resin, was prompted by the war of 1861, which cut off supplies from the east. The legislature in 1862, *Cal. Statutes*, offered premiums as an incentive. J. W. Jacobson gained the first, and in 1864 fully 350,000 lbs. of crude pitch was collected, from which 3 distilleries made over 7,000 gal. of turpentine, and 1,150 barrels of resin, each tree yielding 3 gal. crude. The cessation of the war reduced the production to small proportions. A small factory opened in S. Diego in 1872 to supply local demand. The camphene distillation, so common before 1860, from North Carolina turpentine, has almost ceased. *Sac. Union*, May 7, Nov. 17, 27, 1863; *Alta Cal.*, May 14, 1863; June 27, 1872; *Scient. Press*, March 20, 1869; *Call*, Jan. 6, 1864; Feb. 14, 1865.

Charcoal has been burned since the early fifties, and is now produced chiefly by Italians, from oak and partly from willow. S. F. used in 1881 120,000 sacks of 60 lbs. each, or 3,600 tons, worth about $65,000. This came chiefly from Sonoma. In Nevada and other mining regions large quantities were used for low-grade ore, at about 28 cents a bushel. *Sac. Union*, Aug. 1, 1855, etc. Peat is gathered in Alameda and other marshy districts. *S. F. Times*, Feb. 8, 1867, refers to a special company to work them. Under all these inroads, favored by the small value of land in early days, there has been a great waste of forest resources, and in spots accessible for shipping and near settlements, as in Santa Cruz and San Mateo, and in the mining belt, there is little timber left, large districts being entirely denuded. Before the U. S. occupation, forest fires regularly devastated large sections, owing to the custom, among Indians especially, of thus gathering insects and other articles of food. This is one of the evident checks to forests in the valleys. Subsequently shepherds and hunters were in the habit of firing large tracts to promote the growth of pastures. Sheep in particular have kept down the renewal of forests by eating the shoots. Yet after all, the inroads upon timber do not affect more than one fifth of the entire area, and most of this is renewing itself, so that the supply is practically inexhaustible. This is notably the case in the redwoods and partly in the mining belt, and it is believed that the Truckee region will also revive. Laws have been passed for the protection of forests, but with little effect. *U. S. Gov. Doc.,* Cong. 41, Sess. 3, Sen. Misc. Doc. 71; Cong. 42, Sess. 2, H. Ex. Doc. 326, p. 218–37; Cong. 45, Sess. 2, Sen. Rept 122; *Statutes,* 89–91; Cong. 47, Sess. 1, H. Ex. Doc. 5, p. 370; H. Misc. Doc. 38, p. 200–2; *Cong. Globe,* 1877–8, 32, 289, etc.; *Cal. Agric. Soc., Trans.,* 1868–9, p. 28; 1872–3, pp. 339 et seq.; *U. S. Land Off. Rept,* 1865, 26, etc.; *Cal. Lumber Scraps,* 43–9. So far the private ownership of land has served best for protection, by rousing private interests to check fires and renew the growth. There is a further compensation in the artificial planting of trees, fostered by the state, and latterly by arbor-day festivals. This is extended not alone to roads and settlements, for shade, screen, and embellishment, but to entire groves of forest dimensions, for fuel and industrial purposes, notably for remedying the lack of hard wood sufficient to supply in due time the demand and to balance destruction elsewhere. The sycamore, willow, and cottonwood grow readily, for fences and fuel, also Lombardy poplar, but the black locust and especially the eucalyptus are most widely planted, the latter promising to prove very desirable for elasticity and hardness. One party planted 100,000 in 1875 near Florence. *Los. Ang. Co. Hist.,* 63. The olive and mulberry will no doubt receive attention. *Noyes' Lumbering,* 1–107; *Sierra Lumber Co., Prosp.; Van Dyke's Stat.,* MS., 8, etc.; *Colusa Annual,* 1878, 80; *Overland,* xiii. 242 et seq.; *Harper's Mag.,* Dec. 1873; Nov. 1878; Jan. 1883, with cuts; *Hawley's Humboldt,* 13–37; *Vischer's Pict. Cal.,* 95–108; *U. S. Land Off. Repts; Kellogg's Forest Trees of Cal.,* 1–145; *U. S. Geol. and Geog. Survey of Territ.,* 9; *Sargent's Forest Trees.*

In connection with lumber manufacture have sprung up a number of planing-mills for preparing frames, casings, doors, sashes, balustrades, cornices, and other ornaments, with special factories for several branches. The redwood is admirable for these purposes in being easily worked, and as it does not warp, crack, or stain. the export demand extends to these manufactures. The first planing-mill is ascribed to Hutton on Market st, S. F., the second to Meiggs at North Beach, both soon after 1850. The first sash and door factory is claimed by Marysville for 1854. There were in 1888 a score of mills, with a capital of $1,000,000, employing 1,500 men, and producing nearly $5,000,000 worth of articles. Petaluma claims a special stair-building factory. The progress of San Diego finds an illustration in the rapid success of the Enterprise planing-mills, although established only in 1885. The founder, Henry Allen Perry, born in Huron co., N. Y., on May 1, 1843, has been connected with the city since 1873 in various contract works. The mills are sustained by the general predilection for wooden dwellings, brick being objected to on account of dampness and a lurking fear of earthquakes, so as to be virtually restricted to business houses, which require greater stability and security against fire. Even in the south adobes are yielding to light and handsome wood buildings. The apparently flimsy yet strong Chicago frame structure is the favorite, with elaborate façades, S. F. being remarkable for the use of bay-windows for catching the sun and enjoying a view in comfort, piazzas and balconies being here too exposed to the windy and chilly atmosphere.

With an extensive and widely settled coast line, full of resources, ship-building received an early impulse. Craft had been constructed for bay traffic before the U. S. occupation, as shown in my preceding volumes. The gold fever, with its attendant unfolding of commerce, gave a start to ship-yards during the winter 1848-9, and in the middle of 1849 S. F. and Benicia became the headquarters, the latter for launching several steamboats, and even Sac. put forth a scow during the late summer. See chapter on commerce. Williams, the builder, *Stat.*, MS., 9, made one at Sauzalito for $2,000, the lumber being hand-sawed. Napa also claimed a launch in 1849, after having constructed craft in 1841 and 1845. *Hist. Napa Co.*, 58; *Sac. Union*, May 19, 1858. Stockton had its first sloop in 1850. In the sixties ship-building became common, and at Lindsay Pt 44 vessels, of which 24 were steamboats, were launched 1864-78. *Hist. S. Joaq. Co.*, 26, 71. Along the coast several places joined in the industry, Sta Cruz since 1848. *Sta Cruz Co. Ill.*, 14. Bolinas, Tomales, Pt Arena, Mendocino, all figured; Humboldt Bay taking the lead, however, and launching in 1854 also a steamer. *Humboldt Co. Hist.*, 145; *Marin Co. Hist.*, 270-1, 295, 303. For operations at S. F., see *Alta Cal.*, 1849 et seq.; *S. F. Herald*, June 8, 10, 1850; Dec. 31, 1854. *U. S. Com. and Navig.*, 1851, et seq., has not very complete records in its ship-building tables. *Mendoc. Co. Hist.*, 384, 438; *Hopkins' Ship B.*, MS., 14-18, has general accounts for the coast. The first ocean steamer built entirely in Cal. is said to be the *Del Norte*, with 187 feet of keel, 18 state-rooms, etc., launched Dec. 14, 1864. The boilers were made also at S. F., but the engine was taken from the *Republic*. Description in *S. F. Bulletin*, March 15, 1865. The *Census* of 1880 credits Cal. with 62 ship-building establishments, with a capital of $1,800,000, employing 534 men, wages $589,000, using 6,700,000 feet of lumber, 3,000,000 lbs. of metal, and producing 221 boats and vessels, made and repaired, valued at $1,800,000. Of these 21 were new vessels of 7,361 tons, valued at $771,000 from 13 establishments, employing 181 men, using 4,000,000 feet of lumber. Repairs to the value of $969,000 were done on 40 vessels. The 200 boats came from 9 establishments, value about $57,500. In 1882 Cal. built 8,000 tons of the 17,000 for the U. S. Pac. coast, the aver-age size of vessels being 250 tons; 4 ocean steamers were launched. The construction is about as cheap here as in the east, for higher wages are bal-anced by cheaper timber, easier to work at least in the timber region. The best lumber at S. F. comes from Puget Sd. For fitting, most of the material must be imported. In 1889 the prospects of this industry were encouraging, several large vessels being completed, including the iron steamer *Pomona* of 1,200 tons. Three-masted schooners, suitable for the lumber trade, could be built in Cal. cheaper than in Me. With larger vessels, however, Cal. was at a disadvantage, the cost of a 1,000-ton ship being about $72.50 per ton against $65 in Me. The railway company at Oakland has a large yard. At S. F. are several. A dry-dock was completed in the summer of 1851 at the foot of Second st, S. F., the brig *Sidi Hammet* entering to receive the first coppering in Cal., the Hawaiian Islands having so far done such work. The subsequent U. S. dry-dock at Mare Island is spoken of elsewhere. In *Alta Cal.*, Apr. 16, 1855, both advertise for vessels. A third is recommended in *Id.*, Dec. 31, 1855, at the foot of Lombard st. Later was constructed the fine stone dock at Hunter's Pt, over 400 ft long, which, with two floating docks, is controlled by a company. There are also several slips for repairing. *S. F. Call*, Apr. 23, July 24, 1868.

Traffic was complemented on land by elaborate stage-carriages and huge freight-wagons. The *Alta Cal.*, Sept. 29, 1856, describes one of 4,000 lbs. in weight, 9 feet high, to carry 15,000 lbs. The Spanish Californians were as a rule content with rude frames on disks of board for wheels, though occasional light wagons were made with the help of foreign sailors in 1797. *Cal. Prov. Rec.*, MS., vi. 79; *Alvarado, Cal.*, MS., 31; *Vallejo, Rem.*, 40. There was a sen-sation when, in 1845, the first American wagon entered S. José, observes *Alta Cal.*, March 3, 1851. A carriage factory was established at Los Angeles in 1849. *L. Ang. Co. Hist.*, 69. In the bay towns several started, Sac., Stock-ton (in 1851), and Marysville following S. F. *Hist. Yuba, S. Joaq.*, and *Mateo.* Sacramento claimed in 1858 nearly 4 score shops, with 340 hands, producing

$750,000 worth. With the decline in mining and the construction of railways, the business fell off. Two large factories of S. F., dating 1851, disappeared, and in 1881 less than half the product of 1869 was manufactured here. In 1870 over 80 establishments existed in Cal., employing 630 men, and producing $1,309,000 worth. The demand for vehicles continues, however, exceptionally large, owing to the general wealth, the lively trade, the value of time, cheap animals and feed, sparse population, and fair roads. Favored by the overland railway, business wagons are mostly brought from Michigan in pieces. Wheels and tongues are frequently made elsewhere, and white oak and hickory must be brought for the light vehicles made here, S. F. with one third of the industry turning out about 500 wagons, 500 buggies, etc. Car-works have sprung up at Vallejo, Sacramento, Newark. *S. F. Bulletin*, July 18, 1863; *Vallejo Rec.*, Nov. 10, 1868; *Sac. and Alameda Co. Hists.* Carriage springs invented and made. *S. F. Times*, Sept. 15, 1868; *S. F. Jour. Com.*, Apr. 25, 1877.

Cooperage is also impeded by the insufficient supply of coopers, and the necessity for importing hoops and staves for superior casks. Much redwood and other soft material is used. The chief demand is for wine, liquor, and beer, and especially for wine-casks. In 1881 there were on the Pac. coast, nearly all in Cal., about 100 shops, with over 500 men, producing some 200,-000 casks and kegs for such liquors, worth $900,000; 350,000 barrels and half barrels for sugar, worth $210,000; 35,000 barrels for provisions, valued at $55,000; and 95,000 powder-kegs, worth $43,000, making a total of $1,206,000. To this must be added the value of ship cooperage, about $40,000, and of lime and cement barrels, $25,000. *Com. and Ind.*, 621. Tubs, chests, and the like were made by 3 wooden-ware factories, two of which were in S. F. and one in Sac., producing nearly $200,000 worth. The first was Elam & Howes' of 1852. Armes & Dallam opened at first in Sonoma 1853, and were alone in 1864 for a time. *S. F. Bull.*, Dec. 1, 1864; *S. F. Times*, Feb. 21, 1867. Trays and axe-handles are imported. Of late 4 establishments manufacture bungs and faucets, one of metal.

Box-making is rapidly growing, with the increase in drying and canning of fruit and fish, and the export of fresh fruit. There are several factories at S. F., and one each at different places. Aside from the above, two fifths of the product is required for soap, candles, sugar, and crackers. There are special cigar-box factories at S. F., turning out nearly 3,500,000 boxes a year, worth over $300,000, 60 per cent being twentieths (to hold 50). In 1881 over 200 workers were employed, a quadruple increase since 1870. A dozen persons made jewelry boxes, worth $25,000. Nearly double the value are imported. S. F. had also 9 trunk-factories, manufacturing $150,000 of leather and wood into $350,000 of goods. The small importation, say one tenth, includes fancy bags, locks, and hinges, and is fully balanced by the export. The wages in this branch average $625 a year. Coffins are made mostly of redwood by 5 special and several other establishments, employing fourscore men, and producing $300,000 worth. In 1860 there was only one maker. The importation of metallic and rosewood caskets has declined. There is a factory at Sta Clara. *S. J. Merc.*, Jan. 1, 1880. The embalming process obtains. *Elko Indep.*, Jan. 7, 1871.

Of willow-ware, the larger proportion, about $60,000 worth, comes from Europe, despite duty and freight. There are 30 men, chiefly Europeans, employed, besides some Chinese. Sac. had a factory in 1855. *Sac. Union*, Feb. 10, 1855. Last-making began in 1864, and in 1888 there were two factories in S. F., with 14 hands, producing 30,000 pieces a year, worth $30,000. Brooms are made by about 50 establishments, fully half in S. F., with 400 hands, half Chinese, producing 80,000 dozen a year, worth $350,000; 2 per cent are exported. Broom corn is cultivated since 1851 in several counties, yielding 4 tons per acre, sufficient for fully 100 dozen brooms. Los Angeles opened a factory 1852. *L. Ang. Co. Hist.*, 133; *Sac. Union*, Dec. 8, 1855; Feb. 28, 1856; *Alta Cal.*, Oct. 3, 1857.

Owing to the scantiness of suitable woods, and the high wages, half of the furniture is still imported, much of it in sections, to be fitted here. One half the wood used comes from Oregon and Washington; Cal. primavera is becoming a favorite for its fine wavy grain. The laurel is beautiful, but used chiefly for veneering. Alaska cedar promises to take a prominent place. Redwood has the advantage, aside from its many good qualities, of receiving almost any stain for imitating dark woods. With this growing appreciation and lower wages, the manufacture is increasing, favored by the high freight and equable clime. The first decided impulse was given by the war of 1861, and S. F. had in 1888 fully 2 dozen factories, employing 1,000 hands, with $750,000 in wages, and producing over $3,000,000 worth. *Wigmore's Stat.*, MS. The *S. F. Chron.*, Dec. 29, 1889, gives only $1,250,000 as the output for that year. Finer moulding and gilding of frames is done here, and partly the silvering of mirrors. Home decoration is exceptionally large, and over a dozen firms supply artists' material.

The manufacture of billiard-tables was early encouraged by the great demand. P. Liesenfeld, the earliest existing firm, began in 1855. In the following year the *Alta Cal.*, March 5, Oct. 21, Dec. 14, 1856, refers to two more, Strahle and Vasselin. In 1860 there were 5, with $30,000 sales. By 1870 the sales had trebled from 6 factories. A dozen years later the figure had risen to $200,000, with a small export. The make is fully equal to eastern. One establishment turns billiard-balls.

Pianos claim nine tenths of the millions annually spent on music instruments. Two thirds are imported, the rest, over 800 pianos, 200 house organs, some guitars, and other instruments, occupy 150 men and a capital of three quarters of a million, in making cases and putting together the parts manufactured elsewhere by special factories. The chief demand is for upright cases of ebonized wood. The first piano is credited to Jacob Zech, a six-octave square piece made at S. F. in 1856. In the same year, *S. F. Bull.*, May 22, 1856, Mar. 20, 1857, June 30, 1863, refers to J. H. Allen as having made one. The first upright piece was turned out by G. Rudolf in 1865. By this time the *S. F. Call*, Jan. 3, 1864, Jan. 3, June 10, 1866, Jan. 3, 1867, Aug. 2, 1868, refers to J. Bender and other makers; *S. F. Mission Local*, Jan. 19, 1877; *Jour. Com.*, Apr. 4, 1877. The demand for organs is only one fourth that of pianos, mostly imported, but the local manufacture is increasing. Church organs were first made by Jos. Mayer, in 1856, followed by the Schöwsteins, the factory of J. Bergström dating from 1864, being the largest and best known. Some 4 score have been constructed, at from $1,000 upward, partly for export. Keys are made by one house, flutes and orchestrions, fully 30 of the latter, by others. Of these minor instruments the annual production amounts to $10,000, or one fourth of imports. Guitars and violins were first made at S. F. by C. Stumcke in 1857.

The first fisheries of California were in connection with the fur trade, particularly for catching otters and seals, and this pursuit has continued in ever-diminishing degree, although the *Census* for 1880 still places its value at $15,700 a year. Nidever, *Life*, MS., 140, engaged therein with a schooner in 1850-1; *Hayes' Ang. Arch.*, v. 55; *Hist. Sta Bárb. Co.*, 254-8; *Pac. R. R. Rept*, vi.; *Newberry's Rept*, 42-51; *Custer's Stat.*, MS.; *Alta Cal.*, July 7-8, 1857, July 11, 1859, relating also to sea-lion catch, locations, etc. Protective laws in *Cal. Statutes*, 1865-5, 633. Trappers entered along the Sac. and other streams to swell the fur supply, especially with beavers, and furs are still bought at country stores for S. F. dealers. Deer, water-fowl, and other game yield additional profits. S. F. is the centre of the Pacific fur trade, with chief sources in Alaska, its total value exceeding $5,000,000, one third controlled by the Alaska Com. Co., one fourth by the Hudson's Bay Co., which ships direct from Victoria—see *Hist. Brit. Col.*, *Northwest Coast*, and *Alaska*, this series. The fur seals constitute two fifths of the total, which in England rises in prepared form to $10,000,000. The local fur sale in S. F. reaches $300,000, mostly goods returned from London. Of other pelts only $15,000 worth are sold. The regular fisheries of Cal., as a special industry, came into consideration shortly after the U. S. conquest. The *Californian*, Apr. 19, 1848, reported that a company was forming to improve the salmon fishery at

Brazoria. The gold fever interfered, and fishery projects were not resumed until the winter of 1849–50. The *Sac. Transc.*, June 29, 1850, March 14, 1851, refers to the operations of the Sac. Fishing Co., which included a catch of sturgeons weighing 200 and 300 lbs. Roder, *Belling. Bay*, MS., 6–7, who bought an interest in the concern in 1851, credits Capt. Webb with starting it. G. Cooper was then also in the business. *Sac. Co. Hist.*, 149. By 1855 three firms were engaged in curing salmon in this vicinity, employing 200 men for several months. *Directory Sac.*, 1856, p. xvii.–xviii.; *Sac. Union*, June 30, 1855. Since then the industry has gradually increased, until the Pacific coast in 1881 canned salmon to the value of $5,000,000 a year. Of this the Sac. canneries, from Vallejo upward, assisted by the propagation efforts of the state, produced nearly 200,000 cases, against little over 60,000 in 1880, and still less in preceding years, according to *Hughes' Circular*. The cases of 24 two-pound cans were valued at $5, or nearly $1,000,000. Eel and Smith rivers added 7,000 and 6,000 cases, respectively. For methods and leading companies in Cal. and northward, see *Com. and Ind.*, county histories of *Sac., Solano, C. Costa; S. F. Herald*, March 20, 1853, etc.; *S. F. Bull.*, Sept. 13, 1859; Nov. 26, Dec. 26, 1878; June 6, 1879; Sept. 17, 1881; *Alta Cal.*, Sept. 13, 1859, etc. There are a dozen canneries on the Sac. alone, and several fruit canneries share the business. Profits are becoming less and more uncertain. The laws for protecting the fish, for gill nets, for covering only one third of the river width, for abstaining from catching in August, are little respected, partly owing to the frequent change of regulations. *Cal. Statutes*, 1853, 54; 1854, 158, 167; 1855, 220; 1872, 1004; 1875–6, ap. 53.

Salmon form the staple of the fisheries, which according to the *Census* of 1880 employed a capital of $1,140,000, 3,090 men, including 1,000 shore men, 49 vessels of 5,200 tons, valued at $500,000, 850 boats valued at $90,000, bringing a total product of $1,800,000. The catch is estimated at 12,000 tons a year, of which 4,000 were from S. F. bay and its tributaries. The Chinese sweep the bay flats to the destruction of fish, and catch large quantities at different points, as at Monterey and the Sta Bárbara isles. Fully threescore deep-sea boats are engaged to supply the S. F. market, almost wholly decked, each with 7 or 8 men, and long trawling lines. A fishing outfit costs from $500 to $1,000. The fishermen are mostly of the Latin race, the Italians leading, who earn fair returns, on shares, but are improvident, with frequent intervals of idleness and dissipation. Chinese are content with less profitable fishing near the shore. *U. S. Gov. Doc.*, Cong. 47, Sess. 2, H. Ex. Doc. xviii. 881; *U. S. Census*, 1860, and 1870; *Price's Two Amer.*, 209–26; *Dixon's White Cong.*, i. 23–7; ii. 251–8; *Sac. Directory*, 1857–8, p. xiv., etc.; *Harper's Mag.*, xlvii. 911; *Hayes' Ang.*, v. 66–72; *U. S. Com. and Navig.*, 1877.

With salmon is caught a quantity of sturgeon, from which about 10 tons of caviare is made annually, worth $5,000. Herring forms the staple of the bay men's catch, notably between Oct. and Jan. preceding the salmon season. The smaller kind is marketed as sardines. This branch, together with smelts, affords chief occupation for 75 boats and 200 men. In 1880 the first special vessel was sent to gather halibut. *S. F. Bulletin*, July 18, 1859; *Alta Cal.*, Sept. 1, 1859; Dec. 29, 1872; *S. F. Call*, Apr. 23, 1871; June 25, 1874. Cod banks were discovered in 1863, in the Northern Pacific. The following year a vessel was despatched to try them. *Alta Cal.*, June 2, 1864. She did so well that 7 sailed in 1865, bringing 700 tons, cured partly on Goat Island. *Id.*, Sept. 27, 1864; *S. F. Call*, June 6, 1868. Since then the fleet has varied between 3 in 1872 and 21 vessels in 1870 and 1878, the latter bringing 1,700 to 1,850 tons. Latterly a few large vessels bring the same amount for three firms, with prospects for a wider demand. The drying grounds and warehouses are chiefly in Marin; 6,000 gallons of cod-liver oil and other material are produced. Whaling was pursued in the Pacific by Americans long before they acquired Cal., until the number of vessels in 1855 reached 500, with chief rendezvous at the Sandwich Islands. After 1865 S. F. became their headquarters, and here were owned in 1888 half a dozen of the 40 vessels to which the fleet had declined by 1881, including 4 steamers, first employed in 1880. The S. F. vessels are worth $15,000 to $40,000 each. Early in the fifties Capt. Davenport, an old whaling master, organized a company at Monterey to pursue the passing whales in boats. His success led to the formation of other parties at different points, notably in 1855 of 17 Portuguese at Monterey, who obtained 24,000 barrels in three years. In 1862 the Carmel Co. was formed. *Mont. W. Herald*, Aug. 1, 1874; *Sac. Union*, June 11, 27, Nov. 14, 1855; Oct. 2, 1856; *S. F. Bull.*, Nov. 12, 1855; *Cal. Jour. Ass.*, 1856, 30–1; 1860, ap. 3, p. 68; *Id.*, *Sen.*, 1860, ap. 3, p. 72; 1867–8, ap. 3, p. 104–7; *Hayes' Mont.*, 137–55; *Id.*, *Ang.*, v. 56–73; *Id.*, *S. Diego*, i. 40–2; *Cal. Agric. Soc.*, *Trans.*, 1864–5, 229; *S. F. Herald*, Nov. 30, 1859; *U. S. Com.*, passim; *L. Ang. Co. Hist.*, 70; *Hayes' Emig. Notes*, 461–4; *Alta Cal.*, Sept. 30, 1856; Nov. 13, 1857; *Savage's Coll.*, MS., iv. 262–3; *S. F. Post*, Nov. 1, 1883, with allusions to stations at Crescent City, Bolinas, L. Angeles, S. Diego. The stations are now restricted to Monterey, S. Simeon, Pt Conception, and San Luis Obispo, each employing about a dozen men and obtaining 500 barrels. The gray whales, which provide the main supply, yield only 20 barrels on an average. Between April and Sept. the men are engaged in farming. The *Census*, 1880, places the total value of Cal. whaling at $202,000. Sharks are caught at Humboldt, Sta Catalina, and Anaheim, chiefly for their fine liver oil. *Cal. Chron.*, May 20, 1856.

Oysters were first brought from Shoalwater Bay, in 1850, by Capt. Feltstead, but spoiled on the way. A. Ludlum succeeded better in 1851, after which the supply became regular. With the opening of the overland railway, fresh oysters were brought for transplanting, or rather for fattening, in the shallows of S. F. Bay, as the spawn does not thrive. In 1888 four companies owned 600 acres of beds, with a capital of $300,000. In the third year they reach the size of 200 to the bushel. Canned oysters are imported to the amount of 400 tons, and the transmission in ice is increasing. The total sales reach $1,250,000 a year. *S. F. Bulletin*, March 13, 1868; Aug. 14, 1871; Jan. 27, 1875; *S. F. Call*, Aug. 1, 1874; March 4, 1875; *Com. and Ind.*, 362–4.

In connection with oyster-planting should be mentioned John S. Morgan, a native of Westfield, N. Y., and a Cal. pioneer. In 1853 he brought to San Francisco the first cargo of oysters from Shoalwater bay, and later explored the entire coast, from Puget sound to the gulf of Cal., for the purpose of finding oysters fit for transplanting. Between 1860 and 1869 his operations were limited to the culture and sale of native oysters from Shoalwater bay; but on the completion of the overland railroad he began the importation and transplanting of eastern oysters.

Nearly 300 species of fish have been reported in Cal., 130 being in S. F. Bay, 25 pertaining to fresh water. Some of them lack the flavor of the Atlantic varieties, of which many of the most desirable are absent. Under the incentive of a congressional act creating a fish commission, to import and distribute food fishes, three commissioners were appointed for Cal. *Statutes*, 1869–70, 663–5. A dozen varieties were accordingly introduced, all of which promise fairly, save the eel. A standing arrangement was made to put from a half to two million salmon every year into the tributaries of the Sac., and a hatching establishment on McLeod River yielded, about 1888, from 600,000 to 10,000,000 fish annually, saving 50 fold above the former rate of survival. It is the most extensive institution of the kind, and sends eggs to every part of the globe. *N. Y. Tribune*, Nov. 16, 1878. It seems that a species of salmon, suitable for warmer waters, is developing. The catfish thrives best of all, and in 1888 was found throughout the state. Of shad, over half a million were placed in the Sacramento prior to 1882, and are fairly abundant, but they need protection. Several rivers have been well stocked with trout. Whitefish was among the early introductions, but is not yet profitably abundant. Shad, bass, lobsters, and carp are promising. The last is bred with success in ponds and lakes for the market, as by the Lenni fish propagation company, which also deal in trout and frogs. *S. F. Bulletin*, Oct. 13, 1881; *Lake Co. Hist.*, 155. See, further, *Overland*, xiii. 228–33, 311–15; xiv. 79–85; *Cal. Jour. Sen.*, 1873–4, ap. 68–9; 1875–6, ap. 3, 53; 1877–8, ap. 21, 54; *Sonoma Co. Hist.*, 461–4; *Fisheries, Rept Com.*, for different years; *U. S. Gov. Doc.*, Cong. 42, Sess. 3, Sen. Misc. Doc. 74; Cong. 44, Sess. 1, food fishes; Cong. 45, Sess. 2, Sen. Misc., iii. 797–810; Cong. 47, Sess. 1, id., iii. 1063–84.

The high quality of Cal. wheat is maintained to a great extent also in the flour, the finest coming from mills at Vallejo and S. F., whose products command 25 cents per barrel extra. Spanish Californians produced grain only for their own wants, and were content to grind it on the household metate, or at best, with arastras, by mules, a machine described under mining. The Americans quickly applied water-power to the mills erected in the early forties in Sta Cruz, Sta Clara, Sonoma, S. Joaquin, and by Sutter, Capt. Smith's combined saw and grist mill possessing the only steam-power before the gold era. Major's mill in S. Agustin had horse-power, and likewise Cooper's in Salinas. *Mont. Hist.*, 109; *Sta Cruz Hist.*, 12. In Sonoma, Hagler's mill dated nearly as early as Smith's. *Son. Hist.*, 213, 375. And Alexander's rose in 1845-6, about the same time as Weber's near Stockton. *Tinkham's Stockton*, 62-3, 382; *S. Joaq. Hist.*, 71, 101. Placer, *Co. Hist.*, 239, claimed one in 1846. Sutter was building his large new mill at Brighton in 1847-8; *Hist. Sac.*, 146; and a small one was then on the Cosumnes, at Daylor's. *Sand. I. News*, ii. 194; *Or. Spect.*, June 10, 1847. After 1849 a number began to rise, largely operated by steam, Sac. alone claiming three in 1850. *S. F. Herald*, Nov. 18, 1850; but only two in 1851. *Culor's Sac. Dir.*, 96-8. For others, see *Alta Cal.*, Nov. 29, Dec. 5, 1852; March 4, Aug. 5, Oct. 5, 1853; Jan. 1, 1854; *Yolo Hist.*, 77; *Herald*, Aug. 12, Sept. 4, 24, 1852; Sept. 1, 1853; *Yuba Hist.*, 69-70; *Sac. Union*, Nov. 1, 3, 7, Dec. 1, 5, 20, 25, 1854, etc.; *L. Ang. Hist.*, 134; *Sutter Hist.*, 48. One established in Colusa in 1852 is still working. L. Angeles obtained a large mill in 1851; Bidwell erected the first near Chico in 1853. *North Enterprise*, Oct. 17, 1873. Siskiyou, *Hist.*, 193, claims one for the same year, yet Crescent City regarded its first mill, of 1856, as the most northerly. *Alta Cal.*, Oct. 24, 1856. In 1853 both Merced, *Hist.*, 142, and Stanislaus, *Hist.*, 100, 118, had mills. Data for 1855-6 in *Cal. Jour. Sen.*, Apr. 5, 1856, and following years. Also *Census*, 1852. In 1854 there were 54 mills, with a capacity of 1,250,000 barrels a year; in 1860 91 mills; in 1870 115. The *Census* of 1880 enumerates 150, with $4,360,000 capital, 190 hands, 455 runs of stone, 58,600 bushels daily capacity, using 8,200,000 bushels of wheat and 3,470,000 of other grain, and producing $12,700,000 worth; 97 mills were operated by steam of 5,770 horse-power, out of a total of 7,440. The largest mill, erected at Vallejo in 1869, has a capacity of 1,700 barrels a day, and storage for 50,000 tons. It grinds about 1,000 barrels a day, and ships more than 1,800 tons monthly to Europe. Cal. in 1881 consumed 1,100,000 barrels, and exported 785,000 barrels against 465,000 in 1867, a maximum for several years, and 644,700 in 1873-4, of which 364,000 to England of high grade. Even China, which ranks next as a market, is demanding more of the high-grade flour. Cent. Am. and Hawaii Isl. follow, Australia taking some at times. High wages and the lack of an outlet for middlings, bran, and screenings are obstacles which keep a number of mills closed. The custom of eastern states to grind for a share or for a rate is not in vogue save in remote districts. The rule is for millers to buy grain and take their chances for selling. The 'high grinding' Hungarian system has not yet gained much favor. Of cracked wheat and oatmeal 3,500 tons each were produced in 1881, the latter largely from Oregon oats. The oatmeal importation from the east, of 4,000 barrels, has declined. In 1852 'Emperor' Norton erected the first rice-mill at S. F.; larger ones rose in 1853, etc. *Alta Cal.*, Jan. 3, 1854; March 15, 1855; *Id.*, Nov. 9, 1855; May 10, 1857; *Sac. Union*, Nov. 10, 1855, refer to two starch factories in Contra Costa and S. F.; and there was one in Sta Clara, but all failed save one of S. F., dating 1854, which produced in 1811 100 tons of the 1,300 tons used on the coast, employing 6 men.

The demand of miners and crews for ship-biscuits led in 1849 to the opening of a cracker factory by W. R. Gorman, followed by Deeth & Hore, the last adding steam machinery. *S. F. Herald*, Sept. 4, 1851; Feb. 21, 1855; Sept. 14, 1860; *S. F. Bull.*, Feb. 8, 1865; *Alta Cal.*, Aug. 10, 1855. Deeth's enterprise stood prominent in 1888. The three of 1860 increased to ten by 1881, with a production of 10,500 tons, worth $1,500,000; prices 3 to 28 cents per lb.; 225 hands employed; imports declining, especially since 1872, while the export has increased to 1,000 tons. There were six macaroni factories; the first opened at S. F. in 1855 by Meuli & Schulthess. *S. F. Jour. Com.*, May 5, 1875; *Alta Cal.*, Dec. 8, 1856; *S. F. Bull.*, Dec. 27, 1864. Forty varieties were made; a small lot from Italian wheat. The annual consumption in 1881 was 145,000 boxes, or 950 tons, worth $200,000; 30 tons being exported.

The annual consumption of confectionery was estimated in 1881 at $850,-000, three fourths was sold at S. F., the wholesale dealings reaching $450,000, one third being imported. The invested capital was $375,000; the hands number 250. I. Regan made the first candy for sale in S. F. in 1849. *Cassin's Stat.*, MS., 7. Syrup, extracts, and cordial factories are mentioned in *Alta Cal.*, Sept. 16, 1857; *S. F. Bull.*, Dec. 14, 1870; *S. F. Post*, Sept. 1, 1877; *Jour. Com.*, June 6, 1877. Yeast was used to the extent of 75,000 cases in 1881, one third imported, with prospective increase. The manufacture was estimated at $225,000, a case being valued at $4.50; 100 hands employed; export 1,600 cases. Chocolate is made at two factories, to the extent of 350,000 lbs., worth $100,000, in 1881; imports 100,000 lbs. The leading factory was established by D. Ghirardelli in 1852. *News Letter*, Apr. 20, 1867. These are combined with coffee and spice mills, first established by W. H. Bovee in 1850. Although groceries in different towns have their own hand-mills and small ovens, yet half the business is done by factories at S. F., turning out 5,700,000 lbs. in 1881. Of spices 250 tons were ground. One firm makes a specialty of mustard. *Sac. Union*, Dec. 9, 1854. *Alta Cal.*, Sept. 25, 1857, refers to a horseradish factory. Chiccory is prepared at two factories, one at Sac., the larger one at Stockton, since 1872; the two produce 500 tons; 300 more comes from Germany. *Id.*, March 14, 26, 1859; May 19, 1872; *Price's Cur.*, June 15, 1855; *S. F. Times*, Jan. 10, 1868; *U. S. Agric. Rept*, 1874, 277; *S. F. Chron.*, Nov. 3, 1872. Vinegar is mostly made from cider in the interior, from malt in S. F., of which 2,300 tons was used in 1881; wine has been found too dear. The total production exceeded 3,000,000 gallons, valued at 25 cents each, fully half being required for canneries; French imports fell to 100 barrels from 500 in 1875. The first factory was opened in 1854 by A. D. Baker. Advertisement in *Merc. Gaz.*, June 26, 1858. The *Census* of 1870 reported only 3 factories, with a production of little over $50,000. *Marin Hist.*, 291-2. Pickle-making is largely combined with the preceding, both branches employing threescore hands each. About 20,000 sacks of vegetables are used. The business was fairly large already in 1855. *S. F. Bull.*, Dec. 1, 1855; Jan. 11, 1856.

Beer, as well as vinegar, was made in colonial days on a small scale, the former being credited to W. McGlone, a sailor, in 1837. *Mont. Cal.*, March 19, 1878. The first regular brewery, however, was the Empire, of W. Bull, recorded in *Kimball's S. F. Directory*, 1850, 42. A. Roy and W. McCoy figure shortly after. *Pac. News*, Jan. 10, 1851. Sutter, *Co. Hist.*, 47-8, claims one in the same year. The Lafayette of S. F. aspires to a similar date. The difficulty of introducing malt liquor in good condition gave zest to the business, and breweries spread in all directions, from Stockton and Marysville in 1851 and 1852 to Plumas and Los Angeles in 1854, and to all larger towns. See histories of *Yuba*, 69; *S. Joaq.*, 71-2; *Plumas*, 464; *L. Ang.*, 69; *El. Dor.*, etc. By 1881 there were about 350 breweries on the coast north of Mexico, with a capital of $3,700,000, and a production valued at $4,500,000, the barrel being calculated at $7.50. Nearly nine tenths of this amount pertains to Cal.; S. F., with 38 establishment figuring for 280,000 barrels, the largest yielding threescore thousand; only two were then making lager beer, one at Boca, but since then this production is increasing; ale and porter amounted to 30,000 barrels more. So far the liquor was mostly quick-brewed, of 3 days' fermentation. The import of 2,500 barrels was fully balanced by the export of 4,000. Over 34,000 tons of grain were used for malting, four fifths being converted by the breweries, yet special malt-houses exist, the largest, established in 1857 by H. Zwieg, producing 5,000 tons. Hops have improved till they equal the best. The leading brewery on the coast is the Philadelphia, the success of which is due to the enterprise of John Wieland, a native of Würtemberg, born Oct. 6, 1829. In 1849 he abandoned

viniculture to seek his fortune in America, and reached California in 1851.
With the money gathered at first as a miner and then as proprietor of the
Union bakery, S. F., he in 1855 bought an interest in Hölscher's brewery, of
which he gained sole control in 1867, and at once took steps to enlarge operations, raising the production from less than 4,000 barrels in 1862 to over
threescore thousand by 1885. In this year his public-spirited career, tinged
with a whole-souled benevolence, was cut short by an accident. His sons
have since displayed marked ability in still further extending the business of
their father.

Cal. possesses 15 of the 28 distilleries on the coast, producing in 1881 over
1,800,000 gallons of whiskeys, cordials, and bitters. Brandy has been mentioned under viniculture. The first is claimed for Sonoma. *Co. Hist.*, 215, in
1851. The Mission Creek distillery is mentioned in *Alta Cal.*, Apr. 5, 1854.
For several others, with new processes, full particulars will be found in
Alta, Jan. 30, 1870; Jan. 10, 1875; *S. F. Post*, Oct. 31, 1873; *S. F. Times*,
Oct. 20, 1868; *U. S. Gov. Doc.*, Cong. 47, Sess. 1, H. Ex. Doc., xiv. 100–2;
Sess. 2, xv. 106–7, 117. The largest made 4,200 gallons of rectified spirits
daily in 1881. *Id.*, p. 81, alludes to illicit stills; *Sac. Union*, Dec. 24, 1872,
to seizures. A little rum was distilled at L. Ang. in 1858–9. A factory
for cordials, essences, etc., existed in 1852. The import in 1881 stood at
24,000 barrels of whiskey, 8,000 of other spirits, and 30,000 cases (2,300 barrels) of bitters and cordials.

The Pacific distillery is mainly controlled by Henry Voorman, a pioneer
of 1849, who stands conspicuous as the promoter of several enterprises of
value to the state. He was born in Hanover, Aug. 58, 1826. An unsuccessful attempt at mining brought him back to the mercantile business, for which
he had been trained, and after keeping store for a few years in S. F. he became a member of the firm of Van Bergen & Sons, with whom he
started the Bay sugar refinery, while associating himself with others to open
the Pacific distillery, to reclaim the swamp-land of Bouldin Island, of the San
Joaquin delta, to found the flourishing Scandinavian colony in Fresno, and to
extend irrigation in this region. His views on matters connected with these
undertakings have proved of great value for my industrial chapters.

Of soda the coast consumed 10,000,000 bottles, worth $330,000. Though
readily manufactured, a number of special works exist, several of which yield
100 to 150 dozen bottles a day. Three were recorded at Sac. in *S. F. Herald*,
Nov. 18, 1850. Cal. consumed 35,000 tons of ice in 1881, one third at S. F.
Alaskan ice was much introduced at one time, *Sac. Union*, Nov. 7, 1854; but
the opening of the overland railway gave access to the Sierra, where heavy
storages are made. One sixth of the total was in 1881 of artificial production.
Over $500,000 capital is invested, employing some 600 men for a season.
S. F. Post, June 18, 1881; *S. F. Herald*, March 19, 1859; *S. F. Bull.*, March
9, 1871; *Yreka Union*, Dec. 27, 1879.

Canning of fruit, and partly of vegetables as well as fish, is a fast-growing
industry, fostered by the excellent quality of certain varieties, their increasing
abundance and cheapness, and their scarcity in other parts of the U. S. In
1889 the entire fruit and vegetable pack was placed, according to the most
conservative estimates, at not less than 1,250,000 cases, and by others at
1,500,000 cases. More than half contained fruit, and fully two thirds came
from S. F. establishments, with large shipments from S. José. The fish canning swells the figure largely, as already shown. See also under agriculture;
for details about canning firms, see *Com. and Ind.*, 240 et seq. A cannery
exchange existed for a time to promote the industry, to check frauds by imitators, etc. *S. F. Call*, June 26, July 3, 1883; county histories of *Butte*, 16;
Sonoma, 16; *Fresno*, 123; *L. Ang.*, 70, 157; *S. Bern.*, 124–35; and *Sta Clara*.

The climate is rather warm for meat-packing, and the consequence is a
heavy salting, especially of pork, which rises as a main objection to the product. At certain places, however, notably S. F., the atmosphere, laden with
sea breezes, preserves meat remarkbly well for several days. Nevertheless,
artificial temperature is largely depended upon, and with this device the operations have been satisfactorily improved, so as to permit 'sweet' curing and

pickling throughout the year. As a result, the coast trade is fast being absorbed. Although the early efforts, since 1853, at salting were not very successful, packing continued to some extent at different places, enough for miners' requirements. *Sac. Union*, Feb. 8, 1855; *S. F. Bull.*, July 26, 1856; *Alta Cal.*, Jan. 26, 1856; *Trinity Jour.*, March 1867; *S. F. Times*, March 23, 1867. The process with beef became profitable only in the seventies, and since then large orders are filled for Siberia, Spanish America, etc., as well as for government and trading fleets. The beef is still too light in weight. Pork succeeded better from the first, and the breed is improving with Berkshire crossing, and with corn and wheat feed; the acorn given in some parts yields a soft, oily, and poor pork. Sugar-curing has reached such excellence that Oregon, a former caterer, now draws on Cal. About 150,000 hogs are killed annually at S. F., two thirds by two leading firms. In 1880, Cal. packed 4,900 tons of bacon, 2,300 of ham, and 1,680 of lard. Imports fell by 1881 to 1,900 tons of ham, with very little lard and bacon. The *Census* of 1880 credits Cal. with 51 wholesale slaughtering and meat-packing establishments; capital, $2,130,000, 490 hands, using 112,000 beeves averaging 1,061 lbs. each, 414,000 sheep of 90 lbs., 236,000 hogs of 211 lbs., all worth $5,923,000. Of this, 7,400,000 lbs. of beef and 9,650,000 lbs. of pork were salted or canned, and 9,970,000 lbs. of pork made into bacon and ham, yielding also 4,390,000 lbs. of lard; total value, $7,950,000. See also, for pork-packing, *Los Ang. Hist.*, 70; *Humb. Hist.*, 146. The Cal. salt is improving so much as to supplant the Lower Californian and English supplies.

Sugar finds a very large consumption in Cal., and the numerous canneries demand an ever-increasing quantity. Of 54,000 tons of raw sugar used in 1881, four fifths came from the fertile plantations of Hawaii, against only 23,500 tons in 1879. Since the reciprocity treaty of 1876, the plantations exceed 50, largely owned by Americans, who employ 9 vessels of from 400 to 700 tons in the trade. Hawaii responds by taking more of Cal. manufactures than any other foreign state. Manila, which used to be the principal source, sent only 8,200 tons, against 20,000 in 1878; from China came 2,300 tons, and a few hundred tons from Cent. America. The cultivation of cane, and efforts to obtain sugar from sorghum, melons, and grapes, have not proved a financial success, as tried at Teleton and Los Angeles; here in the fifties and in 1880. *S. F. Call*, Dec. 1, 1863; *S. F. Bull.*, Aug. 31, 1876; *L. Ang. Hist.*, 70–1. Beet was tried with poor results in 1857, at S. José. *Sac. Union*, March 18, 1857; at Alvarado in 1870, *Cal. Farmer*, Dec. 1, 1870; *Alam. Gaz.*, Nov. 1870; whence the factory was moved to Soquel. *Monterey, Democ.*, Nov. 10, 1877; *Lassen Advoc.*, Nov. 11, 1876; county histories of *Sta Cruz*, 51; *Sac.*, 145, 221; *Sutter*, 48; *Alameda*, 26; *Nordhoff's Cal.*, 210–13; *S. F. Call*, Jan. 23, 1869; Aug. 13, 1870. A Sac. factory was in 1879 moved to Alvarado, *Alam. Argus*, Dec. 18, 1879; the only one working in 1882, and under judicious management it has made a promising start, producing in 1881 some 700 tons of sugar, worth $150,000 besides pulp and syrup. The beet is growing richer in sugar, and encouraging other mills. The first refinery, the S. F., was opened in 1855. *S. F. Bull.*, Oct. 31, 1856; *Sac. Union*, Nov. 28, 1857. It began promisingly, but is now closed, overshadowed by two larger establishments, both founded by C. Spreckels, one in 1863, and subsequently sold to C. A. Low, and the other in 1869, *S. F. Times*, Apr. 4, 1869, to which a million-dollar establishment was added in 1881. *S. F. W. Call*, June 2, 1881; *S. F. Post*, Dec. 24, 1881. The total product rose from $1,600,000 in 1860 to $4,000,000 in 1870, over $7,000,000 in 1881, and nearly $11,000,000 in 1889. There was still in 1881 an importation of 3,300 tons of refined sugar from the Atlantic states, partly offset by a growing export of 1,400 tons, some of it to the sugar-producing countries. For cane syrup, see under agriculture. The manufacture of blood albumen was begun, but discontinued in 1881.

Although the Culp process of preparing and improving Cal. tobacco has failed to meet expectations —see the chapter on agriculture—the manufacture of cigars and other tobacco from imported leaf has assumed vast proportions, chiefly with aid of Chinese labor, which, indeed, is able to underbid eastern rates so to permit a small export. In 1881 the revenue office reported 251

cigar factories in Cal., 216 being at S. F., paying for stamps over $900,000.
Of the 150,000,000 cigars consumed, 98 per cent were made here, valued at
$5,000,000, of which 38 per cent pertained to material, 33 to labor, and the
rest to duty and profit. Some of the leading establishments employed 250 to
350 operatives, and produced from 5,000,000 to 7,000,000 cigars annually,
mostly by piece-work. In 1882 only one factory made light-pressed tobacco
in different styles. Cigarettes and pipes are for the most part imported. The
growing agitation of white operatives against Chinese, who in 1882 formed
four fifths of the total force, served rather to cast more of the trade into
Mongol hands, to the injury of white operatives and factories.

The first textile fabrics of Cal. were the coarse blankets made at the missions, to replace the scanty fibre weft of the unconverted Indians. The production disappeared with the fall of these institutions. *Davis' Glimpses*, MS.,
7. During the gold excitement the meat of the now reduced flocks of sheep,
formerly of little value, became the only desirable substance, and pelts were
even thrown away, till junk-dealers began to collect them. *Alta Cal.*, June
15, 1854. The resumption of weaving would have been long delayed by the
high wages but for the influx of cheap labor in the form of Chinese. In 1859,
accordingly, a regular mill was opened, the Pioneer, by Heyneman, Peck, &
Co. It proved fairly successful with coarse goods, so much so that when destroyed by fire in 1861 a company was formed to rebuild it on a larger scale at
Black Point. At the close of 1859 the mission mills started, to be merged 14
years later in the Pioneer, which is now the largest on the coast. The civil
war increased the demand, and before 1888 production rose to over a million.
Id., Jan. 14, 1861; *S. F. Herald*, Dec. 3, 1861; *S. F. Bull.*, Jan. 20, 1860;
Oct. 18, 1865; *Hayes' Agric.*, 97–8; *Rusling's Across*, 307. The foothold obtained by these mills, and the increase of labor, led to the formation of other
establishments, at Marysville in 1867, *S. F. Times*, March 13, Aug. 5, 1867;
at Merced falls, 1867; at S. José in 1869, one remaining out of two; *Sac.*,
1870; Stockton, 1870; Los Angeles, 1872; Sta Rosa, 1877; a third at S. F.
1880, and others at Petaluma, in Humboldt, and in S. Bernardino. *Id.*,
March 13, June 13, 1868; *S. F. Call*, Feb. 19, Aug. 23, 1868; Dec. 20, 1870;
Oct. 8, 1872; Nov. 1, 1875; *Petal. Argus*, Sept. 4, Oct. 16, 1878; *Langley's
Trade*, i. 6–8; *S. Bern. Times*, July 20, 1878; *S. F. Post*, Aug. 6, 1875;
July 31, 1876; county histories of *Yuba*, 70–1; *S. Joaq.*, 40, 72; *Sonoma*,
16, 439; *L. Ang.*, 70; *Sta Clara*, 12–16; *Merced*, 117; *Sac.*, 157–8. The
Census of 1880 enumerates 9 mills, with $1,680,000 capital, 835 hands, re-
ceiving $334,000 in wages, 60 sets of cards with 7,240 lbs. daily capacity,
230 looms, 138 knitting-machines, 18,740 spindles, using 3,560,000 lbs.
crude wool, with a small quantity of foreign wool, camel and buffalo
hair, cotton, etc., $73,000 of chemicals, producing 81,800 pairs of blankets,
633,000 yards of cloth, etc., 1,453,000 yards of flannels, and 13,900 shawls;
wholesale value $1,635,000. Since then the number of mills and the
production have increased, *Com. and Ind.*, 437, raising the total to nearly
$3,000,000, and the hands to 1,600. Little more than one fifth of the wool
product was retained on the coast in 1881, but this is changing, in Cal. at
least; for the fineness of its wool, and the substantial nature of the blankets,
cloths, and flannels, have acquired a wide fame, sustained by premiums and
gold medals, so that a considerable amount is exported. The cloth fabrics
are as yet remarkable for strength rather than fineness, and while the local
mills have since 1865 almost driven out foreign goods in their line, the
above deficiency assists to sustain the imports of woollens at about $5,000,000.
Hosiery was knitted at several of the mills to the value of $200,000 in 1881, but
a special factory opened in that year with great success. Of the exported
wool, nearly all was sent unscoured till 1877. Since then several firms have
entered the business at S. F. with 100 hands, and in 1881 28 per cent of the
clip on the coast was scoured, or 8,000 out of the 19,000 tons shipped. The
consequent saving of two thirds of the weight is a great item when shipments
are made chiefly by rail.

Although cotton was raised to a small extent in colonial times, no spinning
was attempted. In 1865 W. H. Rector & Son built a cotton-mill at Clinton in

East Oakland. *Oakl. News*, Nov. 1865; *S. F. Bull.*, Sept. 4, Nov. 29, 1865; Jan. 16, 1867; *Halley's Alam.*, 208–9. The production in 1867 was 50,000 yards per month, chiefly for flour-bags and sheeting. *Cronise's Cal.*, 151–2. It failed to pay, however, and was in 1869 converted into a bag and jute factory. *S. F. Herald*, March 27, 1859; *S. F. Bull.*, Nov. 26, 1867; June 27, 1868; Dec. 16, 1875; *Cal. Farmer*, March 17, 1870. This employed 800 hands in 1881, nearly all Chinese, without whom operations would be economically impossible. The first Scotch operators soon got better employment. The 120 looms each produce 90 yards of burlap daily, nearly all of which is made into more than 5,000,000 bags, on the premises. *Alam. Hist.*, 22. Several other firms, including a farmer's coöperative company, make bags, employing 100 hands; some dating since the early fifties. *Yuba Hist.*, 69; *Alta Cal.*, Sept. 4, 1857; July 31, 1858; *Sac. Union*, June 6, 1855; *S. F. Chron.*, Oct. 3, 1873; Jan. 12–13, 1875; *S. F. Post*, Aug. 15, 1873; Sept. 12, 1874; Jan. 25, 1875; July 24, 1882, with allusions to a linen company and to the jute factory opened in S. Quentin prison in 1882 with 100 looms.

Silk in 1888 was promising better than cotton, although several of the half-dozen establishments for its manufacture had failed. The first was opened by Newman at Sta Clara in 1867, and revived after a brief stoppage. *Cal. Agric. Soc., Trans.*, 1866–7, 198–200; *S. J. Merc.*, Dec. 12, 1867; *Alta*, June 22, Dec. 18, 1867; Oct. 3, 1871; *S. F. Call*, Nov. 8, 1867; Oct. 20, 1872; *S. F. Times*, Apr. 16, July 6, 1868; May 20, 26, 1869; *S. F. Post*, June 4, 1872. The *Census* of 1880 credits Cal. with $7,645 worth of silk textiles, and enumerates two factories with engines of 52 horse-power. The principal factory in south S. F. spun 20,000 lbs. of raw silk in 1881, worth $150,000, chiefly for twist and coarser goods, yet of good quality. The reel silk was largely imported. Over 100 hands were employed, mostly women and children. *S. F. Bull.*, Feb. 16, 1882; *Stockton Indep.*, Apr. 27, 1881, with allusion to a new local company. *S. F. Post*, Dec. 18, 1873, alludes to a ribbon factory in Oakland, and *Alta Cal.*, Jan. 14, 1872, to one in S. F. The total value of all textile fabrics on the Pacific coast was in 1882 estimated at nearly $12,000,000, produced by 6,000 hands, earning $2,500,000, and using nearly $6,000,000 of material, while the report for 1870 gave only 1,700 operatives, and a production of $3,750,000, an increase for a dozen years of more than threefold. Cotton fabrics in 1888 were imported to the extent of $10,000,000, but cotton could be brought by rail from Texas at nearly as low a rate as to Lowell; so that with available cheap labor, factories could readily be established. Unfortunately the labor market is so uncertain, especially in face of the agitation against Chinese, that capital will not hazard the experiment, as shown by the comparatively small development of woollen mills under far more promising conditions. The abundance of available labor is otherwise demonstrated by the fact that a large amount of the imported cotton fabric is made into overalls, underwear, and similar goods, and sent back to eastern states at a profit. Nevertheless, the production of textiles to the invested capital stands only at 3 to 2 as compared with 6 and 9 to 2 in many other industries.

In clothing, there has been an abatement in the importation to the coast, when compared with the increase in population, from 7,000 cases in 1876 to 5,700 in 1878, 1879, and 1880, and 7,500 in 1881, the last year showing also a largely augmented local manufacture, reaching about $3,500,000 by nearly 2,000 hands, of which $1,500,000 from home fabrics. Yet no organized clothing factory can be said to exist. In 1882 only two substantial firms devoted themselves to ready-made suits, but the work was given out by contract, as was the case with a number of smaller houses. Most of it was done by Chinese firms, and a portion by small coöperative bodies of whites. Eastern factories have the advantage of subdivided labor. Of ducks and denims, $750,000 worth are made, against $75,000 imports. There was an overall factory running in 1888. The foreign export, 553 cases in 1881, is increasing. The demand for oil clothing is limited by the dry weather, and by rubber competition, to $60,000 for the coast, 90 per cent of which is made at S. F., partly with aid of two patents for imparting black color and incombustible properties. *S. F. Bull.*, Oct. 9, 1875. Of the $10,000,000 worth of cotton fabrics imported, somewhat over half may be classed as 'domestics,' most of which is made into garments at S. F., and the rest imported, including the finer grades of women's goods. Dry-goods and other shops control the contract work, yet there are several shirt factories, where the larger proportion of labor is white, 450 out of 650. The production is fully 37,000 dozen, worth $600,000, about half to order; imports, three fourths more. The introduction of neckties reach the large sum of $1,000,000, only one eighth of which is made at S. F., by 4 factories, with 30 to 35 hands. The material is imported for these as well as for the $20,000 worth of suspenders made by two young houses. There was a hoopskirt factory in the sixties. *S. F. Call*, March 12, 1864; March 30, 1867. Hats were manufactured in the early fifties, and a premium granted at the first agricultural fair in 1851. *S. F. Herald*, Nov. 14, 1851; *Alta Cal.*, Feb. 13, 1853; July 3, 1856; Apr. 29, 1857; also in Sacramento. *Sac. Union*, Oct. 10, 1856. But few are made beyond silk plush hats, and these have been subject to many fluctuations, chiefly owing to the favor enjoyed by stiff felt hats. In 1882 barely two dozen hands were engaged on silk hats, producing $100,000 worth. Sustained by a guild, they keep up prices. Caps for railway men, boys, etc., are made to the value of $40,000. Two straw-works existed in the sixties. *S. F. Call*, Jan. 3, 1866; May 12, 1870; *S. F. Times*, Aug. 26, 1868. But the production is limited to 3,000 dozen a year, chiefly men's hats, worth $15,000. The material is chiefly Chinese. For women the main work is to renovate. One factory employs 25 hands during the season; another makes buckram and stiff net frames. There are several dyeing and scouring establishments. *Com. and Ind.; Sac. Union*, Jan. 1, 1881.

Parasols were made to the value of $55,000 in 1881, and umbrellas, $35,000, the imports being somewhat more than double, including material for the manufacture, which employs threescore hands, connected with eight establishments in S. F. The large number of fraternal societies on the coast calls for regalia to the amount of $50,000 annually, all manufactured here, save 5 per cent, chiefly by two firms and about 30 hands. D. Norcross began the business in 1852. *Alta Cal.*, Sept. 11, 1857; *S. F. Call*, Jan. 5, 1865. He also prepared flags, although two other firms give more attention to this branch, selling in the centennial year fully $50,000 worth. *Prices Cur.*, Oct. 22, 1853; *S. F. Herald*, Jan. 23, 1869, alluding to the first silk flag. Fringe and tassel making is connected with the preceding business to some extent, yet of dress trimmings barely a fifth of the $375,000 in use comes from home source. Of upholstery trimmings $35,000 worth are made at S. F. Both classes occupy about 90 hands belonging chiefly to 4 firms.

The abundance of wealth in the community gave impulse to a taste inherited in the colder eastern states for home comforts and embellishments. This applies rather to the towns, for in the country the out-door life fostered by the climate gives another direction to the taste, as noted especially among Spanish Californians. In early days a rich harvest was reaped by upholsterers, and by 1860 a regular factory opened for superior upholstery. The union war decided numerous well-to-do persons to remain permanently in Cal. and the subsequent mining speculation fostered lavish expenditure, till the demand for fine goods has here become larger in proportion to the population than in other states. The business in 1888 was still controlled by furniture manufacturers, and most of the material was imported, but the high freight on such goods insures the local industry. The better furniture is stuffed with curled hair and moss, inferior with gray hair, soap-root, or Eureka hair, excelsior, wool, and tow. Only two of these are produced here, the shoddy or patent wool, in 1881 to the amount of more than 400 tons, and 300 tons of soap-root fibre, resembling horse hair when prepared, and recommended as cool, lasting, and healthy, but cheaper substitutes prevail. Pulu has also been supplanted. The total value of the material for filling exceeds $400,000, of which nearly two thirds are from local sources. S. F. employs about 350 hands on mattresses and bedding, producing goods worth at least $1,000,000, including perhaps $100,000 worth of pillows, although most of the feathers used are imported from the east or from Germany. Of late years most of the springs for mattresses are prepared by three S. F. firms, employing in 1881 two dozen hands, using 600 tons of imported wire, worth $120,000, and producing springs to the value of $200,000. One firm makes woven wire mattresses. Comforters are gaining in favor, owing to their lightness and cleanliness. One factory produces $2,500 worth per month, one tenth of the total in use; the filling is cotton batting. Two houses clean feathers, mostly imported, by distinct patent processes, and make pillows.

The first factory carpet, three-ply, was made at the S. F. Mission mills in 1864, but like ingrain carpets, their manufacture proved unprofitable. Of rag carpets the largest S. F. house produces only 10,000 yards a year. Factories have been described at Vallejo and Red Bluff. *Red Bluff People's Cause,* Apr. 17, 1879; *S. F. Post,* May 12, 1875; *S. F. Bull.,* Jan. 19, 1872. For carpet lining, tule matting is used to some extent, but cotton batting saves the carpet more. The sand-laden breezes of S. F. assist to sustain several carpet-beating houses.

There was a rope-walk in 1856, and others opened subsequently, but there was only one establishment in 1882, at S. F., supported by proximity to sources of supply for raw material and by orders. It employed about 100 hands, and produced 2,000 tons of rope and cordage a year from Manila and Sisal hemp. Sail-making occupies threescore men, belonging to several firms, the annual value amounting to some $200,000. In 1870 an oakum factory opened at S. F., which produces nearly 80 per cent of the bales annually required, employing two dozen hands. Old rope and imports from Liverpool supply the material. Less than one tenth of the $40,000 worth of fishing-tackle used on the coast is made here to order. *S. F. Jour. Com.,* Aug. 23, 1876; *Soc. Union,* Dec. 7, 1858; *S. F. Bull.,* Jan. 7, 1857; *S. F. Call,* Aug. 27, 1865; May 10, 1872; *S. F. Herald,* Dec. 6–8, 1857; *Berk. Advoc.,* Dec. 29, 1877.

Leather manufactures have been favored by the excellent quality of tanned products, and in some branches by the cheap Chinese labor. The possession of raw material led the missionaries to introduce tanning, but only for local wants. The export of hides was a simpler process, and it continued until the disastrous seasons of 1862–4 checked cattle-raising, and till home consumption retained its share. The latter grew so fast as to require the importation in 1881 of nearly 80,000 hides, and double as much in 1885. Nevertheless, the railway then carried east 1,600 tons of dry hides of certain quality, valued at over $600,000. An American, P. Sweet, began to tan at Sta Cruz in 1843. *Hist. S. Cruz Co.,* 11, 74. Sutter opened a tannery about the same time. *Sac. Co. Hist.,* 157. Smith had one at Bodega in 1851, and by 1852 a number were in operation. *Yuba Co. Hist.,* 70; *Census,* 1852; *S. Joaq. Co. Hist.,* 71; *El Dor., Id.,* 114; *Los Ang., Id.,* 69, 157; *Cox's Annals Trin.,* 22; *Matthewson's Stat.,* MS., 3. The war of 1861–5 gave impulse to the industry, and by 1881 the production exceeded 8,700 tons, valued at over $3,700,000; the hides and skins cost $1,900,000; the 28,000 cords of bark, $560,000; 600 tons tallow, 3,600 gallons oil, 550 tons gambier and sumach, $140,000. Of the $2,000,000 capital invested, S. F. held $800,000, the tanneries being here chiefly found in Islais Valley. The *Census* of 1880 enumerates 77 tanneries, with a capital of $1,750,000, employing 630 men, using 22,000 tons of oak bark, and producing 510,000 sides of leather and 1,300,000 skins, worth $3,740,000. The curried leather branch is assigned to 63 establishments, capital $427,000, 230 men producing 266,000 sides of leather and 466,000 skins, worth $2,000,000. The bark of the chestnut oak in Sta Cruz, Mendocino, and Humboldt contains double the usual amount of tanning matter, but imparts strength and other qualities rather than weight. It increases 100 lbs. of hides to 140 lbs. of leather, while the eastern hemlock bark produces 170–200 lbs. of hide. It is becoming less abundant, and tanners are turning their attention to the black wattle of Australia, which presents the advantage of renewing its bark. Gambier and sumach are also imported, the latter growing to some extent in S. Diego. What effect the change will have on the leather is problematic. So far it is the chestnut tan which prompts the growing demand for Cal. leather. In 1881 Cal. exported 920 tons, largely above the shipments of former years, and far in excess of imports of certain qualities. Leather for saddles and harness is sought by Spanish America. Wool-pulling has been long connected with tanning, but is becoming a separate business. The pelts yield 2 to 2½ lbs. of wool worth about 36 cents a lb., while the skins range from 10 to 15 cts, large quantities being sent away in pickle. Of pulled wool S. F. exports fully 1,200 tons a year, two thirds coming from two establishments. By the Napa tan process, skins are now rendered strong yet soft, resembling buckskin. There are six glue factories in Cal., employing twoscore hands, but the profits are far below those obtained in 1870 when only two existed. The Pioneer factory advertises in *Alta Cal.*, Feb. 18, 1857. Cal. saddlery is in demand all over the Pacific slope and in Spanish America, yet 40 per cent of the material is imported, and also $50,000 worth of certain qualities of saddles, wrappers, and harness. The large firm of Main & Winchester has existed since 1849. In 1850 a number of smaller rivals entered the field. *Yuba Co. Hist.*, 71; *Golden Era*, Dec. 18, 1853. By 1870 the *Census* enumerates over 200 establishments, producing $1,070,000 in goods. In 1881 about 1,000 hands were employed, and the trade of S. F. was estimated at nearly $2,000,000. Chinamen are learning the business. In 1881 there was only one whip factory on the coast, and the home production, by three dozen men, was valued at $40,000, little more than the imports. The pioneer factory is mentioned in *Cal. Farmer*, Oct. 7, 1863. The first organized manufacture of boots and shoes is credited to the senior partner of the firm of Porter, Slessinger, & Co., who in 1863 engaged convict labor for making coarse-grade goods. Buckingham & Hecht, later the leading house, entered the field soon after. Account of the pioneer factory in *S. F. Bull.*, Jan. 21, 1870; *Alta Cal.*, Apr. 2, 1869; *Mining Press*, June 23, 1886, refers to a boot-nailing machine. The *Census* of 1880 has 81 establishments, with 2,500 hands, using $2,000,000 worth of material and producing 247,000 pairs of boots, including ladies' lace boots, and 1,600,000 pairs of shoes, value $3,650,000 against $1,400,000 in 1869. By 1889 there was a large increase to over $5,000,000, it is claimed, nearly all produced in S. F. Chinese formed two thirds of the force employed for low-grade goods and slippers, but white workmen have been gaining a firmer foothold again. They can make an average of $16 a week on their piece-work. This high rate, and the necessity to import three fourths of the material, aside from sole leather, gives an opening for the continued importation of one third of the total manufactured goods; but this is nearly balanced by the export of $1,600,000 worth in 1881, with prospects of an increase. The giant seam for heavy water-proof goods is a Cal. patent, supplementary to the sewing and screw machines from the east. At Benicia is a shoe-stock factory aided by a patent water-proof paste. In 1855 a party is said to have collected old boots and shipped $3,000 worth of boot-legs to Europe.

Glove factories were not started prior to 1860, and the *Census* of 1870 reports a production of only $62,000 from six. By 1881 this had risen to half a million, at 16 factories, employing 250 hands, and producing 400,000 pairs of gloves, three fourths being common grades, consuming 250,000 skins of buck, goat, etc. The export amounted to $150,000, due to the excellent tanning and sewing, for the price was enhanced by wages one third above eastern. Kid gloves are little made except to order from imported skins; of other kinds less than $100,000 worth are brought. The hose and belting business has been sustained chiefly by the superior strength and quality of Cal. leather, which resists a high pressure. The eastern rubber hose is now preferred by the S. F. fire dept, but interior towns retain the cheaper and more lasting leather. Belting continues in demand for the mines. The first factory is alluded to in *Alta Cal.*, May 25, 1855; Oct. 3, 1857. In 1881 there were four at S. F., producing 200,000 feet of belting, 6,000 of hose, and 175,000 of lacing, worth $250,000, employing 40 hands. The import of $30,000 was more than balanced by growing export of $50,000. The fulling process of Roger adds greatly to strength and pliancy. Of rubber goods two companies import $1,000,000 worth, manufacturing only a few articles to order. Bellows were first made by C. Van Ness in 1859. *S. F. Bull.*, Dec. 2, 1864. Later there were two factories, with a dozen men, producing 1,800 pairs annually, worth $36,000, leaving a surplus for export. The bellows are marked by two patents for reversible nozzle and safety-valve. Trusses and surgical appliances are made by over a dozen persons, to the value of as many thousand dollars, an equal quantity being imported.

The abundance of tallow led early to the manufacture of soap, Carpenter figuring in 1834 as preparing it for market, at Los Angeles. *Co. Hist.*, 69; *Alvarado, Hist.*, MS., ii. 73–4; *Hijar*, 14. Yet J. J. Bergin claims to have in 1850 opened the first factory for the trade, in S. F. *Culver's Sac. Direct.*, 96. The oldest existing factory is J. H. Heilmann's, established at Sac. in 1850, removing to S. F. in 1855. *Alta Cal.*, June 28, 1852; Apr. 16, 1855; *Sac. Union*, Feb. 8, 1885; Nov. 28, 1856. In 1856 some Frenchmen began to make toilet soaps, but failed. The largest, in West Berkeley, has a capacity for 7,000 tons a year. Of the $1,000,000 invested in the business on the Pacific coast, the neighborhood of S. F. controls three fourths, employing over 400 hands. The *Census* of 1880 credits Cal. with a production of over 11,000,000 lbs. worth $524,000; a little fish, olive, cocoa-nut, and palm oil supplant the tallow material; and Nevada supplies most of the caustic soda. Before the introduction of kerosene, whale-oil was refined by four factories; now there is only partial occupation for one small house. Of linseed-oil, the coast uses 1,500,000 gallons, partly pressed from home-produced seed, partly from East Indian. The first factory opened in 1866. Painters are the large consumers. The *Census* of 1880 credits Cal. with 50,000 gallons of castor-oil, and 395,000 lbs. glycerine. Dried cocoa-nut meat is brought from Hawaii to be pressed for oil, S. F. producing nearly all of the 90,000 gallons used on the coast. There is one special mill, at Alameda, supplied by three schooners. The material from which the oil has been pressed is fed to cattle, and so is linseed. S. J. Capistrano mission had an oil-press in early days. *Cal. Dept. St. Pap.*, xviii. 53. Concerning modern mills, see *Ventura Co. Pict.*, 9; *Sta Barb. W. Press*, Dec. 7, 1878; *S. J. Merc.*, Dec. 4, 1879; *S. F. Call*, Aug. 20, 1868; *Alta Cal.*, Jan. 3, 1867; *Sutter Co. Hist.*, 48; *Los Ang. Id.*, 70. S. F. manufactures candles for the entire coast, to the extent in 1881 of 135,000 boxes, worth $325,000; 98,000 boxes, $235,000, being imported, and 20,000 shipped; 150 hands employed. The *Census* of 1880 gave the home manufacture at $375,-000, but it has been fast decreasing since 1875–8, when the imports alone amounted to 5,000 tons for the mines, which continue the chief consumers. *Culver's Sac. Directory*, 96, claims a factory for Sac. in 1851. By 1855 several existed, *S. F. Herald*, Feb. 10, 1855, *Alta Cal.*, Apr. 16, 1855, offering moulds for sale. *Sac. Union*, Feb. 8, 1855; *S. F. Bull.*, March 9, June 11, 1856. S. F. also makes 150 of the 200 tons of axle-grease used on the coast, the rest is imported, together with the resin and some oil; 25 tons are shipped; 10 hands find employment; total value $45,000; first factory dates 1852. *Alta Cal.*, March 30, 1855; one more exists.

The fast-extending settlement, and the general use of wooden buildings, call for $2,000,000 worth of paint and varnish on the coast, of which 5,000 tons of white-lead cost about $800,000. This and the varnish are chiefly made at S. F., but the preparation of other pigments, though existing, has not proved profitable. The *Census* of 1880 credits Cal. with 4,000,000 lbs. white-lead, worth $260,000; other salts of lead, $65,000. The only special factory employs 150 men. One establishment failed a few years ago. Averill's paint, against heat and moisture, employs one factory, which at times produces 500 tons a month, by secret process; it also makes 150 tons of putty, and 250 tons of pigment. Of rubber paint, against moisture, 80,000 gallons are used from another factory. A similar quantity of varnish is required, chiefly for furniture; 20,000 gallons of fine quality comes from England; the rest is made by several factories, one dating 1857. *S. F. Visitor*, Sept. 25, 1875; *Alta Cal.*, March 10, 1872; *S. F. Bulletin*, March 3, 1871; March 22, 1873; Apr. 12, 1879; *Scient. Press.*, Jan. 11, 1873.

Of $500,000 worth of perfumery used on the coast, one fifth is made at S. F., by 15 hands, chiefly children. The extracts for it are imported. *S. F. Times*, May 7, 1858; *Scient. Press*, Aug. 22, 1868; Jan. 6, 1872; *S. F. Call*,

Nov. 11, 1871; Jan. 22, 1873. *Cal. Farmer*, June 11, 1868, refers to sponge-beds in Cal., and to the preparation of special sponges. The manufacture of brushes is increasing, of late even in finer grades, despite the cheaper eastern competition and the necessity to import most of the material, for bristles here are short. Of $350,000 worth in use on the coast one sixth is made, the first factories rising in 1856 at S. F. and Sac. Soap-root fibre provides valuable material.

Favored by the demand for peculiar machinery, for mining and field operations, not well understood in the eastern states, and by the distance from these sources, as well as by freight, duty, and other charges, the iron industry received a strong impulse in face of such obstacles as the importation of most of the material, even coal, and high wages. The local coal is not suited for castings, and that in use costs three times more than in Penn. Wages are one third higher; yet men can work better in the S. F. climate. Iron ore is abundant, and owners of furnaces promised in 1881 to lay down iron at S. F. for about $24 per ton, or somewhat less than imported material would cost. Of this 14,000 tons came annually during the latter half of the seventies, after which the import declined. The chief demand so far, however, is for machinery rather than plain casting, and this on an average comes to $5 per 100 lbs. The total production rose to $6,000,000 in 1871, and to nearly $20,-000,000 ten years later, under the energy and enterprise which are gradually supplanting eastern goods and gaining new fields beyond the state, as in Hawaiian sugar machinery and mining outfits for Mexico, Arizona, and Nevada. It must grow still further with the unfolding of iron deposits, and the increase of railways and factories, farming, and quartz-mining.

The eager demand for mining implements after 1848 brought forward blacksmiths and machinists, and in 1849 the Donahue brothers established the first iron-works, now known as the Union. *Donahue's Stat.*, MS.; *Woodward's Stat.*, MS., 14; *Sayward's Stat.*, MS., 4; *Mining Press*, July 3, 1875; *S. F. Herald*, Nov. 23-4, 1857. E. Anthony of Sta Cruz, *Co. Hist.*, 29, claims to have made the first mining pick and cast-iron plough in Cal. In *Pac. News*, Dec. 20, 1849, J. P. Hudson advertises his ship-yard, and offers to work iron. In 1850 rose the Vulcan and Pacific foundries, and the Sutter iron-works. *Sac. Transc.*, Sept. 30, 1850; *S. F. Herald*, Sept. 17, 1850; *S. F. Post*, Aug. 21, 1872; *U. S. Census Rept*, 1851-2, 157. In 1851 the Eureka offered its specialties in railings, balconies, etc. At Sacramento, Woodcock & Burnett began to make mining implements in 1850, *Sac. Transc.*, May 29, 1850; and Stow & Carpenter opened iron-works in the fall. Neither lasted. In 1851 the Eureka foundry was established, and in 1852 the Sac. iron-works. *Direct. Sac.*, 1856, p. xx.; *Culver's Dir. Sac.*, 96; *S. F. Herald*, Dec. 25, 1851. Marysville had a foundry in 1852, *Yuba Co. Hist.*, 70, when the Pac. M. S. S. Co. operated one at Benicia. *Alta Cal.*, Nov. 30, 1852. This place had special iron-works soon after. *Id.*, March 29, 1855; *Prices Cur.*, Apr. 7, 1854; *Sac. Union*, July 24, 1855; *Alta Cal.*, June 29, 1852; Jan. 4, June 18, 1853; Jan. 1, 1854, with allusions to other early works, which spread rapidly to leading towns. See county histories, as *Amador*, 219, etc. The interest fluctuated with those of the mines, and many foundries opened, only to collapse after a brief existence, as in 1861-2, owing to lack of means to tide over dull seasons. In 1860 S. F. had 14 foundries and machine-shops, with 220 men, producing $1,200,000 worth of machinery. In 1881 about 1,200 men were employed, producing $4,000,000 from the larger works, three fourths for mines, the rest for marine and agricultural purposes, etc. By 1889 the output had increased to about $7,000,000, and the number of hands in proportion. For mining machinery, the S. F. foundries stand unsurpassed, sustained by long experience and special appliances and inventions. The variety of mines and their increasing depth tax constantly inventive and mechanical skill to meet the difficulties. For pumps, engines of 700-horse power have been made; the famous Dickie pump, for the Chollar-Norcross mine, which lifts 1,600 gallons of water per minute 800 feet, in one stream, with aid of higher water pressure; and the Union mine pump, costing $500,000. *S. F. Bull.*, Nov. 25, 1867. Of small household pumps, only $200,000 worth are made, at about $11 each; quadruple the number is imported. Cables—special factories noted in *S. F. Times*, May 22, 1861—are still drawn largely from England. Cal. possesses numerous improvements in drills, crushers, and means for saving fuel, lessening friction, etc. Patent drills are worked with compressed air for purifying the atmosphere below. Combination amalgamating pans cost about $500. Smelting and assaying are treated under mining, but special metallurgical works have been erected in the leading bay towns. *S. F. Bull.*, July 2, Aug. 15, 1856; *S. F. Herald*, Nov. 30–Dec. 5, 1857. Boilers are made at several of the foundries, besides the special establishments. About 700 are made annually, valued at $700,000. Horizontal tubes made at these places are preferred. One firm alone has fully three dozen in hand at a time. J. Donahue made them in 1853. *Alta Cal.*, June 18, 1853. Peter Donahue, the pioneer foundryman of California, was born at Glasgow on Jan. 11, 1822, of Irish parentage. Brought to America at the age of 11, he was placed as apprentice at the machine-shops of Paterson, N. J., and after some experience at other foundries, he went to Peru in 1847, as assistant engineer of a gunboat, passing thence to S. F. in charge of *Oregon's* machinery. His brother James, a boiler-maker, encountered him here, and jointly they opened a smithy on Montgomery st, in 1849, moving in the following spring to the Happy Valley region, to form the beginning for the present Union iron-works. Taking into partnership their brother Michael, a moulder, thus forming a union of three leading arts in their craft, they made the first castings in the state, constructed the first steam-engine, later in use on the *Tiburon*, the monitor *Camanche*, and other important works. Michael returned east, and became thrice mayor of Davenport, Iowa. Peter entered with zest into a number of enterprises, assisting to establish the S. F. gas-works in 1852–4, the Omnibus street-railway, the first of its kind in S. F., and the S. F. and San José railway, the profits and sale money from which enabled him to build the S. F. and North Pacific railway. His zeal for industrial undertakings hastened his death, which occurred Nov. 26, 1885, and held him back from political and other honors, although he accepted the position of lieut-col on Gen. Cobb's staff, and for a time the presidency of the society of Pioneers. There is room for many imitators of Col Donohue's successful career, as may be instanced by one of the youngest firms in this branch, Rifenburg & Hughes, of the S. Diego Standard iron-works, started in 1885. W. G. Rifenburg was born in Cortland co., N. Y., Jan. 3, 1836, and became noted for his fortunate experiments in fruit culture.

Much of the material for the foundries comes from a local rolling-mill. A portion of the old iron was formerly exported at a profit; to the larger neglected part rails were in due time added which might with little labor be reconverted into useful material. This gave rise in 1866 to a rolling-mill, the Pacific, to which was granted a tract of land at Potrero Pt, S. F. It opened in July 1868, and has gradually increased its capacity, with the aid of gas-furnaces, so that it now employs about 800 men, often night and day, half a dozen engines, as many hammers, and other machinery. It contains depts for puddling, for bars and beams, for iron and steel rails, the latter since 1881 for engine forgings, for car and ship iron, for bolts, nails, and washers, for coil chains, for repairs, etc. Another rolling-mill has been opened at the railway shops in Sacramento. The *Census* of 1880 credits the one rolling-mill then existing with $1,000,000 capital, 320 men, 3 puddling furnaces, 5 hammers, 4 trains of rolls, with a capacity for 100 tons a day, and a total product of 14,000 tons, worth $780,000, the material being placed at $535,000, and the wages at $177,700. *S. F. Bull.*; May 26, 1866; *S. F. Times*, Feb. 27, 1868; *S. F. Chron.*, Jan. 17, 1881.

The first railway locomotive was made in 1865 at the Union works, for the S. José road, and so well that a dozen have since been ordered there. *S. F. Bull.*, July 18, Aug. 7, 1865. But an earlier locomotive engine was turned out by the Vulcan works in 1862, for Oregon. *Sac. Union*, May 22, 1862; *Alta Cal.*, May 18, 1862; Oct. 13, 1871. A toy engine made by Chinese was exhibited in 1856. *Id.*, March 5, 1856. In 1881 the railway shops at Sacramento produced 7 locomotives, 100 cars, nearly 10,000 wheels, and a mass of castings; 1,200 men are employed. The rolling-mill was added in 1881; boiler, copper, and tin shops exist. *Watson's Stat.*, MS., 1–3. Robertson's Track Laying Mach. Co. was formed in 1869. *S. F. Call*, Apr. 21, 1867. Architectural iron-work forms a large branch, one house casting ornamental pieces, another producing wrought girders, beams, railings, vault material, and shutters. The last is noticed in *Alta Cal.*, Apr. 29, 1853. The business amounts to half a million a year. The second branch of importance for iron-workers lies in the increase of agriculture, for which over $4,000,000 worth of implements are annually bought. According to *U. S. Census*, 1880, barely $600,000 worth was made here by 21 establishments, with 290 nands, including 6,000 ploughs. *Com. and Ind.*, 674–5, doubles these figures. The eastern factories have the advantage, in patents, specialties, duplication of sections, and good ready material, but Cal. is gaining more and more of the work. The Benicia Agric. Works are among the largest in the U. S. Jackson, of the firm of Jackson & Truman, leads as an inventor in this line, of improved thrashing-machines, with self-feeder and distributor, portable derrick, with horse and steam fork, etc., by which the cost of thrashing has been reduced one half since 1870. Windmills are widely used, owing to the prevailing sea wind and the absence of rain, and most large towns have factories, usually of self-regulating mills. Eastern are not so well adapted to this climate. The first is ascribed to W. I. Tustin of Benicia, 1849. Stockton, the wind-mill city, now excels. *S. Joaq. Co. Hist.*, 71.

Of stoves, the imports amount to $1,000,000. The local manufacture reaches only one fourth as much, under the advantages possessed by eastern factories in controlling patents. The Alvarado stove-works employed 30 hands in 1882, and was progressing. *Scient. Press*, Jan. 13, 1872, etc. There is only one chain factory, Gordon's, employing from 5 to 15 men. The demand from mines and cable-cars increased the manufacture of wire. A. S. Halli-die has the most important wire-drawing and rope works, started by G. Dennis in 1854. He controls several patents for cable roads, and makes all classes of wire articles; among other shops, some devoted to barbed wire. *Alta Cal.*, Aug. 1, 1858, March 26, Sept. 26, 1859, refers to S. & J. Tristam's wire-works. *S. F. Call*, Aug. 18, 1868; Apr. 9, 1872. *Starr's Merchand.*, MS., relates to a nail factory. Of the annual sale of $300,000 worth of wagon springs, Cal. makes only one seventh, in one factory, the Betts, started in 1868. Elevators are little used outside of S. F., where are held the best hydraulic and other patents, covering the best motive power. The elastic wire rope is the favorite. A few score are made annually, and the demand is steadily increasing.

Of tools only a small stock of local manufacture is kept, production depending largely on orders, which are filled by different factories, some for leather workers, others for smiths, miners, etc. Needle factory noticed in *S. F. Call*, Jan. 29, 1873. The Pac. Saw Manuf. Co., the only one of the kind, was started in 1866, with coöperation of N. W. Spaulding, whose adjustable tooth for circular saws has had a great influence on lumber manufacture. The annual out-turn amounts to $100,000, a portion representing 3,600 dozen cross-cut saws. *S. F. Bull.*, Sept. 18, 1875; *Mechanics' Fair Press*, Aug. 13, 1868. Files were manufactured here by three factories some 15 years ago, but the overland railway opened the gate for eastern goods, and now little else in done than recutting old files. Cutlery in general suffers under similar disadvantages and little more than special orders are filled. Hugh McConnell made large knives in 1852. A sword was sent hence in 1859 to Victor Emanuel. *S. F. Bull.*, June 17, 1859. The annual production is estimated at $80,000. Nautical and mathematical instruments have been made here since 1849, and surveyors' outfits, scales, etc., have increased the out-turn to fully $40,000, besides repairing. Spectacle lenses are made. J. Tennent figures as instrument-maker. *Alta Cal.*, June 15, 1853; Dec. 21, 1856; Feb. 23, 1858; Sept. 11, 1864; *S. F. Call*, Jan. 1, 1865; Jan. 12, 1866; Dec. 2, 1870, with allusion to telescopes, trusses, etc. Fire-arms are limited to a few special orders, yet some cannon have been cast, *Alta Cal.*, July 2, 1859, and many guns put together. *Tehama Co. Hist.*, 97, prides itself upon a noted local factory. Several inventions in this line are recorded. *Alta Cal.*, Oct. 6, 1856; *Stockton Indep.*, Nov. 1866; *S. F. Call*, Jan. 1, 1865; Nov. 29, 1866; Oct. 2, 1870; *S. F. Bull.*, Nov. 5, 1879; *Post*, July 31, 1876; *Merc. Gaz.*, Dec. 8, 1865; *S. F. Times*, Jan. 25, 1867. And so with locks, *Alta Cal.*, Sept. 11, 1867; but the only factory, Adams', of 1875, failed. Special safes were made in 1888 by but one man.

In other metal branches, a dozen coppersmiths turn out articles with over $250,000, whereof sufficiently is exported to balance the small import. J. Macken opened the first shop about 1852. A number of brass foundries produce a large variety of metals, to the value of $300,000 at S. F. alone, by 300 hands. W. T. Garratt started the first works in 1856. His sinking and steam pumps are well known. The largest bells on the coast came from his shop. The first bell of 1851, described in *S. F. Herald*, Dec. 11, 1855; *Alta Cal.*, Jan. 3, 1853; Jan. 20, 1855; Sept. 7, 1858; *Jour. Com.*, May 2, 16, 1877. Lead-works were first opened by T. H. Selby in 1865, stimulated by the abundance of lead and antimony. *S. F. Bull.*, Apr. 10, 1867; Sept. 1, 1868. In 1881 the production of sheets, bars, pipes, wire bullets, etc., exceeded 5,000 tons, worth $800,000; 150 hands were employed. In the plumbing business, about $750,000 is invested, with products half as much larger and equivalent to the imports of chandeliers, hardware, etc. The plumbing work of the Palace hotel cost $350,000. The sale of tinware equals that of plumbers' products, two thirds being local ware. The tin comes from Australia, which sent 750 tons in 1881, a doubling of former imports due to increased canning operations. For the latter branch alone 150 men were employed, one half Chinese. Fully half the tinware is made in S. F. since 1860, prior to which Sacramento employed nearly 100 hands, sustained by the mines. G. H. Tay & Co., established in 1848, own the largest factory. Of galvanized iron only small articles are made here, by two dozen hands. Cornices and other architectural ornaments consume some 700 tons of coated sheet iron annually, and employ at times over 150 hands. Japanning work does not exceed $40,000, the imports being equal. Metallic signs represent $10,000. The Cal. electrical works were the sole manufacturers on the coast, in 1881, of telegraphic and electrical instruments, to the value of nearly $75,000. Nickel plating is done. Electrical works are now increasing in number. Gilding and silvering are done to the value of $100,000, largely for battery plates, employing three dozen hands. The nickel plating is worth $15,000. J. Martell produced hand-plated articles in 1857. *S. F. Times*, Sept. 3, 1868. Plated ware proper is imported to the value of about $750,000. The gold-beating factory of 1853 has alone survived the shops since opened, and it produces only a small part of the $150,000 worth of leaf sold.

The manufacture of jewelry was fostered toward the close of the forties, by miners who desired specimens polished, set, or made into chains and rings. Abalone shells and quartz soon became a specialty sought by all visitors. Barrett & Sherwood sent quartz-work to the world's fair at N. York in 1853. Of the total jewelry sales, $3,000,000, only one fourth represents local manufacture, which is of admirable design and workmanship. Owing to the growing demand for plated goods, the sale of silver-ware is limited to $200,000, fully one half imported. Nevertheless, a few establishments work up 50,000 or 60,000 ounces a year of silver. Half a score of shops do lapidary work, valued at $150,000, exclusive of material. A watch-case factory was advertised in 1860; now several makers exist. *Sac. Union*, June 2, 1860; *S. F. Bull.*, Jan. 24, 1860; *Alta Cal.*, March 25, 1853; March 17, 1855. A watch factory was started in 1874, but it soon failed. *S. F. Post*, Dec. 24, 1873; Dec. 12, 1874; Jan. 16, 30, 1875; Feb. 12, 1876. There was but one clock factory in 1880, which held a patent for pneumatic regulators.

The general preference for wood, and its cheapness, have limited the use of other material for building purposes and for household ware. Settlements have not yet developed sufficiently to warrant the establishment of costly factories for other than common goods.

The buildings of Spanish Californians were almost exclusively of adobe, or sun-dried brick. Brick proper was first burned by G. Zins at Sutterville, in

1847, when 40,000 were produced, followed by 100,000 in 1848. See my chapter on cities, in vol. vi.; *Sac. Co. Hist.*, 146. Yet Tyler, *Mormon Battalion*, 286–7, claims the first burning for S. Diego, in 1847. After 1848 brick-yards multiplied under the cost of transporting timber, and the frequent conflagrations. *S. F. Herald*, June 8, July 10, Oct. 18, 1850; July 18, 1851; *Alta Cal.*, July 10, 1851; June 27, 1852; March 6, Aug. 22, 1856; county histories of *Sac.*, 146, 219; *Yuba*, 69; *L. Ang.*, 69; *S. Joaq.*, 26, 71–2; *S. Mateo*, 29; *Alam.*, 25; *Fresno*, 122; *Tinkham's Stockton*, 189; *Cal. Census*, 1852. Of the many that have risen, the *U. S. Census* of 1880 reports only 50 as remaining, employing 840 men, receiving $210,000 in wages, producing 63,400,-000 common brick, 1,140,000 pressed and fire brick, $60,000 worth of tiles, $1,000 of pipe, total value $516,000. The convicts of S. Quentin made 6,500,000 brick in 1878. Fire-brick are still imported, as ballast, over 700,000 in 1881. The demand in general has increased largely since 1870, with growing stability, though fluctuating with the direction of settlement and the money market. In 1881 over 120,000,000 were reported. The Hoffman process is gaining in favor, by using cheaper coal and producing brick within two days by baking in furnaces. *S. F. Post*, Aug. 5, 1878.

While not abundant, lime is found in many places, notably along the Sierra slope from Auburn to Mariposa, and in Sta Cruz, the latter suppling more than half the total requirement. A kiln was opened here in 1851, or shortly after. *Sta Cruz Hist.*, 28. Other kilns are noted in *Alta Cal.*, May 20, Oct. 18, 1852; Oct. 26, 1855; Jan. 23, 1857; *S. F. Bulletin*, Apr. 23, 1859. El Dorado had 8 kilns in 1855. *Co. Hist.*, 253. Of hydraulic cement 100,000 barrels are used, one third of which is prepared by a factory with a dozen men, at Benicia. *Hist. Solano*, 181. For pipe this cement is mixed with New York brands, clean beach sand and gravel being added. About 125,000 feet are annually called for, value $40,000; made by half a dozen men. Several companies have failed in the production of artificial stone, owing to inferior quality or excessive cost. Marble-works, opened at Oakland in 1871, promised well for a time. Obstacles have gradually been overcome, and both the Ransom, since 1868, and Shillinger processes are now meeting with favor, the latter chiefly for pavements, the other, an English invention, for walls, foundations, pipes, statuary, etc. The annual production reaches $400,000, giving employment to more than 100 hands. *Scient. Press*, Sept. 24, 1870; *S. F. Call*, Aug. 26, Sept. 4, 1868; Jan. 9, 1874; *S. F. Post*, July 13, Sept. 5, 1872; Apr. 21, 1874, with allusions to statuary for the capitol; *Alta Cal.*, Oct. 1, 1864, records the first mosaic flooring; *S. F. Times*, May 30, 1868; *S. F. Bulletin*, May 19, 1873; *Yolo Democ.*, Feb. 27, 1879; *L. Ang. Hist.*, 70–1; *L. Ang. Exp.*, Apr. 28, 1877. Real stone pavements were not laid till 1856. There is one mill for the manufacture of plaster of Paris, opened in 1874 at S. F., yet plaster has been made since 1861. *Merc. Gaz.*, Aug. 30, 1861; *S. F. Bulletin*, Jan. 26, 1865. Since 1875 imports have fallen from 20,000 barrels to less than 5,000 in the early eighties. The annual consumption is 100,000 barrels of 285 lbs., three fourths for buildings. Plaster decorations, for ceilings, etc., employ two dozen hands, belonging to four establishments. One of them makes $3,000 worth of statuary. Sculptured figures and designs, and the cutting of marble and granite, employ more than 100 firms and 600 hands, whose productions exceed $1,250,000. Ornamental pieces are mostly of Italian marble. The import of carved and rough pieces is valued at $150,000, and chiefly controlled by an Italian house, which also saws most of the stone. The leading firm in monumental pieces produces $70,000 worth a year. *Alta Cal.*, Dec. 3, 1852; March 30, 1853; Jan. 1, Dec. 22, 1854; April 8, 1857; *Golden Era*, Dec. 18, 1853; *S. Joaq. Hist.*, 71–2, refer to early marble cutting and carving. An asphaltum mine in S. L. Obispo supplies much of the material for covering roofs. *Alta Cal.*, Aug. 28, 1856; Jan. 21, 1857; *S. F. Call*, Aug. 18, 1868, concerning concrete roofing. *Cal. Census*, 1852, refers to a pitch well in L. Angeles used for roofing.

California possesses the best beds of potters' clay on the coast, notably in the centre of the great valley, and in Contra Costa, where it is worked in connection with coal-mining. The factories number 10, employing over 200 hands,

one third Chinese, and produce pipe, tile, brown earthen-ware, jugs, and other
coarse goods to the amount of about $250,000, yet 4,000 packages of crockery
are imported. The Sewery Pipe Association has adopted a uniform scale of
prices for S. F. One firm makes floor tiles, and another has tried glazed yellow ware. The manufacture of fine articles is augmenting. Early works are
noticed in *Sac. Union*, Nov. 15, 1854; July 30, 1855; Nov. 6, 1856; *S. F.
Herald*, June 13, 1856; *Alta Cal.*, June 1, 1856. Terra-cotta made at Oakland. *S. F. Post*, June 25, Nov. 7, 1874. Porcelain at L. Angeles. *L. A.
Herald*, Sept. 1875; *S. F. Call*, Oct. 4, 1875; *C. Costa Gaz.*, June 20, 1868;
S. F. Times, Nov. 18, 1867; June 22, 1868; *Red Bluff P. Cause*, May 20, 1879;
Alam. Hist., 22; *Oroville Merc.*, July 23, 1880.

High freight and large breakage encouraged the opening of a bottle factory in 1858, after a trial in 1855, but it failed to produce good glass. In
1859 two other parties made the attempt, with similar ill success. *Alta Cal.*,
July 11, Nov. 2, Dec. 14, 1859. In 1862 a third and successful effort was
made by the Pacific glass-works, so much so as to lead to the opening in 1865
of the S. F. works, which soon absorbed the other. *S. F. Bull.*, July 13, Nov.
5, 1859; June 17, 1863; June 11, 1864; July 25, 1865, etc.; *S. F. Times*, July
24, 1868. In 1881 rose a coöperative factory. *S. F. Chron.*, Aug. 5, 1881.
Mont. Democ., May 4, 1878, records a project in its vicinity. The consolidated
firm is the only one recorded in *U. S. Census* for 1880, with a capital of $75,000,
2 furnaces, 7 pots, 125 hands, wages $46,000, material $48,000, product
$140,000. Subsequently, it claims increased capacity and yield, with flint-
glass works for lamp-chimneys, vials, etc. Bottles and fruit-jars are the chief
goods; most other ware is imported to the value of $2,500,000, one fourth of
which consists of window-glass, the rest being mostly table-ware. The sand
is brought from Monterey, the lime from Auburn, the manganese and oxide
from other places in Cal. Ornamental and bent glass employs four firms
with a score of men; product, $75,000. There is also a special lamp and glass
reflector factory. Mirrors are prepared at two places, chiefly with plate
from Europe; 20,000 sq. feet are covered yearly, value $160,000. In 1860
only one man was engaged in this business. *S. F. Bull.*, Oct. 11, 1866.

Soda is consumed to the amount of 6,000 tons, value $350,000, of which
70 per cent comes from England, mostly soda-ash, and 1,000 tons are made
at S. F. at one factory, with a score of hands, in the form of sal-soda, bicar-
bonate, crystals, and washing-powder. The material is drawn from Nevada.
The annual consumption of cream of tartar is about 150,000 lbs., value
$60,000, of which three fourths is refined from French argol, chiefly for yeast-
powder, but the collection of the crude material is increasing among wineries.
The first production was by E. Vacht of Los Angeles in 1860.

Although explosive powder-works were projected in the middle of the
fifties, *Alta Cal.*, Aug. 10, 1855, *Sac Union*, Oct. 11, 1855, *S. F. Herald*,
Feb. 1, 1858, referring to saltpetre discoveries, yet not till 1863 was the
pioneer company formed which created the Cal. powder-works on S. Lorenzo
Creek near Sta Cruz. *Pájaro Times*, May 1863; *Merc. Gaz.*, May 22, 1863;
S. F. Bull., May 5, 1863; Oct. 31, 1866; *Hist. Sta Cruz*, 49–50. The company expanded till it owned 21 mills, 10 shops, 6 magazines, and an entire
village, although the ordinary force is only 60 hands; capital $1,500,000. It
makes the only military and sporting powder on the coast; the first production dating 1864. A branch work at Pinole Pt makes Hercules powder.
There are a number of other mills for the manufacture of high-grade explosives, which have, after some opposition by miners, almost superseded the
ordinary black powder for blasting. These mills are mostly known by the
compound prepared, as tonite, giant, vigorit, safety nitro, granite safety,
thunder, vulcan. *Alta Cal.*, Apr. 22, 1867; Jan. 2, 1872; *S. F. Times*, Dec.
14, 1868; *Mech. Fair Press*, Sept. 11, 1868, referring to Hafenegger powder;
S. F. Call, Aug. 17, 1867, March 5, 1881, Jan. 22, 1883, referring also to explosions; *S. F. Chron.*, July 3, 1881; *C. Costa Hist.*, 17, 419–22; *Marin Hist.*,
281. Of high explosives, 1,500 tons were used in 1881, of black powder over
2,000 tons, total value $2,400,000. Cal. exported nearly 1,000 tons, the im-
port of sporting and cartridge-powder being only 150 tons. The industry

employed nearly $3,000,000 capital, and 300 men. The *Census* of 1880 credits Cal. with 1,250,000 lbs. nitro-glycerine, and 395,000 lbs. of glycerine. There is sulphur in Nevada, but much, as well as other ingredients, is imported. There were three fuse factories, dating from 1863-8, employing 40 hands and supplying the coast, even Montana and Mexico. *Scient. Press*, Apr. 25, 1868, July 2, 1870, refers one to 1863. *S. F. Times*, Jan. 29, 1867. Fire-works have been made since 1852. The opening of this decade found two factories at S. F., one established in 1853, with 20 hands, producing $40,000 worth of goods, the Chinese adding somewhat to the amount. Exports balance imports. *Com. Herald*, Jan. 22, 1874. Of match factories, S. F. contained eight, though many more have existed since 1855. *Merc. Gaz.*, Sept. 11, 1857; *Alta Cal.*, May 29, 1858; Aug. 26, 1859; *Vall. Chron.*, July 13, 1878; *Marys. Appeal*, Jan. 17, 1879; *Mech. Fair Press*, Aug. 17, 1865; *Hist. L. Ang.*, 70, referring to others in Eureka and Oakland. The wood comes from Port Orford, the sulphur, etc., from England and N. York. The entire production reached 500,000 gross, mostly in blocks, four fifths from S. F., and employed about 125 hands, one fifth by Chinese; 60,000 gross were exported. Gas-works exist in all large towns, though partly superseded by electric lighting. S. F. consumes 400,000,000 feet annually, and the rest of the state half as much. The capital invested is about $15,000,000, employing nearly 600 men. In smaller towns and a few large buildings gas is made from petroleum. Gas lighting began at S. F. in 1852. *S. F. Herald*, May 17, 1852; Jan. 4, 1856; and see my chapters on S. F., and on cities; also county histories. All the best systems of electric lighting are now represented in S. F., with two manufactories and several supply companies.

The requirements of mining alone demand large varieties of acids, which are supplied by five factories, one in Nevada, producing altogether 15,000 tons of nitric and sulphuric acids, and from 400 to 500 tons of muriatic, sulphate of copper and iron and Prussian blue, valued at $1,500,000; over 100 hands are employed. Imports are limited to a little Prussian blue. The nitrate of soda comes from Peru. The oldest factory dates from 1854. *Sac. Union*, Dec. 13, 1854; Nov. 28, 1857; *S. F. Herald*, Nov. 26-8, 1857; *Nev. Co., Gaz.*, Feb. 1867; *S. F. Bull.*, Feb. 28, 1867; Dec. 7, 1870. The *Census* of 1880 places the total value of chemical products at $3,180,000. Bisulphide of carbon is made by one factory, to the amount of perhaps 1,000 lbs. daily during the season, for destroying squirrels and other pests. Two factories prepare 4,000 tons of bone charcoal and kindred substances, for sugar refining and agricultural uses. *S. F. Call*, March 23, 1878, etc. Of inks, mucilage, and blacking, usually made at the same establishments, to the amount of $80,000, imports reach $30,000, and the export 500 cases; 15 hands are employed. *S. F. Bull.*, March 29, 1867; *Com. and Ind. Hayes' Miss. B.*, 118, refers to a native berry from which the padres made ink. Printing ink is manufactured at one factory, with half a score of hands, to the amount of $60,000, 150 cases being exported, and very little introduced.

Leads and slugs were made in 1850 by the firm of Jobson, Sterett & Painter, and in 1853 a type foundry was started by E. Pelouze. The business acquired importance only in 1866. *S. F. Bull.*, Aug. 25, Dec. 11, 1866; *S. F. Times*, Jan. 1, 1868; *Com. Herald*, Dec. 30, 1867; and now sustains four establishments, with 60 or 70 operatives, producing type to the value of $70,000, so that few imports are required save of patent and display types. Refined lead and antimony are obtained in Cal. Of printers' material, nearly half is imported. There were two electrotype establishments in 1888, the chief one being that of the Filmer-Rollins Co. Lithographic printing is alluded to in *Alta Cal.*, Apr. 25, 1853; *S. F. Herald*, Dec. 26, 1850. Photographers were numerous by 1850. *Pac. News*, Dec. 29, 1849; Jan. 19, May 8, 1850; Jan. 29, 1851.

The first paper-mill was built by V. B. Post and S. B. Taylor in Marin, and completed early in 1857, driven by water-power, and sustained successfully. *S. F. Bull.*, Apr. 1, 1857; *Alta Cal.*, Aug. 3, 1852; Feb. 21, Dec. 10, 1856; Sept. 8, 1858; *Sac. Union*, Apr. 10, Nov. 30, 1855; Jan. 17, June 26, Oct. 17, 1856; Apr. 23, 1857, with allusions to earlier projects for Sonora, San

Antonio, Alta, Dentville, and Folsom. The *Census* of 1880 enumerates 5 more mills, at Alviso, Saratoga, Soquel, Corralitos, and Stockton, with $610,000 capital, 160 hands, $87,600 wages, using over 4,000 tons of straw, 865 of rags, 562 of old paper, 512 of manila, $56,700 worth of chemicals, producing 1,280 tons of printing-paper, 2,590 of wrapping, with some pasteboard, etc.; value $386,000. Since then there has been an increase, yet not sufficient to supply even half of the printing-paper required, while no writing-paper is made. Fully 8,000 tons of printing-paper are required on the coast, of which about one fourth, with 5,000 or 6,000 tons of other kinds, are produced here. Writing-paper is entirely imported. *Stockton Indep.*, March 22, 29, 1879; *S. J. Merc.*, Apr. 24, Nov. 13, 1879; *Com. Herald*, June 8, Oct. 22, 1874; *Tinkham's Stockton*, 384–5; county histories of *L. Ang.*, 70; *Sta Cruz*, *Sta Clara*, 16; *S. Joaq.*, 72; *Marin*, 133, 279; *Mendoc.*, 377–9, etc. Newspapers abound, and in 1882 were issued from 400 of the 700 printing establishments on the coast, fourscore using steam-power. In 1889, 524 newspapers were published in Cal. The annual value of the newspaper and literature business is placed at $4,500,000, the book and job printing at $3,000,000, employing fully 2,500 compositors. There are more than two dozen book-binderies in Cal., two thirds of them at S. F., doing in 1881 $550,000 worth of work.

Among Cal. manufacturers, the following are worthy of special notice:

Claus Spreckels, who has a national reputation as one of the prominent business men of Cal., was born at Lamstedt, Hanover, July 9, 1828. In 1857 he started the Albany brewery in S. F., and in 1863 organized the Bay Sugar Refining co. Two years later he sold his interest, and going to Europe studied the manufacture of sugar in all its aspects. Returning to Cal. he engaged more extensively than ever in business, having large interest in manufactures and shipping, both in Cal. and in the Hawaiian islands. His sons, John D., Adolph B., and C. August, assume an active management in his extensive business, which reaches all parts of the world.

Charles Kohler, the first to make wine on a large scale, was born in Mecklenburg-Schwerin in 1830, receiving a business education. In 1850 he emigrated to New York, coming to S. F. in 1854. In 1857 Kohler, Frohling, and Geo. Hansen planted in vines a large tract, selling shares among a number of Germans, from which the colony of Anaheim was stated. Kohler was a member of the S. F. vigilance committee in 1856, and one of the original incorporators of the cable-road system in S. F., besides the German Savings bank and S. F. Fire Insurance co. He died in 1888.

James Donahue was the youngest of three brothers—Michael, Peter, and James—natives of Glasgow, Scotland. They all came to Cal. during the flush times, the Union Iron works being the keystone of their fortunes, which industry was closely followed by gas-works and other important enterprises. James died at his country seat near San José in 1862, leaving a name respected by the entire community.

Conspicuous among the early industries of S. F. was the brewery of John Wieland. A native of Wurtemburg, born Oct. 6, 1829, he came to Cal. in 1851, and after mining for a short time, began business in S. F. Later he visited Europe, and with his son Herman made an inspection of the leading establishments in his line in the U. S. His death occurred Jan. 2, 1885. The deep, strong, and warm-hearted nature of Mr Wieland had gained the hearts of the community, and his body was followed to the Masonic cemetery by a large concourse of mourners.

Caleb S. Hobbs, a native of New Hampshire, came to Cal. in 1853, first being employed as a pattern-maker, afterward making boxes by hand until he organized the firm of Hobbs, Gilmore & Co., the first box factory on the Pac. coast. A planing and saw mill was operated in connection with the box factory from 1855 to 1873, when the partnership of Hobbs, Pomeroy & Co. was formed, continuing under that style until 1880, when it became Hobbs, Wall & Co. Mr Hobbs was connected with many other enterprises.

Domingo Ghirardelli, a native of Italy, came to Cal. in 1849, first engaging in mining and afterward in mercantile business. In 1851 he opened a coffee saloon, and selling it, began in the confectionery business, afterward manufacturing chocolate and conducting a general merchandise business.

CHAPTER VI.

FOREIGN COMMERCE.

1848–1889.

Early Trading Vessels—Effect of Gold Discovery—Fluctuations in Prices—At the Mines—Folly of Eastern Shippers—First to Arrive—Influx of Vessels—Alternate Scarcity and Plethora of Merchandise—Revival of Mining—Wages and Prices—Imports and Exports—Social Influence and Trade Revolutions—Treasure Export—Trade Channels—Abandoned Vessels of the Argonauts—Advent of Clipper Ships—Ocean Steamers—Later Developments.

THE sudden unfolding of wealth in California led naturally to a corresponding development of commerce. The congregation of people in a hitherto desert quarter, and the immense influx from abroad, called into existence fresh avenues and means for traffic, and new implements and larger supplies for a novel field of enterprise, while the abundance of gold bred a wasteful extravagance which greatly swelled the demand.

Hitherto trading vessels had been peddling their cargoes along the coast, and occasional supply ships from Mexico provided for the easily estimated wants of a small and steady population. The people relied, indeed, too much upon this ready source, for many articles were purchased which could have been produced at small cost from resources within reach, such as dairy produce and lumber.[1] When the gold excite-

[1] Instance pressed candles bought at 75 cents a pound when tallow was sold for 5 or 8 cents; flour brought from Chile and Oregon at $4 or $6 per cwt., while wheat was offering at 50 cents a bushel. And so with dairy produce and lumber, although the farms and hills abounded with live-stock and trees. Thus local resources were neglected; and even direct trade, to the

ment opened the eyes of local traders to their possible
share in the wealth, several hastened to despatch
orders to Hawaii, Chili, and other customary resorts,
and to keep a close watch for stray trading vessels,
with many a ruse to anticipate competitors.[2]

Under the increased demand from a fast-growing
multitude, the neglect of local farmers, and the cost of
transportation, prices for everything rose immensely,[3]

benefit of entrepôts like Hawaii and Chili. *Cal. Star*, March, Apr. 1,
1848, etc.

[2] Larkin, *Doc.*, MS., vi. 167, sent to Mexico for a cargo in Aug. 1848.
Men were stationed on the hills to signal vessels, and boats lay ready to convey the trader to them, with fast rowers to elude pursuing rivals. Then a
spirited bidding for the whole cargo, including much useless materials. Mel-
lus & Howard bought $15,000 worth in May 1848. *Id.*, 111. Later enterpris-
ing men went to meet emigrant trains across the Sierra to buy their surplus
animals. *Barstow's Stat.*, MS., 13. Imports for 1848, chiefly in last half,
amounted to about $100,000; for the six months ending March 31, 1849, to
$1,000,000. *U. S. Gov. Doc.*, H. Ex. Doc. 5, i. 158, Cong. 31, Sess. 1.

[3] In March 1848 the rates were: flour $4 per cwt.; beans $1.37 per bushel;
wheat 62½ cents per bushel; beef $2 per cwt.; beef cattle $5 to $8 per head;
sheep $2; horses $15 to $30; butter 50 cents; pickled salmon $8 to $9 per
barrel; tallow 5 cents per lb.; lumber $40 to $50 per thousand feet; coffee
32 cts; sugar 6 to 12 cts; Cal. whiskey $40 per barrel; tobacco 30 to 62½ cts;
cotton 8 to 14 cts a yard. *Californian*, March 15; *Cal. Star*, March 18, 1848,
etc. Many articles, like implements, jumped at once in May to high figures;
others advanced gradually, till in Dec. the rates stood: for flour $25 to $27
per barrel; wheat $6 per fanega; beef $20 and pork $60 per barrel; sugar 20
to 25 cts; lumber $125 per thousand. *Id.*, Dec. 16. At the mines goods
brought from 300 to 500 per cent profit, writes Larkin, *Doc.*, vi. 74, 161–3.
See also his much-quoted letters to Washington of June 1st and 28th. At the
Dry Diggings, remote from the easier river traffic, prices in Aug. were double
the rates ruling on the Yuba, where they were twice as high as at Sutter's
Fort. Flour being here $18 in Aug. and at the Yuba $30 to $40. Biscuits
rose $1 to $2 a lb. *Findla's Stat.*, MS., 4–7. Medicine $16 a dose. *Burnett's
Rec.*, MS., i. 375, 404. The French consular report places flour, sugar, and
rice in July at $1 a lb.; liquors $8 a bottle; fresh meat 12½ cts. *Ferry, Cal.*,
320. Flour $50, and shovels $10, in Oct. at S. F., says Buffum. In Nov. he
found flour $60 and pork $150 a barrel at Sutter's. *Six Months*, 55. Prices
fluctuated during the autumn, under arrivals from Oregon, etc. By the middle
of Dec. they fell greatly, partly under a lessened demand for the mines,
from which diggers were returning. Flour $12 to $15; brandy $8 a gallon,
while gold-dust brought only $10½ an ounce.

This was merely a temporary relapse, for early in 1849 they rose again, to
continue high until the autumn. Board cost $20 a week and upward, a meal
at any decent restaurant coming to several dollars; bread, 50 cts for a small
loaf; eggs $9 to $24 a dozen; potatoes 50 cts and upward; apples $3 each;
milk $1 a quart. Lumber rose to $600 per thousand, and in Jan. 1850, $1,000
was paid for fine flooring. *Williams' Stat.*, MS., 4–5; *Ross, Stat.*, MS., 12.
Unskilled labor was $1 an hour; artisans obtained $12 to $20 a day; picks and
shovels were $15 each. Washing was so costly that men preferred to throw
away soiled linen. Doctors charged $25 and upward for a visit. The rent
for a one-story central house for business was $3,000 a month. See further,
on this point, the chapter on S. F. in vol. vi. In the mines prices varied
in accordance with facilities for access and the momentary amount of supplies.

so that flour and beef, which in March 1848 cost $4 and $2 per hundredweight, respectively, reached in December $27 and $20, with pork at $60 a barrel. By the middle of 1849 they were quoted at more than double these rates. For certain articles, like eggs and apples, $2 and $3 each were frequently demanded; tacks, scales, cotton cloth, brought fancy prices. Saleratus, which cost four cents a pound in the east, rose to $16, as a substitute for baking-powder. Lumber cost $600 per 100 feet, and a brick house could be estimated at $1 for each brick. Common labor was $1 an hour; artisans received from $12 to $20 a day. The cheapest boarding-house demanded $20 per week; a drink cost fifty cents, and nothing less than this amount could be offered for the slightest service, while twenty-five cents was for a long time the smallest sum recognized by traders.

Prices at the mines depended greatly on the nature of the roads; for rains, floods, and mountain ridges tended to raise the charges of the costly supply train, and even to cut off communication for weeks at a

Even at Stockton, flour and potatoes rose at times to $1½ a lb. *Randolph's Stat.*, MS., 8. Yet here and at Sacramento rates ranged little above those at S. F. On the Yuba during the winter most necessaries were $1 a lb., though rising to $2 a lb. for pork and $300 a barrel for flour. *Alta Cal.*, Dec. 15, 1849, etc. And so at Coloma, where Little, *Stat.*, MS., 3–6, also obtained $16 a lb. for powder; blankets 2 ounces of gold; boots the same. At the southern mines prices rose to $40 for blankets and boots, liquor $20 a bottle or $2 a drink, in Feb., on the Stanislaus. *Bauer's Stat.*, MS., 314–15; *Buffum's Six Mo.*, 96; *Schenck's Vig.*, MS., 15–20. American horses brought $500 to $600. *Sayward's Pioneer*, MS., 6. Yet this varied with the condition of arriving overland trains. Coleman sold two yoke of oxen for $450. *Vig.*, MS., 141–2; *Boynton's Stat.*, MS., 1. Saleratus for bread $12 to $16 a lb. *Low's Observ.*, MS., 3; *Little's Stat.*, MS., 3. Additional references at the end of this chapter. At the mines, and even at certain Sac. saloons, drinks were $1. Articles on the north branch of the American bring $5 a pound, writes the *Pac. News*, May 17, 1850; *Cal. Courier*, Dec. 23, 1850, quotes flour on Feather River at $2.40. Confirmation of above figures, with curious instances, may be found in *Fay's Hist. Facts*, MS., 3; *Brown's Early Days*, MS., 11; *Connor's Early Cal.*, MS., 2; *Matthewson's Cal. Aff.*, MS., 9–10; *Henshaw's Events*, MS., 4–10; *Sutton's Exper.*, MS., 1, 10; *McCollum's Cal.*, 36, 64; *Neall's Vig.*, MS., 5, 13, 22; *Willey's Per. Mem.*, MS., 99; *Barstow's Stat.*, MS., 12; *Boynton's Stat.*, MS., 1; *Armstrong's Exper.*, MS., 8, 11, 13; *Garniss' Early Days*, MS., 10–17; *Miscel. Stat.*, MS., 18; *Dean's Stat.*, MS., 4; *Dow's Vig.*, MS., 2; *Coleman's Vig.*, MS., 142–3, 150–5; *Mayhew's Rec.*; *Hancock's Thirtien Years*, MS., 118–35; *Fernandez' Cal.*, MS., 175; *Janssen's Vida*, MS., 205; *Kirkpatrick's Jour.*, MS., 32–4.

time. At river towns, therefore, rates ruled lower, but in the interior fancy prices prevailed, with an average of $1 a pound for most articles of necessity in the nearer camps, and the same rate for the indispensable drink of whiskey; although even here $1.50 for flour and $2 for a pound of pork were common enough, while in some places $5 a pound was asked.

The news of these prices roused as much excitement in the commerical circles of the world as the gold discoveries among the fortune-hunters. The spirit of adventure and speculation was abroad. A host of men were seized with the vision of enrichment; of sharing in the spoils of El Dorado, if not by personal participation, by the indirect methods of trade. Anything being deemed good enough for such a wilderness, old and shop-worn goods were raked from dusty shelves and sent off, without regard to suitability or the state of the market. The prudent calculations that usually govern merchants as to supply and demand, and the requirements of the new field, were cast to the winds; and while many articles of prime necessity were omitted, others of no value filled their places, as broadcloth and silk hats, instead of blankets and sombreros; fine linen and shoes, in lieu of woollen shirts and cow-hide boots; female apparel, domestic utensils, and costly furniture came where family life was unknown; bibles, perchance, when men demanded playing-cards.[4]

The first shipments to arrive, especially from the near-lying South American ports, naturally realized enormous profits,[5] even on less needful merchandise; for midst the prevailing dearth and wild inflation everything turned into gold. But the aspect changed as the Atlantic cargoes began to pour in, till the ships in

---

[4] Much of this foolishness was due to a deficient knowledge of the new country, its climate, and the conditions of mining life. Of the many companies formed at various points to despatch goods and passengers, those of Paris, as advertised in the *Journal des Debats*, 1849-50, stood first in extravagant promises. Pianos were advertised in *Pac. News*, Dec. 27, 1849.

[5] *Smith's Report*, Apr. 5, 1849.

the harbor were counted by the hundreds. There
were few wharves and warehouses, and these were
quickly occupied; lighterage and storage cost enor-
mously;[6] money was rated at ten per cent per
month, and meanwhile ship-masters clamored for their
freight. The only recourse was to sell the cargoes at
auction. And here ensued another scramble to be
first in the market before the prices dropped to nothing under the inflowing consignments. To this, indeed, it did come. Goods became unsalable.[7] Some
were left to rot with the deserted vessels; others
were thrown out from the warehouses to serve for
sidewalks and street fillage.[8] Toward the end of the
year came heavy rains to close interior traffic and increase the stagnation, until flour fell below $7 per
hundredweight, and other supplies in proportion.
Failure followed failure; real estate was cast upon
the market to be sacrificed at one tenth its cost; fires
came to ruin others, and in September 1850 a commercial panic was in full blast.[9]

[6] And this in itself interfered with distant storage. At S. F. storage in
1849 was from $2 to $10 per ton monthly, and lighterage $3 to $4. *U. S. Govt
Doc.*, Cong. 31, Sess. 1, H. Ex. Doc. 17, p. 31–2; *Hunt's Mag.*, xxiv. 631–2;
xxvi. 489; xxxi. 111–12, with brokerage, etc. Teamsters' rules in *S. F. Herald*, July 19, 1850.

[7] F. F. Low, *Stat.*, MS., 5. Agents from the east were often present, but
unprovided with money to check the crash. *Neall's Vig.*, MS., 15; *Bartlett's
Stat.*, MS., 7; *Velasco, Son.*, 308.

[8] As described in chapter on S. F., vol. vi. See also *Garniss' Early Days*,
MS., 14; *Johnson's Cal.*, 101–2; *Sutton's Exper.*, MS., 7; *Olney's Stat.*, MS., 1.
Most of them speak of choice tobacco, beans, metals, etc., buried in the mud
of S. F. streets. Dow, *Vig.*, MS., 1–3, instances two ship-loads of heavy
Spanish wine and brandy, which landed at North Beach, covered an acre of
ground. Liquors were abundant at most times. Imported houses helped to
reduce the value of lumber, of which millions of feet lay in the bay lacking
purchasers. *Placer Times*, Feb. 23, 1850; *Pac. News*, Dec. 6, 1849; Jan. 10,
1850. Later, when sailors could be obtained to move the ships, much useless
merchandise was sent back to the Atlantic states.

[9] *Cal. Courier*, Sept. 9, 1850; *S. F. Picayune*, etc. The prices in *Alta Cal.*
for May 1850 are: flour $6.70 per cwt.; bread 2 to 9 cts per lb.; rice 8 cts;
jerked beef 3½ to 5 cts per lb.; mess beef $14 to $16 per barrel; pork $25 to
$35; coffee 28 cts per lb.; sugar 27 to 50 cts; whiskey 70 cts per gallon—
yet Dow, *Vig.*, MS., 1–3, declares that large lots were sold about this time
for 25 cts, wines in proportion, although by regular dealers; tobacco from 10
cts upward; blankets $2.50 to $5 a pair; lumber $40 to $60 per thousand.
By April 1851, after several fluctuations, flour fell below $6 per cwt., with pros-
pects of a further decline, says *Pac. News*, Apr. 17, 1851. Pork sank to $15,
sugar to 5 cts, and coffee to 12 cts, while rice, tobacco, etc., were steadier.
By Dec. 1851 beef and pork stood at $10 per barrel, and rice and sugar as low

The forced and ruinous sales in the autumn of 1849 served to cool the ardor of importers, and by the following autumn the market grew steadier under somewhat reduced supplies. But the gold-fever continued; and in view of the large emigration for the gold-fields, the slightest prospect of improvement sufficed to reanimate speculators to fresh orders and consignments, heedless of past lessons and of prudent admonitions. Boston banks remonstrated, and refused to grant credits to California shippers.[10] The news of fresh shipments brought prices lower than ever in 1851, until flour in July was quoted at $9 for the 200-pound sack, and beef and pork touched $10 per barrel in the following January, while rice and beans fell to two cents a pound, coffee to nine cents, sugar and dried apples to four cents, and coal shortly before to $10 per ton.[11] In order to properly grasp the ruinous nature of these rates, it is necessary to consider the high freights ruling, owing to the demand for vessels on the California route, their detention here through the desertion of crews, and the cost of handling merchandise. The crash did not, however, reach so far as to condemn merchandise for street fillage, as had happened during the preceding spring; for with fleets liberated by the return of sailors, relief could be found in reshipments. Yet most ventures proved a

as 2 and 4 cts, respectively, while flour, etc., had risen somewhat; anthracite coal jumped from $8 to $20. *Prices Current.* Even the interior responded in many directions to the decline. Along the San Joaquin, flour could be had in August 1850 at $15 per cwt.; sugar 40 cts; potatoes 16 cts; coffee 40 cts; boots $8–10. At remote Georgetown flour stood in July at $17, pork 28 cts a lb., coffee 80 cts, beans 30 cts. Yet at Sonora flour was 75 cts, pork 50 cts, sugar 62½ cts a lb., and at other places much higher. *Cal. Courier,* July 11–12, Sept. 11, Oct. 18, 1850; *Pac. News,* Dec. 13, 29, 1849; *S. F. Picayune,* Aug. 6, Dec. 18, 1850. At Sac. beef was 15 cts and pork 20 cts in July; *Sac. Direct.,* 1853, 9; yet milk remained at $1 a quart, butter $2.50 to $3, liquor $1 a glass. Officials' accounts for 1851 place board in private houses at $25 to $30 a week; shaving 50 cts; washing $6 per dozen. *U. S. Gov. Doc.,* Spec. Sess. 1853, Sen. Doc. 4, p. 54; Cong. 33, Sess. 2, Sen. Doc. 16, vi. 22–7; *Williams' Rec.,* MS., 4–5; *McCollum's Cal.,* 65; *Sac. Transcript,* June 29, 1850. Fortunes could have been made by reshipments to N. York, says Schenck, *Vig.,* MS., 15–18. He refused coffee at 5 cts because lighterage was too high. Indeed, the cost of handling goods alone kept up regular market rates.

[40] *S. F. Picayune,* Aug. 9, 1850, etc.

[11] It rose to $32 by Jan. 1852.

loss, in some instances totally so, owing to the cost of storage, with the alternative of forced sales. A main cause was the unprecedentedly small rainfall during the season 1850–1, which obliged a general retrenchment, and spread such discouragement that many abandoned the country as doomed.

The loss fell upon individual importers, and chiefly upon eastern and foreign consigners, who in their wrath and despair threw the blame on the country and their agents, without reflecting that it was due to their own recklessness. True, there were several conditions which here interfered with reliable calculations, notably the distance, which involved a period of about eight months between the sending of an order to the eastern states and the arrival of the goods by way of Cape Horn. The ship which under unfavorable circumstances came first into port to supply existing deficiencies might bring a fortune to its patrons, and leave only loss and ruin for those following.[12] Shipments were, moreover, made from all quarters of the globe, of which merely imperfect notice could be gained.[13] Lack of rain, obstructed roads, and the frequent movements of the population affected the market. The several sweeping fires in San Francisco and elsewhere created sudden gaps and demands, while the fear of such disasters caused many a forced sale. Local jobbers, and the people at large, were gainers, for they kept only small supplies at ordinary seasons, while able to buy largely during a decline, and to keep their goods

[12] This is shown by the violent market fluctuations. Smiley, *Vig.*, MS., 16–18, relates that a small consignment of tacks saved a tottering firm by bringing extraordinary prices after the fire of 1851. Two shipments of flour and whiskey by the *Damascus*, in 1850–1, would have realized a fortune for the former and an utter loss for the other, if the ship had arrived on time. As it was, mishaps kept her back for several months, and the result was reversed. Schenck, *Vig.*, MS., 15–18, Coleman, *Vig.*, MS., 151–3, Burnett, *Rec.*, MS., ii. 204, Garniss, *Early Days*, MS., 15, instance rapid fluctuations.' Howard bought flour for $50 and sold it at $5 before landing. *Findla's Stat.*, MS., 8.

[13] The wide practice of N. Y. shippers at one time to hide the nature of their consignments under vague terms did harm to many without corresponding gain to themselves.

until, in the course of trade, a more favorable market should prevail.

The severe warning of 1851 naturally checked consignments and relieved the market, which also felt in some degree the demand created by the gold excitement in Australia, whither many undesirable characters betook themselves. The improvement was strengthened by copious rains; and during the latter half of 1852 prices advanced, under small supplies and increased consumption, until flour, pork, and other staples rose to four or five times the rates ruling a year before, rice from two cents to thirty cents a pound.[14] Again came prompt response from shippers, with the consequent sharp fluctuations, according to the momentary ability of the market to meet a sudden demand, and to climatic and other influences upon supply and distribution,[15] such as storms and contrary winds on the ocean, obstructed river navigation and roads in the interior, or the rush of miners to a new district, opening fresh markets and routes. By this oscillation, so marked for several years, nearer-lying sources, like Chili, Hawaii, and Oregon, were the chief gainers, while the remote supply stations of the Atlantic borders had to depend mainly on chance for their ventures.

In 1853 mining received a decided impulse, partly from the development of quartz veins and other means, until the yield exceeded any previous record, and that with every prospect of a still greater advance. Meanwhile farming was rising into prominence, with

[14] Compare prices in the list following.

[15] Flour, for instance, fell below $8 in May, while beef rose suddenly to $30. The latter movement was due to the delay of vessels by storms. Freights ruled at 60 to 100 cents per foot. Chili, being nearest, sent in so large a supply of flour as to drive the price below $10 by May 1853, when rice also touched 3 cts, coffee 11½ cts, sugar less than 7 cts, and coal $13. The Atlantic states being less prompt to respond, owing to distance, the prices for salt meat, etc., were longer sustained; but in the latter part of the summer fleets poured in, and beef tumbled from $28 to below $12 during the winter, and pork declined steadily to below $17. Flour, rice, coffee, etc., fluctuated widely, influenced to a great extent by the demand during the spring from the mines, with which communication had been cut off for some time by flooded roads.

large crops, so that the year proved most prosperous for the entire country. San Francisco felt the improvement, and responded with fresh enterprises, particularly in real estate and substantial building operations, attended by increased wages. Unfortunately, success led as usual to excess with wild specution. The reaction came in 1854, marked by tenantless houses and falling rents, till the latter stood at one tenth the rate ruling four years before. Under abundant stocks, well-supplied interior markets, and delayed autumn rains, the depression culminated in the severe monetary crisis of February 1855. The consequently forced sale of several incoming cargoes tended to check the improvement created by a reviving demand from the mines, and prices for certain articles fell more than fifty per cent; flour, for instance, under the prospect of a large home crop, touched the hitherto unexampled figure of $5.50.[16]

After this the market became less subject to disastrous fluctuations; for the experiences of 1854–5 had served to establish a more correct standard. With increased warehousing facilities, and cheaper lighterage and wages,[17] merchants were able better to manipulate

[16] Per 200 lb. bag to $5½. Rice fell to 5 cts, coffee to 13 cts, coal to $15, etc.; a decline of about 100 per cent for flour, 50 per cent for beef, etc. Under reduced arrivals and continued mining prosperity, stocks diminished sufficiently to raise prices by autumn to about January rates, which led to several orders for supplies from abroad, and these, again, to a number of less advisable consignments.

[17] Wages ruled in 1849–50 at about $1 an hour for laborers, as we have seen. In the mines $12 a day, with food, was common, or $16 without board. Artisans obtained one fourth to one half more; yet in the winter of 1849–50, Williams, the builder, Rec., MS., 4, successfully resisted a carpenters' strike from $12 for $16. Washing was over $6 per dozen, or even $1 for a shirt. Burnett's Rec., MS., i. 375, 404. Clerks obtained from $200 to $500 per month. Instances of early wages in Larkin's Doc., MS., vi. 74, 111, 144, 161; Little's Stat., MS., 13; Fernandez Cal., MS., 180–2; Barstow's Stat., MS., 1; Wood's Sixteen Mo., 76; Garniss' Early Days, MS., 13; Findla's Stat., MS., 4; Bartlett's Stat., MS., 4–5; Armstrong's Exper., MS., 10; Coleman's Vig., MS., 143–6; Moore's Pioneer, MS., 6. At Benicia the government paid laborers $16 in 1849. Sherman's Mem., i. 78. Sailors then received $150 and $200. Friend, Dec. 1, 1849. Early in 1848 wages were only from $1 to $3 a day. Californian, July 15, 1848. In 1850 masons struck against $12 for $14 a day. In July 1853 strikes were frequent, longshoremen securing $6 for 9 hours' work against $5 for 10 hours; masons $12 against $10; carpenters had $8; firemen $100 a month. In 1854 common labor fell to $3, artisans getting $5 to $6. In Jan. 1855 the quotations stood: masons $8, carpenters $6, laborers $3, deck hands $60 per month. A year later they had declined to $4 or $5 for masons and carpenters, and $2 to $2½ for laborers, deck hands

stocks, and to control prices in accordance. It was also becoming manifest that the rapidly growing products of California must enter more and more into the calculations of shippers, for she was already producing grain beyond her own requirements. That this industrial revolution was not foreseen was, indeed, a main cause for recent losses, and for the excessive speculation which led to the reaction at San Francisco in 1854–5. Instance the importation in 1853 of grain and flour, representing about eight million dollars, which was entirely dispensed with three years later; and compare the reduction in other commodities within the same period, as shown in the list of imports, with only a slight compensating increase in a few other directions. Observe also the corresponding decline in maritime traffic, and in the business and profits of traders, warehousemen, and handlers of freights, and we find an

receiving $40 to $50, and sailors $20 per month. *Prices Current*, Jan. 1, 1855; *Merc. Gaz.*, Jan. 1, 1857; *S. F. Bulletin*, Jan. 5, 1857, etc. The government paid $3 for laborers in 1854. *U. S. Govt Doc.*, Cong. 33, Sess. 1, H. Ex. Doc. 82; *Id.*, Sess. 2, Sen. Doc. 16, pp. 22–6. Many were then unemployed. *Montgomery's Remin.*, 2–3; see also *Alta Cal.*; *Sac. Union*, etc.

PRICES FOR STAPLES, 1851–6.

	Beef. Mess. ℘ bbl.	Pork. Mess. ℘ bbl.	Flour. ℘ 200 lbs.	Rice. Chinese. ℘ lb.	Beans. Chile. ℘ lb.	Coffee. Manila. ℘ lb.	Sugar. Manila. ℘ lb.	Dried Apples. ℘ lb.	Coal. Anthracite. ℘ ton.
	$	$	$	Cts.	Cts.	Cts.	Cts.	Cts.	$
Jan. 1851....	13–16	14–17	17–15	4–6	6–5	14–16	6–8	8–12	14–15
July........	12–14	14–15	9–11	5	3–4½	12–13	4–5	7½–5	10–11
Jan. 1852....	10–12	10–12	11	2–3	2–3	9–11	4–5½	4–5½	30–32
May.......	30–25	20–23	7¾–9	5	4–4½	13–13½	9–10	9	42–35
Sept...... ..	16–17	35–48	32–30	30	10	20–21	8–8½	10	40
Dec.........	16–17	45–35	41–30	12½–15	5–4	20½–19	6	10–12½	19–22
May 1853...	25–28	28–21½	9½–10½	4–3	5½–7½	11½	6¾–7	9½	13–18
Aug........	25–16½	28–24	19–18	4½–7½	5	16–14½	10–11	10–10½	24
Jan. 1854....	15–12½	16½	10½–10	6–4½	7½–5½	20–11½	9–7¼	9–6	32–38
March......	11–16	19	7–9	4½–4	6½–5¼	14–13½	7¼–8	6¼–8	26–25
May........	18–22	26	9¼–8½	6–6½	7–6½	13½	8¾–9½	11–10	30–40
Sept........	11–20	16½	7½–7¼	5–4¼	6–7	18	8¼–8½	9½–10¾	21–32
Jan. 1855....	23–16	19	9–11	10–8	6	14	10–11	11	21–18
May........	14–15½	17	5½–6	5–7	7–5½	14–13	8¾–8¼	9¼–8½	15–19
Oct.........	22–24	38	9½–9	9–7	8–8¼	18	9–9¼	20–24	25½–19
June 1856 ..	16	24	9½–10½	7–8	6¼	13½	8½	10	19–20
Dec.... ...	16	37	7 (Cal.)	6¾		13½	8	12–12½	16

Sheeting, blankets, whiskey, tobacco, corresponded more evenly with eastern prices, usually at a fair advance. Lumber ruled at $60 per thousand feet at the close of 1850, and continued to decline till it touched $15 in the middle of 1855, after which it rose, during 1856, to about $25, average low rate. Refined sugar is rated about double above prices, and Carolina rice was at first worth double the Chinese grade.

explanation for the reaction following the metropolitan excitement of 1853, which was based on the increase of mining and business in that year. The growth of dairy and stock-raising interests threatened to rapidly reduce other imports, and give the distribution to different interior places, while in due time large exports promised to fill the gap. The imports of 1856 were still in excess of the demand; but owing to the easy financial condition in the eastern states, which required no forced sales, and to the control of the market by consignees, disasters were obviated. The average result was negative, with prices closing at $7 for flour, and other goods in near proportion. Although fluctuations had now been greatly checked, any excess of receipts over three months' requirements was apt to disturb values, as it was the habit of many eastern shippers to invoice goods under the vague term of merchandise. Hitherto the abatement in navigation on the upper rivers, during the dry autumn, diminished supplies in many quarters, and gave activity to early winter operations. The interruption by rains to road traffic was followed by a further increase of trade. Now, with augmenting agriculture came an enlarged spring demand, followed by a busy autumn.

As imports are usually governed by social condition, it is not difficult to estimate the nature of those required for California. As the quiet pastoral people of the forties bought in exchange for their hides and tallow the manufactured goods of the civilized centres which guided their tastes and aspirations, so the teeming miners of 1849 and the early fifties, similarly remote from the world, but without any direct resources, demanded food, clothing, and supplies of a class suited to an almost exclusively male population. While rude camp-life required, above all, staples like salt meat and flour, beans and hard bread, coffee and sugar, with dried apples as the readiest substitute for fruit, the abundance of wealth called for luxuries of every description, the supply of all fluctuating with mercantile speculation and the controlling climatic and social influences. With the growth of family relations, a larger variety of goods came into use, for women and domestic purposes; while the expansion of mining in quartz and hydraulic branches brought forward new adjuncts and requirements. The simultaneous development of agriculture and other industries, partly at the expense of mining, created still wider openings for machinery, seed, timber, and other materials for establishing farms and homes.

The revolution in trade becomes strongly marked after 1853, when home products augment so rapidly as to supplant imported cereals within the following two or three years. Rice alone is sustained by a growing Chinese population. Thus the importation of grain falls from 740,000 bags in 1853 to nothing in 1855, and flour from 500,000 bags to one tenth of that figure, hard bread suffering equally. Salted and cured meats are supplanted more gradually, pork diminishing from over 50,000 barrels in 1853 to 20,000 in 1856. The slower decline in dairy products is due partly to the cost of labor, partly to the preference for vaster and more speculative operations in grain and stock-raising.[18] Other articles, notably coffee, tea, sugar, tobacco, liquors, articles of dress, and powder, which could not as yet be produced at home, offer a certain compensation for the above reductions through the demands of an increasing population. Native fruits and wines begin to compete, however, and the lessened consumption of champagne serves to indicate the wide retrenchment attending the change from the flush mining days to an era of more sedate occupations.[19]

[18] The decline in other effects belongs to a later period.

[19] The change in trade values can be better appreciated when it is borne in mind that the grain, flour, and beans imported in 1853 were worth over eight millions, and that this amount, together with other large sums represented by salt meats, bread, etc., passed away from shippers within two or three years. Ship-owners were also heavy losers, for freights which in 1853 amounted to $11,700,000 fell by 1855 to about $4,000,000, from reduced rates as well as cargoes. The imports of 1850 continued large, partly because the news of falling prices could not arrive in time to stop shipments for the early

In the following decade two important modifying factors appear, affecting shippers as well as prices.

months, partly because the continued rush of gold-seekers buoyed speculation in many quarters. Thus flour reached 300,000 bags of 200 ℔s., of which three fourths was from Chili; 23,000 bags of Central American coffee arrived; of tea, 7,700 chests; sugar, 194,000 quintals; pork, 55,000 barrels; lard, 58,000 kegs, etc.; butter, 55,000 kegs. Records for early times are not wholly reliable, owing to the destruction of the custom-house with its books in 1851. The *Sac. Transcript*, Feb. 1, 1851, *Hunt's Mag.*, xxiv. 544, reproduced among other journals the above statement. In addition came $1,700,000, chiefly in coin for circulation. The subsequent flow of merchandise can be readily understood by comparing the number of vessels arriving annually, and also the rise and fall of prices, as exhibited in the respective tables. It must be borne in mind, however, that after 1849 the proportion of merchandise is greater as compared with the number of arriving ocean vessels, owing to the absorption of passenger traffic by the steamship lines. With 1853 so marked a change begins in the kind and quantity of goods that the details of the appended table of imports of staple commodities cannot fail to prove interesting:

	Year 1853.	Year 1854.	Year 1855.	Year 1856.
Grain, bags.................	740,000	190,000		11,700*
Flour, sacks and barrels.....	499,000	218,000	49,300	36,700
Rice, bags..................	420,000	168,700	198,000	348,000
Beans, bags and bbls........	103,000	43,000	45,000	61,000
Bread, casks................	23,700	8,300	800	
Bread, cases	35,300	6,200	800	
Apples, dried, bbls..........	10,500	7,700	6,800	3,400
Apples, dried, pkgs.........	5,300	4,000	5,400	36,000
Raisins, boxes....	49,000	19,300	38,600	63,000
Coffee, bags	128,500	66,500	85,000	97,400
Tea, chests.................	162,200	53,000	53,400	87,400
Sugar, ref. and domes., bbls..	40,000	34,700	70,000	92,700
Sugar, foreign and raw, bags.	167,000	118,000	126,000	157,600
Beef, barrels...............	16,300	10,500	4,600	9,000
Pork, barrels...............	51,200	32,700	12,900	28,500
Bacon, tcs and bbls.........	9,100	9,500	3,800	5,300
Bacon, boxes	9,400	5,200	1,600	1,900
Hams, casks................	41,000	29,800	21,300	22,900
Butter, casks...............	93,700	40,400	38,000	9,000
Butter, cases....	28,700	10,600	4,500	57,900
Lard, kegs	83,000	34,400	20,000	41,000
Candles, boxes.............	173,900	86,000	133,600	273,000
Tobacco, bales.............	2,100	1,000	1,700	2,100
Tobacco, cases.............	29,000	20,300	26,000	29,000
Liquors, alcohol, casks......	13,500	7,500	10,000	11,800
Liquors, cases	16,500	6,000	7,300	18,000
Whiskey, bbls..............	20,000	13,000	12,000	30,000
Brandy, casks	21,700	9,500	11,900	7,000
Brandy, cases..............	8,000	7,100	7,700	56,000
Wine, bbls.................	11,500	6,700	16,800	17,300
Wine, cases................	157,000	59,200	123,700	130,300
Champagne, cases...........	34,000	16,300	26,000	20,000
Dry goods, bales...........	35,200	18,500	17,000	36,300
Dry goods, cases..	36,600	20,500	19,000	31,600
Blankets, bales.............	4,000	1,900	1,300	2,000
Shoes, cases................	67,500	60,700	82,000	87,400
Powder, kegs...............	15,000	9,000	35,600	35,500
Lumber, thousand feet †.....	58,000	62,000	32,000	38,400
Lumber, pieces.............	400,000	182,000	66,000	2,230
Coal, tons..................	82,000	67,500	86,000	65,000

* Oregon wheat.   † Not including shingles, clapboards, etc.

First the union war of 1861–5, which disturbed the production of raw and refined staples, retained a larger amount for home consumption, and checked the shipment of the surplus, at least in American vessels, which were the prey of confederate cruisers. The state was accordingly thrown more upon its own resources, to the development of much neglected wealth, and had in other respects recourse to the comparatively cheaper foreign products. These were favored, moreover, by the fast-growing wheat export, especially in English ships, which could, therefore, afford to bring merchandise at a low freight. A few years later the opening of the overland railway assisted to revive the demand for American goods, notably of a costlier grade, with a gradual increase in finer articles under the improved quality of eastern and home manufactures.

The opening of the Central and Union Pacific railroads was not followed, as might have been expected, by a considerable decrease in the volume of importations by sea, though to the same result tended, in later years, the completion of the Northern Pacific, the Southern Pacific, the Canadian Pacific, and other lines making connection with the Atlantic states. On the contrary, under the increase of population and wealth, and the rapid growth of industries, our foreign imports by sea increased from less than $20,000,-000 in 1869 to more than $50,000,000 in 1889.[20]

Among notable imports are 230,000 bricks in 1856, of a special grade; for by this time the reduced price of labor permitted the manufacture of such articles. There are also 5,000 crates of crockery. Glass, paper, hardware, etc., form part of staple imports. The imports for this year may be valued at $36,000,000. In *Com. and Navig.* for 1854–6, the foreign imports for these three years are placed at $8,408,000, $5,951,000, and $7,289,000, respectively, $2,063,000 of the latter being duty free.

[20] The foreign imports at S. F. after 1856 are placed by *U. S. Com. and Navig.*, passim, at $8,985,000 in 1857–8, $11,156,000 in 1858–9, $8,366,000 in 1861–2, followed by a rise to $20,300,000 by 1864–5, during the war; then a fall to $15,570,000 in 1865–6, after which a gradual rise to $20,390,000 by 1870–1, with a jump to $39,420,000 in 1872–3, due to mining excitement; then a rise from $29,700,000 in 1874–5 to $44,670,000 in 1880–1, and $51,640,000 in 1881–2. Of the last amount $41,000,000 was merchandise, and $10,640,000 coin and bullion. S. Diego, the other port of entry, received during 1881–2 $679,000 in merchandise. The total introduction of merchan-

The gold discovery had interposed a check on the export trade, which under the stimulating efforts of American settlers was slowly expanding beyond the former narrow limits of hides and tallow.[21]　Cattle came to be slaughtered solely for the meat, which suddenly came into active demand from being a mere refuse or surplus commodity.　Gradually, however, the neglected hides[22] crept back into notice, quicksilver rose to a leading article of export, and San Francisco became an entrepôt for the reshipment of eastern and European merchandise to different Pacific ports, partly from her overstocked markets.　Soon native grain and flour entered the list, and in 1855 they together exceeded in value any other export article, always excepting treasure.　Exports in 1855 amounted to $4,200,000, and in 1856 to $4,300,000, of which quicksilver constituted $976,000 and $883,000, respectively; flour followed, at about $816,000 and $760,000 for the two years; then came grain, hides, tallow, and wool, reshipped goods forming a minor proportion only.　All this gave little occupation to shipping, however, and return cargoes for the in-

dise for 1881 is estimated at $67,600,000, of which $38,600,000 from foreign countries, paying $7,450,000 in duties. Of the rest, from eastern states, $16,400,000 came by railway, $12,000,000 by sailing vessel, and $500,000 by Panamá steamer. Of the foreign goods, $11,000,000 came from China and Singapore, $6,870,000 from Japan, largely silks, $6,400,000 from Hawaii, chiefly sugar, $3,850,000 from England, $1,880,000 from Central America, $1,700,000 from the East Indies, $1,100,000 from Australia, $1,000,000 from B. Columbia, and $840,000 from France. The figures for following years correspond more with those of 1880-1 than 1881-2. Hawaiian imports have come to the front, reaching over $10,000,000 for 1886, Japan following with over $8,000,000, then China $5,000,000, and England nearly $3,000,000. Of the treasure import, exceeding $5,000,000, half came from Mexico and one fourth from Australia. The nature of the imports will be further explained by a comparison with the chapter on manufactures; with *U. S. Com. Rel.*, annual reports; *U. S. Bureau of Statistics; S. F. Merc. Gaz.; Hunt's Merch. Mag.; S. F. Com. Assoc.*, 1869, etc.; *S. F. Chamber Com.*, 1851.

[21] In 1846 1,000,000 feet of lumber, 10,000 fanegas of wheat, and $10,000 worth of soap were added to the 60,000 arrobas of tallow, 80,000 hides, 1,000 barrels of brandy and wine, and $20,000 worth of furs. See *Hist. Cal.*, v. 570, this series. The exports and imports of S. F. for the last quarter of 1847 amounted to $49,600 and $53,600, respectively.

[22] Hides have so far been thrown away, writes one in the *Sac. Transcript*, Jan. 14, 1851, but soon a ship-load is to be sent from Sacramento.

pouring fleets had to be sought in other latitudes and even on Asiatic shores.[23]

By adding treasure, we reach, according to manifest figures, the respectable export of some $330,000,-000 by 1856, or an average of over $40,000,000 for the eight export years 1849–56, to which can safely be added one fourth more for unrecorded values. With a lack of reliable banking and express facilities in early years, it is but natural that miners preferred to carry away their dust privately; but after 1850, this habit decreased until the secretly exported treasure fell below ten per cent of the recorded amount. The latter corresponded to the importation of goods for a growing population,[24] to remittances by departing persons and interested absentees, and to the withdrawal of capital for relieving money pressure abroad, while the surplus left by increasing home productions permitted the retention of larger sums for circulation, plate, and jewelry.[25]

[23] Exports of California products other than treasure:

	Year 1854.	Year 1855.	Year 1856.
Wheat, bags..........	5,000	83,000	23,000
Oats, bags........	3,200	49,000	13,000†
Barley, bags........ ...	15,600	73,000	5,000
Flour, bags and bbls	58,000	116,000	74,000‡
Grits and bran, bags....	.....	12,000	5,000
Potatoes, bags	20,000	12,000	
Hides, no....	44,000	112,000	170,000
Skins, bales..........	.....	1,600	5,000
Tallow, bbls..	.....	500	1,700
Wool, bales...........	1,100	2,500	4,000
Lumber, thousand feet*..	3,200	2,500	1,200
Quicksilver, flasks......	21,000	27,200	23,700‖

* Besides large quantities of shingles, etc.
† Chiefly to Peru.
‡ Chiefly to Australia.
‖ Over half to Mexico, rest to Peru, China, and New York, and a little to Australia. In 1853, 18,800 flasks were shipped.

Although the above staples include a small portion of imported goods, they may be essentially called California products. In 1855 they formed considerably more than half the value of exports, excluding treasure. The remainder included iron-work and other California manufactures, so that the proportion of mere reëxports was not large. In 1856 the value of produce shipped fell off somewhat, but the large increase in both years over the exports of 1854 show the nature of the industrial revolution then beginning. *S. J. Pioneer*, March 3, 1877, claims for Peebles and Wadsworth the first wheat shipment from Peeble's farm. *Alta Cal.*, June 11, 1853, records the first salmon shipment to Australia. *Sac. Union*, Oct. 13, 26, 1855. Crary, *Stat.*, MS., 2–3, alludes to earlier flourings, and later ones in *S. F. Bulletin*, Apr. 24, 1856.

[24] Compare with figures given under imports.

[25] For making estimates of actual gold yield, J. Ross Browne assumes that

Metals formed the main feature of exports for many years, even to foreign countries; but in this respect a change took place before the close of the fifties, with the increase of wheat shipments, which have since assumed the preponderating lead, although checked occasionally by droughts, as in 1863–5. By 1881 they

$200,000,000 may be added to the export figures for the 16 years following 1848, which is evidently nearer the truth than the not uncommon estimate of $40,000,000 for the nine years ending in 1856. Yet I prefer to be less sweeping in my calculations. It must be borne in mind that the unrecorded amounts carried away gradually decrease with the establishment of banks and reliable expresses; that the abatement in certain imports had great effect, though counteracted by the demands of a growing population in other directions, by the drain through absentees, by home circulation and absorption for manufactures, and by monetary disturbances, as in 1855. While export figures must form the basis for estimates, I find them unsatisfactory, owing to the destruction of early custom-house records by fire, and the contradictions presented by official documents for different years. Some, for instance, give the steamer shipments and neglect wholly or partially the remittances by sailing vessels, or to less prominent destinations. Ross Browne and others correct their earlier figures, and still exhibit oversights. Not feeling myself warranted in going outside of these sources, I can only select those amounts which appear best supported in their details, using the statements of the Pacific Mail S. S. Co.; of Butler King, in *Cal. Jour. Sen.*, 1852, 650; reports from custom-house; estimates of L. A. Garnett of the S. F. refinery; *J. Ross Browne's Report*, 1867, p. 50; 1868, p. 292; *Merchants' Mag.*, xxiv. 547, etc.; *Cal. Register*, 1857, p. 112; *Blake's Product. Prec. Metals*, 20–1, a somewhat mixed estimate; the more acceptable *Del Mar's Hist. Prec. Metals*, 166; *Phillips' Mining*, 66; *Hittell's Resources*, 240; the hasty *Bowie's Hydraulic Mining*, 288; *Balch's Mines*, 697, etc.; and reports in *Alta Cal.*, *S. F. Bulletin*, *Prices Current*, and *Mercant. Gazette*.

Treasure export:

	As Recorded.	Estimated Yield.
1848	$2,000,000	$10,000,000
1849	4,900,000	40,000,000
1850	29,400,000	50,000,000
1851	42,600,000	60,000,000
1852	46,600,000	60,000,000
1853	57,300.000	65,000,000
1854	52,000,000	60,000,000
1855	45,200,000	55,000,000
1856	51,000,000	56,000,000
Totals	$331,000,000	$456,000,000

The receipts at eastern mints up to Jan. 1854 have been given at $210,-000,000, with variations of ten per cent from this figure. The Pac. Mail Co. claimed to have carried $15,100,000, in bullion, between Apr. 11, 1849, and July 1, 1850, *Sac. Transcript*, July 3, 1850, charging 5 per cent for freight and insurance. *Alta Cal..*, Dec. 15, 1849.

Of the shipments in 1853, about $48,000,000 went to New York; $5,000,-000 to England; $900,000 to China. In 1854 $46,500,000 went to New York, etc.; $3,800,000 to England; $1,000,000 to China. In 1855 $38,700,000 went to New York, etc.; $5,200,000 to England; $900,000 to China. In 1856 $40,000,000 went to eastern U. S.; $8,700,000 to England; $1,500,000 to China; $800,000 to Panamá, Pacific islands, South America, East Indies, Australia, etc.

reached nearly 1,000,000 tons, worth $31,000,000, though decreasing, with some fluctuations, to about 675,000 tons, worth nearly $20,000,000, for the cereal year ending June 30, 1889. This amount was supplemented by flour worth nearly $5,000,000, by barley, fruit, canned goods, and wine. Refined sugar, explosives, and lumber are among goods which help to swell the total export from San Francisco to over $100,000,000, half of it in domestic merchandise, and one sixth in bullion, for aboard. The rest goes inland and to the Atlantic states, in which last direction bullion sustains itself at the head; for although the yield of the California mines has steadily declined to below $20,000,000, yet gold and silver totals stood, as late as 1877, at $70,000,000, under consignments from Nevada. Since then the latter have declined to less than the California production. The causes which are tending to diminish imports, such as reduced wages and increasing industries, help also to augment the surplus for export. To this end have likewise contributed the mining discoveries in California and adjoining states and territories, by bringing an army of workers and enlarging the markets. Increased railway competition promotes the same object, in opening wider, not alone the eastern portals, but those of several intermediate regions.[26]

[26] After 1856 the exports of S. F. follow approximately the variations indicated under imports. According to *U. S. Com. and Navig.*, passim, they are valued at about $12,000,000 of domestic goods and bullion, and $2,200,000 to $3,500,000 of foreign goods and bullion, for 1856–7, 1857–8, and 1858–9; in 1859–60 they fell to $7,400,000 and $2,900,000, for domestic and foreign, rising to $11,700,000 domestic, although only $1,900,000 foreign, in 1861–2; and in 1863–4 to $48,200,000 domestic and $2,200,000 foreign, under the strictures imposed by the war. A decline followed to $23,800,000 domestic and $3,133,000 foreign in 1867–8; after a fall to $20,800,000 domestic and $2,860,000 foreign in 1870–1, came a rise to $43,500,000 domestic and $4,400,000 foreign in 1876–7, then a decline below $40,000,000 till 1881–2 when the domestic reached $55,900 and the foreign $2,860,000. Of these last two amounts, the merchandise stands for nearly $53,000,000 domestic and $700,000 foreign, and the coin and bullion for $3,000,000 domestic and $2,150,000 foreign. San Diego is credited with $516,000 domestic and $15,000 foreign merchandise. The export of merchandise and treasure to the east and abroad stood in 1859 at $6,000,000 and $48,000,000, respectively; in 1861 at $10,000,000 and $41,000,000; in 1864 at $13,000,000 and $57,000,000; the merchandise export rose to $23,000,000 in 1868, while the treasure shipments declined to $33,000,000 in 1870, both falling in 1871 to $14,000,000 and $17,000,000; in 1873 they stand at $31,000,000 and $25,000,000. Mer-

The direction of trade, which at first sought near-lying ports along the Pacific for urgent supplies,[27] fell quickly into the main channel flowing from New York and other large cities of the United States, whence came the main supplies of merchandise, under a protecting tariff which hampered foreign competition. This trade reached its maximum in 1852–3, after which the growing home productions of California rapidly eliminated cereals, then salted provisions, and gradually different products, till the number of cargoes diminished from 344 in 1853 to 128 in 1856.[28] The traffic with Chili,

chandise continued to increase in amount to $55,000,000 in 1882, declining to $35,300,000 in 1885, all exclusive of transit goods, since when it is again rising. The staple export was wheat, which during the war diminished from 100,000 tons in 1861 to 14,000 in 1865, owing to drought, and then sprang to 250,000 tons in 1867 and following years, falling to 100,000 in 1872 and rising to 600,000 in 1877 and to nearly 1,000,000 tons in 1881, valued at $30,800,000. In 1885 it stood at $16,100,000, and rose again before 1888. A large proportion went to England. The flour export rose to $5,300,000 in 1884. Of the total, $4,700,000, in 1886, England and China took more than $1,500,000 each. Wool shipments advanced steadily to 28,000 tons for 1876, but had by 1886 declined to 17,000, worth $5,500,000. Quicksilver declined in production fully one half after 1881, when shipments reached $1,000,000. Horticultural products were rapidly increasing, on the other hand. In 1886 the wine export by sea stood at more than 750,000 gallons, chiefly to N. York, to which must be added considerable consignments by land. Canned goods are growing in favor. Barley, refined sugar, borax, powder, lumber, are among noteworthy exports, ranging from $500,000 downward. While agricultural products have taken the lead in this gold land, to the overshadowing of its once all-important treasures, the export of the latter was nevertheless maintained at the head till the latter part of the seventies, reaching $58,000,000 in 1877; but this was due to the Nevada mines, which burst into prominence early in the sixties, with a yield increasing to over $50,000,000 in 1877, but fell off by 1881 to less than a dozen millions, with subsequent further decline. The yield of Cal. had continued to steadily diminish from $51,000,000 in 1857 to $17,000,000 in 1881, yet it reached a trifle higher in 1886, when the shipments by sea stood at $18,200,000, of which $11,200,000 to China and $2,000,000 to Japan, both mostly in silver. Inland remittances stood $29,700,000. For additional leading authorities, see notes under imports.

[27] Even in 1852 large quantities of flour, rice, etc., were bought at various ports for the rising market at S. F., with large profits, as Crary, *Stat.*, MS., 2, relates. Hawley in Feb. 1850 bought 2,500 barrels of potatoes and almost cleared the Islands of produce; but the cargo was destroyed by fire. Half of it had been sold for $250,000. *Stat.*, MS., 6–7. Exports to Hawaii in 1848, $12,800; in 1849, $131,500; in 1850, $306,000, according to the *Friend*, vii. 14; *Polynesian*, vi. 141; vii. 149; *Star and Cal.*, Nov. 25, 1848. Concerning Chili flour ventures, Schenck, *Vig.*, MS., 20, Belden, *Stat.*, MS., 60–1, Roach, *Stat.*, MS., 16, give some interesting facts. Even the Farallones were ransacked for eggs, as described in *Harper's Mag.*, xlviii. 622–5. See also *Coleman's Vig.*, MS., 151–2; *Fay's Facts*, MS., 9–10.

[28] The arrivals from the U. S. Atlantic ports, which in 1853 stood at the high figure of 344 vessels with a tonnage of 260,000, fell rapidly in 1854 to

as the chief flour warehouse for California, declined in a more striking degree, during the same period, from 127 cargoes to 11.[29] The imports from Mexico, China, the Pacific islands, and East Indies, consisting of sugar, tea, rice, fruit, and the like, not being among the growing home productions, the trade was sustained. And so with Australia, although here with a partial reversal, for many articles, like flour, once introduced, were now returned to supply the antipodal gold-fields.[30] The steady intercourse with Panamá and Nicaragua was maintained by the leading steamship lines, but with a shrinkage, due on the one hand to the withdrawal of rival lines, on the other to Walker's invasion. England, France, the Hanse towns, and other European contributors had been greatly supplanted by the eastern United States, through which most California immigrants passed.

These different curtailments were balanced numerically, although hardly as to tonnage, by the growth of the coast traffic, which in 1855 employed a tonnage of 190,000.[31] It had been fostered primarily by the ex-

153,000 tons, and in 1856 to 140,000 tons, covered by 128 vessels, evidently of a superior class. Few cleared direct for the east, but sought return cargoes elsewhere.

[29] The 127 vessels entered in 1853 measured 37,000 tons; in 1854 came 39, and in 1856 only 11, of barely 4,000 tons. Peru participated largely in the decline.

[30] *Sac. Transcript*, Aug. 30, 1850, comments on the fine quality of flour then brought from Australia.

[31] The following list exhibits the extent of the export trade in different directions for 1856: To New York, 132,000 hides, 3,900 bales wool, skins, oil, mustard seed, etc., besides 2,400 flasks of quicksilver; value $1,114,000. Australia, 63,400 barrels flour, 32,500 bags grain, 250 flasks quicksilver, etc.; value $1,123,000. Mexico, 13,500 flasks quicksilver, 2,600 cases wine, etc.; value $781,000. Peru, 4,500 flasks quicksilver, bags, etc.; value $338,000. Hawaii, shoes, biscuits, etc.; value $249,000. China, 4,200 barrels flour, 3,000 flasks quicksilver, etc.; value $240,000. Russian N. W. Possessions, various store supplies, $128,000. Chili, $117,000; Society Islands, $62,000; New Granada, $43,000; Vancouver Island, $23,000; Costa Rica, $12,000. Total export value, $4,271,000.

Early in 1849 I find only three consular representatives in Cal., even England not being represented, in spite of the urgings in parliament. *Hansard's Parl. Deb.*, c. ii. 567, 1327; *Alta Cal.*, Jan. 25, 1849; *Polynesian*, v. 159; *Star and Cal.*, Nov. 25, 1848. But there were enough in 1852, being consuls for Austria, Great Britain, Bremen, Belgium, Chile, Denmark, France, Hamburg, Hanover, Hawaii, Mecklenburg, Mexico, Netherlands, Sweden and Norway, Nicaragua, Oldenburg, Peru, Portugal, Prussia, Spain, Switzerland,

tension of mining northward, and gradually by the ever-augmenting flow of supplies and passengers to and from the expanding settlements in different directions. While eastern lumber was at first supplanted by the timber from Puget sound and northward,[32] California developed this and other resources within her own territory, and so in due time with articles like ice, which coming first from Boston was supplanted by the fields of Alaska,[33] and finally by

and Sardinia. Soon after came additions for China, Central America, Ecuador, Nueva Granada, and Russia.

DISTRIBUTION OF SAN FRANCISCO'S TRADE.

	1853.				1854.				1855.		1856.			
	Arrivals.		Clearances.		Arrivals.		Clearances.		Arrivals.	Clearances.	Arrivals.		Clearances.	
	Vessels.	Tonnage.	Vessels.	Tonnage.	Vessels.	Tonnage.	Vessels.	Tonnage.	Tonnage.	Tonnage.	Vessels.	Tonnage.	Vessels.	Tonnage.
U. S. Atl. ports.	344	260845	25	30580		153313	14	8637	147870		128	149370	7	6002
U. S. Pac. ports	110	64668	726	137860			586	138100	189635		1034	138149	860	137456
Whalers.	11	2545	7	1835	3	650	7	1921	3609	2535	12	2879	18	3855
Rus.N.W.ports	6	1883	5	1481							5	2527	9	4797
British Colum.	20	3695	21	4654	21	3765	24	4976			3	537	5	638
Mexico	44	7177	72	16369	26	3077	36	8065	3626	15043	38	5531	43	8873
Nicaragua..	32	30262	28	26472	26	31614	25	28957			13	15574	14	18052
Cent. America.			3	797							1	182	2	349
N. Gran., Pan.	45	54526	39	53850	34	54121	33	52994			26	49903	26	50627
Ecuador			2	446										
Peru	11	2117	269	169022	4	689	124	82458			7	879	59	56573
Chile	127	37137	126	40921		12336	39	13492	6409		11	3985	21	8502
Australia	9	3179	52	14428	19	6854	40	10292	5986	15309	11	3375	29	12558
Manila	6	2402	21	15930							7	2031	19	17620
Hawaii	47	7052	56	16479	40	8426	52	13893	10169	10720	31	6683	42	15555
Other Pac. isl's	21	2439	28	5600	15	2551	14	2287	3705	2913	22	2522	15	1971
East Indies	9	3683	68	41750							10	3983	34	28805
China	55	24329	95	58207	58	31160	117	91987	17626		43	27110	79	72734
Erazil	1	392	2	686							5	2049		
Spain	1	181												
Italy	1	369												
France	31	10415				4562					18	7619	1	900
Great Eritain..	81	35334				22114			25833		21	11729		
Holland	6	3417				3080								
Hanse towns..	15	8399									7	2815		
Denmark..	1	330												

[32] British Columbia supplies of timber and salmon were largely supplanted by those of the adjoining U. S. territories.

[33] Operations began here by the American-Russian Com. Co., and in March 1853 the *Consort* arrived with the first cargo. Only 1,200 tons were brought that year; but depôts were formed at Sitka and Kodiak, with brick ice-houses at the leading trading towns in Cal., with capacity ranging from 400 to 1,300 tons, to be supplied by monthly vessels. Details in my *Hist. Alaska.* First eastern cargo, sadly wasted by equatorial heat, reported in *Cal. Courier,* July 13, 26, 1850. Growth of ice trade in *Sac. Union,* Nov. 3, 1855; Jan. 7, 14, 17, March 13, May 16, June 3, 1856; *Alta Cal.,* Oct. 26, 1854.

the Sierra. With the return of cheaper prices, whalers, which once resorted to the bay, began again to show appreciation of the facilities here offered for repairs. San Francisco naturally remained the objective point for ocean traffic, and consequently the great depôt in this respect; but for home products different distributary places arose to wrest from her this profitable business, and cloud her prospect for a time.

With the growth of wheat shipments, England became the leading customer, by taking one half of the total export to foreign countries, and returning about one sixth in direct imports. Hawaii stands next on the list, by contributing one fourth of the imports, nearly all in raw sugar, and receiving fully one fourth of its value in provisions and manufactures. China takes a large proportion of the flour, and most of the silver coin sent from here, returning chiefly tea and rice; while Japan shares in the silver and manufacturing export, and offers especially silk in exchange. Mexico requires mostly mining machinery and quicksilver; Central America requires flour, and in Australia canned fish find a market; while wood and iron manufactures compete with English ware. The position of San Francisco as the importing centre for the coast, and the exceptionally rich and varied productions of the state, and its superior advantages for many manufactures, have resulted in a coast trade, which during the two decades, 1856–76, grew sixfold in tonnage.[34]

The sudden rise of San Francisco in 1849–50, from an almost unknown village to a centre of maritime trade, stands unprecedented in the annals of navigation. The entries of vessels at the custom-house during the nine months ending December 1849 being over 700, and for the year ending June 1851 more than 850.[35]

[34] Compare notes for shipping, exports, and imports.

[35] A statement of the collector at S. F. on Nov. 10, 1849, places the arrivals since April 1st at 697, of which 401 were American, with a tonnage of 87,494, and 296 foreign, tonnage 32,823, including some vessels which made more than one visit, such as mail steamers and coasters; several men-of-war

Most of those arriving during the first twelve months
were left to swing at anchor in the bay, untenanted,
also entered. Only 312 vessels were then recorded as lying there, while the
gov. agent, King, hastily placed the number in June at over 300. Between
Apr. 12, 1849, and Jan. 29, 1850, 805 vessels were reported, of which 487 were
American; and for the year ending Apr. 15, 1850, 1,113 vessels, 695 being
American. For the year ending June 30, 1851, the entries were 861, with a
tonnage of 258,128, of which 379 were American, while the clearances were
1,330, mostly American. See third note following; *U. S. Gov. Doc.*, Cong. 32,
Sess. 1; *Sen. Rep.*, i. pt. xiv. 3–4; *Id.*, Cong. 31, Sess. 1, Sen. Doc. 3, v.;
Pioneer Arch., 169–82; *King's Rept*, 7; *Buffum's Six Mo.*, 124; *S. F. Her-
ald*, June 12, Dec. 25, 1850; *Alta Cal.*, 1849–50, passim; *Pac. News*, Dec.
1849, and passim; *S. F. Directory*, 1852, 10–11, 14; *Niles' Reg.*, lxxv. 400;
Lancey's Cruise, 87; *Willey's Per. Mem.*, MS., 82–4; *Winans' Stat.*, MS., 4;
Dean's Stat., MS., 1–2; *Amer. Q. Regist.*, ii. 115–20; *Polynesian*, v. 166; *Pan.
Star*, i. no. 1, etc.; *Friend*, vii., passim; *Williams' Early Rec.*, MS., 12; *Sayward; S. F. Picayune*, 1850, passim. *Hunt's Merch. Mag.*, xxii. 208, gives the
departures from U. S. Atlantic ports by Dec. 25, 1849, at 775. Nearly 60
sails entered during the 48 hours ending Nov. 24th. *Sac. Transcript*, Nov. 29,
1850. S. F. was in 1850 the fourth city in the U. S. by tonnage entries. *Cal.
Jour. Sen.*, 1852, 653–4.

Arrivals and departures at San Francisco for the civil years 1851–6, from
custom-house reports and summaries in *Prices Current, Mercantile Gazette, Alta
Cal., Herald, Bulletin*, and other journals.

	Arrivals.		Clearances.	
	Vessels.	Tonnage.	Vessels.	Tonnage.
1851. Totals.......................	847	245,678	1,315	422,043
1852. American arrivals from abroad...	346	188,575	405	216,642
Foreign arrivals from abroad....	450	229,603	387	121,340
Coasters, domestic and whalers..	351	196,282	833	115,462
	1,147	514,460	1,625	453,444
1853. U. S. from abroad..............	179	112,066	481	338,407
Foreign from abroad............	381	119,000	416	131,433
Coasters, etc..................	466	327,036	756	170,232
	1,026	558,102	1,653	640,072
1854. Totals.......................	620	406,114	1,193	515,861
1855. U. S. from abroad..............	210	127,321	328	254,575
Foreign from abroad............	135	50,166	145	54,019
Coasters, etc..................	479	234,599	548	133,193
	824	412,086	1,021	441,787
1856. U. S. from abroad..............	168	109,919	283	255,771
Foreign from abroad............	113	39,698	115	42,783
Coasters, etc..................1,174		290,498	885	147,313
	1,455	440,015	1,283	445,867

The marked differences between some of these numbers is due partly to
the destruction of the earlier custom-house records, the neglect to duly distinguish coasting vessels from domestic arrivals, or even to record them, and
mistakes in summaries. Thus *Alta Cal.* and *Merc. Gazette* assign for 1853,
1854, and 1855 arrivals of 1,902, 1,893, and 1,606 (or 1,520), respectively.
And for the year ending Dec. 20, 1850, the *S. F. Herald*, Dec. 25, 1850, gives
598 American and only 58 foreign arrivals.

for the gold-smitten crews hurried off to the mines, regardless of wages or remonstrances. In July 1850 fully 500 abandoned vessels lay rocking in front of the city, some with cargoes undisturbed, for it did not pay to unload with costly labor upon a glutted market. A number were accordingly sent up the Sacramento and San Joaquin rivers, where it was hoped to sell the goods, while saving transport charges.[36] Many were sold for port dues and broken up for building material; others were hauled ashore and converted into stores and lodging-houses; still others rotted and sank at

	Arrivals.		Clearances.	
	Steamers.	Tonnage.	Steamers.	Tonnage.
1852. U. S. from abroad............ 69		72,441	66	68,511
Foreign from abroad........... 1		389	2	778
Coasters 57		46,046	90	57,758
1853. U. S. from abroad............ 66		82,415	64	82,088
Coasters..... 38		41,025	108	69,305

Arrivals and departures in California, according to the *U. S. Commerce and Navig. Reports,* for the year ending June 30th, chiefly San Francisco:

	Entries.				Clearances.			
	U. S. Vessels.	Tonnage.	Foreign Vessels.	Tonnage.	U. S. Vessels.	Tonnage.	Foreign Vessels.	Tonnage.
1849–50....	140	47,950	355	82,914	303	104,266	320	75,862
1850–1 * ...	379	115,779	482	142,349	815	293,435	515	136,735
1851–2 † ...	342	145,893	376	115,459	486	233,810	420	127,062
1852–3 ‡ ...	216	120,211	444	137,817	456	297,110	465	149,391
1853–4 § ...	184	123,351	271	97,835	418	328,511	301	104,335
1854–5 ‖ ...	208	128,713	135	52,220	379	266,703	160	61,414
1855–6 ¶ ...	194	125,137	127	46,003	312	259,042	127	49,216

* Of which 12 entered and 13 cleared from S. Diego, and 2 entered and cleared from Monterey.

† The entries at other ports were 29 at S. Diego, 6 at Monterey, and 1 at Sacramento; the clearances were 13 from S. Diego and 4 at Monterey.

‡ Outside entries were 3 at S. Diego and 1 at Monterey; the clearances, 3 and 4, respectively.

§ Entries, at S. Diego 1, Monterey 9; clearances, 6 from Monterey.

‖ Entries at S. Diego 3, Monterey 1, Sonoma 7; clearances, 5, 7, and 6, respectively.

¶ Entries, at Sonoma 4, S. Pedro 1; clearances, 3 and 2, respectively.

[36] At S. F. 526 are said to have been counted at anchor in the early part of 1850, and 120 in or near the two upper rivers. Threescore at Benicia, says the *Solano Co. Hist.*, 164; *Findla's Stat.*, MS., 9; *Pierce's Rough Sketch*, MS., 108–10. The list in *Alta Cal.*, of July 1, 1850, places the number then in the harbor at 512, of which 149 were full-rigged ships, 158 barks, 128 brigs, 70 schooners, and 3 steamers. The greater proportion were registered in the U. S., New York claiming 60 and Boston 57. Of foreign vessels, Gt Britain claimed fully a score, including Irish hulks; Australia about the same number, including New Zealand; East Indies 2, China 2, Hawaii 9, Chili 11, Peru 12, Central American states 4, Mexico 4. As for the European continent, almost every maritime county was represented: Portugal 1, Italy 1, France several, Austria 1, Holland 2, Germany half a score, Russia 2. From other countries passengers had come by way of England and the U. S. Besides this number, about 100 were lying at the upper ports of the bay. The *Saratoga*, with 2,400 tons of freight, stood in the front rank of early large ships. *S. F. Picayune*, Aug. 24, 1850. *Cal. Courier* reports on June 1, 1850, at S. F., 635 vessels, and

their moorings.[37] Toward the close of 1850, the return of disappointed miners permitted the engagement of crews with which to spread the long-folded sails.[38]

The decline in immigration and placer mining had their effect on shipping, which fell off rapidly after 1853, until it reached the low figure of 147,000 tons for 1857–8; but with the gradual increase of population and the development of resources, especially the growth of cereals, it began to rise again, until over 1,000,000 tons stood recorded for 1881–2, but with a decrease to less than 700,000 tons for 1888–9. The civil war, the overland railway competition, and other causes served as a check on American vessels in favor of foreign. This is mainly due to the increase of the wheat export, for in other respects the preponderance is in favor of the United States. The coast traffic has encouraged the acquisition of vessels, of which 887 were enrolled and registered by 1882, including 170 steamboats. The constancy of the winds on this coast favors the use of sails.[39]

148 at Sac. and other bay and river ports. *Hunt's Mag.*, xxiii. 324. In Feb. 1851 the *Sac. Transcript*, Feb. 14, 1851, reports 547 vessels at S. F., of which 374 were American and 90 British.

[37] As instanced in the chapter on S. F. *Placer Times*, May 13, 1850, and *Sac. Transcript*, June 29, 1850, show that out of more than 80 vessels entered there, 33 were used for stores; while the *Annals S. F.*, 208, 223, 355, claims 148 store-ships at S. F. in Oct. 1851. Concerning condemned vessels, see *U. S. Gov. Doc.*, Cong. 31, Sess. 1, H. Ex. Doc. 17, 800, 928. Vessels were sold for ridiculous prices. *Polynesian*, vii. 34; *Henshaw's Events*, MS., 9. Concerning harbor obstruction by sunken vessels, *S. F. Bulletin*, Jan. 27, 1857. By the spring of 1851 over 250 vessels had been transferred to owners at S. F. *Cal. Jour. Sen.*, 1852, 653–4.

[38] Hence the large excess of clearances, 1,330, over entries, 861, as shown in a preceding note. Yet even in Aug. 1850 sailors demanded $100 a month. *S. F. Herald*, Aug. 9, 21, 1850. Action of captains, etc., *Alta Cal.*, Dec. 15, 1849; *Pac. News*, Aug. 21–2, 1850; *Pierce's Sketch*, MS., 112.

[39] The variations in arrivals at S. F. from foreign countries show a decline in tonnage to 147,200 for 1857–8, followed by a sudden increase to 221,500 in 1858–9, with a fairly steady advance to 321,300 in 1864–5, to 443,700 in 1868–9, and after a decline to 353,500 in 1870–1, to 548,500 in 1872–3, to 720,400 in 1874–5; then several fluctuations between 621,000 and 724,000, and a sharp rise to 806,700 in 1880–1, and to 1,117,000 in 1881–2, under the large wheat shipments, followed by an abatement for three seasons, to which succeeded another rise. In 1885–6 the figure was 767,600 tons. The figure for 1881–2 includes 398 American vessels of 454,200 tons, and 524 foreign vessels of 662,700 tons, or 922 vessels in all, of which 83 in ballast. In 1885–6 there were 438 American and 259 foreign vessels. San Diego swells the amount for

The stimulus imparted to trade by the gold rush, while affecting all other carrying routes by the diversion of vessels, especially of whalers, led to a strong demand for fast sailers, owing to the distance and the high prices ruling at the new market. American builders responded by an adaptation of their clipper models, hitherto used only for smaller craft, to large ships, whose shapely outlines, with sharp bows, tall masts, and spread of canvas, eclipsed all rivals in beauty and speed. Several of them reduced the passage from New York to less than three months, and paid for themselves in one or two trips.[40] Steam-

1881–2 with 60 American and 29 foreign vessels of 62,700 tons. The clearances at S. F. for 1881–2 stand at 461 American and 531 foreign vessels, of 1,200,000 tons; at San Diego, 63 vessels of 26,000 tons. Of steamers S. F. received 123 American of 242,100 tons, and 84 foreign of 170,600 tons, clearing 199 of 401,600 tons. S. F. shared the bay cargoes with a number of towns. Of the 356 vessels laden with grain and flour, 103 loaded at S. F., 97 at Vallejo, 84 at Port Costa, 33 at Oakland, 31 at Benicia, and the rest elsewhere. Of this fleet 191 were British, 123 American, 22 German, 14 French, 3 Norwegian, 2 Italian, and 1 Dutch. Arrivals from Atlantic domestic ports declined to 110,000 tons, rising to 157,000 in 1859, falling off under the union war to 91,000 tons in 1865. By 1869 they had advanced to 161,000, but now with the opening of the overland railway came a diminution to 68,000 by 1871, after which the growth of population assisted to raise the figure to 150,000 in 1877. The subsequent additional railway competition has naturally tended to check shipments by sea. Coast traffic, on the other hand, shows a steady increase from 158,000 tons of shipping to 320,000 in 1866, to 625,000 in 1871, 941,000 in 1876, and still further subsequently, although with some fluctuations, due partly to increasing railway communications. There has consequently been a rapid increase in the control of vessels, so that in 1881–2 their number stood at 887, of 211,100 tons, of which 188 were registered, 574 enrolled, and 125 licensed; 656 were sailing vessels, 170 steamers of 75,400 tons, and 61 barges of 8,200 tons. *U. S. Com. and Navig.*, passim; *S. F. Cust.-Ho. Lists; S. F. Directories;* Harbor-master's Reports, in *S. F. Municip. Reports*, 1859 et seq.; *U. S. Bureau of Statistics.*

[40] The passage of the average vessel was 150 days from the Atlantic U. S. ports, *S. F. Trade List*, Jan. 14, 1853, hence it proved a revelation when, in 1851, the *Flying Cloud* made the passage from N. Y. to S. F., 13,610 nautical miles, in 89 days, sailing 374 miles in one day. In 1853, the *Flying Dutchman* made the voyage from N. Y. to S. F. and back in six months and 21 days, including the time occupied in discharging and loading. The *Trade Wind* sailed from S. F. to N. Y. in 75 days. The voyage from S. F. to Sydney was made in 38 days in 1875, from S. F. to Liverpool in 86¾ days in 1860, etc. *McCarty, Annual Statistician*, 1880–1, 566; *Alta Cal.*, Aug. 2, 1852; Jan. 17, 1853; Sept. 29, 1854; *Hunt's Mag.*, xiv. 64; *S. F. Herald*, July 3, 1850; June 1, 1852; *Placer Times*, Sept. 15, 1851. Races were frequent. *S. F. Whig*, July 23, 1853. The freight demanded by them ruled for a long time at $50 per ton on certain goods, which was three or four times the rate that had been paid for such distances. Their names were frequently suggestive, as shown above. Concerning the fate of the early clippers, see under wrecks, and in *S. F. Call*, Apr. 28, 1886.

ers, which had so far entered little into freight traffic on the ocean, began to join in the competition, a number being especially built for this trade, besides those of the Pacific Mail Steamship company, which opened regular communication in February 1849, as described elsewhere. Early in 1851, fourscore steamers, measuring 19,600 tons, were connected with California, twenty-three plying on the ocean, fifteen running southward, chiefly to Panamá, and seven northward, including three of the semi-monthly Oregon mail line. In 1852, the southern lines were increased by four steamers of the Nicaragua route, after which no material change took place in the foreign steamship traffic for a considerable time,[41] yet several lines were proposed for China, Australia, and Hawaii, of which only the last obtained a partial realization during this period.[42] Meanwhile, sailing packets maintained a steady connection with these and other countries.[43]

Steamers could always be found for occasional trips in different directions. In 1866 a line opened to the Hawaiian Islands,[44] which subsequently became a way-

[41] The *Alta Cal.*, March 15, 1853, enumerates 83 steamers, of which 60 belonged to the inland fleet, including tow-boats, consuming over 2,000 tons of coal monthly. On Dec. 23d, no less than 14 steamers were lying at Central wharf. *Id.*, Dec. 24, 1850; *S. F. Picayune*, Oct. 16, 1850. A rival line was projected in 1850. *Pac. News*, Jan. 10–12, 1850. In 1853 there were 18 ocean steamers. *Annals S. F.*, 494–5. *S. F. Directory*, 1852, 25, names 20, embracing three lines to Panamá, of which two had only three steamers. See also advertisements in *S. F. Trade List*, 1852–3.

[42] Three steamers preparing for experimental voyage to the Islands, the first link toward China, as *Sac. Transcript*, Feb. 28, May 15, 1851, expresses it. See also *Placer Times*, Nov. 30, 1851; *Polynesian*, vii. 158. The first left Dec. 23d, says *S. F. Herald*, Dec. 16, 1851. Steam communication with China was advocated in 1848 in connection with the Panamá line, *Hunt's Merch. Mag.*, xviii. 467–76, xxix. 549–59, and repeatedly pressed before congress, although for several years in vain. An English steamer came from China in Oct. 1849. *Williams' Rec.*, MS., 12; *U. S. Gov. Doc.*, Cong. 31, Sess. 2, H. Com. Rept 34; H. Ex. Doc. 1, pp. 208–9, with favorable reports; *Cal. Jour. Ass.*, 1854, 671; Speeches, etc., in favor, *Thompson's Mem.*, 1–16; *Latham's Speech*, 1855, 1–15; *De Bow's Rev.*, Oct. 1855, 456; *Alta Cal.*, Apr. 7, 14, Aug. 2, 1854; Nov. 9, 1855. The last-named authority has remarks also upon an Australian line.

[43] Instance the irregular vessels from China in 1850–1, in *Sac. Transcript*, Oct. 14, 1850; Feb. 28, 1851; *Polynesian*, vii. 150, with passages as low as 34 days; *Daily Balance*, Jan. 30, 1851. A regular packet for China began in 1852. *S. F. Herald*, Sept. 24, 1852; July 26, Aug. 3, 1850; Hawaiian and Mexican packets, in *Alta Cal.*, Sept. 4, Oct. 6, 1856; New York packets, etc.; *Coleman's Stat.*, MS., 166.

[44] By the Cal. Navig. Co., monthly, *S. F. Bull.*, Jan. 12, 1866; a failure, *Hayes' R. R. Arch.*, v. 165.

station for Australian packets, and has, since the treaty of 1875, been provided with an additional special line.[45] The filibuster war in Nicaragua cut off the only powerful rival of the Panamá line, leaving it soon in almost undisputed control of the profitable traffic with the Atlantic states and Mexico. A subsidy from the postal service encouraged it to inaugurate in 1867 a monthly connection with China by way of Japan, which soon expanded into a traffic[46] so remunerative as to bring a rival upon that route. A subsidy contract with the Australian governments maintained the branch line to Australia.[47] The opening of the overland railway proved a severe blow to the Isthmus traffic. Then come disasters, stock jobbing, and bribery further to reduce its importance.[48]

[45] The Oceanic, which extends to Australia, besides sailing lines. *Hayes' Pac. Interests*, pt. i.-ii.; *Hawaii Almanacs*, and *Customs Statistics, Spreckel's Pac. Lines*, MS.; Treaty, in *U. S. Statutes*, 1874–5, 69–71; *McCorkle's Speech on Annexation*, Wash., 1852.

[46] Especially in carrying coolies. This raised an outcry from anti-Chinese parties, and the subsidy was lost after a few years. *S. F. & China Communic.*, 1–7; *U. S. Govt Doc.*, Cong. 41, Sess. 2, Sen. Misc. Doc. 34, 128, on growing profits; Cong. 43, Sess. 1, Sen. Rept 286, Misc. Doc. 102; H. Id., 74, 213, 275; H. Rept 598; Sess. 2, Sen. Rept 674; H. Rept 268, Sen. Misc. Doc. 83, all with pro and contra arguments. *Congress. Globe*, 1874–5, 120; *S. F. Chamber Com.*, 1870, 28–30. Petitions for such a line, in *U. S. Govt Doc.*, chiefly Misc. Doc. since Cong. 35; Acts 1865, 14–15; *Latham's Speeches*, 1–13; *Cal. Steam Mail*, 3–104; *S. F. Times*, Dec. 31, 1866; Jan. 3, 1867. The Occidental and Oriental S. Co. a few years later opened a monthly rival line in connection with the overland railway. Treaty with Japan, in *Perry's Exped.*, i. 379; *U. S. Govt Doc.*, Cong. 33, Sess. 2, Sen. Doc. 10; Cong. 36, Sess. 1, Mess. & Doc., i. 8–9; *S. F. Times*, Aug. 3, Sept. 2, 1868.

[47] Supplanted in 1883 by the Oceanic line, under a new contract with New South Wales and New Zealand. See under mails; *S. F. Call*, Jan. 22, 26, 1882; May 25, 1871. The first through-mail had come in 1870. *S. F. Alta*, May 6, 1870; *S. F. Post*, Nov. 1, 1873; *Cal. Jour. Sen.*, 1869–70, ap. 56.

[48] Its vicissitudes are depicted in *Roberts' Navig.*, MS., 5 et seq.; *Williams' Pac. Mail*, MS.; *Simpson's Stat.*, MS.; *Lloyd's Lights*, 423–7; *Hayes' Cal. Notes*, iii. 116; *Com. and Ind.*, 200–2. Concerning additional Mexican steamers and treaties, see *Hist. Mex.*, vi., this series. Steamer lines to Alaska are treated under coast traffic. *U. S. Com. Rel.* contain the best annual account of foreign trade.

CHAPTER VII.

INLAND AND OVERLAND TRAFFIC.

1848–1888.

DURING Mexican times, traffic along the coast was
conducted by foreign trading vessels. This privilege
was not permissible under United States laws, but
owing to the lack of other vessels the military government countenanced it[1] during 1849. On the bay a
few whale-boats and sloops had maintained regular
communication with different settlements, especially
Sutter's Fort.[2] With the rush for the mines anything
available for navigation was impressed, and several

---

[1] Petitions in *Cal. Star and Cal.*, Dec. 16, 1848. Collector Collier in Nov.
1849 notified the authorities that he must revoke the coast-trade license of
foreign vessels. *U. S. Gov. Doc.*, Cong. 31, Sess. 1, H. Ex. Doc. 17, p. 35; *Id.*,
Sen. Doc. 47, viii. 86.

[2] A small schooner manned by six Indians made tri-weekly trips from S.
F., and two smaller craft joined at times. The schooner was the *Sacramento*,
bought from the Russ.-Amer. Co. It was converted later into a roofed house
for salmon fishers. The other two were the *Indian Queen*, a sloop of 10 tons,
and the *White Pinnace*, an open yawl, which occasionally brought down hides,
etc., from Feather River, and ascended to the Stanislaus in the other direction. *Placer Times*, May 13, 1850. Cordua advertised in the *Californian*, Apr.
26, 1848, a monthly launch for Feather River. The *Stockton* traded weekly with
Sonoma, and launches passed up to Napa, all touching at way-places, and
some connecting with wagons for interior ranchos. There was a ferry across
Carquinez. *Id.*, Feb. 16, 1848; *Richardson's Explor.*, MS., 11–12; *Dean's Stat.*,
MS., 4; *Cal. Star*, Feb. 26, 1848.

craft made lucrative trips to Sacramento[3] until the
steamboats sent out by enterprising eastern firms absorbed at least the conveyance of passengers.

The pioneer of this class was a tiny side-wheel craft,
brought from Sitka in 1847, and wrecked within a few
weeks.[4] The next appears to have been the *Washington,* launched in August 1849 at Benicia, which
met a similar fate after a few trips below and above
Sacramento. She was followed by the *Sacramento,*[5]

[3] Men gladly paid $50 for the privilege of working their passage, or even
$200, says Crosby, *Stat.,* MS., 14–15; *Cassin's Stat.,* MS., 5. Barges for han-
dling freight sold for $4,000, while a ship was worth $30.000. *Williams' Stat.,*
MS., 9; *Dean's Stat.,* MS., 3; *Sac. Directory,* 1853, 5. Passage rates were at
times below $20. Incidents of trips in *Kip's Sketches,* 13–16.

[4] Fully described in *Hist. Cal.,* vol., v., 575–9, this series It ran subse-
sequently as the yacht *Rainbow* on the Sacramento.

[5] Concerning the second bay steamer there is much dispute. The *S. F.
Annals,* 235, followed with slight variation by a number of writers, including
Hittell, *Cal.,* ii. 731, claim the credit for the *Pioneer,* an iron boat brought
from Boston and launched at S. F., 'the first that had penetrated so far into
the interior,' as the Sac. River. *S. F. Directory,* 1852, 11, places the launching in Oct.; the others intimate Sept. But from the contemporary evidence
of journals, it appears that the claim must be awarded to a little side-wheel
boat, 80 feet by 18, with an engine of twelve-horse power, and drawing 20
inches, which was launched at Benicia early in August 1849. In *McKinstry's
Papers,* MS., 19, she is called the *Pioneer.* She reached Sac. Aug. 17th.
Placer Times, Aug. 18, 1849. After two trips to Sac. she was sold, and put
on the route between this town and Marysville, but was wrecked on a snag
in Feather River in Sept. This wreck is identified in the contemporary
Placer Times of Oct. 5, 1849, as the *Geo. Washington,* returning from Vernon
to Sac., the name becoming confused with the *Lady Washington,* a steam
scow, which a widely quoted pioneer writer in *S. F. Bulletin,* Feb. 21, 1868,
also declares to have been the second steamboat, although he has her launched
at Sac. in Sept. She was the first to ascend above Sac., going to Coloma.
She was raised and renamed the *Ohio.* In *Solano Co. Hist.,* 159, the first Benicia boat is called *New England,* and by Moore, *Exper.,* MS., 2, the *Colusa.*
The name *Pioneer* may have been attributed to her afterwards, from being a
pioneer boat. Still others identify her with the *Edward Everett, Jr,* a wheeled,
flat-bottomed boat, brought out from Boston by the company which arrived
in the *Edward Everett,* and launched at Benicia on Aug. 12th. Reached Sac.
on Aug. 11th, says Culver, *Sac. Directory,* 74. In July, it is intimated in
the contemporary record of the *Polynesian,* vi. 71. After three trips the
engine was sold to Nevada miners, and the hull for a ferry at Fremont. *S. F.
Chronicle,* Aug. 22, 1878; *Wilmington Journal,* Apr. 8, 1863; *Preble's Hist.
Steam Navig.,* 404. The *Solano Co. Hist.,* 159, declares this boat to have
been the second or third launched at Benicia, and in *McKinstry's Pap.,* 19, a
second is alluded to as on the stocks when the *Pioneer* was floated. Ball, in
Sac. Directory, 1871, 103, upholds J. Van Pelt as the first steamboat captain
on the river, and the *Sacramento* as the first steamer, launched at Sacramento
in Sept. *Placer Times,* Aug. 18, 1849, distinctly mentions this boat, under
Van Pelt, as subsequent to the Benicia boat. She was placed on the S. F.
route, but too weak to face the bay waves, she connected at New York of
the Pacific with the schooner *John L. Day,* the total trip taking from 18 to
32 hours, freight $50 per ton, fare $30. *Sac. Illust.,* 8. He applies also the
name *Sacramento* to the next steamer, 'the *Pioneer* of the *Ed. Everett* com-

also plying on the river of that name to the head of
steamboat navigation, until the appearance in Octo-

pany,' while others confuse the *Pioneer* with Ball's *Sacramento*. The latter
was a ferry at Sac. as late as Jan. 1851. The *Placer Times* vaguely alludes
to a *Sacramento* prior to Van Pelt's, but it looks doubtful. Benicia undoubtedly
launched the first steamer, and as one was evidently running below Sac.
when the *Washington* was wrecked, at least two must have existed before Oct.
Further, as this *Washington* was made the pioneer boat above Sacramento,
after having performed a few trips on the lower and more important part of
the river, she must have been replaced by another, namely, Van Pelt's craft,
which may therefore be placed third. The next place is contested by the
Yuba, a scow intended for dredging, but used for traffic on the upper river,
and sold for $40,000. *Ball*, ubi sup. However this may be, there are clear
records in Oct. for the three most notable of early steamboats, the *Mint*, a
small, careening, yet fast craft, which made its trial trip on Oct. 9th from S. F.
to Sac.; the *McKim*, of 400 tons, by ocean from New Orleans, which left S. F.
on Oct. 26th, and arrived at Sac. in 17 hours. *Placer Times*, Nov. 3, 1849.
She made $16,000 in one trip on this route, but was sold in 1855 for $600,
S. F. Bulletin, Dec. 26, 1855; and the famous *Senator*, a still larger and faster
vessel, which reached Sac. on Nov. 8th. *Id.*, Nov. 10th. During the first
year her net profits exceeded $60,000 a month. *Matthewson's Stat.*, MS., 2;
Ryckman's Vig., MS., 6–7; *Cal. Assoc. Pioneers*, N. Y., 1875, 45–6; *Williams'
Stat.*, MS., 12; *Alameda Gaz.*, March 8, 1873, and other journals. Among
other early boats were the *Merrimac*, first to reach Stockton, *S. Joaq. Co. Hist.*,
23; the second place being disputed by *Gen. Sutter, Mint,* and *M. White;*
the *Lawrence*, which followed in Nov., and then passed to Marysville; the
propellor *Hartford*, appearing in Dec.; the *Linda*, put in Dec. upon the
upper Sac. route; the *El Dorado*, arriving at Sac. in Jan. 1850; the *New
World*, which had escaped from the sheriff at New York; the *Firefly*, April
1850; the *Ætna*, claimed by *Placer Times*, Apr. 22, 1850, to have first ascended the American; the *Gold Hunter*, May 1850, later on the Oregon route;
Lucy Long, which first ascended above Feather River, *Ben. Tribune*, Feb. 14,
1874; *Jack Hays*, first to reach Tehama in May, *Placer Times*, May 22, 1850,
S. F. Bulletin, Feb. 21, 1868; the *Capt. Sutter*, a Stockton trader; the *Napa
City*, trading to the place of that name; the *Major Thompkins*, which exploded
Jan. 1851; the *Santa Clara, Fashion, Phœnix, West Point, N. B. Reading;
Mariposa*, sunk Oct. 1850; *Gov. Dana*, of the spring of 1850; *Confidence, Cali-
fornia, Georgina, Maunsel White; Butte*, to run to Butte City in May 1850,
*Placer Times; Antelope, Wilson G. Hunt, Benicia, H. T. Clay, Erastus Corning,
Star, Tehama, Wm Robinson;* and the *Sagamore*, exploded Oct. 1850. To
these are added the *Union, Missouri, Ion, Chesapeake, C. W. Grinnel, Martha
Jane, Libertad, Com. Jones, New England, Kennebec, Gen. Warren, Victor Constant, New Star, San Joaquin, Jenny Lind*, and *New Orleans*, by a special letter
of Jan. 1851 to *Hunt's Merchants' Mag.*, xxiv. 545–6, 549, which states that
270 other craft were engaged in the river trade. Of the regular lines in Dec.
1850, 8 boats were running from S. F. to Sac., 7 to Stockton, 3 to San José,
3 from Sac. to Marysville, others going less regularly beyond, in different directions. I will not pass beyond 1850 for further names, but may add that
the *San Joaquin* claims to have first reached Red Bluff, in 1853, the *Express*
meanwhile trading to Monroeville. *Sac. Bee*, Aug. 24, 1869; *Alta Cal.*, May
1, 1854. The first Oakland ferry was the *Hector*, the Contra Costa Ferry Co.
being subsequently organized, with *E. Corning* for ferry. *Alameda Gaz.*, May
31, 1873. Klamath navigation was projected in 1850. *Sac. Transcript*, Oct.
14, 1850. Borthwick, *Cal.*, 95–7, and Farwell, *Stat.*, MS., 1–3, explain con-
cisely how Cape Horn was weathered by the first steamers. The names of
the steamers, etc., are found in *Alta Cal., Pac. News, Cal. Courier, S. F. Herald*, and other journals for the time, especially the *Placer Times*. See also
Boyton's Stat., MS., 1; *Sac. Directory*, 1853–4, 18; *Carson's Early Rec.*, 23;

ber of the large steamers *McKim* and *Senator*, which
absorbed this passenger traffic, and drove inferior
boats of the now fast-growing fleet to minor routes
within the bay, and the light-draught ones up the
river and into the American, the Feather, and the
Yuba. The head of navigation on the Sacramento
was rapidly extended to Colusa. The *Jack Hays* ascended, in May 1850, to Trinidad City, close to Red
Bluff, which became the head soon after,[6] and the San
Joaquin was navigated for 150 miles above Stockton,
at high water.[7] With a monopoly of routes for a time,
several of the boats made fortunes, as well they might,
with passenger rates averaging $25 to Sacramento, and
freight $50 a ton.[8] Yet by September 1850, competi-
tion offered to reduce the fare to even $1,[9] and Cali-
fornia builders were beginning to increase the number
of boats navigated round Cape Horn, or brought in
sections as cargo, so that before the close of 1850 the
inland fleet embraced some four dozen steamers.[10] In

Wakeman's Log, 114–38, 220; *Stockton Indep.*, Aug. 3, 17, 1878; *S. F. Call*,
Nov. 29, 1885; *Crosby's Stat.*, MS., 54; *Wood's Pioneer*, MS., 13; *Connor's
Stat.*, MS., 6; *Warren's Dust*, 146; *McCollum's Cal.*, 64. The *New World* re
duced the trip to Sac. to 6 hours and 3 m. *Alta Cal.*, Jan. 10, 1852. *Id.*, of
Aug. 31, 1849, has a long list of sailing vessels running up the Sac. and S.
Joaq. Crary, *Stat.*, MS., 1–3, gives the history of the Union steam line.

[6] See preceding note. Yet Marysville was, in the autumn of 1850, deprived
by low water of its steamers, which lay too deep. *Sac. Transcript*, Aug. 30,
1850.

[7] Navigated by steam to Fresno, observes *S. F. Bull.*, June 8, 1859. The
Mokelumne was early ascended by boats and sailing vessels. In 1862 the
steamboat *Pert* reached Lockeford, and a company formed to continue the
traffic, aided by a river improvement franchise, charging 10 cents per ton on
freight. but the railway soon came to check the enterprise. *S. Joaq. Hist.*,
36–9, 134.

[8] *Taylor's Eldorado*, ii. 46–7. To Stockton $40, says *Bauer's Stat.*, MS., 3.
From Sacramento to Marysville, in Jan. 1850, the *Lawrence* charged $25 fare,
and 8 cents per pound for freight. *Marysville Direct.*, 1855, p. v.

[9] *S. F. Picayune*, Sept. 19, 1850. By the end of 1849, says Buffum, *Six
Months*, 123–4, there were 10 or 12 bay steamers. A year later, about 50
steamers were employed in the river trade of the state, according to *Sac.
Transcript*, Jan. 14, 1851, of which 15 plied above Sac. in the spring of
1850, *Id.*, Apr. 26, 1850; and 9 between Stockton and S. F. by Nov. *Cal.
Courier*, Nov. 16, 1850.

[10] Culver enumerates 9 running between S. F. and Sac., and 10 above Sac.
Sac. Directory, 84. *Alta Cal.*, March 15, 1851, mentions 60 inland boats, including tow-boats. Steamboat-building in Happy valley, says *Pac. News*,
Apr. 30, 1850, the material being introduced. Williams, *Rec.*, MS., 13, declares *Capt. Sutter* as the first boat built on the bay. Trial trip, Nov. 16,

1854, the leading owners combined to form the California Steam Navigation company, with the view to better control the traffic and earnings, while appeasing the taxed public with at least a superior system.[11] For two decades the bay and river steamers flourished, till the opening of railways reduced most of them to mere freight carriers, with diminished profits and importance.

This system extended also to coast traffic, which, aside from sailing vessels, had been supplied by the Panamá mail line, and after 1851 also by the Nicaragua packets, on the route south of San Francisco, and northward to the Columbia, by connecting steamers. Rivals were ever prepared to meet additional demand for service, and finally a special regular line was opened to Humboldt Bay, Trinidad, and Crescent City, and still earlier, in 1851, one to San Diego and San Pedro, touching at Santa Bárbara, San Luis Obispo, and Monterey.[12]

1849. The *Paul Pry*, launched here in Dec. 1856, was perhaps the first steamer of exclusively Cal. manufacture. In my preceding vols are allusions to early ship-building, even on the Sacramento.

[11] Capital $2,500,000, in shares of $1,000. Incorp. Feb. 22, 1854. The corporation absorbed the bulk of the bay traffic during this and the following decade, with profits that enabled them to pay in dividends as much as 3 per cent monthly. The fare established to Sacramento and Stockton was $10 for cabin, $7 for deck; freight $8 and $6 per ton; to Marysville, $15 per ton. The public protested against the monopoly, but it proved all-powerful. Report upon its condition in 1855, in *Cal. Jour. Sen.*, 1856, ap. xxi. 1–12; *S. F. Argonaut*, June 22, 1878; *Observations*, MS., 5 et seq., by Low, one of the directors; also a later chapter. See also *Prices Current*, Sept. 9, 1854.

[12] This one, long owned by Wright, was in 1856 transferred to the Cal. Steam Navig. Co., which then controlled, besides two bay steamers, the Crescent City line. *S. F. Directory*, 1856, 128. The pioneer of the southern line was the *Ohio*, Jan. 1851, followed by the *Sea Bird*, as the most regular, both running for several years. The *Goliah, Southerner, Isthmus, Fremont, America, Republic*, and *Senator* shared in the traffic, some as rivals, others as substitutes. *Hayes' Angeles Arch.*, MS., v. 330–67; *Hawley's Angeles*, 23. In Dec. 1850 the *Goliah, Chesapeake*, and *Gen. Warren* were running to Gold Bluff. *Hunt's Mag.*, xxiv. 545. In 1851 there were seven steamers on the northern coast, including the Oregon mail packets. *Alta Cal.*, March 15, 1851. Among them were the *Gold Hunter* and *Sea Gull. Pac. News*, Jan. 15, 1851; and *Hunt's Mag.*, May 1850, 545. In 1854 efforts were made to establish a line to Puget Sound. Concerning Mudd's scheming, see *Crane's Past*, 34–5. The Pacific Mail S. S. Co. sold its Oregon branch line, and gave the Oregon R. R. & Navig. Co., jointly with the Pacific Coast S. S. Co., plying more than a dozen steamers from San Diego on one side to Alaska on the other, touching at B. C. ports. A Humboldt and S. F. line was also started, and there were in 1888 a few independent steamers, one formerly belonging to the Eel River

The sudden and great expansion of maritime traffic upon waters little explored could not fail to be attended by many deplorable accidents. A large proportion of the vessels engaged in the California trade being old hulks, some of them entirely unfit for the voyage, it was only to be expected that several should collapse before a half-year's buffetings. Others suffered from the absence of good charts, and often from the inexperience and carelessness of inefficient captains. Notwithstanding this increase of unfavorable causes, the disasters to sailing craft were not so frequent as might have been expected. Much more startling were those connected with the comparatively few steam-vessels, which rose between 1849–54 to a score for the ocean lines, and of which seven were on this coast. The Vanderbilt company alone lost five, while the Pacific Mail company, with a much larger but finer fleet, had its first wreck only in 1853. This unprecedented record for steam navigation becomes the more glaring when we add the misfortunes of the river boats, embracing another score during the same six years, and with frequent loss of life, ranging above fifty. Some came to grief upon snags, some yielded to the flames, others collided, and still others exploded through the reprehensible passion for racing, the inferior boiler material, and the lack of efficient engineers.[13]

Co. Steamers began running to Alaska in 1867, the *Oriflamme* being the first. *S. F. Bull.*, Apr. 13, 1867. A regular line opened to Coos Bay in 1879. *Or. D. Zeitung*, Apr. 12, 1879. Act for a line to Crescent City. *Cal. Statutes.* 1863–4, 105–7. First descent of Klamath River. *Alta Cal.*, June 13, 1853. Steamer on Klamath Lake launched. *S. F. W. Call*, July 21, 1881. Steamer *Comet* on Lake Tahoe. See *Preble's Hist. Steam*, 253. Steamers plied on the Colorado in the fifties, *Hayes' S. Diego*, i. 181–3, 192–3, and a co. organized in 1865 for its navigation. *S. F. Call*, June 24, 1865; *Roberts' Navig.*, MS., 6 et seq.; *Woodward's Stat.*, MS., 22–3; *Moore, Pio. Exp.*, MS., 23–7.

[13] In the U. S. law of 1852, providing for steamboat inspectors, California was omitted as a district, and the local inspectors subsequently appointed had to refer decisions to New Orleans. *Crane's Past*, 31. In my preceding volumes are allusions to several wrecks along the coast, although at rare intervals, since so few vessels touched here; but with 1849 the list swells rapidly. All are not recorded, and I will name only the more noted instances. *Tonquin* and *Ascension*, in 1849; *Popmunett, Friendship, Crown Princess*, a foreign vessel, *Utica, Mary Jane, Frolic, Somerset, Marshall*, and *Brothers*, burned in 1850; *Arcadia, Buen Dia*, 1851; *Oxford, Sea Gull*, 1852; *Vandalia, Jenny Lind, Aberdeen, Willimantic, Carrier Pigeon, Eclipse*, 1853; *Golden Fleece*,

Navigation was long fettered, until hydrographic
and cognate surveys marked the way, and till improvements could be effected in harbors and rivers,

Walter Claxton, San Francisco, 1854. Losses in sailing vessels, involving
life as well as cargoes, may be placed at more than $3,000,000, additional
interest being attached to disasters suffered by the proportionately smaller
number of steamers. This list may be made more complete, and extended
even to casualties beyond the actual coast limit when involving California
ships. Their navigation began really in 1849, and so did their misfortunes,
headed by the propeller *Edith,* of the U. S. navy, which struck near Point
Concepcion in Aug. In May 1850, the *Commodore Preble* was wrecked near
Humboldt Bay; in July 1851, the *Union,* on the Lower California coast; in
Oct. 1851, *Chesapeake,* in Jan. 1852, *Sea Gull,* both near Humboldt Bay; a
week later the *Gen. Warren,* on the Oregon coast, with the loss of twoscore
lives. These five belonged to independent lines, and were valued at $50,000
each, except the *Union,* which was worth three times that sum. In Feb. and
Aug. 1852 Vanderbilt's Nicaragua line lost the *North America* and *Pioneer,*
below the California coast, involving values of $150,000 and $250,000, respectively. In Oct. 1852 the N. York and S. F. line lost the *City of Pittsburg,*
near Valparaiso, value $250,000, and in the same year was wrecked the *Com-
modore Stockton,* of the independent line, value $60,000. In 1853 Vanderbilt
lost three more steamers, the *Independence, S. S. Lewis,* and *Washington,* in
Feb., March, and April, respectively; the first at Margarita Island, the second
off S. F. Bay, the third off Mexico, the value of these inferior vessels being
about $70,000, $150,000, and $40,000, and the loss of life 150. In March
1853 the Pacific Mail S. S. Co. lost the *Tennessee,* off S. F., value $300,000, the
only important disaster met by this company during these early years. The
Winfield Scott, of N. Y. and S. F. line, value $290,000, was lost in Dec. 1853.
For the following year are to be recorded the disasters to the *Golden Gate*
(which suffered also in 1855), near Panamá, the *Yankee Blade,* near Point
Concepcion, the *Southerner,* near Columbia River, *Arizpe,* etc. See *Alta Cal.,*
and contemporary papers, for above years. Partial lists are in *Prices Current
and Ship List,* Apr. 29, 1853; *Helper's Land of Gold,* 28; *Hayes' Cal. Notes,*
iii. 78; *Hawley's Humboldt,* 29–30; *Scott's Speech,* 1858, 2–4. Among river
steamers a still larger number of casualties occurred, beginning in June 1850,
when the *Gold Hunter* ran into and sank the *McKim,* near Benicia. For
disasters of later years I refer to *Com. Rev.* and *U. S. Life Saving Service,*
annually. Other notable collisions took place between the *Mariposa* and *West
Point,* in Oct. 1850, near New York of the Pacific, the former sinking; between
the *J. Bragdon* and *Comanche,* in Jan. 1853, in the Carquinez strait, with loss
of life. Several similar accidents were recorded in the following years. In
Feb. 1851 three river steamboats, the *Missouri, Yuba,* and *Jack Hays,* were
snagged on the Sac., the first a total loss. In Jan. 1853 the *Comanche*
sank near Benicia, and in 1854 the regular Sac. boat *New World.* Two
steamboats, the *Santa Clara* and *Hartford,* were burned at Central wharf,
in March 1851, the former totally; in June 1855 the *America* succumbed in
the same manner at Crescent City. More startling and deplorable were the
explosions which destroyed so many steamboats, and always with loss of life,
in some instances over 50. The first to blow up was the *Sagamore,* at S. F., in
Oct. 1850, with fourscore killed and wounded; the *Major Thompkins,* in Jan.
1851, 2 killed; the *R. K. Page,* formerly the *Jack Hays,* in March 1853, two
dozen casualties, both on the Sacramento; the *Jenny Lind,* April 1853, on
S. F. Bay, south, casualties over 30; the *American Eagle* and *Stockton,* both
in Oct. 1853, on the San Joaquin, twoscore casualties on the former; the
Ranger, at Alameda, the *Secretary,* on the northern part of the bay, the *Helen
Hensley,* at S. F., all three in Jan. 1854; the *Secretary* had over 30 casualties.
Among the disasters in 1855–6 may be mentioned the *Pearl* and the *Belle,*
with over 50 and 30 casualties, respectively.

the latter filled with snags that caused many a disaster.[14] The expedition under Wilkes in 1841 did make a partial exploration, and the naval officers of 1846–8 extended it somewhat. In the latter year the war department directed a joint commission of officers to promptly explore the Pacific coast harbors and rivers for determining needful defences, depots, mail stations, and safeguards for navigation.[15] The California legislature and private enterprise coöperated in different directions, stimulated by the rewards of trade and the appeal of citizens.[16] Sacramento river attracted special attention owing to débris obstructions deposited by hydraulic mines in particular, which have stopped navigation and ruined farming land in many quarters. The ocean line was intrusted to the coast survey department, which began operation in 1849 under two parties, although the organization of the Pacific branch properly dates from the advent in 1850 of George Davidson and his party, whose services under adverse circumstances are marked no less by well-attested skill than by heroic devotion.[17]

[14] *Sac. Transcript,* Feb. 14, 1851; *Placer Times,* Oct. 5, 1849.

[15] *U. S. Govt Doc.,* Cong. 31, Sess. 1, H. Ex. Doc. 17, 266–71, 800–1; *Id., Sen. Doc.,* x.

[16] Instance the early improvements in the San Diego and Colorado rivers by the federal gov. *Id.,* Cong. 33, Sess. 1, H. Ex. Doc. 1, i. pt. iii.; *Hayes' Miscel.,* 80; *Id., S. Diego,* i. 31–2, 127–31, 178; the bills in *Cal. Jour. Sen.,* 1850, pp. 1302–6, for opening and improving different streams; the examination of Humboldt bay for a port whence to supply Trinity River mines and the subsequent founding of towns there. Details in *S. F. Journ. Com.,* Apr. 25, 1850; *Humboldt Times,* Feb. 7, 14, 1863; Apr. 15, 1876; *Overland,* i. 144–5; *West Coast Signal,* Feb. 14, Apr. 3, 1872; Jan. 10, 1877; *Pac. News,* May 22, Sept. 7, 1850. In connection with improvements of the San Joaquin, as instanced in *Cal. Jour. Ass.,* 1858, *Sen.,* 1860, ap. iii. 38, came the idea of a ship-canal to Stockton, which remained a project. *Stockton Indep.,* May 1870; *S. F. Call,* May 24, 1870; *U. S. Gov. Doc.,* Cong. 43, Sess. 1, H. Misc. Doc. 137. The débris agitation is considered elsewhere. A new outlet was proposed for the Sac. in 1867, and Capt. Eads came to plan a system similar to that of the Mississippi. The govt held aloof, however, until the débris question should be settled. *Id.,* Cong. 45, Sess. 2, Doc. 17; *Cal. Jour. Sen.,* 1867–8, ap. 80; *Eads' Report.* It was proposed in 1874 to turn San Diego River into False Bay, which was done. Concerning the lakes and their navigation, see *U. S. Gov. Doc.,* Cong. 47, Sess. 2, Sen. Misc. Doc. 46, p. 59; *Wheeler's Survey,* 1876, p. 189; 1877, p. 1287; *Savage's Doc.,* MS., ii. 124–7.

[17] The hydrographic labor began in 1849 under Lieut P. McArthur, U. S. N., and shore duty under Capt. J. S. Williams, assistant; but the anomalous conditions of the time, with high prices and desertion, gave little opportunity for work, and that chiefly by McArthur. The mouth of San Francisco

Among the results of these efforts were the light-houses, which from the first edifices in San Francisco bay spread in due time along the coast, although with provoking slowness.[18]   This harbor naturally received the earliest attention.   Buoys[19] began to be placed in

Bay and Mare Island harbor were examined, and the coast from Monterey to the Columbia River.   This ill success obliged the sending out of younger officers, stimulated by ambition to make a record.   Geo. Davidson accepted the responsibility, was raised to assistant in charge, and selected for aids James S. Lawson, A. M. Harrison, and John Rockwell.   Finding S. F. too costly, Davidson selected Point Concepcion for the opening task, including survey for a light-house.   Thence he passed to Point Pinos, San Diego, and to the Columbia river, declining the brilliant offers made for laying out towns and other private work, and struggling honorably on the scanty pay allowed, which for his assistants was only $30 a month, while their cook received more than four times as much.   The Pacific appropriation for the fiscal year of 1850–1 was $190,000, most of it for a steamer to be built; the following year $150,000 was demanded, and the service now permitting of greater extension, Harrison was detached with Lawson for separate work, and R. D. Cutts was ordered to replace Williams.   The results attained are shown in the annual reports of the *Coast Survey.*   A special valuable history of the service, with interesting details not there found, I possess in the *Autobiography*, MS., 1–104, of James S. Lawson, who reviews 30 years of his connection with the service, wherein he stands connected with some of its most brilliant achievements.   See also *Bache's Notices; U. S. Govt Doc.*, Cong. 31, Sess. 1, Acts 122; *Gwin's Mem.*, MS., 68–9; *S. F. Chron.*, Nov. 7, 22, 1858; *Hayes' S. Diego*, i. 70–1; *Ringgold's Corresp.*, 1–15; *Belknap's Deep Sea Soundings N. Pac.*

[18] On Sept. 20, 1850, $90,000 was appropriated for six light-houses: on Alcatraz Island, and at the entrance of S. F. bay, on the Farallones, at Monterey, Point Concepcion, and San Diego.   On March 3, 1851, $15,000 more for a tower at Humboldt bay.   These appropriations were about threefold geater than for the Atlantic side, owing to the high cost of labor.   The first two were the earliest completed, although the entrance light was interfered with by fortification works.   Monterey and Point Bonita came into operation after 1854, the rest following at the snail-pace consonant with the government red-tape system.   *Alta Cal.*, Oct. 23, 1855.   Buoys, at from $500 to $2,000, were provided by order of March 3, 1853, four for S. F. bay, one each for Sacramento River, Humboldt Bay, and the Umpqua.   Subsequently a beacon was added to Humboldt Bay.   On March 3, 1853, $25,000 was appropriated for light-houses at Point Bonita and San Pedro; on Aug. 3, 1854, $100,000 for Santa Cruz, Santa Bárbara, Point Lobos, Punta de los Reyes, Crescent City and Trinity Bay.   By the close of 1856 there were in operation light-houses at Pt Loma, San Diego, Santa Bárbara, Point Concepcion, Point Pinos of Monterey, South Farallones Island, Pt Bonita, Fort Point, and Alcatraz, Humboldt bay, and Crescent City; description of each in *Cal. Register*, 1857, p. 140–4; *Coast Survey*, 1850 et seq.; *Light-House Board Reports; U. S. Gov. Doc.*, Cong. 32, Sess. 1, Sen. Doc., 66, ix.; Id., 22, 80–95, 111, v.; Cong. 32, Sess. 2; Id.; Cong. 33, Sess. 2; H. Ex. Doc. 3, p. 307–8, ii.; Id., 10, 288–7, 402–20, iv.; Cong. 34, Sess. 1; also *Finance Repts* for these years; *Alta Cal.*, June 4, 1853; June 12, Aug. 24, 1854; March 16, Aug. 10, Nov. 7, 1855; *S. F. Herald*, March 23, 1853.   In *Hayes' Monterey*, 44, is a description of the buildings.   Concerning navy-yard, see chapter on towns under Vallejo.

[19] Under the survey of Ringgold, U. S. N.   See preceding notes; *Coast Survey*, 1856, 119–20.   The harbor has been improved by the removal of the Rincon and other rocks.   *U. S. Gov. Doc.*, Cong. 40, Sess. 2, Sec. War, ii. 51, 507; Cong. 43, Sess. 1, H. Ex. Doc. 189; Chief Eng. Rept, 1868, p. 73, 883; *Alta Cal.*, ap. 24, 1870; *Overland*, xv. 401–7, with remarks on deposits.   The

1849, signal stations were established, and regulations issued for pilots[20] and harbor-masters.[21]

Owing to the political changes in California, from a Mexican province to an Anglo-American territory, under military rule, and subsequently to a recognized part of the United States, but for a time without regular revenue system, custom-house affairs became somewhat mixed, with variations according to the mood of the ruling power and the pressure of circumstances,[22] with a predominance of Mexican rules. Foreign vessels and cargoes were in 1849 admitted under protest as an indispensable convenience, the United States tariff of July 1846 being henceforth applied, with its several grades of ad valorem duties from five to forty per cent, with one of a hundred for spirits.[23] By act of March 3, 1849, California was

extension of Oakland pier has enabled many vessels to discharge coal here, and to load grain direct from the railway cars. A breakwater protects the dredged approach to her inner harbor, San Antonio, used chiefly by a few bay steamboats. Vallejo became a large shipping place, and of late years Port Costa has acquired a similar prominence for the San Joaquin Valley.

[20] Naval officers joined in offering services. *Frémont's Travels*, 99. The organization was left for the legislature. *U. S. Gov. Doc.*, Cong. 31, Sess. 1, H. Ex. Doc. 17, p. 864. Sacramento received its quota in 1850. *Sac. Transcript*, May 29, 1850. By 1852 pilotage fell to $10 per foot from beyond the bar. Tonnage dues were 4 cents a ton; dockage 3 to 6 cents a ton daily. *Prices Current*, Dec. 31, 1852. Vessels entering or leaving S. F. harbor, unless engaged in whaling, fishing, or coast trade, paid $5 per foot draught. Pilotage is 4 cents per ton extra for vessels exceeding 500 tons. Vessels discharging paid from $5 to $23.50 per day, for sizes ranging between 225 and 2,100 tons; half-rate while loading or doing nothing. The wharfage toll on goods was 5 cents per ton. A shipping commission was created in 1872.

[21] *S. F. Manual*, 169–83; *Cal. Jour. House*, 1850, p. 1340; *Cal. Polit. Code.* Prior to this, military and local authorities had appointed temporary officers. *Vallejo Doc.*, xxxv. 259. The registration of vessels was at first referred to Washington. *Californian*, Oct. 7, 1848. Charges against harbor-master of S. F., in *Barry's Up and Down*, 114. Concerning wharves, etc., see the chapter on S. F.

[22] Civil collectors were retained at S. F., Monterey, Santa Bárbara, San Pedro, and San Diego, till Oct. 1847, when military collectors entered a while. Certain staples were in March 1847 admitted free of duty, together with cargoes from the U. S., while other foreign goods had to pay 15 per cent on value. In Oct. 1847 the latter rate was increased to 20 per cent, and in April 1848 extended to 20 and 30 per cent for two classes of goods. In Aug. 1848 civil collectors were reappointed. W. Richardson was replaced by E. Harrison as collector at S. F., Gilbert having been considered. Concerning changes and rules, see *U. S. Gov. Doc.*, Cong. 31, Sess 1, H. Ex. Doc. 17, p. 687–95, 719–20, 781, 833, besides my preceding vol. v. 572–5.

[23] Under 40 per cent were embraced notably preserves, dried fruits, spices, wines, fabricated tobacco; under 30 per cent, weapons, beer, jewelry, fresh

declared a collection district, with San Francisco for
port of entry, and delivery ports at Monterey, San
Diego, and on the Rio Colorado,[24] and James Collier
was appointed collector.[25] He took possession in
November 1849, at first in the old custom-house on
Portsmouth square.[26] With less discretionary power
than the military rulers, he proceeded to suppress certain privileges so far allowed to foreign vessels, in the
coasting trade and in the landing of effects, despite indignant protests.[27]

fruit, apparel, medicine, manufactured goods of leather, iron, hair, glass, etc.,
paper, sugar, leaf tobacco; under 25 per cent, silk, cotton, and woollen fabrics;
under 20 per cent, lumber, bricks, leather, certain fruit, certain grain, meat,
etc.; under 10 per cent, certain dyes, soap, etc.; under 5 per cent, certain
metals, etc.   Tariff changes since then have been numerous.

[24] Subject for the present in revenue matters to the courts of Oregon or
Louisiana. *Cal. Statutes*, 1850, 37–8.

[25] His pay, $1,500, as per act, with $1,000 for deputies at delivery ports;
his commission, three per cent on duties, yet not over $3,000 a year to be re-
tained from emoluments as collector, and $400 for services in other capacities.
An inspector can be appointed as aid at S. F., pay not over $3 a day; also
temporary inspectors.   Recognized coins alone to be received for duties.
Further details, *U. S. Gov. Doc.*, Cong. 31, Sess. 1, H. Ex. Doc. 17, p. 12–15.
Concerning his subappointments, see *Id.*, 16–23, 79Q.

[26] On Nov. 12th.   Removal in Jan. 1850. *Alta Cal.*, Jan. 25, 1850.   In accordance with proposals in the east to erect fire-proof warehouses at S. F., to
be rented at $7,000 a year, arrangements were made for a four-story building
of brick and iron, 25 feet by 100, to be leased for 15 years from Sept. 1, 1850;
rent to be settled later. *Id.*, 18–22.   This rose on the s. w. corner of Cal. and
Montgomery streets, but was burned May 4, 1851. *S. F. Herald*, Aug. 1,
1850, Feb. 20, 1851, refers to arrival of sections for it, etc.   The next custom-
house site was on the corner of Kearny and Washington, whither King, the
new collector, removed the treasure of about a million dollars on May 28th,
with such excessive precautions as to evoke general ridicule. *Alta Cal.*, May
29–30, 1851. *Id.*, May 8, 1852, refers to new plans for one.   See *U. S. Acts*,
Cong. 31, Sess. 1, 170, on earlier orders for.   In Nov. 1853 was occupied the
so-called custom-house block of three stories, costing $140,000, exclusive of
land, and standing on s. E. corner of Sansome and Sacramento sts.   The
bonded warehouse, which partly caved in April 1854, stood on Battery and
Union st. *Alta Cal.*, Jan. 5, 1870; *Annals S. F.*, 334, 473, 529.   In 1854 the
state made partial gift to the U. S. of a site on which a permanent custom-
house and appraisers' store were erected. *Cal. Jour. Sen.*, 1855, 27, 70–2; *Id.*,
Ass., ap. 24.   Progress, appropriations, etc., *U. S. Gov. Doc.*, Cong. 33,
Sess. 1, H. Ex. Doc. 15, v., Doc. 118–19, xiv.; Cong. 34, Sess. 1, Doc. 10, iv.
228, 235.   Collier had rented Starkey, Janion, & Co.'s warehouse on Cal. st.
Pac. News, Dec. 20, 1849, and countenanced use of vessels for storage.   He
met with great inconvenience, owing to the high prices ruling, and as the
officials were resigning—Doc. 17, p. 24–6, 31–2, 55–9, ubi sup.—he was obliged
to incur extra expenditures, concerning which, as well as his own increased
claims and pay, he had trouble afterward.   See *Dickinson's Speeches*, i. 407–39,
defending him.   He claimed half of $94,700 worth of seized goods.   He was
replaced in 1851 by T. B. King.   When M. S. Latham entered in Sept. 1855,
Sac. Union, Sept. 24, 1855, the pay was $10,400; deputies, $3,000 to $4,000,
with fees.

[27] Brandy in bottles he confiscated because the tariff referred only to casks.

Personal gain appears to have prompted this strict-
ness, although precautions were needed to check the
smuggling, which, fostered under a heavy Mexican
tariff and tax supervision, took advantage of the irregular official service in the early flush days.[28]
Owing to the strife for port of entry privileges
among different coast and bay towns, congress conceded them to Sacramento, Benicia, Stockton, Monterey, San Pedro, and San Diego, as a test for final
decision;[29] but their trade proved insignificant, and the

He seized a British vessel for bringing goods both from Puget sound and
Vancouver Island without the formality which he thought necessary, and so
forth. See Doc. 17, pp. 29–33, as above; and protests by French and English
traders, and condemnation by others. *Shaw's Golden Dreams*, 236; *Kelly's
Excurs.*, ii. 250; *Ferry, Cal.*, 246; *S. F. Herald*, June 8, 1850; *Auger, Voy.*,
222–4.

[28] Collier found great looseness at San Pedro. In Feb. 1849, rumor reached
Col. Mason of the proposed landing of several cargoes on the coast, and in June
Gen. Riley reported landings in the bays of San Simeon and San Luis Obispo.
Goods came by way of Sonora. Doc. 17, pp. 496–8, 696, 771; *Pac. News*,
May 14, 1850. Wines, etc., were landed at Humboldt bay and brought
down by coasting vessels. Collier pleaded for a cutter in addition to the
Lawrence in use Nov. 1849, to guard the coast. Also in 1853, in *U. S. Gov.
Doc.*, Cong. 32, Sess. 2, H. Ex. Doc. 51, vii. The *W. L. Marcy* was in service
in 1856. Opium and silks form the chief contraband by ocean route, and the
Mexican and B. C. frontiers favor illicit trade.

[29] Most were created in the second session of the 31st congress. Gwin,
Mem., MS., 70, who promoted the experiment, sought to add Humboldt.
S. Pedro gained the privilege in 1854. The foreign entries and clearances at
these ports were, for 1851, San Diego 12 and 13 respectively; Monterey 2 and
2; for 1852, S. Diego 29 and 13; Monterey 6 and 4; Sacramento 1 entry; for
1853, S. Diego 3 and 3; Monterey 1 and 4; for 1854, Monterey 9 and 6; S.
Diego 1 entry; for 1855, S. Diego 3 and 5, Monterey 1 and 7, Benicia 7 and
6; for 1856, Benicia 4 and 3, San Pedro 1 and 2. *U. S. Com. and Navig.*,
1851–6. The value of imports in 1854 was, at S. Diego $105,800, at Benicia
$8,200, at Monterey $23.800. The gross revenue in the same year was, at
S. Diego, about $18,100, Monterey $6,000, Benicia $2,900, Sacramento $700,
Stockton $300, San Pedro's was smaller. *U. S. Gov. Doc.*, Cong. 34, Sess.
1, Sen. Doc. 83, xiv. San Diego lost the port of entry privilege in 1862, but
regained it in 1872. *Cong. Globe*, 1873, iii. ap. 293; *Hayes' Misc.*, 51. In 1881
its foreign imports amounted to $351,000, two thirds being railway material.
The exports reached $234,000. Wilmington received goods from 35 foreign
vessels, one being very large, and 20 were loaded there, with 17,000 tons of
wheat. *L. Ang. Herald*, Jan. 10, 1880, et seq.; *Banning's Wilmington*, MS.,
12–13; *Com. and Ind.*, 214. Collier favored Santa Bárbara as a port, and
recognized the importance of San Pedro. *Id.*, H. Misc. Doc. 85, ii.; *Id.*, Cong.
33, Sess. 1, Laws, 345. The progress of S. Pedro is depicted in *Hawley's Los
Ang.*, 21–6. The mercantile trade of other ports is alluded to in the chapter
on towns in my preceding vol. Sta Bárbara, Mendocino, Humboldt, Trinidad,
Crescent City, all strove to obtain harbor improvements and privileges, as
instanced in *Cal. Jour. Sen.*, 1851, p. 1826, 1853, ap. 62; 1867–8, ap. 34–6;
1869–70, ap. 45, 91; *Ass.*, 1875–6, 279, etc.; *Hayes' Monterey*, 33; *Id., Los
Angeles*, iv. 22; v. 281 et seq.; *McPherson's Los Angeles*, 47–8; *Los Ang. Arch.*,
iii. 268–71; *S. F. Picayune*, Oct. 8, 1850; *Coast Survey*, 1854, ap. 35; 1875, p. 61

privileges lapsed. Yet San Diego regained the position, while Los Angeles strove to obtain a part for herself, the best claim centring in Wilmington harbor, on which large sums have been expended. San Francisco remained the indisputably supreme entrepôt for the state as well as for adjoining territories, as shown by the traffic and custom-house revenue. The latter increased from about $20,000 for the first half of 1848 to $175,000 for the second half, and to $4,-430,000 for the fiscal year ending June 1852. The total receipts from August 1848 to the end of 1856 were a little over $17,000,000, and the expenses about one fourth of that amount.[30] By 1880 the annual receipts reached nearly $6,000,000, rising in 1881 to more than $7,400,000.

Communication by land before Anglo-American times was carried on by the usual Mexican system of mule-trains and horseback conveyance, which, being

et seq.; *Eureka Times*, April 15, 1876; *West Coast Star*, Dec. 30, 1875. The *U. S. Gov. Doc.*, Cong. 42, Sess. 2, H. Misc. Doc. 143, Cong. 44, Sess. 1, Doc. 102, 161, contain petitions for improvements at Crescent City, Trinidad, and Mendocino, and reports on plans and work are given in *Id.*, Cong. 40, Sess. 2, Sec. War, ii. 507–18; Cong. 41, Sess. 2, H. Misc. Doc. 98; Sen. Doc. 25; Cong. 42, Sess. 3, Sec. War, ii. 97, 998–1009; Cong. 43, Sess. 2; *Id.*, ii. pt i. 118, pt ii. 368–85; Cong. 45, Sess. 3, H. Ex. Doc. 22, extending over S. Diego, Wilmington, San Buenaventura, Sta Bárbara, and S. L. Obispo; *Id.*, Sess. 2, iii. pts ii. 985–1009; Chief Eng. Rept, 1868, 886–9; *Hawley's Los Ang.*, 13–20; *Banning's Wilmington*, MS., 8–9; *Sta Monica, The Coming City*, 8–9; *Davidson's Coast Pilot*, with complete account of all harbors.

[30] The receipts during military rule from Aug. 6, 1848, to Nov. 12th, when Collector Collier took possession, were $1,365,000; during Collier's administration till Jan. 14, 1851, $2,684,500, of which $1,980,000 for duties, $43,380 for tonnage and lights, $23,570 for hospital, $551,660 special deposits, $10,-970 fines, $2,350 storage, $57,900 proceeds of seized goods, $5,661 rents. *U. S. Gov. Doc.*, Cong. 32, Sess. 1, Sen. Doc. 103, x. 3. The gross revenue from Nov. 12, 1849, to June 30, 1850, was $998,720; for the fiscal year 1850–1, ending June 30, 1851, $1,672,870; for 1851–2, $4,429,810; for 1852–3, $2,391,100; for 1853–4, $2,256,580; for 1854–5, $1,590,020; for 1855–6, nearly $1,850,000. The annual receipts at the minor ports, as in preceding notes, formed in total little over one per cent of these figures. *Id.*, Cong. 34, Sess. 1, Sen. Doc. 83, xiv.; *Id.*, Cong. 31, Sess. 1, H. Ex. Doc. 5, i. 11, 95, 157–94, passim; *Id.*, Doc. 72, ix. 13; *Id.*, Sen. Doc. 47, x. 79–81; *Governor's Mess.*, Cal., 1857. The expenditures from Nov. 12, 1849, to June 30, 1856, were about $4,200,000, including hospital expenses, or an average of $6,000,000 a year. Owing to the scarcity of coin, deposits in gold-dust were received until currency could be obtained, as proposed by the *Californian*, Aug. 14, 1848. Collier was removed in 1851 for mismanagement, the charges being that he was careless in keeping accounts, that he loaned money to banks, etc., at good interest, that he pocketed money for rents on government land. *U. S. Sen. Doc.*, 5 Spec. Sess., 1853.

due chiefly to the lack of roads, did not encourage the opening of anything beyond rude and circuitous trails. Under United States control these multiplied in a more direct and expeditious form, to be quickly followed by regular roads, which were constructed partly by private companies, partly by local and state authorities, and extended within a few years to the remote northern frontier. Costly blasting and filling, corduroy and planking, with imposing suspension bridges, marked the substantial nature of the work,[31] and regular and bustling traffic sprang up where shortly before roamed only wild beasts and savages.

Under Mexican rule mails depended on the irregular arrival of supply vessels and couriers and the convenience of commandants. The United States military authorities improved upon this by the establishment of a regular service between their posts, open also to the public,[32] and by sending occasional messengers to

[31] Ferries were rapidly replaced by bridges. Little, *Stat.*, MS., 12–13, built several in 1850, one of which, at Coloma, costing $20,000, paid for itself within 90 days. Murderer's bar had a wire-rope suspension bridge in 1854. *Hist. El Dor.*, 126. Concerning some costly bridges in the mining region, see *Placer Times*, May 27, 1850; *Sac. Union*, Jan. 29, Apr. 10, May 10, June 14, July 3, Aug. 7–8, Nov. 19, 1855; *Alta Cal.*, Oct. 6, 1856, etc. In 1856 it was even proposed to bridge S. F. bay, a project revived several times. *S. F. Call*, Oct. 15, 22, 27, Nov. 4. Several private plank roads existed, one being opened between S. F. and the mission early in 1851; another from Sacramento toward Auburn later. *Id.*, March 1, 1853. By 1856 there were about 117 bridges, costing over half a million, and $300,000 was invested in ferries. *Cal. Routes and Roads*, 15–16. Concerning turnpike roads, see *Sac. Union*, Jan. 16, Feb. 20–1, Sept. 25, 1855. In May 1850 a road was cut to Georgetown from Coloma, *Pac. News*, May 29, 1850; and in 1852 the legislature agitated for a road from Sac. to the northern counties, so as to keep trade within Cal., and subsequently asked congress for $150,000 to open a military highway. *Cal. Jour. Ass.*, 1852, p. 528; *Statutes*, 1852, 305; *U. S. Gov. Doc.*, Cong. 34, Sess. 1, Sen. Misc. Doc. 8. A Sacramento-Yreka wagon-road was much used in 1856. For later roads, see reports of surveyors in *Cal. Jour. Ass.*, app., and under railways for routes eastward. In *Sac. Union*, Apr. 30, June 3, 30, Dec. 23, 1856. It was then proposed to open another between Humboldt Bay and Petaluma. *S. F. Bulletin*, May 31, Aug. 27, 1856; *Mt Herald*, Dec. 2, 1854; *Pac. R. R. Rep.*, vi.; *Abbot's Rept*, 54; *Hayes' Misc.*, 59; *Alta Cal.*, May 28, 1853, with allusions to other long roads. Early legislative steps for such in *Cal. Jour. Sen.* and *Ass.*, 1850, and following years. The road eastward across the Sierra will be considered under the transcontinental railroad surveys. For leading Cal. branches of it, see *Hist. Placer* and *El Dorado*. List of leading roads in *Cal. Register*, 1857, 151–2. Roads to Mt Diablo and Yosemite were completed in 1874.

[32] *Cal. Star*, Apr. 17, May 29, 1847; *Californian*, June 5, 1847. Bimonthly to San Diego, two soldiers meeting half-way and exchanging mails. It took a fortnight for each to go and return. Irregularity crept in after Aug. 1845,

Washington city. Private enterprise prepared in 1848
to inaugurate an overland mail by the emigrant route,
and the newspapers actually despatched an express in
April,[33] but the gold excitement interrupted the service. In February 1849 arrived the first steamer of
the Panamá mail line, under a monthly contract, which
in 1851 was extended to a semi-monthly service,[34] at
a total cost of $700,000 or $800,000 a year, for Atlantic and Pacific ocean routes and Panamá transit,
while the receipts, amounting to $529,000 for the fis-
cal year 1850–1, fell in 1852–3, under reduced postage,
to $263,000. After this the gain was slow. It was

but in May 1849 the semi-monthly connection was ordered to be restored and
extended to Sutter's Fort, Stockton, and Sonoma, which had not at first
enjoyed the benefit. *U. S. Gov. Doc.*, Cong. 31, Sess. 1, H. Ex. Doc. 17, p.
876–86, 905–6.

[33] *Cal. Star*, Feb. 12, March 1, 1848. *New Helvetia Diary*, Apr. 15, 1848, records its departure thence. Letters were carried for 50 cents, and the newspapers for 12½ cents. On Apr. 22d, it announced another express for June
20th, and offered to contribute toward a weekly interior service. Also *Californian*, March 1, May 3, 10, 1848, which announced an overland mail for
May. *Polynesian*, v. 186.

[34] Already bargained for in the original contract with the P. M. S. S. Co.;
and the amount so far allowed, $199,000 a year, was accordingly increased by
75 per cent to $348,250, at which it remained for many years. The Atlan-
tic line, from New York to Chagres, started from the first under a semi-
monthly contract for $290,000. The transport of mails across the Isthmus
was at first taken charge of by the New Granada government, then transferred
in 1851 to the Panamá R. R.; but the charge by weight, which from a cost
of less than $50,000 in 1850–1 had by 1856–7 risen to $160,000, was now
changed to an annual allowance of $100,000. *U. S. Gov. Doc.*, Cong. 32, Sess.
1, H. Ex. Doc. 2, ii. pt ii. 417–46, 470–87; *Id.*, Cong. 34, Sess. 1, i. pt iii.
317 et seq.; *Id.*, Cong. 35, Sess. 1, ii. pt iii. 961 et seq. Reports of postmaster-general 1850 et seq., passim. A weekly service was agitated in
congress, but failed to pass. *Congress. Globe*, 1849–50, ap. 19; 1850–1, p. 385,
403, and index. The rate for letters, at first fixed at 40 cents, papers 3 cents,
interior letters 12½ cents, was reduced in 1851 to 6 cents, and half that amount
for the Pacific states. The number of letters in Sept. 1850 was 112,000, to
and fro on this line; in Sept. 1851, 119,000. The postage paid for the fiscal
year 1850–1 was $529,341, which under cheaper rates fell off to $263,137 in
1852–3, and to $316,477 in 1854–5, on 2,828,946 letters and 3,814,077 papers,
while the ocean service cost nearly three times the former sum. During the
year 1856–7 the letters carried by ocean numbered 2,227,780, and the papers
4,215,222, the postage amounting to $314,343, whereof $42,152 was for papers
at 1 cent. An extra direct line to Chagres ran for a time, for which the government was asked to grant compensation. *U. S. Gov. Doc.*, Cong. 38, Sess. 1,
Sen. Com. Rept, 30. Rival bidders stepped in partly for the route via Mexico
and Nicaragua, but with little success, chiefly owing to their unreliability.
See *Id.*, Cong. 33, Sess. 2, H. Ex. Doc. 47, v.; Cong. 33, Sess. 1, Doc. 1, i. pt
iii. 722 et seq.; *Mex. Ocean Mail Co.*, *Repts*, 3–44, 3–22; *Savage's Coll.*, MS., iii.
138–9; *Pac. Mail Co.*, *Mem.*, 1–18; *Crane's Past*, 34–5; *Latham's Speech China
Mail.*

not until 1858 that the government extended to a regular overland mail the limited service so far maintained by way of Los Angeles and the United States military posts to St Louis.[35]

The first contract for semi-weekly trips cost $600,000. Owing to the civil war, it was transferred in 1861 to the central or Salt Lake route, which had long been used in some degree, and extended to six trips a week, reducing the three weeks' journey by two to four days. The southern route subsequently revived. In 1869 the completed overland railway supplanted as mail and passenger carrier both stages and Isthmus steamers, diminishing the expense, while lowering the transit time to one fourth.[36]

[35] The cost of which to California was about $143,000 a year for 1853-7, Oregon paying less than $40,000 and New Mexico somewhat over $30,000. In May 1859 the letters by this route numbered over $15,000. *Hunt's Mag.*, xli. 37; *Sac. Union*, July 19, 1855. Utah participated in this service, the cost ascribed to her growing from about $2,600 in 1853 and 1854, to $14,800 in 1855, and $32,500 in the following years. A contractor carried the Salt Lake mail by way of Carson, at $14,000 per month. *Id.*, 984-5. An express also connected with Salt Lake, as advertised in 1855. *Hayes' Ang.*, v. 74, 363-5.

[36] In 1857 G. H. Giddings established a mail line from San Antonio, Texas, to El Paso, New Mexico, whence J. C. Woods assisted to extend it to San Diego, the first arrival here being on Aug. 31, 1857. *Hayes' Emig. Notes*, MS., 270; *Alta Cal.*, Sept. 12, 1857. Meanwhile Butterfield and partners were arranging for a regular semi-weekly service by this route from the Mississippi, the contract for which was signed in Sept. 1857, giving them $600,000 a year. Text in *U. S. Gov. Doc.*, Cong. 35, Sess. 1, H. Ex. Doc. 2, ii., pt iii., 986 et seq. The routes from St Louis and Memphis joined at Fort Smith. The first stages left St Louis and S. F. on Sept. 15th, taking 23 days for the trip. A line was also maintained by way of Placerville and Salt Lake, which at the close of 1860 was running semi-monthly from Julesburg. *S. F. Bull.*, Oct. 13, 1858; March 19, Dec. 8, 1860. The first arrival at Placerville was on July 21, 1858, and the first departure July 24th, to reach St Louis Sept. 1st. *Alta Cal.*, Aug. 5, 1858. The overland acquired such favor that most letters began to turn in this direction, and Butterfield accordingly proposed to carry a daily mail in 17 days. In accordance with congress, act of March 2, 1861, for discontinuing the southern route, and to arrange with the same company for 'a six-times-a-week mail by the central route,' a contract was signed for three years ending July 1864, at $1,000,000 per annum, to embrace the entire letter mail, to be carried through within 20 days for 8 months, and within 23 days for the other 4 months, from St Joseph to Placerville, via Salt Lake, with branch lines to Denver. When the Union war began, Omaha and Ft Kearny supplanted St Joseph as distributing point. *Id.*, Cong. 37, Sess. 2, Postmaster-Gen. Report, 560-1. The first stage left St Joseph July 1, 1861, and arrived at S. F. July 18th, with a passenger. *S. F. Bull.*, July 18, 1861; Dec. 17, 1866; *Hooker's Stat.*, MS. In 1865 congress authorized a weekly mail from San Bernardino to Santa Fé, via Prescott, connecting eastward. In Dec. 1866 the route via St Louis was changed to Chicago, to avail itself of the railway. The contract expiring in 1868 reduced the time between Atchison and

A striking episode of this service appeared in the
pony express, by which for nearly two years a light
letter mail was conveyed across the continent by solitary riders. They relieved each other at intervals of
about 75 days, and heroically pursued their path, regardless of snows and storms, of savages and beasts
of prey, yet not without the sacrifice of life.[37]   Between 1867 and 1875 regular mail connections were
opened with China and Japan, the Hawaiian Islands
and Australia, partly sustained by subsidies.[38]

S. F. to 16 days in summer.   Changes continued to be made as the railway
advanced, the Union Pacific R. R. earnings growing from $7,290 in 1866–7 to
$82,950 in 1867–8, and $226,100 in 1868–9. *U. S. Gov. Doc.*, Cong. 42, Sess.
2, H. Ex. Doc. 151.   The last overland stage contract was awarded to Wells,
Fargo, & Co., on Oct. 1, 1868, for $1,750,000 per annum, with deduction for
carriage by the railway, which being completed in May 1869 took mails and
passengers from stages and steamers.   The Central Pacific R. R. carried 5,300
lbs. daily of mail matter in March 1870   The Union Pac. R. R. earned from
$272,000 in 1869–70 to $283,800 in 1871–2.   In 1882–3 the Central Pac. R. R.
received $343,900 upon its leading overland contract.   The mail route via
Panamá was discontinued after June 1870.   Latterly it had received $150,000
for tri-monthly services, carrying chiefly printed matter. *Id.*, Cong. 35, Sess.
2, Sen. Doc. 48; H. Ex. Doc. 2, ii. pt iv. 718–844; Cong. 41, Sess. 2, Sen.
Misc. Doc. 35, 62, 86, 105; Cong. 42, Sess. 3, H. Ex. Doc. 151; Postmaster-
Gen. Reports, passim; *Giddings' Case*, 1–39; *Overland Mail Service*, 1–45; *Id.*,
Memorial, 1–7; *Id.*, *Observ.*, 1–7; *Hayes' S. Diego, Arch.*, ii. 27–107; *Id.*,
Ang., v. 379–418.

[37] In the winter of 1859–60 W. H. Russell, of St Louis, and others, arranged
for a special semi-weekly service on horseback to carry 15 lbs. of letters at $5
per half-ounce.   Stations were erected about two dozen miles apart; each
rider to span three stations at about 8 miles an hour.   The first messenger
left S. F. Apr. 3, 1860, and the first arrival, on the 14th, was enthusiastically
received.   The time for letters from N. York was reduced to 13 days; the
actual ride took 10½ days; telegraph stations shortened message time to 9
days.   The high charges prevented the line from being profitably patronized;
it seldom carried over 200 letters, and at times less than 20; the best pay
came from a mail contract.   Indian troubles brought interruptions.   With
the completion of the overland telegraph in Nov. 1861, it was abandoned; yet
the mail contract of 1868 stipulated for a partial pony service till the railway
was opened. Details and incidents in *Sac. Union, Alta Cal.*, and *S. F. Bull.*,
March 30, Apr. 3, Dec. 29, 1860, et seq.; *U. S. Gov. Doc.*, Cong. 37, Sess. 2,
Sen. Misc. Doc. 54, 85.

[38] The Pacific Mail S. S. Co. inaugurated the line to Japan and China in
Jan. 1867, and the postage grew from $3,556 in 1867 to $15,327 in 1869.
U. S. Gov. Doc., Cong. 41, Sess. 2, Sen. Misc. Doc. 125.   Pro and anti Chinese
resolutions came pouring in during 1869–75 concerning the $500,000 subsidy,
and finally it was replaced by a mere postage allowance, which in 1882–3
amounted to only $3,925. *Id.*, Postmaster-Gen. Reports, 1869 et seq.   For
the Hawaii service $75,000 was allowed in the sixties, soon also to be stopped.
The Australian line opened in 1874, and was for several years sustained by
the New Zealand and N. South Wales govts with a subsidy of $400,000 for a
monthly service.   This has been somewhat reduced, for N. Zealand is the
only real gainer in time by this route.   The postage granted by the U. S.

The interior postal service was for a long time utterly inadequate to the demand, owing to the small pecuniary allowance to meet the ruling high prices.[39] Postmasters could afford neither to engage the needful assistance nor to decline the outside emoluments that were within the reach of their office.[40] Routes were accordingly opened slowly, and as late as June 1851 there were only 34 offices in the state, even populous central counties having to be content with one weekly mail.[41] But the attempt to limit local ex-

amounted in 1882-3 to $12,500. *Id.* The railway into Mexico has affected the steamer mails in that direction.

[39] Agent Allen undertook in 1849 to appease public clamor by extending routes, but was rebuked with an order to limit expenditure to net revenue. *Id.*, Cong. 31, Sess. 1, Doc. 17, p. 974-5.

[40] The first mail agent, W. Van Voorhees, coming with the first steamer, appointed C. L. Ross temporary postmaster of S. F. till the following month, when J. W. Geary replaced the latter. *Williams' Stat.*, MS., 7-9. See also the chapter on S. F. concerning post-office sites. Voorhees, being unable to carry out his instructions for establishing routes and postmasters, owing to the high cost of everything, was replaced in the middle of 1849 by R. T. P. Allen, and J. B. Moore was appointed postmaster of S. F., but this did not remove difficulties. Instructions and correspondence in *U. S. Gov. Doc.*, Cong. 31, Sess. 1, H. Ex. Doc. 17, p. 956-76; *Cal. Statutes*, 1850, 37, revenue. The first interior offices were established in June–July 1849, at Benicia, Sacramento, Stockton, San José, Vernon, Coloma, and Sonoma, all with weekly mail by water, except the last two places, which received it by horseback. Names of postmasters in Doc. 17, p. 969-72, as above.

[41] Instance El Dorado, with 25,000 souls, while Butte co. had not even a post-office. *Sac. Transcript*, Jan. 14, Feb. 14, March 14, 1851. Yet Placerville and Coloma were this year granted a tri-weekly service from Sac. As late as Sept. 1850, places on the main route of traffic, like Benicia, Stockton, and San José, had only a tri-weekly mail; but in 1851 daily delivery was extended to several, while others continued to be neglected, San Luis Obispo, for instance, complaining in 1855 that only 8 mails had been received in 18 months, and Los Angeles had had no mail for six weeks. *Los A. Star*, Jan. 22, 1853; *Little's Stat.*, MS., 15; *Sherwood's Cal.*, MS., 25-6; *Garniss' Early Days*, MS., 28-9; *Sherman's Mem.*, i. 46; *S. F. Herald*, June 27, 1850, speaks of the first daily mail to Sacramento; *S. F. Picayune*, Sept. 19, 1850; *Cal. Courier*, Sept. 20, 1850; *Alta Cal.* reviews contracts and irregularities, Jan. 12, 1850; March 28, June 22, Nov. 14, Dec. 16, 1853; May 29, 1855; *Ev. Journal*, Jan. 24, 1855; *Sac. Union; S. F. Bulletin*, etc.; *Hayes' Angeles*, v. 330-76, on south Cal. mails; *U. S. Mail Scraps*, 6-10. Among the irregularities may be mentioned the neglect of the Panamá steamer to touch at San Diego, and the lack of accommodation by mail carriers, *Hayes' Angeles*, v. 340-50; the unwillingness of postmasters to forward letters by mail to applicants, chiefly with a view to favor express agents from whom they were receiving a good revenue. This and other abuses were to be checked, so as to gain public favor and increase receipts, observes the postmaster-general in his report for 1853-4, p. 705-6. Of the 34 offices in 1851, only 5 were rated at $2,000 salaries, and 4 at about $1,000; 15 ranged between $25 and $100. *U. S. Gov. Doc.*, Cong. 32, Sess. 1, H. Ex. Doc. 2, ii. pt ii. 419. Postmasters had therefore to seek extra income.

penditure by receipts and by eastern rates was soon abandoned before the pressure of public demand; and transportation, which for the fiscal year 1850-1 amounted to $130,270, was by 1852-3 greatly extended, although at such reduced prices that the cost did not exceed $174,243. In 1854-5 the number of offices had been augmented to 256, and contracts were renewed in many instances at half the former rates, permitting an increased frequency of service, so that in 1856-7 routes 3,084 miles in length, involving a transit of 847,614 miles, were covered by $143,797. The charges for transportation against California stood, however, at $245,831, to which must be added $114,022 for salaries and incidentals, giving a total expense of $359,853, while the receipts amounted to $256,994. The real deficit was still larger, for the Panamá service, costing three quarters of a million dollars, was a Pacific coast item.[42] The balance still remains against California, and although the revenue has increased to more than a million and a quarter of dollars from about 1,000 offices, yet the expenditure exceeds this figure by about one fifth. Steamers and railways cover as yet little more than a fifth of the total route mileage.[43]

[42] Yet several central eastern states appeared with large deficits, as New Jersey, with receipts placed at $117,903, against $151,070 for expenses; Maine, $154,565 receipts, $186,159 expenses; Utah stood lowest, with $1,383 receipt, against $68,874; Mew Mexico followed close behind, and Oregon's expenses were nearly triple the receipts. *Id.*, Cong. 35, Sess. 1, Doc. 2, ii. pt iii. 1095, 1053, etc. Concerning California for 1850-1, see *Id.*, Cong. 32, Sess. 1, Doc. 2, ii. pt ii. 418, 434, 470-2, 488, etc., wherein the cost of transport by water is given at 12 cents per mile; by land at 21 cents. For 1854-5 the transportation is placed at $135,386, and the receipts at $234,591. *Id.*, Cong. 34, Sess. 1, Doc. 1, i. pt iii. 431, etc. Concerning the extension of routes, offices, etc., see also intermediate reports of the postmaster-general. *Armstrong's Exper.*, MS., 15-16; *Vallejo, Doc.*, xii. 220; xii. 19, etc.; *S. D. Arch.*, iv. 352; *Charpenning's Case*, 1-56, with contract claims; *Churchwell's Ocean Mail*, 1-29; *U. S. Mail Scraps*, 10 et seq.

[43] When the overland railway opened in 1869 Cal. had 469 offices; the routes extended over 7,384 miles, of which 865 were covered by steamboats, at a cost of $62,000, and 775 miles by railways for $196,500, the rest by stages, etc. The total cost was $673,358, 3,200,000 miles being travelled annually. For 1882-3 the postmaster-general reports 971 offices, with rapid increase under expanding colonies. Of these 57 were presidential offices, and 154 issued money-orders. The revenue amounted to $1,241,600, or 2.77 of the total for the U. S., and the expenses to $1,518,619, or $277,000 in excess

The many short-comings of the postal department obliged the public to seek other facilities for letter delivery, notably by private express lines, which under liberal patronage assumed large proportions, with relays of conveyances and wide-spread agencies, until they became a prominent feature of trade and intercourse. Indeed, the enterprise of the people was in no way more manifest than in this branch of business, marked as it was, not alone by bulk and extent, but by the speed and endurance brought out by competition for public favor.[43] Several express agents rose in the latter part of 1849, among them the firm of Adams and company, which absorbing several minor houses rapidly increased its interoceanic business by

of receipts. The transportation figured for $930,940; postmasters' salaries for $268,770; clerks, rent, etc., for $146,500; route agents and carriers for $172,400. At S. F. the receipts were $558,000, against $100,500 expenditures; here were 72 carriers, handling 24,700,000 pieces, at a cost of $65,500. Post-office orders amounted to $5,000,000. For references, see indices. *S. F. Chamber Com., Report on Post.; U. S. Mail Scraps*, passim; also account of mails in my histories of *Oregon, Wash., B. Col.*, and *Alaska*, this series.

[43] Express agents had for a long time the habit of paying 25 cents for each letter to postmasters for the privilege of obtaining mails in advance of regular office delivery. In April 1855 the Nevada agents determined to save the fee by taking their places in the line of ordinary applicants. This withdrawal inflicted a loss of several hundred dollars to the postmaster. Indeed, the revenue from agents, letter-boxes, and other incidentals alone induced the postmasters of early days to accept office. *Randolph's Stat.*, MS., 9. On the other hand, the encroachments of the expresses upon the postal business caused a serious loss of revenue to the government, Adams & Co. going so far as to carry letters, even from New York, at half the government rate. Postmasters clamored for restrictions, but the public, recognizing the benefit of these enterprising companies, resolved to uphold them, if only to stir the slow official machinery. Even the Cal. legislature of 1855 paid to expresses $24,900 in postage, and only $2,067 to the post-office. Political influence played here its part. During the rainy season especially, the express agents performed feats which officials never dreamed of undertaking, facing pitiless storms, plunging through rushing streams, and braving robbers and wild beasts. On important occasions, notably during elections, their relays of fast horses and wagons enabled them to equal the average time by many a later railway route. In transmitting the president's message, on Dec. 30, 1853, Wells, Fargo, & Co. claimed to have surpassed even the boasted speed of Adams & Co., whose men traversed the distance from S. F. to Weaverville, 330 miles in 30 hours. Their agents leaving S. F. at midnight, reached Stockton at 10.40 A. M., Sonora at 7.30 P. M., Marysville, 8 P. M. *Alta Cal.*, Dec. 11, 1852; Jan. 1-3, 1854, etc. On such occasions money was not spared in the charter of a steamer or other accommodation, and when it came to outstrip a rival agent, ruse and bluster were added to gain a vantage, as Todd says. *Miscel. Stat.*, MS., 27-8. Ballou, *Advent.*, MS., 2, relates one of his daring encounters with robbers, on the Downieville route, when he and the driver repulsed 13 assailants, and saved the treasure-box with $35,000. The two heroes received an ovation at Marysville, with substantial presents.

establishing branches in every promising town and
camp, with assaying and banking departments, until
it stood indisputably supreme, with yearly profits
exceeding half a million dollars.[44]   Rivals of local and
general character sustained themselves, however, particularly Wells, Fargo, & Co., established here in 1852,
which, by tiding successfully the financial crisis of
1855 that overthrew Adams & Co. with several
others, was enabled to assume the leading position,[45]

[44] The claim to the first express in California is made for C. L. Cady, who
announced a weekly service between S. F. and Sutter's Fort in the *Californian*,
July 24, 1847; but it was short-lived. The business subsequently rose from
among the agents and messengers sent from camps or business houses to the
main or branch post-office for letters. *Soulé's Stat.*, MS., 4. The first regular
express is said to have been started by Ballou, *Advent.*, MS., 1, for the southern mines, late in 1849; but Alex. H. Todd shows in his *Stat.*, in *Miscel. Stat.*,
MS., 21–8, that he began the business in July 1849, by registering miners'
names at $1 each, and going down to S. F. for their mail and charging as
much as $4 for delivering letters or papers in the southern camps. He quickly
gained their confidence, and undertook to carry gold-dust and packages, charging five per cent on dust from Stockton to S. F. This soon grew into a banking business, with a charge of from one half to one per cent on deposits. T. R.
Hawley claims the first organized express, advertised in Oct. 1849 as Weld
& Co., and changed some time after to Hawley & Co., which continued till
Dec. 1850. *Alta Cal.*, July 10, 1866. Ballou writes that after himself, about
Dec. 1849, Upman, formerly a messenger for Harnden, the pioneer express-
man of the U. S., started a line between Sacramento and S. F. Both were absorbed by Adams & Co., whose manager, D. H. Haskell, had arrived on Oct.
31st, to found a branch house. He opened in Nov., *Williams' Stat.*, MS., 13,
and at first limited his operations to a mere interoceanic business, with lines
only to Stockton and Sac., where he connected with Freeman's northern and
Newell's southern expresses. These also were absorbed. Additional local and
general lines sprang up, however, to share in a business from which the above
leading house made over half a million profits yearly. Those with oceanic
routes in 1849–50 were Gregory & Co., Haven & Co., and Livingston & Wells;
Kelsey, Smith, & Risley, agents for Miller & Co.'s U. S. & Cal. Express; Independent Mail Co. of Pac. States and Cal.; and Dodge & Co. Bedford &
Co. maintained a daily connection with San José; Hawley & Co. with Sacramento and the northern mines, in which direction Gregory also claimed lines;
and Todd & Co., the chief agency for the southern mines, closely followed by
Randolph. Palmer & Co. rivalled Freeman & Co. on the Sacramento route,
and Bowers Bros. had the Nevada City line. In the interior almost every
district obtained rival lines within a year or two. Ballou joined Langdon in
the Yuba express; Stockton had several forwarding agencies; C. J. Brown
had the Columbia route; Wood & Bro. had a letter express; Cram, Rodgers,
& Co. opened in due time between Shasta and Weaverville, and so forth.
Pac. News, Nov. 6, 22, Dec. 4, 18, 27, 1849; Jan. 1, 5, Oct. 22, 26, 1850;
Alta Cal., Dec. 15, 1849, etc.; *Cal. Courier*, Nov. 18, 1850; *S. F. Directory*,
1850, 125–6; *Grass Val. Directory*, 1856, 20.

[45] The firm was incorporated in 1851–2, under New York laws, with a capital of $300,000, to extend the Pacific business of Livingston & Wells. Col
Pardee was sent out to manage it, and despite rivalry he made good progress,
aided by the failure in 1852 of Gregory & Co., whose agents and lines he
hastened to secure. The failure of Adams & Co. enabled the company to
distance such competitors as the Pacific and Union expresses, the former

and gradually to gain undisputed control of the entire field, with only local rivals.

The intimately associated stage lines sprang into existence about the same time,[46] multiplying with the spread of mining camps. They centred in Sacramento, as the chief point of distribution for the mines, and in the beginning of 1853 a dozen lines were owned there, with from three to twelve coaches each and numerous relays, valued at a third of a million dollars,[47] and with connection to all parts of the state. Their consolidation shortly after into the California Stage company, while operating against the public by checking com-

started by Adams & Co.'s late employees. Under the management of Louis McLane several new features were introduced, such as stamped government envelopes with W., F., & Co.'s express mark, which soon sold at the rate of $140,000 monthly, at 10 cents. The overland express was perfected. The capital of the company, increased to $2,000,000, came with the ensuing current of success quickly back into the pockets of the share-holders. In 1866 the business was sold to the Holladay Overland Express Co., with increased capital, now limited. In 1869 the Pacific Express Co. rose in formidable rivalry, backed by railway privileges, but it was consolidated with W., F., & Co. In 1881 this company had offices in more than 800 towns, employed some 1,300 men, transported goods to the value of $250,000,000 a year, sent messengers regularly by all stages over 7,000 miles of route, by 8,000 miles of railways, and by 12,500 miles of ocean routes. It is an unobjectionable monopoly, and the few independent firms in the business are mostly confined to small districts and auxiliary to it. *Wells, Fargo, & Co.'s Instruc. to Agents*, 1–69; *U. S. Mail Scraps*, 47 et seq.; *S. F. Call*, June 27, 1876; *S. F. Bulletin*, Dec. 31, 1878; *Sutton's Exper.*, MS., 1; *S. F. Directory*, 1856, p. 108, shows six express at S. F.

[46] Transcontinental stages were advertised at St Louis in 1849, fare $200, but they did not prove a success. *McCall's Cal. Trail*, 35; *St Louis Repub.; Placer Times*, Oct. 13, 1849. The rush of miners in 1849 produced a demand for conveyances to the camps, and Jos. Birch is credited with establishing the first line, *Sac. Transcript*, Feb. 28, 1851, from Sac. to Mormon island, beginning in Sept. 1849, fare $16 to $32 according to times. *Sac. Co. Hist.*, 206. This was extended through Placerville to Georgetown, says *Placer Times*, Apr. 13, 1850. In the mining district the stage traffic increased so that river towns like Marysville had land competition in July 1850. *Delano's Life*, 290. Ramsey opened a line from Stockton to the Calaveras in 1849. *Taylor's Eldorado*, i. 79. In 1851 Stockton had seven stages daily. *S. F. Herald*, June 16, 1851. The entrepôt town, Benicia, started one in 1849, *Solano Co. Hist.*, 155; but the first line to San José opened only in April 1850, time 9 hours, fare two ounces; yet competition sprang up, reducing the fare that same year to $10. *Cal. Courier*, Aug. 26, 1850; *Pac. News*, May 20, Oct. 29, 1850; *Hall's Hist. S. José*, 236–7. Los Angeles received its first stage in 1852. *Los Ang. Hist.*, 55. In the same year a line began running between Marysville and Shasta. *Northern Enterprise*, Oct. 17, 1873; *Id., El Dor.*, 126–7; *Hawley's Tahoe*, MS., 3.

[47] *Alta Cal.*, March 22, 1853, assigns from 35 to 150 horses to each line, and places the total value at $335,000. *Sac. Directory*, 1853–4. The termini were Coloma, Nevada, Placerville, Georgetown, Yankee Jim's, Jackson, Stockton, Shasta, and Auburn, some with rival lines.

petition, served to promote a superior system, with greater regularity, extension, and comfort.[48] This corporation, as well as the overland line dating from 1857, disappeared before the railways which occupied the leading routes, and relegated the stages, as well as wagon and mule trains, to mere tributaries of the rail routes. That valued agent of intercourse, the stage-driver, whose self-reliance has been fostered by varied contact with men and the control of brutes of all tempers, developed in California to the highest perfection, and displayed a dash, skill, and gallantry that drew the admiration of travellers from all nations, and has been so frequently described in the writings of tourists and travellers.

The most indispensable and earliest of the expresses were the freight trains, started by traders for the different camps, and following their movements to new fields. They consisted mainly of wagons, usually the large vehicles brought by immigrants, and known as prairie-schooners, carrying from 5,000 to 16,000 pounds, and requiring sometimes a dozen yoke of

[48] The consolidation was effected in 1853, with Birch, the stage-line founder, for president. The new management began operations on Jan. 1, 1854, with a capital of one million, *Alta Cal.*, Jan. 3, 1854; and introduced several reforms and extensions, among which was a line across the Sierra, a trial trip by way of Honey lake being made in May 1857. The company flourished, since it was better able to suppress competition; its stock paid as much as five per cent monthly dividends. *Sac. Union*, Jan. 30, Feb. 20, Apr. 24, May 2, June 26, 1855, etc.; *Mayhew's Recol.*, MS. In 1860 the Cal. Stage Co. controlled 8 lines northward, the longest extending 710 miles to Portland, with 60 stations, 35 drivers, and 500 horses, 11 drivers and 150 horses pertaining to the rest. There were 7 independent lines, covering 464 miles, chiefly east and south, the longest to Virginia City. *Sac. Union*, Jan. 1, 1861. The Cal. & Oregon Stage Co. incorporated in 1867, *S. F. Call*, Sept. 29, 1867, taking the leading place in this branch. Overland stages are described above, in connection with mails. *Garniss' Early Days*, MS., 30-1, refers also to Washoe staging; *Burnett's Rec.*, MS., ii. 238-40; *Benton's Cal. Pilgrim*, 169. Los Angeles claimed half a dozen lines in 1855. *Hayes' Angeles, Arch.*, v. 365. Stage vehicles varied from common mud wagons to luxurious Concord coaches, with from 4 to 6 horses, carrying 9 inside and from 2 to 5 outside, and making 10 or 12 miles an hour on good roads. The drivers of California have been extolled by every visitor. 'These men I consider the finest whips in creation,' exclaims Major Sir Rose L. Price. *Two Amer.*, 197; *Conway's Early Days*, MS., 2-3; *Hutchings' Mag.*, iv. 364, 419. In *Los Ang. Hist.*, 55, the first carriage in California, aside from an old-fashioned vehicle of the friars, is said to have been a rockaway, sold in Jan. 1849 by Capt. Kane to Temple & Alexander of San Pedro.

oxen, or mules.[49] For the southern mining region,
with its steeper ridges and abrupt ravines, pack-mules
presented the only possible means of transport; and
indeed, until the extension of roads they were widely
used in different directions. The train numbered a
score of mules and upward, each laden with from 200
to 400 pounds of merchandise, which had to be secured
and balanced with great nicety to withstand the in-
equalities of the trail. Patient and watchful, the
animal would guard his load against projecting crags
and drooping branches, and signal by a stop when
anything went amiss. Freight charges were regulated both by the demand and the prevailing high
price for labor, so that for a time one dollar per pound
for a distance of 100 miles was no uncommon rate.[50]
The danger from robbers, especially on return trips
with treasure, tended to sustain prices.

As compared with the lumbering, creaking wagons,
dragged wearily along by dilatory oxen, the mule
train presented a striking appearance as it advanced
in winding file, now climbing a ridge, now fringing
some precipitous slope, now disappearing in the wood-

[49] Wagons were made which measured 6 feet in depth of hold and 17 feet
in length on top. Their cost ranged between $8,000 and $1,500, harness $300
to $600, mules $500 to $1,000 a pair, so that an outfit would often exceed
$5,000. *Sac. Union*, Nov. 11, 1856, instances some huge teams. Carson, ubi
sup., describes the unwieldy *carretas* of the Spanish Californians, with wheels
formed of but blocks from the buttonwood-tree, 20 inches thick.

[50] *Barstow's Stat.*, MS., 3; *Henshaw's Events*, MS., 2; *Little's Stat.*, MS., 12.
Even the early launches from S. F. to Sac. demanded 50 or 75 cents per
pound, observes Carson, *Early Rec.*, 37-8. A man paid $1,140 for yokes,
wagons, and expenses, and made $2,200 freight on 2 tons in one trip. *S. F.
Bulletin*, Sept. 26, 1877. In 1848 the rate to Coloma was only $10 per 100
lbs. *Californian*, July 15, 1848. By Dec. 1852 the freight from Stockton to
Sonora had fallen to $20 per cwt. *Alta Cal.*, Dec. 15, 1849; Nov. 25, Dec. 8,
1852, with subsequent greater decline. In the fall of 1850 were counted 70
wagon teams and over 200 pack-mules on the road between Stockton and the
Stanislaus. *S. F. Picayune*, Sept. 19, 1850; *Barstow's Stat.*, MS., 12. For
muleteers and their trains, I refer to the commerce chapters in *Hist. Mex.*,
iii. vi., this series. Borthwick, *Cal.*, 196-8, also describes them, and *Hutchings' Mag.*, i. 241; *Lord's Naturalist*, ii. 202-10; *Dunraven's Gt Divide*, 139;
Frignet, Cal., 118-20; *Sac. Union*, Jan. 18, 31, Feb. 2-6, 15, March 6, 1856, etc.,
on different express features; also *Sutton's Exper.*, MS., 1; *Moore's Pioneer*,
MS., 8. Goods were carried in *porfleshes*, pockets of hides, over pack-saddles
to prevent tearing against branches, etc. The horses dragged long trail ropes
to facilitate catching them. *Brooks' Four Mo.*, 49-50. Banning, *Wilmington*,
MS., 4-5, gives an account of the first goods train to Salt Lake from this
coast.

clad vale, at its head the leader, usually an old horse, the musical tingle of whose bell found response in the pricking ears of his followers. Along the line rode, centaur-like, the dusky Mexican muleteers, in picturesque garb, rousing echoes from the cliffs with monitory cries to their beasts. Twenty-five miles usually intervened between the camping-grounds, which, selected on some grassy river plat, lay outlined by the unpacked loads ranged with military precision, while around browsed the liberated animals. The flickering fire at first stimulated to enlivening chat and song, but the noise of voices was soon hushed by the absorbing excitement of the monte game, or the slumbers of advancing night.

Communication within California was further accelerated by the construction of telegraph lines, the first to be completed, in September 1853, extending merely from the business quarter of San Francisco to the entrance of the bay, for signalling vessels.[51] During the previous year, however, work had begun on the line of the first telegraph company, the California, connecting with Marysville by way of San José, Stockton, and Sacramento, which, after several interruptions, was completed on October 24, 1853. By this time several other lines were foreshadowed, and one was undertaken between San Francisco and Nevada, by way of Auburn, Placerville, and Sacramento, from which, like the other, branches extended in succession.[52]

[51] It was constructed by Sweeney & Baugh, of the Merchants' Exchange, who controlled the signal station on Telegraph hill, and the first report came on Sept. 11th, *Alta Cal.*, Sept. 12, 1853; although the formal opening dates from Sept 21st *S. F. Herald*, Sept. 23, 1853; *Prices Current*, Sept. 24, 1853.

[52] The Marysville line was projected in 1852, by O. E. Allen and C. Burnham, who, on May 3, 1852, obtained a franchise to this end. The line was to be constructed within 18 months, and pay to the state three per cent on the net profit after three years. *Cal. Statutes*, 1852, 169-70. The California State Telegraph Co. was now organized, and reorganized in the following year with W. B. Ransom as superintendent, and W. M. Rockwell for contractor. The erection of poles began in 1852, *S. F. Herald*, Sept. 28, 1852; *Hayes' Angeles*, MS., v. 419; *Los Ang. Star*, Dec. 4, 1852; but fire and other misfortunes interfered, and the wire party of six men, under Jas Gamble, later telegraph manager, did not start till Sept. 13th. It made amends, however, by laying from five to seven miles of wire daily. From Belmont the first test message was sent, and at San José the first station was established. *S. F. Herald*,

Yreka was reached in 1858, and the overland line, begun in the same year, was completed in 1861 with

Oct. 15, 27, 1853. Gamble relates in the *Californian*, Apr. 1881, 321-2, how the mystified natives watched for a visible message along the wires, regarding the armed poles as crosses to ward off evil spirits. Beyond San José heavier wire retarded progress, but a party working from the other end met them, and on Oct. 24th the line was completed a week within the franchise time. The rate charged was $2 for ten words to Marysville; and half that sum to San José. In 1855 the company declared monthly dividends of one per cent. *Sac. Union*, Apr. 19, 1855. Before its completion other men awoke to the value of telegraph investments, and several lines were projected, that of the Alta Tel. Co., between Nevada and S. F., by way of Auburn, Placerville, Mormon island, and Sac., being far advanced in Sept. 1853. *Alta Cal.*, Sept. 24, 1853. Rivalry began; within two years cables were laid under the waters of the bay, and by 1856 the leading counties in the state were in connection. Lines were then actively planned even to distant Yreka on the north, and to Carson on the east. *Id.*, Nov. 28, 1856; *Sac. Union*, Jan. 27, May 1, Oct. 26, 1855; June 19, Oct. 21, 28, 1856; *S. F. Bulletin*, May 26, July 26, Sept. 15, Oct. 23, 30, Dec. 11, 1856; *Golden Era*, Jan. 6, 1855. The line to Yreka was completed in 1858, after a vain effort in 1854. *Alta Cal.*, Aug. 6, 1858, et seq.; *Hist. Siskiyou*, 167. This success gave zest to the project for a connection with the Atlantic slope. In 1858 two companies were in the field. Act in *Cal. Statutes*, 1858, 73-4. The Pacific and Atlantic Co. was pushing a line southward along the Butterfield overland mail route, via San José, and reached Los Angeles in 1860, there to halt. *S. F. Herald*, Oct. 10, 1860. A central line was started by the Placerville and Humboldt Co., which planted the first pole on July 4, 1858, and reached Carson in the spring of 1859, and soon after Fort Churchill. Cal. offered $6,000 a year as an inducement for the first overland line. *Cal. Statutes*, 1861, 344-5. Now eastern companies awoke to the emergency, and congress was in 1860 persuaded to grant an annual subsidy of $40,000 for ten years, and a quarter-section of land for every 15 miles of line, against a free transmission of govt messages to the above amount, the rate for any message being limited to $3 for 10 words. The Western Union Co. secured the grant, and offered to divide with Cal. if the Pacific companies would consolidate for coöperating with the eastern ring. This was done. The Cal. State Tel. Co., with a capital of $1,250,000, gained control of the Pacific system, covering over 1,600 miles in Cal. and Oregon, with threescore stations. The Overland Tel. Co. was now formed with a similar capital, as a branch of the preceding, and it undertook to perfect and extend the Placerville line to Salt Lake City, reaching this point Oct. 24, 1861. The Western Union, under the title of the Pacific Tel. Co., capital $1,000,000, carried its line via Omaha to the same point, arriving here Oct. 19th. On Oct. 24th the first message was transmitted. *S. F. Bull.*, Apr. 6, Oct. 23-5, Nov 7, 1861; *Alta Cal.*, Oct. 7, 1858; *Hayes' Cal. Notes, Arch.*, v. 39 et seq. The Western Union soon acquired a controlling interest in the Cal. lines and leased them, and so became the largest telegraph co. in the world. Portland having been brought into connection, the co. in 1865 prepared to extend the line from Fraser River through Alaska to Siberia, to connect with Europe, but it proved so costly as to forbid competition with the Atlantic cable, and it was abandoned in southern Alaska. Act to aid it in *U. S. Gov. Doc.*, Cong. 38, Sess. 1, Acts 350-2; *Id.*, Cong. 44, Sess. 1, Acts 201, to encourage a trans-Pacific cable; *Latham's Speeches*, 27-31; *Gwin's Mem.*, 122; *S. F. Bull.*, March 6, 1865. An ocean cable was projected in 1858. *Sac. Union*, Oct. 5, 1858; June 14, 1859. See also my histories of *Oregon, B. Col.*, and *Alaska*, this series. Humboldt county obtained its branch line 1864. *Alta Cal.*, Oct. 11, 1864. Mendocino took steps for extension in 1871. *S. F. Chron.*, Jan. 21, 1871. S. Diego, which had projected a line in 1853, *Marysv. Herald*, Jan. 27, 1853, obtained it only in 1870, *Alta*

subsidies from legislature and congress, and with the
coöperation of the state companies, consolidated for
the purpose, and of the Western Union, which soon
acquired control of the Pacific system, and extended
it rapidly in all directions.   An attempt in 1865 to
carry a line through Alaska to Siberia and Europe
proved a failure, but a trans-Pacific cable cannot be
long deferred.

Cal., Aug. 21, 1870; when it was extended also to Sta Bárbara. *Bodie Standard*, May 15, 1878, announces its arrival at Bodie.   A few local independent lines exist, in S. F. the District (with improved signal-boxes) and Gold Stock telegraphs. *S. F. Call*, July 11, 1875; *S. F. Post*, June 8, 1878; *S. F. Chron.*, Apr. 17, Aug. 6, 1878; *Nat. Tel. Co., Art.*, 1–10; *Com. and Ind.*, 192–3.   The telephone was introduced in 1877, and within 4 years 5,000 came into use, half the number at S. F.; the extension continues fast.   G. S. Ladd devised the telephone exchange system through the central station.   The Western Union absorbed many lines, while the Mackay-Bennett overland line entered into formidable competition.

CHAPTER VIII.

BUSINESS METHODS AND CHARACTERISTICS.

1848–1888.

CHANNELS OF TRADE—AUCTION HOUSES—BUSINESS ORGANIZATIONS—INSURANCE—BANKING—DISASTERS AND REVIVALS—SAVINGS INSTITUTIONS—GOLD DUST AND ASSAY OFFICES—PRIVATE COINAGE—VARIATIONS IN VALUES—THE MINT—SPECULATIVE SPIRIT OF THE FLUSH TIMES—INTERIOR TRADE—CREDIT SYSTEM—COMMERCIAL CATASTROPHES AND FAILURES—EXPRESS AND BANKING HOUSES—ADAMS AND COMPANY FAILURE—MINING STOCK GAMBLING—ITS POWER AND INFLUENCE—ITS FALL AND ATTENDANT DISASTERS.

THERE were no distinctly marked channels of trade in the early days, such as we find connected with old established firms and accumulated capital; nor business ancestry to hedge the path. The field lay open to any one to enter upon any trade or undertaking, and to create his own fortune. The general and brilliant success of dealers before the autumn of 1849, and the subsequent tempting fluctuations, lured hosts of ambitious speculators into the fold, some to be favored by fortune, but most to become involved and overwhelmed by the flood of competition, by financial eddies and ebullitions, by fires and other disasters. Firms succeeded firms in rapid succession, rising on tottering ruins and falling with the crumbling mass; thrifty and observant clerks stepping into the shoes of their principals; employés changing places with employers. Yet with all this absence of conservatism, middlemen were quick to resent any disregard of their claims by outsiders,[1] and in due time each branch of commerce became affected by exclusiveness.

Business drifted quickly into recognized localities. Commission merchants, auctioneers, and bankers settled in Montgomery street; wholesale traders followed the extending water-front into the cove, retail shops centred along Kearny street, dry-goods dealers grouped round Clay street, Chinese bric-a-brac collections began in Sacramento street, professionals and caterers, while scattered in between, had also their nuclei.[2]

Owing to the lack of buildings to accommodate the early influx of people, valuable merchandise was exposed; not only sheds and tents, but street stalls abounded.[3] Even when regular stores and offices increased, few of the occupants owned them. Money with them was too valuable to be tied up in real estate, and their plans were too ephemeral.[4]

A prominent feature of business at San Francisco presented itself in her auction-houses, which were well adapted to the California temperament, by their open proceedings, readiness of access to all parties, and prompt and time-saving methods. The chief reason for their existence here lay in the sudden rise of commerce, with the consequent absence of reputable consignees, in the lack of warehouses for storing goods, and in the instability of affairs from fires, panics, and migrations. Auctions proved valuable vent-holes during these ever-threatening disasters, and within their shanty walls entire cargoes were disposed of at a moment's notice, and millions changed hands in the course of a month.[5] They also afforded excellent

[1] In 1852 the captain and consignees of the *Victory* sought to evade middlemen and license by pedling their goods in small lots for cash. Their posters were torn down, and traders combined against them with effect

[2] As shown in the chapter on S. F. in 1848-50.

[3] Hawley, *Observ.*, MS., 4, began with many others to sell valuable goods in this manner.

[4] The lucky speculator, with a sudden excess of means, or the returned digger, usually anchored his surplus in this way.

[5] As business became settled, with warehouses and credit, they declined in importance. In the preceding chapter on S. F. in 1849-50, I have mentioned the leading auctioneers, among them Bleaker, Van Dyke, & Co., one of whose partners sold his interest in the firm for $200,000 in 1850.

opportunities for those who had been overtaken by such calamities to repair their losses, as happened, for instance, to a gentleman who now ranks among the leading citizens of Los Angeles, named Prudent Beaudry, who, after losing nearly all that he possessed by the conflagrations of 1850–1, was thus enabled to secure the means whereby he has largely contributed to the growth of the southern metropolis.[6]

While strongly independent in disposition and enterprise, Americans possess in a high degree the ability to associate labor, skill, and capital for a common object. Among purely business corporations I will refer to insurance companies and bankers. The combustible nature of California towns, and the frequent fires, kept back insurance agents,[7] and it was not till the autumn of 1852 that the first one became established.[8] With high premiums, prudent selection of risks, and improved fire departments, the profits grew so large as to quickly attract a number of eastern and foreign companies, for marine risks[9] as well as fire and life.

[6] Prudent Beaudry, a native of Canada, passed the earlier years of his life in the eastern and southern states, where he conducted a dry-goods business. Reaching San Francisco in 1850, after meeting with the reverses above mentioned, he removed in 1852 to Los Angeles, and there engaged in his former business until 1865, when he turned his attention to real estate. In 1875, in partnership with four others, he incorporated the Lake Vineyard Land and Water association, its object being to improve and place on the market 6,000 acres of land in San Gabriel valley, including the present sites of Pasadena and Alhambra, these lands being now worth from $500 an acre to $800 a front foot. This well-matured scheme was crushed by an adverse decision of the supreme court, coupled with the scarcity of money caused by the failure of the bank of California, whereby he lost the control of property now worth several millions. Nevertheless, there is no one to whose enterprise and public-spirited policy Los Angeles is more indebted for her development from a struggling village in 1852, to its present position as the metropolis of southern California.

[7] A few risks were covered abroad at exorbitant rates. *Schmiedell's Stat.*, MS., 6. See also the S. F. chapter on fires.

[8] J. P. Haven, for the Liverpool, London, and Globe. *S. F. Herald*, Sept. 8, 1852. He charged five per cent, and accepted only fire-proof buildings.

[9] The North American of Phil. had the first marine agency in 1853, but it soon retired. Haven, as prominent marine adjuster, *S. F. Directory*, 1852, 31, acted for it. The rival adjuster, Capt. Hoyt, was duped by many swindlers. *Sayward's Stat.*, MS., 19–26. In 1854 C. K. Garrison represented two small companies, the Hudson and Franklin. *Coast Rev.*, x. 188–9. The

but owing to the personal liability imposed by the
constitution on stockholders in corporations,[10] local
organizations did not venture into the field for many
years.[11] The first successful San Francisco company was the California of 1861,[12] followed by a score
more, of which eleven remained at the close of 1888,
with 159 eastern and foreign companies, the business
transacted for that year including $353,000,000 of fire
insurance, with $6,100,000 in premiums, and $3,050,-
000 in losses; $134,000,000 of marine insurance, with
$1,750,000 in premiums, and $950,000 losses; and
$70,500,000 of life insurance, with $2,800,000 premiums, and $1,200,000 losses and endowments.

Mercantile houses attended to the banking business
in California until 1849, when the increase of commerce called into existence special banking firms, as
Naglee & Sinton, Burgoyne & Co., B. Davidson,
T. G. Wells, Wright & Co., and James King of William,[13] whose operations soon expanded from dealings

National Life and British Com. Life existed in 1854. *S. F. Directory*, 1854,
p. 234.

[10] Which were, moreover, restricted to organize under general laws. Art.
iv., sec. 31–6; *Hittell's Codes*, sec. 5322; *Cal. Laws Insurance*, 1–128.

[11] The Pacific Marine Ins. Co. was organized in Dec. 1850, by Macondray
and others, *Alta Cal.*, Dec. 21, 1850; *Pac. News*, Dec. 19, 1850; but like more
than one subsequent attempt, did not succeed. A German mutual association
alone held out.

[12] First known as the Cal. Mutual Marine, but reorganized to take fire
risks. It was quickly followed by the S. F. Fire, discontinued in 1866; the
Cal. Lloyds, an unincorporated association of capitalists, merged in the Union
in 1867; the Merchants' Mutual Marine of 1863 discontinued in 1874; the
Pacific, the Fireman's Fund, the Cal. Home, the Home Mutual, all of 1863.
By 1881 there were 148 companies and agencies on the coast, of which 9 were
Cal. corporations, carrying risks for $68,000,000 on fire, $2,750,000 on marine, and a large sum on life; 70 U. S. companies with about $75,000,000
risks; and 69 foreign companies, 35 being British, with risks exceeding
$138,000,000. The average fire loss to the companies between 1876 and 1880
was $1,175,000, on $2,526,000 worth of property destroyed. Cal. paid in
1881 $3,108,000 in fire and marine premiums to foreign companies, and re-
ceived for losses $1,084,000, leaving them nearly two thirds for expenses and
profits. A board of fire underwriters embraces most of the insurance companies, and it has greatly promoted the efficiency of the fire dept, which is paid
in the leading towns. At S. F. the loss on $2,680,000 of insured property
was restricted in 1879–80 to $212,000. *Coast Review*, passim.

[13] The first two opened on Jan. 9th and June 5th, the others in Sept. and
Dec. Sinton soon retired and left Naglee to continue the business till the
crisis of Sept. 1850, when he closed, as did Wells & Co. (late of T. G. Wells)
on Oct. 3, 1851. Wright & Co. also disappeared; the others maintained
themselves. Their capital being small—Wright & Co. advertised a capital
of $200,000. *Pac. News*, Nov. 17, 1849; *Sutton's Stat.*, MS., 11—mercantile

in gold-dust and deposits to more important transactions. In 1850 D. J. Tallant, Page, Bacon, and Company, and F. Argenti and Company joined the list, followed by a number of others in this and following years, notably Drexel, Sather, and Church, and Adams and Company.[14] The last, as the most wide-spread express agency on the coast, extended banking facilities to every town and camp of importance.[15] While banks in California were somewhat fettered by corporation laws and the prohibition to issue paper money, they enjoyed in other respects vast opportunities, from the immense yield of gold, the large import and traffic, the speculative spirit of the people, and the rapid development of resources and settlements. The purchase of gold-dust alone was for a long time highly profitable, owing to the low prices paid as compared with mint values.[16] Methods differed widely at first from those ruling in long-established business centres, chiefly owing to the scarcity of reliable securities and firms of good standing, towns being combustible and uncovered by insurance, and fires, floods, and panics ever pending. One result was exorbitant rates of interest, which ruled at ten per cent per month even

houses continued to act as bankers for some years. Instance Gildemeester & De Fremery, who advertised as bankers. *Pac. News*, Jan. 5, 1850; *S. F. Herald*, July 1, Sept. 14, 1850. King of Wm and Wells represented eastern banks. Davidson was Rothschild's agent.

[14] Bolton, Barron, & Co., E. C. Dunbar, and W. F. Young figured in 1850, as did S. Beebe, Ludlow, and Godeffroy, Sillem & Co., agents for New York and Hamburg banks. *Merchant's Mag.*, xxiv. 548. The list in *S. F. Directory*, 1852, p. 94, adds Delessert, Cordier, & Co.; J. W. Gregory, express; McNulty, Carothers, & Co.; Robinson & Co., savings bank; California Savings Bank; F. G. Smith, savings bank; R. Rodgers; Sanders & Brenham; Todd's Express; Wells, Fargo, & Co., express. G. Ward figured also as banker in 1850. *Garniss' Early Days*, MS., 16; *S. F. Herald*, July 1, 13, Sept. 14, 1850; *Bankers' Mag.*, Apr. 1877; *Cal. Courier*, Feb. 21, 1851. In *S. F. Directory*, 1854, p. 232, several of the above are no longer found, but Abel Gay, Lucas, Turner, & Co. managed by Sherman, later general, Palmer, Cook, & Co., Timmerman & Co., savings, J. L. Woolsey & Co., savings, and A. S. Wright, savings and exchange, are added. *Sherman's Mem.*, i. 92, 100.

[15] Leading towns early obtained special banks. At Sac. several mercantile firms opened special banking departments, Barton Lee and Baker & Co. being the most prominent. *Wheaton's Stat.*, MS., 9; *Sac. Transcript*, May 29, 1850, names also Warbass & Co.; Hensley, Merrill, & King, and Henley, McKnight, & Co. *Placer Times*, March 2, 9, 1850.

[16] Soon, however, this trade was abandoned to brokers, among them Sayward, who gives interesting information concerning it. *Pioneer*, MS., 12-19.

after 1849, or even double that for short loans.[17]   In 1852 it declined to three and soon after to two and one and a half per cent per month, at which it stood for some time, while operations adjusted themselves more and more to eastern forms.   The wide prevalence of advances for mining and agricultural purposes, dependent largely on seasons and yield, the enterprise stirred by the fast-developing resources of a new country, and the speculative character of the people, require more liberal concessions from banks than in the settled east, as marked also by the higher banking rate still maintained here.[18]   This requirement was more pressing in early days, and corporations which hesitated to enlarge their risks had to retire.[19]   The new generation of banks largely accepted mining stock as security, especially in the seventies, although with the wide margin called for by their rapidly fluctuating values.[20]   Notwithstanding these hazardous operations, failures were comparatively few, and not until 1877 was a panic precipitated by the collapse of inflated mining stocks, assisted by the general impoverishment through speculation therein, and by business stagnation, which again fostered a communistic and anti-Chinese agitation.   Confidence had also been shaken by the temporary suspension, in 1875, of

[17] Money is from 8 to 10 per cent per month, and there have been loans at from 12 to 20 per cent, observes *Sac. Transcript* as late as Jan. 14, 1851. Commercial paper, 1 per cent per day discount.   The leading bank at Sacramento paid ten per cent interest on deposits in 1850. *Wheaton's Stat.*, MS., 9; *S. José Pioneer*, June 2, 1877.   In 1849–50, 15 per cent was a common rate for sums even above $5,000. *Schmiedell's Stat.*, MS., 2.   The attempts of the legislature to check usury, etc., by enactments could do no good save at exceptional periods, for which they were not intended. *Cal. Jour. Sen.*, 1856, 248–51.   Comments in *Sac. Union*, Jan. 26–8, Feb. 5, 20–6, March 3, 18, 1856; *Alta Cal.*, March 30, 1858, etc.   High interest goes hand in hand with demand and prosperity; restrictions are reactive and foster fraud.   People can be trusted to manage money as they do other things.   With declining rates and pressing competition, prudent bankers found the risk growing beyond profits.   See *Sherman's Mem.*, i. 103, etc.   Gold-dust was after 1852 brought mostly direct from the camps.   Deposits were drained by every fortnightly steamer.   Adams & Co. alone used to send home $500,000 every month for miners.

[18] Reported at 6 to 7 per cent in S. F., in 1889, and 8 to 10 in the interior.

[19] Like Lucas, Turner, & Co.   Several firms, like Palmer, Cook, & Co., disappeared under the frown raised by a neglect to promptly fulfil obligations.

[20] The Nevada Bank, with a capital of $10,000,000, opened in Oct. 1875, advanced money on mining stocks.

the bank of California, the leading institution in the
state, brought about by the imprudent operations of
its president.[21]
The panic brought down a number of lesser establishments, but it gave a salutary check to stock speculation and reckless loans. The depression continued
for some time, however, partly owing to the new constitution of 1879, which, by calling for largely increased
taxation on capital, drove away some rich men, imposed a restraint on investments in many directions,[22]
and diminished deposits at the savings banks. After
1880 a revival became perceptible, as shown by the
augmented clearances at the clearing-house, from
$486,000,000 in 1880 to $844,000,000 in 1889. In
July 1889 there were 117 commercial banks, with resources placed at over $108,000,000, paid-up capital
$37,600,000, and $50,600,000 due depositors.[23] The

[21] W. C. Ralston. With marked business ability and tact, he had, as member of the Garrison and other banking firms, won the confidence of the community by judicious advances to houses of standing. This influence enabled him
in 1864, after a decade of success, to enlist D. O. Mills and other capitalists in
the establishment of the Bank of Cal. *Alta Cal.*, June 16, 1864. His experience and energy speedily gained for him the sole control of its affairs, finally
as president. Of this position he took advantage to indulge in speculations
of his own, and to promote undertakings of doubtful promise, thus absorbing within a few years nearly the entire paid-up capital of the bank, amounting to $5,000,000. This state of affairs was long hidden by the exhibition
of borrowed bullion on examination days. Nevertheless, the disclosure
came on Aug. 26, 1875, and on the very same day Ralston found his
death in the bay. His lavish patronage of industrial enterprise and
plans for public improvements, his generosity and princely hospitality, had
made him a favorite with a certain class, which rose in defence of his reputation when assailed at his death. See *S. F. Chron., Call*, and other journals
of the day; special disclosures in *S. F. Bull.*, July 27, 1876, and *Matthewson's
Stat.*, MS., 11–12. No bank so heavily involved has perhaps ever recovered,
but the stockholders, including several millionaires, feared that greater loss
would follow abandonment than resumption, and foresaw litigation touching
their responsibility, and headed by D. O. Mills, they promptly subscribed the
capital, and restored the bank to its old position.
[22] The bank of Nevada reduced its capital from $10,000,000 to $3,000,000,
and others followed its example. The $75,000,000 deposits at the savings
banks in 1878 melted by 1881 to less than $50,000,000; the commercial banks
lost $8,500,000 in capital and surplus. One effect was to draw the masses
from stock-gambling, which had reached an average of $150,000,000 for sev-
eral years, and to diminish their debt to the banks, notably on mortgages;
but this was not an unalloyed benefit, since it also indicated a stagnation in
business. The consequent decline in ra..es of interest led to large investments
by banks and individuals in U. S. bonds.
[23] Other liabilities about $7,000,000; cash on hand, $16,000,000; surplus
and reserve, $13,400,000. There were also 35 national, 34 private, and 5

savings banks, which properly date from 1857, had increased to 28 stable concerns, with $96,000,000 in resources, and over $87,000,000 in deposits. The first one was the San Francisco Savings and Loan Association, founded in 1854 by Albert Miller and Henry Meiggs, its interests being incorporated, three years later, with the Savings and Loan society,[24] of which E. W. Burr was president and Miller vice-president.

The fluctuations in the price of gold, varying from $10 in 1849 to $17 [25] in 1851, was long ignored by traders, and this neglect, together with the prevailing liberal disregard for a pinch more or less in disbursements, favored many tricks and frauds.[26] Although gold-dust passed

branches of foreign banks. In 1880 the banking establishments of the state numbered 111. Of these, 74 were incorporated companies, not subject to national banking law; 8 national banks, and a number of foreign establishments. The commercial proper numbered 54, and the savings institutions 20. The 74 companies had on July 1, 1881, a paid-up capital of $24,000,000, $11,000,000 in surplus and reserve funds, $14,870,000 in U. S. bonds, $11,000,000 in cash, and $82,700,000 belonging to depositors. The S. F. clearing-house, dating 1876, the only one on the coast, exhibited the amount of $486,000,000 for 1880, against its maximum figure of $844,000,000 in 1889. Reports of bank commissioners; periodical reviews in journals; special information in *Burnett's Recol.*, MS., ii. 330–66, 412–38; *Mills' Stat.*, MS.; *Sherman's Mem.*, i. 132–8; *Bankers' Mag.*, x. 276; *Frisbie's Remin.*, MS., 37–8; *Coleman's Vig.*, MS., 166–8.

[24] The first stable institution of this class. It was at first able to pay 18 per cent in dividends. The rates charged ranged from 17 per cent in 1860 to 6 or 7 in 1889, though the rate was gradually reduced until for 1889 savings banks dividends were about 4 per cent for ordinary, and 5 to 5½ per cent for term deposits. The Savings and Loan was followed by the Hibernia and others, till they numbered 28, with $75,000,000 deposits at the close of 1877. Then banks were placed under govt supervision, which reduced the number to a score, weeding out the weaker ones, and reviving the confidence shaken by the disastrous crisis of 1877. See reports of bank commissioners and of the different banks. The 28 savings banks, in operation on the 1st of July, 1889, had a paid-up capital of $5,100,000; surplus and reserve, $3,100,-000; cash on hand and in other banks, $4,600,000; loans on real estate, $64,300,000; loans on stocks and bonds, $7,000,000; investments in stocks and bonds, $17,250,000. The average deposit in 1878 was about $700, and was somewhat larger by 1889. See reports of bank commissioners. *Hewlett's Stat.*, MS., 11-12; *Overland Monthly*, xi. 267–72; *S. F. Chron.*, Dec. 29, 1889.

[25] At a meeting in 1848. In many interior places it fell far below $10. *Simpson's Narr.*, 6; *Vallejo Doc.*, MS., xxxv. 68; *Unbound Doc.*, 143; *Dally's Narr.*, MS., 51–3. The price was formally advanced in 1851 to $17 and $17.40, at which it long remained. *Crosby's Events*, MS., 20. Brannan bought gold from his Mormons as low as $5 per ounce. *Breen's Mem.*, MS., 69; *Cal. Chron.*, May 20, 1856.

[26] Admixtures of black sand, etc., were common; spelter and packages with

as currency, the demand for stamped coin became so imperative for custom-house payments and general convenience,[27] that several private establishments began to coin money,[28] from pieces of two and a half dollars to

spurious dust and coin were passed. *S. F. Picayune*, Oct. 14, 1850. Gold from low-grade districts was transferred to others for admixture with higher qualities. Scales were tampered with, weights were made light, pans were waxed to seize upon gold. Y. Bey and W. Dusugeau manufactured spurious dust in 1855. *Larkin, Doc.*, MS., vii. 28; *Miscel. Hist. Pap.*, MS., doc. 34; *Placer Times*, Apr. 24, 1850; *Sac. Transcript*, Jan. 29, 1850.

[27] See complaints in *U. S. Govt Doc.*, Cong. 31, Sess. 1, H. Ex. Doc. 17, p. 643, etc.; *Revere's Tour*, 254. Indians gave frequently an ounce of gold for a silver dollar.

[28] At first rectangular bars worth $20 and $50; then gold pieces of $2½, $5, $10, $20, $25, and $50, resembling national coins, with eagles and other designs, but bearing the name of the coiners, and usually the initials S. M. V. —standard mint value—although mostly somewhat below this. The alloy was generally silver, which imparted a grassy tint. One third were fully equal to the U. S. issues, some without alloy, several more were near enough to pass unchallenged by traders, but the rest had to submit to a discount of from 50 cts to $2 for every ten dollars. The difference between the price of dust at $16 or $17 and the face value left the coiners sufficient profit. The Philadelphia mint reports in 1851 upon the coinage of fifteen private California mints, with from one to four denominations of coin each. 1. A neatly executed coin marked N. G. & N., with an eagle encircled in stars, and the date San Francisco 1849; on the reverse, 'California gold without alloy,' very nearly sustained its claim to the full weight of a half-eagle, assaying without the silver, which constituted 2½ per cent, from $4.83 to $4.89. 2. Two good denominations, eagles and half-eagles, were issued by the Oregon Exchange company. 3. The Miner's bank issued a plain ten-dollar piece, worth from $9.75 to $9.87. 4. Moffat & Co., in 1849 and 1850, imitated the national five and ten dollar pieces with an average value of $9.97. 5. J. S. O. made a ten-dollar piece worth $9.37. 6. Templeton Reid made a twenty-five-dollar piece worth without the alloy $24.50, and a ten-dollar piece valued at $9.75. 7. The Cincinnati Mining and Trading company, 1849, coined five and ten dollar pieces, worth $4.95 and $9.70, respectively. 8. The Pacific company, 1849, coined irregular and debased five and ten dollar pieces, worth about $4.48 and $7.86. 9. A pretty five-dollar piece debased with copper was made by the Massachusetts and California company, 1849. 10. Baldwin & Co. issued four varieties—a five-dollar piece, 1850, and a ten-dollar piece, 1851, in imitation of the national coinage, a twenty-dollar piece, and a ten-dollar piece, 1850, the latter stamped with a mounted caballero handling a lasso. 11. Dubosq & Co. imitated the national coinage in tens and fives averaging par value. 12. Shultz & Co., 1851, imitated national five-dollar pieces, worth $4.97. 13. The Mormon coin was executed in Utah, though composed of Californian gold. There were four denominations, two and a half, five, ten, and twenty dollar pieces. They were irregular in weight and fineness, averaging about $8.50 to the ten dollars. 14. Dunbar & Co.'s imitation of the national five-dollar piece assayed about $4.98. 15. The fifty-dollar piece or slug of the United States assayer at San Francisco, Augustus Humbert, appointed by act of congress in 1850, was fully up to its alleged value when coined, but not being hardened by copper the wear was rapid. This piece was octagonal in shape, stamped 880 and 887 fine, the former weighing two and three quarters ounces. Stamped ingots were also used as currency in those days. The inconvenience arising from the use of the slug, or fifty-dollar piece, induced Wass, Molitor, & Co. to issue in January 1852 a new five-dollar piece, surrounded by a raised milled edge, and superior in finish to

fifty-dollar 'slugs,' which found general circulation for some years. Some proved of even higher value than the legal coin, but others were defective and suffered rebate. Silver coin was imported in large quantities from different parts of the world by shrewd traders, who relying on the unscrutinizing extravagance of these days passed inferior denominations at some twenty per cent or more above their real value. Indeed, silver was frequently raked into the drawer without counting or inspection, and anything approaching in size and appearance a half or quarter dollar piece was accepted as such, and smaller pieces for a bit.[29]

any hitherto made in California. It was a fac-simile of government coin, except on one side was stamped 'W. M. & Co.,' and on the other, 'In California gold.' The value of this coin was four cents more than that of the government, having a uniform standard of 880 fine, and weighing 131.9 grains, with no other alloy than that of the silver which combined naturally with the gold. Their coining machinery was in Naglee's building on Merchant street, afterward for 13 years occupied by the author as a part of his book and stationery establishment. They could coin seven or eight thousand dollars a day, including correspondingly good ten-dollar pieces, which were all readily received on deposit by the banks. Some of the coining machinery brought out by different trading companies found its way to Sacramento, where J. S. Ormsby & Co. struck coins for miners. According to the *S. José Pioneer*, May 5, 1877, their royalty was 20 per cent. Bankers resolved in 1851 to decline all private coins; but Adams & Co. insisted on their accepting those of Wass, Molitor, & Moffatt, and traders found it good policy to countenance many more. By raising the price of dust to $17, the banks did, however, interpose a check, as did the attempt of the government in 1852 to refuse even the slugs issued under its auspices, a step which for a time placed legal coins at a high premium, as had been the case in 1848–9 for custom-house duties. The legislature passed an act to prevent private coinage, but repealed it on March 25th, and issued another on Apr. 21st, obliging coiners to mark the actual value on their issues, and redeem them with legal money. *Cal. Statutes*, 1851, 171, 404. The establishment of the mint in 1854 proved the best restraint, and in 1856 the final condemnation was passed on private coins. *Alta Cal.*, March 28, Apr. 1, 1851; Oct. 24, 1352; Oct. 5, 12, 1854; Apr. 10, 1856; Nov. 28, 1868; *Pac. News*, May 9, Sept. 21, Nov. 11, 1850; Feb. 1, Apr. 5, 9, 17, 1851; *Cal. Courier*, March 6, 1851; *S. F. Herald*, Feb. 8, Oct. 15, 1851; Jan. 17, 1852; *Sac. Union*, Apr. 30, 1855, etc.; *Polynesian*, vi. 126; vii. 130; *Garniss' Early Days*, MS., 12; *Placer Times*, Feb. 23, 1850; *Mountain Democ.*, Nov. 25, 1854; *Hunt's Mag.*, xxix. 236, 743. *Dickeson's Amer. Numismatic Man.* contained engravings of California coins. In Mexican times hides, cattle, etc., had to supply the lack of coin.

[29] A trader imported $100,000 Austrian zwanzigers at 17 or 18 cts and passed them for 25 cts. *Fernandez, Cal.*, MS., 175–6. Stout found 15-ct coins passed for 25 cts. *First S. S. Pioneers*, 120; *Smiley's Vig.*, MS., 19. Francs, English shillings, Danish, East Indian, and other coin circulated. San Franciscan precautions drove the debased foreign coinage after·some years to the interior, where it still commanded a premium, even after Stockton banks in Oct. 1854 resolved to recognize francs only at 20 cts and other coins in proportion. Soon afterward the 5-ct piece began to circulate; yet to this day dealers accord it only partial acknowledgment.

In 1850 the government provided for an assay office at San Francisco, and although a merely semi-official establishment was opened,[30] it rendered good service in checking inferior coinage and correcting irregularities with gold-dust. Two years later an appropriation was granted of $300,000 for a branch mint,[31] which

[30] The agent in charge, A. Humbert, made contracts with private firms to issue slugs, etc. Crane, *Past*, 28–9, condemns it as a 'shaving shop.' The legislature passed an act Apr. 20, 1850, for the appointment of an assayer. *Placer Times*, May 22, 1850. Kohler was appointed. *Soc. Transcript*, June 29, 1850.

[31] For measures to this end since 1850, see *U. S. Gov. Doc.*, Cong. 31, Sess. 2, H. Ex. Doc. i., p. 10; Cong. 32, Sess. 1, Doc. 92, v., Doc. 132, xiii.; *Id.*, H. Miscel. Doc. 60; petitions, in *Unbound Doc.*, 136–7; *Hayes' Mining Arch.*, MS., i. 5; *Id.*, *Pub. Laws*, 11–13; *Pac. News*, May 13, Nov. 1, 1850; comments of Gwin, *Mem.*, 67, 81, who introduced the bill. *N. Am. Rev.*, lxxv. 410–24; *Alta Cal.*, Apr. 13, 1852. The absence of a mint was estimated to cause a loss of $10,000,000 a year to the state. Curtis & Perry, assayers on Commercial st, contracted with the government to make certain additions to their establishment and put in the necessary machinery for the sum of $296,000. The contractors turned over the mint to L. A. Birdsall, the superintendent, and all was ready for the reception of gold-dust the 3d of April, 1854. The new machinery was manufactured in Philadelphia, under the supervision of George Eckfeldt of the U. S. mint, and put up conjointly by himself and his son, John M. Eckfeldt, the first coiner. J. R. Snyder was the first treasurer, John Hueston, melter and refiner, A. Haraszthy, assayer, and there were some 25 assistants. For assaying and running into bars, the then prevailing local charge of one half of one per cent was made. For assaying and refining, the rate was 11 cents an ounce, or six tenths of one per cent. Half of one per cent additional was charged for coining, thus making the whole cost for turning gold-dust into coin 1.10 per cent. Seven eighths of one per cent was the Philadelphia rate. At this time only one private coining establishment was in operation here, that by Kellogg & Richter. It is estimated that only one fourth of the gold so far produced had been coined in S. F. A description of the mint is given in *Alta Cal.*, Apr. 5, Sept. 25, 1853; Jan. 4, March 28, Apr. 4, May 16, 1854, and other papers; and a view in *Annals S. F.*, 526. For cost and later appropriations, with salaries, see *U. S. Gov. Doc.*, Cong. 33, Sess. 2, H. Ex. Doc. 3, ii. 357; Cong. 34, Sess. 3, Doc. 32, v.; *Hunt's Mag.*, xxxi. 228; xxxiii. 353–5; *Golden Era*, Dec. 18, 1853; *Hayes' Mining*, i. 90. Operations were temporarily suspended on several occasions within the following three years. P. Lott succeeded as supt in 1853, salary $4,500. *S. F. Bulletin*, Nov. 14, 1855, Oct. 10, Nov. 1, 1856. In 1857 several charges of embezzlement were preferred against employés. The coinage for 1854–6 amounted to $9,731,574, $21,121,752, and $28,516,147, respectively, of which $164,075 and $200,609 were in silver for 1855–6, mostly quarter-dollars, and about half as many fifty-cent pieces. The gold embraced over 2,000,000 double eagles, some 200,000 eagles, 150,000 half-eagles, some three-dollar, quarter-eagle, and dollar pieces, besides some $12,000,000 in bars. *U. S. Gov. Doc.*, Cong. 35, Sess. 2, H. Ex. Doc. 3, i. 72–80. The pressure of business under the growing silver production led congress in 1864 to appropriate $300,000 for a more commodious structure. Additional appropriations were granted, and in 1874 was opened the new edifice on Fifth st, whose hollow parallelogram, in two stories, covers an area of 160 by 217 feet. It is in Doric style, with brick walls faced with blue-gray sandstone. Inauguration in *S. F. Call*, Nov. 1, 6, 1874; *Alta Cal.*, May 25, 1870; *Taylor's Gates*, 174–91. The coinage, which in 1860 had fallen to $12,000,000, ranged between $14,000,000

opened in April 1854, and gave quick relief to legal currency by issuing over fifty-nine millions by the end of 1856, of which two thirds were in double eagles alone. In 1886, with a coinage of $25,000,000, half-eagles formed this proportion. Attempts to circulate paper notes met with little favor; and subsequently a special legislative act prohibited such money,[32] greatly to the benefit of the community; for by leaving to California a purely metallic currency the financial convulsions ever threatening a field so speculative have been greatly softened. The eastern crisis of 1851 was greatly mitigated by gold shipments from California. Even treasury notes were restricted to a small circulation under the specific-contract act of the state.[33]

Early California speculations partook in a marked

and $22,000,000, during 1863-73. After this, the Nevada yield increased it to $50,000,000 by 1877. For the fiscal year ending June 30, 1885, it fell to about $24,000,000, and after some fluctuations, stood at nearly the same figure for the year ending June 30, 1889. *U. S. Mint Reports; Hayes' Mining Arch.*, i. 92, 110. Comment on silver and currency, and their effect on trade, *S. F. Chamber Com.*, 1873, 15-29; *Cal. Remonetization*, 1-91; *Buttemer's Coinage*, 1-18.

One of the ablest and most esteemed mint superintendents was H. L. Dodge, the descendant of a family which traces the departure of its founder from England in 1629. Born at Montpelier, Vt, Jan. 31, 1825, he was educated at the state university. While preparing for the profession of law, the gold fever carried him away to S. F., where he as clerk of the court and council took a prominent part in the development of the city during 1849-50. Two years later he was here admitted to the bar and gathered a large clientage, but soon abandoned it to join his brothers in establishing the wholesale provision house of Dodge, Sweeney, & Co. After a brief term as supervisor, he was in 1862 and following years sent successively to the legislative assembly and senate. In 1877 he accepted an appointment on the U. S. treasury commission and the superintendency of the mint, which he left with a rarely equalled record for judicious and honorable management. He subsequently served on the U. S. Mint Assay commission, as president of the chamber of commerce and of the pioneer society.

[32] *Cal. Statutes*, 1855, 128. Banks were already prohibited by the constitution from issuing paper money. F. Marriott issued notes in Dec. 1851, for one and five dollars, under the name of 'cash orders,' but none would accept them. The common use of gold created a contempt for less tangible currency.

[33] Under which contracts define the currency to be paid. Many patriots raised an outcry against the discrimination, but metal prevailed, and remains the medium in 19 out of 20 instances, although greenbacks have here recovered from their position practically of merchandise, and deprived gold-note banks of their vantage. The period of 1861-5 proved a golden harvest for merchants dealing with the east. The present amount of coin on hand within the state has been calculated at $80,000,000, of which five sixths is in mint, treasuries, and banks.

degree of the gambling spirit connected with mining, and the bizarre, capricious extravagance produced by the sudden unfolding of wealth. An independence and daring prevailed, which soared above petty haggling, and revelled in dashing operations and great projects. Partnerships and contracts were accepted on the spur of the moment.[34] Gold was taken by liberal pinches. Prices were regulated by an elastic conscience, guided by a keenness sharpened with experience. Men preferred to speculate at great odds rather than endure irksome stagnation, and stoical as to the immediate results, they were ever buoyed by the hope of a happy turn. They met the mockery of chance with cheerful energy and recuperative power, and if overwhelmed one moment by some sweeping financial crash or obliterating conflagration, they were on their feet the next, planning fresh undertakings, and constructing new buildings.[35]

Although accident rather than perseverance brought fortune[36]—the happy speculation on the turn of the

[34] And without knowing anything about the partner or parties, adds White, *Pioneer*, MS., 194, 201.

[35] Hawley, *Observ.*, MS., 7–8, writes that he was burned out six times within less than a year and a half; and Neall, *Vig.*, MS., 15–16, four times within 14 months. Of course many succumbed. James Phelan was engaged in trade at Cincinnati when the gold fever induced him to transfer his general merchandise to S. F., and there establish himself in Aug. 1849 with his brother, under the firm J. & M. Phelan, for which a third brother, John, a merchant of N. York, acted as Atlantic agent. Fires and mismanagement by partners made inroads in time, but Mr Phelan turned to the rescue and continued as sole trader till 1869, to devote himself to his interest in banking and real estate, the latter distributed in different sections of the coast, and including one of the most conspicuous buildings of S. F. In 1870 he helped to organize the first national bank, as president, acting also as director of the national bank of San José. He also participated in forming the Western Fire and Marine Insurance Co., and in pushing operations on the Panamá canal. By all who knew him he was acknowledged as one of the most enterprising of our Cal. pioneers, and as one to whom the state was indebted for much of its early prosperity.

[36] One class of goods in an invoice would frequently bring a fortune, while the rest proved a loss. Instances by Coleman, *Vig.*, MS., 155–65; *Dean's Stat.*, MS., 3. In 1850 four firms contracted with a Chile house for 100,000 to 200,000 barrels of flour at $14, each firm assuming responsibility for $700,000, with a forfeit of $100,000. The market rose, they speedily made several hundred thousand dollars, and could have retired with a large surplus after paying the forfeit, but they continued to accept the flour, which fell and swallowed much more than the profits. *Hittell's S. F.*, 213–14. Cheney & Hazeline of Sac. made a profit of $350,000 on $80,000 invested in flour.

market, or the fortunate possession of goods to meet a demand—yet shrewdness and observation were profitable. The dealer could feel the market by advancing his prices upon each successive purchaser; he could sell one class of goods on condition that certain undesirable effects should be taken;[37] he could buy at forced auction and send the merchandise to better inland markets, or sell it out on the street corners at great profit.[38]

The cost of handling goods and the combination of traders tended to maintain retail prices within certain limits, especially in the interior, with its numerous points of distribution, so that the miners gained only in a measure by the decline at San Francisco. They were, for that matter, the golden geese, to be plucked primarily by the store-keepers who followed their trail, and indirectly by merchants, carriers, and manufacturers.[39] By maintaining agents at the chief mart, and communication with the camps, dealers at the interior entrepôts could do a safe and profitable trade,[40] and camp stores, with their small and varied stock, ran little risk. Competition naturally caused great fluctuations also here, within the bounds assigned by the cost of local transportation, but if one camp was well provided, the supply train would usually distribute its cargo in small lots at different diggings. Although flour sold during the middle of 1850 at fifteen and

Crary's Vig., MS., 3. Schwartz, opposite Sac., from the sale of melons, realized that year (1849) $30,000. Burnett's Rec., MS., ii. 132-3. White of San José had a patch of onions which netted him over $12,000 in 1849. Crosby's Events, MS., 128; Wood's Sixteen Mo., 171.

[37] If only to save storage. The price for goods would often differ widely at different shops. Schmiedell's Stat., MS., 1-2.

[38] Smiley, Vig., MS., 17-22, sold some crockery at $5 a crate, and found the buyer retailing it at $5 a piece. Boots purchased at auction for $10 to $16 a pair were sold on the street at $50 to $100, and so with wines, etc. Coleman's Vig., MS., 155-65. Butter at 20 cts was sent to Coloma to sell for 80 cts, etc.; Oakland Transcript, March 12, 1874; Neall's Stat., MS., 7-9. Unsalable japanned waiters were transformed into valued tom-irons for miners; the emptied bottles of seltzer water sold for more than the original cases.

[39] Helper, Land of Gold, 140-1, bestows a wail over the drones.

[40] Sac. Transcript, Jan. 14, 1851, instances a successful firm of Sac., which in 8 months sold $450,000 worth of goods.

seventeen dollars per hundred-weight in certain interior stations, with other articles in proportion, yet in these early days the rate was usually kept above twenty-five cents a pound. The increase of light river steamers tended mainly to reduce the cost of transport, for they penetrated into most of the tributaries, and in the mountain districts the abundance of game served as a check on traders. Nevertheless, if these were restrained in certain directions, they could always rely on one prolific source of revenue, in the extravagant and convivial habits of the miners, most of whom spent all their golden winnings at the bar if not at the counter. The simple-minded Indians and the prodigal Mexicans were even more welcome customers.[41]

The risk attending early California commerce was increased by the absence of civil government and laws to enforce the observance of obligations, midst the general disorganization. This had to be left to the honor of the parties; and at first the method worked well, partly because the readiness with which wealth presented itself reduced the temptation to defraud. Misfortune always met with consideration, while summary justice[42] was apt to be meted to suspicious parties. With growing pressure and strange admixture of men, trickery and rascality grew apace. The distance from foreign and eastern claimants was great, and evasion easy, with frequent conflagrations, and pliant or fictitious partners to cover any manipulation.[43]

[41] The Indians were found to be good customers from their lack of appreciating the value of money, and the readiness with which they could be imposed upon, especially to purchase baubles and inferior articles. Buffum, *Six Months*, 93–4, Coronel, *Cosas Cal.*, MS., 142–3, give striking instances. Spanish-Americans proved no less profitable from their extravagance and readiness to spend money, as Belden, *Stat.*, MS., 53–5, found in his dealings with them.

[42] There was no time to hunt rascals; but those within reach were liable to summary chastisement. Garniss relates that a vacillating party to a contract was promptly reminded of duty by having his attention called to a group of armed men who were evidently awaiting orders. *Early Days*, MS., 13.

[43] After great fires it was common enough to feign or magnify losses. One partner would sell to another, and when he failed, buy back the interest at a nominal sum. For false entries and transfers the case of Cronin & Markley of 1851 affords a striking instance. Fraudulent brokers, bankers, insurance

The credit system of California was fraught with much hazard, aside from the prevalent spirit of speculation which required it; instance merely the climatic influence on mining, particularly on so-called dry diggings, where the realization of many months of labor depended upon the brief rainy season, a season which again closed operations and intercourse in other quarters. Payments were also largely connected with the success of prospectors, so that camp traders had to count upon many risks, which in turn extended from them, as the chief and primary agents,[44] to all branches of business. The organization of the Chamber of Commerce in 1850[45] brought early remedies for many difficulties, but nothing save bitter experience could check the recklessness and over-confidence which stamped flush-time trading.

The main causes of commercial disasters were the excessive and badly selected shipments which periodically, upon slight encouragement, flooded the markets,[46] to the ruin of merchants. Then came a series of devastating fires to undermine additional numbers,

agents, etc., posed a while till their net was filled. How high interest could rapidly eat away a large capital may be seen from the case of Gladwin, Hugg, & Co., in *S. F. Bulletin*, Sept. 29, 1858. Adulteration of flour led to strong measures. *Id.*, Apr. 28, 1856; *Alta Cal.*, Feb. 14, 1852. Certain defects and losses were ascribed to rats. *Neall's Vig.*, MS., 17. Notwithstanding a prohibition act against lotteries, *Cal. Statutes*, 1851, p. 211, these apertures for deception and for unsalable effects continued to flourish for several years, as shown in my preceding chapter on society. There was an outcry against them in the legislature as early as 1854. *Cal. Jour. Sen.*, 1854, pp. 324-6, ap. 7; 1855, pp. 47-9; 1856, pp. 514-19, ap. 21.

[44] To refuse credit was not politic among so fraternal a class as miners. *Fernandez, Cal.*, MS., 178. Culver laments in 1851 the uncertainty of repayments. *Sac. Directory*, 74. An unjust attachment law, which gave property to creditors according to the date of their levies, exposed to seizure also unpaid goods in possession of the debtor.

[45] On May 1, 1850; incorporated Nov. 3, 1851. *Pac. News*, May 10, 1850; Nov. 27, 1849, etc.; *S. F. Herald*, June 5, 1850; *Com. Herald*, Nov. 18, 1867. Its location was in the merchants' exchange, which had opened in Dec. 1849. See *Alta Cal.*, Dec. 15, 1849; *S. F. Bulletin*, Nov. 10, 1859; *Neall's Vig.*, MS., 18-20. Its annual reports have proved valuable for the present chapter; likewise those of the S. F. Commercial assoc., aiming to protest against frauds.

[46] California traders were less to blame for this rush. They suffered also from unprincipled shippers, who would take hints from orders received and forward them by slow vessels, while sending consignments of their own by faster sailers, and so forestall the customer.

and affect every inhabitant in San Francisco. Under such circumstances it is strange that so few panics are to be recorded. The first, in September 1850, attended by a 'run' upon the banks, resulted in the suspension of the pioneer banking establishment. About the same time the three leading banks of Sacramento collapsed with a shock that was felt throughout the mining region.[47]

The second and greater monetary crisis occurred in 1855, after brewing for several years. A revolution had gradually taken place in the industrial and commercial condition of the state. The diggings were declining, and although nearly balanced by the development of quartz veins, mining was passing largely into the hands of companies and employers, to the exclusion of a host of humble miners, who were cast adrift to swell the labor market, and lower incomes in every direction. Their chief recourse was agriculture, with the effect of increasing the yield of wheat and barley alone from less than 30,000 bushels in 1850 to over 8,000,000 bushels in 1856, and decreasing to a mere trifle the import of staple provisions, which during the early years had almost all been introduced from abroad. The change in occupation and income produced, moreover, additional contractions from retrenchment and home production. Yet commercial circles remained stupidly blind to the variation, hugging themselves with the delusion that local mishaps and ephemeral causes were accountable for a depression that must be temporary. And so over-trading, speculation, and extravagance continued, with growing indebtedness, glutted markets, and a dulness which at San Francisco was soon manifested in declining tonnage, tenantless houses, and falling real estate values.

The convulsion began in 1855 with the news that the St Louis parent house of Page, Bacon, and Company, leading bankers of San Francisco, had suspended.

[47] Barton Lee made an assignment on Aug. 5th, with liabilities over $1,000,000; the firms of Henley and Wabass followed shortly after.

The first manifestation was a run upon this bank, which succumbed on February 22d, followed by the suspension of a large number of establishments, notably Adams and Company. This was an express and banking-house, with branches in almost every town and mining camp on the coast. It had grown up in the confidence of the people, and among its depositors were many who had entrusted their all to its keeping. When this institution fell, faith in bankers seemed for the time destroyed. A financial storm swept over the country, leaving in its track disaster, ruin and confusion. In San Francisco alone, two hundred firms failed that year, with liabilities exceeding eight millions, and assets estimated at less than one-fifth of this amount; and yet the city numbered scarcely 40,000 inhabitants. Of firms established before 1850 not one in ten survived. On the 22d of February, not then a legal holiday, a quiet run was made upon Adams and Company, and it was said that $250,000 and upwards was withdrawn. Still the general feeling was that the bank would maintain itself, and during the run, while eager demands were made by some patrons, others came to express confidence and to extend the time on their deposits. The officers of the bank, however, looked with alarm upon anothers day's run; for while it seemed certain that its assets were sufficient, much of its funds were held in different branch offices. Without this help, which could not be had in time, because there was no railroad communication with any of these offices, and telegraphic lines to only two or three of them near the city, another day's run would be a catastrophe.

A consultation with the best legal talent on the Pacific coast was had ; the whole night of the 22d was spent in efforts to meet the crisis. I. C. Woods, partner and manager of the bank, was of the opinion that the coin would give out early in the day, and in this event it was a question whether excited and suspicious depositors would accept gold-dust. Trenor

W. Park insisted that it would be a hazardous experiment to offer gold-dust. Others tried to prevail upon Woods to open the bank and pay out gold-dust if necessary, because it was fairly current, and because also it would be more acceptable with whatever discount, than to undergo the expense and uncertainty of litigation. But Park prevailed. In what way then could the bank be closed? What legal form invoked? Superior counsel pointed out to Woods that a petition in insolvency to liquidate the debts of the bank *pro rata* had better be made. But finally it was determined to appoint a receiver, and the man selected was A. A. Cohen, who after some demur consented, his bonds of $1,000,000 being immediately furnished and approved.

Before proceeding further, it should be here remarked that as to Mr Cohen's receivership, I have in the main followed his own statement, in the absence of conclusive evidence to the contrary, taking him at his word.

It was suggested that, owing to the excitable character of the population, an attack would doubtless be made upon the bank and the funds carried away; therefore it might be advisable for the receiver to remove the coin, gold-dust, and valuables. Cohen acted upon this advice; but owing to the limited time, it was impossible to have the coin counted and the gold-dust weighed; besides, it was not necessary, as Woods assured him that two employés of the bank had already taken an account of the contents of the vaults, which were then hurriedly removed and deposited with Alsop and Company, private bankers of San Francisco. This same morning the bank of Adams and Company was surrounded by a threatening and angry mob of creditors, who demanded payment of their various claims. Similar scenes were enacted around all the branch offices in the state.

In those days we were without railroads, and except one or two near points, without telegraphic connection.

It was therefore difficult to communicate with the
agents of the company, only a few near offices answer-
ing the demand of the receiver by sending coin and
dust. The creditors in the interior, immediately they
learned of the suspension of the bank, attached whatever they could get, while sheriffs and constables
broke open safes and vaults of the company, and took
away in every case much more than sufficient to pay
the amounts covered by the writs of attachment in
their hands; in many cases the original demands
were less than twenty dollars, the costs of these
amounted to four times that sum. It was not possible to get possession of the scattered assets of Adams
and Company.

It became apparent to the receiver that Adams and
Company could not resume business, and upon making
an examination of the books which came to him from
the San Francisco office, he found that the money
which he had actually received was considerably less
than the amount which the books showed he should
have on hand. It was ascertained that when the
stoppage of the bank had been resolved upon, and
before the receiver had been notified, a large amount
of gold-dust and coin had been removed from the
office of Adams and Company to the private assay
office of Kellogg, Hewston and Company, and that
the gold-dust which had been received from the interior on the evening of the 22d of February had
been taken to the same place. These funds had been
dissipated, whether rightfully or wrongfully, and without remedy. Part of the amount was covered by
cash checks, while the gold-dust abstracted, it was
claimed, was not the property of the bank, and was
held for the account of those who had shipped it
through the company as an express agent. Finally
the attorneys of Adams and Company, realizing that
there was no possibility of winding up the affairs of
the firm through a receiver, and not being able to
induce any one to accept this office who could at the

same time give the necessary bond, adopted the idea, first suggested by John T. Doyle, of settling the estate by a proceeding in insolvency. It may here be remarked that this gentleman, elsewhere quoted as authority in my *California*, has been, since the early days of this state, a very conspicuous and reputable jurist; recognized not only as among the ablest lawyers on the coast, but as one who can be depended upon to maintain the honor and dignity of the bar; and withal, a scholar of rare culture and refinement.

The court entertained the petition, and three assignees were appointed to take charge of the estate and administer it. Thereupon Cohen did not immediately press his application to be discharged as receiver, but awaited the election of the assignees to whom he might turn over his accounts. Those selected were Richard Roman, Edward Jones, and A. A. Cohen. At once turning over to the assignees all moneys and property of every description, the receiver took a receipt for the same, and thereupon pressing his application to be relieved, the court appointed William G. Wood referee to examine his accounts. Wood made his report, showing that Cohen had fully and fairly accounted for everthing; and now the court made an order directing that his bonds be cancelled and he be relieved.

Soon afterward great confusion was caused by the decision of the supreme court that all proceedings in insolvency were void; for the creditors of Adams and Company thereupon brought suit to attach the funls of that firm, now deposited in the banking house of Palmer, Cook and Company, and garnished all the debtors who owed them money.

The court then required Cohen again to take charge of this property as receiver, which he refused to do, on the ground that he had been discharged and his bonds cancelled. Meanwhile, during his temporary absence in the eastern states, the court had seen fit to order his removal from the receivership, and to appoint to that place Henry M. Naglee. Cohen, being required by the court to account for the missing funds of Adams and Company, set forth the facts as above narrated, showing that he had lost all authority and control over the same, and that he had no power to account for them, and was altogether unable to surrender the same to the court. A suit was then commenced through Naglee, on account of Adams and Company, against Cohen. It was a most vexatious suit. A great deal of excitement prevailed, and the press of San Francisco preferred to lay all blame upon and to criminate the most convenient person for use in its articles, and manifested neither the disposition nor the capacity to consider the embarrassing circumstances under their legal aspect. Cohen was temporarily made the scapegoat for all in the court-house. The verdict agianst him, by which he was attached and required to give bond, was really ineffective, and remained *in statu quo.* Various motions were made, exceptions taken, divers proceedings were instituted, but no judgment was entered, as it was necessary for a further accounting before any final judgment could be rendered.

After waiting until 1862, soliciting investigation at all times, and vindicating himself whenever opportunity was allowed, at last, feeling that to permit adverse record against him any longer was not only doing an injustice to himself, but was doing himself and his friends an injury, Cohen, through his attorneys, insisted that whatever prosecution was to be made against him should be made and finished forthwith. Hence, after he had been imprisoned for six months, awaiting trial in the district court of the fourth judicial district of the state of California, on the 30th of June, 1862, it was ordered by the court that this suit be forever dismissed.[48]

[48] Alfred A. Cohen was born in London July 17, 1829. His father was a coffee planter in the West Indies, who failed as the result of the emancipation act of 1838, and was unable to complete the education of his son, who

The litigation which followed the first proceedings
in the failure of Adams and Company lasted for nearly
a decade, and swallowed up their assets.   Under the
law a bank could not avail itself of its insolvency act,
nor could its creditors demand an equitable distribution.   The amount received depended upon the grasp,
more or less forcibly fixed and tenaciously maintained,
by lawyers who divided the spoil with their client ?,
and not upon the just amount of the claims.   The
poorer depositors, who were not able to fight against
heavy odds, realized nothing.   But from first to last
the public never understood how disaster occurred, or
where the money went which should have been in the
bank to meet the claims of its patrons.   The newspapers
could only recite those matters which were made
known through the courts, the courts were not free
from the imputations of fraud, the rage of the business
community against them, exhibited later by the proceedings of the Vigilant committee, compelled the
judges to vacate the bench, and all was confusion.

The effect was continuous, assisting in 1856 to drag
down over one hundred and forty firms,[49] but with lia-

was put to the study of the law, but at the age of fourteen went to Canada
to start in life for himself.   In 1847 he went as clerk to Jamaica, and in
1849 left New York for California, where he arrived in 1850, engaging in the
business of a commission merchant in Sacramento and San Francisco.   In
1857 he was formerly admitted to the bar, and shortly after was appointed
justice of the peace for Alameda county, occupying himself also with farming
and horticulture.   In 1862 he retired from practice.   He was the builder of
the San Francisco and Alameda railroad, which was completed in 1864, and
afterwards extended to Haywards.   In 1865 he obtained control of the San
Francisco and Oakland railroad, and built the steamers *El Capitan* and
Alameda — the first double-enders on the coast.   In 1869 he sold out his railroad interests to the Central Pacific company.   In 1867 he was admitted to
practice before the Supreme Court of the United States.   From 1876 to 1883,
when he retired almost entirely from practice, he took only cases involving
large results, and was usually successful, being for several years employed
as attorney for the Central Pacific.   He died suddenly while en route late
in 1887 from New York to his home in Alameda.

[49] On Feb. 17, 1855, the steamer brought news of the suspension of the
St Louis firm of Page, Bacon & Co., and a run ensued upon this bank.   This
was well sustained with nearly $1,200,000 in the vaults, but five days later
the firm announced its suspension.   Sherman, *Mem.*, i. 109–16, had been
warned of danger with regard to the firm in 1854, and he states that the
managing partner objected to freely exhibit the condition of the bank during
the crisis.   It paid out some $600,000 before closing on Feb. 22d.   Business
was resumed, but further bad news from St Louis forced it into liquidation

bilities of hardly three and a half millions. The most serious was the failure of the bank of Palmer, Cook and Company, which involved a number of officials,[50] and shook the credit of the state. Then, with a misunderstood uprising of popular power, California sank into disgrace abroad. But it was only for a time. In view of the apparently reckless way of doing business, California has been remarkably free from financial convulsions, and these misfortunes, the only great disasters during flush times, were brought upon her primarily through her connections.

The crisis of 1855–6 was but the clouded change from the magnificent disorder of the golden period to the better regulated tenor of a setttled era; from the speculative mania of general mining to the sedate habits of broad industrial expansion. On the ruins of mushroom firms rose the substantial houses of men trained and purified by varied experience; men who had helped to raise reliable safeguards against hurtful fluctuations, and established standards for more legitimate business, under which San Francisco was to retain the high position gained as the fifth commercial city in the union, and the foremost on the Pacific.

in May. Nine years later there was still half a million owing, besides interest, with a residue of barely five per cent to meet it. Meanwhile the run extended to other banks, among them foremost Adams & Co. The failures for the year, chiefly connected with this crisis, numbered 197, with liabilities over $8,300,000, and assets estimated at only $1,500,000. Among these figured Markwald & Caspari with about $268,000 liabilities, J. B. Bidleman $261,000, A. J. Tobias $250,000, E. Vischer $192,000, J. Middleton $180,000, Chapin & Sawyer $180,000, Gibbs & Co. $166,000, T. F. Gould $145,000, A. S. Wright $145,000, C. H. West $144,000, R. H. Chenery $140,000, J. A. McCrea $131,000, F. Vassault $119,000, M. A. Correa $116,000, T. Sherry $115,000, Lepien, Schultz & Co. $112,000. Lucas, Turner & Co., B. Davidson & Co., and Drexel, Sather & Church sustained themselves under heavy pressure; Palmer, Cook & Co., and Tallant & Wilde were considered sound enough to escape the fury; Wells, Fargo & Co. suspended only temporarily for lack of ready coin; but Wright's Miners' Exchange bank succumbed, as did Robinson & Co.'s savings bank. Other savings banks are mentioned elsewhere.

[50] Who had intrusted it with large sums of public money on the strength of the surety offered for them. Its liabilities as bondsmen for state officials alone were placed at $583,000. *Sac. Union*, Oct. 17, 1855; July 1856; *S. F. Bulletin*, Nov. 28, 1855; July 30, 1856; *Alta Cal.* In June 1856 the firm failed for the second time to pay the interest on the state bonds at N. York, and to meet their own drafts there. Among the leading bankrupts were Clifford & Simmons for $355,000, Friedlander & Kirchner $285,000, H. A. Breed $132,000, H. B. Pomeroy $107,000, E. S. Perkins $108,000.

The Frazer river excitement of 1858 placed a temporary check on revival, and the civil war, while imparting greater stability to Californian enterprise, deranged the order of affairs to some extent. Financially, it proved a golden harvest for dealings with the eastern states, where a depreciated paper currency prevailed, while sales here commanded coin. Distance and uncertainty concerning the duration of the struggle impeded the nearer adjustment of values which the overland railway helped to establish after 1869. The effect on trade by railway communication was at first depressing; it cut off many industries, and ruined many firms. Under diminishing imports by sea, and the opening of the interior to direct eastern sources, San Francisco suffered in particular. She had, moreever, to share the growing export, notably wheat, with several bay ports. But compensation in due time arose in the general increase of trade, due to growth of population, and expansion of settlement, stimulated by mining and agricultural developments throughout the state and in adjoining territories. These remain tributary to the bay city as the only good harbor except that of San Diego along a coast line of thirteen degrees of latitude, at the gate of the richest valleys on the Pacific slope, and consequently the main distributing point for an ocean traffic which extends from Alaska to South America, from Australia to China. The railway systems concentrating at this outlet are subsidiary channels to fresh fields in adjacent states and on the Atlantic slope, while a growing competition facilitates the introduction of supplies for local manufactures. The manifold resources of California, which exceed those of any Pacific coast region, and her superior advantages in many important industries over countries in the south and in the orient, hold out the prospects of an ever-widening range of markets.

So far the proportionately greater wealth among the Pacific coast population, marked by higher wages, and their enterprising and open-handed disposition, fostered by recent settlement and climatic conditions, has tended to promote a lively trade, far above the average for eastern states. This was stimulated by the frequent renewal of mining excitements, through the opening of fresh deposits in and beyond the state, which, on the other hand, tended to keep alive in a great measure the speculative spirit of the flush times, and to stimulate a demoralizing gambling in mining shares. By this means a large class was impoverished, and taxed, moreover, with assessments to feed tricky managers, who gained control of mines purely for fraudulent manipulations on the stock market.[51] Such operations could not fail to affect commercial morality to a certain degree, and to endanger the standing of the numerous banks and firms connected therewith.

This state of affairs, the wide collapse of mines, the failure of crops, and the inflated value of real estate, contributed to bring about the financial crisis of 1877, the solitary one for a long period, attended by bank failures and a threatening attitude on the part of the laboring classes, directed particularly against the Chinese.[52] With the reaction came a more sound condi-

[51] Favored by loose state laws, unscrupulous speculators could practise their swindles with impunity. They would acquire the management of mines by election tricks, and then use their position to 'bear and bull' the shares to their own gain, concealing valuable discoveries made by the diamond drill, or other means, until the share could be depreciated by damaging reports and secured; or when lodes gave signs of exhaustion, to unload the shares upon a duped public dazzled by unwarranted dividends. The directors contracted with themselves as owners of quartz-mills, timber-land, and teams, to crush ore which often was too poor to pay the expense, or to do other needless or costly work, employed their tools at high salaries. For all of which the deluded public had to pay in assessments or deductions from profits. The chief men in these transactions usually disguised their rascality by holding their shares in the name of trustees, who frequently knew not the actual owner. Within 22 years fully $70,000,000 was thus extorted in assessments alone. In 1872 the sale of shares amounted to $200,000,000, and this was by no means the maximum figure. The levy was largely for worthless mines, gilded by reflections from such glittering sources as the Crown Pt and Belcher mines, which yielded over $40,000,000 in three and a half years, and those of the still richer Consolidated Virginia. For a history of the stock exchanges, see especially *Mining Review*, 1878–9, 5–21; periodical reviews by different journals; references in the chapter on mining.

[52] The direct loss by the drought was some $20,000,000. The two leading Comstock mines alone shrank $140,000,000 in value within two years, and many disappeared from view, ingulfing scores of supposed millionaires.

tion of business, purged of many objectionable features. Impressed by the lesson, the masses widely abandoned stock-gambling for more provident habits, and their increased means, applied to home building and comforts, gave a material prop to legitimate trade, which by 1881–2 rose to unequalled proportions, and continued to acquire strength for the bright future assured to it.

California occupies a position of rare importance, and her influence reaches far beyond the limits of the Pacific coast. Through her the United States have been placed a half-century in advance of other nations in mercantile enterprise. Her gold yield, while changing the value of this medium of exchange, as the early Spanish discoveries did that of silver, has stimulated throughout the world an industrial and commercial activity never before imagined.[53]

[53] Among the leading bankers, insurance, and business men of this state the following are worthy of note:

William Alvord, ex-president of the bank of Cal., was born at Albany, N. Y., Jan. 3, 1833, came to Cal. in 1853, conducted the hardware business of Alvord and Haviland, Marysville, for two years, after which he continued the business in San Francisco under the name of William Alvord & Co., until 1866, and was one of those who in that year organized the Pacific Rolling-mill co. Among the many positions of honor and trust held by Mr Alvord were, trustee of the college of Cal.; president of the S. F. art association; president of the Philharmonic society; vice-president of the Loring club; Golden Gate park com.; police com.; and mayor of S. F.

Darius Ogden Mills, who came so opportunely to the rescue of the bank of California, was a trained banker before reaching this coast. He was also fortified by early self-reliance; for although his father was a land-holder and justice of the peace at North Salem, N. Y., where Darius was born Sept. 5, 1825, he was left to make his own way sooner than expected. By 1847 he became cashier and partner in the Merchants' bank of Buffalo, but seized by the spirit of adventure, he started in 1848 for California, and at once launched into trade at Sacramento. Within a few months he had cleared $40,000, and soon after opened a bank under his name. In 1864 he lent his aid to found the bank of California, holding the presidency till 1873, after raising the institution to the first rank.

Among interior bankers may be mentioned Oliver S. Witherby, president of the consolidated bank of San Diego, into which were merged the bank of S. D. and the Commercial bank, with the rank of national bank. His career exhibits a wide range of experience. Born at Cincinnati Feb. 19, 1815, and educated at Miami university, he entered the legal profession, only to yield to the thirst for military glory by sharing in the Mexican war as a lieutenant of volunteers, and then, after a brief career as editor, to join the Mexican boundary commission as quartermaster, in which character he reached San Diego in 1849. Here he settled, and was chosen to represent the county in the first and subsequent legislatures. In 1850 he was judge of the first judicial district, then collector of customs, and finally he embarked in business, and became a banker.

A colleague and contemporary pioneer is E. Weed Morse, born Oct. 16, 1823, at Amesbury, Mass, and who came to Cal. in July 1849. Stricken shortly after by fever while mining, he sought the climate of San Diego, even then noted as a health resort. Here he successfully engaged in general trade, and took position as a representative citizen. In 1852 he was elected associate justice of the court of sessions, and soon after a city trustee and secretary. In 1856 he was admitted to practice in the district court. On resuming trade, he received the agency for Wells, Fargo & Co., and moved in 1869 to new San Diego, assisting there to organize the bank of S. D., and continuing as director of its successor, identified, moreover, with road and railway building, and holding office as public administrator and county treasurer.

Another colleague is Bryant Howard, born at Buffalo, May 17, 1835, who settled at San Diego in 1867, and became the first cashier of the bank of S. D., taking the position in 1879 of president of the Consolidated bank, which he filled with honor. He has taken a prominent part in the building up of the city, figuring as founder of the Benevolent society, as member of the citizens' railway committee, treasurer of the Central Market co., and the Masonic building association, president of the free library, and since 1880 as city treasurer. He is also a director and founder of the Savings bank of South. Cal. at Los Angeles, where he has other business interests.

To A. Pauly credit is due as one of the founders of the chamber of commerce at San Diego, of which he became the president. He was born at Lebanon, Ohio, May 24, 1812, and reached Cal. as a pioneer of 1849, engaging first in general trade in Butte, and then in stock-raising till 1869, when he moved to S. D., landing the first goods on Horton's wharf for his general store. Since 1875 he has devoted himself to real estate business, and to the duties of tax collector.

A striking instance of southern progress is presented in Santa Ana, which within a few years has risen from a rancho to a town of 2,500 inhab. Wm H. Spurgeon was mainly instrumental in laying out this place, where he opened the first general store, still the leading establishment, under the firm name of Spurgeon bros. He was born in Henry co., Ky, Oct. 10, 1829, and came to this coast in 1852. After mining for four years, he returned home, but could not long resist the attractions of California.

James R. Toberman, a native of Va, came to Cal. in 1859. After engaging in several branches of business in different places, he became interested in banking at Los Angeles, and entered politics, being elected to the office of mayor of Los Angeles in 1878. With the prosperity of Los Angeles Mr Toberman prospered.

Another prominent banker of Cal. is E. F. Spence. Born in Ireland in 1832, he came to Cal. at the age of 19, and embarked in the drug business at Nevada city, where he continued for fourteen years. In 1869 he made a tour of Europe, and on his return went to San José, where he first became connected with the banking business through the San José savings bank. In 1871 he went to San Diego, and was one of the organizers of the Commercial bank; three years after he went to Los Angeles to organize a bank, bought property, for which $500 per foot for the lot was paid, and helped to organize the Commercial bank of Los Angeles. In 1881 it was changed from a state to a national bank, Spence becoming its president. He became connected with eight banks in southern Cal., being president of two of them. During the time he was at Nevada city he filled the offices of city trustee and county treasurer, and in 1860 was elected to the legislature on the republican ticket, serving a term also as mayor of Los Angeles in 1885.

One of those who in 1859 organized the Hibernia savings and loan society was the late Edward Martin, who was also one of the first trustees, and later secretary and treasurer, which offices he held until his death. A native of Ennescorthy, Ireland, where he was born March 3, 1819, he came to Cal. in Sept. 1848, and soon afterward engaged in the real estate business. In 1863 he established the wholesale liquor business of E. Martin & Co., and soon afterward became one of the largest land-owners on the coast, with 450,000 acres of farming, grazing, and timber lands in eastern Oregon.

Albert Miller, a native of Hanover, came to San Francisco in 1851, and a few years later became a partner in a leading dry-goods firm. In 1862, in conjunction with John Archbald and James de Fremery, he established the San Francisco Savings Union, of which he has ever since been president or vice-president. In 1888 he was one of those who incorporated the Sather Banking company. He is also agent and manager of the Central Gas company, and is connected with other leading enterprises, in the management of which he takes an active part.

Among the leading bankers of southern California is Major George H. Bonebrake, who in 1883 organized and is still the president of the Los Angeles National bank. He also aided in organizing the First National banks at Pasedena, Pomona, Riverside, Santa Ana, and Santa Monica, the state bank at Santa Paula, Ventura co., and others, which, like the above, are in a sound and flourishing condition. A native of Preble co., O., after graduating with distinction at the Otterbein university, serving with greater distinction almost throughout the civil war, after practising law at Winchester, in partnership with General Thomas M. Browne, in 1878 he came to Los Angeles on account of his wife's failing health, and 'there he has ever since resided.

One of the directors of the Los Angeles co. bank is Hugh Livingston MacNeil, a native of Perth, Can., where he was born Aug. 9, 1850. In 1876 he came to Cal. for his health's sake, and in Jan. following was appointed teller and book-keeper, and three years later cashier of the bank, which position he held until 1886. Meanwhile he invested in country and city lands, and with such success that, though still almost a young man, he is now worth $1,500,000.

Prominent among the bankers, business men, and stock-raisers of Siskiyou co. is Jerome Churchill, a native of Elizabethtown, N. Y., who came to Cal. in 1849, and after following various occupations, in 1851 established general merchandise stores at Yreka and Humbug city, engaging also in the freighting business. He is president of the Yreka bank, and the owner of three large ranches, on which he raises horses and beef-cattle.

Chauncey H. Phillips was in former years a leading banker in San Luis Obispo co., first in partnership with H. M. Warden, and afterward as cashier and manager of the bank of San Luis Obispo. A native of Medina co., O., he came to this coast in 1864, and after filling various positions, engaged in ranching and real estate operations. In 1886 he was one of the five men by whom was organized the West Coast Land co., of which he was the projector.

By David Burris was established, in 1875, the bank of Sonoma, of which he has ever since been president. To him also is due the organization of the Santa Rosa bank, some years before that date. A native of Mo., Mr Burris is a pioneer of 1849, and has made his fortune principally by stock-raising in Tulare co., in which occupation he is still engaged.

Among those of central California is John D. Stephens, by whom was organized, in 1868, the bank of Woodland, which under his able management has paid nearly $1,000,000 in dividends. A native of Cooper co., Mo., but of Virginian parentage, Mr Stephens is one of our pioneers, his first occupation being stock-raising in Yolo co., where he was also the first to introduce sheep husbandry. By him Woodland and its neighborhood were furnished with a plentiful supply of cheap water and gas, and otherwise, especially in educational matters, he has largely aided this section of the state.

Prominent among insurance men is William D. Garland, for many years the manager of the Equitable Insurance co. of N. Y. Born Sept. 27, 1828, in Penobscot co., Me, where, except for a year or two, his youth was passed, he arrived in this state in Aug. 1850. Within 17 months he made a small fortune at the mines, and returning east increased it largely in the lumber trade, but was one of those who suffered financial shipwreck in the panic of 1857. Coming back to this coast, after some further mining experience in Nev., he was appointed in 1863 an insurance agent for the Mutual Life Ins. co. of N. Y., and from that position rose to be general agent and manager of the Equitable. In 1887 he retired from active business with a stainless reputation and a reputed income of $15,000 a year.

Among our prominent business men was Andrew J. Bryant, a native of New Hampshire, who came to Cal. in 1850, when he was 18 years of age. In 1851 he was doing business in Benicia, where he was twice elected city marshal, afterward establishing a business in Sac., and in 1860 in S. F., continuing in business until he was appointed naval officer. In 1870 he became general agent on the Pacific coast of the Brooklyn Life Insurance co., and was for many years manager of the State Investment and Insurance co. Mr Bryant was chairman of the Union party in 1864, and afterward held the same position on the democratic state central committee. In 1875 he was elected mayor of S. F., which he held for two years. He died in 1888.

The name of William F. Babcock has ever been prominent among San Francisco business men. Mr Babcock is descended from a long line of English ancestors, the family in the new world being as conspicuous as in the old world. He was born in Mass in 1820, and entered a counting-house in New York city at the age of 16, removing thence to New Orleans in 1845, and coming to Cal. in 1852, conducting here the extensive business of Davis, Brooks & Co., with which he had been associated in New York and New Orleans, and taking charge of their steamers on the Pacific, finally becoming associated with A. B. Forbes in the agency of the Pacific mail steamship company. In Feb. 1864 he was made president of the Spring Valley water works, and in 1866 became a partner in the house of Alsop & Co. Mr Babcock in 1850 married Miss Kate Duer Babcock, a second cousin. He died Sept. 22, 1885, highly respected.

A. B. Forbes was born in New Jersey July 15, 1824, and came to Cal. in 1849. He was purser on the steamer *California*, and later was made agent of the line at S. F., in company with Mr Babcock. Mr Forbes was always a public-spirited man, interested in the welfare of the city.

Thomas H. Selby was born in New York city May 14, 1820, entered the dry-goods houses of A. T. Stewart & Co. at the age of 17, after engaging in business with two brothers on their own account. He married Miss Jane Williams of Stockbridge, Mass, who was the mother of Clara W. and Prentiss Selby, and who died in 1848. In 1849 Mr Selby came to Cal. and engaged in the metal business in S. F., where to the day of his death he remained one of San Francisco's most honored merchants. He was early city alderman, and later mayor. In 1853 Mr. Selby married in S. F. Mrs. Henrietta I. Reese, who bore him six children, four surviving. Mr Selby died June 9, 1875.

Henry M. Newhall was a native of Saugus, Mass. After a sailor trip to the West Indies, he entered an auction house in Phila, and conducted business on his own account in Nashville, Tenn. Coming to Cal. in 1849, after a short experience in the mines, he engaged in the auction business in S. F., where he soon took the lead. He invested heavily in landed property, and founded the town of Newhall in southern Cal. He was twice married, first at Nashville to Sarah White, by whom he had three sons, Henry G., William, and Edwin, who succeeded to the business upon the death of the father, which occurred in 1882. His second wife was Margaret White, sister of the first wife, by whom he had two sons, Walter S. and George A. Mr Newhall was a man of strong character and sterling integrity.

Almer I. Hall, a native of Wallingford, Connecticut, came to San José in 1849, where he began the hotel business, the chambers of his hotel being used for the senate of the first legislature of Cal. In 1850 he removed to S. F., where he engaged in the auction business, and was burned out in 1851, afterward becoming the New York agent for Newhall & Co. After the death of Mr Newhall, he established the firm of A. I. Hall & Son of S. F. He married Miss Mary Hall in 1853, and had three children.

Charles M. Plum, one of our leading merchants in the line of furniture and upholstery, was born in New York city Dec. 31, 1827, and came to Cal. in 1849. He was president of the Mechanics' Institute, member of the school board, and one of the trustees of the Lick fund.

Among the commercial houses of the Pac coast none rank higher than the great hardware firm known as the Huntington-Hopkins co., in connection with which should be mentioned the president of the corporation, Albert Gallatin. Born in N. Y. state Dec. 10, 1835, Mr Gallatin passed his boyhood on his father's farm, attending the district school as opportunity offered. After several changes of occupation and residence, he came to this state in 1860, and in the following year found employment in the Sacramento store, at that date the only store of Huntington, Hopkins & Co. Beginning as a porter, he displayed such ability and zeal that in 1868 he was admitted to a junior partnership, and in 1888 was elected president of the company in which the business of the firm was merged.

One of our leading business men and viniculturists is Gustave Niebaum, who began life as a sailor boy in the service of the Russian American co., remaining for the most part in their employ until the transfer of the territory in 1867, before which date he had been promoted to the captaincy of a steamer. After the transfer, he determined to try his fortune in seal-hunting, and on Christmas eve of the same year landed at St Paul island. During the ensuing season he gathered about 10,000 seal-skins, with which he came to S. F., and entered into partnership with Hutchinson, Kohl & Co., the firm in 1872 transferring their interests to the Alaska Commercial co., of which Mr Niebaum was general manager. Later he embarked in various branches of business, in 1880 purchasing a ranch of 11,000 acres, and engaging in wine-making, in which he was very successful, his vintage for 1884 being 110,000 gallons.

In the wool business the most prominent man is John H. Wise, of the well-known S. F. firm of Christy and Wise. Born in Accomack co., Va, July 19, 1829, and a graduate of the university of Ind., he began life in the employ of the Atlantic coast survey. Coming to S. F. in 1853, he found employment in the custom-house, and in 1861, having meanwhile passed some years in Washington, where he was chief collector, first turned his attention to the wool business, taking into partnership Simeon P. Christy, whose interest was transferred in 1876 to James Denigan, from the first an employé of the firm. By this firm is now handled about one half of the entire wool crop of the state. As president of the Commercial Insurance co., the Pacific States Savings and Loan co., and other associations, Mr Wise is also well known in business and financial circles.

There are few among the merchants of San Francisco whose memory is so much respected as that of the late John Deane, formerly a partner in the wholesale dry-goods house of Murphy, Grant & Co. A native of co. Mayo, Ireland, in 1851 Mr Deane came with his father and his elder brother Coll to Philadelphia, and in 1864, after some years of service at the headquarters of that firm in New York, was promoted to a partnership in the S. F. branch, which position he retained until his decease on the 27th of April, 1885.

Among our leading business men in the line of high explosives is Julius Bandman, a native of Hamburg, where he was born July 24, 1825. After receiving his education and gaining an insight into business in that city. where he was in the employ of one of the largest firms, he came to this country in early manhood, and in partnership with Hans Nielsen, introduced Alfred Nobel's high explosives, for which the firm were general agents. He afterward became one of the largest stockholders in the Atlantic Dynamite co., which has now the most extensive business in this line. For a number of years he conducted the selling department of the Giant Powder co., which position he still retains.

One of the most prominent merchants and pioneers of San Francisco was the late Joseph Emeric, a native of Nouelles, in the south of France, who, after receiving a thorough business training in his native land, came to this coast in Feb. 1849. After engaging in various occupations, he began farming on the San Pablo ranch, near Berkeley, where he soon became the owner of 2,500 acres of land, now worth nearly $1,000,000. He was also a member of the finance committee of the board of supervisors for Contra Costa co. In 1869 he established in S. F. a general commission house, importing largely of French goods and wines from Mediterranean ports. On his decease, in June 1869, the bulk of his ample estate was left to his son, Henry F. Emeric.

In the lumber business one of the most prominent men is Asa M. Simpson, who was born in Brunswick, Me, in 1826, and came to this state in Apl 1850. After working for a time at the mines, he began shipping lumber from S. F. to Stockton and Sacramento, and in 1852 started the manufacture of lumber at Astoria, gradually enlarging his operations on the Columbia river and elsewhere, though still with his headquarters at S. F. By him was established at Gray's harbor a ship-yard, at which have been built a number of sailing vessels and steamboats.

Harry N. Morse was born in New York Feb. 22, 1835, attending the public schools until he was ten years of age, when his parents consented for him to become a sailor. In 1849 he came to Cal., and after various changes of residence he removed in 1854 to Oakland and started in business. He was elected sheriff in 1864, holding the office consecutively for 14 years. In 1855 he married Miss Heslap, who bore him seven children, three surviving.

Another successful man was the late David L. Beck, who was born in New York city Sept. 26, 1814; in 1841 he became a partner in the establishment of Hoyt & Bogart, came to S. F. in 1850, engaging in general merchandising and commission business. He afterward established himself in the commission business under the firm name of D. L. Beck & Sons. For two or three years before his death, in 1884, he did not take an active part in business, it being carried on by his sons. He was an advocate of the people's party, and one of the early founders of the fire department, and of the presbyterian church. In 1841 he married Miss Wardle, and had four children, two surviving.

A successful business man of Oakland has been Frederick Delger, a native of Prussia. Edward F. Delger, his son, was born in S. F. Oct. 24, 1859, his parents shortly afterward removing to Oakland, where he attended school, continuing his studies in Europe. Marrying Miss Prior of S. F. in 1885, he engaged in business in Oakland, taking also an active interest in politics.

In Sacramento one of the leading merchants is Eugene J. Gregory, who was born in S. F. Aug. 15, 1854, and finished his education at the Santa Clara college. In 1874 his father died, leaving a large business, which he conducted until 1882, when it passed into the hands of himself and brother, under the firm name of Gregory bros. He was also elected and served a term as mayor of Sac. city.

Eugene Germain, a native of Switzerland, came in 1869 to Los Angeles. Here he engaged in the mercantile business, and by close attention and economy he was enabled to extend his operation from time to time until he became president of the Germain Fruit co., the largest fruit shippers of southern Cal., and also president of the Los Angeles board of trade, and the Cal. Fruit and Produce Shippers' association. Germain was also president of the Produce Exchange for two years, and is a firm believer in the future greatness of Los Angeles.

The French consul at Los Angeles is L. Loeb, a member of the dry-goods firm of Stern, Cahn & Loeb, proprietors of the City of Paris store, the largest in the southern metropolis. Leaving France in 1865, he settled at Los Angeles in Feb. of the following year, and gradually won for himself the position which he now occupies as one of her leading business men and most public-spirited citizens.

Among the merchants of San José should be mentioned T. W. Spring, who came to this coast in 1849 as a member of Magruder's battery, and to S. F. in 1851, when he made the acquaintance of the late H. M. Newhall, to whom he owes his start in life. Though meeting with strong opposition, he gradually won his way to a foremost rank among the business men of the 'garden city.'

Prominent among the authorities that have been consulted in preparing the preceding chapters are the United States government documents, of which, with reference to the respective indices, the most important are the agricultural, industrial, census, and land-office reports; the reports of the secretaries of the interior; the *H. Ex. Doc.*, and *Misc. Doc.;* the *Sen. Ex. Doc.*, *Sen. Misc. Doc.*, and *Sen. Com. Repts;* also *Public Laws, Mess. and Doc.*, *Coast Survey, Patent Off. Rept*, and *Cong. Globe.* To which must be added California official documents: *Cal. Sen. Jour.*, and *Assem. Jour.*, *Cal. State Agric. Soc., Trans.*, and reports of the different departments. Also among general authors: *Burnett's Recoll.*, MS., i. 373; ii., passim; *Alameda Co. Hist.*, *Atlas: Alexander, Mendel, etc., Rept*, passim; *Annals S. F.; Bay Dist. Horticult. Soc., Trans.*, 1872, 1–40; *Cox's Annals of Trinity Co.; Brereton's Rept*, 1–11; *Amador Co. Hist.; Dow's Tour*, 37–52, 182–4; *Dye's Recoll.*, MS., 5, 29; *Barnes' Or. and Cal.*, MS., 15; *Balch's The Mines, etc.*, 569–71, 575, 577; *Owens' Sta Clara Val.*, 1 9, 20 1; *Barton's Hist. Tulare*, 12 *Brace's New West*, 218–329, 430; *Frere's Antipodes*, 518–29; *Boynton's Statement*, MS., 1–3; *Anderson's Silver Country*, 11, 84–6, 93; *Appleton's Guide*, 363, 369–75, 382; *American Naturalist*, i. 337–42; *Lux' Pastoral Life*, MS.; *Boyer's Orient to Occident*, 124–38; *Player-Prowd's Cal.*, 40–7, 58, 65–84, 130–50, 153–7, 162–4; *George's Progress and Poverty; Helper's Land of Gold*, 16–20, 34–5, 58–9, 101–3, 138–42, 162–3; *Hittell's Res. Cal.*, 25–6, 79–80, 151–237, 240; *Id., S. F.*, 128–488; *Codes Cal.*, ii. 1660, 1861; *Yosemite*, 35–6, 40–2; *Commerce and Industries*, 143, 148; *Fay's Facts*, MS., 3–10, 14, 17; *Fields' Reminis.*, MS., 12, 14–15, 138–42, 208–12; *Hayes' Col.*, including agriculture, mining, and industries, natural phenomena and material relating to the history of cities and towns in California; *Fisher's Cal.*, 2–9, 19–27; *Faithful's Three Visits*, 237–42; *Foster's Statement*, MS.; *Id., Gold Region*, 17–22; *Fowler's Bear Party*, MS., 7; *Baxley's West Coast Amer.*, 413; *Gordon's Great Geysers*, 1–53; *Gwin's Speeches on Land Titles; Id., Memoirs*, MS., 67–73, 81, 122, 178–85; *Gift's Cal.*, 13, 19–32; *Bartlett's Narr.*, MS., 3–8, 54; *Gunnison's Rambles*, 127–56, 159–78; *Hilgard's Phys. and Agric.: Roach's Stat.*, MS., 5, 13, 16; *Rose's Stat.*, MS., 3–20, 24–30; *Ross' From Wis. to Cal.*, 125–7; *Butler's Res. Monterey Co.*, 14–21; *Hayden's Surveys; Hyatt's Grape Cult.*, 226, app. 1–6, 27–9; *Haraszthy's Cult. Grapes*, 1–21, 85–6; *Browne's Resources*, 275–80, 439; *Id., Min. Res.*, 1868, 432–41; *Brown's Stat.*, MS., 11, 15–16; *Revere's Keel and Saddle*, 165; *Id., Tour of Duty*, 254; *Lowe's The Laborer*, 58; *Gonzales' Stat.*, MS.; *Humboldt Co. Hist.; Hall's Cal.*, 4–7, 8–11, 25, 113–14, 193–4; *Lord's Naturalist*, 88, 230, 238–44; *Lancey's Cruise of the Dale*, 87, 189–90; *Lake Co. Clerk Rept*, 68–71; *Ross' Stat.*, MS., 9–13; *Hastings' Emig. Guide*, 124–6; *Harrison's Guide*, 50; *Cal. Commis. for Land Claims*, 1–20; *Howe's Winter Homes*, 18–37, 216; v. 124; *Bauer's Stat.*, MS., 3, 7, 14–15; *Bancroft's Jour. to Or.*, 19–20; *Id., Guide Pac. States*, 3–6, 150–6; *Hollister's Stat.*, MS., 2–4, 8–12; *Harston's Silver Coinage; Lawrence's Reply, etc.*, passim; *Bowles' Pac. R. R.*, 78–90; *Beadle's Undevel. West*, 255–89; *Id., Western World*, 112–14, 141–61; *Fresno Co. Hist.; Hawley's Los Ang., etc.; Id., Humboldt Co.; Hayden's Great West*, 374–81; *Butte Co. Hist.*, 7, 12–17, 206–9, 227–8, 248, 252–3, 259–60, 263; *Rowley Wood, etc., Mem.*, passim; *Larkin, Doc.*, MS., vi. 74, 107, 111, 144, 161, 163, 167; *Hinton's Ariz.*, 22–4, 33; *Bunnell's Yosem.; Langley's Trade Pac.*, i. 4–5, 13–15; *Monterey Parr.*, 15–31; *Hutchings' Yosem.*, 1877, 3–102; *Barry's Up and Down*, 111–14; *Los Ang. Hist.; Belden's Stat.*, MS., 51, 60–1; *Davis' Glimpses*, MS., 7, 111–12; *Bits of Travel at Home*, 44–51, 87–139; *De Bonnemain's Stock Raising*, MS., 10–12; *Kelly's Excursion*, ii. 14–16, 243, 250; *Kern Co. Hist.; Barstow's Stat.*, MS., 1–14; *Lambertie's Voy.*, 298–9; *Kneeland's Yosem.*, 26–7, 30; *Douglas' Speeches*, June 26–8, 1850; *Krull's Stat.*, MS.; *Cal. Digger's Hand Book*, 27, 32–4, 37, 49; *Kohler's Wine Prod.*, 3–22; *Clark's Reminis.*, MS., 2–5; *Cooke's Treatise; Dunphy's Stat.*, MS.; *Calistoga Hand Book; Insects Injurious to Fruit Trees; Cal. Irrigation; Froebel, Aus Amer.*, ii. 521–2; *National Alm.*, 1864, 434–5; *Campbell's Notes*, i. 71, 78–80; *Frisbie's Reminis.*, MS., 37–8, 40; *Cal. Squirrel Law; Denison's Yosem. Views; Avery's Cal. Pictures; Purisima Miss. Arch.*, MS., 33–4; *Chaboya vs U. S.*, 1–120; *Rusling's Amer.*, 307, 457, 490–1; *Cal. Mineral Springs, Scraps*, 1–6, 28;

San Luis Ob. Co. Hist.; Morris & Bennett's Manuf. Int., 1–46; *Tyson's Geol.*, etc., *of Cal.*, 79–80; *Tyler's Bidwell's Bar*, MS., 6–7; *Sutil y Mex.*, 168; *Pearson's Recol.*, MS., 3–5; *Peirce's Rough Sketches*, MS., 108, 110, 112; *Mofras' Cal.*, 365; *Zabriskie's Land Laws; Yuba Co. Hist.; Sherman's Mem.*, i., passim; *Shippee's Stat.*, MS.; *Cerruti's Ramblings*, 39–40; *Crosby's Events in Cal.*, MS.; *U. S. Mails, Scraps*, 5–19, 27–54; *Sherwood's Pocket Guide*, 25–6, 75; *Scribner's Mag.*, vi. 641–51; x. 278; xvii. 644–52; *Semi-Tropic Cal.*, iii. 1 et seq.; *Mayhew's Recol.*, MS.; *Todd's Stat.*, MS., 21–8; *Velasco, Sonora*, 308; *Willey's Personal Mem.*, MS., 82–110; *Williams' Rec. Early Days*, MS., 4–5, 9, 11–16; *Id., Pac. Mail Steam. Co.*, MS.; *Id., Mam. Trees Cal.; Id., Pac. Tourist*, 214–19, 248; *Simpson's Gold Mines*, 6, 24–5; *Tyler's Mormon Bat.*, 286–7; *Trask's Geol. Cal.*, 14–18; *Savage, Col.*, iii. 128, 138–9; *Id.*, MS., iv. 43–4, 52, 262–3; *Carson's Early Recol.*, 6–50; *Turk's Son. Wines*, 2–14, 22–6; *Wood Bros' Live Stock Move.; Stebbins' Eighty Years*, 37–68, 81; *Schlagintweit, Cal.*, 101–42; *Montgomery's Reminis.*, MS., 2–3; *McCollum's Cal.*, 36–40, 64–5; *Yolo Co. Hist.; Staples' Stat.*, MS., 5–17; *Strobel's Stat.*, MS.; *Vischer's Pict. Cal.; Stephenson's Stat.*, MS.; *Shuck's Repres. Men of S. F.*, 1015–20, 1077; *Yosem. and Big Trees; Wigmore's Stat.*, MS., 1–2; *McKinstry's Papers*, 19; *Starr's Merch. Pac.*, MS.; *Currey's Incidents*, MS., 11–12, *Cronise's Cal.; Woods' Pioneer Work*, 12–13, 16, 22–3; *Id., 16 Months*, 76, 88, 171; *Smyth's Law Home.*, 45, 467; *Soc. Mex. Geog.*, vi. 77; *Skellenger's Reminis.*, MS.; *Schott's Precip.*, 74–7, 116–17; *Id., Distributions*, 12–15; *Century Mag.*, July 1882, 388; Nov. 1883, 27; *Simpson's Stat.*, MS.; *Ventura Co. Pen Pictures*, 9–10, 21–3; *Weed's Cal.; Spreckels' Pac. Steam. Lines*, MS., 1–149; *Stearns' Stat.*, MS., 17–19; *Nidever's Life and Advent.*, 140–2; *Wakeman's Log*, 114–38, 220–1; *Soule's Stat.*, MS., 4; *Sutton's Stat.*, MS.; *Serrano, Apuntes*, 139, 146–8, 153–4; *White's Pict. Pioneer Times*, MS., 194; *N. Amer. Rev.*, lxxv. 410–24; *Shaw's Golden Dreams*, 236; *Smiley's Vig. Com.*, MS., 16–22; *West Shore Gaz., Yolo Co.*, 137–58; *Sac. Illus.*, 8–9; *Wilder's Cal.; Walton's Min. Springs; Whitney's Mt Heights*, 4–6; *Sac. Directory*, 1853–4, 1856, 1857–8, 1871; *Sac. Co. Hist.; Stanislaus Co. Hist.; Van Buren's Remarks*, March 1852, 1–8; *Winan's Stat.*, MS., 4–16; *Tembley's Meteor. Oakland; Noyes' Redwood and Lumber. in Cal.; Sutter Co. Hist.; Siskiyou Co. Hist.; Id., Affairs*, MS., 27, 29; *Woodward's Stat.*, MS., 14, 18–23; *Powers' Afoot*, 274–6; *Peto's Res. Amer.*, 153, 306; *Solano Co. Hist.; Sonoma Co. Hist.; Powell's Land of Arid Reg.*, 47–56; *Schmiedell's Stat.*, MS., 1–2, 6; *Neall's Vig. Com.*, MS., 5, 7–9, 11–22; *Proceed. 1st Nat. Conv. Cattlemen; Schenck's Vig. Com.*, MS., 15–22; *Warren's Dust and Foam*, 146; *Tex. Alm.*, 1859, 139–50; *Turrill's Cal. Notes*, 18–21, 87–95, 177–8, 232; *Sayward's Personal Reminis.*, MS.; *Tiffany's Guide*, 36, 72; *Cal. Bureau Labor Statistics*, 1883–4; *Californian*, 1881, April, 1–20; Aug., 321–6; *S. F. Manual*, 169–83; *San Bernardino Co. Hist.; Treasury of Travel*, 103–4; *San Luis Obispo Co. Hist.; Whitney's Yosem.*, 9–15, 24–46, 113–55; *Santa Clara Val. Res.*, 22, 24; *San Gabriel Libro de Mis.*, MS., 9–10; *Thompson's Law of the Farm; Wheeler's Surv. Rept*, 1875–1877; *Santa Barbara Arch.*, i. 74, 129; ii. 65–6; v. passim; vi. 53–5; ix. 598–9; x. 495–8, 502–6; *Santa Barbara Co. Hist.; San Diego City*, 12–16; *Twain's Roughing It*, 70–2; *Tuthill's Cal.*, 324–45, 351–7; *San Joaquin and Kings River Irrig. Co.; Wheaton's Stat.*, MS., 9, 38–9; *San Joaquin Co. Hist.; Id., Directory*, 1878, 42–4; *Id., Val. Agric. Soc., Trans.*, 1861, 4–150, 168–71; 1863, 62–77, 107–96; *Vallejo's Reminis.*, MS., 34–5, 39–40; *Van Allen's Stat.*, MS., 29–31; *Santa Clara Co. Hist., Atlas*, 10–17; *Santa Cruz Co. Hist.; Van Tramp's Advent.*, 306; *Taylor's Spec. Press; Id., Cal. Notes*, 58–60; *Id., Between Gates*, 146–65, 174–92, 239, 268–9; *Id., Cal. Life Illus.*, 248–9; *Id., Eldorado*, i., ii.; *San Mateo Co. Hist.; Van Dyke's Stat.*, MS., 8–9; *Throckmorton's Min. Rept*, 1–15; *Vallejo, Docs.*, iii. 228–30; xii. 320; xiii. 19, 37, 179; xxviii. 98–101; xxix. 48; xxxiii. 263; xxxv. 68; *Baudin, Doc.*, 2, 3, 4; *Beadle's Monthly*, Nov. 1866; *Bryant's Cal.*, 304, 449. Moreover, a multitude of newspapers and periodicals published in California and elsewhere, too numerous to specify, have been examined. Mention can only be made of a few; namely, the *Alta, Evening Bulletin, Chronicle, Morning Call, Evening Post, Herald, Times, News Letter, Golden Era, Examiner, Scientific Press, Daily Stock Exchange, Argonaut, Abend Post*, and *La Sociedad*, all issued in San Francisco.

CHAPTER IX.

CRIMINAL AND JUDICIAL.

1849–1879.

CREATION OF COURTS—THEIR POWERS AND POSITION—LEGISLATORS, LAW-
YERS, JUDGES, AND GOVERNORS, THE ENEMIES OF THE PEOPLE AND THE
FRIENDS OF CRIMINALS—EARLY JUDGES—AND YET THERE HAVE BEEN
HONEST MEN ON THE BENCH—WEAK AND UNPRINCIPLED GOVERNORS—
CALIFORNIA THE MURDERERS' PARADISE—THE NOBLE PROFESSION OF
HIGHWAYMAN—CALIFORNIA BANDITTI—JUDGES WHO SHOULD HAVE
BEEN HANGED—PROSTITUTION OF THE PARDONING POWER.

THE constitution of California vested the judicial
power in a supreme court, district courts, county
courts, and justices of the peace; and the legislature had power to establish such municipal and other
inferior courts as might be necessary. The supreme
court had appellate jurisdiction in matters in dispute exceeding $200, and decided questions of law
concerning tax, toll, import, and felony cases. The
district courts had original jurisdiction in law and
equity in all civil cases where the amount exceeded
$200. · In criminal cases, not otherwise provided for,
and in all issues of fact joined in the probate courts,
their jurisdiction was unlimited. The county courts
were also probate courts; and the county judge, with
two justices of the peace, constituted a court of sessions, with such jurisdiction as the legislature should
confer; but the county courts had no original
jurisdiction.

The first legislature established the superior court
of San Francisco, consisting of a chief justice and two
associate justices. This court had the same original

jurisdiction as conferred upon district courts. Either of the justices might hold court for the trial of causes, and different trials might take place at the same time before different judges; but all points reserved and issues of law were argued before at least two of the three justices. ' The superior court had no power to send any process beyond the limits of the town, except to subpœna witnesses, and in such cases as those in which district courts might issue final process beyond their limits. A cause might be transferred from the district court of San Francisco to the superior court. Each of the justices had the power to issue writs of habeas corpus at the instance of any person held in actual custody, and had in fact the same powers as district judges. The judges in all the courts of the state were to be chosen at the general election, except those first appointed by the legislature.[1] Superior judges held their offices three years, one being appointed each year, as vacancies occurred; district judges for two years, and supreme justices for six years. Thus the machinery of justice seemed provided for, and it was only by its numerous failures that its weakness was discovered.

The end sought to be attained by a state government, which was the prevention and punishment of crime, the regulation of landed property, and general good order of society, was defeated by a number of causes, the chief of which were found to be the defective laws enacted, and imperfect organization of the courts; the incompentency of the district attorneys, who were generally young men without an adequate knowledge of the law; the want of secure prisons;

[1] The legislature of 1850 appointed P. H. Morse chief justice of the sup. court of S. F., and Hugh C. Murray and James Caleb Smith associates. The state was divided into nine districts, numbered from San Diego toward the north, S. F. co. being the 4th, and Sac. and El Dorado the 6th. The judges appointed by the first legislature were, for the 1st district O. S. Witherby, 2d Henry A. Tefft, 3d John H. Watson, 4th Levi Parsons, 5th Charles M. Creaner, 6th James S. Thomas, 7th Robert Hopkins, 8th William R. Turner, 9th W. Scott Sherwood. *Cal. Jour. Leg.*, 1850, 283–4, 256–65; *Cal. Stat.*, 1850, 93.

the expense of keeping prisons and convicts, the difficulty of enforcing the attendance of witnesses, and
the impossibility of securing good jurymen, especially
in the principal towns where there was a large proportion of idle, reckless, disappointed, and desperate
men, ready to be summoned, and more than willing
to be bribed.

It has been many times remarked that crime was
much increased in frequency after the adoption of a
state government, as if the laws were chargeable with
the crimes; but the truth was that the laws were
not chargeable with the punishment; and the discovery of this fact emboldened a constantly increasing
criminal element, which took upon itself to still further defeat the ends of justice by corrupting elections,
and placing its own creatures in public offices. In
the first grand jury report, in San Francisco, were
eight indictments, two of which were for murder; all
of them were quashed on some technicality of the
law. Crime, they said, stalked abroad in open day,
and they were instructed by the court that they could
not take cognizance of it.

In his message to the legislature, in January 1851,
Governor Burnett urged the necessity of amending
the criminal laws, pointing out that the original jurisdiction in felony cases was confined to the district
courts, which were required to be held only at certain
periods, with long intervals between, while there were
few prisons in which to detain the offenders. He
suggested conferring criminal jurisdiction upon the
court of sessions for some counties, and requiring
them to hold frequent terms, with called terms when
necessary to try a criminal, giving the right of appeal.
He recommended that for grand larceny and robbery
the punishment should be death until the state should
be provided with county prisons and a penitentiary.
"The crime of grand larceny, in stealing horses and
cattle, has become so common in many places," says
the message, "as to diminish their value fifty per

cent. In some instances whole bands of tame cattle have been stolen, and farmers have lost all their teams, and been compelled to abandon their business in consequence." This condition of affairs led to the creation of a class of judges not before known to legal parlance, who were denominated Judges of the Plains, whose duties were to attend rodeos, and to decide disputes concerning ownership. An appeal might be taken to a justice of the peace of the township, provided it were taken within twenty-four hours after the decision. These officers were appointed by the court of sessions. In 1857 this act was amended so as to empower the judge of the plains to make arrests, and take before a magistrate any persons suspected of stealing, hiding, or killing cattle or horses. "We believe," said one of the public journals, "that there are over 1,000 men in California who make horse-stealing a regular business." But it disapproved of hanging for stealing, as a disgrace to the statutes, saying a jury would not condemn a horse-thief to death. It, however, declared the courts not summary enough, straw bail too common, peace officers not sufficiently responsible. Murders, it said, might be nightly committed in saloons with impunity had the victim no friend present. Officers executed warrants as they pleased, before pursuing a fleeing criminal asking the price of county scrip.

Concerning the number of assassinations, another authority says, "There was no crime for which immunity could not be bought. Many times have I met in the street a man who was known to be guilty of murdering his companion for $2000, half of which distributed among his judges had obtained him a full acquittal." Murder was even more lightly judged than robbery, for a man carried his life about with him, and was generally esteemed capable of taking care of it; but property was the object of living, and was often defenceless; crime against property, therefore, was taken more notice of than crime against life, except where murder was committed in a stealthy and treacherous manner.

Taking note of these things, and considering the governor's suggestions, the legislature in 1851 performed some tinkering of the laws affecting the courts, leaving them no more effective than before. The original statute fixed the time of holding the district courts absolutely; the amended law left the times of holding terms in the most important counties entirely to the judges, without increasing the number of terms. Some additional power was conferred upon the court of sessions in criminal cases. The act concerning crimes and punishments was amended so as to leave it to the discretion of the jury whether to bring in a verdict of death for robbery or the former extreme penalty of ten years in prison. Grand larceny was defined as feloniously taking any property of the value of fifty dollars or more, and was punishable by imprisonment from one to ten years, "or by death, in the discretion of the jury." [2] But few cases of hanging occurred under this law, demonstrating that the normal impulse of the people was toward ordinary clemency,[3] a jury at this period fixing the penalty.

By the original law, judges of the supreme, district, and superior courts were forbidden to absent themselves from the state without the consent of the legislature, if in session, or of the governor, who was required to appoint to the vacancy. This guard on the administration of justice was repealed by the legislature of 1851, which first granted leave of absence to the judges of the 2d, 5th, and 7th judicial districts, then opened the door to the others. There was no

---

[2] *Gov. Ann. Message*, 1851, 15–16; *Cal. Jour. Sen.*, 1851, 22–3; *Staples, Statement*, MS., 12; *S. F. Picayune*, June 11, 1851; *S. F. Alta*, June 12, 1851; *Sac. Transcript*, Feb. 4, 1851; *West Shore Gazette*, Yolo co., 23; *Augur*, 208; *Cal. Stat.*, 1851, 406–7.

[3] A burglar in Grass Valley was hanged for taking a silver watch in 1852. This was the first capital punishment in this district. There was also the case of one Tanner, taken in the act of stealing a wagon-load of goods from a warehouse in S. F. The vigilance committee handed the culprit over to the courts, where he was convicted and hanged. *F. F. Low*, MS., 8–9.

provision in the law for requiring the district judges
or superior judges to attend court, except at their
pleasure, and the sheriff had power to adjourn the
court until the next term, should a judge of a district
be absent for three successive days, the matters pending being continued over, and the same latitude extended also to the superior judges. It is needless to
point out the effect of this lax judicial system, when
combined with the conditions of society already mentioned. In the elective system was an evil of still
greater magnitude, for the very worst men sought
office, and were supported by those who intended to
use them for nefarious purposes. Says one authority,
there were those " holding offices of trust and dignity
whose moral life would disgrace the lowest resorts of
the most degraded beings in human form." [4] A
Botany bay convict was a town constable ; the county
judge was a drunkard and debauchee ; his successor
could not spell correctly. A man caught in the act
of committing grand larceny was tried and acquitted
on a quibble. A dozen years later this man was
elected county judge of one of the best counties, and
pronounced sentence upon similar offenders in the
presence of the lawyer who had defended him.

To the 8th judicial district, in 1850, the legislature
appointed a southerner from the lone-star state, one
who had, together with a narrow mind and bitter
prejudices, the bowie-knife manners of that border-
land. Therefore, when an attorney from New York [5]
sent him a package of New York papers, as a very
proper attention, he became enraged at an article in
the *Evening Post*, and made war on this young lawyer, fining, imprisoning, banishing him from court,
and ruining his business. He went still further and
sent the sheriff to arrest the county judge, [6] who was

⁴ *Farnham, Cal.*, 464–7; *Hutchings*, i. 409. The people of Martinez demanded the resignation of George F. Worth, as he was unfit to hold the office
of county judge. *S. F. Bulletin*, Dec. 24, 1855.
    ⁵ Stephen J. Field. See *Field's Early Days in Cal.*, 41–55.
    ⁶ Haun, who was appointed U. S. senator in Broderick's place, was judge

sitting in court at the time.   The judge reminded
the sheriff of his duty, at the same time pointing a
navy revolver at him when he retreated.   The sheriff
was fined $200 for contempt; but such was the in-
fluence of the Texan that the county judge, Haun, being also a pro-slavery man, was forced to apologize
to him for having behaved in a friendly manner toward the disbarred attorney.   The supreme court ordered the lawyer rienstated, but the Texan refused to
obey the mandate, and threatened violence.   After
carrying a pair of revolvers for some time to defend
himself, the lawyer was luckily elected to the legislature, where he employed himself "reforming the
judiciary," one part of his reform being the banishment of the southerner by so arranging the judicial districts that he was sent to the wilds of Trinity
and Klamath, which counties were made to constitute
the 8th district.   He also moved his impeachment,
whereupon B. F. Moore, another southerner, made
him the subject of disparaging remarks, with the apparent intention of provoking a duel, which was happily averted by the interposition of friends, Moore
apologizing before the assembly.   A brother of the
judge, soon after the adjournment of the legislature,
attempted to assassinate this northern "abolitionist"
in a public saloon,[7] but was fortunately prevented.

of Yuba co.   Attorneys J. O. Goodwin and S. B. Mulford were expelled
from court along with Field.   Turner relates these incidents in his *Documents,
etc.*, MS.   He says that Field's friends fired 10 or 12 shots at him during the
time Field was in confinement.

[7] Field relates how on two occasions Broderick befriended him, even to
saving his life.   The first was when he felt he must offer to fight Moore, but
could find no one willing to act as his second on account of the provision
against duelling in the constitution.   'Whilst thinking the matter over,'
says he, 'I happened about 9 o'clock in the evening to walk into the senate
chamber, and there found Mr David C. Broderick, afterwards U. S. senator,
sitting at his desk, writing.   He was at that time president pro tem.   I had
known him for some time, but not intimately; we were mere bowing ac-
quaintances.   As I entered he looked up and said, "Why, Judge, you don't
look well; what is the matter?"   I answered that I did not feel well, for I
had not a friend in the world.   He replied, "What is it that worries you?"
When the matter had been explained, Broderick said, "My dear Field, I
will be your friend in this matter; go and write at once a note to Moore, and
I will deliver it myself."'   Drury Baldwin was Moore's "friend," and upon

Upon such slender threads hung the lives of great and small in this epoch of crime.

Among the dangers by which men were perpetually surrounded was that of being murdered for their money or property.[8] To mention even a small pro-

him Broderick called for the answer to Field's note. Baldwin replied that his principal had given up doing anything further in the matter. Broderick then said that Field would rise in his seat in the house, and after giving a statement of all that had passed, call Moore a liar and coward. 'Then,' said Baldwin, 'Judge Field will get shot in his seat.' 'In that case,' rejoined Broderick, 'there will be others shot.' When the house met, Field took his seat prepared to do as Broderick had said, who sat behind him with several of his personal friends, all armed. Just as Field rose, Moore also rose, and the speaker recognized him first. He made a complete apology, and that put a stop to southern badgering for that term. But in May following, Field being in San Francisco, and visiting Broderick at his hotel, while taking wine together at the bar, Broderick suddenly threw himself before him, and with great violence pushed him out of the room. To Field's astonished and indignant question, 'What does this mean, Mr Broderick?' he received for reply that V. Turner, a well known desperado, had drawn from beneath his Spanish cloak a navy revolver, and levelled it at Field, seeing which Broderick threw himself between them and carried off the intended victim. *Early Days in Cal.*, 77–83; *Yuba Co. Hist.*, 51–2.

[8] There were 3 classes of acknowledged criminals—the native Californians, who stole horses, and lassoed travellers; the 'Sydney ducks,' who committed grand larceny in the towns, and killed the successful miners returning to S. F. to ship for home; and those from the states, who were either professionals, or through ill luck and evil associations had become inducted into crime. The victims of robberies were almost always killed, whether or not murder was necessary to the consummation of the robbery. Of the Mexicans, there were some who were thieves only, but who paid the penalty of their crimes 'at the discretion' of a miners' jury by strangulation. *Dew's MS.*, 3–5; *Bothwick*, 226–7; *Popular Tribunals*, this series, passim. The miners being much troubled by this class. took advantage of the amended criminal law to rid themselves informally of the dangerous men who prowled in the vicinity of their camps, but particularly of the natives of Mexican origin. There existed for 10 or 15 years after the conquest, among the ignorant, half-Indian, native population, a hatred of Americans which they nourished as patriotism, and justified upon the ground that as the Americans had taken the country, with the gold in it, away from them, it was quite fair to take the lives of the intruders, and repossess themselves of the treasure stolen from their country. Hundreds of murders on the highway in every part of the state were committed by these assassins. About 1850 they began to form banditti, formidable for their number and crimes. At first they operated chiefly in the southern counties, but soon infested all the mining portions of the state, and the roads in every direction. There were several Mexican robber bands even in 1849. One was headed by Andreas Armijo, and another by Tomas María Carrillo, a disbanded soldier of the late Californian army. *Brooks, Four Months*, 168–9, 187–8. Still another celebrated bandit was Salomon Pico, who committed a great many crimes. *Ord.* in *Misc. Docs*, 1–9; *Green, Life and Adventures*, 19. Pico ranged in the region of Monterey. In April 1851, he fixed upon a day to visit the Escobar rancho, 6 miles from town, in charge of an American, Josiah Swain, who was to be killed, but one of his band refusing to take part in the murder was threatened, and deserted, ex-

portion of the outrages perpetrated upon the industrious by the profligate class would convert history
into a police report. Justice did not reach the
offenders, and the people became sheriff, jury, judge,
and executioner. Lynching became common, and was
often justifiable, for what was to be done with a red-
handed murderer or a highwayman by a community
which had no prison, and whose sheriff, for anything
they knew to the contrary, might be in collusion with
the criminal. Possibly they sometimes hanged an innocent man; but the district courts were liable to error,
as in the case of Thomas Burdue,[9] where mistaken

posing his former confederates. A company was raised in Monterey, and
the robbers intercepted on the 18th. Five were arrested, and two discharged
for want of evidence. Pico, Cecilia Mesa, and William Otis were tried by a
people's court, and sentenced to be hanged, but the legal authorities interfered. Mesa was discharged. State senator de la Guerra became bail for
Pico, who ran away, when Guerra refused to be made responsible. Otis,
whose alias was Bill Woods, but whose real name was William Otis Hall,
having no friends, languished in prison for some time, but finally escaped.
He was retaken, and hanged by the people. The newspapers and books of
travel and adventure of the period record a fearful list of felonies.

According to the proclamation of the governor of Sonora, there was a
band of American highwaymen, 300 strong, ranging about the crossing of
the Colorado for the purpose of robbing returning miners. The governor
directed an investigation to be made, and the proceedings sent to him.
Pinart, Coll., no. 1077. On the other hand the California newspapers attributed the same robberies to banditti from Mexico, which was more probable.
S. F. Pac. News, Aug. 1, 1850. During May 1851, a band or robbers, under
the leadership of John Irving, a Texan, raided the county of Los Angeles,
striking terror into the hearts of the native population, many of whom fled to
the camp of the militia maj.-gen., Joshua H. Bean, who was at Cajon pass
in pursuit of the Indian murderers of eleven men who kept a ferry on the
Colorado river. Irving had threatened the ranchos of several Spaniards in
Los Angeles co. who fled before him, leaving their property to be pillaged.
Irving was finally killed with 10 of his men, by Juan Antonio, a chief of
the Cohuilla tribe, and an alcalde in his district, who with his people followed and fought the banditti. In his turn Antonio, alarmed at a rumor
that 200 white men were about to attack him in revenge for Irving's death,
fled to the mountains, two of his children being lost in his flight, who were
not recovered for several days. The grateful inhabitants soon found means
to reassure Antonio, and return him to his home at Apolitan, on the San
Bernardino rancho. There was a scandal connected with Bean's command
to the effect that some of the volunteers were in sympathy with Irving, and
mutinied because they were not permitted to punish the Indians, breaking
up the command. *Gov.'s Amer. Message*, 1851, 9; *Hayes' Scraps, Indians*, i.
61-5, 68; *Id. Angeles*, i. 106-12. Bean was assassinated in Nov. 1852, at
Los Angeles, by three Mexicans who were tried and hanged by the people
Dec. 11.

[9] Berdue petitioned the legislature in 1853 for indemnity to the amount
of $4,000 for the injury to his feelings, person, and estate, suffered in his
imprisonment and trial. The report of the judiciary com. on the subject

identity was proved and the innocent man narrowly
escaped.

In May 1851, state senator S. E. Woodworth was
commissioned by Governor McDougal to raise a company of rangers to capture horse-thieves in Monterey
county.   Only one of the band was caught, who after
confessing, and inculpating others, endeavored to escape and was shot.   The expedition cost the state
$9,000.[10]   One of the singular features of this epi-
demic of crime was that men in good standing became
infected ; and not only the low and depraved were
engaged in robberies, but those who had previously
sustained good reputations.   They behaved like people at a shipwreck or a fire, who carry off what does
not belong to them to prevent other people from so
doing.

Nor was this period confined to the first three or
four years of excitement and foreign immigration.   It
reappeared, over and over again, notwithstanding
criminal laws, and vigilance committees, and notwithstanding that laws were passed against convict immigration, making it a misdemeanor for any master of
a vessel or other person knowingly to land a felon
or convict upon California shores.   It was not that
so many confessed outlaws had immigrated to the
new state, but that the conflict of races, of ideas, of
customs, and of the principles of the world's future
government, taking root in the soil of the Pacific,
and steeped in the crude semi-civilization of Spanish
territories, produced this strange crisis in morals.

was a refusal, with the remark that in society the innocent often were wrongfully accused, and he should be rejoiced that the laws afforded him protection when wrongfnlly accused. *Cal. Sen. Jour.*, 1853; *App. Doc.*, 37.   The
history of the Burdue case is given in full in vol. i. of my *Popular Tribunals.*

[10] *S. F. Alta*, May 14 and June 3, 1851.   The same paper of March 21,
said that Pacheco's rancho, at the foot of Pacheco pass, San Joaquin valley,
had lost 900 head of horses about the 10th of that month.   Pacheco had
been robbed of $15,000 in gold a short time previous.   Salinas valley was
raided.   Theodore Gondolez lost most of his stock.   Juan Anser of St John
valley lost all of his; around Mission Soledad 160 were taken, and a reign
of despair existed among the rancheros, whose business demanded the service
of many horses.

"What then shall cleanse thy bosom, gentle earth, from all its painful memories of guilt? The whelming flood, or the renewing fire, or the slow ranges of time? That so at least the horrid tale of perjury and strife which we call history may seem a fable, like the inventions told by poets of the gods of Greece."

The miners occasionally framed municipal regulations within the limits of their camp or district, excluding gamblers; gambling generally being a prelude to robbery and murder. At a camp in Placer county, in 1853, the miners lost one of their number at the hands of a gambler, who shot the man in simulated anger, for detecting a false play. The sound of his pistol was hardly stilled before he found himself seized and pinioned. In another half hour he was swinging stark on the limb of a neighboring oak tree. The following day the sheriff of the county, a friend of the dead gamester's, appeared with a posse to arrest the persons concerned in the hanging ; but the miners having decided upon a course of action in such an event, were prepared, and on a concerted signal surrounded the officer of the law, and accusing him and his posse of being confederates in evil of the man they had executed, gave him five minutes to consider the propriety of withdrawing from the camp, or suffering the alternative of being lynched with his lieutenants. The sheriff could only submit.[11]

In this case the letter of the law was violated, both in the unauthorized hanging of the gambler, and resistance to the sheriff. Yet the murderer only met his just deserts, and the miners were right to prevent his executioners from falling into the hands of those whom they suspected of having no regard for the law, while they used it as a cloak for their crimes. This same camp afterward made and enforced a regulation against gambling, but again violated the law in so do-

---

[11] *Life in the Mountains or Four Months in the Mines*, 30–32. The author of this brochure signs himself S. Weston, and says he was many years principal of a public grammar school at Providence, R. I.

ing, as only a license was required by the statutes to make gambling legal.

Highwaymen, as well as criminals of a higher social position, perceived the weakness of the laws and their ineffectual operation. Force could be met only by force; hence the vigilant sytem, and ubiquitous Judge Lynch. In the meantime business men and well-disposed people were in despair, and by an uprising in 1856 gained a temporary relief, especially for San Francisco and the principal towns. But upon the highways leading from camp to camp, from town to town, safety had not been secured. With the establishment of mail and stage lines into the mountains, and particularly with the opening of the Pioneer stage line to Carson valley, and the overland line from St Louis, via New Mexico, Sonora, and San Diego, to San Francisco, there sprang up a new class of highwaymen whose business it was to rob coaches of treasure in transit, and to pillage travellers by stage. Murder did not always accompany a robbery, but was not infrequent. This form of brigandage came up about 1859, and is not quite done away with to this day. An armed guard, and a coach full of armed travellers were generally unable to prevent the plundering of the express company's treasure-box, the mails, and the passengers themselves, owing to the suddenness with which the order was given to "halt! hold up your hands," enforced at the muzzles of several rifles. Resistance was seldom offered, although occasionally shooting occurred, and one or more persons were killed; at other times drollery or mock generosity was indulged in by the robbers.

Chinamen were very often losers. They usually walked to the mines, or travelled on Indian ponies; but returning, if they had treasure, they took the coach, and by this means frequently lost a whole season's profits. The express companies were the heaviest sufferers. The state had no banking system or medium of exchange between the interior towns and the metropolis of San Francisco, except coin and gold-dust; hence large amounts were frequently carried over the roads on Wells, Fargo & Co.'s coaches, which sums were greatly augmented by the opening of the Comstock lode about this period. Such was the loss and danger resulting from brigandage that the governor, in 1860, recommended that it should be punished with death.[12]

After the expulsion of the foreign convict class, in 1856, the banditti of the state were predominantly Mexicans, or native Californians,[13] for the next ten

[12] *Knox, Underground*, 854–7; *Pac. Monthly*, xi. 834–5; *Red Bluff Independent*, Feb. 14, 1866; *Grass Valley Union*, July 31, 1866; *Nordhoff's Cal.*, 234; *Cal. Jour. Assem.*, 1861, 384.

[13] Among the Californians was Joaquin Murieta, a young Sonoran, who was chief of a considerable company of natives. He told a romantic story of wrong and oppression heaped upon him by the Americans in Calaveras co. His robberies were innumerable, and usually accompanied by murders. His followers thought nothing of riding up to a miner' tent and shooting the inmates before they realized their danger. Travellers received a ball in the back of the head. Ranchos were invaded and pillaged. Chinamen were killed as hunters kill a covey of quail. Many attempts were made to capture Murieta, but he had the fleetest horses in the country with relays in the hands of confederates, and was never approached nearer than half a mile by pursuers. This gave him the advantage of being personally unknown. The counties he ravaged were Calaveras, Tuolumne, and San Joaquin. At length the governor offered a reward of $1,000 for his capture, dead or alive, which was increased to $5,000. Being in Stockton in disguise and seeing the handbills offering this reward, he wrote underneath in pencil 'I will give $10,000 myself, Joaquin.' The reward offered by the government proved sufficient to hunt him down, and he was finally surprised, and after a desperate resistance killed in 1853, and his head sent to Stockton together with the hand of Three-fingered Jack, a well-known member of his band. The legislature passed an act giving the reward of $5,000 to Henry Love, who effected the capture. Joaquin's true name was Carrillo, of a respected Mexican family, and J. M. Covarrubias, when the bill offering a reward for the capture of the bandit chief was before the committee of which he was chairman, reported against it, on the ground that to set a price upon the head of any individual who had not been examined and convicted, is to proceed upon an assumption of his guilt.' *Cal. Jour. Assemb.*, 1853, 700. H. C. Miller, 'the poet of the sierras,' obtained his soubriquet of Joaquin from the versified story of the robber's life. Harry Love was a noted mountaineer, and is described as resembling Walter Scott's black knight. He sometimes wore a sword presented to him by a wealthy Mexican, whom he rescued from the savages during his mountain life. He appeared at a Fourth of July celebration at Santa Cruz in 1865, when the *Pajaro Times* spoke of him as of a 'tall, manly figure, with sparkling eyes, long curling hair falling far down his shoulders, with his knightly sword hanging by his side.' But others, who hated almost everybody connected with the repression of crime, said he looked more like a large-sized ape than a man, that he was illiterate and a coward. *S. F. Post*, April 12, 1879. Much has been written about Joaquin Murieta to give him a chivalric character resembling Robin Hood.

years, after which there was an influx of the outlaw
class from the states in rebellion, who naturally took
to the highways, making a pretence of having public
grievances to adjust by private reprisal.   It required

A few of his men were captured with him, and several were afterward
taken and executed in southern Cal.

A Mexican named Claudio was a contemporary of Murieta, perhaps a
little earlier.   During 1852 he kept the southern mines in a state of terrorism.
He was captured in 1853 on his way to Monterey with 6 of his men by H.
Cocks, justice of the peace at Salinas, who headed a party of 8 resolute men.
Claudio and 5 of his men were killed in the fight with Cocks' party.   The
one who escaped was afterward hanged by the people. *San Joaquin Valley
Argus*, June 13, 1874; *Hayes' Scraps, Cal. Notes*, v. 71; *Streeter's Recoll.*, 155;
Janssens' Vida y Av., 221.   Francisco Garcia was the next famous robber, at
the head of a mixed company of Mexicans and ruffianly Saxons. *S. F. Alta*,
Oct. 22, 1854; *Hayes' Scraps, Monterey*, 112–13.   He was wounded by his own
lieutenants in a quarrel over the spoils.   One of these, Sebastian Flores, •
quarrelling with the other, Beas Angelino, turned state's evidence, and had
Angelino hanged.   Garcia, after a bloody career of 17 years, was tried on an
old indictment at San José, Flores being detained as a witness.   The case was
put off, and at the next session of court Garcia was acquitted. *San José Patriot*,
Oct. 18, 1879.   Anastasio Garcia, another of this band, was sentenced to
state prison for horse-stealing, and on regaining his freedom, in 1856, hastened to Los Angeles to revenge himself upon the informer.   While hiding
in the hills he fell in with another evil-doer, and in a brief time had gathered
to himself a dozen kindred spirits, most of whom were Angelenos.   Among
them were Pancho Daniel, Juan Flores, Espiñosa, Andres Fontes, Varela,
'El Chino,' Pigumini, 'El Tuerto,' Faustino Garcia, Juan Cartabo, and Ar-
dillero, 'el huero.'   They called themselves 'los Manilas,' and used pass-
words, etc.   Their trade was horse-stealing, with its attendant incidents.
Anastacio Garcia and his manilas dogged the steps of the informant to San
Juan Capistrano, but the man escaping, they murdered the storekeeper at
that place, and robbed the place of goods, spending the night in drunken
revelry.   Word being sent to Los Angeles, Sheriff James Barton, with six
well-armed men, two of whom were constables, William H. Little and
Charles R. Baker, set out for San Juan.   They were ambuscaded at the
Barranco de los Alisos, and Barton and the two constables killed, the remainder of the party escaping back to Los Angeles. *Hayes, Angeles*, i. 647–8.
This occurrence greatly alarmed the Angelenos, as the bandits were all native
Californians, and the Americans and other foreign-born residents feared that
the Californians sympathized with the criminals.   The excitement ran high,
and the feeling of insecurity became so great that an armed defensive attitude was mutually maintained.   But confidence was restored when several
prominent Californians took horse at the head of 40 of their countrymen, and
pursuing the outlaws captured most of them in the Sierra de Santiago, and
brought them to Los Angeles, where, after a trial by the people, they were
hanged.   Tomas Sanchez, who, with Andreas Pico, was active in making
these captures, was afterward sheriff, and maintained a party of mounted
men until all the manilas had been taken and executed.   This action on the
part of the Californians restored confidence between the two races. *Coronel,
Mena*, 204–9.   Varela, a person who was well connected, was pardoned, and
at the breaking out of the civil war joined the confederate army, but returned
to Los Angeles, and lived conformably to the laws. *Kraszewski,*,1–17; *Sta
Barbara Press*, March 9, 1878.   Sato and Senati were two other native bandits, notorious about 1856. *Dixon's White Conquest*, i. 67–74, 110.   Tiburcio
Vasquez figured at a later period.   His pride was to surprise large parties;

nerve to attack these outlaw organizations. Valuable lives were lost in attempts to make arrests, but occasionally a man attained to fame by his daring in pursuing banditti. The general government was frequently appealed to for aid down to 1877.[14]

Banditti, such as swept through the southern counties while the population was sparse, can no longer exist. Rebels against labor and order now tramp about the country in the rôle of mendicants, but so watched and suspected that they are powerless, the law having asserted itself everywhere. Occasionally one bolder than his comrades in distress waylays a country stage and "holds up" the passengers; or some

35 men were bound and robbed at Kingston, Fresno co., by 13 of his gang, who escaped with their booty. He was finally captured by the officers of Los Angeles co., in May 1874, and hanged in 1875. His obliging guard one day asked him if there was anyone he would like to have visit him. 'Who is that little Irishman—the poll-tax collector?' asked Vasquez. 'Mike Madigan,' replied the guard, 'would you like to see him?' 'No,' said Vasquez, 'but he is a funny little fellow. I was riding alone in the cañon de los Verdugos when I met him driving in a buggy. He asked in a very important manner whether I had paid my poll-tax. I said no, and he asked if I would pay it then. I answered that I would, for I was a good citizen, and always paid my taxes. He drew a book and pencil from his pocket, and swelling up like a turkey-cock inquired my name. When I said Tiburcio Vasquez, his hand shook so that he could hardly write the receipt. I paid him the $2, and without saying good-bye he whipped up his horse, and kept whipping as far as I could see him.' There is almost as much literature about this rogue as about some earlier ones, as *Career of Tiburcio Vasquez*, being scraps from newspapers; *Cerruti, Ramblings*, MS., 147; *Vasquez, His Career*, in *S. F. Call*, Oct. 25, 1873; *S. F. Bulletin*, Jan. 5, 1875; *S. F. Post*, May 15, 1874; *S. F. Alta*, April 21 and May 15, 1874; *Hayes, Memorabilia*, 123–5; *Cal. Crimes and Society Scraps*, 100–1; *San Diego Union*, May 21, 1874; *Salinas City Democrat*, May 25, 1874. Santos Sotello, the successor to the honors of Vasquez, was sent to prison in 1877, and was the last of the robber chiefs of Mexican birth who have troubled the border counties. Sotello was arrested, single-handed, by a young Californian, Rafael Lopez, who thereby acquired an honorable reputation. Chavez, one of his lieutenants, was captured and killed a little earlier, and these losses broke up the band. There was a claim for his capture before the Cal. legislature in 1877–8. Of the Anglo-Saxon robbers, Tom Bell, born in Albany, N. Y., figured in 1856, and was executed by the people with a number of his followers. Jack Powers was another well-known robber of 1856–7. In 1858, San Luis Obispo and San Diego were terrorized by organized bands of outlaws. *S. F. Alta*, June 14 and Aug. 27, 1858. The civil war drew a good many of this class away, and the close watch kept upon all kinds of outlawry during 1862–5 was a decided check to crime. *Sta Barbara Gazette*, 23–33, 61–70, 87–109.

[14] Such a man was Stephen Venard, a detective employed by Wells, Fargo & Co., who made several important captures, and killed half a dozen highwaymen. *Ukiah Press*, Nov. 16, 1871; *Grass Valley Union*, May 16, 1866; *Healdsburg Flag*, in *S. F. Bulletin*, Jan. 9, 1880; *U. S. H. Doc.*, 13, p. 202–3, 45 cong. 1 sess.

desperate rogues plan the capture of railroad trains, in which enterprises they have sometimes been successful. As the certainty of punishment becomes more evident, the number of offences gradually lessens.

I have given considerable space to outlawry, yet have only outlined it. Without presenting this picture it would be difficult to represent fairly the responsibility resting upon the courts and officers of the law. Add to the crimes of banditti the individual crimes committed from various impulses, the reckless shooting by gamblers and drunkards, the vendetta,[15] bur-

[15] An instance of the vendetta, in Monterey co., resulting in 10 murders and a number of wounded, illustrates a phase of society in southern counties. José María Sanchez was accidently drowned in 1852, and left an estate worth from $60,000 to $90,000. William Roach administered upon the estate, and Lewis Belcher was his bondsman. Roach obtained possession of all the money and property, and Belcher quarreled with him for a share in it. Mrs Sanchez had married a Dr Sanford, who sided with Belcher in the quarrel, and legal proceedings were commenced against Roach, who was arrested and lodged in Stockton jail. But Roach persuaded his jailer to liberate him, and fly with him to Monterey. Here he defied the law, and gathered about him a following of personal friends on whom he could rely. Belcher also had a party on his side, and a body-guard, among whom was Anastacio Garcia, before mentioned, who was living at the Carmel mission. He determined to take Roach, and the feud was at a white heat. McMahon, a brother-in-law of Roach, meeting Sanford in a bar-room, both men fired, and both fell dead. A brother-in-law of Sanford, named Atwood, in the excitement of these proceedings blew out his own brains. Two friends of Roach, Isaac B. Wall, collector of the port of Monterey, speaker of the assembly in 1853, and Thomas Williamson, late of Tenn., set out for San Luis Obispo with pack mule and arms. They had not proceeded many miles when they were assassinated, as it was supposed by Belcher's tool, Anastacio Garcia. The sheriff went to Garcia's house to arrest him with a posse, 3 of whom were killed by Garcia, who escaped. On the 18th of June 1856, Belcher, standing in the barroom of the Washington hotel was shot by some unknown person on the outside, and died next day. In his dying deposition he said he believed that Roach, Garcia, and others whom he named, were his assassins. But as there was no proof on examination, nothing could be done. After Belcher's death Roach retired to his farm in Santa Cruz co. and lived quietly. Garcia, however, was arrested and thrown into prison, for the murder of Wall and Williamson. Some persons obtained access to his cell and hanged him there, it was said lest he should confess and implicate them. After a time Roach too was assassinated near Watsonville, it was alleged, on the ground that he talked too freely about past occurrences for the safety of his former confederates. In this feud, arising from the efforts of two men to rob a woman of her estate, eleven persons were killed—Gomez says 13—and several wounded. Meantime the woman had married George Crane, who persuaded her to deed all the property to him, which he spent in a short time, and going east died, and the object of these dozen murders was accomplished, namely, robbing a widow. *S., F. Herald,* June 21, 1856. The only one of these criminals punished was Garcia, and he was hanged by his friends and not by the law.

glaries, larcenies, and other felonies, with the great burden of civil suits of all kinds, and the labor of disposing of all appears Cyclopean. Says one who had every opportunity of knowing, "People from 1850 to 1858 complained of corruption in the courts, but the accusations were unfounded. The courts, as a general rule, administered the law to the best of their ability."

It cannot be denied that the courts were often crippled in their action by juries who decided, not according to fact, but to expediency; who, instead of inquiring did the prisoner commit the crime, asked did the murdered man deserve to be killed? A distinction which, if not good law, was sometimes good justice. But it was the general opinion that the courts and juries erred on the side of clemency. The prisoner might have friends on the jury; or a juror might have sensitive qualms; or he might be affected with the moral disease about him. Such things are not unknown even now; but probably the infection referred to was the most dangerous, because the most subtle enemy with which the law had to contend, for when a judge or juror condones a crime, he is an accessory after the fact, as far as the moral of it goes.

I have no means of determining what was the proportion of punishment to crime, but the judges received a large amount of blame, and the press, which but echoed the public sentiment, fell under the displeasure of the courts in several instances. A certain judge of the 4th judicial district suggested to the grand jury which met in March 1851, "the propriety of inquiring into the conduct of the press, and, if it transcended certain limits, of presenting it as a nuisance." The editor of a San Francisco journal of respectability was arrested for contempt of court, in commenting on the judge's charge to the grand jury, and without the benefit of jury, the judge himself sitting in judgment, was sentenced to pay a fine of $500 or in default of payment to go to prison. An indignation meeting of citizens was thereupon held at the plaza, speeches

made condemning the action of the judge, and resolutions of censure passed, with talk of impeachment
and a complaint to the president of the United States,
who had nothing to do with it, since the state legislature had elected the judges. The grand jury for the
following term gave even more cause for displeasure,
since it censured the judge officially, and in no mild
terms, insomuch that he was constrained to move the
court of sessions to strike out from their report the
stinging paragraphs.[16]

The judge of the 10th judicial district, which then
consisted of Yuba, Nevada, and Sutter counties,[17]
was spoken of as the most dissolute man that ever
wore the ermine of justice,[18] a gambler, and associate
and protector of gamblers. Great effort was being
made to have laws enacted against gambling by
men and women, and trenchant articles were written
for the press in all parts of the state; but this
infamous jurist only gave encouragement to the sporting fraternity, and became, according to one of the

---

[16] *Currey Incidents*, 10–11; *S. F. Alta*, March 9 and 10, 1851. The report
concerned the vigilance committee of 1851, and read as follows: 'When we
recall the delays, the insufficient and, we believe with much truth it may be
said, corrupt administration of the law; the incapacity and indifference of
those who are its sworn guardians and ministers; the frequent and unnecessary postponement of important trials in the district court; the disregard of duty and impatience while attending to perform it, manifested by
some of our judges having criminal jurisdiction; the many notorious villains
who have gone unwhipped of justice lead us to believe that the members of
that association have been governed by a feeling of opposition to the manner
in which the law is administered, and those who have administered it,
rather than a determination to disregard the law itself.' *S. F. Herald*, Aug.
3, 1851.

[17] The legislature of 1851 increased the judicial districts to 11. The
11th consisted of Yolo, Placer, and El Dorado counties. *Cal. State*, 1851, 12.

[18] *Nevada Gazette*, Dec. 9, 1864. The judge challenged Field to fight a duel,
but made it appear that he was the challenged in order to secure the choice
of arms. He selected bowie-knives and colt revolvers; the fighting to be
done in a room 20 feet square, the principals to be placed with their faces to
the walls, and to turn and fire at a given signal, then to advance with their
knives. Field accepted, believing this a device of a coward, and so it proved,
for the judge first modified his mode, and then withdrew altogether from the
fight, screening himself behind his judicial office. He threatened, however,
to kill anyone who should assault him. Hearing that his course had been
ridiculed, he attempted to shoot Field from behind, the latter being unarmed.
Field's Early Days, 100–107. The judge was indicted in 1854 for a criminal
offence, but continued in office from 1852 to 1858.

judges of the court of sessions in Yuba county, "the head of the hell-concocted junta, headed by the judge of the 10th district, and tailed by a noted gambler of Marysville." Some libel suits grew out of this freedom of speech, but public sentiment sustained the press, as did also the courts in general.[19]

The grand jury of San Francisco, at the September term, 1851, wished to resign, because the governor had pardoned a certain notorious character who had been convicted of a brutal assault and sent to prison; but Campbell, who had succeeded Murray on his promotion to the supreme bench, refused to discharge them. The jury represented in their report, that if the judgment of the courts and the lives and property of the people were to be set at naught by the executive, their acts as grand jurymen were not required. But this was only the temporary disgust and despair which overcame the people when the highest officials failed in their duty. In 1856 the grand jury had become less sensitive. Its bill for expenses for a single term was almost $1,000.

The organization of a county, or the establishment of a new judicial district, was the occasion for the swarming of the office-seekers, who were thereupon hived by their leaders. In 1852, the Tulare valley was explored by an expedition under Indian Agent Savage, the legislature having divided Mariposa county by act of April 20, 1852, named the southern portion Tulare, and provided for an election in July for choosing county officers. As the new county was inhabited solely by Indians, Savage and company were the first "settlers." They proceeded to hold an election the day after arriving, at Poole's ferry, on King river, and at a place called Woodville, on the Kaweah river, from a trader named Wood, who had established a

---

[19] The first libel suit against a newspaper was *in re* Melhado *vs.* Crane & Rice. The verdict of the lower court was against the defendants, but Judge Murray declared it contrary to law and fact, and granted a new trial. *Sac. Transcript*, Feb. 28, 1851.

post there, but whom the Indians had killed. The
number of votes polled at both places was 109, but
from this population the requisite officials were chosen,
a certain major being elected county judge. Next
day most of the electors and elected returned to
Mariposa. Shortly after he qualified as judge, the
major killed Savage in a quarrel,[20] and under circumstances which caused people to regard the death of
the Indian agent as the result of a conspiracy to vacate
his position. The major had only organized the court
of sessions, and his own arrest was the first in Tulare
county. He was permitted to go free, but public
sentiment being much against him, he left the country, and Thomas Baker was appointed in his place.

But the wrong-doing was not by any means all on
the side of the courts. In Napa, in 1851, J. A. Sellers, justice of the peace, nonsuited a certain person
for being absent. Meeting the justice in a public
place, the other endeavored to provoke a quarrel, which
the justice equally endeavored to avoid, but finally, being irritated, said that if he really wished to fight, he
would send a negro to fight him, whereupon he was
stabbed in the breast, and died in a few minutes.[21]
The legislature passed an act within a week providing
for a special term of district court in Solano county
to try the murderer of Sellers, but he escaped punishment. In 1850 a Sacramento judge was publicly
whipped by a man whom he had not long before sentenced. There were none to interfere, and the judge
resigned his office. Such examples were not encouraging to the administration of justice. Judge Wilson
of the Sacramento court of sessions, in 1852, was as-
saulted on leaving the court-room by two men, one
of whom was a prominent lawyer of that place,

[20] Cal. Courier, Sept. 10, 1851; S. F. Alta, March 14, 1856. Savage was
the 3d man of the expedition who was killed before the year was out.
Barton, Hist. Tulare, 3.
[21] Sac. Transcript, March 14, 1851; Hartnell, Convention, MS., pt 18, 1–4.
Another man attempted to kill Judge McCabe, but was pardoned. S. F.
Alta, March 17, 1855.

while both had figured in the squatter riots, and also owed him a grudge. Wilson defended himself with a cane-sword, which he thrust into the lawyer's left lung. A sheriff named McDonald interfering, disarmed the judge, whereupon the latter was shot at, but the sheriff, in endeavoring to shield Wilson, received the bullet in his own person. A great excitement arose, and the vigilance committee was called together. The offender was taken in charge, and placed on the prison brig, and the committee demanded an immediate trial. Chief Justice Willis could not preside at the case because the affray took place at his rooms. Aldrich, the district judge, could not try him until he was indicted. It was decided, however, to let the law take its course, and the wounded man recovering, the affair blew over. Grand juries were extremely negligent in bringing evil-doers to trial, frequently ignoring assaults with intent to kill, and manslaughter. Men of criminal reputation often went free for years, committing numerous crimes against life without being punished.[22]

The difficulty in bringing a cause to trial where the parties charged with crime were of southern antecedents, and especially if they occupied official positions, was illustrated by the ease with which Terry eluded the law for the killing of Broderick. A change of venue to a district where the judge was also a southerner and sympathizer, a trick to delay witnesses, a

[22] The Lloyd family were an example. Edward Lloyd shot and killed Thornton, a teamster, in 1861, at Oroville. He was tried and sentenced to 10 years in state prison, but through a decision of the supreme court was released. In 1862 he was killed by T. N. Smith, in the fight between steamboat runners in Sacramento. Smith remained in the county jail six months, when the grand jury ignored the charge against him. Within an hour after his discharge he was killed by George Lloyd, who was tried and acquitted; but was killed in a quarrel over mining claims in Nevada, the murderer being supposed to be his brother-in-law, Coleman, who was also shot and killed at Pioche, by Barney Flood, in 1867, the grand jury refusing to indict Flood. Thomas Lloyd shot and killed a man in S. F. in 1865, and was sentenced to 10 years in prison. Sears, an intimate of the Lloyds stole a horse, was pursued and killed. Not long after the owner of the horse was assasinated, presumably by the Lloyds, or their friends. Four other deaths resulted from the violence of this ruffianly association, making 12 in all, yet the only one punished by the law was Thomas Lloyd. *S. F. Alta*, April 15, 1871.

dismissal of the case, and all was settled. No, not all, for the legislature in the case of certain criminals passed ex post facto amendments to the laws for their benefit.[23]

A case which may be here recorded, comprehending all these judicial and legislative artifices, occurred in 1861. A feud had grown up between a Baltimorean and a Kentuckian, both citizens of a certain town in Placer county, of which the latter had been mayor. The quarrel arose concerning some personal remarks made first by the Kentuckian's wife, who was a sister of the judge of the 16th judicial district, and replied to in kind by the other. Something of a political aspect was given to the hostilities, the Baltimorean being a Douglas democrat, while the Kentuckian was of the Lecompton order. The former, who was a newspaper publisher, went to San Francisco to purchase stock for his office. He was followed by the judge and the ex-mayor, who did not conceal their intention of killing him should they meet him, which they did in the forenoon of New Year's day on Sacramento street. The Kentuckian at once attacked with a bowie-knife, and soon his victim lay dead on the ground. With his accomplice, who was close at hand, he then walked arm-in-arm to the police station, and was introduced by his companion to the chief of police, who locked the murderer up, safe away from vigilance committees, or any honest man who might hurt him. A writ of habeas corpus was issued by Robinson, judge of the Sacramento county court, which required the prisoner to be brought before the 12th district court, Campbell, judge. His attorney applied for change of venue, but the application was denied. The ex-mayor then petitioned the legislature to pass

[23] An act to amend an act entitled an act to regulate proceedings in criminal cases, passed May 1, 1851. *Cal. Stat.*, 1860, 71. This amendment provides for granting a change of venue, and was passed after the Terry fiasco. In 1857 it was proposed to pass an act requiring a judge to grant a change of venue, but the judiciary committee to whom it was referred repudiated it.

an act directing the court to grant a change of venue to Placer county, and such was the influence of the southern minority in that body that a bill was actually passed by a large majority, requiring the submission of Campbell to legislative interference with his duties. The governor vetoed the bill, but nevertheless it was passed over his head, through the exertions of lobbyists who persuaded some of those who had voted against it to pair off, and leave the bill to its supporters. The constitutionality of the act was argued before Campbell, who decided against it on many grounds, but particularly because it was a special act to liberate the assassin.

The opinion of Campbell being conclusive, instead of appealing to the supreme court, the murderer's friends again applied to the legislature to enact a general law covering all similar cases as well as this one. Certain public journals had commented from time to time upon the case, and the same influence which had procured the special act for the relief of a murderer, caused the introduction of a bill declaring "it unlawful to print in a newspaper the testimony or facts, or the probable testimony or facts, or any statement whatever of the testimony, facts, or circumstances, or anything purporting to be such evidence or statement of facts or circumstances relative to any crime or misdemeanor in this state, under a penalty of from $50 to $500 for each offence;" but the publication of the general nature of an offence with the name of the accused, or the proceedings after trial, was not prohibited, nor the publication of evidence of an offence of a political or insurrectionary character, or of the wrongful acts of public officers. Murder, only murder, was to be so sheltered and defended, that the bowie-knife chivalry might have their safety in their own hands, whatsoever lives they might choose to take.

The legislature did not, however, venture upon this further outrage to public sentiment. As for the chief instigator of the acts above related, he was indicted for the murder of the Baltimorean by the grand jury of San Francisco, and arrested at Sacramento on the 28th of March, on the ground that he was an accessory before the fact, and in the eye of the law equally guilty with the other. A habeas corpus was issued by Baldwin, judge of the supreme court, returnable before Judge Robinson of Sacramento, who declined to have anything to do with it. A writ was then issued returnable before Judge McKinstry of the 7th district, who also declined jurisdiction. Still another writ was made, returnable before Judge McKune of the 6th district. About the middle of April the supreme court rendered an opinion that the special act of the legislature was constitutional, and Judge Campbell made the order transferring the assassin to the 11th district court in his own county, which acquitted him. His accomplice was soon again seated upon the judicial bench, and the doctrine that homicides could be cleared by the legislature was soundly engrafted upon California jurisprudence. In 1863, the ex-mayor having knocked down an agent of Wells, Fargo & Co. at Virginia City, Nevada, was shot, and died from the wound. The judge was impeached upon charges of malfeasance in office, of uttering disloyal sentiments, and language unbecoming his high position. W. H. Badgely succeeded him as judge of the district.

While it is extraordinary that so many men chosen to administer the law in criminal courts should prove themselves criminal, they were after all the exceptions.[24] California had forty-three counties, each with its county court, and court of sessions; eighteen judicial districts with a judge for each; the superior court of San Francisco, with three justices; lower

---

[24] *S. F. Bulletin*, March 22, 1861; *Cal. Jour. Assem.*, 1862, 566–72, 609–11, 653–6, 753; *S. F. Bulletin*, March 30, 1861. Yet there were in California model judges, impartial and decorous, men of whom any people might be proud. There were Edward Norton of the 12th district, afterwards supreme judge; John S. Hager of the 4th district, and Shattuck of the superior court of S. F. Campbell of San Francisco was an able and honest judge in early times.

municipal courts in towns with as many justices as required; a supreme court, and a United State circuit court. It would seem that with so much legal machinery, order should have reigned. But it took the strong hand of the general government to evolve order out of the discordant element in California; and in that respect the civil war was a blessing.

From 1849 to 1854 inclusive, 4,200 murders were committed in California.[25] In San Francisco there were 1,200, and only one conviction. In 1855, 538 persons died by violence out of a population embracing 110,223 voters.[26] One wishes to turn away from such wholesale blood-letting, and yet if we consider the character of the population and the infrequency of punishments, we have no reason to be surprised at this enormous proportion of homicides.[27] In the county of Sacramento during thirty years, from 1850 to 1880, there were 21 legal executions. The record of San Francisco from 1852 to 1882 shows that there have been but 16 legal executions, and 139 convictions for different degrees of manslaughter which were punished with imprison-

[25] Helper in his *Land of Gold*, 29, gives a list of lives lost: murders 4,200; killed by Indians en route to Cal. 1,600; perished of want, and accident, and by Indians in Cal., 5,300; wrecked and lost at sea, en route, 2,200; suicides 1,400; became insane 1,700; total 16,400.

[26] Of these 357 were white persons; 133 Indians; 32 Chinamen; 3 negroes. Exclusive of Indians there were 405 homicides. The particulars are not always given but the following are known: found murdered, 46; executed by mobs, 47; executed according to law, 9; killed by sheriffs or police, 10; killed by collectors of miners license, 6; killed by Indians, 32—civilization is far before savagism in human butchery—in justifiable homicides, 17; in quarrels about mining claims, 12; in gambling disputes, 8; for robbery, 16. *Hittell, Resources*, 375-7; *S. F. Alta*, March 19, 1855. The *Weekly Gazette* of Sta Bárbara, June 7, 1855, says that according to the calendar published in the *Chronicle*, there were 152 murders committed in the state during the first four months of the year; two were hanged by the sheriff; 14 by the excited mob, and 8 convicted.

[27] The first man hanged under Cal. laws was a Mexican in Mariposa county. *San Joaquin Republican* in *S. F. Alta*, June 9, 1851. The first in San Francisco co. was a Spaniard, José Farmi, who was hanged on Russian hill in 1852. There was no legal execution in Monterey until 1858, when José Anastacio was sentenced by Judge Hester and hanged. *Monterey Herald*, Oct. 23, 1875.

ment.   Of these 31 were sentenced to imprisonment
for life.   The total of 155 convictions for the thousands of lives taken in over thirty years, gives us a
sense of something peculiar in the laws themselves,
or in their administration.   What it is, let the student of law and social science determine; the fact remains that an average of 25 homicides has taken
place yearly in this city for the last decade, during
which none of the exciting causes of the first twenty
years have existed, and that out of the 250 or more
homicidal crimes, only four have been punished capi-
tally, and seventy-seven by imprisonment.   In all the
other cases the juries probably agreed that the victim
deserved to be killed, the attorney for the defence
usually being chosen for his skill in proving murder
justifiable, and his patience in exhausting the privileges of all the courts.   In 1871, when people wished
to have hanged Laura D. Fair for the murder of her
paramour in the presence of his family, the crime being augmented by the social eminence of the man,
they were restrained in the expression of this feeling
by a sense of the shame it would be to make an example of a woman, when they allowed four out of five
men to escape.   But of the several atrocious public
assassinations by men of social standing since that
event, not one has resulted in conviction.

The combined operation of all of the courts in the
state, even in this laxity in administering the laws,
furnishes a large number of prisoners to the penitentiary.   The whole number received at the state prison
from 1851, when it was first occupied, until 1880, when
the new constitution went into effect, was 9,320, of
whom 7,756 had been discharged, and 1,564 remained.
In the first decade so many prisoners escaped [28] that the

[28] In 1856 the convicts confined in the prison brig at Sac. conspired to
murder the officers and escape, but were suspected, and the first plot frustrated.   A second attempt was discovered to the officers by one of their
number under sentence of death, for which service the governor commuted
his sentence. *Sac. Union*, June 3, 1856; *S. F. Alta*, Sept. 27, 1856.   In the
spring of 1857, 4 convicts escaped from San Quentin in an open boat, but

pardoning power was not called into exercise to any great degree. The disposition to pardon felons has since increased to such an an extent as to make the trying and sentencing them appear an official farce. In 1861 the governor pardoned 41 convicts out of the penitentiary. In 1862–3 there were 26 pardons. From 1863 to 1865 the number was reduced to an average of eleven pardoned yearly by Governor Low. But from 1865 to 1867 the governor liberated 83 state prisoners, and 17 from county jails. From 1867 to 1869 were pardoned 42 out of the state prison and two out of jail; and from 1869 to 1871 the governor freed 70 from state prison and 13 from jail. From

were retaken. In the following November, some convicts being on a wood-boat, which they were unloading, moved the boat onward, as they afterward alleged, by the order of the person having them in charge; but a guard standing by a 6-pound gun seeing the movement, and remembering the late escape, fired on the prisoners, killing 3 and wounding 5. *S. F. Bulletin*, Nov. 9, 1857. The conduct of the prison under the contract system was highly discreditable to the state. The state was robbed, and the prisoners were starved and ill-treated. Escapes were frequent. It used to be said of criminals that they 'might as well have been freed, for if the courts do not turn them loose, Estill will.' *S. F. Bulletin*, March 2, 1857. In 1858, Gov. Weller took forcible possession, for the good of both state and prisoners, and began the reform which has culminated in a thoroughly good system of prison discipline and management, although the policy of legislation forbidding prison labor to compete with outside manufactures has deprived one third of the prisoners of the benefits of employment. *Rept Dir of Cal. State Prison*, July 1, 1879. When Gov. Weller instituted his reforms there were 585 convicts crowded into a building which could not comfortably accommodate more than 350. At present, with more than twice the number, the arrangements for healthfulness, moral training, religious instruction, reading, and schools for the younger prisoners, are admirable. In May 1859, 14 convicts escaped from San Quentin, and in June another attempted escape was planned, in the execution of which 5 were killed. In Oct. there was still another daring effort made to secure freedom, but the prisoners were this time safely recommitted. The great revolt occurred in 1862, when the lieut-gov. was visiting the prison. He was seized by a body of nearly 200 convicts, who bore him before them around the walls, and compelled him to signal to Fort McClellan not to fire on them. The officers, however, managed to get in one shot without hitting the lieut-gov., which partially disbanded them, and through the assistance of the citizens of San Rafael the main body of them were captured and returned to prison. Ten were killed and 30 wounded. *San Rafael Journal*, July 26, 1862; *Marin Co. Hist.*, 130–2; *S. F. Bulletin*, July 23, 1862. In 1864, while the prisoners at San Quentin were at work in the brick-yard, an effort was made to escape by scaling the wall and taking post No. 4. The guard was assailed with every sort of missile at their command, and to prevent the prisoners using the cannon, spiked them. After a hard battle between the 4 guards at the post and 23 convicts, the latter were compelled to return to the prison, 4 being killed, 8 wounded, 3 mortally. *S. F. Bulletin*, April 4, 1864.

1871 to 1875 were liberated 80 from the state prison, 18 from jails, and commuted the sentences of 12 convicts. Pacheco, who held the office of governor only from February to December 1875, released 60 state prisoners, 16 county prisoners, and commuted the sentences of five. Irwin followed in 1876–7 and 1878–9, with 109 pardons for state prisoners and 21 for county prisoners, beside 25 commutations of sentence. Thus in nineteen years, after society had recovered from its first fermentative state, there were deliberately liberated in its midst 536 state criminals and 81 prisoners confined in county prisons, while 42 had their sentences commuted. In these 660 cases were the grand juries mistaken ? Did the witnesses perjure themselves, were the judges mistaken in the law, or unduly severe in their decrees? These are seldom urged as reasons for exercising the pardoning power. A petition for the release of a prisoner, containing certain statements to account for his incarceration, and favoring his liberation, to which is appended a long list of names, among them being often those of the prosecuting attorney who convicted and the judge who sentenced him, is the evidence which undoes all that the former testimony had effected. These petitions are signed by persons who know nothing of the merits of the case, and who do not even stop to inquire the contents of the paper to which they subscribe. This part of a dangerous act may be attributed to a reprehensible carelessness; but when those who administer the laws petition to have their operation set aside, the conclusion is soon arrived at that the majesty of the law has departed. As for the governor, he is but an instrument, and if the lawmakers and law-administrators counsel him to return so many electors to their forfeited privileges, what then? It would be curious if the evil-disposed should show greater respect for the government which fails in respect for itself.

In the report of the board of prison commissioners

for 1879, with the governor's name at the head, was the following paragraph which should have some meaning: "I would use the pardoning power ten times where it is now used once; would not use it absolutely but conditionally. The governor may impose any condition he pleases; he may confine one man to the limits of a particular town; another to a county or a farm, or he may send him out of the state or the United States, or he may pardon him upon condition that he pay a sum of money for the support of the prison, or that he furnish beef for the prison for a certain time. There are at least 100 prisoners here who ought, in my judgment, to be pardoned; and there are at least 200 serving excessive, unheard of, inhuman sentences.[29] Then, again, there are at least 200 prisoners here, under short sentences, who should either have been sent for life, or long terms." The legislature was requested to devise some plan for the equalization of sentences, which was certainly only proper, to prevent the state of things here represented; but making the governor a pardon-broker, with unlimited powers, would have been strange legislation.

In the next chapter I shall have particular reference to courts of appeal, their constitution, history, and decisions.

[29] The governor may have found some cases like this one: a Mr Levy, in 1855, was sentenced to a year in state prison, and a forfeit of $30,000, for smuggling cigars. _S. F. Alta_, Nov. 6, 1855. This, while murderers went free! The report of the assembly com. on prisons for 1881, gives a list of 26 prisoners convicted of robbery, whose sentences vary all the way from one year to life, five being in for their natural lives.

CHAPTER X.

THE JUDICIARY.

1850-1872.

The First Supreme Court—Personnel of the Judges—Influence on Opinion—Evils of an Elective Judiciary—Character of Cases to be Determined, and Influence on Industry—Land and Mining Interests—Effect of the Amended Constitution—Federal Courts in California—The Municipality and the Consolidation Act—Pueblo Lands—Compilation of the Laws.

The supreme judges elected by the legislature in 1850 were S. C. Hastings, chief justice, and H. A. Lyons and Nathaniel Bennett, associates. Hastings served his term of two years. Lyons became chief justice by seniority in 1852, but resigned in April. Bennett had resigned in October 1851. Thus, in the course of a little more than two years, the whole supreme bench was changed. Solomon Heydenfeldt was the first elected supreme judge to succeed Hastings. To fill vacancies, Hugh C. Murray was appointed vice Bennett; A. Anderson vice Lyons. At the general election of 1852, Murray was chosen to fill the unexpired term of Bennett; and in 1855 he was re-elected, to a full term, but died before the end of his term. At the same election Alexander Wells was chosen for the unexpired term of Lyons, and in 1853 he was elected for a full term, but died in October 1854. Charles N. Bryan was appointed to the vacancy until September 1855, when David S. Terry was elected to the unexpired term of Wells, ending in 1859. Heydenfeldt served until January 1857, when he resigned, and P. H. Burnett was appointed to the vacancy. Thus in seven years there were ten

judges on the supreme bench, and the intent of the
constitution in classifying the first three appointments
so that the election of justices for long terms should
be the more quickly secured, was defeated.

Questions of law arose among the judges on the
supreme bench. The temporary absence of one of
the three judges made a decision impossible in the
case of a disagreement between the remaining two.
In February 1852 the legislature granted Heydenfeldt leave of absence for six months, and in March
passed an act authorizing the governor to fill temporary vacancies by appointment. The governor offered the place left by Heydenfeldt to Burnett, who
declined, deeming the act unconstitutional. Wells,
however, accepted. The constitutionality of the act
was tested on an agreed case. Murray decided
against, and Anderson in favor of it. There being
therefore no decision, Wells remained upon the bench
until Heydenfeldt's return, when Murray's opinion
was concurred in, and his occupancy by appointment
during a vacancy occasioned by the voluntary absence of a judge who had not resigned, was declared
to be unconstitutional. His subsequent election soon
restored him to his place on the supreme bench.
When Murray took his seat in 1856 for the beginning
of a new term, he claimed that by virtue of his appointment in 1851, and election in 1852, he was the
senior justice in commission. Heydenfeldt, who was
elected in 1851, was entitled to the place, but not
liking to have a quarrel, yielded his right.

Murray dying in September 1857, Burnett, then
serving as associate justice, was appointed to that
vacancy, and Stephen J. Field to the place left vacant by Burnett's promotion. Field was at that time
associate justice elect, to succeed Heydenfeldt in
January 1858. Murray's successor was Joseph G.
Baldwin, elected to fill the unexpired term, ending in
January 1862. By the expiration of Heydenfeldt's
term, Terry became chief justice. He resigned just

before his time expired by limitation, and W. W. Cope was elected to succeed him, Field, who had been only a little more than one year on the bench, taking the chief-justiceship. Baldwin's successor was Edward Norton, pioneer lawyer of San Francisco.

The constitution of California said that the justices of the supreme court should be elected for six years; yet Murray, Wells, Terry, and Baldwin were elected for unexpired, or short terms, varying from two, to four, and five years. The constitution said that the governor should have power to appoint, when any office became vacant, from any cause, but the commission should expire at the end of the next legislative session, or at the next election by the people. The constitution had not provided a mode for filling a vacancy in the supreme court. The governor therefore appointed, temporarily, and issued a proclamation for an election of a judge, or judges, at the next general election, but "for the unexpired term"; and neither the bench, the bar, nor the people found fault with this interpretation, although it plainly defeated the evident intent, and the letter of the constitution. The governor, also, as in the case mentioned above, appointed when there was no actual vacancy, the judge being still in commission, and only absent for his own pleasure.

The administration of justice, particularly of the higher courts, is beyond everything the most important part of the government. By the degree of enlightenment in the jurisprudence of the country, its advancement in national greatness is to be estimated. But it is irrational to expect of an elective judiciary, nominated in party conventions, taking part in exciting campaigns, cognizant of, and sharing in the personal abuse of the rostrum, that dignity, purity, or learning which constitute an enlightened judiciary. The judicial ermine which has been dragged through the political pool in any state must have lost its whiteness. What then of the immaculateness of

elected judges during the first decade of California
judicial history ? The framers of the constitution in
their honest dependence upon the virtue supposed to
reside in the exercise of the electoral privilege, lost
sight of the peculiar conditions likely to accompany
that franchise in California. But who shall say that,
had the elective power been conferred upon the legislature, the welfare of the people would have been
more safe than in the hands of the judges elected by
themselves ? for the legislatures were not much above
political conventions.

In the older, agricultural states, settled slowly by
industrious and conscientious men, with parents and
grandparents, brothers and sisters, wives' and children,
each in their way influencing legislation, the purity of
the ballot-box, and the honesty of the law-makers
might be depended upon for a generation at least.
But in California, overrun by adventurers from every
land under heaven, with the scum of the great sea of
humanity floating to its shores, until earth, air, and
water shared the contamination, the body politic could
not be healthy, nor its soul pure ; least of all should
we look for that highest expression of social integrity
and culture, a perfect judiciary.

Yet we should be justly surprised not to find among
the aspirants to positions of trust, who have secured the
favor of a majority of the electors, some, even many,
who deserved that favor ; for even a political convention may respect the prejudices of the better portion
of society sufficiently to put forward its most respectable material, intellectually, or otherwise, to be voted
for. And so it fell out, that in the rudest times of
the rude epoch of California history the superior and
supreme judges, with certain marked and most infamous exceptions, made themselves respected.[1] But

---

[1] None more so than Orville C. Pratt, a native of Ontario co., N. Y.,
where he was born April 24, 1819. After practising as a lawyer, first at
Rochester, N. Y., and later at Galena, Ill., he was appointed associate judge
in Oregon, where he rendered excellent service in the Whitman massacre
cases, and in the famous location controversy of 1851-2. In 1856 he re-

they could not always make the constitution and laws respected, because some faults in both interfered with their satisfactory interpretation, a matter to which I shall again refer.

The difficulty of keeping the private opinions of a judge out of the legal decisions was illustrated by Burnett in the case of the negro Archy, related in another place. Burnett decided that Stovall, who claimed Archy, was not entitled, under the law of the state, to have possession of him; but that "there were circumstances connected with the particular case that may exempt him from the operation of the rules we have laid down," and being "not disposed to rigidly enforce the rule for the first time," Stovall might have the negro, though this decision was not to be a precedent for the future, in similar cases. The critical, and by no means reverent California public, openly ridiculed the opinion of one whose prejudices and amiability together had led him to commit a judicial blunder, of which much worse judges and men would not have been guilty. In this judgment Terry, of course, concurred.

As I have before said, it was the law, more than the judges, which was at fault, though the latter were also to blame. For a considerable period in

moved to San Francisco, where after practising for three years in partnership with Alex. Campbell, he was elected judge for the twelfth judicial district. His decisions are among the classics of the law, and as a jurist he has won a reputation second to none on the Pacific coast.

The first chief justice of California, Hastings, was a native of Jefferson co., N. Y., at the time 36 years of age, tall and powerful frame, genial manner, and some legal lore. He was elected to congress in 1846, and appointed chief justice of the supreme court of Iowa in 1848, but resigned to come to Cal. the following year. He retired from public life in 1853, having served one term as attorney-general. Of his associates, Lyons and Bennett, the same might be said. Bennett was also a New Yorker, born in 1815, and educated at Hamilton college. He came to Cal. in 1849 by sea. Murray was of Scottish descent, but was born in St Louis, and reared in southern Ill. He joined the 14th infantry regiment at the age of 21 to fight in the battles under Scott in Mexico, winning the commission of a lieut. Coming to Cal. in 1849, he was elected one of the associate justices of the superior court of S. F., created by the legislature of 1851. J. Caleb Smith of Va was his associate, and Morse presiding judge. Sac. Union, Sept. 19, 1857. It is said that being asked what he knew about law, he replied, 'I do not know much about it, and am too indolent to study. If I am elected I shall acquire

1856 no supreme court was held. Heydenfeldt was absent from the state; Terry was in confinement by the vigilance committee; and Murray utilized the period while the people usurped his powers, to visit some springs and remain in seclusion away from the shadow

knowledge without effort. Every lawyer who comes before me will be a compulsory teacher, giving me the benefit of his midnight cramming and tedious search after authorities.' *Calistoga Tribune*, Aug. 8, 1872. Such was the activity of his intellect and the power of his memory, joined to a naturally judicial mind, that he soon became a good judge of law, and was appointed to the supreme bench to fill the place made vacant by Bennett's resignation; was elected to it in 1852 by the democrats, and reëlected in 1855 by the know-nothings. For five years—a lifetime in effect to many whose fortunes hung upon the supreme bench decisions—this magistrate ruled the chief court in Cal. and even the others by appeal.

The associate justices who occupied the bench for the greatest length of time with Murray were Heydenfeldt and Terry. Both were democratic politicians, Heydenfeldt being Weller's manager in the senatorial contest in 1857. He did much to support the reputation of the state, and although often included in the denunciations hurled against the supreme bench, was certainly the least deserving of censure of either. Terry was a southern man, of acquirements, with a Texan experience, a typical chivalry judge, given to assaulting those who offended him, even when practising in court, and exhibiting a warm friendship for those who pleased him—a man of extremes. During vigilance committee times, he descended from the dignity of his high office to go to S. F. at the instance of a brother of Billy Mulligan, who was to be brought by them befcre the judge on a writ of habeas corpus for which the prisoner had not asked. When the committee sent an officer to take Mulligan, he resisted the arrest, fomented a quarrel, and stabbed the officer, being himself arrested. The vigilance committee detained him prisoner for 6 weeks, and released him at last, more out of respect for the office he degraded than out of their sense of justice to the man. Terry was one of a party of about 40 men which left Texas for Cal. in April 1849. Two other parties, one from La and one from Miss., travelled in company. After his arrival in Cal. he had a political dispute with M. R. Evans, attacking him with a pistol and beating him until he was senseless. *San José Telegraph*, July 8, 1856. During Terry's incarceration in 1856, the Texan legislature addressed a memorial to congress praying the govt to interfere to protect him; and afterward also passed resolutions of esteem and admiration toward the committee for the fair trial granted to him. He had probably a narrow escape, for if Hopkins had died, he would certainly have been hanged. He was not without friends. Frink relates that there was a movement in Sac. to come down 200 strong, and take Terry by a coup d'etat. Ten thousand men could not then have taken him. Sac. in those days was strongly southern in sentiment, which accounts for the disposition to serve Terry. Every effort was made to save Hopkins' life by friends and foes alike. Perhaps no man in Cal. has had more written about him than Terry, whose fame cannot, with it all, be considered a happy one. The works in my library which refer to him are numerous, of which the following are some: *Coleman, Vig. Com.*, MS., 109–17; *Truett, Vig. Com.*, MS., 3; *Cole, Vig. Com.*, MS., 7–8; *Crary, Vig. Com.*, MS., 9–10; *Rogers, Vig. Com.*, MS., 12; *Bluxome*, MS., 17–18; *Olney*, MS., 18–21; *Dempster*, MS., 4–11; *Ryckman*, MS., 18; *Durkee, Vig. Com.*, MS., 3–5; *Daw's Vig. Com.*, MS., 8; *Manrow, Vig. Com.*, MS., 9; *Farwell, Vig. Com.*, MS., 22–3; *Smiley, Vig. Com.*, MS., 10–12; *Watkins, Vig. Com.*, MS., 22–3; *Gillespie*, MS., 10; *Lloyd, Lights and Shades*, 25–6; besides the report of his trial, and all the newspaper articles.

of their displeasure. The chief justice, for reasons of his own, was somewhat shy about coming in contact with the people's police while they held entire control of the city and were in a dangerous humor. But the people had a proper regard for appearances, and left their supreme court to the judgment of the world, from which there is no appeal, whose verdict no bribery can reverse. Terry was discharged with the admonition that the state desired his resignation, which he heeded not, resuming his seat upon the bench until he stepped from his pedestal in 1859 to kill Broderick. Murray died in September 1857, at the early age of thirty-two, expiating thereby, it would seem, the failings of his life, for bar, press, and pulpit paid to his memory the tributes due to goodness and greatness, as lavishly as they had only a few months before censured him for his infirmities.

Yet, it would be altogether unfair to withhold from Murray and his associates the credit of having done much, while dispensing justice, to frame the judicial system of California, which became for equity and soundness unsurpassed by any of the older states. Upon the supreme court, during the first half-dozen years of its existence, devolved the task of testing the constitution and laws of the new commonwealth, cases of appeal from the courts beneath being very frequent, and many of great importance in themselves, and as establishing precedents in similar cases; Mexican law, federal law, and the laws of California, concordant or conflicting, increasing the difficulty of arriving at correct decisions. The study of these knotty questions, whether aboriginal, or by the help of the ablest members of the bar, rapidly developed the jurist, so that California in a few years had acquired, in spite of the drawbacks above cited, a high legal reputation.

The act of 1851 defining the jurisdiction and powers

of every judicial officer in the state was the production of Field, then a young practitioner smarting under the tyranny of the district judge, and recently elected to the California legislature. It was not likely therefore that he would be guilty of an infraction of the law which had emanated from his own brain. He became chief justice on the resignation of Terry, which position he retained until 1863, when he was promoted to the bench of the United States, and assigned to the circuit of the Pacific states.[2] At the time Field came to the bench in California there was a vast amount of litigation growing out of land questions, and he did much by way of evolving out of chaos a system which could be understood, to bring these claims to a settlement. He held, in the first place, that the obligation on the part of the United States was imperative to protect, according to the treaty of Guadalupe Hidalgo, Mexican grantees, in the enjoyment of their lands. In the second place, that they were entitled to possession, and to recover in ejectment, until their claims had been passed upon by the agents of the government; and when the grant was not a mere float, but was defined by boundaries embracing a greater amount than specified, that the grantee could retain possession of the whole against intruders, until the measurement had been determined by the government surveys. Such decisions, although evidently just, were denounced by a large class of squatters, and others, who asserted in no qualified terms that the judges so deciding were in the interests of monopolists and land-grabbers.

Decisions in cases of government lands, whether

---

[2] Stephen J. Field was born in Conn. in 1816, his father removing to Stockbridge, Mass., soon after. He was educated at Williams college and in European schools. He came to Cal. in 1849, settling at Marysville, where he was first alcalde, and justice of the peace. He did not always escape censure, though by impartial observers it has generally been admitted that his administration was one of the purest in the earlier records of our California judiciary. His later reputation, at least, has not been attacked, perhaps for the reason that his position removes him from politics.

mineral or agricultural, offered less difficulty, and were
accepted with greater approbation. The mining
statutes of California, from which the mining laws of
the more recent states and territories were chiefly
borrowed, provided that in suits for mining claims,
brought in magistrate's courts, the customs and regulations of the miners in the vicinity should be put in
evidence, and when not in conflict with the constitution and laws of the United States, should govern the
decision. Thus the miners became their own law-
makers, the same principle being adopted in all the
courts. The first appropriator of a claim was considered to be the owner, from whom title could be acquired by another.

This principle was applied to possessory rights in
all the public lands, the government, which owned
the lands, not interfering. To interfere in all these
cases, as a party to the suit, would have produced in-
describable confusion; but the court proceeded as if
a grant really existed to the first claimant of mines,
water-privileges, or lands.

In the early years of mining, an opinion of the supreme court gave weight to the belief entertained by
some, that gold and silver belonged to the state, by
virtue of her sovereignty; that the state had the sole
right to authorize the mines to be worked, to frame
laws and regulations, to license miners, and to affix
such terms and conditions as she might deem proper
to the freedom of their use. Under this decision the
lands of private proprietors were invaded for mining
purposes as freely as public lands. This brought on
numerous suits for intrusion on private property
claimed under United States laws, and the supreme
court was forced to modify this opinion, and to decide
that "an invasion of private property in order to enjoy a public franchise would require more specific legislation than any yet resorted to." This right to
invade private lands in search of gold was first repudiated in 1859, by Judge Field, he finally establishing

the doctrine that gold and silver belonged to the land, like any other product, or any property fixed to its surface. This opinion is now never seriously denied; but the supreme court, as in other cases, was much maligned by the laboring class, who believed that the court was governed in its decision by the influence of capital.

Titles to land in San Francisco led to incessant trouble; and the decisions of the courts constantly occasioned bitterness of feeling. Under Mexican laws San Francisco was a pueblo, entitled to four square leagues of land, which the municipal magistrates were authorized to apportion in small quantities, to the inhabitants. The city of San Francisco succeeded to the landed proprietorship of the pueblo, and lots were sold by the alcaldes during the military government of California, for trifling sums. But many immigrants treated the land as belonging to the United States, claiming any vacant lots they conveniently could, their claims being resisted by others, the result being never-ending controversies, emphasized sometimes with bloodshed, and employing the whole legal learning of the city in their settlement.

In 1850 San Francisco was incorporated, and with a recklessness characteristic of the times, contracted more debts than she was able to pay. Executions were levied upon the city's lands. That portion of the population which denied the city's right to the pueblo lands laughed at the sheriff's sales; but suits of ejectment followed rapidly. Property of great value was sold on execution for merely nominal prices, and the supreme court soon had to decide upon the validity of the sales. Its decision confirmed among others the validity of the Peter Smith sales. In 1855, Van Ness being mayor, the city council passed an ordinance which bears his name, and of which he was the author. It relinquished the city's interest to lands within its corporate limits, as defined by charter, with certain exceptions, to the persons in actual possession

on or before January 1, 1855, provided they were
still in possession in June of that year, when the ordinance would be introduced into the common council, and to all persons holding under grants made by
the alcaldes before July 7, 1846, or by virtue of a
grant subsequently made by those magistrates, if the
grant had been properly entered in a book of record
in custody of the recorder of the county, previous to
April 3, 1850. This ordinance was approved by act
of the legislature in 1858, and by a test case brought
before the supreme court, settled definitely the land
cases within the city limits, the court confirming the
titles under the ordinance. Millions worth of property belonging to the city was rescued from speculators, and thousands of homes saved from the spoiler;
yet such was the hatred incurred by the judges from
disappointed contestants, that if ever they had enjoyed
any rose-hued visions of the dignity of their office,
such illusions were dissipated, often to give place to
dread of assassination.

There was another part of the city land question
which had to be adjudicated upon. This was the
right of the city to the whole of the four square
leagues belonging to the pueblo. The board of land
commissioners created in 1851, by act of congress at
Gwin's suggestion, confirmed that portion embraced
within the charter limits only. The city appealed to
the district court, but the case remained undecided
until September 1854, when it was by congressional
act transferred to the circuit court of the United
States, and decided by Justice Field as it had been
when he was on the supreme bench by Baldwin, that
the city had succeeded to the whole of the pueblo lands.
This decision was the occasion of an attempt on Field's
life above referred to.[3]

[3] 16 Cal., p. 572; *Hicks* vs *Bell*, 3 Cal., p. 219; *Steaks* vs *Barrett*, 5 Cal., p.
37; *Field's Early Days*, 140; 2 Cal., pp. 524-57. In 1866, when on the sup.
bench of the United States, Field received a package at his rooms in Washington containing a torpedo. In the appendix to *Early Days in Cal.*, exhibit
K, pp. 243-5, is an account of the circumstance by Judge Lake, who was

As a matter of fact, the injury which certain persons, justly or unjustly, sustained by the decision of the United States circuit court was due to Field, he having been the author of those parts of the congressional act previously alluded to, which authorized the district court to transfer to his court the cases pending, in which the title to lands within the corporate limits of a city or town were undetermined, and which relinquished the right of the United States to any of the land within such limits, in trust to the city and its successors, for the uses specified in the Van Ness ordinance, except such reserves as the government had made for military or other public uses.

It might reasonably be questioned whether a judge should be allowed so far to interfere with matters originating in another court as to procure an act of congress transferring it to his own court; but most men are reconciled to irregular proceedings instituted to result in better order. So nature travails, while a mountain or a mouse is born, and thenceforth throughout the ages mountains and mice abound, the former regulating the winds that cool, and the waters that fertilize the earth, the latter adding their quota to the sum of vermin without which the universe would remain unfinished. This society, oppressed for long years with unbearable wrongs, is suddenly aroused in all its majesty, and, ignoring law and the machinery of justice, exacts and obtains a justice higher than the law.

The decision here referred to was rendered in October 1864, but a motion for a rehearing kept it in court until May 1865, when the decree was finally entered. The United States appealed from it to the

present, and cautioned Field not to open it. When it was finally opened, after being well soaked in water, it was found to have pasted inside the cover a newspaper slip as follows: 'Monday, Oct. 31, 1864. The City of San Francisco vs United States. Judge Field yesterday delivered the following opinion in the above case. It will be read with interest by the people of this city.' It may have been to kill somebody; it may have been a harmless joke.

supreme court, in toto, and the city from that part of
it which reserved certain quantities of land to be designated by the president within a given time.   The
appeal not being likely to be reached in the supreme
court for a long time, and the secretary of war being
consulted as to reservations, and not finding any
necessary, Field drew a bill which the California delegation[4] took in hand and carried through both houses
of congress, quieting the city's title to all the land
embraced within the decree of confirmation.   This act
was signed in March 1866.   The appeals were dismissed, and the city was finally at rest on the subject
of titles.   The municipal authorities took measures to
set apart lots for public buildings and schools, and
reserved for a park that generous quantity of land
now rapidly being made one of the finest of pleasure
resorts, overlooking the Golden Gate, and within
sound of the sea's unending melody.[5]

The city of San Francisco, after going through all
the courts for a long series of years, during which the
value of property had increased extraordinarily, was
at length placed upon a footing similar to that of
towns upon public lands of the United States, under
the town-site laws;[6] that is, it held its lands in trust
for the occupants, to be conveyed to them upon such
terms as the legislature might prescribe.   If it took
possession of any lot or parcel already occupied for
public purposes, it assessed those occupants to whom
title had passed upon agreement, and raised the money
required to make reasonable compensation to the dispossessed.[7]   Instead of the insecurity of titles which

---

[4] Senator John Conness and Representative McRuer had charge of the
bill.

[5] Frank McCoppin, elected mayor of the city in 1867, was the prime
mover in the improvement of the park lands.

[6] Act of May 23, 1844; of March 2, 1867; and of June 1868.

[7] To the distinguished author of *Early Days in Cal.* I am indebted for the
candid statement of his part in the labor of adjusting land matters in California, for while wading through *Cal. Reports* and U. S. supreme court decisions may convey elaborate information, it fails to impress the reader like
the narrative of the actors in the strife.

for fifteen years prevented permanent improvements, a disputed title is now as rare as it was once common.

Baldwin, on the bench of California with Field, was an able lawyer. He was from Alabama, although of Connecticut stock,[8] and his Yankee shrewdness was toned down by the more genial southern temperament. He arrived in San Francisco in 1854, and making friends with the Murray fraternity, "as a legitimate consequence," one says, "he was soon overwhelmed with great cases, some of which involved the public interests." These cases were chiefly city suits, dragging through the courts from year to year, to the profit of the lawyers and the ruin of client.

In 1862, the constitution was amended in its legislative, executive, and judicial departments. The supreme court was made to consist of a chief justice and four associate justices, the presence of three being necessary to the transaction of business, except such business as might be done at chambers, and the concurrence of three justices was made necessary to pronounce a judgment.[9] The offices were still elective, but

[8] J. G. Baldwin was a kind of prodigy. At the age of 12 years he performed the duties of dept. dist court clerk; at 17 he conducted a newspaper. At 21 he went to Ala., and was soon in the legislature. In 1844 he canvassed the state for the whig ticket; in 1849 he was beaten for congress by S. W. Inge. He wrote the *Flush Times in Alabama*, being a picture of local character, and *Party Leaders*, a history of politics under the management of such statesmen as Jefferson, Hamilton, Jackson, Clay, and Randolph.

[9] First were the city slip cases, involving $80,000. A corrupt common council in 1853 sold at auction certain water lots set apart for a public dock, for an average price of $9,784, or a total of $1,193,750, one quarter paid down, half in two months, and the remainder in four months. Two wharf companies threatening to enjoin the sale, on the ground that their wharves were built on the faith of the ordinance setting aside these lots for a public dock, the council passed an ordinance to quiet these objectors, allowing them $185,000 indemnity for the injury sustained. Soon after the sale, property declined rapidly, and several of the purchasers of the city slips were anxious to draw back from their bargain, and were shown by their lawyer, Baldwin, a way to do it, which was to have their titles attacked, and on being declared invalid, to sue the city for judgments. Test cases were prepared, and after tedious delays, Burnett and Terry decided for the city, Murray dissenting. These cases were again opened in 1860, Baldwin being now on the bench, his decision that no title passed making the city liable to return $800,-000 cash for the scrip paid in on account of the slip purchases. The city still contested the judgment, and the matter was kept in court, at enormous

by a special election, at which no officer, other than judicial, except for the superintendent of public instruction, should be chosen. Their term was, moreover, increased to ten years from the 1st of January next after their election, except those elected at the first election, who should be so classified among themselves by lot that one should go out of office every two years, the justice drawing the shortest term to be chief justice.

Under this amended law, the justices elected under the former one were legislated out of office, namely, W. W. Cope and Edward Norton,[10] Field resigning in May 1863, and E. B. Crocker being appointed to the vacancy. The justices elected under the amended constitution, and on the republican ticket, were Silas

costs, until an entirely new set of officers were on the bench, and the property had so enhanced in value that 35 of the purchasers of the city slips deciding to keep the lots, the city consented, and gave bonds for $1,000,000 to be paid. Six others brought suit later, and were beaten by a legal quibble as absurd as the first, which saved the city $190,000.

In the case of Biddle Boggs vs. the Merced Mining Co., brought to test the right of Frémont to the gold in the land of his Mariposa grant, argued for Frémont by Baldwin, before Burnett and Terry in 1858, it was decided that the gold belonged to the U. S. gov't, the Alvarado grant being for the land only. In 1859 the decision was reversed by Field and Cope—Baldwin not sitting—and Frémont, or his creditors, were adjudged to own the contents of the land. Another important suit lost by Baldwin as a lawyer, and revived while he was on the bench, was that of McCauley vs. The State Controller, involving the prison contract, of which mention has been made in a previous volume. In 1860 the court reversed the decision of Burnett and Terry, and the controller was served with a mandamas for $40,000, which, under the advice of Terry, now acting as counsellor, he refused to obey. A compromise was effected, the state paying $270,000, ten per cent. of which went to McCauley's lawyers. One of the projectors of the bulkhead scheme which so troubled S. F. for so many years, was Felton, the quondam partner-at-law of Baldwin; and one of its supporters was John Conness, then assemblyman from El Dorado co., who afterward was elevated to the U. S. senate. What more natural than that people should say that Felton labored to place Conness where he could assist Field in settling land questions agreeably to Baldwin, and his former clients? These are some of the features of an elective judiciary.

[10] W. W. Cope, of Amador, was a southerner. Field speaks of him as 'possessed of a superior mind, and genial nature. He made an excellent judge.' Later he continued the practice of the law in S. F. 'Norton,' says the same authority, was 'learned, patient, industrious, and conscientious; but he was not adapted for an appellate tribunal. He had no confidence in his own unaided judgment.' Early Days in Cal., 118–19. Tuthill says that while Norton was judge of the 12th district court he was particularly averse to criminal trials, but that he was an excellent man.

W. Sanderson,[11] who drew the short term, Lorenzo Sawyer, John Currey, Augustus L. Rhodes,[12] and Oscar L. Shafter.[13] Sanderson was reëlected to succeed himself, but resigned in 1869, when Jackson Temple was appointed by the governor, and obtained a nomination in 1871, but was beaten by Addison C. Niles, for the unexpired term. Currey,[14] who was chief justice for two years, went out in 1868, and was defeated for reëlection by William T. Wallace.[15] Sawyer's[16] term expired in 1867, and he was defeated

[11] Sanderson was a native of Vt., born in 1824, and educated at Williams college, Mass, and Union college, N. Y., where he graduated in 1846. He was admitted to the bar at Albany in 1849, and began practice in Florida, but came to Cal. in 1851, settling in El Dorado. Although a whig, when there was a whig party, he was elected district attorney in 1858 by the democrats. In 1862 he was elected by the Union party to the assembly, where he distinguished himself by becoming the author of the Specific Contract Act. 'As a judge he knew no politic's creed, color, nationality, influence, or wealth.' At the expiration of his term he was elected for ten years.

[12] A. L. Rhodes was born in Oneida co., N. Y., in 1821, educated at Hamilton college, and after studying law migrated to Green co., Ind., whence he came to California in 1852. He settled at San José, being district attorney, and state senator in 1859. As a member of the judiciary committee, he urged the amendments which were afterwards adopted.

[13] O. L. Shafter was born in Vt., in 1812. His parental grandfather fought at Bunker hill, Bennington, and Saratoga, and was afterward for 25 years a member of the Vermont legislature. His father was county judge, member of the constitutional convention of his state in 1836, and several times a member of the legislature. He was educated at Wilbraham academy and the Wesleyan university, graduating in 1834, after which he studied law at the Harvard law school, under Judge Story. He came to Cal. in 1854, practicing his profession until elected associate justice of the supreme court. He resigned on account of failing health, and went abroad: but recovery was impossible, and he died in Italy in 1873.

[14] John Currey was a native of Peekskill, N. Y., where his family had been established for a century. He was born in 1814, and educated at his native town, Vermont academy and Middletown college, Conn., studying law with William Nelson of Peekskill, and being admitted to practice in 1842. He came to Cal. in 1849, and passed through the stormy political period of the following 10 years without ever soiling his fame as an honest and pure man. He was one of the first to make headway against the Lecompton democracy. Williams college, Mass., conferred on him in 1870 the title of L.L.D.

[15] William T. Wallace, born in Ky., in 1828, was bred to the profession of the law, having just completed his studies when he moved to Cal. in 1850. Settling at San José, he formed a partnership with Burnett and Ryland; and soon married Ronertte, daughter of Ex-gov. Burnett. He was a candidate in 1868 for the U. S. senate, and also for presidential election. He owed his election as judge of the supreme court in 1869 to the democratic party.

[16] Lorenzo Sawyer was born in Le Roy, Jefferson co., N. Y., in 1820, his father Jesse Sawyer and his grandfather being among the pioneers of the

by Royal T. Sprague,[17] who died in February 1872,
when Isaac S. Belcher was appointed in his place, his
successor, E. W. McKinstry, being chosen in 1873.
Rhodes' term expired in 1871, when he was reëlected.
Shafter resigned in December 1867, Joseph B. Crockett being appointed, and in 1869 elected for the short
term, to succeed him.   Sawyer was chief justice in
1868–9, Rhodes in 1870–1, Sprague in 1872, succeeded
by Wallace the same year, who being in for ten years,
remained chief justice until the adoption of a new constitution again legislated out of office the supreme
judges.

Both parties in 1869, by their ballots, declared the
existence of a long and short term, and again in 1871,
when Rhodes was chosen for the long term, and Niles
for the short term.   But Justice Crockett, who was
elected for an unexpired term of four years, when it
was ended contended that he had been chosen for ten
years, and he was sustained in his opinion by the
bench.   It was evidently the intention of the legislature in amending the constitution in 1862 to
prevent the frequent recurrence of judicial elections, and to separate them as much as possible
from politics, yet the politicians were as ready as

Black river country. On the maternal side he was related to the Col Prescott who led the American forces at Bunker hill, and to the historian of that
name.   Lorenzo lived upon a farm until 16 years of age, but being studious,
acquired the rudiments of a good education at home, and at the Black river
institute in Watertown.   He went to Ohio in 1840, and studied for a time at
the Western Reserve college, after which he read law with Gustavus Swan,
and Noah H. Swayne now on the U. S. supreme bench.   On coming to Cal.
in 1850, he located himself at Nevada city, but soon removed to S. F.   His
practice was large and profitable.   He was one of the organizers of the
republican party of Cal.   In 1869 when his term expired on the supreme
bench of the state, he was made U. S. circuit judge of the 9th circuit, which
he took in 1870.   In 1877 Hamilton college, N. Y., conferred upon him the
honorary degree of L.L.D.   His supreme court reports fill 15 vols, and his
circuit court reports 5 vols.

[17] T. Sprague was a native of Vt., whence he removed to Ohio, where he
acquired his legal knowledge.   He migrated to Cal. in 1849, making his residence in Shasta co.   He was elected to the state senate for 1854–55, but
declined reëlection and devoted himself to his profession.   Of him, as a
judge, chief justice Wallace declared that 'no judicial officer ever possessed
in a higher degree that absolute independence of soul which acknowledged
accountability to none save God and his own good conscience for the motives
by which his course here was actuated and determined.'

before to avail themselves of a vacancy to introduce short terms.

After eight years trial of the amended judicial system, the legislature of 1869–70 proposed again to amend so as to establish courts of exclusive criminal jurisdiction in cities or towns; to abolish special elections of supreme and district judges, and to confine a judge elected to fill a vacancy, to the unexpired term only. Any judicial officer wilfully absenting himself from the state for thirty days forfeited his office. The judges already in office should hold for their full term, after which one justice should go out and his successor be elected every two years, the judge having the shortest term to be chief justice; but this change appears not to have been made at that time.

Congress in 1855 established a circuit court of the United States, which had appellate jurisdiction over the federal courts of the northern and southern districts. This act removed from the United States district courts the special jurisdiction before vested in them over the board of commissioners for the settlement of land claims. The circuit judge was also required, from time to time, to form part of and preside over the federal district courts when either was engaged in the discharge of appellate jurisdiction over the board of commissioners. He had no seat on the supreme bench of the United States, but his office was exclusive to the Pacific coast.[18] The first and only judge of this court, Matthew Hall McAllister,[19] resigned in 1862, and the court was abolished soon after. The subsequent elevation of Field to the supreme bench of federal judges, with the circuit of the Pacific states, revived its powers.

[18] Crane mentions this with indignation, being the only state in the union without a judicial representative at Washington. *Past and Present*, 36.

[19] M. H. McAllister was born in Savannah, Ga., in 1800, and educated at Princeton college, N. J., after which he was trained in the law, to which his father was also bred. He practised in Savannah 29 years, and was U. S. atty for the southern dist of Ga. As a legislator, and judge of law, he was equally distinguished. He died in S. F in 1865, universally regretted.

The United States district courts, as the reader
will remember, were two in number, a northern and
southern.   In 1866 the southern district was abolished, and its jurisdiction conferred on the court of
the northern district.   The ostensible reason for dispensing with one of the federal courts was that there
was not enough business to give it constant occupation.   But while this was true, it was equally true
that many land titles were still unsettled, which had
been thrown into litigation by the United States
and not by the claimants.   Many claimants were
already ruined by endless law-suits; and now the remainder were required to travel with their witnesses
several hundred miles to San Francisco, and to incur
an expense they were unable to bear.   It had been
bad enough going to Monterey to attend court, but
this was an additional infliction.

A petition praying for a restoration of the southern district, and a term of the court annually at the
city of Los Angeles was forwarded to congress, the
business of the federal courts having increased beyond their capabilities.   An effort was made by
Senator Stewart of Nevada to have the Nevada
judicial district joined to the southern district of California.   Nothing however was done during the twenty
years from 1866 to 1886, when a new district was
formed, but congress failing to provide the means to
set the court in operation, no judge was appointed.
Ogden Hoffman long remained upon the bench where
he was placed when a young man in 1851.[20]

[20] *Los Angeles News,* Jan. 22 and 25, 1867; S. F. *Com. Herald* and *Market
Review,* Feb. 18, 1868; *Cal. Judiciary Scraps,* 3–8; *S. F. Chamber of Com. Rept.*
1870, 24–7; *Monterey Democrat,* Feb. 8, 1868.   Isaac S. K. Ogier was the first
incumbent of the U. S. dist bench in southern Cal, Judge Jones having died
soon after his appointment.   He died of apoplexy at Bear Valley, May 21,
1861.   He was formerly U. S. atty for the southern district.   Ogier was succeeded by Fletcher M. Haight, who also died in office, and the place remained vacant for several years. According to the *S. F. Chronicle* Jan. 30,
1869, the efforts made at Washington to have a certain obnoxious individual
elevated to the position of U. S. district judge, was the cause of the abolish-
ment of the district—to be rid of persistent and disgusting importunities.
However that may be, there was much difficulty to secure its re-establish-

If the federal and supreme courts were crowded with business the inferior courts were even more so. The 6th district court, which opened in May 1850, at Sacramento, had in October 450 cases on its docket. The business of the most populous districts was retarded, and became sometimes ruinously involved through the interference of the higher courts with the lower. In 1854, Judge Heard, of Sacramento county court, on an appeal from a justice's court, decided that where the matter in dispute exceeded $200 it was unconstitutional for the justice's court to take cognizance of them. As a result the county court was inconveniently crowded with cases on appeal, being continued from time to time, waiting for an opinion of the supreme judges who failed to agree, until by the death of one of them, a change in the constitution of the bench was brought about.

The constitutionality of the superior court of San Francisco was also called in question in 1855. The supreme bench decided in its favor; but in the following year it declared that this court was merely municipal in its jurisdiction, and its authority must be confined to the territory for which it was created. By this decision the superior court became virtually disabled, and the litigants seriously injured.

Another difference of opinion arose between the supreme court and the United States district courts

ment. Of U. S. attys for the southern dist, Alfred Wheeler was the first. He wa born in New York city, April 30, 1822, and came to Cal. in 1849. He was succeeded in office by Ogier, and he, on his promotion, by Pacificus Ord, who held the office under him. B. C. Whiting was U. S. attorney during Haight's term. The first U. S. marshal for this district was Pablo Noriega, of San José; the second, Edward Hunter, of same place, and A. S. Taylor clerk; third, Henry D. Barrows. The U. S. attorneys for the northern dist were, Calhoun Benham, S. W. Inge, and Wm. H. Sharp; the marshals were David F. Douglass, William H. Richardson; clerk, John H. Monroe; third, James Y. McDuffie, and Chas. W. Rand. Delos Lake was appointed U. S. district attorney in 1863. Lake was born in Otsego co., N. Y., in 1820. He was admitted to the bar at the age of 21. The following year he practised before the supreme court, and settled in Utica, where he became city attorney, but was drawn away from a good practice to Cal. in 1850. In 1851 he was appointed district judge, to fill a vacancy, but resigned in 1855 to return to the business of a lawyer. He was one among those who maintained a spotless reputation while on the bench.

in regard to jurisdiction; the state supreme court holding in the face of the highest authority, that no cause could be appealed from the state courts direct to the United States court, Judge Lake of the 4th district, and Judge Shattuck of the superior bench having made orders on motions to remove cases from their courts to the United States district courts.[21] There was established in 1855 a circuit court of the United States, in and for California, with appellate jurisdiction over the other federal courts. Affairs were growing daily more unsatisfactory, when the great uprising occurred in 1856, which would never have happened had the courts discharged their duty to the public. In April 1856 there were absent from their places, McAllister, of the United States circuit court; Heydenfeldt, of the supreme court; Ogier, of the United States district court; and Hager, of the 4th district. Their places were partly filled by substitutes, but not in the manner demanded by the people. Early in the year, Shattuck, of the superior court, had petitioned to have this tribunal abolished, owing to the decision of the supreme court that it was incompetent to protect its own receiver, or send its final process out of the city. Defendants in certain cases, on account of this opinion, refused to comply with the order of the superior judge to surrender property, and the course of justice was impeded in proportion to the amount of business thus obstructed.

Such was the condition of the judiciary of San Francisco and the state, when the revolution occurred which resulted in an improved administration of justice. Only a few months before this revolutionary movement, there was passed by the legislature the consolidation act, by which the city and county gov-

---

[21] Shattuck was commanded to revoke the order removing a case to the U. S. district court, and refused to comply. *Sac. Union,* March 10, 1855. Should he obey the mandate, the U. S. court could imprison him for not sending the case as ordered; and should the supreme court choose to notice his refusal, it could punish him for disobedience. It was plain that the superior court must give way.

ernments of San Francisco were merged in one. By
this act, which went into effect in July, the superior
court was abolished, a county and police judge and
twelve justices of the peace constituting the local
judiciary.

Had it not been for the change in the city government at this juncture, it is difficult to see how the
reforms brought about in criminal matters by the
vigilance committee could have been made permanent,
nor how the courts could have purified themselves
from former practices. But the law going into effect
in July, and an election of a new set of officers taking
place in the autumn, gave an opportunity for the carrying out of the reform measures. Previous to this
change every city and county office was in the hands
of despoilers. Taxes were exorbitant; yet the streets,
wharves, and public buildings were neglected and de-
caying. The money, if ever it reached the city
treasury, was immediately spirited away. Those who
had claims against the city for labor or material, were
forced to accept scrip, which was nearly worthless;
and soon they charged the city five prices for services
or property, heaping up a debt which the new government was compelled to extinguish. But the new
law enjoined the old officers while they remained in
office from contracting any further debts, and when
the new incumbents came into power, so poor was the
city government that there were no funds in the
treasury with which to pay for lighting the streets,
or purchasing furniture for the court-room of the
police judge,[22] who was presented with a docket by a
benevolent citizen,[23] and who bought candles at his

[22] H. P. Coon, a native of Columbia co., N. Y., educated at Williams college, Mass., and a practitioner of medicine, who came to Cal. in 1852, was
chosen and urged to accept the office of police judge, which he held for four
years. He became part owner in the chemical works established to supply
the mint, soon after coming to S. F., but when not in office practised his profession. He was chosen mayor in 1863. Under his administration the city
was well governed.

[23] This was Dr Samuel Merritt. *Coon. Annals, S. F.*, MS., 10.

own expense to hold his evening sessions, as well as
stationery for the use of the court. In less than a
year the men nominated by the People's nominating
committee, and elected by the People's party, had
so changed the complexion of things, that there was
money in the treasury, and a new prosperity apparent
everywhere.

The consolidation act was exceedingly stringent.
Definite salaries were fixed, only a few officers elected
under the old county government being allowed to
retain their fees until the legislature could be brought
to eliminate them, after the law had been tested. No
more public money went into the keeping of the "political bank in Kearney street." A police department
was created which became famous for its efficiency
and men, and women too, were safe to go everywhere
in the city by day or night. The consolidation act
had, however, to undergo the scrutiny of the supreme
court, where it was sustained. But it often gave the
people a shock, as, for example, when it was decided
that the state debt was unconstitutional, and therefore that the credit of the state was ruined; and that
when the people determined that the debt should not
be repudiated, the legislature acted unconstitutionally
in recognizing the indebtedness. The legislature was,
however, permitted to shift the responsibility upon
the electors, the adoption of such a debt by the state
not being provided for in the constitution. It would
be too much to expect, even in a supreme court, to be
always consistent.

In 1859 Hoffman of the United States district
court made a decision in regard to the banishment of
a certain obnoxious person by the vigilance committee
of 1856. This person, one Martin Gallagher, who
among his other accomplishments, encompassed that
of ballot-box stuffing, sued the captain of the *Live
Yankee*, on board which vessel he was placed by the
committee—an alternative to save him from hanging
—for damages, the case being decided in his favor by

the court, which awarded Gallagher $3,000. Aside
from the annoyance to the committee of having these
disturbing questions re-opened in San Francisco, its
friends contended that the captain of the *Live Yankee*
had no option, any more than Gallagher, the city being under a revolutionary government, and he forced
to obey the committee, and transport the exile to a
foreign shore, namely the Hawaiian Islands; also that
Gallagher was really benefited, as it saved his life,
which would have been taken had he not been conveyed out of the country. The press of San Francisco, moreover, charged the author of the decision
with an intention to irritate and annoy, a grave
charge when applied to a judge of a high court of the
United States, and illustrative of the antagonism between the courts and people.

The confirmation of the Limantour and Santillian
claims, of so much importance to the city of San
Francisco, to the state, and United States, by the
claim commissioners, was a source of justifiable discontent. For some time the citizens of San Francisco
regarded these claims as having been instigated with
the purpose of levying black-mail, and gave them
little attention, but when they saw them confirmed,
their alarm became proportioned to the injury about
to be inflicted. The general government, also, fear-
ing for the presidio lands, custom-house, mint, and
other United States property, appropriated $200,000
for the purpose of defending its rights, and defeating
fraudulent claims, as they should come up in the
United States district court. This amount was expended in opposing the Limantour claim, which was
proved to be a forgery, and little resistance was offered to the Santillian claim, which was hastened
through this court almost unchallenged, to a complete
confirmation.[24] Owners of property then became dis-

[24] This claim was bounded on the north by the southerly line of the Yerba
Buena village, corresponding with what is now California st, on the south by
the Buri Buri rancho, sweeping across the peninsula for the entire width,

turbed, and some government officials displayed their opposition by entering an appeal to the supreme court at Washington.

At this point in the history of the case, and when the claimants were confident of a victory, a few citizens who feared for the result, the claimants having the record in their favor, called a public meeting, and sought to arouse the people to a realization of their peril. A committee of twenty was appointed to resist land frauds in the city and county of San Francisco, of which Police-judge Coon was chairman, and became somewhat famous in this connection. The chief difficulty being the procurement of funds, Coon applied himself to securing contributions. A memorial to congress was proposed by William J. Shaw, praying that the case might be remanded back to the United States district court for re-trial on its merits, offering to show the pretended grant a fraud, and setting forth particulars. Care was taken to bring this memorial to the attention of all the United States judges, including the supreme bench. The attorney employed was Nathaniel Bennett, who presented an able printed argument against the claim in the United States supreme court,[25] and finally through these measures, the case being fairly brought to the attention of the highest tribunal, the claim was rejected. But for this action on the part of the people the Santillian claim would have been confirmed.

I have already spoken of the settlement of the pue-

and over that part of the city west of Stockton st. Some of its supporters however, for the purpose of quieting opposition, alleged that the claim affected property only south of a certain fictitious line called Vallejo line. To the Philadelphia Land Company, however, which purchased the claim, it was represented as embracing all outside of the little Spanish village bounded by California and Stockton streets. Limantour was a Frenchman, long resident in the city of Mexico. When the fraud—which was detected by discovering that the seal of the state of Mexico was counterfeit—was exposed he deposited $30,000, the amount of his bail, with his bondsmen, and fled the country. *Gwin, Mem.*, MS., 66. Santillian was a half-mendicant priest, who never owned any land. *Coon. Annals, S. F.*, 15.

[25] Coon says that the U. S. atty-gen. has since been 'proved to have been deeply interested in the claim, and strove hard to prevent this printed argument from reaching the hands of the judges.' *Annals S. F.*, MS.. 19.

blo and government titles by the supreme court of California, and by the Van Ness ordinance. It only remained for the city to extend the provisions of the Van Ness ordinance over the lands lying outside of the charter line of 1851, and provide for the proper distribution of these lands according to the act of congress. This was done by a municipal regulation known as the Outside Land ordinance, which made provisions for granting deeds to such persons as were entitled to them. A committee of the board of supervisors, called the outside land committee, determined this question and extended the deeds.

The city slip cases mentioned in the previous chapter entered into politics as late as 1863. In the first place, the money derived from the sale of the city's lots went into that vortex where all the people's money went, from 1851 to 1856. Next came the attempt on the part of the purchasers to compel the city to pay back the purchase money with interest for ten years. In 1863, when the People's nominating committee began its sessions, the course of the city-slip owners and the city attorney was being freely discussed in the daily press, and it was discovered that the candidate for mayor was among these speculators, when he was hastily dropped, and H. P. Coon, a friend of the city, substituted. One of his first official acts was the acknowledgement of service of a mandate from the supreme court of California, commanding him and the board of supervisors to pay the city-slip judgments. Finding on examining the matter that there could be no escape from ultimate compliance with the final judgment of the court, he proposed a plan for settlement which was carried into effect. But for this there would have been no compromise, and the city would have been greatly embarrassed.

So many causes of discontent as the foregoing history has revealed, could not long be borne without

creating a feeling of rebellion against the constitution
and laws of the state, which permitted them.   As
early as 1856 the necessity of immediate constitutional reform was urged, and a long bill of indictments
brought against the organic law of California.   Gross
defects, especially in the judiciary, were apparent.   A
large part of the people were in favor of a territorial
government; but the dread of slavery [26] had urged
them on to organize a free state, and they had no alternative but to erect their structure upon a hastily im-
provised legal foundation.   Since that time the same
dread had kept them from re-modelling the constitution, knowing that to call a convention would open
the door to a division of the state.

No provision was made in the organic law for the
certain and prompt punishment of official or of judicial misconduct, and to impeach an officer under it
was an expensive and ineffectual proceeding.   Judges
were treated as superior to legislators, and the constitution "almost completely surrendered into their
hands the very rights of justice itself, of which they
are the mere servants." [27]   "The clothing of judges
with an official importance beyond other mortals," said
the complainants, "has no sound arguments to support
it; and it may be questioned whether it does not lead
to the very abuses it is designed, if there be any design in it, to prevent.   In ages past English judges exercised the power, now boldly employed by the California judiciary, of making laws upon the bench; but all
the English judges combined could not prevent an
appeal to the upper branch of the legislative power.
"Who are our judges?" they asked.   "What would they

---

[26] Speech of Wm J. Shaw in the state senate in 1856.

[27] The supreme court decided on the eve of the general election of 1855,
the case being one where application was made to the supreme court in
a hypothetical case, that naturalization papers could not be taken out in any
courts of the state except district courts, not even in the U. S. courts.   Ex
parte Frank Knowles, application for naturalization. *Sac. Union*, Aug. 14,
1855.   A former decision had been that a voter could not be required to
show his naturalization papers; hence of what effect was one court more
than another. *Id., The People vs. Gordon and Warren.*

be off the bench ? What were they before ascending
it ? Do cushioned chairs and scarlet curtains change
their character ? Are we fools, to give up to names
what belong only to entities, and take for wisdom and
learning the vaunting of conceit ? Are we freemen,
and willing to give the department authorized to
administer the laws, the power to change them with
impunity ?" In the superior court two men, being a
bare majority of three, may condemn a man to death,
or deprive him of his property, or his liberty ; but the
senate, consisting of more than ten times as many,
could not convict a judge, a state attorney, or a surveyor, by less than a two-thirds vote.

Everybody knew that the laws of California made
no distinction between cases in equity or chancery,
and cases in common law ; and no distinction as to
the mode of ascertaining the facts in issue had ever
been tolerated between equity and law cases. The
legislature had provided that all matters of fact arising in such cases in the district courts should be disposed of by juries. But the supreme court, " having
become fond of power, and grown bold in its usurpa-
tions," had decided that in chancery cases, district
judges should be chancellors, and the litigants not entitled to trial by jury. It was not denied that the
jury system needed re-modelling, but it was asserted
that the court of last resort had no right to deprive
the people of trial by jury in the lower courts. These
defects of the judicial system under the constitution
of 1849 were strongly urged as a reason for its
abolition.

At length, in 1861, certain amendments affecting the
judicial, as well as the executive and legislative departments of the government, were proposed, consented to by the electors in 1862, and went into
effect in 1863. By this change the supreme bench
was made to consist of five judges, to be elected at
special elections, and to hold office for ten years. The
state was divided into fourteen judicial districts, sub-

ject to alteration from time to time, the judges to be chosen at the special election provided for judges of the supreme court, and to hold office for six years. The legislature was deprived of the power to grant leave of absence to any judicial officer; but any such officer who should absent himself for more than one month should be deemed to have forfeited his office. County judges should hold office for four years, and should have the power to issue naturalization papers. A probate judge was allowed for the city and county of San Francisco, whose term should be four years. The jurisdiction of each of the courts was distinctively defined, as well as the duties of the district attorneys and clerks.

The period when these changes were made being that of the rebellion, loyalty to the government was required to be sworn to by all judges and court officers. Lecompton democracy, with its office-seeking, its rapacity, and its political tyranny, was pushed aside, and ordered to be silent, while loyalty and devotion to principle dominated the hour. No faithful historian but would declare the change was for the better, or that the judgment was a righteous one which required the chivalry to step down and out.

Reckless legislation during the reign of the chivalry often obstructed justice, as I have pointed out in individual cases, and was fruitful of crimes. Attorney-general Williams in 1859 and 1860 made a number of suggestions in his report to the governor,[28] concern-

---

[28] Among other matters, he recommended the repeal of all that portion of the act of 1851 concerning attorneys and counsellors at law, after section 12. According to the letter of this act any outrage or contempt may be committed against the courts, other than the supreme court, without remedy, except by the dilatory process of application to the latter court. A felon, or any one who has heaped every imaginable insult upon a district or other lower court, may continue practising in such court until application shall have been made to the supreme court for his expulsion, such application made, and a judgment fully rendered. This is manifestly wrong. In addition to the injustice which may be inflicted upon the lower courts, without a speedy remedy, the statute under consideration may be liable to two constitutional objections: First, it gives the supreme court original jurisdiction of a proceeding in its nature criminal, when that court, under the constitu-

ing legislation on crimes, and criminal practice, as well as civil practice. He urged the propriety of appointing a commission to codify the laws. "The delays and difficulties attendant upon ill-digested legislation," he said, "have cost this state more than the expense of many such commissions, and yet the injury sustained by the state, as such, has not been a tithe of that of her citizens." In March 1868 an act was passed providing for the revision and compilation of the laws of California, with their publication, J. B. Harman, John Currey, and Henry P. Barber being appointed commissioners to meet in San Francisco, and complete their work by the first of July, 1869. The commission was unable to finish its labors before the meeting of the next legislature, when another act was passed, April 4, 1870, authorizing the governor to appoint three commissioners to meet in Sacramento and organize as a board for the prosecution of this purpose, continuing the labor of the first commission. The work was revised by Charles A. Tuttle and Sidney L. Johnson, and finally by a committee consisting of Creed Haymond,[29] John C. Burch, and Charles A. Tuttle. By an act approved in March

tion, can only exercise appellate jurisdiction. Secondly, it interferes with the inherent right of self-protection which rests in every court, etc.

[29] Creed Haymond was born in Beverly, Randolph co., Va, April 22, 1836, his father being W. C. Haymond, a lawyer of prominence. At the age of 16, young Haymond came to Cal. overland, and engaged in mining, packing, merchandising, and ditching, until he had laid up some money. He then studied law, and became eminent. It is claimed that California had the first complete code ever adopted by any state of the union, or any English-speaking people. Haymond was chairman of the code committee, and connected with many great civil cases, and many noted criminal ones. He defended Shepardson, charged with highway robbery in Shasta co., and the More murderers in San Buenaventura, saving all these villains from their just deserts. He was captain of the Sierra Grays, a militia company, serving under Col Jack Hays in the spring of 1860, against the Indians in Nevada, after the Pyramid lake massacre, and for some time col of the 1st artillery regt, National Guard of Cal. In 1882, he became attorney for the Central Pac Railway co., and in the railroad tax cases raised for the first time the question of the protecting influence and power of the 14th amendment of the U. S. constitution against the exercise of the discriminative power by a state, contending that the state could not discriminate in the matter of taxation between citizens holding the same class of property, nor as to property of the same class because of its ownership by citizens or associations of citizens. This position was affirmed by the U. S. circuit court in Cal., and by the highest courts of several other states.

1872, parts of the penal, political, and civil codes went into effect.[30]

The expense of the code commission was not less than $50,000, but it was of the greatest value to the state in pruning the laws of that unwholesome redundancy which had given shelter to ill-omened birds of prey ever watchful of the unwary. But once having begun to charge whatever was wrong in affairs to the constitution and laws, the idea of change became a point with politicians. The state had grown fairly in population, and made strides in the direction of industries, commerce, transportation, social, religious, and educational matters; but along with this growth had run a reactionary tendency—a sort of undertow from the whelming tide of early affluence which had dizzied the brain and bewildered the moral sense of those who, for a time, had been borne upon the flood's crest. A dozen years after the amendment of the constitution and codification of the laws, a demand arose for a radical change, the history of which must follow the recital of the events which led up to it.

[30] *Cal. Proceed. of Commis. for Revision of Laws*, 8 pp.; *S. F. Bulletin*, Oct. 31, 1871; *Cal. Jour. Sen.*, 1871–2, app. No. 41–3, iii.; *S. F. Alta*, Nov. 16, 17, 18, 20, 21, 1872; *Cal. Jour. Sen.*, 1873–4, app. No. 17, 59–60, iv., vi.; *S. F. Alta*, July 11, 1873; *S. F. Call*, Feb. 4, and Dec. 14, 1873.

Worthy of note among the former members of the judiciary is R. M. Widney of Los Angeles, a native of Ohio, who set forth westward in 1855. After studying law and engaging in various pursuits, among others the real estate business, he was appointed district judge by Gov. Booth to fill the unexpired term of Judge Morrison, deceased. He was the originator of the system governing the university of southern California, of which mention is made in a later chapter. Through his bravery, coolness, and determination at the time of the Chinese riot at Los Angeles in 1871, he was largely instrumental in checking a wholesale slaughter. In this good work he was aided by his brother, J. P. Widney, who came to California in 1862, and after studying at the Toland medical college, S. F., and serving for two years in Arizona as assistant surgeon in the U. S. army, in 1868 settled at Los Angeles, where he practised his profession. He was also one of the promoters and is still a trustee of the university of southern California.

Among the former leaders of the San Francisco bar may be mentioned the late James Parker Treadwell, a native of Ipswich, Mass, who after graduating at Harvard and practising law in Boston came to this state in 1851. He was known as a man of great and varied information, of strong reasoning powers, and as one who would never espouse a cause or question that he believed to be wrong.

CHAPTER XI.

LOYALTY, OR DISUNION AND A PACIFIC REPUBLIC?

1860.

The Legislature—Gwin-Weller Combination—Latham's Policy and Administration—Federal Dissolution and State Division—Lecompton and Other Conventions—A Political Crisis—Federal Parties and Politics—Fight for Breckenridge—The San Francisco Bulkhead Scare—Change of Constitution and Division of the State—New Election—The State Loyal to the Union

The legislature elected in 1859, which convened January 2, 1860, was the last in which the element of chivalry and Lecomptonism prevailed. Had Broderick's death occurred before instead of after the election, it would not have had a pro-slavery majority. Nemesis was already shadowed in the air, albeit invisible to her victims.

The Gwin-Weller combination, which had so long retained its power, was broken by the choice of Latham[1] for governor, who, while a Lecompton democrat, was regarded as a friend of San Francisco, which had suffered so much from former administrations. He was, indeed, pledged to use his influence against the obnoxious bulkhead scheme,[2] which at that juncture

---

[1] Milton S. Latham was born in Ohio, May 23, 1829. his father being a native of Va. and his mother of N. H., both being originally of old New England stock. He graduated from Jefferson college, Pa, in 1846, soon after going to Ala where he studied law, and was appointed clerk of the circuit court of Russell co. He came to Cal. in 1850, and soon after arriving was elected dist atty for the judicial dist of Sac and El Dorado cos. In 1851 he was elected congressman and remained in this office until 1856, after which he was appointed collector of the port of San Francisco. His senatorial aspirations and election to the executive office have been recorded in the preceding volume. The sec. of state, under the administration was Johnson Price, a native of Ky, and an officer of Ky vols in the Mexican war.

[2] The legislature of 1863 created a board of harbor commissioners consisting of 3 members, one to be elected at the election for assemblymen, one by

threatened the city and state with a heavy tax upon its commerce, and the growth of a giant monopoly to rule for fifty years. A majority of the legislature,

joint convention of both houses of the legislature, and one by the electors of the city and county of San Francisco. Term of office, 4 years. They were authorized to take possession of and hold all that portion of the bay of San Francisco lying along the water front to a distance of 600 feet into the waters of the bay from the line of the water front, as defined by the act of 1851, together with all of the improvements, rights, privileges, and appurtenances appertaining thereto, except such portions as were held under valid leases, and of those as soon as the leases should expire. This board was to have the entire management of the state's property in the harbor, to collect rents, tolls, etc., which were to be paid into the state's treasury, and drawn therefrom to construct the improvements required by commerce. They were to provide, out of the surplus funds, for the construction of a sea-wall along the water front from Harrison st to Vallejo st, and after the completion of this portion as much further as should be found necessary to the protection of the harbor, and consistent with the state of the fund. William J. Lewis was the first civil engineer employed on the sea-wall. In 1872, the legislature granted to the city and county of S. F. 'all the streets and alleys in the city and county of San Francisco which lie within the exterior boundaries of certain salt, marsh, and tide lands donated by the state to the Southern Pacific R. R. Co. and the Western Pacific R. R. Co. for terminal purposes,' by an act of 1868; and also 'all streets and alleys within the exterior boundaries of lands lying within the boundaries of said lands not donated to said railroad companies, but reserved for market places, and known as Produce Exchange and Market Place,' and 'the lands set apart by the board of tide-land comm'rs for basins known as China and Central basins,' with full power to regulate, manage, donate, or dispose of the same for railroad or other commercial purposes, on condition that any lands thus donated should revert to the state if at any time the railroad company holding should cease to use them. This power to sell or in any manner to alienate this property was revoked by the legislature of 1874, which left the city only the right to lease it. In 1878 another act was passed dedicating to public use the basins in the harbor, and providing for the construction by the harbor commissioners of a sea-wall, and a thoroughfare 200 feet in width, from the east line of Taylor st to the boundary between the city and county of San Francisco and the county of San Mateo. The means to be used in its construction were to be derived from rents, wharfage, and tolls, and the sea-wall was declared to be for public use, together with the land created by filling in the lots formed by running the line of the sea-wall straight from point to point. In 1886 the value of this new land amounted to $1,300,000. Various suggestions were offered as to the use to which it should be devoted by the state. It was once proposed by the chamber of commerce that free grain warehouses should be erected upon these lots, but it was found that this would necessitate a railroad, which was not practicable. Some persons proposed making public parks of the state land; others that it should be held for high prices, and sold; and still others that it should be sold as fast as wanted, and the proceeds devoted to the more rapid extension of the sea-wall. After much discussion and consultation between the state and city authorities, a proposition was made to have the whole sea-wall property transferred to San Francisco, upon condition that the system of tolls should be abolished, and bonds issued by the city to the amount of $4,000,000 for the completion of the sea-wall, the money to be recovered by the lease of the made land, and the land to remain unsold. A railroad to connect the wharves and warehouses along the sea-wall is also talked of. The legislature and the freeholders who form the new city charter will probably soon decide the question of sea-wall and bonds.

it was well understood,[3] could be purchased, and upon
the governor depended in a great measure the prevention of this iniquity.

There was universal surprise and disapproval, therefore, when, on the day after his inauguration, the
legislature went into joint convention, and elected
Governor Latham to the seat in the United States

[3] The senate for 1860 was composed of Andres Pico, Los Angeles, San Ber-
nardino, and San Diego; P. de la Guerra, Sta Bárbara, San Luis Obispo;
J. H. Watson, Sta Cruz and Monterey; R. A. Redman, Sta Clara and Ala-
meda; S. H. Sharp, T. G. Phelps, A. C. Peachy, S. H. Parker, S. F. and
San Mateo; S. A. Merritt, Tulare, Fresno, Mariposa, and Merced; J. J.
Franklin, I. N. Quinn, Tuolumne and Stanislaus; G. W. Dent, Contra Costa
and San Joaquin; R. C. Clark, James M. McDonald, Sac.; H. Edgerton,
Solano, Napa and Yolo; Jasper O'Farrell, Marin, Sonoma, and Mendocino;
J. P. Haynes, Klamath, Del Norte, and Siskiyou; Jonathan Logan, Colusa,
Shasta and Tehama; J. M. Vance, S. A. Ballou, Butte and Plumas; H. P.
Watkins, E. D. Wheeler, W. H. Parks, Yuba and Sutter; S. H. Chase, C.
J. Lansing, Nevada; T. J. Leet, James Anderson, Placer; W. B. Dickinson,
R. D. Crittenden, A. S. Denver, I. S. Titus, El Dorado; J. A. Eagan, B. T.
Bradley, Amador and Calaveras; M. Kirkpatrick, Sierra; James T. Ryan,
Humboldt and Trinity. Officers of the senate: J. N. Quinn, pres't pro tem.;
J. R. Beard, sec.; D. J. Williamson, asst sec.; Cyril Hawkins, enrolling
clerk; W. S. Tetcher, engrossing clerk; W. H. Bell, sergt-at-arms; J. Mc
Clenchy, asst sergt-at-arms.

The assembly was composed of: P. C. Johnson, John Bowman, Amador;
P. K. Shattuck, Alameda; John Lambert, Butte; P. A. Gallagher, Samuel
Wilson, H. A. Shelton, Calaveras; E. A. Stevenson, Colusa; Cornelius
Yager, Contra Costa; John Daggett, Del Norte; John Conness, D. C. Patten,
D. Fairchild, W. H. Stone, Asa H. Hawley, Jack C. Bell, G. H. Watson,
E. Dunlap, El Dorado; T. M. Heston, Fresno, Tulare and Buena Vista; L.
M. Burson, Humboldt; A. J. King, J. J. Warner, Los Angeles; Samuel
Lewis, Marin; J. B. Hammond, Mariposa; F. F. Jenkins, Merced; Mariano
Malarin, Monterey; Nathan Coombs, Napa; Henry Hayes, Samuel T. Cur-
tis, C. F. Smith, Philip Moore, M. P. O'Conner, Nevada; S. W. Lovell,
D. S. Beach, J. S. Mackin, J. W. Harville, Placer; T. B. Shannon, P. O.
Hundley, Plumas; Henry Starr, D. W. Welty, B. Ellis, L. C. Goodman,
Sac.; W. A. Conn, San Bernardino; Robert W. Groom, San Diego; Abner
Phelps, J. C. Schmidt, Daniel Rogers, Jasper Babcock, Samuel L. Theller,
B. T. Tate, F. A. Sawyer, S. S. Telton, San Francisco; W. B. Maxon, San
Mateo; W. L. Campbell, Thomas Laspeyre, San Joaquin; B. M. Henry,
San Luis Obispo; J. M. Covarrubias, Sta Bárbara; J. M. Williams, D. B.
Bailey, Santa Clara; J. L. Halstead, Sta Cruz; John White, Shasta; James
A. Johnson, T. J. Halliday, Sierra; Charles McDermitt, Siskiyou; Thomas
M. Swan, Solano; Charles P. Wilkins, Sonoma; Miner Waldron, Stanislaus;
J. L. Smith, Sutter; A. C. Lawrence, Trinity; G. W. Bailey, F. Yaney, E.
A. Rodgers, Robert Howe, Tuolumne; H. Gwinn, Yolo; C. H. Kungle,
Benjamin T. O'Rear, Benjamin P. Hugg, J. M. Crowell, J. Westcott, Yuba.
Officers of the assembly: Philip Moore, speaker; J. M. Anderson, chief
clerk; R. K. Weston, asst clerk; C. W. Tozer, sergt-at-arms; William New-
som, asst sergt-at-arms; E. W. Casey, engrossing clerk; H. C. Kibbe,
enrolling clerk.

senate[4] left vacant by Broderick, and filled temporarily by Haun. The whole appeared to be a trick, and people said in their wrath that Latham had sold himself, or had been elected to the senate by the arch-plotters to get him out of their way for infamous purposes.[5]

The legislature of 1859 had passed an act authorizing the people of the six counties of San Luis Obispo, Santa Bárbara, Los Angeles, San Diego, San Bernardino, and a part of Buena Vista, or all that part of the state south of the 36th parallel, to vote upon the question of separation from the state, with the design of being relegated to a territorial condition. The Lecomptonites, taking advantage of the fact that the native Californians had always been opposed to being taxed for the support of a state government,[6] that they complained of the inequality of taxes as between agriculturalists and miners, and maintained their right to carry slaves into any territory, had fixed upon this means of consummating their purpose of bringing slave property to the Pacific coast. By shrewdly fanning the flame of discontent in the southern counties, they managed to secure a two-thirds

---

[4] Says Tuthill: 97 of them, democrats, went into caucus together, and on the 1st ballot ex-governor Weller had 38 votes, ex-congressman Denver 31, Judge Baldwin 11, Collector Washington 9, and Gen. McDougall 8. They tried it again on an early ensuing evening; Baldwin was withdrawn, Denver stepped aside, and the first ballot showed Latham 51, Weller 43, Washington 2. The two houses met in joint convention on the 11th of January. A Sac. member nominated Latham, a San Franciscan nominated Oscar L. Shafter, and John Conness for the anti-Lecomptonites nominated Edmund Randolph. The first ballot gave Latham, who the day before was inaugurated governor, 97, Randolph 14, Shafter 3.

[5] One obnoxious scheme was the Omnibus Wagon Road bill, which provided for the construction of several different roads over the Sierra, in the same direction, and at a great expense, to give contracts to political friends. This the governor vetoed. Another bill vetoed was for changing the venue in the murder case related in cap. ix., pp. 212–14, of this vol. But the legislature of 1861 passed it over his head. *Cal. Stat.*, 1861, 47–8; *Quigley, Irish Race*, 308.

[6] *Val. Doc.*, MS., 35, p. 262, and 13, pp. 39–45; *Sta Bàrbara Archives*, MS., 8, pp. 229–30, 233; *Cota, Call*, MS., 25–36; *Parkes' Letter-book*, MS., 93; *Hayes' Constit. Law*, i. pp. 47–8; *Hayes' Scraps, Angeles*, iv. 125; *Sqc. Union*, Feb. 15, April 14, May 11, Sept. 15, 1855; *Cal. Jour. Assem.*, 1858, 564–5; *Californian*, Feb. 1881, pp. 124–7.

majority for the division.   But there being a question
of the right of a state to take such a step, Latham
had employed some of his leisure in preparing an argument in its favor, for the perusal of the president
which on his inauguration he presented to the legislature for its consideration.   "The origin of this act,"
he said, "is to be found in the dissatisfaction of the
mass of people in the southern counties of this state
with the expenses of state government.   They are an
agricultural people, thinly scattered over a large extent of country.   They complain that the taxes upon
their land and cattle are ruinous, entirely dispropor-
tionate to the taxes collected in the mining region;
that the policy of the state hitherto having been to
exempt mining claims from taxation, and the mining
population being migratory in its character, and hence
contributing but little to the state revenue in proportion to the population, they are unjustly burdened;
and that there is no remedy, save in a separation from
the other portion of the state.   In short, that the
union of southern and northern California is unnatural."

A resolution of the assembly was passed jointly by
both houses to instruct senators and representatives
in congress to oppose the execution of the act of 1859
dividing the state.   This resolution, together with
the governor's division document, was referred to the
committee on federal relations, a majority of which
reported in favor of the legality of the act, and against
the resolution.   But a minority report was presented
which answered the governor's arguments by others
in nowise less logical.[8]   It contended that there was
no authority in the constitution of the state for the
action of the previous legislature, no precedent in the
history of the United States, no consent given by the
whole people of the state, but, instead, a protest from

---

[7] *Cal. Division of State* (pamphlet, 1860); *Cal. Jour. Assem.*, 1860, p. 125.
[8] The majority report was signed simply Chas P. Wilkins, chairman, but
the minority report was signed by J. R. Williams of Santa Clara, E. A.
Rodgers of Tuolumne, P. C. Johnson of Amador, and J. W. Harville of
Placer.

one of the counties included in the dissevered portion, and, in case they should be set off, inextricable confusion imminent in the courts, and all county business, including the collection of their portion of the state debt.[9]

"The strongest barrier we have against the encroachment of federal power would be broken down, and it would be only necessary to secure the legislatures of the various states by money or political favors, in order to centralize all power, and consolidate all government." Thus spoke the minority, and as 'state rights' was one of the hobbies of the party in power, they could not but pay some heed to the suggestion.

The matter was debated with much warmth in the assembly, and some pointed criticisms were uttered concerning the "governor of the day" who had felt it his duty to declare in favor of a law which he admitted was opposed to the sentiment of the state at large, which was overwhelmingly against it. The interest created at home by these debates was overshadowed at the national capital by more important interests, and passed as merely an incident of these uneasy times. Whatever the California delegation had to say about its ex-officers does not appear in the proceedings of congress.[10]

Before the adjournment of the legislature, which remained in session until April 30th, the political cauldron was set boiling, in which was destined to go ingredients more full of horrible witchery than was dreamed of even by the jugglers themselves. In January the Lecompton state central committee held a meeting at Sacramento and made its appointment, taking the highest vote cast for any candidate at the

[9] The act of 1859 declared that a commission should be appointed to adjust the financial affairs between Cal. and the new govt, and to determine the amount of the new govt to Cal. on account of the state debt, the expenses of the said comm'rs to be borne equally by the two govts, but no plan of payment of the debt was even suggested. *Cal. Stat.*, 1859, 310–11. The name proposed for the contemplated territory was Colorado. *Sac. Union*, April 18, 1855.

[10] There is a mere mention in *U. S. Miss. Doc.*, 2, 36 cong. 1 sess.

state election, and appointed February 29th for a convention.   The anti-Lecompton democratic state central committee followed suit, and held a meeting on the same and following days; resolving that the 're-enunciation of his federal heresies by James Buchanan, demanded that they should renew their adherence to old principles, namely, those expressed in the Cincinnati platform, and to the "great doctrine of popular sovereignty,[11] as expounded in 1856." It was decided by the anti-Lecompton democrats not to send delegates to the national convention to be held at Charleston, hence not to hold a convention.   The republicans, who were silently gaining ground, and who felt that the hour had come for action, held their state convention February 23d, to choose delegates to the national convention at Chicago, to be held June 15th, instructing them to vote for W. H. Seward, or in case the convention could not agree upon him, for whomever it should agree upon.[12]

The delegates chosen to attend the Chicago convention were T. P. Tracy of San Francisco, Leland Stanford of Sacramento, A. A. Sargent of Nevada city, D. W. Cheesman of Butte, and D. J. Staples

[11] A writer in the *Nevada Journal*, Oct. 5, 1860, makes the distinction between popular and squatter sovereignty. 'We understand, by squatter sovereignty, a so-called inherent right of the people in an unorganized territory to govern themselves.   The doctrine of squatter sovereignty is that preached by Pugh, Broderick, and the *Sac. Union*, that the people of a territory have a right of themselves to organize a government, and the constitution of the U. S. does not extend over them until, at their option, sanctioned by congress.   It is the doctrine taught in Lieber's work on political ethics. By popular sovereignty we understand the exercise of the right of government by the people of a territory after an enabling act has granted the permission.   That is the phase of the doctrine taught by Douglas....He asserts that a government like that undertaken by Cal. in 1849 is irregular and revolutionary.   The case of Cal. is one of squatter sovereignty, not popular sovereignty.'   The terms are often used, even by politicians; but popular sovereignty, as here defined, was the principle for which Douglas and Broderick contended in discussing the Kansas question.

[12] Samuel H. Parker was pres't of the republican state convention for the choice of delegates to the national convention; vice-pres't, J. F. Chilles of Trinity; T. G. Phelps of San Mateo; J. S. McLean of Yuba; William W. Belshaw of Amador, and G. W. Towle of Santa Clara.   The secretaries were Dr William Rabe of S. F., and William M. Lyon of Sonoma.   From the proceedings it appears that the republican ranks received important accessions from the anti-Lecompton democrats.

of San Joaquin. The alternates chosen were J. C. Hinckley of Shasta, a recruit from the anti-Lecompton ranks, Isaac M. Baldwin of Sonoma, John B. Yan of San Francisco, Francis Snyder of Calaveras, and James Churchman of Nevada.

The democratic state convention was a stormy one, being distracted by the absence of any one leader of power to control it, and having for every would-be leader an antagonistic pretender. Philip Moore was elected president. The two prominent factions were the Gwin-Weller combination, and the Latham-Denver opposition. In the choice of delegates to the Charleston convention the opposition were triumphant, electing seven out of eight of their nominees. The man of most prominence among them was John Bidwell of Butte; the others being G. W. Patrick of Tuolumne, John S. Dudley of Siskiyou, William Bradley of San Joaquin, Newell Gregory of Monterey, John A. Dreibelbiss of Shasta, Austin E. Smith of San Francisco, John Raines of San Bernardino. So long had the Gwin-Weller alliance been in power that only men connected with it were familiar figures in politics, and this was the beginning of a new dispensation. The delegates were instructed to vote for Daniel S. Dickinson as California's first choice, but if he should not receive the support of a majority of the states, to do their best for the democratic party, without regard to choice.

Both republicans and democrats felt that a great crisis was upon the nation. The southern wing of the latter party had openly declared that the election of a republican president would be ground for the secession of the southern states. Senator Gwin had said, in a speech delivered December 12, 1859, in the senate chamber, "I believe that the slave-holding states of this confederacy can establish a separate and independent government that will be impregnable to the assaults of all foreign enemies," and had gone on to show why they should, and how they could, exist as a separate government. He had also said that if the southern states went out of the union "California would be found with the south;" but he was careful to expunge this and other similar remarks from the official report of his speech. It was intended for the senate and not for the ear of California; but it was wafted on the wings of newspaper gossip, and was known before either of the conventions met to choose a course for the future.

Latham challenged Gwin's declaration that California would go with the south, to which the latter replied that he had never said so; that the statement was destitute of truth. "I hope, Mr President," said the suave politician, "that this union will be imperishable, but if it is ever broken up, the eastern boundary of the Pacific republic will be, in my opinion, the Sierra Madre and the Rocky mountains." There was no little talk thenceforth about the Pacific republic and Gwin's designs, but people were not yet quite ready to believe there was anything in it.

Broderick, lest he should become a republican, was removed from earth. Douglas, because he held to his popular-sovereignty beliefs, was removed from the position of chairman of the committee on territories. The same influence accomplished both ends. Gwin himself relates that it was through his management, as chairman of the sub-committee of democratic senators, who reported to the democratic caucus nominees for the various committees, that Douglas was removed.[13] It was only another instance of that "insidious tyranny" of which Broderick complained.

[13] *Gwin, Mem.*, MS., 165. In the controversy between Gwin and Douglas which followed, and in speeches in the senate at the beginning of the 36th congress, it came out how near Douglas had been to yielding his position, which he would have done but for Broderick. According to the correspondent of the *Sac. Union*, Jan. 2, 1860, this fact was common talk in Washington. Says F. F. Low, in his *California Affairs*, MS., 19, John Hickman, hearing that Douglas intended to back down, and yield the fight to Buchanan, went to Broderick's room and told him of it. Broderick, thunderstruck, raged like a lion. He refused, at first, to believe the story, then in his imperious way, he ordered Hickman to find Douglas, and bring him to his room. When Douglas came he found Broderick pacing the floor.

Latham now proceeded cautiously. He said in reply to Gwin's disavowal, that he was glad to have his impression corrected; that Mr. Gwin knew that California possessed resources not belonging to any other state of the union, and the most energetic population on earth, and "why should we trust to the management of others what we are abundantly able to do ourselves? Why depend on the south or the north to regulate our affairs? And this, too, after the north and south have proved themselves incapable of living in harmony with one another."[14] Here was more, but impartial independence of the federal government.[15]

California was still the elf-child of the union, never regularly baptized into the family of states, one which felt the isolation of her foreign blood, the pride of her dreamy ancestry, and the self-assurance of unquestioned native resources. Many things could have been forgiven her had she needed forgiveness, which, to her glory be it spoken, she never required, although her mistaken representations would often have persuaded the federal sisterhood it was her purpose to betray them. Said Latham, following the lead of Hammond of South Carolina, who denominated the white laboring class as the "mud-sills of society,"

'Mr Douglas,' said he, 'I hear you propose to abandon the fight.' Douglas answered, 'I see no hope of success; they will crush us; and if they do, there is no future for any of us, and I think we can agree upon terms that will virtually sustain ourselves.' Broderick replied: 'You came to me of your own accord, asking me to take this stand. I have committed myself against this infernal Lecompton constitution. Now, if you desert me, (with an oath) I will make you crawl under your chair in the senate'. Douglas at once resolved to stand firm, and not to support the English bill on which he was wavering. In the republican convention at Sac. for the choice of presidential electors, A. H. Myers said: 'A more noble, open, glorious, manly statesman never lived than David C. Broderick. The proudest act of my life will have been to canvass this state with him; and I tell you I would rather live in retirement all my life than to vote for Stephen A. Douglas, the professed friend, who vilely betrayed him, and the man who voted for the confirmation of the appointment of Calhoun Benham, one of the seconds in that fatal duel, as United States district attorney for California.' Sac. Union, June 21, 1860.

[14] Gwin, Mem., MS., 175–6.

[15] Dempster tells us in his MS., 3–4, that in vigilance committee sessions, independence of the federal government was broached, but discountenanced by the majority. Coleman MS. refers to the same thing.

and as "white slaves"[16]—"the political institutions
of a country have very little to do with the relative
position of capital and labor." This his opponents
construed into a declaration that the majority everywhere, which represented labor, should never be
anything but servants to the minority, which represented capital, and should never be granted equal
political rights. The men who had elected him
governor, and their representatives who chose him
to sit in the United States senate, were chiefly
those who labored with their hands, but who
never expected to be classed with slaves, or with
the laboring classes of India or Europe; much less
to be presented as an apology for slavery in the
south, or as saying to the north, " As long as you
make the slavery question the battle-cry of your sectional adherents it is impossible for the south to trust
you, or to look upon your proceedings with indifference. Abandon it, and the south will again unite
with us upon all questions concerning our common
welfare. The south claims nothing but her constitutional rights." [17] This was equivalent to saying that
the south had the right to carry slavery into all the
territory of the United States not organized under
state government, from which it would in time drive
free labor ; it meant that the millions of freemen
being born every year in the federal union should be
confined to northern territory or become like the
" poor white trash" of the south, which the very
slaves despised for their enforced poverty and ignorance. The enunciation of these sentiments, in obedience to the Lecompton senatorial rule, roused that
portion of the democratic party in California which
was not distinctly pro-slavery to take a stand against
Lecomptonism.

What the California senators did not accomplish by
way of alienating the northern democracy of California,

[16] Cong. Globe, 1857–8, pt. 2, p. 962.
[17] Latham's Speech, in Cong. Globe, 1859–60, pt 2, p. 1727; Sac. Union, May
9, 1860.

the delegates to the Charleston convention did. They obeyed their instructions so far as to vote for Daniel S. Dickinson on the first ballot, after which they went over to the ultra-southern pro-slavery democracy, forsaking the Cincinnati platform, the Pacific railroad, and everything they had been intrusted to labor for, following the seceders even to Richmond. In doing this, and forsaking the northern democracy, they had gone directly counter to the best interests of their state. But they were infatuated. "What is it?" asked the Sacramento *Union*, "which has so bewitched the California representatives, from senator to delegates to the convention?" The answer was not far to find. It was that "insidious tyranny" which terrorized and flattered alternately, which broke up the Charleston convention, seceded a second time from the Baltimore convention, and threatened the ruin of the democratic party, should not the ultra wing be permitted to dictate to the national party.

The long and bitter contest ended by the nomination of two tickets: Stephen A. Douglas of Illinois, with Herschel V. Johnson of Georgia, for the nationals, and John C. Breckenridge of Kentucky, with Joseph Lane of Oregon, for the Lecomptonites. The latter party dared not put forward a candidate from the gulf states for fear of being considered sectional, knowing the northern democrats had set their hearts on Douglas.

> 'There are hills beyond Pentland,
> There are friths beyond Forth:
> If there are lords in the southland,
> There are chiefs in the north,'

quoted a Maine delegate in the Baltimore convention. The southland dared not place upon their ticket its lordliest lords. The nationals boldly supported their chief.

The surprise of the Californians at the rejection by the eastern republicans of their foremost leader, Seward, was only equalled by their dissatisfaction. The distance, and the time occupied by mail transit, even with the pony express, just established,[18] prevented that perfect knowledge of the situation at the centres of political agitation which could render satisfactorily accountable the action of either of the great parties. Why Lincoln, then little known, should be preferred to men of national reputation, did not at first appear. It did not occur to them that to be too prominent is to be in danger of destruction from the cross-fire of factions with past grievances to redress. Although doubtful of the result, the names of Abraham Lincoln of Illinois, and Hannibal Hamlin of Maine, were placed before the republicans of the state for president and vice-president. Still another presidential ticket was in the field, that of the Americans, or as they now called themselves, the constitutional union party, who might more properly be named conservative republicans, and whom the regular republicans had at first hoped to receive in their convention; but they met at Baltimore and nominated John Bell of Tennessee for president, and Edward Everett of Massachusetts for vice-president.

With regard to slavery, the republicans contended that it could exist only by virtue of municipal law, that no such law existed in the territories, nor any power to enact one. Congress could not establish or legalize slavery, and was bound to prohibit it in any federal territory, whenever there was a necessity for such exclusion. The Douglas democracy declared that slavery or no slavery in any territory was optional with the people, and neither congress, nor any other

[18] In several parts of my history I have given some account of the Pony Express. It was a private enterprise, undertaken by Russell Majors and Co., owning the central stage line route, via Salt lake and Carson valley, and carried a mail weekly from St Joseph to Sac., time 8 days. The first mail received by pony arrived in Sac. on the afternoon of the 13th of April, 1860, and was received with wild enthusiasm. It brought 80 letters for S.F. and half a dozen for Sac. Public news of importance was printed upon tissue paper almost without weight, and by this means full reports of the political conventions were received long before the arrival of the steamer mails. This mail was interrupted by Indian hostilities in the Carson and Humboldt valleys in the month of June, occasioning much discontent, but soon resumed. The first pony mail bound east left Sac. April 4th, carrying 70 letters.

part of the union, had a right to intermeddle. The Breckenridge democracy claimed the right to carry slaves, as property, into any territory, and that congress was bound to protect such property when necessary, whether or not the territorial legislature sanctioned it, or the majority of the people approved. All the parties in California favored a transcontinental railroad, that being the sine qua non of support with the people of the Pacific coast, who just then were more troubled about transportation and mails than about ethical politics,[19] but who received neither from the out-going administration.

[19] The majority of the people of Cal., as I have mentioned in the preceding volume, preferred the central to the southern route for mail transit. The central route was gradually opened, first from Salt lake to the Missouri river, then by wagon from Placerville to Carson valley, and finally to Salt lake, connecting there with the mail to St Joseph. George Chorpenning owned the western division, but his means were limited and the management bad.   Broderick endeavored to procure the adoption of the central route by the government in place of the southern or Butterfield route, established in 1857, and thereby incurred the hostility of Gwin and the southern influence. The exposure of Gwin's methods had the effect to cause him to withdraw his opposition to the central route, but he did so then only when he fancied he saw an opportunity to make capital for himself out of it. Senator Hale, of N. H., introduced a bill which could have been passed, which would have given California a daily mail over the central route.   But Gwin had several motives for preventing the passage of this bill.   One was that he was retained in the interest of the steamship company; another that he would do nothing so pleasing to the republicans as to allow this republican bill to pass, thus overshadowing him; and again, that he reserved to himself the glory of appearing as the author of the contract for a tri-weekly mail over the central route.   He introduced another bill to embarrass Hale's, and allowed neither to pass.   But this plank, on which he hoped to stand when the next U. S. senator should be chosen in Cal., slipped away from him when, going to Postmaster-general Holt, after the close of the session, that official flatly refused to carry out the terms of the bargain between them, In this manner Cal. was deprived of mail service, except over the Butterfield route, until the secession of the southern states and a change of administration caused the suspension of this line, and the establishment of the central route. *Sac. Union*, June 15, 26, and July 23 and 28, 1860. Latham offered some amendments to Hale's bill when it was before the senate, but they were defeated with the rest.   He presented some figures which are interesting.   From Sept. 1858 to and including March 1860, there were 685,960 letters sent over the Butterfield route, the postage on which was $71,378.63; and over the route via Salt lake 15,725, the postage on which was $865.51. The Butterfield contractors received $600,000 for tri-weekly service. This was one of the profitable contracts given to southern men by the consent of California senators, but the service performed was never complained of. The Pacific Mail Steamship company in 1860 refused to carry express packages containing mail matter, or to carry the newspaper mails, which could not go overland, the object of the refusal being to force congress, with the help of California's senior senator, to give the mail contract to Vanderbilt's company.

The platforms being settled and nominations made, there began the most remarkable struggle for principles ever decided by ballot. The whole congressional delegation returned to California early in August to support the Breckenridge ticket; but they were met with reproaches which augured ill for their political preferment hereafter. The San Francisco *Bulletin* and the Sacramento *Union* bore hard upon Gwin for his treachery to the interests of the state, and his complicity in the Lime Point sale to the government, reported to be just consummated, by which $200,000 was paid for a point of barren rock at the Heads, which the state would have sold for $2,000, or whatever price a jury empanelled by the district court should declare it to be worth.[20] They quoted from his speech in the United States senate, where he had said: "The northern states are laboring under a delusion if they think that the southern states cannot separate from them, either violently or peaceably—violently if necessary. They can take possession of all the public property within their limits, and prepare against any aggression of the non-slave-holding states, or any power that may choose to infringe upon what they conceive to be their rights."[21] These were alarming utterances, whether it was believed or not that the south could succeed in parting from the union.

As for the junior senator, who had been elected governor only a few months before, as one whom the people could trust, he shared the opprobrium of having neglected the state's interests,[22] and having taken

[20] The legislature of 1859 passed a law intended to meet cases of this kind, that is, where the govt required a piece of land, and the owner was a minor or non-resident, or for any reason refused to sell the land, a jury should appraise it, and the sheriff of the county should execute a deed to the U. S. *Cal. Stat.*, 1859, 26–7.

[21] *Cong. Globe*, 1859–60, pt. 1, p. 125.

[22] The legislature of 1860 had passed a concurrent resolution instructing the Cal. senators and representatives to use their influence to procure the passage of a law by congress donating to actual settlers 160 acres of land for homesteads, title to be given after a residence of 5 years or more. *Cal. Stat.*,

sides with the bolters from the regular democratic party, who by their action imperilled its existence. Such was the political situation in California in July, followed by a peremptory marshalling of clans, and an exciting campaign. A number of national democrats, chiefly those who had been, or who hoped to be federal office-holders, under democratic administrations, went over to the Lecomptonites. These politicians published a lengthy manifesto to show that by the two-thirds rule adopted at the Charleston convention, Douglas had not received the nomination. They did not attempt to show that Breckenridge had been regularly nominated, but only claimed the right to be regarded as the real democratic party, because their principles had been indorsed by "every certain democratic state," or in other words every slave state. Ex-governor Weller declared his devotion to party principles, and emphasized the declaration with the avowal that he had been compelled by his fealty to party to vote for "a gambler of thirty years standing to be high sheriff of San Francisco," instead of a better man who was opposed to him. His example was offered as an instance of those high sentiments of duty entertained by the chivalry in party matters.[23]

1860, p. 419. Johnson of Tenn. introduced a homestead bill in the senate in Dec. 1859. It occupied much time, being opposed by southern senators, and frequently amended, but was finally passed by a vote of 44 to 8, June 10, 1860. President Buchanan vetoed it upon the ground that it was unjust to the old settlers who had paid $1.25 per acre for their lands, and to other classes of people, not agriculturalists, who had an equal interest in the common inheritance of all the people. An amendment was offered by Gwin, and supported by Latham, giving miners a right to occupy public mineral lands without being considered trespassers. Gwin was artful enough always to have some popular measure pending, but his colleague had not so much tact. The first bill before the senate, embodying homestead principles, was introduced by Gwin in 1850-1. At the next session he spoke in favor of a house and homestead bill, introduced separately. This measure was kept in the prospective down to 1860, and finally passed, doubtless with the knowledge that it would be vetoed. It served the purpose of flattering the people, while the more important objects of mail and railroad communication suffered neglect, and the Lime Point swindle was perfected, in which a handsome bonus was believed to have been paid to the venal senators. Congress enacted a homestead law in 1862; and in 1866 an act similar to the mining-law amendment offered by Gwin in 1860 was passed.

[23] A Breckenridge meeting was held in S. F., July 28, 1860, when the fol-

The Douglas men were not attracted by the prospect of being forced to vote for gamblers, embezzlers, or other swindlers, and did not obey the call.[24] They also published a manifesto in which they claimed the nomination of their chief to be regular; and accused the Breckenridge democracy of being revolutionists, disunionists, and conspirators. At a meeting of

lowing officers were chosen: R. A. Thompson, pres't; O. C. Pratt, B. F. Washington, G. W. P. Bissell, R. McMillen, S. Heydenfeldt, Thomas Hayes, V. E. Howard, R. R. Provines, L. Ryan, C. H. Hempstead, G. O. McMullin, J. E. Addison, A. Hollub, T. J. Haynes, A. Phelps, W. H. Moore, J. H. Bosworth, Hall McAllister, A. C. Peachy, J. H. Cutter, F. A. Benjamin, John Roach, W. L. Higgins, C. L. Weller, Jacob Cramer, R. P. Ashe, G. B. Grant, A. Churchill, J. B. Schaffer, B. Schloss, G. D. Naglee, A. Wasserman, Fred. Griffin, vice pres'ts; J. C. McCeny, Alex. P. Green, J. Frank Lawton, sec'tys. The meeting was addressed by R. A. Thompson, ex-gov. Weller. V. E. Howard, and Calhoun Benham. *S. F. Bulletin,* July 30, 1860. These and others signed the Breckenridge address, with the exception of Naglee and Peachy.

[24] The Douglas manifesto was signed by John G. Downey, Joseph P. Hoge, J. Mora Moss, Wm M. Lent, Owen McMahon, Richard P. Hammond, H. W. Halleck, John Parrott, James A. McDougall, James T. Ryan, William S. Long, Frederick Billings, Eugene Casserly, Samuel M. Wilson, Sol. A. Sharp, George Wallan, N. K. Masten, Charles Hosmer, Charles de Ro, Wm H. Rogers, George A. Harris, Charles F. Hamilton, J. P. Gervey. A. Hayward, James Denman, Wm V. Garvey, A. J. Hotalling, George O. Ecker, Leander Ransom, John Reynolds, Isaac Hartman, E. P. Peckham, L. B. Mizner, Jasper J. Papy, J. W. Hawkins, Louis McLane, Wm R. Garrison, H. J. Bowie, George F. Sharp, John S. Williams, William D. Chapman, H. A. Cobb, H. P. Heintzelman, R. C. Mathieson, Robert C. Page, C. M. Brosnan, C. McC Delaney, C. S. Whitney, A. J. Bryant, Ira A. Eaton, Terrence Faley, Elisha Cook, Wm C. Hoff, B. M. Henry, Charles Ruehl, J. Gundlach, Herman Hertzer, D. Clement, Joseph Campe, Frederick Epting, W. G. Barneman, Jacob F. Haehnlen, John Pforr, Jacob Knell, J. Startz, Wm Huefner. L. Shearer, C. J. Eaton, R. H. Lloyd, C. T. Emmett, H. J. Labatt, Joseph J. Labatt, E. D. Sawyer, Thomas N. Cazenean, Henry Gregory. Daniel Welcom, J. P. Buckley, Wm G. Wood, Amos Noyes, James Donohue, James Sharkey, H. F. Williams, Wm Wright, James Graves, John Whipple, Wm Hammond, H. C. Moore, John A. Richart, Nat. L. Braughton, John Vandewater, Charles L. Wilson, F. O. Dennis, J. O. Callahan, W. D. Fordham, Cornelius D. Sullivan, John Kelley, Jr, Francis O'Farral, Richard S. Haven, John Flannagan, D. J. Oliver, James Hayden, Alfred T. Beall, Pierre B. Cornwall, Joseph J. Babcock, C. F. McDermott, Wm Hayes, John McLellan, Daniel T. Murphy, Lewis L. Aldrich, J. H. Blood, Thomas C. Browne, F. S, Wensinger, Charles H. Parker, P. Riley, A. F. Sawyer, P. A. Owens, J. S. Jenkins, Fred. K. Collier, George F. Price, Frankiin L. Jones, C. T. Ryland, Robert Pollock, George C. Parkinson, F. Vassault, John C. Leach, Myron Norton, W. Porter, Wm G. Ross, H. L. Barker, T. W. Freelon, Anthony Ludlum, S. P. Bowman, David Scannel, R. H. Sinton, J. N. Daniels, Samuel Purdy, F. Kingsbury, Henry Gerke, J. E. Nuttman, E. B. Mastick, James P. Ames, P. H. Owens, David Jobson, W. H. Harvey, S. T. Leet, C. H. Shear, P. Hunt. On the anti-Lecompton side were J. W. Denver, S. W. Inge, E. D. Wheeler, J. R. Roseborough.

the state central committee in San Francisco on the 31st of July, J. P. Hoge being chairman, an effort was made to harmonize the two wings of the old party by resolving that each might select two presidential electors for whom the united party should vote, the electors being pledged to cast their votes in the electoral college for the democratic candidate receiving the majority in the presidential election. But to this the Breckenridge delegates would not agree, and Hoge withdrew from the committee, Charles Lindley of Yuba being chosen chairman in his place. The result was a split, and the nomination of two sets of electors by two separate conventions.

This would seem to have left a clear field for the republicans, but they also had their difficulties. Ever since the adoption of the charter of 1856, and the rule of the vigilance committee in San Francisco, the municipal officers of the consolidated county and city were nominated by a People's nominating committee irrespective of the political bias of the nominee, and dependent wholly on his fitness for the office. Under this order of affairs the city had prospered and enjoyed honest administration. The republicans who had so far aided now wished to absorb the people's party, its efforts being regarded with disfavor by many of the best citizens. Besides, the state was still strongly democratic, and not favorable to republicanism which had so far done nothing for California, except once or twice to hold a scheming legislature in check. But clubs were rapidly formed both in country and city, and their organizations grew apace.[25]

[25] The names which appear as officers of the central republican club of S. F., are William Sherman, pres't; M. S. Whiting and B. F. Perkins, sect'ys; Alpheus Bull, treas'r; Peter Witbeck, marshal; D. C. McRuer, Alexander Campbell, A. T. Lawton, T. J. L. Smiley, Henry Seligman, R. Marton, William Ireland, J. Regensburger, H. J. Rogers, N. C. Lane, B. T. Case, F. G. E. Tittle, George C. Waller, Joseph Weed, H. C. Squire, William H. Culver, C. W. Howe, Andrew Walker, C. H. Dexter, George Amarige, C. L. Hobbs, John Swett, H. A. Sontag, P. W. Shephard. Other prominent republicans were E. B. Crocker, S. B. Mulford, E. Lander, L. Stanford, Louis R. Lull, H. H. Haight, C. Webb Howard, R. B. Swain, O. F. Willey, A. J. Pope, Seth H. Wetherbee, Alfred J. Ellis, Ira P. Rankin,

The Bell and Everett men took the name of the
union party, and held their convention for the nomination of presidential electors. They were chiefly of
the conservative class,[26] and lacked the eager spirit of
the republicans, many of whom were young men desirous of attaching themselves to a party with principles on which they could rely to build up the state,
and satisfy personal ambition at the same time. In
San Francisco the republican central club won the
applause of the better class of citizens by consenting
not to run a municipal ticket, but to allow the people's
nominating committee to make up a non-partisan
ticket which they would support; but a faction per-
sisted in making a race for the offices by bringing
out a straight republican ticket.

These matters settled, the campaign was prosecuted
with enthusiasm[27] on all sides, the republicans, notwithstanding some rough treatment in those districts where
the pro-slavery population was in the majority, making
good progress, and in November giving a plurality
for Lincoln over Douglas of 700, although Douglas
received 3,000 more votes than Breckenridge. Bell
had a meager 6,049 votes. Lincoln received the four
votes of the state in the electoral college.[28]

J. M. Batchelder, C. C. Webb, Frank M. Pixley, William C. Talbot, Alfred
J. Ellis, James Laidley, Caleb Burbank, Thomas Fitch, Captain Frank
Folger, Dr Wm Rabe, E. R. Hawley, E. Harte, George W. Tyler, Harvey
S. Brown, William H. Weeks, Cyrus Palmer, John P. Taylor.

[26] The Bell and Everett delegates of S. F. to the Union State convention,
were D. O. Shattuck, J. E. Wainwright, Capt. Samuel Card, James Dawes
H. B. Livingston, J. H. Gardner, L. J. Wilder, Mark Brumagim, J. B.
Crockett, Wm Taffee, L. L. Treadwell, Thomas H. Selby, John S. Bray, E.
C. M. Chadwick, Wm N. Coghill, Wm Alvord, Henry B. Brooks. From
Sac'to, G. W. Bowie, A. P. Catlin, H. O. Beatty, R. H. McDonald, V. J.
Fourgoud, John H. Gass, David Meeker, B. F. Wallace, E. M. Chemault,
Benjamin Orrick, J. Beam, James Maddux, Cyrus S. Coffin, James Queen,
Alfred Morton, J. Neely Johnson, L. A. Booth, Daniel Moore, P. H. Lee,
Robert M. Folger, D. S. Hayden, J. H. Shirley, L. F. Reed, Seth R.
Kneeland, George Griggs, Edward Stockton, G. W. Whitlock, James Scott,
Jesse Morrill.

[27] Of the domestic newspapers in the state 24 were for Douglas and 22
for Breckenridge. The republicans were represented by only 7, and the
Union party by 3. The *Bulletin* explains the large number which declared
for Breckenridge by showing how many had been purchased for the campaign, by sums varying from $500 to $10,000.

[28] The republican presidential electors were Charles D. Tuttle, northern

The revolution which had occurred was directly chargeable to the pro-slavery wing of the democratic party. It was the result, so far as Breckenridge was concerned, of the killing of Broderick by Terry. It was the consequence, so far as Douglas was concerned, of the impression upon the anti-Lecompton mind in California that Douglas had been untrue to Broderick. It was the use made by the republicans of the action of the California senators in dragging the state into the quarrel between the north and south, against which the whole population, except the Lecomptonites, had always protested, and of the fact of their having grossly neglected the welfare of the state while giving aid and comfort to disunion agitators. Only one year before, the chivalry had exulted over the defeat of free principles in California; one year, and they had by their own acts put an end to all their greatness, turning a majority of nearly 21,000 to a defeat.

The legislature elected in 1860 was not so largely republican as the presidential vote might lead one to expect. The hold-over senators were eighteen in number, eleven of whom were Douglas democrats, six Breckenridge domocrats, and one republican. The senators elect were divided between Douglas democrats eight, Breckenridge democrats five, republicans four. In the assembly there were thirty-eight Douglas democrats, twenty-two Breckenridge democrats, union one, and republicans nineteen. Thus the legislative power was wrested from the chivalry by the anti-Lecompton democrats. There were two issues on which the legislature had been elected; one the

dist; W. H. Weeks, central dist; C. H. Washburn, S. F.; Antonio Maria Pico, southern dist. The electors chosen by the Union party were J. B. Crockett and G. W. Bowie, at large; Phineas L. Miner, Tehama; James Lander, Los Angeles. Alternates, A. M. Roseborough, of Siskiyou; William R. Langley, of Placer; Dr E. Gibbons, of Alameda, R. H. Daly, of Mariposa. The Douglas democrats chose Humphrey Griffith, of Yolo; Richard B. Hammond, of Stockton; Pablo de la Guerra , of Santa Bárbara; G. F. Price, of Yreka. The Breckenridge choice for electors, were V. E. Gieger, of Tehama; A. P. Dudley, of Calaveras, Zach. Montgomery, of Sutter, Antonio F. Coronel, of Los Angeles.

defeat of a proposition of the preceding legislature to
hold a convention for the revision and change of the
constitution, and the other to prevent the passage of
a bulkhead act. Although it was acknowledged that
the organic law needed revision, the people feared to
incur the danger of a convention lest the southern
counties should be separated from the state. And as
to the fifty years' monopoly of the water-front of San
Francisco, for which the bulkhead conspirators were
still plotting, that must be defeated.

The legislature[29] did not disappoint its constituents

[29] The hold-over senators were J. A. Eagan, James M. Vance, John P.
Haynes, W. B. Dickinson, R. D. Crittendan, James T. Ryan, S. H. Chase,
G. T. Leet, T. G. Phelps,* Solomon A. Sharp, R. C. Clark, John H. Watson,
Pablo de la Guerra, Andres Pico, J. Logan, Henry Egerton, J. J. Franklin,
H. P. Watkins. Senators elect, A. L. Rhodes,* Alameda and Santa Clara;
Richard Irwin, Butte and Plumas; P. A. Gallagher, Calaveras; A. St Clair,
Denver; O. Harvey, El Dorado; A. Merritt, Mariposa, Merced, Buena Vista,
and Tulare; William Watt, Nevada; Phil. W. Thomas, Placer; Caleb Bur-
bank,* James McM. Shafter,* S. F,; E. H. Heacock, Sac'to; F. M. Warm-
castle, San Joaquin and Contra Costa; H. I. Thornton, Sierra; Dr Hill,
Sonoma, Marin, and Mendocino; C. V. Williamson, Tuolumne and Stanislaus; William H. Parks, Yuba and Sutter; C. E. De Long, Yuba. The officers of the senate were Pablo de la Guerra, pres't; Richard Irwin Pres't,
pro tem; Charles W. Tozer, sec.; D. J. Williamson, ass't. sec.; George C.
Gorham, enrolling clerk; George A. Gillespie, engrossing clerk; William F.
Williamson, serg't-at,arms; C. A. Uhrig, ass't serg't-at-arms.

The assembly consisted of, Frank Fargo,* Alameda; R. Burnell, T. M.
Hornell, Amador; W. P. Tilden, P. H. Harris, Butte; B. E. Lippincott,
William Childs, Thomas O'Brien, Calaveras; Dr Durst, Colusa and Tehama;
C. B. Porter,* Contra Costa; W. L. Buell, Del Norte and Klamath; John
Conness, Theoran Foster, James J. Green, Robert Henderson, Alexander
Hunter, William Coleman, Samuel Hill, C. W. Coltrin, El Dorado; O. K.
Smith, (Union,), Fresno and Tulare; W. B. Hagans, Humboldt; Murray
Morrison, Abel Stearns, Los Angeles; N. M. Gordon, Marin; Daniel
Showalter, Gregory of Mariposa; Martin Baechtel, Mendocino; A. W.
Blair,* Monterey; J. B. Scott, Napa; E. F. Spence,* J. M. Avery,* E. W.
Councilman, J. E. Eastman, N. C. Miller, Nevada; L. G. Smith; W. J.
Harrison, P. Munday, D. W. Harriman,* Placer; A. Wood, Plumas; N.
Greene Curtis, Joseph Powell, Amos Adams, Charles Crocker,* Sac'to;
Charles W. Percy, San Bernardino; D. B. Kurtz, San Diego; S. S. Tilton,*
John W. Cherry,* Alvan Flanders,* F. G. E Tittel,* Robert Clark,* Alex-
ander Campbell,* J. A. Banks,* O. F. Willey,* L. R. Bradley, Thomas
Laspeyre, San Joaquin; C. E. Johnson, San Luis Obispo; James G. Dennis-
ton, San Mateo; J. M. Covarrubias, Santa Barbara; H. W. Briggs,* J. H.
Morgan,* Santa Clara; Charles Ford,* Santa Cruz; John White, Shasta;
J. Dougherty, Thomas Wright, Sierra; F. Sorrel, Siskiyou; D. B. Holman,
Solano; William Ross, Sonoma; Waldram of Stanislaus; Z. Montgomery,
Sutter; F. Walters, Trinity; G. W. Patrick, M. Y. Gillett, Fleming Amyx,
T. J. Chandler, Tuolumne; W. C. Wood, Yolo; Lloyd Magruder, E. Lalor,
J. H. Harrison, D. L. Hann, C. H. Kungle, Yuba.

The assembly was ten days ballotting for a speaker, and at last elected
R. Burrell. For chief clerk, J. M. Anderson; ass't clerk, J. W. Scobey;

in these important issues.   It declined to approve of the proposal for a convention by submitting it to the people, but instead offered several amendments to the constitution, which were adopted in 1862, and which made the legislative sessions biennial, the governor's term of office four years in length, and changed the judiciary system, as I have elsewhere fully explained. There was a good deal of legislating about railroads, and a number of franchises granted, with more liberality than foresight, but the general character of the acts passed was an improvement upon the work of their predecessors.

Among the resolutions passed in the early part of the session was one expunging that passed by the legislature of 1859, censuring Broderick for not supporting the administration, and requesting him to resign.   The new resolutions declared that "the people of the United States have by a very large majority endorsed the course of D. C. Broderick against the Kansas policy of the late president," and that the former resolutions were "unjust to his character while living, and derogatory to the honorable and patriotic fame which a true and faithful record of his acts will always accord to his memory ;" and further, that they were "not true in fact, and were not sanctioned by the people of California, but on the contrary, the people of this state will cherish with profound respect the memory and character of the late Broderick, adorned as his character eminently was by integrity, firmness, and patriotism."   The events of the winter of 1860–61 caused a resolution of fidelity to the union to be passed, declaring that "California is ready to maintain the rights and honor of the national government at home and abroad, and at all times to respond to any requisition that may be made upon her to defend the republic against foreign or domestic foes."   So it was

serg't-at-arms, M. Gray; ass't serg't-at-arms, J. H. Leese; engrossing clerk, E. Corbett; enrolling clerk, H. C. Kibbe.   The republicans in both houses have been marked with an asterisk, as it is not unimportant to know the pioneers of a great political movement.

that this digging, delving, half-foreign, rich young state was not after all able to keep out of the quarrel between the north and south. As the mails brought reports of the disunion speeches of pro-slavery senators, and the disloyal acts of southern people, her nerves tingled, and her blood was up. Disunion? Never! A Pacific republic? Never!

Upon this question of loyalty or disloyalty turned the choice of a senator to succeed Gwin, who was now politically dead. The Douglas democrats in caucus chose James A. McDougall,[30] a few votes being given to Edmund Randolph, Henry Edgerton, and Humphrey Griffith. The republicans chose Timothy G. Phelps. The Breckenridge democrats could not for some time obtain a caucus. In joint convention, on the first ballot, Weller received twenty-seven votes, McDougall twenty-seven, Phelps twenty-three, Nugent nine, Denver sixteen. The Breckenridge members ten days afterward fixed upon John Nugent for their nominee. Nugent was former editor of the San Francisco *Herald*, a democratic newspaper which had come out for Breckenridge in the late campaign, but after he had become disconnected with it by selling out to the Lecomptonites. When Nugent was made candidate by choice, the votes stood on the twenty-second ballot, McDougall fifty-six, Nugent forty-seven, Weller six, Phelps one, and Creanor one. The number required to elect was fifty-seven, and Phelps changed

[30] James A. McDougall was born in Albany co., N. Y., in Nov. 1819, receiving a grammar school education at Albany. While still a youth, he assisted in the survey of the first railroad in the state of New York—that between Albany and Shenectady. He then turned his attention to the law and studied with enthusiasm. In 1837 he migrated to Pike co., Ill., and in 1842 was elected attorney-general of that state, being reëlected in 1844. During this period of his life he became acquainted with Baker, Pratt, and Hoge, all afterward, like himself, prominent in California politics. In 1849 he came to Cal., overland, from the headquarters of the Rio del Norte, where he had been exploring for the precious metals with a party from Ill. He settled in S. F., and began the practice of the law, in which he soon became distinguished for wit, sarcasm, and classicism. He was elected attorney-general of Cal. in 1850, and member of congress in 1853. His talents were undoubted, though his motives have been sometimes impugned. He died in 1867 in his native state.

his vote to McDougall, who was thereby elected. The republicans used their votes to secure a loyal senator, even though he were not of their party. McDougall was the only candidate professing union sentiments who could be elected by a democratic legislature with twenty-seven Breckenridge members in it voting solidly for their nominee.

Gwin and Latham returned to Washington, where they quarreled over the action of the former in attempting the final defeat of the house bill for an overland daily mail by the central route. When Gwin found his treachery exposed he changed his tactics, and adroitly placing himself at the front, stole Latham's laurels. But California was too glad to get a daily service to care whence it came. Latham took back his assertion concerning the independence of his state in the event of disunion, and confessed that he had been mistaken in his estimate of the loyalty of the majority. When congress adjourned in the spring of 1861 he returned to California, and spoke for the cause of the union, acting with the administration party in the senate for that year; but in 1862, the last year of his term, his southern sympathies assumed ascendancy, and he denounced abolition like a born slave-holder.

McDougall came into the senate at a time when the administration was overwhelmed with the responsibility of suppressing rebellion, and he made no opposition; but gave a half-hearted support which failed to satisfy his state, and was repudiated by the legislature of 1864 in concurrent resolution.

CHAPTER XII

PERIOD OF CIVIL WAR.

1861-1865.

THE legislature of 1861 had not declared for the
support of the federal government without some
prompting. The generations of fealty to party to
which the democracy of the country had been trained
rendered it painful to the "regular" to discard his
factioned brother. It was against party usages, also,
for a democratic legislature to pledge its support to
any other than a democratic administration. But the
times were out of joint. California's representatives
in congress, and the president himself appeared to be
somewhat indifferent to the welfare of the Pacific
states, and this neglect tended to make them disloyal.
Lane of Oregon, following in the path marked out by
his superior, Gwin, abandoned the interests of his
state, whereby he brought condemnation upon his
head, even more marked than that of California toward
her senators. His course, almost more than any other
cause, turned the thoughts of the Oregonians toward
their danger and their duty, and prepared the way for
the incoming of the republican party to power in that
state. Baker, only a short time in California, had
given them the benefit of his rhetoric, and been

elected to represent them in the United States senate, in place of Lane. When he returned to San Francisco, on his way to Washington, he aided in arousing union sentiment in California. In a speech at the American theater, in October, 1860, he talked of liberty—though why he should now have inflicted this discourse on his audience I know not, unless it be that the tongue of the American stump-speaker cannot withhold itself from such indulgence. "As for me, I dare not, I will not be false to freedom. Where the feet of my youth were planted, there, by freedom, my feet shall stand. I will walk beneath her banner. I will glory in her strength. I have watched her, in history, struck down on an hundred chosen fields of battle. I have seen her friends fly from her; her foes gather round her. I have seen her bound to the stake; I have seen them give her ashes to the winds. But when they turned to exult I have seen her again meet them face to face, resplendent in complete steel, brandishing in her right hand a flaming sword, red with insufferable light. I take courage. The people gather round her. The genius of America will at last lead her sons to freedom."

In December South Carolina seceded, and Fort Moultrie was evacuated by the federal forces for the stronger position of Sumter. In January the newspaper press of California was still undecided what course ought to be pursued. Union meetings were hinted at by the loyal journals, but many influential business men thought that nothing California could do would have any effect upon the result of the national controversy, and counselled neutrality as the most safe and comfortable course. To this the press replied that, isolated though she was, California had a duty toward the loyal states to perform, by proclaiming her fidelity to the bond of federal union, and influencing the votes of her delegation in congress. If the cotton states were allowed to believe that their withdrawal from the union would be followed by the

organization of a Pacific republic, they would thereby
be greatly encouraged in their course.   "The repudia-
tion of the Pacific republic notion by California," said
the *Bulletin,* "and her declaration against secession in
any form, may therefore prove an important step toward restoring harmony to the country." If the union
were to be dissolved, what was to become of the Pacific railroad? No portion of the country had so
much to gain by the preservation of the union as California, and both people and legislature should take
immediate action ; such was the conclusion arrived at.

But the California representatives had already declared their convictions, each in his chosen manner,
Gwin and Latham in the senate, Scott[1] and Burch in
the house of representatives.   An attempt to pass
resolutions of loyalty and support to the federal government by the California legislature called out the
forensic talent of that body,[2] while it betrayed the
lurking fear of being beforehand with its duty.   To
keep the union sentiment up to a safe and proper point
a mass meeting was arranged to take place on the 22d
of February.   This meeting, intended for a test, was
attended by fully fourteen thousand people.   The day
was fine; flags fluttered from house-tops and windows;

[1] Scott wrote a letter to the chairman of the state central democratic committee, Charles V. Lindley, in which he said, 'If this union is divided, and
two separate confederacies are formed, I will strenuously advocate the secession of California, and the establishment of a separate republic on the Pacific slope...If California links her destiny with the northern government,
crippled and ruined as she must necessarily be by the separation and withdrawal of her southern allies, California, instead of being benefited, and receiving aid from the northern confederacy, will be heavily taxed to carry on
the machinery of their government.' *Address of Charles L. Scott of California
to his constituents on the constitutional right of secession,* in *Hayes' Cal. Pol.,* 1861–
2, vol. iii., p. 54.   Burch, his colleague, declared in favor of union; but
should the union be dissolved, he favored a Pacific republic.   Gwin, the
power behind the throne, remained discreetly silent, while Latham boldly
corrected his blunder of the previous session.

[2] I allude to speeches in the senate from Edgerton of Napa, in favor of
coercion; Thornton of Sierra, against coercion; Crittenden of El Dorado, in
favor of reconstruction, or secession; to speeches in the assembly by Durst
of Colusa, on the preservation of the govt; Kungle of Yuba, in defence of
slavery; Morrison of Los Angeles, in favor of letting the rebellious states
take their own course, because they were 'brothers' to the loyal states, and
should have kind treatment; and Conness of El Dorado, on the duty of sustaining the govt.

bands discoursed brilliant music; the streets were
thronged with glad-visaged men and women, and enthusiasm for the support of the government everywhere displayed itself. Speeches were delivered by
Edward Stanley, Delos Lake, J. B. Crockett, Thomas
Starr King, and James Shields. Union clubs which
were forming in the city and country increased from
this time on. But it required the overt act to fix the
determination of union men to support, at all hazards,
the execution of the federal laws, and the power of
the federal government. That motive was furnished
when in April Fort Sumter surrendered, and blood
was spilled. The news was received in San Francisco
April 24th. A call was made for the republican clubs
of the campaign of 1860 to meet for the purpose of
organizing as Administration Union clubs on the 27th.
The response surprised those who made the call, so
great was the attendance.[3]

An address was presented to the People's nominating committee on the 26th, signed by more than
one thousand business men of San Francisco, requesting them to assemble and make their nominations for
city and county officers. The republicans followed
with monster petitions to the republican county committee to make nominations. Both parties professed
the utmost devotion to the union ; but the republicans
plainly meant to demand recognition as the administration party, and to strive for the city and county,
as well as the state offices, against the people's party
to which they resigned their rights in 1860.[4]

[3] Four companies were formed out of the clubs in the 12 districts. Each
company was officered by a marshal, two aids, a sec'y and treas'r. An
executive committee of 12, one from each district, was appointed by the
pres't of the meeting, William Sherman, which should have a general supervision, and appoint such general officers as should be deemed expedient.
These clubs constituted a thoroughly organized military police during the
years of the civil war, no more relaxing their vigilance than did the famous
committee of 1856.

[4] The republicans nominated the following ticket: for mayor, Caleb T.
Fay; for treas'r, Asa L. Lawton; for recorder, Charles W. Rand; for asses-
sor, Thomas D. Matthewson; for sheriff, James Laidley; for surveyor, Milo
Hoadley; for harbor master, N. Proctor Smith; for supt of pub. schools,

On the 11th of May business was suspended in San Francisco that a loyal demonstration might be made. The city was swathed in national colors, and one lone palmetto flag, raised by a daring Breckenridge man named Nash, was lowered by the people in an emphatic manner.[5] Several prominent citizens of dubious tendencies took their stand openly for the federal government against secession. Senators Latham and McDougal, generals Shields and Sumner, and others made speeches in favor of coercion. At this date John G. Downey,[6] as lieutenant-governor, had succeeded to the executive office vacated by Latham.

The rapid growth of union sentiment throughout the state decided the legislature to pledge the support of the government, which it did on the 17th.[7] The

John H. Brewer. In *Fay's Historical Facts*, MS., which is an autobiography chiefly, it is mentioned that in the elections of 1860 he received but 1500 votes, but that in 1861 he came within 500 of an election. Fay was born in Southboro, Mass., and came to Cal. by sea in 1849, as one of a company of 22, calling itself the Northwestern Association of Boston, owning the vessel in which they sailed. He went into business in the mines, and afterward in S. F.

[5] *S. F. Bulletin,*, May 11, 1861. A Pacific republic flag was hoisted on board a surveying schooner at Stockton Jan. 16th, creating much feeling. In S. F. the palmetto flag was raised in Feb., and hauled down again. In May the Bear flag was raised at Los Angeles. This flag was raised at Sonoma and at San Bernardino. It was simply a secession demonstration, and was not allowed to float any length of time. *S. F. Alta*, June 22 and July 9, 1861; *Sac. Union*, June 24, 1864.

[6] A native of county Roscommon, Ireland, and of distinguished ancestry, Gov. Downey came to California in 1849 with $10 in his pocket, and after a varied experience opened at Los Angeles in 1850 what was then the only drug-store between San Francisco and San Diego. Here he accumulated $30,000 within three years, and then engaged in stock-raising and real estate operations, whereby he accumulated a handsome fortune, purchasing about 75,000 acres near the present site of Downey, Wilmington, San Pedro, and elsewhere. Among his possessions is the Santa Gertrudes rancho, noted for its beauty and mineral springs. His administration as governor was universally commended, and as a private citizen, and one to whose enterprise and liberality is largely due the prosperity of southern California, he is no less widely esteemed.

[7] On the authority of Gen. Wool, Floyd, the secretary of war, placed, for safe-keeping, in southern arsenals 135,430 government arms from the Springfield, Mass., U. S. armory alone, with ordnance and military stores. This was independent of the quota of these states. To Cal. 7,000 were sent to which the state had no claim. The whole number of arms surreptitiously sent to Cal. was 50,000, of which 30,000 was returned in 1861. About the 1st of Feb. 1861, Crittenden, assemblyman from El Dorado, said in effect that 30,000 men in Cal. would take up arms in defence of secession, if the government attempted to enforce the federal laws in this state. Rumors

militia law had already been thoroughly revised, the
state militia being organized in six divisions and twelve
brigades, with a full staff of officers for each, and for

were afloat that the presidio and the forts on Alcatraz island would be captured, with the custom-house, mint, post-office, and all U. S. property, after
which the rebels would proceed to invade Sonora, to add that territory to
the Pacific republic. Officers were named. The Mexican vote was counted
upon, and it was hoped to catch the Irish. The catholic vote was counted
upon, because both these men were of that faith, and so the French. It
appears from revelations made at a later period that Floyd sent in all
75,000 muskets to Cal. without the knowledge of congress. About the time
a man named Street was postmaster at Shasta. His successor discovered
among a lot of waste papers a number of letters from a brother of this man,
Charles R. Street, editor of the *Marysville Express*, the same one who afterwards conducted disloyal newspapers in Idaho and other territories. These
letters came into the possession of Judge Goodwin of Yuba. They revealed
much of the plan, with some of the names of the conspirators, but only a
portion of them were published, in the Stockton *Independent* of Aug. 31,
1863. One of these letters dated Dec. 27, 1860 at S. F. declares that the
writer Charles R. Street, had a talk with several men here about what California would do in the event of a separation between the northern and southern states. "Mr Guthrie of the *Herald* declines to publish the letter of Mr
Burch for the present—wants to wait for further news from the east, at
least until the arrival of one pony. The fact is he is afraid of the issue,
and perhaps not without reason....I saw Gen. Shields this morning and
had quite a talk with him about the matter....and I will predict here that
if any great effort is made to separate from the east, he will be the leader of
the movement....He intimates that it had been proposed to him to take the
initiative in this thing, but that he had replied as Benton had replied on
a certain occasion. 'No, I will not do it; it is useless to shoot at the moon.'
Yet I could not help perceiving that he thought circumstances might arise
before the trouble works itself out, that would turn the current of opinion
in favor of a separate republic. In this correspondence Street said that
congressman Burck declared all the representatives of Oregon, Washington,
and Arizona in favor of the movement, and that Latham approved it.
Latham afterward retracted. So did I. I. Stevens of W. T., but Lane
blindly ruined himself by it. Downey is mentioned as uncertain. Dosh, of
the Shasta *Courier* was named as favorable. 'I will keep you posted,' said
Street to his brother, 'as far as I am able, of events and purposes here, and
advise you to caution and secrecy.' 'We have not the least doubt,' said the
editor of the Stockton *Independent*, 'that Gwin was at the head of this conspiracy; not the least doubt that Johnston was sent to the command of this
department at the request of the conspirators, and for the express purpose
of doing their executive work.' Whatever intention the conspirators may
have entertained, there is still an honorable doubt of Johnston's complicity.
Probably they hoped to use him for their purposes; but the arrival of Sumner at too early a moment prevented the consummation of any project to
secure the public property in and about S. F. The conspirators had confided
in Doane, the sheriff of S. F., whom they believed to be a secessionist, but
who was a union man, and who consulted with the chief of the fire department, who entered into his plans, several of the fire companies being also
military companies that would number 1,000 men, who could be called together at a given signal of the fire-bell, armed and equipped. This matter
being arranged there was held an interview with Gen. Johnston, who denied
all knowledge of the plot. The *S. F Bulletin* of Feb. 2, 1861, contains an
editorial, headed Needless Alarms, declaring 'there are 100,000 men in California who would have to be put to the sword before any secession tricks or

regiments and battalions, with provision for their equipment and regulations for drilling and calling them into service.

News was received every ten days by pony. That coming by the Butterfield route was double the time; what came by steamship was from three to four weeks old when it arrived. In the spring of 1861 the Apaches on the southern route attacked and delayed the mails. It was the pony to which every one looked for intelligence; men prayed for the safety of the little beast, and trembled lest the service should be discontinued. Telegraphic dispatches from New York were sent to St. Louis, and thence to Fort Kearney, whence the pony brought them to Sacramento, where they were telegraphed to San Francisco. Great was the relief of the people when Hale's bill for a daily mail was passed, and the service changed from the southern to the central route, as it was early, in the summer. News by the daily mail was eighteen days old at the shortest, but it was regular and consecutive at short intervals, which was far more satisfactory than the former arrangement. After all it was to the flying pony that all eyes and hearts were turned; and to the praise of the St Joseph company be it recorded that they kept up the service, at a loss, until the the telegraph was completed across the continent in October, 1861. Their first object was to exemplify the practicability of a mail, or railroad line, on or about the 41st parallel. After that was demonstrated, they had no further interest in the pony express, except through patriotism.

The Pacific republic idea which had always haunted the southern brain had assumed some definiteness, or was at least more openly broached, when the southern states seceded. The California senators had proclaimed

Pacific republic forces could be successfully practiced on this coast.' Notwithstanding its tone of affected security, when Sumner unexpectedly arrived in April, the same paper declared that it breathed more freely, and that the general's arrival would be 'a cordial to all union men.'

it in Washington in 1860 to intimidate the north, and it continued to be talked of in a threatening manner during the winter of 1860–1. The inside workings of the conspiracy were not divulged. There was a secret movement, with a history, carried on by an order called Knights of the Golden Circle. And there were other organizations. Even at the time enough was known at Washington to cause the president to dispatch, with every effort at secrecy, General Edwin A. Sumner to the Pacific coast to relived General Albert S. Johnston of the command of the military department. But with all the caution observed in this transaction, Johnston received information by pony express in time to resign before Sumner arrived. Not an hour was lost when the general landed before taking command, but Johnston was evidently not surprised. He yielded gracefully, no doubt gladly, and was soon on his way overland, via Texas, with other officers and volunteers for the southern confederacy.[8] He was a Kentuckian, and was imbued with that devotion to state, instead of general government, which was the political religion of the south. He gave his sword to the "lost cause," and laid down his life at Shiloh as a proof of his loyalty to an idea.

The officers in command at San Francisco when Sumner arrived were Captain Stewart, a Kentuckian, at Alcatraz Island; Colonel Merchant, a New Yorker, at the presidio; and Major Austin of Connecticut at Fort Point. Probably they were soon ordered east among other regular officers. Early in May, the president having called for seventy-five thousand troops, volunteering was begun in California, and drilling of the militia by officers assigned by Sumner,

[8] Johnson was joined by a company of officers who had also resigned, namely, lieuts R. H. Brewer, 1st drag.; F. Mallory, 3d inf.; E. B. Dudley Riley, and A. Shoaf, 4th inf.; and M. Wickliffe, 9th inf. U. S. A. They were escorted by 18 secessionists, Alonzo Ridley, of Los Angeles, was captain of the company and escort, and remained with Johnson until his death. Afterward he went to Texas, and killed Commander Wainwright, with his rifle, at the taking of the *Harriet Lane*. He subsequently served in the Texan cavalry.

Lieutenant John Hamilton, 3d artillery, being made military instructor of the second division of the state troops, and now the military spirit ran high.

Meantime each latest arrival of intelligence from the east added fresh fuel to the flame of loyalty now brightly blazing on the Pacific coast. Pacific republic schemes had small opportunity to develop, and plots were invariably found out and frustrated. Even Edmund Randolph, though a Virginian, until his state seceded and he became half demented,[9] was loyal, and was said to have given the president warning of the conspiracy to take California out of the union. Perhaps there was something hysterical on both sides. At all events, a great moral crisis had arrived, of which all men were strongly conscious.

It was not in California only that Californians were under excitement.[10] Much fear was entertained on

[9] Randolph, who unexpectedly appeared in the Breckenridge convention, in July, was tempted to make a speech, though suffering from illness. He said, in a frantic manner: 'To me it seems a waste of time to talk. For God's sake, gentlemen, tell me of battles fought and won. Tell me of usurpers overthrown; that Missouri is a free state, no longer crushed under the armed heel of a reckless, odious despot. Tell me that the state of Maryland lives again; and, oh! gentlemen, let us read, let us hear, at the first moment, that not one hostile foot now treads the soil of Virginia. If this be rebellion, then I am a rebel. Do you want a traitor? then I am a traitor. For God's sake, speed the ball, may the lead go quick to his heart, and may our country be free from the despot usurper that now claims the name of president of the United States.' This outburst of Randolph's reveals the early inception of the conspiracy against the president's life.

[10] Immediately after the president's call, April 21st, the following notice was placarded in the streets of New York: 'Californians—to arms! California steamers in danger! Rally Californians, the federal capital is in danger. Californians, Oregonians, coast men, and men who have seen service, attention! A meeting will be held at Metropolitan hotel at one o'clock to-day, Sunday, in order to form a California regiment. None but men accustomed to work are requested to attend. Over $25,000 on hand to equip the regiment, and sustain it.' There were present upon this hasty summons about 200 Pacific coast men. J. C. Birdseye was chairman; William T. Coleman, C. K. Garrison, J. Y. Halleck, D. L. Ross, Folger, Leonard, Eugene Kelly, J. P. F. Wentworth, S. W. Bryant, Minor Frink, W. S. Denio, E, D. Baker, Charles Watrous, D. W. Cheeseman, Samuel Gamage, Kinzer, Martin, Ira P. Rankin, S. H. Parker, James Satterlee, all residents of Cal., on a visit to the east. W. B. Farwell, J. J. Arrington. and Ross Irish, of Maryland, were secretaries. Baker addressed the meeting, followed by Gilpin and Parker, who had been appointed postmaster at S. F. The organization of a regiment was begun on that day. Baker was elected col; Brainard, lieut-col; Lemon, major—killed at South mountain—Ross A Fish, capt.—imprisoned twelve months by the rebels. The reg't was armed and

both sides of the continent that rebel cruisers would capture some of the mail steamers laden with treasure. Insurance rose to three per cent—before the close of the war going up to seven per cent—and despatches were received in April to stop the shipment of gold, as insurance was suspended. With the completion of the telegraph line much of the inconvenience attending the transaction of business was overcome.

In October, Sumner, much to the regret of loyal men, was called east[11]; but colonel George Wright was

equipped in six weeks, and in camp near Fort Ellsworth on Staten island; the camp being named after California's new senator, McDongall. This reg't drew on the union defence committee for only $1,505. Baker was tendered a brigade and resigned. R. Matheson being elected col—killed at South mountain—Baker. afterward accepted the command of the 71st Pa reg't, and through his known connection with the Cal. reg't this Pa organization was mistakenly called the First Cal. reg't. *Sac. Union*, May 10, 1861; *S. F. Call*, Feb. 11, 1864; *S. F. Bulletin*, June 19, 1861.

[11] Either by accident or design, Gen. Sumner and staff sailed on the same vessel with Senator Gwin and Calhoun Benham. Gwin had returned to Cal. in June, and remained until Oct., but found no opportunity to carry out any of the confederate designs against the public property, and was now departing on the *Orizaba* to prosecute them elsewhere. Just before reaching Panamá, on learning that some of his officers had been approached, Sumner arrested Gwin, Benham, and J. L. Brent on a charge of treason, compelling them to accompany him to New York and Washington. On the evidence it appeared that Gwin expected to meet Slidell and Mason, the confederate com'rs to Europe, at Habana, and proceed with them abroad. Had not his plans been frustrated, he must have been arrested in their company and confined in Fort Warren. As it was, they had a brief residence in Fort Lafayette, and were released. Benham and Brent joined the confederate army at the first opportunity, and Gwin spent some time in Miss. before going to France to labor for the recognition of the confederacy. Sumner did not seem to realize that he had it in his power to discover all the plans of the conspirators on the *Orizaba*. He simply sent for them to come to the captain's office, when he placed them under arrest, but not in confinement. They retired to their rooms, and threw overboard a quantity of maps and papers, a fact unknown for half an hour afterward. At this point Gwin disappears from the political history of Cal., whose senator he had been for 10 years. Like Lane of Oregon, to whom his example was fatal, he betrayed his state and his country. It remains now only to briefly relate his subsequent career as he has himself recorded it in his *Memoirs*, MS. in my library, He was the son of a methodist preacher, and was born in Tenn. in 1805, was educated at Transylvania university, Ky, and for several years practised medicine in Tenn. and Miss. He was appointed marshal of Miss. about 1833, and relinquished his profession. In 1841 he was elected to congress. In 1847 he was appointed to superintend the erection of the U. S. custom house at N. O. His love for political life led him to come to Cal., and take a leading part in the affairs of the Pacific coast. That he was already imbued with the sentiments of disunionists, his record sufficiently proves. He possessed in a peculiar degree that smooth self-assertion and readiness at extricating himself from embarrassing positions without blame which is known as diplomatic talent. That it did not save him from severe humilia-

placed in command, whose conscientious discharge of duty in his whole department was of the greatest value to the government and the state. Nothing escaped his observation, and at every turn the disaffected were met with stern reproof.

To keep public sentiment up to the point of ardent patriotism during the reverses of the first eighteen months of the war was the care of loyal men of influence, of the pulpit, the press, the military, and of all good men—for it was not admitted that a good man could be a sympathizer with rebellion. The patience

tions, or from displaying a revolting degree of sycophancy in his dealings with a foreign aristocracy, his own narrative is evidence. Before proceeding to the closing chapter of his public career, I cannot refrain from giving his statement concerning his influence in the conduct of national affairs. Seward, he says, was made sec. of state through his, Gwin's, representations to Lincoln that it would be agreeable to the south; and that he had immediately written to Jefferson Davis that Seward was to be secretary, and there would be peace. But the south was opposed to Chase as sec. of the treasury, and when his appointment was officially announced, he was forced to telegraph the news to Davis to expect war, or bear the opprobrium of having misled the south. The despatch was shown to Seward, who altered it to read that Chase's selection would be favorable to peace. It was taken to the telegraph office by a mutual friend, who, he believes, copied it, and used it to obtain a perilous influence over Seward, who, he says, continued to use him, Gwin, as an intermediary between himself and the southern commissioners. But when they demanded something more than polite verbal messages, Seward fell ill of lumbago, and could see no one. Gwin accepted his dismissal, and left Washington, having discovered that two could engage in the game of dissimulation when necessary. *Memoirs*, MS., 186–200. After his arrest, as related above, he went to Paris, where his family resided for several years, while he labored for the recognition of the confederate states, the emperor being in favor of it, but the French people against it. Had Slidell and Mason consented to address a note to the emperor's minister of foreign affairs, stating that in the event of achieving indepenence the confederacy would pass laws looking to the emancipation of slaves in 10, 20, or any number of years, the confederacy would have been recognized. Instead of entertaining this proposition, Slidell was so violent in his language as to affront the Marquis de Montholon, who offered it. *Gwin, Mem.*, MS., 202–3.

Success no longer attended his best laid schemes, and the latter part of his life was spent in retirement in Cal. The subject of his disloyalty is carefully avoided in his memoirs. That he dreamed at one time of establishing an aristocratic government, in which he was to figure prominently, there can be no doubt. He died in New York in the autumn of 1885, and was buried at San Francisco. Of his private life little has been said, and that little not interesting. In public affairs he was avaricious, heartless, and devoted to his own aggrandizement, *N. Y. Tribune*, of Oct. 1885; *Marysville Herald*, Sept. 26, 1854; *Crosby's Statement*, MS., 66–7; *N. O. Republican*, March 18, 1871; *Torres Perip.*, 76; *S. F. Alta*, July 3, 1851, and Nov. 12, 1863; *U. S. Foreign Affairs*, Mess. and Doc. p 111, p. 417, 519–21; *39 cong*; 1 sess; *Soule, Hun.* S. F., 790–3; *Contemp. Biog.*, i. 234; *S. F. Bulletin*, Dec. 20, 23, 1856, and Jan 4, 1857; *Gwin, Congress. Record*, 16 pp; *Sonora Periodicio Official*, Nov. 3, 1865, p 3; *Diario del Imperio*; *Pinart Coll.*, MS. passim.

of the people was sorely tried when a presbyterian
minister changed his form of prayer, calling God's
blessing on the presidents of these American states,
instead of the president of the United States. Ministers generally were haranguing heaven for curses on
the confederacy, notwithstanding their master had
told them to bless their enemies. But, in truth, it
made little difference. Trying as it was, however, to
know that Jefferson Davis was prayed for in a San
Francisco pulpit by a fashionable preacher, no public
demonstration occurred until the reverend doctor
voted 'no' to some loyal resolutions offered in a meeting of the presbytery by another preacher.[12] The proceedings appeared in the newspapers, and the following
Sunday morning a United States flag floated from
the top of Calvary church, where it had never before
been seen, and from each lamp-post in front of the
edifice other flags were flying, while from the window
of a building opposite dangled an effigy placarded "Dr.
Scott, the reverend traitor." A large crowd collected
about the church, and filled it to overflowing during
the service. All ears were strained to catch the wording of the morning prayer, which on this occasion
contained no reference to presidents in the plural. The
minister after service reached his carriage in safety,
though not without jostling from the dense crowd.
Though there had been no actual violence, the scene
was too suggestive to bear repetition, and resigning
his ministry, Doctor Scott with his family soon after
took steamer for Europe. His friends spoke of him
as a martyr, while they filled his pockets with gold
for the journey. This was one phase of the subject.
A different view was that presented by another

---

[12] Archbishop Alemany, of the Roman church, published a pastoral letter
against divorces and duels, which he condemned—and ended by calling attention to the national divorce and duel, which of course came under the
same condemnation. *S. F. Bulletin*, Feb. 25, 1861. Of the career of this
well-known and much respected prelate, whose decease occurred in 1889, it
is unnecessary to make further mention in these pages, except for his connection with the church, which will be noticed in a later chapter.

preacher, Thomas Starr King, whose lectures became largely attended. Small of stature, delicate in health, with a soft and luminous brown eye, betokening his gentleness of disposition, he was yet, when aroused, able to sway multitudes. All through the most doubtful and trying period of the civil war his voice encouraged and animated the people, whom his eloquence fascinated. He was invited as far as Oregon to deliver one of his famous lectures. He lived long enough to see victory perched upon the union banner, but not to see the end, dying in the spring of 1864, of diphtheria. From the roof of his church the national flag was kept flying during the four years' struggle. Indeed, to hang his banner on the outward wall became the ambition of many householders.

In October the propriety of maintaining a coast guard and training artillerymen was discussed in the public prints. It was urged, with truth, that the harbor of San Francisco was poorly defended, and that against a single privateer no effectual resistance could be made with the guns of Alcatraz and Fort Point, the danger from which to a ship in passing would be momentary, whereas the peril of the town would be imminent, and might be fatal. Temporary fortifications and water-batteries were suggested by the state adjutant-general, and the legislature was recommended to avail itself of the aid of Colonel de Russy, a competent engineer at that time on the coast. Nothing, however, was undertaken, although alarms frequently existed, and more than one danger was averted by discovery.[13] The government occasionally

[13] Several efforts had been made by certain parties to purchase fast-sailing vessels upon a pretence of wishing to convey munitious of war to the assistance of Mexico against the French, and to enjoy a trade in such articles. So plausible were these representations that loyal merchants, notwithstanding federal and state laws intended to prohibit the exportation of military supplies, were prevailed upon to sell privately a cargo of mixed goods, arms, powder, etc., to one Ridgely Greathouse and his agents, to be placed on board the fast-sailing clipper schooner, the *J. W. Chapman*, which arrived out from New York in Feb. 1863, and was sold to Greathouse. The movements of her purchasers had not escaped the observation of the naval authorities in the harbor, and at the moment when she was ready to quit the

sent an armed vessel into the Pacific, and finally fitted
out two cruisers for the protection of the coast, beside dispatching to San Francisco an iron monitor in
sections, to be put together by a local firm whose long
dalliance with the contract caused them to be accused
of treachery, the *Aquilla*, which had the plates, being
sunk at her wharf without apparent cause. So long
was the completion of the *Monitor* postponed that
she was never of any service to the state or to the
Pacific coast.

port she was boarded by boats from the man-of-war *Cyane* lying in the
harbor, and her officers and crew placed under arrest. The *Chapman* was
found to have on board, besides her cargo of miscellaneous goods, shipped by
merchants to Manzanillo, cannon, arms and ammunition, and a party of
armed men concealed in the hold. Search revealed a supply of uniforms
provided for the intended pirates, the oath of secrecy to be taken before going into an engagement, and other papers of importance showing the nature
of the undertaking. Upon a separate examination of the prisoners, it was
ascertained that the purpose of the conspirators was to throw overboard the
cargo on getting to sea, and take on board further supplies at a rendezvous
on the southern coast, to which they had been sent to avoid suspicion. After
that the vessel was to lie in wait for the steamship *Oregon*, capture her,
transfer the armament of the *Chapman* to the steamer, and use the latter to
capture two or more of the treasure-laden steamers from S. F., after which
the pirates would repair to Victoria, V. I., to divide the spoils. In connection with this piratical scheme was a plan to form secret associations of men
favorable to the confederacy in every community, who were to be secretly
armed, and when their numbers were deemed sufficient to meet at Sac., cut
the telegraph wires, seize a steamboat, run down to Benicia, secure the
arsenal, take by surprise Fort Point and Alcatraz, which three objects being
accomplished, they would declare Cal. out of the union, and one of the confederate states. The conspirators besides Greathouse were Alfred Rubery,
an Englishman; W. W. Mason, of Alabama, nephew of the confederate
comm'r to England, and a disorderly fellow; Asbury Harpending, a violent
secessionist, and author of the enterprise; Albron T. Crow, late of the confederate army; John E. Kent, a sympathizer, from Ill.; Wm C. Low, of
New York, commander, who offered to turn state's evidence; Lorezo L.
Libby, 1st officer; Thomas Reole, Joseph W. Smith, alias Snyder, of Ky;
Alfred Armond, Ottawa, C. W.; Henry C. Boyd, of Del.; R. H. Duval, of
Florida; William D. Moore, J. W. McFadden, William W. Maron, D. W.
Brown, John Fletcher, James Smith, George W. Davis, M. H. Marshall, five
sailors, and cabin boys. The principals, who proved to be Greathouse,
Harpending, and Rubery, were convicted on trial, sentenced to ten years im-
prisonment, and to pay a fine of $10,000, each, and confined in Fort Lafa-
yette. The president pardoned the Englishman, at the solicitation of John
Bright, and Greathouse was 'released by Judge Hoffman's strict construction of the amnesty proclamation.' Some authorities say that he escaped
and went to Europe. A plot to take Mare island and the Navy-yard was
discovered only a little later than the *Chapman* affair. The steamboat
Guadalupe, in Napa creek was to be taken by a force of 200 men who were
to cross over to Vallejo, take the works and gov't shipping by surprise, and
with the vessels and arms obtained, the plotters were to make an assault on
S. F. The discovery of the conspiracy was its defeat; but it was of sufficient
importance to detain the U. S. steamer *Saginaw* from leaving the harbor.

That portion of the population which gave the most trouble was in the southern counties, requiring volunteer companies to be stationed at some points, which perhaps did not pour oil on the troubled waters. The Tulare *Post* was the organ of the fire-eaters, whose diatribes stirred up the ire of the "blood-hounds of Zion" as the union men were denominated. The quarrel was carried into local politics, the anti-coercionists electing their candidate to the legislature, as well as filling the county offices. The *Post* became the *Equal Rights Expositor*, more fire-devouring, if possible, than its predecessor. Finally its publishers were arrested by the commanding officer at Camp Babbitt, and imprisoned at that post. One of them took the oath of loyalty, the other refused, and was discharged by order of General Wright. Both returned to the publication of the disloyal journal, which was destroyed by the troops after two of the volunteers had been killed in some of the quarrels, which were of daily occurrence. This state of affairs lasted throughout the war. There was never a moment when the advocates of secession and anti-coercion did not assert their freedom from any allegiance to the government.[14] Soon after the rebellion closed, and the union was restored, it took several years for this class to learn that they could not still control public affairs in these counties.

Congress required passports to be taken by immigrants from the east to California, to prevent insurgents from embarking for England and France via Aspinwall. But immigration from California overland into the rebel states was comparatively secure, and in the early months of the war was frequent. This way went Terry, Daniel Showalter, and other noted secessionists. To check seditious adventures General Wright made Fort Yuma a strong post and military prison, threatening disloyalty with condign punishment. In this solitary citadel Showalter and a number of his associates were confined in the winter of 1861–2 for several months, but finally liberated, representation being made to General Wright by Showalter that the incriminating letters and papers upon which the arrests had been made were known to him alone, and that there was no organization, as had been believed, of recruits for the southern confederacy, but merely an accidental meeting of persons travelling in the same direction. Showalter, at least, made use of his liberty to join the confederate army. Passports were afterward required to be granted by the commander of the department before travellers could pass the frontier of California in the direction of Texas. The conduct of certain army officers in Arizona, and a rumor that secessionists under Van Dorn were marching upon California led Sumner in the early part of September 1861 to publish a general order: "No federal troops in this department of the Pacific will ever surrender to rebels;" which laconic hint was not disregarded by plotters in and out of the state.

With military encampments on every hand for the training of the state and volunteer troops, California developed a readiness in the pursuit of war which could not have been expected of a community seemingly devoted to mining, commerce, and agriculture. That portion of the people heretofore engaged in managing the politics of the state found their occupation gone and their power passed away. They were unable to elect more than a small minority to the legislature, and the state and federal offices had slipped from their grasp. The death of Douglas, in June 1861, left the Douglas democracy without a leader. The Breckenridge party, which still held together, and which dared not bring out a decided secession platform, adopted the principle that California could not be neutral in the pending conflict, but must either remain in the union or go out of it, and the party intended it should remain in; the duty of California, moreover, was to contend in congress for peace. If

peace could not be had with union, then the southern
states should be allowed to depart .without an effort
being made to subjugate them. Before announcing
these principles the Breckenridge men had offered to
fuse with the regular democratic party, which, however, rejected them.

The republican party, having achieved a great victory in 1860, was reluctant to relinquish any of its
honors, and so declined the overtures of the union
men irrespective of party in the democratic ranks,
and in 1861 enjoyed the satisfaction of a victory in
the election of a republican state ticket. Leland Stan--
ford, one of the founders of the republican party in
California, was elected governor. It was alleged that
he would have been elected without the help of
political opponents who voted for him to make sure of
a union governor.[15] The republicans carried the election by a great majority, but they said little about
their gains, knowing that it was a desire to save the
union, and prevent revolution in California, which
had so swelled their ranks.[16] In 1862 they acknowledged the propriety of this action by dropping the
name of republicans, and coming out as a union party
to which all loyal men might belong.

The congressmen elected by the republicans in
1861, were Aaron A. Sargent, Timothy G. Phelps,
and Frederick F. Low.[17] Sargent was from Massa-

[14] *McDaniel's Early Days*, MS., 44–5; *Staples' Statement*, MS., 14; *U. S.
Sen. Doc.*, 4, vol. iv, 37 cong. 2 sess.; *S. F. Alta*, Feb. 5, 1862; *Doc.*, 22;
Misc. Hist. P.

[15] The Breckenridge men called themselves the regular democrats, and
nominated John R. McConnell of Nevada. The union democrats nominated
John Conness; the settlers, a local Sac. ticket, nominated Conness also.
The republicans, Stanford, and for lieut.-gov., J. F. Chelles of Trinity,
Stanford received nearly 53,000 votes or almost double that of either of the
other candidates. Wm H. Weeks of Sac. was elected sec. of state; Gilbert
R. Warren, of Stockton, comptroller; D. R. Ashley, of Monterey, treasurer;
Frank M. Pixley, of S. F., attorney-general; J. F. Houghton, Sac., surv.-
gen.; John Swett, supt. pub. inst.; W. C. Kibbe, ajdt.-gen; Benjamin P.
Avery, of Marysville, state printer. Edward Norton was elected supreme
judge in place of Baldwin, term expired.

[16] *Dwinelle, Notices of Cal.*, ix.; *Hayes' Scraps, Angeles*, vi.; *S. F. Alta*,
July 1, 1862.

[17] The U. S. act allowing Cal. three congressmen had not been passed,

chusetts, had been a printer, and was one of the
"argonauts," as well as one of the founders of republicanism in California. He labored for the construction of a Pacific railroad, and with marked success,
as will appear in the later chapters of this volume.
Starr King was asked to enter the race with Sargent,
Conness, Hoge, Shurtleff, and others, but declined;
his ways were not as their ways.

It was the hope of good men that with the retirement of the party which had so long ruled California,
certain political practices, such as lobbying, bribery,
extravagance and dishonesty in office, with similar
evils, would be abandoned, and that the new party in
power would set an example of reform. I cannot say
that all of them did so conduct themselves. Like other
victors, they claimed the spoils. The public journals
still complained of venality in the legislature. "And
why not?" said the new men. "The democrats have
enjoyed these privileges and perquisites for many
years, why should not we?" Millions for spoils, and
not one cent for reform. But their legislation after
all was not really bad, and they were intensely loyal!
And how could it be possible, when heaven itself is
set before us as a reward, and not as a sequence, of
our actions, that a man who serves his country should
not want office? or that the new president should not
be overwhelmed with applications for places under the
government? Baker, who had only gone to Oregon
to be made a senator of the United States, to be
nearer his former intimate friend, Abraham Lincoln,
and who felt himself at heart a Californian, could not
help suggesting to the president his choice of men to
fill important places. The intrusion upon their pre-
rogative was quickly resented by the Californian delegation, and Lincoln, with his usual good sense, put an
end to the quarrel by giving the Californians their

but was passed at the 29th sess. 37 cong., see p. 102 acts of that session.
For Low's arguments on his right to a seat see *U. S. H. Misc. Doc.*, 4 and 19,
37 cong. 2 sess.

choice.[18] Soon afterward, Baker left the senate
chamber for the battle-field, on whose bloody plain he
was stricken down in October 1861.   The first through
despatch on the completed overland telegraph brought
the intelligence of his death.

The winter of 1861–2 being the season of a great
and destructive inundation of the Sacramento valley,
the legislature, and the government in all its departments, was forced to adjourn to San Francisco in January, at which place the session was continued to its
close.[19]   The Sacramentans feared this might be

[18] The most important appointments of the president in 1861 were as
follows: collector at S. F., Ira P. Rankin; appraisers, S. J. Bridge and B.
W. Mudge; collector at Benicia, S. M. Swain; at Monterey, John F. Porter;
at Stockton, S. W. Sperry; at San Diego, Joshua Sloan; at San Pedro, Oscar
Many; at Sta Bárbara, S. B. Brinkenhoff; supt. of the mint, R. S. Stevens;
coiners, William Schmalz and Conrad Wiegand; sub-treasurer, D. W. Chees-
man; post-master, S. H. Parker; register of land-office at S. F., George B.
Tingley; receiver of public moneys, R. H. Waller; register at Los Angeles,
Antonio María Pico; receiver, Louis Sperry, register at Stockton, George
D. Webster; at Visalia, Henry W. Briggs; at Humboldt, John W. Eddy;
at Marysville, A. J. Snyder; receiver at Visalia, George M. Gerrish; at
Marysville, J. Compton; at Humboldt, William Pratt; postmaster at Sac.,
George Rowland; William Rabe, U. S. marshal of the northern dist; William
B. Sharp, U. S. atty; George M. Hanson, Ind. supt.; Henry D. Barrows,
marshal; Kimbell H. Dimmeck, att'y; Minor Frank, Ind supt of the
southern dist.
[19] The senate of 1862 was composed of the following members: hold-over
senators, A. L. Rhodes, Richard Irwin, P. A. Gallagher, A. St Clair Denver,
O. Harvey, S. A. Merritt, William Watt, Phil. W. Thomas, James McM.
Shafter, E. H. Heacock, F. M. Warmcastle, John H. Hill, C. V. Williamson, William H. Parks, C. E. De Long; republicans 3, union democrats 9,
secessionists 3.   Elected in 1862: J. C. Bogart, San Diego and San Bernardino; J. R. Vineyard, Los Angeles; R. Pacheco, Sta Bárbara and San Luis
Obispo; Thomas Baker, Tulare and Fresno; G. K. Porter, Santa Cruz and
Monterey; B. W. Hathaway, Samuel Soule, R. F. Perkins, J. A. Banks,
San Mateo and S. F.; A. M. Crane, Alameda; C. H. Chamberlin, San Joa-
quin; L. Quint, Tuolumne and Mono; William T. Lewis, Calaveras; R. Bur-
nell, Amador; A. B. Nixon, Sac.; O. B. Powers, Solano and Yolo; William
Holden, Napa, Lake, and Mendocino; W. D. Harriman, Placer; Joseph
Kutz, Nevada; William Kimball, Sierra; R. C. Gaskell, Butte. J. G. Dall,
Tehama and Colusa; Benjamin Shurtleff, Shasta and Trinity; W. Van Dyke,
Humboldt, Klamath, and Del Norte; George B. Oulton, Siskiyou.   Repub-
licans 14, union democrats 7, secessionists 4.   The officers chosen were J.
McM. Shafter pres't pro tem., Thomas Hill sec., A. A. De Long ass't sec.,
Archibald G. Turner serg't-at-arms, Charles E. Abbott minute clerk, W. F.
Heustis journal clerk, H. C. Kibbe enrolling clerk, George A. Gillespie en-
grossing clerk, George C. Harriman, C. B. Bonestel copying clerks; three
porters, 4 pages, and a paper-folder.
The assembly was composed of S. B. Bell, J. M. Moore, Alameda; G. W.
Seaton, W. A. Waddell, Amador; J. M. Kunnard, George W. Printy, Butte;
Thomas Campbell, J. W. Griswold, Thomas O'Brien, Calaveras; C. B. Por-
ter, Contra Costa; Seneca Dean, J. Frasier, J. H. Dennis, H. G. Parker, El

taken advantage of to create a movement for a permanent change of capital, but the following winter saw the legislature reëstablished in the legal seat of government. The session of 1861–2 was a long one, the members sitting as a high court of impeachment to try Hardy, judge of the 16th district, upon charges of disloyalty and violation of his oath of office. His sentence was dismissal from the bench. It must be admitted, I think, that while the evidence was sufficient to convict on the counts, the trial was brought on quite as much by the recollection of previous defiance of law and travesties of justice[20] as by the more recent offences.

Among the concurrent resolutions passed was a renewed pledge of loyalty, and one authorizing the governor to notify by telegraph the secretary of the United States treasury of the intention o. California to pay at once the direct tax of $254,538, apportioned to the state by congress, as her share of the interest on the public debt. There was no niggardliness. Money was poured out in every way that could help the gov-

Dorado; James Smitn, Fresno; G. W. Werk, Humboldt; S. P. Wright, Klamath and Del Norte; James A. Watson, Murray Morrison, Los Angeles; A. C. McAllister, Marin; J. G. McCullough, Mariposa; T. W. Lane, Merced and Stanislaus; T. M. Ames, Mendocino; Juan W. Cot, Monterey; Edward Evey, Napa and Lake; J. M. Avery, James Collins, William H. Sears, Reuben Leach, Nevada; John Yule, E. W. Hillyer, C. C. Dudley, Placer; T. B. Shannon, Plumas; J. E. Benton, W. H. Barton, J. H. Warwick, R. D. Ferguson, J. B. Saul, Sac.; Benjamin Barton, San Bernardino; D. B. Hoffman, San Diego; S. S. Tilton, William Lowry, James Otis, George Barstow, J. W. Van Zandt, George B. Reeve, W. W. Battles, George Amerige, Caleb T. Fay, B. Dare, William T. Reese, S. C. Bigelow, S. F.; John Thompson, Samuel Myers, San Joaquin; C. W. Dana, San Luis Obispo and Sta Bárbara; S. Tilton, San Mateo; Charles Maclay, Joseph E. Brown, John Zuck, Sta Clara; T. Eager, Sta Cruz; George W. Woodman, Shasta; D. Love, E. B. Smith, Sierra; William Irwin, C. N. Thornbury, Siskiyou; J. M. Dudley, Solano; W. A. Ellason, G. W. Reed, J. G. Dow, Sonoma; C. E. Wilcoxon, Sutter; J. W. Thompson, Tehama and Colusa; J. H. Matthews, Trinity; J. C. Pemberton, Tulare; T. N. Machin, C. W. Kendall, B. K. Davis, Tuolumne and Mono; I. N. Hoag, Yolo; J. C. Sargent, E. Teegarden, T. O. Jackson, Yuba. Republicans 41, union democrats 29, secessionists 10. Officers of the house: George Barstow speaker, John Sedgwick, W. N. Slocum, W. G. Wood, H. H. Fellows, Sheldon Allen, George A. Hill, George C. Hough, C. T. Jennings clerks, H. J. Clayton, Jeremiah Watts serg'ts-at-arms. *Cal. Jour. Assem.*, 1862, 25–6.
    [20] Notably the failure to try Terry for the killing of Broderick. See *Sen. and Assemb. Jour.*, 1862, *App. Rept*, 37, p. 703; *Cal. Stat.*, 1862, 613.

ernment. The encampments with which the state was charged cost the treasury $200,000 in 1863. The United States sanitary commission, from first to last, received from California $1,234,257.31.[21] Fortunately for the liberal desires of the people, the mines of Nevada, owned chiefly by Californians, were yielding at this period an amount of bullion which seemed to justify a prodigal generosity.

The number of electors in the military service of the United States caused the legislature of 1863 to pass an act requiring the adjutant-general of the state to make out a list of their names, from which separate lists should be sent to the commander of each regiment in camp, with ballot-boxes, that the volunteers might not be deprived of the privilege of voting at the election of that year. This law was called in question by certain candidates who were beaten by volunteer votes, and the courts, district and supreme, declared that the soldiers' ballots should be excluded from the count,[22] judges Sawyer, Shafter, and Rhodes agreeing, and Currey and Sanderson dissenting. The legislature asserted its superiority to the courts by renewing the act in 1864, and volunteer votes were not again questioned.

The invitation of the republicans to the loyal democrats to join them in a union party, irrespective of old

[21] The movement for sanitary help began in 1862, in S. F., when in one evening $6,600 was subscribed by a few persons, and it was proposed to systematize the work of collecting funds. The matter was taken up by the board of supervisors, and public meeting appointed for Sept. 10th, when a committee was chosen consisting of M. C. Blake, Eugene Casserly, R. G. Sneath, D. C. McRuer, and S. H. Washburn, afterward increased to 13. Before the middle of Sept. $160,000 had been subscribed and remitted in one bill of exchange. Two weeks later another $100,000 was sent, and before the close of the year the third $100,000. Up to the time that Cal. opened her long purse the work in the east was insignificant; after that it became an institution, and during the duration of the war was carried on in a liberal spirit, but nowhere so generously as on our Pacific coast. The pres. of the U. S. sanitary commission, W. Bellows, paid a visit to S. F. in the spring of 1864 to address the people; $200,000 was paid to him, and as said above the total amount contributed was over a million dollars. Nevada, Oregon, and other west coast territories contributed $234,506 25. *Steele, Hist. U. S. Sen. Com.*, 197–243 and app. No. 5.

[22] *Cal. Sup. Court, Soldier's Vote*, pp. 24; *Sac. Union*, Feb. 8, 1864.

party lines, and its acceptance, was the distinguishing feature of California politics in 1862. To it was added the intimation that there would be a departure from established practices in the matter of political bribery by the new party. The constitutional amendments, making the governor's term of office four years, the legislative sessions biennial, and changing the judicial system, were adopted by the people in 1862, and confirmed by the legislature in 1863.[23]

[23] The senators elected in 1862 for the legislature of 1863, the last under the annual rule were, besides the hold-over members elected the previous year, J. G. McCullough, Merced, Mariposa, and Stanislaus; Joseph S. Wallis, Sta Clara; Alexander G. Abell, G. W. Clark, M. S. Whiting, S. F.; C. B. Porter, Contra Costa and Marin; Joseph M. Cavis, Tuolumne and Mono; William Higby, Calaveras; O. Harvey, A. H. Sexton, El Dorado; Newton Booth, Sac.; James H. McNabb, Sonoma; T. B. Higgins, Placer; J. C. Birdseye, Nevada; Francis Anderson, Sierra; William H. Park, Yuba and Sutter; Lewis Cunuingham, Yuba; Thomas B. Shannon, Butte and Plumas. All were chosen on the administration ticket. The officers of the assembly chosen were: A. M. Crane, pres't pro tem; John White, sec.; H. G. Stebbins, asst sec.; George I. Lytle, E. W. Councilman, sergt-at-arms; John E. VanDaren, W. F. Heustis, J. B. Reed, Robert Henderson, L. M. Foulke, Holland Smith, clerks.

The assembly was composed of Thomas Scott, Henry Robinson, Alameda; A. B. Andrews, E. M. Simpson, Amador; F. M. Smith, J. G. Moore, Butte; Teuton G. McDonald, James Barclay (Thomas Campbell, elected, died), Calaveras; T. G. Butler, Colusa and Tehama; T. G. Wright, Contra Costa; S. W. Sanderson, Thomas Fitch, J. R. Clark, James Burr, El Dorado; James Smith, Fresno (elected, died); Stephen G. Whipple, Humboldt; S. P. Wright, Klamath and Del Norte; E. J. C. Kewen, J. A. Watson, Los Angeles; Robert Torrence, Marin; J. W. Wilcox, Mariposa; T. M. Ames, Mendocino; James W. Robertson, Merced and Stanislaus; M. A. Castro, Monterey; Chancellor Hartsan, Napa and Lake; James Collins, William H. Sears. John M. Rule, Seth Martin, Nevada; C. C. Dudley, John Yale, N. W. Blanchard, Placer; M. D. Howell, Plumas; W. H. Barton, M. M. Estee, Amos Adams, J. H. Warwick, Charles Duncombe, Sac.; R. S. Allen, San Bernardino; George A. Johnson, San Diego; George Barstow, Henry L. Dodge, O. P. Sutton, John E. Kincaid, Cyrus Palmer, Jacob Duth, James A. Banks, John F. Swift, Hugh Farley, Benjamin Dore, Andrew J. Gunninson, William R. Wheaton, S. F.; T. J. Keys, Samuel Myers, San Joaquin; Ramon J. Hill, San Luis Obispo and Sta Bárbara; James G. Denniston, San Mateo; J. J. Owen, J. W. Owen, D. W. Harrington, Sta Clara; I. C. Wilson, Sta Cruz; J. N. Chappell, Shasta; E. B. Smith, James Crawford, Sierra; William Irwin, B. T. Varney, Siskiyou; J. M. Dudley, Solano; E. F. Dunne, W. M. Rider, J. B. Beeson, Sonoma; C. S. Harwell, Sutter; M. W. Personette, Trinity; J. W. Freeman, Tulare and Buena Vista; T. N. Ma n, N. M. Orr, Frederick Lux, Tuolumne and Mono; Edwin Patten, Y , J. C. Sargent, O. F. Redfield, D. O. Adkinson, Yuba. All were electe on the union administration ticket, except 10 union democrats who would not fuse, and 7 secessionists. On a joint ballot there were 94 administration, 15 union democrats, and 11 secessionists from the southern counties. The officers of the assembly were: T. N. Machin, speaker; James Collins, speaker pro tem.; N. G. Worthington, W. N. Slocum, W. G. Wood, James G. Smith, G. H. Marble, George A. Hill, H. Polley, E. M. Lynde, clerks; Thomas Eager, A. H. Winn, sg'ts-at-arms. *Sac. Union*, Jan. 5, 1863; *Cal. Jour. Sen.*, 1863,20.21.

By every act possible, except one, the state of California, through its legislature, declared its devotion to the government. It appropriated $24,260, which State-treasurer Ashley had saved to the treasury by paying the federal tax in legal tender notes instead of the gold collected, to the purpose of aiding recruiting officers in filling up the volunteer regiments. It appropriated $5,000 out of the general fund for the relief of the family of Colonel Roderick Matheson, who was killed at the battle of Crampton Gap October 2, 1862. For placing the coast in a more efficient state of defence it appropriated $100,000; and $600,000 was set aside as a separate fund, to be known as the Soldiers' Relief Fund, for the purpose of paying a compensation to volunteers in the service of the United States over and above their regular army pay. It enacted the law in reference to soldier's election privileges already mentioned, which a majority of the supreme bench pronounced unconstitutional. It declared by act secession flags and insignia a nuisance, to be abated by the sheriff and destroyed; made the arming and equipping of vessels for piratical purposes[24]

[24] This law was intended to stop the practice of exporting ammunition and arms under the pretence that they were required in Mexico, toward which, in its struggles for freedom from a foreign invader, Americans entertained sympathy. That these supplies did not always go to Mexico was more than suspected. The schooner *Live Oak*, in Jan. 1863, sailed from S.F. with 10 tons of powder on board, whose destination was unknown at the time, and never since explained. In the spring of 1864, there was much sensation over the discovery of a plot to capture the Cal. mail steamers, as follows: S. R. Mallory, sec. of the confederate navy, in May of this year ordered acting master T. E. Hogg to proceed with the men under his command from Wilmington, Del., by the shortest and safest route, to Panamá, there to take passage on board the *Guatemala* or *San Salvador*, steamers trading between Panamá and Realejo, and to devise means to capture the vessel, after reaching the high seas, in the name of the confederate govt. Having secured the steamer, he was to take measures to arm her, and 'proceed to cruise against the enemy in the Pacific,' and to endeavor to strike a blow against the Cal. trade, and the whalers in the north Pacific. Hogg went to Habana, where he betrayed his mission to Thomas Savage, American consul at that port, and later one of my most valued assistants, who took care that the officers of the threatened steamers should be informed through U. S. Admiral Pearson at Panamá. A watch was kept, and when the agents of the confederate govt appeared, they were arrested and brought to S. F., where they were tried by a military commission which sentenced them to be hanged. McDowell commuted their sentence to imprisonment for life for Capt. Hogg, and ten years' confinement for E. A. Swain, John S. Hiddle, W. L. Black,

a felony, punishable by imprisonment for not more
than twenty nor less than five years, or by death, as
the jury might determine; excluded secessionists and
alien enemies from courts of justice; required attorneys
to take an oath to support the constitution of the
United States and the state of California, and declared
that denunciation of the government, and wishing evil
to it, was a criminal abuse of the freedom of speech,
to be punished by imprisonment in the county jail for
one year, or a fine of $1000, or both. Resolutions
were passed thanking Colonel Connor and the volunteers of the 2d cavalry of California for their gallant
action at Bear river, in Utah. It renewed its resolutions of loyalty, and declared itself a "union league to
sustain the administration;" expressed regret at the
death of Sumner, "by whose prompt and decisive
action the state was saved from anarchy, and the hor-
rors of civil war." Lastly, the emancipation proclamation of Lincoln was approved, and California
pledged to the support of the measure

T. J. Grady, R. B. Lyon, and Joseph Higgin, his associates. They were
tried as belligerents, violating the rules of war. Foiled in this undertaking,
the rebel cruiser, *Shenandoah*, was sent to the whaling grounds of the north
Pacific via China, thus escaping our cruisers, and succeeded in destroying
the following vessels, at or near Ascencion island: April 1st, the *Edward
Carey*, Capt. Baker; *Harvest*, Capt. Eldridge ;*Pearl*, Capt. Thompson; *Hector*,
Capt. Chace; May 27th, *Abigail*, Capt. Nye; June 21st, *Euphrates*, Capt.
Hathaway; June 22d, *William Thompson*, Capt. Tucker; *Sophia Thornton*,
Capt. Smith; *Uriah Swift*, Capt. Williams; June 23d, *Susan Abigail*, Capt. F.
S. Redfield; June 25th, *General Williams*, Capt. Benjamin; June 26th, *Nimrod*,
Capt. Clark; *Catherine*, Capt. William H. Phillips; *William C. Nye*, Capt. P.
A. Cootay; June 27th, *Gipsy*, Capt. Orlando G. Robinson; *Isabelle*, Capt.
Hudson Winslow; June 28th, *Hillman*, Capt. Macomber; *J. Howland*, Capt.
Ludlow; *Nassau*, Capt. Green; *Brunswick*, Capt. Potter; *Waverly*, Capt. Holly;
Martha 2d, Capt. Macomber; *Congress*, Capt. Wood; *Favorite*, Capt. T. G.
Young; *Covington*, Capt. Jenks. Four other vessels captured were sent to
Honolulu and S. F. with the crews of the plundered and destroyed vessels.
They were the *Milo*, Capt. Hawes, June 22d; *General Pike*, Capt. H. M.
Crowell, New Bedford, June 27th; *Nile*, Capt. Fish, New London, June 28th;
and *James Maury*, New Bedford, June 28th. Capt. Nye, of the *Abigail*, who
was put on board the *Milo*, taking advantage of a dense fog, manned a whale
boat, and went to warn the fleet, succeeding in saving two vessels. The loss
of the whaling fleet was a serious blow to the business of the S. I. as well as
ruinous to the private fortunes of New England and other owners. The
value of a vessel and cargo would average $45,000, making the loss about
$1,500,000. There were at this time 7 U. S. men-of-war in the Pacific, but
all too busily employed to go cruising after the *Shenandoah*. The total loss
sustained by Cal. from cruisers on both oceans was $2,000,000, of which the
claimants received by award about seven per cent.

But the one thing California rebelled against was the idea of accepting United States legal tenders as currency. In the east, business was based upon the value of the bills of specie-paying banks, which, with gold, formed the currency.[25] In California there were no banks of issue, and business was based solely on a gold and silver standard of values. In the east gold was treated as merchandise and purchased with legal tenders, which fluctuated in value with the news from every battle-field. In California government paper was merchandise, purchased at a very profitable rate of exchange with gold, which circulated as currency, while legal tenders did not, except at the discount which every day's bulletins announced. No merchant would risk being paid in legal tenders, dollar for dollar, for goods purchased with gold, and sold at gold prices. To avoid losses of this nature it was necessary to make contracts, naming the kind of money in which debts were to be paid; and then it was necessary to enact a law enforcing the observance of these contracts. Such a law, called the specific contract act, was accordingly passed by this legislature, about one year after the notice of suspension of specie payment by the eastern banks and the federal government. As a matter of fact, gold payments were not entirely suspended by the government until about March 1863. There had been much discussion of the subject during this year, and two classes of opinions were held. While the judge of the 4th district decided that a plaintiff must receive "greenbacks," instead of coin, in satisfaction of a judgment,

---

[25] Sec. Chase, and McCullough, his successor, were of the opinion that the Cal. gold law was against sound policy, and advised repeal. The latter, in a letter to Thompson Campbell of this state, declared the specific contract act in opposition to a necessary war measure, and that thereby it assailed the national credit, but acquitted the people of any such design. It was the opinion of the secretary that the effect in Cal. of a purely metallic currency was injurious to her own prosperity, because no country could long prosper where money commanded so high a rate of interest. Immigration, he thought, would be checked, manufactures prevented, and commerce crippled until Cal. had a sound banking system, such as provided by the national currency act.

another authority contended that paper money issued
by the government was unconstitutional; and Attorney-general Pixley, always pronounced in his loyalty,
condemned as traitors those who refused to take greenbacks at their face value. To settle this vexed question the specific-contract act was deemed necessary,
and proved satisfactory, although objections continued
to be raised that the state was disloyal as well as short-
sighted in a business point of view, in excluding cheap
money. But all attempts to repeal the act failed.
The supreme court decided that the government notes
were constitutional, and also that the specific-contract
act was equally so. These decisions smoothed the
public temper, and California, while making a handsome profit on importations from the east purchased
with greenbacks and sold for specie, returned a good
share of this difference to the nation at large.   Oregon
and Nevada followed her example, and passed specific-
contract laws, and the questions raised concerning the
validity of such acts was finally settled by the federal
supreme court, which held that a contract to pay in
any kind of legal tender was valid, whether written
or not.   Some hostility was exhibited toward government paper as late as 1868, when the legislature
was asked to pass two bills intended to exclude it
from circulation in California, but which failed through
the opposing report of the judiciary committee.

Another tender point with the people of California
was the taxation of the mines, which they had always
resisted.   They alleged that the state furnished the
gold to sustain the nation's credit, and although the
mineral lands belonged to the government, it was unwise to impose any tax upon the product of the mines
which would tend to embarass them in any degree.
Yet when in 1864 a levy of one half of one per cent
was placed upon gold and silver bullion, it was
promptly paid as due to loyalty.

Assemblyman Dudley, of Placer, introduced a bill
proposing an amendment to the constitution, exclud-

ing colored persons from the state. Hartson of Napa, chairman of the judiciary committee to which it was referred, reported an amendment excluding traitors. "It is self-evident," said the report, "that if it is necessary or proper to exclude any class of people from the state, it is, first and above all, those entirely overlooked in this bill, but described in the amendment—those of bloody hands and black hearts, and therefore your committee recommends its passage as amended."

Something of this spirit showed itself in the collisions which now and then occurred between union men and confederate sympathizers. Yet it was chiefly men with nothing at stake who were boisterous secessionists. The way in which General Wright sought to hold secession in check was by excluding disloyal newspapers from the mails, and by declaring the estates of secessionists subject to confiscation by the government. To this congress added the suspension of habeas corpus by the president when emergency required it within the Pacific department. It was in this manner that California fought the battles of the union.

The new departure in politics instituted by the union party, that bribery was to be discountenanced, furnished the rock on which two senatorial aspirants were wrecked, and gave an unexpected turn to the legislative choice. Both Sargent and Phelps, congressmen, desired to step across the vestibule leading to the senate chamber, but during the preliminary caucus a friend of Phelps was so indiscreet as to approach an adherent of Sargent with an offer for his vote. This being exposed by Sargent's friends ruined Phelps' prospects, and Phelps' friends, in revenge, frustrated Sargent's hopes. One of the consequences was that John Conness, who had not been popular with the republicans, and could not be made governor in 1861, was elected to the United States senate in 1863, to succeed Latham, who had fallen out with the administration, and no longer truly represented his state.

The proneness of California senators to political backslidings forms one of the curiosities of history, unless we accept as true the theory that peculiar influences were brought to bear that were not applied to senators of other free states. One of them, who had been chosen for his declared loyalty and devotion to the state, had become so infatuated with the pleasures of Washington life that he had not once returned since taking his seat to learn what were the wishes of his constituents, for which apparently he cared very little. On this and other grounds he was brought to book by his colleague, who very plainly declared that he misrepresented the sentiment of California, and betrayed the trust reposed in him by reason of his own professions. The debate was upon the constitutionality of confiscating rebel property, which the other denied. For this and other reasons he was censured, as many thought unjustly, by a resolution of the legislature of 1864.

The constitution, as amended, required the election in 1863 of a governor for four years, a legislature, a part of whose senators should hold over for four years, a new bench of supreme judges to hold office for ten years, and an entire corps of state officers, the legislature elect to meet in December, when the new government would go into operation. In view of the condition of the country, the fact that the new officers would be in for four years, and the certainty that every effort would be made to secure some political strength by secessionists, the election was regarded as one of unusual importance. Nor was this view an exaggerated one, the length of the war, its cost, hardships, reverses, and the necessity of a draft, being made the ground of backsliding among the weaker sort of union democrats, who gave a moral support to rebellion by opposing the vigorous prosecution of the war. This faction, defined as "copperheads" by the

more strictly loyal men, had never as much comparative strength in California as in the older states, but
its existence was an important factor, and one which
had to be considered in electing state officers; all the
more, too, that the following year would bring on another presidential campaign, with its momentous issues.

Sargent, who had been disappointed in being beaten
for senator, wished to be made governor, and had no
rival this time in Phelps, who did not want the office.
There would have been no difficulty with the people
in either of these cases, but Senator Conness, following the traditions of the democratic party, to which
he belonged, took the management of the union nominating convention in his hands, and made up the
state ticket, with the help of those he was able to
reward.

The system always obtaining in the state, of primary
elections, made it possible for an active politician, by
the use of money and by voting the same men several
times over, to secure any nomination he chose. The
primaries, conducted in this manner, determined
who should be brought forward in county conventions,
and informed the wire-pullers of the number of votes
that could be depended upon in the state convention.
Our formulas of government are by no means perfect.
The same system prevails to-day, and an honest election is an impossibility, candidates being placed before
the people for whom the political "bosses" alone are
responsible, and in whom the people take little interest.   Hence it is that the best citizens stay away from
the polls, except in some great crisis.

Senator Conness performed the duties of "boss" in
1863, making up his slate unalterably, and having his
candidates elected. They were F. F. Low, late
United States collector at San Francisco, for governor; T. N. Machin, of Tuolumne, for lieutenant-
governor; B. B. Redding, of Sacramento, secretary
of state; Romaldo Pacheco, of San Luis Obispo,
state treasurer; George Oulton, of Siskiyou, state

controller; John G. McCollough, of Mariposa, attorney-general; W. D. Harriman, of Placer, clerk of the supreme court; O. M. Clayes, of San Joaquin, state printer; J. F. Houghton, of Solano, surveyor-general; Charles L. Taylor, of San Francisco, harbor commissioner; and for congressmen, Thomas B. Shannon, of Plumas; William Higby, of Calaveras; and Cornelius Cole, of Santa Cruz. Cole was the only spontaneous choice of the convention. All the elect were firm union and war men. The election of the union candidates was a foregone conclusion from the first, but the copperheads ran a ticket at the head of which were several well-known politicians, John G. Downey for governor; E. W. McKinstry, for lieutenant-governor; John B. Weller, John Bigler, and N. E. Whitesides, for congressmen; and Beriah Brown, for state printer. The majority of Low over Downey was 19,-831, and for Machin over McKinstry 21,120. The curiosity of the election was the bolting of the independent unionists of San Francisco city and county, who made up their own legislative ticket, and elected two to one of San Francisco's delegation without injury to the union state ticket.

On the 21st of October occurred the special election of the judiciary, according to the amended constitution, when the five supreme judges selected by the convention, namely, O. L. Shafter, Lorenzo Sawyer, S. W. Sanderson, John Currey, and A. L. Rhodes, were chosen, together with fourteen district judges,[26] forty-two county judges, and other judicial

[26] The district judges elected by the union party were: 1st district, Pablo de la Guerra; 2d, W. T. Sexton; 3d, S. B. McKee; 4th, E. D. Sawyer; 5th, James M. Cavis; 6th, J. H. McCune; 7th, J. B. Southard; 8th, William R. Turner; 9th, E. Garter; 10th, I. S. Belcher; 11th, S. N. Brockway; 12th, O. C. Pratt; 13th, J. M. Bouderant; 14th, J. B. McFarland. The 13th dist alone elected a copperhead judge. This was composed of the counties of Tulare, Mariposa, etc. The legislature created another district, the 15th, at the session of 1863-4, when S. H. Dwinelle was chosen judge. *Cal. Rept*, 24, 1864; *Hayes' Scraps, Cal. Notes*, iv. 15-92. De la Guerra had made a speech in the state senate on a bill that threatened Mexican claims, and this speech had great influence in electing him over Benjamin Hayes, copperhead, in a copperhead district. Hayes was the collector of the numerous vols of

officers.   The state was now completely loyalized, so
far as its public servants were concerned.

The legislature elect,[27] met on the 7th of Decem-

scraps referred to under different heads in this work.   His patience and fore-
thought in saving these helps to the historian has proved invaluable.   He
was for a long time judge of his district, but when the rebellion broke out
sympathized with the secessionists with whom he was associated.   He was
pure-hearted and high-minded in every respect.

[27] The senate was composed of the following members: W. W. Crane,
jr, Alameda; R. Burnell, Amador; R. C. Gaskill, T. M. Smith, Butte and
Plumas; Joseph Shepard, W. H. Leonard, Calaveras; J. A. Rush, Colusa
and Tehama; C. B. Porter, Contra Costa and Marin; S. P. Wright, Del
Norte, Humboldt, and Klamath; A. C. Henry, F. L. Maddux, El Dorado;
J. W. Freeman, Fresno and Tulare; Chancellor Hartson, Lake, Napa, and
Mendocino; H. Hamilton, Los Angeles; W. S. Montgomery, Mariposa,
Merced, and Stanislaus; George S. Evans, J. W. Haskin, Mono and
Tuolumne; W. E. Lovett, Monterey and Sta Cruz; Joseph Kutz, E. W.
Roberts, Nevada; John Yule, J. E. Hale, Placer; James McSnafter, J. H.
Reddington, H. L. Dodge, J. P. Buckley, Horace Hawes, S. F.; E. H. Hea-
cock, J. A. Benton, Sac.; Samuel Myers, San Joaquin; M. C. Tuttle, San
Bernardino and San Diego; J. Y. Cot, San Luis Obispo and Sta Bárbara;
W. S. McMurtry, Sta Clara; John P. Jones, Shasta and Trinity; J. W.
Nayle, Sierra; L. M. Foulke, Siskiyou; J. T. Hall, Solano and Yolo; George
Pierce, Sonoma; Lewis Cunningham, C. S. Haswell, Yuba and Sutter.
Pres pro tem. of the senate, R. Burnell; sec., Charles Westmoreland;
asst sec., A. W. Bishop; serg'ts-at-arms, John Helmsley, James A. Stidger;
clerks, J. S. VanDorn, W. F. Heustis, Albert Clark, M. A. Gelston, F.
Hallowell, W. A. Plunkett.

The assembly consisted of Thomas Scott, Asa Walker, Alameda; A. C.
Brown, W. B. Ludlow, Amador; George S. Sumner, A. C. Buffman, Butte;
S. N. Parker, L. Langdon, B. Dyer, Calaveras; T. J. Wright, Contra Costa;
S. Jennison, Colusa and Tehama; R. P. Hurst, Del Norte and Klamath. T.
Fraser, P. Tearse, F. A. Dow, J. S. Campbell, El Dorado; J. N. Walker,
Fresno; A. Wiley, Humboldt; W. R. H. Dodson, Lake and Napa; E. J. C.
Kewen, J. Sepulveda, Los Angeles, S. Johnson, Marin; J. W. Wilcox, Mari-
posa; L. Wilsey, Mendocino; W. S. Dickinson, Merced and Stanislaus; Freder-
ick Lux, Otis Perrin, E. F. Mitchell, Mono and Tuolumne; Estevan Castro,
Monterey; W. H. Sears, J. W. Rule, S. Martin, A. A. Smith, Nevada; M. C.
Winchester, J. D. Pratt, E. H. Snyder, Placer; R. A. Clark, Plumas; Francis
Tukey J. P. Rhodes, W. B. Hunt, Alexander Badlum, Jr, J. R. Watson,
Sac., George J. Brooks, James Bowman, C. F. Mebins, Charles Clayton,
Nathaniel Gray, John Lynch, John S. Hittell, Henry Dutton, L. W. Mc-
Collian, Thompson Campbell, Joseph Wood, J. W. Cherry, S. F.; E. H.
Allen, J. E. Perley, San Joaquin; J. J. Owen, William Erkson, J. D. Van
Schaick, Santa Clara; O. H. Hoag, M. Whellon, J. Smith, Sonora; R. C.
Scott, S. L. Litchfield, Siskiyou; R. S. Weston, S. H. Allay, Sierra; Van
Leuven, San Bernardino; Kendrick, San Diego; Ramon J. Hill, San
Luis Obispo and Santa Bárbara; H. Devoe, Santa Cruz; J. N. Chappel,
Shasta; A. T. Green, San Mateo; Milton Wasson, Solano; M. Boulware,
Sutter; M. W. Personette, Trinity; S. C. Brown, Tulare; J. B. Hartsough,
Yolo; O. F. Redfield, L. Hubbard, J. H. Beaman, Yuba.   Officers of the
assembly: Williams H. Sears, speaker; J. J. Owen, speaker, pro tem; O.
C. Wheeler, R. H. Daly, Martin Rowan, J. H. Marple, A. N. Gambill, L.
S. Taylor, H. A. Leese, Nicholas Moritz, clerks; William Rider, J. F. Hol-
loway, serg'ts-at-arms. Cal. Jour. Assem, 1863-4.   35 out of 40 senators,
and 72 out of 80 assemblymen were unionists.   The seat in the senate of
Hamilton of Los Angeles, secessionist, was contested by R. P. Ramirez, on

ber, and in its adminstrative zeal had nearly repealed
the specific contract act; but Governor Low [23] and the
public press presented so many good reasons for the
law as it was, that the bill failed to pass. Strong
union resolutions were adopted. An investigation,
which was found to be necessary, was held as to the
cause of the destruction by fire of the carriages of
seven guns furnished the state by the United States,
but with what motive could only be suspected. Three
thousand dollars was appropriated to remount the
guns. The federal government was asked to establish
a naval depot and force in the bay of Monterey, to
mount cannons on the old fort, and to construct additional fortifications on water-line batteries for the protection of the harbor. The poll-tax of two dollars a
head was remitted to volunteers, and a bounty was
granted to men enlisting thereafter for three years or
during the war, of $160 in installments to be paid
every six months; and to honorably discharged veterans reënlisting, an additional sum of $140, paid in
like manner. To meet these obligations the treasurer
was directed to prepare bonds of the state to the
amount of $2,000,000, to redeem which a tax of
twelve cents was levied on each $100 of valuation of
real and personal property in the state, estimated at
$174,000,000. Yet no loyal citizen thought of pro-
testing, although the state was then paying two per
cent monthly on a large portion of the current expenditures. The debt of the state, including the soldiers'
bounty bonds, was $5,365,640.71, and the money in
the treasury was less than it should have been by a

the ground of disloyalty, being an Englishman, and not eligible. The evidence of disloyalty was complete, but it was determined that Hamilton was
legally elected.

[23] Frederick F. Low, ex-congressman, collector of the port of S. F., governor of Cal., and minister to China, was born in 1828 at Frankfort, Maine,
and came to Cal. in 1849. After a period at mining he engaged in business
in S. F. and Marysville. He was one of the incorporators of the Cal. Steam
Navigation co., and established a banking house at Marysville.

considerable amount, owing to the defalcation of G. R. Warren, republican controller elected in 1861.[29]

The great contest was approaching of the presidential election, which would be governed chiefly by the conduct of the war, as the copperhead element in politics was gaining ground in the eastern states with the necessity of providing substitutes to fill the places of drafted men. There was no draft in California, her volunteers exceeding her quota, and being needed where they were, and her treasure flowing freely to support men in the field. But there was a democratic peace-on-any-terms party and press, which was putting forth its strongest efforts in opposition to the union-administration party, and encouraging disloyalty by studied misrepresentation of the aims of the government.[30] In the southern counties it was impossible to hold a primary election at which true union men could vote, copperheads calling themselves unionists taking possession of the polls by various devices, among others, postponing a meeting, and when the honest voters had gone home, opening the polls for half an hour to allow the conspirators to choose delegates.[31]

On the 24th of March the union state convention met at Sacramento, W. H. Sears president, to elect delegates to the national convention at Baltimore, and selected Thompson Campbell, a lawyer of San Fran-

[29] The embezzlement amounted to $12,217.92, and was taken from the stamp account. Warren fled, and his sureties were made to pay the deficit, the first instance in the history of Cal., where bondsmen had been held to the responsibility of such a debt. *Cal. Jour. Sen.*, 1865–6; App., no. 5, p.4, i.

[30] Of this class of journalists was Beriah Brown, a Vermonter, He first established the *Republican*, in Stockton, which was removed to Sac.; and finally he conducted the *Democratic Press*, of S. F., a bitter anti-administration journal. He was one of that class selected by secession leaders to promulgate disunion under the pretence of only demanding constitutional rights. Being condemned by the public sentiment of S. F., he first went to Guaymas, Mexico, to join Gwin, who failing him, he removed to Oregon, and then to Washington Ter., where he established a successful journal at Seattle after the close of the war. The Marysville *Express*, Stockton *Beacon*, Merced *Democrat*, Napa *Pacific Echo*, Tulare *Post*, *Equal Rights Expositor*, and other newspapers were engaged in covertly aiding the confederacy.

[31] *Savage Doc.*, ii. MS. 102–12.

cisco; M. C. Briggs of Sacramento, a methodist preacher; John Bidwell of Butte, a landed proprietor; and Phineas Banning of Los Angeles, a loyal business man, to represent the state at large. The district delegates were Nathan Coombs of Napa; Robert Gardiner of Yolo; William Ritter of Sacramento; O. H. Bradbury of Tuolumne; James Otis of San Francisco, and William S. McMurty of Santa Clara. There was nothing very remarkable recorded of these men; but California had gone through some disagreeable experiences with her brilliant men which made the usefulness of others apparent. They were instructed to vote for Lincoln.

The democratic copperhead state convention met in San Francisco May 10th, having for president John B. Weller. Among the delegates elected to the Chicago convention were the president, and three other ex-governors, Bigler, Downey, and McDougal,—four governors, and four Johns—but McDougal declining, Thomas Hayes was substituted. The district delegates were C. L. Weller and William J. Whipple of San Francisco; J. B. Stevens of Calaveras; Clayton Wetherill of Tuolumne; J. J. Berry of Butte, and C. D Semple of Colusa.

C. L. Weller was the copperhead candidate for sheriff of San Francisco, and was beaten at the city and county election, H. L. Davis, people's candidate, having a majority over him of 4,244 votes. Whether or not his defeat embittered him, he was arrested in July, by order of General McDowell, for language calculated to discourage enlistment and incite to violent resistance to a draft, should one be made in California. He was confined in Alcatraz until the middle of August when he offered to take the oath of allegiance, and was released at the solicitation of his family and friends. A mass meeting was held at Hayes park during his incarceration, which violently denounced the military authorities and federal government for the arrest; and Weller as soon as liberated

gave utterance, at public assemblages, to language
scarcely less objectionable than that for which he
was imprisoned. A few others were arrested for similar offences. Had these Hotspurs had their head,
there might have been civil war on the Pacific in 1864.
McDowell, however, while issuing orders as placable
as possible, said succinctly: "No armed organizations
will be suffered in the department, save those sanctioned by competent constituted authority."

The methodist church south formed a factor in
anti-war, anti-administration, and pro-slavery politics,
and had its emissaries in the rural districts, extending
as far north as the Columbia river in Oregon. Thus
it happened that Bishop Kavanaugh, of Georgia, who
had introduced himself into the state under a pass
from the confederate authorities only, was arrested on
suspicion, but released on his assurance that his visit
was made in obedience to the commands of the church,
and had no political significance, while he would willingly take the oath of loyalty.

Yet that disloyalty was more outspoken in 1864
than it had been since the beginning of the war notwithstanding the vigilance of the authorities, the
watchfulness of union leagues, and the unremitting
teachings of the loyal press, was not to be denied.
This was partly owing to the effect upon an illiterate
southern population of the tirades indulged in by the
copperhead press, partly to the virulence of feeling
induced by sympathy with relatives and neighbors in
the southern states whose fortunes had been ruined
in the long strife, but chiefly, after all, to the selfish
partisanship of northern men whose insane ambition
was to be still recognized as representatives of the
"chivalry" of former days. Encouraged by their
seditious utterances, the class just referred to became
more and more disposed to violate all law, and actually in some instances attempted to inaugurate a

system which would have ended in guerrilla warfare,
had it not been promptly checked.[32]

The intelligence received in June that Lincoln was
renominated excited extraordinary enthusiasm. The
remainder of the summer was a political joust,[33] in
which there was much confident anticipation on one
side, and some rather feeble attempts to seem confident on the other. Frequent processions were indulged in, and almost any night, as the election drew
near, the democratic broom-rangers of San Francisco,
as they were facetiously named, paraded the streets,
following after a band playing Dixie Land, Johnny
Comes Marching Home, or other popular songs of
the confederates during the war. Then came the
momentous days of the presidential election. Every
precaution had been taken to prevent any disturbance
at the polls. Business was suspended, drinking-places
closed, and additional police placed on duty. The
city was dressed in the national colors, and the
weather being bright presented an inspiring appearance. Every face met upon the streets wore a look
of earnest and suppressed feeling. Even ordinary
conversation was carried on more quietly than usual.
There was no doubt of California, but there was
anxiety about the east, for the copperhead influence
had been increasing there also. Late in the day the

[32] An organization was formed among the farmers and residents in Santa
Clara county for procuring volunteers for the confederacy, and also the
money to support them. Several robberies were perpetrated on the stage-
line from Placerville to Carson in Nevada. In June 1864, two coaches were
robbed by a party of eight men, who secured eight sacks of bullion, and a
box of treasure. Their captain sent a receipt to Wells Fargo, & Co., for
$——— cash, signed 'B. Henry Ingram, com'd'g co., C. S. A.' Dep't sheriff
Staples, of El Dorado, was killed in arresting some of the gang. Sheriff
Adams, of Santa Clara co., and a Mr Conney, were wounded in the capture
of others. Thomas B. Poole was tried and hanged for killing Staples.
Mountain Democrat, Sept 30, 1865. A number of the organization were arrested at a democratic meeting in San José in Aug. *Hays Cal. Pol.*; vii. 72.
Three union men in Tulare co., were killed because of their union sentiment.
Among 100 guests at some springs in Santa Bárbara co., were only two
union men. One left to avoid trouble, and the other, a Carolinian, who had
left his state to avoid rebellion, was killed. Four other union men who accompanied him as far as Texas, were murdered there for their loyalty.

[33] *Dartini Reflec. Hispan. Amer.*, 1-4.

indications of California's 30,000 majority[34] for Lincoln over McClellan began to come in from such portions of the state as could be heard from by telegraph. The excitement was as tense as it was quiet. The city waited breathless, far into the night, for the first news from east of the Missouri, and while it waited windows were illuminated and few households thought of sleep. Toward midnight there began to move through the principal streets a solid column of 4,000 of San Francisco's chief citizens, singing in one grand chorus the Battle cry of Freedom and other songs of the war, not forgetting John Brown's body lies mouldering in the grave, etc., while women crowded the balconies and windows waving handkerchiefs and flags, laughing and weeping together in a contagion of exultant emotion; for then it was known that the president whom all trusted was to remain in his place, and his policy, which was believed to be wise and right, carried out.

What a different scene was that which San Francisco witnessed on the following 15th of April. The city was in gala dress in honor of victories on the field and in the cabinet. A waving sea of starry banners flooded every house-top with a crimson radiance, and a glad light was reflected on thousands of faces. Suddenly the crimson sea was calmed, the banners, drooped and lowered, were darkened by bands of crape —the shadow of a monstrous crime, and a nation's despair. Shudderingly the bells of the city tolled forth the dread intelligence. On every face the gladness was quenched beneath a pallor such as blanches the cheeks of strong men seldom in a lifetime. Grasping each others' hands, looking in each others' eyes, unable to syllable the emotions of grief mingled with horror and rage which possessed them, the citizens,

[34] The vote of S. F. was 21,024, while Boston with a population nearly double, returned 20,807 votes. The preponderance of adult males is not sufficient to account for the vote of S. F., and even the absence of a registry law in addition, is hardly sufficient to do so. There was an increase of 6,- 000 in one year.

forsaking all business, congregated on the streets, or
wandered restlessly about, benumbed by the unparalleled calamity of the tragedy at Washington.

But soon hot blood began to stir. Terrible denunciation and threats of retribution passed from quiver-
ing lip to lip. Nothing more fitting could be thought
of than that those newspapers which had encouraged
treason should be destroyed, and to this work the people lent themselves with a will. Four years of patient tolerance of too great freedom of speech was
revenged by demolishing a number of newspaper offices. It was a spontaneous expression which was not
checked until the *Democratic Press*, owned by Beriah
Brown; the *Occidental*, owned by Zachariah Montgomery; the *Monitor*, a disloyal, catholic journal,
owned by T. A. Brady; the *Franco–Americaine*, and
the *News Letter*, were destroyed. The *Echo du Pacifique*
would have received the same treatment but for the
fact of its press being in the *Alta* building, which
would have shared in the loss.[35] As soon as possible
the military were called out to assist the police in
suppressing the riot, but only a few arrests were made.
Public feeling would not condemn the demonstration,
although to prevent bloodshed it was necessary to
check the proceedings. Addresses were made by Mc-
Dowell and others, and 5,000 men were placed under
arms to patrol the streets. By the next morning quiet
was restored.

But public confidence was much shaken. It was
feared that the war would be reopened in the east,
where it was confidently expected the loyal troops
would avenge the president's death by the slaughter
of confederates. Greenback currency, the national
barometer, went down to thirty-three. Before the 20th,
however, when the obsequies of the president were to
be celebrated, the people had been brought back from

[35] Brady of the *Monitor* applied to the legislature of 1865–6 for relief, and
a bill was introduced for that purpose, but the S. F. delegation, to whom it
was referred, reported against it. *Cal. Jour. Sen.*, 1865–6. App. No. 62, iii.

their implicit reliance on one man to realize that the
government was not of men, but of laws, and that
irreparable as was their loss, the nation remained, and
the laws would be executed.   Then they paid their
last sad tribute of respect and love in a grand funeral
pageant, in which the whole city participated amid
the tolling of bells, the booming of guns, the measured beating of muffled drums, and the music of
bands playing solemn marches.   Fourteen thousand
people were said to have been in the procession which
followed the catafalque to the Mechanics' pavilion,
where the literary services were conducted.   Among
these were the reading of Lincoln's second inaugural
address, the devotional tenor of which made it peculiarly appropriate to the time and scene; Horatio
Stebbins, Starr King's successor in the Geary street
unitarian pulpit, delivered the address; Frank Soulé
read an original poem; the Bianchi opera troop rendered an anthem; but the most thrilling effect was
produced when all the thousands present sang in
chorus the Battle cry of Freedom, as it had not
been sung since that night in November when it celebrated the triumph of the nation's chief at the polls.
It was a happy augury then; it was the revival of
hope now.

As suddenly as it began the war was ended, and
with the exception of some secession outrages [36] in

[36] The growing offensiveness of secession in the pro-slavery districts was
exhibited by the rejoicings at the death of the president, and other acts.   In
Solano co., at Green valley, there were open rejoicings.   The military at
Benicia being notified, a company was sent to that place, the confederates
firing upon them, having fortified themselves in the house of one David
James.   The fire was returned, and two of them wounded, when the party
surrendered.   They were David James and two sons, William P. Durbin and
son, Charles Ramsey and son, A. O. Laramel and son, and John Stiltz.
They were brought to Benicia to be tried for treason.   They had threatened
to shoot Capt. Robinson of the volunteers for recruiting in that district.
This neighborhood contributed J. Milton Jones to the *Chapman* piratical
crew, and offered others.   In Tehachapi valley a band of guerrillas occupied
themselves, in the spring cf 1865, in robbing union men of horses and other
property, and committing occasional murders.   The military were appealed
to, but no troops could be spared for that service.   During the first week in
May 1865, the inhabitants of San Bernardino were greatly alarmed by the
rumor that in their vicinity were 300 to 700 guerrillas from the confederate

certain localities for a time, there was no occasion to
entertain further anxiety.   It was some months before
the California volunteers were released from the duty
of holding forts and guarding routes of travel.   It
has been said that California cut no figure in the war,
which assertion most assuredly was not true.   California had few men on the battle-fields where most
blood was spilt, not because they were not offered,
but because they were not wanted there.   The population of the whole Pacific coast of the United States,
including Utah and Colorado, was not equal to one
quarter of the population of the single state of Pennsylvania.   Yet to the volunteers of this sparse population was entrusted the labor of aweing avowed
secession at home, guarding against foreign interference, and fighting numerous Indian tribes from Oregon to New Mexico.   The readiness with which war
taxes were paid, the cheerful contributions to the
sanitary fund, and the loyal expressions of every
legislative body, were a moral as well as material
support, without which the war must have been indefinitely protracted, or the union dismembered.   The
attitude of California discouraged rebellion, which had
relied upon seizing the west coast of the continent
whereon to found an empire for the perpetuation of
slavery.   In common with the other Pacific states,
California poured forth like water her mineral treasure, without which the government would have been
well-nigh bankrupt, and her currency selling probably
at ten dollars to one of gold.   For these services in the
contest for freedom she should share in the glory of
having helped to preserve the integrity of the union.

army, who proposed to sack and pillage that town, and proceed thence to
Lower California.   The settlers flocked into the place, and every citizen was
under arms.   See *Los Angeles News*, May 6, 1865; *Marysville Appeal*, May 14,
1865; *Pajaro Times*, May 20, 1865; *Hayes' Scraps*, *S. Cal. Wilm.*, 56.   San
Diego was also threatened. *S. F. Alta*, May 9, 1865.   These alarms resulted
in nothing more than the loss of stock, and some personal encounters, and
terminated in a few months, when the confederates were compelled to take
the oath of loyalty

CHAPTER XIII.

PARTY CHANGES.

1865-1868.

CALIFORNIA had never more reason to regret the adoption of primary elections, than in 1865. The practice was begun by the democracy as early as March 1850, when a meeting was held at Portsmouth square for the purpose of organizing the county of San Francisco, and a county committee was appointed which a year and a half later called a primary election for December 23d, to elect delegates to the Sacramento state convention, who were to appoint others to the national convention for the nomination of president of the United States. The committee, to keep control of the organization, selected but one polling place in the city and county of San Francisco, and allowed but six hours for receiving votes. John A. McGlynn, chairman of the county committee, was appointed inspector, and his associates were Edward McGowan and T. A. Lynch. A large number of democrats protested, claiming the right of the people to set themselves in motion without any delegated authority, and published a call for the democratic electors of each ward and precinct of the city, to meet

in their respective localities on the 24th, for the purpose of appointing inspectors of election, and determining the time and place of holding primaries at
which all democrats might have an opportunity of
voting, with the object of effecting a re-organization
of the party.

Notwithstanding this movement by the majority,
the county committee held its election, at which 841
votes were polled out of 3,000 democratic electors,
and a full list of delegates declared elected. The pro-
testing democrats held their meetings on the 24th to
appoint inspectors, and held their primary elections
on the 26th, at which 2,900 votes were cast, the committee's men voting a second time. Gross frauds
were charged against the committee, but the protestants elected a majority of the delegates to the county
convention which was to choose delegates to Sacramento. When the county convention assembled, the
committee attempted to elect McGowan chairman,
pro tem., but were outvoted, and John W. Dwinelle
was chosen. In an attempt to force their choice on
the convention after the election of Dwinelle, the
committee had recourse to riotous demonstrations,
and a scene of disorder occurred most disgraceful to the
party and the city. There was a division, the protestants withdrawing, and holding their convention, while
the county committee went on with its proceedings,
both electing a list of delegates to the Sacramento
convention. When that body met, the struggle was
renewed, and continued for two days, or until the
delegates of the protestants were declared admitted
by the majority of the delegates from the other
counties.

Similar scenes were enacted on many succeeding
occasions. At state conventions the country delegations had it in their power to rebuke the rowdy democracy of San Francisco; but the city was powerless
in their grasp until the vigilance committee brought
about a reform, and the people's party, a purely local

organization, took the government of the city and county in its hands. But the primary elections still governed the city's relation to state politics, and always prevented anything like harmony between San Francisco and the state. The custom established of a few professional politicians naming candidates for all offices descended from one dominant party to another, and was not abandoned by the union party in its time of strength.

The most important question in politics in 1865 was the election of a United States senator. There were a number of candidates, but Governor Low and John B. Felton, a successful lawyer with a large income, hitherto unknown as an aspirant for office, were the leading favorites. The Low party were called Short Hairs, and the anti-Low party Long Hairs. When these two factions of the union party met in county convention at Sacramento, July 25th, exactly the same scene occurred as that which disgraced the democratic party in 1861. The short hairs finding themselves in a minority, and unable to control the convention, resorted to the exercise of muscle, and inflicted severe personal injury upon a number of their opponents, whereupon the convention divided, and the long hairs chose another place of meeting. Soon after this exhibition of the uses of primary elections, Governor Low published a card, withdrawing from the senatorial contest, and disavowing any connection with the short hairs, who had used his name without leave. This course, although commended by union men as maintaining the dignity of the executive office, gave his opponent a free course in the primaries.

The short hairs were the democrats who, now that the union was preserved, eagerly returned to the pursuit of politics as a trade. The question of loyalty, vital during the period of the war, was now caught up by a demagogue press, which aimed to procure the repeal of the specific-contract law, or by pointing out the friends of the law charge them with disloyalty for resisting the change to a paper currency, and thereby accomplish their political ends. The importance of national banks was not, however, denied by the advocates of gold currency. The act of congress apportioned to California but $3,000,000 for a circulating medium, whereas there was fully $35,000,000 in gold employed as money. The three millions could not take the place of thirty millions, but it could be used to develop the resources of the country as far as it would go, and being cheaper than gold could be used more profitably for such purposes. That proposition was not disputed, but the hard-money advocates would not consent to bankrupting the state by a sudden change of the currency. So hard pressed were they, however, by the politicians, that the people's nominating committee was overawed by it, and driven, unwisely, to adopt a resolution offensive to the better class of democrats who had hitherto voted with them, that no candidate before them could be nominated who had not voted for Lincoln and Johnson at the election in 1864.

Public meetings were held in San Francisco, and resolutions passed declaring that a public and unconditional endorsement of the specific-contract law would be required of every candidate for any legislative office. An independent call was made for a reorganization of the union party, and signed by about two thousand citizens of good standing, who named delegates to a union county convention and solicited them through the press to act as such, by this means obviating any primary election. Upon those men, selected by responsible citizens, devolved the duty of appointing a union county committee for the year; of appointing delegates to the judicial convention for that year, under the amended constitution, and of nominating candidates for the state senate and assembly. They repudiated the doings of the county committee above spoken of, and known as 'the boys,' and declared their wish that in the nomination of candidates for the legislature the convention should select men of the "highest capacity, purest integrity, and most devoted loyalty;" that they should be left unpledged and free in regard to senatorial perferences; and that in selecting delegates to the state convention, and in the choice of a county committee the same principles should be observed. But when they came to meet the boys and the long and short hairs in convention at Sacramento, the independents were not recognized, and withdrew. The moral effect of their presence was not altogether lost, and the convention performed its duties in a manner leaving nothing to complain of except the defeat of a proposition from James M. McShafter to vote on the question of primaries or no primaries at the next general election.

S. W. Sanderson was renominated for supreme judge, and elected by a majority of 6,000 over H. H. Hartley, but only such candidates of the people's union party, represented by the independents, as had great strength personally, were elected this year, and in 1867 the sceptre passed away completely,[1] since which time primaries and bosses have ruled the hour in the metropolis. Between factions and fusions the political muddle was often unintelligible. In San Francisco, in 1865, the boys, or short hairs, fused with the democrats; in Sacramento they did the same, but there was, nevertheless, a working majority of union members in the legislature,[2] which performed some good

[1] *Coon's Annals of S. F.*, MS., 27.

[2] The state senators elected in 1865 were Henry Robinson, Alameda; G. W. Seaton, Alpine and Amador; J. W. Freeman, Fresno and Tulare; P. Banning, Los Angeles; A. L. Tubbs, William J. Shaw, J. S. Hager, S. F.; P. W. Murphy, Sta Bárbara and San Luis Obispo; W. J. Knox, Sta Clara; L. E. Pratt, Sierra; E. Wadsworth, Siskiyou; L. B. Mizner, Solano and Yolo; George Pearce, Sonoma; E. Teegarden, Sutter and Yuba. S. P. Wright, a hold-over senator from Klamath, Humboldt, and Del Norte, was chosen pres't. The sec. elected was John White, ass't sec. Charles W. Gordon, clerks Martin Rowan, W. F. Heustis, Albert Hart, M. E. Gelston, E. B. Edson, Bart. Morgan; sergts-at-arms, John Moran, James Lane.

The assembly was composed of John L. Wilson, Thomas Eagan, Alameda; Miner Frink jr, Harvey Lee, Alpine and Amador; W. P. Tilden, George E. Smith, Butte; Isaac Ayres, M. M. Collier, N. G. Sawyer, Calaveras; William S. Long, Colusa and Tehama; F. A. Brown, Contra Costa, L. H. Murch,

service, among which was the passage of a registry
law for the purification of the ballot-box, and also a
law for the protection of primary elections. In view
of President Johnson's policy toward the states late
in rebellion, resolutions were passed endorsing that
policy so far as to declare that those states had no
right to resume domestic government, or send representatives to congress before they had fulfilled certain conditions in determining the terms, of which
they should have no voice, but denying the right of
the executive branch of the government to determine
those conditions. On the contrary all questions pertaining to the status of the states late in rebellion
should be left to congress; and any other course
would be dangerous to republican liberty. The second
clause of the constitutional amendment, empowering
congress to abolish slavery, would become a dead
letter with a congress composed of the late masters
of those whose freedom the amendment contemplated
to pass upon the measure. California senators were
requested to give their full support to the amendment,
to the end that the rebel states when admitted should

Del Norte and Klamath; J. S. Campbell, J. S. Kidder, E. L. Smith, Ed. F.
Taylor, El Dorado; R. P. Mace, Fresno; S. Cooper, R. J. Heustis, Humboldt;
John M. Coghlan, Lake and Napa; J. D. Goodwin, Lassen and Plumas; W.
H. Peterson, E. C. Parrish, Los Angeles; D. Olds jr, Marin; J. W. Wilcox,
Mariposa; William Holden, Mendocino; R. H. Ward, Merced and Stanislaus;
J. E. Goodall, L. I. Hogle, Otis Perrin, Mono and Tuolumne; M. G. Ireland,
Monterey; John Pattison, George D. Darrin, Reuben Leech, H. L. Hatch,
Nevada; John Yule, William Sexton, John Bosquet, Placer; Dwight Hollis-
ter, William B. Hunt, Thomas Hansbraw, J. M. Maholmb, P. J. Hopper,
Sac.; J. W. Satterwhite, San Bernardino; D. B. Kurtz, San Diego; Charles
Clayton, James Bowman, C. L. Wiggin, S. C. Bugbee, Henry Dutton, David
Dwyer, J. A. McClelland, M. A. Brayley, Michael Hawkins, George Hearst,
Samuel L. Lupton, E. J. Chase, S. F.; C. H. Chamberlain, W. E. Green,
San Joaquin; R. J. Hill, San Luis Obispo and Sta Bárbara; George M.
Howard, San Mateo; John Zuck, J. M. Corey, A. B. Hunt, Sta Clara; Wil-
liam Anthony, Sta Cruz; J. N. Chapelle, Shasta; M. A. Singleton, G. Meri-
deth, Sierra; Thomas H. Steele, J. K. Tutrell, Siskiyou; James M. Lemon,
Solano; O. H. Hoag, A. C. Bledsoe, J. L. Downing, Sonoma; Francis Hamlin,
Sutter; J. C. Dorr, Trinity; J. C. Brown, Tulare; Charles F. Reed, Yolo;
T. J. Sherwood, A. J. Batchelder, Orrin Stewart, Yuba. Yule was elected
speaker, and Wilcox speaker pro tem.; Marcus D. Boruck, John H. Roberts,
J. M. Wood, J. E. Youngberg, B. S. Marston, John Drum, E. L. Selfridge,
J. C. Breen, clerks. Benjamin Dore, Charles Roberts, sergts-at-arms; M. C.
Briggs, chaplain; J. H. Hathaway, watchman. *Cal. Jour. Sen. and Assem.*,
1865-6.

be reduced to an equality, as to representation, with the loyal states. The adoption of this amendment, and possibly others, should precede the restoration of civil power to the states late in rebellion. The Freedman's Bureau bill[3] was approved, and the president's refusal to sign it declared "totally indefensible, and an assumption of dictatorial power justly calculated to awaken the gravest apprehension in the minds of a people jealous of their liberties." In the proper sentiment and action of congress the utmost confidence was expressed.

The repeal of the specific-contract act was attempted, but failed, and that law remained upon the statute book notwithstanding that the supreme court of the neighboring state of Nevada had decided against it, and that the new secretary of the federal treasury, McCulloch, gave it as his opinion that California would have been more prosperous with paper money than with gold currency. California felt that she might please herself in the matter of her currency so long as she paid her full share of federal taxes, and bought liberally of United States bonds, quite as much out of patriotism as with an eye to business.[4] In truth, the state needed the money for its own devel-

[3] *Cal. Stat.*, 1865–6, 288–301. There was a convention of the colored population of Cal. held in Sac. in Oct. 1865. The report showed, in Colusa county, black pop. 21, churches none, schools none, valuation of property $22,300; Tehama, pop. 73, churches none, schools none, prop. $69,500; Santa Clara, pop. 175, churches 1, schools 1, prop. $75,000; Napa, pop. 48, churches none, schools 1, prop. $51,290; Mariposa, pop. 72, churches none, schools none, prop. $26,000; Merced, pop. 27, schools none, prop. $30,000; Sac., pop. 620, churches 2, schools (49 pupils) 1, prop. $141,895; S. F., pop. 1850, churches 3, schools, day and evening, 4; prop. $750,000. Total of wealth represented in the convention, not including Solano, Sta Cruz, and Contra Costa cos, $1,417,585, belonging to a population of 3,425. In some of the counties just named there were 7 schools, and, including Contra Costa, 11 churches.

[4] *Cal. Stat.*, 1865–6, 909–11. In 1864 Cal. dug out of the ground and paid to the federal govt for war customs duties $6,378,384 in gold. She also paid $3,000,000 war taxes in paper, worth $1,500,000 in gold. There was disbursed by congress for all expenses on the coast, overland mail included, $9,670,656 in legal tenders, or $4,481,000 in gold, leaving $3,497,384 net contribution of the 16-years-old state to the support of the govt, besides taking several millions of the govt loan at a much less rate of interest than the same amount would bring if invested in this state.

opment, which was retarded by the prodigality of its offerings in the cause of the whole country.

The consciousness of being regarded in a false light by congressmen and others in the older states caused the legislature by a concurrent resolution to request the president to give a seat in the cabinet to a citizen of the Pacific coast,[5] and subsequently to recommend Frederick Billings of San Francisco to the president's notice, should the request be favorably received. No appointment was made of a cabinet officer from the Pacific coast until 1871, and then not of a Californian.

Early in the session the election of a successor to McDougall in the United States senate took place without any excitement, Cornelius Cole[6] being chosen on the first ballot, W. T. Coleman being nominated with him. This was the first senatorial election in California not governed by cliques for the succession or parcelling out of offices for years to come. The acceptable record of the early part of the session was clouded later by the passage of bills taxing the state heavily for the benefit of the railroad companies, and for the increase of fares on the street railways of San Francisco. The direct tax was vetoed by Governor Low, but the indirect tax became the law. Money was freely used in the passage of these bills, and in the endeavor to induce the legislature to grant to individuals large tracts of state lands on the waterfront of San Francisco and Oakland, which, however, failed through exposures made by the press.

[5] *Cal. Stat.*, 1865–6, 899, 905. The Nevada legislature reported against petitioning for the admission of a Pacific coast man to the cabinet or other representation. *New Jour. Sen.*, 1866, 157. The first appointment of a presidential adviser from the Pacific states was George H. Williams, senator from Oregon, to be attorney-general.

[6] Cornelius Cole was born at Lodi, N. Y., in 1822, and educated at the Wesleyan university, Conn. He studied law, and was admitted to the bar, but came to Cal. in 1849, working for a year in the gold mines, after which he commenced the practice of his profession. He was district attorney of Sac. from 1859 to 1862, a member of the national republican committee from 1856 to 1860, was a representative in the 38th congress, and elected to the U. S. senate as a union republican in 1866, for a term of 6 years, from March 1867 to March 1873. *Poore, Cong. Dir.*, 40 cong. 5–6.

About this time it became apparent that the Central Pacific railroad was becoming a power in the land. There were many who declared that the directors would dictate who should be elected to the legislature, and through the legislature who should be chosen United States senator; in short, that the state was about to pass under the rule of a dangerous monopoly. But as a fact they interfered but little in politics, and then only to secure their rights or the passage of such measures as were necessary to the completion of their enterprise. It was at this time that Senator Conness appeared upon the scene, and assumed control of union primaries and conventions, with the result that the party was divided and fell.

The governor proposed by Conness was George C. Gorham,[7] a politician by no means popular in San Francisco, on account of his attitude as to the water-front question in 1859–60, and the obnoxious railroad-tax bills in 1865–6, whereby, but for the governor's veto, the state would have been forced to donate to railroad companies an amount equal to about $3,000,000, a percentage of which would have gone to his account for services rendered. After the ticket made up by the union convention, against which the independent press of the state energetically protested, was published, a second convention was held, which revised the nominations, placing on the ticket the name of John Bidwell for governor, and changing three other nominations

[7] Geo. C. Gorham was born in New London Ct. in 1833, and came to Cal. in 1849. *Vallejo Recorder*, June 29, 1867; Marysville *North Californian*, June 17, 1869. Another and perhaps better authority says he was born in Greenport, L. I., in 1832, and removed to New London in 1833. On arriving in Cal. he settled at Marysville, and became clerk in the office of the alcalde, Field, which position he held until American courts were established. In 1853 he visited the east, returning to Cal. in 1855, and was employed to edit the *Herald* at Marysville. In 1856 he was elected city clerk, and in 1859 nominated county recorder. In 1860 he edited the *S. F. Nation* for a short time, soon purchasing the Marysville *Democrat*, and in 1861 became associated with the Sac. *Union*. He was appointed supt of the state reform school in 1862, and in 1863 clerk of the U. S. circuit court. He served as private secretary to Gov. Low in 1864. In 1867 he aspired to be governor. See further San Andreas *Register*, Aug. 3, 1867; *Colusa Sun*, April 11, 1874.

to state offices.[8] These changes were made upon
principle by those union men who were formerly republicans, and who viewed with dismay the union
party, which had so clean a record, being prostituted
to place and money-getting without reference to the
welfare of state or nation by men who made noisy
pretensions to patriotic sentiments, yet whose acts be-
lied their declarations. These seceders now re-allied
themselves to the national republican party.

Bidwell, however, declined the nomination, pre-
ferring, perhaps, the quiet and profit of his estate to
the doubtful honors to be derived from being beaten
by a division in his own party. The candidate substituted for the ex-congressman was Caleb T. Fay,[9]
who accepted with a full knowledge that he would
probably be beaten. His letter of acceptance, and
speech on the occasion of his nomination were remark-

[8] These were William H. Parks, for sec. of state, changed to J. G. Mc-
Callum; Josiah Howell, controller, changed to William Jones; and D. D.
McCarthy, state printer, changed to E. G. Jeffries. McCallum was formerly
state senator from El Dorado, serving with distinction. He was also presidential elector in 1864, carrying the certified vote of the state for Lincoln to
Washington. Jones was from the same county where he settled in 1850.
He was a mechanic, had been mayor of Placerville, and was a colonel in the
2d regt Cal. vols. in the union army, having enlisted as a private. Jones
was a native of N. Y. In 1873 he was the candidate of the independents
for state senator. In 1875 he was the republican candidate for assemblyman
but was beaten by G. J. Carpenter, dem. In 1867 he was again a candidate
for the same position, but died before the election was officially decided, at
the age of 60 years. Jeffries was one of the original publishers and proprietors of the *Sacramento Union*, a good printer and a good man.

[9] Caleb T. Fay, a native of Mass., born in 1821, came to Cal. in 1849, on a
vessel which, with the cargo was owned by the Northwestern association
of Boston as the emigrants to the land of gold styled themselves. George
W. Denny, pres't of the Granite bank of Boston, was pres't of the association, and the company was composed of the sons of prominent men. The
vessel was commanded by Capt. Moore, of the U. S. navy. Fay soon drifted
into a profitable business. He ran for mayor of S. F. on the republican
ticket in 1860, and took a prominent part in forming that party. Only 1500
votes were given for the republican ticket for mayor in 1860, but in 1861 he
came within 500 votes of an election. In the autumn of the same year the
republicans elected their whole legislative ticket, and in 1862 elected Fay
mayor of S. F. as a unionist. In 1867 he was defeated for governor. In
1872 he opposed the claim of the Central Pacific R. R., to the possession of
Goat island, and was appointed a commissioner to proceed to Washington
in company with Gen. Alexander and Prof. Davidson of the coast survey, to
represent the matter to the gov't, and succeeded in defeating the claim.
This placed him in antagonism to the railroad supporters in Cal., and was a
point in the campaign of 1867. *Fay's Hist. Facts*, MS., 1–23.

able for their propriety of principle and diction, and considering the character of some of California's executives, it was to many a source of regret that a candidate so manifestly possessing the firmness and dignity required for the position should be sacrificed to circumstances so untoward as those attending this campaign. He was not unknown in politics, having served in the legislature, and as federal assessor in the 1st California district. He was spoken of for governor by the best men in the union party before the division, but was found too inflexible for the approval of the Conness-Gorham management.

The democratic candidate for governor was H. H. Haight,[10] a man who enjoyed an excellent reputation, though one long accustomed to politics and place. The contest under these conditions, with the existence of a party at stake on one hand, the success of deep-laid schemes on the other, with a third party striving to return to power, was the most bitter and exciting of the many exciting political campaigns witnessed by this politician-ridden state.[11] It ended, as might have been expected, in the triumph of the democratic third party, and the extinction of the union organization, composed originally of the best men in the commonwealth, but

[10] Henry H. Haight was born in Rochester, N. Y., in 1825. His father, Fletcher M. Haight, was judge of the U. S. Dist court, for the southern dist of Cal. The son came to Cal. in 1850, from St Louis, having graduated at Yale, studied law, and been admitted to the bar in that city. The father followed in 1854, and together they practised law in S. F.

[11] The ticket of the Conness-Gorham union party contained the following names: For congress, 1st dist, T. G. Phelps; 2d dist. William Higby; 3d dist, C. Hartson; governor, George C. Gorham; lieut-gov., J. P. Jones; sec. of state, William H. Parks: controller, Josiah Howell; supreme judge, John Currey; att'y-gen., John G. McCullough; sur.-gen., Charles F. Reed; treas., Romualdo Pacheco; harbor com'r, Charles Clayton; clerk of sup. ct., R. H. Farquahar; state printer, D. O. McCarthy; sup. of public instruc., John Swett. The revised ticket, as before stated, changed four of these candidates. The democratic ticket contained the names of the following candidates: for congress, 1st dist, S. B. Axtell; 2d dist, James W. Coffroth; 3d dist, James A. Johnson; gov., H. H. Haight; lieut-gov., William Holden; sec. of state, H. L. Nichols; controller, Robert Watt; treas., Antonio F. Caronel; sur.-gen., John W. Bost; att'y-gen., Joseph Homilton; harbor com'r, James H. Cutter; clerk of sup. ct, George Seckel; state printer, D. W. Gelwicks; sup't pub. instruc., O. P. Fitzgerald; judge of sup. ct, Royal L. Sprague.

now being used to promote the personal aims of
aspiring politicians.[12]   " In some respects," said the
Sacramento *Union*, "it is the strangest chapter in
the strange political history of California."

The union party for four years had been guided
and directed by pure men and patriots, but with the
coming of peace the old hungry brood of place-hun-
ters, basing their claims to public favor on the actions
of better men, now paraded their spurious patriotism,
and demanded their reward, while the more modest
real benefactors of their country were artfully retired
from observation by the tricks of primaries and conventions.   The tricksters had forced many of the
best men out of the union party.   The seceders had
exposed their methods, the small vote drawn by the
republicans only adding to the democratic majority of
9,546 for Haight, and a proportionate majority for

---

[12] Said Gorham: 'And now in relation to the bill to grant aid to the
Western Pacific Railroad company. . . I knew some of the parties interested, and holding no public office, and being under no obligation whatever
to represent the state's side of the question, I, as a private citizen, did just
as I had a right to do, namely: I seconded the application of the company
for aid. Was it immoral for them to ask for a bounty at the hands of the
government? Was it immoral in me to join in this request? Ought the
company to have opposed the bill? Ought I, as a friend, to have opposed
it? We did not say the state owed anything to the company. We said:
"Give, if you please." Was there anything dishonest in this? It so happened that I did not own any interest in the Western Pacific railroad, or in
the contract to build it. . . . It would have been in perfect accordance
with good morals, I suppose, for me to have owned an interest. Well, the
bill passed, and was vetoed. Since that time the W. P. R. R. co., have
sold out to the Central Pacific company.' *Letter to D. M. Kelsey,* in *Sac. Union,*
Aug. 1, 1867. In 1863 a bill passed the legislature authorizing San Francisco
to subscribe $400,000 in aid of the Western Pacific. The subsidy was voted
for, but the supervisors refused their consent. The matter was compromised
by a grant of $200,000 in bonds. As to Conness, the *S. F. Flag* newspaper
had this elegant charge: 'If a popular citizen is suggested as a suitable
person for a certain office, he cannot be nominated without having been first
chalked out on Conness' slate; he must express his readiness to pack sand
and eat dirt for the Great Senatorial Manipulator. If we require a member
of the legislature, he must be a friend of our 'only sober senator.' If we
want a sheriff, the Great Western Prestidigitateur pours him out of a magic
bottle. If we desire a justice of the peace, the Great First Cause creates
one directly. If we would have a head schoolmaster, that eminent scholar
sets his traps and catches one. If a special policeman be required, Senator
Conness springs his rattle and presto! we have one of his friends.'

the whole democratic ticket,[13] except in the case of Higby reëlected to congress.[14]

It was with unfeigned sorrow that the founders of the union party beheld it in extremes ; not because their political hopes went down with it, but because it represented the most unselfish, patriotic, and pure-minded political organization which the state had ever known. For a short time they flattered themselves that at the judicial election in October their candidates might be elected, but such was not the result, and the conviction was settled that the "dear old party" was dead. The first impulse was to lay all the blame at the door of the self-constituted party managers; but unscrupulous as they had shown themselves, this was not all the cause. There were no longer any but local issues except the one of the quarrel between congress and the president, and the democrats sympathized with the latter. To strengthen their party they had taken up the cause of the workingmen, who were clamoring for an eight hour law. This forced the unionists to adopt this plank in their platform also. But as the majority of workingmen belonged primarily to the democratic party, this was little to the advantage of the opposing party. As to other issues, they were chiefly those which affected San Francisco, in which the voters in distant counties felt little interest. Thus the politics of the state were settling back into their ante-rebellion footing.

The legislature of 1867–8 consisted of seventy democrats and ten republicans.[15] It selected Eugene

[13] Haight's majority over Gorham was 8,546; Fay's vote was only 2,088.

[14] The congressmen serving from 1865 to 1867 were John Bidwell, William Higby, and Donald C. McRuer. Higby was born in Essex co., N. Y., in 1813, educated at the university of Burlington, Vt, and read law for a profession, practising in his native co. until 1850, when he came to Cal., settled himself in Calaveras co., and was elected dist att'y in 1853; holding his office until 1859. In 1861 he was a Douglas democrat, and aided in forming the union party in 1862, which elected him to the state senate. In 1863 he was chosen member of congress from the state at large; in 1864 he was reëlected, and for the third time in 1867, participating in the action of congress through the most interesting period of its history.

[15] The senators elect were E. L. Brady, Placer; Horace Beach, Yuba and

Casserly,[16] an Irish lawyer of prominence, to succeed
Conness, Thomas A. Brown of Contra Costa being
the next most popular candidate. Casserly, like
Haight, was a man of pure private character, and also
of varied talents and accomplishments, superior to Conness as a man, but inferior to him as a manager of party

Sutter; William A. Conn, San Diego and San Bernardino; N. Greene Curtis,
Sac.; John Conly, Butte, Plumas, and Lassen; J. N. Chapelle, Shasta and
Trinity; Janson J. Green, Contra Costa and Marin; George W. Hunter, El
Dorado; H. Kincaid, S. F. and San Mateo; James Lawrence, Mariposa,
Merced, and Stanislaus; E. J. Lewis, Colusa and Tehama; F. A. McDougall,
Monterey and Santa Cruz; J. W. Mandeville, Inyo, Mono, and Tuolumne;
D. L. Morrill, Calaveras; L. H. Murch, Del Norte, Humboldt, and Klamath;
J. E. Perley, San Joaquin; William Pendergast, Lake, Napa, and Mendo-
cino; E. W. Roberts, Nevada; A. H. Rose, Amador and Alpine; John H.
Saunders, S. F.; Charles Tweed, Placer. Republican majority of two.
Officers of the senate: L. Mizner (hold-over), president; John White, sec.;
Wilbur F. Heustis, asst sec.. C. E. Barnes, John E. Dent, W. H. Frink, W.
L. Hawkins, A. W. Perley, B. S. Marston, George W. Dixon, clerks; F. S.
Tarduer, T. Mahoney, sergts-at-arms.
    The assembly was composed of W. C. Agney, C. T. Ryland, John H.
Moore, Sta Clara; Thomas J. Ables, Marin; Isaac Ayer, L. S. Beaver, Otto
Mentzell, Calaveras; Thomas A. Brown, Contra Costa; E. B. Bird, Charles
Gildea, Hugh Newell, Stephen Willetts, El Dorado; J. R. Buckbee, Plumas
and Lassen; Marion Biggs, Paschal Coggins, A. Comte jr, Bruce Lee, Charles
Walleb, Sac.; T. S. Battelle, J. W. Downer, Sierra; B. J. Broderson, Mat-
thew Canavan, David W. Connely, Thomas E. Farrish, Samuel Lupton,
John Middleton, Frank Mahone, J. J. O'Malley, Jasper S. Papy, A. G.Russ,
Frank Scudder, Thomas Wand, S. F.; J. C. Brown, Tulare and Kern; A. J.
Batchelder, L. B. Clark, J. K. Smith, Yuba; A. M. Church, John W. Dwin-
elle, Alameda; John C. Crigler, Napa and Lake; R. M. Cochrane, W. M.
Ord, Butte; William H. Cureton, Mendocino; William Caldwell, S. M. Mar-
tin, J. B. Warfield, Sonoma; J. M. Days, G. D. Dornin, H. G. Rollins, John
D. White, Nevada; Perry Dyer, Sierra; W. A. Davies, M. Meagher, B. A.
Mardis, Tuolumne, Mono, and Inyo; Asa Ellis, A. J. Watson, Los Angeles;
John B. Frisbie, Solano; J. A. Fairchild, Elijah Steele, Siskiyou; J. B.
Gregory, George Payne, Amador and Alpine; W. S. Green, Colusa and Te-
hama; Francis Giltner, Mariposa; Benjamin Hayes, San Diego; John M.
James, San Bernardino; T. E. Jones, Trinity; John M. Kelly, Yolo; R. P.
Mace, Fresno; L. J. Morrow, Warner Oliver, San Joaquin; R. L. Mattingly,
San Mateo; W. T. McElhany, Sta Bárbara and San Luis Obispo; J. W.
Newsom, Merced and Stanislaus; George Pardee, Sta Cruz; Thomas H. Rec-
tor, Klamath and Del Norte; C. G. Spencer, C. A. Tuttle, M. Waldron,
Placer; B. R. Spillman, Sutter, E. C. Tully, Monterey; Charles Westmoreland, Humboldt. Democratic majority 22. Officers of assembly, C. T. Ryland, speaker; J. J. O'Malley, speaker pro tem.; John A. Eagan, Newton
Benedict, D. F. Beveridge, R. M. Clarkian, H. G. Siebert, W. S. Croper, J.
de la Guerra, clerks; John K. Luttrell, William H. Peterson, sergts-at-arms;
T. H. B. Anderson, chaplain.
    [16] Eugene Casserly was born at Mulligar, county Westmeath, Ireland, in
1822, his family being a branch of the O'Conners. His father was a man of
culture, and on arriving in New York was engaged as a teacher of the
classics. The talents and superior training of Eugene recommended him to
the attention of prominent men, especially as editor of a democratic newspaper, the *Freeman's Journal.* He abandoned editorial life for the study of

politics, if, indeed, he were not above the business. A republican senate and democratic assembly holding each other in check, fewer obnoxious bills were enacted into laws than usually happened. The Central Pacific railway company made an effort at this session to obtain a gift from the state of a large portion of the tide-lands at San Francisco, with the result of securing a conditional grant of one hundred and fifty acres; the condition being that the land should be used solely for the purposes of a terminus, or otherwise revert to the state. The company could not demand or receive any wharfage or other revenues from the possession of this land.

During the presidential canvass of 1868 the usual excitement occurred. The republican party, which in California still loved to call itself the union party,[17] met in convention at Sacramento on the 1st of April to choose delegates to the national convention at Chicago, Frank M. Pixley being chosen president.[18] Ten delegates were selected, two from each congressional

the law, which he pursued in the office of John Bigelow, afterwards U. S. minister to France. In 1844 he was admitted to the bar, and in 1850 came to Cal., bringing with him the materials of a printing office, and starting, in connection with Benjamin R. Buckalew, the publication of a daily paper, the *Public Balance*, from which the latter withdrew in a few months, when the name of the paper was changed to *True Balance*, and subsequently to the *Standard*. He was elected state printer by the first legislature; but the fire of 1851 swept away all his office material. His library, however, was saved, and he returned to the practice of law, and united himself to the democratic party. During the civil war he was a unionist, but when it was over rejoined his former party.

[17] The call for a state convention was issued as a call for a 'union state convention.' *Sac. Union*, March 27, 1868.

[18] Frank M. Pixley was born in Oneida co., N. Y., in 1825, of a race of farmers of English descent. He received an academic education, after which he studied law, and moved to Mich.; but being of an adventurous disposition, set out for Cal. in 1848, wintering in Mo., arriving in the mines in 1849, and settling himself in S. F. in 1851. He was elected city attorney; in 1858 became a republican, and was elected to the assembly, where he fought the Parsons bulkhead bill successfully. In 1861 he was elected atty-gen. Subsequently he was active in politics, and although defeated in 1868 for congress was widely known for his political opinions uttered from the platform, and with much vigor in the editorial columns of the *Argonaut*, to which his writings gave a strong individuality. He has had many enemies, and has been often assailed; but his disposition is both generous and pugnacious, and in order to be himself he was usually to be found on the weak or unpopular side of any question.

district, and four from the state at large.[19] They
were instructed to vote for Grant for president, and,
as might seem best, for either Wade or Colfax for
vice-president.   The meeting adjourned after choosing
a state central committee

The democratic state convention met in San Francisco April 29th, lieutenant-governor Holden presiding, and elected to the national convention to be held
in New York one delegate at large, and three from
each congressional district.[20]   Presidential electors
were also chosen, although the presidential nominations were yet to be made, every elector being an
anti-war democrat.   Upon many propositions the democracy were purer and sounder than other parties
which had more recently been corrupted by power.
Their ideas were certainly sound when they resolved
"that it is not only the patriotic duty but the deliberate purpose of the democratic party never to submit
to be governed by negroes, nor by those claiming to
be elected by negro suffrage ; and we do earnestly
recommend the adoption of this resolution by the national convention of the democratic party which shall
assemble in July next."   Now, if in this resolution
the low Irish could have been included, the political
millennium, indeed, were at hand.   But the party depended upon this element for its strength.

The Chicago convention met in May, nominating

[19] The delegates at large were P. E. Conner, James Casy, John Stratman,
and James Green.   Alternates, Joseph Benrimo, John C. Byers, B. N. Bugbee, and John O'Brien.   The district delegates were William E. Lovett and
Williams H. Sears, 1st dist; J. M. Days and Charles Higby, 2d dist; Thomas
Spencer and J. S. Rogers, 3d dist.   Alternates, C. E. Allen and Benj. Dore,
1st dist; Henry G. Rollins and Abijah Baker, 2d dist; C. F. Reed and T. G.
French, 3d dist.

[20] Thomas Hayes was elected delegate at large, with two alternates.
The district delegates were: A. Jacoby, James Roberts and R. C. Page, 1st
dist; Richard Heath, H. Rose and John Bigler, 2d dist; S. C. Fairfax,
Thomas H. Steele and Woodward, 3d dist.   Alternates: John Buckhalter,
B. T. Myers and J. M. Martin for the three districts in the order named.
The presidential electors chosen by the democratic convention were E. J.
Kewen and T. J. Henry, for the state; W. T. Wallace, A. B. Dibble and
George Pearse, for the 1st, 2d and 3d dists.   The alternates being Francisco
Pico and John R. Kittrell for the state; and John Buckhalter, B. F. Myers
and J. M. Martin for the 1st, 2d, and 3d dist.

Grant and Colfax.   The New York convention met
in July, nominating Seymour and Blair.   In August
California republicans nominated Pixley for congressman from the 1st district, Sargent from the 2d district,
and Hartson from the 3d district, and chose their
presidential electors.[21]   The democrats chose for congressmen S. B. Axtell, James W. Coffroth, and James
A. Johnson,[22] in the order named.   The election was
close, both parties exhausting argument and resources.
The republicans recovered from the democrats ground
enough to give the state to Grant by a majority of
506 out of a total vote of 108,000, and to elect one
congressman, Sargent;[23] Axtell and Johnson being
elected in the 1st and 3d districts.

The election of Grant to the presidency of the
union established the republican party upon a sure
footing, and made it the great party for good and evil
of the age.   For twenty years it remained in power,
and during that time California steadily cast her vote
for a republican president, whatever victories the democracy accomplished in state politics.   It will be remembered that the union-republican majority of 1864

[21] The republican electors were Hoffman of San Diego, Redington of Sac.,
and Westmoreland of Humboldt for the three cong. dists, and for the two
sen. dists J. B. Felton, S. F., and La Grange, Alameda.   Alternates, senatorial, G. W. Tyler and Walter Van Dyke; congressional, Lewis Schloss, S.
F., C. A. Tweed, Placer, James H. McNabb, Sonoma.

[22] Samuel B. Axtell was born in Ohio in 1819, educated at Western Reserve college, and studied law.   James A. Johnson was a native of Spartan-
burg, S. C., born in 1829, received a common school education, and studied
law and medicine.   In 1859–60 he was a member of the legislature of Cal.
Poore's Cong. Dir., 1868, 6.

[23] Sargent, who was a printer, had at one time been compelled to walk
the streets of Phil., being unable to find employment and having no money.
He was born in Newburyport, Mass., in 1827, and came to Cal. in 1849,
locating himself in Nevada co., and engaging in mining.   He also conducted
a whig newspaper.   In 1854 he was admitted to practise law, and the following year was chosen dist atty.   He took an active part in the formation of
the republican party, but was defeated in 1857 for atty-gen'l.   In 1861 he
presided over the republican state convention, and was first elected to congress; in 1863 he was a member of the republican state central committee.
In 1872 he was chosen U. S. senator.   As a politician he became powerful as
master of a 'ring,' and placing or displacing men according to the will of a
syndicate.   He was appointed minister to Germany in 1882.   See *Grass Valley
Union*, May 23, 1874; Waite, in *Bowman's Newspaper Matter*, 51; *Solano Press*,
in *Downieville Mountain Messenger*, May 13, 1865; *Watsonville Pajaro Times*,
May 13, 1865; *S. F. Chronicle*, March 14, 1882, and Nov. 16, 1884.

was over 18,000. In four years it had dwindled to
500; but national politics had less to do with this remarkable change than local issues, of which I shall
speak presently. The election of 1872 was somewhat
remarkable, inasmuch as Greeley, a republican, was endorsed by a democratic nominating convention for
certain favors shown toward distinguished confederates,[24] but the democratic party as a whole rejected
him, failing to vote, and the republican majority was
13,302, notwithstanding that even more republicans
than democrats neglected to go to the polls. In 1872
the trial of strength was legitimate, and the republican majority had fallen to 2,900. The party was
divided on railway and corporation issues soon afterward, the democrats electing their state ticket, but in
1876 it gave a majority for Hayes. In 1879 it
was again divided on local issues, but elected the
governor by a plurality, but by a vote of 23,849 less
than a majority over all. In the very next year, however, the party recovered all but about 200 of the
majority against it in the election of Garfield, and
succeeded in electing half the congressmen, and a
majority of the assemblymen, which gave them the
United States senator, thus grasping the substance of
a republican victory while their opponents secured
the shadow. In 1884 the party had so far recovered
itself as to achieve a majority of nearly 8,000. The
fluctuations during non-presidential years, returning
when a national election takes place to the supremacy,
shows how the state has been swayed by municipal
agitations, while the true sentiment of the American-
born population, at least, was republican.

The local causes which led to so much variation in
the political atmosphere may be named under the
general heads of taxation, corporate monopolies, Chi-

[24] The Bailing of Jefferson Davis, an article in the *Century* magazine for
Feb. 1887, explains Greeley's action in this matter; but it was, after all, a
mistake excelled only by the greater one of running for the presidency.

nese. Imigration, and labor demands. The extravagant habits which the early mining period engendered in California private and public life remained after the period had passed in which they originated, and more in public than in private. The state debt had been allowed to go on increasing, while legislatures expended upon themselves and a numerous retinue of attachés the money wrung from the people, or voted it in appropriations, either wisely or unwisely, creating additional burdens. The complaints of the people caused the legislators to attempt pacification by pretending to shift the burden of tax from borrower to lender by exempting $1,000 worth of property of widows and orphans from taxation; exempting the land claims of new settlers for one year; and remitting the tax upon growing crops, vines, and mining claims, all of which was in violation of the constitution, which declared that taxation should be equal and uniform.

In 1866 property to the amount of $80,000,000 was thus exempted from taxation, and yet there was a cry of hard times. The savings banks contained more deposits per inhabitant than any state or country on the globe; but the prosperity was more apparent than real; for, whereas in other states the owners of a bank account were of the class who had some sort of permanent homes enabling them to keep and increase their capital, in California the money was often withdrawn to meet painful emergencies arising from the unsettled condition of society and the greater expense of living, with the decrease in gold-production.

As early as 1865, owing partly to the influx of unemployed persons after the war, there began a movement among the laboring classes looking to the improvement of their condition. Among the demands of laborers was the reduction of their hours of employment without any corresponding reduction of pay, and toward this purpose numerous trades-unions were formed. To this demand was soon added that

of increased wages.   As soon as trades-unions were
organized political parties began to seek the votes of
these organizations, and the eight-hour law was a
sop thrown out by a democratic legislature to secure
the adhesion of the unions.   These same legislators,
however, in making contracts for public works, required ten hours labor to be performed daily.[25]

[25] Caius T. Ryland, the speaker [of the assembly in 1867-8, was born
June 30, 1826, in Howard co., Missouri, working on a farm during the summer, and attended school during the winter.   In 1849 he started across the
plains for Cal., finally settling at San José, where he began the practice of
law, having previously been admitted to the bar in Missouri.   He was appointed clerk of the court of first instance in S. F., which office he afterward
resigned, going back to San José.   When the first legislature met he was
appointed private secretary to Gov. Burnett, and in 1854 was elected to the
legislature from Santa Clara co., where he was the author of the first appropriation bill passed in the state for a wagon-road over the Sierra Nevada into
El Dorado co.   Mr Ryland's health giving way in 1869, he gave up his law
practice, and engaged in banking.   He married Letitia M. Burnett, a daughter of Gov. Burnett, one of the pioneers of 1843.

CHAPTER XIV.

CHINESE, THE LABOR AGITATION, AND POLITICS.

1868–1877.

Coming of the Mongolians—Not Welcome in California—Attitude of the Miners—Disgusting and Altogether Damnable—Long but Powerless Legislation Against Them—Treaties and Commissions—Our Masters of the Hod and Shovel—Kearneyism—Monopolists Denounced—Sand-lot Speeches—Riots and Arrests—Safety Committee—Labor Organizations—The Workingmen's Party becomes a Power—Decline of Communism—More Elections, Legislatures, and Representatives.

Ship-loads of paper and printer's ink had been spoiled, and breath enough wasted to sail those ships in reiterating the proposition of aliens of other lands congregated in California that "the Chinese must go," although according to some authorities the western shore of the continent was theirs by right of discovery.[1] They were frequent visitors to and residents of Mexico,[2] and were employed at ship-building or other labor in Lower California within historic times, from 1571 to 1746, and even in Los Angeles, Alta California, in 1781.

See *Vol. III.*, *Native Races*, chap. ix.. this series.

[2] Chevalier fancied he saw about Acapulco the evidences of many intermixtures. In the *Historie Chretienne de la California* mention is made of a Chinois ship-carpenter. Villa-Señor y Sanchez in his *Theatro Americano*, 1746, relates that the Chinese were numerous in and around Acapulco. The Japanese in 1681 were ordered out of Mexico, and were forbidden to carry away more than 2,000 ducats each, from which it appears they were successful tradesmen. The Chinese themselves assert in their year-book, that certain Buddhist priests crossed into Alaska, explored the coast to Mexico, and penetrated to the Aztec empire, 1,000 years before Cortés. President Porter, of Yale college, places the number of Chinese arrivals in the U. S. between 1820 and 1840 at 11, and between 1840 and 1850 at 35. This refers to immigrants to eastern ports. For facts and opinions concerning the Chinese I have consulted some hundreds of volumes and thousands of newspapers, as well as the official report ordered by the state senate at a recent period.

The first immigrants from China to modern California were two Chinese men and one woman, who arrived by the clipper bark *Eagle* in 1848. The men went to the mines, and the woman remained as a servant in the family of Charles V. Gillespie, who came hither from Hong Kong. In February, 1849, the number of Chinese men in California had increased to 54 ; and in January, 1850, to 787 men and 2 women. A year later there were 4,018 men and 7 women ; and in January, 1852, 7,512 men and 8 women. By May they had increased to 11,787, of whom only 7 were women. Like other immigrants some died and some returned, the whole number of both amounting to 476. By August, 1852, there were not less than 18,026 men and 14 women added to the Chinese population of California, brought chiefly from Hong Kong in British ships. Statistics show that at the time the labor troubles commenced in California, or about the year 1876, there were 116,000 Chinese in California, and probably 151,000 in the United States, the most of whom were on the Pacific coast. Of the entire number 6,000 may have been women.

These people were truly, in every sense, aliens. The color of their skins, the repulsiveness of their features, their under-size of figure, their incomprehensible language, strange customs, and heathen religion,—containing though it might the base of all true godliness, the virtues of the Christian decalogue, —conspired to set them apart had they not themselves exhibited a disposition to hold aloof from the white race. Their camps were always removed to a comfortable distance from the camps of the white miners, as much from choice as from recognition of the unfriendliness visible in the looks and acts of their American or European neighbors.

This unfriendliness was manifested by injustice, by insolence, and by oppression. The placers the white miners had abandoned were usually occupied by Chi-

nese who were content with five or eight dollars a
day, while a white man wanted sixteen or twenty.
When such returns failed, the Mongolians were often
assailed by other miners with no better rights, and
driven away from the diggings heretofore despised by
these men, who complained to the legislature, which
at every session endeavored to make the laws so oppressive to the detested race that they should cease
to immigrate.[3]

It was proposed in 1852 to hold Chinamen as ap-
prentices; and in 1853 a senate resolution asked the
president to appoint a commissioner to China in the
person of Edmund Randolph who should negotiate
with the emperor on this subject. This artifice to introduce the coolie system in place of slavery failed,
as I have noticed in an earlier volume. In 1854 a
resolution was passed urging congress to authorize
the California legislature to impose. a capital tax on
the Chinese and Japanese, to be paid before landing
by the vessel bringing them. It was enacted by the
legislature of 1855 that masters, owners, or consignees of vessels bringing to this coast any persons
incompetent to become citizens under our laws should
pay a fine of $50 for every such person landed, and
commissioners of immigration were appointed to enforce this statute; but a suit being brought under it,
the court declared the act unconstitutional. The foreign miners' license was raised this year to $6 a month,
from October, 1855, to October, 1856, and an act
passed increasing the tax to $8 per month for 1857,
$10 for 1858, and so on, each successive year.

[3] The legislature of 1850 enacted a law against all foreigners—Mexicans
and Indians not included—which required a license to be taken out at $20
per month. This tax, together with the uncertainties of mining was equivalent to a prohibition, and the law became to a considerable extent inopera-
tive, and was repealed in 1851. In 1852 the cost of a foreign miner's license
was fixed at $3 a month, but the act was repealed in 1853, when it was raised
to $4. An appropriation of $600 was made for translating the law into Chinese and and printing 4,000 copies. In 1855 the law excluding from the
courts negro and Indian evidence, was amended to include Chinese, and obstructions were thrown in the way of procuring bondsmen, so as to make it
difficult for Asiatics charged with crime to procure bail.

Driven from good to poor or exhausted diggings, even with their frugal habits the Chinese found it difficult to pay these sums, more in the nature of a fine than a tax, and the collectors were unable to extort from them the amount exacted by the law, the effect of which was to impoverish them, while the revenue of the state was not increased ; for rather than submit to the extortion, first of the Chinese companies[4] which brought them out, and then of the government of California, a considerable number returned to China in October of this year.

Already the cry was raised against them that their presence in the country tended to injure the interests of the working classes and degrade labor.   It was argued that no good could come from allowing an inferior race, not in a state of bondage yet not citizens, to compete in the labor markets.   They simply, by their numbers and by taking less wages than white men, deprived the latter of the money they should have earned, and instead of investing it in the state carried it to China.   In a word, they were human leeches, sucking the life-blood of the country.   The only voices raised in their defence came from the universal philanthropist, often the world's greatest blunderer, the merchant who had something to sell that Chinamen would buy, and, of course, the employer of cheap labor.

To drive them from the mines deprived the state of the revenue derived from their licenses, amounting, even at $4, to about $200,000 monthly.   Again, to forbid mining would force them in great numbers into the towns and agricultural districts, to steal or to starve, for it would be impossible to return them

<hr />

[4] *Cal. Stat*, 1855, 216–17; *Nevada Journal*, Oct. 26, 1855. The Chinese six companies which imported laborers under contract for passage money, and a certain percentage of earnings, were known severally as the Ning Yung, 75,000; Hop Wo, 34,000; Kong Chow, 15,000; Yung Wo, 12,000; Sam Yup, 11,000; Tan Wo, 4,300. The figures here represent the number of coolies belonging to the several companies in 1876. It is easy to see how profitable must have been their business.

en masse to China, as had been proposed, or to convey
them in less than 200 vessels, each carrying 250 passengers, or five vessels a month for four years. The
marine to perform this service not being at hand, the
proposition to return them to China was untenable.

It became necessary then to consider the Chinese
question from some point of view having a wider
range than that belonging to the mere ground of race
prejudice Of white labor there was not enough in
California to develop its resources as was desirable, or
furnish house servants or factory operatives. Neither
could improvements be carried on to any extent with
wages at the standard demanded by white labor. The
monuments of civilization were in no land raised except by cheap labor. But California had not reached
the monumental period of development. Her workmen had first to dig ditches, build roads, sow grain,
plant vines and orchards, and erect manufactories.
To turn the wheels of progress the Chinaman, quickly
perceptive and willingly industrious, might be used
to advantage. Thus the political economists.

The opposition to Chinese immigration was in the
first place almost purely southern, and arose from the
antagonism of men accustomed to regard themselves
as masters toward races to which there attached any
suspicion of servitude. To work at all was a sad
coming down for them, but to work beside a pig-tail,
whom even a wild Indian despised, was abasement
intolerable.[5]

Next to a man who has been a master, one who
has been a servant is the most exacting and super-
cilious. Thus it happened that as the mines attracted
to the state other foreigners of low extraction, the
Chinese became subject to the hatred of another class
of white men, who without being in any sense Amer-

[5] The legislature in 1858 enacted a law forbidding Chinamen to land upon
this coast, except driven by stress of weather; and any captain landing such
should pay a fine of from $400 to $600. or be imprisoned not exceeding one
year; said law to be made known in China and California. *Cal. Stat.*, 1858,
295-6.

ican in spirit, were admitted to citizenship and enjoyed political privileges with native-born electors. They, from the novelty of their position as 'sovereigns,' were unduly anxious to exercise their prerogatives, and sought to influence legislatures by certain noisy demonstrations, which, meaning votes, had a certain weight with politicians, enough, at all events, to procure local legislation [6] inimical to the Chinese, and frequent appeals to congress to remove this abomination from the land.

For that many of the habits and practices of this people were abominable could not be denied. They were as far from observing the maxims of Confucius as nominal Christians are from imitating Christ. With that air of perfect docility which comes from centuries of enforced subserviency, they won the confidence of employers whom they, in some unguarded moment, treacherously murdered for gain. Chinese murders, however, were not more frequent than European murders, not so frequent as Mexican or native Californian murders, and they were no more abhorrent, though frequently accompanied by a breach of trust, coolly planned and brutally executed. Their opium dens were scenes of disgust and horror. While apparently not much given to concupiscence, they had no regard for chastity, and subjected their women to a revolting slavery for the profit to be derived from prostitution. But then did not our own people do these things, the difference being that the Chinamen used less disguise?

Ineffectual laws were enacted against this vice, and against Chinese gambling games, as also to correct

---

[6] In 1862 a law was enacted which provided for taxing Mongolians over 18 years of age—except those who paid a monthly miner's tax—$2.50 as a monthly capitation tax, to be known as the Chinese police tax. But the sup. ct declared the law unconstitutional. In 1863 the sup. ct sustained the law excluding Chinese witnesses in suits where white persons were parties. They were also excluded from the public schools, together with negroes and Indians, but separate schools might be provided for either. In 1866 this law was so modified that they might be admitted to schools where no objection was made by the parents of white children.

the uncleanliness of the Chinese quarter; for the
Mongolian, while he might wear immaculately white
clothing, and have every appearance of personal neat-
ness, had no prejudices against sleeping, sardine-like,
as many as could be crowded into the space,[7] or to
living surrounded by filth that smelt to heaven. To
matters like these the attention of congress was every
now and then directed by the legislators of California,
but without result.

In 1867 emigration schemes were organized by
means of which Chinese coolies were to be supplied
by the six companies to work on sugar and cotton
plantations in the gulf states ; but the contractors
failed to pay, and the Mongolians retired from the
engagement. In 1870 the legislature was again moved
to impose a penalty of not less than $1,000 nor more
than $5,000, or imprisonment, upon any one bringing
to these shores any subject of China or Japan without first presenting evidence of his or her good character to the commissioner of immigration, but the
supreme court decided against its constitutionality.
The same year the municipality of San Francisco
passed an ordinance forbidding the employment of
Chinese on public works of any kind; and in 1876,
in an act to create an irrigation district in the counties
of Alameda, Contra Costa, San Joaquin, Stanislaus,
Merced, Fresno, and Tulare, it was forbidden to employ Chinese labor in the construction of any canal or
ditch provided for in the act. In 1878 a law was enacted forbidding aliens debarred from citizenship to
acquire title to real estate ; and another withholding
business licenses from the same class. Laws of this
description served to pacify the other alien element,
and gave the courts some labor in setting aside afterward. The supervisors of San Francisco even ex-

[7] The legislatnre in 1876 made it a misdemeanor, punishable by a fine of
from $10 to $50, for any person to let or occupy any apartment within the
limits of an incorporated city, which contained less than 500 feet of space
in the clear to each person. This law was sustained by the sup. ct.

cluded Chinese granite from use in the public works; and passed an ordinance which required that the hair of any convicted male prisoner should be cut within one inch of the head in order to sacrifice the queues of the Chinese convicts—a greater indignity than if their ears had been cut off. This was celebrated under the name of the Pig Tail Ordinance, and was vetoed by the mayor as barbarous and malicious. In 1876 the supervisors required a license of $2 per quarter from a laundry using a one-horse vehicle, and $4 per quarter for a two-horse vehicle; but charged laundries using no horses—meaning those of the Chinese—$15 per quarter. The courts again interfered to prevent this injustice.

In the meantime the Chinese, protected by the better sentiment of the intelligent and right-minded, and the decrees of the supreme court, held their ground, and were constantly employed. Gardening, farming, viticulture, horticulture, laundrying, cooking, and general housework were monopolized by them to a great extent. Railroad companies employed them to build their roads; and they worked in mines, in lumber districts, and in the great fisheries. They came at last to engage in some manufactures, such as shoemaking, cigarmaking, and a few other trades, but remaining in every sense aliens. In 1865 a steamship line to China, carrying the mails monthly between San Francisco and Chinese ports, was authorized by congress, and established in 1867, thus recognizing the importance of the trade with China and Japan.[8]

Anson Burlingame, the American minister to China from 1861 to 1867, being taken into the confidence and friendship of the regent of the empire, Prince Kung, was authorized by that potentate to frame

[8] Gwin as early as 1851 advocated a China mail, and prided himself on being the projector of the enterprise; but the scheme was advocated in congress by Benton in the 40's, and outlined even earlier by Jefferson. They, however, started their line from the Columbia river.

treaties of amity with European nations as the representative of China, and also to amend the existing treaty with the United States.[9] From this amended treaty sprang the strong hostility to the Chinese which marked the laws and ordinances above referred to; for the clauses added by Burlingame agreed to the mutual protection of the citizens of China or the United States on each others' soil; to freedom in religious opinions and exercises; to the right to reside in either country at will, with all the privileges accorded to the most favored nations, with the right to enact penal laws for the prevention of involuntary immigration, to establish an international system of currency and commerce; and to enjoy the privilege of admission to the public schools of the United States, or the establishment of American schools in China.

Against this liberal and intrinsically just policy, the anti-Chinese party in California protested; and as the years passed, rebelled more and more strenuously, the outcry being increased by the obscurity of the naturalization laws, the act of 1804 confining the privilege to free white persons, and the law of 1870 extending it to persons of African nativity and descent. The Revised Statutes of 1873 dropped the words, "being free white persons," by clerical error as it was alleged, and a few Asiatics took advantage of the wording to become naturalized. This advance upon the privileges of white and black men roused renewed hostility, public sentiment generally being against incorporating into our civilization these alien pagans, and in 1875 Mongolians were excluded from naturalization rights. The importation of Chinese women for illicit purposes was made punishable by a

[9] A treaty was negotiated with China in 1844 by Minister Cushing, which was modified in 1850, by Minister Reed in 1858, and further modified by Burlingame in 1868. The U. S. law of 1862 prohibited the importation of coolies, and the treaty also. In 1870 congress declared that no tax should be imposed by any state upon persons immigrating thereto, which was not enforced upon every other immigrant to such state from any other foreign country. Thus California was properly held in check by the general gov't.

penalty of $5,000 and five years' imprisonment, by act of congress ; but the law was declared unconstitutional, and the only bar to this species of immigration was a fine of $2,000, and one year's imprisonment for bringing to the country any person compulsorily. The importation of laborers under contract, was also made subject to a penalty of $500, and a year in prison for each person so brought to the country.[10]

But none of this legislation was likely to eradicate the evils of which the workingmen of California complained, the greatest of which was that China was absorbing the industries of California as fast as its busy population became inducted into our methods, to the exclusion of the white workmen. This exclusion was of two kinds: voluntary, where white men refused to work beside Chinamen, and involuntary, where employers preferred to avail themselves of Chinese cheap labor.

In April 1876 the state senate appointed a committee to take testimony upon the effect, moral, social, and political, of Chinese immigration, and $5,000 was authorized by the legislature to be expended by the city of San Francisco, in sending a delegation to Washington to procure such a modification of the Burlingame treaty as to prevent the coming of certain classes to our shores. The commission sat from October 18th to November 18th, their investigations filling 173 printed pages, but practically the subject remained where it had been, nothing new being elicited. Congress in 1877–8 so far yielded to the pressure as to lay a per capita tax of $2.50 on each Asiatic arriving in the country, officials excepted, any evasion of the law subjecting the offender

[10] The Chinese six companies were really contractors and importers, although they attempted to pass themselves off as benevolent organizations. They governed and controlled with an iron hand all the Chinese in the country, and sustained a secret organization of highbinders, who were not only a detective police, but secret avengers of any infraction of the companies' rules. So swift and mysterious were their blows that the S. F. police seldom succeeded in capturing a highbinder who had exacted 'blood atonement' in the Chinese quarter.

to five years' labor in the state prison, the act to take effect in January 1879

When congress came to take hold of the subject, although not sharing in the prejudices of California workingmen, or the California delegation in congress, it found a knotty question to be solved. Alien against alien, one as bad as the other, the national traditions being a country free, open to all, and the ignorant white and the ignorant black having been accepted, how could the ignorant yellow be kept away at the modest request of the ignorant white? In 1877–8 it was proposed to limit the number which might come by any single vessel. Another proposition was to punish contracting here or elsewhere for the importation of Chinese; and still another contemplated colonizing those already here on government land. During the spring of 1878 a special agent was sent to California to make a quiet investigation into the subject.

It had been said by Californians in congress that revolution would result from a longer delay in complying with the demands of the majority in the state who desired the expulsion of the Chinese. It was no new thing, indeed, for attacks to be made upon their camps in mining regions, whether the mines were in placers, quartz, or coal; but after the futile efforts to change the Burlingame treaty, the threats of violence increased and riots occurred in various places,[11] as in Los Angeles, Chico, and San Francisco, where an attack was made upon the Chinese laundries, some of which were sacked and burned in 1877.

The California delegation in congress found themselves in the position of being suspected of having a hysterical mania on the Chinese question. Grave senators of New England insisted upon extending to a half-civilized nation the constitutional privileges

[11] See *Los Angeles Star*, Aug. 1871, and April 7, 1877; *Truckee Republican*, Dec. 1879; *S. F. Alta*, March 17, and April 2, 1877; *San Diego News*, July 27, 1877; *Ross from Wis. to Cal.*, 95, 99, 101, 106–7, 127–8.

which the authors of our organic law provided for
the people of enlightened nations,[12] and they insisted
that the majority of people in this state, of all classes,
were as much governed by jealousy and prejudice as
was a disorderly alien element whose doings had been
bruited by a sensational press at home, and freely
criticised by the press abroad. It was in vain that
the report of the investigating committee was spread
before them, and commented on by such men as Sargent, Page, Miller, Farley, and others—men of sound
enough minds and arguments when common-sense
was on the side of profit, but whose professed views
had to be taken with allowance when any other attitude was to them political death. Arguments were
advanced to show that certain manufactories could
not be operated with profit except by Chinese cheap
labor; that railroads could not be built without it;
and that house-servants could not be obtained except
from among this people. This position was sustained,
so far as the railroads were concerned, by the attitude
of the Central Pacific. White labor, by refusing to
descend to the level of yellow labor, was held at a
higher figure in California than many employers
could well afford. This was peculiarly true of domestic service. A Chinaman would do more and better work in the kitchen than the female cook. On
farms he was almost indispensable, being the only
available help for the hard-worked housewife.[13] At
the same time, with this peculiar competition, wages
in California did not as elsewhere follow the general

[12] Senator Hoar maintained that 'the function of the American people,
the duty which God had committed to them, is to work out in practical
history the truth that whenever God has placed in a human frame a human
soul, that which is created is the equal of every other like creature on the
face of the earth—equal, among other things, in the right to go everywhere
on this globe, and to seek and enjoy the blessings of life, liberty, and the
pursuit of happiness at his own will.'

[13] The amount of opium which paid duty at S. F. from 1873 to 1877, inclusive, was 269,712 pounds; and the amount confiscated for smuggling and
sold in the same time, realized $120,175. What amount escaped detection
cannot be known. *Rept Custom-house Comm'rs*, 1877, p. 6–8.

law of supply and demand, but adapted themselves to the changing condition of the country.[14]

Meanwhile, the restriction or prohibition of Chinese immigration continued to be agitated. In 1879 President Hayes vetoed an act passed by congress on the subject, but conflicting with the terms of the Burlingame treaty. The following year the president appointed three commissioners, James B. Angell of Michigan, John F. Swift of California, and William Henry Trescott of South Carolina, to proceed to China for the purpose of forming new treaties. The commissioners were eminently successful, finding the Chinese plenipotentiaries, Pao Chum and Li Hungtsao, willing to concede to the United States the control and regulation of immigration, the emperor never having been desirous of expatriating any of his numerous subjects; and on the 17th of November, 1880, it was agreed that whenever, in the opinion of the government of the United States, the interests of the country were endangered by the coming to or residence in it of the Chinese, such coming might be suspended for a time, the limitation to apply only to laborers, and not to other classes. The Chinese already in the country were accorded "all the rights, privileges, immunities, and exemptions accorded to citizens of the most favored nation." This treaty was

[14] As an example of a poster issued by a Chinese laundry association when one of its rules was broken by one of their countrymen, who established a laundry within a prohibited distance of another wash-house, is the following, translated by Condit, a Chinese scholar: 'Because here a country has laws and customs which they observed, afterward families also mutually follow, how much more have come down to us for a long time—each man doing his duty dares not not observe them. At this time Wong Yee Nui, on Second street, Orleans laundry, secretly has opened business, so broken rules, resting on his own force, cannot oppose him, therefore assemble in hall. We men, one heart, put forth exertion mutually to aid, must clean him out and avoid after trouble. Therefore deliberate the following particular: In our companies number of friend who has ability first to kill Wong San Chee, thankfully give him 2000 round dollars. Afterward also take Wong Yee Nui, destroy his name, thankfully give him 600 round dollars. If only wound him, not kill, also give him one half in his hand. At this time what trouble comes cannot tell. If he cannot get away, is seized by foreigners, and put in jail, then our company manage the whole affair. Do not swallow our words; this poster is put up as evidence. Kwong Sui, first year, fifth month. Lucky day fixed. Kwong Hong Tong, put forth.'

ratified by the senate on May 5th, 1881, and ratifications exchanged at Peking, July 19th of the same year. A supplemental treaty concerning commerce agreed to prohibit the importation of opium by Chinese subjects.

Congress was now at liberty to enact such laws as should satisfy the better sense of the inhabitants of the Pacific coast, if not silence the clamor of the foreign residents of European birth. The first bill which was passed was voted by President Arthur, who considered twenty years too long a time to suspend immigration from China, and who had, besides, some technical objections. Several other bills were introduced, and finally, on the 6th of May, 1882, the president approved of an act which had passed both houses suspending immigration for ten years, but not interfering with the Chinese already in the country. This act also denied that people the right to become naturalized.

So far from being displeased by the prohibition of immigration, the Chinese already here were fully satisfied, being quite as much opposed to competitors as the Europeans, and raising the price of domestic service immediately thereafter. During the ninety days before the prohibition went into effect several shiploads of Mongolians were landed, showing the readiness of this people to grasp any opportunity. Their cunning in evading the law against opium importation continued to give occasion for the closest scrutiny; but it must be admitted that the infringement of the law is not confined to the Chinese.

Closely allied to the Chinese question, and in a measure proceeding from it, was the labor agitation of 1877–8, when, for the first time in California, labor arrayed itself against capital. Partly it was a natural result of the existing condition of affairs, and partly it was forced by that jealousy of classes which the naturalized citizen is rapidly engrafting upon Amer-

ican republicanism. In Europe the war of the laborer
is upon the government; in the United States upon
capital, or what is the same thing—power. During a
certain period California had been producing money
freely, and paying liberal wages. During and following the civil war the inflation of currency kept wages
up to a value hitherto unknown in this or any other
country. Later, the building of the Pacific railroad
introduced a surplus of laborers, until some new enterprises should be set on foot to furnish employment.
At the same time the productiveness of the mines
had decreased, and with the return to hard money
circulation in the east there had been a contraction
in expenditures which had closed manufactories and
thrown operatives out of employment. The reduction of wages and discharge of workmen were then
followed by strikes and riots.

In California, from 1865 to 1875, and especially in
San Francisco, there was a large number of foreign-
born laborers and artisans, who were temporarily unemployed, or not employed satisfactorily to themselves;
yet there was no great reduction in the price of labor.
Even the influx of Chinese laborers made no perceptible change in the labor market for a period of from
six to ten years, and then not because labor was too
abundant, but because money was more scarce The
wages of mechanics were kept, however, at higher
figures than in the east.

But with the first signs of a change in the condition of "the foreigners paradise," there arose a protest against the decline. Trades' unions began to
form, and strikes to occur. In May 1867 the workingmen of San Francisco held a convention, and one
of the concessions required from employers was that
eight hours should constitute a day of labor.[15] In
June there was a grand demonstration in favor of the

[15] Compare *S. F. Times*, Mar. 23 and May 13, 1867; *S. F. Bulletin*, Mar.
11, 1867; *S. F. Californian*, Mar. 2, 1867; *S. F. Call*, May 23, 30, and June
4, 1867; *Cal. Stat.*, 1867–8, 63, 145–6, 543; *Cal. Jour. Sen.*, 1867–8, 379–81.

eight-hour rule.   A free labor exchange was established in San Francisco in 1868.   The legislature also
passed an act making eight hours a legal day's work,[16]
the demand being made not only to secure leisure for
so-called improvement, physical and mental, but in
order to give employment to a greater number of
persons.   It would have seemed reasonable that with
fair pay [17] and reduced labor the workingmen should
have been satisfied to adapt themselves to the existing condition of affairs.   But the discontent continued to grow ; there were occasional strikes, and also
occasional new enterprises undertaken with encour-

[16] Among the occupations enumerated, the employé being sometimes found
in board, amalgamators received $100 per month, apprentices $25 to $28,
apothecaries $40, bakers $30 to $40, barbers $60 to $100, bar-tenders $30 to
$45, bed-makers $30 to $35, blacksmiths $50 to $100, boiler-makers $35 to $60,
book-keepers $35 to $100, boot-makers $35 to $75, bottlers $35 to $40, brewers
$50, bridge-builders $75, brick-makers $35 to $60, butchers $35 to $60, butter-
makers $30 to $40, charcoal-burners $35, cheese-makers $30 to $40, clerks
$40 to $100, coachmen $30 to $50, coat passers $30, confectioners $40 to $60,
cooks $35 to $80, dairymen $30 to $35, deck hands $40, dishwashers $20 to
$30, druggists $60, dyers $40 to $50, engineers $60 to $125, farm-hands $26
to $46, filers $45 to $50, firemen $50 to $60, flour packers $30, fruit-peddlers
$30 to $35, fruit-packers $25 to $30, gardeners $30 to $40, general helpers $20
to $70, gilders $50, glue-makers $35 to $50, grave-diggers $50, grooms $30 to
$45, harness-makers $40 to $75, herders $25, hop-growers $30, housekeepers
$30, interpreters $30, laborers $25 to $50, laundrymen $30 to $40, local re-
porters $50, lumbermen $35 to $70, man and wife $50 to $80, mattress-makers
$50 to $70, milkers $30 to $40, miners $40 to $60, nurses $25 to $35, ox-
drivers $35 to $45, pantrymen $35, ploughmen $30, porters $30 to $40,
potato-diggers $30 to $35, printers $60.   Day wages were in proportion, and
monthly wages where the laborer was boarded his wages of course were
less.   Quartz miners received $40 to $60 per month, quarrymen $40 to $50,
salesmen $35 to $50, sawyers $40 to $90, shepherds $25 to $30, shoemakers
$35 to $45 and by the piece, smelters $60 to $150 and found, stewards $30 to
$40, stove men $30 to $35, sugar packers $80, street sweepers $35, tanners
$35 to $45, teamsters $30 to $65, track-layers $2 per day and found, trunk-
makers $2.50 and found, undertakers $80, wagon-makers $50 to $80, or $3 to
$5 per day, waiters $20 to $40 per month, warehousemen $60 to $70, watch-
men $50 to $75, wheelwrights $60 to $80, woodchoppers $40 to $60.   Workmen paid by the day received more: blacksmiths from $2 to $4, boiler-makers
$3 to $4, brick-layers $5 to $6, cabinet-makers $3 to $4.50, carpenters $3 to
$4, ship carpenters $3 to $5, carriage-makers and painters, $3 to $4, carriage-
trimmers $3 to $4.50, gun-smiths $3 to $5, hod-carriers $2.50, iron-moulders
$3.50 to $4, machinists $3.50 to $4.50, marble-cutters $4, masons $4 to $5,
tin-roofers $4, tinsmiths $3 to $4, upholsterers $3 to $4, whitewashers $3, etc.

[17] The printer's strike which occurred in 1880 was in the nature of a conspiracy against employers.   It was kept a profound secret until within seven
hours of the consummation.   Even prominent members of the printers' union
were kept in ignorance of the movement until the last moment, when they
were given the alternative of breaking faith either with their employers or
the union.   While complaining of the hardship and injustice of being thus
compelled to stop earning wages without notice, they adhered to the union.

aging success.[18]   But the causes which I have already
enumerated began gradually to tell upon the labor
market, until when the crash in mining stocks came,
there was distress, real or fancied, among the unemployed workingmen of San Francisco.   These were,
almost to a man, of foreign birth, and rarely of much
intelligence.   Nice questions of the relation of labor
to capital they were neither able nor inclined to dis-
cuss.   They could understand that one man had more
than he needed and another less, and toward the
former they entertained nothing but envy and hatred.
Among them, however, were some shrewd philoso-
phers, who directed their chief efforts against Chinese
and convict competition, who restricted apprentice-
ships, and who insisted on the observance of the
eight-hour law.   Finally, in 1877, the agitation on
the subject of labor and the duties of capital reached
to an alarming height.   There were at that time
twenty-five trades unions in the city, with a membership of 3,500, several organizations being branches
of national and international associations.   Later
there was hardly a branch of labor that had not its
union.

It would be idle to assert that the workingmen had
no real grievances.   Might is right in every human
society, and it is only by occasional revolutions in
which the higher law is asserted that society advances in the recognition of its mutual relations.
There was truth in what was alleged, that the presence of the Chinese in California reduced the chances
and earnings of citizen laborers, while it strengthened
the power by adding to the wealth of capitalists.   It
was true, as alleged, that the enormous monopolization of land by a few men, who refused to sell at a
fair value, hindered the settlement of the country,
thereby inflicting the double injury of preventing the

[18] Reference is here made to the Woman's Co-operative Printing union,
and Shoemakers Co-operative union, both of which became prosperous
associations.

poor from acquiring cheap homes, and checking the employment of farm and other laborers. The farms in California were usually large, but the proprietors, owing to the perfection of agricultural implements, required the services of comparatively few men, and those only at certain periods of the year. Owing to the mildness of the climate, farm-hands were not provided with as good quarters as in the older states, but were temporarily lodged in barns, and fed in messes separate from the families they served. Tramps abounded, ready to work a few days at any price, and then to march on. Thus country life was robbed of its charms, and the small savings of a season's work were squandered in idleness in some town. There was cause of complaint, also, in the fraudulent values put upon mining stocks, in the wild gambling operations of 1875-6, which had impoverished thousands of families, emptying into the coffers of men already rich the lifelong savings of honest toil, and that without making any return, present or prospective, for the robbery. They had a just cause of complaint in that the men who had made the greatest amount of money by monopolies, and treacherous mining operations, took a large part of it out of the state—ten times as much as the Chinese carried away—and spent their time in New York, Washington, London, and Paris, instead of investing in business enterprises in California, which would help the people to recover from their losses.

That there was destitution also in the year 1876 was true, 7,000 being relieved by the San Francisco Benevolent association, which, from May to December disbursed $19,000. In May 1877 over 1,000 persons were relieved, and in February 1878 the association and the churches fed over 2,000 persons daily. After this period, when the number of idle men was estimated at 15,000, the calls for help decreased. The majority of the unemployed attributed their distress to the encroachment upon their trades of Mongolians, particularly in shoe and cigar-making. In the former trade the Chinamen out-numbered them four to one, and earnings had declined from an average of $25 a week in 1870 to $9 in 1878.

For these grievances no remedy had been provided, nor any effort made to secure a better condition beyond holding meetings on the Chinese question, and petitioning the state and national legislatures for redress. The failure of the latter means exposed to them their weakness in the political arena, and opened their eyes to another evil. They had left the government to men who made a business of politics, and having flattered and bribed the lately naturalized citizen into voting as desired, dismissed him from their thoughts. Those bills were most sure to be passed which were lobbied through the legislature; privileges were to be purchased at the expense of the public, which paid a large per cent of its income in taxes to support a government recklessly extravagant. Corruption and favoritism were the rule and honesty the exception; at least, so they were told by those who pretended to be their friends, and I am not able to say that they were far wrong in the indictment.

A conference of workingmen on the 21st of July, 1877, resolved to call a mass meeting for the 23d on the then vacant lot on the Market street side of the city hall. Precautions were taken by the police, who feared an outbreak, and the national guard assembled at their armories. During the progress of the meeting, which was presided over by James F. D'Arcy, organizer of the workingmen's party of the United States, and advocate of an eight-hour law,[19] an anti-

[19] The resolutions passed expressed sympathy for those who had been shot in the late riot at Pittsburg; denounced the grasping policy of the moneyed and governing classes; declared that no further subsidies should be granted to steamship and railroad lines; declared that the military should not be employed against strikers; asserted that the reduction of wages was a part of the conspiracy for the destruction of the republic; that the non-enforcement of the eight-hour law had over-crowded the labor market; an evil which the gov't should take immediate steps to remedy; and that all railroad property in disaffected districts should be condemned to public use, allowing the owners a just compensation therefor.

coolie club formed on the outskirts of the assembly,
and incited to riot a portion of the workingmen, who,
in the course of that and the two succeeding evenings,
destroyed a large number of Chinese laundries.   In
the struggle between the rioters and the police, aided
by a committee of safety led by William T. Coleman,
several persons were killed.   These acts of the lower,
communistic element of the workingman's association,
were repudiated by the more intelligent, who in large
numbers joined the committee.   Considerable alarm
was felt in Oakland, on account of a meeting of 12,000
of the malcontents, threats having been made against
the property of the railroad company in that city, unless the Chinese in their employ should be discharged.

It now became apparent that some political power
could be obtained by divorcing that section of the
workingmen's party in California from the Chicago
centre, and the leading spirits determined upon effecting the separation.   Among these was an Irish dray-
man, named Dennis Kearney, who had made his first
public appearance a few months previous at a lyceum
for self-culture, and subsequently as a member of a
committee appointed by the Draymen and Teamster's
union, to lay before Senator Sargent certain trade
grievances.   Having been accorded a not very gracious reception, Kearney was stirred to wonder why
he could not become as great a man as Sargent, and
thereupon set about making himself such by constituting himself orator at his own and other unions.

On the 18th of August, at a meeting of workingmen, Kearney took preliminary steps to organize a
party, which held a meeting on the 22d under the
title of the Workingmen's Trade and Labor union,
J. G. Day being chosen president, and Kearney secretary, but no effective organization resulted.   In the
meantime other trades unions in different parts of the
state were acting in sympathy with those of San
Francisco.   At Sacramento they advocated the abol-
ishment of all national banks, and the withdrawal of

the present bank currency in favor of full legal tenders issued only by the United States; the exemption from execution and taxation of $1,000 upon every homestead; all property to be assessed at its full value, and the percentage of taxation to be graduated from one to ten; the unconditional abrogation of the Burlingame treaty; and the fees of office-holders to be reduced to the prices paid for skilled labor.

Not to be outdone in reforms, the San Francisco Trade and Labor Union held a meeting September 12th, at which it was resolved to sever all connection with existing political parties, and organize under the name of the Workingmen's Party of California, with the following objects: The abolition of all assessments on candidates for office—the people to own the offices, not the incumbents; holding state and municipal officers to a strict accountability for their official acts; the establishment of a bureau of labor and statistics; the reduction, and periodical regulation thereafter, of the hours of labor; and the creation by the legislature of a convention on labor, with headquarters in San Francisco.

This was the beginning of a party which was to overturn the government of the state. On the following Sunday, the first of the regular sand-lot meetings was held. On the 21st, the workingmen assembled at Union hall, on Howard street, to consider means for the relief of the unemployed. State senator Roach addressed the meeting upon the Chinese trouble and political corruption, calling for united action to obtain legislation for the poor, to which Kearney added that every workingman should procure a musket, and that a little judicious hanging of capitalists would be in order. Subscriptions for the destitute were ordered to be paid to the mayor.

Day proved too temperate a president to please the turbulent element of the party. When at a meeting on the sand-lot, Kearney broke forth with the declaration that San Francisco would meet the fate of

Moscow should the condition of the laboring class not be soon improved, and that bullets were not wanting to enforce their demands, Day interrupted him, and declined to preside at a meeting where such sentiments were uttered. Kearney was applauded and Day yelled down, whereupon there was a division. On the 5th of October a permanent organization of the workingmen's party was effected, with Dennis Kearney president, J. G. Day vice-president, and H. L. Knight secretary

The principles adopted proposed to elevate the working class at the expense of every other.[20] They found ready acceptance among a class who envied the aristocrat rolling in wealth which their hands had gathered, who hated the encroaching Chinamen, and who detested the politician as a betrayer and parasite. They were dazzled by the glittering prospects which

[20] The following were the principles declared: 'The object of this association is to unite all the poor and working men and their friends into one political party for the purpose of defending themselves against the dangerous encroachments of capital on the happiness of our people, and the liberties of our country. We propose to wrest the gov't from the hands of the rich and place it in those of the people where it properly belongs, We propose to rid the country of cheap Chinese labor as soon as possible, and by all the means in our power, because it tends still more to degrade labor and aggrandize capital. We propose to destroy land monopoly in our state by such laws as will make it impossible. We propose to destroy the great money power of the rich by a system of taxation that will make great wealth impossible in the future. We propose to provide decently for the poor and unfortunate, the weak, the helpless, and especially the young, because the country is rich enough to do so, and religion, humanity, and patriotism demand we should do so. We propose to elect none but competent workingmen and their friends to any office whatever. The rich have ruled us till they have ruined us. We will now take our own affairs into our own hands. The republic must and shall be preserved, and only workingmen will do it. Our shoddy aristocrats want an emperor, and a standing army to shoot down the people. For these purposes we propose to form ourselves into the Workingmen's Party of California, and to pledge and enroll therein all who are willing to join us in accomplishing these ends. When we have 10,000 members we shall have the sympathy and support of 20,000 other workingmen. The party will then wait upon all who employ Chinese, and ask for their discharge; and it will mark as public enemies those who refuse to comply with their request. This party will exhaust all peaceable means of attaining its ends; but it will not be denied justice when it has the power to enforce it. It will encourage no riot or outrage, but it will not volunteer to repress or put down, or arrest, or prosecute the hungry and impatient who manifest their hatred of the Chinaman by a crusade against John or those who employ him. Let those who raise the storm by their selfishness suppress it themselves. If they dare raise the devil let them meet him face to face. We will not help them.'

arose like a mirage before them, picturing shady groves and cooling fountains to the exhausted traveller in the desert. The infection spread; men came to listen to the fiery harangues, and went away more or less converts to the seductive theory. Clubs with active leaders were formed in every ward. Kearney spoke every night at one or more of them, and urged unity of purpose, and the formation of military companies. Nothing more warlike, however, was indulged in than vituperative bluster,[21] to which his followers were well pleased to listen.

Kearney now devoted himself to agitation. Of some of his mad pranks I have spoken in my *Popular Tribunals*. Such was the alarm created by his incendiary speeches and threats that on November 3, 1877, he was arrested and confined in jail, a martyrdom to which he aspired as a means of spreading his fame. It delighted him to know that the militia and committee of safety thought him of sufficient consequence to keep under guard.[22]

[21] Some of Kearney's sayings were in the highest degree imflammatory, and occasioned much uneasiness. He frequently expressed himself able to effect anything with his followers, from lynching a railroad magnate to destroying a city. At a meeting in Dec. 1877, he promised in the course of his customary tirade against 'thieving millionaire and scoundrelly officials,' 'If I don't get killed, I will do more than any reformer in the history of the world. I hope I will be assassinated, for the success of the movement depends on that.' On another occasion he said, 'Judge Lynch is the judge wanted by the workingmen of California. I advise all to own a musket and 100 rounds of ammunition.'

[22] Kearney was born in 1847, at Oakmount, County Cork, Ireland, the 2d in a family of 7 boys. At the age of 11 he went to sea as a cabin boy, sailing principally under the American flag, and gaining rapid promotion, so that when he arrived at S. F. in 1868, he was first officer of the clipper ship *Shooting Star*, a position which he continued to occupy on coast steamers for 4 years. It was here he acquired the air of domineering command which was of service to him in the role he had assumed. He was temperate and industrious, saving enough to purchase a draying business in 1872 which prospered until 1877, when the merchants withdrew their patronage on account of his incendiary speeches. He was not devoid of means, while drawing support from his followers, in collections taken up at the Sunday meetings on the sand-lot. He married in 1870, and had several children, whom he raised in the catholic faith. He was not naturalized until 1876. His oratory was earnest and forcible, partaking of the epigrammatic, and showing a smattering of historical knowledge, with a pronounced brogue in the utterance, and shallowness of argument. His ideas of political economy were crude and illogical, and his conceit as towering as his ambition. For example, when he came into power he would decree a minimum pay of $3 or

The course pursued by the agitators was not one to melt the hearts of the city fathers toward the workingmen's woes. But two days after Kearney's incarceration a public meeting was held to consider the condition of the distressed, and collection agents appointed, who gathered from the citizens $20,000, of which $12,000 was set aside for a free labor exchange, and the remainder distributed among charitable institutions for the benefit of the needy. To check incendiary speech' the supervisors issued an ordinance against it known as the 'Gibbs' gag law.' Kearney remained in jail about two weeks, during which time he addressed a letter to the mayor, stating that he had been unfairly reported by the press, and was willing to submit to any proper measures to allay the agitation, upon which the charge against him was dismissed. He, however, immediately availed himself of his liberty to repeat his outrageous attacks upon the police, the judges, and the supervisors. At a ward meeting a resolution was passed that " if any officer or leader in the workingmen's movement lagged behind, or proved recreant to his trust, he should be hanged to the nearest lamp-post." Kearney's impris-

---

$4 per day for any kind of labor, the expenditure of which sum was to create extraordinary development in the country. Every man should own a homestead. Poverty was to be abolished, but great wealth was to be prevented by laws under which manufacturers and traders could not retain more than a fixed amount of profits, the surplus to go to the erection of public works and institutions. By his admirers he was compared to the first Napoleon, to Cæsar, and to Christ. In personal appearance he was below medium height, compactly built, with a broad head, slight mustache, quick but lowering blue eyes, and nervous temperament. J. G. Day, the vice-pres't had seceded, though he again joined Kearney's following. He was a Canadian carpenter, of Irish extraction, 6 feet in height, with a reddish beard. He was industrious and temperate, with a common-school education. His language was good, and his ideas thoughtful, and the opposite of incendiary. H. L. Knight came of a Yorkshire family in England. He was short, squat, with a round face, twinkling gray eyes, and small gray mustache. He had a strong proclivity for reforms, any kind being better than none. In 1842 he immigrated to the U. S. and settled himself in Mo. where he was admitted to the bar. He served through the Mexican war, coming to Cal. in 1852, where he engaged in mining for three years. gave some attention to law, finally becoming a social parasite. The situation of secretary to the Kearney organization fitted him well. Among other leading members of the association was another Irishman, T. H. Bates, a house-painter, with the air of a sporting man; and Charles C. O'Donnell, afterward city coroner.

onment had increased his following, and on Thanksgiving day 7,000 workingmen, representing every ward and trade in the city, held a grand parade. Nothing disorderly occurred, and it terminated at the sand-lot in so-called literary exercises, C. C. O'Donnell acting as president of the meeting, and William Wellock [23] vice-president. After resolving to wind up the national banks the assembly dispersed.

An attempt had been made to form a central body of delegates from the city and county organizations. Failing in this, Kearney resolved to push the scheme in the interior, and set out with Knight to stump the southern counties, and organize clubs, his expenses to be paid from the Sunday collections at the sand-lot. From the farmers not much encouragement was received; but in the principal towns were large numbers who eagerly listened to and applauded his presumptuous talk, made up largely of denunciation of and threats against the wealthy classes, and the administration of the government, and boastings of his dictatorship. [24]

[23] William Wellock was a Yorkshire man, and a shoemaker by trade. He was likewise an evangelist and bible expounder. Landing in the U. S. in 1873, he worked at his trade in various places, reaching S. F. in 1877, where he was naturalized. He was tall, with a long, narrow head, high forehead, full, short beard, and nervous temperament. Having married a widow with some means, he could afford that luxury of low foreigners, American politics. Not entirely devoid of culture, and possessing considerable dry humor, he was not altogether unattractive as a public speaker, although the frequent use made of bible quotations smacked of cant, and gave him the soubriquet of Parson Wellock. Indeed, he had played chaplain to the party before assuming the vice-presidency, and discoursed upon bible texts at the sand-lot. Like Kearney, he was not unappreciative of his own importance. At a mass-meeting in Dec. he promised that when he and his colleagues had cleared Cal. of demagogues, they would do the same for the other states, until the whole republic should be purified, after which they would go to England and pull down the monarchy. When that was done his work would be ended. Speaking of monopolists he would say, ' These men who are perverting the ways of truth must be destroyed. In this book, called the bible, the lord is said to be a consuming fire. When he commands, we must obey. What are we to do with these people that are starving our poor, and degrading our wives, daughters, and sisters? And the lord said unto Moses, "Take all the heads off the people and hang them before the lord." This is what we are commanded by a supreme being to do with all that dare to tread down honesty, virtue, and truth.' Rather hard on the supreme being.

[24] It was proposed at a ward meeting in S. F. to make him dictator, when he eagerly accepted the office, saying that he was the voice of 40,000 people,

On the 12th of December the workingmen of Oakland sent an address to the president of the United States, petitioning for the abrogation of the Burlingame treaty, which was transmitted to the senate, but without effect. On the 3d of January, 1878, Kearney led several hundred unemployed men to the city hall to demand "work, bread, or a place in the county jail." On the march the column swelled to 1,500, and halting before the mayor's office created no little alarm in the treasury office. The men demanded that the capitalists of the city should establish an industrial colony, or take other means for relief. To compel such a measure was, of course, out of the mayor's province. A bill was introduced in the legislature authorizing the city of San Francisco to employ 2,000 laborers for three months, of which, however, the supervisors took no notice.

Soon afterward Kearney, Knight, and Wellock were several times arrested for incendiary language and terrorism.[25] Threats to blow up the Pacific Mail Steamship company's dock and steamers, to drop dynamite from balloons into the Chinese quarter, to make infernal machines with which men might be secretly destroyed, were supplemented by advice to bring guns and bludgeons to the sand-lot. Military companies were formed, but only those of the 10th and 11th wards were able to procure arms. The city authorities took note of these proceedings, and on the 16th of January the incendiaries were again locked up, the national guard called out, and a man-of-war sent to protect the mail docks. A committee was appointed to visit Sacramento, to lay before the legis-

and would remain dictator until deposed by their will. One ward proposed to crown him with a coronet of $20 pieces, taken from the rich men on Nob hill.

[25] Kearney was charged with saying at a meeting of cooks and waiters, 'I am glad to see you making preparations for the fish-balls—that is, you make the balls and we will fire them. If the members of the legislature overstep the limits of decency, then I say, hemp! hemp! hemp! That is the battle cry of freedom.' He defied the grand jury, and said if imprisoned he would work out of jail and 'annihilate every one of these hell-hounds in the state of California.'

lators there assembled the condition of affairs. That body immediately passed an act authorizing the arrest of incendiary speakers, and the dispersing of doubtful assemblages.[26]

A workingman's convention was held on the 21st, which continued for several days. On the second day Kearney and Knight were acquitted on the indictment of inciting a riot, and released on bail pending the trial of other charges. The same day came the news of the triumph of the workingmen at the Alameda election, where they claimed to have secured a senator from that county.[27] There were 150 delegates in attendance upon the convention. A state central committee was formed, with five members from each senatorial district, and one representative from each trade union. The storm of dissent against the riot act in the convention caused the legislature to appoint an investigating committee, which, after attending a sand-lot meeting, whereat the usual tirades were softened so as to come within the statute, and taking the testimony of a large number of witnesses on both sides, presented a report, showing that the workingmen's party had not been engaged in the July riots, that their language required to be interpreted with regard to surrounding circumstances, that the Chinese were a curse to the country; and, in short, that no serious charges could be sustained against the workingmen. It now became evident that the workingmen's party was strong enough to become a powerful factor in the politics of the state. Their

[26] Ferral, judge of the S. F. police court, testified at a later period that he regarded the act as unjust and despotic, the existing laws being sufficient to provide for any emergencies specified by it.

[27] This was John W. Bones, elected to fill a vacancy. He repudiated the Kearneyites, who, he said, had nothing to do with the law-and-order convention of workingmen which nominated him. Nevertheless Kearney proceeded to Alameda and brought the senator—the first fruits of the agitation —to exhibit him at the convention. At the Sept. election, out of 7,118 votes in this county, 118 were polled by the workingmen, the main vote being about equally divided between republicans and democrats. At the Jan. election the whole vote was 4,340, of which the workingmen carried 2,730, the republicans 2,038, and the democrats 572, showing from which party the workingmen had been drawn.

leaders had used the temporary depression in business to engage the public attention, and they had alternately amused, disgusted, and terrorized the city of San Francisco, until it began to be seen that there was something more in their movements than blind passion or brute force. They began in February to visit the different counties for the purpose of influencing municipal elections. In Oakland and Sacramento the workingmen elected several of their candidates, whereupon the press of the state began to recognize them as not only a party, but a powerful one; and perhaps the strongest proof of the influence attained in politics was contained in the rumor that Kearney's palm was now crossed with railroad money, and that the bonanza bank flung him a few gold pieces occasionally. However absurd these statements, he assumed the air of a potentate, and introduced himself where he had never before been recognized.[28] He even advanced the idea in ward clubs that he was opposed to Americans being admitted to the organization, and although nominally a catholic, retorted upon Archbishop Alemany, who reproved his church members for seditious language—that the constitution of the United States made it sedition to interfere in people's religious affairs. He was invited east in the spring of 1878, where he was not received as a hero, and where I will leave him, although he afterward figured as an inmate of the house of correction in San Francisco

To return to the course of state political affairs in

[28] An attempt by the legislature to pass a bill for the sale of the Spring Valley water-works to the city of S. F. for $15,000,000 created a unanimous outcry, and on the 16th of March a meeting of property-holders was called to denounce the scheme. At this meeting appeared Kearney with a large escort, and proceeded to take a place on the platform, When reminded that he had not been invited, he insisted on his right, as the representative of the workingmen, to share in its deliberations, calling on his adherents for a show of hands, and declaring himself elected chairman, carried matters with a high hand, entirely routing the property-holders. A set of resolutions was then passed, instructing the city representatives in the legislature to vote against the bill, a deputation being dispatched to Sac., to present them to the governor and legislature.

1868, the administration of Governor Haight was acceptable, although he gave his adhesion to President Johnson and not to congress. Legislators who were not satisfied with the pay received from the people, but who looked for an additional income from the lobby, received the check of frequent vetoes, and monopolies were not encouraged. In 1869–70 he objected to the fifteenth amendment to the constitution of the United States, with the same hostility to the black man that he had shown in his message two years before. The legislature [29] followed his lead,

[29] *Cal. Jour. Assem.*, 1867–8, 92–102. *Cal. Jour. Assem.*, 1869–70, 168–76, 947–8. The legislature, which met in the new capitol at the 18th session, consisted of 26 democrats, 11 republicans, and three independents; the assembly of 66 democrats, 11 republicans, and three independents. The senators elect were E. M. Banvard, of Placer; John S. Hager, R. J. Betze, Thomas M. Wand, S. F.; William Burnett, Sonoma; A. Comte, Jr, Sac.; J. T. Farley, Alpine and Amador; Thomas Fowler, Fresno, Kern and Tulare; William M. Gwin, Jr, Calaveras; S. C. Hutchings, Yuba and Sutter: William Irwin, Siskiyou; Charles Maclay, Santa Clara; William Minis, Solano and Yolo; M. P. O'Connor, Nevada; N. M. Orr, San Joaquin; George C. Perkins, Butte, Lassen and Plumas; Edward Tompkins, Alameda; R. T. Turner, Sierra; Stephen Wing, Tuolmne, Inyo and Mono; B. D. Wilson, Los Angeles; Romualdo Pacheco, Santa Luis Obispo and Santa Bárbara; E. J. Lewis, (hold-over) was chosen pres't; Joseph Roberts, sec.; B. A. Mardis, ass't sec.; J. B. Stevens, J. J. la Guerra, L. Keplan, E. K. Phipps, Edward Curtis, N. S. Cooper, George N. Morton, clerks; Nat. Boice. J. J. Thomas, serg'ts-at-arms; chaplain, Rev. W. R. Gober.

The assembly consisted of F. D. Luelling and Daniel Inman, Alameda; J. M. Johnson, A. C. Brown, Alpine and Amador; J. C. Martin, Marion Biggs, Butte; A. R. Young, E. L. Green, W. S. Williams, Calaveras; L, Searce, Colusa and Tehama; J. R. Carothers, Contra Costa; J. E. Murphy, Del Norte and Klamath; Charles Gildes, J. H. Miller, J. D. McMurray, H. B. Newell, El Dorado; P. C. Appling, Fresno; J. J. DeHaven, Humboldt; J. C. Crigler, Lake and Napa; John Lambert, Lassen and Plumas; M. F. Coronel, R. C. Fryer, Los Angeles; W. J. Miller, Marine; D. M. Pool, Mariposa; G. W. Henley, Mendocino; Miner Walden, Merced and Stanislaus; J. A. Blankenship, Monterey; W. A. King, B. F. Hawley, T. A. Slicer, S. T. Oates, Nevada; M. H. Power, M. H. Calderwood, M. Waldron, Placer; M. S. Heran, R. D. Stephens, I. F. Freeman, John A. Odell, J. Duffy, Sac.; J. W. Satterwhite, San Bernardino; William N. Robinson, San Diego; E. A. Rockwell, Joseph Napthaly, J. C. Griswold, Thomas P. Ryan, Michael Hayes, George R. B. Hayes, George H. Rogers, T. J. Maynihan, J. L. Romer, Charles McMillan, H. W. Fortuus, W. O'Connell, S. F ; C. G. Hubner, J. S. Thurston, San Joaquin; A. G. Escandon, San Luis Obispo and Sta Bárbara; S. J. Linney, San Mateo; W. B. Shoemaker, B. D. Murphy, T. R. Thomas, Sta Clara; F. A. Hahn, Sta Cruz; A. R. Andrevs, Shasta; B. J. Sammons, John Kautz, Sierra; William Shores, R. M. Martin, Siskiyou; R. C. Haile, Solano; B. B. Munday, Thomas Hudson, Barclay Henley, Sonoma; C. P. Berry, Sutter; John McMurray, Trinity; W. E. Doss, Tulare and Kern; E. W. Eichelroth, J. S. Mooney, F. York, Tuolumne, Inyo, and Mono; J. M. Kelly, Yolo; George Merritt, C. McClaskey, J. E. Brewer, Yuba. George H. Rogers was chosen speaker; C. Gildea, speaker pro tem.;

only a minority of the federal relations committee reporting in favor of the amendment, which was rejected by a senate joint resolution.

The chief idea in state politics at this period was resistance to the monopolies of land, railroad, water, gas, and other companies. The republicans lost ground in 1867 by being the party which favored railroad construction and the granting of subsidies; but they recovered it in time to elect for governor Newton Booth, anti-monopolist, in 1871, with three congressmen,[30] and a large majority[31] in the lower house and in joint convention of the legislature.[32]

Robert Ferral, Newton Benedict, D. F. Beveridge, Fenwick Fisher, A. L. Henshaw, J. C. Edwards, T D. Murphy, clerks; Dan'l Perkins, J. M. Shannon, sergts-at-arms; J. G. Johnson, chaplain.

[30] The congressmen were Houghton 1st dist, Sargent 2d dist, and Coghlan 3d dist, elected on the republican ticket in 1871. In the following year there was another split in the republican party, which, however, had a majority over the democrats. The legislature, by act, ordered an election for congressmen in 1872, when Page was chosen in the 2d dist, Luttrell in the 3d, Houghton in the 4th, and Clayton in the 1st; all republicans but Luttrell, who was elected by the liberals.

[31] The election of this year was marked by invention of the historic 'tapeworm ticket,' the legend of which runs as follows: The navy yard at Mare island had remained since the war under the control of the republican party, and the large number of employés were in the habit, previous to a general election, of enrolling themselves as members of republican clubs; but it was observed at the counting of ballots that an extraordinary number were democratic. To prevent scratching and pasting, the republican county committee had a peculiar ticket printed for Vallejo, the same being long and narrow, with the names of candidates printed without spaces, filling the paper entirely, the lines running from end to end. These tickets were printed and distributed, but it was found on counting and examining them that 128 of these intricately contrived ballots were altered by democratic voters. Of course the object of the tape-worm ballot was intimidation, and the disgrace of the attempt to make all government employés vote the republican ticket was commented upon even in the U. S. senate.

[32] The senators elected in 1871, were David Boucher, Butte, Plumas and Lassen; Barlow Dyer, Calaveras; John Boggs, Colusa and Tehama; David Goodale, Contra Costa and Marin; J. J. DeHaven, Del Norte, Humboldt and Klamath; H. J. McKusie, El Dorado; W. W. Pendergast, Lake, Napa, and Mendocino; T. J. Keys, Mariposa, Merced and Stanislaus; Thomas Beck, Sta Cruz and Monterey; M. P. O'Conner, Charles Kent, Nevada; Jacob Neff, Placer; James A. Duffy, Sac.; James McCoy, San Bernardino and San Diego; George Oulten, W. T. Garratt, S. F.; S. J. Trinity, S. F. and San Mateo; George S. Evans, San Joaquin. To fill vacancy: James P. VanNess, Sta Bárbara and San Luis Obispo; John McMurray, Shasta and Trinity; to fill vacancy, B. T. Tuttle, Sonoma; M. C. Andross, Tuolumne and Mono; L. T. Crane, Yuba. President of the senate pro tem., J. T. Farley; sec., Robert Farral; asst sec., T. J. Shackleford; clerks, J. B. Stevens, J. J. de la Guerra, E. L. Crawford, Ted Robinson, A. Sites, E.

The party, however, was too much under railroad influence, and split upon that test in 1873, pending the election of a legislature which was to choose a successor to United States senator Cole, whose term expired in March. The seceders called themselves independents, but were facetiously named Dolly Vardens. Their avowed principles were to destroy the power of monopolies, regulate railroad fares and freights, and devise an irrigation system for the benefit of the whole state. The independents received much of their strength from the order of grangers which was extensively organized about this time, and who, as patrons of husbandry, were naturally interested in the proposed reforms. The party proved strong enough to control the election of 1873, secure a majority in the assembly, and with the other branch of the republican party, the control of the legislature.[33]

Gallagher, J. P. Cunningham; sergts-at-arms, J. W. Hawkins, J. M. Shannon; chaplain, J. H. Bonte. Democrats 21, republicans 18, independents 1. The assembly consisted of Cyrus Coleman, J. A. Eagan, Alpine and Amador; E. H. Pardes, E. T. Crane, Alameda; J. N. Turner, W. N. Dettaven, Butte; C. L. Y. Brown, J. L. Gibson, L. M. Schrack, Calaveras; Loomis Ward, Colusa; Joseph W. Gallaway, Contra Costa; T. H. Rector, Del Norte and Klamath; J. Burkhalter, Kern and Tulare; Samuel H. Center, William Barklage, Robert Chalmers, A. J. Bayley, El Dorado; I. N, Walker, Fresno; Joseph Russ, Humboldt; N. W. Stillwagen, Lake and Napa; T. D. Mott, Asa Ellis, Los Angeles; J. B. Rice, Marin; John W. Wilcox, Mariposa; George B. Mathers, Mendocino; J. B. Sensabaugh, Merced; H. M. Hayes, Monterey; Henry Everett, Robert Bell, J. M. Days, S. Barker, Nevada; Jacob Welty, O. H. Lee, Henry Long, Placer; B. W. Barnes, Plumas and Lassen; C. G. W. French, E. B. Mott jr., P. J. Hopper, O. Harvey, William Johnson, Sac.; F. M. Slaughter, San Bernardino; George W. Daniels, San Diego; Giles H. Gray, T. B. Shannon, W. T. James, W. A. Aldrich, A. D. Splivalo, Charles Goodall, David Meeker, Charles Jost, William R. Wheaton, John Seibe, Samuel McCullough, H. R. Reed, S. F.; R. C. Sargent, F. J. Woodward, San Joaquin; Milton Mason, Sta Bárbara; Curtis Baird, San Mateo; J. P. Sargent, F. E. Spencer, H. C. Frank, Sta Clara; G. W. Brockus, Sta Cruz; A. R. Andrews, Shasta; D. L. Whitney, B. J. Sanders, Sierra; J. K. Luttrell, W. A. Little, Siskiyou; M. J. Wright, Solano; E. C. Henshaw, William Caldwell, R. B. Munday, Sonoma; C. P. Berry, Sutter; H. J. Tinnin, Trinity; P. B. Bacon, George A. Whitney, W. C. Connolly, Tuolumne, Mono and Inyo; J. C. Bradley, T. R. Lofton, William Edgar, Yuba; F. S. Freeman, Yolo. Speaker of the assembly, T. B. Shannon; speaker pro tem., B. J. Hopper; clerks, M. D. Boruck, G. W. Dixon, Martin Rowan, I. R. Wilber, J. H. Reed, Alfred Thompson, Isaac Ayer, Frederick Creque; sergts-at-arms, A. J. Rhoads, G. Meredith. Republicans 55; democrats 24; independents 1. [33] The state senators elected in 1873 were C. W. Bush, Los Angeles; W. J. Graves, San Luis Obispo, Sta Bárbara, and Ventura; Tipton Lindsley, Fresno, Kern, and Tulare; T. H. Laine, Sta Clara; Washington Bartlett,

On the 28th of November, Casserly resigned his seat in the national senate, which unexpected action rendered necessary the choice of another senator to complete his term.   The place was filled by John S. Hager,[34] democrat, and anti-monopolist.   The choice

Philip A. Roach, S. F. and San Mateo; Edward Gibbons, Alameda; R. Hopkins, Calaveras; J. T. Farley, Amador and Alpine; Thomas Fraser, El Dorado; Henry Edgerton, Sac.; H. E. McCune, Solano and Yolo; B. F. Tuttle, Sonoma; N. Martin, Placer; M. P. O'Connor, Nevada; H. K. Turner, Sierra; S. Spencer, Yuba and Sutter; George C. Perkins, W. C. Hendricks, Butte, Lassen, and Plumas; William Irwin, Siskiyou.   Irwin was chosen pres't, T. J. Shackelford sec., J. B. Chinn, Ira H. Reed, ass't secs; Newton Benedict, A. F. Thompson, A. H. Estell, Daniel Fenton, A. J. Starling, Fred. Creque, clerks; J. W. Hawkins, C. J. Burns, sergts-at-arms; George F. Beveridge, postmaster; C. E. King, Joseph McBayle, George Ellery, Bcn. W. Day, pages; George W. Hansbrow, paper-folder; H. Clock, Ed. Duffy, S. J. Eddy, porters.   The senate comprised 18 republicans, 14 democrats, and 8 independents.

The assembly consisted of Ammerman, W. J. Gurnett, Alameda; W. H. Steerer, L. Miller, Alpine and Amador; J. B. Clark, J. C. Gray, Butte; W. P. Peck, George Gilman, M. Fahey, Calaveras; John Simpson, Colusa and Tehama; A. W. Hammalt, Contra Costa; J. J. Murphy, Del Norte and Klamath; G. E. Williams, G. W. Sempers, G. H. Ingham, N. Gilmore, El Dorado; J. J. Ferguson, Fresno; B. S. Hurlbut, Humboldt; W. Canfield, Kern and Tulare; S. K. Welch, Lake and Napa; J. D. Byers, Lassen and Plumas, A. Higley, J. S. Venable, Los Angeles; T. J. Abies, Marin; J. W. Snyder, Mariposa; R. S. McCallum, Mendocino; H. B. Davis, Merced and Stanislaus; C. Tully, Monterey, A. J. Pelham, G. W. Griffin, D. C. Northrup, W. Hill, Nevada; W. C. Norton, W. Raush, S. B. Burt, Placer; P. Coggins, P. H. Russell, R. Kercheval, J. N. Barton, W. E. Bryan, Sac.; N. C. Pishon, San Bernardino; W. W. Bowers, San Diego; M. M. Estee, D. Rogers, J. F. Swift, John Hamill, W. A. Aldrich, C. C. Terrill, James Patterson, B. C. Vandell, G. C. Wickware, D. Friedenrich, J. F. Cowdery, Robert Howe, S. F.; Samuel Myers, A. C. Paulsell, San Joaquin; A. G. Escandon, San Luis Obispo, Sta Bárbara, and Ventura; James Burns, San Mateo; Thomas R. Lea, F. C. Frank, Alexander Hay, Sta Clara; C. L. Thomas, Sta Cruz; R. Klotz, Shasta; S. Winchell, W. R. Morgan, Sierra; J. McBride, W. C. Cressler, Siskiyou; L. H. Heald, Solano; W. S. M. Wright, J. Dixon, W. H. Northcutt, Sonoma; A. L. Chandler, Sutter; J. W. Tinnin, Trinity; J. W. Summers, J. E. Parker, A. J. Long, Tuolumne, Mono, and Inyo; F. S. Freeman, Yolo; J. C. Bradley, J. C. Carter, Martin Knox, Yuba; 19 republicans, 28 democrats, and 33 independents, or in joint convention rep. 37, dem. 42, ind. 41.   M. M. Estee was chosen speaker; Robert Howe, speaker pro tem.; D. T. Laofbourrow, John Webber, J. A. Brumsey, T. S. Harris, B. F. Jeffries, Mrs J. P. Biggers, Walter Ferral, Richard Brown, clerks; William M. Cratcher, J. M. Ingraham, sergts-at-arms; W. H. Copper, Charles Weltz, J. Nicholson, John S. Wilkins, porters; Samuel Alexander, Robert Craig, William Dunlevy, J. O'Niel, pages; C. E. Street, postmaster; Frank Morse, P. O. page; W. J. Hawkett, paper-folder.

[34] John S. Hager was born in Morris co., N. J., in 1818, and educated at Princeton college.   He came to Cal. in 1849, and after mining for a short period commenced the practice of law in S. F.   In 1852 he was elected to the state senate, serving in 1853-4.   I have already spoken of his high character as judge of the fourth dist court from 1855 to 1862.   Many important suits, including the litigation growing out of the failure of Adams & Co.

for the long term fell upon Booth,[35] who resigned the executive office to accept the greater dignity. Pacheco filled out the governor's term, ending in December 1875.

In the latter year there were four candidates in the field for governor, namely, William Irwin,[36] T. G. Phelps, John Bidwell, and William E. Lovett, representing the democratic, republican, independent, and tax-payers parties. As the independents and tax-payers were mainly offshoots from the republican party, the democrats carried the election for governor and lieutenant-governor, and two out of four congressmen.[37] Irwin received a majority over Phelps of 29,587, and over Bidwell of 31,647. Phelps received a majority of 1,808 over Bidwell. J. A. Johnson[38] was elected lieutenant-governor by a majority of 25,119 over Pacheco, independent; and Pacheco 7,273 over J. M. Cavis, republican. Thus the reform party collapsed in 1875[39]

and Page, Bacon & Co. were disposed of in his court. In 1871 he was appointed a regent of the university of Cal. He died March 19, 1890.

[35] Newton Booth was born in Salem, Ind., in 1825 and educated at Asbury university, after which he studied law at Terre Haute was admitted to the bar, and removed to Cal. in 1850, engaging at first in mercantile pursuits at Sac. He returned to Ind. in 1857, remaining in Terre Haute three years, when he once more yielded to the attractions of the west coast, and settled at Sac. a second time, where he resided when elected governor. To his reputation for integrity and ability he added a fine fortune, and may be reckoned among California's most successful men.

[36] Irwin was a native of Ohio, had been a professor in a college, and edited the *Yreka Union* previous to his election. He was a man of no great repute, though had been a member of the assembly and state senate several times.

[37] Page was again elected by 1,400 maj. over Henry Larkin, dem. and C. A. Tuttle ind., in the 2d dist. W. A. Piper, dem., beat Rankin and J. F. Swift; Pacheco beat D. P. Wigginton dem. by one vote in the 4th dist; and J. K. Luttrell, dem., beat C. B. Denio and C. F. Reed in the 4d dist. Luttrell was of Santa Rosa and carried a good deal of weight. He was born in Tenn. in 1833, coming to Cal. in 1853. He educated himself, studied and practised law, although a farmer, was elected to the legislature in 1863, 1865-6, and 1871-2. He was twice elected to congress.

[38] Johnson was born in Spartenberg, S. C., in 1829, and was educated at Jefferson Medical college, Phila. He came to Cal. in 1853, and was elected to the assembly in 1859, and again in 1860. After serving as lieut-gov. he was twice elected to congress.

[39] The state officers elected in 1875 were Thomas Beck, sec. of state; J. W. Mandeville, controller; I. G. Estudillo, treas.; Jo. Hamilton, atty-gen.; William Minis, surv.-gen.; D. B. Woolf, clk. sup. ct

The agitation arising from those interests which had rendered a reform desirable had reopened the question of a change of constitution, not only to amend the form of the organic law in some respects, but to introduce new subjects of legislation coming from a change in affairs arising from the development of the state by railways, agriculture, the necessity for different corporation laws, municipal and otherwise, and a judicial system which should secure justice with less cost and delay.

The legislature of 1873–4 recommended to the electors to vote at the next general election for or against a revision of the constitution by convention, but the political managers not having thought proper to put this question upon their tickets at the election of 1875, the legislature following [40] again recommended a vote

[40] The members of the senate of 1875 newly elected were James Beazell, Alameda, E. J. Lewis, Colusa and Tehama; Paul Shirley, Contra Costa and Marin; John Montgomery, Mariposa, Merced, and Stanislaus; Robert Mc-Garvey, Mendocino, Humboldt, and Del Norte; Creed Haymond, Sac.; J. W. Satterwhite, San Diego and San Bernardino; T. McCarthy, J. Craig, Edward Nunan, M. J. Donovan, W. M. Pierson, Robert Howe, Frank Mc-Coppin, S. F.; George H. Rogers, San Mateo and S. F.; George S. Evans, San Joaquin; W. Z. Angney, Sta Clara; Thomas Flint, Sta Cruz, Monterey, and San Benito; W. J. Tinnin, Trinity, Modoc, and Siskiyou; S. G. Hillborn, Solano; William McPherson Hill, Sonoma, Napa, and Lake. B. F. Tuttle (hold-over) was chosen pres't pro tem.; T. L. Shackelford, sec.; E. L. Crawford, ass't sec.; Newton Benedict, George B. Cosby, William F. Howell, P. H. Ryan, George W. Canaway, Edward Gallagher, clerks; James W. Hawkins, J. B. Snyder, sergts-at-arms; Hiram Clock, James Watson, Edward Duffy, porters; Hyman Jacobs, H. M. Edwards, W. P. Dolan, J. H. Parsons, pages; J. C. Bernstein, postmaster; John M. Kilgariff, paper-folder; James Saulty, night watchman.

The assembly was composed of T. F. Boggs, D. W. Gelwicks, M. W. Dixon, Alameda; F. H. Carter, Thomas Dunlap, Amador; T. J. Jenkins, E. S. Ruggles, Butte; J. B. Reddick, Calaveras; L. J. Hart, Colusa and Tehama; Charles Wood, Contra Costa; James E. Murphy, Del Norte and Klamath; G. J. Carpenter, El Dorado; S. A. Nott, El Dorado and Alpine; J. D. Collins, Fresno; Jonathan Clark, Humboldt; M. Griswold, Inyo and Mono; J. A. Patterson, Kern and Tulare; R. V. S. Quigley, Lake; J. R. McConnell, Frederick Lambourn, Los Angeles; George M. Burbank, Marin; J. W. Wilcox, Mariposa and Merced; J. M. Covington, Mendocino; S. C. Abbott, Monterey; George N. Cornwall, Napa; S. L. Blackwell, Thomas P. Blue, G. W. Giffen, Nevada; W. M. Crutcher, Placer; John S. Chapman, Plumas and Lassen; Marion Biggs jr, T. J. Clunie, A. D. Patterson, Sac.; G. M. Roberts, San Benito; Henry Suverkrup, San Bernardino; J. M. Pierce, San Diego; T. N. Barber, William Broderick, R. M. Clarken, James V. Coffey, James G. Carson, J. W. Harding, J. W. Jourden, John Kennedy, J. C. Murphy, Thomas McInerny, William McMann, M. McCarthy, James G. Maguire, W. O'Connell, H. Rankin, Frederick Raisch, D. C. Sullivan, S. E.

upon this subject, which was acted upon at the election of 1877–8, as I shall further show in the next chapter, merely remarking here that while the proposition of revising the constitution was being canvassed, the subject of a division of the southern from the northern portion of the state was again brought forward, and endorsed by the press of that portion of California.

Wetherill, George A. Young, S. F.; John Patterson, N. C. Sargent, Martin Lammers, San Joaquin; R. M. Preston, San Luis Obispo; John Garrettson, San Mateo; W. A. Hayne, Sta Bárbara and Ventura; Cyrus Jones, S. I. Jamison, Lawrence Archer, Sta Clara; N. Rice, Sta Cruz; John Kautz, Sierra; G. F. Harris, Siskiyou and Modoc; T. M. Swan, Joseph McKenna, Solano; Walter Ferral, James Samuels, E. C. Henshaw, Sonoma; J. J. Scrivner, Stanislaus; C. P. Berry, Sutter; J. M. Briceland, Shasta and Trinity; T. C. Birney, Tuolumne; Jason Watkins, Yolo; J. C. Bradley, D. A. Ostrom, Yuba. G. J. Carpenter was chosen speaker, and J. E. Murphy speaker pro tem.; Robert Ferral, W. M. Ord, C. W. O'Neil, J. W. McCarthy, J. A. Martin, J. P. Rodgers, T. C. Morris, Matt. D. Carr, Charles Gildea, clerks; Dana Perkins, T. O'Connor, sergts-at-arms; John Kofod, William Lugg, John Hickey, H. Whitaker, porters; Joseph O'Neil, Bertie Worthington, Robert Hood, Willie Beveridge, E. J. Rodda, pages; S. Dunlap, postmaster; Frank Morse, paper-folder; Richard Pratt, chaplain. Of the senate elect there were 16 dem., 3 rep., 2 ind. Of the assembly, 62 dem., 15 rep., 1 ind.

For eight years, beginning with Jan. 1868, when he first took his seat in the state senate, Chas Maclay was one of its acknowledged leaders. A native of Concord, Pa, and of Irish descent, at eighteen he began his career in the ministry. In 1851 he was sent as a missionary to Cal., and appointed to the Santa Clara methodist circuit. On account of failing health he resigned his position, and in 1861-2 served in the state legislature, and later in the state central committee. While in the upper house he was chairman of several committees, and introduced a number of important measures, among them being a bill to encourage the early construction of the Southern Pacific, and one to establish the university of California.

HIST. CAL., VOL. VII. 24

CHAPTER XV.

THE NEW CONSTITUTION.

1878-1879.

MORE than once, as in 1857, 1859, 1860, and 1873, the legislature had recommended to the people to vote upon the question of a constitutional convention, and each time the proposition had been rejected. But the agitators had found so much amiss, that by the help of a popular newspaper in San Francisco, and the methods known to politicians, they were able to unsettle the minds of the people regarding the organic law.

It was discovered that all the regulations concerning taxation, contained in it, "did not occupy four lines." Any legislature might impose any tax which in its judgment, or want of regard for the tax-payers, it might decide to require of the people, and so infamously had the neglect been taken advantage of, that hundreds of capitalists had left the state to invest their money elsewhere. The constitution was dumb on the subject of finance, which the legislature might regulate at pleasure, borrowing from one fund to squander in another, with no check upon its acts.

With regard to salaries, no limit was imposed upon the legislature, which might allow its members and officers any amount. No guard had been established against extravagant fees, which the laws, in consequence, allowed for the most ordinary official services. The legislature was not restrained from disposing of the entire public domain and property of the state, without obtaining the consent of the people; nor did the constitution prohibit that body from funding or from otherwise forcing the people to pay illegal demands against the state, or its lesser communities. It made no provision for separate senatorial and assembly districts, whereby the people might be specifically represented. The members elected at large from the more populous counties controlled the legislature, while there was no exclusive responsibility resting upon them. The number of assembly-men was limited to eighty and of senators to forty. The assembly had already its full complement, though counties existed which had no representation in the house. Another serious fault was the unrestricted pardoning power of the governor, which should never form any appreciable link in proceedings in criminal punishment. To sum up in one all the counts against the constitution, as experience revealed its defects, the case was this: that the whole political duty and power of the people under it was to vote into place the men who would legislate away their substance—the constitution gave them no remedy.

The complainants asserted that the state required a constitution peculiarly her own, suited to its geography, topography, resources, commercial requirements, and the character of its population, and not to the wants of the purely agricultural states after which the constitution of 1849 was copied.

Undoubtedly there was some truth in all this, although much exaggerated. At the bottom of the discontent was a cause more pregnant than the incongruity of the constitution with the natural, commercial, and political condition of the country. Along with the rather phenomenal growth of the state, there had run a reactive tendency, an undertow from the tidal wave of early affluence which had dizzied the brain and bewildered the moral sense of those who for a time had been borne upon its crest. Many of those who had esteemed themselves favorites of fortune when the tide was at flood, now found themselves stranded on barren sands. They had lost the ability to return to the monotonous groove of their pre-California lives; and having also lost their place in the ranks of progress here, were falling out by the wayside. Their youth was fled, their shoulders bent, their locks thin and gray; they could no longer dig, had gold been as plenty as in '49; but they still had the restless, aspiring, projective spirit, and were unwilling to go down to oblivion. These men believed, or affected to believe, in the efficacy of a new constitution to cure the ills from which they suffered.

Another numerous class was made up of later arrivals of foreign birth, who were disappointed at not finding either a fortune or political preferment for the asking. To these were added the labor unions, and a large proportion of the agricultural class, who looked to a new constitution to lighten taxation and modify the mortgage laws. The judicial system was still unsatisfactory, and the courts overcrowded with business. Lastly, the hard times following the collapse of mining stocks from a value in 1875 of $300,000,000 to $30,000,000 in 1887, prepared the public mind to accept any change which promised the recovery of the state from the depression into which business had been thrown.

The opportunity for the workingmen and their chiefs was too good to be lost. It was pointed out by their leading journal that the mines and farms of the state together had yielded in five years $750,000,-000. But the wealth of the country was in the hands of about 150,000 persons, a dozen of whom were millionaires several times over, while 700,000 other individuals were struggling for existence, Out of 850,000 population, less than one quarter lived upon farms, and not over one half were supported by productive industries. Much of the earnings of that half had gone to build up the colossal fortunes of the few, and when an attempt was made to legislate against stock-gambling they opposed the reform with the might of their capital.[1] The whole amount of money in the state in 1878 was $25,000,000. The value of credits amounted to $200,000,000, of which $133,277,640 was banking capital. The real and personal property of the state, less the money, was $580,000,000. Averaging the riches of the state by the number of inhabitants, there was still a larger amount of property value to the individual than in many of the older commonwealths. But its unequal distribution, artfully dwelt upon by the agitators, was the source of the discontent and turbulence described in the foregoing chapter, the result of all of which was to create a majority vote in favor of a constitutional convention in 1878, and to revolutionize the state government, a consummation certainly not looked for by the legislatures of 1873–4 and 1875–6[2] when they recommended a convention. An appropriation of $150,000 had been made by the legislature to defray the expenses of a convention, and a special election for delegates, as well as for the adoption or rejection of the new instrument was ordered.

Finding the issue not to be avoided, an attempt was made, in April 1878, to fuse the best elements of the democratic, republican, and workingmen's parties into a non-partisan organization,[3] which at first was

---

[1] By advancing large sums of money to stock-brokers in return for their political influence, though of course charging them good interest on the amount.

[2] *Cal. Stat.*, 1873–4, p. 732, and 1877–8, 759–65; *Nov. Mess.*, 1877–8, pp. 33–5.

the 30 non-partisan candidates 19 were American born, 10 Irish, and

not successful; but in May a fusion was effected between a majority of republicans and democrats. Nevertheless there were many who preferred adhering to their own organizations, and finally, the workingmen refusing, there were three parties in the field with their delegates, besides the three tickets of the different labor organizations, namely, the Kearneyites, or workingmen's party of California, the national labor party, and the anti-workingmen. Before election, however, two of the tickets were withdrawn, the nationals fusing with the non-partisans. Even the offer of a delegateship to Kearney, Wellock, and one other, was not a bribe sufficient to catch the workingmen, and to prevent desertion through these influences, the rule was adopted that no member of their representative assembly should accept a nomination as delegate.

The convention of 152 delegates was to meet on the 28th of September, and the election was held in June. The workingmen carried the city and county of San Francisco, with 50 delegates; the non-partisans the state, with 85 delegates; the republicans had nine and the democrats eight in the convention.[4]

Under the circumstances, one might have looked for the expression of European socialistic ideas in this assemblage, but there cropped up in discussion the less advanced American one of state rights instead,[5]

3 Germans; 19 had been on the register ever since the passage of the registry law in 1868. On the Kearney ticket, 19 were foreign born; 15 out of 30 non-taxpayers; and only 4 had been on the register since 1868.

[4] *S. F. Alta*, June 26, 27, 1879; *S. F. Chronicle*, June, 27, 1879.

[5] In the debate on adoption of the 3d section of the declaration of rights, the majority refused the usual language ' the constitution of the United States is the charter of our liberties,' and adopted ' the state of California is an inseparable part of the American union, and the constitution of the United States is the supreme law of the land.' Said the *Sac. Record Union*, of June 29, 1879, ' the ignorant communistic, alien section, fraternized with the unconstructed rebel section, and Americans who love their country were compelled to submit to the bitter humiliation of hearing its fundamental law repudiated, alike by foreign demagogues unable to speak the English language correctly, and by apostate Americans whose only claim to notoriety is that in their country's hour of danger they were on the side of her enemies, and aided and abetted the plot for her destruction.' The phrase ' charter of our liberties ' was rejected by Volney E. Howard, elected on the

for the reason, perhaps, that the advocates of socialism were more skilled in throwing cobble-stones than defining principles. There may be crises in the world's affairs when the art of hurling paving-stones is not to be despised. So now, the doltish determination of the workingmen was not without value in giving direction to the ideas of constitution-makers. As for a parliamentarian to govern the proceedings, an accomplished presiding officer was found in Joseph P. Hoge.[6]

The convention sat 156 working days, and produced an instrument which its critics objected to as a code. Such in truth it was meant to be, a code which could not be altered at every session of the legislature, formed to secure labor against the tyranny of capital. While native American political philoso-

democratic ticket. He was born in Maine in 1809, bred to the profession of the law, and went to Miss. where he became southernized, was elected to the constit. conv. and sent to congress; and lastly he came to Cal. in 1853 where he aspired to the U. S. senate, was one of those who rejected 'the charter of our liberties.' *S. F. Post*, April 14, 1879. Another delegate who rejected this phrase was P. B. Tully, born in Tenn. in 1830, and bred a farmer, his father removing with him to Arkansas during his boyhood. Afteward he went to Texas, and came from there to Cal. in 1853. He settled in Mariposa, but removed to Gilroy where he studied law, and where he married Miss Mary Martin, whose father immigrated to Cal. in 1843 from Mo. In 1863, being admitted to practice, he established himself in Santa Clara co., where he became noted in his profession. He was elected on the non-partisan ticket. Still another was Patrick T. Dowling, born in Tuam, County Galway, Ireland, in 1849. He migrated to the U. S. in 1865 and to Cal. in 1866, where he had acquired considerable property. He was elected on the workingmen's ticket, and was intelligent enough to lead his party vote which prevailed, and the language used in the section named was 'the supreme law of the land.' Law being statutory, unless in the form of a charter, it was of course subject to alteration by legislation.

[6] Joseph P. Hoge was born in Pa in 1813, educated in Ohio, and practised law in Galena circuit, Ill., being three times elected to congress from his district. He came to Cal. in 1850, and resided in S. F. He was elected president of the convention by a vote of 74 against 73 for his opponent, W. J. Tinnin of Trinity. W. J. Tinnin was born in Miss. in 1829, came to Cal. by sea in 1849, mined in several counties, and finally settled as a merchant at Weaverville, Trinity co., where he was prosperous, and from which he was elected to the assembly in 1871 and 1873, and to the senate in 1875 to fill an unexpired term. He was a democrat, elected on the non-partisan ticket. V. E. Howard and Henry Larkin were also proposed for the office of president of the convention. Larkin was a native of Madison co., N. Y., born in 1826. He came to Cal. in 1847, and was deputy sheriff of El Dorado co. from 1852 to 1855, when he was appointed census marshal. In 1869 he was elected to the stated senate, and in 1875 was a candidate for congress. By occupation he was a farmer. He was elected delegate to the convention on the workingmen's ticket, but belonged to the democratic party.

phers were discussing the propriety of a property qualification for voters, by means of which an impecunious and purchasable rabble could not at their pleasure vote money out of the pockets of the prudent and thrifty, the cobble-stone throwers entered in their bill of rights : "No property qualification shall ever be required for any person to vote or hold office." It summed up with the declaration that, "The provisions of this constitution are mandatory and prohibitory, unless by express words they are declared to be otherwise."

The legislative department of the government was subjected to many restrictions in the matter of time,[7] pay, place,[8] rules of the legislative body, and other matters. The governor might veto a bill, but a two-thirds vote of each house should pass a bill over the governor's veto. The assembly alone should have the power to impeach, but all impeachments should be tried before the senate. The governor and all the state officers, with the judges of the superior, and justices of the supreme courts, being liable to impeachment, judgment in such cases extended only to removal from office and subsequent disqualification for office ; but the person so tried and punished was liable to the ordinary process of law. Embezzlement by one in the service of the United States should render the guilty person ineligible to any office in the state, and the legislature must pass laws for the punishment of this crime as a felony. Appropriations of money from the state treasury, or grants of property, for the use of corporations or institutions not under the exclusive control of the state, were forbidden ; except that aid might be granted to orphanages,[9] or homes

[7] Sessions were made to commence the first Monday after the first day of January, to avoid the holiday week, during which legislative business was neglected.

[8] No more changing of the capital during sessions.

[9] Most of the orphanages, especially those demanding state aid, are institutions under the charge of the catholic church, and most of the indigent requiring public aid are of foreign birth, and usually of the catholic faith; therefore this section must be set down to the Kearney workingmen under

for the indigent, by a uniform rule proportioned to the number of inmates. Special legislation was forbidden in a large number of cases, including any affecting the action of courts of justice, the collection of taxes, granting divorces, changing the names of persons or places, declaring a minor of age, or enabling him to encumber his property, chartering ferries, roads, or bridges, etc. Lotteries should be prohibited ; laws should be passed to regulate or prohibit the buying or selling of shares of the capital stock of corporations in any stock board, exchange, or market under the control of any association ; and all sales of stock on a margin, or to be delivered at some future day, should be void. Neither the legislature, nor any municipal corporation, county, or school district, should ever make an appropriation from any public fund, or grant anything to or in aid of any religious sect, or help to support any school, or college, or hospital controlled by any religious creed, church or sectarian denomination, but as before excepted in aid of orphanages and homes for the indigent. The legislature should have no power to lend or authorize the giving or lending of the credit of the state, in aid of persons, associations or corporations, municipal or otherwise ; nor to make gifts of any public money or thing of value to individuals or corporations ; nor to authorize the state or any sub-division thereof to subscribe for stock, or to become a stockholder in any corporation whatever. The legislature should enact laws limiting the charges of telegraph and gas companies, and the charges for storage and wharfage. Any person attempting to influence the legislature by bribery, intimidation, or other dishonorable means, should be guilty of lobbying, which was declared to be a felony, for which the legislature should provide a punishment ; and any member accepting a bribe

the guidance of the Romish church. While the protestants were barred under this section, the way to the public treasury was left open to the catholics.

should be guilty of a felony, and in addition to his punishment be disfranchised, and disqualified from holding any office or public trust.

The changes in the executive department were slight. The governor might convene the legislature on extraordinary occasions; but it should have no power to legislate upon any subject other than that specified in the proclamation of the executive. The power to appoint a secretary of state was taken away from the governor, and the office made elective by the people. The legislature might abolish the surveyor-general's office. Pardons, reprieves, and commutations of sentence might be granted by the governor, subject to certain restrictions to be provided by law; but a person twice convicted of a felony could not be pardoned except upon the written recommendation of a majority of the judges of the supreme court. The governor should not, during his incumbency, be elected a senator of the United States.

In the judiciary department there were more important changes. In the first place, in the declaration of rights a blow was administered to the jury system. The right of trial by jury was secured, but in civil actions three-fourths of a jury might render a verdict. Trial by jury might be waived in criminal cases not amounting to felony, both parties consenting in open court; or in civil cases, the parties consenting in a manner to be prescribed by law. In civil cases the jury might consist of any number less than twelve, on which the litigants should agree. Offences heretofore requiring to be prosecuted by indictment might be prosecuted by information and commitment by a magistrate, or by indictment. A grand jury should be summoned but once a year in each county. The freedom of the press was to be maintained without any fear of its influence on a jury. The judicial power of the state was vested in the senate sitting as a court of impeachment, in a supreme court, superior courts, justices of the peace, and such inferior courts

as the legislature should establish in incorporated
cities or towns, or city and county. The supreme
court should consist of a chief justice and six associate justices. The court might sit in departments or
in bank, and should be always open for the transaction of business. It should be divided into two departments, numbered one and two, the chief justice
assigning three judges to each and changing them
from time to time; but they might interchange with
each other by agreement. Each department should
have power to hear and determine causes or questions
arising therein, subject to provisions made in relation
to court in bank. The presence of three justices was
necessary to the transaction of any business in either
department, except such as might be done at chambers, and the concurrence of three justices was necessary to pronounce a judgment, one of them sitting as
presiding judge. The chief justice should apportion
the business to the departments, and might order any
cause to be heard and decided by the court in bank,
and the order might be made before or after judgment
pronounced by a department; but the order must be
made within thirty days after such judgment be concurred in by two associate justices, and should have
the effect to set aside the judgment. Any four justices
might order a case to be heard in bank before or after
judgment by a department; but the order must be
made within the prescribed time, after which a judgment became final, and could not become final in less
time unless approved by the chief justice in writing,
with the concurrence of two associate justices. The
chief justice might convene the court in bank at any
time, and must preside over it. The concurrence of
four justices present at the argument was necessary
to pronounce a judgment; but if they could not agree,
then all the justices should hear the argument, and at
least four should agree to a decision. All decisions
of the supreme court should be rendered in writing,[10]

[10] The sup. ct rendered many decisions without giving any reason, written

and the grounds of the decision stated. In the event of the illness or absence of the chief justice the associate justices might choose one of their own number to exercise the powers of chief during such period.

The chief and associate justices should be elected at the general state elections, and should hold office twelve years; but the six associate justices should at their first meeting so classify themselves by lot that two of them should go out of office at the end of four, two at the end of eight, and two at the end of twelve years. Should a vacancy occur, the governor should appoint a person to the office until it was filled by election, and the judge then elected should hold for the remainder of the unexpired term. The jurisdiction of the supreme court was not made to differ essentially from the same under the old constitution; but each of the justices should have power to issue writs of habeas corpus to any part of the state upon petition by or on behalf of any person held in actual custody, and could make such writs returnable before himself, or the supreme court, or any superior judge or court in the state.

The superior courts took the place of county and district courts, and held original jurisdiction in all cases civil and criminal not assigned to inferior courts, and possessed the power of naturalization and appellate jurisdiction in cases arising in justices' and other inferior courts in their respective counties. These courts, like the supreme court, should be always open for business, legal holidays and non-judicial days excepted, and their process should extend to all parts of the state; but cases affecting real estate should be begun in the counties in which such land was situated. They should also have power to issue writs of every kind, including habeas corpus, in the same manner as the supreme court, and might issue and

or verbal. The legislature, to remedy this, enacted that the ct should give a written reason—sec. 657, Practice act—for all its decisions, but the ct decided the law unconstitutional. *Heuston* vs *Williams*, 13 Cal., p. 24.

serve injunctions and prohibitions on legal holidays and non-judicial days.

One of these courts should be organized in each of the organized counties, or cities and counties, of the state, for each of which at least one judge should be elected at the general state election; but in the city and county of San Francisco twelve superior judges should be elected, any one or more of whom might hold court. There might be as many sessions, at the same time, as there were judges, and a presiding judge might be chosen or removed by the remaining eleven at their pleasure, but he must distribute the business of the court among the judges, and prescribe its order. The judgments, orders, and proceedings of any session of the superior court, held by any one or more of the judges, should be as effectual as if all had been present. Several of the more important counties had two superior judges, while Yuba and Sutter had but one between them. The term of office of the superior judges was fixed at six years, except in the case of San Francisco, whose judges must classify themselves so that four should go out of office at the end of two years, four in four years, and four in six years. Vacancies should be filled as in the case of supreme judges. Whenever there was more than one judge of the superior court in a county, other than San Francisco, they might hold as many sessions as there were judges, and apportion the business among themselves; and a judge of one county might, by request, hold court in another, or the governor might direct him to do so. A cause might also be tried in a superior court by a judge pro tempore, who must have been a member of the bar, and agreed upon by the litigants or their attorneys, and sworn to try the cause.

The legislature was denied the power to grant leave of absence to any judicial officer, and should he absent himself for more than sixty consecutive days he would be deemed to have forfeited his office; but the legislature might increase or diminish the number of judges in a county, or city and county, provided no judge already in office was dislodged. The manner prescribed of removing justices of the supreme and judges of the superior courts was by concurrent resolution of both houses of the legislature;[11] but the senate might remove all other judicial officers, except justices of the peace, on the recommendation of the governor, the ayes and noes being entered on the journal. The number of justices of the peace, their powers and duties, were left to be fixed by the legislature, except the limiting their jurisdiction to cases involving amounts under $300.

As to salaries, the state should pay the judges of the supreme court and half the salaries of the judges of the superior courts, the remainder being paid by the counties for which they were elected. During the first term under the new constitution the supreme court justices should receive $6,000 each per annum. The superior court judges should receive $3,000 per annum, except in San Francisco and some of the more populous counties, where the salary was $4,000, but the legislature might change these amounts. Salaries were made payable monthly, and no judge of the supreme or superior courts should be allowed to draw his pay, unless he should subscribe an affidavit before an officer entitled to administer oaths, that no cause in his court remained undecided which had been submitted for decision for a period of ninety days. No person was eligible to the office of justice of the supreme or of the superior court who had not first been admitted to practice before the supreme court of the state.

Thus the convention labored to cure the evils which California had suffered through its various courts; to secure continuous sessions, speedy trial, and early de-

---

[11] This was a weak point in the judiciary article, as a legislature could remove the entire bench, and substitute creatures of its own. *S. F. Call,* May 2, 1879.

cisions, with the reasons therefor. In point of expenditure it was a more costly system than the old one, but it was argued that penuriousness in this department of the government was not true economy.

The subjects of taxation and corporations received much attention, and elicited much criticism. The article on taxation, as adopted, declared that all property should be taxed according to its value, to be ascertained as provided by law, and property was declared to include "moneys, credits, bonds, stocks,"[12] dues, franchises, and all other matters and things, real, personal, and mixed, capable of private ownership;" but growing crops,[13] public school property, United States and state property, or property belonging to any municipal corporation in the state, should be exempt. Land and the improvements thereon should be assessd separately. Land, cultivated or uncultivated, if similarly situated and of the same quality, should be assessed at the same value;[14] and every tract of over 640 acres which had been sectionized by the federal surveyors should be assessed, for purposes of taxation,

[12] The legislature of 1881 added a section to the political code declaring that shares of stock possessed no intrinsic value over and above the actual value of the property of the corporation which was assessable and assessed.

[13] To assess growing crops, it was argued, would be to discourage planting and sowing.

[14] This section was aimed at railroad companies, and other large landholders, who paid but a small amount of taxes on uncultivated land. The report of the surveyor-general for 1877 gave the whole area of California at 100,500,000 acres, of which 50,000,000 acres were fit for cultivation. But in 1876 only 6,319,864 acres were enclosed, and 3,576,366 in cultivation; in 1879 there were 8,000,000 acres enclosed, and 5,000,000 cultivated. In 1876 there were 24,058,349 acres assessed for taxes; in 1877, 24,706,162 acres assessed, being an increase in one year of $2\frac{1}{3}$ per cent. An equal rate of increase would have given in 1879 25,858,940 assessed for taxes—that is to say, 5,000,000 acres in cultivation, and 20,858,940 uncultivated, belonging and assessed to large land-owners. The owners of the 5,000,000 acres were probably taxed 8 or 10 times as much as the owners of the 21,000,000. The average assessment value of lands held in tracts ranging from 5,000 to 125,000 acres was not much, if any, above $1.80, while their market value averaged not less than $15. In 1877 the real estate outside of San Francisco was assessed at $203,803,446, of which $41,000,000 was on town lots, the remaining $162,803,446 being on lands. Of this, the small farmers paid at least $125,000,000, while the remaining $37,803,446 was paid by the large owners, who produced little, and held the land for speculation, or leased a part to cultivators at three times as much per year as it was valued for taxes, and who, it was alleged, built few roads, towns, school-houses, or churches.

by sections or fractions of sections, and the legislature
should provide by law for assessing in small tracts un-
sectionized lands.[15]

Mortgages, deeds of trust, contracts, and all obligations whatever by which debts were secured, were
treated as an interest in the property, and taxed accordingly; but the owner of the property mortgaged
should be taxed its full value, less the mortgage,[16] in
the city or county in which the property was situated.
In the case of railroad property, the franchise, roadway, road-bed, rails, and rolling stock should be assessed by the state board of equalization, and the tax
apportioned to the counties, cities, towns, townships,
and districts through which the road passed. The
state board of equalization should consist of one member from each congressional district, elected at the
general elections for a term of four years, the state
controller being ex officio a member of the board. The
supervisors of the several counties should constitute
county boards of equalization; and these boards, state
and county, were empowered to increase or reduce
the entire assessment roll, or any part of it, to make it
conform to the money value of the property taxed.
Incomes might be assessed to and collected from individuals, corporations, joint-stock associations, or companies resident, or doing business in the state, in a

[15] It was objected to this provision that it would cost $1,000,000 to estab-
lish the surveys so as to render the assessment in small tracts practicable.

[16] The sup. court had decided in some cases in favor of taxing mortgages
under the existing constitution and code of California. People v. McCrury,
34 Cal. Repts, 432; and People v. Eddy, 43 Cal. Repts, 331; People v. Gerke,
35 Cal. Repts, 677; People v. Black Diamond C. M. Co., 37 Cal. Repts, 54;
People v. Whartenby, 38 Cal., 461. These decisions were rendered previous
to 1872. In 1876 the Hibernia bank appealed from a similar decision by the
3d district court of S. F., when McKinstry, judge, reversed the decision,
giving as his reason that credits were not property in the sense in which the
word property was used in article XI. of the existing constitution, Wallace
and Crockett concurring, and Rhodes objecting, all of whom had previously
decided that credits were property. The Hibernia bank held mortgages to
the amount of $11,366,934.50, the tax levied on these credits amounting to
$77,460.48. The persons owning the real estate had already paid taxes upon
the actual property without deducting the value of the mortgages, and the
judge held that it would be double taxation to assess the evidences of these
debts of the owners. It was natural that, under the circumstances, the

manner to be prescribed by law.[17]   An annual poll-tax of not less than two dollars should be collected from every male inhabitant of sound mind, except Indians, between the ages of twenty-one and sixty years, which tax should be paid into the state school fund.   The legislature might provide for the payment of taxes upon real estate by installments.   The power of taxation should never be surrendered or suspended by any grant or contract to which the state should be a party.

Corporations could be formed only under general laws, and not by special act.   Each stockholder should be individually liable for such proportion of all debts and liabilities, incurred while he was a stockholder, as the amount owned by him bore to the whole of the capital stock.   The directors or trustees were made jointly and severally liable to the creditors and stockholders for all money embezzled or misappropriated by officers of a corporation or joint-stock association during their term of office; and the term corporation included all associations having any of the powers and privileges of corporations not possessed by individuals or partnerships; and they had the right to sue and be sued in like cases as natural persons.

The legislature could not grant a charter for banking purposes, but companies might be formed for banking under general laws.   No corporation could issue or put in circulation any but lawful money of the United States.

The exercise of the right of eminent domain should never be abridged so as to prevent the state from subjecting the property of individuals or incorporated

people should regard this decision with some distrust, as being made to favor capitalists.   But after much discussion, the convention settled the matter by deducting the amount of mortgages from the property taxed, and assessing mortgagees for the amount.   In the end it only increases the rate of interest.

[17] The general sentiment against an income tax, so long as all the means by which it was obtained were taxed, has so far prevented the legislature from levying any assessment on incomes.   When the U. S. was collecting an income tax as a means of meeting the unusual expenses of the rebellion, it was not taxing land.

companies to the public use; nor should the police power of the state ever be so abridged as to permit corporations to infringe the rights of individuals or the well-being of the state. No corporation should engage in any business other than that expressly authorized in its charter, or hold for a longer period than five years any real estate not necessary to carrying on its business;[18] the legislature should not pass any laws which would tend to relieve the property held under a franchise from its liabilities; no corporation should issue any stock or bonds except for actual payment in money, labor, or property; all fictitious increase of stock or indebtedness should be void; no increase could be made without the consent of the holders of a majority of the shares, at a meeting called for the purpose on a sixty days' public notice, at which every stockholder should have the right to vote in person or by proxy, and directors could only be elected in the same manner—except in the case of coöperative societies; but every stockholder could vote all his shares to one candidate, or distribute them among as many as he should think fit; and the books of the corporation should be open for inspection by every one interested therein, and by legislative committees. No corporation, organized outside of the limits of the state, should be allowed to transact busi-

[18] This section appears to have been intended to prevent the railroad companies from acquiring town-sites and other valuable real estate for speculative purposes. As for instance, the state granted to the Western Pacific, subsequently absorbed by the Central Pacific, and to the Southern Pacific 30 acres each in Mission bay, for terminal purposes, upon condition that a certain amount of money should be expended upon the grant within a specified time, in the erection of depots and warehouses. The Central Pacific obtained control of the property, and as the time after being extended by the legislature was finally allowed to expire without making the improvements agreed upon, the land reverted to the state. During Gov. Booth's administration a suit was instituted against the railroad corporations to declare the land forfeited. The companies moved to dismiss the suit because it was not properly brought, and the motion was denied. They demurred to the complaint, and the demurrer was overruled. The case was on the calendar for trial while the constitutional convention was in session. The prohibition in reference to other business was aimed at the alleged intent of the Central Pacific to engage in warehousing and grain business on the land granted for terminal purposes; but this is the merest surmise.

ness within the state on more favorable conditions than if organized under the laws of California.[19]

All railroad and other transportation companies were declared to be common carriers, subject to legislative control. They should have a right to connect at the state line with the railroads of other states, and every railroad should have the right to intersect, connect with, or cross, any other railroad, and they should receive and transport each others' passengers, tonnage, and cars, without delay or discrimination. No officer, agent, or employé of any railroad or canal company should be interested in furnishing material or supplies[20] to such company, nor in the business of transportation over the road, except such as flowed from the ownership of stock therein. No railroad or other transportation company should grant free passes, or tickets at a discount, to any person holding any office of honor, trust, or profit in the state; and the acceptance of any such pass or ticket, by a member of the legislature, or any public officer, other than railroad commissioner, should work a forfeiture of his office.

Railroad companies were forbidden to combine with navigation companies or any common carrier,[21] to the end that the earnings of the one doing the carrying were to be shared with the other not doing the carrying. And whenever a railroad corporation should, for the purpose of competing with any other common carrier, lower its rates for transportation of passengers or freight, such reduced rates should not be again increased without the consent of the authority in which the government vested the power to regulate fares and freights; and no discrimination should be made

[19] This prohibition referred to foreign insurance and other companies doing business in California without paying taxes.

[20] This was probably aimed at the Western Development company, organized in 1874, and soon after the framing of the new constitution merged into the Pacific Improvement company. To the former were transferred the interests of the Contract and Finance company, as will be spoken of in a later chapter.

[21] The only effect of this prohibition was to force these corporations to purchase steamer lines.

in charges or facilities for transportation of passengers or freight within the state, or coming from or going to any other state; but persons and property should be delivered at any station, landing, or port, at charges not exceeding the rates to any more distant station.[22]

The state was to be divided into three districts, in each of which one railroad commissioner should be elected at the regular gubernatorial elections, whose term of office should be four years, and whose duty it should be to establish rates for the transportation of passengers and freights by railroad or other common carriers, and publish them from time to time, with such changes as they might make; to examine the companies' books, records, and papers, for which purpose they should have power to issue subpœnas and all necessary process, to hear and determine complaints against railroad and other transportation companies, to send for persons and papers, to administer oaths, take testimony, and punish for contempt of their orders and processes, in the same manner and to the same extent as courts of record, and enforce their decisions and correct abuses through the medium of the courts. A uniform system of accounts to be kept by all such corporations should be prescribed by them. Any transportation company which should fail or refuse to conform to the rates established[23] by

[22] Here we have one of the weakest points in the new constitution. Although there are many precedents in American and European legislation for regulating in detail the charges of railroads, they have seldom been found to work to advantage. In this connection the following remarks, taken from the report of a parliamentary committee held in London in 1872, may be of interest, as they apply equally to all except government railroads: 'Legal maximum rates afford little real protection to the public, since they are always fixed so high that it is, or becomes sooner or later, the interest of the companies to carry at lower rates. The attempt to limit rates and fares by the principle of fixing a maximum has almost always failed in practice, and is almost always likely to fail, for the simple reason that the parliamentary committees and authorities, by whom such limits are decided, cannot do otherwise than allow some margin between the actual probable rate, as far as they can forecast it, and the maximum rate; and cannot foresee the contingencies of competition, of increase in quantities, of facilities or economy in working, or of alteration of commercial conditions.'

[23] The Pacific Coast Steamship company refused to recognize the authority of the board, and commenced suit in the U. S. circuit court to restrain the board from in any way interfering with the business of the company. *Rep't of R. R. Commissioners in App. to Jour. Sen. and Assem.*, 1881, No. 3.

the commissioners, or charge rates in excess thereof, or fail to keep their accounts in accordance with the system prescribed by the commission, should be fined not exceeding $20,000 for each offence, and every officer, agent, or employé of such corporation who should demand or receive rates in excess of those prescribed by the commissioners should pay a fine of not more than $5,000, or be imprisoned in the county jail not exceeding one year. The rates established by the commission should always be deemed conclusively just and reasonable; and in any action against a railroad company for damages on account of excessive rates, the plaintiff might, in addition to actual damage, recover, in the discretion of the judge or jury, exemplary damages. The legislature might, in addition to the penalties already named, enforce this article of the constitution by forfeiture of charter or otherwise, and might confer further power on the commissioners if necessary to the performance of their duties. Vacancies in office should be filled in the same manner as in the case of other state officers. The commission should make an annual report to the governor.[24]

The railroad, mining, and banking corporations, through the press and their agents, strongly opposed the article containing so many restrictions upon their methods of doing business, and the convention itself was divided, capitalists holding out a threat of abandoning the state and withdrawing their money. "Let them go," said the advocates of restriction, "they cannot take with them the houses, farms, or railroads which they have acquired with our money. We will, in one year, dig out of the mines as much gold as they will take away, and produce in two years ten times the amount; and the sooner the bankers go the bet-

[24] The first board of commissioners elected consisted of Joseph S. Cone, 1st dist; C. J. Beerstecker, 2nd dist, and George Stoneman, 3d dist. Cone was chosen pres't. The secretary of the com. was W. R. Andrus; bailiff, T. V. Steinman. The board was organized in May 1880. In December an attempt was made to assassinate Beerstecker, the supposed cause being political jealousy. Both B. and his assailant belonged to the workingmen's party.

ter.[25]   They cannot frighten us with circulars[26] declaring that if the new constitution is adopted they must materially increase the interest on loans." Thus the restrictionists; but the alarm was nevertheless quite real and wide-spread lest the business of the state should be seriously affected by the new fundamental law, if adopted; and, indeed, it was already restricted to a considerable extent in anticipation of a revolution which as yet nobody seemed to comprehend.

In the matter of Chinese labor and immigration the constitution declared that the legislature should prescribe all necessary regulations for the protection of the state, and every part of it, from the evils arising from the presence of aliens who were or might be vagrants, from mendicants or criminals, who were infected with contagious diseases, or who were in any way dangerous or detrimental to the well-being or peace of the community; also to impose conditions upon which persons might reside in the state, and provide the mode of, and means for their removal in case of their failure or refusal to comply with such conditions.   The presence of foreigners ineligible to become citizens of the United States was declared to be dangerous to the well-being of the state; and it should be the duty of the legislature to discourage their immigration by every means in its power. Asiatic coolyism was pronounced a form of human slavery, which was forever prohibited in the state, and all contracts for coolie labor should be void.   All companies for the importation of such labor, whether formed in California[27] or in a foreign country, should be subject to such penalties as the legislature might prescribe, which should also delegate to incorporated cities and towns power to remove Chinese without their boundaries, or to certain prescribed limits, and

---

[25] S. F. Chronicle, March 16, 1879, and April 3, 1879.

[26] The Sacramento savings bank published such a circular, for which see Sac. Record Union, in S. F. Chronicle, March 14, 1879.

[27] A prohibition to prevent railroad companies particularly from making contracts with the Chinese companies.

should provide the necessary legislation to prohibit
the introduction of Chinese into California. No corporation existing or to be formed under the laws of
the state should, after the adoption of the constitution, employ directly or indirectly, in any capacity,[28]
any Chinese or Mongolians; nor should any Chinese
be employed on public work, except in punishment for
crime.[29]

The article on education did not allow of quite
such revolutionary changes as the preceding ones.
The school-money was placed where it would most
benefit the working classes; that is, for the use only of
the primary and grammar schools, leaving the legislature to provide for schools of a higher grade, or the
municipalities to raise a revenue for this purpose from
other than the fund arising from the sale of the school-
lands granted to the state by congress. The state
board of examiners was abolished, the local board
having control of teachers' examinations and granting of certificates. Sectarian doctrines should not be

[28] Workingmen have gone about in S. F. warning families who employed Chinese servants, both before and after the constitutional convention; and even since the restriction of immigration by congress, a bill for
which was at that time before congress, and which finally passed. The
legislature had no power to prohibit Chinese immigration while the treaty
with China was in force; nor at any other time without the consent of
congress.

[29] Stuart, of Sonoma, hits hard the low foreigner in his speech on the Chinese question: 'Who are they who desecrate the sabbath?' he says; 'who form
our rioters and hoodlums? Who fill our almshouses? Who are plotting to
overthrow our common schools? Who stuff our ballot-boxes? Who are
plotting to overthrow our government, and to utterly stamp out liberty,
that depotism over conscience, mind and muscle may rise upon the ruins?
Who constitute the Molly Maguires? Who burn our railroad depots? Who
threaten the lives of our best citizens? Who are plotting to despoil our
wealthy men? Who claim two-thirds of our public offices? Not Chinamen.'
Charles V. Stuart, elected on the non-partisan ticket, was born in Pa. in
1819, in which state his parents, Charles and Mary Stuart were also born.
He was bred a farmer, and educated at Owego acadamy N. Y., after which
he wandered over the state west and south until 1849, when he came to Cal.
overland in command of a company. He settled himself on ten acres of
land at Mission Dolores, and was elected on the first board of aldermen of
S. F. in 1850. He leased the New Almaden mine for 21 years from the
Barryessa family, supposing them to be the true owners, but after years of
unproductive labor sold it. He built the first brick house in S. F. in 1851,
but 8 years afterward removed to Sonoma valley where he was one of the
first viniculturists.

taught directly or indirectly in any of the common schools of the state.[30]

The university of California was to be a public trust which should continue in the form and character prescribed in the act creating it,[31] subject only to such control by the legislature as secured compliance with the terms of its endowments and the safety of its funds. It should be non-sectarian in the administration of its affairs. The interest of the money derived from the lands donated by congress should be used as an endowment for the support of at least one agricultural college; and the legislature should pro-

---

[30] This was meant to prohibit bible-reading in the schools, to which catholics objected. It was double-edged, and cut both ways.

[31] The act creating the university of Cal. was passed March 23, 1868, the constitution of 1849 having provided for a university in anticipation of a grant from the general govt for such a purpose, which grant was made according to a general law giving to each state a certain amount of land for educational purposes. Cal. received in 1853, besides her common-school lands, 72 sections 'for seminary purposes,' and in 1862 150,000 acres for the establishment and maintenance of an agricultural college. The state law of 1868 creating the university of Cal. combined with it the agricultural college, and made that the first to be erected by the means derived from the state funds. But it also accepted for the state the gift of the college of Cal., which became a college of letters in the university. This college was founded at Oakland as a college school by Henry Durant, becoming an incorporated college in 1855. It acquired property and prospered under the management of Durant and Bushnell, who selected the location at Berkeley, which became the site of the university of Cal., containing 200 acres of land, a part of which was devoted to experimental farming. The donation to the university of the college of Cal. was a great help. There were 7 colleges in existence in 1879, namely, of letters, agriculture, mechanics, mining, engineering, chemistry, and medicine. To the last a donation was made by H. H. Toland of S. F., whose name was conferred upon that college by act of legislature in March 1881. To the law college S. C. Hastings donated $100,000 in 1878, and this college was named after him. Military instruction was required by the congressional act of donation, and the students were organized into a body of cadets. The resources of the university were the seminary fund and public building fund granted to Cal. by congress; the property received from the college of Cal., as stated; the site at Berkeley; the fund received from the congressional land grant in 1862, the tide land fund, appropriated by the state; specific appropriations by the legislature for buildings, current expenses, etc.; and the gifts of individuals. The care of the university and its finances was entrusted to a board of regents, including the gov., lieut-gov., speaker of the assembly, supt of public instruction, pres't of the state ag. society, pres't of the Mechanics' institute of San Francisco, the pres't of the university, and 16 others. This govt was continued by the new constitution. Some jealousy was exhibited by the farmers in the convention lest the agricultural interest should be injured by the attractions of the other colleges, for which reason they insisted on the inviolability of the appropriation made for the support of a college of agriculture, but without excluding other scientific and classical studies, and including military tactics.

vide that if, through neglect or other contingency, any
portion of the fund so set apart should be lost, the
state should replace it so that the principal should
forever remain undiminished. No person should be
debarred admission to any of the collegiate departments of the university on account of sex.[32]

State indebtedness could not be incurred for a
greater amount than $300,000, unless in case of war,
invasion, or insurrection, except for a single object
for which ways and means had been provided, exclusive of loans, the debt not to run more than twenty
years, and the people to vote upon the proposition to
incur it.

The legislature should protect by law from forced
sale a certain portion of the homestead and other
property of the heads of families. The holding of
large tracts of land should be discouraged as against
the public interest. Lands belonging to the state,
suitable for cultivation, should be granted only to
actual settlers, and in quantities not exceeding 320
acres to each settler, under such conditions as should
be prescribed by law. All property, real and personal, owned by either husband or wife before marriage, and that acquired by either of them afterward
by gift, devise, or descent, should be separate property. No contract of marriage, if otherwise duly
made, should be invalidated for want of conformity
to the requirements of any religious sect.[33] Eight

[32] There was in 1879 both curiosity and interest felt in the application of
Mrs Clara S. Folz, who had studied law and been admitted to practise in the
20th district court, but who was refused admission by the directors of the
Hastings law college, where she wished to pursue her studies and graduate.
Laura de Force Gordon was also preparing to practise before the courts, and
had the same difficulty.   Mrs Folz petitioned the 4th district court to compel the directors of the law college to admit her as a student, and Morrison,
judge, issued a writ of mandate to that effect.   Congress had just passed an
act authorizing women to practise law, and a woman had been admitted to
the U. S. sup. court.   Under these circumstances, and knowing that the
new constitution declared for equal educational and business rights, the directors submitted. See *S. F. Post*, Jan. 28 and Feb. 11, 1879; *S. F. Chronicle*,
Jan. 30 and Feb. 11, 14, 1879, and March 6, 1879.

[33] This same declaration was in the constitution of 1849, and in the Cal.
code. In the Hill-Sharon divorce case, commencing in 1883, it was the
foundation of the application for divorce and alimony. Sullivan, of the su-

hours were made to constitute a day's work on all public contracts.   Any citizen who should fight or assist at a duel should be disfranchised.   The right of eminent domain was declared to exist in the state to all frontages on the navigable waters of the state; and the right of way to such water, should not be excluded by individuals or corporations claiming or possessing the tidal lands fronting on any navigable bay, harbor, or inlet.   All the tide lands within two miles of any incorporated city or town fronting on the waters of any harbor, estuary, or bay, used for navigation, should be withheld from grant or sale.

The use of all water already appropriated, or that might thereafter be appropriated, for sale,[34] rental, or distribution, was declared to be a public use, and subject to the rule and regulation of the state; but the board of supervisors of city, town, or city and county government might fix the rates for which it should be furnished to the inhabitants under pain of penalties for neglect; and any company collecting any other than the established water-rates should forfeit its franchise and water-works to the city and county, or city, or town where the collection was made for the use of the public.

No article provoked more comment than that relating to cities, counties, and towns; because San

perior ct, gave judgment for the plaintiff.   The case was appealed to the sup. ct, when the plaintiff made a motion to dismiss the appeal, on the ground that, as to the judgment itself the ct had no jurisdiction to entertain appeals in action for divorce; and as to the order awarding alimony and counsel fees, that such orders were not appealable.   The ct in bank decided in favor of the appellant, the justices concurring, except Chief Justice Morrison who took no part in the decision, and Justice McKee, who dissented from the opinion.   On a rehearing Morrison joined with the five other judges. Suit was then brought in the U. S. circ. ct, to compel Mrs Hill-Sharon to give up the contract, refusing which she was confined a day or two in jail for contempt.

[34] The question of riparian rights was an important one in Cal., on account of the necessity for irrigation.   The war between the farmers and hydraulic and other miners, had been long carried on in the courts and the legislature.   The attempt of corporate companies to appropriate all the water of unnavigable streams was another source of trouble.   Gov. Stoneman called an extra session of the legislature to please a few men who wished to have repealed the article on water rights; but they failed.

Francisco, from which the workingmen's delegates were elected, was chiefly affected by it. No county could be established with less than 5,000 inhabitants, or divided when the population was less than 8,000; nor should the dividing line pass within five miles of the county seat. Counties were to be classified according to population, and the legislature should provide a uniform system of county governments under general laws regulating the compensation of county and municipal officers, who were to be held to a strict accountability.

Corporations for municipal purposes should not be created under special laws, but should be organized under general laws which should provide for their incorporation and classification; and cities and towns heretofore organized should be incorporated under these laws whenever a majority of the electors voting at a general election should so determine.

City and county governments might be consolidated —as in the case of San Francisco—into one municipal government. In consolidated city and county governments of more than 100,000 population there should be two boards of supervisors or houses of legislation, one of which, to consist of twelve persons, should be elected from the city and county at large for a term of four years, so classified that after the first election only six should be elected every two years; the other to consist of twelve persons elected every two years for a two years' term; vacancies occurring to be filled by the mayor or other chief executive officer. Any city of more than 100,000 population might frame a charter for its own government by choosing fifteen freeholders at any general election to prepare a charter, said freeholders to have been qualified voters for five years. The qualified electors should receive thirty days' notice of the submission of the charter for approval, when, if approved, it should be submitted to the legislature for confirmation. Amendments to a charter should not be made oftener

than once in two years.   Counties, towns, and cities
should pay proportional taxes to the state; but the
legislature should not have power to impose taxes for
municipal purposes; yet it might vest the power in
the corporate authorities to assess and collect taxes
for such purposes.   The legislature should not delegate to any special commission, private corporation, or
individual any power to control, appropriate, super-
vise, or in any way interfere with any county, city,
town, or municipal improvement, money, property, or
effects, whether held in trust or otherwise.

No state office should be continued [35] or created in
any municipality for the inspection, measurement, or
gradation of any merchandise, manufacture, or commodity; but the city should be authorized by general
law to appoint such officers.   Private property should
not be taken or sold for the payment of the corporate
debt of any political or municipal corporation.   All
moneys collected for the use of any such corporation
should be immediately deposited with the treasurer
or other legal depository.[36]   The making of profit out
of public money, or using it for any purpose not authorized by law by any officer having possession or control
of it, should be prosecuted and punished as a felony.
No city, county, town, township, board of education,
or school district should incur any liability exceeding
the income provided for each year,[37] without the assent
of two-thirds of the qualified electors voting at a
special election, or without providing for the interest
and sinking fund to extinguish such indebtedness
within a limited time.[38]   No public work or improve-

[35] This prohibition referred to the practice of legislatures in creating such
offices as state inspectors of flour. *Cal. Stat.*, 1852, 129, and 1853, 272; and of
beef and pork. *Cal. Stat.*, 1856, 232; *Id.*, 1860, 116; gauger of wines and liquors. *Cal. Stat.*, 1852, 131; harbor commissioners, and other boards of commissioners for S. F. *Cal. Stat.*, 1874, 910, who assessed the merchants heavily,
or received benefits from the state.

[36] And not spirited away to a bank in collusion with a dishonest official,
as in bygone years.

[37] The interdict as to debt was inconveniently exhibited in 1882, when for
two or three months the city was in darkness, there being no money in the
treasury to pay gas bills, and the city prohibited from going in debt.

[38] This prohibition arrested the completion of the new city hall, on which

ment of any description should be made in any city, the cost of which should be made chargeable upon private property by special assessment,[39] unless after an estimate of such expense had been made, and an assessment levied in proportion to the benefits to be effected on the property had been levied, collected, and paid into the city treasury.

There was much prophesying of evil in the event of the city of San Francisco having to adopt a charter under the new constitution. While it could not be denied that there was evident a wise intent to make fraud and extravagance impossible, and to restrict the power of the legislature to interfere in municipal affairs, there was believed to be too complete a transfer of the responsibility of the government of the city from the legislature to the popular vote of the citizens. "Municipalities," says an eminent authority, "are merely an agency of government;" and again, "There ought to be careful and effectual restrictions by the state upon its municipalities."[40] The new constitution removed all restrictions and left the city, except as to the payment of a state tax, and some obligations in the matter of general and salary laws, to do as best pleased it in all affairs. And what it pleased to do would depend upon the kind of charter which fifteen freeholders of certain political tendencies, at the date of some election at which they should be chosen, might be able hastily to create ; and upon the popular vote upon it, which would be a partisan

about $5,000,000 had been spent. It has stood, during eight years, only partially habitable, a ruin in appearance, rather than a handsome edifice. There will probably be provided, in the charter about to be created, some plan whereby this costly structure may be finished.

[39] Private property had been burdensomely taxed for state improvements, and where the grades were heavy, on the hills, had been sold for assessments in former times, but no such abuses existed when the new constitution was formed. On the contrary, the charter under which San Franciscans were then living, made it necessary that property owners should petition to have street improvements made, before it was undertaken, and when the contract was let they had the privilege of taking it themselves at the lowest bid. The property being assessed and the assessment paid, the payer of the tax lost all control over his money.

[40] Thomas M. Cooley, of Michigan.

demonstration, followed by the approval of a partisan legislature.

The San Franciscans had come to love their municipal government, faulty though it might be, under which the city had prospered for twenty-five years. There were expressions in the articles on counties and cities in the new constitution, which looked as if the city of San Francisco might become an independent state,[41] like Venice, Genoa, Pisa, Florence, and other free cities of the middle ages, whose histories are in the past. The city was to have "two houses of legislation;" it was to have a mayor, or "other chief executive officer." Was there to be another line of doges, or was King Kearney to rule? There was no power in the legislature, the judiciary, nor any of the departments of state, to interfere with whatever charter San Francisco might adopt under general laws. On the contrary, the electors of the city and county decided that matter; and the secretary of state, the courts, and the heads of every department were required to keep a copy of this charter on file in their offices, and to govern themselves accordingly. Was not this imperialism? Every advocate of the measure complained of the abuses practised by boards of supervisors in the past; yet proposed to place the city entirely in the hands of the very class of which they complained, and cut it off from state aid in correcting abuses. Was not this secession? Would not the legislative power of San Francisco over-top every other, and the city-hall issue its edicts to 300,000 people, and more or less to the state? An important question, too, was whether the framers of the constitution deliberately proposed thus to capture the city, with ulterior designs, looking to the future, or was this simply the reaction from abuses of power by the state legislature in the past? This the wisest could not answer, although both theories had their advocates.

[41] *Sac. Record Union*, Jan. 23, 1879.

As to the constitution in general, the objections offered to it were, that it hurried the state business too much by limiting the legislative sessions; hampered legislation with too many restrictions; introduced a new and untried plan of judiciary; created a triple-headed and dangerous supreme court, a court of delays and expenses which would defeat the poor appellant and give the case to the rich respondent,[42] and of extraordinary power which might open up its decisions on its own motion; prohibited the sale of tide lands to a more than questionable extent;[43] provided for removing the Chinese contrary to the restrictions of state power by the federal constitution; provided for taxing credits, choses in action, and stocks, in addition to tangible property, thus favoring non-resident holders; took from the legislature the power to regulate fares and freights and gave it to three commissioners who would become an easy prey to railroad corporations, whose passes and hospitality they were permitted to accept; made void every office in the state, without justice or discrimination, requiring elections for which the people had no time to make a proper choice of candidates; it legislated and experimented too much; was too long and loose; was not dignified; showed the weapons of the contending forces, lampoon and broadsides by the majority, stealth, craft, and ambuscade by the minority; and, in short, that much of the good to be obtained by it could be accomplished by legislation, but none of the evils proceeding from it could be thus remedied. It was only, said its enemies, a democratic platform elaborated.

Child of the workingmen's party though it was, such was the agitation and doubt upon the subject of the new constitution, that when it came to the vote,

[42] Rich respondents, if anything is to be learned by reading the Cal. law reports, generally do get the case. *Pickett, Anti-Plunderer's Pamphlet.*

[43] This was done with a view to retain, as far as possible, control of the water-front of cities.

San Francisco, the home of the chief instigators of
the change,⁴⁴ rejected it by a majority of 1,592 out of
38,034. The state, however, through the support of
the agricultural class, which hoped for an easing of
taxation, gave a majority for it of 10,820, out of
145,088 votes, and it went into effect at twelve o'clock,
meridian, on the 4th day of July, 1879. That is to
say, on the 7th of May one provision of the constitution—that which decreed that all existing charters,
grants, franchises, special or exclusive privileges,
under which a bona fide organization had not been
commenced, should thereafter have no validity—went
into effect. On the 4th of July it became effectual
as to officers and their terms. On the first day of
January 1880, it became in a general sense the organic law of the state, all laws inconsistent with it
being repealed at noon that day. On the first Monday after the 1st of January, which fell upon the 5th,
all the officers elected at the general election in September, 1879, took their places, except the governor,

⁴⁴ Only one public journal in S. F., the *Chronicle*, supported the new constitution or the Workingmen's party. Out of the whole press of the state
the opposition had a majority of ten, but the *Chronicle* performed yeoman's
service for the party it advocated, and to its influence may be attributed the
success of the movement. It abandoned the Kearneyites when this matter
was accomplished, and through political quarrels which grew to be personal
feuds, the senior proprietor, Charles De Young lost his life. He was killed
by I. M. Kalloch, the son of I. S. Kalloch, pastor of a baptist church, a
supporter of the sand-lot fraternity, and enemy of the Chinese, who was
elected mayor of S. F. by the workingmen. In the heat and turbulence of
political strife, I. S. Kalloch's former life was freely related in the *Chronicle*. Kalloch, the elder, replied by attacking De Young's family in a speech
in front of the Metropolitan Temple, where he preached. Next morning De
Young called him out to a carriage in which he was sitting, and shot him,
inflicting a wound severe but not dangerous. A few months afterward, De
Young was fatally shot in his business office by Kalloch's son, also a minister, who was tried for murder and acquitted. The episode, however, put an
end to the public career of father and son. The *Chronicle*, by its persistent
war upon oppressive corporations, incurred the enmity of the capitalist
Spreckels, whose son, goaded by the *Chronicle's* imputations against his
father, attacked M. H. De Young with a pistol. He also escaped punishment. In fact, it may be said that few persons of wealth or position were
ever punished for crime in the courts of Cal. No change of constitution
will make the people law-abiding where the courts cannot be depended
upon to administer justice according to the intention of the statutes of
the state.

who could not be inaugurated until a speaker of the assembly was elected. Between the 1st and 5th there was a period when there were no courts in California, except the inferior local courts. On the 4th of July, 1880, all laws inconsistent with the provisions of the new constitution, and not altered or repealed, became a dead letter.[45]

And with all this revolution in the midst of an organized community of free people, the sky refused to fall—refused because the people were free—free, if this experiment failed, to profit by the failure. The real American, aware of the fact that the half Americanized foreigner, trying his skill at making laws for a people accustomed to the utmost liberty consistent with good government, infallibly exhibits a desire to bear rather more heavily upon this people than upon himself, good-humoredly assents to the check as an incident only of his political history, from which possibly he may derive some useful lesson. It is well known to him that the uneducated and just naturalized immigrants from Europe see in the millionaires of the republic only another aristocracy which they are prompted to pull down; and that these throne-levellers are more sensitive to the alchemy by which ballots are changed to quarter or half eagles than any other class; therefore, that their hostility to any measure may be softened by placing in their palms at election these shining testimonials to their power. Between monopolists and socialists, with free institutions, wit, and money, he hopes to hold the balance even, and if ever he yields to a doubt on the subject, it vanishes before a conviction, born with him, that in the nation's vocabulary there is no such word as failure. Change, amendment, even disaster, there may be, but total miscarriage, not at all.

[45] There was another period set to the old laws—that on the 1st of Jan., 1882, the practice of letting out convict labor at the state prison must cease. The workingmen would have no competition of that kind, but the prisoners might labor for the state only.

In this spirit the new constitution was adopted.[46]
When the change came, the state had been for two
years in a tumult between the labor agitation, four
general elections, and other exciting issues, the people

[46] The constitutional delegates were J. P. Hoge, S.F. pres't; B. A. Shurtleff,
Napa, born in 1821, in Mass, educated at Harvard, physician, came to Cal.
in 1849; S. J. Farrell, S. F., born in Boston in 1853, public school education,
came to Cal. in 1861, lawyer; A. H. Chapman, Chico, b at Niagara Falls in
1827, came to Cal. in 1861, lumber dealer; W. W. Moreland, Healdsburg, b
in Johnson co., Ark., in 1845, came to Cal. in 1859, teacher; C. S. Ringgold,
S. F., b in Cecil co., Md, in 1832, came to Cal. in 1852; W. F. Heustis,
Eureka, b in Buckingham co., Va, in 1836, came to Cal. in 1849, lawyer;
George Ohleyer. Yuba, b in Alsace, France, in 1831, came to U. S. while an
infant, to Cal. in 1852, farmer; H. Davis, Truckee, b in Nelson co., Ky, in
1809, came to Cal. in 1849, business man; Edward Barry, Downieville, b in
Australia in 1847, came to Cal. in boyhood, lawyer; W. J. Sweasy, Eureka,
b in London in 1805, came to U. S. in 1840, to Cal. in 1851, farmer; T. B.
McFarland, Sac., b in Pa. in 1828, educated at Marshall college, came to
Cal. in 1850, lawyer; Lucius De Witt Morse, San Mateo, b in E. Poultney,
Vt, in 1822, educated at the N. Y. university, physician; S. G. Hilborn,
Vallejo, b in Mass in 1835, educated at Tufts college, Somewell, came to Cal.
in 1861, lawyer; J. A. Harvey, Vallejo, b in Herkimer co., N. Y. in 1838,
educated at Fairfield academy, came to Cal. in 1859, lawyer; J. A. Eilcher,
Auburn, b in Burlington, Ia, in 1845, came to Cal. in 1858, educated at Cal.
Normal school, teacher and editor; George Steele, San Luis Obispo, b in
Delaware co., N. Y., in 1825, came to Cal. from Ohio in 1856, land owner,
cheese maker, and county judge; G. W. Hunter, El Dorado, b in Ill. in 1829,
came to Cal. in 1850, farmer; W. J. Tinnin, Trinity; A. A. Noel, Lakeport,
b in East Tenn. in 1832, came to Cal. in 1854, lawyer; W. A. Gregg,
Bakersfield, b in Burlington, Ia, in 1844, educated at Iowa Wesleyan and
Michigan university, came to Cal. in 1867, lawyer; D. C. Stevenson, Shasta,
b in Ohio in 1821, came to Cal. in 1852, farmer, lumber manufacturer, furniture dealer; A. C. Freeman, Sac., b in Ill. in 1843, came to Cal. in 1861,
lawyer; John Thomas Weeks, Grass Valley, b in Baltimore in 1836, came to
Cal. in 1852, teacher; Presley Dunlap, Sac., b in Pa in 1817, came to Cal. in
1849, lawyer; Marion Briggs, Butte, b in Mo. in 1823, came to Cal. in 1850,
and again in 1864, agriculturalist, and pres't of State Agric. Soc.; Hugh
Walker, Marin, b in Nova Scotia in 1843, came to Cal. in 1864, cooper and
merchant; J. F. McNutt, Yuba, b in Tenn., in 1815, came to Cal. from Mo.
in 1850, carpenter; G. V. Smith, Bakersfield, b in Ky in 1855, lawyer; Rush
McComas, Sta Clara, b in Va in 1830, came to Cal. from Mo. in 1861, farmer;
Clitus Barbour, S. F., b in Ill. in 1838, left Knox college to come to Cal. in
1854, lawyer and editor; C. F. Reed, Yolo, b in Mass in 1826, educated at
West Point for civil engineer, came to Cal. in 1849 through Mexico, pres't
Agric. Soc. for 9 years, farmer, miner, and grain dealer; H. C. Rolfe, San
Bernardino, came to Cal. in 1851, when 16 years of age, lawyer and dist
judge; Charles J. Beerstecher, S. F., a native of Germany in 1851, came to
U. S. in 1852, educated at Lewisburg, Pa, came to Cal. in 1877, lawyer and
socialist; Engene Faucett, Sta Barbara, b in Ohio in 1845, came to Cal. in
1871, lawyer and dist judge; John G. McCallum, Oakland, b in Ind. in 1830,
educated in the Ind. university, came to Cal in 1854, lawyer; C. C. O'Donnell, S. F., b in Baltimore in 1834, came to Cal. in 1850, physician; A. P.
Vacqural, S. F., b in Paris in 1841, came to U. S. in 1858, and to Cal. in
1866, civil engineer, soldier, sailor, and communist; W. H. Prouty, Amador,
b in Ohio in 1837; came to Cal. in 1852 from Ia, farmer; James Caples, Sac.,
b in Ohio in 1823 came to Cal. in 1849 from Mo., farmer; John A. Eagan,
Amador, b in Va in 1827, came to Cal. in 1851 from Ohio, lawyer; Thervald

being surfeited with politics, if not nauseated with
the quality of the feast so long forced upon unwilling
stomachs.   So far as its practical workings are concerned, it has achieved nothing which a few amend-

Klaudius Nelson, S. F., a native of Norway in 1849, came to U. S. in 1852,
to Cal. in 1873, wood-turner, and carver of meerschaum pipes; G. A. Johnson, Sta Rosa, b in Md in 1829, educated at Yale college, prof. of ancient
languages at the Western Military Institute of Ky in 1853–4, came to Cal.
in 1873, lawyer and mayor of Sta Rosa; W. P. Grace, S. F., b in East Tenn.
in 1837, came to S. F. in 1868, architectural draughtsman; P. B. Tully, Gilroy; H. M. Lampson, Tuolumne, b in Vt in 1852, physician; Henry W.
Smith, S. F., b in Me in 1838, came to Cal. in 1863, plumber; P. T. Dowling, S. F.; Henry Larkin, El Dorado; John D. Condon, S. F., b in Ireland
in 1846, came to U. S. in 1858, to Cal. in 1868, cabinet-maker and car-
builder; C. W. Cross, Nevada city, b in Syracuse, N. Y. in 1848, educated
at Northwestern university, came to Cal. in 1870, lawyer. Joseph C. Gorman, S. F., b in Ireland in 1844, came to U. S. in 1848, to Cal. in 1868 as a
civil engineer on the N. P. R. R,, and took up the business of tinner; A. R.
Andrews, Shasta, b in Ky in 1829, came to Cal. in 1849 from the battlefelds
of Mex., farmer; Peter Bell, S. F., b in Glasgow in 1845, came to U. S. in
1862, served in union army, came to Cal. in 1867, house-pointer; B. F.
Kenny, S. F., b in S. F. in 1854 of Irish parentage, educated at the Jesuit
college of St Ignatius, telegraph operator; Justice Schamp, San Joaquin, b
in Ohio in 1855, farmer; E. P. Soule, Susanville, b in Ohio in 1828, educated
at Marietta, came to Cal. in 1853, mill-wright and wagon-maker; W. P.
Hughey, S. F., b in Ky in 1831, confederate captain in Longstreet's corps,
came to Cal. in 1875, house-painter; Josiah Boucher, Chico b in Pa in 1819,
came to Cal. in 1851, stock-raiser and capitalist; Charles Swenson, S. F., b
in Denmark in 1847; came to Cal. in 1866, sailor, wood-chopper, restaurant
keeper; T. H. Estey, Marine, b in Mass in 1826, came to Cal. in 1849,
dairyman; B. B. Glascock, Colusa, b in Mo. in 1843, came to Cal. in 1855,
farmer; P. M. Wellin, S. F., b in Ireland in 1836, came to U. S. in 1852,
studied drawing at Cooper Institute and Union, came to Cal. at the close of
the war in which he served, carpenter; H. C. Boggs, Lakeport, b in Mo. in
1820, came to Cal. in 1850, farmer; James O'Sullivan, S. F., b in Cork, Ireland in 1825, came to U. S. in 1841, joined Stevenson's reg't in 1846 for Cal.,
printer and editor; A. P. Overton, Sta Rosa, b at Independence, Ms in 1830,
came to Cal. in 1850 from Tex. and Mex., lawyer, county judge, and banker;
L. F. Jones, Mariposa, b in N. Y. in 1821, lawyer; J. R. Freud, b in N. Y.
of Hungarian parentage, came to Cal. in 1864, educated in the public schools
and Cal. university, merchant; John Mansfield, Los Angeles, b in N. Y. in 1822;
J. M. Dudley, Solano, b in N. Y. in 1830, came to Cal. in 1852 from Ind.,
teacher and farmer; Thomas Harrison, S. F., b in Eng. in 1837 of Irish parents,
came to Cal. in 1858, potter, grain broker, sailor, rigger; G. W. Schell, Modesto,
b. in N. Y. in 1837, came to Cal. in 1861, dept. col. int. revenue 1864–9, county
judge 1874–6, lawyer; J. C. Steadman, S. F., b. in S. F. in 1851, educated
at Sta Clara college, conveyancer and searcher of records; T. D. Heiskell,
Stanislaus, b. in Va in 1842, came to Cal. in 1849 from Tenn., farmer and
stock-raiser; Henry Neunaber, S. F., b. in Oldenburg, Germany in 1838,
came to U. S. in 1860, to Cal. in 1861, grocer; J. S. Reynolds, S. F., b. in
N. Y. in 1831, came to Cal. in 1854 from Wis., established the *Idaho Statesman* in 1864, settled in Cal. in 1872, lawyer, helped Barbour defend the
rioters of the workingmen's party; Rufus Shoemaker, Grass Valley, b. in
Copiah, Miss., in 1830, came to Cal. about 1855, editor and county clerk; F.
Lindow, S. F., b. in Prussia, came to U. S. from Eng. in 1861, to Cal. in
1864, tailor; Conrad Herold, S. F., b. in Germany in 1831, came to U. S. in
1857, to Cal. in 1859; grocer; Hugh M. La Rue, Sac., b. in Ky in 1830, came

ments would not have done. Those objects which it particularly aimed at it failed to achieve. The effect upon corporations disappointed its authors and supporters. Many of them were strong enough still to defy state power and evade state laws in protect-

to Cal. in 1849, sheriff and farmer; M. M. Estee, S. F., b. in Pa in 1833, came to Cal. in 1853, lawyer; J. J. Ayres, Los Angeles, b. in Scotland in 1830, came to Cal. from St Louis in 1849, started with others the *Morning Call* in 1856, which was sold in 1866, when Ayres went to Los Angeles to take charge of the *Evening Express*, printer; Edmund Nason, San Benito, b. in Stafford co., N. H., dairyman; I. S. Belcher, Marysville, pres't pro tem. of the convention, b. in Vt in 1825, educated at the Vt university, came to Cal. in 1853, dist atty, judge of dist, and sup. judge; H. C. Wilson, Tehama, b. in Ky in 1827, came to Cal. in 1849 from Texas, farmer; John M. Kelly, Woodland, b. in Mo. in 1825, came to Cal. in 1849 from Mex., farmer; W. H. L. Barnes, S. F., b. in Mass. in 1832, came to Cal. in 1862, lawyer; Patrick Reddy, Inyo and Mono, b. in N. Y. in 1839, came to Cal. in 1861, notary public, lawyer, and politician; D. H. Cowden, Marysville, b. in Pa in 1839, came to Cal. in 1860, lawyer and probate judge; Byron Waters, San Bernardino, b. in Ga. in 1849, came to Cal. in 1869, lawyer; John P. West, Los Angeles, b. in Ireland in 1825, came to U. S. in 1828, served in 14th Ia inf. vols, came to Cal. in 1875, farmer; Alexander Campbell, Oakland, b. in Jamaica, W. I., in 1820, came to Cal. in 1849, lawyer; J. E. Murphy, Crescent City, b. in Me in 1846, came to Cal. from Minn. in 1860, lawyer; J. McM. Shafter, S. F., b. in Vt in 1816, came to Cal. from Wis., lawyer; Daniel Tuttle. Sta Cruz, b. in Ohio in 1823, came to Cal. in 1852, farmer; C. R. Kleine, S. F., b. in Prussia in 1830, came to U. S. in 1850, to Cal. in 1854 from St Louis, shoemaker; C. V. Stuart, Sonoma; Raymond Lavigne, S. F., b. in France in 1848, came to Cal. 1868, lithographer; Edward O. Smith, San José, b. in Montgomery co., Md, in 1817, came to Cal. in 1853 from Ill., farmer and trader; H. K. Turner, Sierra, b. in Me in 1828, educated at Bowdoin college, came to Cal. in 1853, farmer; J. E. Hale, Auburn, b. in Pa in 1824, came to Cal. in 1849, lawyer, county judge, and sup. ct reporter; C. G. Finney, San Buenaventura, b. in N. Y. in 1830, son of the founder of Oberlin college, where he was educated, came to Cal. in 1874 from Wis., lawyer, editor, and horticulturalist; R. S. Swing, San Bernardino, b. in Ohio in 1845, educated at Mich. university, came to Cal. in 1872, lawyer; William Van Voorhies, Oakland, b. in Tenn. in 1820, educated at Jackson college, came to Cal. in 1849 as bearer of despatches to Gen. Riley, and was appointed postal agent for the coast, law partner of Edmund Randolph, sec. of state under three governors, surveyor of the port of S. F., etc.; Eli T. Blackmer, San Diego, b. in Worcester, Mass., in 1831, came to Cal. in 1873, school supt; Dennis Willey Herrington, Sta Clara, b. of German and Irish parents in Ind. in 1826, educated at Asbury university, came to Cal. in 1850, lawyer; C. Brown, Tulare, b. in Ky in 1821, educated at Louisville college, came to Cal. in 1850, sheriff, lawyer, and politician; Edward Evey, Los Angeles, b. in Md. 1813, came to Cal. in 1854, owner of the White Sulphur springs of St Helena; Daniel Inman, Livermore, b. in E. Tenn. in 1827, came to Cal. in 1849 from Ill., hotel-keeper and farmer; S. A. Holmes, Fresno, b. in Wilmington, N. C., in 1830, came to Cal. from Miss. in 1868, farmer; N. G. Wyatt, Salinas, b. in Mo., educated at St Joseph college Bardstown Ky, came to Cal. in 1859 from Ia via Denver, Idaho mines, Salt Lake and San Bernardino trail, farmer; Joseph R. Weller, Sta Clara, b. in N. J. in 1819, educated in the N. Y. state normal school, came to Cal. in 1850, farmer and stock-raiser; Thomas McConnell, Sac., b. in Vt in 1827, came to Cal. in 1850, editor, banker, sheep-raiser, land-owner; J. M. Charles, Petalumn, b.

ing their interests, and this they did without scruple. The relation of capital and labor is even more strained than before the constitution was adopted. Capital soon recovered from a temporary intimidation, and

in Pa in 1809, educated at Marietta, O., came to Cal. from Mo. in 1854; J. W. Winans, S. F., b. in New York in 1820, educated at Columbia college, came to Cal. in 1849, with a company owning their vessel, prominent politician and lawyer; Eugene Casserly, S. F.; Thomas H. Laine, Sta Clara, b. in Mo. in 1832, came to Cal. in 1847, finishing his education at the university of the Pacific, lawyer; J. R. W. Hitchcock, San Joaquin, b. in Va in 1825, educated at the baptist college of that city, came to Cal. in 1849, machinist and farmer; F. O. Townsend, Mendocino, b. in N. Y. in 1845, came to Cal. in 1851 from Canada West, farmer; D. S. Terry, Stockton, b. in Miss. in 1827, came to Cal. in 1849 from Texas, politician, lawyer, judge, etc.; S. B. Burt, Placer, b. in Chemung co., N. Y., in 1828, educated at Alfred college, came to Cal. in 1850, teacher, lumber-dealer, quartz-miner; Henry Edgerton, Sac., b. in Vt, came to Cal. in 1853, orator and lawyer; J. B. Hall, Stockton, b. in Md in 1819, educated at St Johns and Jefferson colleges, came to Cal. in 1850, lawyer; J. H. Keyes, Yuba and Sutter, b. in Ct in 1831, educated at Worcester, Mass., came to Cal. in 1849, farmer, prime mover in the 'slickens' suit against the Little York Gold Mining and Water co. for depositing mining debris on farming lands; John Berry, Yreka, b. in O. in 1826, educated at Wyandotte, came to Cal. in 1849, merchant, miner, lawyer; W. J. Graves, San Luis Obispo, b. and educated in Va, came to Cal. in 1849 from the Mex. war, lawyer; M. R. C. Pulliam, Butte, b. in Salinas co., Mo., came to Cal. in 1850, lawyer and miner; W. F. White, Watsonville, b. in Ireland in 1822, came to U. S. in 1823, came to Cal. in 1849, merchant, farmer; E. Martin, b. in Eng. in 1833, came to Cal. in 1851, stationer, post-master, notary public; J. N. Barton, Humboldt, b. in Ohio in 1830, educated at Cincinnati, came to Cal. in 1850, merchant, stock-raiser, miner; David Lewis, San Joaquin, b. in Vt in 1828, came to Cal. in 1849, as a member of a Boston mining company, carpenter, miner, land-owner; J. V. Webster, Alameda, b. in Tenn. in 1830, came to Cal. in 1853, from Ill., with a party of young men who walked from Salt Lake to Placerville, fruit-grower; J. E. Dean, Placerville, b. in R. I. in 1837, educated at Niantic, came to Cal. in 1859, served in Co. G, 4th inf. Cal. vols, miner; J. B. Garvey, Calaveras, b. in Pa in 1843, educated at St Mary's college, Niagara, N. Y., came to Cal. in 1865, school sup., under-sheriff; W. S. Moffatt, San Mateo, b. in Roxbury, N. Y., in 1818, came to Cal. in 1849, miner and farmer; J. F. Miller, S. F.; John Walker, Tuolumne, b. in Wilmington, N. C., in 1825, came to Cal. in 1850, physician; John McCoy, Nevada, b. in Erie co., Pa, in 1837, educated at Galesbury college, Ill., came to Cal. in 1853, miner; J. M. Strong, Mariposa and Merced, b. in Ga. in 1831, came to Cal. in 1850 from Miss., farmer and sheriff; Peter J. Joyce, S. F., b. in Ireland in 1839, came to U. S. when a boy, learned shoe-making and cabinet-making, served in the civil wrr, went to Ireland on a Fenian mission, participating in the demonstration on Chester, Eng., and heading an expedition against Wicklow in 1867, the Eng. gov't offering a reward for him he returned to U. S. in 1868 and came to Cal.; Volney E. Howard, Los Angeles; Hiram Mills, Contra Costa, b. in Hudson, N. Y., in 1830, educated at Alleghany college Pa, and at the law institute of Ballston Spa, N. Y., came to Cal. in 1851, dist att'y for 20 years; Robert Crouch, Napa, b. in Ohio in 1823, educated at Hopedale, came to Cal. in 1850, physician, lawyer, county clerk, county judge; Walter Van Dyke, Oakland, b. in N. Y. in 1823, educated at the village academy of Tyre, read law in Cleveland, came to Cal. in 1849, dist att'y of Klamath co., editor of *Humboldt Times*, settled himself

returned to a land where it could earn high interest. Labor, still uneasy, was also still subject to the inexorable laws of supply and demand. Legislators were still to be approached by agents of railroads and other corporations, as might be seen by the reports of investigating committees. Chinese were still employed digging and grading. The state board of railroad commissioners was a useless expense to the commonwealth, being as wax in the hands of the companies it was set to watch. The new constitution was framed to make the rich pay their share of taxation, to control corporations, to correct the revenue system, and to equalize the rights of the people altogether. In each of these designs it failed. But it also failed to check the advancement of the state, which, purely by its resources, climate, and generally favorable conditions for comfort and wealth, progressed in spite of political blunderings. By and by the people may have time to consider what is best to be done with laws, lawmakers, and law-breakers.

at Oakland in 1868, U. S. att'y; Smith B. Thompson, S. F., b. in Dutchess co., N. Y., in 1821, educated at the Quaker school of Mechanicsville, came to Cal. in 1860, business man, school director; John S. Hager, S. F.; J. West Martin, Oakland, b. in Washington co., Md, in 1822, educated at Prospect Hill academy, came to Cal. in 1853 from Tenn., agriculturalist and stock raiser, regent of the Cal. university, pres't Union Savings Bank of Oakland; S. M. Wilson, S. F., b. in Ohio in 1824, came to Cal. in 1853, lawyer; Luke Doyle, S. F., b. in Ireland; W. L. Dudley, Stockton; J. M. Rhodes, Woodland, b. in Ohio in 1817, came to Cal. in 1850, banker with Sturges and Purdy at Sac. until 1857, when he purchased the rancho Cañada de Capoy in Yolo co. and became a farmer. The secretary of the convention was Asbury Johnson, b. in Joliet, Ill., in 1833, educated at Beloit college, came to Cal. in 1864, teacher and editor of *Santa Barbara Press*, one of the judges at the Phila Cent. Exposition of 'national and elected state exhibits' and historian of the exposition, owner of the *Daily Times* of Oakland. The clerks were George A. Thornton of Santa Rosa, Edwin Frederick Smith of Sac., George McStay of Stockton, Ellison L. Crawford of El Dorado; sergts-at-arms, Thomas J. Sherwood of Marysville, Benjamin Chambers of Modesto; post-master, Michael Barnes of Chico.

CHAPTER XVI.

POLITICAL HISTORY.

1879-1889.

Under the New Constitution—State Elections—San Francisco Charter—Municipal Matters—Our Imported Rulers—Legislation
under the New Régime—Irrigation and Riparian Rights—An
Elective Judiciary—Extra Session of the Legislature—Party Issues—Grave Questions—Contest for the United States Senator-
ship—Brief Period of Quiet—California as a Type—Disturbance
of the Public Mind—Names of Counties—Finances—Federal Expenditures—Industrial Enterprise—Immigration—New Era of
Development.

Smarting under the sense that thirty-five foreign-
born delegates had been chosen to sit in the constitutional convention of an American state, and that almost
one half of San Francisco's delegation had also been
of this class, the republicans made an effort at the
general election in September to redeem the state
from this unnatural domination. The result was hard
to prognosticate with four municipal tickets in the
field, and a bewildering re-organization of parties; for
the Kearney workingmen held aloof from the Workingmen's party of California, the new constitution
party had dropped the labor[1] element, which was

---

[1]The workingmen were inclined to believe that the adoption of the new
constitution was due to their movement, as the convention had been. But
this was not so. A revolution had taken place among the former labor organizations, and there had also been a change of sentiment brought about by
the debates on the constitution which were published from day to day. The
workingmen carried two municipal elections in Oakland, and in the special
election for state senator in 1878 polled 52 per cent of the popular vote; yet
Oakland gave 1,496 majority against the constitution which they assumed to
be theirs. Santa Clara co., which elected the workingmen's candidate for
assemblyman in 1878, gave a majority of 679 against the constitution. San
José also, which had elected workingmen to the municipal offices, gave 574
votes against the constitution. Similar changes occurred in Gilroy and other
places. The workingmen's two tickets at the municipal election in Sacra-

divided between the democrats and republicans, and much independence was exercised in the indulgence of individual preferences.

Upon the state ticket the republicans elected for governor George C. Perkins, a prosperous business man, a native of the state of Maine; for lieutenant-governor John Mansfield; for secretary of state D. M. Burns; for treasurer John Weil; for controller D. M. Kenfield; for attorney-general A. L. Hart; for superintendent of public instruction Frederick W. Campbell; for surveyor-general James W. Shanklin; and for clerk of the supreme court Frank W. Gross. The whole congressional delegation was republican, namely, Horace Davis, Horace F. Page, Joseph McKenna, and Romualdo Pacheco,[2] of the first, second, third, and fourth districts, in the order named. On the other hand, the chief justice and the whole supreme bench with a single exception[3] were elected by the democratic and workingmen's parties. The bench

mento, in March 1878, polled 49½ per cent of the total vote, the Kearney wing electing nearly all the officers. The same strength was shown in voting for delegates to the constitutional convention, yet that city gave 1251 majority against the constitution. At Marysville the same reversal occurred, and in all the leading cities, showing that the workingmen had changed. On the other hand, a change in the general sentiment toward the constitution had carried it by a large majority. *Workingmen's Party in Cal., Its Rise and Fall*, 1876-8.

Horace F. Page was born in Orleans co:, N. Y., in 1833, came to Cal. at the age of 20, worked in a saw-mill, then in a livery stable, and drove stage. He became a successful business man. A republican in politics, he was nominated for the state senate when the defeat of his party was certain, but did not shrink from the ordeal. In congress he was a working member. His principal achievements during his first term were securing the passage of a bill which made a saving of $3,000,000 in the mail service without decreasing its efficiency.

[2] Romualdo Pacheco was born in Cal. in 1831. His father came from Guanajuato, Mexico, in 1825, with Echandia, military governor and general in command of Alta California, and was killed in a skirmish between Echandia and Victoria, who had been appointed in his stead, but whom he refused to recognize. He had married Ramona Carrillo of San Diego, and his son was born at Santa Bárbara. Romualdo was sent to school at the Sandwich islands at the age of seven years, where he remained until 1843, forgetting his native tongue, but acquiring English and French. After this he had a private tutor, and his mother having married John Wilson of Dundee, Scotland, a sea-captain, he was sent to sea with his tutor to learn navigation. When the country passed into American hands he became a politician.

[3] Ross was republican. The new constitution party had nominated Nathaniel Bennett for chief justice, and the republicans A. L. Rhodes, but the workingmen secured all but Ross.

consisted of Chief-justice Robert F. Morrison[4] and associates E. W. McKinstry, J. D. Thornton, Samuel B. McKee, M. H. Myrick, E. M. Ross, and J. R. Sharpstein. Of the three railroad commissioners Burstecher was elected by the workingmen, Stoneman by the workingmen and the new constitution party, and Cove by the republicans. The state board of equalization, consisting of one member from each of the congressional districts, was composed of Warren Dutton, T. D. Heiskell, M. M. Drew, and James L. King, with ex officio member, the state controller, two of whom, if not more, were republicans. The state senate consisting of forty members had a majority of four republicans, without counting the fusionists who had belonged to the party.[5] The assembly of eighty mem-

[4]Robert F. Morrison was born in Ill. in 1826, served in the Mexican war as a non-commissioned officer in the reg't of his brother, now a prominent lawyer of St Louis, and with whom he studied law before and after the war. In 1852 he came to Cal. His brother, Murray Morrison, also a lawyer, was practising at Sac., and here he was admitted to the bar, and formed a partnership with J. Neely Johnson. He was elected dist atty of Sac. co., and afterward removed to Virginia city, Nev., where he resided two years. From there he removed to S. F. in 1862. In 1859 Morrison was the candidate of the southern wing of the democratic party for state senator, but was defeated by the know-nothing candidate, Robert C. Clark, who was for many years county judge and superior judge of Sac. co., and who died on the bench in 1883. In 1870 Morrison was elected judge of the 4th dist court for 6 years, was reëlected, and served until the change in the constitution, when the workingmen's convention chose him for chief justice for a twelve years' term. At the end of seven years his labor ended, his death occurring March 2, 1887.

[5]The first senate under the new constitution was composed of the following republicans: E. H. Pardee, S. G. Nye, Alameda; W. A. Cheney, Butte, Plumas, and Lassen; W. H. Sears, Contra Costa and Marin; W. H. Brown, El Dorado and Alpine; Chester Rowell, Fresno, Tulare, Kern, Mono, and Inyo; William George, B. J. Watson, Nevada and Sierra; S. B. Burt, Placer; Grove L. Johnson, William Johnston, Sac.; A. T. Hudson, San Joaquin and Amador; George F. Baker, James C. Zuck, Santa Clara; J. F. Wendell, Solano and Yolo; E. A. Davis, Yuba and Sutter; W. W. Traylor, John H. Dickinson, Paul Neuman, Theodore Hittell, John S. Enos. Democrats: B. B. Glasscock, Colusa and Tehama; W. L. Anderson, Napa, Lake, and Sonoma; D. M. Pool, Mariposa, Merced, and Stanislaus; W. W. Moreland, Sonoma. Workingmen: Joseph C. Gorman, San Francisco. New Constitution party: B. F. Langford, San Joaquin and Amador; R. M. Lampson, Calaveras and Tuolumne; J. P. West, Los Angeles (and workingmen); W. J. Hill, Monterey, San Benito, and Santa Cruz; J. W. Satterwhite, San Diego and San Bernardino; Warren Chase, Ventura, Santa Bárbara, and San Luis Cbispo; Robert Desty, San Francisco and San Mateo; J. H. Harlan, Solano and Yolo; Martin Kelly, T. K. Nelson, Thomas Kane, San Francisco; Pierce H. Ryan, Del Norte, Humboldt, and Mendocino. The assembly was composed of republicans: Charles N. Fox, W. W.

bers consisted of thirty-four straight republicans,
twenty-three democrats and workingmen, and twenty-
one fusionists or new-constitution members. Upon
each of the several tickets used at the election was
printed in conspicuous lettering "Against Chinese."
In San Francisco out of 40,259 votes only 229 were
for allowing the Chinese to remain in the country.
The plurality of Perkins [6] for governor was nearly

Camron, G. W. Tyler, Alameda; R. C. Dawees, L. Brusie, Amador; Max
Brooks, W. W. Durham, Butte; T. Fraser, El Dorado; Cyrus Goleman, El
Dorado and Alpine; C. D. Estey, Marine; Charles Mulholland, Plumas and
Lassen; J. R. Finlayson, T. H. Murry, W. B. May, H. A. Gorley. L. J.
Hardy, Jr., J. F. Cowdrey, San Francisco; H. Y. Stanley, San Luis Obispo;
Rush McComas, J. L. York, D. Frink, Santa Clara; W. R. Leadbetter, San
Joaquin; C. N. Felton, San Mateo; F. A. Leach, A. Bennett, Solano; James
Adams, Sonoma; A. L. Chandler, Sutter; Daniel Dimond, Tuolumne; J. P.
Brown, Yuba; T. L. Chamberlain, Placer; Seymour Carr, J. N. Young, El-
wood Bruner, Sacramento; H. M. Streeter, San Bernardino.   Democrats:
H. A. Messenger, Calaveras; C. G. Sayle, Fresno; James Hynes, H. K.
Brown, Sonoma; J. D. Spencer, Stanislaus; R. F. Del Valle, Los Angeles;
W. F. Coffman, Mariposa and Merced; C. J. Sayle, Fresno; J. B. Cook,
Siskiyou and Modoc.   Workingmen's Party: E. S. Josselyn, Monterey; W.
J. Sinon, W. W. Cuthbert, S. J. Garibaldi, S. R. Finlayson, G. B. Ward, J.
J. McCarthy, G. Picket, J. J. McCalian, S. Braunhart, J. J. McDade,
Michael Lane, John Burns, P. T. Gaffey, S. Maybell, A. B. Maguire.   New
Constitution Party: D. N. Sherburne, Contra Costa; W. P. Matthews,
Colusa and Tehama; L. F. Cooper, Del Norte; C. L. Stoddard, Humboldt;
A. P. McCarty, Lake; L. G. Morse, Mendocino; J. Levee, A. M. Walker,
J. O. Sweetland, Nevada; C. C. Watson, San Diego, Milton Wason, Santa
Barbara and Ventura; Elihu Anthony, Santa Cruz; J. J. Harris, San
Benito; E. J. McIntosh, H. J. Corcoran, San Joaquin; J. S. P. Bass, Trinity
and Shasta; D. N. Hershy, Yolo; T. H. Carr, Yuba; A. B. Du Brutz,
Tulare.   There appears to be two vacancies or only 78 members elected.

    In this assembly James Adams, member for Sonoma, whose decease oc-
curred in 1888, was one of the most prominent men, serving on many important committees with rare ability and zeal.   An Irishman by birth, he
embarked for Quebec in 1846, removing soon afterward to Phil., and in 1852
to Cal.   After farming for some years in Humboldt co., he engaged in the
real estate business, in which he was remarkably successful.   In 1869 he was
elected supervisor, in 1871 sheriff, and on being relieved from the shrievalty
engaged in viticulture and stock-raising in the Sonoma valley.   In 1857 he
was married to Miss Sarah Elizabeth Cameron, a native of Phil., who died
some five years before him.   Of their surviving children, James E., the eldest, was married to Frances Isabel, daughter of Governor Perkins.

    [6] The N. C. P. candidate was Hugh J. Glenn, of Colusa, who received
46,851 votes; the workingmen's candidate, William F. White, received 44,-
436 votes; the republican, Perkins, 67,619. *S. F. Chronicle*, Sept. 15, 1879.

    A native of Maine, Gov. Perkins began life as a sailor boy, at the age of
sixteen coming to Cal., where, after a brief mining experience, he found
employment in a store at Oroville.   By close economy he saved enough to

21,000, and this extraordinary reversal of the vote on the adoption of the new constitution was with difficulty accounted for except by supposing that powerful agencies had been at work to bring about this result in order to modify as far as possible the strenuous interpretation of the constitution by the first legislature. Moreover, to the result which the new constitution party deplored, the inexperience of many of its former supporters contributed by dividing instead of consolidating their forces. All attempted political reforms, where the unthinking and uneducated are used as a power, as in the adoption of the constitution of 1879, incur the danger that the appeal of any demagogue, and especially of a demagogue whose palm when it grasps the hand of a voter has a trick of shedding gold, may make a breach in its ranks. Such breaches had been easily and quickly effected in the new party, so that it might be said that in six months after the adoption of the constitution the party which had just carried the state was practically defunct.

In San Francisco the result of the municipal vote was even more indicative of interference than elsewhere in the state, the republicans and workingmen carrying the city against the new constitution in the cradle of its party. Of twelve superior judges five were republicans and seven workingmen.[7] Eight of the twelve were on the new constitution ticket, also,

purchase the business, which he gradually increased until his sales amounted to $500,000 a year. In 1872 he was admitted into partnership with Goodall & Nelson. Later he became connected with a number of prominent enterprises, among others the Arctic Oil works, of which he is president, the Pacific Steam Whaling company, and the West Coast Land company, of both of which he is vice-president. In 1869 he was chosen state senator for Butte co., and in 1873 to fill the unexpired term of Sen. Boucher for Butte, Plumas, and Lassen.

[7] The judges elected to the superior bench in S. F. were, rep: T. K. Wilson, John Hunt, Jr, J. M. Allen, John F. Finn, James C. Carey; W. D. and N. C. T. W. Freelon, W. P. Daingerfield, Rob't Ferral, O. P. Evans, Howard Smith, M. A. Edmonds, Jeremiah F. Sullivan.

which made their election sure. But the mayor, I.
S. Kalloch, a baptist preacher, was chosen by a plurality[8] of 1,528 by the workingmen, while his competitor on the new constitution ticket was upon the
democratic ticket also. The inference was plain that
republican votes had assisted to place at the head of
the city government a man whose presence there was
regarded by the public and press a reproach to the
city, no less than to the church which he rendered
notorious by his ministrations.[9]   So far, indeed, from
being in sympathy with the class whose candidate he
was, he had denounced them unsparingly ın the labor
agitation of 1876–7.[10]   But now he was Kearney's
choice for mayor, and Kearney himself was openly
accused of having been purchased.

It will be observed that no election was held in
1879 for freeholders to form a charter for San Francisco to supersede the consolidation act.   When the
legislature met in January, 1880, at the request of
the board of supervisors of San Francisco, which had
been advised that the force of the consolidation act
would expire on the 4th of July,[11] it passed " an act to

[8] The candidate for mayor on the rep. ticket was Brilsford P. Flint; and
on the N. C. and Dem., Walcott N. Griswald.

[9] I have myself heard Kalloch urge violent measures against the Chinese in
his Sunday evening service, which consisted of 15 minutes devoted to religion
and 45 to politics.   Admission tickets were sold at an office in the vestibule,
as at a theatre, by the speaker's colored servant and confidant; price ten
cents.   The house was always well filled, and had quite the air of a theatre.
This sort of entertainment seemed extremely well adapted to the taste of a
certain class, who enjoyed hearing that the 'Chinese must go,' and who rev-
elved in the startling, if not polite, remarks of the Rev. mayor upon the
views of the non-conservative classes.

[10] Kalloch published a little paper called the *Evangel*, in which appeared,
June 8, 1876, the following: 'The Chinese furnish cheap and efficient labor
as house-servants, both in town and country.   They do well in our manufactories and our railroads.   They fill an important niche in society in their
wash-houses and huckstering.'   In a speech he said: 'These howling de-
claimers are not laborers.   They are incendiaries.   They are weatherkites.
They are mercenaries.   They ought to be suppressed....The best argument
for them is the bayonet and the Gatling gun.'   *S. F. Call*, Nov. 12, 1877.

[11] Such was the opinion of some of the best jurists in S. F. See *S. F.
Chronicle*, Nov. 16, 1866.

provide for the organization, incorporation, and government of merged and consolidated cities and counties of more than 100,000 population, pursuant to the provisions of section seven, article eleven, of the constitution of this state," [12] under which it was thought the city might be governed until a freeholders' election could be held, and a permanent charter adopted by submission to the people. The legality of this legislative act was at once questioned, being construed to be in the nature of special legislation which the constitution expressly forbade, and so the supreme court inferentially decided. In the meantime, a special election was held for the purpose of choosing freeholders to form a charter, which body sat from April 12th to June 28, 1880, another special election being held September 8th to decide upon its adoption. Although a good instrument, two causes operated against it, causing its rejection ; first, party selfishness, the new instrument greatly lessening the opportunities for jobbery and corruption; and second, the opposition of the catholic clergy, on account of an article prohibiting cemeteries within the city limits. The issuance of a pastoral letter against the so-called sacrilege determined the vote of the catholic voters. They threw their influence against the charter, and fully half of the electors, neglecting their duty, voted not at all, on account of which combination of circumstances San Francisco was left to struggle on without any legal charter. In 1882, when another election of freeholders took place, and another charter was framed, which in its general features was much like the consolidation act, it was rejected by the people at an election held March 3, 1883, the majority against it being no more than 32. No further effort to secure a charter for San Francisco was made until 1886, when at a general election in November fifteen

[12] *Cal. Stat.*, 1880, 137–229. This was called the McClure charter.

freeholders were elected from her leading citizens,[13] to whom was delegated the important duty of framing a charter which might be more acceptable to the people than the consolidation act, which had, by frequent amendments, become a more-than-ever consolidated instrument. The committee completed its labors in March 1887, and the election was ordered for April 12, at which time a special election was to be held to allow the people to vote upon amendments to the constitution. But whether weary of elections or indifferent to the change, few votes were cast on the amendments, which were defeated ; and notwithstanding that the merchants of San Francisco published an address to the electors of the city, appealing to them to accept the new instrument, which they very much praised, it was beaten by default, and San Francisco was again left to the untender mercies of political freebooters. Thus on several occasions have the citizens of our western metropolis declined to avail themselves of the protection afforded by a charter.

The election of 1879 was the last held in odd-numbered years, the new constitution ordering that the terms of the first officers chosen after its adoption should be one year shorter than those fixed by law, in order to bring elections in the even-numbered years. But this change necessitated an election in 1880--- the year of the presidential campaign of Garfield and Hancock—for the choice of congressmen, state senators, and assemblymen, as well as presidential electors. Judicial officers and the superintendent of public in-

---

[13] Russell J. Wilson, A. H. Loughborough, George R. B. Hayes, E. R. Taylor, George T. Marye, S. G. Murphy, D. A. MacDonald, Ralph C. Harrison, A. G. Booth, A. S. Hallidie, John McKee, Thomas Magee, Charles Holbrook, Jacob Greenbaum, D. C. McRuer were chosen. The instrument framed by them furnished a concise and complete form of government; gave a responsible head to affairs; provided a prudent and economical administration; permitted the city to vote to make, when occasion demanded, an unusual appropriation; placed the city's money in the treasury and kept it there; increased the authority of the auditor; provided a system of drainage much needed in the city; increased the efficacy of the police, fire, and school departments, and provided an election system removing opportunities for fraudulent voting. *S. F. Chronicle*, April 10, 1887.

struction were also to be chosen at the same time with state officers.

The San Franciscans also entertained the idea of putting municipal tickets in the field, and electing a new set of city and county officers; but upon a question arising as to the construction to be placed upon the new organic law, the supreme court decided that no municipal election was called for or legal except as to five superior judges of San Francisco whose terms would expire, according to their classification, in January, 1881.[14] This opinion united the two branches of the democratic party in the city, and gave to the presidential contest something of the enthusiasm of long-past political battles. The result was a meager majority for Hancock of 198 votes.[15] The democrats secured five of the six presidential electors,[16] and two congressmen, but the republicans elected two congress-

[14] This decision, sustained by the working of the organic law, was by some not well received for divers reasons. A petition for a review of the decision was filed in the court by James A. Waymore and Walter Van Dyke, republicans, upon the ground that the people who voted for the new constitution had not so construed it, and had therefore not approved it. 'The heavy cost, the constant annoyance, the turmoil and the demoralization of annual elections' was what they had wished to avoid, and for which they sought remedy in the new constitution, whose framers had solemnly promised to give them that relief, and whose announcement that they had done so had been accepted as final. To deny the city the right to elect at the general election would be to compel it to go through with the excitement and incur the same expense in 1881 which attended all elections, etc. Whatever truth and justice there was in this appeal, there was the equally strong motive of the petitioners to relieve the city of the official presence of its shameless and infamous mayor. It was equally the policy of the workingmen and democracy, by whom the majority of the superior judges had been elected to keep him in office. It was certainly the democrats who raised the question.

[15] Through five presidential elections from 1860 to 1880, California had cast her vote for the republican candidates. In 1857 the democratic plurality for Buchanan was 17,200; the opposition majority divided between Fillmore and Frémont was 3,491. The state was not then democratic by a majority of all the votes. It became so 4 years later; yet curiously, the democrats, although having a large majority of the votes, were beaten by Lincoln, republican, by a small plurality. After that, until 1880, whatever the combinations, the republican presidential candidate had a majority. In spite, however, of the presidential loss this year, there was a republican gain of 23,500 over the majority against the year before.

[16] The presidential electors chosen were William T. Wallace, J. C. Shorb, W. B. C. Brown, Barclay Henley, R. F. Del Valle. David S. Terry was on the democratic ticket for the 6th place, but ran behind his ticket, and Henry Edgerton rep. was elected. Terry, the year before ran for the office of state attorney-general on the N. C. ticket, and was defeated.

men,[17] and secured a working majority in the assembly,[18] with a decided majority in the joint convention which would elect a senator of the United States. They gained also the re-districting of the state for senators and assemblymen nnder the new constitution, which forbade any further change in the districts for ten years. San Francisco republicans lost their choice for congressman, Horace Davis, and the democrats elected W. S. Rosecrans.[19] Of the judges of

[17] W. S. Rosecrans, dem., was elected in the 1st dist; Campbell P. Berry, dem. in the 3d dist.; H. F. Page, rep. in the 2d dist., and R. Pacheco, rep. in the 4th dist.

[18] The senate of 1881 remained the same as in 1880. The assembly was composed of the following members: Valentine Alviso, L. B. Edwards, Alameda co.; R. E. Arick, Kern; J. E. Baker, W. C. Van Fleet, J. N. Young, Sacramento; (died in May, during the extra session) F. E. Baker, Yolo; T. C. Birney, Tuolumne; J. W. Bost, Merced; C. L. Branch, Stanislaus; J. P. Brown, Yuba; John Burns, P. Garrity, W. G. Gavigan, D. Geary, J. H. Gilmore, J. G. Hoitt, M. B. Howard, H. J. Jackson, Ed. Keating, M. Lane. Oscar Lewis, W. B. May, J. J. McCellion, David McClure, J. W. McDonald, J. G. Noonan, T. O'Conner, L. J. Pinder, H. G. Platt, J. D. Siebe, San Francisco; W. W. Camron, Alameda; A. L. Chandler, Sutter; C. Coleman, Alpine; J. F. Crank, R. F. Del Valle, Los Angeles; H. J. Crumpton, Lake; J. F. Cunningham, Santa Cruz; John Daggett, Siskiyou; G. L. Estey, Marin; C. N. Felton, San Mateo; Thomas Fraser, El Dorado; J. C. Wertsbaugher, L. D. Freer, Butte; H. M. Gay, John Reynolds, C. Wentz, Santa Clara; E. J. Griffeth, Fresno; J. E. Hale, Placer; C. Hartson, Napa; E. W. Hendrick, San Diego; E. C. Hinshaw, James Samuels, E. L. Whipple, Sonoma; William Holden, Mendocino; J. P. Jones, Contra Costa; W. W. Kellogg, Plumas; P. Kilburn, Monterey; F. E. Leach, E. E. Leake, Solano; W. D. Long, Thomas Mein, J. B. Patterson, Nevada; W. B. Mason, Del Norte; W. P. Matthews, Tehama; J. H. Matthews, San Benito; J. N. McMurray, Trinity; G. C. Mudgett, Humboldt; P. W. Murphy, San Luis Obispo; W. H. Parks, Yuba; John Patterson, R. C. Sargent, C. C. Paulk, San Joaquin; J. B. Reddick, Calaveras; H. M. Streeter, San Bernardino; C. B. Swift, C. Warkins, Amador; M. Wason, Ventura; Joseph Wasson, Mono; George Wood, Sierra. *Cal. Jour. Sen.*, 1881, 43-4.

[19] Rosecrans was born at Kingston, Ohio, in 1819, graduated at West Point in 1842, and was for one year executive officer of the engineering department of Fortress Monroe. In 1843 he was asst prof. of civil and military engineering; in 1844 asst prof. of natural and experimental philosophy, including physics and astronomy; in 1845-6 1st asst prof. of civil and military engineering; nine months on coast duty, acting as post quarter-master and commissary at West Point, and engineer-in-charge of construction of cadet barracks. In 1847-52 he was engineer-in-charge of fortifications, lighthouse, etc., at Fort Adams, Newport, R. I., and surveying New Bedford and Providence harbors, and Taunton river. In 1854 he resigned, and became a civil engineer at Cincinnati, also engaging in the manufacture of kerosene oil. At the breaking out of the civil war he became voluntary aid-de-camp to Gen. McClellan, remaining in the volunteer service until 1866. In 1865 he was offered the nomination of the union party for governor of Ohio, bnt declined, and came to Cal. by sea, and was offered the nomination for governor in 1867. Two years later he received the same offer from the democrats of Ohio. Also declined the nomination for member of congress from Nevada in

several superior courts, the republicans elected all but one.[20]

The choice of the legislature for United States senator to succeed Newton Booth was John F. Miller,[21] elected by a large majority over William T. Wallace and Henry George.[22] His course in the senate against the Chinese, and in laboring for the ratification of the modified treaty with China, which gave the American congress the right to pass laws for the regulation of

1876. He accepted the nomination to congress in 1880, with the object of reuniting the workingmen and democrats. *Letter of W. S. Rosecrans to Author*, 1886. The vote on his reëlection to congress in 1882 stood 22,733 against 14,847 for A. Neumann rep., 67 for H. S. Fitch, and 33 scattering.

[20] Three judges were reëlected on the republican ticket, namely T. K. Wilson, John F. Finn, and M. A. Edmonds. On the opposition, F. W. Lawler, and Robert Y. Hayne, elected to fill an unexpired term. There was a greenback ticket, made up of both national parties, but chiefly of democrats, who were anxious to have the interest on the U. S. bonds saved to the government. This party in California nominated for congress, S. Maybell; supported the republican judiciary nominees; and otherwise ran a ticket of their own, which only served to divide the others' strength.

[21] John F. Miller was born in Ind. in 1831, educated at South Bend, came to Cal. in 1853. Returned to Ind. in 1856, and was elected state senator. He served in the union army from 1861 to 1865 as brig.-gen., and retired a maj.-gen. by brevet; coming to Cal. the same year. For four years he was collector of the port of S. F.; afterward pres't of the Alaska Commercial co., and connected with other enterprises of a commercial nature. In 1872 and 1876 he was chosen elector at large on the Grant and Hayes ticket; and was elected member at large for the state to the constitutional convention. He was elected by the legislature of 1881, U. S. senator, and died in Washington in 1886.

[22] Henry George was born in Pa, in 1839, and received a common school education, and entered counting room at the age of thirteen years. Having a taste for sea-going, he shipped before the mast two years later, on a voyage to Australia and India. After this he learned the printing trade, but again went to sea, and finally, in 1858, visited the Fraser River mines in B. C., but returned to S. F., and resumed printing, becoming a member of the Eureka Typographical union, and working for several years as compositor on the daily papers. During this time he read and studied, becoming occasional reporter, and in 1867 was promoted to be the chief of the editorial staff of the *S. F. Times*. In the winter of 1868 he went to New York to arrange the telegraphic business of the *S. F. Herald*. Soon after he began writing for the *N. Y. Times*, on the Chinese question, and attracted considerable attention to himself by his manner of treating the subject. Returning to Cal. he inaugurated the eight-hour labor movement. *Our Land Policy*, *Progress and Poverty*, and other writings, were published, presenting arguments in the interest of the laboring class. He started the *S. F. Evening Post* in 1871, which he edited until 1876, when he withdrew from it to rewrite in a more extended form his *Progress and Poverty*, which was republished in England, where he made speeches on the questions involving the rights of 'enslaved labor.' His course has been steadily forward, and at the election of mayor in New York city in 1886 he received 65,000 votes as the apostle of labor. His doctrines appear, in the light of history, to be impracticable.

immigration from that country, was applauded by the
opponents of Chinese labor.

The legislature of 1881 was the first elected and
held under the entire provisions of the new constitution. As I have pointed out, it was republican by a
bare majority in the assembly and a larger one in the
joint convention. But in the early part of the session
the democrats obtained, by political trading, the control of the assembly, and gave the state a reminder
of the legislation of an earlier period of the state's
history.[23] It contained, as every large body elected
by the people must contain, a few men zealous for
their country's good; but a much greater proportion
were demagogues, or worse, were bent upon defeating
the ends and aims of the constitution which it should
have been their object to render acceptable and beneficial to the commonwealth.

With a view to shorten legislative sessions and prevent extravagance, the constitution had, as far as possible, prohibited special enactments. Deeming sixty
days sufficient for the business necessary to be done,
it fixed the length of a session at that limit, denying
compensation for any time in excess of that to which
legislators prolonged their proceedings. But the constitution proved neither guide to the duty nor obstacle
to the official criminality of this body. Lobbying,
which was made a felony by the organic law, was
openly encouraged. It wasted its time in bickerings
over matters affecting bargain and sale,[24] and in pre-

[23] *Concurrent Res.*, passed May 5th by the legislature. *Cal. Stat.*, 1881,
127–8. Mass meeting Res. in S. F., April 30, 1881, in *S. F. Chronicle*, May
1, 1881.

[24] The legislature of 1880 passed a drainage act making an unconstitutional levy of 5 cents on every $100 for the purposes contemplated in the
act, and the payment of a state and asst engineer, and for construction of
works connected with the control of water used in mining, and of the
'slickens' or debris from hydraulic mines. In order to save this act from
repeal a few republicans from districts interested in drainage entered into a
bargain with the democrats to defeat the apportionment bills; and did so
defeat them, at the expense of their party, and in violation of their obligation to observe the constitution, which forbade them to pass any special law
for the assessment of taxes, and commanded them to pass an apportionment
act based on the then population of the state. *Cal. Stat.*, 1880, 123–131; *S.*

venting an apportionment by the republicans. It adjourned at the end of sixty days without an apportionment having been made, although such an act was mandatory, and the census of 1880 was made the basis for fixing and adjusting the legislative districts. It failed to pass a general appropriation bill, to levy the rates of taxation, or authorize the state board of equalization to fix an ad valorem rate, to enact a general road law, or to send appointments to the senate for confirmation.

For the purpose of completing the neglected legislation and allow the government to go on, Governor Perkins called a special session, fixing the limit at twenty days The members reassembled April 4th, and remained in session 39 days, passing appropriation bills and no other, except to authorize the state board to fix such an ad valorem rate of taxation as should furnish the means to meet these demands, among which was the unconstitutional pay for the extra session of 39 days. In such ways, and by increasing rather than diminishing the expenses of the government, its enemies sought to bring into contempt the new law, as they had corrupted and disobeyed all law.   These

F. Chronicle, May 7, 14, 1881. The supreme court decided 'in bank, that the drainage act was unconstitutional, Judge Sharpstein only dissenting. *Cal. Repts*, 58, 624–659. The legislature also, either by design or otherwise, failed to specifically levy a tax upon railroad property, but simply delegated the power to do so to the state board of equalization. On this ground the railroad companies contested the collection of taxes. To meet the objection the legislature of 1881 inserted in the tax-levy bill the words, 'and the same is hereby levied;' yet when the bill was engrossed these words were omitted, whether accidently or not it was impossible to know. The governor signed the bill without discovering the omission; and was strongly-minded when it was pointed out to convene the legislature for the third time, but on consultation with the attorney-general and supreme judges abandoned the idea. The C. P. co. brought suit against the board of equalization upon the ground that the Cal. law was in conflict with the 14th amendment to the U. S. constitution, which provides that no state shall 'deny to any person within its jurisdiction the equal protection of the laws.' The supreme court decided that the provisions applied only to natural persons, and not to corporations or artificial persons; that 'person' had no relation to the assessment of the property of railroad corporations; that the franchise of the C. P. R. was property subject to taxation, and not exempt by reason of its being a means employed by congress to carry into operation the powers of the general government. *Cal. Rept*, 60, 35.

acts, as well as points in the constitution itself, kept
employed the bar and courts of the state.

A question had arisen in 1880 concerning the duration of the terms of service of officers elected in a
city, or city and county under the constitution. The
term of a mayor in San Francisco had ever been two
years. The republicans, anxious to be rid of Mayor
Kalloch, as were most of the better class of democrats, wished to apply that section which declared that
the terms of all officers chosen at the first election
should be shorter by one year than those fixed by
law or by the constitution, the object being to bring
all the elections in the even-numbered years. Application was made for a writ of mandamus to Kalloch
and the remainder of the board of election commissioners to comply with the law, which was refused,
and the case came before the supreme court, which
decided that the offices referred to in the constitution
were not county and municipal offices, and that San
Francisco was, until the legislature enacted laws upon
the subject, governed by the regulations under which
its officers had formerly been chosen. To this decision
the people bowed, and prepared for a municipal election in 1881; but the legislature in March of that
year passed an amendment to the existing code which
was construed as fixing city elections on the even-
numbered years, by which their wishes were seemingly
frustrated. Again the courts were called upon to in-
terpret, and decided that the amendment was of a
general nature, and that the act under which San
Francisco had held municipal elections ever since 1866
had not been repealed. A mandamus was granted
compelling the commissioners to issue an order for an
election, which was held in September, and at which
the republican reform ticket was triumphant, Maurice
C. Blake succeeding Mayor Kalloch, and every office
but two in the city and county being filled by republicans.

But as the law just mentioned, while it permitted,

with the help of the supreme judges, an election to
be held in 1881, required one to be held in 1882, and
every two years thereafter, the benefits of the September victory were shortlived.   By one.of those sudden
changes in the wind of politics which overturn so
many partisan air-castles, the city and county went
solidly democratic in 1882, from the governor elect,
George Stoneman,[25] down to ward supervisors.[26] The
congressmen elected in the first, second, third, and
fourth districts respectively, were W. S. Rosecrans,
James Budd, Barclay Henley, and Pleasant B. Tully.[27]
Two representatives at large were Charles Allen
Sumner and John Ragland Glascock.[28]

[25] Stoneman graduated at West Point in 1846, and served in the Mexican
war under Col, afterward Brig.-Gen., Kearney.   He came to Cal. with Gen.
A. J. Smith's command, and continuing to reside in this state, though he
fought in the Ind. war of Oregon, as I have related, being then a captain.
[26] The republicans nominated M. M. Estee, a determined opponent of
the Central Pacific, while the greenback party's candidate was R. H. Mc-
Donald, and the democrats nominated railroad commissioner Stoneman, who
was believed to be more or less favorable to the railroad interest, which
elected him.   For the rest of the state officers, John Dagget was chosen
lieut-gov.; T. L. Thompson, sec. of state; John P. Dunn, controller; W. A.
January, treasurer; E. C. Marshall, atty-gen.   Marshall came to California
in 1850, and was elected to congress in 1852.   H. T. Willey, sur.-general;
J. W. McCarthy, clerk sup. ct; W. T. Welcker, supt pub. instruction; E.
M. Ross, J. R. Sharpstein, associate justices sup. ct; W. P. Humphreys,
W. W. Foote, G. J. Carpenter railroad com'rs.   In S. F., Washington Bartlett, city politician since 1849, was elected mayor; James V. Coffey, F. M.
Clough, James G. Maguire, and D. J. Toohy were chosen superior judges;
over James A. Wayward, Columbus Bartlett, J. M. Troutt, and James M.
Allen.   Hale Rix, police judge; James Lawler judge of police ct no. 2.
Rix was the only rep. elected to the bench of any court.   He had served
about 20 years.
[27] Rosecrans ran against A. Neuman; Budd against H. F. Page; Henley
against J. J. De Haven; Tully against George L. Woods.   Budd was born
at Janesville, Wis. in 1851, and educated at the university of Cal., lawyer, res. Stockton; received 20,229 votes against Horace F. Page, rep.
U. S. H. Jour., 1884–5, 873.   Barclay Henley, born in Ind. in 1842, came to
Cal. in 1853, returned to be educated at Hanover college, lawyer, res. Santa
Rosa, was dist att'y of Sonoma co., member of the state assembly, presidential elector in 1880, etc; received 21,807 votes against 19,473 for J. J. De
Haven, rep.
[28] Sumner was born in Great Barrington, Mass in 1835, and educated at
Trinity college, Hartford, lawyer, S. F.; received 87,234 votes against 73,-
749 for W. W. Morrow, rep., and 2,786 for Yarnell.   Glascock, of Oakland,
born in Miss. in 1855, educated at the university of Cal.; and the university
of Va; lawyer, and dist att'y of Alameda co.; received 87,259 votes against
73,434 for Henry Edgerton, rep., and 2,786 for Hotchkiss, U. S. H. Jour.,
1884–5, 892. Sumner ran against W. W. Morrow; Glascock against Henry
Edgerton.

The constitution provided that all the senators elected in 1879 should hold office three years. This regulation rendered necessary the choice of a whole senate in 1882, half of whom were required to vacate their seats in 1884, after which a senatorial term would be four years. This circumstance gave an opportunity for the democrats to secure an almost exclusively one-party legislature, 33 out of 40 senators and 65 out of 79 assemblymen being democratic.[29]

[29] The senate consisted of John Wolfskill, San Diego and San Bernardino, R. F. Del Valle, Los Angeles; George Steele, Sta Barbara and San Luis Obispo; Patrick Reddy, Fresno, Tulare, Kern, Mono and Inyo; J. D. Spenser, Mariposa, Merced and Stanislaus; Benjamin Knight, Monterey, San Benito and Santa Cruz; C. H. Maddox, Santa Clara; J. Lynch, S. F. and San Mateo; T. McCarthy, D. McClure, G. H. Perry, E. Keating, T. K. Nelson, J. T. Dougherty, Martin Kelly, F. J. Sullivan, W. Cronan, S. F.; H. Vrooman, Alameda; W. B. English, Contra Costa and Marin; B. F. Langford, F. T. Baldwin, San Joaquin and Amador; C. D. Reynolds, Calaveras and Tuolumne; J. Routier, Frederick Cox, Sac.; J. M. Dudley and J. E. Kelley, Solano and Yolo; D. Spencer, Napa Lake and Sonoma; G. A. Johnson, Sonoma; J. A. Filcher, Placer; T. Fraser, El Dorado and Alpine; C. W. Cross, H. W. Wallis, Nevada and Sierra; A. L. Chandler, Yuba and Sutter; W. W. Kellogg, Butte, Plumas and Lassen; P. H. Ryan, Del Norte, Humboldt and Mendocino; C. W. Taylor, Siskiyou, Modoc, Trinity, and Shasta; C. F. Foster, Colusa and Tehama. Pres't, pro tem, Del Valle; sec. Edwin F. Smith; ass't sec's, J. J. McCarthy, A. T. Voglesang; serg't-at-arms, J. S. Messee; ass't serg't-at-arms, J. B. Snydor; minute clerk, A. A. Taylor; journal clerk, W. J. McGee; engrossing clerk, George W. Tuttle; post-master, Mrs J. V. David. *Cal. Jour. Sen.*, 1882, 1–7.
Members of assembly: L. H. Carey, W. B. Clement, L. H. Brown, Alameda; Robert Stewart, Amador; L. C. Grange, T. R. Fleming, Butte; George T. Carter, Contra Costa; A. R. Wheat, Calaveras; Reuben Clark, Colusa and Tehama; W. A. Hamilton, Del Norte; C. F. Irwin, Dl Dorado; Thomas B. Rowland El Dorado and Alpine; Frank Wharton, Fresno; J. H. G. Weaver, Humboldt; J. M. Keeler, Inyo and Mono; A. B. Moffatt, W. W. Head, Los Angeles; H. J. Crumpton, Lake; W. L. Smith, Mariposa and Merced; S. C. Bowers, Marin; Archibald Yell, Mendocino; Thomas F. Faw, Monterey; F. E. Johnston, Napa; J. L. Lewison, A. Walrath, J. O. Sweetland, Nevada; P. McHale, Placer; Calvin McCloskey, Plumas and Lassen; E. A. Gaussail, William J. Sinon, J. J. Callaghan, Thomas F. Barry, B. F. McKinley, A. G. Booth, J. H. Culver, C. A. Murdock, B. A. Rawle, Sidney Hall, Peter Wheelan, Thomas E. Healy, Patrick Plover, M. R. Leverson, T. N. McDonald, James J. Flynn, Charles A. Hughes, D. H. Bibb, Thomas M. Murphy, E. J. O'Conner, S. F.; F. D. Ryan, H. M. Larue, Gillis Doty, Sac.; Edwin Parker. San Diego; Truman Reeves, San Bernardino; J. H. Hollister, San Luis Obispo; C. A. Storke, Sta Barbara and Ventura; A. B. Hunter, J. H. M. Townsend, Adam Rhiel, Sta Clara; Lucien Heath, Santa Cruz; J. H. Matthews, San Benito; S. L. Terry, C. S. Stevens, J. W. Kerrick, San Joaquin; J. V. Coleman. San Mateo; M. Farley, Sierra; E. B. Beard, Stanislaus; Joel A. Harvey, D. G. Barnes, Solano; John T. Campbell, S. M. Martin, John Field, Sonoma; S. R. Fortua, Sutter; J. M. Briceland, Trinity and Shasta; F. D. Nicol, Tuolumne; D. N. Hershey, Yolo; W. M. Cutter, N. D. Coombs, Yuba. Larue, speaker; Campbell, speaker, pro tem; chief clerk, M. C. Haley; serg't-at-arms, James M. Farrelly;

Strictly construed, their election was not constitutional by reason of the neglect of their predecessors to apportion the representation of the two houses; but they proceeded to district the state, and remove this disability for the future, as also to define six congressional districts, beginning with the northern portion of the state and proceeding south, San Francisco comprising the 4th and a portion of the 5th congressional divisions. They displayed great readiness in appropriating the state's revenue, and a fair amount of industry in introducing bills in one house which were rejected in the other,[30] if not at first hand.

In March, 1884, Governor Stoneman called an extra session, unlimited, the extraordinary occasion for which was the refusal of the railroad companies of the state to pay taxes which, they alleged, had been illegally imposed. Actions had been instituted against them to enforce collection, which had been on various grounds delayed, but had finally been terminated by the decision of the court that while nothing was legally collectible from these corporations, the state might accept whatever they were willing to accord.[31] But the people were loath to accept this decision, and more effective measures for securing revenues from the railroads were imperatively demanded. The plan of electing railroad commissioners by districts had not proved satisfactory, for they had failed to agree on a tariff of fares and freights, and a thorough revision of the constitution and laws on this subject was demanded; hence the call for an extra session. It was recommended to propose to the people to amend the sections of article XIII. which

ass't serg't-at-arms, James P. Martin; ass't clerks, G. W. Herbert, Julius Reimer; minute clerk, Thomas Cleary; journal clerk, George W. Peckham, engrossing clerk, Charles A. Griffin; enrolling clerk, C. B. Swift.

[30] Among the more important measures were those brought forward by Senator Chandler, to provide against the accumulation of mining débris. Augustus L. Chandler, a native of Johnson, Vt, came to Cal. in 1852, and engaged in various occupations, mainly agriculture and stock-raising. He rendered good service to the Yuba city grange, the Farmers' union, and kindred associations. In 1873 he was chosen assemblyman for Sutter co.

[31] Governor's proclamation in *Cal. Jour. Sen.*, 1884, 1–2.

dealt with railroad and mortgage assessments; to
abolish the railroad commission system, for which the
legislature would substitute some better laws ; and to
amend the constitution so that the state board of
equalization should assess railroad property, including
mortgages, deeds of trust, contracts, and other securities, in the same manner that the property of individuals was assessed by local assessors. The legislature
should enact laws providing for delinquent sales of
railroad property; for the prevention of any writ for
hindering or preventing the collection of revenue; for
the appointment of a receiver when property should
be sold for delinquent taxes; should declare by law
that the people of California had not authorized and
did not ratify any compromise nor any judgment
theretofore rendered by consent in any action for the
collection of revenues by which a less amount was
recovered than the sum due by law; should enact
laws more clearly defining the powers and duties of
the attorney-general, district attorneys, and boards of
supervisors with reference to the collection of delinquent taxes. They were to propose to the people,
also, an amendment to fix a maximum rate of charges
for transportation of passengers and freight on all
railroad lines in the state, according to a classification
in length, gauge, and income; and laws were to be
passed appointing penalties for discrimination by the
railroad companies.

The legislature met March 24th, and adjourned
May 13th. It spent $83,000 of the people's money,
passed four bills, two appropriating pay to themselves,
one amending the constitution, touching the state
board of equalization, and one providing for funding
the indebtedness of counties in certain cases. This was
the sole outcome of the governor's proclamation
against the so-called recalcitrant railroad companies.
Naturally, the people were somewhat irritated against
the legislature, and also, though without apparent
cause, against the railroad, taking no heed of the
fact that the latter paid into the state treasury more

than $1,000,000, for which they were held by no legal obligation.

In the autumn of 1884 the general state and presidential elections being commingled, there was more than ordinary disturbance of the public mind; for men will make sacrifices to elect a chief of the federal government, who sit quietly at home while a foreign rabble make and unmake the officers and the offices of the state in which they live. Good men, sick of the name of politics, and wearied with ever-recurring elections, were more and more inclined to neglect registration as required by law, and to abandon with a sigh the responsibilities of electors. Of what avail, during this long period of political demoralization, and the ever-increasing prostitution of American free government, of what avail the votes of the few leading men of wealth and intelligence on whom the burdens of government fall, as against the imported European rabble, and the unthinking masses easily swayed by bribing monopolists and designing demagogues? Two causes, however, united to bring out a full vote in 1884; first the choice of a chief magistrate of the republic, and second, to prevent the reelection of the last state legislature. The result of the contest was a republican majority over all of 7,855, for president, the election of five out of six congressmen,[32] the control of the state legislature, and in San Francisco a gain in municipal officers,[33] although

[32] The exact figures were, for Blaine, rep., 102,406; for Cleveland, dem., 89,225; 2,960 for St John, prohibition (of liquor-selling); and 2,010 for Butler, greenbacker; total vote of the state, 196,957. Rep. presidential electors, Henry Edgerton, A. R. Conklin, J. D. Byers, J. B. Reddick, Charles F. Reed, Horace Davis, Marcus H. Hecht, Chester Rowell. In the 1st cong. dist a democrat, Barclay Henley, was elected over Thomas L. Carothers, rep., by 145 maj.; in the 2d, Louttit, rep., over Sumner, dem., by 119 maj.; in the 3d, McKenna, rep., over Glascock, dem., by 3,643 maj.; in the 4th, Morrow, rep., over Hastings, dem., by 4,490 maj. (plurality over all 4,461); in the 5th, Felton, rep., over Sullivan, dem., by 1,064 maj.; in the 6th, Markham, rep., over Del Valle, dem., by 409 maj. The state board of equalization elected consisted of 3 dem., Charles Gildea, C. E. Wilcoxon, and John Markley, and one rep., L. C. Morehouse, being the board of 1882. The former dem. board of railway commissioners was also reëlected, viz., G. J. Campbell, W. W. Foote, and W. P. Humphreys.

[33] Of the superior judges elected, 2 were rep., John Hunt and D. J.

Bartlett was reëlected mayor, and several important places were filled by democrats.

An important phase of this election was the adoption of three amendments to the constitution;[34] not important because the amendments were so, but as an illustration of the ease with which this manner of making legislation binding could be practised. Only about one-fifth of the electors voted on the amendments, and it may be doubted if the other four-fifths knew anything of their nature; but a majority only of the qualified electors voting was required to amend.

The legislature elect, which assembled in January, 1885,[35] took up the subject of railroad taxation, and

Murphy; and 2 dem., J. F. Sullivan and T. H. Reardon.   Hale Rix and W. A. S. Nicholson, rep., were elected police judges.

[34] Two were proposed by the legislature of 1883, and concerned privileges of individuals to lay water-pipes in cities; and provided that the state board of education should compile, or cause to be compiled and adopted, a uniform series of text-books for use in the common schools.   The 3d was the proposal of the extra legislature to amend sec. 9 of art. xiii., not as Gov. Stoneman had recommended, but continuing the then present board in office until 1886, dividing the state into 4 districts corresponding with the former congressional districts, and providing that no board should raise any mortgage, deed of trust, contract, or other obligation by which debt is secured, money, or solvent credits, above its face value.   Weighty and ironical legislation!

[35] The senate of 1855 was composed of A. P. Johnson, San Bernardino; R. F. Del Valle, Los Angeles; George Steele, San Luis Obispo; P. Reddy, Mono; J. D. Spenser, Stanislaus; Ben. Knight, Santa Cruz; James R. Lowe, A. W. Saxe, Sta Clara; J. Lynch, George C. Parkinson, Egisto Palmieri, D. McClure, George H. Perry, Daniel J. Creighton, Edward F. Drum, J. T. Dougherty, M. Kelly, John M. Days, John L. Boone, S. F.; H. Vrooman, G. E. Whitney, Oakland; F. C. De Long, Marin; F. T. Baldwin, B. F. Langford, Stockton; A. B. Beauvais, Tuolumne; Fred. Cox, J. Routier, Sac.; W. B. Parker, Martin J. Wright, Solano; D. Spenser, Napa; G. A. Johnson, Sonoma; J. A. Filcher, Placer; Henry Mahler, El Dorado; G. W. Cross, Nevada; H. W. Wallace, Sierra; A. L. Chandler, Sutter; W. W. Kellogg, Plumas; E. G. Hurlburt, Humboldt, C. W. Taylor, Shasta; C. F. Foster, Tehama.   John Daggett, pres't; Edwin T. Smith, sec.; J J. McCarthy, F. J. Saxe, asst secs; I. G. Messec, sergt-at-arms; J. Pinch, asst sergt-at-arms; Ray J. Falk, minute clerk; Guy H. Salisbury, asst minute clerk; John F. Meagher, journal clerk; P. M. Sullivan, enr. clerk; George F. Tuttle, eng. clerk.

Members of the assembly: J. K. Johnson, Siskiyou; J. H. G. Weaver, Joseph Russ, Humboldt; John Yule, Trinity; Thomas A. Roseberry, Modoc; George Wood, Sierra; John Ellison, Tehama; Allen Henry, J. M. Ward, Butte; Robert Barrett, Colusa; Whit. Henley, Mendocino; E. W. Brit, Lake; W. H. Parks, Yuba; Austin Walrath, C. F. McGlashan, Nevada; George H. Colby, Placer; E. H. Watson, El Dorado; W. J. Davis, C. T. Jones, Dwight Hollister, Sac.; C. B. Culver, Yolo; H. A. Pellett, Napa; W. T. Mears, S. I. Allen, M. E. C. Munday, Sonoma; D. G. Barnes, R. C. Carter,

an amendment was proposed, Heath of Santa Rosa
being the author of the bill which removed several of
the most objectionable features of the constitution,
touching the manner of taxing the railroad corporations of the state. It so changed article XIII. as to
include growing vines and fruit-trees among taxable
property, to provide for taxing ships and vessels or
their net earnings, and to prohibit double taxation in
any form. It excepted railroad owners from the obligation of making a sworn statement of all their
property, real and personal; but all corporations and
persons owning or operating a railroad or any portion
of one in the state should pay to the state treasurer
on or before the first day of July of each year two
and one-half per cent upon the gross earnings of the
year next preceding, ending in December, which tax
should be in lieu of all other state and county taxes
upon the material and property of such roads, including mortgages, deeds, contracts, etc. All other
property owned by such corporations or persons should
be assessed and taxed according to law. The gross
annual earnings of railroads were to be ascertained
and declared by the state board of equalization. Any
corporation or person failing or refusing to pay the
tax provided by the amendment should be deemed to

Solano; Joseph Almy, Marin; James H. Daly, E. C. Kalben, Peter Deveny,
Joseph Franklin, W. B. May, F. W. Hussey, N. T. Whitcomb, John Lafferty,
M. J. Sullivan, W. B. Hunt, Charles H. Ward, Julius Buhlert, H. C. Fire-
baugh, V. C. McMurray, Eugene F. Loud, Frederick Lovell, Hugh K. Mc-
Jenkin, Thomas H. McDonald, Charles D. Douglas, Frank French, S. F.;
James V. Coleman, San Mateo; Lucien Heath, Santa Cruz; Joseph F. Black,
Thomas C. Morris, F. J. Moffitt, W. M. Heywood, W. H. Jordan, G. W.
Watson, Alameda; G. W. T. Carter, Contra Costa; Hugh J. Corcoran, F. J.
Woodward, San Joaquin; U. S. Gregory, Amador; Mark S. Torrey, Cala-
veras; W. G. Long, Tuolumne; W. F. Patterson, J. W. Cook, D. M. Pyle,
Santa Clara; E. B. Beard, Stanislaus; G. G. Goucher, Mariposa; Maurice T.
Dooling, San Benito, S. N. Laughlin, Monterey; A. M. Clark, Fresno; E.
De Witt, Tulare; R. J. Van Voorhies, Mono; Arza Porter, San Luis Obispo;
Alex. McLane, Sta Bárbara; R. I. Ashe, Kern; J. Banbury, H. T. Hazard,
E. E. Edwards, Los Angeles; Truman Reeves, San Bernardino; T. J. Swayne,
San Diego.   W. H. Parks, speaker; Frank D. Ryan, chief clerk; C. F. Long,
Aaron Smith, Ed. J. Smith, asst clerks; Thomes E. Atkinson, R. D. Cannon,
minute clerks; Frank J. Brandon, Frank W. Marston, journal clerks; Jacob
Shaen, eng. clerk; Jerome Porter, A. F. Chapman, sergts-at-arms. *Cal. Stat.*,
1885, xviii.-xx.

have waived the right to operate their railroads within the state ; and the taxes should be a lien upon the property, which might be enforced by law. An ad valorem tax for school purposes should also be levied upon railroad property situated within any common-school district. Income taxes might be assessed and collected from persons, corporations, companies, or joint-stock associations doing business in the state. No court within the state should have power by injunction or otherwise to interfere with, hinder, or delay the collection of any tax laid under the form of law, unless it be shown that the same property had been taxed more than once for the same purpose in the same year, and then only upon the payment to the collector or into court of a sum equal to the amount of one of the taxes laid upon the property in question; but actions might be maintained against a tax collector to recover taxes paid under protest, if begun within thirty days after payment; and it should be the duty of courts to give precedence to cases of this kind. Nothing in this amendment was to be permitted to affect any penalty theretofore incurred, or any action or right of action. The first levy and payment of railroad taxes under the amendment should be made in 1886 upon the gross earnings of 1885, but it should not affect the taxation for the previous year. The real object of this amendment was to permit the ruling railroad corporation to settle with the state upon its own terms, the rates fixed being about one-sixth of that paid by the average tax-payer. This amendment was rejected in 1886.

Another question of paramount importance to the agriculturalists of the state—the proper distribution of water and its reasonable cost—had also become the subject of legislation. The movement did not emanate from the people, but was projected by political conspirators, who, while feigning to make all water which had been or might be appropriated a public use, subject to the control of the state in a manner to be prescribed by law, provided that in fixing the rates of compensation to be collected by any person or corporation for the use of water supplied to any city, town, or irrigation district, a net return of seven per cent per annum upon the cost of construction and maintenance of the necessary works should be secured to the owners. While declaring every neutral stream the property of the public, and dedicated to the use of the people, subject to appropriation, diversion, and use for irrigation and other beneficial purposes, prior appropriation[36] was allowed the better right, and should be exercised under legislative regulations. As in the Heath amendment, the courts were forbidden to intermeddle by injunction, and all suits pending against the diversion of water from any natural stream were to be stayed by the passage of the amendment until the plaintiff's right had been established by a recovery of damages in an action at law.

These innocent-sounding sections contained the germ of a mighty monopoly, and were conceived for the benefit of a few men[37] who had become, or meant to become, prior appropriators of all the waters in the southern portion of the state, for the use of which the farmers were to pay them at the rate of not less than seven per cent upon their expenses in perpetuity, or until this part of the constitution should be

[36] According to *Cal. Civil Code*, 1873, p. 302–3. As between appropriators, the one first in time is the first in right. 'The rights of riparian owners are not affected by the provisions of this title.' The supreme court followed the old English law in deciding upon riparian rights. *Vrooman*, MS., 12.

[37] The instigators of this movement were denounced in the public press, persons in interest, as a matter of course, becoming greatly worked up about it. Judge McKinstry had decided some time previously that a riparian owner was entitled to the full flow of streams traversing his property, and could not be compelled to divide with non-riparian owners, or with owners nearer the source of the stream (*i. e., prior* appropriators). Most people thought this bad law—it was founded on English common law—for California, and expected a reversal of the decree whenever the supreme bench should be changed. Meantime, the 'water-grabbers,' as they were called, had the law on their side, but found injunctions and law-suits expensive and uncertain, and devised this new plan of gaining control of the coveted water-supply.

abolished. Such a monopoly would be far more oppressive than that of railroads, which could be checked by competition; whereas the people could not create new water supplies when all the springs, lakes, and rivers of the state had been pre-empted, and converted to the use of the prior appropriators. The people demanded free water, not water belonging, according to the court, to riparians, or as monopolists intended, to themselves.

For the purpose of defeating the unwelcome judgment of the supreme court, the appropriators prevailed upon Governor Stoneman, though with some difficulty, to call an extra session of the legislature in July, 1886, to propose amendments to the constitution. They failed of their purpose, the senate refusing to be brought into the scheme for giving away the water of the state, and taxing the people heavily for the benefit of a few wealthy and interested men. The assembly, after becoming aware of the real animus of the call, also became recalcitrant, and the scheme fell through.

Another object was to abolish or at least to reorganize the supreme court. One of the chief advocates of a change was David S. Terry, whose private, no less than his professional interests, had suffered through the interference of the higher court with the decision of the superior court. He brought charges of physical and mental incompetency against two of the justices whose decisions were adverse to his interests, and procured an investigation before a committee, which ended in nothing except a bill of costs. The supreme court had other enemies, and the governor in his proclamation calling the extra session had declared that under its present cumbrous system it had failed to realize the aims and accomplish the results intended by the framers of the constitution. To meddling with the judiciary, the body of lawyers in the state opposed their united influence, and this attempt also miscarried.

The evils of an elective judiciary were made strikingly apparent in the political maneuvers of this year, strong efforts being made to prevent the reëlectlon of the most capable judges, by those whose several schemes had been, or were likely to be, frustrated by their decisions. On the other hand, the election of at least one justice to the supreme bench was undoubtedly secured[38] by the judgment rendered in the case above referred to, by a judge of the superior court. The lawyers who, with Terry, endeavored to have the entire supreme bench removed were, like Terry, democrats, and spared no pains to accomplish their purpose. They opened political headquarters during the state conventions, and secured votes for their favorite, whom they were to elect to the supreme bench, while the case was still pending upon motion for a new trial, and was entirely in his hands. I do not know whether this spectacle, or the other, of certain clergymen appearing upon the floor of a political convention to urge the choice of their candidate, should be regarded as most reprehensible. It is at least impossible to defend a system which, instead of placing the supreme court beyond reach of political influence, makes, unmakes, and sometimes uses judges at will. I can see in it only the lowering of the national standard of right, and the degradation of American pride of character.

It was next suggested to this legislature that it not only could, but should, elect a United States senator to succeed John F. Miller, republican, whose death occurred in the spring of 1886, and whose place had been temporarily filled by the appointment of George Hearst, democrat. This republican legislature had elected Leland Stanford senator of the United States in 1885, to succeed James T. Farley,[39] democrat, chosen by the legislature of 1877–8. It had

[38] One whom, in common with most men, I believe to have been perfectly honest, by whatever means his election was brought about.

[39] Farley was born in Va in 1829, educated in the common schools of

long been Stanford's wish that the choice should fall
on A. A. Sargent, and this selection he constantly
urged on his friends. Only after frequent protests
and remonstrances did he agree to accept the appointment, in deference to the consensus of his party's
opinion.

In the meantime, as I have just mentioned, on the
death of Miller, Governor Stoneman[40] had appointed
Hearst, who had with his family been but a few
months in Washington when he found himself deprived of his seat by senator-elect A. P. Williams.[41]
Thus the extra session had accomplished nothing except to unseat the appointee of the governor, and by
creating a prejudice against the executive in both
parties, to defeat his hopes of reëlection. The expense

Missouri, and migrated to Cal. where he studied law, and began practise in
1854. He was member of the assembly in 1855, and in 1856 was speaker of
that house. He served 8 years as state senator, and was pres. pro tem. one
session. Residence, Jackson, Amador co.

[40] George Stoneman was born in Busti, Chatauque co., N.Y., and educated
at the Jamestown academy. He studied surveying with an idea of going
west, but changed his views, and sought an appointment to the military
academy at West Point, graduating thence in 1846. He was assigned to a
2d lieutenantcy in the 1st U. S. dragoons, company C, Capt. Moore, and
proceeded to Fort Kearny, where he was detailed to conduct an ammunition
train and battery of heavy artillery to Santa Fé. From Santa Fé he
marched across the continent, acting as asst qrmaster to the Mormon battalion, arriving at San Diego in Jan. 1847. He served until the spring of
1853 on the Pacific coast in Cal., Or., and Ariz., when he was assigned to
the command of an escort which accompanied a R.R. surveying party from
Benicia to San Antonio, Tex. Following this duty, he was appointed aid-
de-camp to Gen. Wool, com'd'g the dept of the Pacific. In 1855 he was
promoted to a captaincy in the 2d U. S. cavalry regt, serving in Texas until
the breaking out of the civil war. When Gen. Twiggs surrendered his command, Capt. Stoneman refused to obey the order, and seizing a steamer
escaped with his command, and was recommended for promotion by brevet
by Gen. Scott. He reached New York in April 1861, and was ordered to
report for duty at Carlisle barracks, Pa, where he remounted his company
and reported to Scott in Washington, this being the first cavalry co. in that
city. His military career during the war is a part of the history of the great
rebellion. *Stoneman, Data,* MS., 1–4.

[41] A. P. Williams was born in Me. in 1832, and received an academic
education, after which he engaged in mercantile pursuits. In 1858 he came
to Cal., and after mining and merchandising for 4 years, settled in S. F.,
where he became a partner in the firm of Livingston and Hickey, after serving them for about 10 years. He began his political life by advocating
republican doctrines in Tuolumne co.,where they were exceedingly unpopular.
In 1880 he was placed on the executive com. of his party, and again in 1882.
In 1884 he was chairman of the republican state central com. In 1886 he
was chosen senator of the U. S. without having sought the nomination.

to the state of this extra session, which was called for ten days, and which remained in session thirty-seven, exclusive of a recess of seventeen days, during which the state conventions of the political parties were making up their tickets for the November election, was $72,383.

A brief interval of comparative quiet in political circles followed the adjournment of the extra legislature before the state election came on, with its absence of any vital issues, and its bewildering multiplicity of tickets and candidates.[42] It resulted in a loss to the republicans, as might have been anticipated from the numerous splittings of its regular ticket. The governor elected was Washington Bartlett,[43] first American

[42] 'Regular Republican,' a vignette at top representing Industry and Labor, a smith standing at his forge and a water-wheel and mill. 'Regular Democratic' was headed by an eagle with outstretched talons bearing a streamer inscribed 'Economy and Reform, and Protection to Labor.' 'Anti-Monopoly, Anti-Sargent and Independent Republican,' had a vignette representing a locomotive impeded by Fort Independence. 'Independent Republicans' headed with a vignette of a broken slate held aloft by Justice. 'Labor Party,' headed by a sunburst, crossed flags, and on either side a pick and sledge. This ticket was printed in two forms for S. F., one with the democratic state nominees at the top, and the other with the republican nominees, to catch voters on either side. 'United Anti-Boss,' bore Hercules holding aloft a sword, and about to strike at a monster representing bossism. The nominees on this ticket were divided between all the other parties. 'Regular Irish-American Democrat,' was headed by a vignette of a blacksmith shoeing a horse held by a farmer, and the motto, 'All public work must be done by days' work.' 'Citizens Independent,' had figure of Labor standing with one foot on the throat of a 'boss,' and in deadly combat with another 'boss.' 'Regular United Labor,' was headed by a likeness of C. C. O'Donnell, who was running for governor on the Irish-American ticket. Another 'United Labor' ticket had a vignette of Cox and Bell, the standard-bearers of the party. The 'Independent Producers,' had a horse's head for a vignette, and also bore the name of O'Donnell, though it was issued in the interest of J. S. McCue who wished to be sent to congress; the other nominees being from the various tickets. 'American Home-Rule,' had simply two U. S. flags at the top, and was a state ticket only. 'Committee of 200,' was headed by the American flag, and beneath 'Our Platform; Honesty and Integrity.' 'Independent Colored Citizens,' headed by a bee-hive surrounded by a swarm of bees. The state nominees were republican. 'Prohibition,' headed by three stars. A German-American spurious ticket was the 16th in the field. There was a great deal of borrowing from each others' lists. A full state and municipal ticket had 84 names on it, and the confusion was appalling to electors and those who counted votes. There were six candidates for the position of governor. Washington Bartlett (D.), John F. Swift (R.), Jerome B. Cox (L.), P. D. Wigginton (A.), Joel Russell (P), C. C. O'Donnell (I.).

[43] Gov. Bartlett, a well known pioneer, was born in Augusta, Ga, Feb.

alcalde of San Francisco, and mayor of the city when
elected, a lifelong democrat. He died soon after, having been in ill health for some time. Elected on the
same ticket were W. C. Hendricks secretary of state,
John P. Dunn controller, Adam Herold[44] treasurer J.
D. Spencer clerk of the supreme court, and Jackson
Temple associate justice of the supreme court for the
unexpired term of Justice Ross. Elected on the republican ticket were R. W. Waterman, lieutenant-
governor, who succeeded Governor Bartlett, after
his death; W. H. H. Hart attorney-general, Theodore
Reichert surveyor-general, Ira G. Hoitt superintendent of public instruction, and two justices of the supreme court for the long term, A. Van R. Patterson
and T. B. McFarland. Out of six congressmen

29, 1824, and resided in Tallahassee, Fla. In Dec. 1848 he determined to go
to California, and failing to procure a passage in the first mail steamer from
New York, shipped at Charleston on the *Othello*, Capt. Galloway, and arrived at San Francisco Jan. 31, 1849. Here he published the *Journal of
Commerce*, first issued in Feb. 1850. The office was destroyed by fire May 4th.
With the material saved the paper was re-issued, but on the 14th of June
another fire destroyed it entirely. With other material which had been
purchased at great cost, the *Stockton Journal* was started, and the state
printing for the first legislature was also performed. After the session the
San José office was removed to S. F., and started the *Evening Journal*, which
he sold out and started the *Evening News* with his brothers Columbus and
Julian, who had followed him to Cal. But when James King of William
started the *Bulletin*, his popularity over-shadowed every other journal. The
True Californian was Bartlett's next and last newspaper enterprise, which
did not run long. In the city's history he has ever been more or less conspicuous.

[44] Adam Herold was born in Bavaria, Germany, in 1842, going to school
until he was 15 years of age, when he was apprenticed to a miller, afterward
entering the German army. In 1869 he came to Cal., where he kept a hotel
for five years in Santa Clara co.; selling it out, he went to Gilroy, bought a
brewery, and operated it until 1886, when he was elected state treasurer.
He then gave up his business and removed to Sacramento, and afterward
purchased land in Placer co.

   McFarland was born in Pa in 1828, of Scotch parents; graduated from
Marshall college, studied law with his uncle, and was admitted to the bar in
the court of common pleas of Bradford co. He came to Cal. in 1850, mining for some time, but returning to his profession in Nevada city, where he
was judge of the 14th district from 1861 to 1863. He removed to Sac. and
was appointed superior judge by Gov. Perkins to succeed Denson who resigned. He was a member of the constitutional convention of 1878, and
voted against the constitution on the final ballot.

   A. Van Rensselaer Patterson was but 37 years of age. He came to Cal.
in 1869 from N. Y. and settled in Stockton. He served as district attorney
in San Joaquin co. and was twice elected superior judge.

   Ira G. Hoitt was born in Lee, N. H., in 1833, brought up on a farm, and
sent to the district schools, entering Dartmouth college in 1857, and grad-

elected, five were republicans.[45] But the legislature, which was to elect a United States senator to succeed Williams, had a democratic majority.

Owing to the irregularity of the election of 1884—for which the state had not been districted according to the constitution—a full senate was elected in 1886, half of whose members would hold over the session of 1889. What would be the course of the legislature in 1887, it was hopeless to conjecture. One thing which it did was to elect Hearst to succeed Williams. It was now six years since the adoption of the constitution, framed under such conditions as I have described, yet under it the machinery of government had not been brought to work harmoniously. Whether it was the fault of the people or of the constitution, let those judge who read. One thing appeared evident to many, that it was time for Americans, and men of sense and education, to take the lead in politics —honest men, desirous of doing something for their

uating in 1860. He removed to S. F. in 1864, and devoted himself to education.

William H. H. Hart was born in England in 1848, immigrated to Ill. in 1852, and to Iowa in 1854. In 1862, at 14 years of age, he joined Hinkley's union scouts, serving two years, and returning home to school in 1864. At 17 he again enlisted for 100 days service, after which he again returned to school. In 1865 he again reënlisted and was mustered out in 1866. He then studied law, was admitted to practise in 1869. Five years afterward he came to Cal. and settled in San Francisco.

Theodore Reichert, born in Ohio in 1839, came to Cal. in 1858, settling in Sac. in grain and commission business, although but 19 years of age. In 1863 he removed to S. F., and afterward to White Pine, Nevada. In 1869 he became clerk in the U. S. sur.-gen.'s office, where he remained until 1886.

[45] The congressmen elected were Charles A. Garter, Joseph Clabaugh Campbell, Joseph McKenna, W. W. Morrow, Frank J. Sullivan, and William Vandever, their districts numbered in the order here given. Sullivan was the democrat. W. W. Morrow was born in Wayne co., Ind in 1843, and educated in Ill. At the age of 16 years he came to Cal. by sea, residing in Santa Rosa from 1859 to 1862, when he went to the mines of E. Or., and entered upon the practise of law at Cañon city. When the civil war broke out he went east to enlist. After serving for a time he was given a place in the U. S. treasury, and in 1865 was sent to Cal. in charge of $5,000,000 in money. He returned to the study and practise of the law, and in 1870 was appointed ass't U. S. attorney for Cal., which position he held for many years. McKenna was a native of Pa, born in 1843. He came to Cal. in 1855, and at the age of 22 was elected district attorney of Solano co. He was a distinguished member of the state assembly in 1875–6; and was elected to congress in 1879 and 1884. Campbell was born in Ind. in 1851, and came to Cal. in 1876, a lawyer, and in 1883 was district attorney for San Joaquin county.

country, and not thinking solely of themselves. It could not be safe to longer endure, condone, or smile at the antics of foreign demagogues, who understood democracy to be a synonym for anarchy, who sought to pull down the institutions nobler men have built up, to glut their greed of plunder by making predatory warfare upon capital which they never could have amassed by their own brain or muscle, and who aspired even to assume the government of a state which had afforded them an asylum from the poverty, ignorance, and debasement of less favored lands.

If one could wonder at anything men may do, the marvel would be that the leaders of these variously styled factions do not perceive that their banner-cries are for the most part dead issues. They were, many of them, never native to the soil, but were imported with fugitives from aristocratic abuses, from Europe. Aristocracy and democracy do not now oppose each other as in the beginning of our government, while republicanism has degenerated to a degraded rule bordering on anarchy. The contest now is entirely between honesty and rascality. The foreigners who insolently seek to rule these American states are neither republicans nor democrats. Their blood is soured by ages of enforced inferiority and discontent. Having always been compelled, they desire to compel others, nominally their equals, but visibly their superiors.

This assumption had gone to such lengths in California, as in some other states, that a considerable number of independent men, particularly young men, "sons of the golden west," and others, left older parties to call themselves Americans. Their platform declared that all law-abiding citizens, whether native or foreign-born, were entitled to the protection of the laws; that the naturalization laws of the United States should be repealed; that aliens or non-residents should not be permitted to own real estate in the United States; that persons not in sympathy with the principles of this government, should be refused domiciliation in the territory of the United States.

This platform, crude as it was, contained ideas which had long been brooding in the American brain.[46] Possibly the day is not far distant when it shall take form and purpose, at least so far as relates to the repeal and amendment of the naturalization laws, and the holding of offices by foreign citizens. Whenever this is resolved upon a different class of men will be found demanding the suffrages of the people, and the laws will be regarded as binding.

To judge California by the history of the state and municipal politics, would be to misjudge her. She is altogether of a noble and generous type, great in her virtues as in her faults and follies. But a short time ago she celebrated the thirty-seventh anniversary of her birth as a state. Her population is roundly 1,-600,000. She has one city of nearly 400,000, and six others of from 20,000 to 75,000. She has 52 counties,[47] embracing all resources of soil, productions, and

[46] A call was made for a convention of Americans to be held at Fresno, on the 28th of September, 1886. Fresno was in the midst of a population largely from the southern states, who were opposed to foreign immigration of all kinds. The call might therefore be regarded with distrust, as not purely patriotic. But it touched a popular chord, and under favorable conditions might have competed for a majority with either of the old parties.

[47] It appears proper here to make mention of the counties in their consecutive order of creation. A number were mentioned in the previous volume, but for the sake of unity they are included in the list. The first sub-division of the state was made in 1850, when 27 counties were set off; beginning with the southern portion, the legislature preserved the names first applied by Junípero Serra and his brethren.

San Diego county was named after the mission town and bay, so called by the fathers in 1769.

Los Angeles, that is to say, The Angels, or more near the original appellation, The town of the Angels, was the name given in 1781 to the settlement near the mission of San Gabriel founded by order of the viceroy of New Spain, Bailio Frey Antonio Bucareli y Ursua, and the county, including the valley of Porciuncula river, with a population of 12,000 to 15,000, was allowed to retain the name.

Santa Bárbara was named after the presidio thus styled by Father Junípero in 1782.

San Luis Obispo took the name of the mission founded in 1772 by Serra and José Cavaller in Bear's glen. The father of M. G Vallejo, then a young man, was present as 'tenedor,' holder, at the birth of the first white child, a girl, whose hand he demanded in marriage immediately he had helped bring

mineral wealth known to the most favored parts of
the earth. The value of her assessable property in
1880, when the constitution was changed, was not far

her into the world. When she was 14 years of age the marriage took place,
which gave to California a valued citizen.

Monterey, signifying king of forests, was thought too beautiful a name
to be discarded. The bay was first named, in honor of Count Monterey, in
1603. The town of the same name became the county seat. It had been
the residence of 14 Spanish governors, Fages, Borica, Arrillaga, Arguello 1st,
Sola, Arguello 2d, Echeandia, Victoria, Figueroa, Chico, Carrillo, Alvarado,
Micheltorena, and Pico.

Santa Cruz, or the holy cross, was first named by the legislature Branciforte, but the name of the mission of Santa Cruz was restored to this division.
In all these counties the seat of justice was fixed at the towns of the same
name.

Santa Clara county was named from the mission founded in 1777, and the
county seat was at San José. The boundary between Santa Cruz co. and
Santa Clara co. was surveyed in 1855.

San Francisco county could take no other name than that of the noble
bay which bounds it, and the patron saint of the order which first founded a
settlement on its border in 1776. The American town of San Francisco became the county seat, town and county being afterward consolidated.

Contra Costa, or the opposite coast, so well described the territory to
which it was applied that it was chosen for the name of that county, and
Martinez the county seat. Monte Diablo, in this county, is an object of
superstition to the native race, but white men do not disdain picking up the
coal scattered about the devil's furnace-fire.

Marin was the name of a chief of the Licatiut tribe, the word licatiut signifying a favorite root used for food. It grew in abundance in the valley of
Petaluma. An expedition into the country by the Spanish soldiery in 1815
or 1816 brought on a battle with Marin, who was captured and taken to
San Francisco; but he escaped, and carried on hostilities, having his refuge
in the Marin islands, at the mouth of the inlet of San Rafael. He was again
captured in 1824, and his spirit being broken, he retired to the mission of
San Rafael, where he died in 1834. This county was at first attached for
judicial purposes to Sonoma county, Sonoma signifying in the Indian tongue
valley of the moon. It was formerly inhabited by Chocuyens, and is a lovely
vale, fronting on San Pablo bay. It will always be noted as the spot where
American filibusters first raised the bear flag. The pueblo of Sonoma was
the first county seat, but Santa Rosa became the seat of justice in 1855. The
boundaries of Marin and Sonoma were altered in 1852, 1854, and 1856.
The commissioners who fixed the present county seat were Charles Lopez,
Gilbert R. Brush, and James M. Neal.

Solano was the second name of the missionary Francisco Solano. The
chief of the Suisunes adopted it, his residence being in the Suisun valley,
bounded by the heights of Suscol. In 1817 a military expedition crossed
the strait of Carquinez, on rafts made of rushes, after the fashion of the
Indians, with the double purpose of exploring the country, and 'reducing
the Indians to christianity.' Led by their chief Malaca, they fought desperately against the intruders, inflicting considerable loss, but the Spanish
soldiery rallied and pursued them to their rancheria, which they set on fire,
men, women, and children perishing in the flames, rather than fall into the
hands of their enemies. Benicia was made the county seat of Solano. Fairfield is the present seat of justice. Boundary settled in 1852.

Napa was the name of a tribe which occupied the valley now known as
Napa valley, in the county of Napa. This was a warlike and brave tribe,
and harassed the frontier posts continually until 1838, when small-pox car-

from $700,000,000.   In 1888 it was over a thousand
million.   The average per capita in the different
counties was $676.05.   The bonded indebtedness of

ried them off in great numbers, reducing them to a handful.   Napa city
has always been the county seat.   Boundary changed in 1852 and 1855.
The highlands at the north end of the co. were called by the natives
Mayacmas.

Yolo is a corruption of the Indian word Yoloy, signifying a place abound-
ing with rushes (tular), with which they constructed Yoloytoy or 'rush-
town,' (Pueblo del tule), situated on the west bank of the Sacramento.
From this town the tribe took its name.   The chief Motti was christianized
—at all events he bore the name of Francisco Solano, after Father F. Solano;
but in 1835 he rebelled, and Father Solano reduced him to submission.   He
was taken to Sonoma and retained a captive until his people were subdued.
The county seat was fixed at Fremont, but was removed to Woodland.

Mendocino was the patronymic of Mendoza the 1st viceroy of New
Spain, who ordered the survey of the coast whereby Cape Mendocino was
discovered, and named in his honor.   The county which very properly per-
petuates his memory was at first attached to Sonoma for judicial purposes.
The county seat was subsequently fixed at Ukiah.

Colusa, spelled Colusi in the act of 1850, and Coluse by some, was the
name of a numerous native tribe on the west side of the Sacramento river.
The county of Colusa was attached to Butte for judicial purposes in the beginning, but the county seat was afterward fixed at the town of Colusa.
Boundary changed in 1856.

Butte, a purely French word, came into use through the French trappers
who traversed the country, and who named many detached mountains and
knolls this and that butte.   The high hills in that part of the Sacramento
valley denominated Butte co. secured it this name.   They were called peaks
(picachos) by Capt. Luis A. Arguello, who led an expedition to the Columbia
river, by order of the governor of California.   The county seat was first
ordained to be selected between Butte or Chico, but in 1851 was fixed at
Hamilton, whence it was removed to Oroville in 1857.

Sutter county was named in honor of John A. Sutter, a conspicuous
figure in the ante-American history of California, proprietor of a Spanish
grant and Fort Sutter and a member of the constitutional convention of
1849.   The county seat was established at Oro in 1851, changed to Vernon.
and subsequently to Yuba city.   The boundaries of the county were changed
in 1854 and 1856.

Yuba is a corruption of Uva, uva silvestres, wild grapes, the Spanish
population pronouncing the word as if spelled with a b.   The county was
named from the Yuba or Uva, by an exploring expedition in 1824, from the
abundance of wild grapes on its banks.   Some have erroneously supposed
that the county took its name from Uber, a person in the service of Sutter.
The county seat has always been at Marysville.

Sacramento, that is to say the sacrament, was the appellation applied to
the river of that name by Lieut Moraga, at an early date.   He called the
branch now known as Feather river, Jesus María.   It was natural the
county situated upon the main stream should be called by its musical name.
The town of Sacramento, which was made the county seat, had already
adopted it.   The county boundary was changed in 1857.

El Dorado was so named from the fancied resemblance of its history to the
wonderful country pretended to be discovered by Pizarro, and celebrated by
his chronicler, Orellana.   It was in this country that gold was first discovered, whence the application of the name.   Coloma was made the county
seat, but it was removed to Placerville in 1856.   The boundary of the
county was changed in 1855 and 1863.

the counties, exclusive of San Francisco, was $5,621,-212, and the floating indebtedness $1,992,932. Taxation for county purposes amounted to $3,486,818, and

Shasta is a corruption of the French *chaste*, pronounced *shas-t*, and was first applied to the mountain of that name, spelled Chesta or Chasta, by early American travellers. Mr Walthell, assemblyman, of the delegation from Sacramento district, proposed the name to the legislature. Its boundary was not established until 1852. The seat of justice was fixed at Reading's rancho in 1850, and at Shasta city in 1851, where it has remained.

Trinity was named from the bay, which received its appellation from having been discovered on the 11th of June, 1775, the festival of the trinity, trinidad, by a Spanish expedition in command of Bruno Heceta and Juan de la Quadra y Bodega. It was in that region called by the English navigators New Albion. Gold was discovered there in 1850. The county was attached to Shasta for judicial purposes. but in 1851 the legislature appointed commissioners G. O. McMullin, David Buck, W. L. Blanchard, C. S. Ricks, and B. Kelsey, who ordered an election for county seat in 1852, which was established at Weaverville. The county boundaries were changed in 1855.

Calaveras signifies skulls, and was applied to the region embraced in this county by the Spanish captain Moraga, who found the ground covered with them. The natives related to him that the tribes who formerly lived on the Sacramento and San Joaquin rivers made war on the tribes of the sierra that came to fish in these waters. In a great battle fought on Calaveras creek, 3,000 were killed—hence the skulls and the name. The first county seat was Pleasant Valley, changed in 1851 to Double Springs, later to Mokelumne, and finally to San Andreas. The pop. in 1850 was 15,000, mostly miners.

San Joaquin was a name given by Moraga in 1813 to a rivulet issuing from the Sierra Nevada, and emptying into lake Buena Vista. The name was carried down to the river, and finally adopted for the county traversed by it. The county seat has been from the first at Stockton, which as early as 1850 had 2,500 inhabitants. The city was named in honor of Com. Stockton. The boundaries of the county have several times been changed by the creation of new counties.

Tuolumne is a corruption of the Indian word *talmalamne*, signifying a cluster of stone wigwams. It was suggested as a name for this county by Benj. S. Lippincott, senator from San Joaquin district. The seat of justice was established at Sonorian camp, alias Stewart. In 1851 it was altered to Sonora—probably the same place—where it has remained.

Mariposa, signifying butterfly, derived its name from the abundance of this insect in the country at the head of the San Joaquin, a tributary being thus named in 1807 by a hunting party. The name being beautiful in sound and significance, was adopted for this famous district. Agua Fria, cold water, was first named as the county seat, but in 1852 it was changed by election to the town of Mariposa, adjoining Agua Fria.

Three counties were created in 1851, first, Placer, named from the gold placers on the American river. The county seat was established at Auburn, where it has remained. The first com'rs were Joseph Walkup, William Gwynn, H. M. Hann, and Jonathan Roberts. Nevada, named from the snowy sierra on the east, county seat at Nevada City, where it remains—first com'rs Henry Miller, J. N. Turner, J. R. Crandall, J. S. Allen, and Amos T. Laird, the boundary being changed in 1856; and Klamath, named from the Klamath—formerly spelled Tlamath—river, which was named from the tribe inhabiting its headwaters. Its county seat was first Trinidad, but was changed to Crescent City in 1854. The first com'rs were Robert A. Parker, W. W. Hawks, Edward Fletcher, Smyth Clark, and B. W. Bullitt. There is now no co. of that name.

Three counties were created in 1852, namely; Sierra, mountain range,

for state purposes other than schools, $1,853,112.
The bonded indebtedness of the four principal cities
of California was together only $7,055,115, of San
Francisco alone, $4,161,500.

with the county seat at Downieville, whence it has never been removed—
first comm'rs, John James, Francis Anderson, John Craycroft, C. E. Smith,
and J. M. Ramsdell. Tulare, taken from the southern portion of Mariposa,
county seat at Woodville, as I have elsewhere related—the name refers to
the reedy nature of the bottom-lands—present county seat is at Visalia.
Siskiyou—the origin of the word Siskiyou and its meaning has often been
given on questionable authority, The only sensible, and reasonable history
of its derivation was given to the legislature by J. R. Snyder, who explained
that when Michael La Frambois and his French trappers in 1832 made an
excursion into Cal., they crossed a stream in the mountains by a ford composed of six large stones—hence the name *six ceilloux* ford or mountain.
The sound of the French words bears out the statement. Snyder however
located the ford on the Umpqua and said he had seen Frambois' map of his
route. But he might easily have been mistaken among the half-a-dozen
ranges which the trail crossed, and the ford may have been on the Klamath
or on the Rogue river, between which streams lie the Siskiyou mountains,
but probably on the former. The first comm'rs of Siskiyou co. were H. G.
Furrls, David Fowry, R. F. Rae, Judge Tutt, and Judge Smith. The
county seat was established at Yreka, where it remains.

Three counties were created in 1853, namely: Humboldt, taken from the
western portion of Trinity—first comm'rs A. H. Murdock, H. F. James,
James Ryan, John Kingsbury, and K. Dobbins—county seat chosen by election, was at Union, but in 1856 the legislature changed it to Eureka, where
it remains. San Bernardino, out of the east portion of Los Angeles; county
seat at the town of San Bernardino, which was incorporated in 1854—first
comm'rs Isaac Williams, David Seely, H. G. Sherwood, and John Brown. Alameda, the name signifying a shaded promenade, when created extended 'east
'to the junction of the San Joaquin and Tuolumne counties.' Its first comm'rs
were James B. Larue, Michael Murry, J. S. Watkins, J. S. Marston, and
Gustavus Harper. They were to meet in the town of Alvarado, which
should be 'known as the seat of justice,' but the same act says that New
Haven should be the county seat. In 1856 it was removed to San Leandro,
and is now at Oakland.

Three counties were created in 1854, namely: Stanislaus, from the west
part of Tuolumne—first comm'rs John D. Patterson, Eli S. Marvin, G. D.
Dickinson, W. Loud, and Richard Horner—boundary settled in 1855 and
county seat established at Knights Ferry, since removed to Modesto; Ama-
dor, cut off from Calaveras by election—comm'rs appointed were William
L. McKim, Alexander Baileau, Alonzo Platt, H. G. Sneath, and P. W.
Gemmill—county seat fixed at Jackson by a vote of the inhabitants, where
its remains. Plumas, cut off from Butte, first county seat at Elizabethtown,
American valley, now at Quincy—first comm'rs H. J. Bradley, W. S. Dean,
John W. Thompson.

Two counties were formed in 1855, namely: Merced, out of the southern
portion of Mariposa—first comm'rs A. Stevenson, William Neal, W. J.
Barfield, Charles V. Snelling, John McDermott, Samuel Lovejoy, and C. F.
Bloodworth—county seat at Snelling, now at Merced. Buena Vista, taken
from the north part of Tulare, not organized.

Three counties were organized in 1856, namely: Fresno, taken from parts
of Mariposa, Merced, and Tulare, with the county seat at Millerton, removed to Fresno City—first com'rs Charles Hart, Ira McRae, James Cruik-
shanks, O. M. Brown, H. M. Lewis, H. A. Canal and J. W. Gilson. Tehama,

The state imported in 1889 goods to the value of $50,000,000, and exported to the value of $35,000,-000, for the most part to foreign ports. The wheat export alone amounted to $20,000,000, and flour to $4,650,000. The wool product of the state was 34,000,000 pounds. The hop crop was 35,000 bales. The wine product received at San Francisco was 10,-150,000 gallons, and the brandy product 489,000 gal-

taken from parts of Colusa, Butte, and Shasta—first com'rs A. G. Toomes, N. Hall, Dennis Dunn, county seat at Tehama, removed to Red Bluff; and San Mateo, formed out of the south part of San Francisco, county seat established at Redwood City in 1858. First com'rs John Johnson, R. O. Tripp, and Charles Clark.

In 1857 Del Norte county was organized from the north part of Klamath co., with the county seat at Crescent City. First com'rs W. B. Freaner, J. T. Basey, Peter Darby, R. B. Marford, P. H. Peveler, who were to give notice of proceedings in the *Crescent City Herald*.

Two counties were created in 1861, namely: Mono, out of those portions of Calaveras, Mariposa, and Fresno lying east of the summit of the Sierra Nevada, with the county seat at Aurora—first com'rs P. J. Hickey, W. M. Baring, E. W. Casey, C. N. Noteware, L. A. Brown, G. W. Bailey, and T. A. Lane—county seat, after the organization of Nevada territory, was in dispute, as I have related in *Hist. Nevada*, it is now at Bodie; and Lake, lying between Mendocino, Yolo, Solano, and Napa. Com'rs William Manlove, Alexander McLean, Woods Crawford. For the selection of a county seat J. N. Pendergast of Yolo, Charles Ramsey of Solano, and Anthony P. Buckner of Colusa were appointed to choose two sites, one of which should be chosen by a majority of the electors in June of 1861, and Lakeport became the capital.

Two counties were organized in 1864, namely: Alpine, from parts of El Dorado, Amador, Calaveras, and Mono—it was attached to Amador for judicial purposes for one year, first com'rs Benjamin Sears, O. F. Thornton, and Frank Cooper, county seat fixed at Markleeville, which was incorporated in 1864; and Lassen, named after Peter Lassen, formed out of the east portions of Shasta and Plumas. The first com'rs were F. Drake, C. Stockton, and N. Breed, who were ordered to 'meet at Kingley and Miller's store in Susanville,' to be sworn in by a qualified officer. They were to appoint three freeholders of the county to select two sites to be voted upon for county seat, the result being the choice of Susanville. The boundary was changed in 1866.

Two other counties were created in 1866, namely: Kern, out of portions of Tulare and Los Angeles, with the county seat at Havilah—first com'rs Michael H. Erskine, Eli Smith, Daniel W. Walser, Thomas Baker, and John Bright—present county seat Bakersfield; and Inyo, out of portions of Tulare and Mono, with the county seat at Independence. The first com'rs were Thomas J. Goodale, Louis F. Cooper, W. A. Greenly, William Baker, and Lyman Tuttle. The county was first attached to Mono for representative purposes, formed a part of the 12th senatorial district, and was attached for judicial purposes to the 5th judicial district. The county seat remains unchanged.

In 1872 Ventura county was created out of a portion of Santa Bárbara, with the county seat at Buenaventura, where it remains. No com'rs were appointed, being elected at a special election, and I have not their names.

In 1874 two counties were created, namely: San Benito, out of the east-

lons.[48] Of fruit, fish, and twenty other merchantable productions there was a due proportion. Of quicksilver the product was about 26,000 flasks. Of treasure exported, $21,000,000. The clearings of the banks for the year amounted to $844,000,000.[49] The duties collected at the port of San Francisco aggregated $9,478,000, and the internal revenue receipts were on a commensurate scale. A large amount of industry and labor, considering the population, is represented by these figures, showing the character of the people—not the politicians. In their enterprise and energy they cannot find time to protest against the greed of those they permit to spend the public money, but the time will come when they or their children will not fail to do so, either peaceably, or by way of terrible retribution.

As we stride through the present, we build churches and pleasure resorts, school-houses and colleges, along with our factories, steamships and railroads, sparing nothing that can help the development of the generations destined to erect a wonderful superstructure upon the foundations of which we are proud to be styled the architects. In other chapters devoted to material progress, the vitality, elasticity, and strength of the first generation of American Californians are so thoroughly illustrated as to need no further commentary in this place.

The benefits of the government to the state in appropriations not in the regular annual list aggregated for various purposes from 1851 to 1886 $15,398,377.-28; as follows: public buildings, namely, custom-house,

ern part of Monterey, with the county seat at Hollister, where it remains; and Modoc, named after the tribe that lived on Pitt river, out of the east part of Siskiyou, with the county seat at Dorrisbridge. Present county seat, Alturas.

By retaining Spanish names in most instances, poetic justice is subserved. The pleasantness of a metrical language is added to the romance of association with a half mysterious and ever piquant history.

[48] There was less than half a crop of grapes in 1885, and about the same falling off in other crops.

[49] This makes San Francisco the 5th city of the union in its volume of exchanges.

appraisers' stores, and post-offices, $2,239,555.91;
river and harbor improvements, $2,038,000; light-
stations on the coast, $1,273,272; United States
mint, $2,629,192.37; arsenals and forts, $6,617,757.
An appropriation was made in the session of 1886–7
of $350,000 toward a new post-office. Los Angeles was
also granted an appropriation for a public building,
and to San Francisco manufacturers was awarded the
contract for building of a government iron cruiser
at a cost of $500,000, followed by others, as will be
mentioned elsewhere in this volume. Other defences will soon be provided for, congress having
taken up the matter recently in a determined spirit.
Congress at the same session appropriated $100,000
for the establishment of a branch of the National
home for disabled volunteer soldiers.[50] But the
money appropriated for public improvements is less
than that paid in salaries to government officials residing in California, and not connected with the army
or navy. These salaries amounted in 1872 to $743,-
992 per annum; to the post-office $126,932; to the
custom-house $289,790; to the mint $196,926; to
the internal revenue office $44,100; to the United
States courts $19,250; to the land-office $26,900; to
the light-keepers, steamboat inspectors, naval recruiting station, military surveys, marine hospital, and
Indian affairs $40,074. The post-offices and light-
houses have since become a much greater expense to
the government; but I have no figures at hand to
show the actual present expenditure or income.

At no period of the state's existence has the immigration exceeded that of 1886–8. The arrivals overland averaged 5,000 a month, many persons of wealth
and refinement coming to remain. When the state
has attained to the age of fifty years it will be more
famed for its agricultural, horticultural, and manufactured productions than for its mining product.

[50] The people of California had already established a soldiers' home in
Napa co., and congress was brought to consent to consolidate with it the plan
for a branch national home.

CHAPTER XVII.

MILITARY.

1848-1888.

CALIFORNIA UNDER MILITARY RULE—DESERTIONS—QUARTERS AND RESERVATIONS—LIGHTHOUSES—COMPANIES FORMED—INDIAN TROUBLES—POSTS ESTABLISHED—DEPARTMENTS—VIGILANCE COMMITTEE MATTEES—WAR FOR THE UNION—COAST DEFNESES.

I HAVE given nothing of the military history of California since the establishment of the United States in possession under the rule of Governor Mason. Influences were present in the geographical and political position of the country at this period which rendered military force a necessity; and the disbanding of the New York volunteers on the declaration of peace in 1848 seriously embarrassed the temporary government,[1] which feared an uprising among the na-

---

[1] From the orders of the military governors I transcribe the names of their appointees. Frémont made few appointments, but reports giving the office of collector of port of San Diego to Santiago Arguillo, and of San Pedro to Pedro Carrillo. Kearney appointed D. W. Alexander collector at San Pedro, William A. Richardson at Monterey, Angel Lebriga at La Paz, and Miguel Chosa at San José, L. C. He also appointed, Feb. 22, 1847, Edwin Bryant to succeed naval Lieut W. A. Bartlett—appointed by Capt. Montgomery of the Portsmouth in 1846—and May 28th, George Hyde to succeed Bryant. He appointed Edward Petty Hartnell to be translator and interpreter to the gov't, March 10th; Walter Cotton judge of admiralty, March 24th; John A. Sutter sub. Indian agent, April 7th; Lilburn W. Boggs to be alcalde of Sonoma in place of John H. Nash, April 10th; M. G. Vallejo sub. Ind. ag't, April 14th; Mariano Bonilla alcalde of San Luis Obispo; and Pablo de la Guerra alcalde at Sta Bárbara. Mason appointed Louis Robideau alcalde of San Bernardino, June 1st; William B. Ide land surveyor, June 7th; William Blackburn alcalde of Sta Cruz, June 21st; Jasper O'Farrell asst surveyor, July 6th; J. D. Hunter sub. Indian agent, San Luis Rey; Miguel de Pedrosena collector at San Diego, July 14th; John Foster alcalde at San Juan, July 14th; Jacob R. Snyder asst surveyor, July 22d; H. W. Halleck sec. of the ter. Cal., Aug. 13th, T. Minor Leavenworth

tive Californians. There remained only the battalion
of 2d dragoons, Major L. P. Graham in command,
in the southern district; Captain A. J. Smith's company C of the 1st dragoons at San Francisco; and
Lieutenant-colonel H. S. Burton's company F of the
3d artillery at Monterey. From these so many desertions took place that it became doubtful if one
whole company would be left in the service. Early
in September the ship *Huntress* arrived at Monterey
with 46 recruits; but as soon as they had recovered

alcalde of the 2d district of S. F. Oct. 2d; Julian Urgua alcalde San Juan
Bautista, Nov. 22d; John Sharmon alcalde dist of San Diego, Nov. 24, 1847;
Robert Cliff, alcalde of San Diego, Dec. 10th. In 1848 he made the follow-
ing appointments: Stephen C. Foster alcalde of Los Angeles, Jan. 1st;
Stephen Cooper alcalde of Benicia, Jan. 3d; William R. Langley 2d alcalde
of Monterey, Jan. 13th; John Price alcalde of San Luis Obispo, Jan. 25th;
P. C. Carillo alcalde of Sta Bárbara, Feb. 8th; Charles White alcalde of
Pueblo San José vice James W. Weeks, resigned; and 2d alcalde Dolores
Pacheco, Feb. 9th; Juan Bandini 1st alcalde dist of San Diego, April 15th;
E. L. Brown 2d alcalde same dist; Isaac Callaghan sub-alcalde Sta Bárbara;
William Byrne 1st alcalde at San José; Miguel Pedrorena collector and har-
bor-master at San Diego; Edward Gilbert ditto at S. F., N. S. Carnes ditto
at Sta Bárbara; Edward H. Harrison, collector at S. F., Sept. 3d; Florencio
Serrano 1st alcalde at Monterey. Riley's appointments in 1849 before the
adoption of the constitution were as follows: Jabez Halleck of Monterey
and Joshua B. Haven of S. F. notaries public, in May; W. M. Eddy and
Addison H. Flint land surveyors in June; A. C. Peachy notary public of S.
F. in June; T. M. Leavenworth, 1st alcalde of the dist of S. F., was sus-
pended, and a commission appointed to investigate charges against him;
Horace Hawes was appointed prefect of the dist of S. F., Aug. 1st; G. D.
Dickerson prefect of San Joaquin, Jose Antonio Estudillo prefect of San
Diego, Joaquin Carillo prefect of Sta Bárbara, C. P. Wilkins prefect of
Sonoma, David Spence prefect of Monterey, William G. Doud prefect of
San Luis Obispo, Antonio M. Pico prefect of San José, in Aug.; E. Crosby
prefect of Sac.; Stephen C. Foster prefect of Los Angeles, in Sept.; Lewis
Dent, J. M. Covarrubias, Pacificus Ord, Peter H. Burnett judges of the
superior tribunal, in Aug.; Richard A. Maupin vice Dent, in Oct.; J. W.
Geary, judge of 1st instance, at S. F., in Aug.; Wm
B. Almond ditto, with civil jurisdiction, in Oct.; R. M. May judge of the
1st instance, with crim. jurisdiction, at San José, in Aug.; J. T. Richardson
ditto, with civil jurisdiction, in Nov.; Ignacio Esquer alcalde of Monterey,
April and Aug., Mariano Malarin judge of 1st instance at Monterey, in
Nov.; Stephen C. Massett notary public for New York of the Pacific, San
Joaquin district; Edward M. Howison, notary public in the dist of San Joa-
quin, in Oct.; George G. Belt justice of the 1st instance in San Joaquin dist,
in Aug.; Raymundo Carrillo ditto in Sta Bárbara, April and Aug.; Manuel
Abrita ditto in San Luis Obispo, in Aug.; Augustin Olivera ditto in Los
Angeles, in Sept.; James C. Thomas ditto, with civil jurisdiction, in Sac., in
Oct.; Stephen Cooper ditto in Sonoma dist, in Aug.; H. F. Page, Theodore
Griswold, John McVickar, Hopeful Toler, Charles C. Moore, Thomas Filden
notary publics in S. F.; John McDougal and William Shaw ditto in Sac.;
Hall McAllister dist atty for S. F., in Sept.; E. A. King harbor-master at
S. F., June 19th; N. Wise and J. Walsh port-wardens, in June. *U. S. H.
Ex. Doc.*, 17, 31 cong. 1 sess.; *Cal. Mess. and Corr.*, 1850, vol. v.

from the scurvy with which most of them were afflicted, they, too, deserted and went to the mines. Efforts were made to recruit in California and Oregon[2] without success, owing to the greater inducement held out by miners, who paid high wages to men willing to be hired to dig for others.

In November, 1848, Colonel Mason asked to be ordered home, and was succeeded in the command of his department by General Persifer F. Smith, who arrived by the first mail steamer, the *California*, which touched at Monterey February 23, 1849, and proceeded with the new commander of the department to San Francisco.[3] He had upon his staff E. R. S. Canby as adjutant, Lieutenant Alfred Gibbs, aid-de-camp, and Major Cornelius Ogden of the engineers. Leaving Canby at Monterey, he took W. T. Sherman for his adjutant on account of his knowledge of affairs gained by a two years' previous residence.

On the 21st of March the government steam propeller *Edith* reached San Francisco with military stores, being the first of a fleet bringing troops for the relief of California and Oregon. There followed in April the ship *Iowa* having on board the new governor, General Bennett Riley, and a part of the 2d infantry regiment. In May the *Rome* arrived with

[2] L. W. Hastings was employed by Gov. Mason in 1848 to endeavor to raise a battalion of American volunteers; but as those had not been paid who served under Frémont, they declined. *S. F. Californian*, March 8 and 22, 1848. *Polynesian*, iv. 182. *Murray's Narr.* 209-10. Major James A. Hardie was sent to Oregon with instructions to enlist 800 men, but here he found the fighting men still in the Cayuse country where they were having an Indian war, or guarding the Willamette settlements from threatened invasion. The object of these attempts at recruiting was not so much the defence of Upper Cal. as the conquest of Lower Cal. but the treaty resigned the peninsula to Mex., and ended that anxiety.

[3] Mason said: 'The war being over, the soldiers nearly all deserted, and having now been from the states two years, I respectfully request to be ordered home. I feel less hesitancy in making the request as it is the second only that I recollect ever to have made, in more than thirty years' service, to be relieved from any duty upon which I have been placed; the first was asking to be relieved from the recruiting service in 1832, that I might join my company in the Black Hawk war.' *U. S. H. Ex. Doc.* 17, 649; 31 cong., 1 sess. He died at St Louis, of cholera, in the summer of 1849. See *Willey's Personal Memoranda*, 32; *Buffum's Six Months*, 115; *Contemp. Biog.*, i., 317; *Burnett Recoll.*, MS., ii. 60-1; *Crosby's Early Days*, MS., 11-12.

another detachment, and, not until July, the *Mary and Adeline* with the remainder of the regiment. Riley's choice of a staff was captains H. W. Halleck and G. C. Westcott, Major E. R. S. Canby, and Lieutenant George H. Derby, known as a humorous writer under the signature of John Phœnix.

The general depot for military property was established at Benicia,[4] the selection of the site being made by a commission composed of majors C. A. Ogden, J. L. Smith, and Danville Leadbetter of the army, and captains Louis M. Goldsborough, J. G. Van Brunt, and Simon F. Blunt of the navy. The same commissioners selected Mare island as a site for a navy-yard. Military headquarters was established temporarily in the old adobe custom-house in San Francisco, but after the arrival of General Riley, who assumed command of the department, General Smith removed division headquarters to Sonoma, and with him went company C, 1st dragoons, A. J. Smith, captain

The different companies were distributed as follows: M, 3d artillery, Captain E. D. Keyes, to the presidio of San Francisco; F, 3d artillery, Lieutenant-colonel H. S. Burton, to the redoubt at Monterey; C and G, 2d infantry, Colonel Silas Casey, to the main depot at Benicia; D and I, 2d infantry, Major S. P. Heintzelman, to San Diego; A, B, and K, 2d infantry, and one company of the 1st dragoons, Major A. S. Miller, to the main crossing of the San Joaquin; E and F, 2d infantry, Major J. J. B. Kingsbury, to a post near Sutter's fort; two companies of the 1st and two of the 2d cavalry, majors L. P. Graham and D. H. Rucker, at Los Angeles and San Luis Rey; the remainder of the infantry, including about 70 recruits, being divided between Monterey and a camp on the

---

[4] Sherman affirms that Gen. Smith, being disinterested, decided on Benicia as the proper point for the city, and where the army head-quarters should be. See also *Larkin Doc.*, vii., 113. The general purchased a mile square of land at Suisun, of M. G. Vallejo, for $25,000. *Vall. Doc.*, xiii., 24.

Stanislaus river.   One of the companies at San Diego was ordered to escort the boundary commission under Major W. H. Emory of the topographical engineers.

In May Los Angeles and San Luis Rey were abandoned as military stations on account of the wholesale desertion of the soldiery who were carried away by the attractions of gold-getting in the mines. Los Angeles had been an important post, but the stores were now sent to San Diego, and the guard-house turned over to the alcalde to be used as a prison, of which the town stood in need.[5]   Desertion had reduced the four companies of cavalry until little more than enough to form one remained; while at San Diego it was feared the boundary commission would be without an escort.   The depredations committed upon the inhabitants by the soldiers, who were unable to carry with them the means of subsistence, were the subject of much concern to the military authorities.   Comparatively few arrests were made, though twenty-five or thirty persons were tried at Monterey and sentenced to be sent east to serve out at hard labor in confinement the remainder of their terms of service;   and until a government vessel should be returning, they were to be kept at hard labor under guard in California.

The severity of the punishment did not deter the soldiers from breaking away from their engagements. An expedition under Captain W. H. Warner of the topographical engineers, ordered to make an examination of the routes from the Humboldt valley to the Sacramento river, and which consisted of 80 men at the offset, had 34 desertions in less than a month. Captain Warner prosecuted his reconnoissance with his reduced force, and was ambushed and killed by the Indians near Goose lake, from which circumstance

[5] *Los Angeles Arjunt Rec.*, 77.   The need of prisons in which to confine offenders was often embarrassing.   Mason in 1848 offered to contribute $1,-000 toward the erection of secure prisons in each of the towns of Los Angeles, Sta Bárbara, San José, Sonoma, and Sutter's Fort; but it does not appear that the offer was accepted.

the Warren range of mountains received its name.
His remains were not recovered until the following
spring, although Lieutenant Davidson was sent in
search of them.

To check the tendency to desertion commanding
officers were instructed to allow furloughs to be
granted to detachments, with other reasonable indul-
gences which might tend to prevent desertion. Nothing, however, could restrain men under the temptation
of gold and freedom. By the end of August there
were no more than 650 officers[6] and men in the department. Under these circumstances little exploration could be carried on, and few expeditions of any
kind[7]. The generals contented themselves with a

[6] There were present in Cal. in 1849, the following officers, exclusive of
those already mentioned, some of whom have since become famous: Lieut-
col Joseph Hooker; majors Justus McKinstry, W. Seawell, (formerly of the
N. Y. reg' t), D. H. Vinton, R. Allen, quartermaster S. F. and civil treasurer; E. H. Fitzgerald, quartermaster at S. F.; P. B. Reading, former pay-
master of Frémont's battalion; H. Hill and H. Leonard, Captain R. Campbell, E. R. Kane, W. G. Marcy, N. Lyon, J. Hayden, N. H. Harris, G. P.
Andrews, C. Q. Tompkins, and R. Ingalls; Lieutenants, C. J. Coutts, C. E.
Jarvis, F. L. Patterson, W. A. Slaughter, J. W. T. Gardiner, Sweeney, J.
Hamilton, E. O. C. Ord, J. W. Davidson, George Stoneman, H. Wager
Halleck, James A. Hardee, M. R. Stevenson, (formerly of the N. Y. reg't),
and Evans. These are all the names that appear in the military correspon-
dence of that year; but John Nugent mentions as being at San Diego, him-
self, Major Caperton, and Hays. Only two surgeons are mentioned, Murray
A. Perry and W. S. Booth. On the 1st of Jan., 1850, Sherman, Ord, and
A. J. Smith returned to the states.

[7] One of the principal expeditions was made by Co. E., 1st Lieut Wilson,
commanding, in search of some Indians. Murders were becoming frequent.
Early in the year a fearful tragedy was performed at San Miguel mission.
Reed was an Englishman, who lived with his native wife and family at the
mission. He had sold a band of sheep in the southern mines, and was followed to his home by a Hessian and an Irishman, who, after killing two
sleeping miners by the way, and picking up three deserters from the Pacific
squadron at La Soledad, called at Reed's and were hospitably entertained
over night. The next morning they murdered every inmate of the mission,
twelve in all, and taking the gold found in the house fled to a secluded cove
on the sea beach. It happened that two travellers were passing the house
at the very hour of the murder, hailed it, and getting no answer, suspected
a crime, and gave the alarm along the road and at Sta Bárbara. The citizens pursued and discovered the retreat of the murderers, one of whom, and
one citizen, were killed in the conflict. Another swam out to sea and was
drowned, and the other three were captured, tried by a temporary court,
found guilty, and sentenced to be hanged. But there being some hesitancy
about executing the sentence of this court, Gov. Mason ordered them shot,
and Lieut Ord, with nine soldiers performed the duty. *Colton Three Years in
Cal.*, 391–2. *Dally Narr.*, MS.; 53–63. *S. F. Alta*, Jan. 25, 1849. Foster,
a dealer in cattle, was killed by a Mexican dealer named Mariano, whose
guilt was proven by Foster's property in his possession. He escaped from

sort of royal progress to the mines and a brief inspection of the different posts. Commanders of posts nearest to the routes of immigration were instructed to furnish assistance and relieve suffering when required.[8] In this manner the military government discharged, as in its judgment seemed best, its duty to the country.

General Smith removed his headquarters in May or June to Sonoma, residing in a house erected by Jacob P. Leese, for which he paid a rental of $400 a month. On his staff were Hooker, Gibbs, and Sherman. In September he went to Oregon to inspect that portion of his department, and remained on the Columbia river for several months,[9] attending to the establishment of forts Vancouver, Steilacoom, Dalles, and a post at Astoria.

The Pacific squadron, which in 1846 had consisted of eight armed vessels, carrying 300 guns, was dispersed, the line-of-battle-ship *Ohio* alone being at San Francisco in 1849. She lay at Sauzelito, and was of use in preventing the entire abandonment of the mail service.[10] Of defences to her coast or com-

the sheriff, but his vaquero and associate in crime were hung. *San Jose Mercury*, Jan. 1, 1882. Arms were issued to the inhabitants in exposed localities to protect themselves.

[8] Major Rucker was detailed by Gen. Smith to conduct the relief to immigrants; and $160,000 was supplied out of civil funds to purchase provisions and hire men and teams for the service. Scurvy had attacked the immigrants, who were now perishing. Rucker remained in the mountains until the last of the immigration had passed into the valley. *Sherman Mem.*, 80–1. *S. F. Alta*, Dec. 15, 1849. I find '$70,000 transferred to Purser Forest, for paying the expenses of bringing immigrants from Lower California,' on a government vessel of course. Lieut Caulto, of the boundary escort, established Camp Calhoun on the Cal. side of the Colorado, where he remained for two months assisting the immigration.

[9] The *Massachusetts*, a gov't propeller, which arrived out in the spring, conveyed two companies of the 1st artillery, to the new forts of Vancouver and Steilacoom. Col Casey was stationed at Steilacoom during the Ind. wars in Washington, and Lieut Slaughter was killed there

[10] The *Warren*, which was at S. F. when the gold fever set in, was deserted, and Capt. A. R. Long was forced to import a crew from Mazatlan to go to sea. The *California* on her first trip lost all her crew, and the *Oregon*, when she arrived, anchored alongside the *Ohio*, and Capt. Pearson sent his crew aboard as prisoners until she was ready to sail. On her second trip she brought a crew for the *California*, guarded in the same way. *Grimshaw's Narr.*, 12–13, MS.; *Folsom Telegraph*, Nov. 9, 1867.

merce California had at this period none that would
have been effectual in case of attack from a foreign
foe.   At San Francisco Major Hardie of the New
York regiment had occupied two companies during
the summer of 1847 in repairing the presidio and removing to it the ordnance and military stores brought
out in the *Lexington* and landed at the town of Yerba
Buena; but the guns, mortars, and carriages, with
the heavy shot and shell, could not be moved across
the hills, and remained near the landing.   There
were some guns mounted at San Pedro, and a field-
battery kept at the fort in Los Angeles.   At Monterey Colonel Mason had caused to be constructed,
under the superintendence of Lieutenant Halleck, a
redoubt in the form of a bastion, on a hill commanding the anchorage and the town, mounting upon it 20
guns carrying 24-pound shot, and four 8-inch mortar
guns on platforms.   Quarters for the artillery companies, consisting of two large two-story log houses,

There was great need of lighthouses and buoys on the coast, and the government, aware of this necessity to a rapidly growing commerce as well as
to its own vessels, authorized Professor Bache in 1848 to organize two parties
for a coast survey, the party for shore duty being in charge of Captain James
S. Williams, assistant, and Joseph S. Ruth, sub-assistant.   The hydro-
graphical party was in charge of Lieut William P. McArthur of the navy,
in command of the schooner *Ewing*.   The *Ewing* arrived at S. F. in the spring
of 1849, but there was little work accomplished.   The men attached to the
topographical work ran away to the mines, and those on board the *Ewing*
had to be placed in irons, and some were hanged for attempting the drown-
ing of Lieutenant Gibson in order to desert.   The *Ewing* ran over to the Soc.
isl. in winter in order to prevent the entire failure of the survey, which in the
spring of 1850 was removed to the Columbia bar and river.   In June of that
year a third party under sub-assistant George Davidson, whose services to
California, begun in those uneasy terms, have been continued through a
generation, was in every way successful after its first hard struggle with
the difficulties besetting science in the gold period.

About the 1st of November there arrived the United States brig *C. W.
Lawrence*, Captain Alexander V. Fraser, all of whose officers and seamen resigned or deserted within a month, being unable to live upon their pay.   A
naval recruiting station was opened at San Francisco in December, but without much relief to the service.   In November also there arrived a collector
for the port of San Francisco, James Collier, who relieved the military
authorities of the care of the customs.   He was escorted by a dragoon company commanded by Captain Thorn, who with three of his men was drowned
at the crossing of the Rio Colorado.   Collector Collier found some things
that surprised and some that displeased him.   The surprise was occasioned
by the amount of business, and the displeasure at finding the goods with
which he had to do stored in nineteen dismantled hulks of vessels in the

were erected, and in the rear of the redoubt a stone magazine. The barracks for the accommodation of other troops were erected in the town. In the summer of 1849 Captain Folsom constructed military store-houses at San Francisco, the presidio was still further repaired, and four 32-pound guns and two 8-inch howitzers were mounted on the old fort at the entrance to the harbor

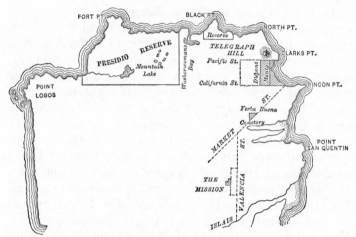

MILITARY RESERVATIONS AT SAN FRANCISCO, 1849.

Thus passed the year of transition, while California was under a rule nominally civil, but really military, yet lacking the power to be wholly either. The local

harbor. Immediate steps were taken to have a custom-house erected, with what result I have already narrated in a preceding volume.

Postal communication in 1847, 1848, and part of 1849 had been by military express from post to post, citizens being permitted to avail themselves of this service without charge, the private expresses patronized in the mines making exorbitant profits. The arrival of William Van Voorhies, special post agent of the United States, by the *California* in March, seemed to promise relief to the military service. Van Voorhies was superseded in a month's time by R. T. P. Allen, who received, if he did not merit, innumerable anathemas from longing and expectant but disappointed miners and settlers, who believed they were entitled to have delivered to them letters that cost forty cents from the states, and twelve and a half cents from any point on the Pacific coast. The agent, however, hardly found time during the summer to select sites for post-offices, and the military and private expresses were even more required than before to accommodate the thousands to whom the monthly steamers brought news from home.

government of San Francisco, which was sanctioned because it could not be abolished, expressed its dissatisfaction with the military power, which retorted, "prove any of your complaints to be well founded, and the guilty officer will be removed or punished." Taking into the account all the novel conditions of the period, I think it must be admitted that affairs were conducted with becoming prudence on the military side.

In 1849, owing to the inefficiency of the army in California, and the condition of society at San Francisco from the importation of foreign criminals as well as the unrestrained freedom of deserting sailors and soldiers, a military company was formed in that place under the name of First California guard. It was an artillery company, but drilled also with muskets, and in the evolutions of infantry. It consisted of 41 members in July, and was increased to 100 by September, on the 8th of which month General Riley commissioned Henry M. Naglee captain, William O. H. Howard and Myron Norton 1st lieutenants ; Hall McAllister and David F. Bagley second lieutenants ; Samuel Gerry surgeon, and R. H. Sinton sergeant. This company continued its existence under the state laws, and was the initial military organization of this commonwealth. At present it is known as company A, light battery, of the national guard. Together with 50 men of Protection Fire company, No. 2, the guards repaired to Sacramento to quell the squatter's riot of 1850. During their sojourn in the capital two military companies were formed, which now belong also to the national guard. Twenty-one companies[11] were organized in San Francisco previous

[11] These companies were organized as follows: Washington Guard, 50 men; Empire Guard, 125 men; Marion Rifles, 65 men; National Lancers, 45 men; Eureka Light-horse Guard, 50 men; San Francisco Blues, 60 men; City Guard, 55 men; Washington Continental Guards, 40 men; Independent National Guard, 70 men; Young America Guard, 35 men; Wallace Guard, 50 men; Independent City Guard, 100; California Fusileers, 60 men; Black Hussars, 42 men; First Light Dragoons, 59 men; Mechanics Guard, 50 men; Schuetzen Verein, 150 men; California Light Guard, 66 men; City Guard,

to the period of the civil war, which greatly stimulated the military spirit. As that period was exceptional it will be treated of by itself.

In 1851 Indian disturbances at San Diego called for troops, and two companies of rangers were organized from the California Guard, Washington Guard, and Empire Guard, the only existing military companies in San Francisco at that time. Before transportation to San Diego could be provided the trouble had blown over. In 1854 six companies then existing in San Francisco were formed into a battalion with a colonel and other officers. No military services were required of them until 1856, when the vigilance committee assumed the government of the city, and the militia were ordered to report for duty to the governor of the state; nor subsequently, except in June, 1871, when on account of a strike among the miners of Amador county a collision between the Miners' League and the mill-owners was feared, and one company each of the national guard and of the Sumner light guard were ordered to the scene of the disturbance; and still later, when in 1877 the three days' labor riots caused the military companies to be placed on duty in San Francisco to guard the armories and prevent the destruction of valuable property. The service rendered on these occasions amply illustrated the benefit to society of these organizations.

I have mentioned in its proper place the early enactment by the California legislature of a militia law. The state was partitioned in 1850 into four divisions with four major-generals, and two brigades to a division, with a brigadier-general to each,[12] a quarter-

60 men; French Guard, 75 men; McMahon Guard, 43 men; Montgomery Guard, 50 men.

[12] Major-generals of the 1st, 2d, 3d and 4th division respectively, were: Thomas J. Green, John E. Brackett, David S. Douglas and Joshua H. Bean. The brigadier generals in the same order were, J. H. Eastland, William M. Winn, Robert Semple, Alex. C. McDonald, John E. Addison, D. P. Baldwin, Thomas H. Bowen and J. M. Covarrubias. Adjutant-general, Therou R. Per Lee. Quarter-master general, Joseph C. Moorehead. *Cal. Jour.*, 1850, 312–22. Many of the appointments were of the former members of the

master-general and an adjutant-general being also elected by joint convention of the legislature. The conflict between the Indian tribes and the miners, and attacks by the natives upon immigrating parties furnished the only occasions on which the militia were called upon to perform military duty, which occasions continued but for a few years, costing the state, however, a considerable sum, for which it received partial indemnity from the general government.

In February, 1851, the legislature passed an act authorizing a loan not exceeding $500,000, payable in ten years, and bearing interest at the rate of twelve per cent per annum, payable semi-annually, to meet the expenses of expeditions against the Indians. Another act was passed in 1852 authorizing a loan of not more than $600,000 with interest at seven per cent, payable annually; and the law bound the state to pay the principal if at the end of ten years congress had made no provision for its liquidation. Congress, in 1854, made an appropriation of $924,295.65 to pay the bonds issued in 1851 and 1852; but the amount ordered to be granted was the sum actually paid by the state of California in the suppression of Indian hostilities prior to January 1854, which the secretary of war was directed at once to ascertain. The amount of the appropriations, had it been immediately available, would have discharged the bonded debt, bnt the delay consequent upon the appointment of a commission, and the transfer of the business to Washington, so increased the interest on the bonds that, when after much legislation the money

New York volunteers. In 1851 James M. Estill was elected maj.-gen. of 2d div. in place of Brackett, and S. M. Miles and S. E. Woodsworth brig.-gens of 1st and 4th div. in place of Eastland and Bowen. In 1852 William C. Kibbe was elected qr-master-gen., also governor's aids, with the rank of colonel of cavalry, as follows: Samuel A. Merritt, Mariposa co.; Alphonso Sutter, Sutter co.; E. C. Cromwell, El Dorado co.; Edward M. Burrows, Butte co.; Andreas Pico, Los Angeles co.; John Watson, Shasta co., 1852; Cave C. Couts, San Diego co.; and J. E. Lawrence, San Francisco., 1853. In 1853 John A. Sutter was elected maj.-gen. at large; J. M. Covarrubias maj.-gen. of the 4th div., and D. B. Kurtz brig.-gen 2d brigade 4th div.

appropriated was applied, the state still owed in September, 1856, $173,322.66, coupons to that amount being cut from the bonds and returned to the respective holders for redemption. The interest upon these coupons being added, the whole amount remaining to be paid when a committee of the house of representatives reported upon the matter in 1883, reached $241,625.82, for which the general government was justly liable to the state for expenses incurred in its defence in 1850–51.

On account of other Indian hostilities the legislature in 1857 again issued bonds amounting to $410,-000 to be paid out of any moneys that might be appropriated by congress to the state to defray the expenses incurred in the suppression of Indian hostilities specified in this act,[13] the bondholders in this instance relying solely upon the general government. I have found nothing to show that these claims were ever paid. The state was reimbursed for its participation in the Modoc Indian war of 1872–3 to the amount of $4,441.33, appropriated by congress in 1883.[14]

[13] This act is a history of volunteer expeditions and losses during several years. It specifies services in Sutter co. in 1850, $5,000; in Nevada co. in 1850 and 1851, $20,000; in Yuba co. in 1850, $20,000; in Klamath co. in 1852, $10,000; in Siskiyou co. in 1855, $14,000; the same co. in 1856, $200,000; Humboldt and Klamath cos in 1855, $110,000; Los Angeles co. 1852–5, $20,000; San Bernardino in 1855, $1,000; Tulare co. in 1856, $10,000. *Cal. Stat.*, 1857, 262–4. These expensive expeditions were undertaken after the failure of appeals to the United States officers in the department, which was ill supplied with troops for the protection of so extensive a frontier; and even as late as 1872–3 it was necessary to call out volunteers to subdue the Modocs on the northern border.

[14] The whole army of the United States in 1849–50 comprised two regiments of dragoons, one of mounted riflemen, four of artillery, and eight of infantry, aggregating with the engineer corps and general staff 12,927 members. All the mounted troops were employed in Oregon, California, Texas, New Mexico, and on the routes leading to the Pacific coast. From the extent of country to be traversed in the event of an outbreak, and which could not be covered by infantry in time to overtake the enemy, it became necessary to increase the cavalry by recruiting the broken companies with tried and trusted men from the east, whose terms of service were nearing the end; and also by increasing the size of the companies from the quota, sometimes as low as 42, to a number not exceeding 74 privates per company. With such troops as were available an expedition set out in the month of May to punish the Indians in the neighborhood of Clear lake, in what is now Lake county, for the murder of citizens in 1849. It consisted of C troop 1st dra-

In 1849 and 1850 the territory on the Pacific had
constituted the third division of Department No. 11;
but on the 17th of May, 1851, the command of departments 10 and 11 were merged in that of the Pa-

goons, commanded by Lieut Davidson, and a detachment of the 2d infantry,
the whole in charge of Capt. Nathaniel Lyon. Davidson having failed of
reaching the Indians the previous year, by reason of their taking refuge on
an island in Clear lake, wagons accompanied the troops, carrying boats to be
used in pursuit. This unexpected movement surprised and alarmed the
Indians, who from being defiant became terrified. They showered their
arrows ineffectually upon the troops, who first drove them from their con-
cealment with a howitzer, and afterward shot them down with their muskets,
until 60 out of 400 were killed, after which their rancheria was destroyed.
The command then proceeded to Russian river, where two settlers, Stone
and Kelley, had been atrociously murdered, and surrounding the Indians in
a jungle, slaughtered 'not less than 75 of them.' In these two engagements
the only damage received was two men wounded. Sending the horses to
Benicia to be rested, the troop then marched to the Goose lake country to
search for Warner's bones and punish his murderers.

While these events were taking place, Gen. Smith was making a tour of
inspection in the south. Finding at San Diego that persons arriving from
the Gila complained that a gang of thirteen lawless men had established a
ferry over the Colorado, in competition with the young Indians, and were
extorting enormous prices from travellers, besides committing robberies and
murders, and being besought to send a command to drive them away, he offered, if a writ could be issued for their arrest, to assist the civil officers in
the execution of their duty. But nothing was attempted to be done by the
authorities, and the gang continued to rob and kill, charging their crimes
upon the Yumas. They killed an Irishman who had set up an opposition
ferry, and destroyed the boats of the Indians. The Yumas retaliated by
killing eleven of the men, including the leaders, for which nobody was sorry,
although Major-general Bean of the 4th Cal. division of militia endeavored
to raise a company to punish the Indians for the murder of the white men,
but failed. The ferry was soon reëstablished, and in order to prevent the
recurrence of such trouble, and to protect the immigration, Gen. Smith ordered Major Heintzelman to proceed as soon as possible to the mouth of the
Gila to establish there a military post. This action was rendered possible by
the arrival at San Diego in the spring of a body of troops under lieut col.
J. B. Magruder, who occupied that station in the absence of Heintzelman.
On the 27th of November, 1850, two companies of the 2nd infantry established Camp Independence at the crossing of the Colorado, which was transferred to the former site of a mission, in March 1851, and was thenceforth
called Fort Yuma. So little were the Indians in the vicinity feared that
the fort was soon left in charge of Lieut L. W. Sweeney and ten men. They
soon, however, began murdering immigrants, and attacked the fort, which
on account of the difficulty of obtaining supplies was abandoned in Dec.,
after being reinforced by Lieut Davidson. It was not again occupied until
in February 1852, when Heintzelman returned to make a permanent establishment at this point, which for many years retained its importance.

The adjournment of the boundary commission on the Rio Grande, in
February, to meet at El Paso in November, left a company of infantry under
Lieut Coults, disposable for garrison duty, in addition to which was a company organized from detachments that had marched across the country on
the Gila route, under Maj. E. Fitzgerald. From these companies, too small
to take distant or exposed posts, Gen. Smith organized three garrisons, sta-
tioning Fitzgerald at the rancho El Chino, in San Bernardino valley, the remainder of the infantry at the Cajon pass, and the dragoons at San Luis Rey.

cific division, Brevet Brigadier General Ethan A.
Hitchcock being placed in command, with headquarters at Sonoma.   The departure of the 2d dragroons
about this time, and the withdrawal from Oregon of

Lieut Derby was sent by Gen. Riley to open a wagon-road from mission
San Miguel to the mines on the Mariposa river; from all of which it appears
that the commanders used their best endeavors to make the military of use
to the country.   Remarking upon the extent of the territory and the nature
of the service, Gen. Smith in his report says: 'To comply with our treaty
obligations with Mexico will require 600 cavalry and 400 infantry on the
line of the Gila, and eastward to the Rio Grande, besides those now on the
two extremities of that line.   The cavalry must be practised dragoons, not
raw recruits that cannot ride.   This country is the best country for dragoons
in the U. S.' He might well say that, when he had himself just ridden 840 miles
from San Diego to Sonoma.   Few changes or improvements were made at
any of the posts on account of the extraordinary cost of labor and material.
From the report of Maj. D. H. Vinton, quartermaster, I learn that at the
post on Bear creek, in what is now Yuba county, to which Maj. Kingsbury
was transferred, and which was maintained until 1852, the troops were required to 'cover themselves by their own labor, with material to be found
in their vicinity,' and that at a post established on Clear lake the same was
required.   For the station on the San Joaquin, iron houses were recommended, while at San Diego barracks, officers quarters, guard-houses, and
hospital were thought necessary.   This was indeed for several years the
most important depot next to Benicia, on account of the necessity of supplying Fort Yuma from this station.   But the work first undertaken was in
the vicinity of San Francisco, at the presidio, and at Benicia, to which place
Gen. Smith designed to remove his headquarters in 1850, or as soon as quarters were erected.

The improvements made at Benicia in 1849–50 consisted of 3 buildings for
officers' quarters, a barrack for soldiers, 2 military store-houses, 3 cottage
farm buildings for quarters for employés, stables, blacksmith shop; cook-
house, bake-house, boat-house, stone corral, steam saw-mill; and house for
employés, with stables, out-houses, and enclosures.   The lumber used in
their construction cost $600 per M., and the wages of mechanics not less than
$11 per day.

From the report of Gen. Smith of March 1851 it appears that the adjutant general of the army had desired to know what reduction in the number of troops could be made in Cal. and Oregon, with safety to the public service.   To this the general replied that it depended upon the choice the government should make, between the regular army and the militia, to protect
an Indian and maritime frontier, each over 1,000 miles in length, adding
some further remarks intended not to be complimentary to the militia, as to
conduct, or cost of service.   It is interesting to compare the civil and military
views of the same subject.   On the page following the rather curt reply of
Smith to the adjutant-general, is a communication from Gov. McDougal to
Pres. Filmore.   The governor asked for arms for the militia, which was not
yet enrolled, but was estimated at 100,000, while the general had just said
that 'whatever arms are delivered to the frontier people here will be lost to
the U. S.,' meaning that they would be sold to anybody who would buy
them.   So well had Senator Gwin pleaded the cause of the new state, however, that the secretary of war had anticipated the governor's requisition
for California's quota, and the arms arrived soon after the requisition had
been made.   As if to justify the opinion of the general just quoted, the
quarter-master general of the state, Joseph C. Moorehead, on the 20th of
April 1851, absconded, having sold or taken with him several hundred muskets without authority of law.   But notwithstanding this unfortunate ful-

the mounted rifle regiment, had reduced the already inadequate force of the division in a considerable degree. In addition to the Indian troubles in California, of which an account has been given in another chapter, a call from Oregon, now almost defenceless, for a strong military post in the south, occasioned General Hitchcock to recommend the establishment of such a station, but from ignorance of the country he selected Port Orford as a suitable point for a fort, whereas, it was separated from that portion of the country threatened by the Coast range, a broken and heavily timbered region, nearly impassable and wholly unexplored. Before the secretary of war could respond, a party of men arriving at Port Orford by sea with the intention of settling there, were attacked and half of them murdered by the Indians. The incident decided the question of troops at this point, and a detachment of 135 men, 50 of whom were to be mounted, the whole commanded by Colonel Silas Casey, proceeded by steamer to Port Orford, with supplies and horses. Beyond furnishing protection to a small and isolated settlement, which had no reason at that period for existing, the post was of no use to the country, and was a heavy expense to the government.

To fill up the skeleton companies in California, 500 recruits from the Atlantic states arrived in February 1852, of whom 101 deserted by the 1st of July. Several new posts were established this year, the whole number in California and Oregon, of all classes, being 17. In August the 4th infantry regiment arrived by the Isthmus route. It had suffered severely from

filment of an unfriendly prophecy, the militia took an active part in the suppression of Indian hostilities in 1851. 'Certain persons,' said Gen. Smith, 'have determined that there shall be a war.' 'The state of Cal.,' said Major McKinstry, acting as quarter-master at San Diego, 'has been involved in a heavy debt, for the payment of which she is unprepared, by our failure to establish a few military posts, the maintenance of which would have been expensive, but beneficial beyond calculation.' Thus opinions differed.

Camp Mojave, the oldest post in Arizona, was established in 1858 to protect the immigration; abandoned in May 1861, and reoccupied in May 1863 by 2 comp. of the 4th Cal. vol. The next posts seem to have been those just

disease contracted in equatorial heat and miasma, and was practically incapacitated for immediate service. This regiment was distributed to the northern posts : to Fort Humboldt on Humboldt bay two companies, Lieutenant-colonel R. C. Buchanan ; one company, Captain B. R. Alden, to Fort Jones in Scott valley ; one company, Colonel George Wright, to Fort Reading on the upper Sacramento river ; two companies, Major C. H. Larned, to Fort Steilacoom, Puget Sound; two companies, Major E. J. Rains, to Fort Dalles, Columbia river; and two companies to Fort Vancouver, the headquarters of the regiment, under command of Lieutenant-colonel B. L. E. Bonneville. In the spring of 1853 the Indians on the Colorado compelled the evacuation of Fort Yuma. While captains Sweeney and Davidson were retreating to San Diego, they were joined by Colonel Craig's expedition coming overland, which escorted them to that place. On his return the following February, Craig was shot and killed by two deserting soldiers whom he was attempting to persuade to return to their duty.

In spite of the presence of a greater number of troops in the country, Indian hostilities were increased, and a number of valuable citizens' lives lost, in addition to the destruction of immigrant life and property, a state of affairs which continued for many years thereafter, as has been shown in the narrative of Indian wars in California and Oregon. In the sum-

mentioned. Breckenridge and Buchanan, established about 1860. Camp Verde was erected by Arizona volunteers, mostly Mexican, in 1861, to protect Prescott co. It was occupied by regular troops in 1866, and site changed in 1871. Fort Bowie was established to protect the road between Tucson and Mesilla valley, in 1862, by comp. G, 5th Cal. vol. It was rebuilt in 1868. Fort Whipple, 24 miles east of Prescott, was erected in 1863, but changed to its present site in 1864, and became headquarters of the district. Camp Lowell was established during the rebellion, 7 miles east of Tucson, in the San Catarina mts. Site changed to present location. Camp McDowell was established in 1865 by 5 comp. of Cal. vols. Camp Apache, first called Goodwin, then Ord, then Mogollon, then Thomas, and last Apache, was established in 1870 by Major John Green with 2 comp. 1st U. S. cavalry. Camp Grant, 2 miles from Mount Graham in the Sierra Bonita, was established in 1873. Most of these posts were occupied until within the last decade, and several are still garrisoned.

mer of 1853 Fort Lane was established in Rogue
River valley, Oregon, by Major G. W. Patten.[15]

On the 9th of January 1854 Major-general John
E. Wool was assigned to the Pacific department, and
relieved General Hitchcock in February following.
Previous to the arrival of Wool military matters in
California had been ably conducted in the main,
though with something of the *dolce far niente* of the
country, but if no great amount of activity had been
displayed, there had been few collisions between the
military themselves, or between them and civilians.
But when General Wool took the command a different state of affairs prevailed. Before he left the
Atlantic coast he had made several suggestions to
the secretary of war, which that official had seen fit
to ignore without comment; but when Wool proceeded to act as if they were doubtless to be adopted,
the secretary ruthlessly demolished such expectations
in toto. Wool's correspondence, though somewhat
voluminous, furnishes very entertaining reading.
His quarrels with the civil authorities on the Pacific coast were continuous, and often on both sides
acrimonious. The secretary more frequently took
sides against him than with him. As to his inten-
tions, I have no doubt of their honesty, though to
some his measures appeared at times to be arbitrary
and ill-advised.[16]

[15] An entire reorganization of the military departments of the United
States took place in October 1853, the country west of the Rocky mountains,
excepting Utah and the department of New Mexico constituting the department of the Pacific, Gen. Hitchcock in command, with headquarters at S.
F. This year the 2d inf. reg. was broken up and assigned to different companies, the officers being ordered east to recruit. Jefferson Davis had
succeeded C. M. Conrad as sec. of war. To him Gen. Scott reported that
another regiment of infantry was needed on the Pacific coast, as well as an
additional regiment of cavalry in the department of the west, to guard the
routes of travel to the coast. Accordingly the third art. reg., the 'gay and
gallant third,' as it was called in the Mexican war, commanded by Lieut-
col J. M. Washington and Maj E. S. Merchant was placed under orders to
proceed by sea to Cal. It left Gov. I., N. Y. harbor, in Dec. and in Jan.
returned in a distressed condition to N. Y., the *San Francisco*, on which it
sailed having been shipwrecked. It was not until midsummer that the several companies of the regiment arrived, and were distributed to the different
posts.

[16] At the time of this appointment to the command of the department, the

At the period of the commencement of hostilities by the south the only fortifications on the coast of California and Oregon were Alcatraz and Fort Point. At the former there were 130 troops under Captain

filibustering expedition of William Walker was in progress. Wool had asked for special instructions from the president, empowering him to interfere with the recruiting of such expeditions, as violations of the neutrality laws; and further, to enable him to check these operations, that two companies then at Fort Hamilton might be ordered to accompany him to S. F. Neither request was granted, and when in his report to the secretary he related the steps taken by him to arrest persons recruiting for Lower Cal. and Sonora, and his efforts to place the harbor of S. F. in a defensible condition, when according to the secretary of war he should have been attending to the suppression of hostilities in his department as his first duty, he was told that he 'manifested a want of definite purpose,' and 'devoted an undue portion of his time to other than the proper duties of his command.' As to the harbor defenses, in May 1854 Gen. Wool directed Capt Stone of the ordnance department of the service to mount on Alcatraz island six 8-inch guns, and six 32-pound guns; also ten 32-pound guns near Fort point, commanding the entrance to the harbor; and that 10 24-pound guns should be brought from Monterey to be mounted on seige-carriages. The reason given for this order was stated in the correspondence of the commanding general to be 'in consequence of the conviction of the Mexican consul, the threats of the French consul, he having lowered the French flag, and the expectation of several French ships-of-war in the harbor of San Francisco, and other causes.' But the secretary thought, inasmuch as fortifications were in progress at the place named, and the batteries would require to be re-mounted, the extra expense of the temporary armament was unnecessary. 'The propriety of erecting the temporary batteries to which you refer,' he said, 'depends upon the necessity.'

The senior engineer in charge of the fortifications at Fort Point was Lieut-col Mason, an eminent officer, who arrived at his post in 1853, laboring under disease contracted on the Isthmus. Anxious for the prosecution of the work entrusted to him, he failed to take sufficient time for recovery, and becoming again prostrated soon died. The officer who was sent to succeed him was Maj. J. G. Barnard. The old Spanish fort at the Point was taken down, and some of the material used in the new works. The final surveys of Alcatraz i. were not made until 1854, when, temporary buildings and a wharf having been erected, the work upon the batteries and excavation of the ditches was completed. The remaining works were forced to wait for appropriations, Fort Alcatraz not being completed until 1858, nor Fort Point until a year later. The authorities at Washington, believing that the removal of headquarters to Benicia would be an economical measure, ordered the transfer; but so far from acquiescing, the department commander gave irrefragable reasons for remaining at S. F., and, moreover, proposed to have constructed a plank road from Fort point to the city via the presidio. To have abandoned the military reservation at that period would have been to have had a squatter war over its possession, for which cause if no other it was urged by the officers stationed here that the presidio should not be vacated. And so the official war continued, Wool grimly effecting his purpose and explaining afterwards.

In the summer of 1855, two companies of the 3d artillery and 85 dragoon recruits left Fort Leavenworth under the command of Brevet Lieutenant-colonel E. J. Steptoe, for the Pacific coast. It wintered at Salt Lake, and arrived in the department in July 1856, the artillerymen at Benicia, and the dragoons at forts Lane and Tejon. Later in the season Steptoe marched for Fort Vancouver via Fort Lane, arriving in Oregon just in time to take part

Stewart. Fort Point was not occupied until February 15, 1861, when, by order of General Scott, it was garrisoned by two companies of the 3d artillery, numbering 160 men, officered by lieutenants Kellogg,

in the Yakima Indian war, which broke out in October, which several times called Wool to Oregon, and was the cause of much angry correspondence between high officials, as I have related in my histories of Oregon and Washington. Wool had more than once insisted upon the need of increasing the army to meet the demands of the extended frontier to be defended, and in 1855 two regiments of infantry were added, the 9th and 10th, the former being intended for the Pacific department, and particularly for service in Oregon and Washington. It numbered 811 men, drilled in Hardie's ·shanghai ' tactics, armed with minie rifles, and trained to travel all day at the rate of five miles an hour. It embarked at Fortress Monroe about the 12th of December, 1855, and arrived at San Francisco and Fort Vancouver in January, by steamers *Great Republic* and *Oregon.* The commanding officer of this regiment was Colonel George Wright, afterwards so thoroughly identified with the Pacific coast. The other commissioned officers were Maj. R. S. Garnett, captains H. M. Black, G. E. Pickett, and D. Woodruff, and lieuts D. B. McKibbin, Churchill, Hodges, and Gentry. They served in the Yakima war, with various fortunes, and were stationed at Vancouver, Fort Bellingham, Fort Townsend near Port Townsend, on the Muckelshoot prairie near Seattle, at forts Simcoe, Walla Walla, and Dalles. They acted an important part in the development of the country, and with their high-hearted commander should be remembered with esteem by those who have fallen heirs to the benefits conferred. The prosecution of Indian wars with foot troops being found generally impracticable, seven companies of the 1st dragoons were ordered from Fort Union, on the Rio Grande, to the Pacific division, arriving late in 1856 at their several posts; four companies, commanded by Maj. J. H. Carleton and captains Davidson, Northrop, and Ewell, all under Maj. E. Steen, took post at Tucson; one company, Capt. Radford (detached), under Lieut Mercer, was posted at San Diego; and two companies, Maj. W. H. Grier and Captain Whittlesey, under Maj. G. A. H. Blake, at Fort Tejon. To this command were attached lieuts Ogle, adjutant, Magruder, quartermaster, and Gregg, Williams, and Pender.

The vigilance committee episode in California history, involved in an unexpected manner the reputation of Wool and an officer then off the U. S. army list of which he is now the head, W. T. Sherman. Sherman had returned to S. F., after an absence of three years, and having resigned and turned civilian and banker, had accepted a few days previous to the murder of James King of William, the position of maj. gen. of the 2nd division of militia, embracing S. F. The action of the committee being in a legal sense unlawful, Gov. Johnson could not do less than endeavor to prevent the hanging of the murderer who had been taken from the hands of the constituted authorities. He therefore issued his proclamation, and while assuming to be performing his duty as a defender of the peace, made his arrangements for the spilling of a good deal of blood, Sherman entering hot-headedly into the plan, and Wool seeming to encourage it. There has always been a controversy over Wool's share in it, Sherman asseverating that he gave his promise to furnish assistance, and Wool denying it. My own opinion is that Wool's first impulse was toward suppression of the committee, but he knew he had not the authority to issue arms and ammunition to the state without the order of the pres't of the U. S., and although so far from the seat of government that he did not know but a general of division might venture to do it, he could not but remember the manner in which the secretary of war had rebuked his forwardness in the matter of the Walker expedition, and besides the Oregon legislature had asked for his removal. There

Kip, and Shinn, and Gibson quartermaster.　At the same time 10,000 stand of arms and 150,000 cartridges were brought down from Benicia and stored at Alcatraz　At the presidio, under Colonel C. S. Mer-

is no doubt but that he misled Sherman and the governor at the first, by an implied readiness to furnish arms to the enrolled militia, from which position he afterward withdrew.　Sherman's plan, as arranged by himself, is given in his *Memoirs*, in which he says: ' I had agreed that if Wool would give us arms and ammunition out of the U. S. arsenal at Benicia, and if Com.. Farragut, of the navy, commanding the navy yard on Mare island, would give us a ship, I would call out volunteers, and when a sufficient number had responded, I would have the arms come down from Benicia in the ship, arm my men, take possession of a 32-pound gun battery at the marine hospital on Rincon point, thence command a dispersion of the unlawfully armed force of vigilance committee, and arrest some of the leaders.'　Application was made by Sherman to Farragut, who very sensibly discouraged ' taking part in civil broils,' and consented only to allow the sloop *John Adams* to drop down abreast of the city, ' for moral effect.'　Sherman then determined to seize a mail steamer to bring down the army; state Quar. Gen. Kibbee opened an office in the city to enroll companies, and the suppression of the vig. com., was firmly decided upon.　In vain the vigilants remonstrated, assuring him there would be a collision, with terrible results; his reply was: ' Remove your fort; cease your midnight councils; and prevent your armed bodies from patrolling the streets.'　Practically this was an order to restore the reign of the roughs, who now sided with the governor and Sherman, and gloried in the name and style of the 'law and order party' —more properly, the newspapers said, 'law-and-murder party.'　Committees of the best citizens expostulated to no purpose; Johnson, Sherman, and Chief-justice Terry, who sat with his hat on, drawn over his eyes, and with his feet on a table, while the 'damned pork merchants,' made a prepared speech, embracing a clear and fair statement of the condition of things in S. F., concluding with the assertion of the willingness of the committee to disband and submit to trial after a certain date not very remote.　Finding that Wool had entirely withdrawn from his real or supposed first intention, and that no arms would be furnished by him, Sherman resigned his commission, and Volney. E. Howard was appointed in his place.　The history of the vigilance committee being fully given elsewhere, need not be repeated here.　Wool's caution in the matter caused the governor's party to charge him with falsehood and deceit, and there ensued one of those controversies on paper for which he was famous.　That the president sustained his policy of non-interference was apparent by the uninterrupted success of the committee.

But there was a rumor of his recall as early as September, although it did not take place until Feb. 1857.　On the 20th of March he left Cal. to take the command of the department of the east, and the command of the Pacific department devolved upon Col Thomas T. Fauntleroy until the arrival of Gen. Newman S. Clarke, col 6th inf.　Gen. Clarke found himself embarrassed not only by the insufficiency of force, but by the policy of his predecessor.　He arrived at Fort Vancouver, the military headquarters for the Columbia region, about the last of June, and without attempting to enforce a peaceable condition of the Indians in the upper country, contented himself with excluding the white men who had commenced its settlement, and leaving the troops in garrison.　Under these conditions there was no war, but neither was there any peace deserving the name.

In May 1858, Colonel Steptoe, feeling that there should be something done to impress the Indians, who were growing insolent and troublesome about the fort, with the power of the U. S., set out to make a reconnaisance

chant, was one artillery company, Captain Landman, and Lieutenants Chandler and Hamilton, with recruits, etc., in all 115 men. At Benicia, Colonel Andrews commanding, the garrison consisted of companies G. and K., 6th infantry, 162 men, lieutenants Corley, Sawtelle, and Moore. The arsenal was in charge of Lieutenant McAllister with 41 men of the

of the country to Fort Colville, with a command of 159 men and a supply train. He was attacked soon after crossing the Snake river by a combined force of several tribes, and forced to fall back, after a hard battle, in which he lost two dragoon officers, Capt. H. P. Taylor and Lieut William Gaston, and a number of men. This affair opened the eyes of General Clarke to the disposition of these tribes, and he determined to subdue them. To accomplish this he was forced to bring together troops from the most distant posts, even from Yuma and San Diego, whence were drawn 3 companies of the 3d artillery, under Capt. Keyes, and officered by 1st lieuts Robert O. Tyler, James L. White, Dunbar R. Ransom, and 2d lieuts Hylase B. Lyon, George B. F. Dandy, and Lawrence Kip. From Umpqua another company of this regiment was taken, commanded by Lieutenant George P. Ihrie and James Howard, making with those at the Columbia river posts six companies, a larger number of this company than had been together since it was wrecked on the *San Francisco* five years before. General Clarke accompanied the troops to Vancouver, where Steptoe and Wright were summoned for consultation. It was not until August that all things were in readiness, when a large force, consisting of dragoons, artillery (serving as infantry), howitzer and rifle companies, with a large train and guards, moved north of Snake river over the route pursued by Steptoe the previous year. On the 1st of Sept., being at Four Lakes in the Spokane country, the Indians attacked, and a battle ensued in which they suffered severely. Proceeding onward to the Cœur de Alêne territory, laying waste the native villages, and capturing and killing the Indian horses, great loss was inflicted, the several tribes engaged in the battle of Steptoe's butte, a point near the present town of Colfax, being utterly subjugated and compelled to sue for peace. The Yakimas also were punished, and a number of the chiefs hanged. The operations of this summer, known as 'Clarke and Wright's campaign,' were in direct opposition to the policy of Gen. Wool, and won for these officers the applause of the inhabitants of Oregon and Washington. But before the intention of Clarke to open the country for settlement had been made known, the department of the Pacific was divided into the departments of Cal. and Oregon, and Gen. William S. Harney placed in command of Oregon, his first act being to issue a proclamation removing the inhibition against the settlement of the eastern part of the territories of Oregon and Washington. For this he received the thanks of the legislature and the applause due to Clarke's design.

The department of Oregon was of brief duration. Harney, for his meddling with civil affairs, and his patriotic zeal in the San Juan imbroglio, creating some anxiety at Washington, being summoned thither in 1860 upon the pretense that his evidence was required in estimating the Oregon war debt, and after some gentle reproof placed in command of the department of the west, relieving Gen. E. V. Sumner. The two departments on the Pacific were soon after consolidated under Clark. Meantime the 6th infantry regiment had arrived in Cal. from Utah in 1858 and been distributed to the different posts. It was strengthened in Dec. 1860, together with the 1st dragoons by 200 recruits from the east who arrived by sea under the command of Lieut-col C. S. Merchant of the 3d artillery, commanding at the presidio of S. F. The territory of Arizona, unorganized, belonged to the

ordnance corps, in all about 500 troops in the vicinity.
In the department were 3,650, of whom 1,725 were
stationed in California, and 1,925 in Oregon and
Washington.

On the 19th of April, General Johnston resigned
his command, and on the 24th arrived, unannounced,
to succeed him, Brigadier-general Edwin V. Sumner,
of Massachusetts birth, and second only below General Scott in army rank.   On the following day the
sententious order was issued: "In compliance with
special order No. 86, war department, adjutant-
general's office, Washington, March 23, 1861, I hereby
assume command of this department.   All concerned
will govern themselves accordingly." The moral effect
of this brief warning was to lift a load of suspense and
apprehension off the minds of loyal citizens.

Pacific department, and on account of the ceaseless hostilities of the Apaches
and other tribes, stood in need of a considerable army; but it had, in fact,
two posts, forts Breckenridge and Buchanan, each about 60 miles from
Tucson, in different directions, and a third, Camp Mojave, on the east
bank of the Colorado, none of which could much more than hold their own
in the Indian country.   Had it not been for them and the California militia,
immigration must have ceased.   In 1858, Edward O. Smith, a citizen,
rescued 120 persons from starvation at the Mojave crossing of the Colorado
where the Indians had attacked them and prevented them moving.   The
Indian war in this quarter in 1859 employed volunteers as well as regulars.
It was expected that sixteen companies from Texas would occupy Arizona
under Lieut-col Pitcairn Morrison, and Reeve; but only four arrived in the
territory before events so shaped themselves that the remainder were called
in another direction.

Late in 1859 Major-gen. Scott arrived in California, whence after a brief
stay he repaired to Puget sound to assert the rights of the United States in
the San Juan dispute with Great Britain.   He returned home in November.
In October 1860 General Clarke died, and for a few months succeeding Col
George Wright commanded the dept of the Pacific, to which about the first
of the following year Brevet Brigadier General Albert Sidney Johnston was
assigned.   Johnston was an accomplished officer and gentleman, about
whose otherwise spotless fame there must ever hang the suspicion, amounting almost to certainty, that he accepted the command of the Pacific department with the intent to deliver the forts into the hands of rebel conspirators.
He resigned his Utah command about the time of the secession of South
Carolina, and although in sympathy with the rebellious states, which should
have prevented him from accepting another command under the U. S.,
allowed himself to be sent where he knew he would be required by the south.
In a certain case to act as a traitor.   That he was saved from the completion
of the scheme was due to the watchfulness of both sides, one discovering
the plot and appointing his successor, and the other warning him of the discovery, so that he could resign before he was superseded.   He served in the
confederate army, and died on the field of Shiloh.   Of this I have spoken
elsewhere.

It was understood that in the event of a war, the
regular troops would be needed at the east, and not
only they, but volunteers also. The First Regiment
California Infantry was a spontaneous organization,
springing into life upon the arrival of the news of the
fall of Fort Sumpter. It was however drilled by
regular tacticians, and its field officers selected from
the army. Captain H. W. Halleck, being appointed
major general of the 2d division of state militia, in
May called on all good citizens in the counties of this
division to form themselves into companies, battalions,
and regiments, promising arms should there be call for
their services. Lieutenant John Hamilton, 3d artillery, was made the military instructor of the 2d
division of California militia, and the military spirit
ran high. The volunteers hoped to be allowed to
serve in the east, the ambition to distinguish themselves upon the battlefield being the great incentive to
enlistment. But in this they were to be disappointed,
and the 1st infantry was even deprived of its proper
place on the roster by the professional jealousy of its
officers, who refused to be superseded by a regular
officer.[17]

[17] Major Carleton of the army being ordered to march with this regiment
into Arizona and New Mexico, and finding it in a rebellious temper, established a recruiting camp named after the adjutant-general of Sumner's staff
Richard C. Dunn, and with a part of the original 1st infantry and such
others as flocked to his standard had an expedition in the field in the autumn,
of which the 1st infantry, as raised by him, was an important part. He
was promoted in April 1862 to be brig.-gen. of vol.. and Joseph R. West
was promoted to the colonelcy first, and Edwin A. Rigg second. His army
consisted besides the 1st of the 5th Cal. inf., Col George W. Bowie, the 1st
battalion, Cal. cav., Lieut-col E. E. Eyre, one company of the 2d Cal. cav.,
Capt. John C. Cremony, and one battery of the 3d U. S. artil , Lieut John
B. Shinn—in all about 2,500 men. The column marched from San Pedro to
the Rio Grande, and performed well the part assigned to it of fighting Indians, and driving back rebels from the frontiers of New Mexico and Colorado. When the 1st and 5th inf. regiments had been three years in the
field, the 1st veteran inf. regiment was formed by a transfer of troops from
these two, in the department of New Mexico, and was commanded by Lieut-
col E. A. Rigg. It performed important service on the line operated on b y
the Cal. column.

Perhaps the most conspicuous regiment of the Cal. vols in the service of
the U. S. on the Pacific coast was the 2d cav., commanded at first by the
experienced cavalry officer A. J. Smith, with whom the reader is familiar as
captain, but who became a brigadier-general a few months after the war be-

gan, when Columbus Sims became col of the regiment, holding the position for little over one year. George S. Evans was then promoted to the colonelcy, but resigned in May 1863 and was succeeded first by William Jones, and second by Edward McGarry. Jones's commission was revoked in 1864. The regiment marched thousands of miles, and skirmished with Indians from New Mexico to Oregon. Col Evans fought a battle near Camp Independence in Owen river valley in the spring of 1862 for which he received particular commendation from his superiors. On the 29th of Jan. 1863, companies A H, K, and M., 2d cavalry, under Maj. Edward McGarry, and K company of the 3d Cal. inf., all under command of Col P. E. Conner, fought the Shoshones, under Chief Pocatello, who had killed many immigrants on the road to Cal., Idaho, and Montana, making a great slaughter.

The 3d infantry regiment of Cal. vol's, numbering 1,634 members, whose col was Patrick E. Connor, renowned for his fighting qualities, was organized at Stockton and Benicia, and was employed in protecting the Central overland route from Nevada, eastward, having a rough, ungrateful service. Connor was promoted brig. gen. March 29, 1863, when Robert Pollock became col. On the expiration of the term of the original members of the regiment, organized into a battalion under Lieut-col William M. Johns, and finally mustered out in July 1866. It was known as the 3d bat. of inf. The 2d inf. reg., consisting of 1,980 men, which should have been the 1st, was organized at Camp Sumner in Sept. 1861, and employed in defending the frontier of California, Washington, and Idaho, about half the reg. being sent to the north, and marching from Puget Sound to Fort Boise, which they established, and from Fort Walla Walla to Fort Colville. The remainder served in the Humboldt country against the Indians, until the expiration of the term of enlistment of most of the men, when in 1864 they were re-organized by col T. F. Wright, and ordered to Arizona by McDowell in 1865. The other volunteer organizations of 1861 were the 1st cav., and 3d, 4th and 5th inf. regiments. The 1st Cavalry organization was effected by Lieut-col B. F. Davis of the regular army, who was killed at Gravelly Ford. It consisted until 1863 of but five companies, whose first rendezvous was at Camp Merchant, in Oakland. It went by steamer to Los Angeles, and marched thence to San Bernardino, where it was mounted. Davis being ordered to join his regiment in the east in Nov., the command devolved upon Maj. E. E. Eyre. In Feb. 1862 the battalion was ordered to Fort Yuma, on its way to the Rio Grande to relieve Canby, and to join the column from Cal. in New Mexico. A second battalion of seven companies was raised in 1863 and sent to join the regiment, of which David Ferguson was commissioned col, Eyre having resigned in Nov. 1862. Ferguson was dismissed for leaving his post, and Oscar M. Brown succeeded him. The regiment took part in the campaign against the Navajoes, who were subdued, and placed on the reservation at Fort Sumner. A part of the reg. also fought the Comanches, and had altogether perhaps one hundred engagements with Indians during the several years it occupied New Mexico and Texas. William McCleave became col in 1866, and the regiment was mustered out at the end of that year, at the presidio of S. F. This regiment numbered 1,830 members. The 4th infantry regiment was organized in Sep. 1861 by Col Henry M. Judah, of the regular army, who resigned in Nov. and was succeeded by Ferris Foreman who commanded until August 1862, when he was succeeded by James F. Curtis. The reg. served in southern Cal. and Arizona. On the expiration of the term of service of the earlier members it was re-organized with five companies under Lieut Col E. W. Hilliyer, and was used to garrison posts until 1866, when it was mustered out. The men of this reg. volunteered in Placerville, Shasta, Auburn, Sac., and San Diego, and numbered 1,639 exclusive of one company, which preserved no register. The 5th inf. reg. was also drawn from the northern part of the state, and composed of young and vigorous men. It was organized at Camp Union, two miles below Sac., by Col John Kellogg of the regular army, who resigned to go east in October, where George W. Bowie accepted the commission tendered him by the governor, and commanded until the expiration of term. The regiment, numbering nearly 1,000 men, was ordered to southern Cal. in the spring of 1862, and a part accompanied Carleton's column to Arizona. Col Bowie held the remainder at Fort Yuma until ordered by Gen. Wright to return to take the command at Drum Barracks, to prevent threatened trouble here. In 1863 these troops marched to New Mexico and El Paso, a continuous march of 1,050. In Nov. 1864 all the men of Company A, whose term of service had not expired, were transferred to the 1st veteran inf., and the regiment was mustered out in the following Jan. The 6th inf. reg., numbering 1,243 men, was organized at Benicia in 1863 by Col Henry M. Black of the regular army, and was stationed chiefly at that place, although several companies engaged in Indian fighting. It was a fine regiment, and was mustered out in Oct., 1865. The 7th inf. was not organized until 1864 by Col Charles H. Lewis. It served in Arizona, and participated in the battle of Chiricahui mountains. It was mustered out in 1866. The 8th inf. was the last Cal. regiment raised under the congressional act of July, 1864, and consisted of ten companies of a total membership of 960. Company A. was stationed at Fort Point until Feb., 1865, when it was transferred to Wash. Ter. until October. Co. B, was sent to Fort Stevens, Oregon, about the same time. The other companies were stationed at Fort Point, Alcatraz, Angel I., and Benicia barracks. The col of the regiment was A. L. Anderson. It was mustered out Oct. 24, 1865. In May, 1863, Lieut-col S. G. Whipple organized the 1st bat. of Mountaineers in Humboldt county, its purpose being to fight the Indians of southern Or. and northern Cal., who took advantage of the civil war to get in some hard blows against American settlers. The bat. was mounted, and consisted of six companies and continued in the service to the close of the rebellion, their commander having been brevetted colonel. Another organization was the 1st bat. of native cav., effected in 1863 by Maj. Salvador Vallejo, Andreas Pico having declined the commission. Vallejo resigned in 1865, and was succeeded by John C. Cremony. The bat. was composed chiefly of young natives, and numbered 476 members, uniformed like the U. S. cavalry, well mounted, and good riders.

All of the above named regiments and parts of regiments served out their periods of enlistment on the Pacific coast, or at least west of the rebel frontier. Their patriotism was of that superior sort which enabled them, while burning with ardor to fight on the more glorious, if fratricidal, fields of the civil war, to suppress their ambition and serve on the outposts of civilization, if the government required such service. But their duty was by no means insignificant. They were charged with the safe-keeping of all the western slope of the continent within United States limits, and with keeping closed the highways against the agents of secession from the Texas line to San Diego. There were, however, some who could not forego the gratification of their zeal, but who must fight for country and glory. Of these was the California Hundred, a select body of young and expert equestrians, organized in San Francisco in 1862 by Lieut-col Ringgold of the regular army. Their captain was J. Sewell Reed, promoted major, and succeeded by Lieut Archibald McKendry, also promoted major and colonel. Reed was killed in action with Moseby's Guerillas at Drainsville, Virginia, in 1864. The Cal. Hundred paid its expenses from the date of the organization of the company until accepted into service in the east. It fought in 23 general engagements, and lost many of its number killed, mortally wounded, and missing. It was mustered out at Fairfax Court House July 20, 1865, its last engagement being at Cedar Creek under General Sheridan. The banner carried by the company was presented by Daniel Norcross, and was a Bear Flag. Upon arriving in Massachusetts the American flag was presented to the company by Miss Abby A. Lord of Charlestown, but it was never borne in the field. Both flags are preserved in the state archives. Following shortly after the hundred was the Cal. bat. of 400 men which went to offer its services to the government early in 1863. They were assigned to duty in the 2d Massachusetts cav., of which regiment the hundred also formed a part of the first bat. The Cal. bat. and Cal. Hundred met in July, 1863, at Centreville, V., and served together thereafter. They were terribly earnest fighters, and won applause from the enemy who made havoc in their ranks. Of the 500 Californians of the Massachusetts regiment only 182 remained to be mustered out at the close of the war. The major of the bat. was DeWitt C. Thompson, one of the founders of the California guard of 1849.

The whole number of troops raised in Cal. during the war was 16,231, or more than the whole of the U. S. army at its commencement, and far in excess of the state's quota. To the instructions given by the regular officers by whose exertions the several regiments were raised, and for a time commanded, the excellence of the service was largely due. From it the militia of the state caught a valuable *esprit du corps* which has descended to the present. From the volunteer army list in Cal. a number of appointments were made to the regular army, notably Stephen G. Whipple, Thomas F. Wright, Robert Pollock, and Ambrose E. Hooker to be 1st lieuts; Samuel Smith, A. Starr, 2d lieuts.

On the mustering out of the troops in the service of the general government, 88 militia companies under various names formed to serve, if required, in their respective localities, or to respond to a call from the governor, were disbanded, and the legislature of 1866 passed an act declaring that the organized uniformed troops of the state should be designated as the national guard of the state of California, not to exceed in all 80 companies, 64 being of infantry, 12 of cavalry, and 4 of artillery, located with regard to the military wants of the state, and means of concentration. The national guard was divided into six brigades, and the tactics prescribed for the regular army was made the practise of the Guard. The number of companies was reduced by the next legislature to 60, and a few changes made, but the morale of the militia remains excellent to this time.

That California enjoyed peace when men were conspiring to erect a Pacific empire was due, if not first, still in a great measure, to the prudence and firmness of generals Sumner and Wright, who while the government was withdrawing the regular troops, one regiment after another, raised up others from the people, trained them, and set them to guard half of the public domain, with the inhabitants thereof. Sumner was called east in Oct. 1861, and Wright placed temporarily in command of the department, with the expectation that Gen. J. W. Denver would be ordered to Cal., an expectation which was not fulfilled, owing to some opposition from Californians. Instead, Wright was commissioned brig.-gen., and placed permanently in command. He was superseded in June 1864 by Major-gen. Irwin McDowell, whose soldierly qualities could not overcome the regret with which Californians suffered the exchange, effected, it was believed, by private enmity. In a farewell letter addressed to the people, Wright hinted at the cause of the transfer: 'Had I for a moment yielded to the insane demands of a radical press and its co-laborers, I should have filled my forts with political prisoners to gratify personal hatred, causing such an outburst of indignation at such a course as to render it almost certain that civil war and bloodshed would have followed.' But to escape the condemnation of some in such troublous times was probably impossible. He was assigned to the command of the department of Oregon in 1865, and perished by the wreck of the steamer *Brother Jonathan* on his way to his post, having served on the Pacific coast for twelve years. Gen. McDowell remained in Cal. until the close of the war, commending himself to the people, as Sumner and Wright had done, by the purest patriotism.

The following is a list of the officers commanding the department of California without interruption to the present: On the 23d of Feb., 1849, the third or Pacific division was established by the war dept, including the tenth and eleventh military departments, Brev. Maj.-gen. Persifer F. Smith, col mounted rifles, assuming command, with headquarters at S. F., which were transferred to Sonoma in June. Gen. Smith was relieved by Maj. Washington Seawell, 2d infantry, assuming command April 29, 1851, which command he retained until July 9th, when Brev. Brig.-gen. Ethan A. Hitchcock, 2d inf., relieved him, and transferred headquarters to Benicia in the following Oct. The name of the command was changed to department of the Pacific in Oct. 1853, and on the 17th of Feb., 1854, Maj.-gen. John E. Wool assumed command, with headquarters at Benicia. He commanded until the 19th of Feb., 1857, when he was relieved by Col Thomas T. Fauntleroy, 1st dragoons, who was relieved April 29th by Brev. Brig.-gen. Newman S. Clarke, 6th inf., who established headquarters at S. F., where they have since remained. The designation of the command was changed to that of the department of Cal. in October 1858. Gen. Clarke died at S. F. Oct. 17, 1860, when Lieut-col Benjamin L. Beall, 1st dragoons, succeeded to the command from that time until Jan. 14, 1861, when he was relieved by Col and Brev. Brig.-gen. Albert S. Johnston, 2d cav., who announced that his command was to be called the department of the Pacific. On the 25th of the following April he was relieved by Brig.-gen. Edwin V. Sumner, who was succeeded Oct. 17th by Brig.-gen. of volunteers George Wright, who commanded until July 1, 1864, when he was relieved by Maj.-gen. of vols Irwin McDowell. Again, Maj.-Gen. Henry W. Halleck being assigned to the command of the military division of the Pacific on the 30th of August, 1865, retained it until June 1, 1869, when it was taken by Maj.-gen. George H. Thomas, who died March 28, 1870, when Maj.-gen. George M. Schofield was assigned to the command, which he held until July 1, 1876, at which time Gen. McDowell was a second time assigned to the command of this division, which comprised also the department of the Columbia, commanded by Brig.-gen. O. O. Howard, and the dept of Arizona, commanded by Col O. B. Willcox, 12th inf., and the dept of Alaska, created in March 1868. In June 1875, so much of the territory of Idaho as lay east of the extension of the western boundary of Utah, and embracing Fort Hall, was detached from the dept of Cal. and added to the dept of the Platte. On the 15th of Oct., 1882, Gen. Schofield relieved Gen. McDowell, and was himself relieved Nov. 30, 1883, by Maj.-gen. John Pope, who retained the command until March 16, 1886, when he retired, and Maj.-gen. Howard was assigned to this division.

The coast defenses of the state are not numerous. At S. F. the principal fortification is at Fort Point projection of the Presidio reservation which forms one side of the entrance to the harbor. It is situated upon the southern side of the channel, and consists of large casemated works, and extensive exterior earthen batteries *en barbette*, for the largest size of guns and mortars. On the opposite side of the channel is Lime Point, where other detached batteries are placed. Lying north of S. F., and almost directly facing Golden Gate is Fort Alcatraz, on a small rocky island, which is completely covered with fortifications of open barbette batteries. This is also the military prison. Angel island, north of Alcatraz, and Point San José north of Point Lamb, were fortified in a temporary manner during the civil war, but were allowed to decay, and have now to be reconstructed. The great improvement in ordnance within a few years has rendered it necessary for the government to make an appropriation of several millions for strengthening its fortifications and providing new guns of more modern size and capacity. The only other harbor furnished with fortifications is that of San Diego, where a small amount has been expended by the gov. for earthworks.

The naval arm of defence has been similarly neglected, with the exception of Mare Island Navy Yard which from first to last has cost the government large sums of money, and is, perhaps, the most commodious work of its kind in the world. But the decline of the merchant marine service, and the small need heretofore of an armed squadron in the Pacific, has made it of comparatively little use in proportion to its cost. Several old government vessels lie rotting in the gradually increasing deposit of river silt, and mining debris which is lessening the depth of water both in the channel and upon the side-flats. There has been some thought of removing the navy yard and allowing the Central Pacific railroad company to acquire the island for the establishment of foundries, workshops, depots, and ship-yards, but no such transfer of a magnificent property has yet taken place, and the government surveyors and engineers report annually very slight changes.

Much is said of the defenceless condition of the city, the navy yard, and the Benicia arsenal. Congress withstood all such criticisms for years, but in 1888 an appropriation of $5,000,000 was agreed to by the senate for the repair of fortifications, but rejected by the house, which left the state in its former condition of practical defencelessness. Whether the predicted misfortune will follow is for the future to determine; but nothing can alter the fact that vast sums have been saved by the neglect, for such has been the improvement in war vessels and heavy ordnance that expensive changes must have been made every few years. At the close of the late war the seacoast fortifications of the United States, and the American navy were quite equal to those of other countries. In the two decades last past, while Europe has made great progress, this country has apparently remained indifferent. Only very recently was California permitted to have a steel cruiser, the contract for which was let to a S. F. firm. Floating batteries will hereafter take a foremost rank in the defences of S. F., the long range of the guns now in use on ships of war enabling them to throw shells quite over the shore batteries, and from a distance which would place them out of reach of the latter. In the meantime, the inventive genius of the country is not diminishing, and our neighbors are at peace with us.

The United States naval force in the Pacific is insignificant, there being few harbors, no detached territory, and a small merchant marine to be protected even in the event of war. In 1862 there was a proposition made to establish a naval academy at San Francisco, which, however, was not carried out. In 1874 an act was passed by the legislature establishing and maintaining a training ship to instruct boys in seamanship and the mechanic arts connected with it, an appropriation being made for that purpose by the city and county of San Francisco, and a vessel furnished by the navy department. By the provisions of this act "any male person under eighteen years of age who shall be convicted of any misdemeanor" might be sentenced to serve his term of imprisonment on board of the training ship. In 1876 the law was amended to exclude convicts from serving out their terms on this ship; and was still further amended in 1878 by receiving boys from any counties to the number of 100, the state paying their expenses. The boys trained for seamen were placed on board merchant vessels when fitted for duty, a good disposition to be made of bad boys. But the change of constitution in 1879 rendered it illegal for the state to appropriate money for the purpose, and the training school was abandoned. Military tactics and drill are taught at several preparatory schools in the state. The history of our institutions, however, leads to the conclusion that except when we have some great object in view we think little about fighting and the glories of war.

CHAPTER XVIII.

EXTERMINATION OF THE INDIANS.

1849-1887.

Beating up the Game—Treatment by Mexicans and Americans—Some So-called Fighting—Congressional Attitude and Action—Outrages and Retaliations—United States Law of Compensation—End of Indian Affairs and End of the Indians.

That part of the early intercourse between aboriginal Americans and Europeans which properly belongs to history may be briefly given. For short work was made of it in California. The savages were in the way; the miners and settlers were arrogant and impatient; there were no missionaries or others present with even the poor pretense of soul-saving or civilizing. It was one of the last human hunts of civilization, and the basest and most brutal of them all.

We do not know why the Digger Indians of California were so shabbily treated by nature; why with such fair surroundings they were made so much lower in the scale of intelligence than their neighbors; but being low, and unsophisticated, in a measure harmless until trodden upon, surely it was not a mark of high merit on the part of the new comers to exterminate them so quickly. They were without houses or dress, with hardly any knowledge of agriculture, and almost devoid of religious ideas, roaming through forest and plain in search of roots and berries, small game and fish, improvident and dependent wholly

(474)

on the products of the seasons. Split into petty
bands, they were kept apart by a confusing multiplicity of tongues.[1]

The professed aim of the early missionaries, to
spread civilization, would appear to have discovered a
prolific field; but indolent in mind as well as body,
the natives offered no encouragement, and the fathers
soon adopted the plan of extending the pupillage system of Mexico into actual serfdom on this remote
frontier. Gathered partly by force from their hunt-
ing-fields and haunts, with their nomadic allurements,
the Indians were set to toil on plantations; not severely, for friar rule was tempered by religion ; but
without any incentives or hopes beyond those of a
slave, and maintained in a politic condition of ignorance
and abjection. The sale and decay of the missions
brought further hardships to the fold. A few had acquired sufficient knowledge of settled customs to remain either as hangers-on of the colonists or to
manage a field or cattle range of their own. The rest
drifted back among their roaming kindred to revel in
savage freedom, with many a fresh vice to poison the
good nature of an abasing indifference. Imbued with
a certain taste for the comforts of their former life,
notably for meat, they found additional incentive for
horse and cattle stealing, partly in retaliation for the
overbearing manners and harsh treatment so often experienced from their Mexican masters. This feeling
had in many directions grown bitter, and during the
conquest by the United States it led to a more men-
acing attitude, marked by atrocities.[2]

In the southern half of the state the wild Indians
were practically restricted to the Coast range and
valleys eastward. On the lower San Joaquin and

[1] Tribal distinctions were especially numerous among the degraded central
hordes, known as diggers. For a list of tribes, with boundaries, etc., I refer
to my *Native Races*, i., iii., v. passim

[2] Such as the massacre of a number of Hispano-Californians. See my
Hist. Cal., v. 567, etc.

beyond, the influence of the missions faded into a still fainter impress left by occasional contact with settled outposts, and with kidnappers from missions and pueblos. The gold discovery brought them a share of affluence,[3] but the increased intercourse with white adventurers led to degrading habits, particularly drunkenness and prostitution, which acquired further virulence from the fostered taste for finery, and the disposition to linger round mining camps to pick up cast-off clothing and refuse.[4] The attendant train of disease produced sadder havoc in their ranks than sword or famine.

The most prominent feature of their contact with the gold-seekers was abuse on the part of white men, and consequent retaliation. A hatred for Indians was acquired on the plains, from which the milder tribes of California had to suffer. Then followed the rush of miners into regions hitherto claimed as tribal ranges, with consequent encounters, and the slaughter or repulse of less strong intruders,[5] many of whom found to their cost that the confidence inspired by the milder natives of the lower Sacramento was misplaced when applied to the fiercer clans of the north and of the hills. The old practice of kidnapping continued in force, partly owing to the high price of labor, partly for immoral purposes.

Race antagonism, for much of which the Mexicans were responsible, brought on many evil complications; later came maletreatment by agents, with embezzlement of presents and property pertaining to the wards,

[3]Partly in working for the white men, partly for themselves, the women being generally set to dig for the men. *Barstow's Stat.*, MS., ii.

[4]They never learned to duly appreciate the value of money. Traders could readily cheat them. Beads and flaming colors took their fancy, and liquor their brains. *Grimshaw's Narr.*, MS., 44–8; *Fay's Stat.*, MS., 15–17; *Cesar, Cosas*, MS., 17. Though women were readily sold, yet husbands proved occasionally strict. *Overland*, xii. 24; *Little's Stat.*, MS., 7; *Matthewson's Cal. Aff.*, MS., 4–7; *Connor's Early Days*, MS., 3–4; *Delano's Life*, 309, et seq.; *Cal. Courier*, Aug. 17, 23, 31, 1850, Feb. 19–20, March 29, 1851; *Pac. News.*, Aug. 23, 26, Oct. 1.

[5] In 1848 the Trinity River Indians drove back prospectors, roused as they were against early trappers.

and disregarded treaties and criminal neglect by the government.[6] The indifference and errors of the latter were a main cause for the many wanton outrages.

Thus it is that the California valley cannot grace her annals with a single Indian war bordering on respectability. It can boast, however, a hundred or two of as brutal butcherings, on the part of our honest miners and brave pioneers, as any area of equal extent in our republic. The poor natives of California had neither the strength nor the intelligence to unite in any formidable numbers; hence, when now and then one of them plucked up courage to defend his wife and little ones, or to retaliate on one of the many outrages that were constantly being perpetrated upon them by white persons, sufficient excuse was offered for the miners and settlers to band and shoot down any Indians they met, old or young, innocent or guilty, friendly or hostile, until their appetite for blood was appeased.

The United States authorities began in 1847 to interest themselves in behalf of their wards by appointing agents,[7] and recommended the people to aid the priests in promoting industry among the Indians in the southern coast counties, without interfering in their internal government under elected alcaldes.[8] The legislature passed a special law April 22, 1850, for their government and care, which confirmed them in possession of their villages, although owners of the land were at liberty to arrange with them for occupying

[6] Official swindlers have been the rule rather than the exception. *Hayes' Indians*, v. 225; i. 76–85. Encroachments on reservations formed later a frequent cause for ill-feeling. *Alta Cal.*, Oct. 6, 1851; *U.S. Gov. Doc.*, cong. 34, sess. 3, *H. Ex. Doc.* 76, p. 127–30.

[7] Vallejo, as sub-agent for the Sonoma region, extending to Clear lake; Sutter for Sac. and San Joaquin, each with $750 salary, and J. D. Hunter as agent for the south, with headquarters at San Luis Rey. They had power merely to admonish and watch over their charges. Kearney in 1849 placed the sub-agents to act till the regular appointees should arrive, Riley recommending three for San Joaquin and Sacramento valleys. *Pres't Message*, cong. 38, sess. 1. i. 171.

[8] *U. S. Gov. Doc.*, cong. 31, sess. 1, *H. Ex. Doc.*, 17, p. 701. Halleck's circular in *Avila, Doc.* 6. This applied particularly to mission Indians. The property reserved for churches and priests should be respected.

some special section of it.   A confined tenancy at the
most, for neither landed rights nor citizen privileges
were accorded.   They might be hired to work under
contract, and by a special provision this was made to
some extent compulsory by enabling the local authorities to arrest all whom they chose to denominate as
vagabonds and beggars, and turn them over to the highest bidder for not exceeding four months.   Any surplus
wages, after providing the victim with clothes, was assigned to a mysterious Indian fund, unless relatives
claimed the money.   In cases of crime juries might be
demanded by either race, but white men could not be
convicted on Indian testimony.[9]   These formal restrictions availed little for the intended purpose, since
they left only the same loop-holes as formerly for
hoodwinking justice, and afforded moreover a legal
cover for enslaving and oppressing the natives.   It
was easy to charge any one with vagabondage, especially by enlisting the potent aid of liquor, and
obtain his condemnation to forced labor.   The im-
pressment generally occurred toward harvest time;
and this over, the poor wretches were cast adrift to
starve, for their own harvest season was by this time
lost to them.   Bondage was also insured or prolonged
by inducing the workers to spend their small allowance on vile drink, in open violation of the law,[10] and
then locking them up as irresponsible.

[9] The justices of the peace, who had jurisdiction in Indian cases, were
given discretionary power, however. *Cal. Statements*, 1851, and *Cal. Laws*,
1850–3, 822–5.   For later projects in behalf of the natives, see *Cal. Jour.
Sen.*, 1850, p. 1299, 1851, p. 1826, 1852, p. 762; *Hayes' Indians*, i. 1–3.

[10] Supt Beale reports in 1852 that Indians were caught like cattle for the
work season near the large towns.   Out of one band turned adrift after the
season 18 died of starvation.   It was also common to kidnap children and
enslave them. *U. S. Govt Doc.*, cong. 32, sess. 2., *Sen. Doc.*, 57, vii. 8–9,
cong. 31; sess. 1, *H. Ex. Doc.*, 5, i. 166, 170.   Indian peons at Los Angeles
would spend their wages in a debauch on Sunday and be driven to a corral
by an Indian foreman.   On Monday they were exposed for sale at from $1
to $3 for the week. *Bell's Remin.*, MS., 9–10.   Staple, *Stat.*, MS., 20, claims,
like Sutter, to have employed Indians largely without trouble or force.   He
treated with the chiefs and held them responsible. *Hayes' Indians*, v. 15.
The officials used freely to infringe the liquor law. *Unbound Doc.*, 235–6.
A later temperance society set a watch upon such offenders. *Sac. Union*, Ap.
7, 1855.   A humorous article in Trinity co. *Monitor*, Feb. 1, 1855, on the

In the more settled or occupied districts, the strength of the white men tended to repress murmurs against injustice, but elsewhere the aspect changed, in particular along the slopes of the Sierra, where a more independent mountain spirit prevailed, and where tribes could count upon numbers further swelled by occasional alliances. Roused by personal injuries from the encroaching miners, who looked upon them as fair prey, and rendered apprehensive by reports of outrages in other directions, the Indians would rise, primarily to repel intruders, not infrequently to retaliate, according to their custom, upon individuals and small parties, and gradually to yield to their desire for blood and plunder. In the spring of 1848, some thirty murders by them were reported in different directions, and parties set out in pursuit, notably one of three score men toward Coloma, which came up with flying Indians, killing a number of them, and recovering some property. Soon after several who were suspected were brought in to Coloma, and tried, the result being the slaughter of thirty.[11] A pursuit toward the Cosumne was marked by the indiscriminate massacre of a band on mere suspicion.[12]

market rate and demand for women was based on actual traffic. 'Good middling' could be had for five oxen, seven deer, and five pair of blankets. *Cox An. Trinity*, 127. Further accounts of treatment in *Kip's Cal. Sketches*, 45; *Henshaw's Events*, MS., 2. Indians were chastised so severely as to cause death. *Sac. Union*, July 28, 1855.

[11] *Sac. Transcript*, June 29, 1850. Ryan, *Pers. Adv.*, ii. 300–1, relates that McKay's party attacked a ranchería of 20 huts, killing about 30 of the 300 inmates, and capturing 7 men and 40 women. Buffum, *Six Mos*, 100, speaks in this connection of Greenwood's party killing 20 men at a Weaver creek ranchería, and capturing 30, of whom 6 were sentenced to be shot. The condemned were allowed a chance to run, but 5 fell. On Dry creek three murderers were captured and hanged. *Placer Times*, May 12, 1849. The notable murders embraced, on the American Fork 7 out of a party of 9, 5 out of 8, and 2 out of 3. *Id.*, Apr. 28, 1849. Little, *Stat.*, MS., 7, had a narrow escape. He blames the men of Stevenson's regiment for drunken outrages and cold-blooded killing.

[12] The lessons already given proved salutary, however; the berry harvest occupied the Indians, and gold-picking the white men, so that the summer and autumn proved quiet. Then came a renewal of trouble, outrages and murder on one side, and robbery and murder on the other. They were followed by expeditions along the different tributaries of the Sacramento, from the American fork to Feather river, and especially on the Yuba, where seven white men and ten times that number of redskins had fallen by the

The upper valley of the San Joaquin had for years been noted as the abode of Indians whose independent spirit delighted in inroads upon the adjoining coast districts;[13] and when, in the spring of 1849 gold-seekers began to enter the country, those of King river among others manifested their objection by several atrocities.[14] Troops were dispatched to recon-

middle of April 1850. The latter exhibited considerable courage and tenacity, assuming at times the offensive against large bodies, even laying siege to entrenchments, and employing tactics which led to the belief in European counsellors. The efficient movement of troops, however, assisted by the militia under General Green, and by numerous volunteer corps, obliged the leading tribes of the Yuba region to accept peace on May 25th, after which comparative security was secured for the summer. But order could not long prevail with so many incentives for outrages in the form of lazy, vicious, and drunken vagabonds at the camps, who took pleasure in abusing the natives, especially in regard to women, or where the Indians presumed to find a desirable gold claim. Appeals for redress being as usual disregarded, there was no resource save retaliation, in murders and plunder. Although no regular combination among the tribes was probable, yet with October 1850 raids and attacks became general, from the head of Sacramento valley downward. The alarm spread, and the government, while believing it best to let each district defend itself, deemed it necessary to order Sheriff Rogers, of El Dorado, to call out 200 men for suppressing the savages along the leading immigrant route. The force, with Rogers as elected colonel, divided into several parties to pursue the marauders. The Indians generally scattered before them into retreats difficult of access to the less active white men, who were, moreover, hampered by baggage, and little inclined for climbing and other exhausting tasks. The ardor of the latter was further checked by finding that when gathered in force the Indians fought desperately, and defended themselves against rifles with glass-tipped arrows, which were so effectively shot as to cause more than one repulse of the militia. Indeed, their exploits were far from brilliant, and were mostly restricted to destroying abandoned rancherías, with their stores of berries and other provender, a measure which could only drive the Indians to other desperate means or starvation. Reports indicating that the El Dorado region had been cleared of the enemy, the governor ordered a reduction, and soon after a disbandment of the troops. At once rose the cry of renewed raids, started by interested traders and their shiftless customers, whose appetite had been whetted for the state's money. The legislature, indeed, was so impressed by the magnitude of the danger as to authorize the governor to raise 500 men. The governor fortunately looked more closely into the affair before encroaching further upon the state's war fund of half a million, and the war party was greatly disappointed. The movements here during the spring of 1851 accordingly fell to small proportions, to be overshadowed by more important events elsewhere.

[13] Those of the Merced and Tulare were expected by the authorities of 1849 to be the most troublesome. In Jan., 1849, the settlers of S. Juan Bautista petitioned for relief against them. *U. S. Gov. Doc.*, cong. 31, sess. 1, *H. Ex. Doc.*, 17 p. 688-9, 907. Naglee had in 1849 pursued stock robbers into Mariposa. *Wozencraft*, 4.

[14] Such as flaying victims alive. This fate is applied to Garner in 1849, and to Wood in Jan., 1851. *Sac. Transcript*, Feb. 28, 1851; *S. José Pioneer*, Nov. 17, 1877. In May, 1849, the Pacheco party was attacked ,by 300 Indians and 6 killed. *Unbound Doc.*, 308-10.

noitre, and volunteers scoured over the country, but with so little effect as to render the enemy bolder than ever. James Savage, who owned two trading posts on the Fresno and Mariposa, and possessed great influence over the tribes, took some of the chiefs to San Francisco to receive a salutary impression of paleface strength, but without avail. The plundering of isolated men and small parties was too tempting to be resisted.[15]

The southern counties had been exposed not alone to raids from the Tulare region, but from the many bands roaming in the deserts east of the San Bernardino range. In the summer of 1849 the Yumas began to harass immigrants and to rob settlers, but an expedition followed by a treaty brought them to terms for the time. In the following April they were roused by the outrageous conduct of some Americans who owned a ferry on the Colorado, and in a night descent eleven of the offenders were slain. San Diego and Los Angeles took alarm and the governor was induced to order out a hundred of the militia to exact punishment and protect the immigrant route. The expedition reached the river in September, under command of Morehead, but finding everything quiet disbanded after remaining a few weeks in observation.[16] Soon after a military post was established

[15] With the avowed intention of driving out the white men they extended their raids so far as to destroy, in December, 1850, also the Fresno station of the friendly Savage. Their action seemed preconcerted, for at the same time tribes were ravaging along the Stanislaus and Tuolumne, within a few miles of Stockton, along the Merced and streams southward, driving the miners from the headwaters of the San Joaquin and slaughtering a large party at Rattlesnake creek. Further down settlements and cattle stations were attacked and demolished, particularly on Kaweah and Kern rivers and toward Owen's Lake, attended by massacre and pillage. Again a number of volunteer companies took the field, to meet with occasional advantages, such as the destruction of a deserted rancheria and the killing of a few warriors, which were magnified into victories; but also to encounter repulses at the hands of the sturdy tribes in ambuscade or in good position, strengthened by captured or purchased arms; or, more generally, to be tired out by fruitless pursuit. The regular troops did not distinguish themselves any more than the bodies called out by the governor, whereof 200 men were to be raised by the sheriff of Mariposa.

[16] The order for raising troops was issued in June, to Gen. Bean of the 4th div. of militia, who entrusted the formation and command of

here by the federal government. The Indian war
which was afflicting the great valley at the close of
1850, made itself felt also in this direction, at first
by incursions from the Tulares, so that the governor
authorized Bean to raise a company.[17]

The hostilities of 1849 served to impress upon
congress the necessity for some arrangement by which
to appease the aboriginal holders of the soil, and so
render more secure the rising settlements. In October 1850, accordingly, the president appointed Redick
McKee, G. W. Barbour, and O. M. Wozencraft Indian agents to figure for a time as peace commissioners, with ill-defined instructions to act for the best in

the party to Morehead, a lawyer formerly lieut in Stevenson's reg't,
member of legislature in 1850, and now styled quarter-master-general. He
was preparing in July and August, but as the alarm had subsided, the citizens objected to furnish supplies for his scrip, whereupon he seized by force
what was required. With levies from emigrant parties he obtained 125 men.
Although quiet prevailed he managed to provoke a quarrel, the result of
which was a skirmish wherein a score of Indians fell. In Sept. the government ordered a disbandment, which had to be repeated before it was obeyed.
Cal. Sen. Jour., 1851, 16–17, 607–9, 734, 1045–7, etc. Morehead's bill
amounted to $76,588. Concerning claims of citizens for seized property, see
Hayes' Angeles, i. 42. etc; *Alta Cal.* Jan. 14; 18, 1851. *Id. Indians*, i., 192–
205.

[17] This precaution proved of value, but in the middle of the following year
disaffection spread to the Yumas and San Luis Rey Indians, the latter in-
censed at the enforcement of taxes from which they had so far been exempt.
In November the Yumas signalized themselves by attacking a party of
sheep drovers, and obliging the troops stationed on the Colorado to withdraw. At the same time the San Luis Rey chief, Antonio Garra, a turbulent
and treacherous fellow, declared war, boasting that some 3,000 warriors
awaited his signal to descend upon the settlements. Consternation spread;
martial law was proclaimed at San Diego, and every man impressed; volunteers mustered at Los Angeles, and appeals for aid went northward. In response a company of troops departed from Benicia, Gen. Bean was ordered
to raise two companies in the south, and volunteers started from San Francisco. These movements and the revelation of the plot served to frighten
many a vacillating tribe, and Juan Antonio, chief of the powerful Cahuillos,
whose attitude at one time appeared suspicious, hastened to proclaim his
loyalty by entrapping Garra and several of his adherents, and surrendering
them to the authorities. The chief was promptly tried and executed, together with several accomplices, including an American and a Californian.
A portion of his tribe which had meanwhile taken the field was promptly defeated at Los Coyotes, and so ended with a few raids an uprising which for
a while alarmed the entire state. Major Heintzelman, who had taken a
leading share in these operations, now marched to the Colorado. The Yumas
proved more stubborn, allied as they were with Arizona tribes and well
armed, and the troops were kept busy throughout the spring and summer.
In August, however, a decisive advantage was gained, followed by the capture and execution of the chief, whereupon comparative order was restored.

conciliating the natives and bind them by written treaties, reporting upon their customs and condition. They arrived in California in January 1851, and as the governor had ordered out 200 men to operate against the Indians of Mariposa region, in conjunction with United States troops, under Captain Keyes, it was resolved that the commissioners should proceed to this quarter and seek to effect a peaceful arrangement, the troops awaiting the issue. Their conclusion was that the aborigines had been driven by the advancing miners and settlers from the fishing and fruit grounds into the less hospitable mountain districts, and were consequently forced, greatly by necessity, to prey upon the flocks and other possessions of the white men. The only preventive seemed to be their restoration to certain unoccupied portions of the plain, with allowances of beef, blankets, and other body comforts as compensation for encroachments upon their hunting ranges, and for keeping them contented and under control.

This campaign with flour in lieu of powder proved effective, for a number of treaties were formed with the Indians throughout the San Joaquin valley, from the Stanislaus to Tejon,[18] setting aside a limited sec-

[18] On March 19, 1851, a treaty was formed with six tribes from the headwaters of the Tuolumne, Merced, and Mariposa. On April 29th a treaty with 16 tribes between the Mariposa and King rivers, numbering 2,000 or 3,000, who agreed to occupy a strip along the lower foothills about 15 miles wide by 50 in length. On May 13th, a treaty was signed with 12 of the warlike tribes of the country between King and Kaweah rivers, though ranging as far south as Kern river, and numbering 4,120 souls, to occupy a small district in this region; May 30th, the treaty with 7 tribes, allies of preceding, between the Kaweah and Tulare rivers; June 3d, with 4 tribes, 1,700 strong, on the Tulare, which were allotted a section of the range; June 10th with 11 tribes, in the southern extreme of the valley, round Kern lake. The Indians southward, in Los Angeles and San Diego, being friendly, no arrangements were then made with them. All treaties in the San Joaquin valley after April were arranged by Barbour alone. For names of above tribes and other data, see *U. S. Gov. Doc.*, spec. sess. 1853; *Sen. Doc.*, 4, p. 81, 93, 207–10, 252–8, etc.; *Id.*, cong. 32, sess. 1, H. Ex. Doc., 2, ii. pt iii. 484, 507–12, etc.; *Alta. Cal.*, May–July, 1851. The commissioners ascribed nineteen-twentieths of all trouble to white aggression or broken promises. It was cheaper to feed the Indians for a year than to fight them for a week. Accounts follow of similar arrangements with the Stanislaus, giving them a section 8 miles by 12; in El Dorado 10 miles by 25 were set apart, including some good valleys, but mostly poor soil; the placer gold would

tion of land within the range of each contracting
group, thus forming a dozen reservations, with suggestions for more, and offering to all who would
settle therein a certain amount of rations and presents, for 1851–2, till more definite arrangements could
be made. A large proportion of the tribes recognized
the futility of resisting terms offered at the point of
the bayonet, and accepted the restricted occupation
with the sugar-coating of provisions.

Only the first treaties were arranged by the commissioners jointly. By April they tired of the mutual
supervision prompted by a natural jealousy. Each

soon be washed out; between Yuba and Bear rivers a piece 12 miles square
was selected; in Colusa 3 miles by 15 along the east bank of the Sacramento,
on the Sutter claim; by the Chico treaty a reservation in the foothills north
of Feather river, 6 miles by 20; by the Cottonwood treaty, 35 miles square
at the head of the Sacramento valley, between Shasta, Nevada, and Coast
ranges. The Sacramento valley treaties were arranged by Wozencraft.
By June 1851, Agent Johnston reported about 1,000 Indians on the reservation between the Stanislaus and Tuolumne; 800 on the Tuolumne and Merced;
1,800 or 2,000 on the Chowchilla-Kaweah. Trading licenses were granted
within these reservations, on the Stanislaus, to Dent & Co. for $1,000; on
the Tuolumne, to G. Belt for $1,000; on the Chowchilla, to Savage & Co. for
$1,200. On the Sacramento reservation three were issued by Wozencraft.
See *Sen. Doc.*, 4, 230, as above. Agent Johnston undertook to award Stone
and Marks $12,000 damages for dispossessing them of their hotel, ferry,
land, and trading post on the Merced; but the chief agent, McKee, who was
one of the few honest agents of the government, reported against it. *Id.*, 109–
11. He had set out for his northern allotment in Aug., escorted by some 36
men under Wessells, and with a drove of cattle for vanquishing Indian appetite and obstinacy. Numerous attendants for the pack trains, etc., were also
engaged at heavy wages. Marching through Sonoma he reached Clear lake
and there effected a treaty Aug. 20th, with eight tribes of about 1,000 souls,
setting aside the lake valley as a reservation. To the same reservation were
assigned four Russian river tribes, numbering somewhat over 1,000 souls,
with whom a treaty was signed Aug. 22d. He passed through the Coast
region, which from Fort Ross to Mud river was estimated to contain 1,700
souls, whom he proposed to settle at the mouth of Eel river, and on Oct. 6th
and 12th, made a treaty with the Indians of lower Klamath and Trinity
rivers, for whom a reservation was proposed near the junction of these
rivers. On Nov. 4th, the Scott valley treaty was concluded with the upper
Klamath, Shasta, and Scott River natives, numbering 3,000 souls in 24, 19
and 7 rancherías, respectively; to these were added 1,000 Upper Trinity
River Indians, the whole 4,000 to be assigned to Scott's valley. For names
of tribes and chiefs, varying estimates of number and other details, see
McKee's reports in *U. S. Gov. Doc.*, spec. sess. 1854, *Sen. Doc.*, 4, 136–228,
239; *Id.*, cong. 34, sess. 1, H. Ex. Doc., 2, ii. pt iii., 498 et seq.; *Id.*, cong.
34, sess. 3, doc. 76, ii. 59–68; *S. F. Morning Post*, Sep. 1, 1851. Further
record of commissioners' movements in *Wozencroft*, 1 et seq.; *Hayes' Indians*,
ii. 118, iv. 13–14, v. 94–7; *Sac. Transcript*, Feb.–Apr., 1851; *Pac. News*, Jan.–
Ap., 1851; *Cal. Courier*, id.; *Alta Cal.*, Jan.–July, Sep. 9, 13, Dec. 29, 1851,
etc.; *Placer Times and Transcript*, Nov. 15, 1851, etc.

longed to figure by himself as arbitrator over the
destiny of peoples, attended by an imposing escort of
soldiers, and with a no mean power among settlers in
offering protection, disposing of lands and dispensing
contracts.   In the latter lay a golden means of enrichment that could not well be gained in company.
And so on the 1st of May the commissioners agreed
to act separately, Barbour retaining by lot San Joaquin valley, with southern California added, Wozencraft taking the Sacramento valley, and McKee all
north of this and west of the Coast range above
latitude 40°.[19]

The Indians could not be blamed for becoming res-
tive under the cumulative injuries now openly fostered
by the government itself in the mismanagement and

[19] No sooner had they turned their faces to the respective allotments than
each entered into heavy contracts for the supply of provisions, mostly beef,
in which different collusions were made for dividing equably their benefit
between the government and the Indians, commissioners and distributing
agents.   In one instance it was proved that only two thirds of a contract
had been delivered; in another, that choice lots were sold at high rates to
the miners.   Similar prices were exacted from the Indians in different directions, for the supposed presents and rations of a paternal government; spoiled
flour was utilized, and as thick or double blankets must interfere with the
free movements of the natives when sent to hunt their rations in the forest,
thinner material was considerately provided for them, or the agent applied
his shears with such calculations as to turn most of the fabric to better advantage in other quarters.   The tact and skill with which these managers
could make available one means for several purposes shone equally resplendent in demonstrating their own disinterestedness in these transactions.   The
government, however, could not be made to reconcile figures with purity of
motives; and in accordance with an act creating a superintendent of Indian
affairs for California, E. F. Beale was, in the spring of 1852, entrusted with
the management.
He endorsed the policy so far pursued with assignment of reservations
and provisions, but condemned the wasteful and gross mismanagement under
which an indebtedness of nearly $800,000 had been formed within little more
than a year.   One result was the resignation or suspension of the agents and
the revision of their contracts, involving reduced and deferred payments.
It was declared unwise to reject the treaties, for this would undoubtedly
lead to bloody and ruinous wars.   Unfortunately the selection of reservations
was in itself injudicious, scattered as they were in so many localities, frequently cutting into the midst of mineral belts, and occupying much valuable
land coveted by settlers.   Strong objections were accordingly made before
congress under legislative auspices, and the treaties were rejected, chiefly on
the ground that under the acquisition of California from Mexico the natives
had no right to the soil, and consequently no claims upon the United States
government.   Nevertheless, an appropriation of $100,000 was made for pre-
serving peace with dispossessed Indians till other permanent arrangements
could be made.

neglect of agents, and in broken promises and disregarded treaties, with consequent threatening spoliation. Even the usually gentle aboriginals of south-west California appeared unquiet, and Los Angeles county was startled by raids from adjoining districts. These did not prove serious, however, owing to the presence of several military companies near Bajou pass, San Luis Rey, Vallecitas, linked with those at Four creeks, King river, and Fort Yuma. In the desert region eastward, with its less forbearing Yumas and Mojaves, the Pintos and other roaming tribes of Nevada were tempted to repeated attacks on emigrant trains, checked only occasionally by some garrisoned detachment or passing volunteer corps. The opening through Arizona of the overland road in 1858–9 was attended by more formidable movements, and the despatch of a special body of troops to establish a crossing on the Colorado. The peace now forced upon the Mojaves prevented any further serious trouble in this quarter; but northward the influx of miners and stock-raisers stirred the hitherto quiet Owen's river natives. Driven into the mountains or more sterile tracts, they were compelled by hunger to raid upon the vast herds of cattle, and to commit attendant outrages, until in 1862 the settlers opened a regular campaign. This served only as a momentary check, and after two more seasons of endurance the exasperated settlers resolved upon a severe retaliation. They marched forth, and in January, 1865, massacred over two score of persons at one village, and a month later over 100 were driven into the corroding waters of a lake, there to meet a terrible death. The lesson proved effective, especially so far as those that were killed were concerned, if it did not serve to thoroughly restrain natives to whom mountain fastnesses and deserts presented so inviting an impunity.[20]

[20] The efforts of the tribes in the lower part of San Joaquin valley to assert their rights against the advancing settlers culminated in the Kern river war of 1856. Northward in the valley the white population spread too rapidly

The most troublesome Indians of California were those of the extreme north, from the headwaters of the Sacramento to the Oregon border, and toward the coast. They had shown their hostility to the early trappers and immigrants, and were more relentless after every contact with the inimical Oregonians, who traversed their country en route for the gold fields. Many an early prospector suffered for his temerity, and when the miners subsequently entered in force they fought their way with little scruple, exacting terrible vengeance for every outrage. Beyond Feather river the Cottonwood bands were among the first noted hostile savages to suffer, and westward those of Humboldt county became exposed to a double fire, for miners were entering in large numbers also by sea. The coast Indians gave just cause for anger by their thievishness, which in a measure justified the destruction of villages and lives that followed.[21]

and overwhelmingly to permit the less spirited natives to exhibit any marked discontent. Cattle stealing and pilfering would occur, however, in obedience to the prevailing Digger instinct, and lead at intervals to armed combinations of the farmers and miners. The last notable uprising took place during the winter of 1857–8, and before it was over there were still fewer savages to suffer hunger and eke out existence on the reduced acorn crop.

[21] Their retaliative attacks led to the Klamath war of 1851–2, marked by several petty expeditions, and by the participation of troops which established a post at Humboldt. Forts had already been erected at Reading and Scott valley for raids upon supply trains, and small parties were by this time frequent throughout the northern counties. During the summer of 1851 the Oregon border region was ablaze with the Shasta war, which despite treaties, continued to break out in occasional hostilities and gave occasion for such atrocities as the massacre by Ben Wright of two score Modocs during a peace conference.

The latter were undoubtedly guilty of murderous raids, but the manner of retaliation has been condemned. In 1853 the widespread Shasta tribes joined anew in the Rogue river war. Their operations did not then assume any magnitude, partly from the recent increase of military posts; but the comparative inaction of the settlers encouraged the natives to relieve the wants created by severe winter seasons. The consequent depredations, chiefly upon cattle, attended by a few murders, provoked brief avenging spring campaigns in 1854 and 1855, the latter directed chiefly against the lower Klamaths, whose rising during the winter created general alarm in Humboldt county. Desultory movements continued throughout the year along the Oregon line, in connection with the Rogue river war, wherein the Shastas took a leading part. The diversion of the regular troops for that campaign, and the seeming security of the mountains, tempted to fresh outbreaks along the Klamath to the border, obliging the governor to send assistance and call out volunteers, first for Humboldt county, and in the summer for Siskiyou. In the former regions two companies of settlers assisted to in-

The incidents of the several wars lay recorded in different sections in long enduring signs of devastation, and in the now harrowing, now boastful, narratives of victims and participants, refreshed by protracted appeals for indemnity from the government, and for reimbursement by the federation of the campaign expenses of the state. Even more impressive was the sad spectacle of the miserable remnants of the abused race, fast sinking under the withering influence and diseases of European civilization, under ever diminishing resources and changed and constrained modes of life.[22]

flict so summary a chastisement upon the lower Klamaths that they quietly accepted the reservation assigned to them, and gave little cause for further anxiety. In Siskiyou the campaign extended till October, before peace could be arranged. The trouble afflicting San Joaquin valley in 1857–9 extended in more virulent form throughout the northern counties, notwithstanding the conciliatory establishment of reservations with attendant offers of rations and other presents. The advance of settlement was everywhere marked by a more or less revolting treatment of the natives. In the contact of antagonistic races, one side was incited by a spirit of maintenance of possessory rights, and often by hunger, as was well instanced in the occupation of Honey Lake valley; the other side was impelled by the demon of unjust and arbitrary domination. Aggravating circumstances existed in the prosperity of the natives for pilfering, which readily expanded into robbery and raids, while among the miners especially a large proportion consisted of reckless ruffians, stimulated by vicious passion and innate cruelty, and at times by a desire to rake up cause for obtaining government aid toward a formal expedition against marauders. The campaign of 1858–9 in the north was sustained by the enrolled state forces under Gen. Kibbe, which operated between October and March on both sides of the Coast Range, killing more than a hundred natives and capturing several hundred for the reservations. The settlers swelled the former figure by spasmodic descents and expeditions, and fanned the incipient movements on Mad and Eel rivers into formidable ravages, marked on one side by slaying of cattle, and on the other by kidnapping of women and children, and crowned by several sickening massacres, involving fully 200 beings of both sexes and all ages, which called forth formal condemnation of the grand jury of the county. The only effective stand in this quarter was made by the Hoopas, who, after a five years desultory struggle, had in August 1864 to be propitiated by a treaty whereby the lower Trinity valley was assigned to them as a special reservation. Simultaneously the settlers in and round Butte swept that region of natives for transmission to reservations. Then followed a comparative lull, until the Pitt river savages opened the campaign of 1867. In this Gen. Crook took the lead, and enforced peace the following year. The Modoc war of 1873 marks the end of serious Indian troubles in California; and this desirable condition of affairs has been fostered by an improved management of reservations, and a more considerate attitude toward outside natives. The growth of settlements tends naturally to awe them into good behavior, while yielding greater jurisdiction to judicial and political authorities, sustained by the more humane sentiments of a cultivated public opinion.

[22] Estimates of the Indian population vary from 10,000 to 30,000, the latter, as a rule, by Indian agents, who had obvious reasons for not placing

While refusing to admit any claim on the part of the California Indians for their land, the United States government recognized that in dispossessing them from their hunting and berrying grounds some compensation must be made, if only out of consideration for the safety of the intruding settlers. Superintendent Beale received instructions accordingly. He approved the reservation plan of the agents and commissioners of 1851–2, yet with improvements. Impressed by the success of the early missions, he proposed a system of discipline and instruction under resident agents and the protecting care of military posts, together with communal farming to promote self-support. This received the approval of congress, which appropriated $250,000 toward the formation of five military reservations. Beale proceeded energetically to his task, although reporting it difficult to persuade the Indians to leave their old homes and hunting grounds for the restraining limits of an uncongenial reservation or to convince the citizens of the necessity for keeping his wards within the state

them too low. The smaller figures are due to early travellers and residents, some of whom evidently went to an extreme in the other direction. The mission padres could not be expected to lower the results of their labors among converts, so that the 17,000 or 20,000 neophytes reported by them during the first decades of the century may be excessive, and include a large number of relapsed fugitives. Nevertheless their reports indicate that in the southern half of California alone the natives must have numbered more than 15,000, perhaps double, while a still larger total is generally allowed for the north. But it is also known that a large proportion, sometimes entire tribes, were swept away by small-pox at different times. Chest diseases and fevers carried off thousands, and a more insidious malady undermined in a slower but equally effectual manner, far more so than wars, whiskey, and other less defined concomitants of foreign civilization. One result was a startling excess of deaths over births in Mexican times. It is not surprising, therefore, that the census of 1852 reported only about 32,000 'domesticated' Indians, and that of 1860 reduces the number to less than 18,000. But these figures evidently neglect the tribes of the north, and those roaming in the mountains, not to mention the bands driven into the adjoining territories before the advancing and aggressive white men. The census of 1870 raises the total to 31,000; yet by 1880 it is again lowered to a little more than 16,000, and this with a detailed enumeration that appears conclusive. The diminution since 1848 is due not alone to wars, diseases and famine, but to the retreat of bands into adjoining territories before the advance of the aggressive settlers. The more humane policy lately in vogue, with greater medical care and attention to bodily comforts, will no doubt prevent any rapid decline, and the growing settled condition, with gradual adaptation to new circumstances, favoring the rearing of female as well as male children, cannot fail to have a beneficial effect.

or to obtain the necessary extent of land without incurring great expense in purchasing existing claims. These obstacles must have sorely perplexed Beale, for he lost sight of the vast northern half of the state, with its unclaimed tracts and its more pressing need for departmental interference under the great influx of miners, and turned his entire attention and funds toward establishing one solitary reservation in the southern extreme of San Joaquin valley, at Tejon pass. His zeal led him, moreover, to make disbursements and estimates for 2,500 swarthy wards, although unable to encounter more than about 700 fit objects for his benevolence. A distant government failed to understand the difficulties with which he had to grapple, and sent Colonel T. J. Henley to replace him. He took a different course in manipulating the liberal allowances of the treasury. Instead of pouring the entire revenue through one glaringly conspicuous channel, he diverted it into several, and dazzled his superiors by establishing, in addition to El Tejon, three reservations: Nome Lacke, on Stony creek, in Colusa, which for its central position and fertility assumed the lead for a time; Mendocino, on the ocean, below the cape of that name, which became the home of 700 Indians, sustained by fishing and potato growing; and the Klamath, along both sides of this stream, which received some 2,000 natives, chiefly devoted to salmon fishing and berrying, for the scanty soil afforded little range for cultivation. Even these selections roused condemnation from different quarters as too good for Indians; and eager to please, especially men whose watchful eyes were upon him, Henley early suggested the planting of a large reservation east of the Sierra, but failed to gain the approval of his superiors.

Henley was a man of broad views and varied expediences; and not intent merely on personal gains, he devised other means whereby the obnoxious presence of his wards might be turned to some benefit for their white masters. There was a number of office-seekers whose persevering patience under frequent rebuff had touched his sympathies. The position of agents and employés upon the reservations was not brilliant, but it presented the allurements of a quiet life, and opportunities for diverting the rations provided by government into better channels than wasting them upon savages. For these a bountiful nature had provided acorns and roots in abundance. It was also understood that as the agent could not well control more than a portion of the Indians under his charge, the employés might foster discipline and industry among the rest by using their labor for private undertakings. As these manifold attractions became apparent the demand for positions grew apace, so that Henley found additional inducements for increasing the number of reservations. His instructions limited them to five, but any number could be established under the designation of farms and branches. A short distance west of Nome Lacke, he accordingly, in 1856, selected a tributary to it in Nome Cult, or Round valley, on the upper Eel river, which in due time became the chief reservation in the state, with about 1,000 occupants, who, at times, raised crops exceeding 20,000 bushels. In San Joaquin valley he opened farms successively at Fresno, King river, and Tule river, for his humane and economic instincts revolted at the cruelty and cost of removing the Indians too far from their ancient haunts. These farms were leased, so that here a double benefit was conferred by providing deserving citizens with a handsome rental from comparatively useless property, while improving it with Indian labor and government funds in the shape of fences, buildings, and irrigation ditches. Others, who had not yet obtained farms, he allowed to select choice slices from the different reservations. And what more commendable aid to progress than to permit untilled land to be converted into fields and gardens ? So secure a foothold

did these squatters obtain as to speedily convince the
government that it would be advisable to relinquish
possession of the small section left to the Indians.[24]

[24] In the first spasm of enterprise Henley had planted large areas in grain,
particularly at El Tejon, supplied by long irrigation ditches, but the enerva-
ting heat prevented his agents from straining their attention beyond 700
acres, and even the crops from this reduced tract, although ever promising
well far into the summer, usually fell to little or nothing. In one case a
flood was credited with the disappearance, but usually drouths bore the
brunt, although, singularly enough, the fields cultivated by Indians for private account yielded well. Similar reverses overtook Fresno. Another
peculiarity was that the population at the different reservations appeared
much larger to the overtasked agents than to visitors. Unable to comprehend these vagaries of a strange climate, the government stooped to listen
to the insinuations of army officers that the Indian management had fallen
into the hands of a ring which manipulated it to their own advantage. One
result was the dispatch of G. Bailey as special agent to examine into the
matter. Disregarding the experience of agents accustomed to the country,
and unconvinced by their demonstrations, supported by long array of figures,
he preferred to take the unsupported evidence of his own eyes, and declared
the reservations to be mere almshouses, wherein a small proportion of the
natives were scantily fed at great cost. The pay and rations of the employés consumed about $100,000, a sum sufficient to sustain more than all the
actual reservation Indians. A still larger sum was annually granted for
clothing and provisions, and another allowance aimed to provide the several
government farms with live stock, implements, and other improvements ;
yet this large expenditure, which so far exceeded $1,170,000, had served to
produce but a scanty crop, valued at less than one-fourth of the salaries
alone. Such was the net result of these proposed self-sustaining establishments, for the gain in civilization lay almost wholly in forcing distasteful
lessons in agriculture upon a handful, and this was fully counterbalanced
by the demoralizing influence of soldiers, servants, and settlers upon bands,
which, if left to their own wild haunts, would have long remained purer and
happier.

The commissioner at Washington came to the conclusion that there were
too many reservations, partly in unsuitable locations, and too many men to
work for the Indians, instead of training them to work for themselves, besides
lack of system, ability, and integrity on the part of the managers. The first
step was to appoint a new superintendent, James Y. McDuffie, with an
appropriation so pitifully reduced as in itself to compel a sweeping dismissal
of servants and the consequent neglect of the reservations, upon which the
dismissed staff and the surrounding settlers combined in a raid of seizure and
spoliation. The knowledge that further changes were pending in congress
did not encourage the new officials to interpose a saving hand. Under an
act of June 19, 1860, California was divided into two Indian districts, the
northern and southern, each under a supervising agent, assisted at each reservation by a supervisor and four laborers to teach husbandry. Indians requiring supervision were either to be brought to the reservation to earn their
living if possible, or situations were to be sought for them among farmers.
As a check on the new régime, an agent was sent to ascertain the number
and disposition of the tribes to be taken under guardianship.

The reservations having by this time fallen into utter dilapidation, the
new officials found it almost a matter of necessity to enter into the new economic spirit by recommending the abandonment of several, and to concentrate
their wards. But while the northern superintendent gained approval of his
plan for selling Nome Lacke, Mendocino, and Klamath, as either unsuitable
or worthless, he was not content with the spacious fertile and secluded
Round valley, but undertook upon his own responsibility to remove some

2,000 northern Indians to Smith river, in Del Norte, and rent farming land at the exorbitant rate of $5 an acre, while strongly urging the purchase of the entire valley. In the south, Fresno and King river farms were abandoned, and in 1863 El Tejon, under the cumulative disadvantages of droughts and rentals. Tule farm became the headquarters for a small proportion of the neglected San Joaquin tribes. The fact was that these Indians had become sufficiently quiet and well-behaved to inspire no further fears, and so they were cast adrift to starve. They might have taken a lesson from their brethren of the Klamath region, who, by pursuing the different course of ravaging, burning, and killing among the settlers, were in 1864, under the Trinity war treaty, rewarded with the special Hoopa valley reservation, bought for them at a considerable sum.

The absurdity of keeping two superintendencies for the diminished government farms of the state led in 1863 to their consolidation, and shortly after the commissioner awoke to the expediency of establishing schools for his wards. He resolved, moreover, to try the effects of missionary labor as an economizing factor, and in teaching the Indians the soothing virtues of meekness under the purifying ordeal of land spoliation and neglect to which their Christian fathers at Washington were submitting them. Notwithstanding all efforts to curtail expenses, the estimates continued to grow, as did the number of pensioners—in the reports—till the government, in despair over the general dishonesty and inefficiency among its agents, in 1869 made a sweeping change, and intrusted the management of the northern and central Indians of the United States to the Society of Friends, and the rest to army officers. Gen. McIntosh accordingly took control in California. But congress objecting to such employment for army men, and as the Friends had proved a success, the president in the following year invited other religious denominations to assume the charge. The methodists were allowed to recommend agents for the three reservations now left in the state, Hoopa and Round valleys and Tule river, and they in due time reported direct to Washington, the superintendent being dispensed with. The religious domination was not entirely a success, yet since then the administration has been more satisfactory, although only a small proportion of the natives enjoy the benefits of the reservations. In San Joaquin valley the Tule farm was abandoned for a sterile expanse of wooded mountain country on the south fork of the Tule, with not over 250 arable acres, selected in 1873, upon which less than one fourth of the agency population could manage to hold out. The rest, in this and other parts of California, had to support themselves elsewhere as best they were able, with occasional aid from the headquarters, or with mere advice from special agents, who undertook to procure them work and fair treatment among the settlers. The most glaring of the general injustice and neglect fell to the lot of the mission Indians, those who had once occupied the missions, and assisted with their labor to transform the southern region from a wilderness into a flourishing colony, with fields and orchards and stately temples. The secularization of the missions in the thirties was a premature act which opened the door for despoiling these, the real owners, of their interest in the mission lands and improvements; and heedless of their rights, the Mexican officials transferred all in vast grants to strangers, including the very ground on which they had reared their humble cabins. The United States courts confirmed the titles, at least without a thought for the natives. For a long time the federal government regarded them vaguely as citizens, and many were such under the treaty of Guadalupe Hidalgo, yet the advantages of citizenship were withheld, notably at the land and registration offices. It required the fear of a bread riot in 1857 to gain attention for them. Soon after they were in a measure recognized as wards by the appointment of agents to assist them with seed, implements, and a weak solution of advice, and in 1870 were assigned to them the valleys of Pala and San Pascual as a reservation. This tardy act of partial justice roused the hatred of the surrounding settlers. A rush was made for these hitherto neglected tracts; the natives were threatened with dire calamities if they

should dare to accept the gift, and their consequent reluctance assisted so
well the appeal to congress that the grant was annulled.   Encouraged by
their success, land-grabbers began to oust the Indians, even from their homesteads, occupied by them for generations, but for which they had failed, as
non-citizens, or through ignorance, to obtain preëmption or other title deed.
Grant-holders also joined in ejecting them, and in removing ancient rancherías to quiet titles and sell the land.   Even their scanty personal property
was sold to cover the cost of such iniquitous judgments.   This satire on justice soothed the government for another decade before it was roused to some
sense of its obligations, and consented to set aside for them a portion of the
comparatively worthless tracts unoccupied by land-grabbers, chiefly in San
Diego, and to give aid toward establishing schools.   Blushing at this stigma
upon the nation, upon humanity, certain fair-minded men undertook to
champion the cause of the oppressed.   They clamored at the doors of justice
for three decades before a hearing was accorded them, and then came a small
concession to the mission Indians, some refuse land on the outskirts of the
valleys which their fathers had transformed into gardens; the rest, nothing.
They might have taken lessons from more savage tribes, which gained
prompt and favorable attention by ravaging the homesteads of white men,
and slaughtering their wives and children, after the manner of the white
men in their outrages upon Indians.   The progress lately exhibited by different California tribes, once among the lowest in the scale of culture, affords
the most flattering hopes for the future, and our duty and interest to assure
their realization are the more concerned when we consider the influence of
soil and climate toward a probable final predominance of the aboriginal type
among dwellers in America.

CHAPTER XIX.

INCEPTION OF RAILWAY ROUTES.

1832–1862.

EARLY TRANSCONTINENTAL EXPEDITIONS—WAGON-ROAD PROJECTS—FIRST RAILROADS IN AMERICA—AGITATIONS AND PROJECTS FOR AN OVERLAND RAILWAY—CARVER, PLUMBE, WHITNEY, WILKES, AND OTHERS —THE STATES MOVING—MEETINGS AND CONVENTIONS—THE QUESTION IN CONGRESS—PACIFIC RAILROAD BILLS—THE ACT OF 1862.

BEFORE the average American statesman began seriously to consider that proposition in our politics called the Monroe doctrine, there were a few sagacious men who foresaw the Americanization of the continent, and discussed it, chief among whom was Thomas Jefferson. The question which presented itself to his mind most strongly after obtaining an acceptable treaty with England giving us a boundary to the Pacific, was how to bind the west coast of America to the territories stretching to the Atlantic on the east. Such a navy as ours could not hold it against the other navies of the world; nor could isolated military stations, such as Spain had used to frighten away sea-rovers, prevent other nations from erecting forts and disputing with us our claim. If we were to be a homogeneous people from the Pacific to the Atlantic, we must have free communication; but how?

This question led to the explorations of Lewis and Clarke in 1804–6, proving that nature had interposed no insurmountable obstacles to the establishment of a road to the mouth of the Columbia river, whence the enthusiastic traveller could almost scent the breezes of far-famed Cathay.

To the establishment of a highway of such length and importance much thought must be given, and the best routes sought out. This led to other expeditions[1] to and through the mountain ranges which ran tranversely to the general direction of such a road. The early surveys of Lewis and Clark, Pike, and Long did not contemplate a scheme for a continent-spanning railroad; for railroads, it is unnecessary to remark, did not come into use until many years after these surveys were in progress.[2] When Jefferson thought of a route to the mouth of the Columbia he contemplated a wagon-road only, and the route to be selected had reference to climate, grass, water, fuel, and safety from Indian hostilities.

It is one of the peculiarities of our institutions that while congress debates upon the propriety of an undertaking, the people get so far along in the prosecution of it that the government feels forced to lend its aid. The wagon-road to the Columbia, which was to give us "the most direct route to the Indies," was established by the people. American fur companies not only opened a track to and beyond the South pass, but by their reports to the government, they

The early expeditions ordered by congress have all been treated of in other volumes, and the whole subject of congressional action in connection with the Oregon question and a route to the Columbia has been considered in my *Oregon I*, and *Northwest Coast II*. Some other surveys will be referred to in their proper places.

[2] The first railroad in America was the Quincy, Mass., railroad built in 1825–6, 4 miles in length, used for carrying quarried stone. The second was. the Mauch Chunk and Lehigh, 13 miles long. The first locomotives were imported from England where Stephenson was experimenting, and used by the Delaware and Hudson Canal company in running from Housedale to the terminus of their canal. In 1827 the Maryland legislature chartered the first railroad company in America, with a capital stock of $500,000. The use of locomotives was not contemplated, but horse power was used, relays of horses being kept at the stations on the road. Hence the name of Relay House at the junction of the main line with the Washington branch, which is still retained. In 1830 Peter Cooper, since of New York, built at Baltimore a locomotive weighing one ton or thereabouts, with which he drew an open car filled with the directors of the road and their friends, at the rate of 18 miles an hour. This was the first locomotive for railroad purposes ever built in the U. S. From this time improvements in railroad construction were rapid, and passenger transportation was carried on in several of the states previous to 1840. In 1844 there were 2,278 miles of railroads in the U. S.

served as explorers and surveyors. The agitation of the Oregon question in congress for years produced no other result than that of prompting the people of the western and south-western states to emigrate; and they finished out the road to the Columbia and the Sacramento valley, begun by the fur-traders. Their road, and the emigration over it, settled the question of how to make manifest the claim of the United States to a frontage on the Pacific. The government had not a mile of road west of Fort Leavenworth in 1849, at which date there were 150,000 Americans in California and Oregon.

Previous to the conquest of California and the settlement of the Oregon boundary, the war department kept some small expeditions traversing the country west of the Mississippi and along the flanks of the Rocky mountains and beyond; but for manifest reasons proceeded economically and quietly with these explorations. Following the conquest and the gold discovery considerable activity was displayed, the exploration of the western half of the continent affording employment for the army, whose forts furnished points of rendezvous or departure at convenient distances, besides offering protection to engineers in the field.

The gold-hunters of 1849 again relieved the government of the obligation of constructing a road and discovering a route to the Pacific, by finding passes for themselves, as good as any which have ever been discovered.[3] Having no further call to consider the subject of wagon-roads, the war department began about this time to order surveys of sections of routes toward the Pacific, reports of which were laid before congress to be studied by the advocates of a conti-

[3] Lassen's and the Truckee routes were opened by immigrant companies in 1846 and 1848. Companies also came into Cal. by the San Bernardino and Warner passes and Fort Yuma. The railroads can do no better to-day. Truckee is also a very important point on the Central Pacific on account of the lumber and timber supplies to the construction of the road.

nental railway.[4] The greater part of the surveys were upon lines west from the rice and cotton states.

The first person to propose a railway for any portion of the Pacific coast was Hartwell Carver of Rochester, New York, who advocated the construction of a track across the continent, whose western terminus should be on the Columbia river, California not having come into our possession at this period. Considering that the first passenger railway in the United States had been put in operation only two years previous, it was remarkable that Carver, who, by the way, was a grandson of the explorer, Jonathan Carver, should have thought of this means of grasping the commerce of Asia and the eastern isles. He published articles in the New York *Courier and Inquirer* in 1832, and memorialized congress on the subject from 1835 to 1839. For a while Asa Whitney gave him support, but finding much opposition in certain quarters, abandoned him, and Carver continued to petition for a charter for fifteen years more, spending forty years of his life and $23,000 of his own money in endeavoring to float the project. He had for his reward in 1869 a free pass over a railway to the Pacific!

Carver's plan was that congress should give him and his associates an exclusive and perpetual charter for a railroad and telegraph line from Lake Michigan to the South pass, with branches to San Francisco bay and the mouth of the Columbia river, with a belt of land the whole distance, and stone, iron, and lead from the public quarries and mines, and the privilege of purchasing 8,000,000 acres of selected lands at a dollar and a quarter an acre, which was to be paid for with the stock of the company as the road became

[4] *U. S. Sen.Ex. Doc.* 64, 31 cong., 1 sess., *Id.*, 56–7; *U. S. Sen. Ex. Doc.* 3, *Spec. Sess.*, March,1851; *Oregon*, ii. 81–3; *U. S. H. Ex. Doc.* 1, 31 cong., 2 sess.; *Brackett's Cavalry*, 126–7; *U. S. H. Ex. Doc.* 5, pt i., 182, 185–6, 188; *U. S.H. Ex. Doc.* 51, 31 cong., 1 sess.; *U. S. Sen. Doc.* 81, 31 cong., 1 sess.; *Carson's Early Recoll.*, MS 50; *U. S. Sen. Doc.* 54 32 cong., 1 sess.; *Pac. R. R. Rept*, xi.

finished. The answer of the people in conventions to this proposition was that congress had no constitutional right to enter into any stock jobbing operations with their means. Carver had good ideas of railroad building and equipment for those times. His road was to be laid upon stone foundations; the time from San Francisco to New York was to be five days; palace sleeping cars sixteen feet long, with saloon and dining cars, were to be attached. Certainly we have only succeeded in elaborating his plans.

Carver was not without rivals. John Plumbe, afterward a resident of Sacramento county, California, but at the period referred to residing in Dubuque, Iowa, advocated the construction of a railroad from Lake Michigan to Oregon, as early as 1836, and a public meeting was held in Dubuque March 26, 1838, for the purpose of considering how this object was to be accomplished. On the anniversary of that meeting, nine years afterward, another railroad meeting was held at Dubuque, which Plumbe addressed, and at which it was resolved, "That this meeting regard John Plumbe, Esq., our fellow-townsman, as the original projector, (about ten years ago,) of the great Oregon railroad." [5] And such he publicly claimed to be, while stating that the project was regarded by most persons as "visionary and absurd." At the Dubuque convention of 1838 a memorial to congress was drafted, Plumbe being chairman of the committee, " praying for an appropriation to defray the expense of the survey and location of the first link in the great Atlantic and Pacific railroad, namely from the lakes to the Mississippi." Their application was favorably received, an appropriation being made the same year, which was expended under the direction of the secretary of war, the report being of a very favorable character.

[5] *Plumbe's Memorial Against Mr Asa Whitney's Railroad Scheme.* Pamphlet, 47 pp., 19; *Iowa News*, March 24, 1838.

At the session of the Wisconsin legislature of 1839–40 Plumbe was present, and drafted a memorial to congress urging the importance of continuing the work, which he carried to Washington, where he used his best endeavors to secure attention to its petition; but the government being absorbed in other subjects, especially the condition of the treasury, did not again respond. He next visited New England, circulating memorials to congress praying for a further appropriation, all of which was of no effect.

Plumbe's plan for securing means to construct the road, was that a sufficient appropriation of the public lands should be made, in alternate sections, on each side of the line of route; that the company to be chartered should consist of all who chose to participate; that the stock should be divided into twenty million shares, valued at five dollars a share; that twenty-five cents a share be paid in as the first installment, producing five millions with which to commence the work; that when this was expended the sale of the lands should produce the next five millions, and so on to the end. The local business of the road would, it was said, support it as fast as completed. But this plan contemplated the building of not more than a hundred miles of road per annum, taking ten years to complete the first thousand miles, or twenty years from the Missouri to the Pacific. This memorial was accompanied by a bill, which was defeated in congress by the southern members, who liked not that the road should go so far north.[6]

These were not the only pretenders to the distinction of having projected a transcontinental railroad.[7]

---

[6] *Or. Archives*, MS., p. 197.

[7] Lewis Gaylord Clarke, in the *Knickerbocker Magazine*, in 1836, claimed to have originated the idea. Lilburn W. Boggs, once governor of Missouri, since a resident of Napa, Cal., wrote an article in 1843 on the subject of a Pacific railroad estimating the cost intended, for the *St Louis Republican*, but which, for some reason, was never published. It is in the possession of his son, W. M. Boggs, of Napa. Benton also predicted in a speech in St Louis in 1844, that men full grown at that time would yet see Asiatic commerce crossing the Rocky mountains by rail.

The most conspicuous for a time was Asa Whitney, of New York. He had passed many years in China, and was thoroughly imbued with a conviction of the advantages to accrue to the United States by becoming the carriers of the great oriental traffic with Europe. Whitney's plan was to connect Lake Michigan by rail, with Puget Sound or the Columbia river, or both. He made an extensive exploration in 1845, of the region between the Mississippi and Missouri rivers, finding no obstacle to railroad building in 500 miles of the route west. But he demanded of congress a strip of land sixty miles wide, along the whole length of the road, or 92,160,000 acres, with their agricultural, mineral, and lumber products. With no other capital he offered to build a road, selling the land to raise the means, but retaining for himself and his heirs all that remained unsold after its completion. As to a tariff, he offered, if the government would allow him to charge one-half cent per ton per mile on ordinary freight for all distances over 200 miles, to carry the same any shorter distances for one-half the price charged on the principal railroads in the United States, to transport Indian corn across the continent for twenty cents a bushel, flour for $1.25 per barrel, and passengers for half the usual price, during the first twenty years after its completion. He also offered to carry the public mails, troops, and munitions of war free of charge for the same period, and after that date congress might make any alteration in the tolls which was deemed expedient.

Whitney's project occasioned much discussion and partisanship, there being able writers among its friends and foes.[8] Some argued against it as threatening a monopoly imperial in wealth and resources, and a standing menace to the government, with power at least to influence congress in the election of representatives, if not to divide the country into sec-

[8] *American Review*, i. 424–32; *Niles' Reg.*, lxix. 105; *Or. Spectator*, Feb. 18, 1847.

tions by a principality through its centre. Others
argued in favor of a national railroad, controlled by
the government; while others still declared it would
impoverish the public treasury to build the road.

Meanwhile another project was started in 1845 by
George Wilkes, which differed from Whitney's in dispensing with a land grant, and requiring the government to construct the road.   He held that the mere
fact of an official survey would so enhance the value
of the public lands that capitalists would hasten to invest money in the enterprise, supplying the means for
working expenses.   The friends of a national railroad
supported Wilkes' scheme.   Whitney's memorial was
presented to the house of representatives in January
1845, and Wilkes' in December of the same year.
The public journals of the country discussed the subject in all its bearings, and according to their lights.
There was mentioned in the *New York Sun* in 1846, a
project by a Canadian company to build a line of railroad from Halifax to Quebec, with a view to its ultimate extension to the Columbia river.   The Canadian
plan contemplated a free grant of all unlocated crown
lands through which the road should pass, together with
the privilege of using timber and other material necessary to the construction of the work; a preëmptive right
to the shareholders to purchase lands in certain situations upon certain favorable terms; and a pledge from
the provincial government, guaranteeing five per cent
interest on all moneys invested.⁹

Soon after the presentation of Whitney's memorial to congress, public meetings began to be held in
different parts of the union, to approve or condemn
the various methods proposed.¹⁰   Congress was disposed to consider the proposition of Whitney; at

⁹ *Or. Spectator*, Sept. 3, 1846.   After the conclusion of the boundary treaty
of June 15, 1846, nothing further was heard of the Canadian project, though
a book was published in London, at a later date, advocating a Pacific R. R.
Sac. Transcript, (*Extr. Ed.*) March 14, 1851.

¹⁰ See account of a large public meeting at Canton, Ohio, Feb. 4, 1846.
Ohio Repository, (Canton), Feb. 12, 1846.

least it found favor with the senate committee of
1846, which brought in a bill; but the friends of a
national road met it at every point and prevented its
passage. The opening of the following year witnessed
a still greater agitation on the subject, as evidenced
by the railroad conventions in the large cities and
smaller towns.[11] The acquisition of a vast amount of
land stretching to, and along, the Pacific to the 49th
parallel, much of which lay in a line with the slave
states, and was adapted to slave labor, gave to the
question a new significance, and aroused the caution
of southern politicians. It was not so much now,
whether the road should be built with the people's
lands,[12] to enrich private corporations, or how much
time would be consumed in building it,[13] as it would

[11] Railroad meetings were held at Galena, Ill., April 2; at Bloomington,
Ind., April 7; and at Burlington, Iowa, April 9, 1847. *Plumbe's Memorial
Against Asa Whitney's Railroad Scheme,* 28.

[12] Wilkes, in a letter to a chairman of a committee of congress, enumerated the main points of his proposal as follows: 1st, that the road be built
and owned by the government; 2nd, that its construction and control be
confided to sworn commissioners to be appointed by the state legislatures, or
elected by the people of the various states; 3d, that it start from the line of
the Missouri in the vicinity of the parallel which strikes the South pass, and
thence run westwardly over territories under the jurisdiction of the general
government; 4th, that its revenues be confined strictly to the measure of
its expenses of attendance and repairs, and that it be open to foreigners and
their merchandise on the same terms as to our own citizens—the latter to be
secured by regulations of debenture, returning all customs charges on such
merchandise on its reshipment. Lastly, that it be built out of the public
treasury, without any allotment of the public lands for sale for that purpose.
' I believe that any measure that would subject the public lands to the reach
and appropriation of speculators, or indeed that would dispose of them to
any but actual settlers, would be highly unpopular, and would excite a wide
and determined opposition throughout the country. I think, therefore, that
the most just as well as most satisfactory disposal of these lands would be
to insert in the bill recommending the road—if such should be the decision of
the committee—securing to each laborer or mechanic who shall have worked
upon it for one year, 100 acres of land along, or contiguous to the line. This
regulation, instead of making a few rich men richer, would make prosperous
land-holders of the most deserving poor, and while it conferred a priceless
population on the west, would perform the highest achievement of republican philanthrophy, by elevating labor to its true importance in the social
scale.' *Speech of William M. Hall, of N. Y., in favor of the National Railroad
to the Pacific, at the Great Chicago Convention of July 7, 1847.*

[13] A committee of Boston men, consisting of William Ingalls, E. H.
Derby, I. C. Dunn, P. P. F. Degrand, and O. D. Ashley, in 1849, propounded
this question to the N. Y. chamber of commerce: Assuming that Whitney
would build ten miles of road this year, take another year to sell the land,
and three years more to get the money, being thus at the end of five years
prepared to build the next ten miles, and so on, would it not take him 850

be laid out on a route far enough south to enhance
the value of lands south of the Missouri compromise
line, and prevent the preponderance of settlement
north of it.

Through this anxiety of the south it was that the
army engineers were so industriously employed in
exploring the territory between the Arkansas and the
Colorado rivers during the administration of President
Polk.   Meanwhile, discussion [14] revealed the difficulties as well as the advantages attending the construction of a Pacific railroad, chief among the former
being the obtainment of capital [15] and labor.   To procure the latter, it was proposed to organize a vast
system of immigration from the eastern states and
Europe, the workmen to be part paid in land, and a
corps to be detailed to prepare a part of each farm for
cultivation, so that when the laborers of the second
year should go forward, they would leave behind them
those of the first as farmers and guardsmen of the
road.   By this process "many millions" of poor and
oppressed people would be raised to the dignity of free-
holding American citizens.   This charitable scheme
in all its simplicity fell through along with the rest.
The discovery of gold following the conquest of Cali-

years to make 1700 miles of road? or if 'by a stretch of imagination,' he
should build ten miles of road, sell his land, and get his pay all in one year,
would it not even then take him 170 years to build 1700 miles !   This objection, remarks Plumbe, should be sufficient to condemn Mr Whitney's scheme.
Plumbe's Memorial, 3

[14] In an article in the *Merchants' Magazine* for Oct. 1847, vol. xvii., p. 385,
the editor presents a letter of Zadock Pratt, of Prattsville, endorsing Whitney's plan, and remarks that he—the editor—in the latter part of 1844 predicted that 'those persons are now living who will see a railroad connecting
New York with the Pacific.'   Here is another person who claims to have
uttered this prophecy in nearly the identical words of Benton in his St Louis
speech on the railroad to the Pacific.

[15] An article in *De Bow's Indust. Res.*, 499–500, makes an estimate, placing
the cost of grading, bridging, etc., west from Lake Michigan at $5,000 per mile
for 2,630 miles, $13,150,000; a bridge across the Mississippi, $800,000; superstructure, single track, depots, turn-out, etc., for 2,730, at $10,500 per mile,
$28,665,000; locomotives, cars, etc., $10,276,600; contingencies, $2,000,000;
repairs upon road until completion, and before earning its own support,
$15,000,000, or a total of $69,891,600.   The figures in De Bow's article are
not quite the same as mine, an error in computing making his figures foot up
$69,226,600.   Less sanguine calculators estimated the entire cost at
$100,000,000.

fornia imparted fresh interest to the subject. In 1848, resolutions began to pour in to congress from the legislatures of the different states,[16] approving of Whitney's plan, and the grant of nearly 100,000,000 acres of the public lands for the purpose of carrying it out. Mr McClelland, from the select committee of the house of representatives appointed to consider the various memorials concerning the proposed railroad, reported a bill, May 3d, to set apart and sell to Whitney a portion of the public lands to enable him to commence the construction of it, which was referred to the committee of the whole on the state of the union, and ordered printed. On the 23d of June, Mr Pollock from the same committee made a report to accompany the bill, which was laid on the table. This bill was the first favorable official act by this branch of the government.

In the senate, June 26th, Mr Borland, from the committee on public lands, on the memorial of Whitney relative to a railroad to the Pacific, reported a joint resolution, providing for a survey and exploration of one or more routes from the Mississippi river, below the falls of St Anthony, to the Pacific, under the direction of the secretary of war.[17] From this

[16] Tennessee and New Jersey set the example in 1848 of sustaining Whitney, which was followed by Indiana, Illinois, New York, Connecticut, Maine, New Hampshire, Vermont, Rhode Island, Georgia, Maryland, Alabama, Ohio, Kentucky, Pennsylvania, and the senate of Michigan; in 11 of the states almost unanimously.

[17] On the 27th of June, Mr Niles obtained the unanimous consent of the senate to introduce a bill to set apart and sell to Whitney a portion of the public lands to enable him to build a railroad from Lake Michigan to the Pacific. The bill was referred to a select committee consisting of senators Niles, Corwin, Lewis, Dix, and Felch. *Cong. Globe*, 1847–8, 903. On the 29th of July, Niles moved to take up the bill granting Whitney a tract of the public land, when senators Hale and Benton spoke strongly against the motion, the latter moving to lay Niles' motion on the table, which motion was carried by a vote of 27 to 21. On the 8th of Aug., Niles made an attempt to bring forward the Whitney bill by inserting it as an amendment to a bill granting right of way and a donation of land for building a railroad from Mobile to the mouth of the Ohio river, but was subsequently induced to withdraw his amendment. *Cong. Globe*, 1847–8, pp. 1011, 1051. On the 29th of Jan., 1849, Niles again moved to take up the Whitney bill, urging the peculiar interests existing in Cal. at that time, and the need there was of quick communication through territory of our own. Borland opposed Niles' motion, and stated that he was directed by the committee on public lands to urge a joint resolution adverse to Whitney, and merely authorizing the sec.

time forward the subject was continually before congress.

Benton, who had formerly been so strong an advocate of the route to the Columbia via the South pass,
had changed his views, according to reports from his
son-in-law, Frémont, and on the 7th of February,
1849, introduced a bill to provide for a central
national road, from St Louis to the Pacific ocean at
San Francisco, with a branch to the Columbia. He
advocated a national road because it was impolitic and
illegal for private citizens to treat with the Indians
for the extinguishment of their title, and impossible
for them to protect the road after it should be built;
and because he questioned the propriety of allowing
individuals to become proprietors of such a road; and
denounced all the schemes presented as stock-jobbing
machines for the markets of Europe and America.[18]

of war to direct surveys to be made to the Pacific to determine the better
route, which could never be known except by the comparison of several.
Finally, however, Niles' motion was agreed to, and the bill taken up, when
Senator Foote offered to amend as follows: That after the crossing of the
Missouri the road should be built in a southwest direction as far as the features of the country would permit, and pass the Rocky mountains at some
point south of the South pass, the terminus being at Monterey; but if no
practicable route should be found in that direction, then the road should run
to the Paso del Norte, and thence to San Diego, keeping within U. S. territory. After this road was completed, Whitney should have power to build
a branch to the Columbia, or north of it, and should have the same grant of
thirty miles on each side of the road that he would have for the main line.
Borland followed by a second amendment to strike out all of the original bill
after the enacting clauses, and insert a direction to the secretary of war to
employ the topographical corps to explore such routes from the lakes, or
from the Mississippi below the falls of St Anthony, to the Pacific as might
be deemed fitting, and to report to congress the result of their explorations
at an early date. *Cong. Globe*, 1848-9, vol. 20, p. 381-2.

[18] His bill appropriated a sum of money to enable the president to conciliate the Indians, and extinguish title to as much land as might be required
for the purposes of the road; and proposed that 75 per cent of the proceeds
of all public lands in Oregon and Cal., and 50 per cent of the proceeds of the
sale of public lands in the states, should be set apart to defray the expenses
of the contemplated railroad. The bill reserved a strip of land one mile in
breadth for the whole length of the railway, for the purpose of maintaining
all manner of roads. 'I propose to reserve ground for all sorts of roads—
railway, plank, macadamized; more than that, room for a track by magnetic
power, according to the idea started, I believe, by Prof. Henry, and, to me,
plausibly pursued by Prof. Page, of the patent office, if that idea ripens into
practicability—and who can undertake to say that any idea will not become
practicable in the present age? But, Mr President, the bill contains another
provision, that there shall be a margin reserved out of this breadth for a plain
old English road, such as we have been accustomed to all our lives—a road

On the 17th of February, 1849, Borland presented a petition to the senate from citizens of Arkansas, asking for aid for the construction of a railroad from Memphis to the Pacific, which was laid on the table; and on the same day Houston asked and obtained leave to introduce a bill authorizing the Galveston and Red river railroad company to construct a railway to the Pacific ocean in California, which was referred to the committee on territories.

In May, Whitney published, in pamphlet form, an elaborate argument against all the other various schemes, and in support of his own, among which he included the improbability of an appropriation of money for such a work, the time it would take to complete surveys under the government, and the difficulty, if not impossibility, of fixing upon a route, because it would be made a sectional question between the north and south, which years of legislation could not adjust; but allowing that this question should be settled, and the work commenced, it would soon become a powerful party engine to agitate the whole country; in fact, it could only be commenced by a party vote, and if commenced at all, would draw the means from one section of the union to be squandered

on which the farmer in his wagon or carriage, on horse or on foot, may travel, without fear and without tax, with none to run over him or make him jump out of the way. I look forward to the time when this whole continent is to be settled from one end to the other, when there are towns and villages upon it, when neighbors will want a convenient road. They may there find a space for them in which they shall not give way to the cars or anything else—a road not to be interfered with.' *Cong. Globe*, 1848-9, 470-4; *De Bow's Indust. Res.*, ii. 498. What romantic dreams, what freaks of fancy, what bubbles of imagination our great men indulged in only forty years ago! The brain of the world was teeming with ill-digested ideas. New discoveries in science, new fields of enterprise and thought marked the period as an extraordinary one, and men, while half understanding whither they were being carried, were unappalled by the most giant undertakings. In the midst of these, Senator Benton could stop to rhapsodize over the grant of a wagon road which could be of use only to those following the line of the railroad from east to west, while the continent on either side of it was as trackless as ever. One thousand feet of ground in breadth should be reserved in like manner along the line of the branch to the Columbia; military posts were to be erected at certain intervals, and a telegraph line stretched from ocean to ocean. It was easy to see that Benton was still largely under the influence of his early Oregon sympathies, somewhat warped and turned aside by southern views, and perhaps looking to the future of his daughter's husband.

in another upon the hirelings of aspirants to office, becoming fifty times more potent and obnoxious than a United States bank, or any other question that had ever excited the people. The business of a thoroughfare so immense would absorb and control the entire legislation of the country. This, and more, said Mr Whitney against a national road, and he clinched his arguments with estimates of cost and comparison of routes which were to the majority of northern readers conclusive.[19] He was sustained, too, by such authority as Captain Charles Wilkes, whose opinion had weight from the knowledge possessed by him of west coast topography, although that had little to do with the political view of the subject.[20] Another naval officer, Lieutenant M. F. Maury, took a different view. While conceding that an interoceanic railroad was of the highest importance, he took the position that geographically Monterey was the point in California most central to the commerce of the world, and therefore the proper point for the eastern terminus was at Memphis.[21]

The people of St Louis held a preliminary meeting in the spring of 1849, at which it was resolved that a national convention, consisting of delegates from every state in the union, should be invited to assemble in that city on the 16th of October, to give expression to the will of the American people. Only fourteen states accepted the invitation, the only southern delegates present being from Louisiana, unless Virginia, Kentucky, and Tennessee be classed as southern. It will be noticed that in none of the public discussions of Pacific railroad matters did the Carolinas take any part, and seldom the New England states. This was partly from sectional apathy, and partly, also, from political prejudices. The 835 delegates present at St Louis in October were chiefly

---

[19] *A Project for a Railroad to the Pacific*, by Asa Whitney, New York, 1849; *Hunt's Merchants' Magazine*, xxi. 72–9.
[20] *Western America*, by Charles Wilkes, Phil., 1849.
[21] *Hunt's Merch. Mag.*, xviii. 592–601.

from the central and western states. As might have been anticipated, Senator Benton was a prominent figure at this convention. He attempted to describe a route across the Rocky mountains for which Frémont had been looking when he became lost in the snow, but which he had never seen, and only took for granted because Frémont's guide had told him of the existence of a pass between the parallels of 38° and 39°. A railroad does now indeed traverse a pass in this latitude, but the route through the cañon of the Arkansas river was not one to be recommended for a great national highway, especially if a wagon-road were to accompany it, as Benton proposed. Unfortunately for his prepossessions, a committee appointed at the mass-meeting in the spring to collect facts had brought in a report of fifty or more printed pages, in favor of the South pass,[22] which he was compelled to present to the convention. "The South pass," said the senator, "though good in itself, has never met the approbation of Mr Frémont for the road to California. It is too far north. He wanted a road three or four degrees further south, and has found it, and gives the country the benefit of it." But John Laughborough, of Missouri, would not accept it, and presented his views so convincingly that he carried the convention with him, and was thanked by resolution. The meeting was adjourned to convene at Philadelphia in April 1850.[23]

[22] Printed in the St Louis *Western Journal*, a periodical of that city.

[23] With regard to the Frémont-Benton route, known as the central, Frémont was deceived by the representations of Maxwell, St Vrain, Beaubien, and Wootten, all of whom had large grants of land on the eastern slope of the great range, in the latitude to which Frémont, upon their description, gave his endorsement. The *Santa Fé Gazette*, Oct. 8, 1853, remarks upon this subject, that Benton's route was not practicable, and a railroad through the passes indicated by him not possible. 'Among the gentlemen from whom we obtained this information was Capt. St Vrain. He stated to us and others during last spring, that the idea of locating a railroad through the country mentioned in Leroux's letter to Col Benton was ridiculous and absurd,' etc. Yet St Vrain had been president of a public meeting in Taos, at which James H. Quinn had said of Frémont's route, 'Our fellow citizen, Richings L. Wootten, has just returned from an expedition to California, on the continuation of the route that Frémont was following. He declares that the route is most excellent, etc. Robidoux, he said, left the Arkansas

510 INCEPTION OF RAILWAY ROUTES.

The next convention occurred at Memphis in October 1849, at which the flowery and fiery advocates of the southern route presented their arguments.[24] New Orleans and Boston had also their railroad mass-meetings and conventions in 1849.

The Boston plan was to secure means by a government loan, and to entrust the construction to a company. The author of this plan was P. P. T. Degrand, who offered to build from St Louis to San Francisco[25] in four years, by employing two sets of laborers relieving each other day and night, and at the most difficult points a third party.

with wagons in 1840, for Cal., but left them at the Caochetopa pass, on account of the difficulty of cutting out the timber, which would be of great advantage to the railroad. *Hayes' Scraps, San Diego*, ii. 122.

[24] The delegates of western Texas presented an address in behalf of a route through the San Saba valley from Memphis to San Diego. After presenting the facts of distance, climate and topography, they say, "Within half a century we will have a population of 25,000,000 on the Pacific slope. That slope is now separated from us by the almost impassable barriers of a mountain and a desert. This mountain must be made smooth—this desert must be made to blossom as the rose. This people, blood of our blood, flesh of our flesh, must be brought to our doors. Social reasons urge it, political reasons require it, commercial reasons imperatively demand it. The east, the gorgeous east, will be opened to our commerce without a rival, a competitor. The east, not more celebrated in song for its perfume-bearing breezes and balmy clime, for its sacred legends and mystic lore, than in more staid and sober history for the splendor of its empires, the gorgeous magnificence of its palaces and temples, the magnitude of its rivers, the grandeur of its mountains, the fertility of its plains, the abundance of its gold and silver, and its precious stones, its gums, its teas, and its spices, the beauty and costliness of its manufactures, the untold variety of its productions, and for the extent and richness of its commerce—a commerce which has been sought by all nations who have risen to commercial greatness as far back as history reaches into the past, and which has always rewarded the search with countless wealth and unrivalled splendor. A commerce which in ancient times caused the cities of Tyre and Sidon, and Balbec and Palmyra, and Alexandria, each in succession, to rise to such a height of general prosperity, commercial greatness, and refinement in the arts as to excite, even to this day, the wonder and admiration of the world. A commerce which in more modern times caused Constantinople, and Venice, and Genoa, and Lisbon, and Amsterdam, each in their turn to attain ¦the very pinnacle of commercial greatness, and caused them, single as they were, each to excel in the splendor of its achievements in arts and in arms, all the kingdoms and empires then upon the earth. A commerce which has caused Britain to 'wrest the very trident from Neptune himself,' and enabled her to utter the proud boast of 'mistress of the seas.' This commerce with all, all its untold wealth, and its limitless future increase, may be ours—will be ours without the fear of a competitor, if we only reach forth our hands and clutch it." Signed by James W. Allen, T. J. Hardeman, M. Erskine, T. Connelly, Wm E. Jones, and E. Bellenger, in behalf of the Gonzalez convention, Oct. 10, 1849, in *Railroad and Steamships*, doc. viii.

[25] 'I propose that a company, composed of men in whose integrity and steadiness of purpose confidence can be reposed by the nation, be chartered

The proposition to take a government loan removed a difficulty as to the constitutional power of congress to furnish funds for the construction of a national road; there could be no doubt of its right to loan the public credit for the purposes of providing for the national defences, transporting the public mail, etc. There seemed, indeed, in a business point of view, more common sense in the Boston plan than any of those proposed; but, alas! Degrand adopted Benton's and Fremont's still undiscovered route, which could not compete for public favor with the South pass or a more southern line.[26]

After so much discussion of routes it appeared that three roads at least would sometime be demanded. Of the most prominent were the Memphis and San Diego, the St. Louis road proposed by Benton, and the South pass and Columbia river road proposed by Whitney. In the midst of all this talk, the people rushing to the gold mines in 1849 pointed out the way from the Missouri river to the bay of San Francisco. I find it called the "new route" in Loughborough's monograph on the Pacific telegraph and railway of December, 1849. It started from St. Louis and followed the route to Independence, nearly in the track of the early emigration to Oregon, thence north westwardly to Big and Little Blue rivers and

by congress to construct a railroad from St Louis to S. F., with a capital of $100,000,000, and that this company, after having paid in $2,000,000, shall have the right to borrow United States 6 per cent stock to such an amount, not exceeding $98,000,000, as may be sufficient to finish the road and carry it into full operation with a double track. I propose that congress give to this company a strip of the public lands, 10 miles wide on the north side of the road, and the land for the bed of the road, and for depots, and the right to take from the public lands wood, gravel, stone, iron, and other materials necessary to construct the road.' *Address to the People of the United States* in *Railroads and Steamships*, doc. xiii.

[26] The associates of Degrand were William Ingalls, E. H. Derby, S. S. Littlehale, James C. Dunn, Robert F. Fisk, O. D. Ashley. Bayard & Co. also proposed to congress to build a railway from St. Louis to S. F. in 8 years, along the 38th parallel or near it. They offered to deposit $5,000,000 in the U. S. treasury as security for their fidelity to their engagements; but the objections to this were the lack of authority in congress to create corporations; the cost of a railway through the mountains south of the South pass, and the necessity involved in this plan of making the road earn dividends for its stockholders. *Railroads and Steamships. Doc.* ix., p. 20.

the Platte; keeping on the south side of the latter stream to the South fork, which it crossed, and again followed the emigrant route to Laramie and the South pass. From the South pass it still kept on the line of the travelled road, via Sublette's cut-off to Bear river, thence to the Humboldt valley, and through the Truckee pass into the valley of the Sacramento.[27] Two other passes through the Sierra Nevada were mentioned; one leading into the Sacramento valley by following Carson river to its source, and descending the American fork of the Sacramento river; and another proceeding from the sink of the Humboldt south into the valley of the San Joaquin. Among 30,000 men there were enough with clear vision and strong will–albeit they required also toughened muscles —to spy out and lay open passes to the gold mines.

After pointing out the advantages of the Platte and Humboldt route, the pamphleteer makes this reference to a difficulty [28] lying in the way of any road at

[27] W. R. Singleton, who had travelled the Humboldt route to Cal., furnished the itinerary of the route to Loughborough in 1849. Before giving it, he says, 'I shall propose a route, the last portion of which, from the Salt Lake to the bay, was discovered by Mr Peter Ogden, a fur trader in the employ of the Hudson's Bay company, as far back as 1811—which has been repeatedly followed since by intelligent bodies of traders—by which a party of men under the orders of Capt. Bonneville proceeded to S. F. bay, which has been traversed by and described by Bryant, Bidwell, and other travellers; which has been surveyed by Col Fremont, and over which emigrants with families and wagons have repeatedly passed, and more than 30,000 men with 6,000 wagons and 100,000 head of stock are now passing.' *Pacific Telegraph and Railway*, 22. The author is a little out in his dates when he places the discovery of the Humboldt by Ogden in 1811. Maj. Carleton in 1849 presented the *Intelligencer* and the *American Quart. Reg.* of July, 1850, with a tabular account of distances, streams, and resources in the way of wood and grass on the two great routes leading from Fort Leavenworth westward, viz.: from Leavenworth to El Paso, via Santa Fé, and from Leavenworth to Fort Laramie, via Fort Kearney; to El Paso 1104 miles; to Laramie 604 miles; from Fort Pierre on the Missouri to Laramie 326 miles.

[28] 'It is the opinion that congress has no constitutional authority to construct works of this character within the bounds of sovereign states. [To overcome this objection the legislature of Mo. passed an act March 12, 1849, to incorporate the Pacific railroad, and a company was organized under the act in Jan., 1850, which petitioned congress for a grant of land to build it.] Whether the opinion be right or wrong, just or fallacious, well or illy fortified by authority, can make no difference so far as we are concerned. It is a fixed fact that it has always existed, (the right?) and has been acted upon by a large number of our public men in their official capacity, and that a very large portion of the American people, perhaps even a majority, sanction its validity. If the friends of a Pacific railway are wise and discreet they

all and remarks: "We are willing to take advantage of the existence of the constitutional difficulty already alluded to, to make a suggestion, which, if acceded to, will unite every friend of a Pacific railway upon one distinct and clear system, and enable them to compel congress to consummate the work at once. This suggestion is that the general government be memorialized to undertake the construction of a railway from a point at or near the mouth of the Kansas river on our western border to the bay of San Francisco, with a branch to the Columbia river or Puget sound; and that congress be further memorialized to donate to the states so much of the public lands within their borders as may be needful to aid them in the construction of three branches of the Pacific railway from the mouth of the Kansas river to the Mississippi river; the first branch to be taken to St. Louis, the second to Memphis, and the third to such point on the upper Mississippi as will most favorably connect with the great lakes and the lines of railway along their southern shores to eastern cities."

Loughborough's pamphlet, with other propositions, had been placed before the St. Louis and Memphis conventions, and had been digested by the country before the meeting of the convention of April 1, 1850, at Philadelphia, which was presided over temporarily by Joseph R. Ingersoll, member of congress from Pennsylvania; and which elected William B. Ogden of Illinois president. Among the letters received from public men not present was one from Thomas J. Rusk of Texas. Said he; " Let this road be constructed, and there will be no north and no south, no

will take advantage of the existence of this opinion to come to a fair understanding instead of permitting it to hang as a millstone about the neck of the project; and we say to them that nothing is easier to do than this, if they will only divest themselves of sectional and personal motives, and resolve to act in good faith for the advancement of the cause. Three important objects should be kept steadily in view in fixing upon the route and the details of the work. The first object is that of empire; the second that of nationality; and the third a revolution in the commerce of the civilized world.'

east and no west, but our country will be everywhere, and every spot of earth on which our hardy yeomen tread will be their home and the home of their brethren.   All the angry passions which have of late agitated the public mind, breathing forth the unhallowed name of disunion, threatening the very existence of our free institutions, and causing the heart of every patriot to beat quick with dread when he reflects on the bare possibility of such a result, will pass away." [29]

Letters were received from Benton, Orin Fowler, John Robbins Jr, Job Mann, Samuel R. Thurston, Joseph R. Chandler, Thomas Ewing, Charles E. Clarke, James M. Porter, John Cessna of the Pennsylvania legislature, and W. Milnor Roberts.   Frémont also sent a letter to the convention, accompanied by a map which was a delineation of the Benton-Frémont route, running from St Louis to Independence, along the Kansas river to Bent Fort on the Arkansas, thence through the great mountain chain, not by the grand cañon of the Arkansas, but south of it where no pass exists, and in a general northwest course to White river, up the Uintah river, and over the dividing ridge separating the waters of the Pacific from those of the great basin, to the foot of Great Salt Lake; thence in a northwest course to Pilot knob at the head of Humboldt valley, and down it, through the Truckee pass into the Sacramento valley. As compared with the South pass route, it was one full of difficulties, and, as the map presented to the convention shows, was one with which its author was not personally acquainted, and for which he had no other authority than hearsay.   It was an effort to establish a line as nearly direct as possible between St Louis and San Francisco; and, perchance, to make political capital thereby.

All the plans ever broached were reconsidered. Stevens, delegate from that state, presented the plan

---

[29] *Proceedings of the Convention in favor of a National Railroad to the Pacific Ocean through the Territories of the United States,* Phila, 1850, 9,

of Rhode Island as agreed upon at a meeting held
March 20th at Providence.   Jacob Dewees, of Pennsylvania, offered a project which included a system of
railroads from the several Atlantic ports to converge
at St Louis as the eastern terminus of Pacific railway.   Delegate Robinson of Indiana spoke in favor
of Whitney's proposition.   Joel B. Sutherland argued
in favor of a national road.   "No man living," said
he "ought to have the power of building this road
vested in him and his heirs—nor should any company
have that grant made to it;" and he gave his reasons,
which do not particularly concern us at this day.

The committee on resolutions resolved that it was
the duty of congress "in some way to apply the ener-
gies of our country," so as to secure the earliest possible completion of a Pacific railroad; that the work
was national and should be constructed by national
means; but to avoid state and local prejudices, the
government should confine its operations to the country beyond the limits of the organized states, leaving
the branches to be constructed by those states; that
liberal appropriations of the public lands should be
made to aid said states; and that congress be memo-
riialized on the subject of a survey by competent
engineers of all the routes considered practicable.

Morrison of Pennsylvania spoke against the resolutions.   He favored Whitney's plan, as it interested
the working classes.   John Biddle, of Michigan, and
S. R. Curtis, of Iowa, sustained the resolutions, favoring a national road, and its immediate commencement.   The resolutions were finally adopted.   Elder
of Pennsylvania offered a resolution, which was lost,
that the president of the convention appoint one
delegate from each of the states present, to present a
report on the most feasible route.   Solomon W.
Roberts moved that the committee recommend to the
American people, in every part of the country, to
urge upon congress, by numerous petitions, to make
an early and ample appropriation for surveys of the

most feasible routes for the construction of a railroad to California and Oregon, from the valley of the Mississippi; which was adopted.

Camp, of New York, offered a resolution that the electors of the United States should be recommended to vote for no man at the ensuing election for members of congress who opposed the construction of a Pacific railroad. This motion proving inadmissible, even when amended by T. B. Florence to the effect that " the people in their primary assemblies " should pass resolutions in favor of the railroad, it was tabled. There was danger enough of the matter getting into politics without resolving it there. President Ogden, in an interesting speech, gave his views of the nation's ability to build the road.[30]

A memorial to congress was adopted, presenting the proceedings of the convention, and calling attention to the subject, but, leaving all definite plans to the wisdom of that body.

The subject of an inter oceanic railroad might be now said to be before the people and congress in all its bearings. So far as the public were concerned, its individual writers and speakers exhibited a commendable degree of interest;[31] but the inertia of great bodies has passed into a problem.

Explorations had been ordered for military posts and routes, with the incidental view of learning more about the country belonging to us, through which we might sometime desire to travel in comfort in railway

[30] Our war with Mexico and the purchase of California had cost us $70,000,000. We owed more than that from 1790 to 1800, when we were, as a nation, very poor, and numbered in population no more than four or five millions. In 1816 our national debt was $127,000,000, and our population less than 9,000,000; but in 1836 this debt was extinguished and we had $40,000,000 surplus in the treasury soon after, which congress distributed among the states for want of some object to apply it to. How trifling then would be a debt of $170,000,000 now, when we had a population of 23,000,000 in an unexampled state of prosperity, even if the outlay were to return us nothing. But judging by the business of the Erie canal, which had been scoffed at in its inception, it would greatly increase the wealth of the country, and that very rapidly.

[31] *Hunt's Merch. Mag.*, xxiii. 123–4; *Id.*, xxii. 149; *Amer. Quart. Reg.*, iv. 590–6; *Rev. Calvin Cotter's Lecture on the Railroad to the Pacific*, Aug. 12, 1850; New York, 1850. *Cal. Past and Present*, 192.

coaches. What more, indeed, could have been reasonably expected before the gold discoveries caused the unprecedented migration of 1849. In his messages of 1849 and 1850, the president made some suggestions to congress concerning overland communication; and in the debates of that body upon the several projects before it, the majority leaned toward Whitney's plan, although Plumbe still urged his scheme, and Benton his route.[32] Several bills were introduced which did not change the outlook for any. De Bow's *Southern Review* for December 1849, commenting on the reports of the committees of both houses of congress, said: "Although we have always been disposed to press a more southern route than that proposed by Mr Whitney, for a railroad to the Pacific ocean, we have never once doubted of the practicability and great commercial value of his, and that in its plan and details it embraces the only constitutional mode of effecting the great work, whether through the agency of that gentleman or through any one else." The writer, after presenting a favorable argument, considered nationally, for Whitney's scheme presented the southern view of the case upon two propositions: 1st, the route proposed was all on free soil; 2nd, the building of the road would greatly accelerate the settlement of the entire line to the Pacific, and it was feared such a result would be prejudicial to the south by increasing a population hostile to its institutions. The question, it was declared, must be settled at the coming session of congress, as after that period the land reformers of the north who were giving away the public lands to make capital against

---

[32] *Review of the reports of congress committee on R. R., with remarks from De Bow's Southern Review,* Dec. 1850, *in Railroads and Steamships,* Doc. i; *Speech of James B. Bowlin, of Mo.,* Wash., 1850; *No. 4 in Speeches Cong.;* Review of route, advantages, resources, cost, etc., *in U. S. House Rep.,* 437, iii. 36 pp., 31 cong., 1 sess., *U. S. H. Ex. Doc.,* i., p. 30, 31 cong., 2 sess; *Frémont's Letter* to Gerhard and others of the Mississippi R. R. convention, on the features and advantages of his route; *Amer. Quar. Reg.,* iv. 558-64.

the south for the presidency, would have left nothing
with which to satisfy Whitney's proposed contract.[33]
The press of California was urgent for quicker communication with the east. Frémont, the first senator
elected by the legislature of the independent, self-constituted first state on the Pacific coast, presented in
one day eighteen bills for the benefit of California,
but among them was no bill for a transcontinental
railroad, although he was charged with the joint resolutions of the legislature, urging congress to construct
a national road,[34] at the earliest possible moment.
Gwin in his *Memoirs* more than hints that he was the
author of the eighteen bills presented by Frémont on
the 13th of September, in which case he was also responsible for the absence of a railroad bill, and for the
failure to present the joint resolution of the legislature, which was not brought to the attention of congress until the last of December, when, Frémont being absent during the entire session, Gwin apologized
for the delay in presenting them, by saying that his
colleague must have forgotten them. It would seem
difficult, in the midst of all the railroad discussion of
that year to forget that California had instructed him
to urge immediate action on this subject. Not that
her demand would be complied with in preference to
others,' but that the apparent neglect to make the demand made weight for the enemies of the road. Gwin's
sympathies being always with the south, he could not

[33] This referred, of course, to that portion of the route between Lake
Michigan and Missouri; and the allusion to the disposal of the public lands
by congress was made in reference to soldiers' bounty land laws.

[34] The resolution reads: '1st, Be it resolved by the senate and assembly
of the state of California, that our senators be instructed, and our representatives requested, to urge upon congress the importance of authorizing as
soon as possible, the construction of a national railroad from the Pacific to
the Mississippi river. 2nd, Resolved, that they be further instructed and
requested to urge upon the national government, with a view to facilitate
the accomplishment of the great work contemplated in the first resolution,
the immediate organization of an efficient engineer corps, to make complete
surveys and explorations of the several routes which have been recommended
to public notice as practicable for the line of said road. 3d, Resolved, that
his excellency the governor, be requested to forward to each of our senators
and representatives in congress, a certified copy of the foregoing joint resolutions.' *Cal. Statutes* 1850, p. 465, *U. S Sen. Misc.*, Doc. 4. 31 cong, 2 sess.
Cal. Jour. Leg., 1850, p. 202, 203; *Cong. Globe 1850-1*, vol. 23, 132.

cordially urge the construction of a central or northern Pacific railway out of the national treasury ; but
having had time to grasp the subject, as it was understood by politicians in Washington, he perceived that
the second resolution which asked for a survey of the
different routes, nullified, for the time being, the first,
and thus made the whole innocuous to the south.   He
particularly urged the survey.   As the artful senator
himself explains, when giving an account of his instru-
mentality in laying the foundation of the magnificent
system of surveys across the continent of America,
that "it brought about the exact result which Mr
Gwin had predicted—that no one route could be
agreed upon."

The history of the Pacific railroad in congress for
several years is a repetition and an elaboration of the
arguments, estimates, opinions, and plans which had
been put forth by individuals and conventions ever
since 1832, and especially since 1847, and would fill
volumes.[35]   It had the effect to stimulate railroad
building in all the states, and to cause a demand for
congressional aid[36] by public land grants; to increase
public intelligence on the subject of railroads to the
Pacific,[37] and to make more hopeless than ever the

[35] *Cong. Globe*, 1850-1, 6, 56; *Senate Jour.*, 377; 31st cong., 2d sess.; *U. S.
H. Jour.*, 602, 662, 1471, 31st cong., 2d sess.   Report of U. S. House Com.
on Whitney's project, urging the attention of congress to it. *U. S. H. Com.
Rept*, 101, 32d cong., 1st sess.; *Cong. Globe*, 1851-2, p, 941.   Bill to set apart
and sell to Asa Whitney of New York a portion of the public lands, to enable
him to construct a railroad from Lake Michigan or the Mississippi to the
Pacific; bill to provide for the location and construction of a central national
railroad, from the Mississippi river to the Pacific; bill granting the right of
way, and making a grant of land to aid in the construction of a railroad from
Lake Michigan to the Mississippi. *Id.*, 2466.   Propositions for two railroads
to connect the Mississippi with the Pacific.

[36] *Cong. Globe*, 1851-2.   Bill and amendments thereto, making grants of
land to several states, to aid in the construction of railroads and for other
purposes, pp. 1536, 1562, 1579, 1595, 1602, 1612, 1616, 1624, 1626.   Bills
granting land to construct railroads, viz., for the construction of the Virginia
and Tennessee railroad; from the copper mines on the shore of Lake Superior
to Chicago; from St Louis to St Paul; from Manétowoc to the Mississippi;
from the Wabash to the Missouri; to the Sunbury and Erie railroad company
of Pa to aid in the construction of their works; proposition for a grant of
land to the South Carolina and Tennessee railroad; bills granting lands to
the states of Me, Mass, Pa, Ohio, Ind., Mo., Ia, Ill., Miss., La, Tenn., Wis.,
Ark., Ala, Minn., Fla, Mich., Ky.

[37] See *Whipple's Rept*, in *Pac R. R. Rept*, xi 76; *Id.*, vols iii , iv.; *Frémont's Rept*, in *U. S. Sen. Misc. Doc.*, 67, 33d cong., 1st sess.; *Pope's Rept*, in

prospect of any single road. At the session of 1852–3
it was proposed by Senator Brodhead of Pennsylvania
to amend the appropriation bill so as to authorize the
secretary of war, under the direction of the president,
to employ such portion of the corps of topographical
engineers and others as might be advisable to ascertain the most economical and practicable route for a
railroad to the Pacific from the Mississippi, and that
$150,000 be appropriated to defray the expenses of
such explorations. The engineers employed were to
be organized into as many distinct corps as there were
routes to be surveyed, and their several reports laid
before congress on or before the first Monday in January 1854. To this motion Gwin added: "And be it
further enacted, that in making such explorations and
surveys the engineers and other persons employed
may be directed to act in concert with any engineers
or other persons employed by any individual or individuals, association or associations, for the same
general object, and the secretary of war is hereby
authorized and required to receive proposals from individuals or associations for the construction of a railroad between the valley of the Mississippi and the
Pacific ocean, and to lay the same before congress at
the next session," and presented the whole to the
senate.[38] Congress adopted the amendment March
3d, and the surveys were begun in the spring of 1853.

U. S. H. Ex. Doc., 129, xviii., pt 2, 33d cong., 1st sess.; *Pac R. R. Rept*, ii.;
Parke's Rept Do., Gunnison and Beckwith's Repts, and in vol. xi., 73–6; *Williamson's Rept*, in *U. S. Sen. Doc.*, 52, vol. viii., 33d cong., 1st sess.; *U. S. H.
Ex. Doc.*, 46, p. 99–118, vol. viii., 33d cong., 1st sess.; *Id. Doc.*, 129, vol.
xviii.; *Silliman's Amer. Jour. Science*, 1858, vol. 25, 317; *Stevens' Rept*, in
Smithsonian Rept, 1854, 80–2; *Id.*, 80–7.
    [38] 'I feel myself constrained,' says this diplomatist, 'to bring forward this
proposition, and I do it with great distrust, under the belief that injury may
result from it.   I am not at all satisfied that we ever can get a national railroad, or any particular route to be designated by congress, because those
sections of the country that are rejected in the report that may be made to
congress will, by combining, prevent the establishment of any.' *Gwin, Memoirs*, MS., 101–3; *Cong. Globe*, 1852–3, 815–40; Debate by Adams, Bell,
Borland, Bright, Butler, Cass, Chase, Douglas, Gwin, Hale, Hunter, Mason,
Pratt, Rusk, Underwood, and Walker. *Arguments of the Hon. William M.
Gwin on the subject of a Pacific railroad in 1854 and 1858; Speech of Gen. H. Wal-
bridge of New York in the House of Representatives*, June 13, 1854.

The surveys occupied a number of years, and were continued under acts of congress of May 31 and August 5, 1854.[39] "They had," says Gwin, "the exact result which I predicted, that no one route could be agreed upon." He avoids saying that the south would not permit the north to have a road, lest a northern population should flow out and absorb the public lands; and the north would not permit the south to have it for fear the iron rails would bind the territory acquired from Mexico, including California, to the slave-holding states.

---

[39] The northern route along the Missouri was explored by Gov. I. I. Stevens of Wash. Ter., and Capt. George B. McClellan of the engineer corps. The route near the 41st and 42nd parallels was explored by Capt. J. C. Frémont, Capt. H. Stansbury, top. eng'rs, and Lieut E. G. Beckwith, 3d reg't artillery. The route near the 38th and 39th parallels was explored by Capt. J. W. Gunnison, top. eng'rs, report by Lieut E. G. Beckwith. The route near the 35th parallel was explored by Lieut A. W. Whipple, top. eng'rs. The route near the 32d parallel was explored by Capt. John Pope, Lieut John G. Parke, and Major William H. Emory, top. eng'rs. Examination of extension of this route from the mouth of the Gila to San Francisco was made by Lieut R. S. Williamson, top. eng'rs. The reports, which fill—with those of subsequent explorations in California, Oregon, New Mexico, and the Pacific coast generally, and which include observations upon the mineralogy, botany, forestry, and fauna of this coast and Indian characteristics and customs—seven quarto volumes, are among the most interesting documents ever published by the government. Vol. I. is devoted to a report of Jefferson Davis, sec. of war, condensed from the several reports of the different expeditions, with a tabulated statement of the distances, altitudes, estimated cost, etc., of the various lines surveyed. I take from this elaborate table a few figures. The northern route, from St Paul to Vancouver, was estimated to be in a straight line 1,445 miles, by the proposed railroad route 1,864 miles, sum of ascents and descents 18,100 feet, cost $130,781,000; route near the 41st and 42d parallels, from Council Bluffs to Benicia, distance in a straight line 1,410 miles, by the proposed route 2,032 miles, sum of ascents and descents 29,120 feet, cost $116,095,000; route near the 38th and 39th parallels, from Westport to S. F. by the Cochetopa and Taheachaypah passes, distance in a straight line 1,740 miles, by the proposed route 2,080 miles, sum of ascents and descents 49,986 feet, cost 'so great that the road is impracticable;' route from and to the same points by the Cochetopa and Madeline passes, distance 10 miles greater, and sum of ascents and descents 56,514 feet, cost same as above; route near the 35th parallel, from Fort Smith to San Pedro, distance in a straight line 1,360 miles, by the proposed line 1,892 miles, sum of ascents and descents 48,812 feet, cost $169,216,265; branch road from the Mojave river to S. F., distance 400 miles, sum of ascents and descents 7,500 feet, cost $19,935,000; route near the 32d parallel, from Fulton to San Pedro, distance 1,400 miles in a straight line, by the proposed route 1,618 miles, sum of ascents and descents 32,784 feet, cost $68,970,000; extension to S. F., distance 440 miles, sum of ascents and descents 10,150 feet, cost $25,100,000. On none of these routes were there more than 670 miles of cultivable land reported; on some not more than 374. *Pac R. R. Rept*, i. 31; *Beechy*, in *Royal Geog. Soc. Proceedings*, 1866, 165.

In the meantime a long projected railroad from ocean to ocean at the isthmus of Panamá was being constructed. It was undertaken by the New York company, consisting of William H. Aspinwall, John L. Stephens, and Henry Chauncey, who had the government contract for carrying the United States mail in steamships from New York to the Pacific coast. By a fortunate coincidence this service began at the very time when gold was discovered in California, the first mail steamers carrying all the passengers that could be accommodated, and who were compelled to cross the Isthmus by boats up the Charges river, and by mules across the mountains, a trying and even perilous journey.

Immediately upon assuming the obligations of their contract the Pacific Mail company recognized the imperative necessity, in their own interest, of improving the route across the Isthmus. The government, too, after the acquisition of California, comprehending the importance of a free and uninterrupted passage at all times and forever across the Isthmus of Panamá, had negotiated a treaty with the government of New Granada, by which the United States undertook, in consideration of such a free and uninterrupted right of way, to guarantee to the public the neutrality of the Isthmus, the authority of Granada over it, and its protection from invasion by foreign powers.[40]

[40] As early as the 17th century a company was formed in Scotland, projected by William Patterson, to improve the advantages offered by the isthmus of Darien and Panamá for trade in the Pacific; but the East India company remonstrating, the project was discountenanced, and the enterprise suspended. Patterson, however, having raised £700,000 and 1,200 men sailed to New Granada to found a colony; but the local government denounced him, and the Spanish soldiery attacked him, while disease decimated his colony, so that the enterprise had to be abandoned. In 1814 Spain revived the project of Isthmus communication with the Pacific, but foreign and domestic troubles rendered her incapable of carrying out the design. Bolivar in 1827 appointed a commissioner to ascertain by actual survey the best line, either by railroad or canal, between the two seas. The report was in favor of the latter, but the death of Bolivar put an end to the prosecution of the scheme. In 1842 the Mexican government under Santa Ana conferred upon José de Garay a grant empowering him to open a communication by steam across the isthmus of Tehuantepec. This grant pledged the honor and faith of the nation to maintain the projector, Garay, as well

The report of the secretary of war on the several surveys made under his direction, having been laid before congress in February 1855, the interest in a Pacific railroad was if possible augmented, though nothing definite was to be learned from it; nor was there anything in it to allay sectional jealousies or quiet free-soil agitation.

The subject of overland communication in the senate was referred to a select committee, which reported a bill providing that there should be granted

as any private individual or company succeeding him, either native or foreign, in the undisturbed enjoyment of all the concessions granted, a part of which was all the vacant land on each side of the line.of communication between the two seas. In 1843 Garay was placed in possession of these lands by Nicholas Bravo, then president of the republic, who declared all lands previously granted to natives or foreigners, but which remained unimproved, included in the concession to Garay. The survey was concluded in October, 1843, and the provincial governors were ordered to furnish convicts to be employed upon the work. The time allotted for constructing the road was extended in 1844 and other privileges added. Revolution at this juncture overthrew the government, which was changed from a central to a federated one under Salas, who again extended the time of completing the work to 1848. By the terms of the contract Garay was authorized to sell his right. This he did in 1846 and 1847 to Manning and Mackintosh, English subjects residing in Mexico, which transfer was approved by the Mexican government. In 1847 President Polk, when negotiating, through Mr Frist, the treaty of Guadaloupe Hidalgo, tendered $15,000,000 to Mexico for the right of way in favor of the U. S. across the isthmus of Tehauntepec; but was assured that no treaty could be had on that subject because the right was already transferred. In the meantime P. A. Hargoies of Pa. had purchased the grant of Manning and Mackintosh, and formed a company in New Orleans to carry on the work; but before commencing it, and while surveying the route in 1851, the Mexican congress declared void the decree under which Garay obtained an extension of time. This piece of punic faith was attributed to jealousy of the U. S.; but the U. S. government while insisting on the right of Garay and his successors was met by the answer that it was entirely a matter of Mexican law; which was the truth, the Mexican gov. reserving to itself the right to abrogate as well as to grant privileges. This gov. in 1853 accepted proposals from a 'mixed company,' all being Mexicans except the principal, A. G. Sloo, to construct a plank-road and railroad across the Isthmus. It proposed, also, to the U. S. to enter into a treaty to protect this highway, similar to the treaty with New Granada. Nothing came, however, of the Tehuantepec project. The Nicaragua route was surveyed by Bailey in 1837-8, under authority of the Nicaraguan gov. He estimated the cost of a canal connecting lake Nicaragua with the Pacific at $30,000,000. The canal was never attempted. Steamers have ascended the San Juan river from the gulf of Mexico, and navigated the lake; but the land travel was unpopular, and the route not much patronized. The Panamá railroad was commenced in 1850 and ran its first train between Aspinwall and Panamá in 1853. It is 47½ miles long, and cost $7,500,000. *Railroads and Steamships. Id. Doc.* xv.; *Hall's speech in favor of a National Railroad, and Review of the Tehuantepec route; Hund's Merchants' Mag.,* 1849. Vol. xx., 269–278.

to any individual or company, or corporation chartered
for the purpose by any state, which might contract
with the United States for the work, every alternate
section of land designated by odd numbers within
twenty miles of each side of the route, and appropriating a sum not exceeding $600 a mile for carrying
the mail daily on the road for a period of not more
than thirty years; the road to be commenced within
three years from the date of the contract, and completed within seven years, one seventh to be finished
each year. The party bidding lowest for carrying
the mail and complying with the other stipulations
would be awarded the contract.

On the 15th of February Gwin offered a substitute
for this bill. It called for three roads to California,
one commencing on the western border of Texas,
another on the border of Missouri or Iowa, and a
third at Wisconsin, to be called the Southern, Central, and Northern Pacific railroads. A telegraph
line was to accompany each road. There should be
set apart for the construction of these roads a quantity of the public land equal to the odd-numbered
sections for the space of twelve miles on each side of
the roads for their whole length, and where the lands
were occupied a selection of lien lands might be made
from any unappropriated lands within thirty miles of
the road, except in California, where the selection
might be made within fifty miles, mineral lands excepted. Immediately on the enactment of the bill,
the secretary of war, the secretary of the interior,
and the postmaster-general were to cause advertisements to be published inviting proposals for the construction of a railroad and telegraph line, each proposition to state the general route selected, the time to
be consumed in the completion of the work, the terms
on which the United States mail would be carried
daily each way, and the charge that would be made
for carrying troops, military and naval stores, munitions of war and government freight of every kind.

The contractor whose proposal should be accepted, should deposit $500,000 with the secretary of the treasury, either in money or United States or state bonds, which could be drawn out $5,000 at a time only on showing this amount had been expended. The road was to be divided into sections of 100 miles, and no land should be conveyed until one of the sections should be completed and in operation, when there would be conveyed by patent of the United States three-fourths of the land pertaining to that section, and so on to the end, when the residue of the whole subsidy would be conveyed to the contractors. On the completion of the first hundred miles of road, and when it should be in full operation in the territories of the United States, the contractors should be entitled to receive an advance of $2,500,000 in government bonds, redeemable at a certain period, and bearing interest at six per centum per annum, payable semi-annually; and the same for every hundred miles of road completed. The bonds so advanced were to be repaid to the United States within fifteen years after the completion of the road, the government to have lien on the road and its equipments until the loan should be fully repaid, which should not exceed $15,000,000. Should the first contractors fail the work might be relet. As soon as the general route should have been selected the public lands on either side for forty miles should be surveyed, the Indian title extinguished, and the preëmption laws extended to the even-numbered sections; but the lands reserved to the government within ten miles of the road should not be sold for less than double the minimum price of the public lands; and those receiving grants under the bill were to sell and convey unconditionally, within five years after receiving their patents, one half of their grant; all that was left unsold at the end of ten years to revert to the United States. The road when fully completed was to be surrendered to the government, free of cost, for the purpose of being again surrendered to the several states then organized, or to be organized, within whose limits it should be located, when it became with their assent, the property of such states, subject to the use of the United States for postal, military, and all other government service, and subject also to such regulations as congress might prescribe restricting the charges for such service.

The absurdity of Gwin's proposition was evident, yet the freinds of a Pacific railroad who had committed themselves to its support could do no less than vote for it. Even Seward, for whose bill it was substituted, was compelled to do so.[41] It was this or nothing, and he meant that a bill should pass. Perhaps he knew, also, that the bill of the California senator was but an artifice to draw attention away from his purpose to defeat any scheme for a northern road; but he was at least as good a diplomatist as Gwin, and concealed his cognizance of the intention. The substitute passed the senate by a vote of 24 to 21, on the 19th of February. It went to the lower house, which took no notice of it. A bill altogether similar was before that body, but failed to pass.

At the next session a number of Pacific railroad bills were introduced, which were referred to the same committee,[42] a committee a majority of whom were opposed to the passage of any of those introduced,[43] but which allowed Weller of California to report a bill similar to that of the last session, except that it called for but one road, and left the selection of the route to the contractors. This bill was laid on the table. In the lower house, the hostility of the southern members to any Pacific railroad legislation was undisguised and aggressive. For several successive sessions, and through all the political excitement which

---

[41] See Seward's remarks in *Cong. Globe*, 1854–5, 808–9.

[42] The following senators constituted the committee: Rusk of Tex., chairman, Douglas of Ill., Bell of Tenn., Seward of N. Y., Geyer of Mo., Evans of S. C., Reid of N. C., Foot of Vt, and Weller of Cal.

[43] See debate in *Cong. Globe*, 1855–6, pt ii., p. 1720,

preceded the civil war, the Pacific railroad question was presented over and over, in every form and with one result, until the session of 1860–1, when the house passed a bill providing for two roads, since it could not get one, but the senate amending it so as to require three, in which form it passed. To this the house would not consent, and it again failed.[44]

The secession about this time of the southern delegations, with the events which followed, gave a new character to legislation. Opposition to one road was withdrawn, and its immediate construction was imperatively demanded, not only as a commercial but a defensive measure. During all the years wasted in fruitless discussion of a transcontinental railroad, the public lands had been developing into territories and states. California, Oregon, Minnesota, and Kansas had assumed statehood; Utah, New Mexico, Colorado, Montana, and Dakota were yet in leading strings, but would soon come to maturity. Congress having long since granted the right of way over the public lands, capitalists had availed themselves of the privilege to build roads in all directions where the population would sustain them, soon discovering that population always followed a railroad, and that it was safe to build anywhere, provided the country would support a settlement.[45]

[44] Gwin says, in his *Memoirs*, MS., 104, that there was a large majority in the senate in favor, and that 'there was an equally large majority in its favor in the house, but the majority of that body determined to defeat its passage then in order to give the credit of inaugurating this great system of transcontinental railroads to the incoming administration of Mr Lincoln.'

[45] The system of land grants to aid in the construction of railroads began in Illinois by a grant from congress of an area equal to 4,055 sq. miles, or 2,595,000 acres. This was the corner stone of the great system of internal trade and travel. The grant was made to the state of every alternate section for six miles on each side of the road with its branches, with indemnity where the sections were not found of other land within 15 miles of the route. The whole line of over 450 miles was under contract in 1852, from Galena on the north to Cairo on the south, with a branch to Chicago, and 10,000 men were employed upon it, at an annual cost of $3,700,000. It was fully equipped in 1861, with over 100 locomotives, 100 passenger, baggage, and express cars, and over 2,000 freight cars. The company had sold $16,250,000 worth of their land, the larger moiety remaining unsold, so that the grant was estimated as amounting to $40,000,000. *Latham's Speech* in *Cong. Globe.* 1861–2 p. 2676.

In May 1862, a bill passed the house of representatives " to aid in the construction of a railroad and telegraph line from the Missouri river to the Pacific ocean, and to secure to the government the use of the same for postal, military, and other purposes." It passed the senate June 20th by a vote of 35 to 5, and became a law July 1st of that year. It chartered a company consisting of men of every northern state, and of Maryland, Kentucky, Kansas, Oregon, California, and the territories of Nebraska, Colorado, and Nevada, associated with five commissioners, to be appointed by the secretary of the interior.

The chief points in the act to which I shall hereafter call attention were first, the name of Union Pacific Railroad Company, given, not as might be conjectured, on account of the union sentiment of the loyal states at that period, but because it was intended to unite several roads in forming a transcontinental line, namely, the Pawnee and Western railroad company of Kansas, which was authorized to construct a railroad and telegraph line from the mouth of the Kansas river to the 100th meridian of longitude west from Greenwich in the territory of Nebraska. At this point, which is about at Elen creek, the Union Pacific proper began, and continued to the eastern boundary of California, where it would connect with the Central Pacific of that state.

The terms and conditions upon which these companies were chartered were that the capital stock of the Union Pacific should consist of 100,000 shares of $1,000 each, of which not more than 200 shares should be held by any one person. No person should be a director who was not a bona fide owner of at least five shares of stock. The right of way through the public lands was granted, with the right to take from them earth, stone, and timber, or other material for the construction of the road and telegraph. The United States should extinguish as rapidly as possible the Indian title along the line; and there was granted

to the company to aid in the construction of the road
and telegraph, "and to secure the safe and speedy
transportation of the mails, troops, munitions of war,
and public stores thereon, every alternate section of
public land designated by odd numbers, to the amount
of five alternate sections per mile on each side of the
railroad on the line thereof, and within the limits of
ten miles on each side of the road not sold, reserved,
or otherwise disposed of by the United States, and to
which a preëmption or homestead claim may not have
attached at the time the line of said road is definitely
fixed; provided, that all mineral lands shall be excepted
from the operations of this act; but where the same
shall contain timber, the timber therein is hereby
granted to said company. All such lands, so granted
by this section, which shall not be sold or disposed of
by said company within three years after the entire
road shall have been completed, shall be subject to
settlement and preëmption like other lands, at a price
not exceeding $1.25 per acre, to be paid to said
company."

When forty consecutive miles of road and telegraph
should be completed and ready for service, no other
than American iron being used in the rails, or in the
construction and equipment of the road, and when
three commissioners appointed by the president should
have examined and accepted it, the secretary of the
treasury should issue to the company bonds of the
United States of $1,000 each, payable thirty years
after date, bearing interest at six per centum, which
interest should be paid semi-annually in lawful money
of the United States, to the amount of sixteen of
these bonds per mile for every mile of the completed
section; the delivery of said bonds, twenty-five per
cent of which were retained until the road should be
completed, to constitute, *ipso facto*, a first mortgage on
the whole line and telegraph, together with the rolling stock and property of every kind appertaining;
and on the refusal or failure of the company to re-

deem its bonds, or any part of them, when required
by the secretary of the treasury to do so, its road and
property might be taken for the use and benefit of
the government; the grants being made upon the
condition that the company should pay its bonds at
maturity, should keep its road and telegraph in repair
and use, and at all times ready for the service of the
government, which should pay a fair and reasonable
compensation for such service, but not more than
private individuals were charged, and this indebtedness of the United States might be applied upon the
bond and interest debt of the company to the government, and after the completion of the road, at
least five per centum of the net earnings should be
annually applied to the payment thereof. The company should file its assent within one year from the
passage of the act, should designate its route within
two years, and should complete its railroad and telegraph within twelve years. On filing a map of its
route, the lands along its line would be withdrawn
from market and surveyed as fast as necessary for the
purposes entertained. The Kansas company should
complete 100 miles of its road within two years after
filing its assent; the Central Pacific company of
California should complete 50 miles within two years;
each road to construct an equal distance each year
thereafter until the whole was completed; and afterwards might unite upon equal terms with the Union
Pacific company to complete what remained of that
road. So also the Hannibal and St Joseph railroad,
or the Pacific of Missouri, might unite with the Kansas company, and in case the latter should reach the
California boundary before the Central Pacific, it
might, with the consent of the state continue on to a
connection with that road; or should the Central
Pacific first reach the boundary of the state, it might
continue on to a meeting with the line from the east.

For 150 miles westwardly from the eastern base of
the Rocky mountains, and for the same distance east-

wardly from the western base of the Sierra Nevada, the number of bonds per mile which might be issued was treble the amount granted for the level sections, and should be due upon the completion of each twenty miles; and between these two mountain divisions the number of bonds per mile to be issued should be double the amount for the level sections, and should issue every twenty miles; but no more than 50,000 bonds should be issued in aid of the whole main line of the road.

The Union Pacific company was authorized and required to construct a railroad and telegraph line from a point on the western boundary of Iowa to the 100th meridian, to connect with the roads converging to a point to be selected by the president on that line of longitude; and was required to build 100 miles of this road within two years, and 100 miles each year thereafter until completed. Whenever a railroad should be constructed through Minnesota or Iowa to Sioux city, the Union company was required to construct a line to connect with it at that place. The penalty for not complying with the terms assented to was that congress should take possession and adopt measures to have the road completed. The government also reserved the right to regulate fares after the receipts of the road should exceed ten per centum upon its cost, exclusive of the five per centum to be paid to the United States.

Although the directors of the Central Pacific did not hesitate to accept the grant, they were fully aware that it was entirely insufficient, and that, without further action on the part of congress, to complete even the first forty miles might be a task beyond their resources. First of all was the depreciation in government bonds and currency attending the civil war, the result of which was then by no means assured. But a more serious drawback was the provision of the act which made the subsidy in bonds a first mortgage on the road, for under such conditions no second mortgage would be accepted by capitalists, without whose aid the first lot of subsidy bonds could never be obtained. Moreover, the land grant in California was of little value, for under the terms of the act less than 200,000 acres of arable land could be obtained between Sacramento and the state line. On these and other representations, on the 2d of July, 1864, congress passed a supplementary act enlarging the subsidy granted two years before, and withdrawing the more objectionable features; but of this mention will be made in the following chapter.

The main causes which led to the granting of government aid for the construction of a transcontinental railroad may thus be briefly summarized: First, it was a political necessity, partly to prevent the threatened withdrawal from the union of the Pacific states. Second, it was a military necessity, one needed to provide against invasion by a foreign power, through the more rapid movement of troops and munitions of war. Third, it would put an end to Indian wars. Fourth, it would furnish cheaper and quicker means of transportation for mails and government supplies. Fifth, it would aid to develop the vast and then almost unpeopled region between the Missouri river and the Pacific ocean, a region covering more than one half the area of the United States.[46]

[46] Before proceeding further with the history of railroads in California, I will here give some account of the former career of those by whom were organized and pushed to completion the Central and Southern Pacific systems. Although frequent mention of them will be made in these pages in connection with railroad matters, it is also fitting that a brief record should be given of their earlier life and of their family antecedents.

Leland Stanford was born near Albany, N. Y., on the 9th of March, 1824, the fourth of a family of seven. His father, who was a farmer by occupation, and whose land adjoined the line of the Albany and Schenectady, the first railroad built in the United States, took an active interest in the work going on around him, as did also his son Leland, some of whose leisure time was passed in watching its progress. At the age of 20 the latter began the study of law, his boyhood having been passed in working on his father's farm in summer and attending school in winter. In 1845, being then admitted to the bar, he began to practise his profession at Port Washington, Wisconsin, where, but for an accident, he might have remained for his lifetime, that accident being the destruction by fire in 1852 of his law library and most of his other property. Thereupon he determined to remove to California, where he arrived in July of that year, soon afterward starting in business at Michigan Bluff, in Placer county, and in 1856 becoming an active member in the firm of Stanford Brothers, one of the most prominent in Sacramento. The later career of Mr Stanford forms a part of the history of the state, and here it remains only to be said that in that state no man is more highly respected, not only as a railroad artificer, but as a statesman, a citizen, and as a philanthropist.

Charles Crocker, whose services as superintendent of construction were invaluable, was a native of Troy, N. Y., his birthday being September 16, 1822. When only ten years of age he began to earn the money with which, a few years later, he helped his father, then in straightened circumstances, to purchase a farm in Indiana, to which state, in 1836, the family removed. Here, after assisting for two years to clear and cultivate the land, he found employment in a saw-mill, and afterward in a forge, where he worked for $11 a month, with his board, and permission to attend the district school in winter. Soon he became a thorough and efficient workman, whereupon he started a forge of his own, which he conducted with fair success. In 1850 he crossed the plains to California, and some two years later, after a brief mining experience, established what soon became the leading dry-goods house in Sacramento. In 1860 he was elected to the state legislature on the republican ticket, and in 1862 gave up the management of his business to devote his fortune, time, and abilities to the Pacific railroad enterprise. His decease occurred at Monterey, on the 14th of August, 1888.

Collis P. Huntington, who was for years the financial agent of the company in New York, was born Oct. 22, 1821, at Harwinton, Connecticut, where his father was a wool manufacturer, and one of the most prominent citizens. At the age of 22 Mr Huntington began business as a general merchant, in conjunction with his eldest brother, at Oneonta, N. Y., where he remained until 1849, when he removed to California, and opened a mercantile house at Sacramento in the line of hardware and miners' supplies. In 1855 he entered into partnership with Mark Hopkins, with whose aid he built up the well-known firm of Huntington, Hopkins & Co. At their store on K street were held some of the meetings at which the railroad associates discussed their plans, with the ways and means of carrying them out. In 1863 he went east with a full power of attorney to employ all the means and credit of his colleagues in furtherance of the great enterprise. It was largely due to his skilful management that all their obligations were promptly met, and that their bonds took rank among the best securities in the moneyed centres in Europe.

Mark Hopkins, the treasurer of the Central Pacific, was the eldest of the railroad quartette, his natal day being Sept. 1, 1813, and his native place Henderson, N. Y., whence, in 1825, the family removed to St Clair, Mich. At the age of 16, his father being then deceased, Mr Hopkins began his career as a clerk in a mercantile firm, first in Niagara co., N. Y., and afterward at Lockport, where he became the leading partner in the firm of Hopkins & Hughes. In 1837 he began the study of law with his brother Henry, one of the leading practitioners of Lockport, not with a view to practise, but for the training which it afforded. After some further changes he removed to California, landing in San Francisco Aug. 5, 1849, and a few months later opened a store at Placerville, bringing his own goods by ox-team from Sacramento. In the following year he established a wholesale grocery business, in conjunction with his friend and fellow-passenger, E. H. Miller, Jr, afterward secretary of the Central Pacific Co. The partnership which he formed with C. P. Huntington in 1855 continued until the time of his death in March 1878. Mr Hopkins has been aptly termed the Mentor of the railroad associates, for whenever difficult problems arose, he was consulted as one who held a comprehensive grasp of the business situation, and whose decisions were seldom at fault.

CHAPTER XX.

1852–1888.

ORGANIZATION AND LEGISLATION—ROUTES AND SURVEYS—ACTION OF CON-
GRESS—FINANCES AND CONSTRUCTION—CENTRAL PACIFIC AND UNION
PACIFIC—STOCK SUBSCRIPTIONS AND SUBSIDIES—OTHER ROADS.

THE pioneers of the American state of California
were not men who had to learn that upon facilities of
rapid transit and transportation depended the development of resources, material, political, and social.
They brought that knowledge with them, and while
enduring heroically the privations of a country naked
from the creation, planned an early deliverance from
the inconveniences of the magnificent distances in
which the new state abounded.

Among the first legislative proceedings were acts
and resolutions in favor of railroads; a joint resolution being passed at the first session instructing the
United States senators thereto elected to urge upon
congress the importance of proceeding at once to the
construction of a national railroad from the Pacific
ocean to the Mississippi river, by ordering surveys of
the routes under discussion in congress. The same
legislative body enacted a general incorporation law,
with a chapter on railroads; and the second legislature passed an act to provide for the incorporation of
railroad companies, which was amended from year to
year to meet the requirements or serve the interests
of the companies chartered. In 1852 an act was
passed granting the right of way to the United

States "for the purpose of constructing a railroad from the Atlantic to the Pacific ocean;" and also a joint resolution urging the California delegation in congress to give their attention to the subject.

The legislature of 1854 repeated this request, and resolved to appoint a committee of three from each house to collect information in relation to routes. The southern democrats in the legislature were united in insisting upon a national road, by which was meant one constructed with money out of the public treasury, and that the route should be a southern one. I have already shown how these demands were met in congress.[1]

As might be supposed, much interest was early exhibited, not only in the ideal great thoroughfare which was to make a pathway for all nations across the continent; but in local railways as well. In 1850 the practicability of a railway from Sacramento to Coloma was discussed in the public press, with the advantage to accrue to the state. Various plans were proposed, and several companies were formed, resulting in nothing but surveys and reports,[2] until the time had expired to which the law limited the preliminaries. Every traveller, and particularly every one crossing the continent, felt called upon to make a statement of his observations for the benefit of future railroad builders.[3] So every local expedition to aid

[1] McDougall of Cal. made a good speech in congress on the need and practicability of a Pacific railroad, May 29, 1854; pp. 16.

[2] Rep't of Route explored from Yreka to Humboldt river, and to the Coast in Cal. Jour. Sen. 1853. App., no. 3, p. 41–2. A petition by D. W. Murphy and others, praying for right of way for a railroad from Benicia to Shasta city. U. S. Sen. Jour., 358, 440; 32 cong, 1 sess.

[3] Froebel in 1852 travelled by the way of the Arkansas valley, and the Cimarron to La Joya, thence down the Rio Grande, via El Paso, to Chihuahua, returning thence to the U. S. in 1853. In 1854 he repeated the journey to El Paso, travelling thence down to Gila, and over the Colorado desert to Los Angeles, in Cal. whence he came to San Francisco. Froebel, Cent. America, 242–85. G. Harris Heap, one of the party accompanying E. F. Beale, first sup't of Ind. Aff. in Cal. wrote an account of the daily marches of the company. They travelled by what was then known as the central route, terminating at Los Angeles, Heap, Central Route,

immigrants or chastise Indians was made the subject of a geographical and topographical report in the interest of railroads.

The first of the several local projects to be attempted, and which finally succeeded, was a line of road from San Francisco to San José, and thence east, its projectors hoped, to the Mississippi river. The scheme was agitated in 1849–50, and subscriptions solicited in 1850–51. In February, 1851, there had been raised $100,000.[4] On the 6th of September a company was organized under the name of the Pacific and Atlantic Railroad company, and soon after surveying was commenced. The engineer's report was published about the close of the year, when an effort was made to get the company's stock on the market in the two cities, but without success. Attempts were also made to negotiate for subscriptions through the agents of banking-houses in New York and England, but as no portion of the road had been constructed the effort failed. Congress was then applied to for aid in the way of land and bonds, but although a bill was passed through one branch of the national legislature, it went no further.

The affairs of the company remained in this unpromising state until October 29, 1853, when it was reorganized under a new incorporation law. The capital stock was then fixed at $2,000,000, and for a brief period the prospects of the road seemed good; but the financial reverses of 1854–5 involving its friends in the disaster, no more was heard of it for a period during which all railroad enterprises languished.[5] The misfortunes attending the first two organizations deterred others from reviving the Pacific and Atlantic railroad until 1859, when a third company was formed and incorporated under the name of San

[4] *Sac Transcript*, (Str. Ed.) Feb. 14, 1851. *Address of Committee* appointed at a public meeting of the citizens of San José in relation to the feasibility of a railroad between San Francisco and San José, adopted June 29, 1851.
[5] The legislature of 1855 extended the time of the P. and A. R. R., and also of the Marysville and Benicia National R. R. *Cal. Stat*, 1855, 144.

Francisco and San José Railroad company, which, profiting by the experience of the pioneer companies, sought to construct at least a portion of its road before offering its stock abroad. The legislature was persuaded to enact a law submitting to the people of the counties through which the road would run a proposition to vote a stock subscription of $900,000. But the San Francisco press opposed the subsidy as a fraud upon tax-payers, and so discouraged the directors that they dissolved their corporation in June, 1860. Their place was filled by a fourth organization in July, with a capital stock of $2,000,000 divided into 20,000 shares of $100 each.

The new company had the same obstacles to encounter. It, however, put the road under construction in October, the contract being let to Charles McLaughlin and Alexander H. Houston, to complete according to specifications within three years for the sum of $2,000,000, of which $500,000 was to be in cash, $500,000 in bonds of the counties through which the road should pass, the legislature having again come to their aid; $500,000 in mortgage bonds of the company payable in ten years, drawing eight per cent interest, and $500,000 in the capital stock of the company. The amount of individual subscriptions obtained was $285,300, of which only $100,000 was paid, the remainder being taken by directors and contractors to prevent the stock going on the market to be at the mercy of brokers and speculators. The road was opened to Mayfield, thirty-five miles from San Francisco, in October, 1863, and completed to San José January 16, 1864, to the great joy of the three counties. It was extended southward to Gilroy in 1869.

The Sacramento Valley Railroad company, which was able to complete its road at an earlier date than the San Francisco and San José company, began operations about the same time, and was the first company to

make a railroad in California an accomplished fact.[6]
It was proposed to run the road from Sacramento
along the foothills east of the American river, and to
branch north and south, passing through Placer and
Sutter counties to Mountain city in the county of
Yuba, a distance of about 40 miles. Ten per cent of
the subscriptions was paid in, amounting to $5,000,
when the company reorganized under the railroad act
of 1853.[7] The president proceeded to Boston and
New York, where he arranged with capitalists to furnish material for constructing the road, and procured
a competent engineer to survey it—Theodore D. Judah, who afterwards projected the Central Pacific.
Grading was commenced in February, 1855, and in
June a vessel arrived from Boston with iron and
other material, so that track-laying began in August.
On the 17th of that month the first platform-cars
were placed upon the rails, and on the 10th of November a party of excursionists was carried ten
miles from Sacramento at one dollar the round trip.
The formal opening of the road to Folsom, 22 miles,
took place February 22, 1856. The cost of the road
was but little less than $60,000 a mile, at which rate
it was not possible to build many or long roads in a
new country.[8] As the capital stock of the company

[6] The directors under the first organization were C. J. Hutchinson, William McNulty, James L. L. F. Warren, J. B. Patch, Julius Wetzler, E. J.
Willis, John Bigler, William H. Watson, J. C. Zabriskie, Lewis B. Harris,
Thomas P. Robb, and T. M. Freeman. *Sac. Val. R. R. Co. Articles of Asso.
and By-Laws.*

[7] On the reorganization, the directors elected were C. L. Wilson, Henry
E. Robinson, R. P. Johnson, John Forsher, C. J. Hutchinson, Ferris Forman, W. H. Watson, of Sacramento; C. K. Garrison, H. M. Gray, Levi
Parsons, James A. Mc Dougall, of San Francisco; A. P. Catlin, of Mormon
island, and Hamlet Davis, of Nevada. The treasurer was T. W. Page; secretary, W. H. Watson; engineer, W. B. Foster; committee of construction.
Henry E. Robinson and Ferris Forman.

[8] Robinson, Seymour & Co. were the contractors, L. L. Robinson being
the principal. They were to take $45,000 per mile, $\frac{1}{3}$ in cash, $\frac{1}{3}$ in bonds,
and $\frac{1}{3}$ in stock of the company. Says one of the directors, 'The whole thing
was sunk. I had 10,000 in it, and sold it for $1,900. *Burr's Early Commercial
Ventures. MS. 5.* The statement of the company in the *Sac. Union* of Dec.
19, 1854, was that the contractors were to build 40 miles of road, and to take
in payment $800,000 in stock, $500,000 in bonds, and $500,000 in cash and
notes, as the work progressed.

would cover no more distance at this rate, the road stopped at Folsom, and its earnings went to pay its debts. No blame attached to the directors', whose sole reward was the glory of having furnished California with her first railroad. The business of the road was good. The tonnage of vessels of every description arriving at the wharves of Sacramento in October, 1855, was 38,327 tons, the largest part of which was for the mines, and made a respectable income for this short railway. It drew to itself in time twenty-one different stage lines at Folsom. It declared in 1864 a profit of $500,000. The following year it was sold to George F. Bragg, agent of the Central Pacific railroad of California, by L. L. Robinson and two other stockholders, Pioche and Bayerque.

A number of railroad companies were organized between 1853 and 1863, some of which never arrived at the dignity of an actual and useful existence, while a fair proportion were constructed either wholly or in part.[10] In March 1863 the Freeport Railroad company, with a capital of $150,000, was organized to construct a branch from the Sacramento valley road, at or near Brighton, ten miles, to a point on the Sacramento river at or near the Russian embarcadero, the object being to make a new landing below Sacramento, and take the business of the older road away from that city, with which it had some quarrel, in which case it was expected to form a combination with some other lines, and to make Freeport the

[9] The officers elected in the autumn of 1855 were C. K. Garrison, pres't; W. P. Sherman, vice-pres't; H. R. Payson, sec'ty; J. P. Robinson, sup't; H. Havens, cashier; C. K. Garrison, E. Jones, W. P. Robinson, Levi Parsons, H. E. Robinson, Theodore F. Mays, J. R. Robinson, E. W. Burr, C. R. Goodwin, and Edward Flint, directors.

[10] Right of way granted to the Petaluma R. R. *Cal. Stat.*, 1860, p. 265. R. R. franchise granted to a company to construct a railroad to the coal mines in Contra Costa co. via Kirker's pass, to a point on the San Joaquin river, or Suisun bay. *Cal Stat.*, 1862, 97. A franchise granted to J. S. Kohn and associates to construct and maintain a railroad from Corral hollow in Alameda co. to a point on the San Joaquin river. *Cal. Stat.*, 1861, 309.

shipping point of the upper country. The track was leased to the Sacramento valley company, which soon after sold out as just stated,[11] together with the leased road.

The first point to which the mining population flowed after Coloma, was to Placerville, at the confluence of several rich ravines. The Mormons of Carson valley found a way across the Sierra to these mines by the pass of the Carson river, which was afterward explored by agents of the government, and pronounced superior to that by the Truckee river. It was adopted by the immigration of 1849, and every year thereafter many persons passed over it.[12] On the discovery of the Comstock lode it became the highway of travel to Virginia city.

As early as 1854 a railroad meeting was called in Placerville, for the purpose of connecting that place with the Sacramento valley road, but the business proceeded no further at that time. Soon afterward there was a decline in the mining interest which threatened, and indeed destroyed much of the trade enjoyed by the Placerville merchants, and a discouraging dullness prevailed until the Washoe excitement revived the spirit of the town. Wagon roads were opened through the mountains by other passes[13]

[11] *Sac. Co. Hist.*, 200. The first directors of the Freeport company were George F. Bragg, J. B. Bayerque, George W. Mowe, J. P. Robinson, and J. Mora Moss. *R. R. Scraps*, 26.

[12] The Cal. newspapers call this the Beckwourth pass; but it was discovered by Lieut E. G. Beckwith, who belonged to the expedition ordered to explore the route near the 38th and 39th parallels. Says the report: 'the survey of the western portion of this route by Lieut. Beckwith has resulted in the discovery of a more direct and practicable route than was believed to exist, from the Great Salt Lake to the valley of the Sacramento. Since his report was made, a brief communication from Brevet Lieut-col Steptoe, commanding the troops in Utah, has announced the discovery of a still more direct line from Great Salt Lake to San Francisco. The new portion of this route passes to the south of Humboldt or Mary's river, and entirely avoiding the difficulties experienced by travellers along that stream, proceeds to the valley of the Carson river, being well supplied with water and grass. From Carson river it crosses the Sierra Nevada by the passes at the head of that river, and descends to the valley of the Sacramento, being practicable throughout for wagons.' *Pac. R. R. Rep't*, i. p. 16.

[13] The first one of those was known as Johnson pass, which was 2,000 feet lower than the old Carson road. The trail followed the exposed southern slopes of the valley of the south fork of the American river, and entered

branching off from the Beckwith pass, one or more of which were 2,000 feet lower, and consequently more free from snow. Competition grew up between the wagon routes where tolls were collected, to the advantage of the travelling public.

A tri-weekly line of stages was established from Placerville to Genoa in Carson valley in 1857, via, Johnson pass; and in 1858 the overland mail from Salt Lake to Sacramento began to be carried over this route. The following year came the Washoe migration, giving the Pioneer stage line enough to do, in fact too much, and a company was organized, which spent $50,000 in constructing a new road via Strawberry valley, having a wide solid bed, easy grades, but short curves. It was the best equipped stage road in the United States; kept sprinkled in summer, and free from snow in the winter. The coaches were of the best, the horses of the fleetest, and the whole outfit, including the foppish knight of the whip, a delight to the eye. The hotels at Placerville were crowded in those days, while the streets were filled with monster freight wagons making ready to cross the mountains with their great loads of merchandise or machinery. In 1863 the tolls on the new roads amounted to $300,000, and the freight bills on mills and merchandise summed up $13,000,000. All this pointed to a railroad to connect at Placerville with wagon transportation. The subject was agitated in 1859, and on the 30th of January, 1860, a meeting was called, at which resolutions were passed, but nothing accomplished in forwarding the enterprise.

For the seeming apathy of Placerville there were

the Carson valley via the south end of Lake Tahoe. It took its name from its explorer, J. A. Johnson, a Norwegian, who carried the mail, on snowshoes, between Placerville and Carson city in the winter of 1857. Another way lay between the Carson and Johnson passes, called the Luther pass. Placerville was 1,755 feet above sea level. Old Carson road, on the highest summit, was 9,036 feet above the sea, and on two other summits over 7,000 feet. Johnson's trail was 6,824 feet above the sea on the highest summit, and less than 6,000 in the Lake Tahoe valley. Luther's pass was 7,185 feet above the sea.

reasons which will appear as I proceed. Already I must have said enough upon the subject to 'impress upon the reader's mind the status of railway enterprises in California during the first twenty years of the commonwealth. Perhaps I should have more prominently brought forward the fact that each corporation held itself to be a link in that coming belt of steel which was to span the continent at some period as yet unknown, but foreordained. The sunburnt immigrant, walking with his wife and little ones beside his gaunt and weary oxen in mid-continent; the sea-traveller pining on ship-board, tortured with *mal de mer*; the homesick bride, whose wedding trip had included a passage of the Isthmus; the merchant whose stock needed replenishing; and the miner fortunate enough to be able to return home—every one, except, of course, the men of the Pacific Mail Steamship company, prayed for a Pacific railroad. And they did nothing else but pray, when it is a well-known maxim that the gods wait for a beginning before they lend their aid.

At length, in September 1859, a Pacific railroad convention was held in San Francisco, in Assembly hall, on the corner of Kearney and Post streets, according to a resolution of the legislature passed April 5th of that year.[14] There were present at this con-

---

[14] Resolved, by the assembly, the senate concurring, that to promote the interest, and insure the protection and security of the people of the states of California and Oregon, and the territories of Washington and Arizona, and especially to consider the refusal of congress to take efficient measures for the construction of a railroad from the Atlantic states to the Pacific, and to adopt measures whereby the building of the said railroad can be accomplished, it is expedient that a convention be held on the 20th day of September, 1859, at the city of San Francisco, in the state of California, composed of delegates from the said states and territories. Resolved, that the people of the several counties of the said states and territories are hereby especially requested to send to said convention delegates equal to the number of the members of the legislature of the said states and territories to which they are entitled to represent them in said convention. Resolved, that his excellency, the governor of this state, be requested to send copies of the foregoing resolutions to the governors of the state of Oregon, and territories of Washington and Arizona respectively. *Cal. Stat.*, 1858, 391; *Pacific R. R. Memorial to the President of the U. S., Heads of Departments, Senate and House of Representatives*.

vention delegates from every county in the state, and from Oregon and Washington. Its president was John Bidwell; its vice presidents were Edward Lander, of Washington territory; Alexander P. Aukeny, of Oregon; E. S. Holden and George W. Crane, of California; its secretaries, W. Rabe, O. H. Thomas, and Henry S. Wells. Thomas H. Pearne, a delegate from Oregon, offered a resolution that the committee appointed to prepare a memorial to congress, asking government to aid in the construction of a road through the territories, to connect at the east boundary of the state with such road as might be constructed in California, should be instructed to set forth the preference of the convention for the central route. A resolution was finally passed declaring the preference of the convention for the central route, the feasibility of which had been demonstrated by the maintenance upon it, summer and winter, of a stage line.

As to the means by which the California portion of the Pacific railway was to be constructed, it was proposed that the states of California and Oregon should create a debt of $15,000,000 and $5,000,000 respectively, to aid in the enterprise; also, that a railroad fund should be created by setting aside funds derived from the swamp and overflowed lands for internal improvements. A preference was expressed for a line from San Francisco via Stockton, to some intersection of the central route between the 42d and 38th degrees of latitude, thus making a selection which congress had never yet ventured to make, or endorse.

At this convention T. D. Judah, the engineer of the Sacramento valley and other local railroads, was present as a delegate from Sacramento city. He was, in fact, the chief promoter of the meeting, being deeply impressed with a belief in the practicability of a Pacific railroad, and possessed of a desire to see the enterprise inaugurated in California; perhaps also, with an ambition to have his name connected with it. For months he pondered over the problem, taking into his confidence a few business men of Sacramento, and urging the formation of a company to venture upon undertaking the California division of a transcontinental railroad. The men who listened most approvingly were Leland Stanford, Collis Potter Huntington, Mark Hopkins, and Charles Crocker.

At length in the spring of 1861, Judah called a railroad meeting at St Charles hotel in Sacramento, at which he made an appeal for assistance in perfecting his surveys of the different passes of the Sierra, which had already been crossed by him twenty-three times in different reconnoissances. He reminded the people of Sacramento that if they desired to have the great highway end with them, they must show some faith in its probability. In response a fund was raised to keep surveyors in the field, and for contingencies; but there was yet no organization.

On the 28th of June, the Central Pacific railroad company of California was organized, under the general incorporation law of the state. Leland Stanford was chosen president, C. P. Huntington vice-president, Mark Hopkins treasurer, James Bailey secretary, and T. D. Judah chief engineer. The directors were those just named, and E. B. Crocker, John F. Morse, D. W. Strong, and Charles Marsh. The capital stock of the company was $8,500,000, divided into 85,000 shares of $100 each. The shares taken by individuals were few, Stanford, Huntington, Hopkins, Judah, and Charles Crocker subscribing for 150 each; Glidden & Williams, 125 shares; Charles A. Lombard and Orville D. Lombard, 320 shares; Samuel Hooper, Benjamin J. Reed, Samuel P. Shaw, 50 shares each; R. O. Ives, 25 shares; Edwin B. Crocker, 10 shares; Samuel Brannan, 200 shares; cash subscriptions, of which ten per cent was required by law to be paid down, realizing but a few thousand dollars with which to begin so important a work as a railroad across the Sierra Nevada.

Indeed, when it is remembered that neither congress, individual states, nor syndicates of capitalists had yet been found willing to lay hold of so stupendous and hazardous an enterprise as that of constructing a Pacific railway at that time, the audacity of the Sacramento corporation in attempting the most difficult portion of it appears an act of madness or of inspiration. Few were found to give material encouragement to the project, and many said that those Sacramento merchants who had ventured upon it would sink their personal fortunes in the cañons of the Sierra.

Of those men, four, at least, have been much before the country. The combination was a fortunate one for its purposes. None of them were rich;[15] all had been accustomed to struggle with hardships in their youth. Stanford was a leader in the republican party just coming to the front in California, and was governor of the state through the most critical period of the formation and launching of the Central Pacific railroad company upon the sea of experiment. He had some practical knowledge of railroad construction, having been in the service of his father, a contractor on canals and railroads. He had also the reading of a lawyer, and had practised in the courts of Wisconsin previous to coming to California. Personally he was strong and enduring, exhibiting great tenacity of purpose and power to execute it, with a certain reserve which indicated unknown qualities behind his massive brows.

Huntington, a native of Connecticut, was one who, as a business man, had few equals in the land of his nativity or adoption. Energetic, quick-sighted, but cool in execution, despising nothing that had a dollar in it, nor any fair means of making a profit, he had saved and gained thirty or forty thousand dollars

[15] I quote from a memorial to congress the sworn statement of Leland Stanford and brother that the value of property owned by the firm in 1862 was $32,950; of Charles Crocker that he was worth $25,000 at the same period; of Mark Hopkins that he was worth $9,700; of C. P. Huntington that he had property amounting to $7,222; and of Huntington & Hopkins that they owned $34,115 in 1862. *Petition of the Stockholders of the Central Pacific R. R.*

since his advent in California.   To him were largely
intrusted the financial management of the company's
affairs, the negotiation of loans, and the purchase and
forwarding of supplies, all of which duties he successfully performed.   For such purposes no better selection could have been made.   Judah was a native of
Bridgeport, Connecticut, who was educated at Rensselaer Polytechic Institute of Troy, New York, and
still a young man, having been born in 1826.   He possessed enthusiasm, and the courage of his convictions.

Charles Crocker loved work for work's sake.   Entirely a self-made man, a man of remarkable energy,
of strong physique and power of will, he had already
become one of the most successful merchants in Sacramento.   He knew how to manage men in gangs, having developed some coal mines in the west before
coming to California.   He knew the value of money,
and to quote himself, was always trying to "make a
dollar buy a dollar and five cents' worth of material."
No danger of wastefulness with him.   E. B. Crocker,
who held ten shares in the company, was an engineer
by education, and afterward a lawyer by profession,
a man of good ability, and one of the most industrious members of the bar.   He was appointed by Governor Stanford to the supreme bench in 1863, to fill
an unexpired term, after which he became counsellor
to the company.

Hopkins' most marked traits were less of the positive sort than those of his associates, by whom he is
described as "one of the truest and best men that ever
lived," and as a balance-wheel in the company.   "I
never thought anything finished until Hopkins looked
at it," says the vice-president, which is praise enough.
Like Stanford and Crocker, his earlier career had
been passed in New York.

Bailey, the secretary, was a jeweller of Sacramento, and a friend of Judah's, who was introduced by him to Stanford, Hopkins, Huntington,
and Crocker.   He was succeeded at one of the early

elections by Edward H. Miller, a partner of Hopkins, and now a director of the Southern Pacific. Together, the railroad associates possessed the combination of business qualities that was required for their gigantic enterprise.

The result of the surveys in progress at the time of organization was, that of the three several routes surveyed, one through El Dorado county, which avoided Placerville; another through Nevada county via Nevada city; and another through Placer and Nevada counties via Dutch Flat, that by Dutch Flat was chosen, the line running from Lincoln via Clipper gap, Illinoistown, Dutch Flat, and Donner lake pass to the Truckee river. The months of August and September were devoted to mapping the surveys, making profiles of the mountains, and gathering information to be laid before congress. In October Judah went with these to Washington to endeavor to secure the passage of a Pacific railroad bill.

If from a financial point of view a better time could have been selected for the great enterprise than 1861, from a political and military standpoint none could have been more favorable. Congress could no longer wrangle over routes, since the south had withdrawn from the contest, and a rebel army held the 35th and 32d parallels. It needed no great forecast to perceive that, cut off from the Atlantic states, undefended, and divided in sentiment, California and Oregon offered tempting opportunities for foreign intervention, as well as domestic disunion, or that the remedy for this peril was railroad communication. It was therefore, as I have said, a fortunate time to come before congress with a bill to supply this need.

The California delegation at this time consisted of Latham and McDougall in the senate, and Sargent, Phelps and Law in the house. Latham had made a speech in favor of a Pacific railroad in January; but it is one thing to show the need of it, and another to point out how to obtain it. Sargent, who was newly elected, travelled in company with Judah, who was thus afforded the best of opportunities during the sea voyage of more than three weeks, shut out from the world, with nothing to divert his attention, while maps of routes were examined by day, and the whole subject talked over in the warm still nights, when the glory of the heavens was rivalled by the phosphorescent fire of the sea through which the steamer cleft her course.   When the people of California get ready to remember their benefactors in statues of marble and bronze, I trust that among them will be found a monument to Theodore D. Judah.

Fortunately, Sargent was assigned to the Pacific railroad committee.   No opportunity offered to get a bill before the house for two months, but when he at last forced its attention he made a decided impression. Then began the labor of shaping a bill so that it should not only meet the views of Californians, but secure the assent of the Atlantic states.   Up to this time all bills but one had been framed creating but one company to construct the whole road.

This one, called the Rollins bill, was adopted for a base on which the superstructure was patiently erected. It proposed in the first place to recognize the Leavenworth, Pawnee, and Western railroad company of Kansas, the Hannibal and St Joseph railroad of Missouri, and the Pacific railroad company of Missouri, as competing companies for the eastern end; while the Central Pacific of California, and the Nevada company of Nevada were authorized to construct the western end of the Union Pacific railroad.   The Perham company of Maine, which had its bills before congress for several sessions proposing to build the Peoples' Pacific railroad, was first put in the house bill, but finally expunged, leaving the middle space open to corporators, as previously shown.   The bill, as it finally passed, was chiefly moulded by Sargent, with the aid of Judah, before the committees of both branches of congress.   Of such value were the efforts of the latter that he received a written testimonial signed by the friends of a Pacific railroad in both houses of congress, a great burden being lifted off the congressional mind by the passage of this bill, July 1, 1862, the chief features of which were given in the preceding chapter.

In July 1862 Judah returned to California, gladdening the hearts of all classes with the news. He made his report, and his company gave notice to the government of the acceptance of the propositions contained in the bill. It was filed in the office of the secretary of the interior December 1, 1862. From this time two years were allowed for the completion of the first division of fifty miles. Forty miles must be constructed and equipped, and the telegraph completed before the issuance of the government bonds— $16,000per mile to the foot of the mountains; $48,000 per mile through the mountainous portion.

To procure the means to construct the first forty miles without injury to their several private interests was the problem that now presented itself, and compelled each officer to assume a specific duty. Huntington became the agent in the east, where he was enabled to procure material for fifty miles of road; [16] Stanford looked after legislation and other interests in California; and Crocker and Hopkins applied themselves to the business details necessary to be attended to.

On the 22d of February 1863 the ceremony of breaking ground at Sacramento took place, Governor Stanford throwing the first shovelful of earth, in the presence of the legislature and other spectators.

[16] The reader must not expect to find every transaction of the Central Pacific railroad explained, nor would it indeed be possible to make such explanation. But such things as have at different times come out in suits at law, and by voluntary admissions, are of course available and proper historical matter. It was represented that the company had been able to dispose of 900 of its bonds 'at rates more favorable than could have been expected.' *Sac. Union*, July 14, 1863. Huntington himself says that one of the ways adopted to raise the credit of the company was to make its members individually and personally responsible for a debt of $250,000. However that may be, it is certain that he shipped home the iron and other material for the 50 miles required.

Addresses were made by the governor, and by J. A. Benton, A. M. Crane, J. H. Warwick, W. H. Sears, Newton Booth, J. T. Morse, and Charles Crocker.

Having determined upon its route, a contract was let for the first eighteen miles, the track to be laid by the middle of August 1863; but it was not so completed until about January 1864. Thirty-one miles were completed by the 16th of September.

Meantime the Union Pacific had not commenced construction at its end of the line, nor did it commence until congress had been prevailed upon to double the amount of aid granted. The bill passed by congress in July 1864 benefited as much the California company as the Union Pacific, although the former appears but incidentally in it. In October 1863, Judah set out a second time for Washington, to ask for further benefits, but was stricken with fever, and died in New York, when Huntington succeeded to his work before congressional committees. He had already been delegated to proceed to Washington to prevent the bill then before congress from requiring the payment of any interest on government bonds for a term of not less than ten years.

The amended act increased the land grant from 6,400 acres per mile to 12,800. The reservation of mineral lands was removed, as far as concerned coal and iron; the time for designating the general route was extended one year, while the amount to be annually constructed was reduced from fifty to twenty-five miles. The reservation by the government of a portion of its lands to be issued to the companies was repealed, and if the chief engineer of either corporation should certify that a certain portion of the work required it, to prepare the road for the superstructure for any section of twenty miles, the secretary of the treasury was authorized to issue a proportion of the bonds which would have been due on completion amounting to two thirds. Either company might, on completion of each section, issue first mortgage bonds

on its road and telegraph line to the amount of the
bonds of the United States to be issued to them on
an even date; and the lien of the government should
be subordinate to that of the bonds of the companies
issued on their roads and equipments; besides which,
the government would issue its bonds to the companies
every twenty instead of forty miles, as in the original
act.   Further than this, the amount to be advanced
by the government to the Central Pacific was largely
increased, owing to the nature of the country through
which the railroad must pass, $48,000 per mile being
allotted to 150 miles of the mountainous portion,
which, as was afterward conceded, began within
seven miles of Sacramento, though there were no
steep grades to be overcome for several times that
distance.   Should the company elect to build east of
the state line, it would be allowed bonds of the government at the rate of thirty-two of $1,000 each per mile,
the understanding being that the whole country between the Rocky range and the Sierra Nevada was
more or less mountainous, although there are portions
of the distance between Carson valley and Salt lake
nearly as level as the Platte valley, where the Union
Pacific received only $16,000 per mile aid in bonds of
the United States.   The contract, which was filed in
the office of the secretary of the interior, was that the
government should pay six per cent interest on these
bonds in semi-annual payments, but that the whole
amount of the loan, principal and interest, should be
repaid in thirty years, less the sum of the value of the
services performed for the government during that
time in carrying mails, transporting troops, and government stores, etc.   The only limitation to the equal
privileges of the Central with the Union Pacific in
the bill was that authority was given only to construct
150 miles of road east of the boundary line of California.[17]   The two companies might consolidate upon any

[17] Says Huntington: ' 150 miles ought not to have gone into the bill; but
I said to Mr Union Pacific, when I saw it, I would take that out as soon as I

terms they might agree upon, with a capital stock not to exceed the actual cost of the roads so consolidated. The only guard set up for the protection of the government's interest in the roads was by the appointment of government directors, increased from three to five in the amended act. The office was a mere sinecure, these extraordinary officials knowing no more about the roads they 'directed' than the real directors might choose to tell them.[18]

The Union Pacific made no movement towards construction until after the passage of the amended act, whereas the Central Pacific of California had been more than a year at work, and had become entitled to receive $1,264,000 in United States bonds by so doing. Up to this point the Central had not felt secure in its undertaking, and had met with much opposition, both from rival corporations and from the San Francisco press, the latter contending from 1862 to 1864 that the company's means were inadequate to the business in hand, and laughing at a railroad company for building a wagon-road from Carson valley to Dutch Flat on their line, as a feeder to their road. They built this road in 1863–4, to divert the Placerville traffic, as well as to draw travel to their railroad; and because the El Dorado county people had organized a company to connect with the Sacramento valley railroad, which was to be brought to Placerville and continued on through Johnson pass to Virginia city before the Central could reach there and secure the trade of that prosperous mining region. This com-

---

wanted it out. In 1866 I went to Washington. I got a large majority of them without the use of one dollar. We still had our means, and wanted to get every vote, so I went into the gallery for votes—one head after another. I sat right there. I examined the face of every man, and I am a good judge of faces. I examined them carefully through my glass. I didn't see but one man I thought would sell his vote. MS., 79.

[18] This, at least, is the company's view of their usefulness after 20 years' experience. 'The U. S. directors of the Union Pacific,' he says, ' go a fishing once or twice a year—they take a car and go a fishing. It costs the company probably $5,000 a year to take them around. They are not worth an iota to the government. Of course there have been one or two exceptions ....When they get tired of it they come back.' *Huntington*, MS., 75-6.

pany was formed in January 1863, but no work upon the line was undertaken until the spring of 1863, when proposals were invited. The estimate was placed too low, but the road was constructed twenty-seven miles to Shingle springs by the middle of June 1865. The company owned no rolling stock, but used that of the Sacramento valley company. In short, after a hard struggle, it came to an end at, nowhere! assisted by the Central Pacific in arriving at that undesirable goal.[19]

[19] There is quite a pathetic history attached to this railroad enterprise—pathetic when it is remembered that upon its success depended the welfare of a once thriving and enterprising community, and that it failed. The first pres't of the company was S. W. Sanderson; chief engineer, Francis A. Bishop. In 1864 Charles E. McLane was chosen pres't; Ogden Squires, vice-pres't; J. M. Douglas, treas.; N. A. Hamilton, sec. El Dorado co. subscribed $200,000, and paid up its first installment of ten per cent. Placerville was also a subscriber to a considerable amount. In March 1864, the S. V. R. R. co., being a partner with the Placerville co., and wishing to assist in the rapid construction of its road, issued to Louis McLane and Danforth N. Barney, a trust mortgage providing for the issuance of 750 bonds of $1,000 each, payable in 60 years, at ten per cent interest, but issuing only 448 of the bonds, which were used in the construction of the Placerville R. R. from Folsom to Latrobe. The interest on the issued bonds was paid, but not on the non-issued bonds. In 1869 the Placerville co. became indebted to Wells, Fargo & Co. $150,000, which was a second mortgage trust conveyance. In 1871 Wells, Fargo & Co. obtained judgment in El Dorado co. against the company, and its property was sold on execution to William Alvord, subject to the trust mortgage. Subsequently to the title being acquired by Alvord, Leland Stanford, Mark Hopkins, and C. P. Huntington acquired three-fourths of the capital stock of the company, as well as the Alvord interest, entering into possession of the property; after which time the Placerville company was an insolvent corporation, transacting no business, and having only a nominal existence. In 1876 Stanford & Co. conveyed the road to the Placerville company, which operated it for account of the Central Pacific, under the name of the Folsom and Placerville Co. On the 13th of April, 1877, the S. V. R. R. and the F. and P. R. R. companies entered into an amalgamation. In the meantime Barney died, and Mc-Lane, the surviving trustee, asked to be put in possession of the road, which the Sac. and Placerville R. R. co. refused to surrender, when the court was asked to appoint a receiver, which was done. The S. and P. R. R. then brought suit to determine whether the district court had jurisdiction to appoint a receiver, and the sup. ct sustained the lower ct. These were but two of the many suits growing out of the affairs of this company. A majority of the stock of the company was in the hands of Louis McLane, in trust for Wells, Fargo & Co., as security for a loan. At the next election he voted the shares he held to elect a board of trustees, who conveyed to him the whole road in trust for Wells, Fargo & Co. All construction was at an end, and Placerville was left to bewail her misfortunes amid the ashes of her hopes. The Placerville stockholders however brought suit to declare the election of McLane's trustees void, on the ground that a trustee has no right to vote. Judge Brockway sustained McLane, but the sup. court reversed the decision, and declared that a board could not perpetuate its power by

The Placerville and Sacramento valley railroad
company was one of the first, after the Central Pacific company, to receive congressional aid. A grant
of land was made in 1866, conditioned upon the road
being completed to Virginia city within a given time.
The grant gave the road ten alternate sections of land,
not mineral, per mile, which if not found in the immediate vicinity of the road could be taken wherever
found within a twenty-mile belt, or if not found there,
beyond that. It was, in fact, a floating grant of ten
sections per mile for the whole distance. The road
not being built to Placerville, and extending but
eighteen miles within the county, the people of this
region protested against the grant being allowed, and
the matter was brought to the attention of the legislature, which in 1872, and again in 1874, requested

giving stock in trust to its friends. In Jan. 1881, the judge of the superior
court of S. F. ordered the Central Pacific company to deposit in court, to
abide the event of actions pending therein, $377,500, within thirty days, or
surrender the possession of the Placerville railroad to Louis McLane, whom
Judge Dwinelle had appointed receiver in the case of McLane v. The Railroad Company. What the company did, under this order, was to remove
its rolling stock, and leave the possession of the road to McLane. This action impelled the supervisors of El Dorado county to employ eminent counsel
to procure a modification of the order of the superior judge, so as to permit
the company to reopen the road, or compel the receiver to do so. In this
attempt they were successful, and McLane had already contracted for a
locomotive, when judgment was given against the company for $26,000, on
account of bonds held by one Kittle, and over $20,000 for costs and expenses,
whereupon the company took an appeal and gave a bond for $70,000, and
the receiver was discharged, liberating the road, which resumed its regular
business in July 1882. The taxes assessed to El Dorado co. on bonds of the
railroad nearly caused its ruin. The unpaid interest in 1873 amounted
to $75,000, which added to the tax levied for ordinary expenses made a total
of $7.25 on every $100 worth of property in the co., the taxable property of
which had been gradually declining for several years with the failure of the
mining interest. The Central Pacific procured a mandate of the supreme
court ordering the supervisors of El Dorado co. to levy the railroad interest
tax; but the supervisors, anticipating this movement, filed their resignation
with the county clerk to take effect a few days previous to the arrival of the
mandamus at Placerville; and as there were then no supervisors in the
county it could not take effect. The Placerville *Democrat* intimated that
the tax would be resisted to a bloody issue. *Sac. Union*, Oct. 29, 1873. These
troubles were finally settled, and Placerville was connected with Sac. by
rail in Dec. 1877; the Sac. valley R. R. co. and the Folsom and Placerville
R. R. co. being consolidated in April 1877. In the meantime her business
men had long before migrated to escape from the blight imposed upon the
county by railroad mismanagement, and she must begin at the very foundation to build up a decayed city.

congress to revoke it, and it was restored to the public domain in April of the latter year.

Hardly a railroad in California—and there were
many companies organized about this time, but received more encouragement from the press of the
state than the Central Pacific, whose directors were
mercilessly assailed in many a bitter paragraph.
Whatever of local jealousy there may have been in
these newspaper hostilities, there was also the pardon-
able fear that the Central company, not having the
means to prosecute so great an undertaking to the
end, would content itself with making connection at
Dutch Flat with its wagon-road to Virginia city, and
become an impediment in the way of other and perhaps
wealthier companies. Such, indeed, it might have
been had not the amended Pacific railroad act lifted
them above the fear of failure. From the moment
of receiving the additional land grant, and permission to mortgage their road as fast as completed, thus
in effect doubling the amount of government bonds
loaned to them, all doubt of their ability to perform
what they had undertaken vanished. Up to that
time they had been upon pretty much the same footing with other California roads, compelled to seek
county subsidies and subscriptions to capital stock,
and to solicit state aid.

No less than seven several acts favoring the Central Pacific company were passed by the legislature
and approved by Governor Stanford in 1863. The
first granted the right of way in the city of Sacramento, and all the overflowed land within the city
limits which had been previously granted to it by the
state; the second authorized the relocation of the
road if found to be expedient; the third gave the San
Francisco board of supervisors leave to subscribe, subject to the will of the people, $1,000,000 to the capi-
tal stock of the Western and Central Pacific companies; the fourth authorized the supervisors of Placer
county to subscribe $250,000 in stock; the fifth au-

thorized Sacramento county to subscribe $300,000 in
stock; the sixth authorized the Sacramento, Placer,
and Nevada Railroad company to sell and convey
to the Central Pacific company its road, property, franchises, rights and privileges; the seventh
declared that whenever the company should have
fully completed twenty consecutive miles of any portion of their road, it should be entitled to warrants
upon the state treasury to the amount of $10,000 per
mile; but it provided that only the first twenty-mile
section should be allowed to draw before it could be
shown that $300,000 had been expended upon the
construction of the road between Sacramento and a
point fifty miles east of the point of beginning; and
further, that for the first two years only $100,000,
with interest at seven per cent, should be paid annually, and $200,000, with interest, each fiscal year
thereafter.   The conditions upon which the company
received this subsidy were, that at all times when it
should be required, it should transport over its road
public messengers, convicts going to the state prison,
materials for the construction of the state capital,
articles for exhibition at the state fairs, and in case of
war, invasion, or insurrection, troops and munitions of
war free of charge.   Placer and Sacramento counties
subscribed as authorized by the legislature and the
vote of the people willingly enough, but San Francisco gave a world of trouble, chiefly owing to the
adverse counsel of the local press.   Here was a company, they said, of a few almost unknown individuals
of an interior town, possessed of insufficient means
to commence with, yet who had spent $200,000 in
killing the Placerville railroad by diverting travel to
the Dutch Flat route; who had purchased another
possible rival;[20] and had converted a third to its own

[20] Reference was here intended to the Sac., Placer, and Nevada R. R., to
run through these three counties, and to be carried eventually across the
mountains.   It had made considerable progress before selling out, having
been organized in July 1859.   James E. Hale was first pres't of the company;

purposes by assigning to it the grant and privileges
derived from the Pacific Railroad act of 1862, and
adopting it into its line to San Francisco.

This latter corporation was the Western Pacific,
which was organized in December 1862,[21] with the
purpose of constructing a railroad from San José to
Sacramento via Stockton, passing through the counties of Alameda, Contra Costa, and San Joaquin.
Congress confirmed the assignment in 1865, "with all
the privileges and benefits of the several acts of congress relating thereto, and subject to the conditions

John O. Jackson, treas.; and F. B. Higgins, sec.; S. G. Elliott made the
preliminary surveys, assisted by M. M. Stangroom, and succeeded by Sherman Day.   The route of this road was from a point on the California Central
—running from Folsom to Marysburg—to Auburn, Grass Valley, and Nevada
city.   The legislature of 1860 passed an act authorizing the people of Auburn
to vote on the proposition to subscribe to $50,000 of the S. P. & N. R. R.,
which they did by a unanimous 'yea.'   The same legislature authorized
elections on the following propositions :   The people of Placer county to vote
for or against subscribing for $100,000 of the stock of the S. P. & N. R. R.;
$25,000 of the stock of the Eastern Extension R. R.; $12,000 toward the construction of a wagon road from Secret springs, in Placer county, to Carson
valley; and $12,000 towards the construction of a wagon-road from Dutch
Flat, in the same county, to Carson valley.   But the people refused to place
their necks under these manifold yokes, and voted 'No' on each proposition.
The directors then carried their subscription books to San Francisco, where
$60,000 was subscribed, which with the $60,000 voted by Auburn sufficed to
grade 13 miles, and the contract was let to Jackson R. Myers.   The work
was greatly impeded by the severe storms and floods of the winter of 1861–2,
but with the aid of the Sac. Valley R. R. in furnishing iron and rolling
stock, the road was opened for business to Wildwood station, seven miles
from Folsom, in April 1862.   Nothing less was expected by the people
than that this road, which connected with the S. V. R. R. and Sacramento
city, would form a section of the transcoutinental railroad.   But the C. P. co.
being named in the Pacific Railroad act of 1862, with the choice made of by
that company of a route, destroyed their hopes, and provoked their hostility.
The legislature of 1862 had again authorized the county to vote on subscribing
$100,000 to the road, but they refused to consider it, and no election was held.
The road continued business until June 1864, when, the Central Pacific being
completed to Newcastle, that place became the depot for traffic instead of
Auburn, and the usefulness of the S. P. & N. R. R. was at an end.   The
S. V. R. R., which held a mortgage upon it for the iron supplied, foreclosed,
and commenced taking up its rails, for the purpose of relaying them on the
Sacramento and Placerville R. R., at that time a rival of the Central Pacific
for the trade of Washoe.   The latter co. procured an injunction against the
removal of the rails, and Placer county was involved in a railroad war,
some of the legal features of which have been alluded to in a previous note
on the Placerville R. R., and many arrests and trials resulted, together with
the calling out of troops to protect the officers of the law against hired fighters from San Francisco, and heavy bills of costs against the county; but at
last the rails were removed and the S. P. & N. R. R. was no more.

   [21] The officers of the W. P. R. R. were T. Dame, pres't; E. S. Holden,
vice-pres't; E. T. Pease, sec.; R. Chenery, treas'r; W. J. Lewis, chief-eng'r.

thereof;"[22] the time within which it must construct
its first twenty miles being one year from July 1,
1865, and the whole road within four years thereafter; but congress extended the time two years for
both.   The aid in bonds extended to the Western
Pacific was $1,975,560.

The $1,000,000 which San Francisco was asked to
subscribe was apportioned in the legislative act, $400,-
000 for the Western Pacific, and $600,000 for the
Central Pacific; and so eager were the people for railroad communication that they voted it, notwithstanding the opposition of the San Francisco newspapers.
But when it came to the supervisors they refused to
take action.   By permission of the legislature, a compromise was entered into between the city and the
companies, whereby, instead of subscribing $1,000,-
000 to the stock of the roads, the Central Pacific
company accepted a proposition to take an outright
gift of $400,000 in bonds of the city and county.   The
main reason for this change was that, under the provisions of the state constitution, the city treasury might
be held responsible in case of the company's failure.
Injunctions were obtained, however, restraining the
issuance of the city and county bonds, and legal proceedings delayed the action of the supervisors for more
than a year.   The court then dissolved the injunction
and ordered the delivery of the bonds, which were
finally handed over to the companies—$400,000 to the
Central and $200,000 to the Western Pacific.   Similar
proceedings were held in Sacramento, and law suits
were multiplied.   San Joaquin county subscribed
$250,000 to the stock of the Western Pacific, and
Santa Clara $150,000.

In 1864 the legislature repealed the $10,000 a mile
act, and substituted another empowering the com-

---

[22] A portion of the supposed land grant of the W. P. R. R. was included
within a Spanish grant over which congress had no right, and the land, on
complaint of settlers, was restored.

pany to execute and issue July 1, 1864, and any time thereafter, bonds in sums of $1,000 bearing seven per cent interest, payable half yearly; the interest to be paid at the state treasury for the first 1500, and the remainder where the company should prefer; the whole amount issued not to exceed $12,000,000, and the bonds to run twenty years, secured by mortgages on the railroad, its rolling stock, fixtures, and franchises; but upon the express condition that the city and county of San Francisco and the counties of Placer and Sacramento should be exempt as stockholders from liability for the payment of the company's bonds, interest, or principal over and above the amount previously subscribed by them. A tax of eight cents on each $100 of the taxable property of the state was to be levied, to be paid in gold and silver coin of the United States, to constitute a fund to be known as the Pacific railroad fund, out of which the coupons for the interest on the 1500 bonds should be paid as they fell due from time to time during the twenty years. If the special fund should not prove sufficient, the interest should be paid from the general fund. The conditions of this grant were the same as in the former act, with the additional one of a deed from the company of a granite quarry in Placer county situated on railroad land. In return the company was to transport without charge troops, supplies, munitions of war, and all convicts and lunatics in charge of state officials. The act was assailed as unconstitutional, for only in the case of insurrection, war, or invasion could the state create a debt of more than $300,000; but the bill was so drawn that the civil war was made the motive.

Not only had legislation in California to be looked after, but also in Nevada. At the constitutional convention held in 1863 Stanford was present to prevent the incorporation in the organic law of a clause permitting the legislature to donate to the first railroad company which should connect Nevada with navigable

waters $3,000,000 in bonds.   He pleaded for the dona-
tion direct to his company, and argued so well that the
obnoxious clause was stricken out.   The convention,
however, voted against the subsidy without conditions,
and it was lost altogether.   The company afterward
took reprisals.   There was a little flurry of competition in this quarter in 1864, when a series of resolutions was introduced in the Nevada legislature, the
tenor of which being that the Central Pacific had
completed but thirty miles of the road, while its
principal effort seemed to have been to reduce the
number of miles ordered to be constructed each year ;
that there was a railroad thirty-eight miles long,[23]
commencing at Freeport, at the head of navigation
on the Sacramento, and extending in a nearly direct
line with the capital of Nevada, which, with reasonable encouragement, would push forward to that point ;
therefore congress was asked to grant in United States
bonds $10,000,000 to the first corporation which
should complete an unbroken line of railway, in perfect running order, from the navigable waters of the
Sacramento to the eastern base of the Sierra.   Had
this subsidy been granted, the warfare which would
have ensued would have retarded the completion of
either road ; but the resolutions were a strong incentive to action

The Central Pacific had certainly an unpromising
commencement of its career in respect to suits at law
and legal proceedings generally.   Even Placer county,
which was to be greatly benefited by the railroad, if
honestly constructed and conducted, and which had
subscribed $250,000 to the company's stock, issued an
order by the board of supervisors to a committee con-

---

[23] The company here referred to was called the San Francisco and Washoe
R. R. co, and contemplated making Reese river its eastern terminus.   It required not much argument to show that congress was not likely to make a
further donation to Pacific railroads in that latitude; or if it should, the effect would be to delay rather than hasten the completion of a transcontinental road. *Speech of C. W. Tozer*, Feb. 6, 1865, pp. 14.   *Speech of D. H.
Haskell* on the same subject, 1865, pp. 16.

sisting of A. B. Scott and D. W. Madden to examine the books of the corporation, to ascertain what truth there was in the charges brought against it of having assumed that the grants made by congress to the Central Pacific company were made to the individuals named in the act as incorporators; and that they had assumed to sell these rights to the company incorporated under California laws, receiving therefor paid up capital stock amounting to several million dollars, such transaction being fraudulent toward the county as a stockholder of the corporation. The committee returned a satisfactory explanation to the charge, absurd in a legal point of view, but showing the suspicion which, however unjustly, attached to the management of this corporation from the beginning. That it should be so was not unnatural, considering the vastness of the interests at stake.

There was also expressed a great anxiety for the public lands. It was frequently asserted that the government having removed its reservation of a certain class of mineral lands, the Central Pacific company would take possession of mining land, and even of town-sites in the mineral regions; and when it became known in 1866 that its company's agents at Washington were asking for patents in Sacramento, Nevada, and Placer counties, which were, in the understanding of the people, mineral lands, it was determined to take action in the matter; and Sargent appeared before the judiciary committee of the California senate to demonstrate that a miner would have no standing in the courts against the holder of a United States patent to the land on which he might be mining; and that, therefore, something must be done to prevent the issuance of such patents to the railroad company. Before the same committee appeared, in December 1865, Stanford, B. B. Redding, secretary of state, and the company's land agent, with E. B. Crocker, attorney for the Central Pacific. The result of the examination into this subject was

that the committee reported in favor of resolutions
requesting the president to withhold his signature
from any patents to lands until a segregation of the
mineral from the agricultural had been made. These
resolutions were jointly passed by both houses of the
legislature, and telegraphed by Governor Low to the
California delegation in Washington on the 31st of
December. The dispatch was not delivered until
January 8th, between which dates patents had been
issued for 450,000 acres in Placer and Nevada counties. It was subsequently shown that the rights of
miners were secured by the law which made the grant
to the Central Pacific company; and as to the delayed
dispatch, why, no harm was done!

The county of Placer paid an annual interest on
its bonds issued to the company for stock of $20,000;
and might be required in and after 1868, if necessary
to raise the amount, to pay twenty-five cents on each
$100 worth of taxable property in the county to pro-
vide a fund for the liquidation of its bonds, which
were to be redeemed as often as the fund contained
$3,000 or more until all were liquidated. Again in
1868 the county as a stockholder applied for some
knowledge of the condition of the company, and its
manner of conducting business; but it does not appear that in either instance the inquiry served any
good purpose.

There were suits-at-law arising from the refusal of
the company to pay what the county conceived to be
a just tax. The first assessment was made in 1864,
when only a part of the road was completed, and was
based upon the company's statement of the length
and valuation of it, which latter estimate was placed
at $6,000 per mile. The district attorney complained
that this was much too low ; and proof being brought,
the assessment was raised to $20,000 a mile ; but
when the matter came before the board of equalization the value was placed at $12,160 a mile, and at
that rate the tax was finally paid,

The following year, through some blundering of the authorities, the assessment was allowed to go upon the company's basis of $6,000 a mile; but in 1866 it was raised to $15,000, which being refused, suit was brought and judgment obtained in the district court for the full amount. There was left, however, a loophole of escape, it being discovered that the revenue law of 1864 was in conflict with the constitution of the state, in some minor requirements, whereupon a compromise was effected, and the county accepted for the years 1866-7 a payment upon the company's terms of $6,000 a mile, "because it seemed clear that there was no reasonable probability of compelling the company, by law, to pay any tax whatever upon its property." Such, indeed, was the fact, and such, as we have seen, was the decision of the supreme court, although when the road was only one hundred miles in length its earnings were already on a very considerable scale.

In 1868 the contest was renewed between Placer county and the Central Pacific company. The case was in court until 1872, when it was finally adjudicated in favor of the county. In the interim the company caused the passage of an act by the legislature, authorizing and requiring the county of Placer to sell to the Central Pacific company of California any and all of its stock owned by the county. It was accordingly sold to the company for $250,000 in gold coin, which was used to redeem the outstanding bonds of the county. The stock held by the county of Sacramento was also recovered in the same manner. The foresight of the company in taking in its stock, which had served the purpose of launching it upon its successful career, was apparent a dozen years later, when, after the consolidation of the Western Pacific, and other roads with the Central Pacific, the county of San Joaquin sued the latter company for its proportion of the dividends earned by the combi-

nation, the amount claimed being about $50,000,000.
The county lost its case in the superior court of San
Francisco, and appealed to the supreme court; but
was finally compelled to accept $300,000 and yield
up its stock. As its subscription had only been to
the amount of $250,000, it does not appear that
after all there were any very serious grounds of complaint.

From the evils of subsidy-giving the country suffered
for many years. The population was shifting, the
available resources of the state few; but notwithstanding there was hardly a county in it that by 1870 had
not burdened itself with a debt of from $100,000 to
$300,000, at a high rate of interest, to run in some
instances for sixty years. Companies incorporated
under a general law besieged the legislature annually
to pass acts authorizing the people to vote on incurring this indebtedness; newspapers paraded the benefits to be received from every new railroad scheme,
often without knowing whether it had any merit.
Thus urged by the legislature and the press, the
people passed under the rod with the greatest unanim-
ity. Some counties have not to this day recovered
from the disastrous effects of railroad enterprises.
Not only did they incur debt and involve themselves
in law-suits, but the franchises granted to the insol-
vent companies left them nothing with which to
encourage a solvent successor. Such was the history
of El Dorado, Placer, San Joaquin, and some of the
southern counties.[24] Yet as,

> "The attempt
> Is all the wedge that splits its knotty way
> Between the possible and the impossible."

[24] The new constitution says: 'The legislature shall have no power to give
or to lend, or to authorize the giving or lending of the credit of the state, or
of any county, city and county, city, township, or other political corporation
or subdivision of the state now existing, or that may be hereafter established, in aid of or to any person, association, or corporation, whether municipal or otherwise, or to pledge the credit thereof in any manner whatever
for the payment of the liabilities of any individual association, municipal or
other corporation whatever; nor shall it have the power to make any gift, or
authorize the making of any gift of any public money or thing of value to
any individual, municipal, or other corporation whatever.'

it cannot be said that these efforts were of no advantage to the state. They were the pioneer enterprises, and shared the common fate of pioneers, the foremost of whom go down to make way for men of happier fortunes who avail themselves of their unrequited services.

The amended Pacific Railroad act of 1864 brought the relief of abundant means to the Central Pacific company. Up to this period of its history it had felt its way with great care. To meet the cost of the first forty miles, required by congress as a guarantee of the purpose and capability of the company, had compelled its financiers to resort to borrowing on their personal security.[25] On that alone, since bonds of an unconstructed road were worthless in the market, the money was procured which was expended on the first thirty-one miles, but as that indebtedness was probably liquidated by the money received from state and county subsidies, it may fairly be said that previous to 1864 California had been paying for the Pacific Railroad. As fast as the line was opened for business it produced a revenue which could be applied upon the company's indebtedness of any kind.

The status of the company was greatly improved by the passage of the act which made the United States "virtually an endorser of the company's bonds for the full amount of its own subsidy" of $48,000 per mile, making $96,000 the available sum to be drawn upon for each mile of the road. "The financial problem has been solved," said Stanford in July 1865, "and the result is abundant financial means to press forward the work to its utmost development."[26]

This new condition of affairs made a distinct change

[25] Says Huntington, in this connection, "We had endorsed paper to one party (Oakes Ames) of $1,250,000, personal security. They said, 'Here, we know you, and while we don't know what you are worth, we are satisfied you would not have endorsed the paper if you were not worth the money.'" On this credit he procured the aid required.

[26] That is, enough had been secured in money and land to build the railroad.

in the policy of the company.[27]   Through the means placed in their hands by the state, and by the general government, they were rendered independent. Instead of selling stock they gathered it in. They dismissed sub-contractors, and under the firm name of Crocker & Company secured for themselves the profits arising from the construction of the road. One of the strongest points in their favor was the fall in the price of gold and the rise in the price of bonds which followed the overthrow of the rebellion, before which event comparatively little work had been done, and

The following showing was made Sept. 16, 1864:

Authorized capital..		$8,500,000
Cash subscribed and issued for work and material....	$723,800	
Placer co. subscription...............................	250,000	
Sacramento co "	300,000	
For iron, cars, etc.,................................	188,000	
Total..		$1,462,500
The debts of the company were its first mortgage bonds issued................................	$1,250,000	
Individual accounts, etc...........................	205,700	
Pay rolls for August..............................	25,000	
Total..		$1,480,700
Assets of the company—Due from stockholders....	$ 203,886	
150 Placer co. bonds...............................	75,000	
327 Sacramento co. bonds..........................	163,500	
San Francisco co. bonds............................	400,000	
Due from the U. S. on completed road.............	1,264,000	
Grant by the state—$105,000 annually—..........	2,100,000	
Survey to the eastern boundary of Cal.............	66,740	
31 miles of first-class railroad.....................		
Uncompleted line above Newcastle................	50,000	
Shops, tools, etc., etc.,............................	25,000	
On hand and to arrive iron for 32 miles, and enough purchased for 20 additional miles, besides chairs and spikes for 53 miles, and ties for 22 miles, passenger cars, and freight and construction cars.		
The levee front in Sacramento city, from K street north, and 30 acres north of I street, granted by the city.		
The value of every alternate section of public land for 20 miles on each side of the road for 31 miles completed.		
The earnings of the road from June 6, 1864, when it was opened to Newcastle, to Sept. 14, less expenses..	38,917.74	
Total known values........................		$4,386,943.74

[27] Huntington, in a dictation given to one of my stenographers, and known in my library as the *Huntington Manuscript*, relates on pp. 9–12 some not un-

thus few of their bonds had been sacrificed at the low values ruling during the years of the war. Fortune indeed appeared to favor them at every turn, but if they were fortunate, they possessed also the ability to grasp opportunity firmly and skilfully and at the right moment. That the directors were far-sighted men, possessing, moreover, the tact and adroitness needed for the accomplishment of their task, their acts abundantly prove, as does also their success, in the face of all difficulties and discouragements. In July 1864, within a year and a half after breaking ground, their assets already amounted to nearly a million and a half; their debts were merely nominal, and they were already in the enjoyment of a good income from the completed portion of their road.

From Newcastle to the state line Crocker & Company built the Central Pacific railroad of California. It was not easy to obtain white labor for railroad work in the state, 500 men being all that were employed in the winter of 1864–5. To these were added during the summer 2,000 Chinamen. At a later date several thousand Asiatics were imported expressly for this labor, and during the last months of the construction period, an army of ten thousand men was in the field. Crocker proved an excellent superintendent and a thorough organizer. The engineering

important facts concerning the early management. He says that at the start a construction company was formed consisting of Stanford, Hopkins, Booth, Marsh, Peel, Judah, and himself. Each man was to furnish one-seventh of the means to build the road to Newcastle, which they were to own equally. But Peel receded from his agreement after the work had been commenced, being afraid to risk his share, $34,000 in gold, worth 30 per cent premium. Huntington then said that Peel must buy him out, or sell out to him; but Peel refused to do either. Huntington had another alternative, which was to stop work, which he did, going along the line and ordering 9 sub-contractors to cease, and pay off the men. These sub-contractors, thinking there was some real cause for this arbitrary action, offered to buy out the company, and build the road for themselves. 'All right,' said Huntington, 'I give you two weeks to do it in.' But the only man they found who was likely to become their capitalist, Charles McLaughlin, when he learned that Huntington was to sell out, declined to furnish the money, as Huntington very well knew he would do. The 9 sub-contractors returned, Peel having sold out, and the road was finished to Newcastle.

was performed by S. S. Montague, chief, and L. M. Clement, assistant, the work being inspected by George E. Gray, who has since remained in the company's employ. Some alterations were made in Judah's survey, and the gradient of 116 feet to the mile was the maximum in the whole line, which followed an unbroken ridge from base to summit of the Sierra, crossing but one river three miles above Dutch Flat, and attaining an altitude of 7,042 feet, but avoiding the second summit. It was slow work, cutting down, filling up, building trestles, tunnels, and culverts, and making a solid roadway for the passage of the heavy locomotives required on the mountains. But taking into account the difficulties, it was rapidly done. "Why," says Crocker, "I used to go up and down that road in my car like a mad bull, stopping along wherever there was anything amiss, and raising Old Nick with the boys that were not up to time." [28] Twenty miles a year was all that was completed in 1863, 1864, and 1865 respectively; in 1866 thirty miles; and in 1867 forty-six miles. A telegraph line, snow-sheds, depots, water-tanks, and all else constituting the perfect equipment of a first-class road, were constructed as the road progressed; and as the army of graders, masons, track-layers, and mechanics, passed by, they left not destruction, but civilization behind them.

In 1867 the state line was reached, but ever since the enactment of the amended Pacific Railroad act, the company had been resolved not to stop there, but push on through Nevada, and meet the Union Pacific as far east as practicable—if possible, at Salt Lake. The 150 mile limit, leaving them in mid-desert, was not to be thought of. If they came east of Carson valley they must make for the trade of Salt Lake valley. Nevada in 1866 granted them the right of way, although she never consented otherwise to aid the corporation.

[28] This vigorous description of his energetic course is from a dictation in my library entitled *Crocker's Railroad Building* MS.

The Union Pacific company made no commencement of construction before 1865, whereas, in July of that year, the Central had made 44 miles, and was at Clipper gap, 2,448 feet above sea-level. Taking into consideration the nature of the work to be done by the California company, and that the Union Pacific had several hundred miles of level country to build in, the advantage would seem to be in favor of the latter. This advantage, however, was more apparent than real; for while the Central was compelled to do a great amount of work to gain a little distance, it was well organized, which the other never was; it had rapid communication with the ships·which brought its manufactured material from the east, had stone, timber, and gravel distributed by nature along its line, could easily obtain subsistence, could command cheap Chinese labor, and was ;receiving an income from the completed portion of its road in addition to the means furnished by government. On the other hand, the Union Pacific company had to transport all its material overland, or by means of the Missouri river, at a heavy expense, no eastern railroad connection existing by the aid of which the vast amount of iron, tools, provisions, locomotives, cars, and all else, even including wood for ties and stone for masonry, of which the country was destitute, could be carried to their disembarkation on the Missouri, or beyond it. Thus, leaving out of the comparison the financial status of the two companies, which was in favor of the California corporation, the difficulties to be overcome were of about equal magnitude. The eastern company could lay down more rails per day over the Platte valley than the western company could in the Sierra; but the lofty Rocky range was to be overcome thereafter, while the Central emerged from the Sierra upon the valley of the ·Humboldt, where it could also make time in grading and track-laying.

It was at this point in its career that the officers of the Central Pacific organized among themselves the Con-

tract and Finance company for the further prosecution
of their enterprises, and under this fresh organization
set out to meet the Crédit Mobilier of America, which
was constructing the Union Pacific. Congress in
1866 had again authorized the Central Pacific company to "locate, construct, and continue their road
eastward in a continuous line" until it should meet
the Union Pacific's continuous line. In the autumn
of 1867 it emerged from its windings among the eternal hills, and entered upon a race for the trade entrepôt of Utah, as well as for bonds and lands. It was
the grandest race that ever was run—to which the
Olympics were a petty play—to complete the most stupendous work that men had ever conceived, and one the
most far-reaching in its results. When Shakespeare's
Puck promised a girdle round the earth in forty minutes, it might have been a prophecy verified by elec-
tricity; but even the inspired bard of Avon never had
a prophetic vision of two thousand miles of railroad
built in five years, bearing not thought only, but the
thinkers, swift as the flight of birds, from ocean to
ocean.

"You will see," said Asa Whitney in 1845, "that
it will change the whole world. . . . It will bring the
world together as one nation; allow us to traverse
the globe in thirty days, civilize and christianize man-
kind, and place us in the centre of the world, compelling Europe on one side and Asia and Africa on the
other to pass through us."

The Union Pacific on the plains had forged ahead.
In 1867, when the Central began the strife for the
goal, it had constructed 550 miles. In 1868 it built
425, and the Central 363 miles. Huntington, in the
east, was well informed of the financial condition of
his rival, Oakes Ames, and this knowledge he did not
fail to turn to account.[29] Thus when his associates

[29] Crawford's *Crédit Mobillier* and Hollister's *Life of Colfax* take exactly
opposite views of Oakes Ames' character in connection with the Union Pacific's affairs. It is certain, however, that the *Crédit Mobillier* ruined and
killed Ames.

wrote to him stating that the Union graders were at work in the Humboldt valley, he bade them not to be alarmed, but to go right along as fast as possible, and to leave a good road behind them.

The Central's advantages were that it had done with the mountains, whereas the Union had still some expensive work to do east of Ogden. The means of the former were ample, and it had a force of quiet, orderly Chinese, easily managed, while the other company employed white laborers, who, when not promptly paid, were refractory, and even hostile.[30]

Straining every nerve, the Union Pacific threw out graders as far west as Humboldt wells, 500 miles from Ogden, 80 miles of which were laid with track ; but the gap between that portion of its work and the continuous track east of it was never filled, and $1,000,000 was wasted. But the Central company took reprisals, and sent its graders east of Ogden; at the same time it filed a map of its route to Echo summit with the secretary of the interior, by whom it was approved, upon which a demand was made for the two thirds of the bonds due on completion, according to a clause in section VIII of the amended Pacific railroad act, which allowed such an advance when the exigencies of the case required it. By that remarkable power of will and ingenuity in presenting an argument, which has ever distinguished the attorney of the Central Pacific company, the president, the secretary of the interior, the attorney-general, and the railroad commissioners were persuaded that it was requisite to issue $2,400,000 in United States bonds to the Central company for this late extension of its road. Some congressmen, however, had become aware of the demand, and had exacted a pledge from the secretary of the treasury that he would not issue the bonds

[30] It was a matter well known at the time that when the U. P. had made connection with the C. P. it was unable to pay its gangs of men, and that Durant was held a captive by them for three days, and able only to make a partial settlement in time to take part in the ceremonies at the uniting of the roads.

before an investigation could be made. The investigation was made, but not until after the bonds had been issued and half of them delivered.

Here was indeed a surprise for the Union Pacific, whose engineers had reported only the year before that they would reach the Sierra Nevada before the Central company could cross the range. Had this been accomplished, the latter would have been left with only a short and difficult piece of road to operate,[31] and would always have been subject to the

[31] Huntington prepared an able pamphlet, addressed to the senate committee, giving reasons why the managers of the C. P. R. R. thought the point of junction should be at Ogden, on account of the trade of Salt Lake valley, and the coal in the Wasatch valley. As they had a hard task getting through the Sierra, they ought to have a larger share of the easier road; and as they had filed their map, and received a partial issue of bonds upon the sections reaching to Ogden, they had acquired the legal right to go there. Meantime the house committee was investigating all the circumstances attending the issue of the bonds on March 3, 1869. If the C. P. co. had all the rights claimed, why, asked the opponents of the C. P., issue the $2,400,000 of bonds during the dying hours of Johnson's administration, against the objections of one member of the cabinet, and in contradiction of the repeated pledges of Secretary McCullough? Why had it passed 50 miles beyond its completed track, and applied for and secured a partial issue of bonds over 180 miles of road beyond, unless to gain an unfair advantage of some kind? How could the partially completed grading of the C. P. R. R. have cost $20,000 per mile, as certified to by the commissioners, when the estimates of the U. P. R. R. co. for fully completed grading were less than $10,000 per mile? The law and the policy of the government being to allow the two companies to build track until they met, why should the U. P. R. R. be stopped to wait for the arrival of the C. P.? Why should the point of junction be crowded back to Ogden, and the U. P. be compelled to pull up its rails and wait for the C. P. to build to Ogden? Could any reasonable explanation be made of the facts that when the C. P. was 434 miles from Echo summit, it procured from Secretary Browning the acceptance of a map to that point, though one that was not as yet even authenticated, and thus reach forward and secure a partial issue of bonds over 80 miles of road, reaching to a point within 50 miles of the track of the U. P. and 230 miles from its own track—and all this in the dying hours of a dissolving administration? *Railroad Scraps*, 703. The testimony before the senate committee showed that there had been no over-issue of government bonds, but that they had been issued in accordance with the law and the facts, and on the opinion of the attorney-general. *N. Y. Times*, March 21, 1869. In view of these proceedings, it becomes of interest to hear Huntington's own version of the matter, given to my stenographer in interlocutory style. Perhaps nothing could better illustrate the quick, incisive manner of the man: 'I went to McCullough .... and said I, "Here's a report I want you to have." He had heard we were working there—meaning among the departments—and he had a talk with Ames. I knew he had agreed not to show me the bonds; but I was determined to have them if I could. I got a report from the attorney-general that I was entitled under the law to those bonds. I got one from the solicitor of the treasury; he asked for that; I was legally entitled to them. I got two cabinet meetings in one week outside of the regular day. The majority of them voted that I should have the bonds. Then he would not let me have

dictation of their rival. In such an event, all the benefit of their work would have been lost, and our carrying trade would have fallen into the hands of men whose interests were not in harmony with those of the Pacific coast. But for the rapid progress made by the Central Pacific during the later period of construction, this is precisely what would have happened.

It was now the object of the Central Pacific to obtain a legal right to make the junction at Ogden, but to that congress would not assent, it being in evidence that the completed track of the Union company was twenty-five miles west of Ogden at the time the Central company was seventy miles west. The two companies finally met with their completed tracks at Promontory point, 53 miles from the coveted point of junction, April 28, 1869. On that day the Central performed the remarkable feat of laying in one day ten miles of road. The disagreement between the two companies continued for some time longer. Huntington offered the Union Pacific company $4,000,000 for that part of their road from Promontory to Ogden. But to this

them. I went there nearly a week. I wanted to get them the day the administration closed....I called at McCullough's office; I sent in my card. McCullough would let me know the next morning....I said, never mind, I will go and see him. I did not know McCullough. I wanted those $2,400,000 bonds. "Well," said he, "you seem entitled to them, but I can't let you have them." I answered, "That is all right; give me the reasons, Mr Secretary, why you won't let me have them." "Well," he said, "you seem entitled to them under the law." Said I, "That is all right; give me the bonds." "Well," he replied, "no, I can't do it." "Well," I said, "I want your reasons. I have men in New York who are interested with me; when I go back, if I don't have the bonds, I want the reason why. You can see for yourself." Finally he remarked, "You do seem entitled to them."

'Well, I was nearly a week. I went in there every day, and asked him to give me the bonds, and asked for the reasons. One day there was a score of men right behind me. "Now," said he, "if you do not let those gentlemen see me, I will decide this thing against you." "Now," I replied, "Mr Secretary, rather than have the sec. of the U. S. do as foolish a thing as that, I will sit here for a fortnight." For half an hour or so I sat down. "Now," said he, "Mr Jordan [he came up just then], Mr Huntington is worrying me to death. He says he wants those bonds; what do you think of it?" Jordan said, "I have given you a written opinion, Mr Secretary, that he is entitled to the bonds under the law." "Well," said he, "he shall have the bonds."....A little after 8 o'clock I went out, and found the bonds in my room.' *Huntington*, MS., 53–4. The exact amount delivered was $1,333,000. *U. S. Ex. Doc.*, 38, vol. ix., 44th cong., 2d sess.

they objected, and after some fruitless negotiation the matter was finally settled by the national legislature, where was introduced into a joint resolution of congress for the "protection of the interests of the United States in the Union Pacific railroad company, the Central Pacific railroad company, and for other purposes," a proviso that the common terminus of the two companies should be at Ogden, or near it, and that the Union Pacific should build, but the Central Pacific should pay for and own, the road from Ogden to Promontory, where the two roads should connect. This proviso settled the matter, and the Central obtained the equal command of the Salt Lake traffic, with access to coal mines, securing at cost price that part of the Union road from Promontory to within five miles of Ogden, which five miles it subsequently acquired under a lease.

The extra expense to the Central Pacific of this speedy completion of the road was very great. Supplies were conveyed for hundreds of miles in advance of the finished sections. Materials, railroad iron, and even locomotives were hauled by teams in winter through the deep snows of the Sierra for the building of the road beyond, since at that season of the year little but tunnelling work could be accomplished in the mountain regions.

At length all was in readiness, and on the 10th of May, 1869, took place the ceremony of joining the roads at Promontory. About 1,000 people were in attendance, comprising the officers, directors, and employés of the two companies, with their invited guests, a delegation from Salt Lake, several companies of the 21st infantry, with a band, from Camp Douglas, and a number of military men of note from the same place. The spot where the joining of the Atlantic to the Pacific took place was a grassy plain, sunken between green hills. The horizon was bounded on the east by the silver-rimmed summits of the Wasatch, whose rosy-violet atmosphere was in harmony with the iridescent hues of Great Salt Lake on which they looked. Overhead the speckless blue beamed warm and gracious. In the immediate vicinity were a few canvas tents. Moving about the ground, mingled in a picturesque confusion, were people from the Occident and the Orient—Mongolian, Celt, full-blooded aborigine, and half-caste Mexican, garbed in national costumes, or innocent of any, mixing freely with American citizens and soldiers, each regarding only the significant preparations. At 11 o'clock a train from the west drawn by a decorated engine approached the gap left between the rails. Soon another train from the east, with no less elegant appointments, drew up on that side of the breach, each debouching some principal actors on the scene.

The "last tie," of California laurel, handsomely finished, and having in the center a silver plate, bearing the names of the officers of both companies, was placed beneath the connecting ends of the rails, and a spike of gold placed in a cavity made to receive it, was driven home by a silver hammer in the hands of President Stanford of the Central Pacific. Other significant and precious articles were displayed, the gifts of neighboring territories. There followed addresses of which everyone will be able to conjecture the import. Congratulatory telegrams were read from cities east and west. The Union company's train, with Durant and friends, passed over the connecting rail and backed upon its own track. The Central company's train ran over it, and also returned, with its face to the front. Cheers, music, and banqueting followed, and the royal marriage was consummated. Next morning there arrived from New York a half-dozen passenger coaches for the Central company, part of which were attached to the president's car on its return to Sacramento, this being the first train to pass over the entire distance from shore to shore. Thus ended in fulfilment the long dream of nearly forty years, a fulfilment that was celebrated in every

city of the north and many of the south with enthusiasm. Especially at Sacramento and San Francisco were the rejoicings loud and earnest. But how
soon do we rise to the greatest event, making it seem
commonplace! Finished and yet not complete, for
the commissioners appointed to examine the road reported that a further expenditure of $4,493,380 would
be required to put in a completed state the 551 miles
east of Sacramento, and especially that part of the
road east of Truckee and in the Humboldt valley.
A clause in section 6th of the original Pacific railroad act declared that "after the said road is completed,
until said bonds and interest are paid, at least five
per centum of the net earnings of said road shall also
be annually applied to the payment thereof." Upon
the report of the commissioners the president ordered
deposited with the secretary of the treasury, in first
mortgage bonds, the four millions and over in which
the road was deficient, and that patents to land should
be withheld where not already issued until the road
should be completed according to law.

In September 1869 the railroad company made
application to withdraw the four millions of bonds,
which was denied. But it appearing a few months
later that the deficiencies had been supplied to a considerable extent, the secretary of the interior allowed
patents for half the lands to issue, and soon after the
withdrawal of the bonds. In March 1871 the secretary again refused to issue patents to the land held
for security, the road still being incomplete in the eye
of the law. In 1874 a bill was pending in congress
providing for giving the company a title to the granted
lands in order that they might be taxed by the states
through which they passed. While the matter was
being taken under advisement by the secretary, a
new commission reported that the road had been fully
completed at a cost of $5,121,037.23. Of this sum
$1,014,681.34 was for wharves and depot buildings at
Oakland and San Francisco; $241,490.87 for im-

provements of depot grounds at Mission bay, San Francisco, and $105,906.60 for the steamer *Thoroughfare*, built for ferrying cars across the bay to and from Oakland. Now in 1875 the courts were occupied with the question as to the meaning of the act, and at what point of completion it became obligatory upon the company to commence paying the five per cent of its earnings on the extinguishment of its indebtedness. The government claimed that on the 15th of July, 1869, when it was opened for business it was "completed" for this purpose, and the Central Pacific that the date of its completion was October 1, 1874. The government, it was said, had barred its claim by its admissions in taking security from the unfinished road; or, if the road was really what was required in 1869, it had been unjustly and unlawfully treated by the government, which had withheld its land patents for five years. But if the government's claim did not commence to run until October 1874, then nothing was yet due when the action was commenced. Such was the decision by which, in 1877, the United States government lost its case in the United States circuit court for the district of California, Judge Sawyer giving the decree. By this decision the Central Pacific would have gained $1,836,-635.10, a small amount, they claimed, when was considered the extra cost incurred by completing the road seven years in advance of the stipulated time. The court of claims in 1878, however, decided in the case of the Union Pacific that the road was "completed" in the sense which the act contemplated in 1869, which decision affects both roads equally.

The trunk line being now in operation, the directors could give redoubled attention to their interests in California, and first of all came the question of a Pacific coast terminus. It was at first supposed that if the cars of the Central Pacific should enter San Francisco, they would do so by way of San José; but another company had already built a road on the most available route between those cities. As a matter of policy, however, something should be done to conciliate the metropolis, as the act of congress granted them exclusive control of a line to be located from the Sacramento river to the Golden Gate. As already stated, therefore, this part of the route, with its share of the subsidies in bonds and lands, had been assigned to the Western Pacific company, whose directors were residents of the several counties through which the road was to run. Thus while disposing of a portion of the line to which they attached but little value, they had retained the exclusive control of all that lay east of Sacramento. By this measure, they had prevented the capitalists of San Francisco from obtaining voice in the control of the company.

The legislature of 1867–8 passed two acts bearing upon the question of a terminus on San Francisco bay. The first, "for the purpose of providing the Terminal Central Pacific Railway company with proper depot and commercial facilities," granted the company the submerged and tide lands situated in the bay, beginning at a point 400 feet northwest of the northwest point of Yerba Buena island, and extending northwesterly one mile, comprising 150 acres, with the right of way, 200 feet in width, from this grant to the Oakland, Alameda or Contra Costa shore, for the purpose of building a bridge or bridges; the conditions of the grant being that the Terminal company should establish its depot upon it and use it for the terminus of the Central Pacific railroad, or railroads, and should commence improvements within one year from the date of filing an acceptance of the conditions, which further required a payment of not less than three dollars an acre, and an expenditure of not less than $100,000, not including bridges, the first year; and that a first-class railroad, with ferry communication, should be established between San Francisco, Oakland and Vallejo within four years; the avowed object of the Terminal company being to construct a railroad from Vallejo to Yerba Buena or Goat island, to bridge the strait of Carquinez, construct a tunnel under it, and to construct a bridge to Yerba Buena from the Oakland shore.

The second act mentioned above gave the governor authority to appoint a board of tide-land commissioners, who should take possession of the salt, the marsh, and tide lands lying under water belonging to the state in the city and county of San Francisco, and have them surveyed and mapped to a point where the depth of water was of a depth of twenty-four feet at low tide; and provided that the Southern Pacific and the Western Pacific companies should have granted to each of them for a terminus thirty acres, without price—the grant lying in the water front of Mission bay, together with the right of way over the state lands to their termini 200 feet in width, the companies to make their own locations. The conditions of this grant were that the governor should issue patents when $100,000 had been expended in improvements, any time within thirty months, after which period, if the improvements had not been made, the grant should lapse; and in the event of the donation being accepted, it should be in lieu of all other grants made or to be made to the company accepting in the city and county of San Francisco at that session of the legislature. The time allowed for making their termini upon the Mission bay lands was extended two years in 1869–70, as was also that of the Terminal Central Pacific company; and it was declared by the act of the legislature that the construction and completion of a railroad from the strait of Carquinez, opposite Vallejo, to the Yerba Buena land grant should be construed as fulfilling the conditions of the original act.

Another terminal organization was the Oakland Water Front company, incorporated in April, 1868, with a capital stock of $5,000,000. It was really a branch of the Western Pacific company, and had for

its object to construct, own, hold, control, and use
wharves, docks, basins, dry-docks, piers, and warehouses in Oakland or elsewhere ; and to lease or sell;
borrow or lend money ; carry on commerce, foreign
or domestic ; in short, transact any business in any
way, and to lease, sell, or convey the submerged and
overflowed lands in front of Oakland.[32] The first
trustees of this company were E. R. Carpentier, Lloyd
Tevis, H. W. Carpentier, John B. Felton, Leland
Stanford, and Samuel Merritt. H. W. Carpentier
was president, and executed a conveyance March 31,
1868, to the Oakland Water Front company of "all
the water front of the city of Oakland," as described
in the incorporation act of 1852, being all the lands
in that city lying beween high tide and ship channel,
with the rights mentioned above. On the following
day the Water Front company agreed to convey to
the Western Pacific railroad company 500 acres of
tide land, in one or two parcels. Some concessions
were made in the matter of streets to the city of Oakland; 25,000 shares in the Water Front company
were promised to H. W. Carpentier; 5,000 shares to
John B. Felton ; and to Leland Stanford the remain-

[32] The town of Oakland was the result of the ' squatting ' of three Americans on the Peralta grant, viz.: W. Carpentier, Edson Adams, and A. J.
Moore, near the foot of Broadway. A writ of ejectment being served upon
them, a compromise was effected by a lease. A town was laid out, and in
1852 incorporated. To provide for the erection of wharves, etc., the lands
lying between high tide and ship channel were granted and released to said
town, provided they were used for these purposes, the board of town trustees having the disposal of the entire water front. Among the first ordinances passed by the board was one giving a grant of the use of it for thirty-
seven years, with the privilege of collecting wharfage to Carpentier, who
erected wharves and docks for that purpose. In 1853 a clamor began to be
raised concerning this robbery of the city; suits and counter-suits followed,
but the ordinance was confirmed by a special act of incorporation in 1862.
In 1867 the W. P. R. R., wanting a terminus at Oakland, the objection was
advanced that Oakland had nothing to offer. The city then commenced suit
to recover title, when a compromise was effected, and the legislature passed
an act to enable the city to carry it into effect, giving the mayor authority to
compromise. In 1880 suit was again brought to grant title to the 500 acres
deeded to the railroad company. At the same time the government, in order
to complete certain improvements to the harbor, required a certain quantity
of land on the line of the channel to Oakland creek, which the company
transferred for that purpose while this suit was pending. The City of Oakland may regret, but never can recall her early action in giving away her
water front.

ing 20,000 shares. On the part of the Western Pacific, that company agreed to construct or purchase and complete a railroad to its land grant at Oakland within eighteen months, and within three years expend not less than $500,000 in gold coin in improvements thereon, or forfeit its rights to the city of Oakland. These benefits were secured before the completion of the Central Pacific.

In 1869–70 a bill was before congress the object of which was to secure certain rights to the Western Pacific railroad company, which was but another name for the Central Pacific, on Yerba Buena island. This attempt greatly alarmed San Francisco, the belief being current that the railroad power designed to seat itself on the island, and by leveling it and constructing a causeway to the Oakland water front prepare the foundations of a commercial city whose business would be entirely controlled by this corporation. Such a scheme, if carried out, would be a fatal blight upon San Francisco, which already felt the influence on her shipping business of the opening of a railroad with its terminus at Vallejo.

This Vallejo railroad was incorporated in 1867 under the name of the California Pacific railroad company, which forthwith commenced to construct its line to Sacramento, with a branch to Davisville and Marysville. It was the successor of the San Francisco and Marysville railroad company, which was itself the successor of the Marysville and Benicia railroad company, organized under the general incorporation act of 1851.[33]

[33] This road was disincorporated, the grand jury of Yuba co. reporting its affairs in an unsatisfactory condition, although the legislature of 1855 extended its time. In 1857 the legislature passed an act authorizing the county of Yuba to subscribe $200,000 to the capital stock of any railroad company which should be formed for the purpose of constructing a railroad between Marysville and Benicia or any point on the Sacramento river, at or near Knights Ferry. *Cal. Stat.*, 1851, 596–300; *Marysville R. R.*, a pamphlet report of the engineers, W. J. Lewis and F. Catherwood, 1853. The S. F. and Marysville R. R. co. was organized as a successor to the M. and B. N. R. R., the legislature of 1858 granting it the privilege of keeping railroad bridges across the Sacramento river and Green valley creek. *Cal. Stat.*, 1858, 265–7. It also granted as an inducement to prosecute the enterprise, one-half mile of the water front on the north-east side of Napa bay, together with one-half

The Central Pacific had spared no effort to prevent the California company from entering Sacramento with their road, the dispute causing great expense and trouble, which sometimes threatened bloodshed. The case was brought before the courts, and during this armistice, on the 29th of January, 1870, the latter landed a load of passengers in the city, amidst cheers and rejoicings. But for this privilege the commissioners appointed by the court awarded the Central company damages to the amount of $360,-680, the award being thrown out by the court as excessive.

The California Pacific's route being shorter than that of the Western Pacific, through a beautiful country withal, and its passengers being transferred to elegant steamers for a charming hour upon the bay,

of all the over-flowed and swamp lands, in alternate sections, lying within the counties of Yolo and Colusa, upon condition that within two years these lands should be reclaimed over a certain district, the road completed to Napa bay within four years, and the remainder of the swamp land reclaimed. The first part of the proposition, which was accepted, not being fulfilled in 1860, the time was extended to 1862, when it was still unfulfilled. The company had, however, graded sixty miles of road-bed, which was seriously washed and damaged by the flood of 1861–2, and the contractors assigned as a reason for the delay, the breaking out of the civil war, and the difficulty of obtaining iron. Another extension of time was obtained from the legislature, but the company relinquished the swamp and over-flowed land grant, retaining only the half mile of water front, and agreeing to complete its road in 1864. At the same session (1861) another bill was passed, authorizing the people to vote upon a proposition to issue $100,000 in bonds of the county of Yuba, devoted to aiding railroad construction, in aid of a rival company, but the supervisors refused to break faith with the S. F. and M. co. In 1863 the legislature again extended the time to 1865, and restored the land grant. The management was unfortunate throughout, and the company was finally dissolved.

Its successor, the Cal. Pacific, had for its first pres't De Witt Clinton Rice, a pioneer of 1840, and a native of Canandaigua, N. Y. He resided at Marysville for many years, removing to San Francisco finally, where he died in 1870. The vice-pres't was John B. Frisbie, and the other directors C. G. Bockins, A. D. Starr, L. C. Fowler, and W. K. Hudson. The contractors were W. F. Roelofson, D. C. Haskin, and J. M. Ryder.

The Cal. Pacific R. R. Extension co. was incorporated April 14, 1869, with the ostensible purpose of constructing a railroad from Napa Junction on the Cal. Pacific to Calistoga, thence to Healdsburg, and through Sonoma co., Santa Rosa, and Russian river valleys to Cloverdale. Its intention was not carried out, and it was accused of securing the credit of the Cal. Pacific co. by false representations, which were connived at by a contractor and stockholder in that co., whereby it was induced to guarantee bonds of the Extension co. to the amount of $3,500,000, which guarantee caused many persons to subscribe to the stock.

was a very popular one, and the road should have been profitable to the stockholders, as with proper management it would have been. In July, 1871, this corporation, by its president, Milton S. Latham, agreed to sell to C. P. Huntington, Leland Stanford, and Mark Hopkins 76,101 shares of the 120,000 shares of $100 each which constituted its capital stock, and three-fourths of the subscribed capital stock of the California Pacific Extension company, in consideration of the sum of $1,579,000 to be paid to Latham in 1600 bonds of the company of $1,000 each, with twenty years to run, at six per cent, secured by mortgage on the road and property, payment to be made on the 1st of October, when, the control of the company having passed into the hands of the Central Pacific, a new board of directors should have been elected, when, also, all the property of the company, including steamers and barges, should be transferred to the Central.

The California Pacific, previous to this transaction, owned, besides its $12,000,000 of capital stock, all the stock of the San Francisco and North Pacific, and the San Francisco and Humboldt bay railroads, to the amount of $8,600,000 each, and the California Eastern Extension stock, which had never been issued. All these roads passed, with the California Pacific, into the control of the Central company.[34]

[34] A company was incorporated in 1868 under the name of the San Francisco and Humboldt Bay R. R. co., which proposed to construct a railroad from Sausalito to Humboldt bay, through the counties of Marin, Sonoma, Mendocino, and Humboldt. After grading ten miles, work was suspended. The *Vallejo Recorder* of June 19, 1869, explained the failure by saying that: 1st, S. F. capitalists were opposed to making improvements on a rival harbor; 2nd, the Cal. Navigation co. were opposed to losing the lucrative trade of Sonoma and Mendocino counties; 3d, Petaluma proper did not desire the road, which would kill that aspiring little city; and 4th, the road would not pay.

However that may have been, the San Francisco and Humboldt railroad passed out of sight. Its successor was the S. F. and North Pacific R. R. co., in which Peter Donahue owned a controlling interest, having purchased a majority of the stock of the old company in Aug. 1870. On the 29th the first spike was driven, with a hammer wielded by Simon Conrad, pres't of the board of trustees; and in Oct. the road was completed to Santa Rosa, when the county supervisors accepted ten miles, and paid over the subsidy, amount-

Previous to the transfer the Central Pacific purchasers obtained another contract with the California Pacific, whereby it was agreed, instead of the delivery of the bonds, that the Central should build for the California Pacific an additional track from Davisville to Sacramento, also strengthening and widening the existing road. But the contract was not performed, and in the winter of 1871–2 that portion of the road was washed away, after which the Central secured a contract for the Contract and Finance company to repair the road, charging $1,600,000 for the job. This sum more than covered the price of the bonds paid to the California Pacific. About the same time the Central Pacific directors sold to Peter Donahue the San Francisco and North Pacific railroad, purchased from him by the California company, for the sum of $1,050,000, less a large amount which they owed to Donahue, which debt was thereby discharged. Soon afterward, in conjunction with other parties, they caused suit to be brought against the California Pacific company, based upon certain advances of the Central company, to meet $500,000 of principal and $300,000 of interest upon the income bonds of the first-named company, and other matters, and obtained a confession of judgment for $1,394,000, which became a lien upon the road, in preference to the claim of the other bond-holders.

With its two hundred miles of road, its control of the shortest route between San Francisco and Sacramento, and of the finest steamers running on the bay, with the support of foreign capitalists and its somewhat aggressive policy, the California Pacific had indeed been one of the most formidable rivals[35] of

ing to $50,000. The town of Donahue was laid out at the creek's mouth, wharves erected, and on the 31st of Dec. the line from deep water to Santa Rosa was opened. This road now extends southward to San Rafael, in Marin co.; and on the north sends off from the main road a branch to Guerneville. In 1875 Donahue offered, for a subsidy of $60,000, to extend the North Pacific R. R. from Cloverdale to Ukiah, in Mendocino co., which road is now in operation.

[35] They had purchased the boats of the California Steam Navigation company, bought up the Napa valley railroad and the Petaluma valley road,

the Central company, until the latter, by its purchase of the stock and its skilful manipulations, became virtually master of its movements, and put an end to all competition in that direction.[36] In doing this, however, it is probable that they may have somewhat damaged the value in foreign markets of their bonds of the California Pacific Extension company.

Finally, in 1876, the Central Pacific leased the California Pacific for a term of twenty-nine years, at an annual rental of $550,000, and three-fourths of the amount of its net earnings; all expenses, taxes, and repairs to be paid by the lessees, and the one-fourth of the earnings belonging to them to constitute a sinking and contingent fund, to pay the interest on its bonds, and meet extraordinary outlay. Having thus obtained entire possession of the California Pacific, the Central proceeded to make it a part of the continental railroad by constructing a branch to Benicia, and controlling all the traffic moving to or from San Francisco.[37]

Such, up to this date, were the main extensions and

begun work on a line from Suscol to Santa Rosa, and announced their intention of building a track from the Sacramento valley to Ogden, thus making connection with the Union Pacific.

[36] The Cal. Pacific Eastern Extension co. entertained a grand scheme, which was no less than a railroad commencing at Davisville, on the Cal. Pacific R. R., proceeding thence northerly through the Sac. valley, thence in a N. E. direction, crossing the boundary of the state near Goose lake, going north to Christmas lake in Or., thence easterly through Or., Idaho, and Utah, to Ogden. Also from Pitt river about the 41st parallel, branching northwesterly to a junction with the Or. and Cal. R. R.; also from Christmas lake westerly to a junction with the Or. and Cal. R. R. at Klamath lake; in all 943 miles of railroad. The capital stock of this company was $50,000,000, in 50,000 shares of $1,000 each. W. F. Rulofson held 250,000 shares, Milton S. Latham, J. Friedlander, R. P. Hammond, A. Gansel, E. L. Sullivan, F. D. Atherton, J. P. Jackson, J. B. Frisbie, Alex. De Faski of London, Eng., W. H. Tillinghast, E. H. Greene, London, each 18,000 shares; Rudolf Sulzbach of Frankfort-on-the-main, 24,000; Julius May, 18,000 shares. Ten per cent of the subscriptions was paid-up capital. By the sale which Latham made to Stanford, Huntington, and Hopkins, the Cal. Pacific's shares in this company went into their hands.

[37] The Napa valley R. R., from Vallejo to Calistoga, was united with, and became a branch of, the Cal. Pac. R. R. in Dec. 1868. The road was built chiefly by county subscriptions of $10,000 per mile, the organization being in 1864. C. Hartson was the first pres't, and A. A. Cohen sec. When it was finished to Napa, Hartson obtained the free gift of the county's $10,000 per mile, which, with private subscriptions, completed the road to Calistoga in Oct. 1868. On the 27th of May, 1869, the N. V. R. R. was sold to Rulofson and Ryder for $500,000, which placed it in due time under the Central Pacific management.

acquisitions of the company in central and northern California,[28] and when we consider the comparative obscurity of its origin, and the opposition or indifference which it encountered at the outset, it is indeed remarkable that the railroad quartette should not only have accomplished their original task, but already have secured for themselves almost the entire carrying trade of the Pacific coast. Though men may differ in opinion as to the policy of the directors, it must at least be conceded that they displayed a similar combination of business ability, together with a remarkable aptitude for harmonious coöperation.

In 1866 Congress granted to the California and Oregon Railroad company, organized in 1863, and reorganized in 1865, to aid in the construction of a railroad and telegraph line from the Central Pacific to Portland, the same amount of land per mile that was granted to the interoceanic roads. The condition to secure this subsidy was that twenty miles of the road should be constructed and equipped in 1868, but failing of that, congress extended the time of the completion of the first section to 1870, and of the whole road as far as it lay in California, to 1880. The capital stock of this company, divided into 150,000 shares, was $15,000,000. In December 1869 it became consolidated with the Yuba Railroad company,[39] organized in 1862 to extend the California Central railroad[40]

[38] They also controlled a fleet of the best steamboats plying on the harbor of San Francisco.

[39] The first officers of the Yuba company were Samuel Brannan pres't, James P. Flint vice-pres't, J. M. Shotwell sec. and treas'r, Charles Dana, H. B. Williams, the other directors. The company was composed of the bondholders of the defunct Cal. Central R. R., who, to make the bonds of the old road available, found it necessary to push the new road through to the Yuba river.

[40] The Cal. Central R. R. was commenced in 1858, to run from Folsom to Marysville, but it was completed no further than Lincoln. Its first officers were J. C. Fall pres't, William Hawley vice pres't, Ira A. Eaton sec., John A. Paxton treas'r, T. D. Judah chief eng'r, John H. Kinkead, H. P. Catlin, S. T. Watts, the other directors. The Central Pacific in 1863 purchased the Cal. Central at sheriff's sale, and that portion between Roseville and Folsom was abandoned. The Cal. Northern, or Northern Central, as it was sometimes called, was incorporated in 1860, with a capital of $1,000,000, for the

from Lincoln to a point at or near Marysville, and in which the Central Pacific had a controlling interest. In 1870 the California and Oregon and the Central Pacific were consolidated, the Contract and Finance company constructing the road to Redding. It was not carried further north than Tehama county until 1886-7, when it was completed to a junction with the Oregon line at Ashland in Oregon.

Other consolidations with the Central Pacific took place in 1870, as the Western Pacific, the San Francisco, Oakland, and Alameda railroad,[41] and the San Joaquin valley railroad[42] companies, which were conjoined under the name of the "Central Pacific railroad" --the words "of California" being omitted after this

purpose of constructing a railroad to Oroville from Marysville, with the intent to extend it eventually to Red Bluff. It was completed to Oroville in 1864. The Yuba company connected with it, making an unbroken line of railway communication 90 miles in length, skirting the oak forests, granite quarries, gardens and vineyards of the foothills, and crossing the Central Pacific 18 miles N. E. of Sac. The officers of the Northern Central in 1861 were M. H. Darrach pres't, J. W. Buffum vice-pres't, D. D. Harris sec., S. Van Orden treas'r, U. S. Watson chief eng'r, Charles De Po, H. M. Smedes, H. B. Lathrop, J. M. Clark, the other directors; Chenery, Burney & Co., contractors.

[41] In 1861 an act of the legislature authorized certain persons to construct a railroad from the westerly end of the bridge leading from the city of Oakland to the town of Clinton, through the streets of Oakland to a point on the bay of S. F., where the shore approached nearest to Yerba Buena island, 'or at such a point as a railroad may be built from to said island,' under or by virtue of an act granting to certain other persons the right to establish and run a ferry between the island of Yerba Buena and the city of S. F., and to construct a railroad from the island to the Alameda co. shore. *Cal. Stat.*, May 20, 1861. This latter corporation was known as the S. F. and Oakland R. R. co. In 1863 the legislature authorized the supervisors of Alameda co. to subscribe $220,000 to the capital stock of the Alameda valley R. R. co. The object of this corporation was the construction of a railroad from the easterly terminus of the S. F. and Oakland R. R. in Oakland through Alameda co. to a point near Vallejo mills, with a view to connecting with the Western Pacific R. R., then incorporated. This company was authorized to keep a wharf at the encinal of San Antonio. It crossed San Antonio creek by a drawbridge, and connected with the S. F. and Oakland railway, constituting together the S. F., Oakland and Alameda R. R. It ran to Hayward in 1865, and was extended to Niles and San José under the C. P. management. The first board of directors was composed of B. C. Horn pres't, Timothy Dame treas'r, George C. Potter sec., William Hayward, J. A. Mayhew, J. B. Felton, and Ed. M. Derby.

[42] The San Joaquin valley R. R. co. was organized in 1868, with the intention of bringing the trade of the valley to Stockton. Its consolidation with the C. P. diverted the traffic to San Francisco by deflecting at Lathrop. It was constructed by one of the Central Pacific's contract companies, and extended south to the Colorado river and beyond. Its subsidies were said to be valued at $3,000,000.

change in the organization. The Stockton and Visalia railroad, commenced in 1870,[43] also came under the control of the Central Pacific, and now constitutes a part of its line to Goshen. Its purpose on organizing was to compete with the trunk line of the Central Pacific, but soon afterward it joined the great consolidation in which were eventually united nearly all of the short California roads. By still another consolidation in 1877 the Stockton and Copperopolis railroad was joined with the Stockton and Visalia, and thus with the Central.

[43] As early as 1852 a railroad was projected from Stockton to Sonora in Tuolumne co. by the San Joaquin R. R. co., which, after organizing and disposing of stock, abandoned the enterprise. No other railroad company was organized in this co. for 10 years thereafter, when the Stockton and Copperopolis R. R. co. was incorporated. The legislature of 1863 authorized the counties of San Joaquin, Stanislaus, Calaveras, and Tuolumne to subscribe $100,000, $25,000, and $50,000 respectively in aid of this road. *Cal. Stat.*, 1863, 102, 310. Copperopolis was, at this period, the centre of a rapidly growing mining industry, but the richest deposits were exhausted in two years, and the prosperity of the region declined. However, in 1865, the Copperopolis company reorganized, and applied to congress for aid. A grant was obtained of 231,000 acres in March 1867, conditioned upon a subscription of $200,000, upon which 5 per cent should be paid in, and the work commenced before March 1869, ten miles to be completed annually until the road should be finished. The officers of this company were E. S. Holden pres't, R. B. Parker vice-pres't, George Gray treas'r, John Sedgewick sec., W. L. Dudley, John H. Redington, Willard Sperry, E. R. Stockwell, and J. K. Doak directors. The failure of the mining industries forced the company, in order to save the franchise and land grant, to transfer their rights to the Cal. Pac R. R. co., which constructed the road as far as Milton. In the mean time the Stockton and Visalia co. was, in 1869, incorporated, and the Cal. Pac took the contract to construct its road. Instead, however, it constructed a branch line from a point on the Copperopolis R. R., 12 miles east of Stockton, to the Stanislaus river, calling it the Stockton and Visalia R. R. By this means it was hoped to save the subsidies, but the legislature requested congress to revoke the land grant, which was done. *U. S. Sen. Misc. Doc.*, 67, i., 43d cong., 1st sess.; *Acts and Res.*, 43d cong., 1st sess., pp. 88-9. The city of Stockton had subscribed $300,000, and the county of San Joaquin $200,000, in aid of the Visalia road. The bonds were issued, and placed in the hands of trustees to be delivered to the company on the completion of the first section of the road. The corporation, without building any part of their road, tendered the short line running from the Stockton and Copperopolis road to the Stanislaus river, built by the California Pacific company, as a compliance with the terms of its agreement, but the trustees refused to deliver the bonds, and protracted litigation followed, the district court deciding for the city and county, and the supreme court reversing the decision. The case was compromised by the city and county paying $300,000. Shortly after the completion of the branch above spoken of, all of the Cal. Pacific's work was turned over to the Central Pacific. San Joaquin county has been unfortunate in the matter of its railroads, whether from a want of energy in its people or other causes. In 1874 a charter was obtained by the Stockton and Ione railroad company to construct a narrow-gauge road from tide-water

Of the railroads in the northern counties [44] but little remains to be said. They have greatly multiplied and extended. The construction of several short roads about the bay of San Francisco has, by con-

at Stockton to the coal-fields in Amador co. The line was surveyed, and its construction commenced, the principal person connected with it being Henry Platt, the projector of the Pacific coast narrow gauge. Several miles of grading were done, about one mile of track was laid, car-shops and depot buildings were erected, and locomotives purchased, when matters came to a standstill. The contractor, it was said, had misrepresented and mismanaged, entangling the enterprise in debt, and finally selling out 'to the enemies of the road and of Stockton by disposing of the bonds extorted from the road.' Construction ceased, and litigation followed. All that remains of the well-planned enterprise is the useless depot and the more useless mile of road. The Stanislaus and Mariposa R. R. co. organized in June 1866, with a capital stock of $1,500,000, was intended to connect with the Copperopolis road 10 miles from Stockton, running thence to Knight's ferry and La Grange, a distance of 50 miles, and to be extended finally to Fort Tejon; but it was never even commenced, owing to the opposition of better organized companies. The San Joaquin and Tulare R. R., incorporated in 1873, is another of these failures.

[44] In 1865 Sonoma co. began to stir in the matter of railroads, and the following companies were formed: In October, 1865, the Petaluma and Healdsburg R. R. co., which failed to do more than raise a few thousand dollars. In 1867 the Vallejo and Sonoma Valley R. R. was proposed as a substitute, which offered to construct a road from Suscol to Cloverdale and Healdsburg; and in 1869 the Petaluma and Cloverdale R. R. co., with a branch to Bloomfield, made a proposition to the county, but none of these came to fruition. The Sonoma Valley R. R. was commenced about 1880, is completed from Sonoma Landing to Glen Ellen, and is the only one in the co. except the S. F. and North Pacific, already mentioned. The first railroad in Mendocino co. was built by the Mendocino R. R. co. in 1875, from Cuffey's Cove 3½ miles into the forest along Greenwood creek. It was a narrow gauge, and its rolling stock consisted of 2 locomotives and 29 flat cars. Its principal stockholder was A. W. Hall. The North Pacific Coast R. R., it would seem, should have been extended to Eureka, on Humboldt bay, which lacked an outlet to the valleys of Cal., and connection with the railroad system of the state. But, instead, the people of Eureka, the town having about 6,000 inhabitants, projected the construction of a railroad called the Eureka and Eel River R. R., to give the people of that valley, southeast from Humboldt bay 15 miles, easy communication with the chief town of Mendocino co. Money was raised among the citizens to pay for the survey of a route, each contributor to have the privilege of subscribing to the capital stock of the corporation, and receiving credit to the amount of said subscription to the preliminary survey. They petitioned the legislature in 1878 to permit the town to subscribe $75,000 in aid of this road, and an act was passed in consonance with their wishes. C. S. Ricks was sent to Sacramento to urge this bill; the representative from Humboldt, Mr Russ, and the senator from that district, Robert McGarvey, were instructed to insist upon the right of the Eureka people to vote money to subsidize a much needed improvement; the democrats voted for it, although no-subsidy was one of their party watch-words. This road now extends 26 miles southeast, and will probably be brought to connect with the North Pacific or with the Sacramento valley system. The Vaca Valley and Clear Lake railroad was incorporated in 1869, and constructed from Elmira in Solano co. to Vacaville in the same co. for the convenience of shippers of fruit and vegetables to San Francisco. In 1876 it was extended to Winters in Yolo co. In 1877 it

nection and combinations, made travel in all directions
from the metropolis easy, agreeable, and popular.
Most of these are under the Central Pacific management. The causeway connecting the Oakland shore

was re-incorporated, and extended to Madison, a distance of 30 miles from
Elmira. Its officers in 1879 were A. M. Stevenson pres't; T. Mansfield
treas'r; E. Allison sec't'y; G. B. Stevenson supt.

In Jan., 1871, the people of Antioch, near the mouth of the San Joaquin
river, conceived the idea of a railroad to Visalia in Tulare co., and organized
a company to construct it. The project never came to fruition; but the two
towns have railroad connection through the lines of the Central Pacific
company.

The railroad from San Rafael to San Quentin was undertaken by the citizens of San Rafael in 1869. At the first meeting, Feb. 19th, A. Mailliard,
J. Short, S. V. Smith, (sen.) P. K. Austin, L. A. Hinman, James D. Walker,
and James Ross were chosen directors. Mailliard was elected pres't of the
company, Charles Stevens sec'ty, and J. D. Walker treas'r. The length of
the road was 3½ miles; capital stock $50,000. As was so frequently the case,
their ambition outran their means, and the project rested until Mr Donahue
took hold of the railroad affairs of Marin co. In 1865 a railroad was constructed from a point on the Central Pacific to the Mt Diablo coal mines in
Contra Costa co.

In 1870 the project of connecting Nevada city and Grass Valley in Nevada
co. with the Central Pacific at Colfax was first agitated. Nothing was accomplished until 1873, when a survey was made for a narrow gauge railroad
over this route, and in 1874 congress granted the right of way. *Zabriskie's
Land Laws, Sup.* 1877, 64. The company was incorporated under the name
of Nevada County Narrow Gauge R. R., and received no subsidies, but was
permitted to charge 10c per mile for passengers and 20c per ton for freight,
with additions for hazardous freight. The officers of the company were
John C. Coleman pres't; John W. Sigourney vice-pres't; George Fletcher
secretary; J. H. Bates chief engineer; William Watt, Edward Coleman, J.
M. Lakenan, Niles Searles, and R. W. Tully directors. Turton and Knox,
contractors, constructed the road, commencing in Feb., 1875, and completing
it to Nevada city, 22 miles,, May 20, 1876.

The Northern Railway company, chartered July 19, 1871, extends from
West Oakland to Martinez, 31 miles, and from Woodland to Tehama, 100
miles, forming important links in the railroad system of the state. It controls branches between Suisun and Benicia, 16 miles; and Martinez to Tracy,
46 miles; all these lines being leased to the Central Pacific.

The California and Nevada R. R. has been constructed from Oakland to
a point above San Pablo. It was originally intended to be carried to the
Nevada state line near Bodie, but later made for Walnut creek, Contra Costa
co. It is a narrow gauge. The Bodie and Benton R. R. is also a narrow-
gauge road, 32 miles long, now running between Bodie, in Mono co., and the
town of Mono. It was chartered in Feb. 1881, and was in operation, with
its branches, in 1882. The Carson and Colorado R. R. runs from Keeler, in
Inyo co., to Mound House, Nev., 299 miles. It is a narrow gauge. The
company was organized in May 1880, and the road completed before 1885.
The Nevada and Cal. R. R. was first called the Nevada and Oregon R. R.
It runs from Aurora, Nev., to Goose lake, Cal., 300 miles, entering Cal. at
the lower end of Plumas co. It is a narrow gauge, and was chartered April
25, 1881. In April 1884 it was sold under foreclosure of a mortgage at U.S.
marshal's sale, and purchased for the account of the bond-holders for
$372,534.21, when it was reorganized under its present name. Only 31
miles are in operation, from Reno, Nev., to a point in Cal. a few miles west
of the boundary.

with the mole at deep water, has been gradually widened and strengthened until it forms a solid peninsula, supporting several tracks, and a very extensive and commodious depot, which replaced the old one in 1881. Elegant double-deck steamers are used for ferry-boats on all the lines terminating at San Francisco, and cable and other lines of street cars, several of which belong to the Central Pacific company, convey passengers to every part of the city with ease and expedition, the cable-road system of our metropolis being acknowledged as one of the most complete and commodious in the world.

Colusa co. R. R. is a narrow gauge extending from Colusa to Williams, on the Central Pacific. The San Joaquin and Sierra Nevada R. R. runs between Bracks, on the Mokelumne river, and Valley spring, in Calaveras co., 41 miles. It is a narrow gauge, chartered in March 1882, and opened in March 1885. The Sierra Valley and Mohawk R. R. co. incorporated in Oct. 1885. It is a narrow-gauge branch of the Nevada and Cal. R. R., being intended to run from its junction with that road through Long valley, in Lassen co., through Beckwith pass, through Sierra valley, and thence along the Middle fork of Feather river to Mohawk valley, in Plumas co., 35 miles, its object being to open up a timber region. Lake Tahoe R. R. is a short line running between Tahoe and Truckee, constructed in 1876.

The Banta branch of the Central Pacific R. R., extending from Banta on the then Western Pacific to Antioch, with a branch to Stewartville, projected in 1871, has since been continued to Martinez, and is a part of the Central Pacific line from Goshen to Oakland and S. F. The two most important of the narrow-gauge railroads have their termini at Sauzelito and Oakland. The North Pacific Coast R. R. was chartered in Dec. 1871, and opened for traffic Jan. 11, 1875, when it also leased the San Rafael and San Quentin road. It extends from Sauzelito to Duncan's Mills, in Sonoma co., passing through many suburban towns, the San Geronimo valley, and the redwoods to Point Reyes, skirting the shores of Tomales bay for 16 miles. The whole route is full of picturesque beauty and remarkable engineering. Until recently its terminus was at Duncan's Mills, in the Russian river country, in the heart of a redwood forest, and its length is 82 miles. The road is a very profitable one, and connects with San Francisco by a fine ferry.

The South Pacific Coast R. R., chartered March 1876, was completed May 15, 1880, from Newark, in Alameda co., to Santa Cruz, 51 miles. From Newark to Alameda point, 25 miles, it was built by the Bay and Coast railway co., and leased to the South Pacific Coast co. A portion of it is through the Alameda and Santa Clara valleys, but it also crosses the Santa Cruz mountains, where much fine engineering was required. Six tunnels on this road aggregate 12,000 feet in length. The road was owned principally by James G. Fair, James L. Flood, and A. E. Davis, the two latter owners selling out to Fair, who extended the line to Oakland, with a view to competing for the street-car travel of that city, but after expending considerable money, he sold out all his interests to the Southern Pacific R. R. co., which now owns and operates it. A fine ferry-house at Alameda point, with a half-hourly line of steamers, and other attractions on the Point make this a profitable line. The Santa Cruz and Felton R. R. is a branch of the S. P. C. R. R., running from Felton to Boulder creek.

Thus the Central Pacific company, in extending its branches and popularizing its roads, has thereby furnished a transportation system which has left little to be desired.[45] Something further of its history will be contained in the following chapter, which could not well be arrived at in this.

[45] In June 1876 a lightning express train made the trip from New York to San Francisco in 81 hours. It left Jersey City June 1st at 1 o'clock and 3 minutes A. M., and arrived at the foot of Market street on the 4th at 9 o'clock 43 minutes and 18 seconds A. M. The excursionists were received by Mayor Bryant with ceremonies befitting the occasion. H. C. Jarrett and Henry D. Palmer were the managers of the party.

Of the career of Peter Donahue, the pioneer manufacturer on the Pacific coast in the line of machine-shops and iron-works, a prominent railroad builder, and one of the worthiest and most public-spirited citizens in his adopted state, mention has already been made in this volume. On the 3d of March, 1890, occurred the decease of his son, J. Mervyn Donahue, who was no less widely respected, and who, on the death of his father in 1885, took charge of the railroad system which bears his name, and under his management became one of the most profitable and best conducted on the coast. A native Californian, he received his education at the St Ignatius and Santa Clara colleges, and later at Stonyhurst, England, whence he was recalled by his father's sickness. In addition to his railroad interests he was identified with a number of enterprises, among others the First National bank and the State Investment company, in both of which he was a director. In the circles of society, and among military and fraternal associations, he was widely esteemed, being colonel of the 5th infantry, a leading member of the Young Men's institute, and a trustee of the Native Sons of the Golden West. In January 1884, he married Miss Belle Wallace, the daughter of Judge Wallace of the superior court. Two children, the result of this union, are deceased. Mervyn's untimely death, which occurred at the age of thirty, and was caused by a severe cold, contracted while inspecting a line for a proposed railroad, was deeply and widely regretted by all classes of the community.

CHAPTER XXI.

RAILROADS—SOUTHERN PACIFIC SYSTEM.

1865-1888.

INCORPORATION AND CHARTER—RELATIONS TO THE CENTRAL PACIFIC—
LEGISLATION—YERBA BUENA ISLAND AS A TERMINUS—CONSOLIDATION
OF RAILROAD INTERESTS IN CALIFORNIA—RELATIONS WITH THE GOV-
ERNMENT—EFFECT UPON BUSINESS AND POLITICS.

THE Central Pacific very soon after the completion of its trunk line began to plan the extension of its system to the southern coast counties which, impatient of their isolation, were attempting by means of local roads to establish communication with the interior, and with each other.

In December 1865 the Southern Pacific Railroad company of California was incorporated, and was authorized by the legislature in April 1866 to receive aid from any of the counties south of Santa Clara; with which roving commission it set out to construct its road from Gilroy south. The articles of incorporation of the Southern Pacific company declared that the company was formed for the purpose of constructing a railroad from some point on the bay of San Francisco, and to pass through the counties of Santa Clara, Monterey, San Luis Obispo, Tulare, Los Angeles, to San Diego, and thence easterly through San Diego county, to the eastern boundary of the state, there to connect with a railroad from the Mississippi river.

In July 1866 congress granted to the Atlantic and Pacific Railroad company, to aid in the construction of its road and telegraph line, from Springfield, Missouri, by the most eligible route to Alberquerque, in New Mexico, and thence by the 35th parallel route to the Pacific, an amount of land equal to that granted to the Central Pacific. By this act the Southern Pacific railroad was authorized to connect with the Atlantic and Pacific, near the boundary line of California, at such point as should be deemed most suitable by the companies, and should have therefore the same amount of land per mile as the Atlantic and Pacific.

The charter of the Southern Pacific being for a line through the coast counties, where also it had taken its land grant, the people of those counties were willing and anxious to aid in its construction.[1] But in

---

[1] The legislature in 1863 passed a bill (it had failed in 1861) authorizing the board of supervisors to subscribe $100,000 to the capital stock of a railroad from Los Angeles to San Pedro, or Wilmington, on the coast. This scheme miscarried, owing to objections against the terminus, which was 4 miles distant from the steamer landing. At length, in 1868, another bill was passed authorizing a subscription by the county of $150,000 toward the capital stock of a railroad between Los Angeles and Wilmington, and the city to subscribe $75,000 further. Upon this the work was commenced Sept. 19th, and rapidly prosecuted. The cars of the company were built at Wilmington, a shipyard established there, and a tug-boat provided for service in the harbor. On the 26th of October, 1869, the road was completed. *Banning's Settlement of Wilmington* MS. in Cal. MSS. E. 139, pp. 7 et seq.; *George, The Subsidy Question*, pp. 7–8; No. 12, *Railroad Pamphlets*. In 1872 the citizens of Los Angeles accepted a proposition from the Southern Pacific company to connect them with their line through the interior to Fort Yuma to connect with the Texas Pacific for a subsidy consisting of 5 per cent upon the entire taxable property of the county, as follows: The county and city stock in the Los Angeles and San Pedro R. R.; bonds of the county at 20 years, bearing 7 per cent interest, $377,000, and 60 acres of land in the city, amounting altogether to $610,000. A branch road to Anaheim was also to be constructed, and both were to be completed within two years. Early in 1874 trains were run northerly to San Francisco and easterly to Spadra. The Anaheim branch was completed in Jan. 1875; and subsequently extended to Santa Ana. On the 6th of Sept., 1876, connection was made between Los Angeles and the main line of the Southern Pacific. As early as 1868 a Santa Bárbara company was organized to build a coast railroad, and applied to congress for a charter and also a land grant similar to that enjoyed by other California roads. The grant was obtained, and a subscription of $50,000 in gold coin to be paid with bonds bearing 7 per cent per annum, to run for 20 years, with a donation of the right of way through private property along the line. About this time the Central Pacific completed its transcontinental line, and commenced the construction of the San Joaquin Valley R. R., running through the middle tier of southern counties to Goshen in Tulare. Soon after there arose a contest, to be referred to hereafter, between the Southern Pacific and its rivals from the east, all of which desired the support of Santa Bárbara. The Southern Pacific pro-

1867 it filed a map with the secretary of the interior, showing its route to be not through the coast counties, but out through the Pacheco pass, east of Gilroy, into and through the interior counties of Fresno,

posed to run a line N. E. through Bakersfield to connect with the Central Pacific's southern extension. The Atlantic and Pacific desired to run a line through the coast counties from S. F. to San Diego, and thence to St Louis; but could only do so in the event of receiving a $10,000,000 subscription to its stock. The Texas Pacific, which had its terminus at San Diego, would like to have a subsidy from the upper counties. Between the solicitations and representations of the rivals, Santa Bárbara became doubtful of the proper course to be pursued, and placed the matter in the hands of a committee of twenty-six. The proposition to donate the county subsidy before named to any company which should connect Santa Bárbara with either S. F. or St Louis being left to a vote of the people, was rejected almost unanimously, because it was generally understood that the Texas Pacific, with its terminus at San Diego, would be the road benefited. After the Southern Pacific had extended its line to Newhall, Santa Bárbara co. asked to be authorized to issue bonds to the amount of $500,000 in aid of any company which would build a railroad connecting it with S. F., or any transcontinental line. This, however, the legislature refused; since which time until the present, the city of Saint Barbara, her face to the sea, has remained sadly dreaming over the uncertainty of railroad affairs, far from the busy commerce of her more fortunate neighbors, disturbed for a moment now and then by a rumor that the Southern Pacific contemplated filling the gap which has so long existed between sections of its line in the coast counties.

San Luis Obispo also shared in the neglect which condemned Santa Bárbara to seclusion, except as to local enterprise. When the S. P. R. R. in 1872 incorporated its branch road, abandoning the line between Tres Pinos in San Benito county and Huron in Fresno county, and adopting a route from Soledad via San Miguel and the Palonio pass in San Luis Obispo county to Lerdo in Kern county; with an additional branch from a point near San Miguel southerly to an intersection with its line running from Tehachapi pass to Los Angeles and Fort Yuma, it was expected that the sleepy old mission town, the adjoining vales and sunny hillsides, would soon echo to the thunder of trains rushing down rocky cañons, or start at the sudden shrieks of locomotives announcing a safe passage and arrival; but in that the waiting people were disappointed, as already demonstrated. However, they agitated a narrow gauge railroad from the town to deep water in the harbor in 1873, which culminated in the organization of the San Luis Obispo railroad operated by horse power. Wharves were built at Port Harford, the end of the road, and business upon them became active. But this was only a suggestion of what should be done, and was followed by the San Luis Obispo and Santa Maria Valley railroad company, chartered in 1874 by capitalists of S. F., who purchased the improvements of the former road from John Harford, its principal owner, and consolidating with it, absorbed it entirely. No more of the road was built until 1881, when it was extended to Arroyo Grande. In Oct., 1882, it was completed to Los Alamos in Santa Bárbara county by the Pacific Coast railway co., with which it was consolidated. The total length is 64 miles. A narrow gauge road through Santa Bárbara co. is in contemplation, with a branch up the Santa Maria and Cuyama rivers, through Emigades and Kern Lake valleys, to Bakersfield, and a branch north to San Miguel.

As for San Diego, it was left nearly as long gazing regretfully upon its pretty but empty harbor as its neighbors further north upon theirs. Its first attempt at railroad construction was as early as 1854, too early, of course, to be successful. A company calling itself the San Diego and Gila

Tulare, Kern, and San Bernardino, to the Colorado river near Fort Mojave. Upon this representation the commissioner of the general land office withdrew from market the odd-numbered sections within twenty miles of each side of the road, covering about 7,500,-000 acres.

Upon this transaction being made known in California, Franklin Steele, a citizen, made application to the secretary of the interior, O. H. Browning, to have the lands restored to the public domain, the withdrawal not being according to law; and an order was so issued in July 1868. The railroad company then asked leave to present evidence of the legality of their proceedings, thereby gaining a suspension of the order for restoration. On the 22d of November, 1869, the new secretary, J. D. Cox, after examining the evidence, declared the action of the company in changing its route illegal, and again ordered the land restored. Although during the same month a rehearing of the case was had, it failed to change the secretary's opinion ; but on the 15th of December the decision was again suspended until a joint resolution then before congress should have been acted upon. This joint resolution, which was passed June 28, 1870, gave leave to the Southern Pacific company to construct its road and telegraph line "as near as may be on the route indicated by the map filed in 1867;" and made the land grant con-

Southern Pacific and Atlantic R. R. co. was organized, and its route surveyed. The project slumbered for the next few years, and was terminated by the civil war. About 1867 it was revived, with the expectation of forming a combination with the Memphis and El Paso transcontinental scheme of John C. Frémont. In 1868, M. C. Hunter visited San Diego as an agent of this eastern company, and agreed to construct the road for the franchises of the Gila company; but before the surveys and maps were completed, the company dissolved. The contract, however, was not rescinded until 1872, when the same property was purchased and presented to the Texas and Pacific R. R. co., with the result elsewhere recorded.

In 1881 or 1882, the Bee Line railroad was projected, to run from San Diego through the peninsula of Lower California, crossing the Colorado near its mouth, and, proceeding through the state of Sonora to the town of Calabazas in Arizona, connect with the Atchison, Topeka, and Santa Fé. That design carried out would give San Diego an outlet, but in the mean time it found it by another route.

formable to that line, "expressly saving and reserving all the rights of actual settlers." The legislature of California, also, in April 1870, passed an act granting the company the privilege of changing its line of road, and also of filing new and amendatory articles of association.

Among the principal inducements for granting to the Southern Pacific its charter and privileges were that it would open up some of the richest agricultural districts in the state; that it would furnish the means of rapid transportation for the semi-tropical fruits of southern California, and that it would help to render available the mineral wealth of Arizona and New Mexico, and thus add largely to the production of the precious metals. There were also many other public interests, both commercial and political, to be subserved by the construction of a railroad through these territories and through Texas, and especially to the people of California, to whose merchants new outlets would be opened, with new markets for her products.

To the Central company, the Southern Pacific, if working in harmony with it, would be rather a benefit than a drawback, by maintaining rates, by increasing rather than diminishing its earning capacity, and above all by keeping eastern competitors out of the field. It was about this time, say early in 1870, that the consolidation of the two lines first began to be rumored; but this was officially denied.[2]

[2] Among the officials of the Southern Pacific should be mentioned A. N. Towne, for many years the general manager and one of the directors of the company. A native of Charlton, Massachusetts, where he was born May 25, 1829, at seventeen he entered the service of his uncle, a sign and carriage painter, and a large employer of labor in the neighboring town of Webster. After engaging in various pursuits, as a farmer, a clerk, a merchant, a brakeman, a train-master, we find him, while still a young man, occupying the responsible position of general superintendent of the Chicago and Great Eastern railroad, and later of the Chicago, Burlington, and Quincy, from which, in September 1869, he was appointed to the same position in the Central Pacific. A few years afterward the entire system of the Southern Pacific was placed under his management.

Meantime the Southern company was negotiating, in
1868, for the purchase of the San Francisco and San
José railroad, which had been extended to Gilroy,
and had proposed to San Francisco to make a gift to
it of 3,000 shares, of $100 each, in the San José road,
which the city owned, worth at that time $120,000.
The city had taken this stock a few years previous in
exchange for $300,000 worth of city bonds sold by
the company for $195,000.   Feeling that railroads
were essential to its prosperity, the city gave up its
stock, but upon condition that the San José railroad
should be purchased and made a part of the Southern Pacific line to the southeastern boundary of
the state.   In 1869 a proposition was made to the
supervisors of San Francisco to donate $1,000,000
in bonds of the city to the Southern Pacific, in
consideration of the construction of 200 miles of
road southward from Gilroy, the bonds to be delivered upon the completion and stocking of each
fifty miles ; and such was the eagerness for communication in that direction that the proposition was accepted by a popular vote.   In all some $4,000,000
was asked for from the southern counties to insure
the construction of the road to Los Angeles, but the
newspapers, except in San Francisco, objected to further subsidies, and the legislature passed an act forbidding the supervisors of any county to issue bonds
until at least five miles of any aided road should be
completed, and then only in such proportionate amount
as the distance constructed bore to the amount of aid
granted.   As late as February 10, 1869, the San
Francisco *Evening Bulletin* asserted that the Southern
Pacific would in all probability locate its road through
all the coast counties as far as Los Angeles, and from
thence go to the Colorado river; and urged that "a
moderate amount of local assistance be given."   It
was difficult, seeing the result to northern counties
of granting aid to railroad companies, to get the

consent of the southern counties; and even more so to procure favorable legislation.

When all had been done that could be to bring the people to a more complacent temper, the railroads revealed their plans. In January 1870 the San Francisco and San José, the Santa Clara and Pajaro valley, and the California Southern railroads[3] were consolidated with the Southern Pacific, and it was soon afterward rumored abroad that the whole were owned by the Central Pacific.

On the 1st of May, 1871, the Contract and Finance company agreed with the Southern Pacific company to construct its road, beginning at Gilroy and continuing thence to the boundary of the state near Fort Mojave, and to furnish it complete with rolling-stock buildings, and every manner of thing necessary to a first-class railroad, including a telegraph line, and to do this at the rate of twenty miles a year, or if required forty miles; the first section to be completed by July 1871, and the whole within the time to which it was limited by congress. The original line was carried no further south than Soledad, in Monterey county, 70 miles; and Tres Pinos in San Benito county, 20 miles. In 1874 construction ceased on this line.

In 1872 a new company, called the Southern Pacific Branch railroad company[4] was incorporated, with the purpose of constructing a road from the Southern Pacific near Salinas in Monterey county, to run to a point in Kern county intersecting the San Joaquin valley division of the Central Pacific south of Tulare

[3] Santa Clara and Pajaro valley R. R. co. organized Jan. 2, 1868, to build a railroad from a point on the Southern Pacific in Santa Clara county to Pajaro in Monterey county. The Cal. Southern R. R. co. organized Jan. 22, 1870, and being consolidated with the S. P. R. R. a few months later, had no history of its own.

[4] The incorporators and stockholders were E. H. Miller, Albert Gallatin, E. I. Robinson, E. W. Hopkins, B. B. Redding, W. R. S. Foye, C. H. Cumming, 5 shares each; Mark Hopkins 2,085, and Leland Stanford 5,085 shares each. *San Luis Obispo Co. Hist.*, 318. This branch was consolidated with the S. P. R. R. co. in Aug. 1873. Of the new Southern Pacific Branch railway mention will be made elsewhere in this chapter.

lake.   It was also to build an additional line from this
branch, commencing near San Miguel in San Luis
Obispo county, and running southerly to an intersection with the line of the South Pacific near Tehachipi
pass.   It had already changed its original line from
San Benito county, to the Salinas valley, in Monterey county, for the purpose, as its opponents asserted, of thereby stopping out any company desir-
ing to run this way to San Francisco.   People upon
the line of the Southern Pacific railroad as previously
located in 1867, believing they were in danger of being deprived of their lands,[5] petitioned congress to
declare the land grant to the Southern Pacific forfeited;[6] and the secretary of the interior having
ordered the commissioner of the general land office to
withdraw from market 12,000,000 acres, congress in
1876 ordered an investigation.   The Southern Pacific Branch. railroad has not yet been constructed;
but the land troubles which followed were of a serious nature, as will be related elsewhere in the present chapter.

Already the Central Pacific, by the. San Joaquin
valley railroad, held that valley as far south as Tulare
lake.   The successor of the latter, the Southern Pacific, held the whole tier of coast counties, and two lines

[5] The land grant of the Southern Pacific covered a large area in San Bernardino, Los Angeles, Kern, Tulare, Fresno, and Stanislaus counties, much
of it requiring only irrigation to produce excellent crops of grain, alfalfa, and
tropical and sub-tropical fruits.   By men who have travelled almost throughout the habitable globe, it has been stated that nowhere did they observe
land better suited for such purposes than for a distance of 100 miles along
the line of the road between San Gorgonio and San Fernando.   On this land
may now be seen some of the most thriving vineyards and orchards, and some
of the most thriving settlements to be found in southern California.

[6] U. S. Sen. Misc. Doc., 74, i., 44th cong., 1st sess.; Id. Doc., 87.   The
petition in this case represents that notwithstanding the long time which had
elapsed since the state had granted the charter of the S. P. R. R., no road
had been built, or was being built, in 1876, upon its line; but that instead,
the company was endeavoring to change the line in such a manner as to release it from any obligation to build over that portion of the route between
Hollister, in Monterey co., and Goshen, in Tulare co., 140 miles.   They
complained that it was a hardship that the R. R. co. should have the lands,
for which they could ask any price they might choose, when their value
depended upon the improvements already made at their own cost by the
settlers.

out into the interior counties. It had the right from congress to build its road to meet the Atlantic and Pacific at the eastern boundary of the state near Fort Mojave; and the right, also from congress, to construct a line from near Tehachipi pass, via Los Angeles,[7] to Fort Yuma on the Colorado river, to meet the Texas and Pacific, provided, of course, that the latter did not get its track down first. But after the training they had received in constructing the Central road, and relying upon the ability of their president, C. P. Huntington, to accomplish whatever was desired in Washington, the Southern Pacific directors had little doubt of being able to prevent any eastern company coming into California.

It is necessary before proceeding further to refer to the part taken by San Francisco in the railroad history of the state. Its position upon the point of a peninsula west of the mainland, from which it was separated several miles by the waters of the bay, made it impossible that it should be a railway center, like Chicago or St Louis. The only railroad having its terminus in the city and county of San Francisco was, and still is, that part of the Southern Pacific which was formerly the San Francisco and San José road. Yet the selection of a terminal point for the transcontinental roads was a matter of much importance to the city. While the California Pacific was independent, with its terminus at Vallejo, and its eastern extension branch promising a new system, it was feared that Vallejo would become the terminal point for the northern roads. Afterward this anxiety was transferred to Oakland, and then to Yerba Buena or Goat island, concerning which latter something should here be said. At Sacramento, at the session of 1871–2, a dispatch, signed by twenty-two state sena-

[7] Huntington to D. D. Colton: 'We ought to get a large amount of land from parties along the line between Spadra and San Gorgonio pass, if we build them a line to get out on.'

tors, was forwarded to the California congressmen, approving the pending bill for the use of Yerba Buena island, requesting California senators and representatives to use all honorable means to secure the passage of the bill, and declaring that the island was the natural western terminus of the Pacific railroad.

The Yerba Buena island project had been very cautiously brought forward, and, when discovered, aroused a strong and combined opposition in San Francisco.   Protests were addressed to congress; government engineers were required to report upon the consequences of closing up the channel between Oakland shore and the island, and military officers upon the importance of retaining it for the defence of San Francisco.   Over and above all these reasons for refusing a lease to the Central Pacific company was the declaration that the company had no good reason for insisting upon a present from the government of a property commercially worth at least $6,000,000, and that a lease would be equivalent to a gift, for once established on the island, with all its connections with the mainland made, it would be impossible to dislodge it.   The bill failed at that session of congress, although the effort to secure the island was not relinquished for some time,[8] but the battle was transferred to San Francisco, where, for a period of twelve months, it raged with a determination proportioned to the interests at stake.

On the 7th of March, 1872, the chamber of commerce took up the matter, and passed a series of resolutions against the proposed cession of Yerba Buena island, or a portion of it, to the Central Pacific railroad company.   In these resolutions the company was handled without ceremony, and especially its friend, Senator Sargent, an able and popular statesman.   A memorial was prepared, addressed to the

---

[8] Huntington was reported as saying that 'Goat island was the proper and only place for the railroad terminus of the Overland and Sacramento valley lines.'

president and vice-president of the United States, the senate and the house of representatives, setting forth the injury to San Francisco, its harbor, and its commerce, which would result from the grant of Yerba Buena island, or a part of it, to the railroad; and the telegraph was called into requisition to convey the substance of the memorial in advance of the mail. These proceedings called out a letter from Mr Stanford, addressed to the board of supervisors of San Francisco, who had appointed a meeting for the consideration of a resolution regarding the cession of the island, in which he declared that the railroad company had at heart the interests of San Francisco, and would in nowise injure it, or its harbor or business; but that the occupancy of the island simply meant the transfer of the business of the Oakland wharves to the island, and better facilities for the transaction of San Francisco's business. This letter had little weight, the public mind being stubborn in its convictions concerning the policy of the Central Pacific managers; and on the 17th of the same month a citizens' meeting was held at Platt's hall, James Otis presiding. In his remarks upon the destructive effect of encouraging monopolies, Mr Otis said: "If they will not come to San Francisco, let them stay there [in Oakland]. Other companies will come to us, and are already knocking at our doors." Resolutions were passed in which it was declared that the representations made to congress by the railroad company, that accommodations had not been afforded by San Francisco such as were requisite, were false, for on the contrary a generous donation of land on the water-front had been made, with a strip of land two hundred feet in width and five miles long for right of way. The statement made in the bill before congress, said the resolutions, that the grant of Yerba Buena island would bring the western terminus as near as possible to San Francisco, was open to question, for that island was only one and a half miles from Oakland water-front, and a bridge to it would increase rather than lessen the time of crossing the bay, as a train would take more time upon a bridge than a ferryboat would require for the same distance.

A committee of five was appointed to visit the legislature in session to procure amendments to a bill, then pending, making the port of San Francisco free of port charges for the commerce of the world, whereby an existing reproach, and an argument of the railroad company, would be silenced; and also to ask the legislature to join in San Francisco's protest against granting Yerba Buena island to any railroad company for any purpose whatever.[9]   A modification of the port charges bill was secured, but no resolution was adopted disapproving the measures of the Central Pacific company.   The following extract from a public speech, however, will serve to show the animus of the company's opponents: "No measure of a public character, founded upon the interests of the people of this city, could obtain a decent hearing, and they were constrained to address themselves to the officers of the railroad monopoly, and ask them if a bargain could be made with them as to the laws the legislature should make; and the president of the companies signs the paper to accept the compromise, and the law is passed in accordance with it."

The committee of six entrusted with the errand to the legislature were also authorized to act as an executive committee in all matters pertaining to the public interests in resisting and defeating the further advance of the railroad power.

Another committee was appointed, consisting of three influential citizens, to proceed to Washington city as rapidly as possible, to oppose the passage of the obnoxious Yerba Buena island bill, with instructions, should the senate have passed it, as the house had done, to earnestly request the president to veto it.   The assemblage which authorized these two com-

[9] The committee was composed of six members—A. B. Forbes, S. C. Hastings, T. B. Lewis, J. C. Merrill, E. B. Perrin, and James Otis.

mittees was called an "indignation meeting against the promoters of the grant," and those public journals which had hitherto been lukewarm in reproving the railroads were included in the indignation.

A fresh source of disquiet was the demand made by the Central Pacific company that the streets running through the sixty acres granted to the Southern Pacific and Western Pacific companies for terminal grounds should be closed, and that portion of the water front known as the China and Central basins should be given to the railroad corporations. With this proposition the city supervisors were occupied for some months. As the city did not own the streets, nor certain market and school blocks in the Mission tract, nor the China and Central basins, it required an act of the legislature to donate these reserved portions to the city before the supervisors were in a situation to refuse or accede to the demands of the railroad corporation. The Central Pacific influence might defeat the passage of a bill giving the city control of these reservations; therefore the executive committee resolved on a compromise with that company.[10]

The proposition entertained was that the Central Pacific, in return for the concessions demanded of the city, should abandon all claim to Yerba Buena island, and should make San Francisco its terminal point. Two railroad bridges were to be constructed by the city across the bay, from a point about twenty miles south of the city, one temporary, the other permanent, to be free to all railroads; the city should also erect a bulkhead in front of, and fill in, China and Central basins, giving to all railroads not less than one hundred miles long occupancy free of charge; and should construct a railroad along the city front north-

[10] The grant of the reserved blocks, the streets, and the basins, was made to S. F., with the understanding that the city would come to some agreement with the railroad corporations for the occupancy of the same. It was, however, expressly mentioned in the act, that in case the companies should cease to use the land donated for terminal purposes, it should revert to the state. *Cal. Stat.*, 1871-2, 722.

ward, having switches into warehouses wherever the public convenience should require, to be free to all railroads for the discharge of freight. In consideration of all these free gifts, the Central Pacific would agree to fix its terminus at Mission bay. Although the arrangement appears to have been in many respects desirable, no final agreement was entered into.

Early in April there was a meeting of about twenty men of influence, who appointed a sub-committee of seven to choose a committee of one hundred, whose purpose it should be to protect the interests of the city in its relations with the Central Pacific. This committee took under advisement the bargain between the supervisors and the railroad power, and all matters connected therewith. Between the committee of one hundred and the directors there was a wide difference of opinion concerning the mutual obligations of San Francisco and the Central Pacific, the latter contending that the city had been niggardly in its aid to the railroad, and the committee asserting that it had been liberal and recounting its several subsidies; $650,000 in city bonds given outright, with the interest for thirty years at seven per cent, amounting, with the principal, to $2,015,000; the interest which it would have to pay on the state subsidy amounting to $800,000; San Francisco and San José railroad stock $350,000; sixty acres on the tide lands of Mission bay—in all at least $4,000,000 absolutely given. And again the committee claimed that the company had not kept the promises, actual or implied, under which these favors had been granted. Thus popular prejudice was aroused against the directors, and the newspapers bitterly and ceaselessly denounced them for disregarding the rights of the people.

On the 26th of April there arrived in San Francisco a deputation from St Louis to consult with the business men of the city upon the encouragement to be given to the Atlantic and Pacific railroad,[11] and to arrange for its connection with San Francisco. There were those in the committee of one hundred who were ready to strike hands with the Atlantic and Pacific people upon their promise to come to San Francisco with their road; others who favored an independent railroad built by the people, to connect with some road coming from the southeast; and still others who talked of purchasing the Southern Pacific, and using it for a commencement of a transcontinental road. It was not considered difficult to raise money for any one of these projects.

There was in all this agitation cause for uneasiness to the Central Pacific and Southern Pacific companies; and while they emphatically denied that they had been guilty of breach of faith, they were perfectly willing to make the proposed improvements upon the Mission bay lands. A memorandum was presented to the committee, August 17th, of an understanding arrived at between Stanford and the city, the terms of which were as follows : That the railroad company should withdraw all pretensions to Yerba Buena island, at the same time placing no obstacle in the way of a grant of the same, or a part of the same, to the city for hospital purposes ; that the Central and Southern Pacific companies should construct, within one and one-half years, a shore-line road from Mission bay to Niles, via a bridge across the bay of San Francisco; that the 60-acre tract in Mission bay should have the streets closed except in certain places where the public convenience required them to be kept open, and China basin should in part be granted to the railroad for commercial purposes ; that the city should donate to the Central and Southern companies $2,500,000 in bonds, payable in twenty years,

[11] This delegation consisted of Joseph Brown, mayor of St Louis; Andrew Pierce, managing director of the Atlantic and Pacific R. R.; Clinton B. Fish, Ozias Bailey, and J. R. Robinson, of Springfield, Mo., directors; George Bain, N. C. Chipman, Hudson E. Bridge, E. O. Stannard, Francis B. Hays, pres't of the A. and P. R. R.; and Columbus Delano, sec. of the interior.

drawing six per cent interest; provided the citizens of San Francisco, by vote at the November election, should approve of the gift; that in consideration of this subsidy the city should have the right to confer upon any other company having its terminus in Mission bay, the privilege of laying its track along that portion of the land donated to the Western and Southern Pacific companies for right of way, and to use the tracks upon the bridge by paying a pro rata charge for their maintenance; that the Central and Southern Pacific companies should make their permanent termini on the Mission bay lands, and the latter road should transact its main business over the shore-line road; the main business of the Central, except such as might be done via Vallejo and Sausalito, and of the San Joaquin valley road, should also be transacted over the bridge route; that the railroad companies did not waive the right, should the growth of business demand some different or better route, of adopting it; that whenever the city bulkhead should be completed continuously from Mission bay to Black point, the railroad companies would lay down a railway thereon, with depot and freight-house facilities, which tracks were to be free to any railroad company operating 100 miles of road. Two of the executive committee, while approving of the agreement in general, declined to sign the report, because, in their opinion, the concessions made by the railroad companies were not commensurate with the amount of subsidy proposed to be given. At the November election the people rejected the proposition which the committee, in their judgment, should not have entertained. By the terms of the agreement the option was left with the Central company to change its route and its terminus, and the effect of such a subsidy would have been to impair the city's ability to secure a railroad of its own.

The results of negotiations with the Atlantic and Pacific company were, in some ways, more promising.

On the 6th of May a public conference had been held between the St Louis delegation and the committee of one hundred, at which it was resolved to accept a proposition from that company to take $15,000,000 of stock in the Atlantic and Pacific, which would give San Francisco several of the directors. But before any definite arrangement could be made it was thought necessary to send a commission to St Louis with the returning delegation to investigate the affairs of that company, and Richard G. Sneath, John S. Hager, and C. T. Hopkins were appointed to this duty. A contract was entered into between these delegates and the St Louis company, which had six months to run before being finally accepted or rejected by San Francisco. The condition of the Atlantic and Pacific company's land grant proved not to be entirely satisfactory to the committee, a portion of the route falling in the Indian territory, and for this and other reasons there was a portion of the one hundred in favor of building a road to connect with the Texas Pacific,[12] whose enterprising president, Thomas A.

[12] A second act in 1872 changed somewhat the charter act, and also changed the name from Texas Pacific, to Texas and Pacific. In the summer of 1872 Scott was in San Diego, and received substantial encouragement from the citizens, in the shape of nearly 10,000 acres of valuable lands within the city limits. Large sums of money were expended by them in purchasing right of way and depot grounds, as well as in assisting to procure congressional aid—but without success—upon the promise of the company to complete the road by July 5, 1876. Ground was broken in 1873, and ten miles of grading done. In 1876 Scott offered to relinquish the San Diego subsidy, as he was in much doubt of securing the necessary aid, without which the road could not be constructed. But the San Diegans did not accept the offer, being still hopeful for the T. and P. co. In 1879, however, the pres't of the board of city trustees, D. O. McCarthy, wrote to Scott, asking for a return of the deed to San Diego lands, that much litigation existing, and in prospect, might be prevented. For answer, Scott returned that, 'No effort had been spared, since the failure of 1873, to secure government aid, but that his bill had failed for want of the active support he had hoped for, and that he still expected to build the road, but pending further proceedings, and having no desire to prevent the city from securing other railroad connections, whenever any responsible company had constructed 100 continuous miles of railway eastward from the city, he would re-convey one-half of the lands, but not so as to embarrass the location of the T. and P. line, or its terminal facilities in San Diego. *San Diego Union*, in *S. F. Bulletin*, Dec. 11, 1879. The route chosen by the T. and P. co., after surveying four several lines, was that by the San Gorgonio pass. It followed the coast north to the mouth of the San Luis Rey river, and up the Santa Mar-

Scott, was in California looking after terminal facilities in San Diego.[13]   Only about one third of the committee advocated the Texas Pacific connection; the majority favoring a road to be owned entirely by California capitalists.

About the 12th of July the San Francisco and Colorado River Railway company organized, with a capital stock of $50,000,000 divided into 500,000 shares of $100 each.   Subscriptions were obtained to the amount of $3,900,000, and several millions more promised.   A subsidy of $10,000,000 was asked for from San Francisco, after obtaining which the southern counties could be relied upon for further contributions. The subsidy was to be voted upon at the election in November, but the people in the mean time had been informed that their $10,000,000 would go to purchase the Southern Pacific which had been largely constructed by subsidies, and they declined to buy a road their own money had helped to build.   Thus, indirectly the Central Pacific management defeated the San Francisco scheme, as, perhaps, it was intended should be done.   It was the end of railroad projects, none of which have been indulged in from that time to the present.   Yet it was, at least on the surface, a good and feasible plan.

In 1874 the Contract and Finance company was dissolved, and in December of that year was organized the Western Development company, to which the contracts of the former were transferred, the stockholders being Stanford, Huntington, Crocker, Hopkins, and Colton,[14] the last an able and enterpris-

garita valley, through Don Juan Forster's rancho, to Temecula, and thence to San Gorgonio. *Id.*, April 20, and May 19 and 29, 1873.

[13] The directors of the Colorado company were John Parrott, Peter Donahue, Henry M. Newhall, W. T. Coleman, Michael Reese, William C. Ralston, J. Mora Moss, John O. Earl, Henry D. Bacon, A. Gause, George H. Howard, Josiah Belden.

[14] In the proportion of two ninths of the stock each to Stanford, Huntington, Crocker, and Hopkins, and one ninth to Colton.

ing business men.[15] With the Central Pacific the business of the new organization was restricted mainly to the execution of repairs,[16] but with the Southern Pacific contracts were entered into for the construction of about 405 miles of road, including the sections between Sumner and San Fernando, and between Spadra and Yuma.

After the failure of the Atlantic and Pacific to secure funds and coöperation in San Francisco, which was followed by the panic of 1873, the Southern Pacific temporarily abandoned the route to Fort Mojave, and concentrated its means on a road to Yuma to prevent the entrance into California of the Texas Pacific, which had already gone so far as to have graded ten miles out of San Diego, and to have shipped there iron, ties, and timber for this section of its road, when the reverses of 1873 crippled it financially, and brought it to the doors of Congress to ask for a subsidy in addition to its land grant.[17]

From this period for years the Central Pacific, through its indefatigable vice-president, who was also president of the Southern Pacific, fought the Texas Pacific, represented by Thomas A. Scott, before railroad committees of both branches of the national

[15] David D. Colton, a native of Monson, Maine, where he was born July 17, 1832, came to Cal. in 1879, and was made sheriff at Yreka. Later he returned to the eastern states, and after a course of study at Albany, N. Y., opened a law office in San Francisco, in partnership with R. C. Harrison. Later he took part in several railroad enterprises in company with the men with whom he had become associated. Writing to him, Nov. 18, 1874, Huntington remarks: 'There is a large field to be worked over in California, to bring about good feeling between ourselves and our enemies, and I think you are the man to do it.'

[16] On the basis of cost, with ten per cent added for superintendence and the use of tools. Evidence of F. S. Douty in testimony before the U. S. Pac. railroad commission in *Sen. Ex. Doc.*, 51, pt vi., 50th cong., 1st sess., p. 2673.

[17] Before the crash came, the T. P. co. had organized and incorporated the Texas and Cal. Construction co., which was chartered by the legislature, for the purpose of building the T. P. R. R. The success of the Crédit Mobilier and the Contract and Finance companies led to this later attempt. But the charter of the T. P. R. R. prohibited any officer of the railroad company from being a member of any construction company; and while Scott was not a member, he loaned his name and credit in aid of the construction company. When the panic arrested operations, the Tex. and Cal. Construction co. had liabilities to the amount of $7,000,000, while its assets were claimed to be $18,000,000.

legislature.   In conjunction with Colton,[18] he defeated
Scott's bill, and opposed him on the ground of subsidies; nay, more than that, he offered to build a railroad east of the Colorado without even a land grant;
and by these methods held in check the Texas Pacific
until his object was accomplished.[19]

The history of the Texas Pacific, unlike that of the
Atlantic and Pacific, forms no part of the railroad
history of California, except as showing how and in
what degree eastern competition in transportation has
been kept out of the state.[20]   It remains only to be

[18] Says Huntington: 'I think the Texas P., or some of their friends, will
be likely to take the ground that the S. P. is controlled by the same parties
that control the Central, and that there must be two separate corporations
that run roads into S. F., and it will be very hard for us to make head
against that argument, and I am disposed to think that Colton had better
come over and spend a few weeks, at least, in Washington.'   Colton vs Stanford et al., xiii. 7480.   Relating to his associates what he has said to com-
mitteemen, he quotes from himself: 'My interest is, of course, with the
Central Pacific, which will not be benefited by the construction of this road;
but the parties who control the Southern Pacific are very anxious to have
this southern line completed at an early day.   And as long as I am acting
as president of the company, I shall do all that I can to carry out their
wishes.'   Huntington was entirely right in his convictions.   The only argument entitled to weight, said the minority of the house committee on railroads, in 1878, was that the Southern Pacific connecting with the ocean at
S. F., and having intimate relations with the Central Pacific railroad, might
enter into combination with that corporation against the public interest, and
that the advantages of competition and of an ocean connection at San Diego
would then be lost.   Com. Repts, 238, pt vi., 45th cong., 2d sess., vol. i.
[19] In the Huntington letters, at p. 9, he writes to Crocker: 'I propose to
say to congress, "We will build east of the Colorado to meet the Texas P.
without aid," and then see how members will dare give him aid to do what
we offered to do without.'
[20] 'Would it not be well,' wrote Huntington, 'for you to send some party
down to Arizona to get a bill passed in the territorial legislature granting
the right to build a R. R. east from the Colorado river, leaving the river
near Fort Mojave; have the franchise free from taxation, or its property,
and so that the rates of fares and freights cannot be interfered with until the
dividends on the common stock shall exceed 10 per cent.   I think that would
be about as good as a land grant.   If such a bill was passed, I think there
could at least be got from congress a wide strip for right of way, machine-
shops,' etc.   Sept. 16, 1875, he wrote: 'I shall do all I can to get the Texas
Pacific act amended so as to allow the S. P. to build east of the Colorado river,
but I much doubt being able to do anything, for if Scott cannot pass his
Texas Pacific bill, he can do much to hinder us from passing ours.   Then the
A. and P. will oppose it with what power they have.   Then, of course, the
U. P. would oppose, under cover, if not otherwise; at least I know we should,
if we were in their place.   Then the politicians would naturally be against
it, as they would think it would do them good to prevent this grant going to
the S. P., as if not, it would be likely to come back to the people.   I shall
do what I can, but you had better make your calculations to build the road
east of the Colorado river on what you can get out of the territories and the

said that on the 1st of December, 1881, the Southern
Pacific met the Texas Pacific at Sierra Blanca, near
El Paso, and opened its line to New Orleans in Jan-
uary 1883, through its connection with the Texas and
New Orleans railroad at Houston, Texas.[21]

As to the Atlantic and Pacific, it suffered in common with other similar enterprises from the financial
crash of 1873, and subsequently entered into a combination with the Atchison, Topeka, and Santa Fé, and
the St. Louis and San Francisco railroad companies,
which gave the Atchison road a half interest in the
charter of the Atlantic and Pacific, owned by the St
Louis company, to which a valuable land grant attached. The two companies constructed, jointly, from
the main line of the Atchison road at Albuquerque
west to the Colorado at the Needles, between 1879
and 1883, with the intention of carrying their road
thence to Los Angeles and San Francisco. But at

road itself. If you expect to get anything in Arizona and New Mexico, I
would suggest that you do not do as we did in Utah, wait until the enemy
was in possession. Of course, you notice the vote of the house yesterday on
subsidies—223 against, 33 for.' April 27th Huntington wrote to Colton:
'Scott has given up all hopes of getting any subsidy this session, and is asking for eight years more time, and I think he will get it against all we can do.
His new bill calls for building 20 miles each year from San Diego this way,
and 50 miles west from this end of the road.'

[21] The Texas Pacific in 1873 endeavored to secure the crossing of the
Colorado at Yuma—the only possible site for a railroad bridge, and the military authorities granted the company, or the Cal. and Arizona division of it,
the right to break ground on the Fort Yuma reservation; but the permission
was revoked by Gen. McDowell, division commander. The T. P. obeyed
the order. But both the T. P. and the S. P., upon application, procured the
permission of the sec. of war to carry their roads, provisionally, through a
corner of the reservation, in Aug. 1877. The T. P., in view of the former
revocation, desired to have the matter settled in congress before going on
with construction, and on Sept. 1st the permission was withdrawn from both
companies pending a decision concerning the respective rights of the companies. Again the S. P. secured a modification of this order, so far as to
gain a permit to continue work to the extent only of preventing waste and
injury to its property. Having secured this, it found means to complete the
building of its bridge, laid its track on the bridge in the night, and ran a
train of cars over the river. The official correspondence growing out of this
transaction is to be found in *U. S. H. Ex. Doc.*, 33, 45th cong., 2 sess.; *U. S.
Sen. Com. Rept*, 491, ii., 45 cong., 2 sess.; *Conklin's Arizona*, 46–8.

Huntington in his *Letters*, 185, relates how he changed the mind of the
sec. of war, and 'got him out of that idea in about twenty minutes. I then
saw three other members of the cabinet; then went and saw the president.
He was a little cross at first; said we had defied the gov., etc.; but I soon
got him out of that belief.'

this juncture the Southern Pacific again stopped the way.

The California Southern railroad was chartered October 12, 1880, to construct a line from San Diego to San Bernardino, and the California Southern Extension company was chartered May 23, 1881, to extend this road to a connection with the Atlantic and Pacific in California, at a point about eighty miles northeast of San Bernardino. The two companies consolidated under the name of the first above mentioned, and the road was completed to Colton in August 1882, and opened from San Diego to San Bernardino September 13, 1883.

Soon afterward the Southern Pacific, obtaining through the purchase of stock a share in the management, secured the extension of the Atlantic and Pacific to the Colorado at the Needles, which compelled it to connect there with the former. This had nearly been a death-blow to the California Southern, which had suffered much, not only by opposition, but by floods in the Temecula cañon, which rendered impassable thirty miles of its track, carrying bridges and ties entirely away, some being seen a hundred miles at sea. It must not only rebuild this thirty miles, but in order to reach the Atlantic and Pacific, must construct 300 miles of new road over mountain and desert, instead of the 80 miles as first intended. For several months the directors hesitated. But finally the Southern Pacific determined to sell to the California Southern the road from the Needles to Mojave, built by the Pacific Improvement company,[22] the successor of the Western Development company. The transfer took place in October 1884, and the California Southern at once recommenced construction and repairs, and in November 1885 opened its line

[22] Organized in Nov. 1878, with A. J. H. Strobridge as president, and F. S. Douty secretary and treasurer, the board of directors including, besides these two, Arthur Brown, W. E. Brown, and B. R. Crocker. Its capital stock was $5,000,000. Testimony before the U. S. Pac. R. R. commission in *Sen. Ex. Doc.*, 51, pt vj., 50th cong., 1st sess., p. 2672.

from San Diego to Barstow. In October 1886, it formally passed under the control of the Atchison, Topeka, and Santa Fé company, and was operated as a division of that road. Thus after ten years of struggle, two of the eastern roads effected an entrance into California.[23]

The Atlantic and Pacific has also another and more circuitous route from the east, made by running a branch from Rincon to Deming, in New Mexico, where it connects with the Southern Pacific. In March 1888 the Cuyamaca and Eastern railroad company was organized at San Diego to construct a railroad to the Needles, intending to connect with the Atlantic and Pacific. The route chosen was nearly a straight line, saving two hundred miles in distance, and opening up the country back of San Diego.

The gap in the original line of the Southern Pacific, left uncompleted in 1872, was still unfilled in 1887, but surveys were then in progress for a new Southern Pacific branch railway to supply this defect. The only coast town reached below Monterey was Los Angeles, which, although twenty miles inland, had been made an exception, for substantial reasons. This was one of the first towns in the state to move in the matter of railroads, and built two,[24] which

[23] Thomas Nickerson of Boston was first pres't of the Cal. Southern as consolidated. The road was surveyed, J. O. Osgood, chief eng'r, through the Temecula cañon. The distance to Colton by the route is 126 miles. J. N. Victor took charge of the road as sup't in Aug. 1882, and continued in charge until April 1888, during which time it met and overcame the obstacles mentioned above. The road grew into a large business. F. F. Perris, the eng'r appointed by the sup't, located the line of the extension through the Cajon pass. The two cañons through which the Cal. Southern, is constructed are among the wildest and most difficult for railroad building on the coast. The Cuyamaca and Eastern R. R. was expected to avoid such passes, which, while dreaded by railroad builders, are a pleasure to the tourist.

[24] In 1875, the Los Angeles people incorporated a company to construct a railway which should unite their town with Santa Monica on one hand, and proceed on the other to San Bernardino, and thence to Independence, in Inyo co. The route to be followed was through the Cajon pass, since used by the Cal. Southern branch of the Atlantic and Pacific; and the capital stock was placed at $4,000,000, in shares of $100 each, over half of which was paid up. The first train between Los Angeles and Santa Monica was run in Dec. 1875. Grading was done east of Los Angeles and in the Cajon pass. Whether the

passed under the control of the Southern Pacific. In April 1887 the tracks of two other roads, namely, the Los Angeles and San Bernardino and the San Gabriel Valley railways, were joined, forming a line from San Bernardino to Los Angeles, and taking the name of the California Central. It is really a consolidation of the Atchison, Topeka, and Santa Fé and the Atlantic and Pacific purchased roads, and admitted that eastern combination to Los Angeles.[25] This combination, exercising the right of eminent domain to obtain right of way through the San Joaquin rancho, a valuable property of 108,000 acres, lying across the line of any road down the coast, encountered the opposition of the Southern Pacific, which was also looking out a route for its coast line to San Diego.

The Southern Pacific, like its older brother, the Central, was a good railroad builder. By its endless

company would have been able to complete their road, owing to its cost, is doubtful; but the main reason of its failure was the opposition of the Southern Pacific, which finally, in 1878, purchased the road to Santa Monica at a low figure, it being in difficulties, and put an end to the hopes of its principal projector and president, U. S. Senator John P. Jones, who had large interests in that quarter. Says Huntington in his *Letters*, p. 166, 'Some of my associates in Cal. seem to think it is no interest to us to control this road. In that I am not agreed, as I believe the difference between making that road for or against us will be every year half what it has cost us.' On p. 172 he says: 'I have paid Jones $100,000, as Crocker telegraphed me it would be safe to do so;' and on p. 181, 'We owe Senator Jones on his road $25,000, and the $70,000 S. P. bonds,' from which it appears that Jones received $195,000 for the Santa Monica road; but he lost his investments in that town, which was ruined.

[25] On the 21st of Sept. 1885 was incorporated the Riverside, Santa Ana R. R. co., to run a line from San Bernardino via Riverside to Los Angeles, 75 miles. Also, during 1886 was incorporated the San Bernardino and Los Angeles R. R., 40 miles to a connection with the L. A. and San Gabriel valley R. R. going east from Los Angeles. Also was incorporated the San Bernardino valley R. R., 10 miles to Redlands and east. Also was incorporated the San Jacinto valley R. R., from Perris, on the Cal. Southern to San Jacinto, 25 miles. Also was incorporated the Los Angeles and Santa Monica R. R., 17 miles from L. A. to Ballona. Also was incorporated the San Bernardino and San Diego R. R., from Oceanside on the Cal. Southern to Santa Ana, 50 miles. Also was incorporated the San Diego Central R. R., from San Diego to Cajon valley, 25 miles. All these roads were organized in the Boston interest, and on the 1st of Jan. 1887 the L. A. and San Gabriel valley R. R. came under the same control, being consolidated with these different organizations April 23, 1887, under the name of Cal. Central R. R., which gives the Atchison system 461 miles of road, actual or early prospective operation. *Victor's Atchison System*, p. 8.

digging and blasting, its tunnelling,[26] trestling, bridging, and track-laying, it has brought into communication the extreme northern and southern portions of
the state, without encountering serious antagonism[27]

[26] One of the greatest railroad tunnels on the continent is at San Fernando,
on the line of the Southern Pacific. The work was commenced in July 1875,
and continued for more than a year, with gangs of men numbering 1,500 advancing from each end toward the centre. The length is 6,964 feet, and the
cost of the work was about $2,000,000. One feature of the tunnel is that it
is approached at either end by a heavy up grade, and has a considerable
stream of water running constantly out of its southern end. It runs under
ridges and cañons, the greatest depth being 600 feet.

[27] One instance of bloodshed only can be recorded, and in that no blame
seems to attach to the company. About 1876 the settlers, 600 in number,
petitioned congress to restore a portion of the land grant to the public, no
railroad having been constructed on the route between Hollister, in San
Benito county, and Goshen, in Tulare co., a distance of 140 miles. They
represented that for a distance of 50 miles the route lay over a level, sandy
waste of little value, until by irrigating canals, constructed at their own expense, it had been reclaimed and made fruitful; that subsequent to these
improvements the railroad company surveyed its line, and asked for patents
to the odd sections, some of which were already occupied. Congressional
committees reported some for and some against a forfeiture of the lands, and
the matter remained undetermined until 1878, eleven years after the land was
granted. In April of that year a mass meeting was called at Hanford, in this
region, where a settler's league was organized. The league expressed itself
as willing to pay the price fixed by the government for railroad lands, namely
$2.50 per acre; but declared the railroad company had no right to their homes
and improvements, nor any right to require payment for the same from
those who had made the improvements. On a demand from the league to
have their land-grader removed, the railroad company brought suits of ejectment against settlers on its patented lands, and obtained judgment in the
U. S. circuit court in December. Previous to this decision, however, 80 or
100 men, with masks to conceal their identity, repaired to the house of Ira
Hodge, a purchaser of railroad land, five miles from Hanford, and ordering
out the family, burned down the dwelling. Another purchaser, Perry C.
Phillips, was treated in the same manner, and a settler placed in possession.
Soon after these acts a military company was formed. In July 1879 a party
of men, mounted and disguised, made a midnight visit to a house where it was
suspected that certain obnoxious persons were lodged. Their visit was taken
as a menace. In May 1880, no compromise having been affected, U. S.
Marshal Poole in undertaking to place purchasers of railroad lands in possession, was resisted by an armed force, and a battle resulted, in which eight
persons were killed or wounded, namely James Harris, Iver Knutson, J. W.
Henderson, Archibald McGregory, Daniel Kelly, and E. Haymaker, settlers,
wounded; Walter J. Crow and M. D. Hartt, purchasers of railroad land,
killed. It was shown at the inquest that at the time of the collision Marshal
Poole, in company with land-grader Clark, and Crow and Hartt, purchasers
of railroad lands, had set out in the street the household goods of W. B.
Braden, and were proceeding to evict other families. The coroner's jury
resolved that 'the responsibility of the shedding of innocent blood rests upon
the Southern Pacific railroad company,' and the feeling throughout the state
was strongly adverse to the company's course. It was shown, however, upon
the trial of those persons engaged in resisting the marshal, that the settlers
had set themselves up as the rightful owners, regardless of the patents held
by the railroad company, and had organized a military force which patrolled
the streets on horseback, with masks over their faces; that they warned

from the people.   It has indeed outgrown its older
brother, in 1885 assuming the control of both systems

away one purchaser of railroad land, turning the occupant out of doors; that
it was not known who was the attacking party on the fateful 10th of May;
but that the settlers deliberately murdered Crow after the first fury of the
fight was over.   But such was the sentiment regarding the right of the
Southern Pacific company to hold the land grant, that the only crime charged
against the men who participated in the tragedy of Brewer's rancho was that
of resisting the U. S. marshal.   For this J. J. Doyle, James N. Patterson,
J. D. Purcell, W. L. Pryor, and William Braden were sent to prison in San
José, January 24, 1881, where they remained several months, during which
time they were the recipients of much kindness and attention from the citizens of that place.   On returning to their houses they were met by 3,000
people assembled at Hanford park to tender their sympathy and approval.
Upon the platform erected for the orators of the day sat the released prisoners
and their families with the families of those killed in the defence of their
homes.   Letters were read from congressmen Berry and Ferrel and Senator
Tinnin of the California delegation in Washington; speeches were made, and
resolutions offered.

Previous to this demonstration the railroad company offered to reduce the
price of land 12½ per cent.   Most of the settlers made application to rent,
hoping that the government would come to their rescue; but the leases when
sent to them contained an agreement to apply the rent of 1880 on the purchase of the land, at the reduction offered, and were rejected by the settlers,
who still warned away the agents of the company.   In April, previous to the
culminating event above described, the legislature passed a joint resolution
asking 'congressional aid in behalf of a large number of settlers upon government land, in what is known as the Mussel Slough district, in Tulare
county, Cal.'   The preamble averred that 'nearly 2,000 settlers, acting in
good faith with the said government, and trusting to its full protection, did
settle upon what, at the time of settlement, was supposed to be, and what
they claim was of right, vacant, unclaimed, unoccupied, and unreserved government land;....and whereas the Southern Pacific railroad company, or a
branch of the same, having obtained a charter to construct a road on a route
entirely different from the one now running through said Mussel Slough district, and having obtained a grant of land from the federal government to
aid in the construction of the same, which said grant could not have been
included in any of the lands of the Mussel Slough country, had the railroad
company adhered to the route first located, did, after the private settlements
referred to above, get a modification of its charter, change its route to the
present one, running through the heart of the Mussel Slough country, so as
to include the lands then and now occupied by these settlers in opposition
to the said railroad company; and whereas the United States court, Sawyer
presiding, has recently decided that the said grant to the railroad company
was *in presente*, and not conditional upon location of route and filing map of
same, in face of the uniform decision of the commissioners of the general
land-office for a number of years; and whereas, as the result of said decision,
about 1,800 innocent settlers, many of whom are poor men, with their wives
and children, are in danger of being turned out of their homes, which they
have built up around them by their indomitable industry and perseverance,
and which have become valuable, not by the building of the said railroad
alone, but principally by the construction of several hundred thousand dollars' worth of canals and ditches, which have been commenced and completed
by the individual efforts of these settlers, unaided from any quarter; be it
resolved by the senate and assembly of the state of California, that our senators be instructed and our representatives be requested, to use their best
endeavors to widen the scope of the bill introduced in congress by S. S.
Cox of New York, February 3d, in relation to railroads, so as to afford the

under its one name, besides extending its operations to the Atlantic states.

The uniformly successful enterprises of the directors show not only that they had money to operate with, but that they were notable financiers. The length of their whole system of roads aggregates nearly 7,500 miles. They control or own, wholly or in part, more than forty railroad corporations in California, besides coal mines, express companies, steamship companies, street railways, hotels, and town-sites, all in their corporate capacity. More than $95,000,-000 were expended for construction in 1880–1884, upwards of $30,000,000·being paid for labor alone.[28]

The railroad associates have, of course, found it less profitable to construct long roads through unimproved sections of the state and adjoining territories, than was the case earlier in their career. Previous to the consolidation of the Western and Central Pacific and other roads in 1870 the Central had earned $20,-238,918.13. Its consolidations brought it $5,000,000. Between 1870 and 1882 it earned $113,464,579.13, about forty per cent being expended in operating the roads. Out of the residue there was paid the interest on the first mortgage and other bonds. About $4,-000,000 went to the purchase of the road from San Francisco to Gilroy and the Los Angeles and San Pedro roads, and an unknown amount into other undertakings. The Pacific Improvement company received for constructing the road from Mojave to the Needles payment in bonds to the amount of $6,062,-000, at the rate of $25,000 a mile, and stock to the amount of $7,275,200, at the rate of $30,000 a mile, for 242 miles, or at an average cost of something over $24,000 per mile. The Southern Pacific of Arizona

relief indicated above, and if this be impracticable, that our congressmen be requested, if possible, to procure national aid through the attorney-general in having the question of the ownership of these lands, as between the settlers and the railroad company, finally determined in the supreme court of the United States.' *Cal. Stat.*, 1880, 250–1.

[28] *A. N. Towne, Railroad Transportation and Construction*, MS., pp. 25, p. 23.

paid to this company $25,000 per mile in bonds, and $199,950 in capital stock—par value of stocks and bonds being $19,995,000.[29]

According to the statement furnished the United States railway commissioners[30] by the president of the Central Pacific, the total receipts of that company from 1864 to 1884 amounted to $277,347,789.67, and the total expenditure to $239,612,278.24, the remainder being a surplus of profits. This estimate includes land sales and all transactions on account of the road, except sales of stock. The capital stock of the Central Pacific was increased from $20,000,000 in 1865 to $100,000,000 in •1878. The first stock sold after the consolidation of 1870 was 20,000 shares to D. D. Colton in 1874. The first sale in the New York market was in 1880, when 50,000 shares were sold to an eastern syndicate.

The capital stock of the Southern Pacific, which in 1870 was $40,000,000, was increased to $90,000,000 before the branch to the Needles was constructed, and is now $150,000,000. Its earnings in 1879 amounted to $2,878,356.60, which went to pay interest on its bonds and taxes,[31] the bonded debt of the road being then $29,000,000.

The weak point in the whole magnificent scheme is the accumulation of indebtedness. But the great railroad builders will be in an excellent financial condition should they succeed in inducing the government to accept their terms in the pending final settlement of their indebtedness to the country. The first real effort of the government to secure payment was by an amendment to the Pacific Railroad acts of 1862 and 1864, made May 7, 1878, establishing a sinking fund into which should be paid half the amount due annu-

[29] Colton vs Stanford et al. *Plaintiff's Ev.*, 368–75.
[30] *Answer of the Central Pacific Railroad Company, submitted by Leland Stanford, President,* July 1887, pp. 129–33.
[31] This is Crocker's evidence. *Id.*, *Def't's Ev.*, p. 9074. He says that neither the Western Development co., the Amador R. R., the Berkeley Branch R. R., the Cal. Pacific R. R., nor the Colorado Steam Navigation co. paid any dividends, unless the last a small one.

ally from the United States for mail and other services, while the other half should be applied to the
liquidation of the interest paid by the government on
its bonds. In addition, twenty-five per centum of the
net earnings of the company were required to be paid
into the treasury, in default of which no dividend
could be voted or received, forfeiture of its franchise
being the penalty of a failure to observe the requirements of the law.

In regard to the question of the Central Pacific
company's indebtedness to the government, and for
several years before the people, it is asked, on the one
hand: Whence came the means by which four men,
with only moderate private fortunes, were enabled to
build, buy, own, and operate all the roads belonging
to the Central and Southern systems? In 1869, before the last spike had been driven at Promontory,
the railroad quartet, besides owning the road, had received as a loan $24,000,000 of government bonds,
forming a second mortgage on the road, together with
$400,000 of San Francisco bonds as an unconditional
gift, $550,000 of county bonds, and $2,100,000, paid,
or to be paid, by the state of California, in the way of
interest, in return for services to be rendered by the
company. All this in addition to the land subsidy of
more than 9,000,000 acres. Granted that more than
eighty per cent of the land subsidy was worthless, as
consisting either of mountain or desert; granted that
when the bonds were issued they could only be converted into gold at a heavy sacrifice; nevertheless the
Sacramento syndicate, after receiving these subsidies,
together with the income on their road, should at least
have fulfilled their obligations to the government.

On the other hand, the directors point, first of all,
to the saving effected to the government in transportation charges. From the completion of the Central
and Union Pacific to the 31st of December, 1885,
the total sum paid to both roads for United States
freight, supplies, mails, munitions of war, troops, and

passengers amounted to $20,963,313, while for the same period of only less than 17 years, the charges at ante-railroad rates would have been $160,311,054, thus making a total saving of $139,347,741. The bonds issued, with accrued interest to date, less what has been repaid by the two companies, would represent, at the latter date, a total of $86,685,907, still leaving in their favor a balance of $52,661,834 in excess of both bonds and interest. Moreover, for transportation services rendered by the railroads nothing is paid by the government, the entire sum being retained in payment of bonds and interest. Nor in this estimate has any allowance been made for the enormous increase in the weight of mail matter, from 1,000 pounds daily, just before the completion of the railroad, to 30,000 pounds in 1885.[32]

As to the present relations between the Central Pacific and the government, it is claimed by the former that, according to the reports of government officials, appointed annually, since 1878, to inquire into the affairs of the company, including that of the Pacific Railway commission, all the legal obligations to the government, arising from the issue of bonds or otherwise, have been faithfully discharged. "But," as the president of the company remarks, "beyond these obligations on either side, which were named in the contract acts and in the laws relating thereto, there were certain implied promises of benefits on either side, on which the terms of the contract as to the loan of bonds, as well as the manner and time of their payment were based. The facts as to these promises and the way they have been fulfilled must receive full consideration in any fair plan that may be proposed, looking to the settlement of the affairs between the company and the United States." [33]

But for the passage of the Thurman act, in 1878,

---

[32] *Relations between the Central Pacific Railroad Company and the United States Government. Summary of Facts. 1889.*

[33] *Id.*, p. 6.

whereby the government assumed control of the company's debt, the directors assert that the bonds and interest would have been fully paid at maturity from the proceeds of a sinking fund established for that purpose. But through injudicious investments of the sinking-fund money in the hands of the secretary of the treasury, a loss has already ensued to the company of more than $2,000,000, and this without any advantage to the government.

Until the maturity of the debt, it was at least implied that the government would refrain from granting subsidies to competitive lines, and by doing so they have largely decreased the earnings of the Central Pacific. Moreover, these earnings have been further reduced by the competition of the Canadian Pacific, a line heavily subsidized by the dominion government, and not under the restrictions of the interstate commerce law. Under such competition the average net earnings of the road have fallen of late considerably below $1,000,000 a year, and thus the value of the government's lien has been seriously impaired.

Such are a few of the statements alleged on either side as to this difficult and long-vexed question. On the one hand, it is asserted that the Central Pacific has disregarded it contracts; that it has denied and still denies its obligations to the government, assuming that in equity it owes nothing, because the country has been so largely benefited by the completion of the first overland railroad. On the other, it is claimed that all the company's obligations and contracts have been duly fulfilled; that the subsidies were granted on the understanding that they should build a road to be managed and owned by themselves, for the individual profit of the stockholders, and that there is nothing in the language of the statutes that will fairly admit of any other construction. While it is not disputed that the several acts of congress might have been draughted more judiciously, it should be remembered that at the time they were enacted it was

the general opinion, not only of congress, but of the
people of the United States, that a transcontinental
railroad was a national necessity, and that unusual inducements should be offered to insure its construction.

In conclusion, let us hear the opinion of the Pacific
railway commission, appointed in April 1887, to inquire into the affairs of the Pacific railroads, and to
report to congress a plan whereby a settlement might
be made between the companies and the government.
"By the act of 1864," say the commissioners, "all of
the bond-aided companies were required to apply five
per cent of their net earnings to the payment of the
interest accrued on their debts to the United States.
By the act of May 7, 1878, the requirement was increased as to the Union and Central Pacific companies
to twenty-five per cent of the net earnings. In the
opinion of the commission, these requirements have
been fully satisfied." And, says its chief accountant,
after a careful examination of the Central's books:
"The company have up to the present time complied
with all the requirements of the laws prescribing payments to the United States, and all demands of the
government have been promptly met."[34]

Whatever may have been the shortcomings of the
railroad associates, now that the dust of controversy
is clearing away, and malice and prejudice are losing
their influence, it will at least be admitted that they
have been men of remarkable enterprise and adminis-
trative talent. In the eastern, no less than in the
southern states, the Southern Pacific has already
secured a foothold, appearing even in Connecticut

[34] *Id.*, p. 15. The labors of the commission extended over some nineteen
months, their report being transmitted to the president Dec. 1, 1888. The
examination of witnesses and documents touching the Central Pacific
was conducted mainly in New York and San Francisco; but as the commissioners state, 'they also examined witnesses at a vast number of local
points, for the purpose of ascertaining the relations existing between the different railroads and the local communities, and of giving full and abundant
opportunity to all persons who had business relations with these roads to
state their views and make known their complaints.'

and Kentucky charters.   By leasing and constructing railroads it controls 1,030 miles between Newport
News and Memphis.   Mr Huntington has constructed
a bridge over the Ohio river costing $3,000,000, and
tunnelled through seven miles of rock on this line—a
most difficult piece of engineering.   The Occidental
and Oriental Steamship company running its vessels
to China, and the Colorado Steam Navigation company on the gulf of California and lower Colorado
river, were among the navigation properties controlled
by the Central and Southern Pacific.   There is now
a line of steamers to Liverpool or Queenstown from
San Francisco, the Huntington line, controlled by the
same companies, and a line of steamers to Brazil from
New York, which pays a handsome dividend on the
stock.[35]

In previous chapters allusion has been made to the
relations between the railroad and the state legislature.   About 1866 the public prints assailed the passenger and freight tariffs as too high, ten[36] cents a
mile being charged for passage, and proportionally
high rates for freight.   The legislature was besought
to interfere and to regulate these charges.   In 1868
a bill was introduced in the state senate for the purpose of establishing certain rates by law, and regulating other matters.   The railroad company argued:
"You have your goods and yourselves carried at all
seasons of the year without delay in one fourth
the time formerly consumed, and at about one fourth
of the expense.   Your property is greatly enhanced
in value, and your homes brought practically to

---

[35] *Huntington*, MS., 46.
[36] *St. Louis Republican*, June 2, 1869.   *S. F. Bulletin*, Oct. 1, 1869.   Other
authorities make the passenger rate, probably on through tickets, eight cents
per mile, and freight $48 per ton from S. F. to Elko, and $70 per ton to Salt
Lake. *Sac. Reporter*, Feb. 10, 1869.   The freight reaching S. F. by cars in
the month of June 1871 was 24,469,693 pounds, of which nearly fifty per
cent was from east of Omaha.   Taking 10,000,000 pounds as a fair monthly
average, there would be 60,000 tons, or enough to load 60 ships of 1,000 tons
each.

San Francisco, the great outlet and inlet of commerce for the state.   Yet, despite these advantages
already reaped, and which are but a foretaste of those
greater ones to be enjoyed on the completion of the
transcontinental road, you complain loudly of charges
only reasonable, when the cost of the road and its
equipments, with all other expenses, are taken into
account.   If the legislature reduces the present rates
one third, as it is asked to do, the company must cease
to build eastward, and derive no profit from the operation of the road already completed."

Others asserted that the legislature had no right
to meddle with the management of this railroad, because it was a national work, congress being the body,
if any, which would be justified in restraining or controlling its action; and the question was raised as to
how California was to legislate, and not Nevada or
other states; and how conflicting legislation by different states was to be reconciled, thus raising the question which many years afterward was settled by the
interstate commission law of congress.   Gradually
fares and freights came to be reduced to a schedule
more near that which the public demanded, but discrimination in freights was complained of at all points
intermediate between San Francisco and Ogden, and
on the Southern Pacific.   In 1876 the legislature
passed an act providing for commissioners of transportation, to be appointed by the governor, to hold
office for two years, whose duty it should be to
examine roads and bridges and report negligence in
repairs; and to notify the company to attend to petitions for the establishment of new side-tracks for the
accommodation of the people, or to bring an action in
case of refusal.   By this law corporations were required to file statements under oath of their tariffs
and rates of freight, passage money, and all manner
of charges, with copies of their rules and regulations
and instructions to employés; and it was declared unlawful for corporations to increase any rates above

those in use on the 1st of January, 1876. They were required to furnish information of the condition of their roads and their management, with copies of leases, contracts, and agreements with express or other transportion companies, all of which were to be laid before the legislature. In this act extortion was defined as demanding or receiving between any two stations more than for the same service was specified in the tariff of fares and freight on file with the board of transportion commissioners; and unjust discrimination as demanding or receiving less than the tariff on file with the commissioners.[37] It was also made unlawful for railroad companies to grant free passes over their roads except to persons in their employ, destitute persons, public messengers, troops, and other persons entitled under the existing laws to be transported free of charge, and to the transportation commissioners. The penalties attached to violations of the law were, for extortion, three times the amount of the damages sustained, with the costs of suit; for discrimination, to pay $1,000 for each offence; for issuing passes, a forfeit of $100 for each offence, one half to go go the state treasury, the other half to the informer; and it was the duty of the commissioners to prosecute these suits.[38] The act was amended in 1877–8.

The chief effect of the several statutes was to bring

[37] Colton, in 1877, wrote to Huntington: 'I do not know what the country is coming to. Last week they passed a bill through both houses of the legislature—which the governor will sign—reducing street railroad fares to five cents.' But he added, as if to console his correspondent, 'I do not think this legislature will hurt us very much, for we looked at that matter in advance; but if we had not looked after the senate, they would try to steal all we had before their adjournment.' Colton vs Stanford et al., 7546.

[38] The material for this chapter was gathered not only from the newspaper files of a quarter of a century, innumerable pamphlets, the government documents, and the state archives, but equally from the testimony of persons employed in confidential relations by the company, and by statements and explanations voluntarily made by the members of the company. I have been greatly assisted by an epitome of the business history of the Southern Pacific company furnished by Mr A. N. Towne, general manager of the Pacific system, and by notes furnished by E. H. Miller, secretary of the Southern Pacific. The constant difficulty has been an excess of matter, rather than a lack of material.

out more prominently the existence of alleged abuses through the reports of the commissioners.

It is a fact in California commercial history that hardly could the reader of a city daily, or a country weekly, open his newspaper, without finding therein some complaint against railroad management, especially applying to freight charges. It was not always that this tariff was too high, especially to the owner of through freight, but it was the system that was rebelled against. In order to increase its business, at was alleged, rates were lower to the eastern shipper, who had more goods to be carried, than to the California shipper, who had less. One effect of this discrimination was to strangle at its birth any manufacturing enterprise which aimed at business outside of the state. Again, a manufactured article might have been imported at a certain rate, and the raw material at half that price; and when some enterprising man thought he saw an opportunity to start a profitable manufacture, and ordered a car-load of the raw material, he found himself charged as much freight as he had formerly paid for the imported manufactured article. It was also a common ground of complaint that much higher rates were charged for short than for long distances, for small than for large quantities, and especially that discrimination was made between competitive and non-competitive points. Not that the company had any design to crush out enterprise, for such a policy would have been suicidal; but that, with too little regard for the merchant or producer, they were apt to fix the rates on a given article at "all it would bear."

On the other hand,[39] the directors answered that they were only doing what for years the merchants

---

[39] 'We are informed,' said the commissioners, 'that the minority commissioner has reported, as proved, an interminable succession of alleged discriminations, preferences, and advantages, granted for corrupt or improper purposes, and violations of duty of a similar character. We must respectfully protest against such conclusion, because it is based on no evidence worthy the name.'

and producers themselves had done, and that in their dealings with the public they were guided by the same motives and considerations as those who denounced them. Just as the merchant sells his goods dearer by the pound than by the ton; asks more when the market is barely supplied than when it is glutted; asks more when he is aware that his customer must buy of him; so the railroad charges higher freights on small than on large shipments; charges more in proportion for short than for long distances, and where goods are conveyed between small, isolated stations, demands a higher rate than between terminal points. Here, it might be said, are simple business propositions, in perfect harmony with business laws and business ethics; and to the railroad man, no less than to the merchant, the producer, or the manufacturer, should be conceded the right to exercise a discriminative judgment.

Such matters, in the opinion of most railroad men, are best left to competition; or at least they form no proper subject for legislation; for legislation of this character is apt to be extremely dangerous, forcing corporations in self-protection into the lobbies of the legislature or the rooms of committees. Moreover, as it has been well remarked, the adjustment of legal fares or freights seldom acts as a remedy for the evils against which such measures are directed, because the maximum is usually fixed so high that it is to the company's interest to establish lower rates. Such attempts, however excellent in theory, are rarely successful in practice, since few can foresee the effect of competition, of increase in production, of facilities in operating, or of the constant changes in commercial conditions. As a rule, it is the conviction of those who have most carefully studied this matter, that the expansion and requirements of trade will always nullify the provisions of special enactments, no matter how skilfully prepared.

He who would endeavor to present the railroad question impartially cannot ignore the benefits which have resulted to the state from railroad development. To those who have built up our railroad system must be ascribed much of the prosperity which is now enjoyed, since by making a public use of a portion of their gains they have given to the people a share in the proceeds of their enterprises. Not to admire the result would be churlish. It is a boon to the state that, even in self-preservation, the Southern Pacific, after choosing a route through the richest unsettled lands in the southern counties, should seek to promote immigration to those sections, and should construct tributary roads to develop their resources and create business for itself.

The older settlers in southern California remember the time—not more than a quarter of a century ago—when a single train would have carried every human being that lived within a score of miles of the present line of the Southern Pacific between Fort Yuma and San Bernardino. Several trains a day are now required to accommodate the traffic of this region. Many portions of the San Joaquin valley were then considered worthless, while anything more than a dollar an acre was considered an extravagant price, even for the choicest tracts. Thousands of square miles, before occupied as sheep and cattle ranges, are now valued at from $20 to $200 an acre, and producing goodly crops of grain and fruit, with facilities for cheap and rapid transportation to market. A space of ten miles on either side of the line would contain about 3,000,000 acres, and since the opening of the railroad its value has been enhanced by at least $50,000,000. Such towns as Fresno and Visalia, which formerly existed only on paper, number their thousands of inhabitants, and already take rank as agricultural and commercial centres.

Said General Sherman, in his report to the secretary of war, in 1883: "No person who has not been across the continent by the several routes can possibly comprehend the change now in progress there. Nearly two thirds of the domain of the United States lies west of the Mississippi, and at the close of the civil war the greater part of it was occupied by wild beasts, buffalo, elk, antelope, and deer, and by wilder Indians. Now, by the indomitable courage, industry, and thrift of our people, this vast region has been reduced to a condition of comparative civilization. Three great railroads now traverse the continent, with branches innumerable, and a fourth is making rapid progress. States, territories, cities, and towns have grown up; neat cattle have already displaced the buffalo; horses and sheep have displaced the elk, deer, and antelope; and crops of wheat, rye, barley, and oats are now grown in regions believed hitherto to be desert or inaccessible. This is the real cause of the great prosperity which now blesses our country and swells the coffers of our national treasury."

Whatever may be the judgment of posterity as to the character and policy of the railroad associates, we who are living to-day cannot deny that to their boldness of enterprise is due, in no small measure, the greatness and prosperity of this our western commonwealth. If they cannot as yet afford to establish such rates as obtain in the more densely peopled sections of the union, the tendency of these rates is steadily downward.

The time has gone by when any single line can entirely crush out competition. The Southern road is already forced to compete for transcontinental travel and transportation, and for a part of the state traffic, which necessity will only increase its efficiency. As railroad builders no company has ever surpassed the Central Pacific under whatever name it chooses to be known. Their works are monumental as well as colossal, the peculiar circumstances attending their beginning giving them a place in history which cannot be ignored.

Within the last few years, and more in 1889 than in any other year, the Southern and Central lines have felt somewhat severely the competition of the Canadian Pacific. Further competition is also in store through the building into this state of the Union Pacific,[40] which has consolidated its Utah lines under a single management, has secured the control of what was formerly known as the Oregon Railway and Navigation, or as more commonly termed, the Oregon short line, and by an agreement with the Chicago and Northwestern, secured a continuous route from Portland to Chicago. At a meeting of the transcontinental association, the Southern company succeeded in having the differentials of its northern competitor reduced; but in the Union Pacific, which was expected to reach San Francisco before the close of 1890, it will have a competing line, asking no differentials, but simply demanding to share in the traffic of the coast. With its vast resources and its enterprising management, the Southern Pacific has thus far held the field against all rivals, except for the dominion line; but this, of course, it could not hope to retain indefinitely.

At the annual meeting of the Southern Pacific company, on the 9th of April, 1890, Senator Leland Stanford resigned the presidency, and was elected chairman of the newly organized executive committee, thus being relieved of much detail work, while retaining a general supervision of the affairs of the road. His successor was C. P. Huntington, with Charles F. Crocker, A. N. Towne, and J. C. Stubbs, respectively first, second, and third vice-presidents, C. N. Lansing secretary and controller, T. Hopkins treasurer, N. T.

[40] The contract for building the first section was let in November 1889. *S. F. Chronicle,* Dec. 29, 1889.

Smith assistant treasurer, and C. T. Krebs assistant secretary.[41]

At Los Angeles four and in San Diego three different companies were formed in 1889 for railroad building to various points. And yet two of the roads already in operation, the Southern California—a consolidation of the California Central, California Southern, and Redondo Beach roads—and the Los Angeles and Pacific were losing money, the latter passing into the hands of a receiver.

Of the San Diego, Cuyamaca, & Eastern railroad, intended to intercept the Sunset line at Los Palmos, and the Atlantic and Pacific at the Needles, thirty miles had been completed in March 1889, and a loan of over $6,000,000 obtained to proceed with the work. During the same year the Los Angeles, San Diego, & Yuma Railway company was organized, and work begun at San Diego in the direction of Fort Yuma, a second line being built to Escondido, and a third to Del Mar. From Los Angeles a road was being built to Port Hueneme, and a second to San Bernardino. But the event of the year was the entrance of the Union Pacific into California. What will be the effect of another overland line it is as yet impossible to foresee; but if it should reduce the rates of fare and freight,

[41] Stanford still remained president of the Central Pacific, with C. P. Huntington, C. F. Crocker, and A. N. Towne, first, second, and third vice-presidents, T. Hopkins treasurer, and E. H. Miller, Jr, secretary and controller. The following were the officials elected for the various branches of the Southern Pacific: Southern Pacific R. R. co. (as distinct from the Southern Pacific co.), C. F. Crocker prest, T. Hopkins v.ce-prest, N. T. Smith treas., and J. L. Willcutt sec.; Geary st., Park, & Ocean R. R. co., C. F. Crocker prest, Adam Grant vice-prest, N. T. Smith treas., J. L. Willcutt sec.; Central R. R. co., C. F. Crocker prest, T. Hopkins vice-prest, N. T. Smith treas., J. L. Willcutt sec.; Market st. R. R. co., L. Stanford prest, C. F. Crocker vice-prest, N. T. Smith treas., and J. L. Willcutt sec.; City R. R. co., C. F. Crocker prest, T. Hopkins vice-prest, N. T. Smith treas., J. L. Willcutt sec.; Cal. Pac. R. R. co., R. P. Hammond prest, N. T. Smith vice-prest, T. Hopkins treas., W. V. Huntington sec.; Northern Railway co., C. F. Crocker prest., T. Hopkins vice-prest, N. T. Smith treas., W. V. Huntington sec.; Terminal Railway co., L. Stanford prest, C. F. Crocker, vice-prest, T. Hopkins treas., W. V. Huntington sec. *S. F. Alta*, April 10, 1890.

especially for the carriage of fruit, it will, indeed, be
a consummation most devoutly to be wished for.[42]

[42] The material for this chapter was gathered not only from the newspaper
files of a quarter of a century, innumerable pamphlets, the government documents, and the state archives, but equally from the testimony of persons
employed in confidential relations by the company, and by statements
and explanations voluntarily made by two members at least of the company
itself.   I have been greatly assisted by an epitome of the business history of
the Southern Pacific company furnished by Mr A. N. Towne, general manager of the Pacific system, and by notes furnished by E. H. Miller, secretary
of the Southern Pacific.   The constant difficulty has been an excess of
matter rather than a lack of material.   I have purposely avoided the discussion of the government claims, first, because it would require an amount of
space which cannot be afforded; and again, because it is a national rather
than a California question.   At present the country is flooded with arguments on the side of the company prepared by Huntington and his able
counsellor, Creed Haymond.   I am prepared to admit that there are some
'equities' on the side of the railroad; but also to deny that if the company
had kept to its agreement from the first, and not expended money and talent
to prevent the payment of its debt, its case would have required the consideration of these equities.   The neglect to provide for refunding the U. S.
railroad bonds at a lower than six per cent has worked a loss to the company
of a large amount; and it must also be evident that the sinking fund established by congress in 1878 has not been so invested by the secretary of the
treasury as to help reduce the indebtedness of the railroad company.

Among others connected with railroad, cable-road, and telegraph lines in
Cal., the following are worthy of mention:

T. L. Nesmith, formerly a director in the Texas Pacific, is a native of
Derry, N. H., and came to San Diego in 1870, being soon afterward appointed
president of the bank of S. D. and acting in many public capacities.   His
son-in-law is known to fame as Lt Greeley, the explorer.

The railway question has been a vital one to San Diego, and Chas S.
Hamilton stands prominently connected with it as the agent through whom
the city reclaimed its lapsed grant to the Texas R. R.   He was born at
Milan, Ohio, Dec. 12, 1847, and came to new S. Diego in 1869, to be connected with its first general store, of which he soon afterward became the
owner, latterly in partnership with his brothers.

By the Towle brothers was constructed a road 20 miles long from the
town of Towles, founded by them in 1862, to connect with the C. P. system,
for which they furnished the lumber for a portion of the road-bed.   Allan
Towle was born at Corinth, Vt, July 26, 1833, and coming to Cal. in 1856,
after three years of mining, engaged in the lumber business, the output of
the mills owned by his firm being from 10,000,000 to 25,000,000 ft of lumber
a year.

One of the leading spirits in the efforts of Los Angeles for railroad communication was Thomas D. Mott, a native of Saratoga co., N. Y., who came
to Cal. in 1849, and in 1852 to Los Angeles, where, identifying himself with
the democratic party, he became one of the party leaders in southern Cal.
In 1871 he was elected to the state assembly, and in 1876 was a delegate to
the national convention which nominated Tilden for president.

Among those who assisted to build the Market st railway, the first one in
S. F., is John Hayes, who was born in Ireland in 1824, was educated in New
York, and came to Cal. in 1850, soon afterward beginning a prosperous busi-
ness career at Sacramento.

In 1888-9 an excellent cable-road system, 21 miles in length, was built up
by the Los Angeles Cable Railway company, under the management of James

C. Robinson, its vice-president. Mr Robinson is a native of Birkenhead, England, in which country, and in Ireland and the United States, he has built a large number of street railways. During the disastrous floods of 1889 –90, he succeeded in keeping his roads in Los Angeles n running order with but slight interruption.

The Second st cable-road at Los Angeles was built by E. C. Burlingame, a native of Minneapolis, who came with his parents to Cal. when 10 years of age, soon afterward working on a farm near Compton, in Los Angeles co., and attending school as opportunity permitted. At 19, he began farming on his own account, but a few years later removed to the southern metropolis, where he is highly appreciated for his sterling business qualities.

One of the organizers of the Alta Cal. Tel. co. and other lines was Henry T. Holmes, a native of Lansingburg, N. Y., and among our Cal. pioneers. After a successful business career at Auburn and Sacramento, he established in San Francisco the H. T. Holmes Lime co., with works in Santa Cruz and El Dorado counties.

CHAPTER XXII.

MINING AND MINING STOCKS.

1851–1889.

ORIGIN AND DEVELOPMENT OF QUARTZ MINING—HYDRAULIC MINING—EF-
FECTS ARISING FROM HYDRAULIC DEBRIS—RIVER-BED MINING—SILVER
MINING—YIELD OF GOLD AND SILVER—COST AND RETURNS—OTHER
METALS AND MINERALS—MINERAL SPRINGS—STOCK BOARDS AND STOCK
GAMBLING.

IN the preceding volume I have given a general
view of gold mining down to 1856. The eight years
previously covered include the period of greatest
productiveness in the royal metal, after which mining
became a more settled occupation, with the slower returns of ordinary industries. Believing that a knowledge of the geology of the country was essential to
promote mining, in the base metals as well as in gold,
the legislature of the state early made appropriations
for this object;[1] but it was ultimately learned that

---

[1] The legislature of 1853 appropriated $2,000 to pay Dr John B. Trask for
a geological report furnished by him, and to enable him to prosecute further
investigations on this subject. *Cal. Stat.* 1853, p. 144. The succeeding legislature appropriated $5,000 to enable Dr Trask to complete his survey to
the 35th parallel. In 1860 the office of the state geologist was created, and
J. D. Whitney appointed to it, with a salary of $6,000 and an appropriation
of $20,000 for the expenses of the survey. Whitney's reports were printed
in 1862 at a cost of $3,000. In 1863 another $20,000 was appropriated for
the geological survey of the state. The legislature of 1864 appropriated
$31,600 for survey and printing. Whitney was reappointed by the legisla-
ture of this year. $30,000 was again appropriated in 1866 for expenses of
survey; $25,000 in 1870. with $2.000 per month to continue it to completion;
and for the years of 1872–3, $2,000 per month. The legislature of 1874 ap-
propriated $5,000 for preservation of the material collected. The cost to
the state of the survey and salaries of geologists from 1853 to 1874 was
$356,400. The first volume of *Whitney's Geological Survey of California* was
published in 1865. It is a quarto vol. of 498 pp., illustrated. Whitney is
the author of several publications on Cal.: *A Lecture on Geology*, 1862, 27 pp.;
The Yosemite Book, published by authority of the legislature, 116 pp., N. Y.,
1868; *Yosemite Guide Book*, 155 pp., 1870; and *Auriferous Gravels of the Sierra
Nevada.*

the exceptions to the rule were the rule itself in this science,[2] and that there was no infallible key to the language of the rocks, nor any true record of their origin and history.[3]

Following the general order of things, quartz-crushing followed placer-digging in California. The first method of extracting gold from quartz in California was the simple one of pounding it into fragments and pulverizing it in large iron mortars with heavy pestles fastened by a pole to branches of trees, the spring of which assisted in raising them. The pulverized quartz was then treated with quicksilver; and by this imperfect means—invented by one Ferguson of Brown

[2] Take for instance the finding of gold in sandstone, in clay, and in or under basaltic rocks, as in different localities of the Pacific coast. Or, as has been contended, if not demonstrated, in a state of solution in water charged with alkalies. See *Balch's Mines and Mining*, 223-7. The famous blue lead was a discovery in geology of wonderful interest, as it was of wonderful wealth, a revelation of the world as it was millions of years ago. The ungathered riches of a mighty river bearing the golden wash of the mountains downward to the sea were suddenly fixed in their place by an immense outpour of lava which filled up the river channel, whose waters disappeared or were diverted to other courses. Ages upon ages were required for the action of the elements to wear away the superincumbent mass and reveal the former channel of a dead river, with its long concealed treasure. Its course has been traced by miners for a long distance by signs which they have learned to understand even upon the surface.

[3] There have been rumors of gold mines worked by the padres of the early missions, but proofs of such mining are not now apparent, although they are confirmed by credible authority. A work published in London in 1818 by Mr Phillips, entitled *Lectures on Mineralogy*, mentioned the existence of gold 'a few inches from the surface' in California. In 1822 Mr Ellis of Boston obtained from here 'a mass of gold and quartz' of considerable amount. Alfred Robinson of Boston in 1830 received $10,000 worth of gold in lumps. In 1832 Capt. John Bradshaw took home to Boston for his employer, Joseph Peabody of Salem, Mass, $18,000 in native gold from the Pacific coast. This gold was taken from the coast counties south of Santa Cruz. *San Luis Obispo Co. Hist.*, 246-7. It is said, also, that in 1847 gold was taken from rock near San Diego. It is unfortunate that these tales are not verified by competent proofs. A quartz ledge was discovered at Brown valley in 1850, which was located by one Johnston of Long bar, who gave it no further attention. In the spring of 1851 a quartz excitement prevailed, and Brown valley furnished claims to many locators, 60 feet being allowed to each member of a company. *Marysville Appeal*, May 12, 1864. Quartz mines were worked in Siskiyou co. in 1851. *Siskiyou Co. Affairs*, MS., 22; *Hayes' Scraps Mining*, iv., 120-43. The Eureka mine in Sierra co. was discovered in 1851, and worked in a feeble manner with an arastra. The original owners sold it in 1858 to a capitalist, who erected 2 mills, one operated by steam, the other by water-power, together running 24 stamps. He sunk a shaft 600 feet, taking out up to June 1866 $1,400,000. One run of 60 days yielded $56,000, and another of 40 days $29,000. The annual expense was $75,000.

valley, Yuba county,—the miner made the not inconsiderable wages of ten dollars a day. Webb & Company, who owned a claim in this valley, erected the first mill for crushing quartz in 1851. It was run by a small engine, working a single stamp each in several large mortars. During the following year Reed and others erected a water-power mill, which was carried away in the flood of the next winter. Quimby & Company in 1853 erected a water-power mill in the valley, which never accomplished much for its owners, although it changed hands several times. By these efforts and failures several persons were stripped of their earthly possessions.

During the latter year the Anglo-Saxon Mining company, Sir Henry Hartley general manager, commenced the erection of a quartz mill in Brown valley, importing the machinery from England. The ore was amalgamated at this mill by large iron balls revolving in a set of pans. The works were not satisfactory, and for one cause and another the owners fell into debt, their mill being sold by the sheriff, and the machinery carried to San Francisco to be used in a flour-mill. The failure of the English company discouraged quartz mining for the time, although it was resumed in 1855 by hopeful experimenters,[4] who, year by year, learned how the precious metals could be extracted from their native gangue.[5]

[4] John Rule in 1855 built a 6-stamp steam quartz mill on Little Dry gulch in Yuba co., which was enlarged to 9 stamps, and made a fair profit for its owner until it was destroyed by fire after several years' work.

[5] In 1855 there was a revival of interest in gold quartz mining. The Kate Hayes mine, half a mile from Grass Valley, was famed for its richness, some of the rock paying $1,800 to the ton. The owner was unable to erect machinery on it, and it was sold for debt. The new owners had their mill destroyed by fire. It subsequently proved very rich. 'Lumps of pure gold hung in clusters all over various parts of the rock.' *Grass Valley Union*, June 28, 1865. Another well known mine of Grass Valley in 1857 was the Allison ranch lead owned by Michael Colbert, James Stanton, John Fay, John Daniels, James Donahue, and Timothy Fields. The mill was started up in July 1856. Its weekly yield was $40,000, to be divided among 5 owners. The average yield was about $200 per ton.

Sierra co. became famous for the number of its gold mines in 1857, and mining was carried on at Chip's Flat, a small town on a bench of the mountain overhanging Kanaka creek, by tunnels, nine of which were in from

When Horace Greeley, the man of intuitions, paid a flying visit to the Pacific coast in 1859, he remarked that the time had not yet arrived for profitable mining in quartz, and that three out of four mines were failures. He placed the average yield of quartz at twenty dollars per ton, or one cent per pound, which

1,500 to 2,300 feet, and paid well. The Independence, Whiskey, Downieville, Louisiana, Iowa, Union, Hazel Green, and Gas co. were paying mines in 1857, some of which divided as much as $150 per week per share. From report it would appear that the tunnels were excavated in rotten quartz and gravel. 'In the American tunnel the pay dirt varies from 18 to 3 feet in thickness.' In this mine there were 17 shares worth $4,000 each; the weekly dividends being from $115 to $120 per share. A rich lead of solid quartz was discovered in tunnelling. In the Union mine a vein of quartz was found containing gold, silver, and copper. Nothing was attempted at that period by way of reducing the quartz of any of these discoveries. At Coulterville in Mariposa co. there was a quartz fever about this period. The deepest mining shaft in Cal. was on the Hayward and Robinson mine at Sutter creek, Mariposa co.—315 feet, with the quality of the rock improving. *Nevada Journal,* April 21, 1858. El Dorado co. had a number of quartz mines in 1857. Tuolumne co., Marin co., Amador co., Butte co., all had their quartz excitements. *Calaveras Chronicle,* May 31, 1873.

In 1858 improvements had been made to reduce the expense of quartz mining and increase the returns. Wages were also lowered. In 1852 drifters were paid $3 a day; in 1857 $3.50 a day; in 1858 $3. In 1852 engineers received $180 a month; in 1857 $100. In 1852 castings laid down in Grass Valley cost 10c per pound; in 1858 8c. The consumption of castings averaged 8 tons a year, the reduction of 2c per pound aggregated $5,280 annually. A mine employing 40 men would now save in labor and castings $153,000 a year. All the ore raised during the first 5½ years in Grass Valley was hauled 2½ miles at an expense of $2 per ton, which was saved in 1858 by the erection of a battery at the mine. There were in 1858 six quartz mills, one with 16 stamps in Yuba co. The continued improvement in quartz mining may be inferred from the frequent mention in the newspapers of successful undertakings. A letter in the *Tuolumne Courier,* May 1858, describing the mines at Cherokee, a mountain town of Tuolumne co., mentions the Turnback and Solsbury quartz mills. The latter mine was owned by 8 men, 6 of whom were of one family—the Solsburys—and each interest was valued at $30,000. Another mine in this vicinity only being prospected was thought to be equal to the Solsbury in richness, and was a much larger vein. 'The quartz has a bluish color, is porous, full of cavities, in each of which is crowded fine flour gold.' In the solid quartz gold was found in sulphurets. A large number of claims were worked in this district. The average yield of a 6-stamp mill —Street and Soulby's—was $100 an hour. On the 1st of May, 1858, they retorted the crushing of 5 days, obtaining 41 pounds of gold. The previous week 52 pounds was obtained. The geology of this region was igneous. At Sonora the formation was metamorphic, the stratified slate superimposing to a great depth the plutonic formation. *Sonora Democrat in S. F. Alta,* Jan. 9, 1860. The Monte Sona quartz district in Nevada co., discovered in 1857, had a high reputation. The Oriental mine and mill, under management of Almarin B. Paul, was the leading property in 1859. Yuba co. quartz mining revived about this time, and mills costing $15,000 and $20,000 were erected on the Donebroge ledge. It was not until 1863, however, that the mines began paying largely. *Marysville Appeal,* May 17, 1864. The first mill erected in Kern co. was in 1859 at Keysville. *Bakersville Southern Cal.,* June 8, 1876; *U. S. H. Ex. Doc.,* 207, 471-730, x. 41 cong., 2 sess.

return would not pay the expense of mining. To this the indignant Californians retorted : " In what country on earth, save California, do mining adventurers expect to reap any returns under from two to five years? In Europe people venture in mines for the benefit of their children, not so much for themselves. In California, no sooner are works started than they must pay." That there was much justice in this reply is evident. Two, three, or five years were a short time in which to overcome the difficulties arising from new conditions, an unknown geology, immense cost of transportation, the absence of practical miners, and the high price of labor. It was a current saying in those days that it took the production of one mine to work another. The wonderful pluck of the California pioneers was nowhere better exhibited than in their early quartz-mining ventures, although the richness of the rock in most cases justified the testing of it.[6]

[6] The Woodside mine at Georgetown, discovered in 1860, was the richest in Cal. down to 1866. Over $50,000 was taken out in two days. So nearly pure gold was the ore that it was chiselled out in a solid mass 3 feet in length. One piece weighed over 100 pounds. The discoverers were poor men, and the claim was not thoroughly worked. It was down 120 feet when this rich ore was found, which 'set the country wild.' *Grass Valley Union*, Nov. 17 and 20, 1866. The Hamp Williams, discovered in 1861 in Kern co. by a prospecting party consisting of H. Williams, Robert Palmer, Blackburn Wyatt, and Ticknor Bromwell, 6 miles west of the south fork of Kern river, yielded $200 per ton by arastras, but was badly managed. It was sold in 1865 to a Rhode Island company, which spent $40,000 in experimenting with a 'fourball quartz crusher,' and finally abandoned. Over 100 locations were made in a month after the discovery of this mine. From this 'mining rush' came the town of Havilah. *Havilah Courier*, Sept. 26, 1866; *Havilah Miner*, Aug. 17, 1872. San Bernardino co. had some good mines in operation in 1864-1872. Hydraulic mining was first successfully carried out at Lytle creek, 9 miles from the town of San Bernardino, water being introduced in ditches in 1867 by Captain Winder of San Diego, agent for Harpending of New York. The ditches were 5 miles in length, which being damaged by heavy rains, the claims were sold to Cleveland with the improvements, who sold them to a French company which made them return $2,000 per week. In Holcom valley, 40 miles from San Bernardino, there was a quartz mill in 1872. The rock in that district averaged $15 to the ton. Hydraulic mining was also followed here. Other quartz mines were situated 33 miles from San Bernardino, belonging to George E. Moore; which averaged $40 per ton in arastras. *Los Angeles Express*, June 17, 1872. In 1865 Nevada co. had a quartz mania arising from the discovery of immensely rich mines near the town of Yuba Dam. The ledges were composed of black rock, giving evidences of the action of fire, and so filled with gold as to appear as if bronzed. *Grass Valley Union*, June 27, 1865; *Nevada Gazette*, Jan. 24, 1865. Placer co. also enjoyed an excitement in 1867 from the yield of a mine belonging to

A little experience showed that a mine of extraordinary apparent richness, that is, where the action of the elements had already disintegrated the rock, leaving the gold free, was seldom more than the blossom

Peter Waldenar, 3 miles from Auburn., He had owned the mine for several years, during which it had made irregular showings of great richness. On the 4th of July of this year it exhibited a streak of almost pure gold, $18,-000 being taken out in 3 days. *Marysville Appeal*, July 20, 1867. The Confidence mine in Tuolumne co. produced in 9 months of 1869–70, with 30-stamp mill, $175,000. The vein was in granite, and the average yield was $25 per ton. But by good management and plenty of stamps for crushing the rock, it was made to pay handsomely. The Eclipse mine on the north fork of the Merced prospected over $100 to the ton. *Mariposa Gazette*, Sept. 23, 1870. The Pine Tree mine, Mariposa, was at this period the most important in the state. It had a tunnel driven into mount Bullion 1,450 feet, and below the tunnel 3 working levels at intervals of 80 feet, carrying the workings down 240 feet. The rock exhibited free gold all through it. San Diego co. furnished the great quartz excitement of 1870. About the 22d of Feb. I. T. Gower and others discovered, 50 miles from San Diego, a lead of reddish gray quartz filled with specks of gold throughout, which was estimated to contain from $3,000 to $7,000 per ton. The lode took the name of the Julian Discovery. About 10 miles from the Julian the Stonewall was discovered soon after, which proved one of the richest of modern times, paying for its development without a dollar of outside money, and making handscme returns. Three quartz mills were created in this district, and with the money produced in the mines the town of Julian was built. *Hayes' Misc.*, 98, 139, 141. About three miles from the center of the Julian district was the Banner deposit of San Felipo creek, discovered by Louis Redman in 1870. It was worked first in the most primitive manner by mortar and pestle, then by an arastra. It was sold to capitalists, and a fine mill erected upon it. The Golden Chariot mine, discovered in 1871 by King, Coyne, Connors, Long, and McLellan, was in 1872 the richest in this district, paying on an average $180 to the ton. *Overland Monthly*, v., 424–7. The Montezuma mine, discovered in 1872 by Matthew Palen in the Ivanpoh region in San Bernardino co., was called a rediscovery of an ancient mine, the vein having an old shaft upon it; but no trace of machinery or tools of any kind was found. At a depth of 53 feet it was filled with rubbish, and its owners resorted to tunnelling in order to reach the rock below the old workings. *San Luis Obispo Tribune*, Oct. 19, 1872. *San Bernardino Guardian*, Oct. 5, 1872. Plumas co. in 1873 had its quartz fever following the discovery of 'a ledge of pure gold,' as it was called, near the summit of the mountain south of Taylorsville, by A. S. Light. The vein lay in a bed of decomposed gneiss, and was from 2 to 6 inches in thickness. A rotten granite rim jutted up on either side of the sedimentary bed in which the ledge reposed. The gold was distributed mainly in pockets, where the quartz 'pinched out' and yielded from $500 to $700 to mortar crushing by one hand. *Plumas (Quincy) National*, Sept. 13, 1873. Another mine promising great riches, in the near neighborhood, was sold to an English company, which, after erecting expensive works, failed. Such were and are the vagaries of fortune in mining countries, or such are the mistakes of inexperienced miners. In Grass Valley the main street was macadamized with refuse quartz from the mines, among which several fine specimens were discovered, and it was jestingly said that the pavement was in danger of being 'located' by the small boys of the town. *Stockton Independent*, Jan. 31, 1874. The North Star mine at this place yielded $35 to the ton at a depth of 750 feet. The Hayward mine in Amador co., which was down 1,250 feet in 1871, was increasing in richness. *Claudet's Gold*, p. 9.

of the century plant to the florist—long looked for and gone in a night. All of the top yield would be wasted in the eager search for more, where no more existed, or where, if it existed, it required dollar for dollar to obtain it.

A quartz miners' convention was held at Sacramento in 1857 as a means of gaining information by mutual conference,[7] and as a means of keeping at home for investment in mining the two or three millions of money which was shipped monthly to the east. There were then in the state 152 quartz mills, built at an expense of not less than $2,000,000, and the total amount of capital invested in quartz mining did not fall short of $5,000,000, while the amount of gold realized from this branch of mining at that date was not short of $7,000,000, without taking into account the product of arastras, and the more primitive methods of reducing quartz, nor of those small rich mines owned by individuals whose names never appeared in the list of companies. Gold-quartz mining had begun to be something more than an experiment[8] when the

I might go on multiplying individual discoveries and their results. All over the state, but principally in the foothill counties, gold mining in quartz was carried on with increasing knowledge and consequent improved returns, rising from a venture to a scientific industry. In *Hittell's Resources of California*, 276, published in 1867, it is stated that the three principal mines in the state were then the Fremont in Mariposa co., the Allison, in Nevada co., and the Sierra Butte in Sierra co. The first had produced $75,000 in one month; the second $60,000; the third $20,000; but the average production of the Fremont mine was $14 per ton; of the Sierra Butte $18; and of the Allison $100. The cost of quarrying, crushing, and amalgamating quartz rock in the best mills was from $5 to $10 per ton.

[7] The quartz miners' association was organized at this convention. There were many questions to be settled by such associations, such as the extent of quartz claims, rules for the regulation of companies, etc. The experience of miners became thus gradually formulated into statistics by the legislature. At first a quartz mining claim was no more than 10 or 20 feet square, according to the miners' laws regulating placer diggings. It soon became apparent that more ground was required to allow for dips, angles, and variations as well as for machinery. In order to secure ground enough for mining operations a number of claimants joined together making a claim of 500 or 5,000 feet in length. This seems to have been the origin of 'companies.'

[8] From the Mexican arastra and Chili mill of the early days of quartz mining Cal., soon advanced to the stamp mill. An avalanche of quartz crushers descended upon the state, heterogeneous masses of iron 'heavy enough,' says one writer, 'to sink our navy; at any rate, heavy enough to

Washoe silver discovery of 1859 introduced new problems, the successful solution of which again required the expenditure—and far more than in the case of gold—of money, brain-power, courage, and patience; but when solved the results applied with equal benefit to the science of deep mining in California and Nevada. A great step forward was taken between 1859 and 1863, since which period there have been few changes made in the modes of obtaining gold from its matrix.

One curious result of six or eight years of experiments in quartz-mining—for all was no more than experiment—was the conviction forced upon those interested of the little value of expert knowledge. No science could be applied to the thousand variations to be found in ores in different districts, each of which had its peculiarity, and some of which exhibited distinct features in different lodes. As for assays, they were worthless to show the actual value of rocks. The practical miner obtained a knowledge far above the theories of the scientist, and this knowledge, the fruit of experience, and dearly bought with millions of money, is being now imparted, as in a great school of mining, to the actual workers in this most special industry of the state.[9] There are at present about 400 quartz mills, each costing from $6,000 to $60,000.

sink the quartz business.' Among them were ponderous wheels running in troughs; corrugated rollers; immense iron balls, some running in inclined beds, others made to whirl with great rapidity; and an odd invention called the toggle-joint. The same crudity of invention was applied to amalgamators, of which there was no end. The expense of trying all this machinery was ruinous to mining as a business until the quartz men finally settled down to stamping, either by the straight battery or the rotary. In amalgamating, the simple riffle, blankets, and copper-plates, the Chili mill, and Mexican arastra proved satisfactory.

[9] It was not thought worth while, notwithstanding, to dispense with scientific knowledge altogether; hence a school of mining was provided for by law in 1866 in an act 'to establish an agricultural, mining, and mechanical arts college' in accordance with sec. 2, article ix., of the constitution of this state, and the provisions of an act of congress of 1862, granting to the state lands for maintaining an agricultural and mechanical arts college. The course of instruction was to embrace 'English language and literature, mathematics, civil, military, and mining engineering, agricultural chemistry, mineralogy, metallurgy, animal and vegetable anatomy and physiology, the veterinary art, etymology, geology, technology, political, moral, and house-

Of the 52 counties of the state 35 make returns to
the mint bureau of their gold production, and in 18
of them mining is the chief industry. It is not always, however, quartz mining or placer mining. The

hold economy, horticulture, moral and natural philosophy, history, book-
keeping, and especially the application of science and the mechanical arts to
practical agriculture in the field and mining.' This institution was to be
supported by the interest accruing from the lands donated by congress for a
seminary of learning. Nothing was done toward founding a school such as
contemplated by the act, and in 1868 the legislature established the University of Cal., which comprises a college of mining. *Cal. Stat.*, 1866, p. 504–9.
The U. S. geological survey has done much to promote intelligence among
the people upon subjects connected with mineralogy. It is now thought
necessary to include mining in the scientific course of all universities, while
technical schools devoted to this subject have been established in several
parts of the United States. Senator Cole of Cal. in 1865 proposed a plan for
a national mining bureau, which, if not carried out according to his suggestions, has been practically realized in the American Institute of Mining Engineers, established in 1871, and the system of reports required to be made
through the office of the secretary of the Interior. Most of this advance is
directly due to California first, and to Colorado and the neighboring territories second. The Cal. state geological society was organized in January
1877, and incorporated under the laws of the state, the object of which was
to make a Pacific coast geological collection to be offered to the state gratis,
upon such terms as the society should determine, and should be agreed to by
the state. A state museum was instituted, which took charge of the collection, which in 1882 comprised 1,327 specimens from all parts of the coast,
and a library of 78 volumes and 25 pamphlets bearing upon geology, mineralogy, mining, and even mining litigation. A state bureau of mining was
created by the legislature in 1880, to be established in S. F., on the motion
of Joseph Wasson of Inyo and Mono counties. This law requires the governor to appoint a person of 'practical and scientific knowledge of mining
mineralogy to the office of state mineralogist,' with a salary of $3,000 per
annum. His duties are to collect and preserve specimens; to make analyti-
cal assays as required; to procure and preserve drawings and models of
mining and milling machinery; to correspond with established schools of
metallurgy; to visit the different mining districts of the state; and to collect a library on mineralogy and kindred subjects, with other co-ordinate
duties. *Cal. Stat.*, 1880, 115–17. Harry G. Hanks was the first state mineralogist, appointed in May 1880. The legislature of 1883 appropriated
$5,000 per annum for the care and maintenance of the mining bureau. Among
other requirements of the law are the study of ethnology and the analysis
of the mineral waters of the state—the latter feature being in the interest
of invalids visiting or to be attracted to the state. So widespread is the influence of the ever-widening circles of the science wave first set in motion by
the pebbles rolled into the pool of investigation by the early miners of
quartz in Cal. The *California Mining Journal*, published at Grass Valley in
1856, was the first distinctively mining publication on the Pacific coast.
There was a magazine called *The Miner* in 1866, which had a brief existence.
The *Mining and Scientific Press* of S. F., first published in 1862, became the
leading journal on all matters connected with mining. Besides the writings
already referred to of Trask and Whitney, and of the early travellers mentioned in other parts of this work, there have been valuable contributions to
the geological and mineralogical history of Cal. by W. P. Blake, Clarence
King, and others. Blake was commissioner of Cal. to the Paris exposition
of 1868. References for this note beside those quoted—*Hayes' Scraps, Min-*

latter, except where it is followed by Chinamen, who work over the abandoned diggings, saving thereby a considerable amount of gold, has been discontinued. Fully two thirds of the production of the state from 1871 to 1879 was from gravel mines in the channels of ancient rivers, now elevated above the present level of the country, and showing evidences of post-glacial denudation. Into these beds of water-worn stones and clay the miner penetrates by a drift, or he washes down the bank by a heavy stream of water from the nozzle of a strong canvas or rubber hose several inches in diameter.

Hydraulic mining began in 1855,[19] with nozzles not more than an inch in diameter; but those now in use vary from four to nine inches. An eight-inch nozzle can throw 185,000 cubic feet in an hour with a velocity of 150 feet per second. The disintegrating force of water under these conditions is easily seen. In the case of large bowlders, blasting powder is used to remove them. But in general water is the agent relied upon, excavating, washing down the detritus,

---

ing, i., ii.; *U. S. H. Ex. Doc.* 211, p. 460–86, vol. x., 42 cong., 2 sess.; *Browne's Resources*, 656–65; *Cal. Farmer*, April 23, 1871; *Balch's Mines and Mining*.

[19] Every kind of mining depends upon water for its success; placer and gravel mining particularly. In 1867 there were 6,000 miles of artificial water courses, including their branches, constructed in Cal. It is stated in *Hittell's Resources*, 1879, p. 306, that owing to the bad engineering and inexperience of the early ditch-builders, to the exhaustion of the placers and other causes, the mining ditches which cost as much as $20,000,000 are now not worth more than $2,000,000. The total number of mining ditches, according to the report of the state surveyor-general in 1871, was 516; their aggregate length 4,800 miles, and their daily supply of water 171,000 inches. Where a sufficient head cannot be obtained by height and distance, or a sufficient supply for the whole season, it is necessary to build reservoirs for storing water. The flumes which conduct the water down the mountains where ditching cannot be resorted to, being constructed of wood, do not last more than from 6 to 10 years. But the extent and position of the aqueducts fill the mind with wonder and admiration at the achievements of man.

A company using 2,000 inches or 40,000 gallons for 100 days, and washing down 1,000,000 cubic yards of gravel containing less than ¼ of a pennyweight to the foot, obtained $32,000, of which $12,000 was profit. The cube of earth washed down was 1,100 feet long, 300 feet wide, and 80 feet deep. In 1879 the number of mining ditches is 640, their aggregate length being 6,585 miles, and the daily supply of water 260,000 inches. As on the average the working time of the mines is equal only to about seven months, the actual consumption of water is 712,940,000 gallons annually, or 1,956,000 gallons for every day in the year.

and with the aid of quicksilver collecting the gold. Hence this is a cheap method of mining, doing away with human labor to a great degree ; and the extent of the deposits to be worked over would take a century to exhaust, at the rate of the production of 1879.

Every method of mining is more or less destructive to the other natural resources, and especially to agriculture. During the most active period of placer-mining, the face of the earth everywhere in the otherwise beautiful foothills, river bottoms, and cañadas, and even in the border valleys, was scarred by the miner's pick, leaving unsightly excavations, with corresponding heaps of earth and stones. The enchanting groves that adorned the sunny slopes were ruthlessly and wastefully sacrificed to the immediate requirements of a houseless population, while the whip-saw was brought into requisition to convert trees into rockers, sluice-boxes, and flumes. When the claim was abandoned these unlovely relics were left upon the ground, adding to the general disfigurement of the scene.

Quartz-mining, although confined to certain localities, had also its unsightly features in the waste rock and the washings after milling, besides the many prospectors' shafts and the tell-tale heap of earth and stone. The effect, too, upon the soil of whole districts, of burying it beneath rock and clay, was to render it unfit for cultivation.

But if placer and quartz mining had these destructive local tendencies, hydraulic mining was more fatal to the whole country. The vast amount of débris washed into the streams which feed the greater rivers, and carried along even to the Pacific, has raised their beds and caused the annual floods to deposit unfertilized sand and clay over immense tracts of the best grass and farming lands. Such was the loss sustained[11] and threatened that the courts were called

[11] The plane of low water in the Sac. river had been raised about 6½ feet since 1849. In 1868 the elevation of this plane above that of 1849 was two

upon to decide the rights of miners to jeopardize the
agricultural interests of the counties through the
danger from mining débris.   After prolonged litigation and much effort to control leglslation by the

feet, the more rapid filling having taken place since that year.   The tide,
which formerly rose two feet at Sacramento, is now unfelt above Haycock
shoals, 9 miles below the city.   Shoals have been formed in Suisun bay, and
large deposits in the straits of Carquinez.   In 1879 Prof. Pettee found the
bed of Bear river at the crossing between Dutch Flat and Little York 97 feet
higher than in 1870, while in the same interval Steep Hollow, between Little
York and You Bet, had risen 136 feet. *Whitney's Auriferous Gravels*, ii., 425.
In 1880 Bear river was filled to a depth of 150 feet, Steep Hollow 250, and
the Greenhorn at the crossing of the Nevada and Dutch Flat road 200 feet.
With the exception of about 11 miles, where the grade is from 80 to 140 feet
to the mile, Bear river is filled from Dutch Flat to the mouth.   Experts estimate the deposits in Bear river at 86,000,000 cubic yards above the plains;
and at 36,000,000 cubic yards below the foothills to the mouth.   Naturally
the heavy bowlders or cobble stones remain higher up, while the sand and
earthy matter are carried below.   A similar condition exists in the Yuba
river, where the deposits in 1879 above the foothills, were estimated by the
state engineer at 48,462,100 cubic yards, principally in a distance of 8 or 10
miles, and below this at 23,284,000, although from more recent information
this estimate appears too low.   Every winter flood spreads abroad the sol-
uble and movable débris.   The Yuba spreads out its sand and gravel over
15,000 to 16,000 acres, rising above the level of the adjoining country.   On
north branch of the American the maximum depth of the detritus is 100 feet,
and is thought to measure 20,000,000 cubic yards.   Now to the results.   The
state engineer estimated from actual surveys made in 1878 that 18,000 acres
of valley land on the Yuba, once the choicest in the state, had been buried
beneath mining débris.   Witnesses before the U. S. land com. in 1879 gave
the following statements: 'Although these lands have been exposed to sun-
shine and rain for years they produce not a blade of grass, nothing but willows and semi-aquatic plants that derive their nourishment chiefly from the
strata of water percolating underneath the surface, not from the soil
itself.   A settler of 1857, who purchased a farm on the Yuba bottom, stated
that at that time the banks of the river were 20 or 22 feet high at low water.
His farm was two miles away from Bear river, and had no water upon it before 1862, when it was under 6 feet of water, which left large banks of sand
and sediment.   The amount has increased from that time until now, when
his 1,030 acres are buried 25 feet deep under sand, which reaches to the tops
of the telegraph poles.   He succeeded in protecting 90 acres of his land
with levees until 1875, when the water rose over them and covered his 90
acres also with sand.   His garden fence is now 5 feet under the surface.   The
house where formerly he lived was completely filled with water in the winter
of 1878-9.   The country which was once filled with farms is now a wilderness; and no man can tell where was the original channel of the river.
Other witnesses testified to similar devastation from mining débris.   The
bed of Feather river was raised 8 feet.   The loss in Yuba co. was estimated
by a resident to be not less than $9,724,000, and in Sutter co. $3,152,000.   The
water of the Sac. overflowed the high banks to a depth of 6 inches in 1849-50;
12 inches in 1852-3; 2 feet in 1861-2; 3½ feet in 1867-8; and 5 feet in 1877-8.
I have not space here to multiply evidences of the ruinous effects of running
mining débris into the rivers.   But it should be stated that the detritus from
the gravel mines is not as injurious as the tailings from the quartz mills,
which do not decompose, and which, under the name of 'slickens,' was
fought in the courts for several years.   Undoubtedly there are other causes
operating to raise the beds of the larger streams, among which is ploughing

ditch and mine owners, as mentioned in another chapter, the practice of dumping waste matter into the rivers has been discontinued, and already there is a marked improvement in the navigability of the natural water courses as well as in their purity ; but the ruin wrought in considerable portions of the foothill region is irremediable.

To cause hydraulic mining to be abandoned would seriously cripple the mining interest in the state. The amount of capital invested in mining in California in 1882 was estimated to be $150,000,000, of which $100,000,000 was in hydraulic mines. As ancient gravel channels exist for at least 200 miles, from Siskiyou county to Mariposa, having a depth sometimes of several hundred feet, and a breadth of from 200 to 2,000 feet, throughout which gold is pretty evenly distributed, it is not probable that the effort to extract the precious metal will cease, although to spread such an amount of débris over the adjacent valleys and in the channels of our rivers would entail incalculable injury, not to say utter ruin upon important agricultural portions of the state. In 1884, after several years of discussion and careful investigation, Judge Sawyer decided the case of the state against the North Bloomfield Mining company by a perpetual injunction. This being a test case, determined the status of hydraulic mining thereafter. The law now confines hydraulic mining to certain narrow limits, and impounds the débris. Klamath, Del Norte, and Siskiyou counties do not yet object, but probably will in time. In the lower counties, especially Sutter and Yuba, the citizens have formed a committee of necessity to enforce the law against washing down gravel banks, although drifting is still profitably carried on

the earth and destroying the grass roots which formerly held together the soil particles which the rains now wash off. As to the influence of river silt in shoaling the straits at the entrance to Suisun bay, and affecting the harbor channel, the deposit here is slight, and there are other causes at work in the harbor of San Francisco, such as the sewerage of the city and the operations of the railroad company in building a causeway and dépot ground far out from shore, diminishing the tidal area to a considerable extent.

in Placer, Nevada, and Sierra counties. As the hydraulic process was an invention of the California
miner, so, perhaps, will be some future feasible method
of saving the riches which, in the changes of the
earth's surface, have lain hidden for thousands of years.

River-bed mining consists in turning rivers wholly
or in part from their channels, and washing their beds
for the gold they contain. It was formerly extensively
practised, the richer portions being worked out; but
a revival of this business has taken place, particularly
on Scott and Klamath rivers, and also on some of the
streams before regarded as exhausted of their treasure.
For diverting water from its channels large tunnels
were driven at eligible sites. One of the longest of
these adits was at the big bend of Feather river, the
total length being 11,200 feet, and draining 12 miles
of the river bed. The Chinese swarm to these claims,
purchasing those which are abandoned by white miners,
and making good wages, as a Chinaman estimates
mining results.

Silver-mining in California has not been followed to
any great extent, although silver was known to exist
from the earliest settlement by the gold hunters.[12]
The first notice of a silver mining company that I
find is in January 1851, when a company was organized in Stockton to work a silver mine near Los Angeles. Silver was discovered near Carson, then
supposed to be in California, in 1850; but little attention was given to such discoveries for reasons readily
suggested by the early difficulties in working gold
mines—gold being a metal which only required freeing
from the rock, while silver was an ore that could only
be extracted by laborious processes after the rock was

[12] A silver mine had been in operation some time near Monterey, said to
be quite rich. Another silver discovery near town. *S. F. Californian*, April
19 and July 15, 1848. Silver mine discovered near San José. *Cal. Star*,
March 18 and April 1, 1848. *S. F. Stock Rept*, May 25, 1876. 'Silver and
iron in abundance.' *Sutter's Diary*, April 1848. In Carson's *Early Recollections*, 58-9, is mention of an expedition to Moore's creek, Cal., in search of
silver.

crushed. There were some Mexican miners in the
country who, after a rude fashion, crushed and amalgamated silver ores. From these the American
miners learned all that they knew or practiced of silver reduction previous to the Washoe discoveries.[13]

Reports of silver discoveries continued to be made,
Monterey,[14] Kern, San Joaquin, San Diego, and San
Bernardino counties being mentioned as silver producing. Even smiling Napa, with its flowery meads
and oak-shadowed hillsides, was turned into a pande-
monium of silver-mad wealth-seekers in the winter of
1858–9. The cause of the sudden mania was the
discovery in a cañon of mount St Helena of a ledge
of pure silver! It was the business of the assay offices to furnish certificates of the value of mines at
$15 a piece. The owner of this wonderful ledge re-
ceived the usual credential, but upon being convinced
subsequently that his mine produced iron pyrites in
great abundance, and of silver hardly a trace, the excitement he had occasioned quickly subsided.

Cotemporary with the Washoe discoveries there
was a sympathetic enthusiasm for silver in California.
The first discovery in Alpine county was made in the
autumn of 1860 by three prospectors, Johnson, Harris, and Perry. In the following June several claims
were located on the same lode.[15] The mines in this
rugged region, lying from 5,000 to 11,000 feet above
the sea, have been found to carry about equal amounts
of silver and gold, and have never yielded largely of

[13] It is said that in 1852 and previously considerable crude silver bullion
was disposed of at Stockton. In 1870 an abandoned silver mine was discovered about a day's ride from Antioch. All the old workings were covered
with a growth of underbrush. A dilapidated house and chimney, apparently used for smelting, stood near; and a stone plat which had served as a
patio. A considerable amount of good ore was covered up with soil, and in
the house were found 600 or 700 pounds of crude bullion. The shaft and
dump were overgrown with large trees.

[14] *Coast Survey*, 1855, 182; *Hayes' Scraps, Monterey*, 157–60.

[15] *Monitor Gazette*, Jan. 14, 1865. The claims were named the Mountain
No. 1, the Mammoth, Silver Creek, Jefferson, Washington, and Astor. The
Napoleon ledge was discovered in 1863 in Slinkard's valley, 6 miles east of
Monitor. It was worked by the Mount Vernon co., and yielded native silver
by roasting in an ordinary fire.

either, partly on account of their altitude and the short working season. They had, besides, to wait for the discoveries in amalgamation to become profitable.

The Inyo county mines were discovered in 1865, and although the region is one of the most elevated in the state or on the coast, it is rich in gold, silver, and other minerals. Within its borders are mounts Whitney, Tindall, and Brewer, on whose lofty brows the snow of eternal winter shines with a white radiance. The principal mine in the county is the Union Consolidated company of the Cerro Gordo mining district, lying in the mountains which form the eastern wall of Owen valley. The ore is reduced by smelting, and has yielded many millions of dollars. In the same district the Ygnacio and San Lucas are rich in silver, and the Palmer in gold. The Kearsarge mines and the Rex Moates are situated in the Kearsarge peak, which is 13,700 feet above sea level, and 12 miles east of Independence. The Kearsarge has been worked ever since 1865. Much of the ore from this district is of so high a grade that it must be shipped to San Francisco to be smelted. The country dependent upon these mines is the Owen and Panamint valleys.

All along the western flank of the Sierra are districts where silver predominates, but in all the mines gold is to be found in some proportion, as it is in the silver mines on the eastern slope.[16] Discoveries are still being made, and will be made far into the future, but while gold remains more easily mined than silver it will be more sought after, by prospectors at least. A table of the production of the state by counties in 1881 will give a better understanding of the comparative mineral wealth of different parts of the state than any description, although changes in these rela-

[16] The Rattlesnake ledge discovered in 1863 by Jacob Moulter and John Fulweiler, three quarters of a mile s. e. of Meadow lake, assayed $54 silver and $9 gold to the ton. The Arizona ledge, near the former, assayed $47.37 in silver and $27.50 in gold. *Meadow Lake Sun*, June 9, 1866.

tive values are liable to take place, either by fresh discoveries or by the introduction of more capital.[17]

The production of 1886 was nearly the same, something over $18,000,000. It will be observed that next to Nevada, Mono county produced more of both silver and gold than any other. This county has had a peculiar history. It was organized in 1861, with Aurora as the county seat; but when the eastern boundary line of the state came to be surveyed it was discovered that Aurora, then a thriving placer mining center, belonged to Nevada. After the loss of the county seat and surrounding mines, and the exhaustion of placers generally, the county lost most

[17] COUNTY.	GOLD.	SILVER.	TOTAL.
Amador	$1,450,000	$1,500	$1,451,500
Alpine	2,000	2,100	4,100
Butte	650,000	1,000	651,000
Calaveras	800,000	1,200	801,200
Colusa	3,500		3,500
Del Norte	60,000		60,000
El Dorado	550,000	900	550,000
Fresno	90,000		90,000
Humboldt	75,000	300	75,300
Inyo	170,000	140,000	310,000
Kern	190,000	14,000	204,000
Lassen	71,000	1,000	72,000
Los Angeles	13,000	39,000	52,000
Mariposa	200,000	1,200	201,200
Mendocino	1,000		1,000
Merced	1,500		1,500
Modoc	20,000	1,500	21,500
Mono	3,385,000	300,000	3,685,000
Nevada	3,700,000	9,500	3,709,500
Placer	850,000	6,500	856,500
Plumas	1,350,000	2,000	1,352,000
Sacramento	425,000	1,000	426,000
San Bernardino	9,000	100,000	109,000
San Diego	60,000		60,000
Santa Barbara	2,000		2,000
Shasta	350,000	85,000	435,000
Sierra	950,000	6,000	956,000
Siskiyou	850,000	1,500	851,500
Stanislaus	63,000	31,000	94,000
Tehama	500		500
Trinity	550,000	1,500	551,000
Tulare	8,000		8,000
Tuolumne	500,000	1,000	501,000
Ventura	500		500
Yuba	800,000	1,300	801,300
Total	$18,200,000	$750,000	$18,950.000

of its population, but in 1877 the Standard mine was discovered, attracting again a mining population, and the investment of capital. Many silver mines were afterward developed. Like Inyo, this county lies among the highest peaks of the Sierra, in the shadows of mounts Dana and Lyell, each over 13,000 feet in altitude.

There is no way of determining with certainty the expense and profit of mining. The output of many mines is swallowed up in their development for a long time, if not altogether. It is impossible to determine whether the assessments levied upon stockholders of incorporated mines are or are not necessary; or whether, if the product of the mines were fairly divided, there would not be something coming to the stockholders. During the year 1889 there was $390,-500 levied in assessments by 27 mines, more than half of which was paid to Mono county mines. As to the dividends, few mines were paying any publicly. Prior to 1889, however, there arose a better feeling among mining companies. Mining shares, which are taken as an indication of the value of the mines they represent, became lower in the market than at any time previous to the great rise and fall in Comstocks from 1875 to 1878; but a part of this depression was thought by some to have been the result of the feeling of insecurity caused by the heavy losses during the wild speculation of those years. Others charged the low market upon the mine owners themselves, who, they said, were endeavoring to buy in all the most valuable stock at their own figures. No one can prognosticate what a few hours may bring forth in the stock market. With all the disadvantages, the cost, and the uncertainty of mining, there stands forth the grand fact that California, between 1848 and 1881, added to the precious metals of the world to the value of $1,178,000,000,[18] of which $14,-914,452 was in silver.

[18] It is interesting to know of the remarkable gold nuggets which have

There were several causes to account for the apparent decline in the mining interests of the state, prominent among which was the increase in the agricultural interest, showing wealth in the soil whose

occasionally been discovered in Cal. In 1854 Samnel N. West took a lump from a placer mine near Columbia in Nevada co. weighing 65 pounds, which he sold for $6,675. Another piece found in the same neighborhood was valued at $8,500. *San José Pioneer,* Feb. 16, 1878. A nugget worth over $4,000 found in 1857. A 'specimen' worth $1,000 found near Shasta. Another piece found by a Chinaman near Yreka worth $225. *Quincy Union,* Feb. 20, 1864. A piece found weighing 20½ ounces. *San Andreas Register,* Jan. 14, 1864. A lump of gold mined weighing 80 pounds. A solid chunk of gold weighing 16¼ pounds taken out of a claim on American river. A nugget found among tailings of the Hope and Despair co. in Sierra co. worth $1,770. The Fellow brothers took to the east with them a nugget shaped like a flat-iron, and about two thirds the size of an ordinary smoothing iron, weighing 67 ounces. *Trinity Journal,* Aug. 13, 1864. James Wilson found a piece of gold weighing over 24 pounds in his claim at Spanish Dry Diggings on the middle fork of American river. *Independent,* Aug. 17, 1865. A ten-ounce piece found at Orleans Bar, Klamath co. *Clear Lake Journal,* Sept. 28, 1865. The Oregon claim in Forest city yielded a nugget worth $508. *Grass Valley Union,* June 6, 1865. A handsome specimen taken from a hydraulic claim below Moore's Flat, Nevada co., was worth nearly $1,000. *Nevada D. Transcript,* June 12, 1866. Another on Greenhorn creek was valued at $182. A nugget taken from a ground sluice at French ravine, Yuba co., weighed 56 ounces, and was valued at $1,000. *Marysville North Californian,* June 10, 1867. Also on Dry creek, Tehama co, a piece worth $1,000 A 10-ounce piece taken from a claim on Douglas hill near San Andreas. *San Andreas Register,* Jan. 12, 1867. A slug of gold weighing $110 was picked up at Black Hawk. *Quincy Plumas National,* Aug. 24, 1867. A nugget weighing 36 ounces found between the north and south fork of the Weber creek. *Placerville Courier,* April 27, 1867. A nugget worth $800 or $900 was found by David Robinson near Volcano in 1866. The same man, in ploughing his farm, turned up a package of gold containing $900 in 1867. *Folsom Telegraph,* May 25, 1867. A nugget taken from the old Spanish diggings in Plumas co. was valued at $500. The owner of the Hines claim at Columbia picked up a piece of gold valued at $5,500. *Sonora Democrat,* July 11, 1868. A lump of gold weighing 240 pounds, and worth $20,000, was found in a claim on Remington hill in Nevada co., which was thought to be the largest lump of gold ever discovered. *Woodland Democrat,* June 29, 1868. A nugget was found in 1859 in the Monumental claim on the Sierra Buttes, 13 miles from Downieville in Sierra co., which weighed 103 pounds. After being cleaned in acid, and all the loose particles removed, it weighed 97 pounds Troy; but neither of these was as large as some Australian nuggets. At Shingle Springs two pieces of gold were picked up weighing 64 and 136 ounces. *Nevada Gazette,* April 17, 1869. Out of a claim on Squirrel creek, near Rough and Ready, was taken a lump of pure gold worth $297. *Nevada Transcript,* April 2, 1869. At Chalk Bluff a nugget weighing 39 ounces and valued at $754 was found in Timmons' diggings. *Nevada Gazette,* May 15, 1869. A nugget valued at $2,000 was found in the New Orleans co.'s claim at Little Grizzly. A gold bowlder worth $3,200 was found in a claim in Shasta co. A claim at Grass Valley in Nevada co. yielded a piece of gold worth $429. *Grass Valley National Gazette,* March 15, 1870. At Baltimore ravine, near Auburn, some Austrians found a nugget weighing 106 pounds, containing 97 pounds of pure gold valued at $19,000. *Nevada National Gazette,* Aug. 13, 1870. An 8-pound piece of gold, and 18 ounces in smaller pieces, were found in one claim, and an 11-pound nugget in a neighboring claim. Near

returns were more certain and easily obtained than the gold and silver of the rocks. Another was the gradual disappearance of the prospector of the earlier period, who lived in the mountains, and spent his life in hunting for gold and silver. To the too often unrewarded toils of these men we owe most of our present knowledge of the minerals of California. Capital does not go in search of mines. It waits for a discovery, and takes it at the lowest price at which it can afterward be obtained. Formerly there were some dishonorable transactions in mining-claim sales, where foreign capital was grievously misled. But all this business was later placed upon a safer footing. The output was not as great, but neither was the cost of living the same ; and as money is only an exchange for what we require, one dollar is as good as ten, if it buys the same amount of life's comforts and pleasures.[19]

Downieville a $1,000 nugget was found in 1870, and in the same ground the following year another weighing 175 ounces. *Grass Valley Union*, Feb. 25, 1871. Some Chinamen finding a 40-pound nugget on the middle fork of Feather river, to avoid excitement, chiselled it up into small pieces and sold it at different times mixed with other dust. A nugget weighing over a ton was found in Plumas co. It yielded ore worth $3,000. *National Gazette*, Nov. 16, 1872. A claim near Placerville yielded several nuggets worth from $1,000 to $2,000. A Chinaman found a piece of pure gold worth $170, which he sold to C. W. Brewster of Placerville, and soon after unearthed another nugget worth $700 in the same locality. *El Dorado Co. Republican*, Feb. 29, 1872. In March 1872 Reese and Depew found at Randolph Flat a stratum of decomposed quartz resembling red and white Castile soap in consistency. From a pit 8 feet long and 3 feet wide they took out $5,000 with a pick, shovel, and pan. From the ground in the vicinity a piece was picked up worth $800. *Nevada Transcript*, March 20, 1872. A Frenchman at Mormon Bar found in the earth of the road a nugget weighing 68 ounces. *Colusa Sun*, March 2, 1871. A chunk of gold weighing 240 pounds and worth $50,000 was found in the claim of a Chinese company at Moore's Flat. *Cloverdale Bee*, Feb. 8, 1873; *Plumas Gazette*, Feb. 1, 1873. A 5-pound gold nugget was taken out of Boulder creek, a tributary of the Sac. above Shasta, in 1874. *Wilmington Enterprise*, Oct. 22, 1874. Big nuggets are still being found in various quarters.

[19] References consulted for mining: *Turrill's Cal. Notes*, 180–1; *Stewart's Min. Res.*, 14; *Mer. Gaz. and Prices Current*, Jan. 4, 1860; *Raymond Min. Res Ann. Rept*, for several years—1869–75—in *U. S. H. Ex. Doc.*; *Wheeler's Surveys*, 1876, 47–69; *Hopkins' Common Sense*, 7–16; *Cal. Agric. Soc. Trans.*, 1860, 80–8; *Cal. Land Off. Rept*, 1869, 191–2, 359–60; *Miner* i. 6–8, 18–23, 28–45, 52, 58–60; *Coast Review*, 1872–9; *Cal. Ann. Min. Review*, 1878, 139–43; *Burchard Min. Produc.*, 1881, 11; 1882, 15; 1883, 705; *U. S. H. Ex. Doc.*, vol. 9, pt 5, p. 505–6, 47 cong., 1 sess., *Com. Herald and Market Review*, July 10, 1867; *McClellan, Golden State*, 312; *Coleman's Ann. Circ. and Market Review*,

As a product indispensable both to gold and silver mining, quicksilver may be deemed of the greatest value to the mining interest after the precious metals. Fortunately for that interest it was discovered before gold.[29] It is found in various kinds of rock, namely,

Jan. 12, 1864; *Simonin Vic Sauterraine*, 386–93; *Mines, Min., Money,* 1878–9, 126–35; *Bowie's Hydraulic Mining,* 78–86, 244–51.

[29] Cinnabar was used by the natives to paint their bodies, both in Cal. and Oregon. In 1824 one of the Robles family, having been informed of the existence of the ore by the Indians, revealed it to Antonio Suñol, who worked it for a short time under the impression that it contained silver. In 1845 a Mexican officer named Andres Castillero was shown some pieces of the ore at the Mission of Santa Clara. Having some knowledge of minerals he detected quicksilver, and remarked to those present, Father Reed and Jacob P. Lease, that if the mine could be proved as rich as those of Spain $100,000 would be paid by the Mexican government for the discovery. In order to secure the title to himself Castillero proceeded at once to take the steps required by Mexican law for that purpose. Possession was given by the alcalde of the district, with a grant of 3,000 yards (varas) of land in all directions from the mine. Castillero divided the mine into 24 shares, 4 of which he gave to José Castro, 4 to the brothers Secundino and Leodero Robles, keeping the remainder for himself, and employing an American from Columbia co., N. Y., to open the mine. This man, William G. Chard, seems to have been a genius from his manner of mining. Taking several gun-barrels, he filled them with bits of the broken ore, stopped the vents with clay, placed the muzzles in a vessel of water, and built a fire around the other end. The heat vaporized the mercury, which, passing into the water, was condensed, and precipitated in the form of metal. Chard next tried a furnace, which proved a failure. His third experiment was with six try-pots used by whalers, capable of holding 3 or 4 tons of ore. By inverting one over the other he formed a furnace, and by the application of heat, and conducting the vapor into water, succeeded in saving about 2,000 pounds of quicksilver. This method continued until August 1846, the Mexican government being informed of the facts. Then Chard and his Indian abandoned the mine. The same year T. O. Larkin forwarded information of it to the U. S. During the winter of 1846–7 Castillero sold a part of his shares to the English house of Barron, Forbes, & Co. of Tepic, Mex., who dispatched an agent, Robert Walkinshaw, to hold the property, who, with a man named Alden, took possession in May 1847. In Nov. came Alexander Forbes with a corps of miners and appliances for mining. Retorts were used until 1850, when furnaces were constructed under the superintendence of H. W. Halleck. It was not until July 1850–1 that the production of quicksilver for the market was commenced, since which time to 1880 the New Almaden mine had furnished, with the Euriguita on the same property, 54,378,418½ pounds of the metal. The mine was closed from 1858 to 1861 by injunction, the legality of the title being disputed. It was, however, confirmed to the English company, who sold it in 1864 to a company chartered under the laws of N. Y. and Pa. as the Quicksilver Mining co., with a capital of $10,000,000, divided into $100 shares. *Niles' Reg.,* lxxvi., 140; *S. F. El Heraldo,* Oct. 25, 1848; *S. F. News,* ii., 166; *Hayes' Scraps Min.,* ix., 10–13; *Whitney's Metallic Wealth,* 186–93, 195–7; *Miscellany,* iv., v., vi.; *Reviews of Com. and Finance,* 1876, p. 71; *Taylor's El Dorado,* ii. 12; *S. F. Cal.,Courier,* Sept. 27 and Nov. 18, 1850; *New Almaden, U. S. vs. Castillero; Sac. Transcript,* Feb. 1, 1851; North Pacific *Review,* Dec. 1862; *Castillo Mem., Azoque,* 57–8; *Harper's Mag.,* June 1863, 25–41; *Peto Res. of America,* 171; *Farayr Explor. Min.,* 23–25; *Coignet, Rapport, sur les Mines de N. Almaden; Ann. Scientific Disc.,* 1852, 298–9; *Hunt's Merch. Mag.,* xx., 557–8.

sandstone, decomposed serpentine or talc, porous basalt, rotten slate, and some harder rocks. The principal quicksilver mine of California is at New Almaden in Santa Clara county, and produces somewhat less than the amount produced by the Almaden quicksilver mine in Spain, after which it was named. The total production of the world in 1881 was 115,600 flasks of a little over 76 pounds each, of which California furnished 60,851 flasks, or more than half, and of this amount the New Almaden yielded 26,060.[21] From the maximum output of 79,396 flasks in 1877, the yield

[21] Among the other quicksilver mines are the Phœnix, situated in the Mayacamas system of mountains N. w. of Calistoga, in Napa co., discovered in 1860 by A. J. Bailey and J. Cyrus. An excitement followed the discovery, and many locations were made. The Phœnix was worked until 1878, when, owing to the low price of quicksilver, it was shut down. The Redington, in the same co., is situated in Sulphur cañon, N. of Berryessa valley. It was incorporated in 1861, and worked continuously. In 1881 it had produced 4,958,315 pounds of quicksilver. The Washington mine in Pope valley adjoins the Phœnix. It is a good mine, but suspended on account of low prices in 1878. The Ætna, in the same valley, was successfully worked for a time, and given up. The Summit mine, opened in 1872 upon the top of the Mayacamas range (the boundary between Sonoma and Napa counties), was in operation in 1881, the furnace having a capacity of 24 tons of ore per diem. The Oakville, on the west side of Napa valley, incorporated in 1868, had furnaces capable of reducing 25 tons daily, but is now lying idle. The Manhattan has a similar history. The Napa Consolidated, situated at the head of Pope cañon, was discovered in 1872. From 1876 to 1881 it produced 1,227,978 pounds of quicksilver. The Ivanhoe, Hamilton, New Burlington, Red Hill, Silver Bow, Overland, Mutual, and Mammoth, are all in Napa co. The Oakland, Cloverdale, Great Eastern, and Mount Jackson are in Sonoma co. The last was continuously worked from 1873 to 1881. Several other discoveries remain unworked in this co. The county of Lake also furnishes several quicksilver mines, of which the Sulphur Bank is the foremost. It was opened in Oct. 1874, with limited means, but produced from that date to Sept. 1876, when prices were good, 12,341 flasks, worth $600,000. The Great Western, in Sonoma, is situated in the range between St Helena and Cobb mountain, on the west side of Loconoma valley, and yields well. Yolo co. has also its quicksilver mine, situated in the N. w. corner, 49 miles from Woodland. The works employ 150 men. Sta Bárbara revealed to the prospector in 1860 and 1874 the ore of cinnabar in Sta Ynez valley, but no reduction works exist. Colusa, San Luis Obispo, Monterey, San Diego, San Benito, Plumas, and San Bernardino have laid claim to discoveries. In Fresno co. is the New Idria quicksilver mine, whose fame has been wafted abroad not more on its own metallic vapor than on the wings of rumor, the property having been in litigation for 13 years. It was located on a pretended Spanish grant, which in the course of its history was fraudulently bought and sold several times. The mine was at last sold to Montgomery Blair of S. F. for $1,000,000. *S. F. Chronicle,* March 19, 1876; *Balch's Mines and Miners,* 540; *McGarrahan, Memorial,* 82; *McGarrahan's Quicksilver Mines of Panoche Grande; U. S. Sen. Misc. Doc.,* 15, 42d cong., 1st sess.; *U. S. Com. Rept.,* 33, i., 40th cong., 2d sess.; *Miscellany,* iii.. No. 7, 249 pp.; *Hayes' Scraps Mining,* i. 93; *Fresno Expositor,* Dec. 11, 1872; *Castillo Mem. Azoque,* 59–64.

of the California mines decreased to 26,000 flasks
in 1888, of which latter amount fully one half was
exported. Even with so few mines of this metal in the
world—the Idria mine of Austria being the third
great producer—the prodution of quicksilver exceeds the demand in Europe and America, and only
by allowing China to purchase the surplus can the
price be kept up to remunerative figures. Its use in
this country, except in mining, is limited, but the Chinese employ it in the preparation of paints and in
other ways. A high tariff is required to keep European quicksilver out of the New York market and
enable California producers to pay the heavy freight
charged by the transcontinental roads.

Iron ore exists in many parts of the state,[22] but
owing to the large amount of capital required in working it, as well as its cheapness, and the greater fas-
cination of the precious metals, it has been neglected.
California must, in the near future, produce the pig
iron consumed in her manufactures, and in supplying
rails for her many railroads. Ore was first discovered
on or near American river in 1848, and later in Placer
county, where it was of such purity that tools were
made from it in blacksmiths' forges. It was not until
1880 that smelting works were put in operation for
turning out pig-iron.[23] These works belong to the
California Iron company, whose location is three miles
from Clipper gap in Placer county, and which owns
13,000 acres of iron and timber lands. The capacity
of the works is 15,000 tons per annum, which amount
was produced in 1886.

Copper was one of the mining manias of California,
like gold, quicksilver, and silver. It was known to

[22] Iron ore is found in Nevada, Placer, Sierra, Calaveras, Santa Clara,
Shasta, Los Angeles, Napa, Humboldt, Alpine, and San Luis Obispo counties. In Sierra co. it is chiefly magnetic ore. The ore of Placer is also
magnetic. Chrome iron is found in San Luis Obispo and Sonoma counties.
[23] As early as 1856 the Gold Hill Mining co. smelted some iron ore which
yielded 60 per cent, apparently as an experiment, as no iron appeared in the
market. The Clipper Gap mines were located and owned by Applegate and
Myres.

exist as early as 1840, having been discovered in Soledad pass, 90 miles north of Los Angeles. It is mentioned in the *Californian* in 1848 as having been discovered "north of the bay." J. B. Trask, who acted as state geologist from 1851 to 1854, found it in nearly every county, his first observation of it being made in Nevada county, near a place called Round Tent. From 1855, when some copper mining was done in the Sierra Nevada, on the old Carson road, to 1860 [24] little attention was given it. Then came on a copper excitement. Men spent their all and risked their lives in searching the mountains for green and blue carbonates, red oxides, and shining yellow sulphurets. The fever originated in Calaveras county, at Salt Spring valley, where the town of Copperopolis is situated, on the Union copper vein, and was communicated to every part of the state. It culminated about 1863, by which time it was found that California had copper enough to supply the world, but that there was not capital enough in the country to entice it from its native gangue; or where, as sometimes happened, it was nearly pure, to extract it in merchantable blocks. Copper is worked in a small way at one or two localities, but the value of the annual output is not more than $100,000.

Borax fields exist in Inyo, San Bernardino, and Lake counties. The annual yield is 5,000,000 pounds from a tract of 10,000 acres in San Bernardino and Inyo.

Salt is produced from the waters of the bay in Alameda county,[25] from springs at the head of the Salinas

[24] The Union mine at Copperopolis was discovered in July 1860, by Reed. The ore was rich, and was sent east for reduction, but the vein was not permanent. About 1867 the Copperopolis works were shut down. *Cal. Mountaineer*, i. 366–8; *Brown's Res.*, 207–19; *New York Sun* in *Panama Star and Herald*, 1876. I find mention of copper works in Plumas co., in 1865, on Queen of Union mine—also in Mariposa co. in 1866.

[25] By John Barton, a native of Leicester, Mass, were built the first and largest salt-works in California. Coming to this state in 1849, nearly twenty years later, he began the manufacture of salt, soon merging his interests in the Union Pacific Salt company, of which he is president. On his recommendation the site selected was Rock Island, at the mouth of Eden creek, Alameda co. The output for 1888 was 14,000 tons, distributed all over the coast, and forming nearly one half of its total product.

river in San Luis Obispo county, and from a salt lake in Los Angeles county. The amount marketed is about 30,000 tons annually.

Sulphur is obtained from the sulphur bank on the eastern shore of Clear lake in Lake county.[26] It is freed from earthy matter by heat alone, being finally purified before passing into the molds by melting in pots. It was first manufactured in 1861. Hydraulic cement is manufactured at Benicia, where the limestone necessary for its production is found. About 1,500 barrels are manufactured monthly.

Tin was discovered at Temescal in San Bernardino county in 1856 by a Mr Sexton, and subsequently reported to be found also in Los Angeles, San Diego, and Siskiyou counties. But it is a pretty well established fact that this rare metal is in such abundance in the first named county as to make the possession of the mine a prize worth contending for. This importance has been the occasion of litigation, which has been prolonged from the discovery to the present time. Ore of the Temescal mine is said to yield 60 per cent of tin. The assay gave 97.9 metallic tin, with traces of antimony, arsenic, sulphur, and iron, and a residue of tungsten. The bar so assayed was made in 1870, and is the first and only bar of tin produced in the United States from native ore. That a tin mine, for the discovery of which congress had offered a bounty of $200,000, should so long remain undeveloped is somewhat of a reproach, no less than a drawback, to the community.[27]

[26] An immense deposit is said to exist in Ventura co.

[27] The history of the Temescal tin mine is as follows: Leonardo Serrano, a native, claimed a grant of five leagues of land known as the Temescal rancho, which claim was rejected by the U. S. land commissioners. In 1859, tin being discovered and Serrano having died, Abel Stearns purchased of the widow whatever right she had to the land occupied by Serrano as a settler. The house of the widow was three miles from the mine, and Stearns appealed from the decision of the commissioners, getting a reversal of it in the U. S. dist court. The locators of the mine then appealed to the U. S. Supreme court, which restored the five league grant to the public lands in 1867. Pioche & co. of S. F. desired to purchase the mine, but failing, bought the San Jacinto rancho, twenty-six miles from the mine, and endeavored to float their purchase to make it cover it. Litigation that seems endless has

Coal has been found in most of the counties near the sea, and in several near the Sierra. It was discovered in 1850 in San Diego, in 1852 in Contra Costa, and in 1854 in Humboldt. The Contra Costa mines were slightly worked in 1855, and in 1859 had begun to produce a fair proportion of the domestic coal used in the market of San Francisco. Their output in 1865 was 120,000 tons; in 1881, 144,000 tons. Other mines may have brought the yearly amount up to the estimate of 239,927 tons; but mines hardly known in the market are not likely to have added so largely to the output of the state. The coal-fields of Contra Costa have their principal veins showing on the north-east side of Mount Diablo. Like the Oregon and Puget sound coals, this is of recent geologic origin, but is superior to them in being a steaming coal of a half bituminous character. The Black Diamond, Empire, and Bruce are the principal mines.

Petroleum has been known to exist in some of the southern counties from the earliest American occupation of the country. During the great oil speculations of Pennsylvania this knowledge was revived, and a petroleum fever seized the community, which resulted in finding it, or some evidence of it, in almost all parts of the state.[28] Numerous experiments with the crude material have been made, proving in general too expensive for profit in a market where the eastern oils are plentiful and cheap. The most successful works are in Ventura county, where there is a steady pro-

followed. In 1880 a company took possession to work the mine, but was soon driven away, and no one yet knows what the end will be.

[28] The counties which have laid claim to oil wells, or to what should be oil wells, are Humboldt, where it was discovered in 1859, and a flowing well in 1865; Placer, disc'd 1859; Sierra, disc'd 1861; Santa Clara, disc'd 1861; Napa, disc'd 1865; San Joaquin made a shipment in 1865; Fresno, Siskiyou, Contra Costa, Kern; Santa Cruz, disc'd 1863, and worked to some extent from 1864 to the present; Los Angeles, disc'd on the first settlement of the country, and worked in 1865; Santa Bárbara, disc'd in 1862; San Luis Obispo and Ventura, disc'd about the same time. Upon the report of Prof. Silliman some eastern parties were induced to purchase the Ojai rancho in Ventura, and several other properties were sold for good prices on account of prospective wealth never realized. There is a spring under the sea off the Santa Bárbara coast from which the oil floats on the water, and can be detected by the odor in the air.

duction, and the crude oil is conveyed for 63 miles in iron pipes to a shipping point on the coast, whence it is taken to Alameda to be refined. There were 8,000,-000 gallons manufactured in 1884 and a larger amount since.

Asphaltum, formed by the evaporation of the volatile part of petroleum, is very plentiful in Santa Cruz, Los Angeles, Monterey, Santa Bárbara, and San Luis Obispo counties. It is called bitumen and tar when found in a half fluid condition, and is used, mixed with sand, in making asphalt pavements in San Francisco. As might be expected, from the presence of the substances above named, natural gas is sometimes discovered in boring artesian wells, but it has not yet been much used for lighting or heating purposes.

Mineral soap—for which no better name has been suggested, possessing, as it does, the cleansing qualities of manufactured soaps—was discovered as early as 1849, and re-discovered in 1855 at Table mountain, two miles from Grass valley in Nevada county, the vein being fifteen feet thick. It is of a grayish color, somewhat rough to the touch, as if composed of sand compacted with some oil, is easily mined, and a really good article of soap, so far as its cleansing qualities are concerned. It has been found also in Sonoma, Santa Bárbara, and Ventura counties. Mineral paint is found in Contra Costa and Sonoma counties, and is an article of commerce. Limestone is not abundant on the Pacific coast, but is found in Contra Costa, Santa Cruz, and San Luis Obispo counties. A coarse marble belt extends along the west side of the Sierra Nevada, from Mariposa to Butte, a distance of 160 miles. Gypsum is found in San Benito, San Luis Obispo, and Alameda counties; alabaster in San Luis Obispo county ; lead in Monterey county ; manganese-black oxide—in Napa, Marin, and Alameda counties; plumbago in Tuolumne and Sonoma counties. The last named was discovered in Tuolumne county in 1853 by F. S. and H. S. Macomber, who left it undeveloped until 1866, when by accident discovering that the fine particles cf the black lead were more buoyant than the earthy matter when in water, they were furnished with the solution of the problem of separating them. The Sonoma mine was discovered in 1878.

Saltpetre was discovered in 1848 in Sonoma county; asbestos in Plumas county in 1873 ; antimony in San Bernardino in 1856; and platinum, a scarce metal, I find mentioned in 1848, and more recently in 1879 ; also magnesia (sulphate) in 1855; and chromium in San Luis Obispo in 1877, besides emery in 1863; and at different times and places, mica, alum, (in Alpine county) chalk, (on the Mokelumne river) silicon, bismuth, zinc, iridium, osmium, obsidian, soda, copperas, chalcedony, jasper, agate, topaz, and diamonds.[29] Lithographic stone was found on the Merced river in Mariposa county in 1867; and at other points porcelain clay, soapstone, slate, sandstone,[30] marble,[31] onyx,[32]

[29] None of the precious stones of Cal. are of great fineness. A good many opals have been found which are marketable. The opal mine on Mokelumne hill was worked in 1865, and the stones sent to Europe, where they were sold for about $20 a piece. A diamond excitement was started in 1872, the field being located in Wyoming or Colorado, for fraudulent purposes. But such diamonds as Cal. has are real and brilliant, although not of a great value. They are included in the catalogue of Cal. minerals at the Paris exposition of 1878, and are frequently mentioned in the Cal. newspapers, and are spoken of in the *Scientific Press* of March 26, 1870, and March 4, 1871. They were found in placer mining claims at Cherokee Flat, 10 miles from Oroville, and at Shaw Flat, in Nevada co.

[30] It was for some time believed that building stone was not abundant in Cal., but a better knowledge of this class of resources reveals an ever-increasing list of valuable material. On Angel island there is a freestone quarry of fine color, homogeneous, and easily worked, which belongs to the govt. At Haywards, in Alameda co., is another quarry, of which the bank of Cal. and Young Men's Christian Association buildings are constructed. These quarries were the earliest in use. Stone quarries are found at Knight's Ferry, in Stanislaus, and near Placerville, in El Dorado counties. In 1873, an immense sandstone deposit was discovered near San Diego.

[31] The first marble worked in the state was by E. R. Roberts of Stockton, who established a marble yard at Columbia, in Tuolumne co., in 1857. A block of this stone was taken out and dressed for the Washington monument in that year. The material for Broderick's monument came from Columbia. These works, probably on account of the cost of transportation at that period, were closed; but there was a rediscovery of marble in the same locality in 1865, and again in 1868. At Iowa Hill, Placer co., a quarry of finely variegated marble was discovered in 1855, and the same year a vein of gray marble in Sierra co.; also about the same time near Suisun bay. Calaveras, Yuba, El Dorado, Amador, Monterey, Los Angeles, and Tulare counties all have their marble beds.

[32] Onyx in bowlders was found first near Suisun bay, where it was worked

granite,[33] fire-clay, and fire-proof stone. California, in common with the whole Pacific coast, is
rich in mineral waters of various healing qualities.
Those best known are the Geysers[34] and Skaggs hot
springs[35] in Sonoma county, the Bartlett springs[36] in
Lake county, the White sulphur springs of St He-

out, and later in San Luis Obispo, where it is more abundant. J. F. Kessler
& Co. of S. F. own the mine, which is in a slate formation. At a still later
period the quarrying of onyx has been carried on in Solano co., five miles
north of Fairfield.

[33] The granite quarries of Cal. are several, but that of Sac. co. was the
oldest. It was opened in 1853 by G. Griffith, who furnished this material
for the fortifications at Alcatraz and Fort Point, and for important buildings
of the period. In 1864, Griffith located the Penryn quarry, situated three
miles from Auburn in Placer co. The quality of this granite is equal, if not
superior, to any in the world, being free from iron, and never changing color.
There are polishing works in connection with this quarry, at which a solid
block of 10 tons can be polished with ease. There are three varieties in this
place, blue or dark, white, and black. The granite quarries at Folsom were
opened in 1856–7, and worked by convicts of the branch state prison. Santa
Cruz, Yuba, and Monterey counties. The miners of Tuolumne co. sent a
block of granite as their contribution to the Washington monument. In
1864 the legistature agreed with the Central Pacific R. R. to grant a certain
subsidy, one of the conditions being a deed of a tract of granite land in Placer
co., but the state never derived any benefit from the acquisition. There are
quarries of building stone in Solano co., of slate in Calaveras and San Luis
Obispo, and of fire-proof stone in Tehama and Sierra counties.

[34] There are two geyser localities, both situated in a deep gorge in Sonoma
co. known as Pluton cañon, about 1,700 feet above the sea. They cover an
area of several acres, and number over 300. The temperature of the water
varies from 200° to 210° Fahrenheit. Four miles up the cañon are the Little
Geysers. Here the water is purer, and the temperature from 190° to 200°.
The springs hold in solution a great variety of salts, the sulphates of iron,
lime, and magnesia predominating. Sulphate of magnesia, tartaric acid,
alum, magnesia, and sulphur are found in abundance, and give the rocks a
peculiarly vivid coloring. These waters are sought to cure rheumatism and
skin diseases.

[35] Skaggs Hot springs are three in number. The first is impregnated
with sulphur, iron, and borax, with a temperature of 128° to 130°. The
second spring contains manganese, iron, sulphur, and soda, with a temperature of 138° to 140°. The third is an iron spring.

[36] The Bartlett springs contain sulphur, magnesia, manganese, potassium,
and calcium. In the same locality is one nearly ice-cold, highly charged with
carbonic acid. Another called the Soap spring, is 25 feet long, 12 wide, and
6 deep, with a natural wall of bowlders all around it. Its tepid waters contain borax, soda, salt, and sulphur. A few feet distant another spring contains iron, soda, and chloride of sodium at a temperature of 85. A quarter
of a mile away is a cold spring, always bubbling with the gas escaping
from it.

Lake co. has also Hot Borax springs or Borax lake, lying east of Clear
lake and separated from it by a low ridge. About a mile beyond the ridge
are the sulphur banks before named, a feature of great interest as showing
the geological formation of the region where solfatara is still going on. The
banks cover an area of about 40,000 square yards, and from beneath them
appear to flow the hot borate springs. *Id.*

lena, and the Calistoga hot springs [37] in Napa county, the California Seltzer springs in Mendocino county, the Pacific Congress, and New Alamaden Vichy springs in Santa Clara county, El Paso de Robles in San Luis Obispo county,[38] Montecito hot sulphur in Santa Bárbara county,[39] Agua Caliente in San Diego, and the San Bernardino hot springs, although this does not exhaust the list of well known mineral and hot springs. Tassajara springs, four miles from Monterey, the Chalybeate springs, near the mouth of Carmel river, and Paraiso springs, near Soledad, are all in Monterey county. The mineral springs at Tehachapi and Mojave in Los Angeles and Kern, the Tolenas springs in Solano county, the sulphur and other medical waters in Colusa and Placer, and the soda springs in Siskiyou are only a part of those which really exist in the mountain regions. They are very suggestive of the near neighborhood of the great laboratories of nature, where are pent up the forces which occasionally exhibit themselves in volcanic eruptions and earthquakes.

[37] Calistoga hot springs, at the town of Calistoga, are situated in the level valley, 500 feet above sea-level, and surrounded on three sides by high mountains. The waters contain sulphuretted hydrogen gas, chloride of sodium, chloride of calcium, carbonate of soda, sulphate of soda, sulphate of magnesia, silica, and alumina. There are similar springs at St Helena in the same county.

[38] El Paso de Robles (meaning White Oak Pass,) hot springs, are situated in a flat valley, without any attractive features; The waters are closely allied to the thermal waters of Aix-la-Chapelle in Rhenish Prussia, possessing the unusual combination of heat, chloride of sodium, sulphuretted hydrogen, carbonic acid gas, and an active amount of alkaline carbonates. It is beneficial in gout, chronic rheumatism, and dartrous skin diseases, in contraction of the joints, and old gun-shot wounds. Newcom white sulphur springs, fourteen miles from San Luis Obispo, and Pecho's springs, fifteen miles from S. L. O. and two from the coast, are all in San Luis Obispo co.

[39] These springs are situated at the head of a cañon four or five miles northeast of the town of Santa Bárbara, 1450 feet above the sea. They are seven in number; four of which are nearest the head of the cañon, having the same properties of free sulphur and sulphuretted hydrogen, with a temperature of 114° Fahrenheit. Another, 100 yards west, has a temperature of 117°, and its principal constituent is sulphate of ammonia, sulphate of iron, soda, potash, and a trace of arsenic. The other two have not been analyzed, but have a lower temperature than the first named. These springs are visited for rheumatism, skin diseases, contraction of the joints, paralysis, and, as an auxilliary in the treatment of secondary and tertiary syphilis.

California went through the excitement of her golden era without a stock exchange. In 1851, when Frémont's Mariposa mine was placed upon the European market, there prevailed a mania for joint-stock mining associations abroad, and numerous companies were formed in London and Paris with princes as presidents, counts and barons as vice-presidents, and names followed by many abbreviations as directors, which caused the stock to be purchased with avidity. Four mammoth companies were advertised in the London *Times*, in one of which 100,000 shares were quickly taken at a pound a share. The Nouveau Monde mining company, with a Paris council of supervision, of which Prince Louis Lucien Bonaparte was president, Count de Lantivy and others vice-presidents, was organized in France, with the object of working the Mariposa mines under a lease from Frémont, the capital being 5,000,000 francs in shares of 25 francs each. But in the United States and California this form of mine manipulation did not come into favor until the Comstock lode of Nevada had been sufficiently prospected to show its character as a true fissure vein, carrying silver and gold in probably vast amount. Nor did the need of an exchange then impress itself on the public [40] for a couple of years, during which time shares, which were then called "feet"—a foot representing a share—were transferred in the same manner that other property was bought and sold. When companies multiplied [41]

[40] The first mining and milling company organized in San Francisco to develop a claim on the Comstock was the Washoe G. and S. Mining co. It was the result of a visit of Almarin B. Paul to that region in March 1860. He agreed with the Succor co. for 35,000 tons of ore, returned to S. F., organized his company, was appointed sup't, and set about constructing a steam mill. His example was imitated, and soon there were several mills on the Comstock, while the list of mines incorporated in Cal. swelled rapidly.

[41] The list of mining companies located in the Washoe district in 1860, were: 'Washoe G. and S. Mining co.,' capital stock $500,000 in 1,000 of $500 each; term of existence five years. 'Chollar Silver Mining co,' capital stock $680,000, in 5,600 shares of $300 each; term of existence 50 years. 'Sierra Nevada Silver Mining co.,' capital stock $1,500,000, in 3,000 shares of $500 each; term 50 years. 'Ophir Silver Mining co.,' capital stock $5,040,000, in 16,800 shares of $300 each; term 50 years.

greatly, as they did in 1861, and sales were attended with a corresponding excitement, feet and inches were sometimes sold at auction, or by the board of brokers, whose business it was to dispose of gas and water stocks, bonds, notes, and other securities.

The rapid increase of mining properties, and the opportunity afforded for deception, with the growing desire of the public to invest in mining shares, suggested the establishment of a stock exchange, where fair and legitimate investments might be made, while the market could not be governed by prices created by the pretended sales of one broker to another, as had been done. Franklin Lawton, secretary of the board already referred to, made the suggestion to some of his associates to form themselves into a board similar to the New York Stock Exchange, though he at first met with opposition from dealers who had found other methods

'Buckeye G. and S. Mining co.,' capital stock $280,000 in 2,800 shares of $100 each; term 50 years. 'Gould and Curry Silver Mining co.,' capital stock $2,400,000, in 4,800 shares of $500 each; term 50 years. 'Scorpion Silver Mining co.,' capital stock $35,000, in 350 shares $100 each; term 50 years. 'Yankee Silver Mining co.,' capital stock $500,000 in 5,000 shares of $100 each; term 50 years. These were all the companies whose incorporation papers were on file in July 13, 1860. as I learn by the *S. F. Alta* of that date. Their aggregate capital was $10,935,000.

There was a trading place for stocks in 1860-1 called Olney & Co's Washoe Stock exchange, where James N. Olney had his first regular auction sale Jan. 14, 1861, although stock had been sold there in 1860. I find a notice of a report made in December of that year as follows: 'Dec. 29, 1860. Mining stocks of all descriptions have been for ten days past quite inactive. The interruption by storms of communication, both by express and telegraph, with the mining locations on the eastern slope, has had much effect in suspending operations in this market. The following may be considered as the present ruling rates for the prominent stocks:

Ophir	$825 to $850 per foot.	Sales limited.
California......	550 to 600 " "	Little offered.
Gould & Curry....................	325 " "	Assess'ts unpaid.
Chollar..........	70 to 75 " "	" paid.
Lucerne	85 to 90 " "	Dull sales.
St Louis........................	50 " "	" "
Boston	20 " "	" "
Hope............................	20 " "	" "
Sucker	14 to 16 " "	" "
Rogers	8 to 10 " "	" "
Lady Bryan.....................	6 to 8 " "	" "

At the first regular sale in January, 1861, 'a very large company was present, and a considerable amount of Washoe and Esmeralda interests were disposed of at fair prices.' None of the principal Comstock stocks were offered, except Gould & Curry at $282 per share of three inches.

profitable, and also from owners of mining property, who feared that speculation would be increased by it.

The first meeting was held on the 8th of September at 428 Montgomery street, when a committee was chosen to draft a constitution and by-laws, namely: John Perry, Jr, T. C. Sanborn, Henry Critcher, Robert C. Page, David Henriques, and Wm W. Lawton.[42] On the 12th the by-laws were reported, and, with some modifications, adopted. This was the beginning of an association which has witnessed the making of many fortunes and the undoing of more; which is revered as the pantheon of the gods, or reviled as an assembly of demons, according as the prices of stocks ascend or descend the ever sliding scale. This is the San Francisco Stock and Exchange board.

In 1872 business had so increased that the eighty members, to which the first exchange was limited, were not considered sufficient to properly conduct all the daily transfers of stock, and a second board was or-

[42] The members of this board were charged a fee of $100, but paid only $50 at first, as they confined their operations to a small room in Montgomery block, furnished with a plain table in horse-shoe form, with desks for the president and secretary. The first members were: J. Perry, Jr, F. C. Sanborn, S. Heydenfeldt, Geo. R. Barclay, H. C. Logan, Robert C. Page, C. H. Wakelee, Joseph Grant, J. B. E. Cavallier, S. C. Bruce, P. C. Hyman, Henry Critcher, P. B. Cornwall, N. A. Watson, Wm L. Higgins, E. J. de Santa Marina, Simon Mayer, Franklin Lawton, D. C. Williams, Henry Schmiedell, H. P. Wakelee, D. W. Teacle, O. Abbott, R. E. Brewster, A. Marius Chapelle, E. Dupré, A. J. Shipley, R. H. Sinton, T. A. Talbert, Wm Willson Lawton, Frank M. Pixley, David Henriques, Wm H. Parker, Wm R. Garrison, J. Downe Wilson, A. Van Lokeren, Charles K. Smith. As business increased new applications for membership were received, and it was resolved to limit the number to 80, and to increase the fee to $250— then to $500—and finally to $1,000. Finding themselves restricted for want of space, after several removes they finally secured a room in the new Merchant's Exchange building on California street between Montgomery and Sansome, taking stock in the building to the amount of $20,000. But even here they were crowded, and again changed their quarters to Duncan's building, 411½ California street, where they remained until Oct. 1877, when they took possession of their present elegant Exchange building on Pine street. The Board room here is 70 feet 6 inches square with the ceiling 55 feet high. It has 100 seats, and a gallery for spectators, and a special one for ladies. In 1876 a surplus of $65,000 was divided among the members. The price of seats previous to 1872 had risen to $3,000; since then it has been as high as $40,000. In the early practices of an inexperienced board no charge was made for entering a mine upon their list, and calling it during a session; but now a fee of $6,000 is required. The style of recording tran-

ganized, called the California Stock and Exchange
board.[43]   In 1875 a third, the Pacific Stock Exchange,[44]
was formed, the former, now defunct, being called "the
little board," to distinguish it from the San Francisco

sactions is shown by the following extract from the books of the board in the
beginning:

Friday, September 26th, 1862.

SELLER	BUYER	QUALITY	STOCK	PRICE	TIME
Perry	Logan	$500.00	Starr	$387.50	....
Marina	Sanborn	10 feet	Chollar	185.00	....
Perry	Pixley	50 shares	Mt. Davidson	8.00	....

Saturday, September 27th, 1862.

SELLER	BUYER	QUALITY	STOCK	PRICE	TIME
Perry	Logan	5 shares	Cal. Navig'n	$39.50	....

Monday, September 29th, 1862.

SELLER	BUYER	QUALITY	STOCK	PRICE	TIME
Perry	Logan	$3,000	S. F. Bonds	$70.50	....
Wilson	Perry	6 feet	Esmeralda	50.00	....

Tuesday, September 30th, 1862.

SELLER	BUYER	QUALITY	STOCK	PRICE	TIME
Logan	Cavallier	50 feet	Dessert	$ 12.50	....
Sanborn	Cavallier	10 feet	Potosi	187.00	....

Wednesday, October 1st, 1862.

SELLER	BUYER	QUALITY	STOCK	PRICE	TIME
Marina	Cavallier	15 feet	Chollar	$175.00	....
E. H. Wakelee	Mayer	10 feet	Sierra Nev.	140.00	....
Perry	Shipley	20 shares	Mt. Davidson	6.50	....
Logan	Perry	10 feet	Merideth	20.00	....
Logan	Hyman	362½ feet	Merideth	20.00	....
Perry	Sanborn	7 shares	Bousley Water Co.	35.00	....

[43] The California Stock and Exchange Board was organized in Jan. 1872,
soon after the development of the Crown Point and Belcher mines, which
caused a lively market, by an association of 40 men, many of whom were
experienced brokers.   The membership was limited to 70, which number of
seats was quickly taken, but reduced afterwards to 62.   The sales during
the first year amounted to $16,000,000.   The total sales down to July 1876
were $80,000,000.   The constitution and by-laws were nearly identical with
the older association.   Seats in this board were valued at from $1,000 to
$2,000. *Id.*, 33.   It suspended operations in 1880. *Mining*, 520–1.
[44] The Pacific Stock Exchange consists of 80 members, each of which paid
in at the start $5,000, making a cash capital of $400,000.   As much as

Stock and Exchange, or "old board." The Pacific board endeavored to associate the most active operators on the coast, and embraced a scheme for loaning money on mining securities. Half the members were selected from the California board, then in the height of its prosperity. The members of these boards are honorable men, and the stock-brokers of San Francisco, whether members of boards or not, are generally honest, although, as in every other business, some men have been sucked into the maelstrom of excitement and gone down, sinking their own and their clients' means in hopeless depths of ruin. It is the privilege of the broker to make a commission, whether he buys or sells, and when he keeps to his commissions he is ordinarily sure to make a fair income.[45] Often he knows no more of the value of a mine than the least informed of his clients; and equally as little of the impending rise or fall of any stock on the list of the boards. In the great gamble[46] going on he is

$10,000 was offered for a seat in this board. It held its first meeting for the purchase and sale of stocks in the Halleck building, on the corner of Sansome and Halleck streets, June 7, 1875. It had already purchased for $325,000 the property now owned by the association, on which has been erected a handsome edifice fronting on Leidesdorff street, extending back to Montgomery, and communicating with an exquisitely ornamented rotunda, and that with a spacious vestibule, elaborately decorated, opening on Montgomery street. It was opened May 15, 1876, and the day's sales amounted to $288,000. The charges for placing a mine on the list of the Pacific Stock Exchange are $500, with a renewal fee of $100, to be paid annually. The constitution and by-laws are the same in effect as those of the San Francisco Stock and Exchange board.
   [45] Schmeidell's Statement, MS., 5.
   [46] There is a perfectly bewildering, and, to the uninitiated, unintelligible scene enacted every day at the stock-boards, something like this: The signal to commence the day's operations is a metallic bang! clang! bang! 'Call the roll,' says the chief magician from his curtained dais. Another metallic banging, then 'Ophir' is shouted by the caller. Instantly there is a rush of brokers to the pit in front of the dais. Shouts, yells, gesticulation, and bellowing go on, for a moment only. What they cry is the number of shares they will sell or buy, and 'sell 'em cash,' 'sell 'em reg'lar,' 'sell 'em seller 30.' To sell for cash means that the stock must be delivered and paid for before 2 P. M. the same day. To sell 'regular' means delivery on the following day. To 'buy or sell 30' means that the buyer or seller has 30 days to deliver or demand the stock. Most brokers buy stocks regular, and hold them as required, charging a heavy interest, the customer paying such 'margin' as the broker demands, from 20 to 50 per cent of the price of the stock. Should it fall, the buyer must put up more money (mud, it is termed) to keep up the margin, or the stock is sold at his risk. Should the stock of a 'buyer 30' rise the day after purchase, he has a right to demand it, or the difference in

merely the irresponsible agent, unless, as is frequently the case, he borrows from the banks to carry the stocks of his customers on a margin, when, if they have a rapid decline, he may become involved with his principal.

There have been many individual fraudulent transactions in mines, chargeable to the greed and rascality of mining impostors, who have even gone abroad for their victims; but this is a matter separate and apart from the "gambling deals" in the stock market. Knowing the wealth hidden in the mineral veins of the coast, the people were always looking for some great development, and were only too willing to be deceived by their hopefulness. The silver mines on the Comstock were at first a great mystery and a great promise. When their managers—manipulators, they are called—caught the hint given by the faith of the people, they conceived the scheme of trading upon it. In 1863 Gould and Curry sold for $6,300 a foot; Ophir $2,700; Savage $4,000; Hale and Norcross $2,100; Chollar $1,000, and so on. These prices were dependent on the reported yield of a rich ore-body in Gould and Curry, and when it was showing signs of exhaustion the better informed threw their stock on the market, creating a panic. This was the cause of loss to thousands who had followed the lead of the rich stockholders in buying, but could not follow it in selling because the market was broken. Losses of this nature usually inspire a desire for retrieval through the same medium, and the lesson of 1863 had little effect in discouraging stock speculation. Again shares were multiplied, until, instead of representing a foot on a vein, a share might only rep-

the price at which he bought it, and the quotation at the board that day. When one stock has been called, the brokers retire, and another is shouted out. Perhaps it is 'Consolidated Virginia.' In an instant Babel is let loose again, and the pit is full of stamping, pushing, pulling, yelling, roaring stock fiends. But only for a moment, and so on, to the end of the list. An hour or less has passed, but millions have changed hands, and the telegraph has flashed the intelligence across the continent, and through the Atlantic to Europe.

resent the thickness of a sheet of paper. But people purchased them nevertheless, paying the prices fixed by the manipulators, and the real gambling spirit showed itself. In June 1871 Crown Point sold for $6,000 a foot. In the previous November it was selling at $3 a share. The discovery was made of a body of ore of fine quality which was afterward found to extend into Belcher, the adjoining mine, but was not announced to the share-holders, until one capitalist had quietly purchased 5,000 shares, and 1,000 shares had been secured by another. Then the news was suffered to be made known, and the price advanced rapidly. The principal buyer, with the object of controlling the board of directors, kept on purchasing all the shares within reach until with the last 4,100 shares at $300 he had paid $1,230,000 for his interest in the mine. There were but 600 feet in the mine, divided into 12,000 shares, and the price paid was at the rate of $6,000 a foot. There was but a fraction of an inch in these shares; whereas, by and by, there was but a line, if that. Being so very attenuated, what did it matter whether there were any mine at all except the name on the stock list? Soon afterward a small body of ore was uncovered in the Savage mine, which is located almost in the centre of the Comstock lode. And now ensued one of the most frantic stock excitements ever witnessed on the Pacific coast. It was believed that, when depth was attained, the ore-body in the Crown Point would be found to extend the entire length of the lode, and the prices of shares advanced accordingly, often rising $20, $30, or even $50 in a day, Crown Point selling for over $1,800 a share, Belcher over $1,500, with others, as Savage at over $700, in proportion. The stock-gambling mania extended throughout every portion of the coast, and pervaded all classes of society, the merchant, the farmer, the mechanic, the laborer, and the professional man all taking part in the frenzied rush for sudden and easily acquired riches. The prices of these lines were very well sustained [47] until April 1872, and then came a crash in which the value of silver stocks declined $60,000,000 in ten days. The capitalist above re-

[47] Here is a table of prices, bullion, assessments, and dividends for the month of October 1869, with comparative totals for the years 1866, 1867, 1868, and 1869 for the same month.

	Highest Price	Lowest Price	Bullion	Assessments	Dividends	Sales of Stock
Alpha.........	$ 15.00	$ 10.00				
Belcher........	16.00	11.00		$ 26,000		
Bullion........	15.00	15.00				
Crown Point....	17.00	11.50		90,000		
Confidence.....	25.00	20.00				
Chollar-Potosi..	17.00	13.50	$108,070		$ 28,000	
Daney. ...-.....	1.00	1.00		8,000		
Exchequer	7.50	3.50				
Empire	36.00	15.00	7,523			
Gould & Curry .	77.50	66.50	28,933			
Gold Hill Quartz	30.00	27.00	2,629			
Hale & Norcross	141.00	116.00	110,116			
Imperial.......	37.00	28.00				
Kentuck.......	180.00	112.50	143,381			
Lady Byron....	13.00	8.00				
Occidental	13.50	9.50				
Ophir..........	22.00	13.00		33,600		
Overman.......	125.00	77.50	12,820			
Seg'ated Belcher	8.50	5.00		6,400		
Savage	51.00	37.50	31,271			
Sierra Nevada..	18.50	7.00	16,100		7,500	
Yellow Jacket .	43.00	35.00	150,000			
Total in 1869...	....	....	$610,843	$164,000	$ 35,500	$69,089,731
Total in 1868...	....	....	535,164	106,000	120,000	115,943,119
Total in 1867...	....	....	1,079,799	205,000	240,000	66,274,577
Total in 1866...	....	....	1,032,713	164,620	167,000	32,835,893

Commercial Herald and Market Review, Jan. 14th, 1870.

In another table I find the statement of the annual product, assessments and dividends for the above years as follows:

Years	Bullion Product	Dividends	Assessments
1869	$ 7,265,378	$1,175,000	$1,419,000
1868	8,499,769	2,415,000	1,825,000
1867	13,626,062	3,991,000	1,296,000
1866	11,732,100	1,754,000	1,194,820

Of the mines which produced over one million in 1869 there were only four, Chollar-Potosi, Hale & Norcross, Savage, and Yellow Jacket. It will be observed that the assessments in this year more than equalled the dividends, notwithstanding the production should have covered all expenses. The discrepancies are not less marked in the other years.

ferred to [48] was credited with a gain of $25,000,000, and a few others with enormous profits.[49]

In this case the rise was due to the actual discovery of a new ore-body in Belcher and Crown Point simultaneously with rich discoveries in the Pioche district, but the fact of these developments could not have affected the market 'to such a degree had it not been for the manipulation of the great dealers, in collusion with the banks. Every preparation was made to lead the credulous public to their fatal plunge. In this the speculators were assisted by certain newspapers, affecting to give authentic reports of the condition and prospects of the mines.[50] But these journals were not in the secrets of the manipulators any more than those to whom they gave false advice.

Early in the history of the Comstock, the bank of California, under the management of W. C. Ralston, sent its confidential agent, William Sharon, to Nevada. The result of the policy pursued was that mining was made possible that otherwise would have been impossible. Money was advanced, and stock taken as security. Before 1872 the bank of California held shares enough to control most of the prominent mines, and by means of this control could govern the operations of the mills, even, it was alleged, loaning money to mill-men, and afterwards refusing to give them the custom of the mines, until they fell into bankruptcy for want of employment. In 1875, Sharon was president of the Union Mill and Mining company, which owned 16 quartz-mills, of a value of from $15,000 to $300,000 each, aggregating $1,200,000. The water-works at Virginia City, valued at $7,000,000, and the

---

[48] Alvinsa Hayward.

[49] Sharon, of the bank of California, was said to have mads $20,000,000, C. A. Low $10,000,000, and J. P. Jones the same.

[50] The *Daily Stock Report* was established in 1863, being the oldest daily paper of its class on the entire Pacific coast. It was small at first, but was a financial success from the start, and is now a large quarto sheet, filled with official lists of the stock sales at all the boards, the latest intelligence from the mines (which may be true or false), and the freshest rumors about stocks. It purports to be conservative. The proprietors in 1887 were Wm M. Bunker and A. C. Hiester.

Virginia and Truckee railroad, worth $3,000,000, were under the control of the president of a bank whose nominal capital was only $5,000,000. What wonder that he fell into the pit he himself had dug for others. The property held as security by the California bank amounted to $25,000,000. The milling business was almost entirely in the hands of the Union Mill and Mining company; the railroad controlled the timber and wood necessary for the mines and mills; and there was little connected with the Comstock that was not owned by the institution presided over by Ralston except the Sutro tunnel. To believe that a stock mania ever came on without being predetermined by the holder of so much mining estate was to be blind and credulous to the point of resigning the reasoning capacity.

But a day of reckoning was at hand for the bank of California; it was to be beaten at its own tactics. In 1873, notwithstanding the tumble of 1872, while Crown Point and Belcher were paying large dividends, the Virginia Consolidated commenced dividing $300,000 monthly among its share-holders. In the following year a drift run from the 1,200-foot level of the Gould & Curry disclosed a large body of rich ore, which further exploration showed to be from 300 to 400 feet in width. In December 1874 a professional expert,[51] and one well acquainted with the Comstock, said: " I assert that there is already shown in the two mines, California and Consolidated Virginia, $1,500,000,000 of ore. I make the assertion, and am willing to stand by it. I think it will be perfectly safe to say that the ore will average $200 per ton; I have examined drifts 150 feet in ore that averaged, ton per ton, as it was taken out, $500. I should say the Consolidated Virginia and California are worth at least $5,000 per share; that is, I have no doubt but that amount of money will be paid out in dividends. I have been

[51] Philip Deidesheimer.

mining twenty-four years, or most of my lifetime. I
am very careful about my statements." It is probable that while thus so vastly overestimating the extent and richness of the bonanza, the expert stated only
what he believed to be the truth. Superintendent Fair
reported at the close of 1874: "The quality of the ore
is of very high grade, and far exceeds in value any ever
removed from the Comstock. The quantity now exposed to view is almost fabulous. . . . The quality
and quantity of ore developed in the mine the past
year far exceeds in value that of any mine which has
ever come under my knowledge or observation."

Seeing endless dividends in prospect, all classes
were eager to possess shares in the great bonanza,
which rose in value $10, $20, and $30 a day, and on
one occasion as much as $100 at a single session of the
board.[52] The oldest operators were deceived, because
the amount of bullion so far produced had really exceeded that of any of the Comstocks, and no one
doubted the integrity of the men who controlled it.
As the event proved, they were themselves greatly
deceived as to the value of the mine. The scenes
at the stock exchanges at this period and for
the first weeks of 1875 were weird in their excitement, the brokers crying one to another, like the un-
seemly harpies of Dante's hell, every cry carrying the
Comstock higher. Not only at the exchanges, but
on the street,[53] the wild bidding for fortune's favors

---

[52] The Consolidated Virginia mine was divided into 10,700 shares, its
length being 1,310 feet. The firm of Flood & O'Brien, Mackay, and Fair
bought up a majority of the shares at $4 to $9. (For a history of the relations of these men, see my *Hist. Nevada.*) The property was divided into
two mines, Consolidated Virginia and California, with 108,000 shares each.
Subsequently the mines were divided into 540,000 shares each. Nobody
cared now about the ground conveyed—it was the object to share in the
division of what the mine contained.

[53] One of the means of stock gambling pursued in S. F. in 1876 was by
puts and calls. A 'put' is a contract with a firm of brokers whereby the
purchaser of the privilege agrees to pay a dollar a share for all that the stock
may fall in the market during the next 15 days, the price started from being
from one to ten per cent below the market price on the day of purchase. A
'call' is the reverse of this; it is the privilege of a rise that is given. But
as the price fixed in either case is so much above or below the market rate
that the buyer has little hope of reaching a higher or lower point, he gener-

went on, and at almost every dining-table in the city the day's advances in stock were canvassed anew.

In January 1875 the receipts from Consolidated Virginia were $1,001,400; in February $1,200,000; in March $1;705,600; in April $1,509,000; in May $1,521,000; in June $1,502,000; in July $1,604,000, or over $15,000,000 in seven months. The prices of all shares on the Comstock were carried far beyond their real value, and although fluctuating, were for a time sustained by the developments in the bonanza mines. At the highest, in January, California brought $780 per share, the stock then being divided into 108,000 shares. Consolidated Virginia brought over $700. In February California was divided into 540,-000 shares, fluctuating for some weeks between $69 and $46. This was a falling off in value from $84,-240,000 to $37,260,000, and then to $24,840,000. Meanwhile Comstock values had declined more than $100,000,000, shrinking $42,600,800 in a single week.

The decline resulted from a variety of causes, chief among which was the natural reaction which inevitably follows undue inflation. A few months later the depression was further intensified by the failure of the bank of California, whose president had long been in the unsuspected agonies of approaching ruin, brought on by his too generous treatment of others and his own unauthorized speculation with the funds of the bank. On the 26th of August, 1875, the bank closed its doors, and on the following day Ralston's dead body was taken from the water at North Beach. The whole city—indeed, the whole state, and Nevada as well—mourned the dead king of the Comstock. Whatever the faults of Ralston, they felt that he had intended to befriend the community in which he lived;[54] but being only mortal, he had not been able

ally loses his investment. However, two S. F. firms were compelled to suspend on account of the extreme fluctuations of this year, which sunk all their capital.

[54] Besides the numerous projects in Nevada in which Ralston was interested, he was instrumental in building the dry-dock at Hunter's Point, Mis-

to keep out of the strong current of speculation, which, like a tidal wave, had swept the fair land of California.

Largely through the efforts of Sharon, the affairs of the bank were rehabilitated, and within a few days the directors had decided to resume business. Meanwhile the stock-boards suspended operations for a period of two months. In October the bonanza firm opened the bank of Nevada in San Francisco, with a capital of $10,000,000—afterward reduced to $3,000,-000—and with Flood for president. The Nevada bank then became the support of the stock market, and for a time confidence was maintained, at least in the Consolidated Virginia and California mines.

While since 1874–5 there have been periodical stock excitements, as that of 1878, when, under pretended developments, Sierra Nevada rose to $280 a share, and Union Consolidated to $170, with others in proportion, the former almost without a ton of pay ore in sight, of late such excitements have grown less frequent and less pronounced. Nor could this well be otherwise when it is considered that, with two or three trifling exceptions, no Comstock mine, apart from Consolidated Virginia and California, has declared a single dividend in all the long interval between 1874 and 1890. Of the two bonanza mines the output of the former, between 1873 and 1880, in which latter year it ceased to be largely productive, was $64,974,816, of which $42,930,000 was disbursed in dividends. Of California, the yield from 1876 to 1880 —the extraction of ore on a large scale beginning in the former year—was $46,742,256, with $31,320,000 in dividends. Thus out of a total product of $111,-717,072 for the two mines, $74,250,000, or about two-thirds of the entire amount, was distributed among the stockholders, a larger proportion than has fallen to their share from any mine on the Comstock, if not on the Pacific coast.

sion woollen mills, S. F. sugar refinery, West coast furniture factory, Cornell watch factory, California theatre, Grand and Palace hotels, and in reclaiming Sherman island, with many minor works of benefit to the public.

A few years after the exhaustion of the great bonanza, the two mines were consolidated, and the number of shares reduced from 1,080,000 to 216,000, as before the subdivision in 1875. Meanwhile, from over $700 in January of that year the stock declined to twenty-five cents in 1885. And now came still another of those transitions which have marked the history of the Comstock lode. Early in 1886 deep mining was for the time abandoned, and the lower levels, some of them being then at a depth of 3,000 feet, were allowed to fill up with water, for the public would no longer pay assessments, nearly every stock on the list selling below a dollar a share. But a few months later, at the very time when every one had lost faith in the future of the great lode, another bonanza was unearthed, and again in the ground of Consolidated Virginia, whose stock rose to over $60 a share, with others in proportion, though followed soon afterward by the usual collapse. From this new ore body several millions had been extracted, and nearly $3,400,000 disbursed in dividends up to the spring of 1890, when the ore body showed signs of exhaustion, or was at least deteriorating in quality. In other mines, as Confidence, and Hale and Norcross, smaller bodies of pay ore were disclosed, and in nearly all was low-grade quartz, long known to exist, yielding from $10 to $20 a ton.

From 1860 to 1890 the total yield of the Comstock, most of its shares being held in California, may be estimated at some $350,000,000, from which has been paid in dividends a total of about $130,000,000, offset by assessments of nearly half that amount.[55]

[55] The legislature of 1877-8 referred a bill 'to encourage mining industry, and to suppress stock-gambling,' to a committee, which reported on these subjects at length. It proposed, among other things, to suppress stock-gambling by breaking up the practice, on the part of mining officials, of keeping secret information about the mines for stock-jobbing purposes, and by requiring dealers in stocks to pay a license upon all purchases and sales of stock, which, it was believed, would operate as a check upon fictitious purchases and sales, 'by which mainly the disastrous stock operations are carried out.' This report says: 'These corporations have become so powerful that they have disregarded their obligations, and seem to act upon

The exhaustion of the old ore bodies and the discovery of others have, of course, been attended with extreme changes in the price of stocks. It may be stated approximately that from a total value of more than $300,000,000 in January 1875, the market price of shares in the Comstock mines, over 6,000,000 in number, sank to $2,000,000 or less in the spring of 1885, rose in the autumn of the same year to $60,-000,000 or $70,000,000, and in April 1890 had declined to $6,000,000 or $7,000,000. There are still those who hold shares in mines which they believe to be in bonanza, but which neither pay dividends nor do anything to put money into the hands of stockholders. This class of traders are anxious for a lively market, no matter how produced, in order to sell above what their shares have cost them. We have only to glance over the columns of the daily journals, where whole pages are filled with notices of mining meetings, assessments, and sales of forfeited shares, to obtain some estimate of the amount of capital furnished by the community for the support of mining companies, few of which make any return.[56]

the theory that they have gained a right by prescription to do wrong. Almost every mining corporation has a *credit mobilier* for milling ores or furnishing supplies at prices fixed at little regard to the interests of stockholders. It is within the experience of almost every citizen of this state, that in the purchase of mining shares he takes a greater risk upon the honesty and efficiency of the management of the corporations than he does upon the product and profit of the mines. Indeed, it is notorious that most of them are manipulated more with a view to making money out of the public than out of the mines. Mines that were reasonably worth a few hundred thousand dollars have been sold at the stock-boards for millions. After the stock has been thus floated, assessments have been levied, month after month, and year after year, ostensibly to develop the mines. In this way the mining corporations formed under the laws of this state have collected within the last three years assessments as follows: 1875, $11,880,000; 1876, $11,608,000; 1877, $11,598,000 = $35,086,000,'—nearly a million a month, or more than all the taxes raised in the state during the same time for state, county, and city governments.

[56] In my *History of Nevada* will be found brief biographies of the bonanza quartet—J. C. Flood, W. S. O'Brien, J. G. Fair, and J. W. Mackay—also of W. Sharon, J. P. Jones, P. Deidesheimer, and others, whose career is more or less associated with the history of the Comstock lode. The following are a few of the more prominent men who are or have been connected with mining, mining companies, and mining stock-boards, though from want of space the names of many, such as W. M. Lent, R. Sherwood, and the late W. B. Bourne, have been omitted from this chapter:

The well-known mining magnate, John D. Fry, or, as his friends preferred to call him, Colonel Fry, in allusion to his early exploits, was born at Ghent, Ky, July 15, 1819, and thrown early upon his own resources. Recognizing his dash and firmness, an uncle, Gen. Fry, sheriff of Green co., Ill., appointed him deputy at the early age of 16. Four years later he was elected to succeed him, and then served as recorder, and was twice chosen for the legislature. In 1849 he arrived in Cal. in the company of Sharon, with whom he formed a lasting friendship, acting as his business partner. He held the position of special agent for the post-office dept of the Pacific coast from 1853 to 1860, when he resigned to devote himself to mining enterprises, to which he brought both theoretic and practical knowledge. In 1868 he was chosen president of the Crown Pt and Belcher mines, which under his supervision yielded their famous 'bonanzas.' In later years he turned his attention to Alaskan mines.

Among others who became wealthy by timely purchases of Crown Point, Belcher, the bonanza, and other mining shares, is E. J. Baldwin, the proprietor of the hotel which bears his name. A native of Ohio, he came to Cal. in 1853, and after a varied experience turned his attention to real estate and mining-stock operations, finding the latter more to his taste. Mr Baldwin is, however, a large real estate owner, his Santa Anita ranch in Los Angeles co., where is his country-seat, being one of the most beautiful in the state. That which men have termed his good luck is, in fact, the result of the rare judgment, foresight, and enterprise with which he is gifted.

To the members of the San Francisco stock-board and to the leading men in financial circles, the name of J. W. Coleman is familiar as that of one who, to use his own phrase, 'has prospered by attending strictly to his own business.' A Kentuckian by birth, he came to this coast in 1854, and after working for three years at the mines in Amador co., was appointed manager of the Alta California Telegraph co. In 1870 or 1871 he formed a partnership with James R. Keene, with whom he entered largely into mining-stock operations. In 1876 he was elected president of the 'old board,' and under his supervision was erected the building on Pine st, already referred to. In 1885 he was chosen president of the North Pacific Coast R. R., and in the same year president of the Union club.

At the outbreak of the Comstock excitement, one of the first to arrive on the ground was George Hearst, a practical miner from Mo., his native state. Coming to Cal. in 1850, he worked at the Placerville mines with indifferent success, but afterward became wealthy through timely purchases on the Comstock. After losing his fortune a few years later, mainly through the dishonesty of his associates, he gradually became a large owner in some of the richest mines in Cal., Utah, and Dakota, among others in the Ontario. On the death of Senator Miller he was chosen to fill the vacant seat, and afterward elected for the full term ending in 1893.

Among the most prominent mining men in northern Cal. is A. C. Busch, a Hanoverian by birth, who came to this state in 1855, and soon afterward purchased an interest in and developed the Gold Bluff quartz mine. In 1870–1 he opened the Rising Sun gravel mine, at Loganville, and in 1883, in conjunction with G. H. O. Sunderhaus, located and began to develop the Young America mine.

G. H. O. Sunderhaus, who is a native of Sierra co., Cal., and of German extraction, his parents being Prussians by birth, has been engaged in mining and milling since the days of his boyhood. From the Young America mine, which he helped to locate and develop, nearly $500,000 had been extracted up to the close of 1885, the ore averaging about $24 per ton.

CHAPTER XXIII.

PROGRESS OF SAN FRANCISCO.

1857–1889.

CITY AND COUNTY—FRASER RIVER EXCITEMENT—TRAFFIC AND IMPROVE-
MENTS—STREET RAILWAYS—EFFECT OF FLOODS, EARTHQUAKES, AND
OVERLAND RAILWAY—EVIL INFLUENCE OF POLITICIANS—STOCK AND
LABOR EXCITEMENTS—INFLATIONS AND DEPRESSIONS—FUTURE OF THE
METROPOLIS.

I HAVE space only for a brief review of the leading
events in San Francisco since bringing the city's
annals down to 1856 in the previous volume. As a
rule, the city more than keeps pace with the country
in material progress, but for some time prior to 1889
there was evidently an inclination to rest, and let the
country display its capabilities, which was done in a
remarkable degree.

As the chief seat of manufacturing industries, and
as the commercial and social capital, not alone of
California, but of the Pacific coast, the city pulsates
in sympathy with the fluctuations around, while exhibiting in particular the effects of changing trade
currents.   Thus, the growing production of food articles, by diminishing imports and traffic with the great
entrepôt, combined with the decline in placer mining
to bring about the crisis of 1854–5.   The wane of
flush times had given an incentive to the disorders
which called into existence the vigilance movement of
1856, and all these served to check the hitherto rapid
advance in population and prosperity.

In 1858 occurred the Fraser river mining excite-

ment,[1] which within four months carried away over
15,000 hardy men, the forerunners of thousands more
prepared to follow.   As it was, many interior towns
lost half their population, some faded utterly away,
and at San Francisco real estate declined fully one
half.[2]   Even the staunchest quailed under the predic-
tion that California would pale before the new El Dorado, where Victoria was rising as the new metropolis
of the coast.   In August began the return of the deluded host of gold-seekers,[3] and the city, which, on
the whole, had been a gainer by the traffic, rapidly
came forward under the reaction in favor of California,
encouraged also by the settlement of land titles within
the city.

The tide of prosperity received another impulse
from the Union war, which brought a large influx of
people from the troubled east, stayed the usual out-
flow, and decided many wavering spirits to make their
home here.   Further, by cutting off many sources for
supplies,[4] it gave the greatest encouragement to establishing and expanding manufacturing industries, which
mostly concentrated at San Francisco, as possessing
the cheapest and largest amount of available labor,
mechanical talent, machinery, coal, and other adjuncts.[5]

The flood of 1862 induced a large number of wealthy
people to settle in this city, and the perfected communication with Oakland, and with San José by rail-

---

[1] The fever raged during April–Aug.; 15,088 left S. F. in 112 vessels, according to *Cust. Ho. Repts*, while *Prices Current* places the number at over
23,000.

[2] In many parts it was offered 'for a song.' *Garniss' S. F.*, MS., 20.   In
the interim an abatement of 80 per cent was common.   Many merchants and
professionals prepared to transfer their business to Victoria.

[3] Who must have lost fully $9,000,000 in direct sacrifices of time and
money, not counting depreciation in estate.

[4] Partly by war prices, and the increased freight and risk for shipments
under the pursuit of cruisers; partly by higher tariff on foreign goods, for
revenue.

[5] Not the least being Chinese labor, without which certain manufactures
could never have been sustained.   This gave the great expansion to Chinatown.   The manufacturing interests of S. F. rose by 1880 to an assessed
value of more than $67,000,000.

way, proved fresh avenues for profit,[6] so that building
operations and improvements of all kinds were rapidly
advanced, notably the water-works,[7] the first street
railway,[8] and soon after a paid fire department, which
has acquired a reputation for efficiency.[9]

After the war came a slight reaction, to which contributed the earthquake of 1865,[10] the imposition of a
considerable debt through official neglect in water-lot
sales of 1853,[11] and the several efforts to despoil the
city of its land and water-fronts, upon the expiration
of the wharf leases.[12]   But the lull speedily ended,

[6] While improved overland communication lessened the isolation and
remoteness.

[7] For which charter and permits were granted in 1857- 8. *Cal. Statutes*, 1858,
254; *S. F. Water-works, Charter; Id., Rates; Cal. Jour. Sen.*, 1875–6, app. 61.
From the so-called Spring valley the sources were extended to Pilarcitos,
San Andreas, etc.   By 1876 the official map recognized 7 distributing reservoirs, the chief being Lake Honda at the almshouse, capacity 32,900,000 gallons; and the College hill, of 15,000,000; total 61,150,000 gallons.   The high
rates of the company led in 1872, etc., to several rival projects, notably to
bring water from Calaveras valley, which was offered by speculators for
$10,000,000, but nothing came of it. *S. F. Municip. Rept*, 1874–5. 613; *Alta
Cal.*, Feb. 1–6, 1872; *Bowman's Water Co.*

[8] The omnibuses to the mission, along the Mission and lower parallel
streets, *Williams' Stat.*, MS., 14, were overshadowed in July 1860 by a steam-
car along Market, which street had just been opened. *Alta Cal.*, Jan. 26,
July 6, 1860; *S. F. Bull.*, July 2, 1860.   The first horse railway was the
Omnibus line, founded in 1861 by P. Donohue. *Stat.*, MS.; *Cal. Jour. Sen.*,
1863–4, app. 34.   Other lines followed rapidly, one to Potrero, across the
bridge in 1867. *S. F. Times*, May 6, 1867.   The Clay street cable-road was
the first of its kind, in 1873. *S. F. Chron.*, Aug. 3, Nov. 1, 1873.   The Market
street cable-line, with its numerous branches to the park and to 28th st, is
now the most extensive.   Railroad to the ocean opened in 1883. *S. F. Post*,
Nov. 26, 1883; *S. F. Chron.*, Sept. 29, 1885.

[9] Serving to ensure confidence in the predominating wooden structures.
The volunteer dept was abolished in Dec. 1866, greatly to the relief of the
city, which had long chafed under the corrupt admixture of vagabonds and
political tools introduced therein of late. *S. F. Bull.*, Apr. 27, 1865; Dec. 3,
1866; *Alta Cal.*, Jan. 7, 1864; Jan. 2, 1884.   Telegraphic alarms were planned
in 1863. *S. F. Call*, Dec. 3, 1863.   Fire patrols are added.   The *S. F.
Municip. Rept* of 1884–5 enumerates 15 engines, 9 hose and 4 truck companies,
with 330 men, receiving $217,500 in pay.   Since then has been an increase.
S. F. Fire Dept Scraps, 14 et seq.; *Coast Review*, passim.

[10] Oct. 8th.   It merely cracked a few weak walls, yet the shock frightened
away many people, and depressed real estate.

[11] See chapter on S. F., preceding vol.

[12] They began to expire early in the sixties, though partly prolonged
against 10 per cent of gross receipts.   For disputes and revenue, see *S. F.
Municip. Repts*, 1859–60, 167–8, 1861–2, 259 et seq.   By 1866 the city had
control of the water front.   The subsequent management is noticed in *Cal.
Jour. Sen.*, 1869–70, app. 10, 38; 1877–8, app. 20, 74; *S. F. Chamber Com.
Rept*, 1870, 15–28, etc.; *Hayes' Cal. Notes*, iii., pt 140; *Moore's Vis.*, MS., 7–
8.   Prior to this the wharf companies had combined to plan a stone bulkhead,

under the large immigration,[13] the rapid unfolding of
San Joaquin valley as a wheat region, and the hopes
buoyed upon the progress of the transcontinental railway, so much so that the earthquake of 1868, the
most serious ever felt at San Francisco, left only a
momentary impression.[14]

The expectations based on the railway proved illu-
sive, however. The city had neglected to manifest
any substantial interest in such enterprises because of
her isolated peninsular position,[15] leaving the Central
Pacific, completed in May 1869, to make its terminus
at Sacramento, with the evident prospect of seeking a
bay port, either at Oakland, through the Western
Pacific, or at Vallejo, through the California Pacific.
The recognition of these facts led to a panic in San
Francisco real estate, which had been rising since
1858 to inflated prices.[16] Vallejo, on the other hand,
rose exultantly, boasting of its superior natural har-

requesting in aid a grant of the water front for 50 years. The legislature
assented, despite the popular outcry, but Gov. Downey fortunately vetoed
the bill. *Cal. Jour. Sen.* and *Ass.*, 1859–60; *S. F. Bulkhead Bill*, etc., a series
of pro and contra arguments, petitions, and reviews; *Parson's Bulkhead*, 1–
96; *S. F. Miscel.*, ii. 6–67, 1–60; *S. F. Bull.*, Feb. 21, Mar. 5–11, 1859; Apr.
18, 1860. One result was several wharf improvements, particularly by the
Pacific Mail S. S. co. In 1867 a stone wall for a part of the water front was
contracted for, and of late years the sea-walls have been constructed near
the mission cove and at North Beach. *S. F. Municip. Rept*, 1866–7, 506 et
seq.; *S. F. Seawall*, 1–36; *Robinson's Rept*, 7; *Cal. Jour. Sen.*, 1867–8, app. 14,
18; 1871–2, app. 12, etc.; *Crane's Rept*, 1–16. The harbor has been improved
by the removal of Blossom rock, in 1870, the Rincon rock, etc. *U. S. Gov. Doc.*,
51st cong., 2d sess.; *U. S. Sen. Misc. Doc.*, 146; *Id.*, 41, 43d cong., 1st sess.;
Id., *Rept Chief Eng.*, 1868, 383, etc.; *Alta Cal.*, Apr. 24, 1870; *Overland*, xv.,
401–7; *S. F. Chron.*, Oct. 11, 1885.

[13] The largest since flush times, 1868 showing a gain of 35,000, of which
S. F. had its share.

[14] A dozen weak buildings were rendered untenable, 5 lives were lost by
falling bricks, and some injuries were received through exaggerated fears.
The shock occurred Oct. 21. See *S. F. Bull.*, *Call*, etc.; *Great Earthquake*,
1–16, with synopsis of damages. The earliest recorded quake here was a
severe shock in 1839, as described by C. Brown, in *S. F. Call*, Dec. 21, 1877.
Shocks in 1851, 1854, and 1856. *S. F. Herald*, May 16. Dec. 27–8, 1851;
Oct. 22, 1854; Jan. 3, Feb. 16, 1856; *Bull.*, Feb. 15, Oct. 11, 1856; *Golden
Era*, Jan. 6, Sept. 1, 1855, May 11, 1856. Slight tremors have been frequent. A full list of all notable quakes is given in *Hayes' Nat. Phenom.*, iii.
66–83; *Id.*, *Emig. Notes*, 678–723.

[15] Yet in 1864 it was decided to subscribe for $1,000,000 R. R. stock; this
was compromised for a gift of $450,000 to the Central and $250,000 to the
Western Pacific, without any stock.

[16] Especially in the suburbs, much of which has not yet recovered. The
panic itself survived still in 1872.

bor,[17] at the outlet of the great valley rivers, of its fine level site, its fertile surroundings, and proximity to the rich interior. These advantages had attracted the attention even of foreign capitalists, who in 1868 opened the road between Sacramento and Vallejo, extended it to Marysville, bought the Napa and Petaluma lines as adjuncts, and also the boats of the California Steam Navigation company, establishing communication with San Francisco of so fast and superior a character as to absorb and retain nearly all its Sacramento traffic. Vessels began to come here in large numbers, and the population increased so rapidly that Vallejo in 1871 had reached the third position in the state, with the prospect of further advances under proclaimed plans for extending railway traffic in all directions.[18] Now, the Central Pacific railway company, taking alarm, purchased a controlling interest in the California Pacific, reduced it to subordinate appendage, gave the preference to the Western Pacific, which in 1869 had been merged in the Central and completed to Oakland, and left Vallejo to stagnation.[19]

The suppression of this rival served only to embolden the other, Oakland. A long pier facilitated connection across the bay, but the railway company proposed to extend it to Yerba Buena island, making this their terminus.[20] The metropolis succeeded in defeating the scheme, which undoubtedly would have been of value to the state and to trade, saving to both

[17] Where ships of any size could unload at the very shore almost.
[18] Even to Salt Lake, to rival the Central Pacific.
[19] When the flood washed away its connection with Marysville this was abandoned in favor of the Central Pac main line.
[20] Congress appeared favorable, and S. F. was roused to strenuous efforts against the bill, supported fortunately by military and coast survey engineers, who exaggeratingly declared the island necessary for military purposes, and a bridge connection a dangerous obstruction to bay currents and tidal area, and consequently, in time, to the bay entrance itself. The Atlantic and Pac co. sought to avail itself of the prevailing fear to obtain a $10,000,000 subsidy from S. F., promising to open a main line to it; but the danger passed. Another counter movement was suggested in a railway bridge across the bay, either from Hunter's Po., to cost $15,000,000, or preferably from Ravenswood, to cost $3,000,000,

much inconvenience and cost, although at the expense of the city at the Gates.

Although Oakland gained one point, in the improvement of her creek harbor,[21] and also in her extraordinary growth as a residence suburb for San Francisco, the latter became practically the terminus, with the aid of superior ferry traffic, which embraced the transport of freight-cars by special boats. The Central Pacific, moreover, planted its offices here. All this was certainly no equivalent for the absorption of residents by neighboring towns, and of trade by the railway, which henceforth carried most of the passengers and finer goods that used to come and leave by steamer, and gave a large part of their distribution to interior points. Several bay harbors joined besides with Vallejo in securing the larger share of the wheat shipments. Nevertheless, the city received its quota of the increasing unfoldment of resources and of an immigration, which, within three years, added 50 per cent to the cultivated acreage of the state.[22] The opening in 1876 of the railway to Los Angeles brought increased tribute to the metropolis, and assisted to check the rival aspirations of San Diego, the only port to the south.

A considerable current of wealth had been flowing since the early sixties from the silver mines of Nevada, the returns of which, being mostly owned by San Franciscans, were applied here to the erection of fine buildings and to the support of trade and art.[23]

[21] Appropriations began in 1874, and amounted by 1881 to over $300,000. So far little use has been made of the harbor, but hope is still entertained, stimulated by the rapid growth in population of all the district adjoining the harbor. See the chapter on Birth of Towns.

[22] In 1875 there was a net gain of 64,000 out of 107,000 arrivals in California, the largest since 1852, when the gain was 44,000. In 1865 and 1866 it had fallen to 4,000, and in 1871 to 10,000. By 1877 it again abated to 18,000.

[23] The comparative fiasco in the White Pine deposits found compensation in Crown Pt and Belcher bonanza, which advanced the market price of the silver stock in 1872 from $17,000,000 to $81,000,000 within 5 months. Yet this was eclipsed by the Consolidated Virginia bonanza, including the California, which rose from little over $100,000 in 1871 to $150,000,000 in 1874. The Comstock paid during the 20 years ending 1880 more than $120,000,000

On the other hand, they fostered a gambling mania which led to the impoverishment of a large proportion of the inhabitants, while keeping them on the verge of hopeful excitement. This contributed greatly to impart a glowing inaugural to the centennial year of the Union, which was also that of San Francisco, cradled in the mission.[24]

Building operations and other signs of prosperity received a rude check from the drought of 1877,[25] associated with a diminished number of visitors, a collapse in the silver mines, and an attendant financial crisis.[26] This tended to inflame the spark transmitted by the contemporaneous labor riots in eastern states, and to rouse the large class of sufferers from the depression to a threatening attitude. Their animosity turned against the competing Chinese, and burst forth on July 23, 1877, into lawless proceedings, which resulted in the burning of one Mongolian laundry and the sacking of several others, amid the threats of agitators to drive out all such cheap workers. Composed as

in dividends, of which over $70,000,000 from Cons. Virginia and Cal., and $25,000,000 from Crown Pt and Belcher. The gross yield was far greater, reaching $90,000,000 for the latter in 1874. But large amounts were levied in assessments, chiefly for comparatively worthless mines, although much of it was retained in S. F. for rents, salaries, and machinery to swell the tribute derived from interior stock gamblers.

[24] The centennial celebration of which was celebrated on Oct. 8th with orations and procession. *S. F. Centennial.* Several conspicuous improvements marked this period, as the Palace hotel, one of the largest structures of this kind in the world, and the foremost of the 27,000 buildings then existing in S. F., of which 4,390 of brick; 1,600 houses were erected in 1876. Montgomery avenue was opened to connect North Beach with the central parts, a measure which should have entered into the original plan of the city, to modify materially her subsequent expansion. In 1877 Dupont st was widened to relieve Kearny st, and open several cross streets to trade. The new city hall was also partly occupied. Details on improvements in *S. F. Municip. Repts,* 1872–3, 488, 1876–7, 1025 et seq; *Palace Hotel,* 1–16. The new mint had recently added its embellishment. Real estate sales reached in 1875 the high figure of $36,000,000 against $27,000,000 and $30,000,000 for 1868–9, the former highest. By 1877 they fell to $19,000,000. Concerning some of the homestead associations which promoted expansion, see *Cal Jour. Sen.,* 1875–6, app. 28.

[25] Which affected most severely the southern counties, with their inflated land valuation.

[26] Affecting several savings banks. Confidence had been shaken in 1875 by the suspension of the bank of Cal., followed by the partial destruction by fire of Virginia city, which caused a loss of $5,000,000, and lowered stocks by $35,000,000. Nearly all fell upon S. F.

the city was of very combustible structures, with some 300 Chinese laundries interspersed, the alarm became general, so much so that the vigilance committee of 1856 was revived, with 6,000 members, whose appearance and patrolling sufficed to restrain the turbulent faction. Little additional damage was done, but the indirect injury to both state and city amounted to huge proportions, in keeping back immigration, reducing the value of real estate, checking improvements, and driving away capital. The depression lasted for several years. In 1881, however, came a sudden trade revival, which contributed to impart a healthy tone to the returning prosperity.

The depression of 1877–80 had roused the workingmen of San Francisco to form a party of their own, aiming at the restriction of competing Chinese and of the power of capital, to which they ascribed most of the existing poverty and corruption, the latter marked by evasion of fair tax rates, venal official representation, and wasteful concession of land, money, and privileges to corporations. Their intention was commendable in the main, but it lacked the high principles and influential leadership of the previous reform movement of 1856, which had transformed the city to a model place for order and economic administration. The people's party then brought forward was of so admirable a character that it maintained itself for nearly two decades, although its nominations were devoid of popular participation.[27]

The city took the lead also in proclaiming the loyalty of the state during the Union war, by suddenly replacing the suspicious politicians by a citizens' majority, and quenching the smouldering scheme of a Pacific republic. She also surprised all other parts of the Union in her contributions to the sanitary fund.[28]

[27] The turbulent were kept in check, and exiled criminals at a distance.
[28] In the latter half of 1862 she sent $300,000 out of the $480,000 from the coast. In 1864 she started a monthly subscription of $25,000. She gave

In 1865 the news came of Lincoln's assassination, which provoked such an ebullition among a mob that several newspaper offices were sacked.[29] Nevertheless, the politicians obtained the upper hand in state and city in 1867,[30] and the wedge had been gradually introduced for a certain proportion of corrupt admixtures. The rings and jobbery thus fostered are illustrated by the new city hall structure, and the gradual increase in the tax rate,[31] besides small additions to the bonded debt, which has, however, been reduced under the sinking-fund process to about a million and a half.[32] Reform was, therefore,

about half of the $1,200,000 sent by Cal. toward the total $4,800,000 collected in the U. S.

[29] For this, the first actual mob outrage on the city, the municipality had to pay. The liberality of her people was even more strongly exhibited during the Franco-German war, when the French contributed about $300,000, and the Germans $138,000, to their respective sufferers at home.

[30] Coon, *Annals*, MS., 26-7, enters into the causes for the change. *S. F. Rept Com. Tax-payers' Union.*

[31] The rise from $1.60 in 1856-7 to 2.56\frac{9}{10}$ in 1859-60 was mainly under pressure from the people who objected to the curtailment of schools, gas, and other essentials. Under the rise of estate valuation from $42,000,000 in 1861-2 to $78,000,000 in 1863-4, the rate was reduced to $1.20, though rising again to $2.10½ in 1871-2. Now the forced-sale valuation was replaced by a cash valuation, under which the assessment advanced from $105,000,000 to $288,600,000 in 1872-3, with a rate consequently lowered to $1. The assessment fell to $217,500,000 by 1879-80, while the tax rate was lifted to $1.69 in 1878-9. In 1880-1 the rate was maintained at $1.57, although assessments advanced under increase on personal property to $444,000,000, so extraordinary an amount as to leave half the tax delinquent. Under a new system with pledges, the rate was maintained between $1.12 and $1.20, and after 1885 at $1, although the latter amount is hardly sufficient. The valuation stood in 1885-6 at $227,600,000, of which $56,200,000 on personal property. The state tax rose to $1.25 in 1864-5, declining with some variation to 45 cents in 1884-5. The total tax levy mounted from $1,200,000 in 1861-2 to $4,300,000 in 1872-3, after which it fluctuated, with one exception, between 4½ and 5½ millions till 1880. In 1884-5 it fell to $3,600,000, yet demands were audited for $4,580,000. Since 1856 the property-owners concerned pay two thirds of the street work. In 1884-5 the street dept obtained from the city $261,900. The expense of the school dept, which fell below $93,000 in 1857, rose to $179,000 in 1863, and then more rapidly to $508,000 in 1867; after this it fluctuated to $989,000 in 1878, and to $317,000 in 1875. The city hall, still unfinished for lack of appropriations, was erected under an act of 1870. The corner-stone was laid 1872. *Alta Cal.*, Feb. 23, 1872; *S. F. Courier*, Dec. 30, 1871; *S. F. City Hall*, 1-13; progress described in *S. F. Municip. Repts*, 1869 et seq., and *Cal. Jour. Sen.*, 1871-2, app. 52-3; 1873-4, app. 27-8.

[32] The amount stood in Jan. 1885 at $2,455,000, interest 6 and 7 per cent; but the sinking fund on hand reached $799,000, with an annual addition of about $193,000. Of the total, the park stood debited for $475,000, the Central and Western Pac R. R. for $307,000, the judgment of 1867 for $246,000, city hall $445,500, old claims of 1858 only $136,500, the rest for schools, hospitals, and house of correction.

desirable, although not exactly with the socialistic tints imparted by the workingmen's party to the new state constitution, and to some of their selections for offices.[33]

One result was the reduction of the city tax to one dollar, and efforts were made to obtain a new charter[34] under which to better enforce an economic as well as just administration.

The cloud overhanging the title of city lands south of Pine street had tended in early days to turn population toward North Beach, and the need for wharves to reach the shipping led the business commnnity to fill up the shallow cove,[35] and build out to the deep water front, while the steep hill ranges of Clay street and Russian hills restrained settlement in that direction. But with the adjustment in 1860 of Mexican claims[36] southward arose so marked a confidence in this section that a perfect rush of settlers ensued, attended by the rapid construction of both residences and factories, stimulated by the Union war, and aided by the opening of several railway lines, and the swift operations of the steam-paddy, which, in the course of 14 years, assisted to convert some 450 acres of mission cove tide and marsh land into solid land.[37]

[33] Instance Mayor Kalloch and Coroner O'Donnell. Concerning the Kalloch–De Young disclosures and homicide, see *S. F. Post*, Aug. 25, 1879; *S. F. Bull.*, Apr. 24, 1880; *Sac. Rec.*, Mch 25, 1881, and other dates.

[34] Several efforts have been made to revise or create a new charter, notably in 1874, 1883, and lastly in 1887. *S. F. Charter Scraps*, 1–40, and journals.

[35] To the extent of more than 320 acres, between Folsom and Broadway. Round Telegraph hill and North Beach the filling has of late assumed large proportions. Concerning the sale of tide land and water lots, see *Cal. Jour. Sen.*, 1865–6, app. 27–9; 1867–8, app. 29; 1869–70, 51–3, app. 56, etc. *Statutes*, 1858, 139, 223; *Id.*, *Ass.*, 1865–6, 850–3; *U. S. Gov. Doc.*, 39 Cong., 1 sess.; *Sen. Doc.*, 24. The two latter relate to state and govt land. Petty squatter riots continued to stir certain quarters, as instanced in *S. F. Call*, Oct. 12, 1867.

[36] As Santillan's and Sherreback's, south of California st, practically overthrown in 1860; P. Smith's, west of Larkin st, and Limantour's, rejected two years before, Dr Haro's Potrero claim being defeated in 1867. See the chapter on land titles.

[37] The fillage continues. The expansion of factories gave expansion to the Chinese quarter, which continuously radiated from the original settlement in Sacramento st, west of Kearny, until it, by 1885, covered some ten blocks, closely packed with some 25,000 souls, nearly all males, with a

In the early seventies, titles west of Larkin became assured,[38] and now this quarter became the choice for residences, assisted by cable-car lines, which transformed the hills into the most desirable locations. The widening of Kearny street in 1866 served to make this the leading avenue for retail shops and promenading, both of which are now shifting into Market street, the evident main channel of the city,[39] leaving Montgomery street to mark the limits for financial and mercantile business.[40] Latterly the construction of a fine sea-wall round Telegraph hill is bringing a business revival to the long stagnant North Beach.[41]

San Francisco has clearly a great future before her, possessing as she does the only good harbor north of San Diego for a coast line of more than thirteen degrees of latitude, at the outlet of the richest valleys on the slope, and as the center of a railway system ex-

sprinkling of loose females. Their expansion hastened the flight of fashion from the Stockton st region to South Park, whence the factories forced it up Rincon hill, which again was ruined by the Second st cut. The long bridge over Mission cove was finished in 1865, and in 1867 it was extended across Islais cove, permitting a street railway to connect with Hunter's Pt dry dock. Butchertown was soon after forced by settlements to remove from Brannan st to the Potrero. A steam railway had opened in 1860 along Market st to the Mission, and the Omnibus R. R. assisted it to build up this quarter.

[38] The city claim here to some 4,000 acres was confirmed in 1866, and by ordinance in 1870, although the actual issue of titles was protracted, and then mostly conferred with prodigal looseness upon a number of large land-grabbers, thus losing millions for the city, which retained little more than the park tract. Fashion assisted to give prominence to the west by clustering round Van Ness avenue, and latterly on California st, or Nob hill. So rapid was the increase of settlement that assessments on property west of Larkin and Ninth sts, and south of Mission creek, rose from $1,200,000 in 1860 to over $50,000,000 by 1876. The southeast became less active, so much so that the prolongation of Montgomery st in New Montgomery proved a failure, and likewise the cutting of Rincon hill to open Second st; but the southwest has been steadily gaining.

[39] By width and length, and as the converging line for all tributary treets from the south and north, and from the east and west in its Valencia t prolongation. The theatres and other attractions are mostly south of 'ine st.

[40] After the completion of the Merchants' Exchange and the bank of Cal. building in 1867, California st became the recognized money center, with lots worth $3,000 a front foot; stock brokers drifted gradually into Pine st. and jobbers and importers are pressing from Front st into Market round Sansome st.

[41] Assisted by the opening in 1875 of Montgomery avenue.

tending, with numerous ramifications, to the Atlantic. This . confirms her as the entrepôt and distributing point, not alone for the state and for several tributary territories, but for an increasing trade with the Orient and Australasia, with Spanish and northwest America. She is also the chief seat of fast-unfolding manufacturing industries, and stands secured by millions of invested capital, and as the great social centre for the entire Pacific slope, with its train of institutions philanthropic and literary, for sciences and fine arts.[42] A favoring cause exists in the bracing climate, which permits work and exercise to an exceptional degree. While inviting to the open air, to parks [43] and promenades, it also encourages the formation of pleasant homes, marked by a varied architecture, yet with a predominance of bay windows.[44]

Although marred by improper planning, and a neglect of public impovements, the aspect of the city itself is striking,[45] rising on one side from out the

[42] To be spoken of later. There are more millionaires in S. F. than in any other city in proportion to the population, to support such institutions. During the early sixties more than 1,000 houses rose annually; after this the number decreased to 600 in 1872. In 1874–6 there was a sudden increase to 1,300 and 1,600, then a slight relapse, and lately a great increase again. In 1885 there were over 5,000 gas-lamps, and electric lights were multiplying. For companies and rates, see S. F. Municip. Reports, 1884–5, 168–75. The police force had been gradually increased to 172 by 1877, then suddenly to 329 in 1878–9, with subsequent additions to 400 and beyond. The U. S. Census places the population at 56,800 in 1860, 149,500 in 1870, and 234,000 in 1880, since when the growth has been large. The Chinese figure for 22,000 in 1880, but have since received additions, under the anti-Chinese feeling in the interior. See, also, chapters on society, trade, manufactures, education, and arts.

[43] The extensive Golden Gate park, reaching to the ocean, is supplemented by the govt presidio grounds along the bay inlet, by public squares, hardly sufficient in number, and by garden resorts, as Woodward's, the predecessors of which were Hayes' park, the Willows, and Russ' gardens, the earliest. The beautiful cemeteries near the park attract many saunterers. The Mechanics' Institute holds an annual fair since 1857. S. F. Herald, Sept. 11, 1857, et seq.; Sac. Union, May 14, 1857; Cal. St. Fair Scraps, 75–81. Then there are bench shows, races, art exhibitions, and museums. The city is indebted for statuary, baths, and other institutions to the phianthropy of James Lick, to whom I refer elsewhere more fully.

[44] Due greatly to the prevailing winds and sudden changes in temperature, which render open balconies less enjoyable. The Chicago frame building is the favorite.

[45] As explained in the former chapter on S. F. The paucity of garden squares is to be regretted, and the neglect to plant trees.

waters of the bay, and overlooking on the other the
ocean.[46]

[46] For a study of the condition of S. F. at different periods since 1856 the
following authorities may be consulted: *Williams' Stat.*, MS., 14, etc.;
Woodward's Stat., MS., 47 et seq.; *Hardy's Through Cities*, 141–2; *Player-
Froud's Cal.*, 22–34; *Seward's Trav.*, 28–70; *Avery's Cal. Pict.*, 239–60; *Nordhoff's Cal.*, 61–67; *Marshall's Amer.*, 260–85; *Lloyd's Lights of S. F.*, wholly
descriptive of the city, while *Hittell's S. F.* is a history of it, the only exhaustive one since *The Annals of S. F.* of 1855; *Hoitt's Guide*, 41–79; *Scribner's Mag.*, July 1875; *Putnam's Mag.*, i. (U.S.) 558–60; *Möllhausen's Journey*,
ii., 353; *Russling's Amer.*, 276; *Prieto Viage*, i. 30–503; *Cronise's Cal.*, 644;
Leslie's Cal., 115–200; *Taylor's Gates*, 71–128, 244; *Jackson's Bits of Travel*,
77–86; *Turrill's Notes*, 38–66; *Hughes' Padres.* 6–7; *Curtis' Dottings*, 29–52;
Cal. Fares, 3–10; *Solano's Future*; *S. F. Municipal Reports*, 1859 et seq., and
its attendant sub-reports from different depts; *S. F. Orders.*

Among the real estate operators who have attained prominence on the
Pacific slope stands the name of Wendell Easton stands as one of the foremost.
Born in Mass in 1848, he came to S. F. in 1854, where he attended school.
At sixteen he obtained work in a real estate office, afterward accepting a
position as secretary of the Crown Point Mining co.; finally he opened a
small real estate office, advertising it extensively, afterward taking Eldridge
as a partner, and adding auctioneering to the business. In 1882 a stock co.
was formed to do business in all parts of the state, Easton being its president; 52 agencies were formed, and $385,000 worth of property sold the first
month.

Among others who have grown rich by real estate investments, is Orville
D. Baldwin, a native of Rensselaerville, N. Y., who landed in San Francisco
in 1860, with fifty cents in his pocket. After a long and bitter struggle with
poverty he was admitted into partnership in a fruit business, and this he
built up until his profits soon amounted to nearly $1,000 a month. After
accumulating some $10,000 he opened a restaurant, first on Montgomery and
then on Geary street, and from the latter quickly acquired a handsome fortune, which between 1886 and 1889 he doubled in the real estate business.
Associated with some of our most enterprising men in building up the Potrero
and in other enterprises, he is himself acknowledged as one of the most enterprising and liberal men in the metropolis.

Adolph Gustav Russ, the proprietor of the hotel in San Francisco which
bears his name, was born at Hildburghausen, Saxony, Jan. 19, 1826. He
came with his family to this state in 1846, as a member of the 7th N. Y. volunteers, organized for service in Cal. On the day after their arrival, Adolph
and his father each secured at the alcalde's office, S. F., the title to a 50-vara
lot, and on one of them built a small cabin with lumber taken from the soldiers' berths. On this site now stands the Russ house.

CHAPTER XXIV.

POPULATION AND SOCIETY.

1849-1889.

THE conglomerate humanity which wended its way
to Coloma, the Mecca of progressive adventures and
unsordid money-lovers, was much akin to the gold in
its casing sometimes of common clay and sometimes
of hard and scintillating quartz. This pilgrimage was
the romance of utilitarianism, and presented striking
instances of human efforts under strong impulses, both
bad and good, in its disorder and extravagance no less
than in its grand and enduring achievements. The
levelling of mountains and the turning of rivers from
their course, were but two features of the process
which opened a new era in mining. The spanning of
the continent with great railways was a means toward
transforming a wilderness into cultivated fields and
gardens. Never before was republicanism so lifted
by self-reliant performance to guide the rapid and
substantial advancement of a community, a shining
example to the world. The most striking peculiarities of this society have been delineated elsewhere in
this series, and we have now only to glance at their
later modifications.

The gold fever abroad continued long after the
eventful year of 1849, and the influx during 1850

proved larger than before.[1]   After a relapse in 1851
it reached the climax in 1852, assisted by the sudden
expansion of the Chinese immigration to 20,000 out
of the total arrivals by sea of 67,000.   The declining
attractions of the gold fields now became marked, although partly offset by the prevailing high wages and
the unfolding agricultural resources.   The crisis of
1854–5, the popular uprising of 1856, and the Fraser
river excitement of 1858, had all a depressing effect;
but the Union war of 1861–5 brought an increased
immigration, particularly from the western border
states, while checking the usual large reflux.   After
1865 both of these currents were reversed awhile, until the construction of the overland railway, which
greatly raised the prospects of California in eastern
estimation, partly by reducing distance, and by offering an easier means of access.   Henceforth, after
April 1869, a fairly correct estimate can be made of
the migration, which by 1875 attained the so far unequalled number of 107,000 arrivals, against 43,000

[1] The climax was reached in 1852, with an arrival of 67,000 by sea, against
36,000 for 1850, and 27,000 for 1851.   The overland current can be only
vaguely estimated, owing to the number of routes followed, from Oregon and
Mexico, and by the central and southern highways from the U. S., which
again branched into several roads to cross the Sierra Nevada.   At Laramie
alone a certain record was kept.   See *Soc. Transc.*, Sept. 30, Oct. 14, 1850;
S. F. Picayune, Sept. 6, Oct. 10, 1850; *S. F. Herald*, July 27, 1850; *N. Y.
Herald*, Apr. 15, 1850; *Pac News*, Aug. 21, Sept. 7, Oct. 29, Nov. 22, 1850.
Probably not over 40,000 came by the central route in 1850, leaving 15,000
to enter through Arizona and from Mexico, the former bringing the most
animals.   The Mexican influx declined under the maltreatment in Cal.
The marked general decline in 1851 was due to a lack of vessels, under their
discouraging desertion at S. F., to reports of dread hardships during the trip
and at the mines, and to conflicting accounts of the gold-field, sustained by
the natural reaction upon the excitement, and by disastrous commercial
speculations, duly magnified by an interested foreign press.   In 1852 came
the rebound, and then the second reaction, which reduced the arrivals to
more even proportions.   Between 1853–67 the number coming by sea ranged
between 23,000 and 41,000, except in 1854, when it stands at 48,000.   In
1852 and 1854 the Chinese form a large proportion of the figures 20,000 and
16,000, respectively, after which they range between 2,000 and 8,000, till
1868, when they rise with white totals. *Cal. Popul. Scraps; Alta Cal.*, Dec.
9, 1851; Aug. 17, 1852; Nov. 2, 26, 1853; Dec. 10, 19, 1854; Oct. 4, 1856, et
seq.; *Jour. Com.*, quarterly and annual reports; *Chinese Immig.*, 171; *U. S.
Com. Rel., Flagg's*, i. 532; *U. S. Gov. Doc.*, cong. 31, sess. 2, H. Ex. Doc. 16,
iv. 43–6; *Cal. Gov. Message*, 1855; *S. F. Herald*, Oct. 26–9, 1852, Dec. 4,
1854, June 7, 1858, etc.; *S. F. Bull.*, Oct. 6–8, 29, 1856; *Hunt's Mag.*, xxxii.
449; *Ebey's Jour.*, MS., iii. 58; *Hayes' Notes, S. Diego*, i. 35, etc.

departures.[2]   The disorders of 1877 proved detrimental, but with the opening of the present decade the expanding resources of the state, notably in horticulture, began to swell the influx once more, assisted by increasing railway competition, by immigration societies, and by a benign climate, which draws not only tourists and invalids but a superior class of settlers.[3]

The railways naturally absorbed nearly all the passenger traffic with the eastern states and Europe, leaving only a small percentage to the Panamá steamship line, which prior to 1869 received the most of it, sharing the profits for a time with the Nicaragua line.[4]

[2] The hopes raised by the railway had in 1868 brought the arrivals by sea to 60,000, and, and after a fluctuation between 38,000 and 52,000, to 70,000 in 1873, and to 85,000 in 1874. This rise was greatly due to business depression in the east. The Chinese proportion had ranged between 10,000 and 18,000 arrivals since 1867, and departures between 3,000 and 8,000. The arrivals by rail during 1870–6 stood at 32,000, 30,000, 34,000, 44,000, 56,000, 75,000 and 61,000, and the departures at 23,000, 22,000, 22,000 33,-000, 25,000, 30,000, and 38,000, which leaves little more than one-eighth to come by sea, excluding the Chinese route. In 1884 the Central Pacific railway alone brought over 50,000, and since then the unfolding resources of the state have drawn larger numbers. *U. S. Gov. Doc.*, cong. 45, sess. 2, H. Ex. Doc. 70, p. 745–61; cong. 46, sess. 3, xvi. 701–5: *Siskiyou Affairs*, MS., 16; *U. S. Bureau Statistics*, 1879–80, 187, etc.; *Hopkins' Sense*, 1–64; *S. F. Chron.*, New Year numbers; *Cal. Popul. Scraps.*

[3] The stagnation following the reaction of 1854 created serious alarm among persons interested in the state, and in 1855 a society was formed to promote immigration, assisted by an effusive local press. A subscription opened with $49,000. *Golden Era*, Aug. 12, 1855; *Sac. Union*, Sept. 11, 1855. Since then similar associations were started by foreigners, by counties, by land-holders, by railway companies, and also under state auspices. *Cal. Jour. Sen.*, 1871–2, app. 25–6; *Bureau of Inform. and Coloniz.*; *Alta. Cal.*, Apr. 19, 1857, Oct. 27, 1858, Sept. 1, 1878, Nov. 27, 1883; *Courrier, S. F.*, Mch. 31, 1871; *Hopkins' Sense*, p. i–xii.; *S. F. Chron.*, Nov. 22, 1881; *Immig. Assoc., Art.*; *Hayes' Notes*, MS., iii. 118; *S. F. Post*, May 18, 1883.

[4] The demand of California led to the building of palatial steamers, especially on the smooth waters of the Pacific. The 2,390 miles between N. Y. and Aspinwall required 10½ days. The isthmus railway reduced the transit to one day. The 3,770 miles from Panamá to S. F., calling at Acapulco, and occasionally other places, took 11½ days, at 11¾ miles per hour, against 9½ on the Atlantic. The Nicaragua route was fully 700 miles shorter, but the less commodious transit consumed from 3 to 7 days. The Tehuantepec route might have greatly reduced the time. *Crane's Report* in *U. S. Gov. Doc.*, cong. 34, sess. 3, *Sen. Doc.*, 51; *Capron's Cal.*, 284–345; *Johnson's Far West*, 9–29; *Coleman's Vig.*, MS., 175-83; *Borthwick's Cal.*, 8–32, concerning expenses, scenery, and life during the voyage. Complaints against the Nic. line, in *Alta Cal.*, July 15, Aug. 8–11, 1852, July 30, Dec. 27, 1856. The latter offered the attraction of finer scenery, but the delay and climatic danger were stronger offsets. Its beginning and end are described elsewhere, under trade and voyages.

The establishment of steamer competition had had a similar effect in diminishing the overland current. Yet poorer people, hardy western men and intending settlers, hampered with families, live stock, and bulky commodities, continued to maintain a respectable migration, braving hardships and dangers, treacherous savages and arid wildernesses, from which they escaped at times only with the aid of relief expeditions.[5]

Such was the influx which increased the population of the state from barely 100,000 at the close of 1849 to 255,000 in the middle of 1852,[6] to 380,000 by 1860, to 560,200 by 1870, and to 864,700 by 1880.[7] The two remarkable features of early days, youthfulness

[5] To assist them in crossing the Sierra and desert at its eastern base. *Cal. Jour. Sen.*, 1852, 761, 1853, app. 8; *Ass.*, 1853, 703, 1861, app. 8, 19; *Cal. Relief Exp.*, 1852, 1–5; *S. F. Herald*, July 27–9, 1850, Aug. 21, 1851; *Cal. Cour*, Aug. 26, 1850; *Alta Cal.*, Oct. 4, 1852, June 30, 1853; *Hollister's Stat.*, MS., 1; *Carvalho's Insid.*, 21–250; *Hickman's Destr. Angels*, 70–80; *Barstow's Stat.*, MS., 12–13; *Delano's Life*, 234–42. The state aided. Waldo was a prominent relief leader. Concerning quick trips and return journey, on *Soc. Transcr.*, June 1, 1851; *Alta Cal.*, Aug. 23, 1854. *Heap's Central Route*, 1–136. Carson valley remained the chief thoroughfare. Reports on the best routes in *Cal. Jour. Sen.*, 1855, app. 22; *Ross' Wisc. to Cal.*, MS., 86,132; and my chapter on railways. After 1855 the current declined to less than half of that coming by sea. In the sixties it spread into intermediate territories, especially Colorado and Nevada, so that less penetrated to Cal. Mormons were accused of waylaying emigrants. See *Hist. Utah*, this series.

[6] The federal census of 1850 has 92,597 for all but three leading counties. The fair estimate for these raises the figure to 112,000, yet a semi-official figure assumes 117,300, excluding Indians. A legislative committee claimed 300,000, and congress allowed 165,000. *U. S. Gov. Doc.*, cong. 32, sess. 1, *Sen. Rep't* 113. Census obstacles are noted in *Soc. Transcr.*, Sept. 30, Nov. 14, 1850. The state census of 1852 raised the total to 264,400, which properly added makes only 255,122; including an estimate for El Dorado of 40,000, based on the votes, which by due comparison with adjoining counties falls to not over 28,000. The difference may, however, be added to the low figure for wild Indians. The total arrivals between the middle of 1850 and 1852 may be put at not over 230,000, and the departures at fully one-half. Indeed, during the decade nearly two-thirds of the number recorded by sea departed, and no doubt one-third of the number by land, many going to adjoining territories. The inducements to stay increased only with the unfolding of industries. Browne, *Min. Res.*, 15–16, justly assumes the increase for the first six years at 50,000 per annum. *King's Rep't*, 15; *Crosby's Events*, MS., 52–3. See also the chapter on Indians. The great decrease among these may balance the increase in births.

[7] Of this number S. F. stands credited with 234,000, Alameda follows with 62,000, Sta Clara 35,000, Sacramento 34,400, Los Angeles 33,400, Sonoma, San Joaquin and Nevada range from 25,000 to 20,000, 16 other counties exceed 10,000, and the rest of the 52 counties range from 3,340, for Lassen, upward, Alpine alone standing at the low figure of 539. During 1861–70 the excess of arrivals by sea over departures was 157,000. The departures assisted largely to form the 36,000 population of Nevada, and partly of Arizona, British Columbia, Oregon, etc.

and paucity of women, which stamped it as a community of young men, have gradually disappeared under changing conditions, as mining, with its roaming life, gave way to agriculture and other industries, with settlements and family ties. According to the census of 1850 more than half the white males ranged between 20 and 30 years of age,[8] and still in 1860 two-thirds were between 20 and 50, but by 1880 this class had fallen below one-half of the total population, while children, under 20, formed considerably more than one-third. The number of females increased from less than eight per cent of the population in 1850,[9] to one-third by 1880. The disproportion in sex as well as age will require considerable time for adjustment under the continued large immigration of young men, notwithstanding the fecundity of certain portions among the inhabitants.

Citizens of the United States quickly established

[8] Of the total male population, 85,600, including 872 colored, 44,770 were between 20 and 30 years, 21,460 between 30 and 40, 7,500 between 40 and 50, 7,800 below 20, leaving little over 2,000 for the other ages. By 1860 the total 273,000 of males, showed 39,900 between 20 and 30, 13,200 between 30 and 40, 28,900 between 40 and 50, leaving only one-third for the other ages, chiefly between 1 and 15. By 1880 the total 864,700 of both sexes revealed a more normal proportion—344,700 under 20, 164,500 between 20 and 30, 143,400 between 30 and 40, 111,200 between 40 and 50, 65,400 between 50 and 60, 26,600 between 60 and 70, and 8,700 above this age, including 67 centenarians. The excess of persons in the prime of life was maintained as yet by the constant immigration.

[9] Of which barely two per cent in the mining counties. In 1852 it had reached a little over ten per cent, or nearly 23,000 in a total of somewhat over 200,000 whites. Among Indians the sexes were more equally enumerated. The foreign females numbered 4,360. In remote counties, as Sierra and Trinity, the percentage fell to less than two. By 1860 the females numbered 106,700, against 273,300 males, 96,400 being whites, 7,200 Indian against 10,600 Indian males, and 1,800 Chinese out of a total 34,900 of Mongols. By 1880 the female proportion had risen to 346,500 against 518,200 males, the whites embracing 332,100 females and 435,100 males and the colored, Indians and Chinese, 14,400 females and 83,100 males, the disproportion being among Chinese. Up to the fifteenth year the sexes are normally equal, but after this the males advance till they form double the female number, between the age of 30 and 45, and the disproportion continues into the sixties, when the males figure at 13,300 against 5,000 females. Now the latter creep upward once more till they equal the males in the nineties. The native population with Spanish blood continued very prolific, and Irish and Germans exceeded in this respect the Americans. See previous notes; *Cal. Popul. Scraps*; reports of assessors in *Cal Jour. Sen.*, app.; *Id.*, 1859, app. 7, and *Cal. Board Health*, 1870-1, app. 102-12 contains remarks on registration laws.

their predominance, numerically as well as in influence. The first large influx of foreigners was offset by the expansion of land and ocean currents from the Atlantic states, and checked to some extent in the only objectionable quarters, Spanish-America and China, by a repelling hostility.[10] Nevertheless, the proportion of foreign-born immigrants increased since 1850 from one-third of the number coming from the United States,[11] until in 1880 it surpassed the latter by nearly one-fifth.   Yet the persons born in the state out-number either, so that the foreign percentage of the total remains almost the same as in 1850.

The aborigines during this period dwindled to less than one-half their strength, under the withering contact with white civilization, and the native Spanish inhabitants have undoubtedly suffered a certain check in their remarkable fecundity from their anomalous position.   They possessed an admixture of Indian blood, for which Americans entertained an undisguised and irritating contempt that was inconsiderately extended to almost any sun-burned complexion.   Add to this the feeling engendered by the war of conquest and the intrusion, usurpation, and other injustice to which

[10] See under politics and mining.   The maltreatment offered in Cal. led to restrictive measures by the governments in those countries.   Yet the Burlingame treaty opened once more, in 1868, the celestial portals.   Europeans were hampered by distance and expense, and intercepted by Atlantic states.

[11] The *Census* of 1850 has 21,800 foreign-born persons against 62,600 from the U. S., and 8,000 natives, excluding Indians.   According to the *Census* of 1852 the foreign residents numbered less than 60,000, and the Indians over 30,000 in a total of 255,000.   That of 1860 places the foreign-born at 146,-500 in a total of 380,000, those born in the state at 77,700.   The Chinese lead with 34,900, Irish 33,100, Germans, 21,600, English 12,200, Mexicans 9,200, French 8,500.   The *Census* of 1880 gives the foreign-born at 292,900 against 571,800 born in the U. S.   Of the latter, 326,000 were born in the state, 16,-300 being Indians, about 1,700 Mongolians, and 1,400 other colored races.   This leaves 245,800 born in other states of the Union, including nearly 3,000 colored, 43,700 from N. Y., 20,700 from Missouri, 19,000 from Massachusetts, 17,800 from Ohio, 17,300 from Ill., 15,400 from Pennsylvania, 14,500 from Maine; also a sprinkling from Pacific territories.   The foreign-born are still headed by 73,500 Chinese, plus 1,700 Mongols born on the coast, and followed by 63,000 Irish, 33,100 English and Scotch, 42,500 Germans, plus 3,000 from Austria, etc.; 9,700 Scandinavians, including Danes, 9,600 French, 7,500 Italians, 5,300 Swiss, 4,700 Portugue·e, and only 600 Spaniards, 8,600 Mexicans, 1,800 South Americans, 2,000 Russians and Poles, 18,900 from British America, and 2,000 Australians.

they were subjected by unscruplous new-comers who
enviously beheld the broad possessions acquired by
long colonization. They were besides allied to the
Latin races in America and Europe, and consequently
exposed to the hostility directed against them, and
encouraged by the government itself in a discriminat-
ing mining tax, with the result of greatly checking
the Latin influx,[12] including the highly desirable contribution from France.[13]

The largest foreign immigration consists of Chinese, whose adverse influence on white labor led to
restrictive measures against them.[14] Next in numeri-
cal order come the hardy, versatile Irish ;[15] the sedate
and plodding Germans,[16] whose traits apply also to
the cognate Scandinavians; the grumbling English,
aptly complemented by the prudent Scotch; the
British-American, in whom the inherited stubborn
egotism has been effaced by a manly independence
tinged with the sparkling Gallic temperament. Add
to these a sprinkling of Mediterranean Latins, Slavs,
and other races, not forgetting the ubiquitous Hebrew, ever to be found in the train of commercial enterprise, and we have a material unequalled for cos-
mopolitan association wherewith to modify the pre-

[12] See note nine. But for this the immigration from western and southern Europe, and especially from Mexico, would have been far larger. Disorders in Mexico and high wages, security and comfort in Cal. were strong
causes for migration. *Pico Doc.*, i. 330; *Sonorense*, March 18, 1853, etc.;
Hayes' Angeles Arch., ii. 279 et seq. Increasing poverty, and the intermar-
riage of the fairest Spanish daughters with Anglo-Saxons, were strong factors in the growth. My *Cal. Pastoral* treats fully of their life and traits,
with anecdotal and romantic episodes.

[13] Especially for horticultural interests and valuable for its vivacity and
politeness as a race admixture. They were largely driven from the mines
in early days to towns and viticultural districts. Few sought naturalization
or assimilation. Lottery schemes, etc., gave an impulse to their migration
to Cal. in 1850–1. *Vallejo, Doc.*, xxxv. 318; *Alta Cal.*, Feb. 13, Apr. 29,
1851, Feb. 10, May 5, Aug. 28, 1852; *S. F. Picayune*, Sept. 20, 1851, etc. A
special history of their condition exists in *Lévy, Les Francais en Cal.*

[14] The proportion of women among them is exceedingly small and mostly
of the low class.

[15] Who display a bent for political agitation, and for crowding into city
suburbs. They have a special coast historian in De Quigley, who in his *Irish
Race in Cal.*, 548 pp., paints their wealth and influence in flaring colors.

[16] Their stronger adherence to national customs and language, as compared
with the Celts, is balanced by a quieter diposition.

dominant American element.[17]   This is assured by its
own growth, which for over a decade has surpassed
foreign accessions, and by a strong national sentiment,
demonstrated by loyal adhesion to the Union in
1861–5, and since bound by closer bonds of communication.   The restriction of Chinese alone suffices to
give to American influx a preponderance which is increasing with the approximation of the western frontier settlements that have so largely intercepted the
westward migration.   The appreciation of the climatic
and horticultural advantages of California is again
drawing onward this current.[18]

The character of the immigration has been greatly
affected by the changing nature of its magnet, from
gold-placers to grain-fields and to vineyards.   This is
strikingly illustrated in the shifting centre of population, which retroceded after 1851–2 from the all-ab-
sorbing mineral belt of the Sierra.[19]   The largest
movement was toward the bay of San Francisco, as
affording the readiest outlet to the best markets for
dairy, field and forest products, and subsequently providing, especially at the metropolis, superior advan-

[17] The Jews have attained a position of unequalled influence.   The preponderance of the immigration from New York has been marked in politics.
Ryckman's Vig., MS., 20.   The larger proportion from the Atlantic coast
states is due to their more dense population, which is ever sending forth
pioneers, and to the ready ocean route.   After the first gold excitement the
inhabitants of the western interior states found less inducements in Cal. to
outweigh those around them.   The Mormon project of 1848 to colonizing Cal.,
dwindled to a few petty settlements and to the more important one of San
Bernardino, estimated by *Los Ang. Star*, Feb. 7, Sept. 1852, at 700 strong,
with mills, etc.   *Hayes' Notes*, MS., 76, 204–5; *Id. S. Bern.*, i. 2 et seq; *Id.,
Aug.*, i. 26–7; with feeling concerning them.   A large tract was bought in
1851 for $75,000.   *Alta Cal.*, May 28, June 17, 1851, June 15, 1852, Dec. 2,
1853.   *Sac. Union* of May 1, 1856, estimates the colony at 2,000 souls, owning
a tract of about 35 miles by 12.   *Olshausen's Mormonen*, 163; *Mormon Politics*, 1–8.

[18] Counter attractions exist in intermediate and adjoining territories, in
even Australia, which in the early fifties drew many gold-seekers.   Drawbacks have been interposed by the disorders of flush times, of 1856 and 1877,
the occasional droughts and earthquakes, and in Chinese competition, but
nearly all have disappeared or faded to insignificant proportions, droughts
being greatly modified by irrigation, for instance.

[19] Compare census figures for agricultural and mineral counties in 1850,
1860, and 1880, showing the great gain of the former, while many of the
latter lost or became stationary.   The mining counties held three-fifths of the
popul. in 1852 and only one fifth in 1880.

tages for fast expanding manufacturing interests. The great valleys adjoining the gold belt, and partly settled from it, received a large influx in the sixties, when the value of the San Joaquin lands for wheat culture was recognized. Of late years the southern part of the state has been gaining on the strength of its horticultural features, and similar advantages are also causing a reflux to the Sierra slopes and filling many other neglected sections with flourishing colonies.[20]

Among counter-actions to the increase of population stands foremost the return migration, by men who had come merely to gather wealth, and who, for a long time, remained blind to the advantages for settling. The hardships of life in the mines and in a new country, sickness, fluctuations in business, and family ties abroad were additional promptings. Thus in early years departures largely exceeded arrivals, and subsequently adjacent territories combined to draw away thousands.[21] The gloomy tales of disappointed and suffering miners created at one time the impression that California was not a healthy region,[22] and the hardships of a digger's life certainly told heavily upon the inexperienced though hardy gold-seekers, in the shape of fevers, intermittent and remittent, rheumatism, catarrh, syphilis, scurvy, and notably diarrhœa and

[20] As in Fresno and San Bernardino. See chapters on agric., mines, birth of towns, and manuf. Horticulture is promoting centralization into cities and villages, in addition to railways, machinery, and other adjuncts of civilization.

[21] Australia drew many in 1851-2, British Columbia in 1858, Nevada after 1860, Arizona, etc. In 1855-7 the arrivals by sea were 80,000 and the departures 63,000. The reflux of the land current was less heavy, however. See *Helper's Land*, 20-1; *Crary's Stat.*, MS., 1; *Cal. Popul. Scraps*, 121; daily, weekly, and monthly records in *Alta Cal.*, and other journals. After the opening of the railway, tourists and business men swell the departures, so as to make the figures deceptive. Comparatively few fortune-seekers now return.

[22] In early days diseases found freer play under the effects of a changed climate and life upon systems strained by the hardships of a trying land trip, or of a sea voyage in badly provided vessels. Then followed hard and exciting pursuits, labor in damp soil or water, under a broiling sun, bad water, poor food and shelter, lack of vegetables and remedies.

dysentery. But circumstances changed rapidly, with increased experience, improved methods and appliances, and the extension of traffic, bringing with it better supplies and remedies.[23] Subsequently the regular habits attending agricultural and other settled modes of life tended to counteract the weakness introduced into our exceptionally youthful and hardy community by an increasing proportion of delicate women and children, so that the death-rate remains much lower than in the eastern cities and Europe.[24] Indeed, the dry, warm atmosphere of the interior, the bracing sea winds, and the equable yet invigorating temperature, form a rarely equalled combination, which has made California famous as a health-resort. The

[23] In 1849 fully 500 graves were dug at S. F. in one month. *Johnson's Cal. and Or.*, 241-2; for S. F. and state, see *S. F. Picayune*, Sept 12 1850; *Cal. Courier*, Sept. 12, 17-18, Nov. 1-2, 1850; Feb. 27, Mar. 3, 17, 1851; *Por. News., Alta Cal.*, etc., monthly, quarterly, and at close of year. The rate fell fast in the interior, until it could be safely placed within one per cent, a low figure due to the youth and hardiness of the community. See military reports in *U. S. Gov. Doc.*, 34th cong., 1st sess., *Sen. Doc.*, 96, XVIII. 442 et seq. The Stockton hospital report for 1852 shows 1064 patients, with 176 cases of intermittent fever, 73 remittent, 42 typhoid, and 32 Panamá fever; diarrhœa 35, dysentery 54, rheumatism 32, pneumonia 25, syphilitic cases over 80, delirium tremens 24. At S. F. co. hospital fevers and digestive troubles ruled higher. *Cal. Jour. Ass.*, 1853, app. 18, 21; *Sawyer's Mortuary Tables*, 1-18; *Stillman's Observ. Medic.*, *Sacramento*, 289 et seq.; also chapter on society of 1849.

[24] In the seventies the average may be placed at about 14 per mille. Taking the *Report of the Board of Health* for 1876 and for 1879-80, we find the rate at Marysville 17.9 and 21.9, Sac. 14.5 and 19.7, Placerville 7.2 and 12.3, Stockton 9.7 and 12, S. F. 19 and 18.6, Sta Bárbara 17.8 and 17.5. Vallejo in 1879-80 stood at 10, Downieville at 9, and San Diego at about 14. The southern San Joaquin figures near 20. These rates do not serve as very reliable guidance, owing to the preponderance of families in some places and of hardy men in others, and to the concourse of invalids into certain places, at Marysville from the mines, at S. F. from all parts, at Los Angeles and other southern towns from the east, the last being chiefly sought by consumptives. Of the 5,800 deaths recorded in above report for 1879-80 consumption carried off 954, largely eastern health seekers, and at S. F. where the climate is severe on the chest and throat, pneumonia 505, bronchitis and other respiratory troubles 234, diphtheria 101, diseases of the stomach and bowels 253, of the liver 126, cholera infantum 100, fevers, typhoid, 142, others 95; diseases of the brain and nervous system stand at the high figure of 519, of the heart at 217, alcoholism at 63, and suicide 109; all explained by the habits of life, excitable temperament, and stimulating climate referred to elsewhere. Fevers, dysentery, diarrhœa, and rheumatism, so prevalent in early years, have declined to small proportions. See also reports from hospitals in *Cal. Jour Sen*, app. annually; *S. F. Munic. Reports*, id.; *Nordhoff's Cal.*, 247-55; *Disturnell's Climate*, 154 et seq.; *Logan's Medic. Topog.*, 5-53; *Pac. Medic. Jour.*, passim; *Cal. Min. Springs; Census* tables. Table of suicides in *S. F. Municip. Rept*, 1859-60, 57-9, etc.

peculiar topography gives, moreover, to the climate a variety of grades, ranging from the temperate to the semi-tropic.[25] Medicinal springs abound, and productions are rich and varied. The above conditions explain why epidemics have found a comparatively feeble foothold,[26] and why nervous diseases present the only unfavorable exception, fostered by the prevailing speculative spirit and stimulating environment.[27]

The generous impulses of Californians, so marked in benevolence, and so strongly exhibited, for instance, in the relief of early immigrant parties, and in unequalled contributions to the sanitary fund during the Union war, stand recorded also in numerous charitable and other institutions, among them being two

[25] Leaving only a few exceptional districts near the heated deserts. Marshy tracts are neutralized in their action by the peculiar dryness of the air. S. F. is not to be recommended for weak-chested people; otherwise it is very bracing and healthy.

[26] Small-pox carried off large numbers of Indians in colonial times and in 1862–3, but has since been very restricted, and so with cholera, which created the only real alarm in 1850 and 1852–3. *Dodson's Biog.*, MS., 3; *Kunkler, Etude*, 1–24; *Hayes' Notes*, MS., 90–1; *Cal. Springs*, 32–9; *Alta Cal.*, Jan. 4, 1851, Sept. 19, 1852, July 16, Sep. 17, 1855; *Hayes' Angeles Arch.*, vii. 86.

[27] After the decline of mining the gambling spirit sought a vent in stock speculation, rash enterprise, and high pressure of work and life, with attendant startling changes in fortune, so that the percentage of insane people stands far above the average for the U. S., or 1 in 346 inhabitants against 1 in 544 for the union, according to the *Census* of 1880. That of 1860 shows 1 in 834 against 1 in 1,300 for the U. S. Poverty and marked religious excitement form here an insignificant cause as compared with the east. The percentage of idiots, blind, and deaf-mutes is below the average. Concerning the formation of board of health and medical societies, see *Cal. Polit. Code*, 433 et seq.; *S. F. Co. Medic. Soc.*, annual; *Cal. Pharm. Soc. Proceed.*, and other reports by such bodies.

[28] The special dept in the Stockton hospital was in 1853 expanded into a separate asylum, to which several additions have been made. The more imposing edifice at Napa was opened in 1875, and has cost over $1,500,000. *Hittell's Code*, ii. 1751–2; and reports in *Cal. Jour. Ass. and Sen.*, especially *Sen.*, 1877–8, app. 9; *Statutes*, 1853, et seq.; *S. Joaq. Co. Hist.*, 73–5; *Pinkham's Stockton*, 273–81; *Cal. Charit. Scraps; Napa Co. Hist.*, 290–2; *Wood's Pio.*, 49–51.

The first resident physician of the Stockton asylum was Dr R. K. Reid, a native of Erie, Penn., a graduate of the university of Penn., and a pioneer of 1849. At the outbreak of the civil war he accepted an appointment as surgeon in the regular army, and after its close retired from professional life. Of special value are his contributions to medical science, including his reports between 1851 and 1856 on the state hospital and state insane asylum. In 1879 he was elected president of the Stockton bank, in which he was then a director and one of the largest stockholders.

insane asylums,[28] a deaf, dumb, and blind asylum,[29] and
a large number of orphan asylums, homes, and hospitals, sustained by cities, counties, and private associations, and partly aided by state subscriptions.[30] In these
acts of charity a prompt and conspicuous part was taken
by fraternal societies, notably the Odd Fellows and
Masons, which was organized in 1849.[31] They were

[29] In Berkeley. See reports in *Cal. Jour. Sen.*, app. and *Reports of Sup.
Pub. Instruc.*

[30] The state made appropriations in 1851, *Statutes*, pp. 384, 500–21, also
act May 3, 1852 and May 19, 1853, for three hospitals at S. F., Stockton,
and Sac.; the last never acquired a footing, that at Stockton was surrendered
two years later, and the S. F. abolished in 1855. *Id.*, 1855, p. 47, 67; *Annals S. F.*, 450–2; *S. F. Manual*, 184–96. The state hospital fund, derived
from passengers, was henceforth distributed among county sick funds.
Cal. Revenue Law, 74–6. By 1856 over $1,000,000 had been expended on
the sick by the state. For aid to asylums, etc., see committee reports in
Cal. Jour. Sen., app. The federal gov't erected in 1853 a U. S. marine hospital at S. F. *U. S. Gov. Doc.*, cong. 32, sess. 1, H. Doc., 133, xiii. It was
so severely shaken by the earthquake of 1868 as to be surrendered for a
sailors' home. The first orphan asylum was the San Francisco, organized by
protestants at S. F. on Jan. 31, 1851. Roman catholics followed the example in March. *Sac. Transcr.*, Mar. 14, 1851; *Cal. Courier*, Mar. 6, 1851;
S. F. Ordin., 1853–4, 51; *Asylum Reports*, passim; *Cal Charit. Scraps*, 92 et
seq. *Municip. Reports*, county histories, directories, special pamphlets, and
periodical reviews in journals give accounts of orphan asylums, foundling and
lying-in hospitals, and homes. S. F. has institutions sustained by more than
half a dozen nationalities. The Magdalen asylum is partly aided by state
and city; a veterans' home exists, a society for prevention of cruelty to
animals, etc. Instances of charitable subscriptions are given in *Hittell's S.
F.*, 384–5, 446–7. See also in *Id.*, bequests by Lick, Hawes, etc.

[31] The Odd Fellows met informally in the autumn of 1847 at Portsmouth
house, S. F., and the journals of 1848 record regular Tuesday gatherings.
Lodge 1 was formally instituted on Sept. 9, 1849, at S. F. Lodge 2 gathered
at Sac. Aug. 20, 1849, and was formally instituted Jan. 28, 1851. By 1853
there were eleven and the grand lodge organized May 17, 1853. For benevolence and progress see *S. F. Reports; Upham Notes*, 299; *S. F. New Age*,
1866 et seq.; *Directories*, etc. The Masonic order found its first lodge in
Oct. 1849 and its grand lodge in April 1850. By 1856 over 100 lodges stood
inscribed in the state. Progress depicted in *F. and A. Masons' Reports;
Williams' Rec.*, MS., 13, by one of the first Masons in Cal.; county histories,
etc. Still faster grew the Sons of Temperance, organized in 1849, revived
soon after, forming on Sept. 9, 1851, the grand division and temple of honor
in 1854, and numbering by 1856 some 7,000 members, largely represented
in the volunteer companies of the fire depts, which at S. F. then embraced
1,000 members. Nationality exercised a powerful influence in drawing men
together. The Hebrews set the brightest example in establishing five societies by 1855, the first dating 1849. The Swiss Benevolent Soc. formed in
1849; a St Andrew's in Nov. 1850; the French Dec. 28, 1851; the Hibernian
Feb. 3, 1852; Sons of Emerald Isle, Mar. 17, 1852; an English gov't hospital
1852, followed later by the British Ben. Soc.; the German Jan. 7, 1854; a
Chinese in 1854; Scandinavians, Latins, Slavs, etc., followed; a Ladies
Relief Soc. Aug. 1853, the Seamen's Friend Mar. 26, 1856. Soldiers of the
Mexican war associated in 1854, a N. England Soc. met in 1850, the Griz-
zlies and others; also protective trade unions, as the chamber of commerce,

quickly followed by a large number of other associations, benevolent, national, military, protective, social, literary, and religious, the precedence among which was accorded to the different pioneer organizations to be found in all counties and large towns.[32]

Next to San Francisco, of whose institutions mention is made in a preceding note, Los Angeles probably holds the first place in fraternal and charitable associations. Prominent among them are the odd fellows and kindred organizations, branches of the ancient order of united workmen and of the American legion of honor, the young men's christian association, the orphans' home, the girls' home, the boys' and girls' aid society, and the secular corporation of the trinity methodist episcopal church. The president of the three last and a liberal contributor to all of them is Moses L. Wicks, whose judicious and free-handed benefactions have aided no less in the social development of the city than his enterprises have contributed to its material greatness.

The generous and fraternal feeling so early and widely manifested points in itself to the healthy tone pervading the flush times, notwithstanding the boisterous and reckless spirit therein engendered. There was withal comparatively little of the selfish and sordid. The vicious and criminal were practically confined to certain lawless elements ; but their suppression by the vigilance committees, notably in 1851

typographical union, riggers and stevedores' assoc., several medical, literary, military, and religious associations. See reports by the different lodges and societies on my shelves; county histories, directories, periodical accounts in journals. Libraries and other commendable institutions are attached to these societies to expand their usefulness.

[32] At the head of all stands the society of Cal. Pioneers, organized Aug. 1850, and reorganized on July 6, 1853, to embrace all residents and arrivals prior to Jan. 1, 1849, with a second class for U. S. citizens extending to Jan. 1, 1850. See their *Reports* and *Constitutions; Pioneer Arch., Vallejo Doc.,* xxxv. 249; *Annals S. F.*, 283–4. For the first year meetings were irregular. By 1858 there were nearly 700 members. Levy, *Francais*, alludes to French pioneers. In 1863 a fine pioneer hall was inaugurated, and in 1886 a still more pretentious building. The limitation of date led to the association of Territorial Pioneers, *Constit.*, 1874, and *First Annual*, to embrace white males residing in Cal. prior to Sept. 9, 1850, when the state was created. Kindred assocs. were formed by descendants, as Native Sons, also in adjoining states and at New York, where a permanent assoc. formed 1875. *Assoc. Ter. Pio., N. Y.*, 3 et seq.; *Upham's Notes*, 566, 575–94; *Hayes' Notes*, iii. 56, 129.

and in 1856, while purifying the country and imparting a feeling of security, served to intensify the bad reputation cast upon California.[33] With more settled conditions and better official supervision this blemish was almost effaced, when the outburst in 1877 of the long smouldering anti-Chinese riot brought out the stain once more, for a time only.

The long and costly journey, the ruling high wages, and the slight cost of subsistence have thus far proved a check to mendicancy. On the other hand, the roaming instinct that brought men to this coast, the wandering life connected with placer mining, and a mild climate, fostered a tendency to idleness and vagabondage, and bred in the country the tramp, in the town the hoodlum, the latter a *genus per se*.[34]

The democratic equality fostered by mining life, and by the ready acquisition of independence and wealth, is still marked, but class distinctions are growing in the cities, and spreading throughout the state, under the gradual equalization of wages with eastern rates, the dearness of land, and the expansion of monopolies. Nevertheless, the influence of workingmen was strong enough, a few years ago, to pass a state constitution of somewhat socialistic stamp, whereby much capital was driven from the country.[35]

[33] Impressed by the exaggerated stories by favorite writers like Bret Harte, Mark Twain, B. Taylor. See former chapters on S. F. society and crime, and my volumes on *Popular Tribunals*. It must be admitted, however, that shooting at sight was not infrequent, and that the law against duelling long remained a dead letter.

[34] Applied to the vicious and low youth. Some derive the term from 'huddle.' A former member of the fraternity says that it was once more respectable, and that one gang of boys adopted the designation Hoodoo, the supposed correct form of negro voodooism, with a language marked by lum endings—hence hoodoolums. A connection may also be traced with the hounds, houndlings, of 1849. In the chapter on manufactures I have pointed to seasons, machinery, and Chinese as additional causes for idleness. Turk, *Sonoma*, MS., 15-19, describes the tramp evil in the country; also *Cal. Crimes Scraps*, 138, et seq. A sparse population and the transport of treasure still tempt highwaymen.

[35] But there was plenty left. The state contains more millionaires in proportion to its population than perhaps any country in the world. The state passed a ten-hour law on May 17, 1853, and an eight-hour law on Feb. 21, 1868. Labor unions are very strong, yet too exclusive for the benefit of the rising youth. A labor exchange received state appropriation. *Cal.*

The influence of woman is strikingly exhibited in California during the transition from the camp era to the present settled condition. As a hush then fell upon the revelling miners at the appearance of a woman in their secluded haunts, so a chivalrous respect surrounds her still wherever she moves.[36] The divine halo which encircled her is not yet faded, and shields even the fallen class, which, once so conspicuous, has been forced back into shadows and by-ways.[37] Husbands, becoming reconciled to the country, sent for wives and daughters, and under their protection came others.[38] Yet the gentler sex had by 1880 risen only to one third of the entire population.

There are as yet no indications that the moral tone of women will, in the near future, attain to puritan rigidity. For this reasons are to be sought in climatic conditions and habits which incline toward gambling, extravagance, and excitements. The lavishness and display sustained by affluence assisted to lessen the attraction of household duties, to loosen the family bond, and invite outside adulation.[39] This was promoted by the inferior quality of the

Statutes, 1869–70, 145–6, 543. A bureau of labor statistics made its first report for 1883–4.

[36] She may travel alone throughout the land, assured of respect and protection; in street cars men frequently rise to offer her a seat; many entertainments are made free to her in order to attract more male patronage; in the courts judges as well as juries appear under her influence.

[37] They were imported in batches from Spanish-America, France, etc., and most females from China are still of that class. Cal. Cour., Oct. 17, Nov. 25, 1850; Cal. Popul. Scraps, 121–5. Efforts have been made to restrict this sisterhood. Memorials, etc., in Cal. Jour. Sen., 1877–8, app. 38; Cal. Board Health, Rept., 1870–1, app. 44–53. At S. F. the police have more than once blockaded and raided their dens.

[38] By 1852 nearly 23,000 Americans of the gentle sex had come, and over 4,300 foreigners. Express companies arranged to bring families. Pac. News, Oct. 18, 1850; Sac. Union, July 26, 1855; Alta Cal., Dec. 19, 1854; Helper's Land, 21–2.

[39] Hence the frequency of divorce. An early instance of desertion by the wife is given in Cal., Apr. 12, 1848. Out of 106 applications for divorce in 1857 only 23 were presented by men. The divorce bill created a stir in 1851. Sac. Transcr., Feb. 14, 1851. Comments on frequency. Cal. Crimes Scraps, 67–8. The first breach of promise before Cal. courts was instituted by Mary Gates vs. C. A. Buckingham in 1854. The married women's rights bill passed in 1852. Roach's Stat., MS., 9–10; Hayes' Notes, iii. 89–94, with account of Dr Cole's rating of Cal. women.

women who sought California, as compared with its men, and the consequently large number of incongruous marriages. Loudness and fastness kept apace, and left their impress on the rising generation. This remark applies especially to the large towns, where domestic aspirations are largely sacrificed to the preference for hotel and boarding-house life,[40] which, though detrimental in many respects, is yet unavoidable in view of modern centralization.[41]

Houses need not be costly or over-substantial in climates which invite to out-door life and to the enjoyment of shady gardens. In San Francisco the simple and light, yet strong, Chicago frame structures predominate, with a pleasing variety of style, yet with a marked prevalence of bay windows, for which the strong breezes are responsible, in rendering the use of balconies less comfortable. Interiors are furnished with a richness commensurate with the general affluence, and the wide-spread taste for music and decorative arts is rapidly developing a tasteful surrounding. A pleasing feature is the love for flowers, and the ever-blooming garden patches with which most houses are adorned. In the country the increase in horticultural colonies and homes of wealthy people, and the expanding current of tourists, are incentives for making homes more attractive.[42] Dress partakes somewhat of the composite character of the people,[43] and exhibits in a still stronger light

[40] Due partly to the expense of houses and servants, and to speculative and unsettled conditions, but also to female distaste for house-keeping. Cal. was called the hotel state. Description of *Palace Hotel*, 1–16, one of the finest in the world; hotel life, in *Overland*, v. 176–81; *Macgregor's Hotels*, 1–45. The proportion of families to the population is fully equal to the average for U. S., but the children per family are only 4.87 against more than 5 for young states.

[41] This finds a favorable direction in Cal. in the increase of horticultural colonies.

[42] Than they were in colonial times and during the long prevailing period of speculative farming.

[43] French and English goods and fashions are general, with a certain additional mixture. Shop-girls and wives of laborers sport silks and imitation jewelry to a striking degree. The explanation lies in preceding male and female characteristics, in the easy acquisition of money, and in the benign climate, which favors a snug yet light costume.

the bent for display, among the lowly as well as wealthy. Indulgence extends also to the inner man, and although the palate is not sufficiently studied under the pressure of speculation and excitement, no restraint is placed upon choice and varied pandering. Thus, California consumes more sugar, coffee, and choice wines and fruits *per capita* than the eastern states or Europe.

Extravagance and frivolity in dress combine with an innate craving for excitement to foster the taste for amusements. In this respect San Francisco, with its hotel life, and its position as the great social centre of the coast, surpasses probably any city of its size. Zest is imparted by the medley of nationalities, with their alluring variety of entertainments, notably the concert and beer halls of the Teuton, the modified form of French café chantant, and the Italian masquerade. To these may be added celebrations in honor of St Patrick by the Irish, of Columbus by the Genoese, of May day by Germans, and of king carnival by the peoples of the Latin race.[44]

At most larger reunions dancing is a leading feature, favored by the chilly evenings, which incite to exercise. The proclivity for drinking and gambling remains strong under the different social and climatic influences. The former is sustained also by the general practice of 'treating,' a liberality to which barkeepers respond by offering the unrestricted use of the bottle, and by spreading free lunches of no mean order.[45] Nevertheless, temperance societies present an imposing array. Gambling has been checked in a measure by laws of increasing stringency,[46] although lurking in corner groceries and more respectable

[44] With less public celebrations of national anniversaries, as by Spanish-Americans.

[45] S. F. has probably more drinking bars to the population than any other large city. Fancy drinks are discussed in *Harper's Mag.*, xlviii. 42; *McDonald's B. Col.*, 378–80.

[46] See *Statutes* for 1852, 1855, 1857, etc.

places, despite spasmodic efforts to abolish it.[47]
Mining stocks provided a legalized vent for the pro-
pensity, and thousands yielded to it, from servant
girls and clerks to wealthy women and merchants,
to the improverishment of large classes.[48] The
collapse of the Comstock mines proved a severe,
yet salutary lesson, although since then lotteries
have been largely patronized. Among admissible
games, billiards take an exceptionally prominent rank
throughout the state.

The interposition of wholesome regulations gave,
in some quarters, a healthier direction to pastimes,
particularly toward the drama. The opening of the
transcontinental railway tended to elevate the drama
by inviting artists of ability, hitherto restrained by
the cost of the journey; but of late years the taste
of the masses is deteriorating under the competition
of free variety and dime theatres, which also enforce
a reduction in rates at other places. The taste for
music[49] promises well for the presentation of operas
and concerts; yet cheaper performances of this
character depend chiefly on German and Hebrew
audiences.

The several efforts made since the early fifties to
secure the religious observance of the sabbath[50] have
not been very successful in the large towns, and Sunday is practically Germanized. Multitudes then pour
out to bask in the sunlit valleys of the surrounding
bay shore, or to promenade to the music at the park,
watching at the same time the throng of carriages on
the way to the ocean beach.[51]

[47] The Chinese are the most inveterate culprits, practising under guards
and intricate approaches and bribery of the police.
[48] By losses and assessments. See chapter on trade and mining.
[49] S. F. has probably more pianos and music teachers proportionately
than any other city in U. S. One cheap place of amusement has sustained
itself purely with operatic pieces for over half a dozen years.
[50] Cal. Jour. Ass., 1852, p. 870, 1853, p. 721; Statutes, 1861, p. 655, 1869–
70, p. 52; law sustained by the court in 1882. S. F. Call, Mar. 11, 1882. 'The
Sabbath is universally desecrated.' Willey's Sermons, 29–40.
[51] Many families give a preference to the pleasure gardens like Wood-
wards' and Ocean View. Cal. Amusement Scraps, 76–436, enters fully into
this topic.

Outdoor life is naturally attractive under this rainless summer sky, and even in breezy San Francisco the main streets are crowded, especially in the evening. For camping trips, few regions present so many favorable conditions. Streams and lakes abound at different altitudes for boating, fishing, and swimming; game is abundant, and the air invigorating.

The bent for sports unfolds naturally in this communion with nature, as manifested in the number of associations for that purpose. Special trains conduct sportsmen, especially on Sundays, to adjacent fields and ranges; boats skim the waters; baseball players mingle with picnic parties. Americans are less addicted to riding than the Spanish race. They prefer driving, and trotting has therefore attracted most attention at the races, which, owing to the common possession of horses, are here more frequent than in the eastern states. Latterly, however, the excellence of the climate for breeding race-horses has been recognized, and led to the formation of numerous stables.[52] Bull-fights have long since been banned by the law; but cock-pits flourish surreptitiously.[53] Pugilism is sustained by a wide circle of admirers from all ranks, and in the large towns sparring matches are an attractive feature among their entertainments.

The preceding observations point to a number of influences, medley of nationalities, a quickening clime and environment, and the peculiar migratory habits, which stamped the Californian with distinctive traits. Distances and other obstacles restricted the inflowing population to picked men, who, in their struggles under strange conditions, naturally developed a self-reliance and energy which verged on audacity,

[52] On earlier races see *Green's Life*, MS., 27–8; *Lloyd's Lights*, 478–82; *Hayes' Angeles Arch.*, vii. 74. Long distance races are favored by Spanish settlers.

[53] Dog and poultry shows occur annually at S. F., and in connection with agric. fairs. Baby shows have been tried. *S. F. Call*, Jan. 15, 1878.

though always of a practical nature. Instance the
advance in mining methods, here revolutionized, with
mountains demolished, and streams turned from their
course; in agriculture, in the reclamation of deserts,
in girding the continent with railroads, and in other
undertakings, which have transformed a wilderness
into a prosperous state.

It was the work of utilitarian enterprise, and of
men with decided adaptability ; men, who, careless of
form and appearance, measured intrinsic value, and
kept in view aim rather than means. Casting
aside the hampering conservatism of old communities,
they sought with flexible originality and subtle per-
ception new and independent channels. The life-time
of a year was here compressed into a month; the
life of a month into a day. Wit and muscle reigned
supreme, and democratic equality levelled class aspirations. With this, however, came a regard for wealth
above culture, moral peace, and all other considerations.[54] The entry into social circles was effected
with a golden key, and sustained with gilding. The rapidity with which millionaires were made
gave no time for covering the crudities of their humble origin.[55] Yet the change was attended by little
vulgar conceit, for the caprice of fortune continued
to show itself in the making and unmaking of men
within the day. Class distinctions gradually acquired
some influence, but they have not yet reached the ab-
surdities common in the east. Character and enterprise take a leading rank, but they must be practical
and promising. Education and intelligence stand, on
the average, higher among the masses than probably
in any other country, owing to the select immigration; but the race for wealth has for the time subor-

[54] Thus, in farming, speculative operations overshadowed the desire for
home-building and comfort.

[55] The contact of different nationalities had left its trace, however, in soft-
ening much roughness, and it has been observed that returning gold-seekers
were far more considerate and orderly than those going to Cal. *Borthwick's
Cal.*, 149. Contented aspirations had their effect.

dinated the desire for wider and deeper mental attainments.[56]

Nevertheless, the quest for gold is not altogether sordid. It is sought rather as a means for power and enjoyment, and as freely used as acquired. The cause lies in the prodigality of early mining times, in the long continuance of rich developments and large profits and earnings, and in a soil and climate at once so stimulating and benign as to preclude poverty. Money-makers rely on easy recuperation, and regard empty pockets with little apprehension or discomposure. If extravagance is becoming more showy and calculating, it yet retains much of the generous element of 1849, which lingers also in the deep-drinking sets of the bar-room, shorn somewhat of early profanity. It is like-wise to be seen in the demonstrative patriotism of national feast-days, and the sustained interest in the affairs of the eastern states, and above all, in the local pride, which magnifies California as the finest and most progressive of countries.[57]

The comparative superiority of the men over the women is explained by the nature of the attraction which drew them hither, for gold and adventure, combined with hardships, were not likely to tear away from civilized comforts the same select grades of both sexes. Nor have the prevailing habits of life produced the same admirable development in women as in men.[58] Yet both were hardy and adaptive, and these qualities have left their impress upon the new generation. Children born even of puny parents are healthy and rosy-cheeked, and spring up large and lusty, with mind and nerve no less precocious than physique. All features partake, more or less, of the southern volup-

[56] In certain circles aspirants of shallow education shrink before the comparison that would be invited by a more liberal admission of literary and scientific men. The professions here stand relatively lower.

[57] Indeed, the industrial achievements of Californians justify greatly their vanity.

[58] The earliest influence of women was beneficial, in the greater order, decorum, respect, and chivalry she imparted, and in the elevating family life. Subsequently she has been prominent in fostering extravagance and vanity.

tuousness and sprightliness,[59] displaying also the strong telluric influence, and raising the question as to its ultimate effect upon the race.[60] California is certainly an exceptional country, and the size and beauty of its productions, the fame of its health-resorts, and above all, its varied topography and stimulating coast climate, seem to favor the development of the highest progressive type in man.[61]

The education of the Mexican half-caste population of California previous to the conquest was furnished entirely by their spiritual teachers, who seldom cared to do more than impart a knowledge of the religious observances required of them. Among the higher Spanish families, the sons were sent to Mexico or the Hawaiian islands, and the daughters were instructed, very inadequately, by the neighboring or visiting priest. Hence illiteracy was the rule rather than the exception.[62]

The first public school after the American occupation was established at San Francisco ; the number of persons in June 1847 under 20 years being 107, of whom 56 were of school age. On the 24th of September of that year the town council appointed a committee consisting of William A. Leidesdorff,

[59] The physical resemblance has been termed English, and the mental as inclining to the French type, but a comparison with the Spanish race as developed in Cal. and southward, refers both to a cognate influence. Fruit is here also large and bright. Girls unfold rapidly and mothers are plump and healthy at 40 years. As in the east the stolid features of the German are becoming sharpened, and the coarse skin and lank hair of the English growing more delicate and dry, so may even more striking variations be expected here.

[60] The nervous, untiring activity in S. F., imparted by the bracing sea winds, differs greatly from the modified energy enforced by the warmer temperature of the interior and the south, and which approaches that of the spasmodic Spanish-American.

[61] Concise and interesting accounts of California society may be found in Overland, v. 77, etc.; Nordhoff's Cal., 137, et seq.; Taylor's Yates, 88, 276; Lloyd's Lights and Shades of S. F.; McCall's Pick., 1–46; Cortambert, Peuples; Hutchings' Mag.; Liking's Six Years; Beadle's West, 290–311; Capron's Cal.; Pilgrim; Borthwick's Cal.; Powers' Afoot; 314–26; Helper's Land (cynical); Fisher's Cal., a study of characteristics; Dixon's Conquest; Saxon's Five Years.

[62] The census of 1850 placed the illiterate population of Cal. at 2,318 white natives, and 2,917 foreigners, chiefly Mexicans and Chilians, in a total of 110,000. At Monterey existed in 1836 a so-called normal school, when a few primary branches were taught as indicated by the petty Catecisms de Ortologia printed for it.

William S. Clark, and William Glover to take measures for the establishment of a public school. A school-house was erected on Portsmouth square, dignified by the name of Public Institute, and on the 3d of April, 1848, a school was opened by Thomas Douglas, a Yale graduate, who received a salary of $1,000 per year. From this beginning has grown, with some interruptions, the public school system of California.[63]

[63] To be historically accurate, it should be stated that a private school had been kept since the preceding April by one Marston, a poorly educated Mormon, who had about 20 pupils in a shanty west of Dupont st, between Broadway and Pacific. As early as 1847 it is said that one Tyler taught a class at Cache creek, and Wheaton soon after taught at Washington. Miss McCord also taught at Trémont. The gold excitement carried all off to the mines, and when next a school was opened in S. F., it was by Albert Williams in April 1849 with 25 pupils. About the last of Dec., J. C. Pelton established a free school, which in April 1850 was taken under the patronage and control of the city. An assistant being required, Mrs Pelton was nominated. The salaries of both together were fixed at $500 a month. A school ordinance was passed April 8th, 1850, prescribing rules and regulations for the public school. One hundred and forty-eight pupils between the ages of 4 and 16 years were admitted the first term, as follows: Americans 77; foreigners 71. The number had increased by Jan. 1851 to 174 pupils, of whom 102 were foreign and 75 were girls, most of the pupils being only above infancy. Frequent fires and other causes occasioned the removal of the school to the various churches which had escaped their ravages. By June 1851 there were 300 children on the school list, requiring two additional teachers. Owing to a misunderstanding concerning salary, Mr Pelton closed his school in Sept. 1851, having given instruction during his term to over 1,100 children. *Pelton's Rept.;* in *S. F. Herald, Aug. 9, 1850, 2d March, 1851. The Pac. News* of Nov. 1, 1850, refers to a children's parade with a banner inscribed "The First Public School of California." *Wood's Pioneer Work,* MS., 9; *S. F. Alta,* Feb. 7 and March 1, 14, 1851; *Cal. Courier,* Sept. 17, 1850; *S. F. Picayune,* Sept. 3, 13, 1850; *S. F. Bulletin,* May 27, 1875; *Sac. Transcript,* March 14, 1851; *Willey's Thirty Years,* 43–4; *Ross' Statement,* MS., 13. A public school was taught in Monterey in 1849 by Rev. Willey, in Colton Hall, *Vallejo Doc.,* xiii. 9. In Sacramento also a school-house was built on I street by Prof. Shepherd in 1849, and occupied in Aug. by C. H. T. Palmer, who gathered up a dozen out of the 30 children in the place. J. A. Benton next essayed a school in Sac. in Nov. with even less success. In the spring of 1850 Ferguson taught a school in the 7th Methodist church in Sac., but also failed. Rev. J. Rogers followed and kept a school for two years. Miss Hart began teaching in the autumn of 1850, and Mrs Spear opened a girls' school in the summer of 1851. *Larkin's Doc.,* vii. 336. See other authorities under 'Sacramento' in the chapter on birth of towns, this vol. The matter of schools was agitated in Stockton in May 1850, C. M. Blake teaching in a building furnished by Weber, but failing. *Pac. News,* May 10, 1850. In the autumn Mrs Woods opened a select school, and early in 1851 W. P. Hazelton started a free school, after which progress became rapid. *Hist. Stockton,* 281–2.

The first school on the Mokelumne was opened in a tent fitted up on the Staples' rancho in 1854, by Mr and Mrs D. J. Staples, and taught by A. A. Wheelock. A singing school and Sunday school was taught there under the auspices of Mrs Staples and Mrs G. C. Halman. *Staples' Statement,* MS., 15.

The state constitution of 1849 provided liberally
for public instruction, but owing to the great expense
of the government, the legislature omitted to frame a
school law until its second and third sessions. In
1853[64] and 1855 this law was revised, and with many

At Los Angeles the first English school was taught in 1851 by Rev. Wicks
and J. G. Nichols. Santa Bárbara in 1850 established a public school with
12 pupils, and one private establishment.

Benicia in 1851 had a public school, and Sonoma also one of 37 pupils.
Even mining camps had schools in 1851. At Grass Valley Miss R. Farring-
ton taught. *Grass Valley Directory*, 1865, 13; or Mrs J. P. Stone, according
to the *National* of March 28, 1868. Other particulars are embodied in report
of state supt. of schools for 1852. Although the census of 1850, p. 374-5,
enumerates but 8 schools outside of the 3 leading counties, with an income of
over $14,000 and about 200 pupils, yet four or five times that number claimed
to attend school.

In 1850 Col. T. J. Nevins organized a free class in Happy Valley, near
Mission and Second, which the town council aided and made a public school
It closed in the spring of 1851, though having 200 pupils, to re-open later under the free-school ordinance. Later Nevins erected a large building at
Spring Valley on the Presidio road and opened a school at which a small fee
was charged. *Pac. News*, Jan. 7, 1851. Besides these, select schools taught
by the clergy of the several denominations were numerous. Osborne's select
school under Presbyterian auspices; Dr Ver Mehr's Grace Episcopal parish
school; Rev. Preveaux, S. F. Academy under Baptist patronage; Congregational church school opened in Sept.; Trinity school advertised to open Jan.
14, 1850, for boys only, terms $100, taught by F. S. Mines and A. Fitch.
Soon after, Miss J. B. Winlack opened a seminary for girls near Clark's
Point (Vallejo st). *Placer Times*, May 22, 1850; *Pac. News*, Jan. 5, 1850;
S. F. Herald, Sept. 4, 1850. An English lady also advertised for pupils.
There were two Catholic schools and several primaries in the city in 1850.

[64] The first school law was drawn mainly by G. B. Lingley, assisted by
J. C. Pelton and J. G. Marvin, supt of public instruction, whose report
appears in *Cal. Jour. Legis.*, 1851, p. 1562. See also *Cal. Stat.*, 1851, 491-
500. The revision of 1852 was done by F. Soule, Marvin, Pelton, and P.
K. Hubbs. The statutes of that year, and of 1853 and 1855 show the improvement made in the law. The state school fund at this time depended on
the sale and rental of 500,000 acres of state land, and on escheated estates,
to which were added the poll-tax and a state tax of 5 cents on each $100 of
assessed property. The local fund was derived from a percentage on property, gradually increased from 3 to 10 cents, and in cities to 25 cents. In
1853 congress made the same grant to California of the 16th and 36th sections of land for school purposes, which had been granted to the states
carved out of the public territory previously derived from the gifts of the
original states to the general government, or purchased from the aborigines.
The sum total of the grants of the act of 1853 was 6,765,504 acres, 46,080 of
which was to be deducted for a state seminary of learning, and 6,400 acres
for public buildings, but adding to the amount left the 500,000 before devoted to school purposes, gave 7,212,924 acres appropriated for the support
of public education; 231,680 acres had already been sold at $2 per acre; and
at the minimum of $1.25 per acre the fund arising from the remainder would
amount to $8,726,555, which at 7 per cent would yield $610,858.85, or with
the sum already realized added to $643,345.22, annual income for the sup-
port of free schools. The value of escheated estates in 1855 was placed at
$1,068,375, which was another source of revenue. *Cal. Jour. Sen.*, 1855, 37-
40; *Cal. Educ. Scraps*, 18-20; *Zabriskie, Land Laws*, 44, 47-8. The reports

modifications and improvements, is now the basis of the school law of California.

of the state school superintendent contain statistics showing the condition of the country to be very unsettled in regard to schools, but that was no more than was to be expected from 1850 to 1860, during the period of the greatest restlessness in the population. The deficiency of public schools was partly supplied by private ones, teachers being numerous. P. K. Hubbs was state supt from 1853 to 1856. He was succeeded by A. J. Moulder, graduate of the Virginia military institute. The report of 1856 shows children of school age in Cal. to number 30,039; enrolled on public school register 15,000; daily attendance 8,495; schools 321; teachers 392. A large number of the children were under private instruction. San Francisco took and maintained the lead by passing the first local ordinance under the school law Sept. 25, 1851, dividing the city into 7 districts, and providing for a free school in each, and for a board of education. This was chiefly due to city supt Nevins, who organized the department, an appropriation of $35,000 having been secured, and in 1852 another of $30,000, and a school tax of one-fifth of one per cent levied for school purposes. The first 3 schools opened in 1851 under the ordinance were the Happy Valley, under J. Denman; the Powell st or North Beach, under J. Tracy in Nov.; and the Washington st grammar school under E. Jones Dec. 22d. In 1852 the Rincon under J. Western, 8th Jan.; the Spring Valley under A. W. Cole, 9th Feb.; Mission grammar under A. Rix, in May; Union grammar at Clark's point under A. Holmes, June 7th. The Spring Valley school was leased to the city by Nevins for 99 years for the nominal sum of $700 for the entire period. There was a constant increase, until in 1856 the S. F. schools numbered 24, viz: 7 grammar, 2 mixed, 6 intermediate, and 9 primary, the daily average attendance being 2,516 out of 3,370 enrolled. Much trouble was had concerning school lots owing to squatters. *S. F. Annals*, 684–5. Until 1854 the city owned but one of the school buildings, but after this a number were erected. *State Supt Rept*, 1864–5, 342 et seq. In order to furnish school houses the city contracted a debt of $60,000 in 1854, and increased the tax rate from 28 cents for city and county to 43 cents. The bad and dishonest financial management of the state officers and legislators affected the public school fund during a period of years.

The first apportionment from the state fund was made in 1854, and its inadequacy is apparent by the following table.

	State Fund	County and City Tax	Subscript'ns and rate bills	Salaries	Expenditure
1854	$52,961	$157,702	$42,557	$ 85.860	$275,606
1855	63,662	119,128	39,395	181,906	334,638
1856	69,961	121,639	28,619	200,941	305,221

It was not until 1856 that a high school was organized in S. F., the lack of it compelling parents to send children away, and to patronize sectarian schools against their judgment; but the first heavy expense of erecting school-houses had first to be borne. The present public school fund is derived from three sources; the state fund, the county fund, and the district or local fund. The state fund is derived mainly from a property tax, supplemented by a poll-tax, and by interest on certain bonds held in trust by the state for the benefit of public schools, and also by interest on balances yet due on school lands purchased from the state. The amount of the state fund apportioned in 1885 was $1,845,883.03; and in 1886 it was $2,012,235.01. The county and local funds made up the remainder the total expenses of the public schools, being for each year over $3,000,000. *Rept of State Supt of Schools for 1887* in *Leg. Jour.*, app. no. 7. According to the school census of

California has her state university at Berkeley,[65] a
normal school at San José, with a branch at Los
Angeles,[66] the university of Southern California with
seven affiliated colleges,[67] and will soon have in
operation, in the Leland Stanford Junior university,
an institution combining the best features of
existing colleges with more practical methods and
branches of education.[68] For a state so young,
California has received some magnificent gifts in aid
of learning. Among them are the Toland medical
college, now transferred to the state university;[69] the

1888 the number of white children in S. F. of school age (5 to 17) was 81,592,
while 17,000 infants were soon to augment this figure. Of this 81,000 and
over, 42,077 were boys, 39,515 girls. Of colored children there were 152
boys and 116 girls of school age—total 82,693. Native-born Chinese, 515
boys, 320 girls. Foreign-born children, 962.

[65] See p. 392, this vol. In the buildings are excellent apparatus, laboratories, museum, machinery, library, and art gallery. In San Francisco are
located the colleges of pharmacy, dentistry, Toland college of medicine, and
Hastings law college. The many endowments of the university aggregate
$1,891,952.75. Other gifts to the institution are valued at $3,861,952.75.
The expenditure of 1882 was $95,000 and the income $98,000. The chief
benefactors have been E. Tompkins, Dr Hugh H. Toland, S. C. Hastings,
James Lick, the college of California, William and Eugenie Hillegass, George
M. Blake, A. K. P. Harmon, H. D. Bacon, Michael Reese, D. O. Mills, F.
L. A. Pioche, Dr Hitchcock, and Dr Cogswell.

[66] The legislature of 1862 ordained the establishment of a state normal
school at San Francisco, 'or at such other place as the legislature may hereafter direct.' It was the outgrowth of a normal school already established
in this city by A. J. Moulder, John Swett, and city supt Henry B. James,
who in 1857, assisted by George W. Minns, Ellis H. Holmes, and Thomas S.
Myrick, opened such a school, Minns being made principal. The branch at
Los Angeles was established in 1881 by act of legislature. Cal. Stat., 1881,
p. 89; Id., 1883, 281.

[67] The president of the university of Southern California is Dr Marion M.
Bovard, a native of Ind. and of French-Huguenot descent. Beginning life as
a physician, he became impressed with the idea that his vocation was to
preach the gospel, and first receiving a thorough college training, came to
Cal. in 1873 as a methodist missionary. After laboring for some years at
Riverside, Compton, San Diego, and Los Angeles, he organized the university in conjunction with Judge Widney and others. In 1889 it had 500
students in attendance, and its property was valued at $3,000,000.

[68] For this institution, founded in memory of his only son, whose decease
occurred March 14, 1884, Mr Stanford donated valuable tracts of land in
Butte, Tehama, Santa Clara, and San Mateo counties, with other gifts, representing in all several millions of dollars. It was the intention to make it
an educational centre adapted to all classes, the course of instruction embracing many departments, from mechanical trades to the higher branches of
art, science, and literature, with colleges of law and medicine, a school of
agriculture, a conservatory of music, a museum, library, etc., and with preparatory schools for elementary training.

[69] Dr Hugh Huger Toland, a native of South Carolina, where he was born
April 17, 1809, came to this coast in 1852, after practising successfully for a
number of years in his native state. He at once took rank among the lead-

Lick observatory; and the Cogswell Polytechnic
school of San Francisco, each accessible to all classes
upon easy terms.[70] Private schools of a high order,

ing practitioners of San Francisco, and was appointed physician and surgeon
to the county hospital, and a member of the board of health, which latter
position he held until his death, Feb. 26, 1880. The Toland medical college
was built in 1862 and largely supported at this own expense. The doctor
was twice married, his second wife, Mrs B. M. Gridley, née Morrison, being
known to the world of letters as the authoress of several beautiful poems of
a romantic and legendary character.

[70] James Lick, in disposing of his estate in his lifetime, gave $700,000 for
an observatory which should surpass any in existence. The trustees secured
the manufacture of a lens 36 inches in diameter, with a magnifying power
of 3,360 diameters, mounted as an equatorial telescope. The observatory has
also a 6-inch and a 12-inch telescope, and is in all respects the most thoroughly equipped in the world. The trustees in 1888 transferred the establishment at Mount Hamilton to the state university. Visitors are permitted
the use of the instruments on certain days of the week. *Deed of Trust of
James Lick*, 1875; *Burnham's Rept on the Observatory*, 1880; *Century*, May
1886.

Lick also gave $540,000 for the establishment of an institute of mechanic
arts at San Francisco. This also will be turned over to the university when
the trust shall be executed. It is proper to mention in this place that the
observatories for astronomical studies are numerous in Cal. Prof. Davidson
of San Francisco has a 6.4 inch object-glass, equatorially mounted, and placed
in a portable observatory at the cor of Clay and Octavia sts, and devoted by
act of the supervisors in 1880 to the use of the coast and geodetic survey as
the standard telegraphic longitude of the Pacific coast. The Chabot observatory, with an 8-inch glass, was donated to the city of Oakland by
Anthony Chabot in 1882, with an endowment of $10,000. It is situated in
Lafayette square bet 10th and 11th and Jefferson and Grove sts. The Buckhalter observatory, with a 10½ inch glass is the property of Charles Buckhalter of West Oakland, situated on Chester st, and is the work of his
hands. The Blinn observatory at Highland Park, East Oakland, is another
private establishment, and contains a 5-inch Clark chromatic, equatorially
mounted, and a 1¾ inch Latimer-Clark transit, with a mean-time and side-
real-time clock.

At the university of the Pacific, San José, a Methodist institution, is a
6-inch telescope and working observatory with several instruments, the gift
of Captain Charles Goodall of San Francisco and David Jacks of
Monterey. Mills College, Brooklyn, is also provided with an observatory
and a 5-inch telescope. The university of California was provided by the
legislature of 1886 with a students' observatory, equipped with a 6-inch
equatorial refractor, and other glasses and clocks necessary to complete the
facilities for astronomical observatories; situated at Berkeley. The elevation of Lick observatory is 4,209; Davidson, 378; university, 320; Blinn, 159.

To the university of the Pacific Mr Jacks also presented a handsome
donation for the erection of new buildings. A Scotchman by birth, and after
the gold discovery one of the earliest settlers at Monterey, where he landed
Jan. 1, 1850, Mr Jacks was formerly one of the largest farmers and stock-
raisers in this section, his estate covering an area of 60,000 acres. To colleges, churches, and charities he has always been a liberal contributor, among
his gifts being one of $29,000 to the methodists, wherewith to establish to
the Pacific grove retreat.

Dr Henry D. Cogswell, besides the aid given to the university of Cal.,
erected a drinking fountain in San Francisco, and latterly a handsome
polytechnic school on 26th and Folsom.

Among private schools, Mills seminary, now Mills college, an institu-

and sectarian colleges and universities [71] are numerous.
The means of education are furnished at the institution for the deaf, dumb, and blind, the orphanages,
and the Industrial school [72] near San Francisco. The
state is also ambitious to supplement practical education with special and general forms of culture. It is
but natural that art [73] should follow science, [74] and but
reasonable that a higher development should be looked
for in both. No better field for the scientist
could be found; nor a more inviting one for
the artist, although the extraordinary heights and
depths of mountain scenery militate against the
production of small and unpretending pictures, and
tend to the bizarre effects of great single objects.
Sculpture in California is not represented by
American artists, and but slightly at all, although

tion for the education of young women, has maintained a high reputation.
It was incorporated as Mills college in 1886.

[71] University college of San Francisco was founded under the auspices of
Calvary church in 1860. It opened in the basement of that edifice under
the direction of Dr Burrows. A lot was purchased at the cor of Geary and
Stockton sts, upon which a suitable edifice was erected, with the intention of
removing in time to a tract of land 4 miles from the city on the San Bruno
road. It is however at present located on Haight st, bet. Octavia and
Laguna sts. The plan of this institution is to give an education equal to
any of the eastern colleges. It is now in the hands of a board of unsecta-
rian trustees. S. F. Theological seminary located on Haight st was opened
in 1871 for students of all denominations. The Jesuit college of St Ignatius
in S. F., opened in 1855, is a wealthy and well-equipped institution, and
the same might be said of the colleges of other catholic orders, whose sec-
tarianism is the means of power. Sacred Heart college had in 1887 700 students. Sacred Heart Presentation convent, opened in 1869, had 600. St
Mary's college, opened in 1863, had 250 students.

[72] In April 1859 the legislature passed an act for the establishment of a
state reform school, and an appropriation was made of $30,000 to erect
buildings on a tract 5 miles from Marysville, which in 1861 was increased
by the further appropriation of $25,000. The institution was broken up in
1868, and the property turned over to the city of Marysville. *Cal. Stat.*,
1860, 200–5. In April 1858 the legislature established the Industrial School
department of the city and county of San Francisco, still in existence. Its
aims are reformatory and punitive.

[73] San Francisco has an academy of design doing very creditable work.
It has not hitherto attracted the attention of men who had money to be-
stow on educational objects, and has struggled along with such support as
pupils and artists have given it. For many years it was under the care of
Virgil Williams, a landscape painter of note, and a conscientious teacher.

[74] The California academy of sciences in S. F. organized April 4, 1853,
first occupied hired rooms, but subsequently moved into the old church at
the cor of California and Dupont sts. There was given to the society by
James Lick a valuable lot on Market st, on which the future home of the
academy will be erected. The membership is at present 350.

here and there a monument rises on public grounds to the memory of national genius or worth.[75]

The subject of California literature has been treated elsewhere in this series; hence I give it little space here. It would be folly to look for any peculiarly local type, such as one might say, "It is English," or "It is French," or "It is German" in thought or style. English, French, German, and American writers have furnished the books which treat of Californian subjects, and there is no really homogeneous Californian literature. That every traveller to this coast in the gold-period and before felt it almost as a duty to give his impressions was but the effect of the general demand for descriptions of the country. Those who came and went wrote books about the coast; those who finally settled down to residence here had incidents and recollections to relate attractive enough to gain readers, although the rhetoric and grammar may have been open to criticism, as was. also the matter, too frequently. The eagerness of the public in the eastern states, and even in England, to consume these narratives led to the exaggeration which became a feature of, if not a factor, in California writings.

Perhaps nothing more cultivates pathetic humor than hardship endured with bravery by ordinarily intelligent men.[76] The resistance of their courage to the assaults of physical pain or suffering causes them to seek amusement in absurd flights of fancy and odd combinations of imagery ; until he who draws the long bow most successfully in a company or commu-

---

[75] James Lick left a fund in trust to be applied to erecting a monument to Francis Scott Key, author of the 'Star Spangled Banner.' It was unveiled July 4, 1888. The artist was W. W. Story. Statuary for the city hall was also provided for in the Lick bequests. The state capitol at Sacramento is adorned with figures by P. Mezzara of S. F.

[76] Instance the remark of the famous mountain stage-driver, Hank Monk, when dying: 'I'm on the down grade, and can't reach the brake !' A more expressive image of certain doom could not have been presented, yet it was smilingly uttered.

nity is admired as a man of genius. Hence tales of
adventure, which simply related, might have been
reckoned no more thrilling than others of common
occurrence, when dressed in quaint language, with
happy hits of pathos or fine points of climax, rise
above the commonplace, and charm even a critical
audience.

Mining life in California furnished inexhaustible
material for the exercise of this talent; and almost
every book produced in the golden era gave specimens
more or less entertaining of the wit and humor developed by the struggle with homelessness, physical suffering, and mental gloom. And when, perchance, a
writer had never heard original tales of the kind he
felt himself expected to relate, he took them at sec-
ond-hand,[77] or invented them for the occasion. In
order to make them more improbable still, he had a
dialect of slang, bad grammar, and blasphemy invented, which, by frequent use, became standard, and
was taken by the outside world as the actual utterances of the men engaged in mining; while the truth
was that men in the mines spoke as they were used
to speak in the state or country from which they
came—no better, no worse. Some were common laborers, some artisans, some farmers, some professional
men, and being from every part of christendom,
could have no dialect such as was imputed to them.
Yet this, if any, constitutes in popular belief the
special characteristic of California literature—a belief
fostered by writers of a later period, who have preferred pandering to it rather than to sustain the dignity of the society of which they were a part.

But it cannot be assumed that there has ever been

[77] Even the most powerful of Bret Harte's stories borrowed their incidents
from the letters of Mrs Laura A. K. Clapp, who under the nom de plume of
'Shirley,' wrote a series of letters published in the *Pioneer Magazine*, 1851–2.
The 'Luck of Roaring Camp' was suggested by incidents related in Letter
II., p. 174–6 of vol. i. of the *Pioneer*. In Letter XIX., p. 103–10 of vol. iv.,
is the suggestion of the 'Outcasts of Poker Flat.' Mrs Clapp's simple epis-
tolary style narrates the facts, and Harte's exquisite style imparts to them
the glamour of imagination.

a California literature, good or bad. For the books of travellers, residents are not responsible. Most of the books produced by resident writers have been called forth by a demand for information upon some local topic. A few lovers of science have furnished monographs on these favorite studies. Books of rather commonplace biography have been produced. Few works calling for an exercise of creative talent, or purely philosophic essays have been attempted; the reason for this being two-fold—the impracticability of endeavoring to compete with the established coteries of eastern magazines in their own field, and the poverty of publishers in a sparsely settled and isolated region, which renders them unable to encourage pure literature, for writers of merit, like other professional people, must be paid for their work. This reduces the authorship of almost any state, when taken by itself, to a minimum, the two or three publishing centres of the United States hardly redeeming the individual states in which they exist from the same reproach of having no literature of their own.

Add to these conditions for California the further fact that the comparatively few persons born in this state, who have arrived at maturity, have furnished it with no marked literary ability, and it is evident that nothing which might be called characteristic has yet appeared to distinguish this from any other community of equal numbers. Those who edit the newspapers and conduct the various periodicals of the state are, from every part of the union, besides coming from Mexico and Europe.

What will be the ultimate result of this admixture of race prejudices, talent, and culture upon the future literature of the Pacific coast can only be conjectured. That a generation or two should be allowed in which to erect some local standards is consistent with reason. From the desultory efforts of the present, little can be judged, although they are not without promise should the native-born and home-educated writers of

the future prove even as industrious and full of resources as those of to-day; for although I have said
there is not yet a California literature, I have not denied that there is an extraordinary number of books,
magazines, and newspapers for the population, or that
a fair proportion of them are written and conducted
with as much ability as the same class of publications
in other countries, or that the material is absent
,which should inspire a local literature of a high order.

For remarks upon particular works the writer is
referred to my *Essays and Miscellanies*.

The advent of Americans, and the gold discovery,
had the effect of saving from final and entire abandonment the Roman catholic missionary field in California. Their religious establishments were secularized,
their pious fund diverted,[78] their converts scattered,
and the priests who remained faithful to their charge
were poor, if not sometimes starving. The mines
opened to them a treasure-house. Their cloth chapels
arose in all the chief mining camps, their blessings
were bestowed impartially when golden *chispas* were
given, and the church became rehabilitated. St
Francis' church of San Francisco was organized in
1849 by Anthony Langlois, and a wooden edifice was
consecrated to its uses in December of the same year
by John McGinnis. In 1850 Joseph S. Alemany
was appointed bishop of Monterey, but tranferred to
San Francisco in 1851, and made archbishop in 1853,
while the lower bishopric was given to Tadeo Amat.
There were fifteen catholic priests in California in
1850–1, the residue of the Franciscan missions, who
claimed 15,000 communicants, 24 churches, and one
college; also the remainder of the former mission system, with the exception of St Francis, and the cloth
chapels before mentioned. Twenty-five years after-

---

[78] The recovery of the lands which the Cath. ch. had possessed under the
Mexican domination, but had been deprived of, was ordered, or indemnified
by lieu lands to the extent of 33,000 acres by the U. S. Govt. *Rossi*, 214.

wards there were three bishops, 93 churches, 16 chapels, 121 priests, 13 convents and academies, four colleges, seven orphanages, five hospitals, and four asylums, supported by 200,000 communicants.

Protestantism was introduced into California from the methodist missions in Oregon in 1846 by William Roberts, and was kept alive by the continued if slight immigration from the border states, and occasional religious services by clergymen of various denominations, temporarily sojourning in the country, and in their absence by the volunteer effort of serious-minded laymen.[79] In the spring of 1849 there was amid the sudden influx of population a fair proportion of professional preachers,[80] few of whom, indeed, lived by

[79] Elihu Anthony was announced to preach in the Public Institute (school house) on Portsmouth square, Sept. 3, 1848. *S. F. Californian*, Sept. 2, 1848. Capt. Thomas, of the *Laura Ann*, being solicited, 'ably officiated' at the Institute for several Sundays in October 1848. On the 1st of Nov, T. Dwight Hunt, of Honolulu, at a meeting presided over by E. H. Harrison, James Creighton, sec., was chosen protestant chaplain to the citizens, with an annual salary of $2,500 to be raised by subscription. A beautiful bible was presented for the chaplain's use by W. F. Swasey. *Id.*, Nov. 4, 1848: *S. I. Friend*, vi. 93; *Polynesian* V., iii.; *S. F. Directory*, 1852–3, p. 9; *Willey's Personal Memoranda*, 88. Sam Brannan sometimes preached to the Mormons. *Findlay's Statement*, MS., 4. On the 1st of Jan., 1849, the sacrament of the Lord's supper was administered for the first time to 12 communicants of 6 different denominations. *Overland Monthly*, June 1873, p. 549. Hunt, in July 1849, organized the First Congregational church of S. F., the 3d church in point of date in the city. Its first place of meeting was at the cor. of Jackson and Virginia sts, but soon a church was erected on the cor. of Dupont and California sts. Later the edifice was placed on the S. E. cor. of Post and Mason.

[80] By the steamship *California*, in Feb. 1849, there arrived 4 clergymen: O. C. Wheeler, baptist; Sylvester Woodbridge, John W. Douglas and S. H. Willey, presbyterians. *Wood's Pioneer Work*, 84, 89. Woodbridge and Willey landed at Monterey where for some time the latter remained. On the 15th of Sept., 1850, he organized the Howard M. E. church, with 4 members, the church being erected on Natoma st, upon land donated by W. D. M. Howard. Willey remained pastor for 12 years. Woodbridge, coming to S F., preached once in Hunt's place, and then repaired to Benicia where he organized a presbyterian church on the 10th of April, probably the first regular church organization among the Americans, and certainly the first presbyterian church. This church flourished for many years; but in 1861 it dissolved on account of political dissensions. Woodbridge paid a visit to Sacramento in April 1849, and preached there the first sermon which its people had heard since the settlement. Douglas went to San José, where he organized a church, but afterwards returned east.

In the meantime, Albert Williams, another presbyterian had arrived, and on the 20th of May organized the First Presbyterian church of San Francisco, holding services in a tent erected for the purpose on Dupont st. The society afterward used a store-room in the custom house, and later, the Superior

their calling alone, but most of whom contributed by teaching, and otherwise, to the advancement and refinement of society in the towns, San Francisco and Sacramento receiving a large proportion of their

court room in the city hall by authority of the provisional legislature of the district. *S. F. Picayune*, Dec. 25, 1850. In 1851, a church edifice framed in the east, and shipped round the Horn on the bark George Henry, was erected on Stockton st near Broadway; but it was destroyed in the great fire of that year. Another edifice, costing $75,000, was erected in 1857 by this society. *S. F. Alta,*Jan. 25, 1850; *S. F. Herald*, Feb. 3, 1851; *Williams' Pioneer Pastorate*, 18–23; *Barton's Statement*, MS., 4; *Kimball's S. F. Directory*, 1850, 127. On the 24th of June, 1849, O. C. Wheeler organized the First Baptist church of S. F., and in July this society erected a commodious building on Washington st bet. Dupont and Stockton. Wheeler was the only minister not sent out by the missionary societies. His congregation, in October, offered him $10,000 for his services, which was accepted. In 1850 he visited Sacramento and Marysville organizing churches, assisted by Rev. Preveaux of the Boston Missionary society. *S. F. Cal. Courier*, Sept. 14, 1850. Rev. Capen took charge of the Sacramento church.

In July 1849, J. A. Benton arrived at S. F. and proceeded to Sacramento, where he arrived on the 14th, and found W. Roberts and Dr Deal attending to the religious affairs of the community. On the 16th of Sept. he organized the First Congregational church of Sacramento. Its first church edifice was erected in 1850, costing $9,000, and was consumed in the fire of 1854. On its ashes arose immediately a handsome church costing $42,000. This also was much injured by the flood of 1862, and repaired at considerable expense in 1863, in which year Benton was dismissed at his own request from the pastorate, and I. E. Dwinell of Salem, Mass., was installed in his place.

Roberts announced to 'a large and respectable' congregation at the cor of K and Third sts, in July 1849, that he had 2 churches under way for Cal. —one to be set up in S. F. and the other in Sac. In August, Rev. Cook, a baptist, arrived in Sac. and preached there. A sunday-school was begun by Prof. Shepherd and taken up by Benton, with the help of two women who formed a library. In October, Isaac Owens took charge of the M. E. society of Sac. and a small church building was sent out by the Baltimore conference, and occupied in Nov. *Morse's Sac. Directory*, 1853–4, p. 8; *S. F. Picayune*, Sept. 4, 1850.

Another minister arrived in July, in the person of Flavel S. Mines, from the diocese of N. Y., who first preached on the 8th of that month in S. F. On the 22d the church of the Holy Trinity was formed with 22 members. On the 29th wardens and vestrymen were elected, who invited Mines to be their rector. He was duly elected Aug. 6th. The following month a contract was let to erect a church, but the agreement was for some reason not carried out, and Mines was absent in N. Y. some months. On his return an iron building was erected on Pine st bet. Montgomery and Kearney, which was opened about Easter 1852. Mines died in Aug. of that year, and was buried beneath the church. He was succeeded by C. B. Wyatt, of N. Y., who arrived in Feb. 1853. The church building was enlarged this year. Wyatt was succeeded in 1856 by S. Thrall, of N. Y. diocese, who continued in charge until Aug. 1861. Wyatt returning at that time. The iron church was abandoned in Dec. 1866, when the congregation removed to a new church on Post and Powell sts. The lot on Pine st brought $70,500 and the lot on Post st cost $30,000. The corner-stone of the new church was laid by Bishop Kip.

During the summer of 1849, Mines visited Sacramento and organized an episcopal society, which Rev. Burnham, in Nov., went to preside over, dying in April 1850.

labors[81] from 1849 ot 1853.   Perfect tolerance was

In Sept. 1849 arrived Ver Mehr, missionary of the episcopal church, who first preached at the American hotel, afterward at the state marine hospital on Stockton st, and later at private residences. On the 30th of Dec. a plain building costing $8,000, was erected on the cor. of Powell and John sts., and called Grace chapel; and in 1850 a parish was regularly organized, E. Bryant and E. D. Turner being first wardens, Ver Mehr being called to the rectorship. The congregation increasing, a larger building was erected in 1851, paid for in part by the proceeds of musical entertainments given by the Sänger-bund and by Signora Elisa Biscaccianti, who sang the *Stabat Mater* of Rossini. Bishop Kip took charge in 1854. Christ church of the same denomination was organized in 1853 and occupied a room over the post-office; John Morgan, pastor. St John's church, 'episcopal,' was organized in Stockton, Aug. 25, 1850, O. Harriman holding the first service. In May 1850, James Woods, who arrived by sea around the Horn at the close of 1849, preached the dedication sermon of the first church erected in Stockton—presbyterian—which cost $14,000.

Among the arrivals of 1849 was Wm. Taylor, methodist, who established the First M. E. church of S. F. on Powell st, of which he was pastor, and in addition preached Sunday afternoons in the open air on Portsmouth square. His preaching was well attended, and his life was devoted to doing good. The first meeting of the S. F. Bible Society was held in 1849 in the M. E. church, Taylor, Ver Mehr, and Williams being elected vice-presidents. Methodist services were also held in 1851 in the recorder's court-room, city hall, by J. Baring of the methodist church south. D. W. Pollock of this church was preaching at Sacramento. A M. E. church was organized in Stockton in 1851, and a church building erected, and dedicated in July. The Cal. annual conference of that year instructed Taylor to form a M. E. society in the south part of the city, and a congregation was organized under the name of the Market st charge of the M. E. church, M.C . Briggs, pastor, which met in the school-house on Market st, and in Music hall on Bush st, until their church was erected on Folsom st in 1853, where they remained until 1862. In 1862–3 the present edifice was erected on Howard st bet 2d and 3d sts.

In 1850 a society of Unitarians held services in Robinson's and Edward's dramatic museum on California st. Joseph Harrington arrived in 1852 but died of Panamá fever. T. F. Gray succeeded him, but returned to Boston, and died in 1855. R. P. Cutler arrived in 1854 and remained until 1859. He was succeeded in 1860 by T. Starr King. On the 17th of July, 1853, a handsome church was erected on Stockton st bet Clay and Sacramento. This building was sold to the Zion M. E. church, colored, and a still handsomer one erected on Geary and Stockton 1862–3. That was also sold, and the church removed farther from the business portion of the city.

The Hebrew Congregation Emanu El was organized in 1851. Its present handsome synagogue was erected in 1866 at a cost of $185,000. There are two other congregations with fine edifices on Mason and Post streets.

Calvary Presbyterian church belongs to the early period, having been organized with 60 members in 1854. A church building was completed in 1865 on Bush st costing $70,000. The first pastor was William A. Scott.

[81] The first church organized at Nevada city was the M. E. society, in 1850, by Rev. Isaac Owen. A rude meeting-house was erected, and Rev. A. Bland settled to preach in it. In the autumn of the same year the M. E. church south was organized by the Revs Boring and Ballock. In 1851 a church edifice was erected for Rev. J. H. Warren. In the same year a catholic church was formed; and in 1855 an episcopal church by Rev. Hill. $35,000 contributed for religious purposes in 1855. Placerville's first church was constructed of poles, roofed with canvas. It was erected for Rev. Kalloch, baptist, father of the afterwards notorious I. S. Kalloch. The first

practised. In 1852 there were 37 churches or chapels in San Francisco. That a community in which being a religious man was considered "not exactly a crime, but only a misfortune," should freely lend its aid to the support of religion is not so paradoxical as it seems, since the fundamental idea of christianity itself is that of vicarious suffering for sin. The average San Franciscan was quite willing to pray by proxy, having his good dollars instead of his good deeds recorded in heaven. Hebrew, Greek, Chileno, Chinaman, Mormon, presbyterian, methodist, or universalist had equal liberty to find a road to heaven for himself. Taking everything into account, there were as many keeping in the straight and narrow way as could have been looked for, and after only forty years of growth the number and condition of religious societies throughout the state, and especially in the towns, will compare favorably with other parts of the United States. The pulpits of San Francisco have been filled, since the days of the argonauts,[82] when heroic men preached without pulpits, with the best talent of the country. Such men as W. Ingraham Kip, William A. Scott, T. Starr King, Joseph S. Alemany, Andrew L. Stone, Horatio Stebbins, and a long list of eloquent, scholarly, and zealous preachers have left their impress upon the thought of the community. There are to-day over a hundred places of regular worship in the city, and two hundred professional clergymen. The value of church property in 1850 was $267,800 for

permanent edifice for worship was erected in 1851 as a 'union church.' J. S. Deihl, methodist, preached most frequently. This not being large enough to accommodate the congregation on the occasion of the visit of Bishop Soule in 1852, services were held in a gambling saloon.

[82] California received six missionaries in 1853 by the ship *Trade Wind*, Weber master. They were S. B. Bell, J. G. Hall, E. B. Walworth, S. S. Harmon, James Pierpont and W. C. Pond. They preached and taught in interior towns, except Pond who was pastor of Bethany congregational church, Bartlett st, S. F. Harmon established a seminary at Washington Corners, Alameda co., and afterwards in Berkeley, where he died. Bell, presbyterian, was the first public preacher in Oakland—March 26, 1853— using the school-house on 4th and Clay for a church. Episcopal service had been held in private houses in 1852. The 1st Baptist church of Oakland was organized in 1854 by E. J. Willis, who became pastor,

the whole state; in 1860 it was $1,853,340; and in 1870 was $7,404,235. The increase in the last eighteen years is unknown, but must have been considerable each decade to keep pace with the growth of the state. Owing to the hold which the catholic church had in the beginning upon the resident population, and the influx of foreigners from catholic countries, this denomination for a long time was in the ascendency, a difference which the recent immigration from the eastern states is probably diminishing. But religious bigotry cannot flourish in a city or state where no church monopolizes the wealth or the intelligence of either, and where in all public affairs the coin—the true test—of one is as good as that of another.[88]

[88] One of the most popular and justly esteemed of divines was the late Thomas Starr King, a native of N. Y. city, where he was born Dec. 17, 1824. After receiving his education at various schools, among others the Bunker Hill grammar school at Charlestown, Mass, and the Winthrop school, he became himself a teacher, and at the age of twenty entered upon his ministry, being called in 1846 to the pastorate of the first universalist society at Charlestown, and in 1848 to that of the Hollis st society in Boston. Removing in 1860 to S. F., where he had accepted a call to the unitarian church, the good work he did in upholding the union cause, at a time when the elements of secession were vigorously at work, cannot be overestimated. To the excessive strain on his system, mainly caused by this work, was due his decease on the 4th of March, 1864.

Foremost among those who have rendered good service to the cause of education should be mentioned the two Le Contes, of whom John, the elder, was born on their father's plantation in Liberty co., Ga, Dec. 4, 1818. Completing his education at the university of Ga, and the college of physicians and surgeons, N. Y., in 1842 he began to practise his profession in Savannah, though devoting more of his time to the preparation of medical and other scientific treatises, reviews, and lectures. After holding professorships in eastern colleges, being meanwhile appointed a member of several scientific associations, in 1868 he accepted the chair of physics and industrial mechanics in the university of Cal., of which in 1876 he was elected president. Joseph, whose birthplace was also the Ga plantation, and whose birthday was Feb. 26, 1823, after attending the same institutions as his brother, studied under Agassiz, and graduated at the Lawrence scientific school. In 1852 he was appointed to the chair of natural science in Oglethorpe university; in 1853 to that of geology and natural history in the university of Ga; in 1857 to the professorship of geology and chemistry in the S. C. college; and in 1868 to that of geology and natural philosophy in the university of Cal. He is also the author of many scientific and philosophical treatises, and a member of most of the societies in which his brother's name is enrolled.

Among those who according to their means have contributed most liberally to the cause of religion, education, and charity was the late Nathaniel Gray, a native of Pelham, Mass, who in 1850 established in San Francisco a branch house in connection with an eastern firm of undertakers. To the S. F. theological seminary, the Mills seminary, the hospital for children and training school for nurses, and to other institutions, he contributed largely of his means, while his private benefactions were no less munificent.

Dr William Fletcher McNutt, long recognized as one of the foremost of the medical profession, is a native of Truro, Nova Scotia, where he was born March 29, 1839. Receiving a thorough medical education, he was appointed assistant surgeon in the U. S. navy, and served through a portion of the war. Then after further study and practice he came to San Francisco in the spring of 1868, and there after a hard struggle gradually won his way, being admitted in 1870 a partner of R. T. Maxwell. The connection lasted four years, after which he built up for himself a large and lucrative practice. He has been a frequent contributor to medical literature, and of special value are his reports to the California state medical society.

Dr Beverley Cole, born at Manchester, Va, Aug. 12, 1829, after graduating at the Delaware college, and the Jefferson medical college, Pa, came to San Francisco in 1852, by way of Panamá, suffering many hardships in his journey across the Isthmus. For many years he has been acknowledged as one of the leading physicians in the Pacific coast metropolis.

Among our leading medical practitioners was also the late Dr Washington Michael Ryer, a native of N. Y. city, where he was born July 24, 1881. After studying medicine at St Louis and New York, he began to practise in the latter city, and afterward served as a staff surgeon in the Mexican war. On reaching Cal. he practised his profession in Stockton and its neighborhood for a number of years. By judicious investments in land, rather than by the gains of his profession, he grew wealthy, among his possessions being Ryer island in the Sacramento river, which he reclaimed with infinite labor and expense.

One of the leading physicians of Los Angeles was Dr William F. Edgar, a Kentuckian by birth, who in 1849 was appointed assistant surgeon in the U. S. army. After serving until 1871, he settled in that city, where for five years he practised his profession, and of which since 1882 he has been a permanent resident. He is one of those who helped to organize the first medical society of Los Angeles, and is or has been connected with several of its leading enterprises and associations.

Among the foremost medical practitioners and statesmen of northern California is Daniel Ream, who was born near Hagerstown, Md, in 1830, removing with his family in early boyhood to Ill., and later to Iowa, where at the age of eighteen he began to practise. In 1852 he came to Cal., and in 1860 settled at Yreka, where he has ever since resided. After serving as coroner and sheriff of Siskiyou co., in 1877 he was elected state senator, and rendered good service during his term, especially as chairman of the committee on hospitals.

Prominent among the members of the legal profession, and at its head in his special department as a patent lawyer, is Milton A. Wheaton, a native of N. Y. state, but of New England ancestry. At twelve years of age, having meanwhile attended the district school in winter and worked in the harvest fields in summer, he found occupation with a farmer, receiving for his six months' work $10 and his board. From his own earnings on farm and in factory he paid for his education in after years, and in 1853 came to Cal. to earn the means to complete it. Two years later he entered the law-office of Carter & Hartley of Sacramento, and early in 1857, being then admitted to the bar, began to practise at Suisun. In 1866 he removed to S. F., and soon afterward turned his attention to patent law, his ability and zeal quickly winning so wide a reputation that he was employed in all the leading patent cases on this coast and in not a few in the eastern states. Mr Wheaton is an odd-fellow, a master mason, and a knight of the Cal. commandry. He has been twice married and has three children, his present wife being a native Californian, and of musical and artistic tastes.

Among our literary men, though for the time being a resident of N. Y., is Clay M. Greene, a native of S. F., where he was born March 12, 1850. After receiving his education at the City college, S. F., the Santa Clara college, and the university of Cal., he became a member of the old board of brokers, in which business he remained until 1879, when he adopted literature as a profession, and especially dramatic literature, among his plays being 'Struck

Oil,' 'Chispa,' 'Hans the Boatman,' and others that have been most favorably received.

As one of our most prominent architects should be mentioned Peter J. Barber, who settling at Santa Bárbara in 1869, has planned most of the handsome buildings that have been erected there within recent years. A native of Nelson, Ohio, Mr Barber came to this coast in 1852, three years later starting in business in San Francisco as a contractor and builder. In 1880 he was elected mayor of Santa Bárbara, in which capacity he rendered excellent service.

Another architect and builder worthy of note is Richard Robert Rubenstein, who was born in 1850 at Stetten, Prussia, and coming to this country at an early age has ever since followed this calling, building in 1888 26 residences in the city of Stockton. In 1878 he was elected public administrator, in 1885, and again in 1887, a member of the city council, and in 1888 to the mayoralty of Stockton.

CHAPTER XXV.

RECENT EVENTS.

1889-1890.

LEGISLATION—THE JUDICIARY—POLICE AND CRIME—GOVERNOR WATER-
MAN'S ADMINISTRATION—PUBLIC IMPROVEMENTS—STATE TEXT-BOOKS—
FARMING—IRRIGATION—FRUIT-RAISING AND FRUIT SHIPMENTS—WINE-
MAKING—RAISINS—STOCK-RAISING—THE IRON-MOULDERS' STRIKE—SHIP-
BUILDING—RAILROAD INDEBTEDNESS—MINING—COMMERCE AND BANK-
ING—REAL ESTATE—PROGRESS AND PROSPECTS.

IT has been remarked that a nation or state is
never so well governed as when there is little that is
worthy of record in its political annals. If such be
the case, then for the last year or two, at least, should
California have been one of the best governed countries on earth. In the thirty-eighth session of the
legislature [1] numerous measures were enacted. Among

---

[1] Members of the senate during that session: F. McGowan, Humboldt and
Del Norte counties; J. M. Briceland, Trinity, Siskiyou, and Shasta; M. H.
Mead, Modoc, Lassen, Plumas, and Sierra; A. F. Jones, Butte; E. M. Pres-
ton, Nevada; A. Yell, Mendocino and Lake; T. Fraser, Placer and El
Dorado; J. Boggs, Colusa and Tehama; F. S. Sprague, Yolo and Napa; E. C.
Hinshaw, Sonoma; G. J. Campbell, Solano; F. H. Greely, Yuba and Sutter;
F. R. Dray, Sacramento; A. Caminetti, Amador and Calaveras; F. C. De
Long, Marin and Contra Costa; F. J. Moffit, W. E. Dargie, and M. W. Dixon,
Alameda; J. W. Welch, T. J. Pinder, W. O. Banks, J. N. E. Wilson, W. H.
Williams, P. J. Murphy, J. E. Britt, T. H. McDonald, J. E. Hamill, and
J. R. Spellacy, San Francisco; A. J. Meany, Merced, Stanislaus, and Tuol-
umne; A. W. Crandall and E. B. Conklin, Santa Clara; J. D. Byrnes, San
Mateo and Santa Cruz; G. G. Goucher, Alpine, Mariposa, Mono, and Fresno;
T. Flint, Jr, Monterey and San Benito; J. Roth, Inyo, Tulare, and Kern;
E. H. Heacock, San Luis Obispo, Santa Barbara, and Ventura; S. M. White
and J. E. McComas, Los Angeles; and W. W. Bowers, San Bernardino and
San Diego. President pro tem., S. M. White; sec., G. W. Peckham; asst
secs, J. J. McCarthy and J. H. Corcoran; sergt-at-arms, G. W. Faylor; asst
sergt-at-arms, H. M. Levy; minute clerk, W. E. Bidwell; journal clerk, J.
A. Galland; enrolling clerk, T. W. O'Niel; engrossing clerk, H. I. Ward.
   Members of the assembly: J. McVay, Del Norte and Siskiyou; J. G.
Murray and G. Williams, Humboldt; T. W. H. Shanahan, Trinity and Shasta;

the more important were acts amending and supplementing the irrigation act of 1887; one establishing a school of industry; one establishing a reform school; certain amendments to the civil code of procedure; and the usual appropriations for public improvements, institutions, and deficiencies, not forgetting the appropriations for the pay and expenses of the legislature.
Among the members of the judiciary some changes had taken place, W. H. Beatty being chief justice, with J. D. Thornton, J. D. Works,[2] J. R. Sharpstein,

J. J. Reavis, Modoc and Lassen; H. K. Turner, Plumas and Sierra; W. P. Mathews, Tehama; C. H. Porter and L. Burwell, Butte; J. C. Campbell, Colusa; J. H. Seawell, Mendocino; C. M. Crawford, Lake; D. A. Ostrom, Sutter and Yuba; J. Sims and J. I. Sykes, Nevada; J. Davis, Placer; H. Mahler, El Dorado; W. M. Petrie, E. C. Hart, and L. H. Fassett, Sacramento; L. B. Adams, Yolo; F. L. Coombs, Napa; F. B. Mulgrew, J. W. Ragsdale, and R. Howe, Sonoma; J. A. Mallaney and J. F. Brown, Solano; J. W. Atherton, Marin; T. Mulvey, J. D. Long, T. J. Brannan, J. Staude, W. E. Dinan, E. J. Reynolds, H. H. Dobbin, C. H. Kiernan, T. Searey, D. S. Regan, J. McCarthy, E. Murray, H. C. Dibble, E. S. Salomon, L. L. Ewing, H. M. Black, H. M. Brickwedel, J. Reavey, G. W. Burnett, and T. C. Maher, San Francisco; L. J. Franks, San Mateo; J. A. Hall, Santa Cruz; J. McKeown, W. Simpson, M. D. Hyde, E. S. Culver, M. C. Chapman, and C. O. Alexander, Alameda; H. Hook, Contra Costa; R. S. Johnson and J. McMullin, San Joaquin; C. T. La Grave, Amador; J. Gardner, Calaveras; L. R. Tulloch, Tuolumne; P. Hersey, J. R. Lowe, and L. A. Whitehurst, Santa Clara; V. E. Bangs, Stanislaus; W. M. Rundell, Merced and Mariposa; E. C. Tully, San Benito; T. Renison, Monterey; E. H. Tucker, Fresno; G. S. Berry, Tulare; C. Coleman, Alpine, Mono, and Inyo; D. W. James, San Luis Obispo; C. A. Storke, Santa Barbara; G. W. Wear, Kern and Ventura; J. R. Brierly, J. M. Damron, and E. E. Edwards, Los Angeles; E. W. Holmes, San Bernardino; and N. A. Young, San Diego. Speaker, R. Howe; chief clerk, E. E. Leake; asst clerks, M. Yager and H. Hart; sergt-at-arms, J. J. Driscoll; asst sergt-at-arms, F. Anaya; minute clerk, B. Pendegast; journal clerk, C. Spelling; engrossing clerk, G. Sheehy. *Stat. of Cal.* 1889, xxvi.–xxviii.
Among statesmen and politicians of whom only passing mention has yet been made is Timothy Guy Phelps, a native of N. Y. state, where he was born Dec. 20, 1824, and a pioneer of 1849, landing in S. F. in Dec. of that year. After a brief but successful business career, in 1853 he disposed of his interests and invested his funds in real estate. In 1856 he was elected to the state legislature on the first republican ticket issued in Cal., and was twice afterward chosen for the state senate. In 1869 he was appointed collector of customs for the port of S. F., which position he held for several years, with credit to himself and satisfaction to the public.
[2] John Downey Works, in 1886 elected judge of the superior court for San Diego co., is a native of Ind., his youth being passed on a farm until the outbreak of the war, when at 17 he joined a cavalry regiment, in which he served for two years, being present at Nashville and at the capture of Mobile. In 1868 he succeeded to his father's practice, in his native state, removing to San Diego in 1883 on account of failing health. His work on Indiana practice, pleadings, and forms and his treatise on the removal of causes from state to federal courts are among our standard law-books.

J. Temple, Van R. Paterson, and T. B. McFarland
as associate judges.   One of the more prominent
cases that occupied the attention of the courts was
the suit of the Spring Valley company[3] against the
city of San Francisco, caused by an ordinance which
passed the board of supervisors in February 1889,
reducing the established water rates, which reduction
the company refused to accept.   By the supreme court
the ordinance was declared invalid.   In our superior
courts, either through pressure of business or for other
reasons, the wheels of justice dragged somewhat
slowly, cases taken on appeal being delayed for a year
or more before a decision was pronounced.

Attention has often been called to the smallness
and inefficiency of our police system, declared by the

James A. Waymire, who was born on the site of the present city of St
Joseph, Mo., Dec. 9, 1842, came to this coast when ten years of age, living
with his grandfather and attending school near Roseburg, in the Umpqua
valley, Or.   Beginning life as a school-teacher, in 1861 he enlisted in the 1st
Or. cavalry, and serving with distinction in the Indian campaigns of 1863-4,
was appointed lieutenant.   Some four years later he accepted a commission
in the regular army, but in 1870 was admitted to the Or. bar and began to
practise law, first at Salem and later in San Francisco, meanwhile acting as
phonographic reporter for the supreme court of Cal.   He rose rapidly in his
profession, was employed in many important cases, and in 1881 became a
judge of the superior court.   Resuming practice at the close of his term, he
has been for may years acknowleged as one of the leaders of the bar.

Another member of the Cal. judiciary was Charles Fayette Lott, whose
second term as judge of the second, formerly the ninth, judicial district
ended in 1876, and whose strict impartiality and sound and lucid interpretation of the law gained for him universal respect.   Of English ancestry, and a
native of Pemberton, N. J., where he was born on the 1st of July, 1824,
after completing his education at the St Louis university and studying law
at Quincy, Ill., Mr Lott was called to the bar of that state in 1848, crossing
the plains to Cal. in the following year.   In 1851 he was elected to the state
senate, and declining a renomination, practised his profession, in partnership
with W. T. Sexton, first at Hamilton, then at Bidwell bar, and later at
Oroville, Butte co.   In 1859 he was elected chairman of the democratic county
committee, which position, though a thoroughly union democrat, he held
throughout the civil war.   Still one of the leading practitioners in his section of the state, he is also largely interested in lands and mines in Butte
and Plumas cos.

[3] The superintendent of the co. is Charles Elliott, who was also supt of the
Bensley co., incorporated in 1857, and in 1865 merged in the Spring Valley
co.   A native of Bath, Me, he came to Cal. in 1851, and after passing three
years in Or., settled in the former state, of which he has ever since been a
resident.

In connection with the co. should also be mentioned its former supt, W.
H. Lawrence, who was born in New York in 1840, and after graduating at
the Fairfield seminary, came to Cal. in 1859, and was employed in making
surveys for the co.   From 1880 to 1887 he was a supervisor of San Mateo co.

chief of police himself to be in San Francisco, in proportion to its size, the smallest and most inefficient of any city in the world. The result is that crime and 'hoodlumism' are still rampant in the metropolis, and almost daily is heard in her streets the sickening iteration of the newsboy's cry: "All about the murder and suicide." In the country the so-called tramp nuisance is no less severely felt, and from all portions of the state come urgent requests that measures be taken for its abolition. Every year great damage has been done by this element through the destruction of property by incendiarism, and already it has increased so largely as to be almost beyond control. No action was taken in the matter by the legislature, though in his biennial message for 1889 the governor urged upon that body the adoption of effective remedies.

Though not marked by any special feature, the administration of Governor Waterman gave general satisfaction to the public, and in his message are many excellent suggestions and remarks. On the question of appropriations he says, for instance: "Legislatures are too apt to be radical and inconsistent rather than firm and conservative. They are too prone to neglect the vital interests of the state and raise the cry of retrenchment and economy. This is no argument; it is simply demagogy." While recommending that provision be made for necessary improvements with unsparing hand, he also recommends the abolition of all needless bureaus and offices, and especially of such as have outlived their usefulness.

Among other public improvements it may be mentioned that in Santa Clara county an asylum for the chronic insane was partially completed and opened for the reception of patients.[4] At the state prison at San Quentin an appropriation was made for the purchase of additional machinery, together with an extra

---

[4] At the Napa asylum the patients are encouraged to work, with excellent results to themselves and the institution. For the year ending June 30, 1888, there were produced 130 tons of vegetables, 222 of hay, and 28 of fruit. *Biennial Message of Gov. R. W. Waterman*, 1889, 18.

building for the manufacture of grain-bags and other jute fabrics; but this expense was obviated by running the present machinery with relays of prisoners every hour in the twenty-four. While it does not appear by what right the state thus tampers with the health of prisoners, the making of jute goods is about the least objectionable of penal occupations, since there is but one jute factory in the state, and in that one Chinamen are almost exclusively employed.

A feature in educational matters within recent years was the act of 1885 providing for the preparation of a series of state text-books, of which some four years later nearly half a million had been sold. It was claimed that the state would be benefited by having a stable and uniform system of school-books, avoiding the constant changes that occured in previous years through the caprice or interest of boards and teachers. By a statute of 1889 a tax was levied of one cent on each one hundred dollars of taxable property for the support of the university of California. The transfer to this institution of the Lick observatory in 1888 has given to it the most powerful telescope in the world, with some of the best appliances for observing and recording the movements of the heavenly bodies. In connection with schools it may here be remarked that the school-lands of California are sold at the unreasonably low price of $1.25 an acre. In few other sections of the union is the value of such lands thus rated, the price in Minnesota being $5 to $6, in Nebraska $7, and in Colorado $3 to $50 an acre. Of our school-lands there were sold during the six years ending with August 1, 1888, nearly 1,000,000 acres, realizing probably but a small portion of their intrinsic value.

In industrial and commercial circles the year 1889 was in the main a prosperous season. To the farmers and fruit-growers of California, it was one of unusual prosperity, the product in many departments being the largest yet recorded, while never before were the shipments east of fresh and canned fruits and vegetables on so large a scale. While it cannot be denied that California first attained to prominence by reason of her mineral wealth, it is no less certain that the position which she holds to-day is due to her agricultural resources, and that except for the potentialities of her soil, the state would never have progressed very far beyond the position occupied during the first decade of her existence. True, there have been many vicissitudes, with occasional seasons of positive disaster; but since the first timid and tentative efforts, well-nigh forty years ago, progress has been steadily onward, until in 1889 California ranked second among the wheat-growing states, the product only of Minnesota being slightly in excess. To produce her enormous crop, variously estimated at from 44,000,000 to 50,000,000 bushels,[5] required, as I have said, about 3,250,000 acres, and if for that crop, delivered at tidewater, our farmers received only $30,000,000, it must, with improved and cheaper methods of working, have been fairly remunerative, even at the low prices then prevailing of $1.20 to $1.30 a cental. To any large product of other cereals, California makes no pretentions as compared with the older sections of the union; but in the yield of fresh and dried fruits, and especially of oranges, grapes, and raisins, in the production of wine and honey, she stands without a rival among all the sisterhood of states.

For the year 1890 the outlook was less promising, on account of excessive rains, and in the northern counties of snow-storms and the severity of the winter weather. For the season of 1889–90 there fell in San Francisco up to the 18th of April, 1890, nearly 43 inches of rain. At some other points there was a

[5] In *The Annual Statistician and Economist*, 1890, p. 196, the yield of Cal. for 1889, as given in the *Rept of the Dept of Agric.*, is stated at 43,781,000 bushels, against 45,456,000 for Minnesota. Other estimates, as mentioned elsewhere, place the product of the former state at 50,000,000, which would make Cal. first on the list.

still greater precipitation, the heaviest being at Bowlder creek, where were 122 inches, and next came Delta with 115 inches. Bridges and roads were washed away, railroads blockaded for days or weeks at a time, and in places the floods were hardly less disastrous than those of 1861–2, though in the recent winter Sacramento was not, as before, the principal sufferer. While in some portions of the state, on account of excessive moisture, the ground could not be ploughed in time to plant a crop, in others an abundant harvest was insured, and if the floods of the past year should be succeeded, as is often the case, by a year of drought, the surface has become so thoroughly soaked that a very few inches of rain would suffice.

It connection with agriculture it may here be remarked that while less than ten per cent of our population are engaged in that pursuit, and less than five per cent are owners of farms, the percentage of large farms, say of from 500 to 1,000 acres, is greater than in any section of the union, with nearly 3,000 farms of larger area.[6]

[6] One of our most prominent agriculturists is John Bidwell, who owns one of the largest tracts in Butte co., on the eastern bank of the Sacramento river. Here he raises several thousand tons a year of wheat, with vast bands of cattle, horses, and sheep. On his property is an orchard and vineyard, and great care has been taken to beautify the grounds about his residence. To him the town of Chico is largely indebted for its homelike and prosperous appearance. Mr Bidwell came to Cal. in 1841, and was one of the first to cross the plains from the Missouri river.

Among other prominent agriculturists of whom no special mention has yet been made is Martin Murphy, who was born in 1807 at Balnamough, Wexford co., Ireland, his ancestry being traced back to the kings of Leinster. In 1820 he took ship for Canada, where his father and other members of the family had for some years resided, at Frampton, near Quebec. In 1842 he removed to English grove, near St Joseph, Mo. In 1844 he crossed the plains to California, in company with his father's family and others, including his wife, née Mary Bulger, and their four surviving children. In the following year he purchased two square leagues of land on the Mocosumne, now the Cosumnes river, and at his homestead was inaugurated the Bear Flag revolution. In 1849 he disposed of this tract and purchased another, now known as the Bay View farm, in Santa Clara co., buying additional tracts, together with city property in San José, as means and opportunity offered. A most hospitable and charitable man, giving freely to the cause of education and of the church, he is one of the most respected citizens of his adopted co. and state. On the 20th of October, 1884, he passed away peacefully and almost painlessly in the seventy-eighth year of his age.

No less respected are his sons, Bernard D. and James T. Murphy, his brother, General Patrick W. Murphy, thrice a member of the legislature, and

Of irrigation mention has several times been made
in this and the preceding volumes of my work; for

other members of the family. Bernard is a graduate of Santa Clara college,
and after studying law and being admitted to practise at the bar, was required, on the decease of his brother, to take charge of his father's estate.
In 1870 he was chosen mayor of San José, and in 1877, and again in 1883, was
elected to the state senate. In 1869 he married Miss L. McGeoghenan, a
a native of N. Y., who is most highly esteemed in the social circles of San
José.

Worthy of mention also among our leading agriculturists is John
Theophil Strentzel, a native of Poland, where he was born Nov. 29, 1813.
He came to New Orleans in 1840, and after some changes of residence and
business, to Cal. by way of the plains in 1849–50, and established a ferry,
hotel, and general merchandise store at La Grange. Later he engaged in
farming and stock-raising on the Merced river, near Snelling's, afterward
settling on his present homestead, near Martinez, where he is president of
the Grangers' Business association and of the Gas and Electric Light co.

To the commerce of San Francisco it is said that J. P. Hale has contributed more than $1,000,000 by drawing from that city all the supplies for his
orchilla fields and other enterprises. Coming to this coast in 1852, after following various occupations he engaged in the orchilla business in Lower Cal.,
and became the owner of 6,500 sq. miles fronting on the Pacific, much of it
being used for stock-raising. He made his home in S. F., where, as elsewhere in Cal., he is also a large owner of real estate.

A leading agriculturist and stock-raiser in Siskiyou co., and also one of
our pioneers, was the late John B. Rohrer, a native of Alsace, where he was
born in 1830, and who crossed the plains to Cal. in 1850, and three years
later took up land and built the first house in little Shasta valley. In
1872 he married Miss Elizabeth Jane de Long, five children, all of them
living, being the result of this union. His decease occurred Sept. 10,
1886.

In the Salinas valley one of the largest agriculturists and stock-raisers is
Jesse D. Carr, who was born in Gallatin, Tenn., June 10, 1814, his education
being obtained in a country school. At the age of 16 he commenced work
in a business house at Nashville, going from there to Memphis, and thence
in 1843 to N. O., spending also a couple of years in north Mexico. In 1849
he came to Cal. by way of the Isthmus, and entered the custom-house, where
he remained until 1850. In 1853 he engaged in farming and stock-raising,
removing to the Salinas valley in 1859, which has ever since been his home.
Mr Carr engaged in staging in 1866, carrying the mails for $190,000 a year,
afterward increased to $218,000, carrying on this business successfully for a
number of years, besides speculating in land. In 1873 he established a bank
at Salinas, becoming its president; also being connected with the bank of
Hollister. Mr Carr was elected to the legislature in 1850, and was also a
supervisor of Santa Cruz co.

Hugh M. La Rue, born in Ky Aug. 12, 1830, was of French ancestors,
came to Cal. in 1849, and began mining; afterward he engaged in farming,
which he has followed ever since. La Rue was elected sheriff in 1873, and
was also elected to the legislature from Yolo co., and chosen a member of the
state board of agriculture in 1868, and again in 1878.

Worthy of note, not only as a pioneer, but as one of the largest agriculturists and stock-raisers in Tehama co., is Henry Clay Wilson, a native of
Floyd co., Ky, where he was born Aug. 19, 1827. His youth was passed in
Ill., and removing thence in 1842 to Tex., where he was one of the Texan
rangers, in Apl 1849 he came to Cal. with $37 in his pocket. On his farm
of 12,000 acres near the town of Corning, he raised wheat, cattle, sheep, and
other live-stock, and many kinds of fruit. In Grant co., Or., he also became
owner of some 40,000 acres, but his home, since 1849, has always been in this
state.

the history of irrigation in this state begins with the history of the state itself. Much as had been already accomplished, it is probable that in 1889 more progress was made than in any previous year, and it was even claimed that when the projects inaugurated in that year shall have been carried to completion, the irrigable area of California will have been doubled. Until the passage of the Wright law, our larger irrigation enterprises were in the hands of capitalists, who, owning vast areas of unoccupied lands, thus hoped to dispose of them to advantage. By the provisions of this act, the lands to be watered from a given source might be included in an irrigation district, when so determined by a majority of the freeholders, the cost to be borne in equal proportions by those who were benefited. The district formed and the cost determined, an election could be held to decide as to the issue of bonds to cover the proposed indebtedness, the principal and interest to be paid from an assessment on the real property of the district, which assessment should form a lien on the property assessed. After some opposition and several lawsuits on the part of those who would neither irrigate their own lands nor assist their neighbors to do so, the courts sustained the legality of the law and of the proceedings taken under it in the several districts. As the result, 26 districts had been formed up to the close of 1889, including more than 2,500,000 acres of land,[7] and thus the long-vexed question of irrigation was at length in a fair way to be solved.

The damage caused to our agricultural interests by the floods of 1889–90 would, it was hoped, be partially offset by an abundant fruit-crop, for which fairly re-

Columbus Hurd, a native of Helena, Ark., where he was born Jan. 21, 1835, became a permanent resident of this state in 1879, after two previous visits caused by the failing health of his wife. In 1880 he settled in the neighborhood of Stockton, purchased land, and engaged in wheat-growing on a large scale. He became director in the Stockton Savings bank, and connected with other prominent institutions; he is acknowledged as one of the most public-spirited men in that section of the state.

[7] For names of districts, with locations and areas, see S. F. *Chron.*, Dec. 29, 1889.

munerative prices were anticipated in eastern markets. It was not until shipments by rail became possible that fruit-growing in California assumed any great importance. Within recent years the progress made in this department is on an enormous scale, shipments of fresh fruits to eastern points increasing from 1,832,310 pounds in 1871 to 53,741,670 pounds in 1888; of canned fruits from 182,090 pounds in 1872 to 39,281,- 340 pounds in 1888; of dried fruits from 548,227 in 1875 to 19,759,140 pounds in 1888 ; and of raisins from 220 pounds in 1874 to 16,884,570 pounds in 1888. Meanwhile freights had been reduced from 3.38 to 1.37 cents per pound on fresh fruits, from 3.51 to .94 on canned fruits, from 2.50 to 1.20 on dried fruits, and from 2.81 to about 1.25 cents on raisins. To these reductions is mainly due the phenomenal increase in this branch of industry, and with the further reductions that must follow the advent of competing lines, still greater development may be reasonably expected. In 1889 the net returns of green fruits shipped to the east were about 2.25 cents per pound, with about the same average for the three preceding years, thus showing that eastern markets have not as yet been overstocked. Says the *New York Sun* of September 22, 1889 : "The California fruit trade in this city has increased over tenfold in three years, and the product of the Pacific slope orchards and vineyards is now competing with the domestic fruit product and beating it out of its boots, so to speak, in spite of the 3,000 miles of disadvantage under which Californians labor in comparison with local growers. There is every indication besides that the California fruit business here is comparatively but in its infancy, and that its future growth, so far as bulk of importations is concerned, will be as startling as that of the last three years." This would appear the more probable when it is considered that the yield of grain-lands averages less than $20 an acre, while that of fruit-lands is more than $100, even allowing for trees not yet in bearing.

Of viticulture and the making of wine a description
has been given in a previous chapter of this volume.
It remains only to be said that with greater attention
to treatment, clarification, blending, storage, and bot-
tling, the quality, if not the price, of California wines
is being constantly improved.   According to the tables
furnished by A. Haraszthy, in 1888 the president of
the board of state viticultural commissioners, the
average price of California wines between 1875 and
1887 was 55.7 cents per gallon, the highest being 62
cents in 1876, and the lowest 45 cents in 1887, the
low valuation of the latter year being due to over-
production and to the fact that the wine trade was
largely controlled by middlemen.   In the earlier years
of this industry, all that was thought necessary was
to plant and harvest a vineyard without regard to
location or constituents of soil, to press out the
grapes, and allow the juice to remain in a barrel,
without regard to fermentation or other methods.
But that day has long gone by, and well that it is so
for the reputation of our western vintages, since there
is perhaps no branch of industry that requires such
technical knowledge, such care and delicacy in handling, as the production of a sound and palatable wine.
In 1869 there was a large increase in the eastern
demand for California wines, while several hundred
thousand gallons of wine and brandy were shipped to
England, to which country, some two years before, a
few small shipments had been forwarded by way of
experiment.   While, during the earlier weeks of the
season of 1889, the prices paid for wine grapes were
exceedingly low, later a series of storms, destroying a
large portion of the crops, caused an advance of more
than fifty per cent, and at the close of the season left
our grape-growers masters of the situation.   A gratifying feature was the medals and encomiums bestowed
at the Paris exposition of that year,[8] fully attesting

[8] Including four gold, eleven silver, and twelve bronze medals, with a
number of honorable mentions.

the recognition which our vintages have earned among the most experienced of connoisseurs.[9]

[9] One of our leading viticulturists was the late Henry M. Naglee, who was born in 1815, in Tenn., was cadet at West Point, served in the Mexican war and in several Indian skirmishes, after which he engaged in banking in S. F. He served in the civil war. In 1852 Gen. Naglee had purchased 150 acres of land, and afterward much larger tracts near San José and elsewhere, and in 1865 he made that city his home. Two daughters were the result of a marriage made in 1865. Visiting Europe, he became interested in the study of choice wines and brandies, and on his return planted a vineyard, and entered upon the manufacture of brandy, which was continued till his death. Gen. Naglee took great pleasure in his two daughters, and withheld no effort or means to give them that culture which they so eminently possess.

At the head of our producers in the line of sparkling wines is Arpad Haraszthy, a son of the late Col Agoston Haraszthy, who aided largely in hte development of California viticulture. Born in southern Hungary June 28, 1840, he came with his family to this state in 1851, but in the same year went east to receive his education, returning in 1862, after studying carefully in France the manufacture and treatment of champagnes. Taking charge of his father's cellars at Sonoma, he gradually extended the business, purchasing in 1879 that of Landsberger & Co., and establishing the present firm of Haraszthy & Co. Between 1878 and 1886 he was president of the State Vinicultural society, and supported by our leading wine-makers defeated the proposed free-trade treaty with France. In 1880 he was elected president of the board of State Viticultural commissioners, composed of practical viticulturists from all portions of the state.

Deserving of mention also is A. T. Hatch, a native of Ind., where he was born Jan. 31, 1837. In 1857 he came to Cal. After following a variety of occupations, he planted a small vineyard and almond grove near Suisun, afterward purchasing land in other localities, as means and opportunity offered, and gradually extending his operations until in his own line of business he is to-day one of the richest and most successful men in the state.

E. Bouton, a native of New York, was a son of Russel Bouton, who served in the U. S. army during the war of 1812, and a grandson of Daniel Bouton of the revolutionary army. At the outbreak of the civil was he was engaged in a commission-business at Chicago, Ill. In the latter part of 1861, under the direction of Gov. Yates of Illinois, he organized a battery of light artillery and was promoted for gallant service at Harrisonburg, Guntown, and Shiloh. In 1868 he came to Los Angeles, and until 1880 was engaged in sheep-raising, afterward becoming largely interested in the Nadeau vineyard tract, containing 3,250 acres. He also purchased the Seritas rancho of 7,136 acres. General Bouton married in 1859 Miss Margaret Fox.

To no one is San Diego more indebted for her marvellous development than to A. E. Horton, who has done perhaps more than any other man to make that city what it is to day, one of the most prosperous on the Pacific coast. A native of Conn., where he was born on the 24th of October, 1813, when two years of age he went with his family to New York, where he remained until reaching his majority. The years between 1834 and 1851 were passed in Wis., where he built up the town of Hortonville, and at the latter date he paid his first visit to Cal., returning east in 1856. In 1861 we find him in San Francisco, where, after an absence of two years in Brit. Col., he opened a store on Market st. In 1867 he removed to San Diego and purchased from 800 to 900 acres in what was afterward known as New Town, at the low rate of 26 cents an acre. Then he went to work to build a city. First of all he returned to S. F., and opening an office on Montgomery st, began to make known the merits of his prospective metropolis. He then began the building of a wharf, which was completed in three months, at a cost of $45,000. In 1868-9 he erected several large buildings, including the city

From 6,000 boxes in 1873 the raisin pack of California increased to 900,000 boxes in 1889, the largest yet recorded, except for the preceding year, although a loss of at least 250,000 boxes was caused by heavy autumnal rains. Prices were satisfactory, and for certain choice brands the demand in eastern markets was greater than the supply. Of prunes about 15,-000,000 pounds were produced, the fruit being large, of excellent quality, and even at the low prices prevailing netting a fair profit to producers. Of honey the product was estimated at 2,200,000 pounds, of walnuts 1,500,000, and of almonds 500,000. During the year 1889 nearly 1,800 car-loads of dried fruits, 900 of raisins, and 60 of honey [10] were shipped to eastern markets, growers and dealers being fairly satisfied, and with excellent prospects for the following season.

To stock-raisers the floods and snow-storms of the past winter were even more disastrous than to agriculturists, the loss of cattle and sheep being in some of the northern counties from one-third to one-half, and in some localities more than three-fourths of the total. Nevertheless at the beginning of 1890 California ranked high among the states as to the numbers and value of her live-stock, with over 4,000,000 of sheep, worth $8,400,000, in this department being second only to Texas, with nearly 1,000,000 oxen, milch cows, and other cattle, valued at more than $19,000,000,

hall, Horton hall, and the hotel called the Horton house, the last being completed and furnished in nine months, at a cost of $150,000. In 1870 New Town had a population of about 1,000; but it was not until some years later that it began to progress rapidly, under Mr Horton's energetic management. He secured for it the transfer of the post-office, of Wells Fargo's agency, and of the court-house, all by judicious donations of land, and to churches of several denominations presented building lots and subscribed toward a building fund. In all, he expended more than $700,000 in aiding to build up the city, in which he is recognized as one of the most successful and enterprising citizens. In 1861 Mr Horton married Miss Sarah Babe, a native of New Jersey. Though never an office-seeker, he has taken his full share in political as in business affairs, and after retiring from active life, passed in well-earned repose the declining years of a useful and beneficent career.

[10] For raisins, prunes, dried fruit, walnuts, almonds, and honey, it is estimated that in 1889 at least $6,000,000 passed into the hands of dealers and producers.

and with over 400,000 horses and mules, worth $27,-000,000, or a total value of at least $54,400,000 for all farm and domestic animals.[11]

[11] *Annual Statistician and Economist*, 1890, pp. 178–80. In the S. F. *Chron.*, Dec. 29, 1889, the value of all live-stock is given at $63,526,000, the difference being in the higher estimate of value, for the number of animals varies but slightly from the above figures.

Among other prominent stock-raisers of whom no special mention has yet been made should be mentioned the late Charles Lux, of the cattle firm of Miller & Lux. An Alsatian by birth, after working at his father's trade as a wheelwright, he emigrated at the age of 16 to N. Y., where he found employment as a butcher's apprentice at $6 a month. Coming to S. F. in 1849, in the following year he started in business, and in 1856 formed a partnership with Henry Miller. In 1880 this firm owned at least 700,000 acres in Cal., Or., and Nev., including nearly all the land for 50 miles on both sides of the San Joaquin river. At that date their live-stock consisted of about 60,000 head of cattle, 100,000 sheep, 5,000 hogs, and 2,000 horses. Since the death of Mr Lux the possessions of his partner have been largely increased.

Among the cattle farmers of the San Joaquin valley should also be mentioned George Washington Trahern, a native of Miss., where he was born in 1825, the youngest of five children. His youth was passed in Tex., on the homestead of his brother-in-law, and in 1842–4 he passed two years of captivity in Mex., being one of the prisoners taken by Ampudia. After serving with distinction throughout the Mex. war, in 1849 he came to Cal. and has ever since been engaged in stock-raising, first on the Calaveras river and afterward in the San Joaquin valley.

One of the largest stock-raisers, agriculturalists, and orchardists in Marin co. was Francis De Long, a native of Vt, who came to Cal. in 1850, and after engaging in business in S. F., in 1856 purchased, in conjunction with J. B. Sweetser, the Novato ranch, adding to it from time to time until it contained 15,000 acres, and in 1879 buying his partner's interest. Here is also one of the finest dairy-farms in the state. In 1882 he was one of those who established the Petaluma Fruit Packing co., whose output is about 100,000 cases a year. Since his death in 1885 the estate has been managed by his son, F. C. De Long.

Another large land-owner and dairy-farmer in Marin co. is Jas Miller, a native of Ireland, who came to Canada with his parents in 1826, and in 1844 crossed the plains to Cal. The first portion of his farm of 3,000 acres was purchased in 1846, and since 1864 he has been engaged in the dairy business. His home in San Rafael is one of the most tasteful residences in that thriving and beautiful town.

John Boggs is one of the largest sheep-farmers in Colusa and Tehama cos, where on his ranches, in all some 40,000 acres, are depastured about 20,000 sheep, with a number of blood-horses and of choice Jersey cattle for dairy purposes. Mr Boggs is a native of Mo., a Cal. pioneer, and was elected state senator for these counties in 1870, and again in 1886.

Among the leading stock-raisers of Santa Barbara co. was Thomas F. Hope, an Irishman by birth, who came to the U. S. in 1840, and to Cal. in 1849. After a brief experience as a miner, and afterward as Indian agent, he settled on the Los Posotas rancho, which he purchased for $8,000. Its present value is at least $500,000. In 1856 he married Miss Delia Fox, and all their six children, the result of this union, have survived him. Mr Hope was known to the community as a man possessing the highest qualities of mind and heart.

Still another prominent stock-raiser, and also one of the most prominent citizens of Woodland, Yolo co., is John D. Longenour, who was born at

In manufacturing circles the feature of the year 1889 was the closing down of the Pioneer woollen-mills in San Francisco, an establishment which employed nearly 1,000 hands, producing goods to the annual value of more than $1,500,000. The cause assigned was the excessive importation of eastern goods, the low price of which made competition impossible, with the prevailing rates of labor, fuel, and capital. In the spring of 1890 occurred a strike among the iron-moulders, from 800 to 1,000 men, including also the laborers and case-makers, thus taking the bread from their own mouths. The cause was mainly due to the moulders passing a law limiting the number of hours in their daily work, and the amount of work to be done in those hours, together with their insistence on certain regulations as to the apprentice system.[12]

Salem, N. C., Nov. 23, 1823, and came to Cal. in 1850, for the purpose, as he relates, of making $1,000 and then returning home. Reaching Hangtown, El Dorado co., with his three brothers, their joint capital being 25 cents and a small stock of provisions, they began digging for gold with their butcher-knives on the south fork of American river. After saving a few hundred dollars they opened a trading post at Yankee Jim. In 1853 John engaged in the cattle trade, and in that and later years acquired large tracts of land in Yolo and Colusa cos.

[12] Fourteen foundries were involved in the trouble. For list see S. F. *Bulletin*, March 3, 1890.

In connection with the Union iron works should be mentioned Irving Murray Scott, since 1863 its general superintendent, and to whose careful management is largely due the success of that establishment. A native of Md, where he was born on Christmas day of 1837, after thoroughly learning his trade as a machinist, and studying mechanical drawing in the eastern states, he was engaged by Peter Donahue, first as draughtsman to the Union works and then as superintendent.

William T. Garratt, a native of Conn., and one of California's pioneers and pioneer manufacturers, came to Cal. in 1850, when twenty years of age, first learning his trade at his father's brass foundry in Cincinnati. After engaging in various occupations, and suffering many reverses, as in the conflagrations which thrice destroyed his property, he built his brass and bell foundry and his machine and hydraulic works on Natoma and Fremont streets, and soon afterward his works on Brannan and Fifth streets, S. F. In his special line he is now acknowledged as the leading manufacturer on the Pacific coast.

Another prominent manufacturer and inventor is Joseph Moore, a Scotchman by birth, an engineer by profession, and a pioneer of 1849. After working at various occupations, in 1855 he was appointed foreman of the Vulcan iron works, and a few years later to the same position in the Risdon works, of which he afterward became superintendent. Under his direction was made the large wrought-iron piping supplied for the Comstock and other mining districts, together with the huge pumps capable of raising 2,000 gallons per minute to a height of 800 feet, whereby deep mining was rendered possible.

In ship-building the year 1889 formed a special era
in San Francisco, for during that year the completion

The hydraulic elevators at the Palace hotel, S. F., were also mainly of his
design.

One of the principal manufacturers of galvanized iron in San Francisco is
Joseph F. Forderer, a German by birth, who came to the U. S. when only
seven years of age, and after serving an apprenticeship to his trade began
business for himself in Cincinnati.   In 1874, when bids were invited for the
construction of the insane asylum at Napa, he secured the contract for the
galvanized iron work, and as it was a very large one, he determined to
remove to this coast.   His handiwork may be seen on some of the most
prominent buildings in San Francisco, and elsewhere in California, as well as
in Nevada, Oregon, and the Hawaiian Islands.

Among the leading manufacturers and merchants of San Francisco is
George K. Porter, a native of Duxbury, Mass, where he was born Feb. 9,
1833.   After working on his uncle's farm for three years, and meanwhile attending the district school, he finished his education at the Partridge academy
at Duxbury, and on Feb. 1, 1849, took ship at Boston for San Francisco, where
he landed nearly 9 months later, being weatherbound for 70 days in the straits
of Magellan.   After a brief mining experience, in 1854 he started at Soquel one
of the first tanneries in California, which, in conjunction with his cousin, and
at times with others, he conducted until 1873, when the two cousins established the wholesale manufacturing and commercial firm of Porter, Blumm
& Slessinger, now Porter, Slessinger & Co.   He is also the owner of large
and valuable tracts of land in several counties of the state.   Among his
other interests are those in the California Lumber co., of which he is president.   In 1860 he was elected to the state senate for Santa Cruz and Monterey counties, the first republican returned by that district.   Among other
measures which he introduced was an act to encourage agriculture and manufactures.

Benjamin F., the cousin of George K. Porter, is a native of Northfield,
Vt, and also belongs to one of the oldest of New England families, his grandfather being a chaplain in the war of 1812.   At fourteen he was placed in
charge of one of his father's farms, meanwhile working in summer and attending the district school in winter, completing his education at the academies of Plainfield and Northfield.   In 1853, on his twentieth birthday, he
landed in San Francisco with $80 in his pocket, which he loaned at three per
cent per month, and went to work at cutting and chopping redwood trees,
soon afterward obtaining a contract for making pickets and shakes.   After
engaging in various occupations, in 1858 he bought a third interest in the
tannery of his cousin.   A few years later the two cousins began the manufacture of boots and shoes, establishing in 1873 the firm mentioned in his
cousin's biography, in which Benjamin Porter disposed of his share in 1879,
being then the owner, in conjunction with his cousin and Senator McClay, of
a tract of 56,000 acres near San Fernando.   His wheat crop for 1886 covered
some 12,000 acres, costing 47½ cents and realizing $1.16 per bushel.   He
also engaged largely in farming and stock-raising in Monterey co., where he
owned over 15,000 acres, with other farming lands in various portions of the
state.   He became a large share-holder and a member of the finance committee
in four prominent banks.   His present home is at Los Angeles, though he has
still large interests in San Francisco and Santa Cruz, in all of which cities he
enjoys the respect and good-will of the community.

One of our first brewers was Matthew Nunan, who was born in Ireland,
came to Cal. in 1855, and engaged in mining.   Visiting the east after 1859,
he married Miss Delia Horan, and took up his residence in S. F.   Here he
established a brewery, which developed into a large business.   In 1875 he
was elected sheriff of S. F., and again in 1877.   Mr Nunan is a man of ability and the strictest integrity.   One son, Frank, and four daughters comprised
the children, who may well be proud of their father.

of the United States cruiser *Charleston*, at the Union iron works, proved beyond doubt the ability of our metropolis to compete with eastern cities in the construction of steel vessels of the larger class. After one or two failures, caused by some slight defect in the working of the machinery, the *Charleston* more than satisfied the test by steaming under a forced draught, over eighteen miles an hour. At the same works another war-ship, the *San Francisco*, was all but completed in May 1890. In July of the preceding year was finished the iron steamer *Pomona*, a merchant vessel, and for this branch of industry the outlook was full of promise, some of the ship-yards having more orders on hand than could be executed within at least a twelvemonth.

To railroad matters sufficient space has already been devoted in preceding chapters of this volume. It remains only to be said that in the spring of 1890 there appeared some probability that the long-vexed question of the Central Pacific company's indebtedness to the government might reach a settlement, a house committee reporting in favor of a bill to fund such indebtedness for a term of seventy-five years at two per cent, and in the case of the Union Pacific, for 50 years at three per cent. As already stated, state subsidies, so far as California is concerned, are now among the issues of the past.[13]

Of mining [14] and mining stocks full mention has al-

[13] One of the strongest opponents of railroad subsidies was the late Governor Henry H. Haight, whose decease occurred Sept. 2, 1878. A native of Rochester, N. Y., and a graduate of Yale, he studied law with his father, and in 1847 was admitted to the bar. In Jan. 1850 he landed in S. F., where his ability soon placed him in the front rank of his profession. He married Miss Anna E. Bissell, the daughter of Capt. Bissell of Mo., and of their five children two boys and two girls are still living. Of his political career mention has already been made in these pages.

[14] To Adolph Sutro the Pacific coast is indebted for the construction of the largest and most costly drain tunnel in the world, 12 ft wide, 10 in height, more than five miles in length, including lateral branches, and costing nearly $5,000,000, its object being to drain and cool the levels of the Comstock lode. Born at Aix la Chapelle April 29, 1830, after completing his education he was made superintendent of his father's factory. In 1850 he

ready been made in these pages. Of coal the output for 1889 was estimated at 111,718 tons;[15] of gold, silver, copper, and lead, the value may be approximately stated at $15,000,000 for California, and $110,-000,000 for the Pacific coast, Montana taking the lead with over $30,000,000, followed by Colorado with about $26,000,000, and Nevada with $13,000,-000. A favorable feature in connection with this industry was the appreciation in the price of silver, which, from $42\frac{1}{8}$ pence an ounce in April 1888, rose in the London market to 48 pence in April 1889, an increase of more than 14 per cent. This was mainly due, as was claimed, to the anticipated action of congress on the silver bill introduced by Senator Jones, whereby the free coinage of silver would be permitted, and the sphere of silver currency greatly enlarged. Whatever be the outcome of congressional action, the rise is of the utmost benefit to the mining industry, and if it should go further may lead to a marked revival in that direction. As matters stood in former years, it is said that the discount on silver caused a greater loss in the Comstock mines than their entire operating expenses. There is, however, little hope that in the markets of the world the price of silver will be permanently enhanced by legislation on the

came to this state and engaged in business in San Francisco and Stockton, erecting, soon after the discovery of the Comstock lode, a small mill at Dayton for the reduction of ores by an improved process of amalgamation. In 1871, after years of fruitless endeavor, he secured the means to build his tunnel, and in July 1878 it made connection with the Savage mine. Mr Sutro is the possessor of the largest private library on the coast, including many rare volumes and manuscripts. On his grounds at Sutro Heights he proposes to erect a granite building for their reception, and to donate both library and grounds to the people of San Francisco.

Among our town-builders should be mentioned the late D. J. Locke, who was born at Langdon, N. H., Apl 16, 1823, and coming to this state in 1849 as physician of the Boston and Newton company of mechanics, founded, in 1862, the town of Lockeford in San Joaquin co. He was known as one of the most public-spirited men in this section of the state, donating lots for public buildings, and spending on improvements most of the fortune which he had amassed by hard work and self-denial.

[15] Including 38,000 and 33,718 tons respectively from the Empire and Pittsburg mines in Contra Costa co., 30,000 from the Ione valley mines in Amador co., and 10,000 from other sources. *Rept of State Mineralogist*, 1889, p. 323.

part of the United States, for silver is merely a commodity, and, like other commodities, its value depends on the inexorable law of supply and demand. If by legislation a silver dollar be declared worth more, and here pass current for more than its value in the commercial world, the effect would merely be to make this country a dumping-ground for the spare silver of all the nations.

In business circles, no less than to farmers and fruit-raisers, 1889 was a favorable year, and the more so because it was free from excitement from such real estate or stock inflations as at times send prices skyward, only to be followed by the inevitable collapse. Prices of most commodities were satisfactory, somewhat higher than those of the previous year, although there was here as elsewhere the usual number of financial wrecks. Prominent among the business failures were those of Belloc Frères and of W. T. Coleman & Company, both of them firms of long standing and excellent repute. For the latter various reasons were assigned, and of the former the cause was their heavy advances to Paris houses. On the 1st of July, 1889, the total banking capital of the state was $52,854,070, a decrease of $3,129,803 on the preceding year; the total of assets and liabilities was $236,297,224, an increase of $10,224,746, and of deposits $160,451,775, an increase of $9,300,248. For the first four months of 1890 the bank clearances in San Francisco were $240,684,822 against $259,-819,858 in the preceding year.

Throughout the state, except where values had been carried to extravagant figures, real estate was in good demand at advancing prices, though without unhealthy excitement. In San Francisco the number of sales for 1889 was 6,700, with a valuation of $33,000,000, against 5,000 and $24,500,000 in 1888, an increase of about one third both as to number and value. In the former year 1,230 buildings were erected at a cost of more than $11,000,000, against

974 costing $6,700,000 in 1888. Among those completed or in course of completion were the First National bank, the Rosenthal building, the Huntington-Hopkins company's building, the Chronicle building, the Catholic cathedral, the Odd Fellows' hall, the Academy of Sciences, the Lick free baths, the Old People's home, the Concordia club, the Cooper Medical college, the Hibernia bank, and the Superior court building.[16] For the site of a new post-

[16] For others see S. F. *Chronicle*, Dec. 29, 1889.

One of the largest land-owners on this coast is Dr E. B. Perrin, who came to this state in 1868 with a view to practise medicine. Visiting the Alabama settlement in Fresno co., he became interested in the irrigation question, and soon afterward, with the aid of the bank of Cal., began the construction of the upper San Joaquin canal, acquiring other valuable water rights, including those of the Fresno canal co. In conjunction with others he also acquired large tracts of land in various portions of the state and in southern Arizona. Among them is the Mammoth ranch of 60,000 acres in Fresno co., all of it suitable for vineyards.

Another successful real estate operator is Mark Sheldon, a native of N. Y. state, where he was born on what was known as the Dry Hill farm, near Watertown, Nov. 21, 1829. Coming to this state in 1851, after the usual mining experience, he established himself in business, first in Plumas co. and then in S. F. In the summer of 1861 he went to Virginia City, where his mining ventures were remarkably successful. After passing a few years in the eastern states, he returned to this coast and engaged largely in real estate operations, making such costly improvements as the well-known Sheldon block, on Market and First streets, one of the most commodious and substantial in the city.

A prominent real estate owner of Los Angeles, and in business matters one of the most successful, is Mark G. Jones, a native of San Francisco, where he was born in 1858, removing with his family to Los Angeles when twelve or thirteen years of age. The estate intrusted to him by his father he has largely increased by investments in city property, building recently on Main street a five-story edifice with 500 rooms.

Among those to whom is largely due the prosperity of southern Cal. was Phineas Banning, born near Wilmington, Del., Aug. 19, 1830, and who came to this state in 1852. A few years afterward he founded the town of Wilmington, Cal., erected warehouses, opened a lumber-yard, and built lighters and steamboats to facilitate its commerce, later establishing a stage line between that town, Los Angeles, and San Bernardino. In 1865 he was elected state senator, and through his exertions the city and co. of Los Angeles were authorized to vote $225,000 for a railroad from that city to Wilmington. He was an able and progressive man.

Another prominent citizen of southern Cal. is Henry Harrison Markham, a native of Essex co., N. H., where he was born Nov. 14, 1840. After serving with distinction almost throughout the civil war, at the close of which he held the rank of colonel, and then becoming prominent as an admiralty lawyer in Milwaukee and other cities, he came to Cal. for his health in 1879, settling himself at Pasadena. The fortune which he brought with him to this state he increased largely by mining and real estate investments. He became a director of the Los Angeles National bank, and was one of those who organized the Los Angeles Furniture co. In 1884 he was elected congressman on the republican ticket, and largely through his efforts liberal appropriations were secured for the harbors of the Pacific coast.

office, so long and urgently needed, $800,000 was appropriated by congress, a selection being made by a committee appointed for the purpose.

One effect of the excessive rains was to deprive of employment a very large number of mechanics and laborers, owing to the cessation of building and other operations. For a week or two about one thousand were employed at the Golden Gate park, subscriptions to the amount of over $30,000 being raised for that purpose by the citizens of San Francisco, and a further amount forwarded from Seattle being refused from a feeling of pride, though perhaps of false pride,

Other prominent men not yet noticed are L. Babcock, born in N. Y. state in 1825, and a Cal. pioneer; T. R. Bard, a banker of Hueneme, and a Pennsylvanian by birth, who came to Cal. in 1864; Dr L. Burwell, a farmer of Oroville, and a native of Va, who came to Cal. in 1853; M. J. Burke, a native of Galway, Ireland, and a leading real estate man of S. F., where he landed in 1853; F. Adams of San Luis Obispo, a native of Penn., and a pioneer of 1850; J. Banbury, an Englishman, and a fruit-grower of Pasadena; E. A. Beardsley, who was born in N. Y. state, came here in 1859, and is now a merchant and real estate man of Los Angeles; H. K. Bradbury, a lawyer of Santa Bárbara, and a native of Me; D. Burbank, a native of N. H., and a leading citizen of Los Angeles; B. F. Branham and his son, Isaac, the former ex-sheriff of Santa Clara co.; G. G. Bradt, born in N. Y. state, and a pioneer resident of San Diego; C. Carpy, a wine merchant of S. F., and a native of France; W. A. Clinton, born in Philadelphia, and a real estate man of Los Angeles; N. Cadwallader, a native of Ohio, and a banker of San José; R. E. Crittenden of S. F., a native of S. C., aud formerly state senator; G. W. Coffin, born in N. Y. state, a banker and ex-mayor of Santa Bárbara; B. Cohn, a Prussian, a merchant and ex-mayor of Los Angeles; J. W. Cooper, a Kentuckian, a pioneer, and a banker and merchant of Santa Bárbara; H. B. Crittenden, a lawyer of San Diego, and a native of Ind.; O. S. Chapin of Poway, a native of N. Y. state; W. E. Carlson, a native San Franciscan, and a real estate man of San Diego; F. E. Brown, an engineer of Redlands, and a native of West Haven, Conn.; H. J. Crow, a Pennsylvanian, engaged in the nursery business at Los Angeles; R. Cathcart, a Los Angeles farmer, and a native of St Louis; J. W. Calkins, a Santa Bárbara banker, and a native of Conn.; H. L. Drew, a San Bernardino banker, and a native of Mich.; W. M. Eddy, a native of N. Y. state, a resident of Santa Bárbara, a pioneer, and one of our most prominent bankers and merchants; G. H. Eggers, a German, and a viticulturist, residing in S. F.; C. Forman, a famous Indian fighter, who came to Cal. in 1853; C. Fernald, a pioneer, and ex-mayor of Santa Bárbara; C. Holbrook, a native of Me, and a leading hardware merchant of S. F., where he arrived in 1850; R. Heath, a pioneer, and one of the most prominent citizens of Santa Bárbara; D. Hunter, a Scotchman, also a pioneer, and one of the most enterprising citizens of the metropolis; A. Leonard, still another pioneer, a native of Mass, and a resident of Sacramento; J. De la Montanya, who came to this coast in 1850, and was one of the first to engage in the hardware business in S. F.; W. L. Merry, a native of N. Y., and one of the leading members of the S. F. board of trade; A. E. Maxey, a native of Mass, a pioneer, and a farmer and stock-raiser of San Diego co.; D. J. Oliver, an Irishman, and until his death, in 1886, one of the leading real estate men in S. F.; C. J. Richards, a prominent real estate man of Los Angeles; and A. L. Tubbs, a native of N. H., and the proprietor of the rope and cordage works in South San Francisco.

for in Seattle's hour of distress, after the fire of 1889, the metropolis was, as usual, most prompt and liberal in aiding the stricken city.

In the so-called eight-hour movement, from which serious troubles were apprehended, but happily not realized, in eastern and European cities, San Francisco took no active part, the demands of most of the trades interested being already conceded by employers.

Notwithstanding some drawbacks, few who have become accustomed to the stir and excitement of California life, to the glories of her scenery and climate, to her boundless opportunities, her wonderful prosperity, would care to exchange for any other the land of their nativity or adoption. It is now little more than four decades since the discovery of gold attracted to this coast the attention of the civilized world, and during that period, little more than the span of a single generation, how marvellous the transformation that many yet living have witnessed! As at the touch of a fairy's wand, the land has been converted from one vast pasture-ground into a region smiling with grain-fields, orchards, and vineyards, from the southern boundary of the state to the valleys overshadowed by the snow-capped peaks of Shasta, and from the shores of ocean to the foothills of the Sierra.

He who would know the utmost that can be accomplished by the energy and intelligence of man should study the history of this state, for nowhere else can be found such comprehensiveness of plan,

One of the oldest and most respected citizens in San Bernardino is John Brown, Sen., a native of Worcester, Mass, where he was born in 1817. After engaging in various occupations, as rafting on the Mississippi, and trapping along the mountain streams from the headwaters of the Columbia to northern Texas, meanwhile suffering shipwreck off the coast of Louisiana, and being present at the battle of San Jacinto, he reached California among the pioneers of 1849. In 1852 he settled at San Bernardino, and was one of those who brought about the separation of that county from Los Angeles, afterward rendering valuable services to the city of his adoption.

Probably our most successful hotel-keeper in S. F. is S. H. Seymour, for more than 20 years the manager of the Russ house, from which it is said his profits have averaged from $30,000 to $40,000 a year. A German by birth, he came to Cal. in 1853, and found employment at the American Exchange, then the leading hotel in S. F., of which in 1860 he became the landlord.

such boldness of emprise, such skill and daring in execution. If as yet we lack the minuteness and thoroughness of eastern and European communities, here are to be found in some departments the most remarkable achievements that have ever been witnessed in the world's industrial career. Here are the largest wheat and dairy farms, the largest stock-farms, the largest vineyards, orchards, and orange-groves, the largest hydraulic-mines, the largest mining-ditches, the most powerful mining-pumps and mining machinery, the highest aqueduct, the largest lumber-flume, and one at least of the largest saw-mills in the United States, or in any country on earth. And yet what has already come to pass, how wonderful soever in our sight, is but an earnest of what may be expected when there are hands enough for the work to be done, and consumers enough for its products.

And to what is California indebted for the position which she holds to-day as the first state in the union in her product of gold and wine and fruit, as the first in variety of agricultural products, as the first in wealth per capita, changing the financial conditions of the world by her enormous yield of the precious metals, changing the conditions of labor, and giving to commerce stimulus and direction? To the genius and enterprise of her inhabitants must these results be ascribed, for whatever has been found most excellent in other lands has been adopted in this state. Nowhere else has been displayed such aptitude in studying and applying the lessons of experience; nowhere has such progress been made in new directions; nowhere have so many appliances been successfully brought to bear on the development of agriculture and mining; nowhere is there so much of pride, and of excusable pride, among her adopted no less than her native-born citizens.

It seems but as yesterday since the Pacific coast metropolis was but a collection of cabins and tents

clustering among the few level acres of ground that
skirted the waters of the bay, the mud-flats and sand-
dunes, the steep, rocky hills, and the swamp-covered
ravines. Never, perhaps, was a more unpromising
site selected, and never did skill and enterprise
achieve so quick and complete a mastery over the
obstacles of nature. To-day those hills and ravines
are covered with a city of over 300,000 inhabitants,
stretching forth east and north to the shores of the
harbor, westward almost to the Pacific, and southward beyond the Mission hills, where in pioneer times
the only wagon-road passed through miles of loose
and shifting sand. Here have been erected some of
the finest public and business buildings, some of the
most tasteful and commodious residences in the
United States; here is one, at least, of the largest,
and more than one of the best-appointed hotels and
restaurants; here are theatres, churches, schools,
and libraries such as are seldom found in cities of
equal size; here are facilities for commerce, for travel,
and communication such as are excelled by few eastern or old-world centres.

And what will be the condition of this state a few
generations hence, when the moral and political
status of the community shall be on a par with her
material greatness; when trickery and demagogism
shall give place to honest and enlightened statesman-
ship; when manly worth and intellectual culture shall
be recognized; and when from the heterogeneous elements of which our western commonwealth is composed
shall be eliminated their impurities and debasing influences? Here, let us hope, will be the favored land,
where social science will find its most fitting sphere;
here the accumulations gathered in the vast store-
house of human experience; here the abode of all that
is best worth preserving in the art, the science, the
literature of the world; and here, if California be true
to herself and her higher destiny, may be found one

of the highest forms of development of which humanity is capable.[17]

[17] I give herewith a few additional biographies, in the briefest form, although many who are here mentioned are no less prominent than those who have been noticed at greater length.

Foremost among the military officers who have done service in the Indian wars of the west, both for popularity and gallant service, stands the name of N. A. Miles. A native of Mass, he received an academic education, and followed a mercantile life until the outbreak of the civil war, when, in 1861, he entered the service, out of which he came a major-general. He was then assigned to duty in North Carolina during the reconstruction of the states, and in 1869 he was ordered west to serve on the frontier. In 1875 the Cheyennes, Kiowas, and Comanches, who had been for years committing depredations, were subjugated. He also took part in other Indian difficulties. He married in 1868 Miss Mary Sherman, a daughter of C. T. Sherman of Cleveland, Ohio.

Among other military men well known on this coast was the late Alanson Merwin Randol, a colonel in the first artillery, and during the civil war in command of the second N. Y. cavalry. A native of Newburgh, N. Y., he graduated at West Point in 1860, and the same year was appointed to the ordnance corps at Benicia, with the rank of second lieutenant. At the outbreak of the rebellion he was transferred at his own request to a battery in active service, and from that time until the close of the war was constantly in the field, taking part in 32 pitched battles and engagements, in addition to numberless skirmishes. In 1881 he was ordered to California, and in the following year was inspector-general on the staff of McDowell. After the retirement of that officer he was successively in command at forts Winfield Scott and Alcatraz, San Francisco, and at Fort Canby, at the mouth of the Columbia river.

Edmond D. Shirland was born in Washington co., N. Y., in 1831, coming with the N. Y. reg. to Cal. in 1847. He served till Sept. 18, 1848, when the co. was disbanded. After various changes he went to Placerville, where he contracted; his health failed him, and he went to S. F. From 1850 to 1856 he was engaged in the cattle business, and on the outbreak of the civil war entered the army, serving until 1863 with the rank of captain. He has since been operating in real estate and mining. He was married in 1859, and had two daughters and a son.

Irvin Ayres was for twenty years resident at Fort Bidwell, where he became familiar with the workings of Indian affairs. He was born in 1832 in N. Y., and came to this coast in 1853, where he engaged in various pursuits. He married in 1872 Miss Annie L. Poor of Belfast, Maine; four boys being born to them. The distinguished soldier, Gen. Romeyn B. Ayres, who came to this coast in 1854, was an elder brother of Irvin Ayres.

Joseph G. Eastland was born in Nashville, Tenn., in 1831, and came to Cal. in 1849 with his father, who entered business in S. F. under the name of Thomas B. Eastland and son. They founded the town of Oro on Bear river, and took part in the Gold lake excitement. In 1851 young Eastland entered the Union foundry, under the auspices of James Donahue, and in 1856 became sec. of the S. F. Gas co., with interests in the gas companies of neighboring cities. In 1870 Mr Eastland married Miss Alice Lander, and in the same year was appointed one of the commissioners of the new S. F. city hall.

John Mallon was born in Ireland March 10, 1828, of French and Celtic ancestors, emigrating in 1832 with his parents to New York, where he obtained his education. In 1843 he was apprenticed to a glass-cutter, and afterward began business for himself. In 1858 he came to S. F., and opened an establishment, from time to time adding new branches until the highest styles known to the art were introduced. In 1847 he married Miss Elizabeth

Hanson, the fruit of the union being eight children, the eldest, Peter L. Mallon, having charge of the business.

Among other prominent citizens of Los Angeles should be mentioned I. N. Van Nuys, who was born in New York in 1835, and in 1865 came to Napa, Cal., where he embarked in the mercantile business. In 1870 he went to Los Angeles county, and with the Lankershims organized the San Fernando Farm and Homestead association, later the Los Angeles Farm and Mill co. In 1880 he was married to Miss Savannah Lankershim.

Among the most successful men of Los Angeles should also be mentioned Hervey Lindley, a native of Indiana, where he was born in 1854, accompanying his parents in early youth to Minneapolis, and completing his education at the high school in that city. Removing thence in 1853 to Waterloo, Iowa, he engaged in the lumber trade until 1855, when he removed to Los Angeles. Here he first loaned on real estate, and established himself as a broker, but finding that his patrons often doubled the amount of their investments, purchased some valuable properties in that city and its vicinity, and became largely interested in the quaker settlement of Whittier, located in 1887 by A. H. Pickering, and of which he is manager. In 1888 he had realized $300,000 from the latter venture, and had the utmost confidence in its future prosperity.

Another leading citizen is Henry T. Hazard, who was born in Illinois on the 31st of July, 1844, and came across the plains to Cal., arriving in 1852, his father having preceded him in 1849, and accumulated the means with which to bring out his family and settle them on a farm near Los Angeles. Young Hazard received his early education at Visalia and San José, proceeding thence to Harvard, and finally being admitted to the bar in Michigan in 1868, when he returned to Cal. and began to practise law. In 1881 he was elected Los Angeles city attorney, serving two years, and in 1884 was elected to the legislature. Later he became largely identified with the interests of Los Angeles. In 1873 he married Carrie Geller of Marysville.

Charles Victor Hall was born in San Francisco in 1852, and commenced his education by studying at home and reciting to a friend. Afterward he attended the university of Cal., paying his own way while there; then in 1875 he engaged in the real estate business at Los Angeles, which he has followed ever since, publishing *Hall's Land Journal* from 1876 to 1880. The journal was originated in Los Angeles and was afterward removed to San Francisco.

Few have done more for southern California than E. S. Babcock, Jr, who came to San Diego in the winter of 1883-4, and at Coronado breach built a hotel which for size, architecture, and arrangement, and as a seaside resort, considering furthermore the climate and other conditions, has not its superior in the world. With Mr Babcock were associated in this enterprise H. L. Story of Chicago, Jacob Gruendike of San Diego, and Joseph Collett of Terre Haute, Ind.

Wm R. Rowland was born at Puente rancho, near Los Angeles; his father, John Rowland, was a cattle dealer, and a pioneer of 1842, and afterward the first wine manufacturer of the state. Young Rowland went to the Santa Clara college for three years, and afterward had a private teacher. He had been managing his father's business up to 1871, when he started in business for himself. He has a rancho of 2,600 acres, on which a 32° gravity oil well has been found, and a pipe line from it to the R. R. was built. He was twice elected sheriff, and was the prime mover in the capture of Tiburcio Vasquez, for which he received a large regard. He married in 1874 Manuela Williams, a daughter of Gen. Williams.

INDEX.

For information concerning pioneers, see also the *Pioneer Register*, vols. II to V.

762 INDEX.

766   INDEX.

For information concerning pioneers, see also the *Pioneer Register*, vols. II to V.

Boots and shoes, manufact., etc., of, vii. 92.

Borax, yield, etc., of, vii. 659.

'Bordelais,' Fr. ship, visits of, 1817–18; ii. 287–90, 373.

Borica, Gov., rule of 1791–1800, i. 530–74, 726–32.

Boring, Rev., church organized by, vii. 729.

Borland, Senator, mention of, vii. 505–7.

'Borodino,' ship, ii. 642.

Boston, Cal. trade with, 1822, ii. 475; value of trade, 1843, iv. 376; R. R. convention at, 1849, vii. 510–11.

Botello, 'manuscript,' i. 55.

Bouchard affair, 1818, ii. 220–49.

Bourne, W. B., vii. 680.

'Boussole,' ship of, i. 428–9.

Bouton, E., biog. of, vii. 745.

Bovard, Dr M. M., biog., vii. 720.

Bowen, T. H., gen. of militia, 1850, vi. 319.

Bowie, Col G. W., nominee for congress, 1854, vi. 690; mention of, vii. 469–70.

Box-making, vii. 80.

Brackett, Capt., at Sonoma, 1848, vi. 20.

Brackett, J. E., gen. of militia, 1850, vi. 319.

Bradbury, H. K., biog., vii. 754.

Braden, W., mention of, vii. 617–18.

Bradley, the gold discov., 1848, vi. 53.

Bradley, H. J., mention of, vi. 492.

Bradt, G. G., biog., vii. 754.

Bragg, G. F., mention of, vii. 539.

Branciforte, Viceroy, offl acts on Cal. affairs; 1784–7, i. 525–6, 531, 543, 550–74.

Branciforte, mission, see also Santa Cruz, founding of, i. 565–70; progress at, 1800, i. 571; events at, 1801–10, ii. 155–7; character of settlers, ii. 155; events at, 1811–20, ii. 390–1; events at, 1821–30, ii. 626–7; list of settlers at, ii. 627; trouble at, iii. 588; events at, 1831–40, iii. 696–7; annals of, v. 641–2.

Brandy, Sutter's manufacture of, iv. 135.

Branham, B. F., biog., vii. 754.

Brannan, S., the gold discov., 1848, vi. 56; pres. Yuba R. R. Co., 1862, vii. 586.

Brass foundries, vii. 97.

Brazil, Stev. reg't at Rio Janeiro, v. 512.

Breckenridge party, attitude of, 1861, vii. 290–1.

Breen, Patrick, 'Diary of,' v. 535.

Brenham, C. H., mayor of San Francisco, 1851–2, vi. 761–4; biog., vi. 761.

Brewster, C. W., mention of, vii. 655.

Brewster, R. E., member S. F. stockboard, vii. 668.

Bricks, manufact., etc., of, vii. 97–8.

Bridge, H. E , mention of, vii. 607.

Bridgeport, mention of, vi. 519.

Bridges, building of, 1816, ii. 416.

Briggs, Rev. M. C., mention of, vii. 729.

Brodhead, Senator, motion of, vii. 520.

Broderick, D. C., biog., vi. 659–62; state senator, 1852, vi. 664–6, 677; quarrel with Estill, vi. 669–70; election bill of, 1854, vi. 681–6; further polit. career, vi. 691–730; character, vi. 709–10, 733–5; challenged by Perley, 1859, vi. 725; duel with Terry, 1859, vi. 731–2; death of, vi. 732–3; obsequies, vi. 736–7.

Bromwell, T., mine discov'd by, 1861, vii. 640.

Brooke, Brig.-gen. G. M., of court at Frémont trial, v. 456.

'Brooklyn,' ship, iii. 73, 82, 137, v. 469, 545.

Brooklyn, town, hist. of, vi. 477–8.

Brooks, J. T., mention of, vi. 72; 'Four months among the gold finders,' vi. 97–8.

Brown, B., biog. of, vii. 307.

Brown, C., mention of, vi. 6.

Brown, E., mention of, vi. 10.

Brown, F. E., biog., vii. 754.

Brown, J., mention of, vii. 607.

Brown, J., biog., vii. 755.

Brown, Col O. M., mention of, vii. 469.

Brown valley, mining excitement at, vii. 637.

Brownsville, mention of, vi. 487.

Browne, J. R., bibliog., ii. 176; reporter to constit. convention, biog., etc., 1849, vi. 286–9.

Bruce, S. C., member S. F. stockboard, vii. 668.

Brushes, manufact. of, vii. 94.

'Brubus,' transport, v. 511.

Bryan, Judge C. N., election of, 1855, vii 220.

Bryant, Mayor, courtesy of, vii. 592; biog. of, vii. 186.

INDEX. 767

For information concerning pioneers, see also the *Pioneer Register*, vols. II to V.

For information concerning pioneers, see also the *Pioneer Register*, vols. II to V.

For information concerning pioneers, see also the *Pioneer Register*, vols. II to V.

For information concerning pioneers, see also the *Pioneer Register*, vols. II to V.

784   INDEX.

For information concerning pioneers, see also the *Pioneer Register*, vols. II to V.

For information concerning pioneers, see also the *Pioneer Register*, vols. II to V.

For information concerning pioneers, see also the *Pioneer Register*, vols. II to V.

794 INDEX.

INDEX.

For information concerning pioneers, see also the *Pioneer Register*, vols. II to V.

Mining, soldiers killed while prospecting, i. 465-6; mines discovered in S. F. dist, 1795, i. 705; Goycoechea's views, ii. 33; early attempts, 1802, ii. 144; Ortega's discovery, 1800, ii. 176; Sola's report on, 1818, ii. 417; discoveries, 1821-30, ii. 666-7; discovery of the New Almaden, v. 3; gold, 1848, vi. 67-81; 1848-56, vi. 351-80; methods and yield, 1848, vi. 85-9, 409-26; geologic theories, vi. 381-5; regulations, vi. 396-402; taxes, vi. 404-6; quartz, 1850-6, vi. 415-18; vii. 636-45; yield, etc., 1848-56, vi. 418-26; statutes and decisions, vii. 228-9; tax on, 1864, vii. 300; effect of speculation, vii. 372-3; improvements in, vii. 639; quartz miners' convention, vii. 641; origin of companies, vii. 642; school of mining, vii. 643; hydraulic mining, vii. 640, 645-8; ditches, vii. 645; débris, vii. 646-8; capital invested, vii. 648; river bed, vii. 649; silver, vii. 649; table of productions, vii. 652; expense and profit, vii. 653; gold nuggets, vii. 653-5; decline of mining, 654-5; quicksilver, vii. 656-9; iron, vii. 658; copper, vii. 658-9; borax, vii. 659; salt, vii. 659; sulphur, vii. 660; tin, vii. 660-1; coal, vii. 661; petroleum, vii. 661-2; asphaltum, vii. 662; mineral soap, vii. 662; limestone, vii. 662; marble, vii. 662; gypsum, vii. 662; lead, vii. 662; manganese, vii. 662; plumbago, vii. 662; miscellaneous minerals, vii. 663-4; stocks, vii. 666-80, 687-8; mining companies, vii. 666; Fraser river excitement, vii. 682.

Mining machinery, manufact. of, vii. 94-5.

Minns, Geo. W., vii. 720.

Mint, bills for establishing, vi. 628-9; establ'd, etc., vi. 629; vii. 167-8; appropr. for, 1852, vii. 167.

Miranda, agent in Spain for Gov. Borica, 1794, i. 728.

Miranda, J., mention of, vi. 20.

Misroon, Lieut, miss. of, 1846, v. 156-9.

Missions, archives of, i. 47-8; S. Diego founded, i. 137; S. Carlos founded, i. 170-1; S. Antonio founded, i. 176-7; S. Gabriel founded, i. 179-80; S. Luis Obispo founded, i 188-9; number of friars at, 1773, i. 200; military force, i.

200; conversions in first five years, i. 201; Serra's report on, 1773, i. 212-13; want at, 1774, i. 220; S. Diego moved, i. 229-30; second ann. report on, i. 238-9; attempt founding S. Juan Cap., i. 248; destruction of S. Diego, 1775, i. 249-55; alarm at S. Antonio, i. 256; S. F. established, i. 292; progress at, 1776-7, i. 298-306; 1791-1800, i. 575-99, 654-9, 671-6; Cuadra presents image to, i. 329; extension plans, 1781, i. 338; new regulations for, i. 374-5; list of friars at, 1783, i. 388; Sola's plan to secularize, i. 394-6; Gov. Fages' report on, i. 408; successor to Serra, i. 416-17; war contributions of, i. 428; La Perouse on, i. 435-8; events at, 1783-90, i. 455-60, 466, 468-70, 473-7; 1811-20, ii. 392-412; 1791-1800, i. 654-9, 671-6, 685-90, 712-15, 722-5; Sta Cruz founded, i. 493-5; search for sites, 1794-5, i. 550-4; S. José founded, i. 555; S. Miguel founded, i. 559-60; S. Fernando founded, i. 561-2; S. Luis Rey founded, i. 563-4; industries at, 1800, i. 617-18; land controversies, 1802, ii. 7; Pres. Tapi's report, 1803-4, ii. 26-9; Sta Ines founded, ii. 28-9; regulations for, 1806, ii. 41-2; agric. at, 1801-10, ii. 104-5; manufactures at, ii. 175; statistics of, 1801-10, ii. 107, 108, 110, 115, 116, 121, 123, 132, 137, 138, 148, 149, 151, 153, 154; 1811-20, ii. 346, 347, 349, 350, 355, 358, 364, 366, 368, 374, 377, 380, 383, 384, 385, 387, 390; 1821-30, ii. 567, 578, 580, 581, 582, 595, 596, 599, 601, 602; iv. 62-4, 616, 619, 620, 622, 624; 1831-40, ii. 552, 554, 556; contributions, 1817, ii. 217; Sola's report on, 1818, ii. 250-2; supplies from, 1818-20, ii. 257-9; 1822, ii. 479-80; 1831, iii. 310; presidents of, 1811-20, ii. 396-8; 1821-30, ii. 657; 1831-3, iii. 338; cession of, in s. Cal., 1817, ii. 407-11; report on, 1822, ii. 460; condition, 1821-30, iii. 655-7; 1836, iv. 42-3; 1841, iv. 194-5; supplies and finances, 1825, iii. 20-3; prefect and pres't, 1826-30, iii. 87; proposed secularization, 1830-1, iii. 301-10; secularization of, iii. 346, 353; iv. 43-4, 546-7; destruction of property, 348; slaughter of cattle, 348-9; acts of authorities, 1836-8, iv.

For information concerning pioneers, see also the *Pioneer Register*, vols. II to V.

For information concerning pioneers, see also the *Pioneer Register*, vols. II to V.

800 INDEX.

For information concerning pioneers, see also the *Pioneer Register*, vols. II to V.

For information concerning pioneers, see also the *Pioneer Register*, vols. II to V.

For information concerning pioneers, see also the *Pioneer Register*, vols. II to V.

For information concerning pioneers, see also the *Pioneer Register*, vols. II to V.

For information concerning pioneers, see also the *Pioneer Register*, vols. II to V.

For information concerning pioneers, see also the *Pioneer Register*, vols. II to V.

reëlection, vii. 310–11; assassination, vii. 311–13; democr. convention at, 1868, vii. 330; the Chinese question, vii. 341–5; labor agitations in, 1877–8, vii. 348–62; the new constitut., 1879, vii. 395–400; charter of, vii. 397; election of, 1879, vii. 411–12; 1881, vii. 415–16; charter of, vii. 412–14; name, vii. 438; clearances at, vii. 443; duties, etc., rec'd at, vii. 443; gov't approprs for, 1851–87, vii. 443–4; R. R. affairs in, vii. 542–4, 556–7, 601–3, 605–8, 685 et seq.; stock exch. board, vii. 666–8; mining excitement at, 1858, vii. 682–3; real estate decline, vii. 683, 685; manufactures of, vii. 683; street car lines, vii. 684; bulkhead bill, vii. 684–5; trade increase, vii. 687; labor troubles, 1877, vii. 687–9; workingmen's party, vii. 689; loyalty to union, vii. 689–90; politics, etc., of, vii. 690; land titles in, vii. 691; Chinatown in, vii. 691–2; future of, vii. 692–4; millionaires in, vii. 693; Golden Gate park, vii. 693.

San Francisco bay, question as to Drake anchoring in, i. 86–7, 90–4; discovery of, i. 159; third exploration of. i. 231–4; explored by Ayala, i. 245–7; Moraga explores, i. 290; Aleuts hunting in, 1808, ii. 81; map of, 1826, ii. 589; Aleuts hunting in, ii. 296; Kotzebue's visit, 1824, ii. 522; surveyed by Beechey, ii. 588; iii. 121; Belcher's survey of, iv. 144.

San Francisco Bible society, vii. 729.

San Francisco Bay R. R. co., vii. 578.

'San Francisco Javier,' ship, ii. 474.

'San Francisco de Paula,' ship, ii. 293, 477.

San Francisco peninsula, Anza's explor. of, 1776, i. 279–880.

S. Francisco rancho, gold discovered on, 1842, iv. 297.

San Francisco Solano, see Solano.

S. F., Oakland and Alameda R. R. co., vii. 587.

S. F. & Humboldt Bay R. R. co., vii. 583.

S. F. & Marysville R. R., vii. 581.

S. F. & North Pacific R. R., vii. 583.

San Francisco and San José R. R. co., organized, etc., 1859, vii. 537, 598.

S. F. & Washoe R. R., vii. 560.

S. Francisquito creek, Anza's camp at, i. 280.

San Gabriel, established, 1871, i. 179–80; troubles at, i. 180–2; want of supplies, i. 187; events at, 1772, i. 189; 1783–90, i. 459–60; 1791–1800, i. 663–5; 1801–10, ii. 113–15; 1811–20, ii. 355–7; 1821–30, ii. 567–9; 1831–40, iii. 641–5; miss. force at, 1773, i. 196; locality of, i. 200; condition of natives, 1773, i. 202; buildings at, 1773, i. 204; agric. at, 1773, i. 205; Anza's exped. at, i. 223; tedious march to, 1776, i. 264; consultation between Rivera and Anza, i. 271–2; Garcés' reception at, i. 275–6; friars serving at, 1776, i. 299; alcalde and regidore chosen, 1778, i. 331; deserters arrested at, ii. 88; trouble with Inds, 1810, ii. 92; attempt cotton cultivation, 1808, ii. 177; hemp culture, ii. 180; earthquake, 1812, ii. 200; Inds troublesome at, 1811, ii. 323–4; Colorado Inds at, 1822, ii. 480; industries at, ii. 665; Duhant-Cilly at, iii. 630; trappers at, 1826, iii. 154; Padres and Hijars colony at, iii. 267; secularization of, iii. 346; slaughter of cattle, iii. 348; Ind. depredations at, 1834, iii. 359; restored to friars, 1843, iv. 369; condition of, 1844, iv. 422; battle at, 1846, v. 391–5; sale of miss. estate, v. 561; local annals, 1846–8, v. 628.

San Gabriel river, name, i. 179; ii. 47.

San Gabriel valley R. R., vii. 616.

San Ignacio rancho, ii. 594.

San Isidro rancho, ii. 594.

San Jacinto Valley R. R., vii. 616.

San José, founded, i. 312; early annals, 1776–81, 312–14; agric., i. 331, 478; settlers at, 1782–3, i. 349–50; map, i. 350; events at, 1783–90, i. 477–80; 1791–1800, i. 715–21; 1801–10, ii. 132–6; 1811–20, ii. 377–9; 1821–30, ii. 602–6; 1831–40, iii. 729–32; 1846, v. 294–5; first school at, i. 642; proposed removal, i. 719; boundary dispute, i. 719–21; pueblo regulations, i. 721–2; boundary dispute, 1809, ii. 135–6; ayunt. at, ii. 461–2, 676; visited by Kotzebue, 1824, ii. 523; crime at, 1821–30, ii. 678–9; Duhant-Cilly at, iii. 129; Jedediah Smith's party at, iii. 158; case of Alcalde Duarte, 1831,

For information concerning pioneers, see also the *Pioneer Register*, vols. II to V.

581-2; 1831-40, iii. 661-4; hemp culture at, ii. 179-81; earthquake, 1812, ii. 201; Ind. revolt at, 1824, ii. 528; secularization, iv. 46; restored to friars, iv. 369; ecclesiastical seminary at, 1844, iv. 403, 425-6; condition of, 1844, iv. 421; value of property, 1845, iv. 550; leased, 1845, iv. 553; miss. estate rented, v. 558; sale of miss. estate, v. 561; local annals, 1846-8, v. 635.

Santa Margarita, meeting of Pico and Castro at, 1846, v. 562.

Santa Marina, E. J. de, member stock board, vii. 668.

Santa Monica, Cabrillo anchors in, i. 71; mention of, vi. 521-2.

Santa Paula, town, mention of, vi. 523.

Santa Rosa, settlement at, 1833, iii. 255-6; murder of Cowie and Fowler near, 1846, v. 160-2; fight near, 1846, v. 164; mention of, vi. 507.

'Santa Rosa,' Bouchard's ship, ii. 226.

Santa Rosa island, Cabrillo at, i. 72; granted to Carrillo, iii. 581; Bancroft hunting at, 1838, iv. 90.

Santa Teresa, campaign of, 1844, iv. 466-70.

'Santiago,' ship, Serra returns on, i. 218-19; built for Cal. service, i. 224; northern voy. of, 1775, i. 241-3; first voy. direct to S. F., i. 296; voyages of, 1778-9, i. 328.

Santiago de Santa Ana rancho, holders of, 1809, ii. 112.

Santillian, claims of, vii. 243-4.

Santillian claim, mention of, vi. 561.

Santo, Bernardo del Espíritu, Bishop of Cal., 1818, ii. 411.

'Santo Tomas,' ship in Vizcaino's expedt., i. 98.

Sargent, A. A., congressman, etc., 1861, vii. 291-2; defeat of, vii. 301; congressman, 1868, vii. 331; biog., vii. 331; mention of, vii. 547; bill of, 1861, vii. 548; in R. R. affairs, vii. 561, 602, 615.

Satayomi, Ind. tribe, ii. 506.

Satiyomes, Ind. fight with, iii. 257.

Sauzal rancho, ii. 615.

Sauzalito, Russ. warehouse at, 1836, iv. 164; 'Portsmouth' anchored at, v. 156; name, etc., vi. 511; mention of, vi. 21.

Savage, explor., etc., of, 1852, vii. 209; death of, vii. 210.

Savage, J. D., mention of, vi. 515.

Savage, mine, stocks, vii. 671-2; output, vii. 673.

'Savannah,' U. S. ship, iv. 459; v. 199, 224, 253-4, 290, 295-6, 318, 320, 226-7, 436.

Savings and Loan Society, vii. 164.

Sawyer, Judge L., election, etc., of, vii. 235; biog., etc., of, vii. 235-6; supreme judge, 1863, vii. 304; mention of, vii. 577.

Scala, bibliog., ii. 67, 299.

Schmiedell, Henry, member stock board, vii. 668.

Schofield, Gen. G. M., in command, 1870, vii. 472.

Schwartz, J., mention of, vi. 17.

Scorpion Silver Mining co., vii. 667.

Scott, A. B., vii. 561.

Scott, C. L., nominee for cong., 1859, vi. 723.

Scott, Dr, excitement against, 1861, vii. 286.

Scott, I. M., biog., vii. 748.

Scott, Thomas A., vii. 609-10, 613-15.

Scott, Wm A., vii. 729-30.

Scurvy, ravages of, 1769, i. 130-2; on the Juno, 1806, ii. 67.

Sea-otter, see fur trade.

Seal Rocks, first drive to, i. 233-4.

Sealing, vii. 81.

Seals, see fur trade.

Searles, Niles, vii. 590.

Sears, W. H., speech of, 1863, vii. 550.

Seawall, Major W., in command, 1851, vii. 471.

Secpe rancho, friars object to grant, 1817, ii. 354.

Secularization, decree of Spanish córtes, 1813, ii. 399-400; decree forwarded to Cal., 1821, ii. 431; padres offered to give up miss., ii. 431; policy of friars, ii. 431-5; indications of, 1823, ii. 487; legislature on, 1825, iii. 17-18; policy of, iii. 100-2; experimental, iii. 102-4; Echeandia's plan, iii. 105-6, 301-5; approved by legislature, iii. 106-7; Echeandia's decree, 1831, iii. 184; decree of, 1831, iii. 305-6; attempt to enforce, iii. 307-8; Duran's comments, iii. 309-10; Figueroa's report, iii. 329-31; views of prefect and pres., iii. 333-5; emancipation advised, iii. 335-6; Figueroa's policy, 1834, iii. 341; Mex. law, iii. 342-4, Hijar instructions, iii. 345; reglamento in practice, iii. 346-7; local

For information concerning pioneers, see also the *Pioneer Register*, vols. II to V.

For information concerning pioneers, see also the *Pioneer Register*, vols. II to V.

For information concerning pioneers, see also the *Pioneer Register*, vols. II to V.